11-13

To My Mother and Father

B. Bernard Cohen   Wichita State University   28043

LITERATURE
FOR
UNDERSTANDING

Scott, Foresman and Company
Chicago   Atlanta   Dallas   Palo Alto   Fair Lawn, N. J.

"Huswifery." Reprinted from *The Poems of Edward Taylor*, Thomas H. Johnson, editor, 1939, by permission of Princeton University Press.

Poems I, XVII, XXIX, L, "Dirge in Woods," "Lucifer in Starlight." Reprinted with the permission of Charles Scribner's Sons from *Modern Love* by George Meredith, 1910.

"Safe in Their Alabaster Chambers," "I Felt a Funeral, in My Brain," "What Soft—Cherubic Creatures," "I Heard a Fly Buzz—When I Died," "Because I Could Not Stop for Death," "A Route of Evanescence." Reprinted by permission of the publishers, *The Poems of Emily Dickinson*, Thomas H. Johnson, Editor. Cambridge, Mass. The Belknap Press of Harvard University Press, Copyright, 1951, 1955, by The President and Fellows of Harvard College.

"The Darkling Thrush," "The Man He Killed." From *Collected Poems of Thomas Hardy* by permission of the Trustees of the Hardy Estate, Macmillan & Co. Ltd., London, and The Macmillan Company of Canada Limited.

"Heaven-Haven," "God's Grandeur," "The Windhover," "Pied Beauty," "The Caged Skylark." From *Poems of Gerard Manley Hopkins* (London: Oxford University Press, 1948).

"Loveliest of Trees," "To an Athlete Dying Young." From *A Shropshire Lad*, 1924, and *Complete Poems*, 1959. Reprinted by permission of The Society of Authors as the literary representative of the Estate of the late A. E. Housman, and Messrs. Jonathan Cape Ltd., publisher of A. E. Housman's *Collected Poems*.

"When Smoke Stood Up from Ludlow." Reprinted by permission of The Society of Authors as the literary representative of the Estate of the late A. E. Housman, and Messrs. Jonathan Cape Ltd., publishers of A. E. Housman's *Collected Poems*.

"The Second Coming," "Sailing to Byzantium." Reprinted with permission of the publisher from *Collected Poems* by William Butler Yeats. Copyright 1924, 1928 by The Macmillan Company; renewal 1952, 1956 by Georgie Yeats. Permission also authorized by A. P. Watt & Sons, London, for The Macmillan Company of Canada Limited and Mrs. W. B. Yeats.

"Richard Cory." Reprinted with the permission of Charles Scribner's Sons from *The Children of the Night* by Edwin Arlington Robinson, Charles Scribner's Sons, 1897.

"Mr. Flood's Party." Reprinted with permission of The Macmillan Company from *Collected Poems* by E. A. Robinson. Copyright 1921 by Edwin Arlington Robinson. Renewed 1949 by Ruth Nivison.

"For a Dead Lady." Reprinted with the permission of Charles Scribner's Sons from *The Town Down the River*. Copyright 1910 Charles Scribner's Sons; renewal copyright 1938 Ruth Nivison.

"War Is Kind." Published, 1930 by Alfred A. Knopf, Inc. Reprinted from *Collected Poems* by Stephen Crane, by permission of the publisher.

"The Listeners." From *The Listeners and Other Poems* by Walter de la Mare (London: The Society of Authors, 1916). Reprinted by permission of The Literary Trustees of Walter de la Mare and The Society of Authors as their representative.

"Home Burial," "After Apple-Picking," "Once by the Pacific," "Bereft." From *Complete Poems of Robert Frost*. Copyright 1928, 1930, 1939 by Holt, Rinehart and Winston, Inc. Copyright renewed © 1956, 1958 by Robert Frost. Reprinted by permission of Holt, Rinehart and Winston, Inc.

"Domination of Black." Copyright, 1942 by Wallace Stevens. Reprinted from *The Collected Poems of Wallace Stevens*, by permission of Alfred A. Knopf, Inc.

"Peter Quince at the Clavier." Copyright, 1923, 1951 by Wallace Stevens. Reprinted from *The Collected Poems of Wallace Stevens*, by permission of Alfred A. Knopf, Inc.

"Humming-Bird." From *Collected Poems* by D. H. Lawrence. Copyright 1929 by Jonathan Cape and Harrison Smith, Inc., 1957 by Frieda Lawrence Ravagli. Reprinted by permission of The Viking Press, Inc.

"Terra Incognita." From *Collected Poems*, 1929, by D. H. Lawrence. Reprinted by permission of Laurence Pollinger Limited and the Estate of the late Mrs. Frieda Lawrence.

"The Bloody Sire." From *Be Angry at the*

Sun and Other Poems, by Robinson Jeffers. Copyright 1941 by Robinson Jeffers. Reprinted by permission of Random House, Inc.

"To the Stone-Cutters." Copyright 1924 and renewed 1951 by Robinson Jeffers. Reprinted from *The Selected Poetry of Robinson Jeffers*, by permission of Random House, Inc.

"Hurt Hawks." Copyright 1928 and renewed 1956 by Robinson Jeffers. Reprinted from *The Selected Poetry of Robinson Jeffers*, by permission of Random House, Inc.

"The Paper Nautilus," "The Mind is an Enchanting Thing." Reprinted with permission of The Macmillan Company from *Collected Poems* by Marianne Moore. Copyright 1941, 1944 by Marianne Moore.

"Preludes," "The Love Song of J. Alfred Prufrock." From *Collected Poems 1909-1962* by T. S. Eliot, copyright, 1936, by Harcourt, Brace & World, Inc.; copyright, © 1963, 1964, by T. S. Eliot. Reprinted by permission of the publishers and Faber and Faber Ltd., Publishers.

"The Equilibrists." Copyright, 1927 by Alfred A. Knopf, Inc. Renewed, 1955 by John Crowe Ransom. Reprinted from *Selected Poems* by John Crowe Ransom, by permission of the publisher.

"The Room," "And If We Kiss." From *Collected Poems* by Conrad Aiken. Copyright 1953 by Conrad Aiken. Reprinted by permission of Oxford University Press, Inc.

"L'An Trentiesme de Mon Eage," "Eleven." From *Collected Poems* by Archibald MacLeish (Boston: Houghton Mifflin Company, 1917-1952).

"next to of course god america i." Copyright, 1926, by Horace Liveright; copyright, 1954, by E. E. Cummings. Reprinted from *Poems 1923-1954* by E. E. Cummings by permission of Harcourt, Brace & World, Inc.

"somewhere i have never travelled, gladly beyond." Copyright, 1931, 1939, by E. E. Cummings. Reprinted from his volume *Poems 1923-1954* by permission of Harcourt, Brace & World, Inc.

"anyone lived in a pretty how town." Copyright, 1940, by E. E. Cummings. Reprinted from his volume *Poems 1923-1954* by permission of Harcourt, Brace & World, Inc.

"Dirge." From *New and Selected Poems* by Kenneth Fearing (Bloomington: Indiana University Press, 1956).

"The Ground Hog," "The Cancer Cells." From *Collected Poems* by Richard Eberhart. Copyright © 1960 by Richard Eberhart. Reprinted by permission of Oxford University Press, Inc. and Chatto and Windus Ltd. of London.

"Gold Glade." © Copyright 1957 by Robert Penn Warren. Reprinted from *Promises: Poems 1954-1956*, by Robert Penn Warren, by permission of Random House, Inc.

"Musée des Beaux Arts," "The Unknown Citizen." Copyright 1940 by W. H. Auden. Reprinted from *The Collected Poetry of W. H. Auden*, by permission of Random House, Inc., and Faber and Faber Ltd.

"Elegy for Jane," "The Exorcism." "Elegy for Jane," copyright © 1940 by Theodore Roethke, "The Exorcism," copyright © 1957 by Theodore Roethke, from *Words for the Wind*. Reprinted by permission of Doubleday & Company, Inc.

"I Think Continually of Those." Copyright 1934 and renewed 1961 by Stephen Spender. Reprinted from *Collected Poems 1928-1953*, by Stephen Spender, by permission of Random House, Inc., and Faber and Faber Ltd.

"Ultima Ratio Regum." Copyright 1942 by Stephen Spender. Reprinted from *Collected Poems 1928-1953*, by Stephen Spender, by permission of Random House, Inc., and Faber and Faber Ltd.

"Colorado." From *In the Rose of Time*. Copyright 1956 by Robert Fitzgerald. Reprinted by permission of New Directions.

"Auto Wreck." Copyright 1941 by Karl Shapiro. Reprinted from *Poems 1940-1953*, by Karl Shapiro, by permission of Random House, Inc.

"The Force That Through the Green Fuse Drives the Flower," "Do Not Go Gentle into That Good Night." From *The Collected Poems of Dylan Thomas*. Copyright 1953 by the author; © 1957 by New Directions. Permission also granted by J. M. Dent & Sons Ltd., London, and the Literary Executors of the Dylan Thomas Estate.

"Boom!," "The Sanctuary." Reprinted by

Preface

In *Literature for Understanding* I have attempted to provide a generous selection of poems, stories, and plays for freshman and sophomore college courses which concentrate on literature. My chief criteria for the choices in this book have been the literary merit of the selections and my evaluation of their teachability. Many of the works have stimulated students and teachers in countless classrooms. The new ones—those never before anthologized or infrequently included in anthologies—will, I believe, evoke lively oral and written discussions of ideas and attitudes and of technical achievements.

Although I have been keenly aware of teachability, I have left this anthology relatively free of apparatus. My annotation, for example, is minimal because I believe that the student should be encouraged to use his dictionary and to consult standard reference books in order to get the most out of his reading. Ironically, we English teachers often stress the value of dictionaries and of research but then supply the student with a literary text so heavily annotated that he has no work to do. More than work is involved here. Only when a student is left to use his own resources can he develop a sense of independence and an intellectual curiosity which impel him to investigate beyond the printed pages of an anthology.

In eliminating apparatus, I have also considered the desires of many teachers. Since some of them prefer to develop their own approaches to the characteristics of each genre, I have omitted the standard kind of introduction to each form. Although in my teaching I am always conscious of the thematic and technical relationships among literary works, I have refrained from imposing arbitrarily my concepts of such arrangements for this book. Rather, I have chosen for each section a simple chronological pattern based on dates of birth of the authors. The teacher may feel free to follow this organization or to rearrange the material to suit his own interests.

In the organization of *Literature for Understanding* I start with poetry, even though most genre anthologies begin with short fiction. I become more and more convinced that the close study of poetry at the beginning of an introductory literature course has some sound advantages. First, it breaks down the superficial reading habits inculcated by an emphasis on plot summary in the student's previous experience. Second, the careful study of poetry develops in the student a sense of language—its concreteness, its conciseness, its figurative nature, and its beauty. Armed with this new awareness of language and poetic style, the student will come to his study of fiction and drama well prepared to acquire more than the story. Poetry, I feel, provides the best medium for us to reach and comprehend the nuances of the literary imagination. However, if a teacher does not agree with my view, he can easily ignore my arrangement and begin the course with stories or plays.

Although no one can solve all of the textual problems which confront an anthologist, I have tried to present reasonably authentic texts for each work. I have left some of the early poems in scholarly form—unmodernized—because I feel that to modernize everything in an anthology leads the student to believe erroneously that his language, the spelling of words, and practices in punctuation are somehow static and homogenized. On the other hand, it would be unreasonable to ask an undergraduate to read a truly authentic or scholarly text of a complicated work like *King Lear*. Although the flavor of Shakespeare's language is retained, the text here, in accordance with current practices, is modernized.

I am grateful to Scott, Foresman and Company and to Professor Hardin Craig for allowing me to use his edition and annotation of *King Lear* as the basis of my text. For the changes I have made in Professor Craig's version I am solely responsible.

I owe acknowledgement to others who have offered generous help and support. Professor John Hagopian of Harpur College made some very valuable suggestions about selections. Mrs. Ann Bugliani, Mrs. Lynda Jackson, Miss Margaret Martin, Mrs. Louise P. Herring, and Verne Reaves—all on the staff of Scott, Foresman and Company—have contributed incalculable assistance and useful advice during the development of this anthology. Mrs. Karla Berry Langton, Marlyn E. Eshelman, Jr., and Daniel B. Grove—students at Wichita State University—gave patient and faithful help with proofreading.

For any project in print that bears my name I owe a special debt of gratitude to my wife Lucian. She is so closely identified with every phase of the work here that I am sure she will share equally with me any praise of its merits and any criticism of its defects.

Finally, for those teachers interested in providing their students with apparatus to accompany the poems, stories, and plays in this anthology, I would call attention to two of my other books: *Writing About Literature* and *Working for Literary Understanding*. Behind the three is a design with definite purposes. *Literature for Understanding* provides the basic literary texts for reading, for class discussions, and for analytical essays. *Writing About Literature* supplies practical information about the interpretation of literature and about the writing of interpretive and critical papers. *Working for Literary Understanding*, which is based on the selections in this anthology, offers the student extensive and vital practice in literary analysis and in coping with problems of writing essays. By carefully chosen questions and through directed work, I have hoped to give the student an opportunity to make his written answers or responses the center of class discussions. Used together, the three books will supply sufficient, but I trust not suffocating, apparatus for both students and teachers.

Contents * *Preface*

* *Poetry*

Contents * *Stories*

Contents * Drama

POEMS

EDWARD

"Why dois your brand sae drap wi bluid,
        Edward, Edward,
Why dois your brand sae drap wi bluid,
  And why sae sad gang yee O?"
"O I hae killed my hauke sae guid,
        Mither, mither,
O I hae killed my hauke sae guid,
  And I had nae mair bot hee O."

"Your haukis bluid was nevir sae reid,
        Edward, Edward,   10
Your haukis bluid was nevir sae reid,
  My deir son I tell thee O."
"O I hae killed my reid-roan steid,
        Mither, mither,
O I hae killed my reid-roan steid,
  That erst was sae fair and frie O."

"Your steid was auld, and ye hae gat mair,
        Edward, Edward,
Your steid was auld, and ye hae gat mair,
  Sum other dule° ye drie° O."   20
"O I hae killed my fadir deir,
        Mither, mither,
O I hae killed my fadir deir,
  Alas, and wae is mee O!"

"And whatten penance wul ye drie for that,
        Edward, Edward?
And whatten penance will ye drie for that?
  My deir son, now tell me O."
"Ile set my feit in yonder boat,
        Mither, mither,   30
Ile set my feit in yonder boat,
  And Ile fare ovir the sea O."

20. **dule,** grief. **drie,** suffer.

"And what wul ye doe wi your towirs and your ha,
    Edward, Edward?
And what wul ye doe wi your towirs and your ha,
    That were sae fair to see O?"
"Ile let thame stand tul they doun fa,
    Mither, mither,
Ile let thame stand tul they doun fa,
    For here nevir mair maun° I bee O."   40

"And what wul ye leive to your bairns and your wife,
    Edward, Edward?
And what wul ye leive to your bairns and your wife,
    Whan ye gang ovir the sea O?"
"The warldis room, late° them beg thrae° life,
    Mither, mither,
The warldis room, late them beg thrae life,
    For thame nevir mair wul I see O."

"And what wul ye leive to your ain mither deir,
    Edward, Edward?   50
And what wul ye leive to your ain mither deir?
    My deir son, now tell me O."
"The curse of hell frae me sall ye beir,
    Mither, mither,
The curse of hell frae me sall ye beir,
    Sic° counseils ye gave to me O."

1552?-1599
EDMUND
SPENSER * Amoretti

XV. Ye Tradefull Merchants
That with Weary Toyle

Ye tradefull Merchants that with weary toyle,
    do seeke most pretious things to make your gain:
and both the Indias of their treasures spoile,
    what needeth you to seeke so farre in vaine?
For loe my love doth in her selfe containe
    all this worlds riches that may farre be found,

40. maun, must. 45. late, let. thrae, through. 56. Sic, such.

if Saphyres, loe her eies be Saphyres plaine,
if Rubies, loe hir lips be Rubies sound:
If Pearles, hir teeth be pearles both pure and round;
if Yvorie, her forhead yvory weene;°   10
if Gold, her locks are finest gold on ground;°
if silver, her faire hands are silver sheene:
But that which fairest is, but few behold,
her mind adornd with vertues manifold.

LXXV. One Day I Wrote Her Name
upon the Strand

One day I wrote her name upon the strand,
  but came the waves and washed it away:
  agayne I wrote it with a second hand,
  but came the tyde, and made my paynes his pray.
Vayne man, sayd she, that doest in vaine assay,
  a mortall thing so to immortalize,
  for I my selve shall lyke to this decay,
  and eek my name bee wyped out lykewize.
Not so, (quod I) let her baser things devize
  to dy in dust, but you shall live by fame: 10
  my verse your vertues rare shall eternize,
  and in the hevens wryte your glorious name.
Where whenas death shall all the world subdew,
  our love shall live, and later life renew.

1564-1616
WILLIAM
SHAKESPEARE * The Sonnets

XVIII. Shall I Compare Thee
to a Summer's Day?

Shall I compare thee to a summer's day?
Thou art more lovely and more temperate.
Rough winds do shake the darling buds of May,
And summer's lease hath all too short a date.
Sometime too hot the eye of heaven shines,

10. **weene,** might be considered.   11. **on ground,** on earth; possibly in earth—a reference
to gold as ore; or perhaps gold against the background of a tapestry.

And often is his gold complexion dimm'd;
And every fair from fair sometime declines,
By chance or nature's changing course untrimm'd.°
But thy eternal summer shall not fade,
Nor lose possession of that fair thou owest;° 10
Nor shall Death brag thou wander'st in his shade,
When in eternal lines to time thou growest.
   So long as men can breathe or eyes can see,
   So long lives this and this gives life to thee.

XXX. When to the Sessions of Sweet Silent Thought

When to the sessions of sweet silent thought
I summon up remembrance of things past,
I sigh the lack of many a thing I sought,
And with old woes new wail my dear time's waste.
Then can I drown an eye, unused to flow,
For precious friends hid in death's dateless night,
And weep afresh love's long since cancell'd woe,
And moan the expense of many a vanish'd sight.
Then can I grieve at grievances foregone,
And heavily from woe to woe tell o'er 10
The sad account of fore-bemoaned moan,
Which I new pay as if not paid before.
   But if the while I think on thee, dear friend,
   All losses are restored and sorrows end.

LXVI. Tired with All These, for Restful Death I Cry

Tired with all these, for restful death I cry,
As, to behold desert° a beggar born,
And needy nothing trimm'd in jollity,°
And purest faith unhappily forsworn,
And gilded honour shamefully misplaced,
And maiden virtue rudely strumpeted,
And right perfection wrongfully disgraced,
And strength by limping sway disabled,
And art made tongue-tied by authority,
And folly, doctor-like, controlling skill, 10

8. **untrimm'd,** stripped of ornaments. 10. **owest,** ownest.
2. **desert,** those who are deserving because of merit. 3. **jollity,** finery.

And simple truth miscall'd simplicity,°
And captive good attending captain ill.
Tired with all these, from these would I be gone,
Save that, to die, I leave my love alone.

CXVI. Let Me Not to the Marriage of True Minds

Let me not to the marriage of true minds
Admit impediments. Love is not love
Which alters when it alteration finds,
Or bends with the remover to remove.
O, no! it is an ever-fixed mark
That looks on tempests and is never shaken;
It is the star to every wandering bark,
Whose worth's unknown, although his height be taken.
Love's not Time's fool, though rosy lips and cheeks
Within his bending sickle's compass come.   10
Love alters not with his brief hours and weeks,
But bears it out even to the edge of doom.
   If this be error and upon me proved,
   I never writ, nor no man ever loved.

CXXX. My Mistress' Eyes Are Nothing Like the Sun

My mistress' eyes are nothing like the sun;
Coral is far more red than her lips' red;
If snow be white, why then her breasts are dun;
If hairs be wires, black wires grow on her head.
I have seen roses damask'd, red and white,
But no such roses see I in her cheeks;
And in some perfumes is there more delight
Than in the breath that from my mistress reeks.
I love to hear her speak, yet well I know
That music hath a far more pleasing sound.   10
I grant I never saw a goddess go;
My mistress, when she walks, treads on the ground.
   And yet, by heaven, I think my love as rare
   As any she belied with false compare.

11. **simplicity,** silliness, folly.

CXLVI. *Poor Soul, the Centre*
of My Sinful Earth

Poor soul, the centre of my sinful earth,
[Thrall to]° these rebel powers that thee array,
Why dost thou pine within and suffer dearth,
Painting thy outward walls so costly gay?
Why so large cost, having so short a lease,
Dost thou upon thy fading mansion spend?
Shall worms, inheritors of this excess,
Eat up thy charge? Is this thy body's end?
Then, soul, live thou upon thy servant's loss,
And let that pine to aggravate thy store;   10
Buy terms divine in selling hours of dross;
Within be fed, without be rich no more.
  So shalt thou feed on Death, that feeds on men,
  And Death once dead, there 's no more dying then.

1572?-1631
JOHN
DONNE * The Canonization

For Godsake hold your tongue, and let me love,
  Or chide my palsie, or my gout,
My five gray haires, or ruin'd fortune flout,
  With wealth your state, your minde with Arts improve,
    Take you a course, get you a place,
    Observe his honour, or his grace,
Or the Kings reall, or his stamped face°
  Contemplate, what you will, approve,
  So you will let me love.

Alas, alas, who's injur'd by my love?   10
  What merchants ships have my sighs drown'd?
Who saies my teares have overflow'd his ground?
  When did my colds a forward spring remove?
    When did the heats which my veines fill
    Adde one more to the plaguie Bill?°

  2. [**Thrall to**], a conjectural reading for a misprint in the sources of the text of this sonnet.

  7. **stamped face,** face stamped on coins. 15. **plaguie Bill,** a list of deaths caused by the plague.

Soldiers finde warres, and Lawyers finde out still
　　Litigious men, which quarrels move,
　　Though she and I do love.

Call us what you will, wee are made such by love;
　　Call her one, mee another flye,
We'are Tapers too, and at our owne cost die,
　　And wee in us finde the'Eagle and the Dove.°
　　　The Phoenix ridle hath more wit
　　　By us, we two being one, are it.
So to one neutrall thing both sexes fit,
　　Wee dye and rise the same, and prove
　　Mysterious by this love.

Wee can dye by it, if not live by love,
　　And if unfit for tombes and hearse
Our legend bee, it will be fit for verse;
　　And if no peece of Chronicle wee prove,
　　　We'll build in sonnets pretty roomes;
　　　As well a well wrought urne becomes
The greatest ashes, as halfe-acre tombes,
　　And by these hymnes, all shall approve
　　Us *Canoniz'd* for Love:

And thus invoke us; You whom reverend love
　　Made one anothers hermitage;
You, to whom love was peace, that now is rage;
　　Who did the whole worlds soule contract, and drove
　　　Into the glasses of your eyes
　　　So made such mirrors, and such spies,
That they did all to you epitomize,
　　Countries, Townes, Courts: Beg from above
　　A patterne of your love!

A Valediction: forbidding mourning

As virtuous men passe mildly away,
　　And whisper to their soules, to goe,
Whilst some of their sad friends doe say,
　　The breath goes now, and some say, no:

22. **the' Eagle and the Dove,** variously interpreted; a paradoxical mingling of strength, fierceness, wisdom, and perhaps love with peace, purity, and constancy.

So let us melt, and make no noise,
    No teare-floods, nor sigh-tempests move,
T'were prophanation of our joyes
    To tell the layetie our love.

Moving of th'earth brings harmes and feares,
    Men reckon what it did and meant,
But trepidation of the spheares,
    Though greater farre, is innocent.°

Dull sublunary lovers love
    (Whose soule is sense) cannot admit
Absence, because it doth remove
    Those things which elemented° it.

But we by a love, so much refin'd,
    That our selves know not what it is,
Inter-assured of the mind,
    Care lesse, eyes, lips, and hands to misse.

Our two soules therefore, which are one,
    Though I must goe, endure not yet
A breach, but an expansion,
    Like gold to ayery thinnesse beate.

If they be two, they are two so
    As stiffe twin compasses are two,
Thy soule the fixt foot, makes no show
    To move, but doth, if the'other doe.

And though it in the center sit,
    Yet when the other far doth rome,
It leanes, and hearkens after it,
    And growes erect, as that comes home.

Such wilt thou be to mee, who must
    Like th'other foot, obliquely runne;
Thy firmnes makes my circle just,
    And makes me end, where I begunne.

9-12. **Moving . . . innocent.** This stanza contrasts earthquakes and vast, yet harmless, movements of the axis of the earth. 16. **elemented,** composed.

Death Be Not Proud

Death be not proud, though some have called thee
Mighty and dreadfull, for, thou art not soe,
For, those, whom thou think'st, thou dost overthrow,
Die not, poore death, nor yet canst thou kill mee.
From rest and sleepe, which but thy pictures bee,
Much pleasure, then from thee, much more must flow,
And soonest our best men with thee doe goe,
Rest of their bones, and soules deliverie.
Thou art slave to Fate, Chance, kings, and desperate men,
And dost with poyson, warre, and sicknesse dwell,   10
And poppie, or charmes can make us sleepe as well,
And better then thy stroake; why swell'st thou then?
One short sleepe past, wee wake eternally,
And death shall be no more; death, thou shalt die.

A Hymne to God the Father

1

Wilt thou forgive that sinne where I begunne,
  Which was my sin, though it were done before?
Wilt thou forgive that sinne; through which I runne,
  And do run still: though still I do deplore?
    When thou hast done, thou hast not done,
        For, I have more.

2

Wilt thou forgive that sinne which I have wonne
  Others to sinne? and, made my sinne their doore?
Wilt thou forgive that sinne which I did shunne
  A yeare, or two: but wallowed in, a score?   10
    When thou hast done, thou hast not done,
        For I have more.

3

I have a sinne of feare, that when I have spunne
  My last thred, I shall perish on the shore;
But sweare by thy selfe, that at my death thy sonne
  Shall shine as he shines now, and heretofore;
    And, having done that, Thou hast done,
        I feare no more.

John Donne   11

1593-1633
GEORGE
HERBERT * The Collar

I struck the board, and cry'd, No more.
              I will abroad.
    What? shall I ever sigh and pine?
My lines and life are free; free as the rode,
    Loose as the winde, as large as store.
           Shall I be still in suit?°
    Have I no harvest but a thorn
    To let me bloud, and not restore
What I have lost with cordiall fruit?
              Sure there was wine   10
Before my sighs did drie it: there was corn
        Before my tears did drown it.
    Is the yeare onely lost to me?
           Have I no bayes to crown it?
No flowers, no garlands gay? all blasted?
              All wasted?
    Not so, my heart: but there is fruit,
              And thou hast hands.
    Recover all thy sigh-blown age
On double pleasures: leave thy cold dispute   20
Of what is fit, and not. Forsake thy cage,
              Thy rope of sands,
Which pettie thoughts have made, and made to thee
    Good cable, to enforce and draw,
              And be thy law,
    While thou didst wink and wouldst not see.
           Away; take heed:
              I will abroad.
Call in thy deaths head there: tie up thy fears.
           He that forbears   30
    To suit and serve his need,
        Deserves his load.
But as I rav'd and grew more fierce and wilde
              At every word,
Me thoughts I heard one calling, *Child!*
           And I reply'd, *My Lord.*

6. **in suit,** waiting for favors or attention.

The Pulley

When God at first made man,
Having a glasse of blessings standing by;
Let us (said he) poure on him all we can:
Let the worlds riches, which dispersed lie,
    Contract into a span.

So strength first made a way;
Then beautie flow'd, then wisdome, honour, pleasure:
When almost all was out, God made a stay,
Perceiving that alone of all his treasure
    Rest in the bottome lay.   10

For if I should (said he)
Bestow this jewell also on my creature,
He would adore my gifts in stead of me,
And rest in Nature, not the God of Nature:
    So both should losers be.

Yet let him keep the rest,
But keep them with repining restlesnesse:
Let him be rich and wearie, that at least,
If goodnesse leade him not, yet wearinesse
    May tosse him to my breast.   20

1608-1674
JOHN
MILTON * The Sonnets

VII. How Soon Hath Time

How soon hath Time the suttle theef of youth,
   Stoln on his wing my three and twentieth yeer!
   My hasting dayes flie on with full career,
   But my late spring no bud or blossom shew'th.
Perhaps my semblance might deceive the truth,
   That I to manhood am arriv'd so near,
   And inward ripenes doth much less appear,
   That som more timely-happy spirits indu'th.°

8. **indu'th,** endoweth.

Yet be it less or more, or soon or slow,
   It shall be still in strictest measure eev'n,   10
   To that same lot, however mean or high,
Toward which Time leads me, and the will of Heav'n;
   All is, if I have grace to use it so,
   As ever in my great task Masters eye.

XIX. *When I Consider How My Light Is Spent*

When I consider how my light is spent,
   Ere half my days, in this dark world and wide,
   And that one Talent° which is death to hide,
   Lodg'd with me useless, though my Soul more bent
To serve therewith my Maker, and present
   My true account, least he returning chide,
   Doth God exact day-labour, light deny'd,
   I fondly° ask; But patience to prevent
That murmur, soon replies, God doth not need
   Either man's work or his own gifts, who best   10
   Bear his milde yoak, they serve him best, his State
Is Kingly. Thousands at his bidding speed
   And post o're Land and Ocean without rest:
   They also serve who only stand and waite.

XXIII. *Methought I Saw My Late Espoused Saint*

Methought I saw my late espoused Saint
   Brought to me like *Alcestis* from the grave,
   Whom *Joves* great Son to her glad Husband gave,
   Rescu'd from death by force though pale and faint.
Mine as whom washt from spot of child-bed taint,
   Purification in the old Law did save,°
   And such, as yet once more I trust to have
   Full sight of her in Heaven without restraint,
Came vested all in white, pure as her mind:
   Her face was vail'd, yet to my fancied sight,   10
   Love, sweetness, goodness, in her person shin'd
So clear, as in no face with more delight.
   But O as to embrace me she enclin'd,
   I wak'd, she fled, and day brought back my night.

3. **Talent.** Compare the parable of the talents in Matt. 25: 14-30.   8. **fondly,** foolishly.
5-6. **Mine . . . did save.** Compare Lev., 12.

1621-1678
ANDREW
MARVELL * *To his Coy Mistress*

Had we but World enough, and Time,
This coyness Lady were no crime.
We would sit down, and think which way
To walk, and pass our long Loves Day.
Thou by the *Indian Ganges* side
Should'st Rubies find: I by the Tide
Of *Humber*° would complain. I would
Love you ten years before the Flood:
And you should if you please refuse
Till the Conversion of the *Jews.*°   10
My vegetable Love should grow
Vaster than Empires, and more slow.
An hundred years should go to praise
Thine Eyes, and on thy Forehead Gaze.
Two hundred to adore each Breast:
But thirty thousand to the rest.
An Age at least to every part,
And the last Age should show your Heart.
For Lady you deserve this State;
Nor would I love at lower rate.   20
    But at my back I alwaies hear
Times winged Charriot hurrying near:
And yonder all before us lye
Desarts of vast Eternity.
Thy Beauty shall no more be found;
Nor, in thy marble Vault, shall sound
My ecchoing Song: then Worms shall try
That long preserv'd Virginity:
And your quaint Honour turn to dust;
And into ashes all my Lust.   30
The Grave's a fine and private place,
But none I think do there embrace.
    Now therefore, while the youthful hew
Sits on thy skin like morning dew,
And while thy willing Soul transpires
At every pore with instant Fires,

7. **Humber,** a little stream in Hull, Marvell's home town.   10. **the Conversion of the *Jews*,** considered to occur right before the Last Judgment.

Now let us sport us while we may;
And now, like am'rous birds of prey,
Rather at once our Time devour,
Than languish in his slow-chapt° pow'r.   40
Let us roll all our Strength, and all
Our sweetness, up into one Ball:
And tear our Pleasures with rough strife,
Thorough the Iron gates of Life.
Thus, though we cannot make our Sun
Stand still, yet we will make him run.

1645?-1729

EDWARD
TAYLOR * Huswifery

Make me, O Lord, thy Spining Wheele compleate.
  Thy Holy Worde my Distaff make for mee.
Make mine Affections thy Swift Flyers° neate
  And make my Soule thy holy Spoole to bee.
  My Conversation make to be thy Reele
  And reele the yarn thereon spun of thy Wheele.

Make me thy Loome then, knit therein this Twine:
  And make thy Holy Spirit, Lord, winde quills:
Then weave the Web thyselfe. The yarn is fine.
  Thine Ordinances make my Fulling Mills.°   10
  Then dy the same in Heavenly Colours Choice,
  All pinkt with Varnisht° Flowers of Paradise.

Then cloath therewith mine Understanding, Will,
  Affections, Judgment, Conscience, Memory;
My Words, and Actions, that their shine may fill
  My wayes with glory and thee glorify.
  Then mine apparell shall display before yee
  That I am Cloathd in Holy robes for glory.

---

40. **slow-chapt,** a reference to the movement of the jaws, and hence to chewing.
3. **Flyers,** a part of the spinning wheel, revolving above a spindle which guides and twists the yarn. 10. **Fulling Mills.** In these mills the cloth is cleansed by fuller's earth, a clay-like substance. The process includes the shrinking and thickening of the cloth. 12. **Varnisht,** smooth and glossy.

JONATHAN
SWIFT * A Satirical Elegy on the Death
of a Late Famous General

His Grace!° impossible! what, dead!
Of old age too, and in his bed!
And could that Mighty Warrior fall?
And so inglorious, after all!
Well, since he's gone, no matter how,
The last loud trump must wake him now:
And, trust me, as the noise grows stronger,
He'd wish to sleep a little longer.
And could he be indeed so old
As by the news-papers we're told?   10
Threescore, I think, is pretty high;
'Twas time in conscience he should die.
This world he cumber'd long enough;
He burnt his candle to the snuff;
And that's the reason, some folks think,
He left behind *so great a s[tin]k.*
Behold his funeral appears,
Nor widow's sighs, nor orphan's tears,
Wont at such times each heart to pierce,
Attend the progress of his herse.   20
But what of that, his friends may say,
He had those honours in his day.
True to his profit and his pride,
He made them weep before he dy'd.

Come hither, all ye empty things,
Ye bubbles rais'd by breath of Kings;
Who float upon the tide of state,
Come hither, and behold your fate.
Let pride be taught by this rebuke,
How very mean a thing's a Duke;   30
From all his ill-got honours flung,
Turn'd to that dirt from whence he sprung.

1. **Grace,** John Churchill, first Duke of Marlborough (1650-1722).

1757-1827

WILLIAM
BLAKE * Songs of Innocence

THE LITTLE BLACK BOY

My mother bore me in the southern wild,
And I am black, but O! my soul is white;
White as an angel is the English child,
But I am black, as if bereav'd of light.

My mother taught me underneath a tree,
And sitting down before the heat of day,
She took me on her lap and kissed me,
And pointing to the east, began to say:

"Look on the rising sun: there God does live,
And gives his light, and gives his heat away;   10
And flowers and trees and beasts and men receive
Comfort in morning, joy in the noonday.

"And we are put on earth a little space,
That we may learn to bear the beams of love;
And these black bodies and this sunburnt face
Is but a cloud, and like a shady grove.

"For when our souls have learn'd the heat to bear,
The cloud will vanish; we shall hear his voice,
Saying: 'Come out from the grove, my love & care,
And round my golden tent like lambs rejoice.' "   20

Thus did my mother say, and kissed me;
And thus I say to little English boy.
When I from black and he from white cloud free,
And round the tent of God like lambs we joy,

I'll shade him from the heat, till he can bear
To lean in joy upon our father's knee;
And then I'll stand and stroke his silver hair,
And be like him, and he will then love me.

HOLY THURSDAY

'Twas on a Holy Thursday, their innocent faces clean,
The children walking two & two, in red & blue & green,

Grey-headed beadles walk'd before, with wands as white as snow,
Till into the high dome of Paul's° they like Thames' waters flow.

O what a multitude they seem'd, these flowers of London town!
Seated in companies they sit with radiance all their own.
The hum of multitudes was there, but multitudes of lambs,
Thousands of little boys & girls raising their innocent hands.

Now like a mighty wind they raise to heaven the voice of song,
Or like harmonious thunderings the seats of Heaven among.   10
Beneath them sit the aged men, wise guardians of the poor;
Then cherish pity, lest you drive an angel from your door.

Songs of Experience

HOLY THURSDAY

Is this a holy thing to see
In a rich and fruitful land,
Babes reduc'd to misery,
Fed with cold and usurous hand?

Is that trembling cry a song?
Can it be a song of joy?
And so many children poor?
It is a land of poverty!

And their sun does never shine,
And their fields are bleak & bare,   10
And their ways are fill'd with thorns:
It is eternal winter there.

For where-e'er the sun does shine,
And where-e'er the rain does fall,
Babe can never hunger there,
Nor poverty the mind appall.

THE CLOD AND THE PEBBLE

"Love seeketh not Itself to please,
Nor for itself hath any care,

4. **Paul's,** St. Paul's Cathedral.

But for another gives its ease,
And builds a Heaven in Hell's despair."

So sung a little Clod of Clay
Trodden with the cattle's feet,
But a Pebble of the brook
Warbled out these metres meet:

"Love seeketh only Self to please,
To bind another to Its delight,   10
Joys in another's loss of ease,
And builds a Hell in Heaven's despite."

A POISON TREE

I was angry with my friend:
I told my wrath, my wrath did end.
I was angry with my foe:
I told it not, my wrath did grow.

And I water'd it in fears,
Night & morning with my tears;
And I sunned it with smiles,
And with soft deceitful wiles.

And it grew both day and night,
Till it bore an apple bright;   10
And my foe beheld it shine,
And he knew that it was mine,

And into my garden stole
When the night had veil'd the pole:
In the morning glad I see
My foe outstretch'd beneath the tree.

1770-1850
WILLIAM
WORDSWORTH * She Dwelt Among the
Untrodden Ways

She dwelt among the untrodden ways
  Beside the springs of Dove,

A Maid whom there were none to praise
  And very few to love:

A violet by a mossy stone
  Half hidden from the eye!
—Fair as a star, when only one
  Is shining in the sky.

She lived unknown, and few could know
  When Lucy ceased to be;
But she is in her grave, and, oh,
  The difference to me!

10

A Slumber Did My Spirit Seal

A slumber did my spirit seal;
  I had no human fears:
She seemed a thing that could not feel
  The touch of earthly years.

No motion has she now, no force;
  She neither hears nor sees;
Rolled round in earth's diurnal course,
  With rocks, and stones, and trees.

The World Is Too Much with Us

The world is too much with us; late and soon,
Getting and spending, we lay waste our powers:
Little we see in Nature that is ours;
We have given our hearts away, a sordid boon!
This Sea that bares her bosom to the moon;
The winds that will be howling at all hours,
And are up-gathered now like sleeping flowers;
For this, for everything, we are out of tune;
It moves us not.—Great God! I'd rather be
A Pagan suckled in a creed outworn;
So might I, standing on this pleasant lea,
Have glimpses that would make me less forlorn;
Have sight of Proteus rising from the sea;
Or hear old Triton blow his wreathèd horn.

10

William Wordsworth 21

Composed upon Westminster Bridge

Earth has not anything to show more fair:
Dull would he be of soul who could pass by
A sight so touching in its majesty:
This City now doth, like a garment, wear
The beauty of the morning; silent, bare,
Ships, towers, domes, theatres, and temples lie
Open unto the fields, and to the sky;
All bright and glittering in the smokeless air.
Never did sun more beautifully steep
In his first splendour, valley, rock, or hill;   10
Ne'er saw I, never felt, a calm so deep!
The river glideth at his own sweet will:
Dear God! the very houses seem asleep;
And all that mighty heart is lying still!

1772-1834
SAMUEL
TAYLOR
COLERIDGE * Kubla Khan

In Xanadu did Kubla Khan
A stately pleasure-dome decree:
Where Alph, the sacred river, ran
Through caverns measureless to man
   Down to a sunless sea.
So twice five miles of fertile ground
With walls and towers were girdled round:
And there were gardens bright with sinuous rills,
Where blossomed many an incense-bearing tree;
And here were forests ancient as the hills,   10
Enfolding sunny spots of greenery.

But oh! that deep romantic chasm which slanted
Down the green hill athwart a cedarn cover!
A savage place! as holy and enchanted
As e'er beneath a waning moon was haunted
By woman wailing for her demon-lover!
And from this chasm, with ceaseless turmoil seething,
As if this earth in fast thick pants were breathing,
A mighty fountain momently was forced:
Amid whose swift half-intermitted burst   20
Huge fragments vaulted like rebounding hail,

22 Poems

Or chaffy grain beneath the thresher's flail:
And 'mid these dancing rocks at once and ever
It flung up momently the sacred river.
Five miles meandering with a mazy motion
Through wood and dale the sacred river ran,
Then reached the caverns measureless to man,
And sank in tumult to a lifeless ocean:
And 'mid this tumult Kubla heard from far
Ancestral voices prophesying war!   30
    The shadow of the dome of pleasure
    Floated midway on the waves;
    Where was heard the mingled measure
    From the fountain and the caves.
It was a miracle of rare device,
A sunny pleasure-dome with caves of ice!

A damsel with a dulcimer
In a vision once I saw:
It was an Abyssinian maid,
And on her dulcimer she played,   40
Singing of Mount Abora.
Could I revive within me
    Her symphony and song,
    To such a deep delight 'twould win me,
That with music loud and long,
I would build that dome in air,
That sunny dome! those caves of ice!
And all who heard should see them there,
And all should cry, Beware! Beware!
His flashing eyes, his floating hair!   50
Weave a circle round him thrice,°
And close your eyes with holy dread,
For he on honey-dew hath fed,
And drunk the milk of Paradise.

GEORGE
GORDON,
LORD BYRON * She Walks in Beauty

She° walks in beauty, like the night
    Of cloudless climes and starry skies;

51. **Weave . . . thrice,** a protection against evil spirits.
1. **She.** Lady Wilmot Horton, Byron's cousin by marriage, inspired this poem when she
appeared at a party in a black mourning dress with sequins.

And all that's best of dark and bright
  Meet in her aspect and her eyes:
Thus mellow'd to that tender light
  Which heaven to gaudy day denies.

One shade the more, one ray the less,
  Had half impair'd the nameless grace
Which waves in every raven tress,
  Or softly lightens o'er her face;
Where thoughts serenely sweet express
  How pure, how dear their dwelling-place.

And on that cheek, and o'er that brow,
  So soft, so calm, yet eloquent,
The smiles that win, the tints that glow,
  But tell of days in goodness spent,
A mind at peace with all below,
  A heart whose love is innocent!

On This Day I Complete
My Thirty-Sixth Year

'Tis time this heart should be unmoved,
  Since others it hath ceased to move:
Yet, though I cannot be beloved,
      Still let me love!

My days are in the yellow leaf;
  The flowers and fruits of love are gone;
The worm, the canker, and the grief
      Are mine alone!

The fire that on my bosom preys
  Is lone as some volcanic isle;
No torch is kindled at its blaze—
      A funeral pile.

The hope, the fear, the jealous care,
  The exalted portion of the pain
And power of love, I cannot share,
      But wear the chain.

But 'tis not *thus*—and 'tis not *here*—
   Such thoughts should shake my soul, nor *now*,
Where glory decks the hero's bier,
   Or binds his brow.   20

The sword, the banner, and the field,
   Glory and Greece, around me see!
The Spartan, borne upon his shield,
   Was not more free.

Awake! (not Greece—she *is* awake!)
   Awake, my spirit! Think through *whom*
Thy life-blood tracks its parent lake,
   And then strike home!

Tread those reviving passions down,
   Unworthy manhood!—unto thee   30
Indifferent should the smile or frown
   Of beauty be.

If thou regrett'st thy youth, *why live?*
   The land of honourable death
Is here:—up to the field, and give
   Away thy breath!

Seek out—less often sought than found—
   A soldier's grave, for thee the best;
Then look around, and choose thy ground,
   And take thy rest.   40

1792-1822
PERCY
BYSSHE
SHELLEY * Sonnet—Ozymandias*

I met a traveller from an antique land
Who said: Two vast and trunkless legs of stone
Stand in the desert. . . Near them, on the sand,
Half sunk, a shattered visage lies, whose frown,

*Ozymandias, the Egyptian king, Ramses II (13th century B.C.).

And wrinkled lip, and sneer of cold command,
Tell that its sculptor well those passions read
Which yet survive, stamped on these lifeless things,
The hand that mocked them and the heart that fed:
And on the pedestal these words appear:
"My name is Ozymandias, king of kings: 10
Look on my works, ye Mighty, and despair!"
Nothing beside remains. Round the decay
Of that colossal wreck, boundless and bare
The lone and level sands stretch far away.

Ode to the West Wind

1

O wild West Wind, thou breath of Autumn's being,
Thou, from whose unseen presence the leaves dead
Are driven, like ghosts from an enchanter fleeing,

Yellow, and black, and pale, and hectic red,
Pestilence-stricken multitudes: O thou,
Who chariotest to their dark wintry bed

The wingèd seeds, where they lie cold and low,
Each like a corpse within its grave, until
Thine azure sister of the Spring shall blow

Her clarion o'er the dreaming earth, and fill   10
(Driving sweet buds like flocks to feed in air)
With living hues and odors plain and hill:

Wild Spirit, which art moving everywhere;
Destroyer and preserver; hear, oh, hear!

2

Thou on whose stream, mid the steep sky's commotion,
Loose clouds like earth's decaying leaves are shed,
Shook from the tangled boughs of Heaven and Ocean,

Angels of rain and lightning: there are spread
On the blue surface of thine aëry surge,
Like the bright hair uplifted from the head   20

Of some fierce Maenad, even from the dim verge
Of the horizon to the zenith's height,
The locks of the approaching storm. Thou dirge

Of the dying year, to which this closing night
Will be the dome of a vast sepulchre,
Vaulted with all thy congregated might

Of vapors, from whose solid atmosphere
Black rain, and fire, and hail will burst: oh, hear!

3
Thou who didst waken from his summer dreams
The blue Mediterranean, where he lay,   30
Lulled by the coil of his crystalline streams,

Beside a pumice isle in Baiae's bay,°
And saw in sleep old palaces and towers
Quivering within the wave's intenser day,

All overgrown with azure moss and flowers
So sweet the sense faints picturing them! thou
For whose path the Atlantic's level powers

Cleave themselves into chasms, while far below
The sea-blooms and the oozy woods which wear
The sapless foliage of the ocean, know   40

Thy voice, and suddenly grow gray with fear,
And tremble and despoil themselves: oh, hear!°

4
If I were a dead leaf thou mightest bear;
If I were a swift cloud to fly with thee;
A wave to pant beneath thy power, and share

The impulse of thy strength, only less free
Than thou, O uncontrollable! If even
I were as in my boyhood, and could be

32. **Baiae's bay,** an ancient resort near Naples. 35-42. Shelley's note: "The phenomenon . . .
is well known to naturalists. The vegetation at the bottom of the sea, of rivers, and of lakes,
sympathizes with that of the land in the change of seasons, and is constantly influenced by the
winds which announce it."

The comrade of thy wanderings over heaven,
As then, when to outstrip thy skiey speed   50
Scarce seemed a vision; I would ne'er have striven

As thus with thee in prayer in my sore need.
Oh, lift me as a wave, a leaf, a cloud!
I fall upon the thorns of life! I bleed!

A heavy weight of hours has chained and bowed
One too like thee: tameless, and swift, and proud.

                    5
Make me thy lyre,° even as the forest is:
What if my leaves are falling like its own!
The tumult of thy mighty harmonies

Will take from both a deep, autumnal tone,   60
Sweet though in sadness. Be thou, Spirit fierce,
My spirit! Be thou me, impetuous one!

Drive my dead thoughts over the universe
Like withered leaves to quicken a new birth!
And, by the incantation of this verse,

Scatter, as from an unextinguished hearth
Ashes and sparks, my words among mankind!
Be through my lips to unawakened earth

The trumpet of a prophecy! O Wind,
If Winter comes, can Spring be far behind?   70

                    To——

Music, when soft voices die,
Vibrates in the memory;
Odours, when sweet violets sicken,
Live within the sense they quicken.

Rose leaves, when the rose is dead,
Are heaped for the belovèd's bed;

57. **lyre,** a reference to the Aeolian harp, an instrument whose strings are played upon by winds. This is a favorite image of some Romantic poets, who see in it the infusion of the divine spirit or the inspiration of the creative mind.

And so thy thoughts, when thou art gone,
Love itself shall slumber on.

1795-1821
JOHN
KEATS * On Seeing the Elgin Marbles*

My spirit is too weak—mortality
  Weighs heavily on me like unwilling sleep,
  And each imagin'd pinnacle and steep
Of godlike hardship tells me I must die
Like a sick Eagle looking at the sky.
  Yet 'tis a gentle luxury to weep
  That I have not the cloudy winds to keep
Fresh for the opening of the morning's eye.
Such dim-conceived glories of the brain
  Bring round the heart an undescribable feud;   10
So do these wonders a most dizzy pain,
  That mingles Grecian grandeur with the rude
Wasting of old Time—with a billowy main—
  A sun—a shadow of a magnitude.

When I Have Fears

When I have fears that I may cease to be
  Before my pen has glean'd my teeming brain,
Before high-piled books, in charact'ry,
  Hold like rich garners the full-ripen'd grain;
When I behold, upon the night's starr'd face,
  Huge cloudy symbols of a high romance,
And think that I may never live to trace
  Their shadows, with the magic hand of chance;
And when I feel, fair creature of an hour,
  That I shall never look upon thee more,   10
Never have relish in the faery power
  Of unreflecting love!—then on the shore
Of the wide world I stand alone, and think
Till love and fame to nothingness do sink.

*The Elgin marbles** are fragments of the frieze and pediment sculptures of the Parthenon. These were sold by Lord Elgin to the British Museum.

Bright Star

Bright star, would I were stedfast as thou art—
  Not in lone splendour hung aloft the night
And watching, with eternal lids apart,
  Like nature's patient, sleepless Eremite,
The moving waters at their priestlike task
  Of pure ablution round earth's human shores,
Or gazing on the new soft fallen mask
  Of snow upon the mountains and the moors—
No—yet still stedfast, still unchangeable,
  Pillow'd upon my fair love's ripening breast,   10
To feel for ever its soft fall and swell,
  Awake for ever in a sweet unrest,
Still, still to hear her tender-taken breath,
And so live ever—or else swoon to death.

Ode to a Nightingale

1

My heart aches, and a drowsy numbness pains
  My sense, as though of hemlock I had drunk,
Or emptied some dull opiate to the drains
  One minute past, and Lethe-wards had sunk:
'Tis not through envy of thy happy lot,
  But being too happy in thine happiness,—
    That thou, light-winged Dryad of the trees,
      In some melodious plot
  Of beechen green, and shadows numberless,
    Singest of summer in full-throated ease.   10

2

O, for a draught of vintage! that hath been
  Cool'd a long age in the deep-delved earth,
Tasting of Flora and the country green,
  Dance, and Provençal song, and sunburnt mirth!
O for a beaker full of the warm South,
  Full of the true, the blushful Hippocrene,
    With beaded bubbles winking at the brim,
      And purple-stained mouth;
  That I might drink, and leave the world unseen,
    And with thee fade away into the forest dim: 20

3

Fade far away, dissolve, and quite forget
  What thou among the leaves hast never known,

The weariness, the fever, and the fret
  Here, where men sit and hear each other groan;
Where palsy shakes a few, sad, last gray hairs,
  Where youth grows pale, and spectre-thin, and dies;
    Where but to think is to be full of sorrow
      And leaden-eyed despairs,
  Where Beauty cannot keep her lustrous eyes,
    Or new Love pine at them beyond to-morrow.   30
                    4
Away! away! for I will fly to thee,
  Not charioted by Bacchus and his pards,
But on the viewless wings of Poesy,
  Though the dull brain perplexes and retards:
Already with thee! tender is the night,
  And haply the Queen-Moon is on her throne,
    Cluster'd around by all her starry Fays;
      But here there is no light,
  Save what from heaven is with the breezes blown
    Through verdurous glooms and winding mossy ways.   40
                    5
I cannot see what flowers are at my feet,
  Nor what soft incense hangs upon the boughs,
But, in embalmed° darkness, guess each sweet
  Wherewith the seasonable month endows
The grass, the thicket, and the fruit-tree wild;
  White hawthorn, and the pastoral eglantine;
    Fast fading violets cover'd up in leaves;
      And mid-May's eldest child,
  The coming musk-rose, full of dewy wine,
    The murmurous haunt of flies on summer eves.   50
                    6
Darkling I listen; and, for many a time
  I have been half in love with easeful Death,
Call'd him soft names in many a mused rhyme,
  To take into the air my quiet breath;
Now more than ever seems it rich to die,
  To cease upon the midnight with no pain,
    While thou art pouring forth thy soul abroad
      In such an ecstasy!
  Still wouldst thou sing, and I have ears in vain—
    To thy high requiem become a sod.   60
                    7
Thou wast not born for death, immortal Bird!
  No hungry generations tread thee down;

43. **embalmed,** perfumed.

The voice I hear this passing night was heard
  In ancient days by emperor and clown:
Perhaps the self-same song that found a path
  Through the sad heart of Ruth, when, sick for home,
    She stood in tears amid the alien corn;
      The same that oft-times hath
Charm'd magic casements, opening on the foam
Of perilous seas, in faery lands forlorn.   70

                        8
Forlorn! the very word is like a bell
  To toll me back from thee to my sole self!
Adieu! the fancy cannot cheat so well
  As she is fam'd to do, deceiving elf.
Adieu! adieu! thy plaintive anthem fades
  Past the near meadows, over the still stream,
    Up the hill-side; and now 'tis buried deep
      In the next valley-glades:
Was it a vision, or a waking dream?
Fled is that music:—Do I wake or sleep?   80

              Ode on a Grecian Urn
                        1
Thou still unravish'd bride of quietness,
  Thou foster-child of silence and slow time,
Sylvan historian, who canst thus express
  A flowery tale more sweetly than our rhyme:
What leaf-fring'd legend haunts about thy shape
  Of deities or mortals, or of both,
    In Tempe or the dales of Arcady?
What men or gods are these? What maidens loth?
  What mad pursuit? What struggle to escape?
    What pipes and timbrels? What wild ecstasy?   10

                        2
Heard melodies are sweet, but those unheard
  Are sweeter; therefore, ye soft pipes, play on;
Not to the sensual ear, but, more endear'd,
  Pipe to the spirit ditties of no tone:
Fair youth, beneath the trees, thou canst not leave
  Thy song, nor ever can those trees be bare;
    Bold Lover, never, never canst thou kiss,
Though winning near the goal—yet, do not grieve;
  She cannot fade, though thou hast not thy bliss,
    For ever wilt thou love, and she be fair!   20

3

Ah, happy, happy boughs! that cannot shed
    Your leaves, nor ever bid the Spring adieu;
And, happy melodist, unwearied,
    For ever piping songs for ever new;
More happy love! more happy, happy love!
    For ever warm and still to be enjoy'd,
        For ever panting, and for ever young;
All breathing human passion far above,
    That leaves a heart high-sorrowful and cloy'd,
        A burning forehead, and a parching tongue.   30

4

Who are these coming to the sacrifice?
    To what green altar, O mysterious priest,
Lead'st thou that heifer lowing at the skies,
    And all her silken flanks with garlands drest?
What little town by river or sea shore,
    Or mountain-built with peaceful citadel,
        Is emptied of this folk, this pious morn?
And, little town, thy streets for evermore
    Will silent be; and not a soul to tell
        Why thou art desolate, can e'er return.   40

5

O Attic shape! Fair attitude! with brede°
    Of marble men and maidens overwrought,
With forest branches and the trodden weed;
    Thou, silent form, dost tease us out of thought
As doth eternity: Cold Pastoral!
    When old age shall this generation waste,
        Thou shalt remain, in midst of other woe
Than ours, a friend to man, to whom thou say'st,
    "Beauty is truth, truth beauty,"—that is all
        Ye know on earth, and all ye need to know.   50

To Autumn

1

Season of mists and mellow fruitfulness,
    Close bosom-friend of the maturing sun;
Conspiring with him how to load and bless
    With fruit the vines that round the thatch-eves run;
To bend with apples the moss'd cottage-trees,
    And fill all fruit with ripeness to the core;

41. **brede,** embroidery.

John Keats 33

To swell the gourd, and plump the hazel shells
With a sweet kernel; to set budding more,
   And still more, later flowers for the bees,
   Until they think warm days will never cease,   10
      For Summer has o'er-brimm'd their clammy cells.

                    2
Who hath not seen thee oft amid thy store?
   Sometimes whoever seeks abroad may find
Thee sitting careless on a granary floor,
   Thy hair soft-lifted by the winnowing wind;
Or on a half-reap'd furrow sound asleep,
   Drows'd with the fume of poppies, while thy hook
      Spares the next swath and all its twined flowers:
And sometimes like a gleaner thou dost keep   ˉ
   Steady thy laden head across a brook;   20
   Or by a cyder-press, with patient look,
      Thou watchest the last oozings hours by hours.

                    3
Where are the songs of Spring? Ay, where are they?
   Think not of them, thou hast thy music too,—
While barred clouds bloom the soft-dying day,
   And touch the stubble-plains with rosy hue;
Then in a wailful choir the small gnats mourn
   Among the river shallows, borne aloft
      Or sinking as the light wind lives or dies;
And full-grown lambs loud bleat from hilly bourn;   30
   Hedge-crickets sing; and now with treble soft
The red-breast whistles from a garden-croft;
   And gathering swallows twitter in the skies.

1803-1882
RALPH
WALDO
EMERSON * Days

Daughters of Time, the hypocritic Days,
Muffled and dumb like barefoot dervishes,
And marching single in an endless file,
Bring diadems and fagots in their hands.
To each they offer gifts after his will,
Bread, kingdoms, stars, and sky that holds them all.

I, in my pleached garden, watched the pomp,
Forgot my morning wishes, hastily
Took a few herbs and apples, and the Day
Turned and departed silent. I, too late,   10
Under her solemn fillet saw the scorn.

1809-1849
EDGAR
ALLAN
POE * Sonnet—To Science

Science! true daughter of Old Time thou art!
   Who alterest all things with thy peering eyes.
Why preyest thou thus upon the poet's heart,
   Vulture, whose wings are dull realities?
How should he love thee? or how deem thee wise,
   Who wouldst not leave him in his wandering
To seek for treasure in the jewelled skies,
   Albeit he soared with an undaunted wing?
Hast thou not dragged Diana from her car?
   And driven the Hamadryad from the wood   10
To seek a shelter in some happier star?
   Hast thou not torn the Naiad from her flood,
The Elfin from the green grass, and from me
The summer dream beneath the tamarind tree?

Israfel*

In Heaven a spirit doth dwell
   "Whose heart-strings are a lute;"
None sing so wildly well
As the angel Israfel,
And the giddy stars (so legends tell)
Ceasing their hymns, attend the spell
   Of his voice, all mute.

Tottering above
   In her highest noon,

Israfel. Poe's motto: "And the angel Israfel, whose heart-strings are a lute, and who has the
sweetest voice of all God's creatures.—Koran."

The enamoured moon
Blushes with love,
    While, to listen, the red levin
    (With the rapid Pleiads, even,
    Which were seven,)
    Pauses in Heaven.

And they say (the starry choir
    And the other listening things)
That Israfeli's fire
Is owing to that lyre
    By which he sits and sings—
The trembling living wire
Of those unusual strings.

But the skies that angel trod,
    Where deep thoughts are a duty—
Where Love's a grown-up God—
    Where the Houri glances are
Imbued with all the beauty
    Which we worship in a star.

Therefore, thou art not wrong,
    Israfeli, who despisest
An unimpassioned song;
To thee the laurels belong,
    Best bard, because the wisest!
Merrily live, and long!

The ecstasies above
    With thy burning measures suit—
Thy grief, thy joy, thy hate, thy love,
    With the fervour of thy lute—
    Well may the stars be mute!

Yes, Heaven is thine; but this
    Is a world of sweets and sours;
    Our flowers are merely—flowers,
And the shadow of thy perfect bliss
    Is the sunshine of ours.

If I could dwell
Where Israfel
    Hath dwelt, and he where I,

He might not sing so wildly well
  A mortal melody,
While a bolder note than this might swell   50
  From my lyre within the sky.

The City in the Sea

Lo! Death has reared himself a throne
In a strange city lying alone
Far down within the dim West,
Where the good and the bad and the worst and the best
Have gone to their eternal rest.
There shrines and palaces and towers
(Time-eaten towers that tremble not!)
Resemble nothing that is ours.
Around, by lifting winds forgot,
Resignedly beneath the sky   10
The melancholy waters lie.

No rays from the holy heaven come down
On the long night-time of that town;
But light from out the lurid sea
Streams up the turrets silently—
Gleams up the pinnacles far and free—
Up domes—up spires—up kingly halls—
Up fanes—up Babylon-like walls—
Up shadowy long-forgotten bowers
Of sculptured ivy and stone flowers—   20
Up many and many a marvellous shrine
Whose wreathéd friezes intertwine
The viol, the violet, and the vine.
Resignedly beneath the sky
The melancholy waters lie.
So blend the turrets and shadows there
That all seem pendulous in air,
While from a proud tower in the town
Death looks gigantically down.

There open fanes and gaping graves   30
Yawn level with the luminous waves;
But not the riches there that lie
In each idol's diamond eye—

Not the gaily-jewelled dead
Tempt the waters from their bed;
For no ripples curl, alas!
Along that wilderness of glass
No swellings tell that winds may be
Upon some far-off happier sea—
No heavings hint that winds have been   40
On seas less hideously serene.

But lo, a stir is in the air!
The wave—there is a movement there!
As if the towers had thrust aside,
In slightly sinking, the dull tide—
As if their tops had feebly given
A void within the filmy Heaven.
The waves have now a redder glow—
The hours are breathing faint and low—
And when, amid no earthly moans,   50
Down, down that town shall settle hence,
Hell, rising from a thousand thrones,
Shall do it reverence.

1809-1892
ALFRED,
LORD
TENNYSON * *Ulysses*

It little profits that an idle king,
By this still hearth, among these barren crags,
Match'd with an aged wife, I mete and dole
Unequal laws unto a savage race,
That hoard, and sleep, and feed, and know not me.
I cannot rest from travel; I will drink
Life to the lees. All times I have enjoy'd
Greatly, have suffer'd greatly, both with those
That loved me, and alone; on shore, and when
Thro' scudding drifts the rainy Hyades   10
Vext the dim sea. I am become a name;
For always roaming with a hungry heart
Much have I seen and known,—cities of men

And manners, climates, councils, governments,
Myself not least, but honor'd of them all,—
And drunk delight of battle with my peers,
Far on the ringing plains of windy Troy.
I am a part of all that I have met;
Yet all experience is an arch wherethro'
Gleams that untravell'd world whose margin fades   20
For ever and for ever when I move.
How dull it is to pause, to make an end,
To rust unburnish'd, not to shine in use!
As tho' to breathe were life! Life piled on life
Were all too little, and of one to me
Little remains; but every hour is saved
From that eternal silence, something more,
A bringer of new things; and vile it were
For some three suns to store and hoard myself,
And this gray spirit yearning in desire   30
To follow knowledge like a sinking star,
Beyond the utmost bound of human thought.
     This is my son, mine own Telemachus,
To whom I leave the sceptre and the isle,—
Well-loved of me, discerning to fulfil
This labor, by slow prudence to make mild
A rugged people, and thro' soft degrees
Subdue them to the useful and the good.
Most blameless is he, centred in the sphere
Of common duties, decent not to fail   40
In offices of tenderness, and pay
Meet adoration to my household gods,
When I am gone. He works his work, I mine.
     There lies the port; the vessel puffs her sail;
There gloom the dark, broad seas. My mariners,
Souls that have toil'd, and wrought, and thought with me,—
That ever with a frolic welcome took
The thunder and the sunshine, and opposed
Free hearts, free foreheads,—you and I are old;
Old age hath yet his honor and his toil.   50
Death closes all; but something ere the end,
Some work of noble note, may yet be done,
Not unbecoming men that strove with Gods.
The lights begin to twinkle from the rocks;
The long day wanes; the slow moon climbs; the deep
Moans round with many voices. Come, my friends.
'T is not too late to seek a newer world.

Alfred, Lord Tennyson   39

Push off, and sitting well in order smite
The sounding furrows; for my purpose holds
To sail beyond the sunset, and the baths
Of all the western stars,° until I die.   60
It may be that the gulfs will wash us down;
It may be we shall touch the Happy Isles,°
And see the great Achilles, whom we knew.
Tho' much is taken, much abides; and tho'
We are not now that strength which in old days
Moved earth and heaven, that which we are, we are,—
One equal temper of heroic hearts,
Made weak by time and fate, but strong in will
To strive, to seek, to find, and not to yield.   70

Tithonus

The woods decay, the woods decay and fall,
The vapors weep their burthen to the ground,
Man comes and tills the field and lies beneath,
And after many a summer dies the swan.
Me only cruel immortality
Consumes; I wither slowly in thine arms,
Here at the quiet limit of the world,
A white-hair'd shadow roaming like a dream
The ever-silent spaces of the East,
Far-folded mists, and gleaming halls of morn.   10
    Alas! for this gray shadow, once a man—
So glorious in his beauty and thy choice,
Who madest him thy chosen, that he seem'd
To his great heart none other than a God!
I ask'd thee, "Give me immortality."
Then didst thou grant mine asking with a smile,
Like wealthy men who care not how they give.
But thy strong Hours indignant work'd their wills,
And beat me down and marr'd and wasted me,
And tho' they could not end me, left me maim'd   20
To dwell in presence of immortal youth,
Immortal age beside immortal youth,
And all I was in ashes. Can thy love,
Thy beauty, make amends, tho' even now,

60-61. **the baths/Of all the western stars.** In the Greek concept of the universe, the earth was surrounded by an outer body of water, into which the stars descended. 63. **Happy Isles,** Elysium, the dwelling place of virtuous people after death.

Close over us, the silver star,° thy guide,
Shines in those tremulous eyes that fill with tears
To hear me? Let me go; take back thy gift.
Why should a man desire in any way
To vary from the kindly° race of men,
Or pass beyond the goal of ordinance   30
Where all should pause, as is most meet for all?
   A soft air fans the cloud apart; there comes
A glimpse of that dark world where I was born.
Once more the old mysterious glimmer steals
From thy pure brows, and from thy shoulders pure,
And bosom beating with a heart renew'd.
Thy cheek begins to redden thro' the gloom,
Thy sweet eyes brighten slowly close to mine,
Ere yet they blind the stars, and the wild team
Which love thee, yearning for thy yoke, arise,   40
And shake the darkness from their loosen'd manes,
And beat the twilight into flakes of fire.
   Lo! ever thus thou growest beautiful
In silence, then before thine answer given
Departest, and thy tears are on my cheek.
   Why wilt thou ever scare me with thy tears,
And make me tremble lest a saying learnt,
In days far-off, on that dark earth, be true?
"The Gods themselves cannot recall their gifts."
   Ay me! ay me! with what another heart   50
In days far-off, and with what other eyes
I used to watch—if I be he that watch'd—
The lucid outline forming round thee; saw
The dim curls kindle into sunny rings;
Changed with thy mystic change, and felt my blood
Glow with the glow that slowly crimson'd all
Thy presence and thy portals, while I lay,
Mouth, forehead, eyelids, growing dewy-warm
With kisses balmier than half-opening buds
Of April, and could hear the lips that kiss'd   60
Whispering I knew not what of wild and sweet,
Like that strange song I heard Apollo sing,
While Ilion like a mist rose into towers.
   Yet hold me not for ever in thine East;
How can my nature longer mix with thine?
Coldly thy rosy shadows bathe me, cold
Are all thy lights, and cold my wrinkled feet

25. **silver star,** the morning star.   29. **kindly,** natural.

Alfred, Lord Tennyson   41

Upon thy glimmering thresholds, when the steam
Floats up from those dim fields about the homes
Of happy men that have the power to die, 70
And grassy barrows of the happier dead.
Release me, and restore me to the ground.
Thou seest all things, thou wilt see my grave;
Thou wilt renew thy beauty morn by morn,
I earth in earth forget these empty courts,
And thee returning on thy silver wheels.

In Memoriam*

XI. Calm Is the Morn Without a Sound

Calm is the morn without a sound,
  Calm as to suit a calmer grief,
  And only thro' the faded leaf
The chestnut pattering to the ground;

Calm and deep peace on this high wold,
  And on these dews that drench the furze,
  And all the silvery gossamers
That twinkle into green and gold;

Calm and still light on yon great plain
  That sweeps with all its autumn bowers, 10
  And crowded farms and lessening towers,
To mingle with the bounding main;

Calm and deep peace in this wide air,
  These leaves that redden to the fall,
  And in my heart, if calm at all,
If any calm, a calm despair;

Calm on the seas, and silver sleep,
  And waves that sway themselves in rest,
  And dead calm in that noble breast
Which heaves but with the heaving deep.° 20

*In Memoriam is a sequence of lyric poems reflecting Tennyson's profound grief caused by the death of his close friend, Arthur Hallam. 19-20. And . . . deep. Hallam's body was brought back to England by ship.

O, yet we trust that somehow good
  Will be the final goal of ill,
  To pangs of nature, sins of will,
Defects of doubt, and taints of blood;

That nothing walks with aimless feet;
  That not one life shall be destroy'd,
  Or cast as rubbish to the void,
When God hath made the pile complete;

That not a worm is cloven in vain;
  That not a moth with vain desire   10
  Is shrivell'd in a fruitless fire,
Or but subserves another's gain.

Behold, we know not anything;
  I can but trust that good shall fall
  At last—far off—at last, to all,
And every winter change to spring.

So runs my dream; but what am I?
  An infant crying in the night;
  An infant crying for the light,
And with no language but a cry.   20

CXXXI. O Living Will That Shalt Endure

O living will° that shalt endure
  When all that seems shall suffer shock,
  Rise in the spiritual rock,°
Flow thro' our deeds and make them pure,

That we may lift from out of dust
  A voice as unto him that hears,
  A cry above the conquer'd years
To one that with us works, and trust,

With faith that comes of self-control,
  The truths that never can be proved   10
  Until we close with all we loved,
And all we flow from, soul in soul.

1. **living will.** Tennyson indicated that he meant man's free will. 3. **spiritual rock,** Christ. See I Cor. 10:4.

Alfred, Lord Tennyson 43

1812-1889
ROBERT
BROWNING * *Soliloquy of the Spanish*
Cloister

Gr-r-r—there go, my heart's abhorrence!
   Water your damned flower-pots, do!
If hate killed men, Brother Lawrence,
   God's blood, would not mine kill you!
What? your myrtle-bush wants trimming?
   Oh, that rose has prior claims—
Needs its leaden vase filled brimming?
   Hell dry you up with its flames!

At the meal we sit together:
   Salve tibi!° I must hear   10
Wise talk of the kind of weather,
   Sort of season, time of year:
Not a plenteous cork-crop: scarcely
   Dare we hope oak-galls, I doubt:
What's the Latin name for "parsley"?
   What's the Greek name for Swine's Snout?

Whew! We'll have our platter burnished,
   Laid with care on our own shelf!
With a fire-new spoon we're furnished,
   And a goblet for ourself,   20
Rinsed like something sacrificial
   Ere 'tis fit to touch our chaps—
Marked with L for our initial!
   (He-he! There his lily snaps!)

Saint, forsooth! While brown Dolores
   Squats outside the Convent bank
With Sanchicha, telling stories,
   Steeping tresses in the tank,
Blue-black, lustrous, thick like horsehairs,
   —Can't I see his dead eye glow,   30

10. *Salve tibi!* "Hail to thee!"

Bright as 'twere a Barbary corsair's?
  (That is, if he'd let it show!)

When he finishes refection,
  Knife and fork he never lays
Cross-wise, to my recollection,
  As do I, in Jesu's praise.
I the Trinity illustrate,
  Drinking watered orange-pulp—
In three sips the Arian frustrate;
  While he drains his at one gulp.   40

Oh, those melons! If he's able
  We're to have a feast! so nice!
One goes to the Abbot's table,
  All of us get each a slice.
How go on your flowers? None double?
  Not one fruit-sort can you spy?
Strange!—And I, too, at such trouble
  Keep them close-nipped on the sly!

There's a great text in Galatians,
  Once you trip on it, entails   50
Twenty-nine distinct damnations,
  One sure, if another fails:
If I trip him just a-dying,
  Sure of heaven as sure can be,
Spin him round and send him flying
  Off to hell, a Manichee?

Or, my scrofulous French novel
  On gray paper with blunt type!
Simply glance at it, you grovel
  Hand and foot in Belial's gripe: 60
If I double down its pages
  At the woeful sixteenth print,
When he gathers his greengages,
  Ope a sieve and slip it in't?

Or, there's Satan!—one might venture
  Pledge one's soul to him, yet leave
Such a flaw in the indenture
  As he'd miss till, past retrieve,
Blasted lay that rose-acacia

We're so proud of! *Hy, Zy, Hine°* . . .
'St, there's Vespers! *Plena gratiâ,*
   Ave, Virgo!° Gr-r-r—you swine!

My Last Duchess

*Ferrara**

That's my last Duchess painted on the wall,
Looking as if she were alive. I call
That piece a wonder, now: Frà Pandolf's hands
Worked busily a day, and there she stands.
Will't please you sit and look at her? I said
"Frà Pandolf" by design, for never read
Strangers like you that pictured countenance,
The depth and passion of its earnest glance,
But to myself they turned (since none puts by
The curtain I have drawn for you, but I)   10
And seemed as they would ask me, if they durst,
How such a glance came there; so, not the first
Are you to turn and ask thus. Sir, 'twas not
Her husband's presence only, called that spot
Of joy into the Duchess' cheek: perhaps
Frà Pandolf chanced to say, "Her mantle laps
Over my lady's wrist too much," or "Paint
Must never hope to reproduce the faint
Half-flush that dies along her throat"; such stuff
Was courtesy, she thought, and cause enough   20
For calling up that spot of joy. She had
A heart—how shall I say?—too soon made glad,
Too easily impressed: she liked whate'er
She looked on, and her looks went everywhere.
Sir, 'twas all one! My favor at her breast,
The dropping of the daylight in the West,
The bough of cherries some officious fool
Broke in the orchard for her, the white mule
She rode with round the terrace—all and each
Would draw from her alike the approving speech,   30
Or blush, at least. She thanked men,—good! but thanked

70. *Hy, Zy, Hine,* either the sounds of vesper bells or the beginning of a spell or curse against
Brother Lawrence.   71-72. *Plena . . . Virgo!* These are the opening words of an evening
prayer: "Hail, Virgin, full of grace!"
Ferrara, a city in Northern Italy. The poem may have as its model the Duke of Ferrara
(1533-1598).   3. Frà Pandolf is an imaginary artist, here represented as a monk.

Somehow—I know not how—as if she ranked
My gift of a nine-hundred-years-old name
With anybody's gift. Who'd stoop to blame
This sort of trifling? Even had you skill
In speech—(which I have not)—to make your will
Quite clear to such an one, and say, "Just this
Or that in you disgusts me; here you miss,
Or there exceed the mark"—and if she let
Herself be lessoned so, nor plainly set   40
Her wits to yours, forsooth, and made excuse,
—E'en then would be some stooping; and I choose
Never to stoop. Oh sir, she smiled, no doubt,
Whene'er I passed her; but who passed without
Much the same smile? This grew; I gave commands;
Then all smiles stopped together. There she stands
As if alive. Will't please you rise? We'll meet
The company below, then. I repeat,
The Count your master's known munificence
Is ample warrant that no just pretense   50
Of mine for dowry will be disallowed;
Though his fair daughter's self, as I avowed
At starting, is my object. Nay, we'll go
Together down, sir. Notice Neptune, though,
Taming a sea-horse, thought a rarity,
Which Claus of Innsbruck° cast in bronze for me!

Prospice*

Fear death?—to feel the fog in my throat,
    The mist in my face,
When the snows begin, and the blasts denote
    I am nearing the place,
The power of the night, the press of the storm,
    The post of the foe;
Where he stands, the Arch Fear in a visible form,
    Yet the strong man must go:
For the journey is done and the summit attained,
    And the barriers fall,   10
Though a battle's to fight ere the guerdon be gained,
    The reward of it all.

56. **Claus of Innsbruck,** an imaginary sculptor.
***Prospice,** "Look Forward."

I was ever a fighter, so—one fight more,
    The best and the last!
I would hate that death bandaged my eyes, and forbore,
    And bade me creep past.
No! let me taste the whole of it, fare like my peers
    The heroes of old,
Bear the brunt, in a minute pay glad life's arrears
    Of pain, darkness and cold.   20
For sudden the worst turns the best to the brave,
    The black minute's at end,
And the elements' rage, the fiend-voices that rave,
    Shall dwindle, shall blend,
Shall change, shall become first a peace out of pain,
    Then a light, then thy breast,
O thou soul of my soul! I shall clasp thee again,
    And with God be the rest!

1819-1892
WALT
WHITMAN * Out of the Cradle
Endlessly Rocking

Out of the cradle endlessly rocking,
Out of the mocking-bird's throat, the musical shuttle,
Out of the Ninth-month midnight,
Over the sterile sands and the fields beyond, where the child
    leaving his bed wander'd alone, bareheaded, barefoot,
Down from the shower'd halo,
Up from the mystic play of shadows twining and twisting as if
    they were alive,
Out from the patches of briers and blackberries,
From the memories of the bird that chanted to me,
From your memories sad brother, from the fitful risings and
    fallings I heard,
From under that yellow half-moon late-risen and swollen as if
    with tears,   10
From those beginning notes of yearning and love there in the mist,
From the thousand responses of my heart never to cease,
From the myriad thence-arous'd words,
From the word stronger and more delicious than any,
From such as now they start the scene revisiting,
As a flock, twittering, rising, or overhead passing,

Borne hither, ere all eludes me, hurriedly,
A man, yet by these tears a little boy again,
Throwing myself on the sand, confronting the waves,
I, chanter of pains and joys, uniter of here and hereafter,   20
Taking all hints to use them, but swiftly leaping beyond them,
A reminiscence sing.

Once Paumanok,°
When the lilac-scent was in the air and Fifth-month grass was
    growing,
Up this seashore in some briers,
Two feather'd guests from Alabama, two together,
And their nest, and four light-green eggs spotted with brown,
And every day the he-bird to and fro near at hand,
And every day the she-bird crouch'd on her nest, silent, with
    bright eyes,
And every day I, a curious boy, never too close, never disturbing
    them,
Cautiously peering, absorbing, translating.   30

Shine! shine! shine!
Pour down your warmth, great sun!
While we bask, we two together.

Two together!
Winds blow south, or winds blow north,
Day come white, or night come black,
Home, or rivers and mountains from home,
Singing all time, minding no time,
While we two keep together.   40

Till of a sudden,
May-be kill'd, unknown to her mate,
One forenoon the she-bird crouch'd not on the nest,
Nor return'd that afternoon, nor the next,
Nor ever appear'd again.

And thenceforward all summer in the sound of the sea,
And at night under the full of the moon in calmer weather,
Over the hoarse surging of the sea,
Or flitting from brier to brier by day,
I saw, I heard at intervals the remaining one, the he-bird,   50
The solitary guest from Alabama.

23. **Paumanok,** an Indian name for Long Island.

Blow! blow! blow!
Blow up sea-winds along Paumanok's shore;
I wait and I wait till you blow my mate to me.

Yes, when the stars glisten'd,
All night long on the prong of a moss-scallop'd stake,
Down almost amid the slapping waves,
Sat the lone singer wonderful causing tears.

He call'd on his mate,
He pour'd forth the meanings which I of all men know. 60

Yes my brother I know,
The rest might not, but I have treasur'd every note,
For more than once dimly down to the beach gliding,
Silent, avoiding the moonbeams, blending myself with the shadows,
Recalling now the obscure shapes, the echoes, the sounds and
     sights after their sorts,
The white arms out in the breakers tirelessly tossing,
I, with bare feet, a child, the wind wafting my hair,
Listen'd long and long.

Listen'd to keep, to sing, now translating the notes,
Following you my brother. 70

Soothe! soothe! soothe!
Close on its wave soothes the wave behind,
And again another behind embracing and lapping, every one close,
But my love soothes not me, not me.

Low hangs the moon, it rose late,
It is lagging—O I think it is heavy with love, with love.

O madly the sea pushes upon the land,
With love, with love.

O night! do I not see my love fluttering out among the breakers?
What is that little black thing I see there in the white? 80

Loud! loud! loud!
Loud I call to you, my love!
High and clear I shoot my voice over the waves,
Surely you must know who is here, is here,
You must know who I am, my love.

Low-hanging moon!
What is that dusky spot in your brown yellow?
O it is the shape, the shape of my mate!
O moon do not keep her from me any longer.

Land! land! O land!   90
Whichever way I turn, O I think you could give me my mate back again
*   if you only would,*
For I am almost sure I see her dimly whichever way I look.

O rising stars!
Perhaps the one I want so much will rise, will rise with some of you.

O throat! O trembling throat!
Sound clearer through the atmosphere!
Pierce the woods, the earth,
Somewhere listening to catch you must be the one I want.

Shake out carols!
Solitary here, the night's carols!   100
Carols of lonesome love! death's carols!
Carols under that lagging, yellow, waning moon!
O under the moon where she droops almost down into the sea!
O reckless despairing carols.

But soft! sink low!
Soft! let me just murmur,
And do you wait a moment you husky-nois'd sea,
For somewhere I believe I heard my mate responding to me,
So faint, I must be still, be still to listen,
But not altogether still, for then she might not come immediately to me.   110

Hither my love!
Here I am! here!
With this just-sustain'd note I announce myself to you,
This gentle call is for you my love, for you.

Do not be decoy'd elsewhere,
That is the whistle of the wind, it is not my voice,
That is the fluttering, the fluttering of the spray,
Those are the shadows of leaves.

Walt Whitman   51

O darkness! O in vain!
O I am very sick and sorrowful.   120

O brown halo in the sky near the moon, drooping upon the sea!
O troubled reflection in the sea!

O throat! O throbbing heart!
And I singing uselessly, uselessly all the night.

O past! O happy life! O songs of joy!
In the air, in the woods, over fields,
Loved! loved! loved! loved! loved!
But my mate no more, no more with me!
We two together no more.

The aria sinking,   130
All else continuing, the stars shining,
The winds blowing, the notes of the bird continuous echoing,
With angry moans the fierce old mother incessantly moaning,
On the sands of Paumanok's shore gray and rustling,
The yellow half-moon enlarged, sagging down, drooping, the face
    of the sea almost touching,
The boy ecstatic, with his bare feet the waves, with his hair the
    atmosphere dallying,
The love in the heart long pent, now loose, now at last tumul-
    tuously bursting,
The aria's meaning, the ears, the soul, swiftly depositing,
The strange tears down the cheeks coursing,
The colloquy there, the trio, each uttering,   140
The undertone, the savage old mother incessantly crying,
To the boy's soul's questions sullenly timing, some drown'd secret
    hissing,
To the outsetting bard.

Demon or bird! (said the boy's soul,)
Is it indeed toward your mate you sing? or is it really to me?
For I, that was a child, my tongue's use sleeping, now I have
    heard you,
Now in a moment I know what I am for, I awake,
And already a thousand singers, a thousand songs, clearer, louder
    and more sorrowful than yours,
A thousand warbling echoes have started to life within me, never
    to die.

O you singer solitary, singing by yourself, projecting me,   150
O solitary me listening, never more shall I cease perpetuating you,
Never more shall I escape, never more the reverberations,
Never more the cries of unsatisfied love be absent from me,
Never again leave me to be the peaceful child I was before what
    there in the night,
By the sea under the yellow and sagging moon,
The messenger there arous'd, the fire, the sweet hell within,
The unknown want, the destiny of me.

O give me the clew! (it lurks in the night here somewhere,)
O if I am to have so much, let me have more!

A word then, (for I will conquer it,)   160
The word final, superior to all,
Subtle, sent up—what is it?—I listen;
Are you whispering it, and have been all the time, you sea waves?
Is that it from your liquid rims and wet sands?

Whereto answering, the sea,
Delaying not, hurrying not,
Whisper'd me through the night, and very plainly before day-
    break,
Lisp'd to me the low and delicious word death,
And again death, death, death, death,
Hissing melodious, neither like the bird nor like my arous'd child's
    heart,   170
But edging near as privately for me rustling at my feet,
Creeping thence steadily up to my ears and laving me softly all
    over,
Death, death, death, death, death.

Which I do not forget,
But fuse the song of my dusky demon and brother,
That he sang to me in the moonlight on Paumanok's gray beach,
With the thousand responsive songs at random,
My own songs awaked from that hour,
And with them the key, the word up from the waves,
The word of the sweetest song and all songs,   180
That strong and delicious word which, creeping to my feet,
(Or like some old crone rocking the cradle, swathed in sweet gar-
    ments, bending aside,)
The sea whisper'd me.

When Lilacs Last in the
Dooryard Bloom'd

1

When lilacs last in the dooryard bloom'd,
And the great star early droop'd in the western sky in the night,
I mourn'd, and yet shall mourn with ever-returning spring.

Ever-returning spring, trinity sure to me you bring,
Lilac blooming perennial and drooping star in the west,
And thought of him I love.

2

O powerful western fallen star!
O shades of night—O moody, tearful night!
O great star disappear'd—O the black murk that hides the star!
O cruel hands that hold me powerless—O helpless soul of me!   10
O harsh surrounding cloud that will not free my soul.

3

In the dooryard fronting an old farm-house near the white-
    wash'd palings,
Stands the lilac-bush tall-growing with heart-shaped leaves of rich
    green,
With many a pointed blossom rising delicate, with the perfume
    strong I love,
With every leaf a miracle—and from this bush in the dooryard,
With delicate-color'd blossoms and heart-shaped leaves of rich
    green,
A sprig with its flower I break.

4

In the swamp in secluded recesses,
A shy and hidden bird is warbling a song.

Solitary the thrush,   20
The hermit withdrawn to himself, avoiding the settlements,
Sings by himself a song.

Song of the bleeding throat,
Death's outlet song of life, (for well dear brother I know,
If thou wast not granted to sing thou would'st surely die.)

Over the breast of the spring, the land, amid cities,
Amid lanes and through old woods, where lately the violets peep'd
  from the ground, spotting the gray debris,
Amid the grass in the fields each side of the lanes, passing the end-
  less grass,
Passing the yellow-spear'd wheat, every grain from its shroud in
  the dark-brown fields uprisen,
Passing the apple-tree blows of white and pink in the orchards, 30
Carrying a corpse to where it shall rest in the grave,
Night and day journeys a coffin.

Coffin that passes through lanes and streets,
Through day and night with the great cloud darkening the land,
With the pomp of the inloop'd flags with the cities draped in
  black,
With the show of the States themselves as of crape-veil'd women
  standing,
With processions long and winding and the flambeaus of the night,
With the countless torches lit, with the silent sea of faces and the
  unbared heads,
With the waiting depot, the arriving coffin, and the sombre faces,
With dirges through the night, with the thousand voices rising
  strong and solemn, 40
With all the mournful voices of the dirges pour'd around the coffin,
The dim-lit churches and the shuddering organs—where amid
  these you journey,
With the tolling tolling bells' perpetual clang,
Here, coffin that slowly passes,
I give you my sprig of lilac.

(Nor for you, for one alone,
Blossoms and branches green to coffins all I bring,
For fresh as the morning, thus would I chant a song for you O
  sane and sacred death.

All over bouquets of roses,
O death, I cover you over with roses and early lilies, 50
But mostly and now the lilac that blooms the first,
Copious I break, I break the sprigs from the bushes,
With loaded arms I come, pouring for you,
For you and the coffins all of you O death.)

Walt Whitman 55

O western orb sailing the heaven,
Now I know what you must have meant as a month since I walk'd,
As I walk'd in silence the transparent shadowy night,
As I saw you had something to tell as you bent to me night after
   night,
As you droop'd from the sky low down as if to my side, (while the
   other stars all look'd on,)
As we wander'd together the solemn night, (for something I know
   not what kept me from sleep,)   60
As the night advanced, and I saw on the rim of the west how full
   you were of woe,
As I stood on the rising ground in the breeze in the cool trans-
   parent night,
As I watch'd where you pass'd and was lost in the netherward
   black of the night,
As my soul in its trouble dissatisfied sank, as where you sad orb,
Concluded, dropt in the night, and was gone.

9

Sing on there in the swamp,
O singer bashful and tender, I hear your notes, I hear your call,
I hear, I come presently, I understand you,
But a moment I linger, for the lustrous star has detain'd me,
The star my departing comrade holds and detains me.   70

10

O how shall I warble myself for the dead one there I loved?
And how shall I deck my song for the large sweet soul that has
   gone?
And what shall my perfume be for the grave of him I love?

Sea-winds blown from east and west,
Blown from the Eastern sea and blown from the Western sea, till
   there on the prairies meeting,
These and with these and the breath of my chant,
I'll perfume the grave of him I love.

11

O what shall I hang on the chamber walls?
And what shall the pictures be that I hang on the walls,
To adorn the burial-house of him I love?   80

Pictures of growing spring and farms and homes,
With the Fourth-month eve at sundown, and the gray smoke lucid
  and bright,
With floods of the yellow gold of the gorgeous, indolent, sinking
  sun, burning, expanding the air,
With the fresh sweet herbage under foot, and the pale green leaves
  of the trees prolific,
In the distance the flowing glaze, the breast of the river, with a
  wind-dapple here and there,
With ranging hills on the banks, with many a line against the sky,
  and shadows,
And the city at hand with dwellings so dense, and stacks of chimneys,
And all the scenes of life and the workshops, and the workmen
  homeward returning.

12

Lo, body and soul—this land,
My own Manhattan with spires, and the sparkling and hurrying
  tides, and the ships,   90
The varied and ample land, the South and the North in the light,
  Ohio's shores and flashing Missouri,
And ever the far-spreading prairies cover'd with grass and corn.

Lo, the most excellent sun so calm and haughty,
The violet and purple morn with just-felt breezes,
The gentle soft-born measureless light,
The miracle spreading bathing all, the fulfill'd noon,
The coming eve delicious, the welcome night and the stars,
Over my cities shining all, enveloping man and land.

13

Sing on, sing on you gray-brown bird,
Sing from the swamps, the recesses, pour your chant from the
  bushes,   100
Limitless out of the dusk, out of the cedars and pines.

Sing on dearest brother, warble your reedy song,
Loud human song, with voice of uttermost woe.

O liquid and free and tender!
O wild and loose to my soul—O wondrous singer!
You only I hear—yet the star holds me, (but will soon depart,)
Yet the lilac with mastering odor holds me.

Walt Whitman 57

Now while I sat in the day and look'd forth,
In the close of the day with its light and the fields of spring, and
the farmers preparing their crops,
In the large unconscious scenery of my land with its lakes and
forests,   110
In the heavenly aerial beauty, (after the perturb'd winds and the
storms,)
Under the arching heavens of the afternoon swift passing, and the
voices of children and women,
The many-moving sea-tides, and I saw the ships how they sail'd,
And the summer approaching with richness, and the fields all
busy with labor,
And the infinite separate houses, how they all went on, each with
its meals and minutia of daily usages,
And the streets how their throbbings throbb'd, and the cities pent
—lo, then and there,
Falling upon them all and among them all, enveloping me with
the rest,
Appear'd the cloud, appear'd the long black trail,
And I knew death, its thought, and the sacred knowledge of
death.

Then with the knowledge of death as walking one side of me,   120
And the thought of death close-walking the other side of me,
And I in the middle as with companions, and as holding the
hands of companions,
I fled forth to the hiding receiving night that talks not,
Down to the shores of the water, the path by the swamp in the
dimness,
To the solemn shadowy cedars and ghostly pines so still.

And the singer so shy to the rest receiv'd me,
The gray-brown bird I know receiv'd us comrades three,
And he sang the carol of death, and a verse for him I love.

From deep secluded recesses,
From the fragrant cedars and the ghostly pines so still,   130
Came the carol of the bird.

And the charm of the carol rapt me,
As I held as if by their hands my comrades in the night,
And the voice of my spirit tallied the song of the bird.

Come lovely and soothing death,
Undulate round the world, serenely arriving, arriving,
In the day, in the night, to all, to each,
Sooner or later delicate death.

Prais'd be the fathomless universe,
For life and joy, and for objects and knowledge curious,
And for love, sweet love—but praise! praise! praise!
For the sure-enwinding arms of cool-enfolding death.

Dark mother always gliding near with soft feet,
Have none chanted for thee a chant of fullest welcome?
Then I chant it for thee, I glorify thee above all,
I bring thee a song that when thou must indeed come, come unfalteringly.

Approach strong deliveress,
When it is so, when thou hast taken them I joyously sing the dead,
Lost in the loving floating ocean of thee,
Laved in the flood of thy bliss O death. 150

From me to thee glad serenades,
Dances for thee I propose saluting thee, adornments and feastings
    for thee,
And the sights of the open landscape and the high-spread sky are fitting,
And life and the fields, and the huge and thoughtful night.

The night in silence under many a star,
The ocean shore and the husky whispering wave whose voice I know,
And the soul turning to thee O vast and well-veil'd death,
And the body gratefully nestling close to thee.

Over the tree-tops I float thee a song,
Over the rising and sinking waves, over the myriad fields and the prairies
    wide, 160
Over the dense-pack'd cities all and the teeming wharves and ways,
I float this carol with joy, with joy to thee O death.

15
To the tally of my soul,
Loud and strong kept up the gray-brown bird,
With pure deliberate notes spreading filling the night.

Loud in the pines and cedars dim,
Clear in the freshness moist and the swamp-perfume,
And I with my comrades there in the night.

Walt Whitman 59

While my sight that was bound in my eyes unclosed,
As to long panoramas of visions.   170

And I saw askant the armies,
I saw as in noiseless dreams hundreds of battle-flags,
Borne through the smoke of the battles and pierc'd with missiles
    I saw them,
And carried hither and yon through the smoke, and torn and
    bloody,
And at last but a few shreds left on the staffs, (and all in silence,)
And the staffs all splinter'd and broken.

I saw battle-corpses, myriads of them,
And the white skeletons of young men, I saw them,
I saw the debris and debris of all the slain soldiers of the war,   180
But I saw they were not as was thought,
They themselves were fully at rest, they suffer'd not,
The living remain'd and suffer'd, the mother suffer'd,
And the wife and the child and the musing comrade suffer'd,
And the armies that remain'd suffer'd.

16
Passing the visions, passing the night,
Passing, unloosing the hold of my comrades' hands,
Passing the song of the hermit bird and the tallying song of my
    soul,
Victorious song, death's outlet song, yet varying ever-altering
    song,
As low and wailing, yet clear the notes, rising and falling, flooding
    the night,
Sadly sinking and fainting, as warning and warning, and yet
    again bursting with joy,   190
Covering the earth and filling the spread of the heaven,
As that powerful psalm in the night I heard from recesses,
Passing, I leave thee lilac with heart-shaped leaves,
I leave thee there in the dooryard, blooming, returning with
    spring.

I cease from my song for thee,
From my gaze on thee in the west, fronting the west, communing
    with thee,
O comrade lustrous with silver face in the night.

Yet each to keep and all, retrievements out of the night,
The song, the wondrous chant of the gray-brown bird,
And the tallying chant, the echo arous'd in my soul,   200
With the lustrous and drooping star with the countenance full of
    woe,
With the holders holding my hand nearing the call of the bird,
Comrades mine and I in the midst, and their memory ever to
    keep, for the dead I loved so well,
For the sweetest, wisest soul of all my days and lands—and this for
    his dear sake,
Lilac and star and bird twined with the chant of my soul,
There in the fragrant pines and the cedars dusk and dim.

Sparkles from the Wheel

Where the city's ceaseless crowd moves on the livelong day,
Withdrawn I join a group of children watching, I pause aside
    with them.

By the curb toward the edge of the flagging,
A knife-grinder works at his wheel sharpening a great knife,
Bending over he carefully holds it to the stone, by foot and knee,
With measur'd tread he turns rapidly, as he presses with light but
    firm hand,
Forth issue then in copious golden jets,
Sparkles from the wheel.

The scene and all its belongings, how they seize and affect me,
The sad sharp-chinn'd old man with worn clothes and broad
    shoulder-band of leather,   10
Myself effusing and fluid, a phantom curiously floating, now here
    absorb'd and arrested,
The group, (an unminded point set in a vast surrounding,)
The attentive, quiet children, the loud, proud, restive base of the
    streets,
The low hoarse purr of the whirling stone, the light-press'd
    blade,
Diffusing, dropping, sideways-darting, in tiny showers of gold,
Sparkles from the wheel.

A Noiseless Patient Spider

A noiseless patient spider,
I mark'd where on a little promontory it stood isolated,

Mark'd how to explore the vacant vast surrounding,
It launch'd forth filament, filament, filament, out of itself,
Ever unreeling them, ever tirelessly speeding them.

And you O my soul where you stand,
Surrounded, detached, in measureless oceans of space,
Ceaselessly musing, venturing, throwing, seeking the spheres to
    connect them,
Till the bridge you will need be form'd, till the ductile anchor
    hold,
Till the gossamer thread you fling catch somewhere, O my soul.   10

1822-1888
MATTHEW
ARNOLD * Requiescat

Strew on her roses, roses,
    And never a spray of yew!
In quiet she reposes;
    Ah, would that I did too!

Her mirth the world required;
    She bathed it in smiles of glee.
But her heart was tired, tired,
    And now they let her be.

Her life was turning, turning,
    In mazes of heat and sound.   10
But for peace her soul was yearning,
    And now peace laps her round.

Her cabin'd, ample spirit,
    It flutter'd and fail'd for breath.
To-night it doth inherit
    The vasty hall of death.

Dover Beach

The sea is calm to-night.
The tide is full, the moon lies fair
Upon the straits;—on the French coast the light
Gleams and is gone; the cliffs of England stand,
Glimmering and vast, out in the tranquil bay.
Come to the window, sweet is the night-air!

Only, from the long line of spray
Where the sea meets the moon-blanch'd land,
Listen! you hear the grating roar
Of pebbles which the waves draw back, and fling,   10
At their return, up the high strand,
Begin, and cease, and then again begin,
With tremulous cadence slow, and bring
The eternal note of sadness in.

Sophocles° long ago
Heard it on the Aegean, and it brought
Into his mind the turbid ebb and flow
Of human misery; we
Find also in the sound a thought,
Hearing it by this distant northern sea.   20

The Sea of Faith
Was once, too, at the full, and round earth's shore
Lay like the folds of a bright girdle furl'd.
But now I only hear
Its melancholy, long, withdrawing roar,
Retreating, to the breath
Of the night-wind, down the vast edges drear
And naked shingles of the world.

Ah, love, let us be true
To one another! for the world, which seems   30
To lie before us like a land of dreams,
So various, so beautiful, so new,
Hath really neither joy, nor love, nor light,
Nor certitude, nor peace, nor help for pain;
And we are here as on a darkling plain
Swept with confused alarms of struggle and flight,
Where ignorant armies clash by night.

1828-1909
GEORGE
MEREDITH * Modern Love

I. By This He Knew She Wept with Waking Eyes

By this he knew she wept with waking eyes:
That, at his hand's light quiver by her head,

15. **Sophocles.** See *Antigone* on pp. 295-322.

The strange low sobs that shook their common bed
Were called into her with a sharp surprise,
And strangled mute, like little gaping snakes,
Dreadfully venomous to him. She lay
Stone-still, and the long darkness flowed away
With muffled pulses. Then, as midnight makes
Her giant heart of Memory and Tears
Drink the pale drug of silence, and so beat   10
Sleep's heavy measure, they from head to feet
Were moveless, looking through their dead black years,
By vain regret scrawled over the blank wall.
Like sculptured effigies they might be seen
Upon their marriage-tomb, the sword between;°
Each wishing for the sword that severs all.

XVII. At Dinner, She Is Hostess, I Am Host

At dinner, she is hostess, I am host.
Went the feast ever cheerfuller? She keeps
The Topic over intellectual deeps
In buoyancy afloat. They see no ghost.
With sparkling surface-eyes we ply the ball:
It is in truth a most contagious game:
HIDING THE SKELETON, shall be its name.
Such play as this the devils might appal!
But here's the greater wonder; in that we,
Enamoured of an acting nought can tire,   10
Each other, like true hypocrites, admire;
Warm-lighted looks, Love's ephemeridae
Shoot gaily o'er the dishes and the wine.
We waken envy of our happy lot.
Fast, sweet, and golden, shows the marriage-knot.
Dear guests, you now have seen Love's corpse-light° shine.

XXIX. Am I Failing? For No Longer Can I Cast

Am I failing? For no longer can I cast
A glory round about this head of gold.

15. **the sword between.** In medieval legend or romances a sword placed between lovers
insures chastity.
16. **corpse-light,** a phosphorescent light found in damp places such as marshes. When
associated with graveyards, this kind of light is said to foretell death.

Glory she wears, but springing from the mould;
Not like the consecration of the Past!
Is my soul beggared? Something more than earth
I cry for still: I cannot be at peace
In having Love upon a mortal lease.
I cannot take the woman at her worth!
Where is the ancient wealth wherewith I clothed
Our human nakedness, and could endow
With spiritual splendour a white brow
That else had grinned at me the fact I loathed?
A kiss is but a kiss now! and no wave
Of a great flood that whirls me to the sea.
But, as you will! we'll sit contentedly,
And eat our pot of honey on the grave.

10

L. *Thus Piteously Love Closed What He Begat*

Thus piteously Love closed what he begat:
The union of this ever-diverse pair!
These two were rapid falcons in a snare,
Condemned to do the flitting of the bat.
Lovers beneath the singing sky of May,
They wandered once; clear as the dew on flowers:
But they fed not on the advancing hours:
Their hearts held cravings for the buried day.
Then each applied to each that fatal knife,
Deep questioning, which probes to endless dole.
Ah, what a dusty answer gets the soul
When hot for certainties in this our life!—
In tragic hints here see what evermore
Moves dark as yonder midnight ocean's force,
Thundering like ramping hosts of warrior horse,
To throw that faint thin line upon the shore!

10

Dirge in Woods

A wind sways the pines,
        And below
Not a breath of wild air;
Still as the mosses that glow
On the flooring and over the lines

Of the roots here and there.
The pine-tree drops its dead;
They are quiet, as under the sea.
Overhead, overhead
Rushes life in a race,   10
As the clouds the clouds chase;
     And we go,
And we drop like the fruits of the tree,
     Even we,
     Even so.

Lucifer in Starlight

On a starred night Prince Lucifer uprose.
Tired of his dark dominion swung the fiend
Above the rolling ball in cloud part screened,
Where sinners hugged their spectre of repose.
Poor prey to his hot fit of pride were those.
And now upon his western wing he leaned,
Now his huge bulk o'er Afric's sands careened,
Now the black planet shadowed Arctic snows.
Soaring through wider zones that pricked his scars
With memory of the old revolt from Awe,   10
He reached a middle height, and at the stars,
Which are the brain of heaven, he looked, and sank.
Around the ancient track marched, rank on rank,
The army of unalterable law.

1830-1886
EMILY
DICKINSON * Safe in Their Alabaster Chambers

Safe in their Alabaster Chambers —
Untouched by Morning
And untouched by Noon —
Sleep the meek members of the Resurrection —
Rafter of satin,
And Roof of stone.

Light laughs the breeze
In her Castle above them —

Babbles the Bee in a stolid Ear,
Pipe the Sweet Birds in ignorant cadence —
Ah, what sagacity perished here!

version of 1859

Safe in their Alabaster Chambers —
Untouched by Morning —
And untouched by Noon —
Lie the meek members of the Resurrection —
Rafter of Satin — and Roof of Stone!

Grand go the Years — in the Crescent — above them —
Worlds scoop their Arcs —
And Firmaments — row —
Diadems — drop — and Doges — surrender —
Soundless as dots — on a Disc of Snow —

version of 1861

I Felt a Funeral, in My Brain

I felt a Funeral, in my Brain,
And Mourners to and fro
Kept treading — treading — till it seemed
That Sense was breaking through —

And when they all were seated,
A Service, like a Drum —
Kept beating — beating — till I thought
My Mind was going numb —

And then I heard them lift a Box
And creak across my Soul
With those same Boots of Lead, again,
Then Space — began to toll,

As all the Heavens were a Bell,
And Being, but an Ear,
And I, and Silence, some strange Race
Wrecked, solitary, here —

And then a Plank in Reason, broke,
And I dropped down, and down —

Emily Dickinson   67

And hit a World, at every plunge,
And Finished knowing — then —   20

What Soft—Cherubic Creatures

What Soft — Cherubic Creatures —
These Gentlewomen are —
One would as soon assault a Plush —
Or violate a Star —

Such Dimity Convictions —
A Horror so refined
Of freckled Human Nature —
Of Deity — ashamed —

It's such a common — Glory —
A Fisherman's — Degree —   10
Redemption — Brittle Lady —
Be so — ashamed of Thee —

I Heard a Fly Buzz—When I Died

I heard a Fly buzz — when I died —
The Stillness in the Room
Was like the Stillness in the Air —
Between the Heaves of Storm —

The Eyes around — had wrung them dry —
And Breaths were gathering firm
For that last Onset — when the King
Be witnessed — in the Room —

I willed my Keepsakes — Signed away
What portion of me be   10
Assignable — and then it was
There interposed a Fly —

With Blue — uncertain stumbling Buzz —
Between the light — and me —
And then the Windows failed — and then
I could not see to see —

Because I Could Not Stop for Death

Because I could not stop for Death —
He kindly stopped for me —
The Carriage held but just Ourselves —
And Immortality.

We slowly drove — He knew no haste
And I had put away
My labor and my leisure too,
For His Civility —

We passed the School, where Children strove
At Recess — in the Ring —   10
We passed the Fields of Gazing Grain —
We passed the Setting Sun —

Or rather — He passed Us —
The Dews drew quivering and chill —
For only Gossamer, my Gown —
My Tippet — only Tulle —

We paused before a House that seemed
A Swelling of the Ground —
The Roof was scarcely visible —
The Cornice — in the Ground —   20

Since then — 'tis Centuries — and yet
Feels shorter than the Day
I first surmised the Horses Heads
Were toward Eternity —

A Route of Evanescence

A Route of Evanescence
With a revolving Wheel —
A Resonance of Emerald —
A Rush of Cochineal —
And every Blossom on the Bush
Adjusts its tumbled Head —
The mail from Tunis, probably,
An easy Morning's Ride —

Emily Dickinson   69

1840-1928
THOMAS
HARDY * The Darkling Thrush

I leant upon a coppice gate
    When Frost was spectre-gray,
And Winter's dregs made desolate
    The weakening eye of day.
The tangled bine-stems scored the sky
    Like strings of broken lyres,
And all mankind that haunted nigh
    Had sought their household fires.

The land's sharp features seemed to be
    The Century's corpse° outleant,   10
His crypt the cloudy canopy,
    The wind his death-lament.
The ancient pulse of germ and birth
    Was shrunken hard and dry,
And every spirit upon earth
    Seemed fervourless as I.

At once a voice arose among
    The bleak twigs overhead
In a full-hearted evensong
    Of joy illimited;   20
An aged thrush, frail, gaunt, and small,
    In blast-beruffled plume,
Had chosen thus to fling his soul
    Upon the growing gloom.

So little cause for carolings
    Of such ecstatic sound
Was written on terrestrial things
    Afar or nigh around,
That I could think there trembled through
    His happy good-night air   30
Some blessed Hope, whereof he knew
    And I was unaware.

                    December 1900

10. **The Century's corpse,** the recently ended nineteenth century.

The Man He Killed

"Had he and I but met
    By some old ancient inn,
We should have sat us down to wet
    Right many a nipperkin!

"But ranged as infantry,
    And staring face to face,
I shot at him as he at me,
    And killed him in his place.

"I shot him dead because—
    Because he was my foe,   10
Just so: my foe of course he was;
    That's clear enough; although

"He thought he'd 'list, perhaps,
    Off-hand like—just as I—
Was out of work—had sold his traps—
    No other reason why.

"Yes; quaint and curious war is!
    You shoot a fellow down
You'd treat if met where any bar is,
    Or help to half-a-crown."   20

1844-1889
GERARD
MANLEY
HOPKINS * *Heaven-Haven*

A nun takes the veil

I have desired to go
    Where springs not fail,
To fields where flies no sharp and sided hail
    And a few lilies blow.

And I have asked to be
    Where no storms come,
Where the green swell is in the havens dumb,
    And out of the swing of the sea.

God's Grandeur

The world is charged with the grandeur of God.
  It will flame out, like shining from shook foil;
  It gathers to a greatness, like the ooze of oil
Crushed.° Why do men then now not reck his rod?
Generations have trod, have trod, have trod;
  And all is seared with trade; bleared, smeared with toil;
  And wears man's smudge and shares man's smell: the soil
Is bare now, nor can foot feel, being shod.

And for all this, nature is never spent;
  There lives the dearest freshness deep down things;   10
And though the last lights off the black West went
  Oh, morning, at the brown brink eastward, springs—
Because the Holy Ghost over the bent
  World broods with warm breast and with ah! bright wings.

The Windhover:

To Christ our Lord

I caught this morning morning's minion, king-
  dom of daylight's dauphin,° dapple-dawn-drawn Falcon,
    in his riding
  Of the rolling level underneath him steady air, and striding
High there, how he rung upon the rein° of a wimpling wing
In his ecstasy! then off, off forth on swing,
  As a skate's heel sweeps smooth on a bow-bend: the hurl
    and gliding
  Rebuffed the big wind. My heart in hiding
Stirred for a bird,—the achieve of, the mastery of the thing!

Brute beauty and valour and act, oh, air, pride, plume, here
  Buckle!° AND the fire that breaks from thee then, a billion   10
Times told lovelier, more dangerous, O my chevalier!°

3-4. **oil/Crushed,** the oil of crushed olives.
  2. **dauphin,** title of the oldest son of various kings of France; hence heir.   3. **rein,** apparently
an indirect image of a horse circling his trainer who holds the reins.   10. **Buckle!** This word
has stimulated much discussion, including opposing interpretations of *join* and *break*.   11. **chevalier,** Christ.

No wonder of it: shéer plód makes plough down sillion°
Shine, and blue-bleak embers, ah my dear,
Fall, gall themselves, and gash gold-vermilion.

Pied Beauty

Glory be to God for dappled things—
    For skies of couple-colour as a brinded cow;
      For rose-moles all in stipple upon trout that swim;
Fresh-firecoal chestnut-falls;° finches' wings;
    Landscape plotted and pieced°—fold, fallow, and plough;
      And áll trádes, their gear and tackle and trim.°

All things counter,° original, spare,° strange;
    Whatever is fickle, freckled (who knows how?)
      With swift, slow; sweet, sour; adazzle, dim;
He fathers-forth whose beauty is past change: 10
          Praise him.

The Caged Skylark

As a dare-gale skylark scanted in a dull cage
    Man's mounting spirit in his bone-house, mean house, dwells—
    That bird beyond the remembering his free fells;
This in drudgery, day-labouring-out life's age.

Though aloft on turf or perch or poor low stage,
    Both sing sometímes the sweetest, sweetest spells,
    Yet both droop deadly sómetimes in their cells
Or wring their barriers in bursts of fear or rage.

Not that the sweet-fowl, song-fowl, needs no rest—
Why, hear him, hear him babble and drop down to his nest,   10
    But his own nest, wild nest, no prison.

Man's spirit will be flesh-bound when found at best,
But uncumbered: meadow-down is not distressed
    For a rainbow footing it nor he for his bónes rísen.

12. **sillion,** a ridge of earth created by ploughing.
4. **chestnut-falls,** chestnuts whose husks have been removed after roasting. 5. **plotted and pieced,** fields divided into various shapes—that is, as the eye sees the landscape. 6. **trim,** equipment. 7. **counter,** unexpected. **spare,** rare.

Gerard Manley Hopkins 73

1859-1936
A. E.
HOUSMAN * *Loveliest of Trees*

Loveliest of trees, the cherry now
Is hung with bloom along the bough,
And stands about the woodland ride
Wearing white for Eastertide.

Now, of my threescore years and ten,
Twenty will not come again,
And take from seventy springs a score,
It only leaves me fifty more.

And since to look at things in bloom
Fifty springs are little room,   10
About the woodlands I will go
To see the cherry hung with snow.

When Smoke Stood Up from Ludlow

When smoke stood up from Ludlow,°
    And mist blew off from Teme,°
And blithe afield to ploughing
    Against the morning beam
    I strode beside my team,

The blackbird in the coppice
    Looked out to see me stride,
And hearkened as I whistled
    The trampling team beside,
    And fluted and replied: 10

"Lie down, lie down, young yeoman;
    What use to rise and rise?
Rise man a thousand mornings
    Yet down at last he lies,
    And then the man is wise."

I heard the tune he sang me,
    And spied his yellow bill;

1. **Ludlow,** a town in Shropshire. 2. **Teme,** a river that flows by Ludlow.

74 Poems

I picked a stone and aimed it
   And threw it with a will:
   Then the bird was still.   20

Then my soul within me
   Took up the blackbird's strain,
And still beside the horses
   Along the dewy lane
   It sang the song again:

"Lie down, lie down, young yeoman;
   The sun moves always west;
The road one treads to labour
   Will lead one home to rest,
   And that will be the best."   30

To an Athlete Dying Young

The time you won your town the race
We chaired you through the market-place;
Man and boy stood cheering by,
And home we brought you shoulder-high.

To-day, the road all runners come,
Shoulder-high we bring you home,
And set you at your threshold down,
Townsman of a stiller town.

Smart lad, to slip betimes away
From fields where glory does not stay   10
And early though the laurel grows
It withers quicker than the rose.

Eyes the shady night has shut
Cannot see the record cut,
And silence sounds no worse than cheers
After earth has stopped the ears:

Now you will not swell the rout
Of lads that wore their honours out,
Runners whom renown outran
And the name died before the man.   20

A. E. Housman 75

So set, before its echoes fade,
The fleet foot on the sill of shade,
And hold to the low lintel up
The still-defended challenge-cup.

And round that early-laurelled head
Will flock to gaze the strengthless dead,
And find unwithered on its curls
The garland briefer than a girl's.

1865-1939
WILLIAM
BUTLER
YEATS * The Second Coming

Turning and turning in the widening gyre°
The falcon cannot hear the falconer;
Things fall apart; the centre cannot hold;
Mere anarchy is loosed upon the world,
The blood-dimmed tide is loosed, and everywhere
The ceremony of innocence is drowned;
The best lack all conviction, while the worst
Are full of passionate intensity.

Surely some revelation is at hand;
Surely the Second Coming is at hand.   10
The Second Coming! Hardly are those words out
When a vast image out of *Spiritus Mundi*°
Troubles my sight: somewhere in sands of the desert
A shape with lion body and the head of a man,
A gaze blank and pitiless as the sun,
Is moving its slow thighs, while all about it
Reel shadows of the indignant desert birds.
The darkness drops again; but now I know
That twenty centuries° of stony sleep

1. gyre. For Yeats the word *gyre*, a spiral turn, relates to cycles of civilization. As the falcon in effect escapes the falconer, the end of the current cycle of civilization is imminent (around 1919, the date of the poem). 12. *Spiritus Mundi*, the spirit or soul of the universe. Yeats linked the *Spiritus Mundi*, to the "Great Memory," which contains all the memories of man and which inspires in the poet symbolic images. 19. twenty centuries, the cycle of civilization before the birth of Christ.

Were vexed to nightmare by a rocking cradle, 20
And what rough beast, its hour come round at last,
Slouches towards Bethlehem to be born?

Sailing to Byzantium

1

That is no country for old men. The young
In one another's arms, birds in the trees
—Those dying generations—at their song,
The salmon-falls, the mackerel-crowded seas,
Fish, flesh, or fowl, commend all summer long
Whatever is begotten, born, and dies.
Caught in that sensual music all neglect
Monuments of unageing intellect.

2

An aged man is but a paltry thing,
A tattered coat upon a stick, unless 10
Soul clap its hands and sing, and louder sing
For every tatter in its mortal dress,
Nor is there singing school but studying
Monuments of its own magnificence;
And therefore I have sailed the seas and come
To the holy city of Byzantium.°

3

O sages° standing in God's holy fire
As in the gold mosaic of a wall,
Come from the holy fire, perne in a gyre,°
And be the singing-masters of my soul. 20
Consume my heart away; sick with desire
And fastened to a dying animal
It knows not what it is; and gather me
Into the artifice of eternity.

4

Once out of nature I shall never take
My bodily form from any natural thing,
But such a form as Grecian goldsmiths make

16. In *A Vision*, Yeats wrote, "I think that in early Byzantium, maybe never before or since
in recorded history, religious, aesthetic, and practical life were one. . . . The painter, the mosaic
worker, the worker in gold and silver, the illuminator of sacred books were almost impersonal,
almost without the consciousness of individual design, absorbed in their subject matter and that
the vision of a whole people." 17. **sages,** possibly the saints pictured in the mosaics on the
walls of the church of Hagia Sophia ("Holy Wisdom") in Byzantium. 19. **perne in a gyre,**
spin around in a spiral. Yeats also associated the gyre with movement from subjective (emotional) to objective (rational) states. For Yeats the subjective was the basis of poetry and
inspiration.

William Butler Yeats 77

Of hammered gold and gold enamelling
To keep a drowsy Emperor awake;
Or set upon a golden bough to sing   30
To lords and ladies of Byzantium
Of what is past, or passing, or to come.

1869-1935
EDWARD
ARLINGTON
ROBINSON * Richard Cory

Whenever Richard Cory went down town,
We people on the pavement looked at him:
He was a gentleman from sole to crown,
Clean favored, and imperially slim.

And he was always quietly arrayed,
And he was always human when he talked;
But still he fluttered pulses when he said,
"Good-morning," and he glittered when he walked.

And he was rich—yes, richer than a king—
And admirably schooled in every grace: 10
In fine, we thought that he was everything
To make us wish that we were in his place.

So on we worked, and waited for the light,
And went without the meat, and cursed the bread;
And Richard Cory, one calm summer night,
Went home and put a bullet through his head.

Mr. Flood's Party

Old Eben Flood, climbing alone one night
Over the hill between the town below
And the forsaken upland hermitage
That held as much as he should ever know
On earth again of home, paused warily.
The road was his with not a native near;

And Eben, having leisure, said aloud,
For no man else in Tilbury Town° to hear:

"Well, Mr. Flood, we have the harvest moon
Again, and we may not have many more;   10
The bird is on the wing, the poet says,
And you and I have said it here before.
Drink to the bird." He raised up to the light
The jug that he had gone so far to fill,
And answered huskily: "Well, Mr. Flood,
Since you propose it, I believe I will."

Alone, as if enduring to the end
A valiant armor of scarred hopes outworn,
He stood there in the middle of the road
Like Roland's ghost winding a silent horn.°   20
Below him, in the town among the trees,
Where friends of other days had honored him,
A phantom salutation of the dead
Rang thinly till old Eben's eyes were dim.

Then, as a mother lays her sleeping child
Down tenderly, fearing it may awake,
He set the jug down slowly at his feet
With trembling care, knowing that most things break;
And only when assured that on firm earth
It stood, as the uncertain lives of men   30
Assuredly did not, he paced away,
And with his hand extended paused again:

"Well, Mr. Flood, we have not met like this
In a long time; and many a change has come
To both of us, I fear, since last it was
We had a drop together. Welcome home!"
Convivially returning with himself,
Again he raised the jug up to the light;
And with an acquiescent quaver said:
"Well, Mr. Flood, if you insist, I might.   40

"Only a very little, Mr. Flood—
For auld lang syne. No more, sir; that will do."

8. **Tilbury Town,** Gardiner, Maine. 20. **Like ... horn.** Roland, a legendary hero of the
Chanson de Roland and other stories inspired by Charlemagne, died in the battle of Roncesvalles in
778 A.D. Only when his forces were almost defeated, did he sound his horn in an appeal for help.

So, for the time, apparently it did,
And Eben evidently thought so too;
For soon amid the silver loneliness
Of night he lifted up his voice and sang,
Secure, with only two moons listening,
Until the whole harmonious landscape rang—

"For auld lang syne." The weary throat gave out,
The last word wavered; and the song being done,   50
He raised again the jug regretfully
And shook his head, and was again alone.
There was not much that was ahead of him,
And there was nothing in the town below—
Where strangers would have shut the many doors
That many friends had opened long ago.

For a Dead Lady

No more with overflowing light
Shall fill the eyes that now are faded,
Nor shall another's fringe with night
Their woman-hidden world as they did.
No more shall quiver down the days
The flowing wonder of her ways,
Whereof no language may requite
The shifting and the many-shaded.

The grace, divine, definitive,
Clings only as a faint forestalling;   10
The laugh that love could not forgive
Is hushed, and answers to no calling;
The forehead and the little ears
Have gone where Saturn keeps the years;
The breast where roses could not live
Has done with rising and with falling.

The beauty, shattered by the laws
That have creation in their keeping,
No longer trembles at applause,
Or over children that are sleeping;   20
And we who delve in beauty's lore
Know all that we have known before
Of what inexorable cause
Makes Time so vicious in his reaping.

1871-1900
STEPHEN
CRANE * War Is Kind

Do not weep, maiden, for war is kind.
Because your lover threw wild hands toward the sky
And the affrighted steed ran on alone,
Do not weep.
War is kind.

> Hoarse, booming drums of the regiment,
> Little souls who thirst for fight,
> These men were born to drill and die.
> The unexplained glory flies above them,
> Great is the battle-god, great, and his kingdom— 10
> A field where a thousand corpses lie.

Do not weep, babe, for war is kind.
Because your father tumbled in the yellow trenches,
Raged at his breast, gulped and died,
Do not weep.
War is kind.

> Swift blazing flag of the regiment,
> Eagle with crest of red and gold,
> These men were born to drill and die.
> Point for them the virtue of slaughter, 20
> Make plain to them the excellence of killing
> And a field where a thousand corpses lie.

Mother whose heart hung humble as a button
On the bright splendid shroud of your son,
Do not weep.
War is kind.

1873-1956
WALTER
DE LA MARE * The Listeners

"Is there anybody there?" said the Traveller,
  Knocking on the moonlit door;

And his horse in the silence champed the grasses
    Of the forest's ferny floor:
And a bird flew up out of the turret,
    Above the Traveller's head:
And he smote upon the door again a second time;
    "Is there anybody there?" he said.
But no one descended to the Traveller;
    No head from the leaf-fringed sill   10
Leaned over and looked into his grey eyes,
    Where he stood perplexed and still.
But only a host of phantom listeners
    That dwelt in the lone house then
Stood listening in the quiet of the moonlight
    To that voice from the world of men:
Stood thronging the faint moonbeams on the dark stair,
    That goes down to the empty hall,
Hearkening in an air stirred and shaken
    By the lonely Traveller's call.   20
And he felt in his heart their strangeness,
    Their stillness answering his cry,
While his horse moved, cropping the dark turf,
    'Neath the starred and leafy sky;
For he suddenly smote on the door, even
    Louder, and lifted his head:—
"Tell them I came, and no one answered,
    That I kept my word," he said.
Never the least stir made the listeners,
    Though every word he spake   30
Fell echoing through the shadowiness of the still house
    From the one man left awake:
Ay, they heard his foot upon the stirrup,
    And the sound of iron on stone,
And how the silence surged softly backward,
    When the plunging hoofs were gone.

1874-1963
ROBERT
FROST * Home Burial

He saw her from the bottom of the stairs
Before she saw him. She was starting down,

Looking back over her shoulder at some fear.
She took a doubtful step and then undid it
To raise herself and look again. He spoke
Advancing toward her: "What is it you see
From up there always—for I want to know."
She turned and sank upon her skirts at that,
And her face changed from terrified to dull.
He said to gain time: "What is it you see,"   10
Mounting until she cowered under him.
"I will find out now—you must tell me, dear."
She, in her place, refused him any help
With the least stiffening of her neck and silence.
She let him look, sure that he wouldn't see,
Blind creature; and awhile he didn't see.
But at last he murmured, "Oh," and again, "Oh."

"What is it—what?" she said.

                    "Just that I see."
"You don't," she challenged. "Tell me what it is."   20

"The wonder is I didn't see at once.
I never noticed it from here before.
I must be wonted to it—that's the reason.
The little graveyard where my people are!
So small the window frames the whole of it.
Not so much larger than a bedroom, is it?
There are three stones of slate and one of marble,
Broad-shouldered little slabs there in the sunlight
On the sidehill. We haven't to mind those.
But I understand: it is not the stones,   30
But the child's mound—"

            "Don't, don't, don't, don't," she cried.

She withdrew shrinking from beneath his arm
That rested on the bannister, and slid downstairs;
And turned on him with such a daunting look,
He said twice over before he knew himself:
"Can't a man speak of his own child he's lost?"

"Not you! Oh, where's my hat? Oh, I don't need it!
I must get out of here. I must get air.
I don't know rightly whether any man can."   40

"Amy! Don't go to someone else this time.
Listen to me. I won't come down the stairs."
He sat and fixed his chin between his fists.
"There's something I should like to ask you, dear."

"You don't know how to ask it."

                              "Help me, then."

Her fingers moved the latch for all reply.

"My words are nearly always an offense.
I don't know how to speak of anything
So as to please you. But I might be taught   50
I should suppose. I can't say I see how.
A man must partly give up being a man
With women-folk. We could have some arrangement
By which I'd bind myself to keep hands off
Anything special you're a-mind to name.
Though I don't like such things 'twixt those that love.
Two that don't love can't live together without them.
But two that do can't live together with them."
She moved the latch a little. "Don't—don't go.
Don't carry it to someone else this time.   60
Tell me about it if it's something human.
Let me into your grief. I'm not so much
Unlike other folks as your standing there
Apart would make me out. Give me my chance.
I do think, though, you overdo it a little.
What was it brought you up to think it the thing
To take your mother-loss of a first child
So inconsolably—in the face of love.
You'd think his memory might be satisfied—"

"There you go sneering now!"   70

                              "I'm not, I'm not!
You make me angry. I'll come down to you.
God, what a woman! And it's come to this,
A man can't speak of his own child that's dead."

"You can't because you don't know how to speak.
If you had any feelings, you that dug
With your own hand—how could you?—his little grave;

84 Poems

I saw you from that very window there,
Making the gravel leap and leap in air,
Leap up, like that, like that, and land so lightly   80
And roll back down the mound beside the hole.
I thought, Who is that man? I didn't know you.
And I crept down the stairs and up the stairs
To look again, and still your spade kept lifting.
Then you came in. I heard your rumbling voice
Out in the kitchen, and I don't know why,
But I went near to see with my own eyes.
You could sit there with the stains on your shoes
Of the fresh earth from your own baby's grave
And talk about your everyday concerns.   90
You had stood the spade up against the wall
Outside there in the entry, for I saw it."

"I shall laugh the worst laugh I ever laughed.
I'm cursed. God, if I don't believe I'm cursed."

"I can repeat the very words you were saying.
'Three foggy mornings and one rainy day
Will rot the best birch fence a man can build.'
Think of it, talk like that at such a time!
What had how long it takes a birch to rot
To do with what was in the darkened parlor.   100
You *couldn't* care! The nearest friends can go
With anyone to death, comes so far short
They might as well not try to go at all.
No, from the time when one is sick to death,
One is alone, and he dies more alone.
Friends make pretense of following to the grave,
But before one is in it, their minds are turned
And making the best of their way back to life
And living people, and things they understand.
But the world's evil. I won't have grief so   110
If I can change it. Oh, I won't, I won't!"

"There, you have said it all and you feel better.
You won't go now. You're crying. Close the door.
The heart's gone out of it: why keep it up.
Amy! There's someone coming down the road!"

"*You*—oh, you think the talk is all. I must go—
Somewhere out of this house. How can I make you—"

"If—you—do!" She was opening the door wider.
"Where do you mean to go? First tell me that.
I'll follow and bring you back by force. I *will!*—"   120

After Apple-Picking

My long two-pointed ladder's sticking through a tree
Toward heaven still,
And there's a barrel that I didn't fill
Beside it, and there may be two or three
Apples I didn't pick upon some bough.
But I am done with apple-picking now.
Essence of winter sleep is on the night,
The scent of apples: I am drowsing off.
I cannot rub the strangeness from my sight
I got from looking through a pane of glass   10
I skimmed this morning from the drinking trough
And held against the world of hoary grass.
It melted, and I let it fall and break.
But I was well
Upon my way to sleep before it fell,
And I could tell
What form my dreaming was about to take.
Magnified apples appear and disappear,
Stem end and blossom end,
And every fleck of russet showing clear.   20
My instep arch not only keeps the ache,
It keeps the pressure of a ladder-round.
I feel the ladder sway as the boughs bend.
And I keep hearing from the cellar bin
The rumbling sound
Of load on load of apples coming in.
For I have had too much
Of apple-picking: I am overtired
Of the great harvest I myself desired.
There were ten thousand thousand fruit to touch,   30
Cherish in hand, lift down, and not let fall.
For all
That struck the earth,
No matter if not bruised or spiked with stubble,
Went surely to the cider-apple heap
As of no worth.

One can see what will trouble
This sleep of mine, whatever sleep it is.
Were he not gone,
The woodchuck could say whether it's like his   40
Long sleep, as I describe its coming on,
Or just some human sleep.

Once by the Pacific

The shattered water made a misty din.
Great waves looked over others coming in,
And thought of doing something to the shore
That water never did to land before.
The clouds were low and hairy in the skies,
Like locks blown forward in the gleam of eyes.
You could not tell, and yet it looked as if
The shore was lucky in being backed by cliff,
The cliff in being backed by continent;
It looked as if a night of dark intent   10
Was coming, and not only a night, an age.
Someone had better be prepared for rage.
There would be more than ocean-water broken
Before God's last *Put out the Light* was spoken.

Bereft

Where had I heard this wind before
Change like this to a deeper roar?
What would it take my standing there for,
Holding open a restive door,
Looking down hill to a frothy shore?
Summer was past and day was past.
Somber clouds in the west were massed.
Out in the porch's sagging floor,
Leaves got up in a coil and hissed,
Blindly struck at my knee and missed.   10
Something sinister in the tone
Told me my secret must be known:
Word I was in the house alone
Somehow must have gotten abroad,
Word I was in my life alone,
Word I had no one left but God.

1879-1955
WALLACE
STEVENS * Domination of Black

At night, by the fire,
The colors of the bushes
And of the fallen leaves,
Repeating themselves,
Turned in the room,
Like the leaves themselves
Turning in the wind.
Yes: but the color of the heavy hemlocks
Came striding.
And I remembered the cry of the peacocks.   10

The colors of their tails
Were like the leaves themselves
Turning in the wind,
In the twilight wind.
They swept over the room,
Just as they flew from the boughs of the hemlocks
Down to the ground.
I heard them cry—the peacocks.
Was it a cry against the twilight
Or against the leaves themselves   20
Turning in the wind,
Turning as the flames
Turned in the fire,
Turning as the tails of the peacocks
Turned in the loud fire,
Loud as the hemlocks
Full of the cry of the peacocks?
Or was it a cry against the hemlocks?

Out of the window,
I saw how the planets gathered   30
Like the leaves themselves
Turning in the wind.
I saw how the night came,
Came striding like the color of the heavy hemlocks
I felt afraid.
And I remembered the cry of the peacocks.

Peter Quince at the Clavier*

1

Just as my fingers on these keys
Make music, so the selfsame sounds
On my spirit make a music, too.

Music is feeling, then, not sound;
And thus it is that what I feel,
Here in this room, desiring you,

Thinking of your blue-shadowed silk,
Is music. It is like the strain
Waked in the elders by Susanna.°

Of a green evening, clear and warm,   10
She bathed in her still garden, while
The red-eyed elders watching, felt

The basses of their beings throb
In witching chords, and their thin blood
Pulse pizzicati of Hosanna.

2

In the green water, clear and warm,
Susanna lay.
She searched
The touch of springs,
And found   20
Concealed imaginings.
She sighed,
For so much melody.

Upon the bank, she stood
In the cool
Of spent emotions.
She felt, among the leaves,
The dew
Of old devotions.

*Peter Quince at the Clavier. Compare Shakespeare's *A Midsummer-Night's Dream*, I, ii. 9. **Susanna.** For the story of Susanna and the elders, read the History of Susanna, a book in the Old Testament Apocrypha.

She walked upon the grass, 30
Still quavering.
The winds were like her maids,
On timid feet,
Fetching her woven scarves,
Yet wavering.

A breath upon her hand
Muted the night.
She turned—
A cymbal crashed,
And roaring horns. 40

3

Soon, with a noise like tambourines,
Came her attendant Byzantines.

They wondered why Susanna cried
Against the elders by her side;

And as they whispered, the refrain
Was like a willow swept by rain.

Anon, their lamps' uplifted flame
Revealed Susanna and her shame.

And then, the simpering Byzantines
Fled, with a noise like tambourines. 50

4

Beauty is momentary in the mind—
The fitful tracing of a portal;
But in the flesh it is immortal.

The body dies; the body's beauty lives.
So evenings die, in their green going,
A wave, interminably flowing.
So gardens die, their meek breath scenting
The cowl of winter, done repenting.
So maidens die, to the auroral
Celebration of a maiden's choral. 60
Susanna's music touched the bawdy strings
Of those white elders; but, escaping,
Left only Death's ironic scraping.
Now, in its immortality, it plays

On the clear viol of her memory,
And makes a constant sacrament of praise.

1885-1930
D. H.
LAWRENCE * *Humming-Bird*

I can imagine, in some otherworld
Primeval-dumb, far back
In that most awful stillness, that only gasped and hummed,
Humming-birds raced down the avenues.

Before anything had a soul,
While life was a heave of Matter, half inanimate,
This little bit chipped off in brilliance
And went whizzing through the slow, vast, succulent stems.

I believe there were no flowers then,
In the world where the humming-bird flashed ahead of creation.   10
I believe he pierced the slow vegetable veins with his long beak.

Probably he was big
As mosses, and little lizards, they say, were once big.
Probably he was a jabbing, terrifying monster.

We look at him through the wrong end of the telescope of Time,
Luckily for us.

Terra Incognita

There are vast realms of consciousness still undreamed of
vast ranges of experience, like the humming of unseen harps,
we know nothing of, within us.

Oh when man escaped from the barbed-wire entanglement
of his own ideas and his own mechanical devices
there is a marvellous rich world of contact and sheer fluid beauty
and fearless face-to-face awareness of now-naked life
and me, and you, and other men and women
and grapes, and ghouls, and ghosts and green moonlight
and ruddy-orange limbs stirring the limbo   10

of the unknown air, and eyes so soft
softer than the space between the stars.
And all things, and nothing, and being and not-being
alternately palpitant,
when at last we escape the barbed-wire enclosure
of *Know Thyself*, knowing we can never know,
we can but touch, and wonder, and ponder, and make our effort
and dangle in a last fastidious fine delight
as the fuchsia does, dangling her reckless drop
of purple after so much putting forth   20
and slow mounting marvel of a little tree.

1887-1962
ROBINSON
JEFFERS * The Bloody Sire

It is not bad. Let them play.
Let the guns bark and the bombing-plane
Speak his prodigious blasphemies.
It is not bad, it is high time,
Stark violence is still the sire of all the world's values.

What but the wolf's tooth whittled so fine
The fleet limbs of the antelope?
What but fear winged the birds, and hunger
Jeweled with such eyes the great goshawk's head?
Violence has been the sire of all the world's values.   10

Who would remember Helen's face
Lacking the terrible halo of spears?
Who formed Christ but Herod and Caesar,
The cruel and bloody victories of Caesar?
Violence, the bloody sire of all the world's values.

Never weep, let them play,
Old violence is not too old to beget new values.

To the Stone-Cutters

Stone-cutters fighting time with marble, you foredefeated
Challengers of oblivion

Eat cynical earnings, knowing rock splits, records fall down,
The square-limbed Roman letters
Scale in the thaws, wear in the rain. The poet as well
Builds his monument mockingly;
For man will be blotted out, the blithe earth die, the brave sun
Die blind and blacken to the heart:
Yet stones have stood for a thousand years, and pained thoughts
    found
The honey of peace in old poems.   10

Hurt Hawks

1

The broken pillar of the wing jags from the clotted shoulder,
The wing trails like a banner in defeat,
No more to use the sky forever but live with famine
And pain a few days: cat nor coyote
Will shorten the week of waiting for death, there is game without
    talons.
He stands under the oak-bush and waits
The lame feet of salvation; at night he remembers freedom
And flies in a dream, the dawns ruin it.
He is strong and pain is worse to the strong, incapacity is worse.
The curs of the day come and torment him   10
At distance, no one but death the redeemer will humble that head,
The intrepid readiness, the terrible eyes.
The wild God of the world is sometimes merciful to those
That ask mercy, not often to the arrogant.
You do not know him, you communal people, or you have for-
    gotten him;
Intemperate and savage, the hawk remembers him;
Beautiful and wild, the hawks, and men that are dying, remember
    him.

2

I'd sooner, except the penalties, kill a man than a hawk; but the
    great redtail
Had nothing left but unable misery
From the bone too shattered for mending, the wing that trailed
    under his talons when he moved.   20
We had fed him six weeks, I gave him freedom,
He wandered over the foreland hill and returned in the evening,
    asking for death,

Not like a beggar, still eyed with the old
Implacable arrogance. I gave him the lead gift in the twilight.
  What fell was relaxed,
Owl-downy, soft feminine feathers; but what
Soared: the fierce rush: the night-herons by the flooded river cried
  fear at its rising
Before it was quite unsheathed from reality.

1887-
MARIANNE
MOORE * The Paper Nautilus

  For authorities whose hopes
are shaped by mercenaries?
  Writers entrapped by
  teatime fame and by
commuters' comforts? Not for these
  the paper nautilus
  constructs her thin glass shell.

  Giving her perishable
souvenir of hope, a dull
  white outside and smooth-
  edged inner surface
glossy as the sea, the watchful   10
  maker of it guards it
  day and night; she scarcely

  eats until the eggs are hatched
Buried eight-fold in her eight
  arms, for she is in
  a sense a devil-
fish, her glass ramshorn-cradled freight
  is hid but is not crushed.   20
  as Hercules, bitten

  by a crab loyal to the hydra,
was hindered to succeed,
  the intensively
  watched eggs coming from
the shell free it when they are freed,—
  leaving its wasp-nest flaws
  of white on white, and close-

    laid Ionic chiton-folds
like the lines in the mane of   30
    a Parthenon horse,
    round which the arms had
wound themselves as if they knew love
    is the only fortress
    strong enough to trust to.

The Mind is an Enchanting Thing

is an enchanted thing
    like the glaze on a
katydid-wing
        subdivided by sun
        till the nettings are legion.
Like Gieseking° playing Scarlatti;

like the apteryx-awl
    as a beak, or the
kiwi's rain-shawl
        of haired feathers, the mind   10
        feeling its way as though blind,
walks along with its eyes on the ground.

It has memory's ear
    that can hear without
having to hear.
        Like the gyroscope's fall,
        truly unequivocal
because trued by regnant certainty,

it is a power of
    strong enchantment. It   20
is like the dove-
        neck animated by
        sun; it is memory's eye;
it's conscientious inconsistency.

It tears off the veil; tears
    the temptation, the
mist the heart wears,

6. **Gieseking,** Walter Gieseking (1895-1956), a German pianist.

from its eyes,—if the heart
has a face; it takes apart
dejection. It's fire in the dove-neck's   30

iridescence; in the
        inconsistencies
of Scarlatti.
        Unconfusion submits
        its confusion to proof; it's
not a Herod's oath that cannot change.

1888-1965
T. S.
ELIOT * Preludes

1

The winter evening settles down
With smell of steaks in passageways.
Six o'clock.
The burnt-out ends of smoky days.
And now a gusty shower wraps
The grimy scraps
Of withered leaves about your feet
And newspapers from vacant lots;
The showers beat
On broken blinds and chimney-pots,   10
And at the corner of the street
A lonely cab-horse steams and stamps.
And then the lighting of the lamps.

2

The morning comes to consciousness
Of faint stale smells of beer
From the sawdust-trampled street
With all its muddy feet that press
To early coffee-stands.
With the other masquerades
That time resumes,   20
One thinks of all the hands

That are raising dingy shades
In a thousand furnished rooms.

3

You tossed a blanket from the bed,
You lay upon your back, and waited;
You dozed, and watched the night revealing
The thousand sordid images
Of which your soul was constituted;
They flickered against the ceiling.
And when all the world came back   30
And the light crept up between the shutters
And you heard the sparrows in the gutters,
You had such a vision of the street
As the street hardly understands;
Sitting along the bed's edge, where
You curled the papers from your hair,
Or clasped the yellow soles of feet
In the palms of both soiled hands.

4

His soul stretched tight across the skies
That fade behind a city block,   40
Or trampled by insistent feet
At four and five and six o'clock;
And short square fingers stuffing pipes,
And evening newspapers, and eyes
Assured of certain certainties,
The conscience of a blackened street
Impatient to assume the world.

    I am moved by fancies that are curled
Around these images, and cling:
The notion of some infinitely gentle   50
Infinitely suffering thing.

    Wipe your hand across your mouth, and laugh;
The worlds revolve like ancient women
Gathering fuel in vacant lots.

The Love Song of J. Alfred Prufrock

S'io credesse che mia risposta fosse
A persona che mai tornasse al mondo,
Questa fiamma staria senza piu scosse.
Ma perciocche giammai di questo fondo
Non torno vivo alcun, s'i'odo il vero,
Senza tema d'infamia ti rispondo. *

Let us go then, you and I,
When the evening is spread out against the sky
Like a patient etherised upon a table;
Let us go, through certain half-deserted streets,
The muttering retreats
Of restless nights in one-night cheap hotels
And sawdust restaurants with oyster-shells:
Streets that follow like a tedious argument
Of insidious intent
To lead you to an overwhelming question . . .   10
Oh, do not ask, "What is it?"
Let us go and make our visit.

In the room the women come and go
Talking of Michelangelo.

The yellow fog that rubs its back upon the window-panes,
The yellow smoke that rubs its muzzle on the window-panes
Licked its tongue into the corners of the evening,
Lingered upon the pools that stand in drains,
Let fall upon its back the soot that falls from chimneys,
Slipped by the terrace, made a sudden leap,   20
And seeing that it was a soft October night,
Curled once about the house, and fell asleep.

And indeed there will be time°
For the yellow smoke that slides along the street,
Rubbing its back upon the window-panes;
There will be time, there will be time

S'io . . . rispondo. This passage is from Dante's Inferno, XXVII, 61-66: "If I believed that
my reply would be to someone who would ever return to the world, this flame would stop
quivering [that is, would not speak]. But since no one ever returned alive from this depth—if I
hear the truth—I answer you without fear of infamy." The words are spoken to Dante by the
flame of Guido da Montefeltro, who is among the evil counselors and distorters of reason in
Dante's imaginative version of Hell. 23. And . . . time. Compare Marvell's "To his Coy
Mistress," p. 15, l. 1.

98   Poems

To prepare a face to meet the faces that you meet;
There will be time to murder and create,
And time for all the works and days° of hands
That lift and drop a question on your plate;   30
Time for you and time for me,
And time yet for a hundred indecisions,
And for a hundred visions and revisions,
Before the taking of a toast and tea.

    In the room the women come and go
Talking of Michelangelo.

    And indeed there will be time
To wonder, "Do I dare?" and, "Do I dare?"
Time to turn back and descend the stair,°
With a bald spot in the middle of my hair—   40
[They will say: "How his hair is growing thin!"]
My morning coat, my collar mounting firmly to the chin,
My necktie rich and modest, but asserted by a simple pin—
[They will say: "But how his arms and legs are thin!"]
Do I dare
Disturb the universe?
In a minute there is time
For decisions and revisions which a minute will reverse.

    For I have known them all already, known them all:—
Have known the evenings, mornings, afternoons,   50
I have measured out my life with coffee spoons;
I know the voices dying with a dying fall°
Beneath the music from a farther room.
    So how should I presume?

    And I have known the eyes already, known them all—
The eyes that fix you in a formulated phrase,
And when I am formulated, sprawling on a pin,
When I am pinned and wriggling on the wall,
Then how should I begin
To spit out all the butt-ends of my days and ways?   60
    And how should I presume?

    And I have known the arms already, known them all—
Arms that are braceleted and white and bare

29. **works and days,** the title of a poem by Hesiod (8th century B.C.).   39. **stair,** an ironic
reference to Dante's vast image of a stairway to heaven.   52. **dying fall,** a phrase from Shakespeare's *Twelfth Night,* I, i, 1-4.

[But in the lamplight, downed with light brown hair!]
Is it perfume from a dress
That makes me so digress?
Arms that lie along a table, or wrap about a shawl.
  And should I then presume?
  And how should I begin?

. . . . .

Shall I say, I have gone at dusk through narrow streets   70
And watched the smoke that rises from the pipes
Of lonely men in shirt-sleeves, leaning out of windows? . . .

I should have been a pair of ragged claws
Scuttling across the floors of silent seas.

. . . . .

And the afternoon, the evening, sleeps so peacefully!
Smoothed by long fingers,
Asleep . . . tired . . . or it malingers,
Stretched on the floor, here beside you and me.
Should I, after tea and cakes and ices,
Have the strength to force the moment to its crisis?   80
But though I have wept and fasted, wept and prayed,
Though I have seen my head [grown slightly bald] brought in
      upon a platter,
I am no prophet°—and here's no great matter;
I have seen the moment of my greatness flicker,
And I have seen the eternal Footman hold my coat, and snicker,
And in short, I was afraid.

And would it have been worth it, after all,
After the cups, the marmalade, the tea,
Among the porcelain, among some talk of you and me,
Would it have been worth while,   90
To have bitten off the matter with a smile,
To have squeezed the universe into a ball°
To roll it toward some overwhelming question,
To say: "I am Lazarus,° come from the dead,
Come back to tell you all, I shall tell you all"—
If one, settling a pillow by her head,
  Should say: "That is not what I meant at all.
  That is not it, at all."

83. **prophet,** John the Baptist. 92. **To . . . ball.** Compare Marvell, p. 16, ll. 41-44. 94.
Lazarus. Eliot mingles the stories of the two Lazaruses in the Bible. See John 11:1-44, and
Luke 16:19-31. Also compare the quotation from Dante which introduces the poem.

And would it have been worth it, after all,
Would it have been worth while,   100
After the sunsets and the dooryards and the sprinkled streets,
After the novels, after the teacups, after the skirts that trail
    along the floor—
And this, and so much more?—
It is impossible to say just what I mean!
But as if a magic lantern threw the nerves in patterns on a screen:
Would it have been worth while
If one, settling a pillow or throwing off a shawl,
And turning toward the window, should say:
    "That is not it at all,
    That is not what I meant, at all."   110

                            .   .   .   .   .

No! I am not Prince Hamlet, nor was meant to be;
Am an attendant lord,° one that will do
To swell a progress, start a scene or two,
Advise the prince; no doubt, an easy tool,
Deferential, glad to be of use,
Politic, cautious, and meticulous;
Full of high sentence, but a bit obtuse;
At times, indeed, almost ridiculous—
Almost, at times, the Fool.

    I grow old . . . I grow old . . .   120
I shall wear the bottoms of my trousers rolled.

    Shall I part my hair behind? Do I dare to eat a peach?
I shall wear white flannel trousers, and walk upon the beach.
I have heard the mermaids singing, each to each.

    I do not think that they will sing to me.

    I have seen them riding seaward on the waves
Combing the white hair of the waves blown back
When the wind blows the water white and black.

    We have lingered in the chambers of the sea
By sea-girls wreathed with seaweed red and brown   130
Till human voices wake us, and we drown.

112. **attendant lord,** possibly Polonius in Shakespeare's *Hamlet*.

1888-
JOHN
CROWE
RANSOM * The Equilibrists

Full of her long white arms and milky skin
He had a thousand times remembered sin.
Alone in the press of people traveled he,
Minding her jacinth, and myrrh, and ivory.

Mouth he remembered: the quaint orifice
From which came heat that flamed upon the kiss,
Till cold words came down spiral from the head,
Grey doves from the officious tower illsped.

Body: it was a white field ready for love,
On her body's field, with the gaunt tower above,   10
The lilies grew, beseeching him to take,
If he would pluck and wear them, bruise and break.

Eyes talking: Never mind the cruel words,
Embrace my flowers, but not embrace the swords.
But what they said, the doves came straightway flying
And unsaid: Honor, Honor, they came crying.

Importunate her doves. Too pure, too wise,
Clambering on his shoulder, saying, Arise,
Leave me now, and never let us meet,
Eternal distance now command thy feet.   20

Predicament indeed, which thus discovers
Honor among thieves, Honor between lovers.
O such a little word is Honor, they feel!
But the grey word is between them cold as steel.°

At length I saw these lovers fully were come
Into their torture of equilibrium;
Dreadfully had forsworn each other, and yet
They were bound each to each, and they did not forget.

24. **But ... steel.** Compare Sonnet I of *Modern Love*, p. 63.

And rigid as two painful stars, and twirled
About the clustered night their prison world,
They burned with fierce love always to come near,
But Honor beat them back and kept them clear.

Ah, the strict lovers, they are ruined now!
I cried in anger. But with puddled brow
Devising for those gibbeted and brave
Came I descanting: Man, what would you have?

For spin your period out, and draw your breath,
A kinder saeculum° begins with Death.
Would you ascend to Heaven and bodiless dwell?
Or take your bodies honorless to Hell?

In Heaven you have heard no marriage is,
No white flesh tinder to your lecheries,
Your male and female tissue sweetly shaped
Sublimed away, and furious blood escaped.

Great lovers lie in Hell, the stubborn ones
Infatuate of the flesh upon the bones;
Stuprate,° they rend each other when they kiss,
The pieces kiss again, no end to this.

But still I watched them spinning, orbited nice.
Their flames were not more radiant than their ice.
I dug in the quiet earth and wrought the tomb
And made these lines to memorize their doom: —

> ### Epitaph
>
> *Equilibrists lie here; stranger, tread light;*
> *Close, but untouching in each other's sight;*
> *Mouldered the lips and ashy the tall skull,*
> *Let them lie perilous and beautiful.*

1889-
CONRAD
AIKEN * The Room

Through that window—all else being extinct
Except itself and me—I saw the struggle

38. **saeculum,** a cycle or period of time.   47. **Stuprate,** ravished or violated.

Of darkness against darkness. Within the room
It turned and turned, dived downward. Then I saw
How order might—if chaos wished—become:
And saw the darkness crush upon itself,
Contracting powerfully; it was as if
It killed itself: slowly: and with much pain.
Pain. The scene was pain, and nothing but pain.
What else, when chaos draws all forces inward   10
To shape a single leaf? . . .

    For the leaf came,
Alone and shining in the empty room;
After a while the twig shot downward from it;
And from the twig a bough; and then the trunk,
Massive and coarse; and last the one black root.
The black root cracked the walls. Boughs burst the window:
The great tree took possession.

    Tree of trees!
Remember (when time comes) how chaos died   20
To shape the shining leaf. Then turn, have courage,
Wrap arms and roots together, be convulsed
With grief, and bring back chaos out of shape.
I will be watching then as I watch now.
I will praise darkness now, but then the leaf.

And If We Kiss

And if we kiss, remember too how time
so many fools with flattering tongue has kissed—
so many kings and kingdoms praised in rhyme,
whose names no more now than the rhymes are missed.
What mountains has he not undone to dust!
What rivers rendered into sea! What space
not changed, obscured, and withered, with his lust,
which, like a hot breath, blasts the beloved face!
My love, what comfort in this dereliction,
for us, who know the ruin which we build—   10
we, the creative and created fiction,
this fiction by ourselves both willed and killed—
except to know, and in the knowing cherish,
that we, the loved and loving, must both perish.

1892-
ARCHIBALD
MacLEISH * *L'An Trentiesme de Mon Eage**

And I have come upon this place
By lost ways, by a nod, by words,
By faces, by an old man's face
At Morlaix lifted to the birds,

By hands upon the tablecloth
At Aldebori's, by the thin
Child's hands that opened to the moth
And let the flutter of the moonlight in,

By hands, by voices, by the voice
Of Mrs. Whitman on the stair,   10
By Margaret's "If we had the choice
To choose or not—" through her thick hair,

By voices, by the creak and fall
Of footsteps on the upper floor,
By silence waiting in the hall
Between the doorbell and the door,

By words, by voices, a lost way—
And here above the chimney stack
The unknown constellations sway—
And by what way shall I go back?   20

Eleven

And summer mornings the mute child, rebellious,
Stupid, hating the words, the meanings, hating
The Think now, Think, the Oh but Think! would leave
On tiptoe the three chairs on the verandah
And crossing tree by tree the empty lawn
Push back the shed door and upon the sill

L'An Trentiesme de Mon Eage, "My Thirtieth Year." Perhaps the specific references in
the poem are best explained by MacLeish's comment: "The curious fact that significance in our
time has fallen from the sun and the stars and the vast words with the resounding vowels to light
upon the minute facets of minute experience—the door knob, the coat buttons, and the bannisters.
And this would not be strange were it not that we retain so strongly the sense of mortality."

Stand pressing out the sunlight from his eyes
And enter and with outstretched fingers feel
The grindstone and behind it the bare wall
And turn and in the corner on the cool   10
Hard earth sit listening. And one by one,
Out of the dazzled shadow in the room,
The shapes would gather, the brown plowshare, spades,
Mattocks, the polished helves of picks, a scythe
Hung from the rafters, shovels, slender tines
Glinting across the curve of sickles—shapes
Older than men were, the wise tools, the iron
Friendly with earth. And sit there, quiet, breathing
The harsh dry smell of withered bulbs, the faint
Odor of dung, the silence. And outside   20
Beyond the half-shut door the blind leaves
And the corn moving. And at noon would come,
Up from the garden, his hard crooked hands
Gentle with earth, his knees still earth-stained, smelling
Of sun, of summer, the old gardener, like
A priest, like an interpreter, and bend
Over his baskets.
                    And they would not speak:
They would say nothing. And the child would sit there
Happy as though he had no name, as though
He had been no one: like a leaf, a stem,   30
Like a root growing—

1894-1962
E. E.
CUMMINGS * *"next to of course god america i*

"next to of course god america i
love you land of the pilgrims' and so forth oh
say can you see by the dawn's early my
country 'tis of centuries come and go
and are no more what of it we should worry
in every language even deafanddumb
thy sons acclaim your glorious name by gorry
by jingo by gee by gosh by gum
why talk of beauty what could be more beaut-
iful than these heroic happy dead   10

who rushed like lions to the roaring slaughter
they did not stop to think they died instead
then shall the voice of liberty be mute?"

He spoke. And drank rapidly a glass of water

somewhere i have never travelled, gladly beyond

somewhere i have never travelled,gladly beyond
any experience,your eyes have their silence:
in your most frail gesture are things which enclose me,
or which i cannot touch because they are too near

your slightest look easily will unclose me
though i have closed myself as fingers,
you open always petal by petal myself as Spring opens
(touching skilfully,mysteriously)her first rose

or if your wish be to close me,i and
my life will shut very beautifully,suddenly,   10
as when the heart of this flower imagines
the snow carefully everywhere descending;

nothing which we are to perceive in this world equals
the power of your intense fragility:whose texture
compels me with the colour of its countries,
rendering death and forever with each breathing

(i do not know what it is about you that closes
and opens;only something in me understands
the voice of your eyes is deeper than all roses)
nobody,not even the rain,has such small hands   20

anyone lived in a pretty how town

anyone lived in a pretty how town
(with up so floating many bells down)

E. E. Cummings   107

spring summer autumn winter
he sang his didn't he danced his did.

Women and men (both little and small)
cared for anyone not at all
they sowed their isn't they reaped their same
sun moon stars rain

children guessed (but only a few
and down they forgot as up they grew
autumn winter spring summer)
that noone loved him more by more

when by now and tree by leaf
she laughed his joy she cried his grief
bird by snow and stir by still
anyone's any was all to her

someones married their everyones
laughed their cryings and did their dance
(sleep wake hope and then) they
said their nevers they slept their dream

stars rain sun moon
(and only the snow can begin to explain
how children are apt to forget to remember
with up so floating many bells down)

one day anyone died i guess
(and noone stooped to kiss his face)
busy folk buried them side by side
little by little and was by was

all by all and deep by deep
and more by more they dream their sleep
noone and anyone earth by april
wish by spirit and if by yes.

Women and men (both dong and ding)
summer autumn winter spring
reaped their sowing and went their came
sun moon stars rain

1902-
KENNETH
FEARING * Dirge

1-2-3 was the number he played but today the number came 3-2-1;
  Bought his Carbide at 30 and it went to 29; had the favorite at
  Bowie but the track was slow—

O executive type, would you like to drive a floating-power, knee-
  action, silk-upholstered six? Wed a Hollywood star? Shoot
  the course in 58? Draw to the ace, king, jack?
O fellow with a will who won't take no, watch out for three
  cigarettes on the same, single match; O democratic voter
  born in August under Mars, beware of liquidated rails—

Denouement to denouement, he took a personal pride in the cer-   10
  tain, certain way he lived his own, private life,
But nevertheless, they shut off his gas; nevertheless, the bank fore-
  closed; nevertheless, the landlord called; nevertheless, the
  radio broke,

And twelve o'clock arrived just once too often,
Just the same he wore one gray tweed suit, bought one straw hat,
  drank one straight Scotch, walked one short step, took one
  long look, drew one deep breath,
Just one too many,

And wow he died as wow he lived,   20
Going whop to the office and blooie home to sleep and biff got
  married and bam had children and oof got fired,
Zowie did he live and zowie did he die,

With who the hell are you at the corner of his casket, and where
  the hell're we going on the right-hand silver knob, and who
  the hell cares walking second from the end with an American Beauty wreath from why the hell not,

Very much missed by the circulation staff of the New York Evening Post; deeply, deeply mourned by the B.M.T.°

29. **B.M.T.**, a subway system in New York.

Wham, Mr. Roosevelt; pow, Sears Roebuck; awk, big dipper;   30
    bop, summer rain;
Bong, Mr., bong, Mr., bong, Mr., bong.

1904-

RICHARD
EBERHART * *The Groundhog*

In June, amid the golden fields,
I saw a groundhog lying dead.
Dead lay he; my senses shook,
And mind outshot our naked frailty.
There lowly in the vigorous summer
His form began its senseless change,
And made my senses waver dim
Seeing nature ferocious in him.
Inspecting close his maggots' might
And seething cauldron of his being,   10
Half with loathing, half with a strange love,
I poked him with an angry stick.
The fever arose, became a flame
And Vigour circumscribed the skies,
Immense energy in the sun,
And through my frame a sunless trembling.
My stick had done nor good nor harm.
Then stood I silent in the day
Watching the object, as before;
And kept my reverence for knowledge   20
Trying for control, to be still,
To quell the passion of the blood;
Until I had bent down on my knees
Praying for joy in the sight of decay.
And so I left; and I returned
In Autumn strict of eye, to see
The sap gone out of the groundhog,
But the bony sodden hulk remained.
But the year had lost its meaning,
And in intellectual chains   30
I lost both love and loathing,
Mured up in the wall of wisdom.
Another summer took the fields again

Massive and burning, full of life,
But when I chanced upon the spot
There was only a little hair left,
And bones bleaching in the sunlight
Beautiful as architecture;
I watched them like a geometer,
And cut a walking stick from a birch. 40
It has been three years, now.
There is no sign of the groundhog.
I stood there in the whirling summer,
My hand capped a withered heart,
And thought of China and of Greece,
Of Alexander in his tent;
Of Montaigne in his tower,
Of Saint Theresa in her wild lament.

The Cancer Cells

Today I saw a picture of the cancer cells,
Sinister shapes with menacing attitudes.
They had outgrown their test-tube and advanced,
Sinister shapes with menacing attitudes,
Into a world beyond, a virulent laughing gang.
They looked like art itself, like the artist's mind,
Powerful shaker, and the taker of new forms.
Some are revulsed to see these spiky shapes;
It is the world of the future too come to.
Nothing could be more vivid than their language, 10
Lethal, sparkling and irregular stars,
The murderous design of the universe,
The hectic dance of the passionate cancer cells.
O just phenomena to the calculating eye,
Originals of imagination. I flew
With them in a piled exuberance of time,
My own malignance in their racy, beautiful gestures
Quick and lean: and in their riot too
I saw the stance of the artist's make,
The fixed form in the massive fluxion. 20

I think Leonardo would have in his disinterest
Enjoyed them precisely with a sharp pencil.

Richard Eberhart 111

1905-
ROBERT
PENN
WARREN * *Gold Glade*

Wandering, in autumn, the woods of boyhood,
Where cedar, black, thick, rode the ridge,
Heart aimless as rifle, boy-blankness of mood,
I came where ridge broke, and the great ledge,
Limestone, set the toe high as treetop by dark edge

Of a gorge, and water hid, grudging and grumbling,
And I saw, in mind's eye, foam white on
Wet stone, stone wet-black, white water tumbling,
And so went down, and with some fright on
Slick boulders, crossed over. The gorge-depth drew night on,   10

But high over high rock and leaf-lacing, sky
Showed yet bright, and declivity wooed
My foot by the quietening stream, and so I
Went on, in quiet, through the beech wood:
There, in gold light, where the glade gave, it stood.

The glade was geometric, circular, gold,
No brush or weed breaking that bright gold of leaf-fall.
In the center it stood, absolute and bold
Beyond any heart-hurt, or eye's grief-fall.
Gold-massy in air, it stood in gold light-fall,   20

No breathing of air, no leaf now gold-falling,
No tooth-stitch of squirrel, or any far fox bark,
No woodpecker coding, or late jay calling.
Silence: gray-shagged, the great shagbark
Gave forth gold light. There could be no dark.

But of course dark came, and I can't recall
What county it was, for the life of me.
Montgomery, Todd, Christian—I know them all.
Was it even Kentucky or Tennessee?
Perhaps just an image that keeps haunting me.   30

No, no! in no mansion under earth,
Nor imagination's domain of bright air,

112   Poems

But solid in soil that gave it its birth,
It stands, wherever it is, but somewhere.
I shall set my foot, and go there.

1907-
**W. H.
AUDEN** ✻ *Musée des Beaux Arts*✻

About suffering they were never wrong,
The Old Masters: how well they understood
Its human position; how it takes place
While someone else is eating or opening a window or just
    walking dully along;
How, when the aged are reverently, passionately waiting
For the miraculous birth, there always must be
Children who did not specially want it to happen, skating
On a pond at the edge of the wood:
They never forgot
That even the dreadful martyrdom must run its course   10
Anyhow in a corner, some untidy spot
Where the dogs go on with their doggy life and the
    torturer's horse
Scratches its innocent behind on a tree.

In Brueghel's *Icarus*, for instance: how everything turns away
Quite leisurely from the disaster; the ploughman may
Have heard the splash, the forsaken cry,
But for him it was not an important failure; the sun shone
As it had to on the white legs disappearing into the green
Water; and the expensive delicate ship that must have seen
Something amazing, a boy falling out of the sky,   20
Had somewhere to get to and sailed calmly on.

The Unknown Citizen

*(To JS/07/M/378
This Marble Monument
Is Erected by the State)*

He was found by the Bureau of Statistics to be
One against whom there was no official complaint,

✻Brussels Museum of Fine Arts, which displays Brueghel's painting "Icarus."

And all the reports on his conduct agree
That, in the modern sense of an old-fashioned word, he was
      a saint,
For in everything he did he served the Greater Community.
Except for the War till the day he retired
He worked in a factory and never got fired,
But satisfied his employers, Fudge Motors Inc.
Yet he wasn't a scab or odd in his views,
For his Union reports that he paid his dues,   10
(Our report on his Union shows it was sound)
And our Social Psychology workers found
That he was popular with his mates and liked a drink.
The Press are convinced that he bought a paper every day
And that his reactions to advertisements were normal in
      every way.
Policies taken out in his name prove that he was fully insured,
And his Health-card shows he was once in hospital but left
      it cured.
Both Producers Research and High-Grade Living declare
He was fully sensible to the advantages of the Instalment Plan
And had everything necessary to the Modern Man,   20
A phonograph, a radio, a car and a frigidaire.
Our researchers into Public Opinion are content
That he held the proper opinions for the time of year;
When there was peace, he was for peace; when there was war,
      he went.
He was married and added five children to the population,
Which our Eugenist says was the right number for a parent of
      his generation,
And our teachers report that he never interfered with
      their education.
Was he free? Was he happy? The question is absurd:
Had anything been wrong, we should certainly have heard.

1908-1963
THEODORE
ROETHKE * Elegy for Jane

My Student, Thrown by a Horse

I remember the neckcurls, limp and damp as tendrils;
And her quick look, a sidelong pickerel smile;

And how, once startled into talk, the light syllables leaped for her,
And she balanced in the delight of her thought,
A wren, happy, tail into the wind,
Her song trembling the twigs and small branches.
The shade sang with her;
The leaves, their whispers turned to kissing;
And the mold sang in the bleached valleys under the rose.

Oh, when she was sad, she cast herself down into such a pure depth,   10
Even a father could not find her:
Scraping her cheek against straw;
Stirring the clearest water.

My sparrow, you are not here,
Waiting like a fern, making a spiny shadow.
The sides of wet stones cannot console me,
Nor the moss, wound with the last light.

If only I could nudge you from this sleep,
My maimed darling, my skittery pigeon.
Over this damp grave I speak the words of my love: 20
I, with no rights in this matter,
Neither father nor lover.

The Exorcism

I
The gray sheep came. I ran,
My body half in flame.
(Father of flowers, who
Dares face the thing he is?)

As if pure being woke,
The dust rose and spoke;
A shape cried from a cloud,
Cried to my flesh out loud.

(And yet I was not there,
But down long corridors,   10
My own, my secret lips
Babbling in urinals.)

II
In a dark wood I saw—
I saw my several selves

Come running from the leaves,
Lewd, tiny, careless lives
That scuttled under stones,
Or broke, but would not go.
I turned upon my spine,
I turned and turned again,   20
A cold God-furious man
Writhing until the last
Forms of his secret life
Lay with the dross of death.

I was myself, alone.

I broke from that low place
Breathing a slower breath,
Cold, in my own dead salt.

1909-
STEPHEN
SPENDER * I Think Continually of Those

I think continually of those who were truly great.
Who, from the womb, remembered the soul's history
Through corridors of light where the hours are suns,
Endless and singing. Whose lovely ambition
Was that their lips, still touched with fire,
Should tell of the Spirit, clothed from head to foot in song.
And who hoarded from the Spring branches
The desires falling across their bodies like blossoms.

What is precious, is never to forget
The essential delight of the blood drawn from ageless springs   10
Breaking through rocks in worlds before our earth.
Never to deny its pleasure in the morning simple light
Nor its grave evening demand for love.
Never to allow gradually the traffic to smother
With noise and fog, the flowering of the Spirit.

Near the snow, near the sun, in the highest fields,
See how these names are fêted by the waving grass

116   Poems

And by the streamers of white cloud
And whispers of wind in the listening sky.
The names of those who in their lives fought for life,   20
Who wore at their hearts the fire's centre.
Born of the sun, they travelled a short while toward the sun,
And left the vivid air signed with their honour.

*Ultima Ratio Regum**

The guns spell money's ultimate reason
In letters of lead on the Spring hillside.
But the boy lying dead under the olive trees
Was too young and too silly°
To have been notable to their important eye.
He was a better target for a kiss.

When he lived, tall factory hooters never summoned him
Nor did restaurant plate-glass doors revolve to wave him in
His name never appeared in the papers.
The world maintained its traditional wall   10
Round the dead with their gold sunk deep as a well,
Whilst his life, intangible as a Stock Exchange rumour, drifted
    outside.

O too lightly he threw down his cap
One day when the breeze threw petals from the trees.
The unflowering wall sprouted with guns,
Machine-gun anger quickly scythed the grasses;
Flags and leaves fell from hands and branches;
The tweed cap rotted in the nettles.

Consider his life which was valueless
In terms of employment, hotel ledgers, news files.   20
Consider. One bullet in ten thousand kills a man.
Ask. Was so much expenditure justified
On the death of one so young, and so silly
Lying under the olive trees, O world, O death?

* *Ultima Ratio Regum,* "The Ultimate Reason of Kings."   4. **silly,** simple, naive, happy.

Stephen Spender   117

1910-
ROBERT
FITZGERALD * *Colorado*

Now the plains come to adore the mountain wall,
Their yellow fields running and bowing like waves
To celebrate in such serene order the fire
And love that bore these stony things. Now fragile
Air, sweet health of a superficial season
Garland a while the majesty of winter.

And I, not long nor with profit hereabouts,
Note merely the blue, the watercolor blue
A descriptive man would like; the rare
And rifted shadowline of trees, the smooth   10
Peaks too cold for the warm west to redden,
Much, or gild them. They remain sharply vague.

It is so, too, I think, with the remote
Population of memory: they stand above
Our imperceptible journeys and indulgence,
Easily unseen by a simple turn of the head,
Impossible to grasp in contour, always a little
Shifting, and the same. Death has engraved them
Lovely and lofty, and my metaphysic
Smiles to align them here, the shadowy ones   20
Tinted so faint, yet luminous as gems.

A property of distance. And distance?
A requisite of the just, which is proportion,
Or holy measure, that the sages loved,
Being so fond of stringed instruments and so
Mild: they liked puppies as well as you;
And saw fit, being profound, not to reflect
Chaos unbounded, but to extract therefrom
Numerous order and magnificence.

So at least I interpret the very thin hostile azure   30
Wherein these stones are dipt, and I imagine
Of time and the great dead, they too
Correctly make a tune with me; let me
Behold by their grave light my minuscule
Part in the swaying and tranquil grandeur here.

118   Poems

1913-
KARL
JAY
SHAPIRO * *Auto Wreck*

Its quick soft silver bell beating, beating,
And down the dark one ruby flare
Pulsing out red light like an artery,
The ambulance at top speed floating down
Past beacons and illuminated clocks
Wings in a heavy curve, dips down,
And brakes speed, entering the crowd.
The doors leap open, emptying light;
Stretchers are laid out, the mangled lifted
And stowed into the little hospital. 10
Then the bell, breaking the hush, tolls once,
And the ambulance with its terrible cargo
Rocking, slightly rocking, moves away,
As the doors, an afterthought, are closed.

We are deranged, walking among the cops
Who sweep glass and are large and composed.
One is still making notes under the light.
One with a bucket douches ponds of blood
Into the street and gutter.
One hangs lanterns on the wrecks that cling, 20
Empty husks of locusts, to iron poles.

Our throats were tight as tourniquets,
Our feet were bound with splints, but now,
Like convalescents intimate and gauche,
We speak through sickly smiles and warn
With the stubborn saw of common sense,
The grim joke and the banal resolution.
The traffic moves around with care,
But we remain, touching a wound
That opens to our richest horror. 30
Already old, the question Who shall die?
Becomes unspoken Who is innocent?
For death in war is done by hands;
Suicide has cause and stillbirth, logic;
And cancer, simple as a flower, blooms.
But this invites the occult mind,

Cancels our physics with a sneer,
And spatters all we knew of denouement
Across the expedient and wicked stones.

1914-1953
DYLAN
THOMAS * The Force That Through the Green
Fuse Drives the Flower

The force that through the green fuse drives the flower
Drives my green age; that blasts the roots of trees
Is my destroyer.
And I am dumb to tell the crooked rose
My youth is bent by the same wintry fever.

The force that drives the water through the rocks
Drives my red blood; that dries the mouthing streams
Turns mine to wax.
And I am dumb to mouth unto my veins
How at the mountain spring the same mouth sucks.   10

The hand that whirls the water in the pool
Stirs the quicksand; that ropes the blowing wind
Hauls my shroud sail.
And I am dumb to tell the hanging man
How of my clay is made the hangman's lime.

The lips of time leech to the fountain head;
Love drips and gathers, but the fallen blood
Shall calm her sores.
And I am dumb to tell a weather's wind
How time has ticked a heaven round the stars.   20

And I am dumb to tell the lover's tomb
How at my sheet goes the same crooked worm.

Do Not Go Gentle into That Good Night

Do not go gentle into that good night,
Old age should burn and rave at close of day;
Rage, rage against the dying of the light.

Though wise men at their end know dark is right,
Because their words had forked no lightning they
Do not go gentle into that good night.

Good men, the last wave by, crying how bright
Their frail deeds might have danced in a green bay,
Rage, rage against the dying of the light.

Wild men who caught and sang the sun in flight,   10
And learn, too late, they grieved it on its way,
Do not go gentle into that good night.

Grave men, near death, who see with blinding sight
Blind eyes could blaze like meteors and be gay,
Rage, rage against the dying of the light.

And you, my father, there on the sad height,
Curse, bless, me now with your fierce tears, I pray.
Do not go gentle into that good night.
Rage, rage against the dying of the light.

1920-
HOWARD
NEMEROV * Boom!

SEES BOOM IN RELIGION, TOO
Atlantic City, June 23, 1957 (AP).—*President Eisenhower's pastor said tonight that Americans are living in a period of "unprecedented religious activity" caused partially by paid vacations, the eight-hour day and modern conveniences.*

"These fruits of material progress," said the Rev. Edward L. R. Elson of the National Presbyterian Church, Washington, "have provided the leisure, the energy, and the means for a level of human and spiritual values never before reached."

Here at the Vespasian-Carlton, it's just one
religious activity after another; the sky
is constantly being crossed by cruciform
airplanes, in which nobody disbelieves
for a second, and the tide, the tide
of spiritual progress and prosperity
miraculously keeps rising, to a level
never before attained. The churches are full,
the beaches are full, and the filling-stations
are full, God's great ocean is full   10

of paid vacationers praying an eight-hour day
to the human and spiritual values, the fruits,
the leisure, the energy, and the means, Lord,
the means for the level, the unprecedented level,
and the modern conveniences, which also are full.
Never before, O Lord, have the prayers and praises
from belfry and phonebooth, from ballpark and barbecue
the sacrifices, so endlessly ascended.

It was not thus when Job in Palestine
sat in the dust and cried, cried bitterly;   20
when Damien kissed the lepers on their wounds
it was not thus; it was not thus
when Francis worked a fourteen-hour day
strictly for the birds; when Dante took
a week's vacation without pay and it rained
part of the time, O Lord, it was not thus.

But now the gears mesh and the tires burn
and the ice chatters in the shaker and the priest
in the pulpit, and Thy Name, O Lord,
is kept before the public, while the fruits   30
ripen and religion booms and the level rises
and every modern convenience runneth over,
that it may never be with us as it hath been
with Athens and Karnak and Nagasaki,
nor Thy sun for one instant refrain from shining
on the rainbow Buick by the breezeway
or the Chris Craft with the uplift life raft;
that we may continue to be the just folks we are,
plain people with ordinary superliners and
disposable diaperliners, people of the stop'n'shop   40
'n'pray as you go, of hotel, motel, boatel,
the humble pilgrims of no deposit no return
and please adjust thy clothing, who will give to Thee,
if Thee will keep us going, our annual
Miss Universe, for Thy Name's Sake, Amen.

The Sanctuary

Over a ground of slate and light gravel,
Clear water, so shallow that one can see
The numerous springs moving their mouths of sand;

122   Poems

And the dark trout are clearly to be seen,
Swimming this water which is color of air
So that the fish appear suspended nowhere and
In nothing. With a delicate bend and reflex
Of their tails the trout slowly glide
From the shadowy side into the light, so clear,
And back again into the shadows; slow
And so definite, like thought emerging
Into a clear place in the mind, then going back,
Exchanging shape for shade. Now and again
One fish slides into the center of the pool
And hangs between the surface and the slate
For several minutes without moving, like
A silence in a dream; and when I stand
At such a time, observing this, my life
Seems to have been suddenly moved a great
Distance away on every side, as though
The quietest thought of all stood in the pale
Watery light alone, and was no more
My own than the speckled trout I stare upon
All but unseeing. Even at such times
The mind goes on transposing and revising
The elements of its long allegory
In which the anagoge is always death;
And while this vision blurs with empty tears,
I visit, in the cold pool of the skull,
A sanctuary where the slender trout
Feed on my drowned eyes. . . . Until this trout
Pokes through the fabric of the surface to
Snap up a fly. As if a man's own eyes
Raised welts upon the mirror whence they stared,
I find this world again in focus, and
This fish, a shadow dammed in artifice,
Swims to the furthest shadows out of sight
Though not, in time's ruining stream, out of mind.

1925-
PHILIP
BOOTH * Cold-Water Flat

    Come to conquer
this living labyrinth of rock,

young Theseus of Dubuque
finds he is mazed without a minotaur,
without his Ariadne in the dark.

He dreams beyond
his steelwalled fear to fields grown
vertical with corn
and hope. Home to this heroic end:
imprisoned in the city of alone;   10

here smog obscures
his visionary victor's world
and streetsounds dulled
with rain reverberate in airshaft hours
where braver conquerors have been felled.

Amazed at night,
stalking the seven maids no sword
can save, he is devoured
in passageways of reinforced concrete,
trapped by his beast, and overpowered   20

in sleepless dead-
end dreams. How now, Theseus? How send
word home you are confined
with neither wings nor lover's thread
in the city that a murderer designed?

STORIES

1803-1870
PROSPER
MÉRIMÉE * Mateo Falcone*

In leaving Porto-Vecchio and going toward the interior of the island, a traveller finds the terrain rising rather abruptly, and after three hours' walk along twisting paths obstructed by huge boulders and sometimes cut by ravines, he comes to the edge of a vast *mâquis*. This is the home of Corsican shepherds and of those who wish to escape the law. It should be understood that, to save himself the trouble of fertilizing his land, the Corsican peasant burns a certain portion of forest; if the fire spreads further than necessary, so much the worse. Whatever happens, he is certain to reap a profitable harvest by sowing this ground fertilized by the ashes of the trees which it produced. Because the straw, which is difficult to gather, 10 is left at harvest time, the protected and unburned roots still in the earth sprout during the following spring into very dense shoots that in a few years reach a height of seven or eight feet. This kind of tangled undergrowth is called a *mâquis*. Different species of trees and shrubs compose it, mingled and intertwined as God pleases. Only with a hatchet can a man cut a path through; there are some *mâquis* so dense and luxuriant that not even wild sheep can penetrate them.

If you have killed a man, go into the *mâquis* from Porto-Vecchio, and with a good gun, powder, and shot you will live there safely. Do not forget a brown cloak and hood which will serve as blanket and mattress. The 20 shepherds will give you milk, cheese, and chestnuts; and you will have nothing to fear either from the law or from the relatives of the dead, except when you must descend into the town to renew your supply of ammunition.

When I was in Corsica in 18—, the house of Mateo Falcone stood half-a-league from this *mâquis*. For that country he was a relatively rich man, living handsomely—that is, without toil—on the profit of his herds, which shepherds, especially nomads, drove to pasture here and there on the mountains. When I saw him, two years after the event which I am about to tell, he seemed to be fifty at most. Picture a small but robust man with 30 jet-black curly hair, a Roman nose, thin lips, large piercing eyes, and a leathery complexion. His skill with a rifle was legendary, even in this country where there are so many good marksmen. For example, Mateo would never have fired at a wild ram with buckshot, but at one hundred and twenty paces, he could send a bullet into its head or shoulders as he chose. He could use his gun as readily by night as by day, and I was told of an instance of his skill which will perhaps seem incredible to anyone

*Translation by B. Bernard Cohen and Lucian A. Cohen.

who has never visited Corsica. At eight paces a lighted candle was placed behind a transparent sheet of paper as large as a plate. As soon as Mateo took aim at it, the candle was extinguished; within a minute, in complete darkness, he shot and pierced the paper three times out of four.

Because of his extraordinary skill, Mateo had earned a great reputation. He was known as a good friend but a dangerous enemy; in addition to being obliging and giving alms freely, he lived at peace with everyone in the province of Porto-Vecchio. But it was said of him that at Corte, where he had found his wife, he had very expeditiously rid himself of a rival who was considered as formidable in love as in war. At any rate, people attributed to Mateo a certain shot which surprised his rival while he was shaving in front of a small mirror hung in his window. After the incident was suppressed, Mateo married. At first his wife Giuseppa bore him three girls, which infuriated him, and finally a son, whom he named Fortunato in token that he was the hope of the family, the inheritor of its name. The daughters were well married; in case of need, their father could count on the daggers and carbines of his sons-in-law. Although the son was only ten years old, he had already shown promise.

On an autumn day, Mateo and his wife left early to visit one of their flocks in a clearing of the *mâquis*. Little Fortunato had wanted to accompany them, but the glade was too far away; besides, someone had to remain in charge of the house. Consequently the father refused; we shall see whether he would have reason to repent this decision.

Mateo had been absent for several hours, and little Fortunato was peacefully stretched out in the sun, looking at the blue mountains and thinking that on the following Sunday he would dine in town with his uncle the magistrate. Suddenly his meditations were interrupted by the reverberation of a rifle shot. He rose and turned toward the side of the plain from which the outburst had come. Other shots followed, fired at irregular intervals, yet always coming nearer and nearer. Finally, on the path which led from the plain to Mateo's house there appeared a bearded man who wore a mountaineer's pointed cap and tattered clothes. Leaning on his gun, he dragged himself along with difficulty. He seemed to have been wounded in the thigh.

This man was an outlaw who, having gone at night to buy some powder in the town, had fallen into an ambush of Corsican soldiers. After a spirited defense he was able to escape, but the soldiers pursued him vigorously and fired at him from rock to rock. He was only a little ahead of the soldiers, and his wound made it impossible for him to reach the *mâquis* before being overtaken.

He approached Fortunato and asked, "Are you the son of Mateo Falcone?"

"Yes."

"I am Gianetto Sanpierro. I am being pursued by the yellow-collars."

Hide me because I can go no farther."

"And what will my father say if I hide you without his permission?"

"He will say that you did right."

"How do you know?"

"Hide me quickly; they are coming."

"Wait until my father returns."

"How can I wait? Damnation, they will be here in five minutes. Come on! Hide me or I will kill you."

Fortunato replied with the utmost composure: "Your gun is unloaded, and there are no more cartridges in your belt." 10

"I have my stiletto."

"But could you run as fast as I can?" He leaped out of the man's reach.

"You are not the son of Mateo Falcone! Will you let me be arrested in front of your house?"

The child seemed moved. "What will you give me if I hide you?" he asked, drawing nearer.

The outlaw searched in a leather pouch that hung at his side and took out a five-franc piece which he had no doubt been saving to buy powder. Fortunato smiled at the sight of the piece of silver; he snatched it and said to Gianetto: "Fear nothing." 20

Immediately he made a large hole in a haystack near the house. Gianetto crouched in it, and the child covered him so as to allow him to breathe a little air, but without giving cause for anyone to suspect that the hay concealed a man. Then, with the cunning of an ingenious savage, he thought of another idea. He brought a cat and her kittens and placed them on the haystack to give the appearance that it had not been disturbed recently. Then, noticing the traces of blood on the path near the house, he covered them carefully with dust, and, this done, he himself relaxed in the sun with the utmost tranquillity.

Several minutes later, six men in brown uniforms with yellow collars, 30 commanded by an adjutant, stood before Mateo's door. The adjutant was slightly related to Falcone. (Of course, in Corsica much more distant relationships are recognized than elsewhere.) His name was Tiodoro Gamba, and he was an energetic man much feared by outlaws, many of whom he had already rounded up.

"Good day, little cousin," he said, approaching Fortunato. "How you have grown! Did you see a man pass just now?"

"Oh, I am not as tall as you, cousin," the child replied with a foolish look.

"You will be soon. But tell me, haven't you seen a man pass by? Tell 40 me."

"Have I seen a man go by?"

"Yes, a man with a pointed velvet cap and a jacket embroidered in red and yellow?"

"A man with a pointed cap and a jacket embroidered in red and yellow?"

"Yes, answer quickly, and do not repeat my questions."

"This morning the priest passed our door on his horse Piero. He asked me how Papa was, and I replied—"

"Ah, little rascal, you are mischievous! Tell me quickly which way Gianetto went, for it is he whom we are seeking, and I am certain that he took this path."

"Who knows?"

"Who knows? I know that you have seen him."

"How could I see passers-by when I was asleep?"

"You were not alseep, you good-for-nothing, the gunshots would wake you."

"You believe, then, my cousin, that your guns make so much noise? My father's rifle makes much more noise."

"May the devil take you! You miserable scamp! I am certain that you have seen Gianetto. Perhaps you have even hidden him. Here, comrades, go into the house and see if our man is there. He could walk on only one foot and he has too much common sense, the knave, to attempt to reach the *mâquis* limping. Besides, the traces of blood stop here."

"And what will Papa say?" asked Fortunato, sneering. "What will he say when he finds out that someone entered his house while he was away?"

"Scamp," said the adjutant Gamba, seizing him by the ear, "do you know that I can make you change your tune? Perhaps when you have had about twenty blows with the flat of a sword, you will finally speak."

Fortunato continued to laugh derisively. "My father is Mateo Falcone!" he announced emphatically.

"Do you know, you little rogue, that I can take you to Corte or to Bastia? I shall have you put in a dungeon, on a pallet of straw, with your legs in irons, and I shall have you guillotined if you do not tell me where Gianetto Sanpierro is."

The child burst into laughter at this ridiculous threat, and he repeated, "My father is Mateo Falcone!"

"Adjutant," whispered one of the soldiers, "let's not get into trouble with Mateo."

Gamba was obviously embarrassed. He talked in a low voice with his soldiers, who had already searched the entire house. It was not a very extensive operation because a Corsican hut consists of a single square room. The furniture comprises a table, a few benches, some chests, and various utensils for hunting and cooking. Meanwhile little Fortunato caressed his cat and seemed to derive a malicious enjoyment from the confusion of the soldiers and his cousin.

One soldier came up to the haystack. He looked at it and carelessly poked his bayonet into the hay, shrugging his shoulders as if he thought the precaution was ridiculous. Nothing moved, and the face of the child did not betray the slightest agitation.

The adjutant and his men were desperate; with some longing they looked out over the plain as if inclined to return by the way that they had come. Yet their chief, convinced that threats would make no impression on the son of Falcone, determined to make one last effort—to use the power of blandishment and of gifts.

"Little cousin," he said, "you seem to be a lively youngster who will probably go far. But you play a shabby game with me, and if I did not wish to avoid trouble for my cousin Mateo, the devil take me if I wouldn't 10 carry you away with me."

"Bah!"

"But when my cousin returns, I shall tell him about this affair, and as punishment for lying to me, he will whip you until he draws blood."

"How do you know?"

"You will see. But look here—be a good boy, and I will give you something."

"My cousin, I'll give you some advice: if you delay any longer, Gianetto will be in the *mâquis*, and then it will take a smarter fellow than you to find him." 20

The adjutant drew from his pocket a silver watch worth forty francs. Noticing that little Fortunato's eyes sparkled as he looked at it, Gamba dangled the watch at the end of its steel chain and said: "Young rascal, you would like to have a watch like this hanging around your neck, and with it you would walk along the streets of Porto-Vecchio, proud as a peacock. People would ask you, 'What time is it?' and you would reply, 'Look at my watch.' "

"When I am grown up, my uncle the magistrate will give me a watch."

"Yes, but your uncle's son already has a watch—not as beautiful as this one, it is true, but he is younger than you." 30

The boy sighed.

Viewing the watch out of the corner of his eyes, Fortunato resembled a cat which had just been given a whole chicken. Afraid that someone might be playing a joke on it, the cat dares not pounce, and now and then it turns its eyes away in order not to succumb to temptation, but all the while it licks its lips as if to say to its master: "How cruel your joke is!"

Although the adjutant Gamba really seemed willing to give away his watch, Fortunato did not hold out his hand but merely said to him with a bitter smile: "Why do you make fun of me?"

"By God, I am not mocking you. Simply tell me where Gianetto is, and 40 this watch is yours."

Fortunato smiled incredulously, and, fixing his black eyes on those of the adjutant, he tried to determine how much faith he ought to put in his cousin's words

"May I lose my epaulettes," exclaimed the adjutant, "if I don't give you the watch on that condition! My men are witnesses, and I cannot go back on my word."

As he spoke, he advanced the watch until it nearly touched the boy's pale cheek. Without doubt Fortunato's face showed the conflict in his mind, a conflict between covetousness and the obligations of hospitality. His bare chest heaved violently, and he seemed almost to be suffocating. Meanwhile the watch dangled, twisted, and occasionally hit the tip of his nose. Little by little his right hand reached toward the watch, and his fin-
10 ger tips touched it; finally its whole weight rested upon his palm, even though the adjutant held the end of the chain lightly. The dial was blue, the case newly polished until it seemed on fire in the sunlight—and the temptation was too strong.

Fortunato raised his left hand, and at the same time he pointed his thumb over his shoulder toward the haystack against which he was lean-ing. The adjutant understood immediately, he dropped the end of the chain, and Fortunato felt himself sole possessor of the watch. With the agility of a deer the boy jumped up and withdrew ten paces from the hay-stack, which the soldiers immediately began to upset.

20 It was not long before the hay moved, and a bleeding man, dagger in hand, came out. But when he tried to rise, his wound prevented, and he fell. The adjutant pounced on him and snatched his dagger. In spite of his resistance Gianetto was soon bound tightly.

As he lay stretched on the ground and tied like a bunch of faggots, Gianetto turned his head toward Fortunato, who had approached him. "Son of ——!" he said with more contempt than anger.

In response the boy tossed him the piece of silver which he had re-ceived from him, feeling that he no longer deserved it, but the outlaw seemed to ignore this action. With much composure he said to the ad-
30 jutant: "My dear Gamba, I cannot walk; you will have to carry me to the town."

"Not long ago you could have run as fast as a doe," replied the cruel captor; "but don't be alarmed: I am so happy to have captured you that I could carry you for a league on my back without getting tired. Anyhow, my friend, we will make a litter for you out of branches and your coat, and on the farm at Crespoli we shall find horses."

"Good," said the prisoner, "but I would also like a little straw in the litter to make me more comfortable."

While the soldiers were busy, some making a kind of stretcher out of
40 chestnut branches and others dressing Gianetto's wound, Mateo Falcone and his wife suddenly appeared on a turn of the path from the *mâquis*. The wife came first, bending laboriously under the weight of an enormous sack of chestnuts, while her husband stalked along, carrying one rifle in his hand and another slung through his shoulder-belt. In this country it

is, of course, considered undignified for a man to carry any other burden than his weapons.

At sight of the soldiers, Mateo's first thought was that they had come to arrest him. But why this idea? Did Mateo have any quarrel with the law? No. He enjoyed a good reputation. He was, as the saying goes, particularly well thought of. But he was a Corsican and a mountaineer, and there are few Corsican mountaineers who, if they search their memories adequately, cannot remember some peccadillo—a rifle shot, the thrust of a dagger, or other such trifles. More than most, Mateo had a clear conscience, for it was ten years since he had pointed a gun at a man; yet at the same time 10 he was cautious, and he prepared to defend himself bravely if it should be necessary.

"Wife," said he to Giuseppa, "put down your sack and be prepared."

She obliged at once. He gave her the gun which had been previously slung in his shoulder-strap and which would have impeded him. Carefully he loaded the gun in his hand and moved slowly toward his house, skirting the trees which bordered the path, ready at the least provocation to throw himself behind the largest tree-trunk, where he could fire from cover. His wife walked at his heels, holding his spare weapon and his cartridge-box. In case of a fight it is the duty of a good wife to re-load her 20 husband's gun.

On his part, the adjutant was most uneasy at the sight of Mateo advancing thus with measured steps, gun in hand and finger on the trigger. "If by chance," he thought, "Mateo is related to Gianetto or is his friend and means to protect him, two of his bullets will hit two of us as sure as a letter goes to the postoffice, and inevitably he will aim at me despite our kinship!"

In this perplexity he assumed a brave front and moved alone toward Mateo to tell him what had happened, at the same time greeting him like an old friend. But the brief distance which separated him from Mateo 30 seemed terribly long.

"Hello, my old friend," he cried heartily. "How are you, my worthy one? It is I, Gamba your cousin."

Without answering, Mateo stood still, and while the other spoke, he softly raised the muzzle of his rifle in such a way that when the adjutant came up it was pointed toward the sky.

"Good day, brother," said the adjutant, offering his hand. "I haven't seen you for a long time."

"Good day, brother."

"I just came by to say good day to you and Cousin Pepa. We have 40 journeyed far today, but we won't complain about our fatigue because we have made a first-rate capture—we have arrested Gianetto Sanpierro."

"Glory be to God!" exclaimed Giuseppa. "He stole a milk-goat from us last week."

These words cheered Gamba.

"Poor devil," said Mateo, "he was hungry."

"The rogue fought like a lion," continued the adjutant, a little discomforted. "He killed one of my men, and, not content with that, he broke Corporal Chardon's arm—but that is of little consequence, since he is only a Frenchman. Finally he hid himself so well that the devil could not have found him. Without the help of my little cousin Fortunato, I would never have discovered him."

"Fortunato!" cried Mateo.

10   "Fortunato!" repeated Giuseppa.

"Yes, Gianetto was concealed in your haystack, but my little cousin revealed his trick to me. I shall speak of him to his uncle the magistrate, who will send him a fine present for his trouble. And both his name and yours will be in the report which I shall send to the Solicitor-General."

"Curse you!" muttered Mateo under his breath.

They had now rejoined the soldiers. Gianetto was already in his litter and prepared to depart. When he saw Mateo in Gamba's company, he smiled strangely; then, turning toward the door of the house, he spat on the threshold and cried, "The house of a traitor!"

20   Only a man ready to die would have dared utter the word *traitor* in connection with Falcone. A quick stroke of the dagger—without the need of a second blow—would have immediately avenged the insult. However, Mateo made no gesture except to place his hand on his forehead like a man overwhelmed.

On seeing his father approach, Fortunato had entered the house. He now reappeared carrying a jug of milk, which, with downcast eyes, he offered to Gianetto.

"Get away from me!" the outlaw cried in a withering voice.

Then, turning toward one of the soldiers, he said, "Friend, give me a 30 drink of water."

The soldier placed a flask in his hand, and the bandit drank the water given to him by a man with whom he had not long ago exchanged gunshots. He then requested that his hands be tied across his chest instead of behind his back. "I prefer," he said, "to lie comfortably."

After his request was granted, the adjutant gave the signal to depart, said good-bye to Mateo, who made no response, and went quickly toward the plain.

Nearly ten minutes passed before Mateo opened his mouth. The child looked uneasily first at his mother and then at his father, who, leaning on 40 his gun, regarded him with an expression of concentrated anger.

"You begin well!" Mateo finally said in a voice which was calm but terrifying to any who knew the man.

"Father!" the boy cried, breaking into tears and moving as if to throw himself on his knees.

But Mateo shouted: "Out of my sight!"

The boy stopped motionless a few steps from his father and began to sob.

Giuseppa approached him. She had just noticed the watch chain dangling out of his open shirt.

"Who gave you that watch?" she asked severely.

"My cousin the adjutant."

Falcone seized the watch and threw it so forcefully against a stone that it broke into a thousand pieces.

"Woman," he said, "is this my child?"   10

Giuseppa's cheeks became brick red.

"What are you saying, Mateo? Do you know to whom you are speaking?"

"Indeed! This child is the first traitor of his family."

Fortunato's sobs redoubled, but Falcone held his lynx-like eyes steadily upon him. Finally he struck the ground with the butt of his rifle, then flung the weapon across his shoulder, and headed toward the *mâquis*, ordering Fortunato to follow. The child obeyed.

Giuseppa ran after Mateo and seized him by the arm. "He is your son," she said in a trembling voice, fixing her black eyes on those of her 20 husband as if to read what was passing through his mind.

"Let go," replied Mateo. "I am his father."

Giuseppa kissed her son and entered the hut weeping. Before a statue of the Virgin she threw herself on her knees and prayed fervently.

Meanwhile, Falcone walked about two hundred paces along the path and stopped at a little ravine, into which he descended. With the butt of his rifle he probed the ground and found it soft and easy to dig. The site seemed suitable for his purpose.

"Fortunato, stand by that large rock."

The child did as he was told, then fell on his knees.   30

"Say your prayers."

"Father, Father, do not kill me."

"Say your prayers," Mateo repeated grimly.

Stammering and sobbing, the child recited the Lord's Prayer and the Creed. In a firm voice the father said "Amen!" at the close of each prayer.

"Are those all the prayers you know?"

"Father, I also know the Ave Maria and the Litany which my aunt taught me."

"It is long, but that doesn't matter."

The child finished the Litany in a faint voice.   40

"Have you finished?"

"Oh my father, forgive me! I will never do it again. I will beg my cousin the magistrate to pardon Gianetto!"

He kept imploring, but Mateo raised his rifle and took aim, saying to him: "May God forgive you!"

The boy made one frantic effort to rise and clasp his father's knees, but he had no time. Mateo fired, and Fortunato fell dead.

Without even a glance at the body, Mateo returned to his house to find a spade with which to bury his son. He had taken only a few steps when he encountered Giuseppa, who had rushed out in alarm at the sound of the shot.

"What have you done?" she cried.

10 "Justice."

"Where is he?"

"In the ravine. I am going to bury him. He died a Christian. I shall have a Mass sung for him. Send word to my son-in-law Tiodoro Bianchi to come and live with us."

1804-1864
NATHANIEL
HAWTHORNE * My Kinsman, Major Molineux

After the kings of Great Britain had assumed the right of appointing the colonial governors, the measures of the latter seldom met with the ready and general approbation which had been paid to those of their predecessors, under the original charters. The people looked with most jealous scrutiny to the exercise of power which did not emanate from themselves, and they usually rewarded their rulers with slender gratitude for the compliances by which, in softening their instructions from beyond the sea, they had incurred the reprehension of those who gave them. The annals of Massachusetts Bay will inform us, that of six governors in the 10 space of about forty years from the surrender of the old charter, under James II., two were imprisoned by a popular insurrection; a third, as Hutchinson inclines to believe, was driven from the province by the whizzing of a musket-ball; a fourth, in the opinion of the same historian, was hastened to his grave by continual bickerings with the House of Representatives; and the remaining two, as well as their successors, till the Revolution, were favored with few and brief intervals of peaceful sway. The inferior members of the court party, in times of high political excitement, led scarcely a more desirable life. These remarks may serve as a preface to the following adventures, which chanced upon a summer night, not far from a hundred years ago. The reader, in order to avoid a long and dry detail of colonial affairs, is requested to dispense with an account of the train of circumstances that had caused much temporary inflammation of the popular mind.

It was near nine o'clock of a moonlight evening, when a boat crossed the ferry with a single passenger, who had obtained his conveyance at that unusual hour by the promise of an extra fare. While he stood on the landing place, searching in either pocket for the means of fulfilling his 10 agreement, the ferryman lifted a lantern, by the aid of which, and the newly-risen moon, he took a very accurate survey of the stranger's figure. He was a youth of barely eighteen years, evidently country-bred, and now, as it should seem, upon his first visit to town. He was clad in a coarse gray coat, well worn, but in excellent repair; his under garments were durably constructed of leather, and fitted tight to a pair of serviceable and well-shaped limbs; his stockings of blue yarn were the incontrovertible work of a mother or a sister; and on his head was a three-cornered hat, which in its better days had perhaps sheltered the graver brow of the lad's father. Under his left arm was a heavy cudgel, formed of an oak sapling, 20 and retaining a part of the hardened root; and his equipment was completed by a wallet, not so abundantly stocked as to incommode the vigorous shoulders on which it hung. Brown, curly hair, well-shaped features, and bright, cheerful eyes, were nature's gifts, and worth all that art could have done for his adornment.

The youth, one of whose names was Robin, finally drew from his pocket the half of a little province bill of five shillings, which, in the depreciation of that sort of currency, did but satisfy the ferryman's demand, with the surplus of a sexangular piece of parchment, valued at three pence. He then walked forward into the town, with as light a step as if his day's jour- 30 ney had not already exceeded thirty miles, and with as eager an eye as if he were entering London city, instead of the little metropolis of a New England colony. Before Robin had proceeded far, however, it occurred to him that he knew not whither to direct his steps; so he paused, and looked up and down the narrow street, scrutinizing the small and mean wooden buildings that were scattered on either side.

"This low hovel cannot be my kinsman's dwelling," thought he, "nor yonder old house, where the moonlight enters at the broken casement; and truly I see none hereabouts that might be worthy of him. It would have been wise to inquire my way of the ferryman, and doubtless he 40 would have gone with me, and earned a shilling from the major for his pains. But the next man I meet will do as well."

He resumed his walk, and was glad to perceive that the street now became wider, and the houses more respectable in their appearance. He

soon discerned a figure moving on moderately in advance, and hastened his steps to overtake it. As Robin drew nigh, he saw that the passenger was a man in years, with a full periwig of gray hair, a wide-skirted coat of dark cloth, and silk stockings rolled above his knees. He carried a long and polished cane, which he struck down perpendicularly before him, at every step; and at regular intervals he uttered two successive hems, of a peculiarly solemn and sepulchral intonation. Having made these observations, Robin laid hold of the skirt of the old man's coat, just when the light from the open door and windows of a barber's shop fell upon both their
10 figures.

"Good-evening to you, honored sir," said he, making a low bow, and still retaining his hold of the skirt. "I pray you tell me whereabouts is the dwelling of my kinsman, Major Molineux."

The youth's question was uttered very loudly; and one of the barbers, whose razor was descending on a well-soaped chin, and another who was dressing a Ramillies wig, left their occupations, and came to the door. The citizen, in the mean time, turned a long-favored countenance upon Robin, and answered him in a tone of excessive anger and annoyance. His two sepulchral hems, however, broke into the very centre of his re-
20 buke, with most singular effect, like a thought of the cold grave obtruding among wrathful passions.

"Let go my garment, fellow! I tell you, I know not the man you speak of. What! I have authority, I have—hem, hem—authority; and if this be the respect you show for your betters, your feet shall be brought acquainted with the stocks by daylight, to-morrow morning!"

Robin released the old man's skirt, and hastened away, pursued by an ill-mannered roar of laughter from the barber's shop. He was at first considerably surprised by the result of his question, but, being a shrewd youth, soon thought himself able to account for the mystery.

30 "This is some country representative," was his conclusion, "who has never seen the inside of my kinsman's door, and lacks the breeding to answer a stranger civilly. The man is old, or verily—I might be tempted to turn back and smite him on the nose. Ah, Robin, Robin! even the barber's boys laugh at you for choosing such a guide! You will be wiser in time, friend Robin."

He now became entangled in a succession of crooked and narrow streets, which crossed each other, and meandered at no great distance from the water-side. The smell of tar was obvious to his nostrils, the masts of vessels pierced the moonlight above the tops of the buildings, and the
40 numerous signs, which Robin paused to read, informed him that he was near the centre of business. But the streets were empty, the shops were closed, and lights were visible only in the second stories of a few dwelling-houses. At length, on the corner of a narrow lane, through which he was passing, he beheld the broad countenance of a British hero swinging be-

Nathaniel Hawthorne   137

fore the door of an inn, whence proceeded the voices of many guests. The casement of one of the lower windows was thrown back, and a very thin curtain permitted Robin to distinguish a party at supper, round a well-furnished table. The fragrance of the good cheer steamed forth into the outer air, and the youth could not fail to recollect that the last remnant of his travelling stock of provision had yielded to his morning appetite, and that noon had found, and left him, dinnerless.

"O, that a parchment three-penny might give me a right to sit down at yonder table!" said Robin, with a sigh. "But the major will make me welcome to the best of his victuals; so I will even step boldly in, and in- 10 quire my way to his dwelling."

He entered the tavern, and was guided by the murmur of voices, and the fumes of tobacco, to the public room. It was a long and low apartment, with oaken walls, grown dark in the continual smoke, and a floor, which was thickly sanded, but of no immaculate purity. A number of persons—the larger part of whom appeared to be mariners, or in some way connected with the sea—occupied the wooden benches, or leather-bottomed chairs, conversing on various matters, and occasionally lending their attention to some topic of general interest. Three or four little groups were draining as many bowls of punch, which the West India trade had 20 long since made a familiar drink in the colony. Others, who had the appearance of men who lived by regular and laborious handicraft, preferred the insulated bliss of an unshared potation, and became more taciturn under its influence. Nearly all, in short, evinced a predilection for the Good Creature in some of its various shapes, for this is a vice to which, as Fast-day sermons of a hundred years ago will testify, we have a long hereditary claim. The only guests to whom Robin's sympathies inclined him were two or three sheepish countrymen, who were using the inn somewhat after the fashion of a Turkish caravansary; they had gotten themselves into the darkest corner of the room, and, heedless of the 30 Nicotian atmosphere, were supping on the bread of their own ovens, and the bacon cured in their own chimney-smoke. But though Robin felt a sort of brotherhood with these strangers, his eyes were attracted from them to a person who stood near the door, holding whispered conversation with a group of ill-dressed associates. His features were separately striking almost to grotesqueness, and the whole face left a deep impression on the memory. The forehead bulged out into a double prominence, with a vale between; the nose came boldly forth in an irregular curve, and its bridge was of more than a finger's breadth; the eyebrows were deep and shaggy, and the eyes glowed beneath them like fire in a cave. 40

While Robin deliberated of whom to inquire respecting his kinsman's dwelling, he was accosted by the innkeeper, a little man in a stained white apron, who had come to pay his professional welcome to the stranger. Being in the second generation from a French Protestant, he seemed to have inherited the courtesy of his parent nation; but no variety of circumstances was ever known to change his voice from the one shrill note in which he now addressed Robin.

"From the country, I presume, sir?" said he, with a profound bow. "Beg leave to congratulate you on your arrival, and trust you intend a long stay with us. Fine town here, sir, beautiful buildings, and much that may interest a stranger. May I hope for the honor of your commands in respect to supper?"

10 "The man sees a family likeness! the rogue has guessed that I am related to the major!" thought Robin, who had hitherto experienced little superfluous civility.

All eyes were now turned on the country lad, standing at the door, in his worn three-cornered hat, gray coat, leather breeches, and blue yarn stockings, leaning on an oaken cudgel, and bearing a wallet on his back.

Robin replied to the courteous innkeeper, with such an assumption of confidence as befitted the major's relative. "My honest friend," he said, "I shall make it a point to patronize your house on some occasion, when" —here he could not help lowering his voice—"when I may have more than a parchment three-pence in my pocket. My present business," con-
20 tinued he, speaking with lofty confidence, "is merely to inquire my way to the dwelling of my kinsman, Major Molineux."

There was a sudden and general movement in the room, which Robin interpreted as expressing the eagerness of each individual to become his guide. But the innkeeper turned his eyes to a written paper on the wall, which he read, or seemed to read, with occasional recurrences to the young man's figure.

"What have we here?" said he, breaking his speech into little dry fragments. " 'Left the house of the subscriber, bounden servant, Hezekiah Mudge,—had on, when he went away, gray coat, leather breeches, mas-
30 ter's third-best hat. One pound currency reward to whosoever shall lodge him in any jail of the province.' Better trudge, boy, better trudge!"

Robin had begun to draw his hand towards the lighter end of the oak cudgel, but a strange hostility in every countenance induced him to relinquish his purpose of breaking the courteous innkeeper's head. As he turned to leave the room, he encountered a sneering glance from the bold-featured personage whom he had before noticed; and no sooner was he beyond the door, than he heard a general laugh, in which the innkeeper's voice might be distinguished, like the dropping of small stones into a kettle.

"Now, is it not strange," thought Robin, with his usual shrewdness,
40 "is it not strange, that the confession of an empty pocket should outweigh the name of my kinsman, Major Molineux? O, if I had one of those grinning rascals in the woods, where I and my oak sapling grew together, I would teach him that my arm is heavy, though my purse be light!"

On turning the corner of the narrow lane, Robin found himself in a spacious street, with an unbroken line of lofty houses on each side, and a steepled building at the upper end, whence the ringing of a bell announced the hour of nine. The light of the moon, and the lamps from the numerous shop windows, discovered people promenading on the pavement, and amongst them Robin hoped to recognize his hitherto inscrutable relative. The result of his former inquiries made him unwilling to hazard another, in a scene of such publicity, and he determined to walk slowly and silently up the street, thrusting his face close to that of every elderly gentleman, in search of the major's lineaments. In his progress, 10 Robin encountered many gay and gallant figures. Embroidered garments of showy colors, enormous periwigs, gold-laced hats, and silver-hilted swords, glided past him, and dazzled his optics. Travelled youths, imitators of the European fine gentlemen of the period, trod jauntily along, half-dancing to the fashionable tunes which they hummed, and making poor Robin ashamed of his quiet and natural gait. At length, after many pauses to examine the gorgeous display of goods in the shop windows, and after suffering some rebukes for the impertinence of his scrutiny into people's faces, the major's kinsman found himself near the steepled building, still unsuccessful in his search. As yet, however, he had seen only 20 one side of the thronged street; so Robin crossed, and continued the same sort of inquisition down the opposite pavement, with stronger hopes than the philosopher seeking an honest man, but with no better fortune. He had arrived about midway towards the lower end, from which his course began, when he overheard the approach of some one, who struck down a cane on the flag-stones at every step, uttering, at regular intervals, two sepulchral hems.

"Mercy on us!" quoth Robin, recognizing the sound.

Turning a corner, which chanced to be close at his right hand, he hastened to pursue his researches in some other part of the town. His 30 patience now was wearing low, and he seemed to feel more fatigue from his rambles since he crossed the ferry, than from his journey of several days on the other side. Hunger also pleaded loudly within him, and Robin began to balance the propriety of demanding, violently, and with lifted cudgel, the necessary guidance from the first solitary passenger whom he should meet. While a resolution to this effect was gaining strength, he entered a street of mean appearance, on either side of which a row of ill-built houses was straggling towards the harbor. The moonlight fell upon no passenger along the whole extent, but in the third domicile which Robin passed there was a half-opened door, and his keen 40 glance detected a woman's garment within.

"My luck may be better here," said he to himself.

Accordingly, he approached the door, and beheld it shut closer as he did so; yet an open space remained, sufficing for the fair occupant to observe the stranger, without a corresponding display on her part. All that Robin could discern was a strip of scarlet petticoat, and the occasional sparkle of an eye, as if the moonbeams were trembling on some bright thing.

"Pretty mistress," for I may call her so with a good conscience, thought the shrewd youth, since I know nothing to the contrary,—"my sweet pretty mistress, will you be kind enough to tell me whereabouts I must seek the dwelling of my kinsman, Major Molineux?"

Robin's voice was plaintive and winning, and the female, seeing noth-
10 ing to be shunned in the handsome country youth, thrust open the door, and came forth into the moonlight. She was a dainty little figure, with a white neck, round arms, and a slender waist, at the extremity of which her scarlet petticoat jutted out over a hoop, as if she were standing in a balloon. Moreover, her face was oval and pretty, her hair dark beneath the little cap, and her bright eyes possessed a sly freedom, which triumphed over those of Robin.

"Major Molineux dwells here," said this fair woman.

Now, her voice was the sweetest Robin had heard that night, the airy counterpart of a stream of melted silver; yet he could not help doubting
20 whether that sweet voice spoke Gospel truth. He looked up and down the mean street, and then surveyed the house before which they stood. It was a small, dark edifice of two stories, the second of which projected over the lower floor; and the front apartment had the aspect of a shop for petty commodities.

"Now truly I am in luck," replied Robin, cunningly, "and so indeed is my kinsman, the major, in having so pretty a housekeeper. But I prithee trouble him to step to the door; I will deliver him a message from his friends in the country, and then go back to my lodgings at the inn."

"Nay, the major has been a-bed this hour or more," said the lady of
30 the scarlet petticoat; "and it would be to little purpose to disturb him to-night, seeing his evening draught was of the strongest. But he is a kind-hearted man, and it would be as much as my life's worth to let a kinsman of his turn away from the door. You are the good old gentleman's very picture, and I could swear that was his rainy-weather hat. Also he has garments very much resembling those leather smallclothes. But come in, I pray, for I bid you hearty welcome in his name."

So saying, the fair and hospitable dame took our hero by the hand; and the touch was light, and the force was gentleness, and though Robin read in her eyes what he did not hear in her words, yet the slender-waisted
40 woman in the scarlet petticoat proved stronger than the athletic country youth. She had drawn his half-willing footsteps nearly to the threshold, when the opening of a door in the neighborhood startled the major's housekeeper, and, leaving the major's kinsman, she vanished speedily into her own domicile. A heavy yawn preceded the appearance of a man,

who, like the Moonshine of Pyramus and Thisbe, carried a lantern, needlessly aiding his sister luminary in the heavens. As he walked sleepily up the street, he turned his broad, dull face on Robin, and displayed a long staff, spiked at the end.

"Home, vagabond, home!" said the watchman, in accents that seemed to fall asleep as soon as they were uttered. "Home, or we'll set you in the stocks, by peep of day!"

"This is the second hint of the kind," thought Robin. "I wish they would end my difficulties, by setting me there to-night."

Nevertheless, the youth felt an instinctive antipathy towards the guardian of midnight order, which at first prevented him from asking his usual question. But just when the man was about to vanish behind the corner, Robin resolved not to lose the opportunity, and shouted lustily after him,—

"I say, friend! will you guide me to the house of my kinsman, Major Molineux?"

The watchman made no reply, but turned the corner and was gone; yet Robin seemed to hear the sound of drowsy laughter stealing along the solitary street. At that moment, also, a pleasant titter saluted him from the open window above his head; he looked up, and caught the sparkle of a saucy eye; a round arm beckoned to him, and next he heard light footsteps descending the staircase within. But Robin, being of the household of a New England clergyman, was a good youth, as well as a shrewd one; so he resisted temptation, and fled away.

He now roamed desperately, and at random, through the town, almost ready to believe that a spell was on him, like that by which a wizard of his country had once kept three pursuers wandering, a whole winter night, within twenty paces of the cottage which they sought. The streets lay before him, strange and desolate, and the lights were extinguished in almost every house. Twice, however, little parties of men, among whom Robin distinguished individuals in outlandish attire, came hurrying along; but though on both occasions they paused to address him, such intercourse did not at all enlighten his perplexity. They did but utter a few words in some language of which Robin knew nothing, and perceiving his inability to answer, bestowed a curse upon him in plain English, and hastened away. Finally, the lad determined to knock at the door of every mansion that might appear worthy to be occupied by his kinsman, trusting that perseverance would overcome the fatality that had hitherto thwarted him. Firm in this resolve, he was passing beneath the walls of a church, which formed the corner of two streets, when, as he turned into the shade of its steeple, he encountered a bulky stranger, muffled in a cloak. The man was proceeding with the speed of earnest business, but Robin planted himself full before him, holding the oak cudgel with both hands across his body, as a bar to further passage.

"Halt, honest man, and answer me a question," said he, very resolutely. "Tell me, this instant, whereabouts is the dwelling of my kinsman, Major Molineux!"

"Keep your tongue between your teeth, fool, and let me pass!" said a deep, gruff voice, which Robin partly remembered. "Let me pass, I say, or I'll strike you to the earth!"

"No, no, neighbor!" cried Robin, flourishing his cudgel, and then thrusting its larger end close to the man's muffled face. "No, no, I'm not the fool you take me for, nor do you pass till I have an answer to my question. Whereabouts is the dwelling of my kinsman, Major Molineux?"

The stranger, instead of attempting to force his passage, stepped back into the moonlight, unmuffled his face, and stared full into that of Robin.

"Watch here an hour, and Major Molineux will pass by," said he.

Robin gazed with dismay and astonishment on the unprecedented physiognomy of the speaker. The forehead with its double prominence, the broad hooked nose, the shaggy eyebrows, and fiery eyes, were those which he had noticed at the inn, but the man's complexion had undergone a singular, or, more properly, a two-fold change. One side of the face blazed an intense red, while the other was black as midnight, the division line being in the broad bridge of the nose; and a mouth which seemed to extend from ear to ear was black or red, in contrast to the color of the cheek. The effect was as if two individual devils, a fiend of fire and a fiend of darkness, had united themselves to form this infernal visage. The stranger grinned in Robin's face, muffled his parti-colored features, and was out of sight in a moment.

"Strange things we travellers see!" ejaculated Robin.

He seated himself, however, upon the steps of the church-door, resolving to wait the appointed time for his kinsman. A few moments were consumed in philosophical speculations upon the species of man who had just left him; but having settled this point shrewdly, rationally, and satisfactorily, he was compelled to look elsewhere for his amusement. And first he threw his eyes along the street. It was of more respectable appearance than most of those into which he had wandered, and the moon, creating, like the imaginative power, a beautiful strangeness in familiar objects, gave something of romance to a scene that might not have possessed it in the light of day. The irregular and often quaint architecture of the houses, some of whose roofs were broken into numerous little peaks, while others ascended, steep and narrow, into a single point, and others again were square; the pure snow-white of some of their complexions, the aged darkness of others, and the thousand sparklings, reflected from bright substances in the walls of many; these matters engaged Robin's attention for a while, and then began to grow wearisome. Next he endeavored to define the forms of distant objects, starting away, with almost ghostly indistinctness, just as his eye appeared to grasp them; and finally he took a minute survey of an edifice which stood on the opposite side of the street, directly in front of the church-door, where he was stationed. It was a large, square mansion, distinguished from its neighbors by a balcony, which rested on tall pillars, and by an elaborate Gothic window, communicating therewith.

"Perhaps this is the very house I have been seeking," thought Robin.

Then he strove to speed away the time, by listening to a murmur which swept continually along the street, yet was scarcely audible, except to an unaccustomed ear like his; it was a low, dull, dreamy sound, compounded of many noises, each of which was at too great a distance to be separately heard. Robin marvelled at this snore of a sleeping town, and marvelled more whenever its continuity was broken by now and then a distant shout, apparently loud where it originated. But altogether it was a sleep-inspiring sound, and, to shake off its drowsy influence, Robin arose, and climbed a window-frame, that he might view the interior of the church. There the moonbeams came trembling in, and fell down upon the deserted pews, and extended along the quiet aisles. A fainter yet more awful radiance was hovering around the pulpit, and one solitary ray had dared to rest upon the opened page of the great Bible. Had nature, in that deep hour, become a worshipper in the house which man had builded? Or was that heavenly light the visible sanctity of the place,—visible because no earthly and impure feet were within the walls? The scene made Robin's heart shiver with a sensation of loneliness stronger than he had ever felt in the remotest depths of his native woods; so he turned away, and sat down again before the door. There were graves around the church, and now an uneasy thought obtruded into Robin's breast. What if the object of his search, which had been so often and so strangely thwarted, were all the time mouldering in his shroud? What if his kinsman should glide through yonder gate, and nod and smile to him in dimly passing by?

"O that any breathing thing were here with me!" said Robin.

Recalling his thoughts from this uncomfortable track, he sent them over forest, hill, and stream, and attempted to imagine how that evening of ambiguity and weariness had been spent by his father's household. He pictured them assembled at the door, beneath the tree, the great old tree, which had been spared for its huge twisted trunk, and venerable shade, when a thousand leafy brethren fell. There, at the going down of the summer sun, it was his father's custom to perform domestic worship, that the neighbors might come and join with him like brothers of the family, and that the wayfaring man might pause to drink at that fountain, and keep his heart pure by freshening the memory of home. Robin distinguished the seat of every individual of the little audience; he saw the good man in the midst, holding the Scriptures in the golden light that fell from the western clouds; he beheld him close the book, and all rise up to

pray. He heard the old thanksgivings for daily mercies, the old supplications for their continuance, to which he had so often listened in weariness, but which were now among his dear remembrances. He perceived the slight inequality of his father's voice when he came to speak of the absent one; he noted how his mother turned her face to the broad and knotted trunk; how his elder brother scorned, because the beard was rough upon his upper lip, to permit his features to be moved; how the younger sister drew down a low hanging branch before her eyes; and how the little one of all, whose sports had hitherto broken the decorum of the scene,
10 understood the prayer for her playmate, and burst into clamorous grief. Then he saw them go in at the door; and when Robin would have entered also, the latch tinkled into its place, and he was excluded from his home.

"Am I here, or there?" cried Robin, starting; for all at once, when his thoughts had become visible and audible in a dream, the long, wide, solitary street shone out before him.

He aroused himself, and endeavored to fix his attention steadily upon the large edifice which he had surveyed before. But still his mind kept vibrating between fancy and reality; by turns, the pillars of the balcony lengthened into the tall, bare stems of pines, dwindled down to human figures,
20 settled again into their true shape and size, and then commenced a new succession of changes. For a single moment, when he deemed himself awake, he could have sworn that a visage—one which he seemed to remember, yet could not absolutely name as his kinsman's—was looking towards him from the Gothic window. A deeper sleep wrestled with and nearly overcame him, but fled at the sound of footsteps along the opposite pavement. Robin rubbed his eyes, discerned a man passing at the foot of the balcony, and addressed him in a loud, peevish, and lamentable cry.

"Hallo, friend! must I wait here all night for my kinsman, Major
30 Molineux?"

The sleeping echoes awoke, and answered the voice; and the passenger, barely able to discern a figure sitting in the oblique shade of the steeple, traversed the street to obtain a nearer view. He was himself a gentleman in his prime, of open, intelligent, cheerful, and altogether prepossessing countenance. Perceiving a country youth, apparently homeless and without friends, he accosted him in a tone of real kindness, which had become strange to Robin's ears.

"Well, my good lad, why are you sitting here?" inquired he. "Can I be of service to you in any way?"
40 "I am afraid not, sir," replied Robin, despondingly; "yet I shall take it kindly, if you'll answer me a single question. I've been searching, half the night, for one Major Molineux; now, sir, is there really such a person in these parts, or am I dreaming?"

"Major Molineux! The name is not altogether strange to me," said the gentleman, smiling. "Have you any objection to telling me the nature of your business with him?"

Then Robin briefly related that his father was a clergyman, settled on a small salary, at a long distance back in the country, and that he and Major Molineux were brothers' children. The major, having inherited riches, and acquired civil and military rank, had visited his cousin, in great pomp, a year or two before; had manifested much interest in Robin and an elder brother, and, being childless himself, had thrown out hints respecting the future establishment of one of them in life. The elder brother was destined to succeed to the farm which his father cultivated in 10 the interval of sacred duties; it was therefore determined that Robin should profit by his kinsman's generous intentions, especially as he seemed to be rather the favorite, and was thought to possess other necessary endowments.

"For I have the name of being a shrewd youth," observed Robin, in this part of his story.

"I doubt not you deserve it," replied his new friend, good-naturedly; "but pray proceed."

"Well, sir, being nearly eighteen years old, and well-grown, as you see," continued Robin, drawing himself up to his full height, "I thought 20 it high time to begin the world. So my mother and sister put me in handsome trim, and my father gave me half the remnant of his last year's salary, and five days ago I started for this place, to pay the major a visit. But, would you believe it, sir! I crossed the ferry a little after dark, and have yet found nobody that would show me the way to his dwelling; – only, an hour or two since, I was told to wait here, and Major Molineux would pass by."

"Can you describe the man who told you this?" inquired the gentleman.

"O, he was a very ill-favored fellow, sir," replied Robin, "with two 30 great bumps on his forehead, a hook nose, fiery eyes,—and, what struck me as the strangest, his face was of two different colors. Do you happen to know such a man, sir?"

"Not intimately," answered the stranger, "but I chanced to meet him a little time previous to your stopping me. I believe you may trust his word, and that the major will very shortly pass through this street. In the mean time, as I have a singular curiosity to witness your meeting, I will sit down here upon the steps, and bear you company."

He seated himself accordingly, and soon engaged his companion in animated discourse. It was but of brief continuance, however, for a noise 40 of shouting, which had long been remotely audible, drew so much nearer that Robin inquired its cause.

"What may be the meaning of this uproar?" asked he. "Truly, if your town be always as noisy, I shall find little sleep, while I am an inhabitant."

"Why, indeed, friend Robin, there do appear to be three or four riotous fellows abroad to-night," replied the gentleman. "You must not expect all the stillness of your native woods, here in our streets. But the watch will shortly be at the heels of these lads, and—"

"Ay, and set them in the stocks by peep of day," interrupted Robin, recollecting his own encounter with the drowsy lantern-bearer. "But, dear sir, if I may trust my ears, an army of watchmen would never make head against such a multitude of rioters. There were at least a thousand voices went up to make that one shout."

10 "May not a man have several voices, Robin, as well as two complexions?" said his friend.

"Perhaps a man may; but Heaven forbid that a woman should!" responded the shrewd youth, thinking of the seductive tones of the major's housekeeper.

The sounds of a trumpet in some neighboring street now became so evident and continual, that Robin's curiosity was strongly excited. In addition to the shouts, he heard frequent bursts from many instruments of discord, and a wild and confused laughter filled up the intervals. Robin rose from the steps, and looked wistfully towards a point whither several 20 people seemed to be hastening.

"Surely some prodigious merry-making is going on," exclaimed he. "I have laughed very little since I left home, sir, and should be sorry to lose an opportunity. Shall we step round the corner by that darkish house, and take our share of the fun?"

"Sit down again, sit down, good Robin," replied the gentleman, laying his hand on the skirt of the gray coat. "You forget that we must wait here for your kinsman; and there is reason to believe that he will pass by, in the course of a very few moments."

The near approach of the uproar had now disturbed the neighbor-30 hood; windows flew open on all sides; and many heads, in the attire of the pillow, and confused by sleep suddenly broken, were protruded to the gaze of whoever had leisure to observe them. Eager voices hailed each other from house to house, all demanding the explanation, which not a soul could give. Half-dressed men hurried towards the unknown commotion, stumbling as they went over the stone steps, that thrust themselves into the narrow foot-walk. The shouts, the laughter, and the tuneless bray, the antipodes of music, came onwards with increasing din, till scattered individuals, and then denser bodies, began to appear round a corner at the distance of a hundred yards.

40 "Will you recognize your kinsman, if he passes in this crowd?" inquired the gentleman.

"Indeed, I can't warrant it, sir; but I'll take my stand here, and keep a bright look-out," answered Robin, descending to the outer edge of the pavement.

A mighty stream of people now emptied into the street, and came rolling slowly towards the church. A single horseman wheeled the corner in the midst of them, and close behind him came a band of fearful wind-instruments, sending forth a fresher discord, now that no intervening buildings kept it from the ear. Then a redder light disturbed the moonbeams, and a dense multitude of torches shone along the street, concealing, by their glare, whatever object they illuminated. The single horseman, clad in a military dress, and bearing a drawn sword, rode onward as the leader, and, by his fierce and variegated countenance, appeared like war personified: the red of one cheek was an emblem of fire and 10 sword; the blackness of the other betokened the mourning that attends them. In his train were wild figures in the Indian dress, and many fantastic shapes without a model, giving the whole march a visionary air, as if a dream had broken forth from some feverish brain, and were sweeping visibly through the midnight streets. A mass of people, inactive, except as applauding spectators, hemmed the procession in; and several women ran along the side-walk, piercing the confusion of heavier sounds with their shrill voices of mirth or terror.

"The double-faced fellow has his eye upon me," muttered Robin, with an indefinite but an uncomfortable idea that he was himself to bear a 20 part in the pageantry.

The leader turned himself in the saddle, and fixed his glance full upon the country youth, as the steed went slowly by. When Robin had freed his eyes from those fiery ones, the musicians were passing before him, and the torches were close at hand; but the unsteady brightness of the latter formed a veil which he could not penetrate. The rattling of wheels over the stones sometimes found its way to his ear, and confused traces of a human form appeared at intervals, and then melted into the vivid light. A moment more, and the leader thundered a command to halt: the trumpets vomited a horrid breath, and then held their peace; the shouts 30 and laughter of the people died away, and there remained only a universal hum, allied to silence. Right before Robin's eyes was an uncovered cart. There the torches blazed the brightest, there the moon shone out like day, and there, in tar-and-feathery dignity, sat his kinsman, Major Molineux!

He was an elderly man, of large and majestic person, and strong, square features, betokening a steady soul; but steady as it was, his enemies had found means to shake it. His face was pale as death, and far more ghastly; the broad forehead was contracted in his agony, so that his eyebrows formed one grizzled line; his eyes were red and wild, and the foam 40 hung white upon his quivering lip. His whole frame was agitated by a quick and continual tremor, which his pride strove to quell, even in those circumstances of overwhelming humiliation. But perhaps the bitterest pang of all was when his eyes met those of Robin; for he evidently knew

him on the instant, as the youth stood witnessing the foul disgrace of a head grown gray in honor. They stared at each other in silence, and Robin's knees shook, and his hair bristled, with a mixture of pity and terror. Soon, however, a bewildering excitement began to seize upon his mind; the preceding adventures of the night, the unexpected appearance of the crowd, the torches, the confused din and the hush that followed, the spectre of his kinsman reviled by that great multitude,—all this, and, more than all, a perception of tremendous ridicule in the whole scene, affected him with a sort of mental inebriety. At that moment a voice of
10 sluggish merriment saluted Robin's ears; he turned instinctively, and just behind the corner of the church stood the lantern-bearer, rubbing his eyes, and drowsily enjoying the lad's amazement. Then he heard a peal of laughter like the ringing of silvery bells; a woman twitched his arm, a saucy eye met his, and he saw the lady of the scarlet petticoat. A sharp, dry cachinnation appealed to his memory, and, standing on tiptoe in the crowd, with his white apron over his head, he beheld the courteous little innkeeper. And lastly, there sailed over the heads of the multitude a great, broad laugh, broken in the midst by two sepulchral hems; thus, "Haw, haw, haw,—hem, hem,—haw, haw, haw, haw!"
20 The sound proceeded from the balcony of the opposite edifice, and thither Robin turned his eyes. In front of the Gothic window stood the old citizen, wrapped in a wide gown, his gray periwig exchanged for a night-cap, which was thrust back from his forehead, and his silk stockings hanging about his legs. He supported himself on his polished cane in a fit of convulsive merriment, which manifested itself on his solemn old features like a funny inscription on a tomb-stone. Then Robin seemed to hear the voices of the barbers, of the guests of the inn, and of all who had made sport of him that night. The contagion was spreading among the multitude, when, all at once, it seized upon Robin, and he sent forth a
30 shout of laughter that echoed through the street;—every man shook his sides, every man emptied his lungs, but Robin's shout was the loudest there. The cloud-spirits peeped from their silvery islands, as the congregated mirth went roaring up the sky! The Man in the Moon heard the far bellow; "Oho," quoth he, "the old earth is frolicksome to-night!"

When there was a momentary calm in that tempestuous sea of sound, the leader gave the sign, the procession resumed its march. On they went, like fiends that throng in mockery around some dead potentate, mighty no more, but majestic still in his agony. On they went, in counterfeited pomp, in senseless uproar, in frenzied merriment, trampling all on an old
40 man's heart. On swept the tumult, and left a silent street behind.

"Well, Robin, are you dreaming?" inquired the gentleman, laying his hand on the youth's shoulder.

Robin started, and withdrew his arm from the stone post to which he had instinctively clung, as the living stream rolled by him. His cheek was somewhat pale, and his eye not quite as lively as in the earlier part of the evening.

"Will you be kind enough to show me the way to the ferry?" said he, after a moment's pause.

"You have, then, adopted a new subject of inquiry?" observed his companion, with a smile.

"Why, yes, sir," replied Robin, rather dryly. "Thanks to you, and to my other friends, I have at last met my kinsman, and he will scarce desire to see my face again. I begin to grow weary of a town life, sir. Will you 10 show me the way to the ferry?"

"No, my good friend Robin,—not to-night, at least," said the gentleman. "Some few days hence, if you wish it, I will speed you on your journey. Or, if you prefer to remain with us, perhaps, as you are a shrewd youth, you may rise in the world without the help of your kinsman, Major Molineux."

1843-1916
HENRY
JAMES * The Pupil

I

The poor young man hesitated and procrastinated: it cost him such an effort to broach the subject of terms, to speak of money to a person who spoke only of feelings and, as it were, of the aristocracy. Yet he was unwilling to take leave, treating his engagement as settled, without some more conventional glance in that direction than he could find an opening for in the manner of the large affable lady who sat there drawing a pair of soiled *gants de Suède* through a fat jewelled hand and, at once pressing and gliding, repeated over and over everything but the thing he would have liked to hear. He would have liked to hear the figure of his salary; but just as he was nervously about to sound that note the little boy came back—the lit- 10 tle boy Mrs. Moreen had sent out of the room to fetch her fan. He came back without the fan, only with the casual observation that he couldn't find it. As he dropped this cynical confession he looked straight and hard at the candidate for the honour of taking his education in hand. This personage reflected somewhat grimly that the first thing he should have to teach his little charge would be to appear to address himself to his mother when he spoke to her—especially not to make her such an improper answer as that.

When Mrs. Moreen bethought herself of this pretext for getting rid of their companion Pemberton supposed it was precisely to approach the delicate subject of his remuneration. But it had been only to say some things about her son that it was better a boy of eleven shouldn't catch. They were extravagantly to his advantage save when she lowered her voice to sigh, tapping her left side familiarly, "And all overclouded by *this*, you know; all at the mercy of a weakness—!" Pemberton gathered that the weakness was in the region of the heart. He had known the poor child was not robust: this was the basis on which he had been invited to
10 treat, through an English lady, an Oxford acquaintance, then at Nice, who happened to know both his needs and those of the amiable American family looking out for something really superior in the way of a resident tutor.

The young man's impression of his prospective pupil, who had come into the room as if to see for himself the moment Pemberton was admitted, was not quite the soft solicitation the visitor had taken for granted. Morgan Moreen was somehow sickly without being "delicate," and that he looked intelligent—it is true Pemberton wouldn't have enjoyed his being stupid —only added to the suggestion that, as with his big mouth and big ears
20 he really couldn't be called pretty, he might too utterly fail to please. Pemberton was modest, was even timid; and the chance that his small scholar would prove cleverer than himself had quite figured, to his anxiety, among the dangers of an untried experiment. He reflected, however, that these were risks one had to run when one accepted a position, as it was called, in a private family; when as yet one's university honours had, pe-cuniarily speaking, remained barren. At any rate when Mrs. Moreen got up as to intimate that, since it was understood he would enter upon his duties within the week she would let him off now, he succeeded, in spite of the presence of the child, in squeezing out a phrase about the rate of
30 payment. It was not the fault of the conscious smile which seemed a reference to the lady's expensive identity, it was not the fault of this dem-onstration, which had, in a sort, both vagueness and point, if the allusion didn't sound rather vulgar. This was exactly because she became still more gracious to reply: "Oh I can assure you that all that will be quite regular."

Pemberton only wondered, while he took up his hat, what "all that" was to amount to—people had such different ideas. Mrs. Moreen's words, however, seemed to commit the family to a pledge definite enough to elicit from the child a strange little comment in the shape of the mocking foreign ejaculation "Oh la-la!"
40 Pemberton, in some confusion, glanced at him as he walked slowly to the window with his back turned, his hands in his pockets and the air in his elderly shoulders of a boy who didn't play. The young man wondered if he should be able to teach him to play, though his mother had said it would never do and that this was why school was impossible. Mrs. Moreen

exhibited no discomfiture; she only continued blandly: "Mr. Moreen will be delighted to meet your wishes. As I told you, he has been called to London for a week. As soon as he comes back you shall have it out with him."

This was so frank and friendly that the young man could only reply, laughing as his hostess laughed: "Oh I don't imagine we shall have much of a battle."

"They'll give you anything you like," the boy remarked unexpectedly, returning from the window. "We don't mind what anything costs—we live awfully well."

"My darling, you're too quaint!" his mother exclaimed, putting out to 10 caress him a practised but ineffectual hand. He slipped out of it, but looked with intelligent innocent eyes at Pemberton, who had already had time to notice that from one moment to the other his small satiric face seemed to change its time of life. At this moment it was infantine, yet it appeared also to be under the influence of curious intuitions and knowledges. Pemberton rather disliked precocity and was disappointed to find gleams of it in a disciple not yet in his teens. Nevertheless he divined on the spot that Morgan wouldn't prove a bore. He would prove on the contrary a source of agitation. This idea held the young man, in spite of a certain repulsion.

"You pompous little person! We're not extravagant!" Mrs. Moreen 20 gaily protested, making another unsuccessful attempt to draw the boy to her side. "You must know what to expect," she went on to Pemberton.

"The less you expect the better!" her companion interposed. "But we *are* people of fashion."

"Only so far as *you* make us so!" Mrs. Moreen tenderly mocked. "Well then, on Friday—don't tell me you're superstitious—and mind you don't fail us. Then you'll see us all. I'm so sorry the girls are out. I guess you'll like the girls. And, you know, I've another son, quite different from this one." 30

"He tries to imitate me," Morgan said to their friend.

"He tries? Why he's twenty years old!" cried Mrs. Moreen.

"You're very witty," Pemberton remarked to the child—a proposition his mother echoed with enthusiasm, declaring Morgan's sallies to be the delight of the house.

The boy paid no heed to this; he only enquired abruptly of the visitor, who was surprised afterwards that he hadn't struck him as offensively forward: "Do you *want* very much to come?"

"Can you doubt it after such a description of what I shall hear?" Pemberton replied. Yet he didn't want to come at all; he was coming because he had to go somewhere, thanks to the collapse of his fortune at the end of 40 a year abroad spent on the system of putting his scant patrimony into a single full wave of experience. He had had his full wave but couldn't pay the score at his inn. Moreover he had caught in the boy's eyes the glimpse of a far-off appeal.

"Well, I'll do the best I can for you," said Morgan; with which he turned away again. He passed out of one of the long windows; Pemberton saw him go and lean on the parapet of the terrace. He remained there while the young man took leave of his mother, who, on Pemberton's looking as if he expected a farewell from him, interposed with: "Leave him, leave him; he's so strange!" Pemberton supposed her to fear something he might say. "He's a genius—you'll love him," she added. "He's much the most interesting person in the family." And before he could invent some civility to oppose to this she wound up with: "But we're all good, you 10 know!"

"He's a genius—you'll love him!" were words that recurred to our aspirant before the Friday, suggesting among many things that geniuses were not invariably loveable. However, it was all the better if there was an element that would make tutorship absorbing: he had perhaps taken too much for granted it would only disgust him. As he left the villa after his interview he looked up at the balcony and saw the child leaning over it. "We shall have great larks!" he called up.

Morgan hung fire a moment and then gaily returned: "By the time you come back I shall have thought of something witty!"
20 This made Pemberton say to himself "After all he's rather nice."

II

On the Friday he saw them all, as Mrs. Moreen had promised, for her husband had come back and the girls and the other son were at home. Mr. Moreen had a white moustache, a confiding manner and, in his buttonhole, the ribbon of a foreign order—bestowed, as Pemberton eventually learned, for services. For what services he never clearly ascertained: this was a point—one of a large number—that Mr. Moreen's manner never confided. What it emphatically did confide was that he was even more a man of the world than you might first make out. Ulick, the firstborn, was in visible training for the same profession—under the disadvantage as yet, 30 however, of a buttonhole but feebly floral and a moustache with no pretensions to type. The girls had hair and figures and manners and small fat feet, but had never been out alone. As for Mrs. Moreen Pemberton saw on a nearer view that her elegance was intermittent and her parts didn't always match. Her husband, as she had promised, met with enthusiasm Pemberton's ideas in regard to a salary. The young man had endeavoured to keep these stammerings modest, and Mr. Moreen made it no secret that *he* found them wanting in "style." He further mentioned that he aspired to be intimate with his children, to be their best friend, and that he was always looking out for them. That was what he went off for, to London and 40 other places—to look out; and this vigilance was the theory of life, as well as the real occupation, of the whole family. They all looked out, for they were very frank on the subject of its being necessary. They desired it to be understood that they were earnest people, and also that their fortune, though quite adequate for earnest people, required the most careful administration. Mr. Moreen, as the parent bird, sought sustenance for the nest. Ulick invoked support mainly at the club, where Pemberton guessed that it was usually served on green cloth. The girls used to do up their hair and their frocks themselves, and our young man felt appealed to to be glad, in regard to Morgan's education, that, though it must naturally be of the best, it didn't cost too much. After a little he *was* glad, forgetting at 10 times his own needs in the interest inspired by the child's character and culture and the pleasure of making easy terms for him.

During the first weeks of their acquaintance Morgan had been as puzzling as a page in an unknown language—altogether different from the obvious little Anglo-Saxons who had misrepresented childhood to Pemberton. Indeed the whole mystic volume in which the boy had been amateurishly bound demanded some practice in translation. To-day, after a considerable interval, there is something phantasmagoric, like a prismatic reflection or a serial novel, in Pemberton's memory of the queerness of the Moreens. If it were not for a few tangible tokens—a lock 20 of Morgan's hair cut by his own hand, and the half-dozen letters received from him when they were disjoined—the whole episode and the figures peopling it would seem too inconsequent for anything but dreamland. Their supreme quaintness was their success—as it appeared to him for a while at the time; since he had never seen a family so brilliantly equipped for failure. Wasn't it success to have kept him so hatefully long? Wasn't it success to have drawn him in that first morning at déjeuner, the Friday he came—it was enough to *make* one superstitious—so that he utterly committed himself, and this not by calculation or on a signal, but from a happy instinct which made them, like a band of gipsies, work so neatly 30 together? They amused him as much as if they had really been a band of gipsies. He was still young and had not seen much of the world—his English years had been properly arid; therefore the reversed conventions of the Moreens—for they had *their* desperate proprieties—struck him as topsy-turvy. He had encountered nothing like them at Oxford; still less had any such note been struck to his younger American ear during the four years at Yale in which he had richly supposed himself to be reacting against a Puritan strain. The reaction of the Moreens, at any rate, went ever so much further. He had thought himself very sharp that first day in hitting them all off in his mind with the "cosmopolite" label. Later it 40 seemed feeble and colourless—confessedly helplessly provisional.

He yet when he first applied it felt a glow of joy—for an instructor he was still empirical—rise from the apprehension that living with them would really be to see life. Their sociable strangeness was an intimation of

that—their chatter of tongues, their gaiety and good humour, their infinite dawdling (they were always getting themselves up, but it took for
ever, and Pemberton had once found Mr. Moreen shaving in the draw-
ing-room), their French, their Italian and, cropping up in the foreign
fluencies, their cold tough slices of American. They lived on maccaroni
and coffee—they had these articles prepared in perfection—but they
knew recipes for a hundred other dishes. They overflowed with music and
song, were always humming and catching each other up, and had a sort
of professional acquaintance with Continental cities. They talked of
10 "good places" as if they had been pickpockets or strolling players. They
had at Nice a villa, a carriage, a piano and a banjo, and they went to
official parties. They were a perfect calendar of the "days" of their friends,
which Pemberton knew them, when they were indisposed, to get out of
bed to go to, and which made the week larger than life when Mrs. Moreen
talked of them with Paula and Amy. Their initiations gave their new inmate at first an almost dazzling sense of culture. Mrs. Moreen had translated something at some former period—an author whom it made Pemberton feel *borné*° never to have heard of. They could imitate Venetian
and sing Neapolitan, and when they wanted to say something very par-
20 ticular communicated with each other in an ingenious dialect of their
own, an elastic spoken cipher which Pemberton at first took for some
patois of one of their countries, but which he "caught on to" as he would
not have grasped provincial development of Spanish or German.

"It's the family language—Ultramoreen," Morgan explained to him
drolly enough; but the boy rarely condescended to use it himself, though
he dealt in colloquial Latin as if he had been a little prelate.

Among all the "days" with which Mrs. Moreen's memory was taxed
she managed to squeeze in one of her own, which her friends sometimes
forgot. But the house drew a frequented air from the number of fine
30 people who were freely named there and from several mysterious men
with foreign titles and English clothes whom Morgan called the Princes
and who, on sofas with the girls, talked French very loud—though sometimes with some oddity of accent—as if to show they were saying nothing
improper. Pemberton wondered how the Princes could ever propose in
that tone and so publicly: he took for granted cynically that this was what
was desired of them. Then he recognised that even for the chance of such
an advantage Mrs. Moreen would never allow Paula and Amy to receive
alone. These young ladies were not at all timid, but it was just the safeguards that made them so candidly free. It was a houseful of Bohemians
40 who wanted tremendously to be Philistines.

In one respect, however, certainly, they achieved no rigour—they were
wonderfully amiable and ecstatic about Morgan. It was a genuine ten-

18. *borné*, limited.

derness, an artless admiration, equally strong in each. They even praised his beauty, which was small, and were as afraid of him as if they felt him of finer clay. They spoke of him as a little angel and a prodigy—they touched on his want of health with long, vague faces. Pemberton feared at first an extravagance that might make him hate the boy, but before this happened he had become extravagant himself. Later, when he had grown rather to hate the others, it was a bribe to patience for him that they were at any rate nice about Morgan, going on tiptoe if they fancied he was showing symptoms, and even giving up somebody's "day" to procure him a pleasure. Mixed with this too was the oddest wish to make 10 him independent, as if they had felt themselves not good enough for him. They passed him over to the new members of their circle very much as if wishing to force some charity of adoption on so free an agent and get rid of their own charge. They were delighted when they saw Morgan take so to his kind playfellow, and could think of no higher praise for the young man. It was strange how they contrived to reconcile the appearance, and indeed the essential fact, of adoring the child with their eagerness to wash their hands of him. Did they want to get rid of him before he should find them out? Pemberton was finding them out month by month. The boy's fond family, however this might be, turned their backs with exaggerated 20 delicacy, as if to avoid the reproach of interfering. Seeing in time how little he had in common with them—it was by *them* he first observed it; they proclaimed it with complete humility—his companion was moved to speculate on the mysteries of transmission, the far jumps of heredity. Where his detachment from most of the things they represented had come from was more than an observer could say—it certainly had burrowed under two or three generations.

As for Pemberton's own estimate of his pupil, it was a good while before he got the point of view, so little had he been prepared for it by the smug young barbarians to whom the tradition of tutorship, as hitherto revealed 30 to him, had been adjusted. Morgan was scrappy and surprising, deficient in many properties supposed common to the *genus* and abounding in others that were the portion only of the supernaturally clever. One day his friend made a great stride: it cleared up the question to perceive that Morgan *was* supernaturally clever and that, though the formula was temporarily meagre, this would be the only assumption on which one could successfully deal with him. He had the general quality of a child for whom life had not been simplified by school, a kind of homebred sensibility which might have been bad for himself but was charming for others, and a whole range of refinement and perception—little musical 40 vibrations as taking as picked-up airs—begotten by wandering about Europe at the tail of his migratory tribe. This might not have been an education to recommend in advance, but its results with so special a subject were as appreciable as the marks on a piece of fine porcelain. There was at the same time in him a small strain of stoicism, doubtless the fruit of having had to begin early to bear pain, which counted for pluck and made it of less consequence that he might have been thought at school rather a polyglot little beast. Pemberton indeed quickly found himself rejoicing that school was out of the question: in any million of boys it was probably good for all but one, and Morgan was that millionth. It would have made him comparative and superior—it might have made him really require kicking. Pemberton would try to be school himself—a bigger seminary than five hundred grazing donkeys, so that, winning no

10 prizes, the boy would remain unconscious and irresponsible and amusing —amusing, because, though life was already intense in his childish nature, freshness still made there a strong draught for jokes. It turned out that even in the still air of Morgan's various disabilities jokes flourished greatly. He was a pale lean acute undeveloped little cosmopolite, who liked intellectual gymnastics and who also, as regards the behaviour of mankind, had noticed more things than you might suppose, but who nevertheless had his proper playroom of superstitions, where he smashed a dozen toys a day.

III

At Nice once, toward evening, as the pair rested in the open air after a
20 walk, and looked over the sea at the pink western lights, he said suddenly to his comrade: "Do you like it, you know—being with us all in this intimate way?"

"My dear fellow, why should I stay if I didn't?"

"How do I know you'll stay? I'm almost sure you won't, very long."

"I hope you don't mean to dismiss me," said Pemberton.

Morgan debated, looking at the sunset. "I think if I did right I ought to."

"Well, I know I'm supposed to instruct you in virtue; but in that case don't do right."

30 "You're very young—fortunately," Morgan went on, turning to him again.

"Oh yes, compared with you!"

"Therefore it won't matter so much if you do lose a lot of time."

"That's the way to look at it," said Pemberton accommodatingly.

They were silent a minute; after which the boy asked: "Do you like my father and my mother very much?"

"Dear me, yes. Charming people."

Morgan received this with another silence; then unexpectedly, familiarly, but at the same time affectionately, he remarked: "You're a jolly
40 old humbug!"

For a particular reason the words made our young man change colour.

The boy noticed in an instant that he had turned red, whereupon he turned red himself and pupil and master exchanged a longish glance in which there was a consciousness of many more things than are usually touched upon, even tacitly, in such a relation. It produced for Pemberton an embarrassment; it raised in a shadowy form a question—this was the first glimpse of it—destined to play a singular and, as he imagined, owing to the altogether peculiar conditions, an unprecedented part in his intercourse with his little companion. Later, when he found himself talking with the youngster in a way in which few youngsters could ever have been talked with, he thought of that clumsy moment on the bench at Nice as 10 the dawn of an understanding that had broadened. What had added to the clumsiness then was that he thought it his duty to declare to Morgan that he might abuse him, Pemberton, as much as he liked, but must never abuse his parents. To this Morgan had the easy retort that he hadn't dreamed of abusing them; which appeared to be true: it put Pemberton in the wrong.

"Then why am I a humbug for saying *I* think them charming?" the young man asked, conscious of a certain rashness.

"Well—they're not your parents."

"They love you better than anything in the world—never forget that," 20 said Pemberton.

"Is that why you like them so much?"

"They're very kind to me," Pemberton replied evasively.

"You *are* a humbug!" laughed Morgan, passing an arm into his tutor's. He leaned against him looking off at the sea again and swinging his long thin legs.

"Don't kick my shins," said Pemberton while he reflected "Hang it, I can't complain of them to the child!"

"There's another reason too," Morgan went on, keeping his legs still.

"Another reason for what?" 30

"Besides their not being your parents."

"I don't understand you," said Pemberton.

"Well, you will before long. All right!"

He did understand fully before long, but he made a fight even with himself before he confessed it. He thought it the oddest thing to have a struggle with the child about. He wondered he didn't hate the hope of the Moreens for bringing the struggle on. But by the time it began any such sentiment for that scion was closed to him. Morgan was a special case, and to know him was to accept him on his own odd terms. Pemberton had spent his aversion to special cases before arriving at knowledge. 40 When at last he did arrive his quandary was great. Against every interest he had attached himself. They would have to meet things together. Before they went home that evening at Nice the boy had said, clinging to his arm:

"Well, at any rate you'll hang on to the last."

"To the last?"

"Till you're fairly beaten."

"*You* ought to be fairly beaten!" cried the young man, drawing him closer.

IV

A year after he had come to live with them Mr. and Mrs. Moreen suddenly gave up the villa at Nice. Pemberton had got used to suddenness, having seen it practised on a considerable scale during two jerky little tours—one in Switzerland the first summer, and the other late in the winter, when they all ran down to Florence and then, at the end of ten days, liking it much less than they had intended, straggled back in mysterious depression. They had returned to Nice "for ever," as they said; but this didn't prevent their squeezing, one rainy muggy May night, into a second-class railway-carriage—you could never tell by which class they would travel—where Pemberton helped them to stow away a wonderful collection of bundles and bags. The explanation of this manœuvre was that they had determined to spend the summer "in some bracing place"; but in Paris they dropped into a small furnished apartment—a fourth floor in a third-rate avenue, where there was a smell on the staircase and the *portier*° was hateful—and passed the next four months in blank indigence.

The better part of this baffled sojourn was for the preceptor and his pupil, who, visiting the Invalides and Notre Dame, the Conciergerie and all the museums, took a hundred remunerative rambles. They learned to know their Paris, which was useful, for they came back another year for a longer stay, the general character of which in Pemberton's memory today mixes pitiably and confusedly with that of the first. He sees Morgan's shabby knickerbockers—the everlasting pair that didn't match his blouse and that as he grew longer could only grow faded. He remembers the particular holes in his three or four pair of coloured stockings.

Morgan was dear to his mother, but he never was better dressed than was absolutely necessary—partly, no doubt, by his own fault, for he was as indifferent to his appearance as a German philosopher. "My dear fellow, you *are* coming to pieces," Pemberton would say to him in sceptical remonstrance; to which the child would reply, looking at him serenely up and down: "My dear fellow, so are you! I don't want to cast you in the shade." Pemberton could have no rejoinder for this—the assertion so closely represented the fact. If however the deficiencies of his own ward-

20. *portier,* janitor or door-keeper.

robe were a chapter by themselves he didn't like his little charge to look too poor. Later he used to say "Well, if we're poor, why, after all, shouldn't we look it?" and he consoled himself with thinking there was something rather elderly and gentlemanly in Morgan's disrepair—it differed from the untidiness of the urchin who plays and spoils his things. He could trace perfectly the degrees by which, in proportion as her little son confined himself to his tutor for society, Mrs. Moreen shrewdly forbore to renew his garments. She did nothing that didn't show, neglected him because he escaped notice, and then, as he illustrated this clever policy, discouraged at home his public appearances. Her position was logical 10 enough—those members of her family who did show had to be showy.

During this period and several others Pemberton was quite aware of how he and his comrade might strike people; wandering languidly through the Jardin des Plantes as if they had nowhere to go, sitting on the winter days in the galleries of the Louvre, so splendidly ironical to the homeless, as if for the advantage of the *calorifère*.° They joked about it sometimes: it was the sort of joke that was perfectly within the boy's compass. They figured themselves as part of the vast vague hand-to-mouth multitude of the enormous city and pretended they were proud of their position in it—it showed them "such a lot of life" and made them 20 conscious of a democratic brotherhood. If Pemberton couldn't feel a sympathy in destitution with his small companion—for after all Morgan's fond parents would never have let him really suffer—the boy would at least feel it with him, so it came to the same thing. He used sometimes to wonder what people would think they were—to fancy they were looked askance at, as if it might be a suspected case of kidnapping. Morgan wouldn't be taken for a young patrician with a preceptor—he wasn't smart enough; though he might pass for his companion's sickly little brother. Now and then he had a five-franc piece, and except once, when they bought a couple of lovely neckties, one of which he made Pemberton 30 accept, they laid it out scientifically in old books. This was sure to be a great day, always spent on the quays, in a rummage of the dusty boxes that garnish the parapets. Such occasions helped them to live, for their books ran low very soon after the beginning of their acquaintance. Pemberton had a good many in England, but he was obliged to write to a friend and ask him kindly to get some fellow to give him something for them.

If they had to relinquish that summer the advantage of the bracing climate the young man couldn't but suspect this failure of the cup when at their very lips to have been the effect of a rude jostle of his own. This 40 had represented his first blow-out, as he called it, with his patrons; his first successful attempt—though there was little other success about it—

16. *calorifère,* the warmth from a hot-air heating system.

to bring them to a consideration of his impossible position. As the osten-
sible eve of a costly journey the moment had struck him as favourable to
an earnest protest, the presentation of an ultimatum. Ridiculous as it
sounded, he had never yet been able to compass an uninterrupted private
interview with the elder pair or with either of them singly. They were
always flanked by their elder children, and poor Pemberton usually had
his own little charge at his side. He was conscious of its being a house in
which the surface of one's delicacy got rather smudged; nevertheless he
had preserved the bloom of his scruple against announcing to Mr. and
10 Mrs. Moreen with publicity that he shouldn't be able to go on longer
without a little money. He was still simple enough to suppose Ulick and
Paula and Amy might not know that since his arrival he had only had a
hundred and forty francs; and he was magnanimous enough to wish not
to compromise their parents in their eyes. Mr. Moreen now listened to
him, as he listened to every one and to every thing, like a man of the
world, and seemed to appeal to him—though not of course too grossly—
to try and be a little more of one himself. Pemberton recognised in fact
the importance of the character—from the advantage it gave Mr.
Moreen. He was not even confused or embarrassed, whereas the young
20 man in his service was more so than there was any reason for. Neither was
he surprised—at least any more than a gentleman had to be who freely
confessed himself a little shocked—though not perhaps strictly at
Pemberton.

"We must go into this, mustn't we, dear?" he said to his wife. He
assured his young friend that the matter should have his very best attention; and he melted into space as elusively as if, at the door, he were
taking an inevitable but deprecatory precedence. When, the next moment, Pemberton found himself alone with Mrs. Moreen it was to hear
her say "I see, I see"—stroking the roundness of her chin and looking as
30 if she were only hesitating between a dozen easy remedies. If they didn't
make their push Mr. Moreen could at least disappear for several days.
During his absence his wife took up the subject again spontaneously, but
her contribution to it was merely that she had thought all the while they
were getting on so beautifully. Pemberton's reply to this revelation was
that unless they immediately put down something on account he would
leave them on the spot and for ever. He knew she would wonder how he
would get away, and for a moment expected her to enquire. She didn't,
for which he was almost grateful to her, so little was he in a position to tell.

"You won't, you *know* you won't—you're too interested," she said.
40 "You *are* interested, you know you are, you dear kind man!" She laughed
with almost condemnatory archness, as if it were a reproach—though she
wouldn't insist; and flirted a soiled pocket-handkerchief at him.

Pemberton's mind was fully made up to take his step the following
week. This would give him time to get an answer to a letter he had dis-

patched to England. If he did in the event nothing of the sort—that is if he stayed another year and then went away only for three months—it was not merely because before the answer to his letter came (most unsatisfactory when it did arrive) Mr. Moreen generously counted out to him, and again with the sacrifice to "form" of a marked man of the world, three hundred francs in elegant ringing gold. He was irritated to find that Mrs. Moreen was right, that he couldn't at the pinch bear to leave the child. This stood out clearer for the very reason that, the night of his desperate appeal to his patrons, he had seen fully for the first time where he was. Wasn't it another proof of the success with which those patrons 10 practised their arts that they had managed to avert for so long the illuminating flash? It descended on our friend with a breadth of effect which perhaps would have struck a spectator as comical, after he had returned to his little servile room, which looked into a close court where a bare dirty opposite wall took, with the sound of shrill clatter, the reflexion of lighted back windows. He had simply given himself away to a band of adventurers. The idea, the word itself, wore a romantic horror for him —he had always lived on such safe lines. Later it assumed a more interesting, almost a soothing, sense: it pointed a moral, and Pemberton could enjoy a moral. The Moreens were adventurers not merely because they 20 didn't pay their debts, because they lived on society, but because their whole view of life, dim and confused and instinctive, like that of clever color-blind animals, was speculative and rapacious and mean. Oh they were "respectable," and that only made them more *immondes!*° The young man's analysis, while he brooded, put it at last very simply—they were adventurers because they were toadies and snobs. That was the completest account of them—it was the law of their being. Even when this truth became vivid to their ingenious inmate he remained unconscious of how much his mind had been prepared for it by the extraordinary little boy who had now become such a complication in his life. Much less 30 could he then calculate on the information he was still to owe the extraordinary little boy.

V

But it was during the ensuing time that the real problem came up—the problem of how far it was excusable to discuss the turpitude of parents with a child of twelve, of thirteen, of fourteen. Absolutely inexcusable and quite impossible it of course at first appeared; and indeed the question didn't press for some time after Pemberton had received his three hundred francs. They produced a temporary lull, a relief from the sharpest pres-

24. *immondes,* vulgar.

sure. The young man frugally amended his wardrobe and even had a few francs in his pocket. He thought the Moreens looked at him as if he were almost too smart, as if they ought to take care not to spoil him. If Mr. Moreen hadn't been such a man of the world he would perhaps have spoken of the freedom of such neckties on the part of a subordinate. But Mr. Moreen was always enough a man of the world to let things pass—he had certainly shown that. It was singular how Pemberton guessed that Morgan, though saying nothing about it, knew something had happened. But three hundred francs, especially when one owed money, couldn't last
10 for ever; and when the treasure was gone—the boy knew when it had failed—Morgan did break ground. The party had returned to Nice at the beginning of the winter, but not to the charming villa. They went to an hotel, where they stayed three months, and then moved to another establishment, explaining that they had left the first because, after waiting and waiting, they couldn't get the rooms they wanted. These apartments, the rooms they wanted, were generally very splendid; but fortunately they never *could* get them—fortunately, I mean, for Pemberton, who reflected always that if they had got them there would have been a still scanter educational fund. What Morgan said at last was said suddenly,
20 irrelevantly, when the moment came, in the middle of a lesson, and consisted of the apparently unfeeling words: "You ought to *filer*, you know— you really ought."

Pemberton stared. He had learnt enough French slang from Morgan to know that to *filer* meant to cut sticks. "Ah my dear fellow, don't turn me off!"

Morgan pulled a Greek lexicon toward him—he used a Greek-German —to look out a word, instead of asking it of Pemberton. "You can't go on like this, you know."

"Like what, my boy?"

30 "You know they don't pay you up," said Morgan, blushing and turning his leaves.

"Don't pay me?" Pemberton stared again and feigned amazement. "What on earth put that into your head?"

"It has been there a long time," the boy replied rummaging his book.

Pemberton was silent, then he went on: "I say, what are you hunting for? They pay me beautifully."

"I'm hunting for the Greek for awful whopper," Morgan dropped.

"Find that rather for gross impertinence and disabuse your mind. What do I want of money?"

40 "Oh that's another question!"

Pemberton wavered—he was drawn in different ways. The severely correct thing would have been to tell the boy that such a matter was none of his business and bid him go on with his lines. But they were really too intimate for that; it was not the way he was in the habit of treating him;

Henry James   163

there had been no reason it should be. On the other hand Morgan had quite lighted on the truth—he really shouldn't be able to keep it up much longer; therefore why not let him know one's real motive for forsaking him? At the same time it wasn't decent to abuse to one's pupil the family of one's pupil; it was better to misrepresent than to do that. So in reply to his comrade's last exclamation he just declared, to dismiss the subject, that he had received several payments.

"I say—I say!" the boy ejaculated, laughing.

"That's all right," Pemberton insisted. "Give me your written rendering." 10

Morgan pushed a copybook across the table, and he began to read the page, but with something running in his head that made it no sense. Looking up after a minute or two he found the child's eyes fixed on him and felt in them something strange. Then Morgan said: "I'm not afraid of the stern reality."

"I haven't yet seen the thing you *are* afraid of—I'll do you that justice!"

This came out with a jump—it was perfectly true—and evidently gave Morgan pleasure. "I've thought of it a long time," he presently resumed.

"Well, don't think of it any more."

The boy appeared to comply, and they had a comfortable and even an 20 amusing hour. They had a theory that they were very thorough, and yet they seemed always to be in the amusing part of lessons, the intervals between the dull dark tunnels, where there were waysides and jolly views. Yet the morning was brought to a violent end by Morgan's suddenly leaning his arms on the table, burying his head in them and bursting into tears: at which Pemberton was the more startled that, as it then came over him, it was the first time he had ever seen the boy cry and that the impression was consequently quite awful.

The next day, after much thought, he took a decision and, believing it to be just, immediately acted on it. He cornered Mr. and Mrs. Moreen 30 again and let them know that if on the spot they didn't pay him all they owed him he wouldn't only leave their house but would tell Morgan exactly what had brought him to it.

"Oh you *haven't* told him?" cried Mrs. Moreen with a pacifying hand on her well-dressed bosom.

"Without warning you? For what do you take me?" the young man returned.

Mr. and Mrs. Moreen looked at each other; he could see that they appreciated, as tending to their security, his superstition of delicacy, and yet that there was a certain alarm in their relief. "My dear fellow," Mr. 40 Moreen demanded, "what use *can* you have, leading the quiet life we all do, for such a lot of money?"—a question to which Pemberton made no answer, occupied as he was in noting that what passed in the mind of his patrons was something like: "Oh then, if we've felt that the child, dear

little angel, has judged us and how he regards us, and we haven't been betrayed, he must have guessed—and in short it's *general!*" an inference that rather stirred up Mr. and Mrs. Moreen, as Pemberton had desired it should. At the same time, if he had supposed his threat would do something towards bringing them round, he was disappointed to find them taking for granted—how vulgar their perception *had* been!—that he had already given them away. There was a mystic uneasiness in their parental breasts, and that had been the inferior sense of it. None the less, however, his threat did touch them; for if they had escaped it was only to meet a
10 new danger. Mr. Moreen appealed to him, on every precedent, as a man of the world; but his wife had recourse, for the first time since his domestication with them, to a fine *hauteur*, reminding him that a devoted mother, with her child, had arts that protected her against gross misrepresentation.

"I should misrepresent you grossly if I accused you of common honesty!" our friend replied; but as he closed the door behind him sharply, thinking he had not done himself much good, while Mr. Moreen lighted another cigarette, he heard his hostess shout after him more touchingly: "Oh you do, you *do*, put the knife to one's throat!"

20 The next morning, very early, she came to his room. He recognised her knock, but had no hope she brought him money; as to which he was wrong, for she had fifty francs in her hand. She squeezed forward in her dressing-gown, and he received her in his own, between his bath-tub and his bed. He had been tolerably schooled by this time to the "foreign ways" of his hosts. Mrs. Moreen was ardent, and when she was ardent she didn't care what she did; so she now sat down on his bed, his clothes being on the chairs, and, in her preoccupation, forgot, as she glanced round, to be ashamed of giving him such a horrid room. What Mrs. Moreen's ardour now bore upon was the design of persuading him that in the first place
30 she was very good-natured to bring him fifty francs, and that in the second, if he would only see it, he was really too absurd to expect to be *paid*. Wasn't he paid enough without perpetual money—wasn't he paid by the comfortable luxurious home he enjoyed with them all, without a care, an anxiety, a solitary want? Wasn't he sure of his position, and wasn't that everything to a young man like him, quite unknown, with singularly little to show, the ground of whose exorbitant pretensions it had never been easy to discover? Wasn't he paid above all by the sweet relation he had established with Morgan—quite ideal as from master to pupil—and by the simple privilege of knowing and living with so amazingly gifted a
40 child; than whom really (and she meant literally what she said) there was no better company in Europe? Mrs. Moreen herself took to appealing to him as a man of the world; she said "Voyons, mon cher," and "My dear man, look here now"; and urged him to be reasonable, putting it before him that it was truly a chance for him. She spoke as if, according as he

should be reasonable, he would prove himself worthy to be her son's tutor and of the extraordinary confidence they had placed in him.

After all, Pemberton reflected, it was only a difference of theory and the theory didn't matter much. They had hitherto gone on that of remunerated, as now they would go on that of gratuitous, service; but why should they have so many words about it? Mrs. Moreen at all events continued to be convincing; sitting there with her fifty francs she talked and reiterated, as women reiterate, and bored and irritated him, while he leaned against the wall with his hands in the pockets of his wrapper, drawing it together round his legs and looking over the head of his visitor 10 at the grey negations of his window. She wound up with saying: "You see I bring you a definite proposal."

"A definite proposal?"

"To make our relations regular, as it were—to put them on a comfortable footing."

"I see—it's a system," said Pemberton. "A kind of organised blackmail."

Mrs. Moreen bounded up, which was exactly what he wanted. "What do you mean by that?"

"You practise on one's fears—one's fears about the child if one should 20 go away."

"And pray what would happen to him in that event?" she demanded with majesty.

"Why he'd be alone with *you*."

"And pray with whom *should* a child be but with those whom he loves most?"

"If you think that, why don't you dismiss me?"

"Do you pretend he loves you more than he loves *us?*" cried Mrs. Moreen.

"I think he ought to. I make sacrifices for him. Though I've heard of 30 those *you* make I don't see them."

Mrs. Moreen stared a moment; then with emotion she grasped her inmate's hand. "*Will* you make it—the sacrifice?"

He burst out laughing. "I'll see. I'll do what I can. I'll stay a little longer. Your calculation's just—I *do* hate intensely to give him up; I'm fond of him and he thoroughly interests me, in spite of the inconvenience I suffer. You know my situation perfectly. I haven't a penny in the world and, occupied as you see me with Morgan, am unable to earn money."

Mrs. Moreen tapped her undressed arm with her folded bank-note. "Can't you write articles? Can't you translate as *I* do?" 40

"I don't know about translating; it's wretchedly paid."

"I'm glad to earn what I can," said Mrs. Moreen with prodigious virtue.

"You ought to tell me who you do it for." Pemberton paused a moment, and she said nothing; so he added: "I've tried to turn off some little sketches, but the magazines won't have them—they're declined with thanks."

"You see then you're not such a phœnix," his visitor pointedly smiled —"to pretend to abilities you're sacrificing for our sake."

"I haven't time to do things properly," he ruefully went on. Then as it came over him that he was almost abjectly good-natured to give these explanations he added: "If I stay on longer it must be on one condition —that Morgan shall know distinctly on what footing I am."

Mrs. Moreen demurred. "Surely you don't want to show off to a child?"

"To show *you* off, do you mean?"

Again she cast about, but this time it was to produce a still finer flower. "And *you* talk of blackmail!"

"You can easily prevent it," said Pemberton.

"And *you* talk of practising on fears!" she bravely pushed on.

"Yes, there's no doubt I'm a great scoundrel."

His patroness met his eyes—it was clear she was in straits. Then she thrust out her money at him. "Mr. Moreen desired me to give you this on account."

"I'm much obliged to Mr. Moreen, but we *have* no account."

"You won't take it?"

"That leaves me more free," said Pemberton.

"To poison my darling's mind?" groaned Mrs. Moreen.

"Oh your darling's mind—!" the young man laughed.

She fixed him a moment, and he thought she was going to break out tormentedly, pleadingly: "For God's sake, tell me what *is* in it!" But she checked this impulse—another was stronger. She pocketed the money— the crudity of the alternative was comical—and swept out of the room with the desperate concession: "You may tell him any horror you like!"

VI

A couple of days after this, during which he had failed to profit by so free a permission, he had been for a quarter of an hour walking with his charge in silence when the boy became sociable again with the remark: "I'll tell you how I know it; I know it through Zénobie."

"Zénobie? Who in the world is *she?*"

"A nurse I used to have—ever so many years ago. A charming woman. I liked her awfully, and she liked me."

"There's no accounting for tastes. What is it you know through her?"

"Why what their idea is. She went away because they didn't fork out. She did like me awfully, and she stayed two years. She told me all about it—that at last she could never get her wages. As soon as they saw how much she liked me they stopped giving her anything. They thought she'd stay for nothing—just *because*, don't you know?" And Morgan had a queer little conscious lucid look. "She did stay ever so long—as long as she could. She was only a poor girl. She used to send money to her mother. At last she couldn't afford it any longer, and went away in a fearful rage one night—I mean of course in a rage against *them*. She cried over me tremendously, she hugged me nearly to death. She told me all about it," the boy repeated. "She told me it was their idea. So I guessed, ever so long ago, that they have had the same idea with you."

"Zénobie was very sharp," said Pemberton. "And she made you so." 10

"Oh that wasn't Zénobie; that was nature. And experience!" Morgan laughed.

"Well, Zénobie was a part of your experience."

"Certainly I was a part of hers, poor dear!" the boy wisely sighed. "And I'm part of yours."

"A very important part. But I don't see how you know I've been treated like Zénobie."

"Do you take me for the biggest dunce you've known?" Morgan asked. "Haven't I been conscious of what we've been through together?" 20

"What we've been through?"

"Our privations—our dark days."

"Oh our days have been bright enough."

Morgan went on in silence for a moment. Then he said: "My dear chap, you're a hero!"

"Well, you're another!" Pemberton retorted.

"No I'm not, but I ain't a baby. I won't stand it any longer. You must get some occupation that pays. I'm ashamed, I'm ashamed!" quavered the boy with a ring of passion, like some high silver note from a small cathedral chorister, that deeply touched his friend.

"We ought to go off and live somewhere together," the young man 30 said.

"I'll go like a shot if you'll take me."

"I'd get some work that would keep us both afloat," Pemberton continued.

"So would I. Why shouldn't *I* work? I ain't such a beastly little muff as *that* comes to."

"The difficulty is that your parents wouldn't hear of it. They'd never part with you; they worship the ground you tread on. Don't you see the proof of it?" Pemberton developed. "They don't dislike me; they wish me no harm; they're very amiable people; but they're perfectly ready to 40 expose me to any awkwardness in life for your sake."

The silence in which Morgan received his fond sophistry struck Pemberton somehow as expressive. After a moment the child repeated: "You *are* a hero!" Then he added: "They leave me with you altogether. You've all the responsibility. They put me off on you from morning till night. Why then should they object to my taking up with you completely? I'd help you."

"They're not particularly keen about my being helped, and they delight in thinking of you as *theirs*. They're tremendously proud of you."

"I'm not proud of *them*. But you know that," Morgan returned.

"Except for the little matter we speak of they're charming people," said Pemberton, not taking up the point made for his intelligence, but wondering greatly at the boy's own, and especially at this fresh reminder
10 of something he had been conscious of from the first—the strangest thing in his friend's large little composition, a temper, a sensibility, even a private ideal, which made him as privately disown the stuff his people were made of. Morgan had in secret a small loftiness which made him acute about betrayed meanness; as well as a critical sense for the manners immediately surrounding him that was quite without precedent in a juvenile nature, especially when one noted that it had not made this nature "old-fashioned," as the word is of children—quaint or wizened or offensive. It was as if he had been a little gentleman and had paid the penalty by discovering that he was the only such person in his family.
20 This comparison didn't make him vain, but it could make him melancholy and a trifle austere. While Pemberton guessed at these dim young things, shadows of shadows, he was partly drawn on and partly checked, as for a scruple, by the charm of attempting to sound the little cool shallows that were so quickly growing deeper. When he tried to figure to himself the morning twilight of childhood, so as to deal with it safely, he saw it was never fixed, never arrested, that ignorance, at the instant he touched it, was already flushing faintly into knowledge, that there was nothing that at a given moment you could say an intelligent child didn't know. It seemed to him that he himself knew too much to imagine
30 Morgan's simplicity and too little to disembroil his tangle.

The boy paid no heed to his last remark; he only went on: "I'd have spoken to them about their idea, as I call it, long ago, if I hadn't been sure what they'd say."

"And what would they say?"

"Just what they said about what poor Zénobie told me—that it was a horrid dreadful story, that they had paid her every penny they owed her."

"Well, perhaps they had," said Pemberton.

"Perhaps they've paid you!"

"Let us pretend they have, and *n'en parlons plus*."°
40 "They accused her of lying and cheating"—Morgan stuck to historic truth. "That's why I don't want to speak to them."

"Lest they should accuse me too?" To this Morgan made no answer,

39. *n'en parlons plus,* let us drop the subject.

and his companion, looking down at him—the boy turned away his eyes, which had filled—saw that he couldn't have trusted himself to utter. "You're right. Don't worry them," Pemberton pursued. "Except for that, they *are* charming people."

"Except for *their* lying and *their* cheating?"

"I say—I say!" cried Pemberton, imitating a little tone of the lad's which was itself an imitation.

"We must be frank, at the last; we *must* come to an understanding," said Morgan with the importance of the small boy who lets himself think he is arranging great affairs—almost playing at shipwreck or at Indians. 10 "I know all about everything."

"I dare say your father has his reasons," Pemberton replied, but too vaguely, as he was aware.

"For lying and cheating?"

"For saving and managing and turning his means to the best account. He has plenty to do with his money. You're an expensive family."

"Yes, I'm very expensive," Morgan concurred in a manner that made his preceptor burst out laughing.

"He's saving for *you*," said Pemberton. "They think of you in everything they do." 20

"He might, while he's about it, save a little—" The boy paused, and his friend waited to hear what. Then Morgan brought out oddly: "A little reputation."

"Oh there's plenty of that. That's all right!"

"Enough of it for the people they know, no doubt. The people they know are awful."

"Do you mean the princes? We musn't abuse the princes."

"Why not? They haven't married Paula—they haven't married Amy. They only clean out Ulick."

"You *do* know everything!" Pemberton declared. 30

"No I don't after all. I don't know what they live on, or how they live, or *why* they live! What have they got and how did they get it? Are they rich, are they poor, or have they a *modeste aisance?*° Why are they always chiveying me about—living one year like ambassadors and the next like paupers? Who are they, anyway, and what are they? I've thought of all that—I've thought of a lot of things. They're so beastly worldly. That's what I hate most—oh I've *seen* it! All they care about is to make an appearance and to pass for something or other. What the dickens do they want to pass for? What *do* they, Mr. Pemberton?"

"You pause for a reply," said Pemberton, treating the question as a 40 joke, yet wondering too and greatly struck with his mate's intense if imperfect vision. "I haven't the least idea."

33. *modeste aisance,* modest means.

"And what good does it do? Haven't I seen the way people treat them —the 'nice' people, the ones they want to know? They'll take anything from them—they'll lie down and be trampled on. The nice ones hate that —they just sicken them. You're the only really nice person we know."

"Are you sure? They don't lie down for me!"

"Well, you shan't lie down for them. You've got to go—that's what you've got to do," said Morgan.

"And what will become of you?"

"Oh I'm growing up. I shall get off before long. I'll see you later."

10 "You had better let me finish you," Pemberton urged, lending himself to the child's strange superiority.

Morgan stopped in their walk, looking up at him. He had to look up much less than a couple of years before—he had grown, in his loose leanness, so long and high. "Finish me?" he echoed.

"There are such a lot of jolly things we can do together yet. I want to turn you out—I want you to do me credit."

Morgan continued to look at him. "To give you credit—do you mean?"

"My dear fellow, you're too clever to live."

"That's just what I'm afraid you think. No, no; it isn't fair—I can't 20 endure it. We'll separate next week. The sooner it's over the sooner to sleep."

"If I hear of anything—any other chance—I promise to go," Pemberton said.

Morgan consented to consider this. "But you'll be honest," he demanded; "you won't pretend you haven't heard?"

"I'm much more likely to pretend I have."

"But what can you hear of, this way, stuck in a hole with us? You ought to be on the spot, to go to England—you ought to go to America."

"One would think you were *my* tutor!" said Pemberton.

30 Morgan walked on and after a little had begun again: "Well, now that you know I know and that we look at the facts and keep nothing back—it's much more comfortable, isn't it?"

"My dear boy, it's so amusing, so interesting, that it will surely be quite impossible for me to forego such hours as these."

This made Morgan stop once more. "You *do* keep something back. Oh you're not straight—*I* am!"

"How am I not straight?"

"Oh you've got your idea!"

"My idea?"

40 "Why that I probably shan't make old—make older—bones, and that you can stick it out till I'm removed."

"You *are* too clever to live!" Pemberton repeated.

"I call it a mean idea," Morgan pursued. "But I shall punish you by the way I hang on."

"Look out or I'll poison you!" Pemberton laughed.

"I'm stronger and better every year. Haven't you noticed that there hasn't been a doctor near me since you came?"

"*I'm* your doctor," said the young man, taking his arm and drawing him tenderly on again.

Morgan proceeded and after a few steps gave a sigh of mingled weariness and relief. "Ah now that we look at the facts it's all right!"

VII

They looked at the facts a good deal after this; and one of the first consequences of their doing so was that Pemberton stuck it out, in his friend's parlance, for the purpose. Morgan made the facts so vivid and so droll, and at the same time so bald and so ugly, that there was fascination in talking them over with him, just as there would have been heartlessness in leaving him alone with them. Now that the pair had such perceptions in common it was useless for them to pretend they didn't judge such people; but the very judgement and the exchange of perceptions created another tie. Morgan had never been so interesting as now that he himself was made plainer by the side-light of these confidences. What came out in it most was the small fine passion of his pride. He had plenty of that, Pemberton felt—so much that one might perhaps wisely wish for it some early bruises. He would have liked his people to have a spirit and had waked up to the sense of their perpetually eating humble-pie. His mother would consume any amount, and his father would consume even more than his mother. He had a theory that Ulick had wriggled out of an "affair" at Nice: there had once been a flurry at home, a regular panic, after which they all went to bed and took medicine, not to be accounted for on any other supposition. Morgan had a romantic imagination, fed by poetry and history, and he would have liked those who "bore his name"—as he used to say to Pemberton with the humour that made his queer delicacies manly—to carry themselves with an air. But their one idea was to get in with people who didn't want them and to take snubs as if they were honourable scars. Why people didn't want them more he didn't know—that was people's own affair; after all they weren't superficially repulsive, they were a hundred times cleverer than most of the dreary grandees, the "poor swells" they rushed about Europe to catch up with. "After all they *are* amusing—they are!" he used to pronounce with the wisdom of the ages. To which Pemberton always replied: "Amusing—the great Moreen troupe? Why they're altogether delightful; and if it weren't for the hitch that you and I (feeble performers!) make in the *ensemble* they'd carry everything before them."

What the boy couldn't get over was the fact that this particular blight

seemed, in a tradition of self-respect, so undeserved and so arbitrary. No doubt people had a right to take the line they liked; but why should *his* people have liked the line of pushing and toadying and lying and cheating? What had their forefathers—all decent folk, so far as he knew—done to them, or what had *he* done to them? Who had poisoned their blood with the fifth-rate social ideal, the fixed idea of making smart acquaintances and getting into the *monde chic*,° especially when it was foredoomed to failure and exposure? They showed so what they were after; that was what made the people they wanted not want *them*. And never a wince for
10 dignity, never a throb of shame at looking each other in the face, never any independence or resentment or disgust. If his father or his brother would only knock some one down once or twice a year! Clever as they were they never guessed the impression they made. They were good-natured, yes—as good-natured as Jews at the doors of clothing-shops! But was that the model one wanted one's family to follow? Morgan had dim memories of an old grandfather, the maternal, in New York, whom he had been taken across the ocean at the age of five to see: a gentleman with a high neck-cloth and a good deal of pronunciation, who wore a dress-coat in the morning, which made one wonder what he wore in the
20 evening, and had, or was supposed to have, "property" and something to do with the Bible Society. It couldn't have been but that *he* was a good type. Pemberton himself remembered Mrs. Clancy, a widowed sister of Mr. Moreen's, who was as irritating as a moral tale and had paid a fortnight's visit to the family at Nice shortly after he came to live with them. She was "pure and refined," as Amy said over the banjo, and had the air of not knowing what they meant when they talked, and of keeping something rather important back. Pemberton judged that what she kept back was an approval of many of their ways; therefore it was to be supposed that she too was of a good type, and that Mr. and Mrs. Moreen and
30 Ulick and Paula and Amy might easily have been of a better one if they would.

But that they wouldn't was more and more perceptible from day to day. They continued to "chivey," as Morgan called it, and in due time became aware of a variety of reasons for proceeding to Venice. They mentioned a great many of them—they were always strikingly frank and had the brightest friendly chatter, at the late foreign breakfast in especial, before the ladies had made up their faces, when they leaned their arms on the table, had something to follow the *demi-tasse*, and, in the heat of familiar discussion as to what they "really ought" to do, fell inevitably
40 into the languages in which they could *tutoyer*.° Even Pemberton liked them then; he could endure even Ulick when he heard him give his little flat voice for the "sweet sea-city." That was what made him have a

---

7. *monde chic,* stylish society.   40. *tutoyer,* be on familiar terms.

sneaking kindness for them—that they were so out of the workaday world
and kept him so out of it. The summer had waned when, with cries of
ecstasy, they all passed out on the balcony that overhung the Grand
Canal. The sunsets then were splendid and the Dorringtons had arrived.
The Dorringtons were the only reason they hadn't talked of at breakfast;
but the reasons they didn't talk of at breakfast always came out in the
end. The Dorringtons on the other hand came out very little; or else
when they did they stayed—as was natural—for hours, during which
periods Mrs. Moreen and the girls sometimes called at their hotel (to see
if they had returned) as many as three times running. The gondola was 10
for the ladies, as in Venice too there were "days," which Mrs. Moreen
knew in their order an hour after she arrived. She immediately took one
herself, to which the Dorringtons never came, though on a certain occasion when Pemberton and his pupil were together at Saint Mark's—
where, taking the best walks they had ever had and haunting a hundred
churches, they spent a great deal of time—they saw the old lord turn up
with Mr. Moreen and Ulick, who showed him the dim basilica as if it
belonged to them. Pemberton noted how much less, among its curiosities,
Lord Dorrington carried himself as a man of the world; wondering too
whether, for such services, his companions took a fee from him. The 20
autumn at any rate waned, the Dorringtons departed, and Lord Ver-
schoyle, the eldest son, had proposed neither for Amy nor for Paula.
    One sad November day, while the wind roared round the old palace
and the rain lashed the lagoon, Pemberton, for exercise and even somewhat for warmth—the Moreens were horribly frugal about fires; it was
a cause of suffering to their inmate—walked up and down the big bare
sala with his pupil. The scagliola floor was cold, the high battered casements shook in the storm, and the stately decay of the place was unre-
lieved by a particle of furniture. Pemberton's spirits were low, and it
came over him that the fortune of the Moreens was now even lower. A 30
blast of desolation, a portent of disgrace and disaster, seemed to draw
through the comfortless hall. Mr. Moreen and Ulick were in the Piazza,
looking out for something, strolling drearily, in mackintoshes, under the
arcades; but still, in spite of mackintoshes, unmistakable men of the
world. Paula and Amy were in bed—it might have been thought they
were staying there to keep warm. Pemberton looked askance at the boy
at his side, to see to what extent he was conscious of these dark omens.
But Morgan, luckily for him, was now mainly conscious of growing taller
and stronger and indeed of being in his fifteenth year. This fact was intensely interesting to him and the basis of a private theory—which, how- 40
ever, he had imparted to his tutor—that in a little while he should stand
on his own feet. He considered that the situation would change—that in
short he should be "finished," grown up, producible in the world of
affairs and ready to prove himself of sterling ability. Sharply as he was

capable at times of analysing, as he called it, his life, there were happy hours when he remained, as he also called it—and as the name, really, of their right ideal—"jolly" superficial; the proof of which was his fundamental assumption that he should presently go to Oxford, to Pemberton's college, and aided and abetted by Pemberton, do the most wonderful things. It depressed the young man to see how little in such a project he took account of ways and means: in other connexions he mostly kept to the measure. Pemberton tried to imagine the Moreens at Oxford and fortunately failed; yet unless they were to adopt it as a residence there
10 would be no *modus vivendi* for Morgan. How could he live without an allowance, and where was the allowance to come from? He, Pemberton, might live on Morgan; but how could Morgan live on *him?* What was to become of him anyhow? Somehow the fact that he was a big boy now, with better prospects of health, made the question of his future more difficult. So long as he was markedly frail the great consideration he inspired seemed enough of an answer to it. But at the bottom of Pemberton's heart was the recognition of his probably being strong enough to live and not yet strong enough to struggle or to thrive. Morgan himself at any rate was in the first flush of the rosiest consciousness of adolescence, so that the
20 beating of the tempest seemed to him after all but the voice of life and the challenge of fate. He had on his shabby little overcoat, with the collar up, but was enjoying his walk.

It was interrupted at last by the appearance of his mother at the end of the sala. She beckoned him to come to her, and while Pemberton saw him, complaisant, pass down the long vista and over the damp false marble, he wondered what was in the air. Mrs. Moreen said a word to the boy and made him go into the room she had quitted. Then, having closed the door after him, she directed her steps swiftly to Pemberton. There *was* something in the air, but his wildest flight of fancy wouldn't
30 have suggested what it proved to be. She signified that she had made a pretext to get Morgan out of the way, and then she enquired—without hesitation—if the young man could favour her with the loan of three louis. While, before bursting into a laugh, he stared at her with surprise, she declared that she was awfully pressed for the money; she was desperate for it—it would save her life.

"Dear lady, *c'est trop fort!*"° Pemberton laughed in the manner and with the borrowed grace of idiom that marked the best colloquial, the best anecdotic, moments of his friends themselves. "Where in the world do you suppose I should get three louis, *du train dont vous allez?*"°
40 "I thought you worked—wrote things. Don't they pay you?"

"Not a penny."

"Are you such a fool as to work for nothing?"

36. *c'est trop fort!* that's too bad!   39. *du train dont vous allez?* at the rate you are going?

Henry James   175

"You ought surely to know that."

Mrs. Moreen stared, then she coloured a little. Pemberton saw she had quite forgotten the terms—if "terms" they could be called—that he had ended by accepting from herself; they had burdened her memory as little as her conscience. "Oh yes, I see what you mean—you've been very nice about that; but why drag it in so often?" She had been perfectly urbane with him ever since the rough scene of explanation in his room the morning he made her accept *his* "terms"—the necessity of his making his case known to Morgan. She had felt no resentment after seeing there was no danger Morgan would take the matter up with her. Indeed, attributing 10 this immunity to the good taste of his influence with the boy, she had once said to Pemberton "My dear fellow, it's an immense comfort you're a gentleman." She repeated this in substance now. "Of course you're a gentleman—that's a bother the less!" Pemberton reminded her that he had not "dragged in" anything that wasn't already in as much as his foot was in his shoe; and she also repeated her prayer that, somewhere and somehow, he would find her sixty francs. He took the liberty of hinting that if he could find them it wouldn't be to lend them to *her*—as to which he consciously did himself injustice, knowing that if he had them he would certainly put them at her disposal. He accused himself, at bottom 20 and not unveraciously, of a fantastic, a demoralised sympathy with her. If misery made strange bedfellows it also made strange sympathies. It was moreover a part of the abasement of living with such people that one had to make vulgar retorts, quite out of one's own tradition of good manners. "Morgan, Morgan, to what pass have I come for you?" he groaned while Mrs. Moreen floated voluminously down the sala again to liberate the boy, wailing as she went that everything was too odious.

Before their young friend was liberated there came a thump at the door communicating with the staircase, followed by the apparition of a dripping youth who poked in his head. Pemberton recognised him as the 30 bearer of a telegram and recognised the telegram as addressed to himself. Morgan came back as, after glancing at the signature—that of a relative in London—he was reading the words: "Found jolly job for you, engagement to coach opulent youth on own terms. Come at once." The answer happily was paid and the messenger waited. Morgan, who had drawn near, waited too and looked hard at Pemberton; and Pemberton, after a moment, having met his look, handed him the telegram. It was really by wise looks—they knew each other so well now—that, while the telegraph-boy, in his waterproof cape, made a great puddle on the floor, the thing was settled between them. Pemberton wrote the answer with a pencil 40 against the frescoed wall, and the messenger departed. When he had gone the young man explained himself.

"I'll make a tremendous charge; I'll earn a lot of money in a short time, and we'll live on it."

"Well, I hope the opulent youth will be a dismal dunce—he probably will," Morgan parenthesised—"and keep you a long time a-hammering of it in."

"Of course the longer he keeps me the more we shall have for our old age."

"But suppose *they* don't pay you!" Morgan awfully suggested.

"Oh there are not two such—!" But Pemberton pulled up; he had been on the point of using too invidious a term. Instead of this he said "Two such fatalities."

Morgan flushed—the tears came to his eyes. "*Dites toujours*° two such rascally crews!" Then in a different tone he added: "Happy opulent youth!"

"Not if he's a dismal dunce."

"Oh they're happier then. But you can't have everything, can you?" the boy smiled.

Pemberton held him fast, hands on his shoulders—he had never loved him so. "What will become of *you*, what will you do?" He thought of Mrs. Moreen, desperate for sixty francs.

"I shall become an *homme fait*."° And then as if he recognised all the bearings of Pemberton's allusion: "I shall get on with them better when you're not here."

"Ah don't say that—it sounds as if I set you against them!"

"You do—the sight of you. It's all right; you know what I mean. I shall be beautiful. I'll take their affairs in hand; I'll marry my sisters."

"You'll marry yourself!" joked Pemberton; as high, rather tense pleasantry would evidently be the right, or the safest, tone for their separation.

It was, however, not purely in this strain that Morgan suddenly asked: "But I say—how will you get to your jolly job? You'll have to telegraph to the opulent youth for money to come on."

Pemberton bethought himself. "They won't like that, will they?"

"Oh look out for them!"

Then Pemberton brought out his remedy. "I'll go to the American Consul; I'll borrow some money of him—just for the few days, on the strength of the telegram."

Morgan was hilarious. "Show him the telegram—then collar the money and stay!"

Pemberton entered into the joke sufficiently to reply that for Morgan he was really capable of that; but the boy, growing more serious, and to prove he hadn't meant what he said, not only hurried him off to the Consulate—since he was to start that evening, as he had wired to his friend —but made sure of their affair by going with him. They splashed through the tortuous perforations and over the humpbacked bridges, and they

---

10. *Dites toujours,* At least say. .. 19. *homme fait,* a grown-up man.

passed through the Piazza, where they saw Mr. Moreen and Ulick go into a jeweller's shop. The Consul proved accommodating—Pemberton said it wasn't the letter, but Morgan's grand air—and on their way back they went into Saint Mark's for a hushed ten minutes. Later they took up and kept up the fun of it to the very end; and it seemed to Pemberton a part of that fun that Mrs. Moreen, who was very angry when he had announced her his intention, should charge him, grotesquely and vulgarly and in reference to the loan she had vainly endeavoured to effect, with bolting lest they should "get something out" of him. On the other hand he had to do Mr. Moreen and Ulick the justice to recognise that when on coming in *they* heard the cruel news they took it like perfect men of the world.

VIII

When he got at work with the opulent youth, who was to be taken in hand for Balliol, he found himself unable to say if this aspirant had really such poor parts or if the appearance were only begotten of his own long association with an intensely living little mind. From Morgan he heard half a dozen times: the boy wrote charming young letters, a patchwork of tongues, with indulgent postscripts in the family Volapuk and, in little squares and rounds and crannies of the text, the drollest illustrations— —letters that he was divided between the impulse to show his present charge as a vain, a wasted incentive, and the sense of something in them that publicity would profane. The opulent youth went up in due course and failed to pass; but it seemed to add to the presumption that brilliancy was not expected of him all at once that his parents, condoning the lapse, which they good-naturedly treated as little as possible as if it were Pemberton's, should have sounded the rally again, begged the young coach to renew the siege.

The young coach was now in a position to lend Mrs. Moreen three louis, and he sent her a post-office order even for a larger amount. In return for this favour he received a frantic scribbled line from her: "Implore you to come back instantly—Morgan dreadfully ill." They were on the rebound, once more in Paris—often as Pemberton had seen them depressed he had never seen them crushed—and communication was therefore rapid. He wrote to the boy to ascertain the state of his health, but awaited the answer in vain. He accordingly, after three days, took an abrupt leave of the opulent youth and, crossing the Channel, alighted at the small hotel, in the quarter of the Champs Elysées, of which Mrs. Moreen had given him the address. A deep if dumb dissatisfaction with this lady and her companions bore him company: they couldn't be vulgarly honest, but they could live at hotels, in velvety *entresols*, amid a smell of burnt pastilles, surrounded by the most expensive city in Europe.

When he had left them in Venice it was with an irrepressible suspicion that something was going to happen; but the only thing that could have taken place was again their masterly retreat. "How is he? where is he?" he asked of Mrs. Moreen; but before she could speak these questions were answered by the pressure round his neck of a pair of arms, in shrunken sleeves, which still were perfectly capable of an effusive young foreign squeeze.

"Dreadfully ill—I don't see it!" the young man cried. And then to Morgan: "Why on earth didn't you relieve me? Why didn't you answer
10 my letter?"

Mrs. Moreen declared that when she wrote he was very bad, and Pemberton learned at the same time from the boy that he had answered every letter he had received. This led to the clear inference that Pemberton's note had been kept from him so that the game to be practised should not be interfered with. Mrs. Moreen was prepared to see the fact exposed, as Pemberton saw the moment he faced her that she was prepared for a good many other things. She was prepared above all to maintain that she had acted from a sense of duty, that she was enchanted she had got him over, whatever they might say, and that it was useless of him to pre-
20 tend he didn't know in all his bones that his place at such a time was with Morgan. He had taken the boy away from them and now had no right to abandon him. He had created for himself the gravest responsibilities and must at least abide by what he had done.

"Taken him away from you?" Pemberton exclaimed indignantly.

"Do it—do it for pity's sake; that's just what I want. I can't stand *this* —and such scenes. They're awful frauds—poor dears!" These words broke from Morgan, who had intermitted his embrace, in a key which made Pemberton turn quickly to him and see that he had suddenly seated himself, was breathing in great pain and was very pale.
30 "*Now* do you say he's not in a state, my precious pet?" shouted his mother, dropping on her knees before him with clasped hands, but touching him no more than if he had been a gilded idol. "It will pass—it's only for an instant; but don't say such dreadful things!"

"I'm all right—all right," Morgan panted to Pemberton, whom he sat looking up at with a strange smile, his hands resting on either side on the sofa.

"Now do you pretend I've been dishonest, that I've deceived?" Mrs. Moreen flashed at Pemberton as she got up.

"It isn't *he* says it, it's I!" the boy returned, apparently easier but sink-
40 ing back against the wall; while his restored friend, who had sat down beside him, took his hand and bent over him.

"Darling child, one does what one can; there are so many things to consider," urged Mrs. Moreen. "It's his *place*—his only place. You see *you* think it is now."

"Take me away—take me away," Morgan went on, smiling to Pemberton with his white face.

"Where shall I take you, and how—oh *how*, my boy?" the young man stammered, thinking of the rude way in which his friends in London held that, for his convenience, with no assurance of prompt return, he had thrown them over; of the just resentment with which they would already have called in a successor, and of the scant help to finding fresh employment that resided for him in the grossness of his having failed to pass his pupil.

"Oh we'll settle that. You used to talk about it," said Morgan. "If we 10 can only go all the rest's a detail."

"Talk about it as much as you like, but don't think you can attempt it. Mr. Moreen would never consent—it would be so *very* hand-to-mouth," Pemberton's hostess beautifully explained to him. Then to Morgan she made it clearer: "It would destroy our peace, it would break our hearts. Now that he's back it will be all the same again. You'll have your life, your work and your freedom, and we'll all be happy as we used to be. You'll bloom and grow perfectly well, and we won't have any more silly experiments, will we? They're too absurd. It's Mr. Pemberton's place— every one in his place. You in yours, your papa in his, me in mine—*n'est-* 20 *ce pas, chéri?*° We'll all forget how foolish we've been and have lovely times."

She continued to talk and to surge vaguely about the little draped stuffy salon while Pemberton sat with the boy, whose colour gradually came back; and she mixed up her reasons, hinting that there were going to be changes, that the other children might scatter (who knew?—Paula had her ideas) and that then it might be fancied how much the poor old parent-birds would want the little nestling. Morgan looked at Pemberton, who wouldn't let him move; and Pemberton knew exactly how he felt at hearing himself called a little nestling. He admitted that he had had one 30 or two bad days, but he protested afresh against the wrong of his mother's having made them the ground of an appeal to poor Pemberton. Poor Pemberton could laugh now, apart from the comicality of Mrs. Moreen's mustering so much philosophy for her defence—she seemed to shake it out of her agitated petticoats, which knocked over the light gilt chairs— so little did their young companion, *marked*, unmistakably marked at the best, strike him as qualified to repudiate any advantage.

He himself was in for it at any rate. He should have Morgan on his hands again indefinitely; though indeed he saw the lad had a private theory to produce which would be intended to smooth this down. He 40 was obliged to him for it in advance; but the suggested amendment didn't

20. *n'est-ce pas, chéri?* isn't that so, beloved?

keep his heart rather from sinking, any more than it prevented him from accepting the prospect on the spot, with some confidence moreover that he should do so even better if he could have a little supper. Mrs. Moreen threw out more hints about the changes that were to be looked for, but she was such a mixture of smiles and shudders—she confessed she was very nervous—that he couldn't tell if she were in high feather or only in hysterics. If the family was really at last going to pieces why shouldn't she recognise the necessity of pitching Morgan into some sort of lifeboat? This presumption was fostered by the fact that they were established in lux-
10 urious quarters in the capital of pleasure; that was exactly where they naturally *would* be established in view of going to pieces. Moreover didn't she mention that Mr. Moreen and the others were enjoying themselves at the opera with Mr. Granger, and wasn't *that* also precisely where one would look for them on the eve of a smash? Pemberton gathered that Mr. Granger was a rich vacant American—a big bill with a flourishy heading and no items; so that one of Paula's "ideas" was probably that this time she hadn't missed fire—by which straight shot indeed she would have shattered the general cohesion. And if the cohesion was to crumble what would become of poor Pemberton? He felt quite enough bound up with
20 them to figure to his alarm as a dislodged block in the edifice.

It was Morgan who eventually asked if no supper had been ordered for him; sitting with him below, later, at the dim delayed meal, in the presence of a great deal of corded green plush, a plate of ornamental biscuit and an aloofness marked on the part of the waiter. Mrs. Moreen had explained that they had been obliged to secure a room for the visitor out of the house; and Morgan's consolation—he offered it while Pemberton reflected on the nastiness of lukewarm sauces—proved to be, largely, that this circumstance would facilitate their escape. He talked of their escape —recurring to it often afterwards—as if they were making up a "boy's
30 book" together. But he likewise expressed his sense that there was something in the air, that the Moreens couldn't keep it up much longer. In point of fact, as Pemberton was to see, they kept it up for five or six months. All the while, however, Morgan's contention was designed to cheer him. Mr. Moreen and Ulick, whom he had met the day after his return, accepted that return like perfect men of the world. If Paula and Amy treated it even with less formality an allowance was to be made for them, inasmuch as Mr. Granger hadn't come to the opera after all. He had only placed his box at their service, with a bouquet for each of the party; there was even one apiece, embittering the thought of his profu-
40 sion, for Mr. Moreen and Ulick. "They're all like that," was Morgan's comment; "at the very last, just when we think we've landed them they're back in the deep sea!"

Morgan's comments in these days were more and more free; they even included a large recognition of the extraordinary tenderness with which he had been treated while Pemberton was away. Oh yes, they couldn't do enough to be nice to him, to show him they had him on their mind and make up for his loss. That was just what made the whole thing so sad and caused him to rejoice after all in Pemberton's return—he had to keep thinking of their affection less, had less sense of obligation. Pemberton laughed out at this last reason, and Morgan blushed and said "Well, dash it, you know what I mean." Pemberton knew perfectly what he meant; but there were a good many things that—dash it too!—it didn't make any clearer. This episode of his second sojourn in Paris stretched itself out wearily, with their resumed readings and wanderings and 10 maunderings, their potterings on the quays, their hauntings of the museums, their occasional lingerings in the Palais Royal when the first sharp weather came on and there was a comfort in warm emanations, before Chevet's wonderful succulent window. Morgan wanted to hear all about the opulent youth—he took an immense interest in him. Some of the details of his opulence—Pemberton could spare him none of them—evidently fed the boy's appreciation of all his friend had given up to come back to him; but in addition to the greater reciprocity established by that heroism he had always his little brooding theory, in which there was a frivolous gaiety too, that their long probation was drawing to a close. 20 Morgan's conviction that the Moreens couldn't go on much longer kept pace with the unexpended impetus with which, from month to month, they did go on. Three weeks after Pemberton had rejoined them they went on to another hotel, a dingier one than the first; but Morgan rejoiced that his tutor had at least still not sacrificed the advantage of a room outside. He clung to the romantic utility of this when the day, or rather the night, should arrive for their escape.

For the first time, in this complicated connexion, our friend felt his collar gall him. It was, as he had said to Mrs. Moreen in Venice, *trop fort*—everything was *trop fort.*° He could neither really throw off his blighting 30 burden nor find in it the benefit of a pacified conscience or of a rewarded affection. He had spent all the money accruing to him in England, and he saw his youth going and that he was getting nothing back for it. It was all very well of Morgan to count it for reparation that he should now settle on him permanently—there was an irritating flaw in such a view. He saw what the boy had in his mind; the conception that as his friend had had the generosity to come back he must show his gratitude by giving him his life. But the poor friend didn't desire the gift—what could he do with Morgan's dreadful little life? Of course at the same time that Pemberton was irritated he remembered the reason, which was very hon- 40 ourable to Morgan and which dwelt simply in his making one so forget

29. *trop fort,* too painful or disagreeable.

that he was no more than a patched urchin. If one dealt with him on a different basis one's misadventures were one's own fault. So Pemberton waited in a queer confusion of yearning and alarm for the catastrophe which was held to hang over the house of Moreen, of which he certainly at moments felt the symptoms brush his cheek and as to which he wondered much in what form it would find its liveliest effect.

Perhaps it would take the form of sudden dispersal—a frightened *sauve qui peut*,° a scuttling into selfish corners. Certainly they were less elastic than of yore; they were evidently looking for something they didn't find.
10 The Dorringtons hadn't re-appeared, the princes had scattered; wasn't that the beginning of the end? Mrs. Moreen had lost her reckoning of the famous "days"; her social calendar was blurred—it had turned its face to the wall. Pemberton suspected that the great, the cruel discomfiture had been the unspeakable behaviour of Mr. Granger, who seemed not to know what he wanted, or, what was much worse, what *they* wanted. He kept sending flowers, as if to bestrew the path of his retreat, which was never the path of a return. Flowers were all very well, but—Pemberton could complete the proposition. It was now positively conspicuous that in the long run the Moreens were a social failure; so that the young man was
20 almost grateful the run had not been short. Mr. Moreen indeed was still occasionally able to get away on business and, what was more surprising, was likewise able to get back. Ulick had no club, but you couldn't have discovered it from his appearance, which was as much as ever that of a person looking at life from the window of such an institution; therefore Pemberton was doubly surprised at an answer he once heard him make his mother in the desperate tone of a man familiar with the worst privations. Her question Pemberton had not quite caught; it appeared to be an appeal for a suggestion as to whom they might get to take Amy. "Let the Devil take her!" Ulick snapped; so that Pemberton could see that
30 they had not only lost their amiability but had ceased to believe in themselves. He could also see that if Mrs. Moreen was trying to get people to take her children she might be regarded as closing the hatches for the storm. But Morgan would be the last she would part with.

One winter afternoon—it was a Sunday—he and the boy walked far together in the Bois de Boulogne. The evening was so splendid, the cold lemon-coloured sunset so clear, the stream of carriages and pedestrians so amusing and the fascination of Paris so great, that they stayed out later than usual and became aware that they should have to hurry home to arrive in time for dinner. They hurried accordingly, arm-in-arm, good-
40 humoured and hungry, agreeing that there was nothing like Paris after all and that after everything too that had come and gone they were not

7. *sauve qui peut,* headless flight.

yet sated with innocent pleasures. When they reached the hotel they found that, though scandalously late, they were in time for all the dinner they were likely to sit down to. Confusion reigned in the apartments of the Moreens—very shabby ones this time, but the best in the house—and before the interrupted service of the table, with objects displaced almost as if there had been a scuffle and a great wine-stain from an overturned bottle, Pemberton couldn't blink the fact that there had been a scene of the last proprietary firmness. The storm had come—they were all seeking refuge. The hatches were down, Paula and Amy were invisible—they had never tried the most casual art upon Pemberton, but he felt they had enough of an eye to him not to wish to meet him as young ladies whose frocks had been confiscated—and Ulick appeared to have jumped overboard. The host and his staff, in a word, had ceased to "go on" at the pace of their guests, and the air of embarrassed detention, thanks to a pile of gaping trunks in the passage, was strangely commingled with the air of indignant withdrawal.

When Morgan took all this in—and he took it in very quickly—he coloured to the roots of his hair. He had walked from his infancy among difficulties and dangers, but he had never seen a public exposure. Pemberton noticed in a second glance at him that the tears had rushed into his eyes and that they were tears of a new and untasted bitterness. He wondered an instant, for the boy's sake, whether he might successfully pretend not to understand. Not successfully, he felt, as Mr. and Mrs. Moreen, dinnerless by their extinguished hearth, rose before him in their little dishonoured salon, casting about with glassy eyes for the nearest port in such a storm. They were not prostrate but were horribly white, and Mrs. Moreen had evidently been crying. Pemberton quickly learned however that her grief was not for the loss of her dinner, much as she usually enjoyed it, but the fruit of a blow that struck even deeper, as she made all haste to explain. He would see for himself, so far as that went, how the great change had come, the dreadful bolt had fallen, and how they would now all have to turn themselves about. Therefore cruel as it was to them to part with their darling she must look to him to carry a little further the influence he had so fortunately acquired with the boy—to induce his young charge to follow him into some modest retreat. They depended on him—that was the fact—to take their delightful child temporarily under his protection: it would leave Mr. Moreen and herself so much more free to give the proper attention (too little, alas! had been given) to the readjustment of their affairs.

"We trust you—we feel we *can*," said Mrs. Moreen, slowly rubbing her plump white hands and looking with compunction hard at Morgan, whose chin, not to take liberties, her husband stroked with a tentative paternal forefinger.

"Oh yes—we feel that we *can*. We trust Mr. Pemberton fully, Morgan," Mr. Moreen pursued.

Pemberton wondered again if he might pretend not to understand; but everything good gave way to the intensity of Morgan's understanding. "Do you mean he may take me to live with him for ever and ever?" cried the boy. "May take me away, away, anywhere he likes?"

"For ever and ever? *Comme vous-y-allez!*"° Mr. Moreen laughed indulgently. "For as long as Mr. Pemberton may be so good."

"We've struggled, we've suffered," his wife went on; "but you've made him so your own that we've already been through the worst of the sacrifice."

Morgan had turned away from his father—he stood looking at Pemberton with a light in his face. His sense of shame for their common humiliated state had dropped; the case had another side—the thing was to clutch at *that*. He had a moment of boyish joy, scarcely mitigated by the reflexion that with this unexpected consecration of his hope—too sudden and too violent; the turn taken was away from a *good* boy's book—the "escape" was left on their hands. The boyish joy was there an instant, and Pemberton was almost scared at the rush of gratitude and affection that broke through his first abasement. When he stammered "My dear fellow, what do you say to *that?*" how could one not say something enthusiastic? But there was more need for courage at something else that immediately followed and that made the lad sit down quickly on the nearest chair. He had turned quite livid and had raised his hand to his left side. They were all three looking at him, but Mrs. Moreen suddenly bounded forward. "Ah his darling little heart!" she broke out; and this time, on her knees before him and without respect for the idol, she caught him ardently in her arms. "You walked him too far, you hurried him too fast!" she hurled over her shoulder at Pemberton. Her son made no protest, and the next instant, still holding him, she sprang up with her face convulsed and with the terrified cry "Help, help! he's going, he's gone!"

Pemberton saw with equal horror, by Morgan's own stricken face, that he was beyond their wildest recall. He pulled him half out of his mother's hands, and for a moment, while they held him together, they looked all their dismay into each other's eyes. "He couldn't stand it with his weak organ," said Pemberton—"the shock, the whole scene, the violent emotion."

"But I thought he *wanted* to go to you!" wailed Mrs. Moreen.

"I *told* you he didn't, my dear," her husband made answer. Mr. Moreen was trembling all over and was in his way as deeply affected as his wife. But after the very first he took his bereavement as a man of the world.

5. *Comme vous-y-allez!* How fast you are working!

1868-1936
MAXIM
GORKI   *   *Twenty-Six Men and a Girl**

A Poem

There were six-and-twenty of us—six-and-twenty living machines locked up in a damp basement, where from morning till night we kneaded dough and rolled it into pretzels and cracknels. Opposite the windows of our basement was a bricked area, green and moldy with moisture. The windows were protected from outside with a close iron grating, and the light of the sun could not pierce through the windowpanes, covered as they were with flour dust.

Our employer had bars placed in front of the windows, so that we should not be able to give a bit of his bread to passing beggars, or to any of our fellows who were out of work and hungry. Our employer called 10 us crooks, and gave us half-rotten tripe to eat for our midday meal, instead of meat. It was swelteringly close for us cooped up in that stone underground chamber, under the low, heavy, soot-blackened, cobwebby ceiling. Dreary and sickening was our life within its thick, dirty, moldy walls.

Unrefreshed, and with a feeling of not having had our sleep out, we used to get up at five o'clock in the morning; and at six, we were already seated, worn out and apathetic, at the table, rolling out the dough which our mates had already prepared while we slept. The whole day, from early morning until ten at night, some of us sat round that table, working 20 up in our hands the unyielding dough, swaying to and fro so as not to grow numb; while the others mixed flour and water. And the whole day the simmering water in the kettle, where the pretzels were being cooked, sang low and sadly; and the baker's shovel scraped harshly over the oven floor, as he threw the slippery bits of dough out of the kettle on the heated bricks.

From morning till evening wood was burning in the oven, and the red glow of the fire gleamed and flickered over the walls of the bake-shop, as if silently mocking us. The giant oven was like the misshapen head of a monster in a fairy tale; it thrust itself up out of the floor, opened wide 30 jaws, full of glowing fire, and blew hot breath upon us; it seemed to be ever watching out of its black air-holes our interminable work. Those two deep holes were like eyes—the cold, pitiless eyes of a monster. They

---

*Translated by Emily Jakowleff and Dora B. Montefiore; revised by Avrahm Yarmolinsky.

watched us always with the same darkened glance, as if they were weary of seeing before them such slaves, from whom they could expect nothing human, and therefore scorned them with the cold scorn of wisdom.

In meal dust, in the mud which we brought in from the yard on our boots, in the hot, sticky atmosphere, day in, day out, we rolled the dough into pretzels, which we moistened with our own sweat. And we hated our work with a bitter hatred; we never ate what had passed through our hands, and preferred black bread to pretzels. Sitting opposite each other, at a long table—nine facing nine—we moved our hands and fingers me-
10 chanically during endlessly long hours, till we were so accustomed to our monotonous work that we ceased to pay any attention to our own motions.

We had all stared at each other so long, that each of us knew every wrinkle of his mates' faces. It was not long also before we had exhausted almost every topic of conversation; that is why we were most of the time silent, unless we were chaffing each other; but one cannot always find something about which to chaff another man, especially when that man is one's mate. Neither were we much given to finding fault with one another; how, indeed, could one of us poor devils be in a position to find fault with another, when we were all of us half dead and, as it were,
20 turned to stone? For the heavy drudgery seemed to crush all feeling out of us. But silence is only terrible and fearful for those who have said everything and have nothing more to say to each other; for men, on the contrary, who have never begun to communicate with one another, it is easy and simple.

Sometimes, too, we sang; and this is how it happened that we began to sing: one of us would sigh deeply in the midst of our toil, like an over-driven horse, and then we would begin one of those songs whose gentle drawn-out melody seems always to ease the burden on the singer's heart.

At first one sang by himself, and we others sat in silence listening to his
30 solitary song, which, under the heavy vaulted roof of the basement, died gradually away and became extinguished, like a little fire in the steppes, on a wet autumn night, when the gray heaven hangs like a leaden roof over the earth. Then another would join in with the singer, and now two soft, sad voices would break into song in our narrow, dull hole of a basement. Suddenly others would join in, and the song would surge up like a wave, would grow louder and swell upward, till it would seem as if the damp, foul walls of our stone prison were widening out and opening. Then, all six-and-twenty of us would be singing; our loud, harmonious song would fill the whole shop; the song felt cramped, it was striking, as
40 it were, against the walls in moaning sobs and sighs, moving our hearts with a soft, tantalizing ache, tearing open old wounds, and awakening longings.

The singers would sigh deeply and heavily; suddenly one would become silent and listen to the others singing, then let his voice flow once

Maxim Gorki   187

more in the common tide. Another would exclaim in a stifled voice, "Ah!" and would shut his eyes, while the deep, full sound waves would show him, as it were, a road, in front of him—a sunlit, broad road in the distance, which he himself, in thought, wandered along.

But the flame flickers once more in the huge oven, the baker scrapes incessantly with his shovel, the water simmers in the kettle, and the flicker of the fire on the wall dances as before in silent mockery. While in other men's words we sing out our dumb grief, the weary burden of live men robbed of the sunlight, the heartache of slaves.

So we lived, we six-and-twenty, in the vault-like basement of a great 10 stone house, and we suffered each one of us, as if we had to bear on our shoulders the whole three stories of that house.

But we had something else good, besides the singing—something we loved, that perhaps took the place of the sunshine.

In the second story of our house there was established a gold-embroiderer's shop, and there, living among the other embroidery girls, was Tanya, a little maid-servant of sixteen. Every morning there peeped in through the glass door a rosy little face, with merry blue eyes; while a ringing, tender voice called out to us:

"Little prisoners! Have you any pretzels, please, for me?"   20

At that clear sound we knew so well, we all used to turn round, gazing with good-natured joy at the pure girlish face which smiled at us so sweetly. The sight of the little nose pressed against the windowpane, and of the small white teeth gleaming between the half-open lips, had become for us a daily pleasure. Tumbling over each other we used to jump up to open the door, and she would step in, bright and cheerful, holding out her apron, with her head bent to one side, and a smile on her lips. Her thick, long chestnut braid fell over her shoulder and across her breast. We, ugly, dirty and misshapen as we were, looked up at her—the door was four steps above the floor—looked up at her with heads thrown back, 30 wishing her good morning, and speaking strange, unaccustomed words, which we kept for her only. Our voices became softer when we spoke to her, our jests were lighter. For her—everything was different with us. The baker took from his oven a shovelful of the best and the brownest pretzels, and threw them deftly into Tanya's apron.

"Be off with you now, or the boss will catch you!" we warned her each time. She laughed roguishly, called out cheerfully: "Good-by, poor prisoners!" and slipped away as quick as a mouse.

That was all. But long after she had gone we talked about her to one another with pleasure. It was always the same thing as we had said yester- 40 day and the day before, because everything about us, including ourselves and her, remained the same—as yesterday—and as always.

Painful and terrible it is when a man goes on living, while nothing changes around him; and when such an existence does not finally kill his

soul, then the monotony becomes with time, even more and more painful. Generally we spoke about women in such a way that sometimes it was loathsome to us ourselves to hear our rude, shameless talk. The women whom we knew deserved perhaps nothing better. But about Tanya we never let fall an evil word; none of us ever ventured so much as to lay a hand on her, even too free a jest she never heard from us. Maybe this was so because she never remained with us for long; she flashed on our eyes like a star falling from the sky, and vanished; and maybe because she was little and very beautiful, and everything beautiful calls
10 forth respect, even in coarse people. And besides—though our life of drudgery had made us dull beasts, oxen, we were still men, and, like all men, could not live without worshiping something or other. Better than her we had none, and none but her took any notice of us, living in the basement—no one, though there were dozens of people in the house. And then, too—most likely, this was the chief thing—we all regarded her as something of our own, something existing as it were only by virtue of our pretzels. We took on ourselves in turns the duty of providing her with hot pretzels, and this became for us like a daily sacrifice to our idol, it became almost a sacred rite, and every day it bound us more closely to
20 her. Besides pretzels, we gave Tanya a great deal of advice—to wear warmer clothes, not to run upstairs too quickly, not to carry heavy bundles of wood. She listened to all our counsels with a smile, answered them by a laugh, and never took our advice, but we were not offended at that; all we wanted was to show how concerned we were for her welfare.

Often she would apply to us with different requests, she asked us, for instance, to open the heavy door into the cellar, to chop wood: with delight and a sort of pride, we did this for her, and everything else she wanted.

But when one of us asked her to mend his solitary shirt for him, she
30 said, with a laugh of contempt:

"What next! A likely idea!"

We made great fun of the queer fellow who could entertain such an idea, and—never asked her to do anything else. We loved her—all is said in that. Man always wants to give his love to someone, though sometimes he crushes, sometimes he sullies, with it. We were bound to love Tanya, for we had no one else to love.

At times one of us would suddenly begin to reason like this:

"And why do we make so much of the wench? What is there in her, eh? What a to-do we make about her!"

40 The man who dared to utter such words we promptly and coarsely cut short—we wanted something to love: we had found it and loved it, and what we twenty-six loved must be for each of us unshakable, as a holy thing, and anyone who acted against us in this was our enemy. We loved, maybe, not what was really good, but you see there were twenty-six of us,

and so we always wanted to see what was precious to us held sacred by the rest.

Our love is not less burdensome than hate, and maybe that is just why some proud souls maintain that our hate is more flattering than our love. But why do they not run away from us, if it is so?

Besides our department, our employer had also a bakery where they made rolls; it was in the same house, separated from our hole only by a wall; but the bakers—there were four of them—held aloof from us, considering their work superior to ours, and therefore themselves better than us; they never used to come into our workroom, and laughed contemptuously at us when they met us in the yard. We, too, did not go to see them; this was forbidden by our employer, for fear that we should steal the fancy rolls. We did not like the bakers, because we envied them; their work was lighter than ours, they were paid more, and were better fed; they had a light, spacious workroom, and they were all so clean and healthy—and that made them hateful to us. We all looked gray and yellow; three of us had syphilis, several suffered from skin diseases, one was completely crippled by rheumatism. On holidays and in their leisure time the bakers wore pea-jackets and creaking boots, two of them had accordions, and they all used to go for strolls in the public park—we wore filthy rags and torn leather shoes or bast slippers on our feet, the police would not let us into the public park—could we possibly like the bakers?

And one day we learned that one of their men had gone on a spree, the master had sacked him and had already taken on another, and that this other was an ex-soldier, wore a satin waistcoat and a watch and gold chain. We were anxious to get a sight of such a dandy, and in the hope of catching a glimpse of him we kept running one after another out into the yard.

But he came of his own accord into our workroom. Kicking at the door, he pushed it open, and leaving it ajar, stood in the doorway smiling, and said to us:

"God help the work! Good morning, mates!"

The frosty air, which streamed in through the open door, curled in streaks of vapor round his feet. He stood on the threshold, looked down upon us, and under his fair, twisted mustache gleamed big yellow teeth. His waistcoat was really something quite out of the common, blue-flowered, brilliant with shining little red stone buttons. He also wore a watch chain.

He was a fine fellow, this soldier; tall, healthy, rosy-cheeked, and his big, clear eyes had a friendly, cheerful glance. He wore on his head a white starched cap, and from under his spotlessly clean apron peeped the pointed toes of fashionable, well-blacked boots.

Our baker asked him politely to shut the door. The soldier did so without hurrying himself, and began to question us about the master. We explained to him, all speaking together, that our employer was a thorough-going brute, a crook, a knave, and a slave-driver; in a word, we repeated to him all that can and must be said about an employer, but cannot be repeated here. The soldier listened to us, twitched his mustache, and watched us with a friendly, open-hearted look.

"But haven't you got a lot of girls here?" he asked suddenly.

Some of us began to laugh deferentially, others leered, and one of us
10 explained to the soldier that there were nine girls here.

"You make the most of them?" asked the soldier, with a wink.

We laughed, but not so loudly, and with some embarrassment. Many of us would have liked to have shown the soldier that we also were tremendous fellows with the girls, but not one of us could do so; and one of our number confessed as much, when he said in a low voice:

"That sort of thing is not in our line."

"Well, no; it wouldn't quite do for you," said the soldier with conviction, after having looked us over. "There is something wanting about you all. You don't look the right sort. You've no sort of appearance; and the
20 women, you see, they like a bold appearance, they will have a well-set-up body. Everything has to be tip-top for them. That's why they respect strength. They want an arm like that!"

The soldier drew his right hand, with its turned-up shirt sleeve, out of his pocket, and showed us his bare arm. It was white and strong, and covered with shining golden wool.

"Leg and chest, all must be strong. And then a man must be dressed in the latest fashion, so as to show off his looks to advantage. Yes, all the women take to me. I don't call to them, I don't beckon them, yet with one accord, five at a time, they throw themselves at my head."

30 He sat down on a flour sack, and told at length all about the way women loved him, and how bold he was with them. Then he left, and after the door had creaked to behind him, we sat for a long time silent, and thought about him and his talk. Then we all suddenly broke silence together, and it became apparent that we were all equally pleased with him. He was such a nice, open-hearted fellow; he came to see us without any stand-offishness, sat down and chatted. No one else had ever come to us like that, and no one else had talked to us in that friendly sort of way. And we continued to talk of him and his coming triumph among the embroidery girls, who passed us by with contemptuous sniffs when
40 they saw us in the yard, or who looked straight through us as if we had been air. But we admired them always when we met them outside, or when they walked past our windows; in winter, in fur jackets and toques to match; in summer, in hats trimmed with flowers, and carrying colored parasols. Among ourselves, however, we talked about these girls in a way

that would have made them mad with shame and rage, if they could have heard us.

"If only he does not get hold of little Tanya!" said the baker, suddenly, in an anxious tone of voice.

We were silent, for these words troubled us. Tanya had quite gone out of our minds, supplanted, put on one side by the strong, fine figure of the soldier.

Then began a lively discussion; some of us maintained that Tanya would never lower herself so; others thought she would not be able to resist him, and the third group proposed to break his ribs for him if he 10 should try to annoy Tanya. And, finally, we all decided to watch the soldier and Tanya, and to warn the girl against him. This brought the discussion to an end.

Four weeks had passed by since then; during this time the soldier baked white rolls, walked out with the gold-embroidery girls, visited us often, but did not talk any more about his conquests; only twisted his mustache and licked his lips lasciviously.

Tanya called in as usual every morning for "little pretzels," and was as gay and as nice and friendly with us as ever. We certainly tried once or twice to talk to her about the soldier, but she called him a "goggle-eyed 20 calf," and made fun of him all round, and that set our minds at rest. We saw how the gold-embroidery girls carried on with the soldier, and we were proud of our girl; Tanya's behavior reflected honor on us all; we imitated her, and began in our talks to treat the soldier with small consideration. She became dearer to us, and we greeted her with more friendliness and kindliness every morning.

One day the soldier came to see us, a bit drunk, and sat down and began to laugh. When we asked him what he was laughing about, he explained to us:

"Why, two of them—that Lydka girl and Grushka—have been claw- 30 ing each other on my account. You should have seen the way they went for each other! Ha! ha! One got hold of the other one by the hair, threw her down on the floor of the passage, and sat on her! Ha! ha! ha! They scratched and tore each others' faces. It was enough to make one die with laughter! Why is it women can't fight fair? Why do they always scratch one another, eh?"

He sat on the bench, in fine fettle, fresh and jolly; he sat there and went on laughing. We were silent. This time he made an unpleasant impression on us.

"Well, it's a funny thing what luck I have with the women-folk! Eh? 40 One wink, and it's all over with them! It's the d-devil!"

He raised his white arms covered with golden wool, and dropped them down on his knees. And his eyes seemed to reflect such frank astonishment, as if he were himself quite surprised at his good luck with women.

His fat, red face glistened with delight and self-satisfaction, and he licked his lips more than ever.

Our baker scraped the shovel violently and angrily along the oven floor, and all at once he said sarcastically:

"There's no great strength needed to pull up fir saplings, but try a real pine-tree."

"Why—what do you mean by saying that to me?" asked the soldier. "Oh, well . . . "

"What is it?"

10 "Nothing—it slipped out!"

"No, wait a minute! What's the point? What pine-tree?"

Our baker did not answer, working rapidly away with the shovel at the oven; flinging into it the half-cooked pretzels, taking out those that were done, and noisily throwing them on the floor to the boys who were stringing them on bast. He seemed to have forgotten the soldier and his conversation with him. But the soldier had all at once grown uneasy. He got up onto his feet, and went to the oven, at the risk of knocking against the handle of the shovel, which was waving spasmodically in the air.

"No, tell me, do—who is it? You've insulted me. I? There's not one
20 could withstand me, n-no! And you say such insulting things to me?"

He really seemed genuinely hurt. He must have had nothing else to pride himself on except his gift for seducing women; maybe, except for that, there was nothing living in him, and it was only that by which he could feel himself a living man.

There are men to whom the most precious and best thing in their lives appears to be some disease of their soul or body. They fuss over it all their lives, and only living by it, suffering from it, they feed on it, they complain of it to others, and so draw the attention of their fellows to themselves. For that they extract sympathy from people, and apart from it
30 they have nothing at all. Take from them that disease, cure them, and they will be miserable, because they have lost their one resource in life— they are left empty then. Sometimes a man's life is so poor, that he is driven instinctively to prize his vice and to live by it; one may say for a fact that often men are vicious out of boredom.

The soldier was offended, he went up to our baker and roared:

"No, tell me, do—who?"

"Tell you?" the baker turned suddenly to him.

"Well?"

"You know Tanya?"

40 "Well?"

"Well, there then! Only try."

"I?"

"You!"

"Her? Why, that's nothing to me—pooh!"

"We shall see!"

"You will see! Ha! ha!"

"She'll—"

"Give me a month!"

"What a braggart you are, soldier!"

"A fortnight! I'll prove it! Who is it? Tanya! Pooh!"

"Well, get out. You're in my way!"

"A fortnight—and it's done! Ah, you—"

"Get out, I say!"

Our baker, all at once, flew into a rage and brandished his shovel. The soldier staggered away from him in amazement, looked at us, paused, and softly, malignantly said, "Oh, all right, then!" and went away.

During the dispute we had all sat silent, absorbed in it. But when the soldier had gone, eager, loud talk and noise arose among us.

Someone shouted to the baker: "It's a bad job that you've started, Pavel!"

"Do your work!" answered the baker savagely.

We felt that the soldier had been touched to the quick, and that danger threatened Tanya. We felt this, and at the same time we were all possessed by a burning curiosity, most agreeable to us. What would happen? Would Tanya hold out against the soldier? And almost all cried confidently: "Tanya? She'll hold out! You won't catch her with your bare arms!"

We longed terribly to test the strength of our idol; we were forcibly trying to persuade each other that our divinity was a strong divinity and would come victorious out of this ordeal. We began at last to fancy that we had not worked enough on the soldier, that he would forget the dispute, and that we ought to pique his vanity further. From that day we began to live a different life, a life of nervous tension, such as we had never known before. We spent whole days in arguing together; we all grew, as it were, sharper; and got to talk more and better. It seemed to us that we were playing some sort of game with the devil, and the stake on our side was Tanya. And when we learned from the bakers that the soldier had begun "running after our Tanya," we felt a sort of delighted terror, and life was so interesting that we did not even notice that our employer had taken advantage of our preoccupation to increase our work by three hundred pounds of dough a day. We seemed, indeed, not even tired by our work. Tanya's name was on our lips all day long. And every day we looked for her with a certain peculiar impatience. Sometimes we pictured to ourselves that she would come to us, and it would not be the same Tanya as of old, but somehow different. We said nothing to her, however, of the dispute regarding her. We asked her no questions, and behaved as well and affectionately to her as ever. But even in this a new element crept in, alien to our old feeling for Tanya—and that new element was keen curiosity, keen and cold as a steel knife.

"Mates! Today the time's up!" our baker said to us one morning, as he set to work.

We were well aware of it without his reminder; but still we became alert.

"Have a good look at her. She'll be here directly," suggested the baker.

One of us cried out in a troubled voice, "Why! as though one could see anything! You need more than eyes."

And again an eager, noisy discussion sprang up among us. Today we were at last to discover how pure and spotless was the vessel into which we had poured all that was best in us. This morning, for the first time, it became clear to us that we really were playing for high stakes; that we might, indeed, through the exaction of this proof of purity, lose our divinity altogether.

All this time we had been hearing that Tanya was stubbornly and persistently pursued by the soldier, but not one of us had thought of asking her what she thought of him. And she came every morning to fetch her pretzels, and was the same toward us as ever.

This morning, too, we heard her voice outside: "You poor prisoners! Here I am!"

We opened the door hastily, and when she came in we all remained, contrary to our usual custom, silent. Our eyes fixed on her, we did not know what to say to her, what to ask her. And there we stood in front of her, a gloomy, silent crowd. She seemed to be surprised at this unusual reception; and suddenly we saw her turn white and become uneasy, then she asked, in a choking voice:

"Why are you—like this?"

"And you?" the baker flung at her grimly, never taking his eyes off her.

"What about me?"

"N-nothing."

"Well, then, give me the little pretzels quickly."

Never before had she bidden us hurry.

"There's plenty of time," said the baker, not stirring and not removing his eyes from her face.

Then, suddenly, she turned round and disappeared through the door.

The baker took his shovel and said, calmly turning away toward the oven:

"Well, that settles it! There's a soldier for you—the low cur!"

Like a flock of sheep we all pressed round the table, sat down silently, and began listlessly to work. Soon, however, one of us remarked:

"Perhaps, after all—"

"Shut up!" shouted the baker.

Maxim Gorki   195

We were all convinced that he was a man of judgment, a man who knew more than we did about things. And at the sound of his voice we were convinced of the soldier's victory, and our spirits became sad and downcast.

At twelve o'clock—while we were eating our dinners—the soldier came in. He was as clean and as smart as ever, and looked at us—as usual— straight in the eyes. But we were all awkward in looking at him.

"Now then, honored sirs, would you like me to show you a soldier's prowess?" he said, chuckling proudly.

"Go out into the passage and look through the crack—do you under- 10 stand?"

We went into the passage, and stood all pushing against one another, squeezed up to the cracks of the wooden partition of the passage that looked into the yard. We had not to wait long. Very soon Tanya, with hurried footsteps and an anxious face, walked across the yard, jumping over the puddles of melting snow and mud: she disappeared into the cellar. Then whistling, and not hurrying himself, the soldier followed in the same direction. His hands were thrust in his pockets; his mustaches were quivering.

Rain was falling, and we saw how its drops struck the puddles, and the 20 puddles were wrinkled by them. The day was damp and gray—a very dreary day. Snow still lay on the roofs, but on the ground dark patches of mud had begun to appear. And the snow on the roofs too was covered by a layer of brownish dirt. The rain fell slowly with a depressing sound. It was cold and disagreeable for us waiting.

The first to come out of the cellar was the soldier; he walked slowly across the yard, his mustaches twitching, his hands in his pockets—the same as always.

Then—Tanya, too, came out. Her eyes—her eyes were radiant with joy and happiness, and her lips—were smiling. And she walked as though 30 in a dream, staggering, with unsteady steps.

We could not bear this calmly. All of us at once rushed to the door, dashed out into the yard and—hissed at her, reviled her viciously, loudly, wildly.

She started at seeing us, and stood as though rooted in the mud under her feet. We formed a ring round her, and maliciously, without restraint, abused her with vile words, said shameful things to her.

We did this quietly, slowly, seeing that she could not get away, that she was hemmed in by us, and we could rail at her to our hearts' content. I don't know why, but we did not beat her. She stood in the midst of us, 40 and turned her head this way and that, as she heard our insults. And we —more and more violently flung at her the filth and venom of our words.

The color had left her face. Her blue eyes, so happy a moment before, opened wide, her bosom heaved, and her lips quivered.

We in a ring round her avenged ourselves on her, for she had robbed us. She belonged to us, we had lavished on her our best, and though that best was beggar's crumbs, still there were twenty-six of us, she was one, and so there was no pain we could give her equal to her guilt! How we insulted her! She was still mute, still gazed at us with wild eyes, and a shiver ran through her.

We laughed, roared, yelled. Other people ran up from somewhere and joined us. One of us pulled Tanya by the sleeve of her blouse.

Suddenly her eyes flashed; deliberately she raised her hands to her
10 head and straightening her hair she said loudly but calmly, straight in our faces:

"Ah, you miserable prisoners!"

And she walked straight at us, walked as directly as though we had not been before her, as though we were not blocking her way.

And hence none of us did actually block her way.

Walking out of our circle without turning round, she added loudly, with pride and indescribable contempt:

"Ah, you scum—brutes."

And—was gone, erect, beautiful, proud.

20 We were left in the middle of the yard, in the rain, under the gray sunless sky.

Then we went mutely away to our damp stone basement. As before— the sun never peeped in at our windows, and Tanya came no more. Never!

1883-1924
FRANZ
KAFKA * The Knock at the Manor Gate*

It was summer, a hot day. With my sister I was passing the gate of a great house on our way home. I cannot tell now whether she knocked on the gate out of mischief or out of absence of mind, or merely threatened it with her hand and did not knock at all. A hundred paces further on along the road, which here turned to the left, began the village. We did not know it very well, but no sooner had we passed the first house when people appeared and made friendly or warning signs to us; they were themselves apparently terrified, bowed down with terror. They pointed towards the manor house that we had passed and reminded us of the knock on the
10 gate. The proprietor of the manor would charge us with it, the interro-

*Translated by Willa and Edwin Muir.

gation would begin immediately. I remained quite calm and also tried to calm my sister's fears. Probably she had not struck the door at all, and if she had it could never be proved. I tried to make this clear to the people round us; they listened to me but refrained from passing any opinion. Later they told me that not only my sister, but I too, as her brother, would be charged. I nodded and smiled. We all gazed back at the manor, as one watches a distant smoke cloud and waits for the flames to appear. And right enough we presently saw horsemen riding in through the wide-open gate. Dust rose, concealing everything, only the tops of the tall spears glittered. And hardly had the troop vanished into the manor courtyard be- 10 fore they seemed to have turned their horses again, for they were already on their way to us. I urged my sister to leave me, I myself would set everything right. She refused to leave me. I told her that she should at least change, so as to appear in better clothes before these gentlemen. At last she obeyed and set out on the long road to our home. Already the horsemen were beside us, and even before dismounting they enquired after my sister. She wasn't here at the moment, was the apprehensive reply, but she would come later. The answer was received with indifference; the important thing seemed their having found me. The chief members of the party appeared to be a young lively fellow, who was a judge, and his silent assist- 20 ant, who was called Assmann. I was commanded to enter the village inn. Shaking my head and hitching up my trousers, I slowly began my statement, while the sharp eyes of the party scrutinised me. I still half-believed that a word would be enough to free me, a city man, and with honour too, from this peasant folk. But when I had stepped over the threshold of the inn the judge, who had hastened in front and was already awaiting me, said: "I'm really sorry for this man." And it was beyond all possibility of doubt that by this he did not mean my present state, but something that was to happen to me. The room looked more like a prison cell than an inn parlour. Great stone flags on the floor, dark, quite bare walls, into one of 30 which an iron ring was fixed, in the middle something that looked half a pallet, half an operation table.

Could I endure any other air than prison air now? That is the great question, or rather it would be if I still had any prospect of release.

An Old Manuscript*

It looks as if much had been neglected in our country's system of defense. We have not concerned ourselves with it until now and have gone about our daily work; but things that have been happening recently begin to trouble us.

*Translated by Willa and Edwin Muir.

I have a cobbler's workshop in the square that lies before the Emperor's palace. Scarcely have I taken my shutters down, at the first glimmer of dawn, when I see armed soldiers already posted in the mouth of every street opening on the square. But these soldiers are not ours, they are obviously nomads from the North. In some way that is incomprehensible to me they have pushed right into the capital, although it is a long way from the frontier. At any rate, here they are; it seems that every morning there are more of them.

As is their nature, they camp under the open sky, for they abominate dwelling houses. They busy themselves sharpening swords, whittling arrows and practicing horsemanship. This peaceful square, which was always kept so scrupulously clean, they have made literally into a stable. We do try every now and then to run out of our shops and clear away at least the worst of the filth, but this happens less and less often, for the labor is in vain and brings us besides into danger of falling under the hoofs of the wild horses or of being crippled with lashes from the whips.

Speech with the nomads is impossible. They do not know our language, indeed they hardly have a language of their own. They communicate with each other much as jackdaws do. A screeching as of jackdaws is always in our ears. Our way of living and our institutions they neither understand nor care to understand. And so they are unwilling to make sense even out of our sign language. You can gesture at them till you dislocate your jaws and your wrists and still they will not have understood you and will never understand. They often make grimaces; then the whites of their eyes turn up and foam gathers on their lips, but they do not mean anything by that, not even a threat; they do it because it is their nature to do it. Whatever they need, they take. You cannot call it taking by force. They grab at something and you simply stand aside and leave them to it.

From my stock, too, they have taken many good articles. But I cannot complain when I see how the butcher, for instance, suffers across the street. As soon as he brings in any meat the nomads snatch it all from him and gobble it up. Even their horses devour flesh; often enough a horseman and his horse are lying side by side, both of them gnawing at the same joint, one at either end. The butcher is nervous and does not dare to stop his deliveries of meat. We understand that, however, and subscribe money to keep him going. If the nomads got no meat, who knows what they might think of doing; who knows anyhow what they may think of, even though they get meat every day.

Not long ago the butcher thought he might at least spare himself the trouble of slaughtering, and so one morning he brought along a live ox. But he will never dare to do that again. I lay for a whole hour flat on the floor at the back of my workshop with my head muffled in all the clothes and rugs and pillows I had, simply to keep from hearing the bellowing of that ox, which the nomads were leaping on from all sides, tearing morsels out of its living flesh with their teeth. It had been quiet for a long time before I risked coming out; they were lying overcome round the remains of the carcass like drunkards round a wine cask.

This was the occasion when I fancied I actually saw the Emperor himself at a window of the palace; usually he never enters these outer rooms but spends all his time in the innermost garden; yet on this occasion he was standing, or so at least it seemed to me, at one of the windows, watching with bent head the ongoings before his residence.

"What is going to happen?" we all asked ourselves. "How long can we 10 endure this burden and torment? The Emperor's palace has drawn the nomads here but does not know how to drive them away again. The gate stays shut; the guards, who used to be always marching out and in with ceremony, keep close behind barred windows. It is left to us artisans and tradesmen to save our country; but we are not equal to such a task; nor have we ever claimed to be capable of it. This is a misunderstanding of some kind; and it will be the ruin of us."

1889-
CONRAD
AIKEN * Life Isn't a Short Story

The short-story writer had run out of ideas; he had used them all; he was feeling as empty as a bathtub and as blue as an oyster. He stirred his coffee without gusto and looked at his newspaper without reading it, only noting (but with a lackluster eye) that Prohibition was finally dead. He was having his breakfast at one of those white-tiled restaurants which are so symbolic of America—with an air of carbolic purity at the entrance, but steamy purlieus at the rear which imagination trembles to investigate. His breakfast was always the same: two two-minute eggs, a little glass of chilled tomato juice, dry toast, and coffee. The only change, this morning, lay in the fact that he was having these simple things in a new 10 place—it was a somewhat humbler restaurant than the one he usually entered at eight-thirty. He had looked in through the window appraisingly, and had a little hesitantly entered. But the ritual turned out to be exactly the same as the others—a ticket at the entrance, where the cashier sat behind a glass case which was filled with cigarettes, chewing gum, and silver-papered cakes of chocolate; a tray at the counter; the precise intonation of "*Two twos, with.*" The only difference, in fact, was that the china was of a pale smoke-blue, a soft and dim blue which, had it been green, would have been pistachio. This gave his coffee a new appearance.

He sat at the marble-topped table near the window, and looked out at the crowded square. A light soft drizzle was falling on the morning rush of cars, wagons, pedestrians, newsboys; before the window bobbed a continuous procession of men and women; and he watched them over the half-seen headlines of his newspaper. A middle-aged woman, walking quickly, her umbrella pulled low over her head, so that the whiteness of her profile was sharp and immediate against the purple shadow. She
10 vanished past the range of his vision before he had had time to see her properly—and for a moment after she had gone he went on thinking about her. She might do for the physical model of his story; but she wasn't fat enough, nor was she blonde, and for some obscure reason he had decided that the heroine must be fat and blonde. Just the same, she was real, she had come from somewhere and was going somewhere, and she was doing it with obvious concentration and energy. The rhythm of her gait was unusually pronounced, each shoulder swayed slightly but emphatically sideways, as if in a series of quick and aggressive but cheerful greetings—the effect, if not quite graceful, was individual and charming.
20 He stopped thinking about her, and recovered his powers of observation, just in time to see a gray Irish face, middle-aged, hook-nosed, under a dirty felt hat, a hand quickly removing the pipe from the mouth, and the lips pouting to eject a long bright arc of spit, which fell heavily out of sight, the pipe then replaced. Such a quantity of spit he could not have imagined—his mouth felt dry at the mere thought of it. Where had it been stored and for how long? and with increasing pleasure, or increasing annoyance? The act itself had been unmistakably a pleasure, and had probably had its origins in pride; one could imagine him having competed, as a boy, in spitting through a knot-hole in a fence. He had trained
30 himself, all his life, in the power of retention; his mouth had become a kind of reservoir.

II

But the "story" came back to him. It had waked him up as a feeling of obscure weight at the back of his head or on the back of his tongue; it had seemed also to be in one corner of the shadowy ceiling above the bookcase, like a cobweb to be removed with a long brush. He had lain in bed looking at it, now and then turning his head to right or left on the pillow as if precisely to turn it away from the idea. It might be Elmira, it might be Akron, it might be Fitchburg—it was a small provincial city, at any rate, the sort of small town that looks its most characteristic in a brick-red
40 postcard of hard straight streets and ugly red houses. But she wouldn't be

Conrad Aiken   201

living in one of these—she would be living in an apartment house of shabby stucco, and the entrance would be through a door of grained varnish and plate glass. It would have an air of jaded superiority. And as for her apartment itself, on the second floor, with a little curly brass number on the door—

The idea had first occurred to him in the lobby of the Orpheum. He had paused to light a cigarette in the passage that led past the lounge, where parrots squawked in cages, and canaries trilled, and goldfish swam in an ornate aquarium, at the bottom of which, dimly seen through the heavy green water, was a kind of crumbling Gothic castle. He was standing there, looking at this, when the two groups of people had suddenly encountered each other with such hearty and heavy surprise. He had caught merely the phrases *"as I live and breathe!"* and *"in the flesh!"* The two men and the two women he had scarcely looked at—the phrases themselves had so immediately assumed an extraordinary importance. They would both, he at once saw, make good titles—it was only later that he had seen that they both had the same meaning. They both simply meant—*alive.*

Alive. And that was the difference between life, as one conceived it in a story, and life as it was, for example, in the restaurant in which he was sitting, or in the noisy square at which he was looking. As I live and breathe—I am standing here living and breathing, you are standing there living and breathing, and it's a surprise and a delight to both of us. In the flesh, too—death hasn't yet stripped our bones, or the crematory tried out our fats. We haven't seen each other for a long while, we didn't know whether we were dead or not, but here we are.

At the same time, there was the awful commonplaceness of the two phrases, the cheapness of them, the vulgarity—they were as old as the hills, and as worn; æons of weather and æons of handshake lay upon them; one witnessed, in the mere hearing of them, innumerable surprised greetings, innumerable mutual congratulations on the mere fact of being still alive. The human race seemed to extend itself backwards through them, in time, as along a road—if one pursued the thought one came eventually to a vision of two small apes peering at each other round the cheeks of a cocoanut and making a startled noise that sounded like *"yoicks!"* Or else, one simply saw, in the void, one star passing another, with no vocal interchange at all, nothing but a mutual exacerbation of heat. . . . It was very puzzling.

He stirred his coffee, wondered if he had sweetened it, reassured himself by tasting it. Yes. But in this very commonplaceness lay perhaps the idea, he had begun to see, as he lay in bed in the morning, watching the rain: and as he wondered about the large blonde lady in Fitchburg, he had begun to see that Gladys (for that was her name) was just the sort of hopelessly vulgar and commonplace person who would pride herself on her superiority in such matters. She would dislike such phrases, they would disgust her. After the first two or three years of her marriage to Sidney, when the romance had worn off and the glamor had fallen like a mask from his lean Yankee trader's face, when the sense of time had begun to be obtrusive, and the deadly round of the merely quotidian had replaced the era of faint orchids and bright bracelets and expensive theater tickets, it was then that she became conscious of certain tedious phrases he was in the habit of using. There was no concealing the fact any longer that they really came of separate and different worlds; Sidney had had little more than a high-school education, he had no "culture," he had never 10 read a book in his life. He had walked straight from school into his father's hardware shop. What there was to know about cutlery, tools, grass seed, lawn mowers, washing machines, wire nails, white lead paint, and sandpaper, he knew. He was a loyal Elk, a shrewd and honest business man, a man of no vices (unless one counted as a vice a kind of Hoosier aridity) and few pleasures. Occasionally he went to the bowling alleys, a pastime which she had always considered a little vulgar; he enjoyed a good hockey match; he liked a good thriller in the talkies (one of the few tastes they actually shared); and now and then he wanted to sit in the front row at a musical comedy. On these occasions, there was a definite sparkle or gleam 20 about him, a lighting up of his sharp gray eyes, which reminded her of the Sidney to whom she had become engaged. This both puzzled and annoyed her; she felt, as she looked at him, a vague wave of jealousy and hatred. It must have been this gleam which, when focused intently on herself, had misled her into thinking him something that he wasn't and never would be.

III

As I live and breathe.
The story might even be called that.
A horse and wagon drew up at the curbstone outside the window. On the side of the wagon was inscribed, "Acme Towel Supply Company." Of course; it was one of those companies which supply towels and napkins 30 and dishcloths to hotels and restaurants. The driver had jumped down, dropping his reins, and was opening the little pair of shabby wooden doors at the back of the wagon. The brown horse, his head down, his eyes invisible behind blinkers, stood perfectly still, as if deep in thought. His back and sides were shiny with rain, the worn harness dripped, now and then he twitched his shoulder muscles, as if in a slight shiver. Why did towel-supply companies always deliver towels in horse-drawn wagons? It was one of the minor mysteries; a queer sort of survival, for which one saw no possible reason. Beyond the wagon and the horse, the traffic was beginning to move forward again in response to a shrill birdcall from the police-40 man's whistle. A man in a black slicker had come close to the window

Conrad Aiken 203

and was reading the "specials" which were placarded in cinnamon-colored paper on the glass. When this had been done, he peered into the restaurant between two squares of paper; the quick sharp eyes looked straight at him and then past him and were as quickly gone. This meeting of his eyes had very likely prevented him from coming in; it was precisely such unexpected encounters with one's own image, as seen in the returned glance of another, that changed the course of one's life. And the restaurant had perhaps lost the sale of a couple of doughnuts and a "cup of coffee, half cream."

The way to get at Glady's character, perhaps, was through her envi- 10 ronment, the kind of place she lived in, her street, her apartment, her rooms. First of all, the stucco apartment house, the glass door, on which the name "Saguenay" was written obliquely in large gilt script, with a flourish of broad gilt underneath. Inside the door, a flight of shallow stairs, made of imitation marble, superficially clean, but deeply ingrained with dirt. Her apartment, now that she lived alone, was small, of course—it consisted of a bedroom, a sitting room, a bathroom, and a kitchenette. One's immediate feeling, on entering the sitting room from the varnished hall-way, was that the occupant must be a silly woman. It was plushy, it was perfumed, there was a bead curtain trembling between the sitting room 20 and the kitchenette, at either side of the lace-curtained window hung a golden-wired birdcage, in which rustled a canary, and on the window-sill was a large bowl of goldfish. The ornaments were very ornamental and very numerous; the mantel groaned with souvenirs and photographs; the pictures were uniformly sentimental—several were religious. It was clear that she doted, simply doted, on birds and flowers—talked baby-talk to the canaries and the goldfish, even to the azalea, and always of course in that offensive, little, high-pitched fat-woman's coo. She would come in to them in the morning, wearing a pink flannel wrapper, brushing her hair, and would talk to them or wag a coy finger at them. And how's my sweet little 30 dicky bird this morning? and have they slept well and been good in the night? and have they kept their little eyes shut tight to keep out the naughty bogey-man? And then at once she would forget them entirely, begin singing softly, walk with her head tilted on one side to the bathroom to turn on the bath, return to the kitchen to filch a cookie from the bread-box, and then go languidly to the front door for the milk and the newspaper.

The newspaper was the *Christian Science Monitor;* she took it, not because she was a Scientist, though she had an open mind, but because it was so "cultured." She liked to read about books and music and foreign affairs, and it frequently gave her ideas for little talks to the Women's 40 Club. She had talked about the dole in England, and its distressing effect on the morals of the young men, and she had made a sensation by saying that she thought one should not too hastily condemn the nudist cult in Germany. Everyone knew that the human body craved sunlight, that the ultra-violet rays, or was it the infra-red, were most beneficial, so the idea was at least a healthy one, wasn't it? And the beautiful purity of Greek life was surely an answer to those who thought the human body in itself impure. It raised the whole question of what was purity, anyway! Everyone knew that purity was in the heart, in the attitude, and not really in the body. She thought the idea of playing croquet in the nude, queer as it might seem to us in Fitchburg, most interesting. One ought to think less about the body and more about the mind.

IV

The towel-supply man seemed to have disappeared; perhaps he was
10 getting a cup of coffee at the Waldorf next door. Or making a round of several of the adjacent restaurants all at once. The horse waited patiently, was absolutely still, didn't even stamp a foot. He looked as if he were thinking about the rain. Or perhaps, dismayed by the senseless noise of all the traffic about him, he was simply thinking about his stall, wherever it was. Or more likely, not thinking anything at all. He just stood.

To her friends, of course, and to her sister Emma (who was her chief reason for living in Fitchburg) she posed as a woman with a broken heart, a woman tragically disillusioned, a beautiful romantic who had found that love was dust and ashes and that men were—well, creatures of a lower
20 order. It was all very sad, very pitiful. One ought to have foreseen it, perhaps, or one ought not to have been born so sensitive, but there it was. If you had a soul, if you had perceptions, and loved beautiful things, and if you fell in love while you were still inexperienced and trusting, while you still looked at a world of violets through violet eyes, this was what happened. You gave your heart to someone who didn't deserve it. But what man ever *did* deserve it? Only the poets, perhaps, or the composers, Chopin for instance, those rare creatures, half angel and half man (or was it half bird?), who had great and deep and tender souls. And how many such men could one find in Massachusetts? It was all so impossible, it was all so
30 dreadful. Everyone knew that in America the women were infinitely more refined and sensitive than the men, you had only to look about you. What man ever wanted to talk about poetry with you, or listen to an evening of the Preludes, or to a lecture about the love affair of George Sand and Alfred de Musset? They wouldn't know what you meant; they wanted to go to the bowling alley or talk about the stock market; or else to sit in the front row of the Follies and look at the legs. They were vulgar, they had no imaginations. And she remembered that time at Emma's when Sidney had got so angry and gone on so in that common and vulgar way and made such a scene—whenever she thought of it she got hot all over. Absolutely,
40 it was the most vulgar scene! And done deliberately, too, just because he

was so jealous about their having a refined conversation. And when she tried to stop him talking about it, he just went on, getting stubborner and stubborner, and all simply to make her feel ashamed. As if any of them had wanted to hear about those cheap drinking parties of his in Ohio. And that dreadful word, burgoo, that was it, which they had all laughed at, and tried to shame him out of, why what do you mean, burgoo, why Sidney what are you talking about, who ever heard such a word as *burgoo*, *burgoo!* And even that hadn't been enough, he got red and angry and went on saying it, burgoo, what's wrong with burgoo, of course there is such a word, and damned fine parties they were, too, and if they only had bur- goos in Massachusetts life here would be a damned sight better. The idea! It served him right that she got mad and jumped up and said what she did. If you can't talk politely like a gentleman, or let others talk, then I think you had better leave those who will. Why don't you go back to your hard- ware shop, or back to Ohio, it doesn't seem this is the right environment for you. Or *anywhere* where you can have your precious burgoo.

But of course that was only one incident among so many, it was hap- pening all the time; anybody could see that Sidney was not the man to ever appreciate her. What she always said was that nobody outside a marriage could ever possibly have any *real* idea of the things that went on there, could they. It was just impossible for them even to conceive of it. All those little things that you wouldn't think of—like Sidney's always leaving the dirty lather and little black hairs in the wash-basin after he shaved. Or the way he never noticed when she had on a new hat or ever said anything nice about the meals she got for him, just simply not notic- ing anything at all. That was a part of it, but much more was his simply not ever being able to talk to her, or to take any interest in intellectual things. And his vulgarity, the commonness of his speech, his manners! Every time she introduced him to somebody he would put his head down and take that ridiculous little confidential step toward them and say, "What was the name? I didn't get the name?" The idea! And if you told him about it he got mad. And as for the number of times every day that he said "as I live and breathe"———!

V

It had begun to rain harder. The sound of it rushed through the open- ing door as a small man, very dark, a Syrian perhaps, came in shaking his sodden hat so that the drops fell in a curve on the floor. A bright spray was dancing on the roof of the towel wagon, and a heavy stream fell splattering from one corner of an awning. People had begun to run, to scurry, in one's and two's and three's, exactly like one of those movies of the Russian Revolution, when invisible machine guns were turned on the crowds. One would not be surprised to see them fall down, or crawl away on their bellies.

Or to see the whole square emptied of human beings in the twinkling of an eye. Nor would one be surprised to see a lightning flash, either, for it had suddenly become astonishingly dark—the whole dismal scene had that ominous look which seems to wait, in a melodrama, for a peal of thunder. The light was sulphur-colored; it was terrifying; and he watched with fascination all the little windshield wipers wagging agitatedly on the fronts of cars—it gave one the feeling that the poor things were actually
10 frightened, and were breathing faster. As for the horse, he stood unmoving, unmoved. His head was down, and he seemed to be studying with an extraordinary concentration the torrent of muddy water which rushed past his feet. Perhaps he was enjoying it; perhaps he even liked to feel all that tropic weight of rain on his back, experiencing in it a renewal of contact with the real, the elemental. Or perhaps he merely enjoyed standing still. Or perhaps he simply *was*.

But the question arose, ought one now to switch the point of view in the story, and do something more about Sidney? What about Sidney? Where on earth was Sidney all this while? and doing what? Presumably,
20 running his hardware shop—and presumably again in Boston—but this was a little meager, one wanted to know something more than that. One ought to give him a special sort of appearance—a pencil behind his ear, a tuft of white hair over his sallow forehead, sharply pointed brown shoes. Perhaps he was something of a dandy, with a vivid corner of striped handkerchief pointing from his breast pocket; and perhaps he was by no means such a dull fellow as Gladys thought. But this *would* involve a shift in point of view, which was a mistake; it was no doubt better to stick to Gladys, in Fitchburg, and to see Sidney wholly as *she* saw him, to think of him only as *she* thought of him. She would almost certainly, from time
30 to time (self-absorbed as she was, and vain, and vulgar, and with her silly small-town pretensions to culture), she would almost certainly, nevertheless, give him credit for a few virtues. He was generous: he had offered her a divorce, as soon as he knew how she felt about it; and he had behaved like a lamb, really, if she did say so, like a lamb, about the separation. He had done everything he could think of to make it easier for her.

In fact, one thing you *could* say for Sidney was, that he was generous—generous to a fault. She often thought of that. She always thought of it especially on the first of the month, when the check for the separation allowance turned up, as punctually as the calendar—sometimes he even
40 sent her something extra. On these days, when she bustled to the bank with the check tucked into her glove to deposit it and pay the rent, she always felt so secure and happy that she had a very special state of mind about Sidney, something that was almost affection. Of course, it couldn't *be* affection, but it was *like* it—and it was just that feeling, with perhaps

the loneliness which had upset her to begin with, which had misled her at last into writing him. It was easy enough now, as she had so often said to Emma, to see what had made her do it; she was sorry for him; but it only went to show how right she had been in the whole idea.

Just the same, it had been natural enough to write to him in that affectionate and grateful way; and when he had answered by so pathetically asking her to let him come to see her she had certainly thought it might be worth trying; even Emma had thought so; perhaps they would find after all that the differences between them were superficial; they could patch things up, maybe she would go back to Boston to live with him. The idea actually excited her—she remembered how she had found herself looking forward to having him come. Emma had offered to put him up for the night, so as to prevent embarrassment. And the thought of having him see her new apartment for the first time, with the canaries and the goldfish and the oriental rugs, and the Encyclopædia Britannica, had given her a very funny feeling, almost like being unfaithful. The day before he came she could hardly sit still. She kept walking to and fro round the apartment, moving the rugs and the chairs, and patting the cushions—and all the time wondering if two years would have changed him much, and what they would say. Naturally, she hadn't held out any real hope to him in her letter, she had only told him she would be willing to talk with him, that was all. He had no right to expect anything else, she had made that clear. However, there was no sense in not being friendly about these things, was there? Even if you were separated you could behave like a civilized human being; Emma agreed with her about that. It was the only decent thing to do. But when the day came, and when finally that afternoon she heard him breeze into Emma's front hall, stamping his feet, and went out to meet him, and saw him wearing the wing collar and the stringy little white tie, and the rubbers, and his little gray eyes shining behind the glasses with the cord, and when the very first thing he said was, just as if nothing at all had ever happened, "Well, as I live and breathe, if it isn't Gladys!"—and then stood there, not knowing whether to kiss her or shake hands—it was just a misdeal, that was all, just another misdeal.

The whole thing went down, smack, like a house of cards. She could hardly bring herself to shake hands with him, or look at him—she suddenly wanted to cry. She rushed into Emma's room and stayed there on the bed for an hour, crying—Emma kept running in and saying for God's sake pull yourself together, at least go out and talk to him for a while, he's hurt, you can't treat him like this; the poor man doesn't know whether he's going or coming; come on now, Gladys, and be a good sport. He's sitting on the sofa in there with his head down like a horse, not knowing what to say; you simply can't treat him like that. The least you can do is go out and tell him you're sorry and that it was a mistake, and that he'd better not stay, or take him round to your apartment and talk it over with him quietly and then send him back to Boston. Come on now.

But of course she couldn't do it—she couldn't even go with him to the station. Emma went with him, and told him on the platform while they were waiting for the train that it was no use, it had all been a terrible mistake, and she was sorry, they were both sorry, Gladys sent word that she was very sorry. And afterwards, she had said it was so pathetic seeing him with his brand-new suitcase there beside him on the platform, his suitcase which he hadn't even opened, just taking it back to Boston where
10 he came from. . . . When the train finally came, he almost forgot his suitcase; she thought he would have liked to leave it behind.

The towel-supply man came running back with a basket, flung it into the wagon, banged the dripping doors shut, and then jumped nimbly up to his seat, unhooking the reins. Automatically, but as if still deep in thought, the horse leaned slowly forward, lowered his head a little, and began to move. A long day was still ahead of him, a day of crowded and noisy streets, streets full of surprises and terrors and rain, muddy uneven cobbles and greasy smooth asphalt. The wagon and the man would be always there behind him; an incalculable sequence of accidents and ad-
20 ventures was before him. What did he think about, as he plodded from one dirty restaurant to another, one hotel to another, carrying towels? Probably nothing at all; certainly no such sentimental thing as a green meadow, nor anything so ridiculous as a story about living and breathing. It was enough, even if one was a slave, to live and breathe. For life, after all, isn't a short story.

1894-
KATHERINE
ANNE
PORTER * The Jilting of Granny Weatherall

She flicked her wrist neatly out of Doctor Harry's pudgy careful fingers and pulled the sheet up to her chin. The brat ought to be in knee breeches. Doctoring around the country with spectacles on his nose! "Get along now, take your schoolbooks and go. There's nothing wrong with me."

Doctor Harry spread a warm paw like a cushion on her forehead where the forked green vein danced and made her eyelids twitch. "Now, now, be a good girl, and we'll have you up in no time."

"That's no way to speak to a woman nearly eighty years old just because she's down. I'd have you respect your elders, young man."

"Well, Missy, excuse me." Doctor Harry patted her cheek. "But I've got to warn you, haven't I? You're a marvel, but you must be careful or you're going to be good and sorry."

"Don't tell me what I'm going to be. I'm on my feet now, morally speaking. It's Cornelia. I had to go to bed to get rid of her."

Her bones felt loose, and floated around in her skin, and Doctor Harry floated like a balloon around the foot of the bed. He floated and pulled down his waistcoat and swung his glasses on a cord. "Well, stay where you are, it certainly can't hurt you."

"Get along and doctor your sick," said Granny Weatherall. "Leave a well woman alone. I'll call for you when I want you. . . . Where were you forty years ago when I pulled through milk-leg and double pneumonia? You weren't even born. Don't let Cornelia lead you on," she shouted, because Doctor Harry appeared to float up to the ceiling and out. "I pay my own bills, and I don't throw my money away on nonsense!"

She meant to wave good-by, but it was too much trouble. Her eyes closed of themselves, it was like a dark curtain drawn around the bed. The pillow rose and floated under her, pleasant as a hammock in a light wind. She listened to the leaves rustling outside the window. No, somebody was swishing newspapers: no, Cornelia and Doctor Harry were whispering together. She leaped broad awake, thinking they whispered in her ear.

"She was never like this, *never* like this!" "Well, what can we expect?" "Yes, eighty years old. . . ."

Well, and what if she was? She still had ears. It was like Cornelia to whisper around doors. She always kept things secret in such a public way. She was always being tactful and kind. Cornelia was dutiful; that was the trouble with her. Dutiful and good: "So good and dutiful," said Granny, "that I'd like to spank her." She saw herself spanking Cornelia and making a fine job of it.

"What'd you say, Mother?"

Granny felt her face tying up in hard knots.

"Can't a body think, I'd like to know?"

"I thought you might want something."

"I do. I want a lot of things. First off, go away and don't whisper."

She lay and drowsed, hoping in her sleep that the children would keep out and let her rest a minute. It had been a long day. Not that she was tired. It was always pleasant to snatch a minute now and then. There was always so much to be done, let me see: tomorrow.

Tomorrow was far away and there was nothing to trouble about. Things were finished somehow when the time came; thank God there was always a little margin over for peace: then a person could spread out the plan of life and tuck in the edges orderly. It was good to have everything clean and folded away, with the hair brushes and tonic bottles sitting straight

on the white embroidered linen: the day started without fuss and the pantry shelves laid out with rows of jelly glasses and brown jugs and white stone-china jars with blue whirligigs and words painted on them: coffee, tea, sugar, ginger, cinnamon, allspice: and the bronze clock with the lion on top nicely dusted off. The dust that lion could collect in twenty-four hours! The box in the attic with all those letters tied up, well, she'd have to go through that tomorrow. All those letters—George's letters and John's letters and her letters to them both—lying around for the children to find afterwards made her uneasy. Yes, that would be tomor-
10 row's business. No use to let them know how silly she had been once.

While she was rummaging around she found death in her mind and it felt clammy and unfamiliar. She had spent so much time preparing for death there was no need for bringing it up again. Let it take care of itself now. When she was sixty she had felt very old, finished, and went around making farewell trips to see her children and grandchildren, with a secret in her mind: This is the very last of your mother, children! Then she made her will and came down with a long fever. That was all just a notion like a lot of other things, but it was lucky too, for she had once for all got over the idea of dying for a long time. Now she couldn't be worried.
20 She hoped she had better sense now. Her father had lived to be one hundred and two years old and had drunk a noggin of strong hot toddy on his last birthday. He told the reporters it was his daily habit, and he owed his long life to that. He had made quite a scandal and was very pleased about it. She believed she'd just plague Cornelia a little.

"Cornelia! Cornelia!" No footsteps, but a sudden hand on her cheek. "Bless you, where have you been?"

"Here, mother."

"Well, Cornelia, I want a noggin of hot toddy."

"Are you cold, darling?"

30 "I'm chilly, Cornelia. Lying in bed stops the circulation. I must have told you that a thousand times."

Well, she could just hear Cornelia telling her husband that Mother was getting a little childish and they'd have to humor her. The thing that most annoyed her was that Cornelia thought she was deaf, dumb, and blind. Little hasty glances and tiny gestures tossed around her and over her head saying, "Don't cross her, let her have her way, she's eighty years old," and she sitting there as if she lived in a thin glass cage. Sometimes Granny almost made up her mind to pack up and move back to her own house where nobody could remind her every minute that she
40 was old. Wait, wait, Cornelia, till your own children whisper behind your back!

In her day she had kept a better house and had got more work done. She wasn't too old yet for Lydia to be driving eighty miles for advice when one of the children jumped the track, and Jimmy still dropped in and talked things over: "Now, Mammy, you've a good business head, I want to know what you think of this? . . ." Old. Cornelia couldn't change the furniture around without asking. Little things, little things! They had been so sweet when they were little. Granny wished the old days were back again with the children young and everything to be done over. It had been a hard pull, but not too much for her. When she thought of all the food she had cooked, and all the clothes she had cut and sewed, and all the gardens she had made—well, the children showed it. There they were, made out of her, and they couldn't get away from that. Sometimes she wanted to see John again and point to them and say, Well, I didn't 10 do so badly, did I? But that would have to wait. That was for tomorrow. She used to think of him as a man, but now all the children were older than their father, and he would be a child beside her if she saw him now. It seemed strange and there was something wrong in the idea. Why, he couldn't possibly recognize her. She had fenced in a hundred acres once, digging the post holes herself and clamping the wires with just a negro boy to help. That changed a woman. John would be looking for a young woman with the peaked Spanish comb in her hair and the painted fan. Digging post holes changed a woman. Riding country roads in the winter when women had their babies was another thing: sitting up nights with 20 sick horses and sick negroes and sick children and hardly ever losing one. John, I hardly ever lost one of them! John would see that in a minute, that would be something he could understand, she wouldn't have to explain anything!

It made her feel like rolling up her sleeves and putting the whole place to rights again. No matter if Cornelia was determined to be everywhere at once, there were a great many things left undone on this place. She would start tomorrow and do them. It was good to be strong enough for everything, even if all you made melted and changed and slipped under your hands, so that by the time you finished you almost forgot what you 30 were working for. What was it I set out to do? she asked herself intently, but she could not remember. A fog rose over the valley, she saw it marching across the creek swallowing the trees and moving up the hill like an army of ghosts. Soon it would be at the near edge of the orchard, and then it was time to go in and light the lamps. Come in, children, don't stay out in the night air.

Lighting the lamps had been beautiful. The children huddled up to her and breathed like little calves waiting at the bars in the twilight. Their eyes followed the match and watched the flame rise and settle in a blue curve, then they moved away from her. The lamp was lit, they didn't 40 have to be scared and hang on to mother any more. Never, never, never more. God, for all my life I thank Thee. Without Thee, my God, I could never have done it. Hail, Mary, full of grace.

I want you to pick all the fruit this year and see that nothing is wasted.

There's always someone who can use it. Don't let good things rot for want of using. You waste life when you waste good food. Don't let things get lost. It's bitter to lose things. Now, don't let me get to thinking, not when I am tired and taking a little nap before supper. . . .

The pillow rose about her shoulders and pressed against her heart and the memory was being squeezed out of it: oh, push down the pillow, somebody: it would smother her if she tried to hold it. Such a fresh breeze blowing and such a green day with no threats in it. But he had not come, just the same. What does a woman do when she has put on the white veil
10 and set out the white cake for a man and he doesn't come? She tried to remember. No, I swear he never harmed me but in that. He never harmed me but in that . . . and what if he did? There was the day, the day, but a whirl of dark smoke rose and covered it, crept up and over into the bright field where everything was planted so carefully in orderly rows. That was hell, she knew hell when she saw it. For sixty years she had prayed against remembering him and against losing her soul in the deep pit of hell, and now the two things were mingled in one and the thought of him was a smoky cloud from hell that moved and crept in her head when she had just got rid of Doctor Harry and was trying to rest a minute. Wounded
20 vanity, Ellen, said a sharp voice in the top of her mind. Don't let your wounded vanity get the upper hand of you. Plenty of girls get jilted. You were jilted, weren't you? Then stand up to it. Her eyelids wavered and let in streamers of blue-gray light like tissue paper over her eyes. She must get up and pull the shades down or she'd never sleep. She was in bed again and the shades were not down. How could that happen? Better turn over, hide from the light, sleeping in the light gave you nightmares. "Mother, how do you feel now?" and a stinging wetness on her forehead. But I don't like having my face washed in cold water!

Hapsy? George? Lydia? Jimmy? No, Cornelia, and her features were
30 swollen and full of little puddles. "They're coming, darling, they'll all be here soon." Go wash your face, child, you look funny.

Instead of obeying, Cornelia knelt down and put her head on the pillow. She seemed to be talking but there was no sound. "Well, are you tongue-tied? Whose birthday is it? Are you going to give a party?"

Cornelia's mouth moved urgently in strange shapes. "Don't do that, you bother me, daughter."

"Oh, no, Mother. Oh, no. . . ."

Nonsense. It was strange about children. They disputed your every word. "No what, Cornelia?"
40 "Here's Doctor Harry."

"I won't see that boy again. He just left five minutes ago."

"That was this morning, Mother. It's night now. Here's the nurse."

"This is Doctor Harry, Mrs. Weatherall. I never saw you look so young and happy!"

"Ah, I'll never be young again—but I'd be happy if they'd let me lie in peace and get rested."

She thought she spoke up loudly, but no one answered. A warm weight on her forehead, a warm bracelet on her wrist, and a breeze went on whispering, trying to tell her something. A shuffle of leaves in the everlasting hand of God, He blew on them and they danced and rattled. "Mother, don't mind, we're going to give you a little hypodermic." "Look here, daughter, how do ants get in this bed? I saw sugar ants yesterday." Did you send for Hapsy too?

It was Hapsy she really wanted. She had to go a long way back through a great many rooms to find Hapsy standing with a baby on her arm. She seemed to herself to be Hapsy also, and the baby on Hapsy's arm was Hapsy and himself and herself, all at once, and there was no surprise in the meeting. Then Hapsy melted from within and turned flimsy as gray gauze and the baby was a gauzy shadow, and Hapsy came up close and said, "I thought you'd never come," and looked at her very searchingly and said, "You haven't changed a bit!" They leaned forward to kiss, when Cornelia began whispering from a long way off, "Oh, is there anything you want to tell me? Is there anything I can do for you?"

Yes, she had changed her mind after sixty years and she would like to see George. I want you to find George. Find him and be sure to tell him I forgot him. I want him to know I had my husband just the same and my children and my house like any other woman. A good house too and a good husband that I loved and fine children out of him. Better than I hoped for even. Tell him I was given back everything he took away and more. Oh, no, oh, God, no, there was something else besides the house and the man and the children. Oh, surely they were not all? What was it? Something not given back. . . . Her breath crowded down under her ribs and grew into a monstrous frightening shape with cutting edges; it bored up into her head, and the agony was unbelievable: Yes, John, get the Doctor now, no more talk, my time has come.

When this one was born it should be the last. The last. It should have been born first, for it was the one she had truly wanted. Everything came in good time. Nothing left out, left over. She was strong, in three days she would be as well as ever. Better. A woman needed milk in her to have her full health.

"Mother, do you hear me?"

"I've been telling you—"

"Mother, Father Connolly's here."

"I went to Holy Communion only last week. Tell him I'm not so sinful as all that."

"Father just wants to speak to you."

He could speak as much as he pleased. It was like him to drop in and inquire about her soul as if it were a teething baby, and then stay on for

a cup of tea and a round of cards and gossip. He always had a funny story of some sort, usually about an Irishman who made his little mistakes and confessed them, and the point lay in some absurd thing he would blurt out in the confessional showing his struggles between native piety and original sin. Granny felt easy about her soul. Cornelia, where are your manners? Give Father Connolly a chair. She had her secret comfortable understanding with a few favorite saints who cleared a straight road to God for her. All as surely signed and sealed as the papers for the new Forty Acres. Forever . . . heirs and assigns forever. Since the day the
10 wedding cake was not cut, but thrown out and wasted. The whole bottom dropped out of the world, and there she was blind and sweating with nothing under her feet and the walls falling away. His hand had caught her under the breast, she had not fallen, there was the freshly polished floor with the green rug on it, just as before. He had cursed like a sailor's parrot and said, "I'll kill him for you." Don't lay a hand on him, for my sake leave something to God. "Now, Ellen, you must believe what I tell you. . . ."

So there was nothing, nothing to worry about any more, except sometimes in the night one of the children screamed in a nightmare, and they
20 both hustled out shaking and hunting for the matches and calling, "There, wait a minute, here we are!" John, get the doctor now, Hapsy's time has come. But there was Hapsy standing by the bed in a white cap. "Cornelia, tell Hapsy to take off her cap. I can't see her plain."

Her eyes opened very wide and the room stood out like a picture she had seen somewhere. Dark colors with the shadows rising towards the ceiling in long angles. The tall black dresser gleamed with nothing on it but John's picture, enlarged from a little one, with John's eyes very black when they should have been blue. You never saw him, so how do you know how he looked? But the man insisted the copy was perfect, it was
30 very rich and handsome. For a picture, yes, but it's not my husband. The table by the bed had a linen cover and a candle and a crucifix. The light was blue from Cornelia's silk lampshades. No sort of light at all, just frippery. You had to live forty years with kerosene lamps to appreciate honest electricity. She felt very strong and she saw Doctor Harry with a rosy nimbus around him.

"You look like a saint, Doctor Harry, and I vow that's as near as you'll ever come to it."

"She's saying something."

"I heard you, Cornelia. What's all this carrying-on?"
40 "Father Connolly's saying—"

Cornelia's voice staggered and bumped like a cart in a bad road. It rounded corners and turned back again and arrived nowhere. Granny stepped up in the cart very lightly and reached for the reins, but a man sat beside her and she knew him by his hands, driving the cart. She did not look in his face, for she knew without seeing, but looked instead down the road where the trees leaned over and bowed to each other and a thousand birds were singing a Mass. She felt like singing too, but she put her hand in the bosom of her dress and pulled out a rosary, and Father Connolly murmured Latin in a very solemn voice and tickled her feet. My God, will you stop that nonsense? I'm a married woman. What if he did run away and leave me to face the priest by myself? I found another a whole world better. I wouldn't have exchanged my husband for anybody except St. Michael himself, and you may tell him that for me with a thank you in the bargain.   10

Light flashed on her closed eyelids, and a deep roaring shook her. Cornelia, is that lightning? I hear thunder. There's going to be a storm. Close all the windows. Call the children in.... "Mother, here we are, all of us." "Is that you, Hapsy?" "Oh, no, I'm Lydia. We drove as fast as we could." Their faces drifted above her, drifted away. The rosary fell out of her hands and Lydia put it back. Jimmy tried to help, their hands fumbled together, and Granny closed two fingers around Jimmy's thumb. Beads wouldn't do, it must be something alive. She was so amazed her thoughts ran round and round. So, my dear Lord, this is my death and I wasn't even thinking about it. My children have come to see me die. 20 But I can't, it's not time. Oh, I always hated surprises. I wanted to give Cornelia the amethyst set—Cornelia, you're to have the amethyst set, but Hapsy's to wear it when she wants, and, Doctor Harry, do shut up. Nobody sent for you. Oh, my dear Lord, do wait a minute. I meant to do something about the Forty Acres, Jimmy doesn't need it and Lydia will later on, with that worthless husband of hers. I meant to finish the altar cloth and send six bottles of wine to Sister Borgia for her dyspepsia. I want to send six bottles of wine to Sister Borgia, Father Connolly, now don't let me forget.

Cornelia's voice made short turns and tilted over and crashed. "Oh, 30 Mother, oh, Mother, oh, Mother...."

"I'm not going, Cornelia. I'm taken by surprise. I can't go."

You'll see Hapsy again. What about her? "I thought you'd never come." Granny made a long journey outward, looking for Hapsy. What if I don't find her? What then? Her heart sank down and down, there was no bottom to death, she couldn't come to the end of it. The blue light from Cornelia's lampshade drew into a tiny point in the center of her brain, it flickered and winked like an eye, quietly it fluttered and dwindled. Granny lay curled down within herself, amazed and watchful, staring at the point of light that was herself; her body was now only a deeper mass of shadow 40 in an endless darkness and this darkness would curl around the light and swallow it up. God, give a sign!

For the second time there was no sign. Again no bridegroom and the priest in the house. She could not remember any other sorrow because this grief wiped them all away. Oh, no, there's nothing more cruel than this—I'll never forgive it. She stretched herself with a deep breath and blew out the light.

1897-1962
WILLIAM
FAULKNER * A Rose for Emily

I

When Miss Emily Grierson died, our whole town went to her funeral: the men through a sort of respectful affection for a fallen monument, the women mostly out of curiosity to see the inside of her house, which no one save an old man-servant—a combined gardener and cook—had seen in at least ten years.

It was a big, squarish frame house that had once been white, decorated with cupolas and spires and scrolled balconies in the heavily lightsome style of the seventies, set on what had once been our most select street. But garages and cotton gins had encroached and obliterated even the
10 august names of that neighborhood; only Miss Emily's house was left, lifting its stubborn and coquettish decay above the cotton wagons and the gasoline pumps—an eyesore among eyesores. And now Miss Emily had gone to join the representatives of those august names where they lay in the cedar-bemused cemetery among the ranked and anonymous graves of Union and Confederate soldiers who fell at the battle of Jefferson.

Alive, Miss Emily had been a tradition, a duty, and a care; a sort of hereditary obligation upon the town, dating from that day in 1894 when Colonel Sartoris, the mayor—he who fathered the edict that no Negro woman should appear on the streets without an apron—remitted her
20 taxes, the dispensation dating from the death of her father on into perpetuity. Not that Miss Emily would have accepted charity. Colonel Sartoris invented an involved tale to the effect that Miss Emily's father had loaned money to the town, which the town, as a matter of business, preferred this way of repaying. Only a man of Colonel Sartoris' generation and thought could have invented it, and only a woman could have believed it.

When the next generation, with its more modern ideas, became mayors and aldermen, this arrangement created some little dissatisfaction. On

William Faulkner   217

the first of the year they mailed her a tax notice. February came, and there was no reply. They wrote her a formal letter, asking her to call at the sheriff's office at her convenience. A week later the mayor wrote her himself, offering to call or to send his car for her, and received in reply a note on paper of an archaic shape, in a thin, flowing calligraphy in faded ink, to the effect that she no longer went out at all. The tax notice was also enclosed, without comment.

They called a special meeting of the Board of Aldermen. A deputation waited upon her, knocked at the door through which no visitor had passed since she ceased giving china-painting lessons eight or ten years earlier. 10 They were admitted by the old Negro into a dim hall from which a stairway mounted into still more shadow. It smelled of dust and disuse—a close, dank smell. The Negro led them into the parlor. It was furnished in heavy, leather-covered furniture. When the Negro opened the blinds of one window, they could see that the leather was cracked; and when they sat down, a faint dust rose sluggishly about their thighs, spinning with slow motes in the single sun-ray. On a tarnished gilt easel before the fireplace stood a crayon portrait of Miss Emily's father.

They rose when she entered—a small, fat woman in black, with a thin gold chain descending to her waist and vanishing into her belt, leaning on 20 an ebony cane with a tarnished gold head. Her skeleton was small and spare; perhaps that was why what would have been merely plumpness in another was obesity in her. She looked bloated, like a body long submerged in motionless water, and of that pallid hue. Her eyes, lost in the fatty ridges of her face, looked like two small pieces of coal pressed into a lump of dough as they moved from one face to another while the visitors stated their errand.

She did not ask them to sit. She just stood in the door and listened quietly until the spokesman came to a stumbling halt. Then they could hear the invisible watch ticking at the end of the gold chain. 30

Her voice was dry and cold. "I have no taxes in Jefferson. Colonel Sartoris explained it to me. Perhaps one of you can gain access to the city records and satisfy yourselves."

"But we have. We are the city authorities, Miss Emily. Didn't you get a notice from the sheriff, signed by him?"

"I received a paper, yes," Miss Emily said. "Perhaps he considers himself the sheriff . . . I have no taxes in Jefferson."

"But there is nothing on the books to show that, you see. We must go by the—"

"See Colonel Sartoris. I have no taxes in Jefferson." 40

"But, Miss Emily—"

"See Colonel Sartoris." (Colonel Sartoris had been dead almost ten years.) "I have no taxes in Jefferson. Tobe!" The Negro appeared. "Show these gentlemen out."

II

So she vanquished them, horse and foot, just as she had vanquished their fathers thirty years before about the smell. That was two years after her father's death and a short time after her sweetheart—the one we believed would marry her—had deserted her. After her father's death she went out very little; after her sweetheart went away, people hardly saw her at all. A few of the ladies had the temerity to call, but were not received, and the only sign of life about the place was the Negro man—a young man then—going in and out with a market basket.

"Just as if a man—any man—could keep a kitchen properly," the ladies
10 said; so they were not surprised when the smell developed. It was another link between the gross, teeming world and the high and mighty Griersons.

A neighbor, a woman, complained to the mayor, Judge Stevens, eighty years old.

"But what will you have me do about it, madam?" he said.

"Why, send her word to stop it," the woman said. "Isn't there a law?"

"I'm sure that won't be necessary," Judge Stevens said. "It's probably just a snake or a rat that nigger of hers killed in the yard. I'll speak to him about it."

The next day he received two more complaints, one from a man who
20 came in diffident deprecation. "We really must do something about it, Judge. I'd be the last one in the world to bother Miss Emily, but we've got to do something." That night the Board of Aldermen met—three graybeards and one younger man, a member of the rising generation.

"It's simple enough," he said. "Send her word to have her place cleaned up. Give her a certain time to do it in, and if she don't . . ."

"Dammit, sir," Judge Stevens said, "will you accuse a lady to her face of smelling bad?"

So the next night, after midnight, four men crossed Miss Emily's lawn and slunk about the house like burglars, sniffing along the base of the
30 brickwork and at the cellar openings while one of them performed a regular sowing motion with his hand out of a sack slung from his shoulder. They broke open the cellar door and sprinkled lime there, and in all the outbuildings. As they recrossed the lawn, a window that had been dark was lighted and Miss Emily sat in it, the light behind her, and her upright torso motionless as that of an idol. They crept quietly across the lawn and into the shadow of the locusts that lined the street. After a week or two the smell went away.

That was when people had begun to feel really sorry for her. People in our town, remembering how old lady Wyatt, her great-aunt, had gone
40 completely crazy at last, believed that the Griersons held themselves a little too high for what they really were. None of the young men were quite good enough for Miss Emily and such. We had long thought of them

as a tableau, Miss Emily a slender figure in white in the background, her father a spraddled silhouette in the foreground, his back to her and clutching a horsewhip, the two of them framed by the back-flung front door. So when she got to be thirty and was still single, we were not pleased exactly, but vindicated; even with insanity in the family she wouldn't have turned down all of her chances if they had really materialized.

When her father died, it got about that the house was all that was left to her; and in a way, people were glad. At last they could pity Miss Emily. Being left alone, and a pauper, she had become humanized. Now she too would know the old thrill and the old despair of a penny more or less.   10

The day after his death all the ladies prepared to call at the house and offer condolence and aid, as is our custom. Miss Emily met them at the door, dressed as usual and with no trace of grief on her face. She told them that her father was not dead. She did that for three days, with the ministers calling on her, and the doctors, trying to persuade her to let them dispose of the body. Just as they were about to resort to law and force, she broke down, and they buried her father quickly.

We did not say she was crazy then. We believed she had to do that. We remembered all the young men her father had driven away, and we knew that with nothing left, she would have to cling to that which had robbed 20 her, as people will.

III

She was sick for a long time. When we saw her again, her hair was cut short, making her look like a girl, with a vague resemblance to those angels in colored church windows—sort of tragic and serene.

The town had just let the contracts for paving the sidewalks, and in the summer after her father's death they began the work. The construction company came with niggers and mules and machinery, and a foreman named Homer Barron, a Yankee—a big, dark, ready man, with a big voice and eyes lighter than his face. The little boys would follow in groups to hear him cuss the niggers, and the niggers singing in time to the rise and 30 fall of picks. Pretty soon he knew everybody in town. Whenever you heard a lot of laughing anywhere about the square, Homer Barron would be in the center of the group. Presently we began to see him and Miss Emily on Sunday afternoons driving in the yellow-wheeled buggy and the matched team of bays from the livery stable.

At first we were glad that Miss Emily would have an interest, because the ladies all said, "Of course a Grierson would not think seriously of a Northerner, a day laborer." But there were still others, older people, who said that even grief could not cause a real lady to forget *noblesse oblige*— without calling it *noblesse oblige*. They just said, "Poor Emily. Her kinsfolk 40 should come to her." She had some kin in Alabama; but years ago her father had fallen out with them over the estate of old lady Wyatt, the crazy woman, and there was no communication between the two families. They had not even been represented at the funeral.

And as soon as the old people said, "Poor Emily," the whispering began. "Do you suppose it's really so?" they said to one another. "Of course it is. What else could . . ." This behind their hands; rustling of craned silk and satin behind jalousies closed upon the sun of Sunday afternoon as the thin, swift clop-clop-clop of the matched team passed: "Poor Emily."

10   She carried her head high enough—even when we believed that she was fallen. It was as if she demanded more than ever the recognition of her dignity as the last Grierson; as if it had wanted that touch of earthiness to reaffirm her imperviousness. Like when she bought the rat poison, the arsenic. That was over a year after they had begun to say "Poor Emily," and while the two female cousins were visiting her.

"I want some poison," she said to the druggist. She was over thirty then, still a slight woman, though thinner than usual, with cold, haughty black eyes in a face the flesh of which was strained across the temples and about the eye-sockets as you imagine a lighthouse-keeper's face ought to look.
20   "I want some poison," she said.

"Yes, Miss Emily. What kind? For rats and such? I'd recom—"

"I want the best you have. I don't care what kind."

The druggist named several. "They'll kill anything up to an elephant. But what you want is—"

"Arsenic," Miss Emily said. "Is that a good one?"

"Is . . . arsenic? Yes, ma'am. But what you want—"

"I want arsenic."

The druggist looked down at her. She looked back at him, erect, her face like a strained flag. "Why, of course," the druggist said. "If that's
30 what you want. But the law requires you to tell what you are going to use it for."

Miss Emily just stared at him, her head tilted back in order to look him eye for eye, until he looked away and went and got the arsenic and wrapped it up. The Negro delivery boy brought her the package; the druggist didn't come back. When she opened the package at home there was written on the box, under the skull and bones: "For rats."

IV

So the next day we all said, "She will kill herself"; and we said it would be the best thing. When she had first begun to be seen with Homer Barron, we had said, "She will marry him." Then we said, "She will persuade
40 him yet," because Homer himself had remarked—he liked men, and it

William Faulkner   221

was known that he drank with the younger men in the Elks' Club—that he was not a marrying man. Later we said, "Poor Emily" behind the jalousies as they passed on Sunday afternoon in the glittering buggy, Miss Emily with her head high and Homer Barron with his hat cocked and a cigar in his teeth, reins and whip in a yellow glove.

Then some of the ladies began to say that it was a disgrace to the town and a bad example to the young people. The men did not want to interfere, but at last the ladies forced the Baptist minister—Miss Emily's people were Episcopal—to call upon her. He would never divulge what happened during that interview, but he refused to go back again. The next Sunday they again drove about the streets, and the following day the minister's wife wrote to Miss Emily's relations in Alabama.

So she had blood-kin under her roof again and we sat back to watch developments. At first nothing happened. Then we were sure that they were to be married. We learned that Miss Emily had been to the jeweler's and ordered a man's toilet set in silver, with the letters H. B. on each piece. Two days later we learned that she had bought a complete outfit of men's clothing, including a nightshirt, and we said, "They are married." We were really glad. We were glad because the two female cousins were even more Grierson than Miss Emily had ever been.

So we were not surprised when Homer Barron—the streets had been finished some time since—was gone. We were a little disappointed that there was not a public blowing-off, but we believed that he had gone on to prepare for Miss Emily's coming, or to give her a chance to get rid of the cousins. (By that time it was a cabal, and we were all Miss Emily's allies to help circumvent the cousins.) Sure enough, after another week they departed. And, as we had expected all along, within three days Homer Barron was back in town. A neighbor saw the Negro man admit him at the kitchen door at dusk one evening.

And that was the last we saw of Homer Barron. And of Miss Emily for some time. The Negro man went in and out with the market basket, but the front door remained closed. Now and then we would see her at a window for a moment, as the men did that night when they sprinkled the lime, but for almost six months she did not appear on the streets. Then we knew that this was to be expected too; as if that quality of her father which had thwarted her woman's life so many times had been too virulent and too furious to die.

When we next saw Miss Emily, she had grown fat and her hair was turning gray. During the next few years it grew grayer and grayer until it attained an even pepper-and-salt iron-gray, when it ceased turning. Up to the day of her death at seventy-four it was still that vigorous iron-gray, like the hair of an active man.

From that time on her front door remained closed, save for a period of six or seven years, when she was about forty, during which she gave lessons in china-painting. She fitted up a studio in one of the downstairs rooms, where the daughters and granddaughters of Colonel Sartoris' contemporaries were sent to her with the same regularity and in the same spirit that they were sent to church on Sundays with a twenty-five-cent piece for the collection plate. Meanwhile her taxes had been remitted.

Then the newer generation became the backbone and the spirit of the town, and the painting pupils grew up and fell away and did not send their children to her with boxes of color and tedious brushes and pictures cut from the ladies' magazines. The front door closed upon the last one
10 and remained closed for good. When the town got free postal delivery, Miss Emily alone refused to let them fasten the metal numbers above her door and attach a mailbox to it. She would not listen to them.

Daily, monthly, yearly we watched the Negro grow grayer and more stooped, going in and out with the market basket. Each December we sent her a tax notice, which would be returned by the post office a week later, unclaimed. Now and then we would see her in one of the downstairs windows—she had evidently shut up the top floor of the house— like the carven torso of an idol in a niche, looking or not looking at us, we could never tell which. Thus she passed from generation to generation—
20 dear, inescapable, impervious, tranquil, and perverse.

And so she died. Fell ill in the house filled with dust and shadows, with only a doddering Negro man to wait on her. We did not even know she was sick; we had long since given up trying to get any information from the Negro. He talked to no one, probably not even to her, for his voice had grown harsh and rusty, as if from disuse.

She died in one of the downstairs rooms, in a heavy walnut bed with a curtain, her gray head propped on a pillow yellow and moldy with age and lack of sunlight.

V

The Negro met the first of the ladies at the front door and let them in,
30 with their hushed, sibilant voices and their quick, curious glances, and then he disappeared. He walked right through the house and out the back and was not seen again.

The two female cousins came at once. They held the funeral on the second day, with the town coming to look at Miss Emily beneath a mass of bought flowers, with the crayon face of her father musing profoundly above the bier and the ladies sibilant and macabre; and the very old men—some in their brushed Confederate uniforms—on the porch and the lawn, talking of Miss Emily as if she had been a contemporary of theirs, believing that they had danced with her and courted her perhaps,
40 confusing time with its mathematical progression, as the old do, to whom

all the past is not a diminishing road but, instead, a huge meadow which no winter ever quite touches, divided from them now by the narrow bottleneck of the most recent decade of years.

Already we knew that there was one room in that region above stairs which no one had seen in forty years, and which would have to be forced. They waited until Miss Emily was decently in the ground before they opened it.

The violence of breaking down the door seemed to fill this room with pervading dust. A thin, acrid pall as of the tomb seemed to lie everywhere upon this room decked and furnished as for a bridal: upon the 10 valance curtains of faded rose color, upon the rose-shaded lights, upon the dressing table, upon the delicate array of crystal and the man's toilet things backed with tarnished silver, silver so tarnished that the monogram was obscured. Among them lay a collar and tie, as if they had just been removed, which, lifted, left upon the surface a pale crescent in the dust. Upon a chair hung the suit, carefully folded; beneath it the two mute shoes and the discarded socks.

The man himself lay in the bed.

For a long while we just stood there, looking down at the profound and fleshless grin. The body had apparently once lain in the attitude of 20 an embrace, but now the long sleep that outlasts love, that conquers even the grimace of love, had cuckolded him. What was left of him, rotted beneath what was left of the nightshirt, had become inextricable from the bed in which he lay; and upon him and upon the pillow beside him lay that even coating of the patient and biding dust.

Then we noticed that in the second pillow was the indentation of a head. One of us lifted something from it, and leaning forward, that faint and invisible dust dry and acrid in the nostrils, we saw a long strand of iron-gray hair.

1908-
MARK
SCHORER * What We Don't Know Hurts Us

The mid-afternoon winter sun burned through the high California haze. Charles Dudley, working with a mattock in a thicket of overgrowth, felt as steamy and as moldy as the black adobe earth in which his feet kept slipping. Rain had fallen for five days with no glimmer of sunshine, and now it seemed as if the earth, with fetid animation, like heavy breath, were giving all that moisture back to the air. The soil, or the broom which he was struggling to uproot, had a disgusting, acrid odor, as if he were tussling with some obscene animal instead of with a lot of neglected vegetation, and suddenly an overload of irritations—the smell, the stinging sweat in his eyes, his itching skin, his blistering palms—made him throw the mattock down and come diving out of the thicket into the clearing he had already achieved.

"Is it hard?"

He looked up and saw Josephine, his wife, sitting on the railing of the balcony onto which the French doors of their bedroom opened. She was
10 holding a dust mop, and a tea towel was wrapped around her head, and her face seemed pallid and without character, as it always did to Charles when she neglected to wear lipstick.

He snorted instead of replying, and wiped his muddy hands on the seat of his stiff new levis. Then he walked over to the short flight of steps that led up to the balcony from the garden, and lit a cigarette.

"It looks as though the ground levels out up there where you're working," Josephine said.

"Yes, it does. Somebody once had a terrace up there. It's full of overgrown geraniums that are more like snakes, and a lot of damned rose
20 vines."

"You've got the pepper tree almost free. It's going to be very nice, isn't it?"

He looked up at the pepper tree, with its delicate, drooping branches and the long gray tendrils that hung down from the branches to the ground. He had chopped out the broom as far up the incline as the tree, and now he could see that a big branch of the eucalyptus at the very edge of the property had forced the top of the pepper tree to grow out almost horizontally from the main portion of its trunk. "Look at the damned thing!" he said.

30   "It's charming, like a Japanese print."

"I'm going to hate this house long before it's livable," he said.

"Oh, Charles!"

"I didn't want to buy a house. I never wanted to own any house. I certainly never wanted to own a miserable, half-ruined imitation of a Swiss chalet built on an incline that was meant for goats." Vehemently he flipped his cigarette up into the pile of brush he had accumulated.

Josephine stood up and shook out the dust mop. "Let's not go into all that again. There was no choice. It's no pleasure for me, either, living the way we are, nor is it for the children." She paused, and then she added a
40 cold supplement. "I sometimes think that your disinclination to own anything is a form of irresponsibility." She turned swiftly and went into the house.

He stood staring after her, frowning a little, for it seemed momentarily that with studied intent she had cracked the bland habit of her amiability. But in a minute she reappeared in the doorway and said matter-of-factly, "I heard on the radio that Boston has had eighteen inches of snow." Then she went back inside.

"Are you trying to make me homesick?" he asked of no one as he started back up the incline, and he remembered the frozen river, snow blowing over the Esplanade, and city lights faint in a blizzard.

He began again to chop at the roots of the broom. All right, he told himself, so he was being unpleasant. He did not like the idea of being pinned down by a mortgage to a place his firm had picked for him. He did not even like the idea of being pinned down by a mortgage. To own some- 10 thing was, to that extent, to be owned, and he did not like the feeling. His idea of a good way to live was in a duplex apartment owned by someone else, in Charles River Square, or, better than that but always less likely, in a duplex apartment owned by someone else, on the East River. He connected happiness with a certain luxury, and, probably, sexuality with elegance and freedom. These were not noble associations, he was aware, and he knew that it was foolish to let impossibilities, as they faded, become forms of minor torture. This knowledge made him chop more angrily than ever at the broom.

It was vegetation with which Charles felt that he had a peculiar inti- 20 macy, perhaps the only thing in California which, in the several weeks they had lived there, he had really come to know. And he loathed it with a violence which he recognized as quite undue, and which, now, made him feel childish and curiously guilty. Yet he could not laugh away his loathing. The stuff was ubiquitous, and sprang up anywhere at all the minute the ground was neglected. If it grew up in a patch, it began a foolish competition with itself, and the thin, naked stalks shot ten and twelve and fourteen feet into the air, all stretching up to the sun for the sake of a plume of paltry foliage at the top. Then the foliage tangled together in a thatch, and when you had managed to chop out the shallow roots of the 30 tree, you still had to extricate its trivial but tenacious branches from those of all its neighbors to get it out of the clump. Once it was out, the wood was good for nothing, but dried up into a kind of bamboo stalk so insubstantial that it did not make even decent kindling. As a tree it was a total fraud, and in spite of the nuisance of its numbers, and of its feminine air of lofty self-importance, it was, with its shallow roots in this loose soil, very vulnerable to attack. Charles beat away at it in an angry frenzy, as if he were overwhelming, after a long struggle, some bitter foe.

He did not hear his son come up the incline behind him, and the boy stood quietly watching until his father turned to toss a stalk up on the 40 pile in the clearing. Then the boy said, "Hi." He said it tentatively, almost shyly, as though his father's responses were unpredictable.

"Hi, Gordon."

"What're you doing?"

"Can't you see? How was school?"

"It stinks," he answered doggedly, his dark eyes half-averted and sorrowful.

Charles felt a twinge of pain for him. "Cheer up. Give it time. You'll get to like it after a while."

"I'll never like it," Gordon said stubbornly.

Charles took up his mattock again. "Sure you will," he said as he began to swing it.

"Nobody likes me."

Charles let the mattock come to rest and, turning once more to the boy, he spoke with an impatient excess of patience. "You say that every day. I've told you it isn't true. You're a new boy in the school, and you came in the middle of the term, and there's never yet been a new boy who entered a school late and made friends right away. You're nearly nine, and you can understand that. Anyway, I'm tired of explaining it to you."

"When can I get a paper route?"

Charles laughed without humor. "My God, boy! Give us a chance to get settled."

"I need money."

"You get an allowance."

"I need more money," the boy insisted. "I want a paper route. How do kids get them?"

"You can work for me. You can get in there with a hedge shears and cut out all those vines."

The boy looked at his father despairingly and shook his head. "No, I need a lot of money."

"You can earn a lot of money working for me," Charles said, swinging his mattock.

"I need a dollar," Gordon said faintly.

His father did not hear him, and he did not turn from his work again until presently he heard his daughter calling him shrilly from the foot of the hill on which the house stood.

"What is it?" he called back. She was climbing the path, and he saw that she had a white envelope in her hand.

Then Gordon broke into rapid, desperate speech. "I need a dollar. I'll pay it back out of my allowance. Remember yesterday I told you about that dollar I found? I have to pay it back."

Charles stared at him. "What dollar?"

Gordon glanced wildly over his shoulder. His sister, holding the menacing white envelope in one hand and her workman's tin lunchbox in the other, was halfway up the hill, coming along the side of the house. Pleadingly, Gordon looked back at his father. "The dollar. Remember? I told you I found it. You wanted to know what I did with it."

"What dollar?"

He sighed. "You didn't listen! You never listen!"

Charles patted his shoulder. "Now take it easy. Don't get excited. Tell me again. I don't think you told me anything about a dollar yesterday."

"The dollar I found. You asked me what I did with it, and I told you I gave it to Crow, and you said I should have brought it home to you."

"That Crow! I thought you were joking."

Penelope, the six-year-old, was behind him now, and Gordon's shoulders sagged in despair. "I wasn't joking," he said almost wearily as Penelope handed his father the letter. "You never really listen." 10

Charles read the precise handwriting on the envelope. "Mr. or Mrs. Dudley," it said, and in the lower left-hand corner, "Courtesy of Penelope." He opened the envelope and read the message:

Dear Mr. and Mrs. Dudley—

Gordon became involved in some difficulty about a dollar today, and I wish you would help me. The dollar was lunch money belonging to a girl who says she left it deep in her coat pocket, in the cloak room, yesterday. When I brought it up with Gordon, he immediately said that he did not steal it. He says that he found it on the floor, and he also says that he told his father about it yesterday and that his father said he should have 20 brought it home to him, and now he is fixed in his confusions. He gave it to an older boy named Will Crow, who spent it, and I have told Gordon that he will have to return a dollar to the girl tomorrow. Gordon is a very worthwhile little personality, but I do not think he has been entirely happy here at the Crestview School, and therefore, if you can help me straighten this out to his own best interest, I will be ever so grateful.

Sincerely yours,

Gertrude Grandjent,

Principal.

Charles groaned in exasperation. "My God, why did you have to drag 30 me into it? What will that woman think?"

Gordon's lips were trembling. "You remember? I did tell you, didn't I?"

"Yes, I remember now. I remember very clearly that you told me you found it on the way to school, and when I asked you what you did with it, and you said you gave it to Crow, naturally I said you should have brought it home. *Listen*, Gordon—" The very simplicity of the boy's strategy infuriated Charles, and it was with an effort that he controlled his temper. He said, "Penny, you go in now and tell your mother you're home."

Penny was staring at her brother. "What did Gordon do?"

"Run along, Penny, as I told you."

She went down the incline reluctantly, staring back over her shoulder, and when she had gone into the house, Charles turned to Gordon again and said, "Sit down."

They sat down side by side on the damp slope. Gordon said, "Will you lend me a dollar and keep my allowance until it's made up? I have to take it back tomorrow."

"We'll talk about that later." Charles tapped the letter with his muddy hand. "Why did you tell me you found it in the street?"

10 Gordon looked away but answered promptly. "I knew if I told you I found it in school, you'd have said I should have taken it to the office."

"So you lied to me instead. That was better?"

Gordon did not answer.

"Answer me."

"Yes."

"Yes, what?"

"I lied."

That was that. Charles started over. "Why did you tell Miss Grandjent that you did not steal it when she hadn't even said that you had?"

20 "I knew that's what she thought."

"How did you know?"

"I just knew."

Charles hesitated. When he spoke again, his voice was warmer, friendly, almost confidential. "What's the little girl's name, Gordon?"

"She's not little. She's in high fourth."

"What's her name?"

"I don't know. Joan, I guess."

"What color is her coat?"

Gordon glanced at his father sharply, "I don't know. I never noticed it."

30 Charles bit his lip in exasperation and stood up. "Let's go inside." He led the way in.

Josephine was standing on a chair in the middle of the living room. She was dusting the hideous chandelier of dark metal and colored glass which hung from the center of the ceiling. It was only one of many distasteful features in the house which the Dudleys hoped to rid it of, but it was hard to find men to do all the necessary work, and none would promise to do it quickly. An electrician had torn away a good deal of plaster and lathing, and a carpenter had ripped out some bookshelves and ugly mantels and taken down most of a wall between the dining room and a 40 useless hallway, but neither had returned, and painters, plasterers, paper hangers had not yet come at all. The Dudleys had decided to leave most of their belongings in storage until the work was done, and to bring nothing out of storage that they cared about. The result was that the house was almost fantastically disordered and bleak and squalid, and while

Josephine managed to keep an even temper under these conditions, Charles, who found them very trying, did not.

He stood in the doorway of the living room now and said to her, "Why do you bother?"

"The light was so dim," she said, and then, seeing his expression, asked quickly, "What's wrong?"

"Another problem." He came heavily into the living room and gave her the letter. She read it standing on the chair, her face expressionless. Then she stepped down and went out into the hall where Gordon was lurking and said, "Come in, dear." 10

There was one old sofa in the room, and Josephine sat down there with Gordon. Charles sat facing them on the single straight chair. Josephine took Gordon's hands and said, "Now tell me everything, Gordon, just the way it happened."

The boy's face was composed in a kind of stolid determination, but when he raised his moody eyes from the bare floor to his father, his chin began to tremble, his eyelids fluttered, and suddenly the dogged expression broke in despair, his body sagged, his head fell back against the sofa, and he burst into harsh sobs. Josephine put her arm around his shoulders and held him close while he cried, and she shook her head sharply at 20 Charles as he jumped up impatiently. He sat down again. Finally Gordon stopped crying, almost as abruptly as he had begun.

"How did it happen, Gordon?" his mother asked.

He straightened up and stared at the floor again. "Nothing happened. I just came in the cloak room and saw it on the floor. I took it and put it in my pocket, and at recess I gave it to Crow."

"Didn't anyone see you pick it up?"

"There wasn't anyone else there."

"In the cloak room? Before school? Why not?"

"I was late." 30

"Late? But why? You left here in plenty of time."

"I stopped on the way and played with a cat."

Josephine frowned. "So there was no one else there at all to see you?" she asked meaningfully.

"No."

Josephine glanced at Charles. He drew his lips apart and, with a heavy satiric edge, said, "Well, Gordon, that's too bad! If there'd been someone else there, you could prove that you hadn't—"

Josephine broke in. "Tell me just where the dollar was, Gordon," she said softly, and her voice had no relation to the look in her eyes as she 40 glared at Charles.

"On the floor."

"But exactly where? Was it near the little girl's coat?"

"She isn't little."

"Was it near her coat?"

"I don't know which coat is hers."

"Was it near any coat?"

"It was on the floor, near all of them. They hang on a rack, and it was on the floor near them."

Josephine paused, and Gordon wriggled his shoulders out from under her arm and slumped in the corner of the sofa, away from her. "When can I get out of here?" he asked.

"When you start answering our questions," his father said sharply.
10 "You insist that you didn't steal it?"

Gordon raised his lids slowly, as if they were very heavy, and stared out at his father from under his brows. "I found it on the floor."

Josephine spoke brightly. "Very well. We have settled that. But Gordon, surely you don't think that because you found it on the floor, it belonged to you? Don't you see that it was just as much stealing it as if you had really taken it from the pocket of the person it belonged to?"

"Not as much," Gordon said.

"But it wasn't *yours!* You knew that."

The boy nodded.

20 "Well, then—"

"Someone else would have found it!"

"But would someone else have kept it?"

"I didn't keep it."

Charles leaped up from his chair. "That's the point! Why in God's name did you give it to that Crow rat?"

"He's my friend," Gordon said with simple defiance, and then he slid off the sofa and lay on the floor.

"Your friend! A fine friend!" Charles shouted in disgust, standing over him. "Get up!"

30 Gordon did not make any effort to move, and Josephine grasped Charles' arm. "Let me," she said quietly. "Sit down."

"Nonsense!" he cried angrily at her, and pulled his arm free of her touch. "I'll take over now." He seized the boy by the shoulders and pulled him up on the sofa. The jerk which he gave his body made the boy's head bob back and forward like a doll's, and he slumped against the sofa back almost as if he had been injured, dull eyes staring out of his pale face. "Now listen to me, Gordon. I don't know if you took that money out of someone's pocket or not, but it looks, from the way you're behaving, as if you did. Anyway, you took it. It didn't belong to you, you
40 knew that, and yet you took it. Do you see that there is no difference between the floor and the pocket as long as you kept it?"

"I didn't keep it," Gordon repeated, but almost listlessly.

"Oh, my God!" Charles ran his hand through his hair, and the rumpled hair gave him a sudden wild look. "Listen," he said as quietly as he could, "we are all having a very hard time here. We are trying to live in a house that isn't fit to live in. I am trying to get used to a new office. Your mother—"

Josephine said, "Don't bother about me."

"I will bother! We are all having a tough time, and Gordon can't think of anything better to do than to get into this mess at school. Of all the friends you could pick, you pick that nasty Crow brat, who is too old for you by three years and is a snide little—"

"Charles!"

Gordon lay back on the sofa. He looked ill and defeated. 10

"Will you admit that you stole that dollar? That taking it from the floor was just as much stealing it as if you had taken it from the pocket?"

"Yes," he answered faintly.

"Speak up!"

"Yes, I *do!*" Gordon cried, and turned his face away.

Then the room was very still. Josephine stood stiffly beside the couch, her eyes fixed on Charles with dismay. Charles sagged a little, as if he, too, were defeated. And Gordon might have been asleep or dreaming, so remote had he suddenly become. Then they all heard a sly noise at the door, and Charles and Josephine swung toward it. Penelope stood 20 there, embarrassed to have been caught. She giggled and said, "Why did Gordon steal money?"

"Go away," Charles said.

"Go to your room, dear," Josephine said, "or go outside."

"But why did Gordon steal money?"

Charles walked to the girl, gave her a little push, and closed the door on her face. Then he came back to the sofa. He sat down next to Gordon, and when he spoke, his voice was nearly lifeless. "You want to earn that dollar. All right, you can, Gordon. First go to your room and write your five sentences. Do them quickly for a change, and then go out into that 30 patch of broom with the hedge shears and cut down all the vines you can find in it. You have an hour left before it gets dark."

Gordon's eyes dreamed over his father's face, and then he slowly got up and left the room. His parents watched him go, and when he had closed the door softly behind him, Charles broke out. "What is it, what stubbornness, that makes that boy so impenetrable? Did he steal that money or not? I haven't the slightest idea. All I could do was force him to admit that there was no difference between the two things."

Josephine was looking at him with studied appraisal.

"Well?" he challenged her. 40

"You forced his admission. Did that gain anything? And what did it lose? How much did it hurt him? Is it of very great importance whether he stole it or not?"

"I don't know what's more important."

"No, I really think you don't."

"Well?"

"What's more important is why he took it, and what he did with it, and why he did that. What's more important is that he's a miserable little boy, and that you haven't made the slightest effort to understand *that*. All you've done is played the heavy parent, shown him that you don't trust him or believe him, and left him with a nice new layer of solidified guilt, and what is he supposed to do with *that?*"

"Let's skip the psychology for a change," Charles said. "There is an
10 old-fashioned principle of honesty and dishonesty."

"There's a more old-fashioned one of simple perception!" Josephine's face was red with anger. She stood in the middle of the bare room and looked rapidly around her, as if she felt a sudden desperate need, a hunger, for objects. But there was only the sofa, the chair, and Charles. Her eyes came back to him.

"Have you thought of his difficulties at all? Just the simple matter of his writing, for example? He came from a school where the children printed, and he printed as well as anyone. He comes here where the children do cursive writing, and of course he's made to feel like a fool,
20 and he has to practice at home to learn it when other boys are playing. Or have you once helped him with that? Have you even suggested a sentence he might write? No. All you've done is to give him the extremely comforting bit of information that new boys, especially if they enter school late, have a hard time making friends! The one friend he has made you deride. No, don't interrupt. I know he's a horrid boy. I don't want Gordon playing with him either. But you haven't the sense to see that what has brought them together is that they are both pariahs. I think Gordon's giving that dollar to that dreadful boy is one of the most touching things I've ever heard of!"

30 "If what you've told me about Crow is true," Charles said quietly, "I won't have Gordon playing with him, and that's that."

"Because Crow taught him some nasty words and told him some nasty, mistaken things about sex! You're perfectly right. But you can't just stand there and say no to him! If you were half a father, you would have told him yourself. *You* should be his friend! You're the one who should be giving him a decent attitude toward those things. You *are* his father, after all."

"Oh, listen—He's not even nine!"

"All right. But he's getting it, isn't he? And all wrong?" And then,
40 without warning, she sat down heavily on the single chair and began to sob, her reddened face lifted, her mouth twisted in sorrow, tears streaming down over her cheeks. "All *wrong!*" she wailed.

Charles went to her quickly and, half standing, half kneeling beside the chair, awkwardly put his arms around her. "Josephine, listen—"

Mark Schorer 233

"Oh, I know!" she sobbed. "We all get in your way. We're all a nuisance that you're saddled with! We all just *bother* you! I know! It just isn't your idea of the way to live. You really hate it, don't you?"

His arms tightened. "Darling," he said, "don't be a damned fool. Listen, I love you, I love the kids. Why, little Penny, I—"

"Oh, yes. Penny, sure! She's tractable! She doesn't raise any problems. That's different!"

"You're crazy. Gordon, too. You. Maybe I'm not much good with him, but that doesn't mean . . . And listen . . . I'll try. I'll go out there now." 10

She dug in her pocket for a piece of Kleenex. She blew her nose and wiped her eyes. She pulled the tea towel off her head and shook out her hair. Then she blew her nose again. "I'm all right now," she said, getting up. She picked up the dust cloth which she had flung over the back of the chair, and she said, "It's probably just this awful house, the way we have to camp. I'm going to get cleaned up and dress, and I'm going to find a table cloth, and we'll have dinner at a table tonight, instead of sitting on the floor with plates in our laps."

He said, "Good girl! I'll go and fix it up with Gordon."

Charles went into Gordon's room. It was empty. He glanced at the 20 table where Gordon worked and saw that there was a sheet of writing there. Then he looked out of the window and saw the boy on his hands and knees in among the remaining broom. He crossed the hall to the bedroom where Josephine was dressing. "I may not be very subtle with him, but I seem to get results," he said. She merely glanced up at him, and as he went out on the balcony, down the steps, and up the slippery incline, he felt no satisfaction whatever in his remark.

"How's it going?" he asked the boy.

Gordon glanced over his shoulder. "All right," he said, and turned at once to his job. The hedge shears made a busy, innocent sound.

Charles found his mattock where he had dropped it, and began to chop 30 at the edge of the overgrowth again. Immediately his nostrils filled with the poisonous smell he had noticed before, his hands began to chafe, and even though the heat of the sun had gone in the late afternoon, sweat broke out with a prickling sensation all over his face and body. Once more he was tense with irritation, and he said, "That awful smell! What is it?"

"I don't know," Gordon replied without looking up.

"Like something decaying."

The boy did not answer, and Charles chopped angrily away at a root. 40 When it came free, he shook the earth off and tossed the slim tree down the slope. "This crazy, piddling stuff!" he shouted, and then reminded himself that it was only a kind of exaggerated weed, a thing that grew everywhere, so futile that it could not even send down a decent root and was hardly designed as a personal affront to him. Or was it? He laughed and started to chop at the next root, but stopped at once. "I'm quitting for today," he said. "Come on, let's go in."

Gordon said, "No, I'll work a while. I want to earn the money."

"Oh, let it go. We'll fix that up."

Gordon stared at him. "I want to earn it," he said, and went on clipping at the rose vines.

10 "All right," Charles said, "but come in soon. You'll have to wash up thoroughly to get that muck off."

He went back into the house by way of the bedroom, but Josephine was no longer there. He went into Gordon's room, but she was not there, either. On the table lay the white sheet of ruled paper covered with the boy's writing, his five sentences in their hasty, uncertain, and very large cursive characters. Charles picked it up. The first sentence was, "I am going to cut vins." The second was, "I am going to ern mony." The third was, "The sun is shining." The fourth was, "When it rains here it rains hard." The last, which seemed to have been written with greater 20 care, with a kind of precision and flourish which his writing had never shown before, was, "You hate me and I hate you."

Charles took a sharp breath and held it, then sagged. After a moment he walked to the window and put his forehead against the cool glass. He stared out into the desolate garden, at the bare earth and the darkening tangle, and tried to think. When he heard Josephine moving on high heels somewhere in the rugless house, he began to fold the sheet of paper, and he folded it again and again, until it was a small hard square. This he stuffed deep into his pocket.

He came into the hall and saw Josephine standing in the center of the 30 barren living room. She looked tall in an old but still handsome black housecoat, a straight, severe garment which hung from the tightly belted waist in heavy folds, and was without ornament or color anywhere. Her hair was pulled tautly away from her face, and her face was smooth and white, and her mouth was painted dark red.

She was detached from the room, from the house, and utterly from him —remote and beautiful, cold in resolution. Never in the ten years he had known her had she appeared so wonderfully in possession of herself. And, helplessly, Charles turned away.

He went into the boy's room again, and looked out to see the boy. But 40 twilight had obscured the garden now, shadows hung about it like veils, and Charles could hardly see into the trees. Then he thought that he saw Gordon's shape, hunched on the ground among the slim trunks, and he went out quickly to find him. Perhaps, even now, after everything, it was the boy who, somehow, could help.

1908-
NANCY
HALE * Rich People

After the shock of seeing that face in San Francisco, it is no wonder my recurrent, dreamlike memory of Clam Harbor, and the days when I was growing up there, enveloped me once more as I lay last night in my narrow bed, awakened by the ghastly laughter of coyotes out in the Arizona desert. But, this time, it seemed to come out differently. . . . I lay there, worrying about the ailing children in my charge, and gradually, instead of them, I seemed to see the old dock, of silvery, splintered boards supported at the corners by the weathered posts called dolphins.

Remnants of last night's fog drift across the dock in gauzy streamers; it is the middle of the morning and everybody has gone sailing except me. 10 But I am nineteen and I would rather be caught dead than out in a boat with those great hearty brutes in their blue jeans, laughing at their wholesome jokes. I am sitting on the edge of the dock with my feet hanging over the edge, and beside me sits the idol of my life, dressed in a dark-red French jersey and tweed skirt, with a string of Chanel pearls around her neck. Mrs. Bogden! She is gazing out to where vignettes of brilliantly blue ocean are framed in the garlands of the mist, and telling me about Paris, Saint-Moritz, and Brioni.

Suddenly—as always in this remembered half-dream—she remarks, "The way to be happy is to be always in love, don't you think?"   20

I nod, and swallow hard, thrilled. Mrs. Bogden lights another of her Balkan Sobranies and turns, toward me, her face with its delightful nose and dark-red lips, bordered by exquisitely arranged gray hair. "Don't you?" she repeats. She seems actually to want to know what I think. "Don't you think it is?"

I could never, before last night, reply; either in real life or in the memory. What could such as I tell a Mrs. Bogden about anything? Mrs. Bogden, on the other hand, had everything to tell me. I was, at that period, desperately in love, myself; and while the condition was making me anything but happy, this present seemed, for me, perpetually on the 30 point of breaking forth into a radiant heaven complete with Vionnet angel-wings and harps that played "That Certain Feeling." I had fallen in love with a Harvard boy from New York, whose family owned a house in London and a château in Newport, who had presented me with a bottle of Guerlain's L'Heure Bleue. Glamour was what I needed to cope with my situation. Glamour was what Mrs. Bogden was compact of.

She was exactly what I wanted—what I needed—to be; down to her long, dark-red fingertips. Sitting within her aura I thought how wonderful it would seem to be my old Winsor schoolmate Carola Bogden, and have such a stepmother; someone who could with easy grace lead the way along the paths of the great world and into the courts of sophistication. My own family seemed to me unsophisticated to the point of imbecility.

A person who never visited Boston in the old days cannot imagine the degree to which simplicity could be cultivated in families like ours. And the sightseer from South Bend who did, perhaps, stare studiously up at our house on the water side of Beacon Street could never have realized
10 that its two bathrooms contained zinc-lined tubs about fifty years old, in which all of us Eliots took cold baths before breakfast straight through the winter; that even the grownups made their breakfasts of whole oranges, whole-wheat porridge, and whole milk; that decisions about the day's subsequent menus were based entirely upon nutritive, not gustatory, values; that such entertainments as we might attend (Symphony and Shakespeare) were selected upon a comparable basis; that for school we girls were dressed invariably, like our mother, in serviceable Scotch tweeds, worn over long woollen drawers, to which we gave a twist before pulling up our cotton stockings and lacing our brown boots. A Fair Isle
20 sweater might constitute the sole lavish note in our daytime wardrobes. For Foster's Dancing Classes at the Somerset, we wore, with inevitability, pink taffeta with a tinsel rose at the hip and low-heeled silver slippers.

All this high thinking and plain living carried with it a faint but definite religious tinge. To Bostonians like us, living in the way that people from New York did—worldly people, rich people—was Wrong. Not that my family was churchy. They were fully liberated Arlington Street Church Unitarians, which meant that they subscribed handsomely and went seldom. But, as good Unitarians, they believed they best served their faith when they were following their private spiritual convictions.
30 For my mother, these involved mountain-climbing. Almost from our infancy, she had hauled my older sister Betsey and me up the slopes of assorted White and Green Mountains. Generally she left us far behind, climbing, steadily with her measured but energetic step. Many is the time I have come, panting and puffing, upon my mother, after she had been long seated on some summit and was gazing off at the magnificence of its surroundings with an austere and serene expression which—years later in the catalogue of a museum—I recognized as akin to that of a sculptured Boddhisatva,° an Enlightened One. When she became aware of my arrival, Mother would turn her faint smile upon me: calm, detached,
40 compassionate. "Sit down, Lucy," she would say, "and try to practice realizing that ourselves and the rest of the universe are of one substance."

38. **Boddhisatva,** a Buddhist deity; a being that compassionately refrains from entering nirvana in order to save others.

I would sit down, but I was never able to get interested in the topic she recommended. My thoughts, as I moved into my teens, ran to formless yearnings for clothes, to fantasies about what the world beyond Boston was like, and to boys. I was well aware that my mother's reflections were worthier ones than mine; I was even, dimly, aware that what animated her was something very remarkable; was, in fact, pure love.

My mother's feeling about all of nature was strongly mystical. At our cottage at Clam Harbor, where we spent the greater part of every summer, Mother taught us to swim and dive by principles a woman from another city might have reserved for dealing with her love life. I can see Mother now—long, spare limbs clad in a gray bathing dress, standing beside the diving board on the raft moored off the beach. She has put on a gray rubber bathing cap, but between it and her long, erect, sunburned neck some loops of sandy hair emerge. "Give yourself to the water!" she cries, as we hesitate before the plunge. When she herself comes to dive, her narrow face, freckled and innocent of make-up, wears an expression of bliss in the instant before she dedicates herself to the sea.

To Mother, there was something Wrong about being separated from the outdoors any more than was necessary. At Clam Harbor we slept out on one long sleeping porch, all four of us, in beds that had tarpaulins for the nights when September equinoctial storms drove pelting rain across them. Our three meals were served on a screened porch that possessed an elevating view over Clam Harbor to Clam Point, and, beyond it, of the Atlantic. Our Irish maids, down from Boston for the summer, viewed this latter custom with a sour eye. It was, of course, nothing to them that our food was cold by the time it reached us, but they did not care for waiting on table mornings when a fresh westerly breeze had sprung up, or evenings when the fog insinuated clammy streamers between the meshes of the screen. Sometimes they asserted their point of view by appearing in some old, raveled sweater, worn over black uniform and white Hamburg-edged apron.

My mother would raise sandy eyebrows. "Bridie," she would say in her ringing voice. "Surely you aren't cold, this splendid day?"

"No, Mum," the maid would always mumble.

Our maids might quit, but they never talked back, for my mother carried about her an aura, unmistakable to everybody, of being in the right. Bridie, or Norah, or Teresa, would appear in another minute or two bearing muffins and sans sweater. But sometimes I would hear her when she thought herself alone, washing dishes after the meal at the copper-lined sink out in the bare, matched-board pantry. "Ah," she would be muttering in exasperation and sheer Irishness. "Aaaah. . . ."

My mother *was* in the right; almost always. She made a study of it. To her it would have been foolish and unintelligent not to. She had trained herself to consider the various aspects of her life in order to determine

what in them represented the true, the good, and the beautiful, and then to choose that and follow it up with assiduity. It seemed clear to her that there was always a better and a worser side to things; a higher and a lower. To choose the best of everything was only what one owed to one-self, one's family, and one's God. Outdoors was more beautiful than in-doors; Nature was vaster than man; love was superior to more transitory emotions; thrift was wiser than waste; life was short, and there was little enough time for good music and great books without wasting any of it on the trivial or the frivolous. I remember my sister Betsey, aged about
10 twelve, making one of our rare stands against the claims of the superior. "But I don't *like* Brahms!" she is insisting. Her face is red, her hands are behind her back, pressed for support against the walnut door of the library in the Beacon Street house. "I can't help it if I don't like him, can I?"

My mother, who sits on the Chippendale sofa, which had come down in her own family, closes the book she is holding, over her thumb, and re-plies without heat. "You can help giving way to nonsense," she says. "You know Brahms' music is great. You can, at least, try to feel what you ought to."
20 My mother was able to admit when she had been wrong, and, by mak-ing a fresh assessment and a fresh judgment, arrive once more at a posi-tion of rectitude. "Coming out was not a success for you," she said in early June of the summer of which I write, looking down at me from her unusual height, with the reasonable gaze that had become to me particularly ex-asperating. If only Mother could be unreasonable once in a while! "You would better have begun Radcliffe at once, after all. I misgauged the matter. A pity. Now, for Betsey, coming out seemed to be almost too *much* of a good thing."

I muttered something. No more than any maid could I have talked
30 back to Mother.

But what a coming out mine was! I suppose Mother would never have countenanced a convention so foreign to fresh air and early bedtimes at all had it not been for some concept of her own about a time of innocent gaiety, meeting jolly boys; a little girlish merriment before settling down to the realities of womanhood. Her own debut, forty years before, seems to have been along such lines. She and my father met first at a dinner at the Crowninshields' house on Marlborough Street. Later they became engaged at the Country Club in Brookline, on the basis of a shared in-terest in butterflies, sailing, and climbing mountains. I visualize them on
40 that momentous occasion, sitting out on the glassed-in porch at the Country Club so long ago—their two serious faces, which by the time I knew them had grown to look curiously alike, turned enthusiastically to one another. What my mother's dress that night was like I don't know, but in her wedding photographs she wears a trailing white gown trimmed

with lace, with a boned collar that comes all the way up her long neck to her ear lobes.

By the time Betsey and I came out, however, enthusiasm and shared interests were simply not enough for a girl to get by with at a dance. Betsey, who came out the year before I did, broke out of the confining circle of our bringing-up by becoming "wild"—one of the wild girls. I doubt whether Mother ever knew how wild; I'm not even sure myself. I know that she danced cheek to cheek, and went out to parked cars during dances to neck. I shared the secret that it was routine for her to spend the night with some old school friend so that she could evade the home ordi- 10 nance about not coming home alone with a boy after a dance. At the period of which I speak, Betsey's solution was a fairly typical one with Boston girls for whom the boiling point of high-mindedness had been reached. In any coming-out year there was always at least one girl who was suspected of having "gone the limit."

"Health" was the word we used to sum up the whole unbearable repression against which such as Betsey rebelled. I can see her now, one night early in her coming-out year; she had come into my room, where I was doing my next day's homework for Winsor, dressed in a pale-blue chiffon dress, with silver beading at the hip to match her slippers. I said 20 something about her looking nice.

"In *this?*" she asked; her voice cracked with fury. "I hate it! *Look* at this healthy neckline, for Pete's sake! Look at these horrible health shoes! It's all so S.S. and G.!" This was the term for sweet, simple, and girlish in our day. "Look at my hair!" she continued. Hers was the same fine, straight, sandy hair as Mother's, done up in crossed bands at the back. Suddenly Betsey started snatching out the pins that held it. She seized my desk scissors and began to slash.

"Betsey!" I cried, aghast.

"I don't care," she said, hacking away. "Now she'll have to let me get 30 it shingled. I will *not* have a crown of glory."

All that was very well for Betsey. Whether because of the necking parties or not, she turned out a great success at dances, and had dozens of invitations to Harvard football and ice-hockey games. But nobody even tried to neck me. The memory of my coming-out party still brings cold sweat to my brow in the night.

It was described in the invitations as "a small dance," and small it certainly was. There were two other dances the same night, and not enough stags turned up at the Women's Republican Club, where mine was held. The decorations were russet chrysanthemums, the season being October, 40 and the orchestra Ted Groves's—not Bert Lowe's or Billy Lossez's—because Father saw no point in putting money into things that did not matter. It would never have occurred to me to argue about it. His attitude toward expense was as much a part of Father as walking every day, rain or shine, across the Public Gardens and the Common to his office on Milk Street, or his espousal of Women's Rights. Or his attitude toward Shakespeare. I can see Father as he used to stand before the fire in the library. He lifts his sandy eyebrows and remarks, "My father always told me, 'My boy, never let anyone persuade you otherwise than that a scholar and a gentleman—Bacon, in short—could have written the plays.' " Father coughs, and the Adam's apple in his long, loose-skinned throat jerks. He glances toward Mother for support of what he has said. She usually did agree; she agreed about Ted Groves's orchestra when Father 10 remarked that it seemed to him to play very jolly music.

To its jolly music I, the debutante, danced round and round with a succession of dutiful partners. I was dressed in white tulle, of course, with healthy neckline and low-heeled white-and-silver brocade slippers. That South Bend sightseer might, next day, have been impressed by the far greater prominence given to my picture and my party's guest list in the public prints than to the other, bigger dances, but my father was put out because, by an inadvertence, the picture had got into the paper at all. Betsey expressed her own and my reactions to the whole affair when she said, "At least nobody could say it wasn't a nice, healthy evening."

20 What I felt myself to be, during that winter, was unequipped, unprepared, unaided, helpless, and suffering. What my contemporaries thought of me as was something known as a pill. The attendants in the dressing rooms of the hotels grew well acquainted with me through those hours when I cowered there, assuming chattiness, rather than let some wretched boy be stuck with me any longer. After the first month of it, I stopped even bothering to invent excuses to the attendants about needing to mend my dress or my stocking. I simply fled to them.

In February, just before the dances stopped for Lent, I fell in love. It began as if it were a mutual rescue of and by two kindred sufferers. I had 30 retreated to the fireplace in the long room at the Country Club when the music stopped at the end of an interminable circling in the arms of the son of one of Mother's friends, whose stiff face softened when I said I had to speak to somebody across the room.

There, leaning against the mantelpiece, stood a slight, wistful-looking young man with red hair. When he moved as I approached, I saw that he was lame. I had intended to stand there for only a moment, to gauge my position and decide whether to beat a retreat, once again, to the familiar upstairs dressing room or to join the hostess's group along the wall. But the strange young man put out his hand and touched my arm. "I say, do 40 you mind talking with me?" he said in an English accent. "I don't dance, you see, and I do feel most awfully solit'ry." He smiled a shy, crooked smile.

I smiled, too. "I'm Lucy Eliot," I offered.

"What a nice name," he said. " 'Lucy Locket lost her pocket.' My name's Giles Wall." We shook hands. He shifted his position with a cripple's clumsiness and went on. "Music is what I'm mad for. Music and ballet. What are you keen on?"

"I think I like pictures the best," I said, struggling to reveal the truth about myself. "But I like music, too." We could almost have been Mother and Father, all those years ago, exchanging enthusiasms.

But before I even so much as left the Country Club that night, the situation I had got myself into was revealed to me. "You were certainly hitting it off with Giles Wall," Betsey said to me as we put our evening wraps on. Betsey still went to some of the debutante parties, as an L.O.P.H., or Left 10 On Papa's Handser. She had managed to screw a white bunny-fur jacket out of the family this last Christmas but my own wrap was that ultimate Bostonian degradation, the family Chinese robe, worn over a sweater for warmth.

"He asked me to have tea with him at the Copley, Friday," I said. I am sure my eyes shone. Inside me a river of stars seemed softly to be flowing.

"Good going," Betsey said. "You'll end up with millions yet, old dear."

"What?" I said, only slightly distracted from the contemplation of the heaven which consists of the cessation of being rejected.

"You know who he *is*, don't you?" Betsey said. "Giles *Wall*. Wall and 20 Wall, in New York. Bucky Sturgis has the room next to him in Claverly, and he told me Giles went to school in England. And his mother ran away and married a Duke. And his father is married to a ballet dancer. And they own about ten houses. Just rolling. Giles isn't a bit popular at Harvard, though. He isn't even in a club. So he's just the thing for you," Betsey added with sisterly candor.

The stars in my river were all exploding. By the time I came down the stairs to the hall, where a milling crowd of stags in tails of black tie waited to say good-by to somebody or to take someone home, and saw Giles—his face greenish-white against his red hair—leaning against the further wall, 30 I could feel the first stab of an agony which was to pierce my growing love like the golden arrow that pierces the red-velvet heart.

There was never again to be, for me, the feeling of easy communication we had when we leaned together against the fireplace, talking. Only my adoration continued to grow; and, along with it, the conviction of my utter inadequacy.

Giles used to come to see me, parking his Lancia at the curb on Beacon Street and limping up the steps, while I watched, hidden behind a glass curtain in the bow window, my heart thumping. I would go down to meet him in the reception room to the left of the front hall, and we would sit 40 on the stiff sofa there while Giles talked about ballet and music; Betsey and her beaux would more than likely have pre-empted the living room, and I never liked to take Giles to the library because Mother was usually there. Giles talked about how fabulously beautiful his mother was, and how his father had never cared for him, and how his leg was broken playing rugger at preparatory school in England and set improperly; how he had later hated Eton, and about the symphony he was writing now. "But *nobody* understands what I am trying to do," he would insist. "Nobody at all, actually."

My heart bled. "I *want* to understand," I cried.

"Do you?" he would say, turning his bemused eyes on me. "Sweet. Sweet Lucy Locket. I say! Couldn't you get your family to let you come abroad this summer, p'raps? I'd adore to have you meet my mother. I'm sure she'd ask you. She's living in France, you know, with that beast Fallchester she married. She's divine, my mother is. Very fair, with a face like an ill white lily. Quite, quite different from Mona." Mona, I had learned, was his father's present wife, his fourth. "Mona's divine too, of course, in quite another way from my mother. Dark, with the serene sort of brow a woman has to have if she's to do her hair in smooth bands. Mona has the perfect ballet face, actually. I wonder how long my father will love her."

"I'd love to go abroad!" I cried when he seemed to wait for a reply to his suggestion. "Maybe Mother *would* let me . . ."

But of course Mother wouldn't.

"I think not," she decided. "This would not be a wise summer for Europe, Lucy. I admit my judgment was off about coming out, for you, but this winter was to have provided your time for gaiety. It's certainly provided nothing else. You must learn to seek a balance, dear. Radcliffe, next year, will give you the intellectual discipline you have lacked the past several months. I think of Europe, too, when you do go, as a place of study; you will, of course, thrill to the masterpieces of art there, as well. But the coming summer should be a time for vigorous exercise after your winter within doors—Besides, Giles's mother hasn't invited you."

"She would, if you'd only say I could go. . . ." But I knew it was no use. Mother's logic and her sense of the fitness of things seemed always irrefutable. She liked Giles. She thought of him as that poor unloved young thing who was, moreover, lame. But she was simply unconscious of those elements in his life that made me feel, underneath all my longing and desire, a sort of terror lest Mother might, after all, let me go to visit the Duchess of Fallchester. I was too unequipped for it. Once again, but differently from in the dark days before the meeting with Giles beside the Country Club fireplace, I felt myself unprepared, unassisted, helpless, and suffering. I had been to good schools, I had learned what my mother had tried to teach me, but I did not know anything that I needed. My need seemed as infinite as the sea.

In late May we moved as usual from Beacon Street down to our huge, gray-shingled house at Clam Harbor, cold as a cave at this time of year. The change that had occurred in me was reflected by my realizing, for the first time, that my childhood's summer home was perfectly hideous. Our healthy summer routine began: a dip in the ocean before breakfast at seven, reading and letter writing till ten, swimming or tennis till luncheon, or sailing for the whole day; and for gaiety, a frequent tea party in somebody's garden to view how beautifully the cosmos and the sweet williams and the calendulas were coming along. My father, home from town by that time of the afternoon, would accompany us, in boater hat with club ribbon and white flannel trousers. Sometimes there was square dancing in the evenings, when we pranced back and forth until the house shook. We had a neighborhood tradition at Clam Harbor, which had come down from the last century, of playing a game of beanbags. Two sides were chosen, their members alternating with each other down two long rows. The beanbags were thrown crisscross by members of each team, and the team that got its twenty beanbags down to the end of the line and back to the start again, won.

Giles was in France with his mother, and wrote me a few short letters: "Sweet Lucy, how is America? We had dinner under the pergola last night and I wished you could one day see the moon rise over the Rhône. My mother is suffering terribly, of course. . . ." Her suffering was nothing to my suffering, I felt; his wish nothing to my own wish—my need—to be somebody entirely different, somebody at home in the great world, whom Giles could love; someone beautiful, sophisticated, and like an ill lily. I could visualize all too perfectly how I looked in my actual person, dressed in the old cotton frocks we kept at Clam Harbor; wearing dirty sneakers; my hair unattractively blown about. I was without glamour and inescapably healthy, because I had never learned how to go about being anything else.

Into my need, like a sail on the horizon of a shipwreck, came Mrs. Bogden. Somewhat breathless whispers of her fame had reached me earlier. Mr. Bogden, a Boston widower, had met the former Mrs. Hurst in London the summer before, as he was starting on the Little Tour with his daughter Carola, who graduated from Winsor the year before I did. After sending Carola home in September to continue her work at the School of the Museum of Fine Arts, he had remained in England to press his suit. In December, he married the American divorcée, and in spring, after a honeymoon in North Africa, brought her home to Boston.

Later, when we had become fast friends, Mrs. Bodgen used to tell me about her flat on Half Moon Street, where she was living at the time of Mr. Bogden's advent—tiny, terribly amusing, really, and not at all expensive as such things go. Nicky Eritsoff had sublet it to her for twenty guineas only. How I could visualize that flat! My ravished imagination supplied color to the French furniture she described, the brocaded armchairs. I could see the delightful little suppers after the theater, before a small coal fire, and breathe in the atmosphere, permeated deliciously

by Houbigant's Giroflée—the scent which I came to know so well and which seemed the essence of my idol. Perfume was another of the elements in that unknown life to which I fearfully aspired. No one in the Eliot family had ever come any closer to perfume than 4711 Cologne. But, for my birthday in May, Giles had presented me with a bottle of L'Heure Bleue. I concealed it from Mother, who I knew would not have let me accept it. All alone, in secret, I would take the big crystal bottle with its handsome stopper out from under a pile of sweaters in my bottom drawer, and sniff the scent, which, more than words and images even, could sug-
10 gest the atmosphere of another world. Sometimes I wept.

The first time I met Mrs. Bogden was early in June, after a day out racing my Lightning, with Carola Bogden crewing for me. A squall had overtaken us in the afternoon, and we had been successively wet through and dried out again by the sun and the chill east wind that followed the rain. By the time we walked up to the Bogdens' cottage, carrying the oars and the sailbag, we must have looked a sight. We went into the house, familiar to me from childhood, and suddenly it was unfamiliar. A Russian icon was hanging on the matched-board wall at the foot of the stairs, a fur rug lay on the hall floor, and in the air was a curious, dry fragrance.
20 We walked into the living room, where a woman with beautifully ar-ranged gray hair was crouching before the fire holding the fire shovel out over the flames.

"Uh—*Maman*," Carola said. "This is Lucy Eliot."

Without rising, Mrs. Bogden turned toward us and smiled, with dark-red lips. "Howd' you do," she said in the same sort of international-British accent Giles had. "*So* nice. . . . Trying to take the awful damp out of the air, darlings, by burning a bit of me perfume. An old London trick —Dare we try for some tea? Life is so difficult," she added, making a face in the direction of the kitchen door.
30 Perhaps I make her sound vapid. She was not. She was intuitive and had a gift for understanding, or if not understanding, for a kind of sym-pathy; putting herself wholly in one's place and surrounding herself with an indignant loyalty that became, for me, like an oasis in the desert. After the first of the times I was invited up to Mrs. Bogden's bedroom I was never again to feel alone in my aspirations, my longing, and my pain. "But of *course*, my darling," she had said earnestly, bending the gaze of her intelligent gray eyes upon me. "Of course you must find a way to attract Giles! I know so exactly your feeling. It must all have been *too* frustrating. We must arrange something."
40 We would often sit in that bedroom to which she had brought, from the other world, a touch of richness, a sense of luxury. The chairs we sat in were low, square, covered in pale satin, without arms; one sank into them. On one table stood Mrs. Bogden's perfume bottles—square, round, tapering, or chunky. On the other were placed signed photographs of her

Nancy Hale   245

friends abroad. *Violet Rutland* was, I learned, the signature of a Duchess. There were pictures of Carol and Madame Lupescu; of Leopold of Belgium; of Otto of Hapsburg; and one signed *Edward P.* These two tables were, to me, like altars to the new god I worshipped.

"But of *course* you must visit his mother next summer," Mrs. Bogden would agree. "We must make you utterly enchanting for her. I used to know Marna slightly when she was Wall. I know she'd adore you, with your pretty eyes and divine skin. We must arrange something that will make a little *more*, p'raps, of your looks." Her eyes would move—not in judgment, I felt, but in compassion—over me, and then across the room that she had made so cozy to the window. They would rest, briefly, on the scene outside—the roofs of the Sturgis cottage next door, the bare rocks of Clam Point in the sunshine, and, beyond, the cold blue sea. Her eyes would return to me. "This fall, p'raps, we must run over to New York? Stay at the angel Carlyle, don't you think? And have a bit of fun in the shops?"

"Oh, yes!" I would reply. Hope had been born again in my heart, and trust where there had been despair. It was Mrs. Bogden who had saved me.

I realize now thirty years later, that, with the egotism of youth, I never tried to turn the talk to any other subject but me. Possibly I would not have thought myself worthy to bring up such a sacred topic as Mrs. Bogden herself. Certainly, in those days, I believed her to be invulnerable. Though I never thought consciously about it at all, unconsciously I must simply have assumed that anyone so wonderful as she must be happy. Her philosophy, as it reached me in its application to my problems, was one of happiness. "But, darling, I know so well!" she often cried. "Life *is* so difficult, and all one wants is to have f-u-n, isn't it?" It occurs to me now that she always put these beliefs of hers in the form of questions, as on the morning when we sat together on the dock in the dissolving mists and, to something I must have said about how unhappy I had been before I met Giles and her, she said, "The way to be happy is to be always in love, isn't it?"

I remember, as well, how she would get to her feet after one of our sessions, and walk away from chair or weathered board step, singing; tall, exquisitely thin, dressed with quite another sort of simplicity from our Boston simplicity—the simplicity of perfection. I think of her in that crimson tweed skirt and jersey, with a string of chunky pearls clasped with a fake ruby; pearls in her ears; on her feet shoes made for her at Hellstern's in Paris, and sheer lisle stockings "for the country," with openwork clocks running up the ankles. Her gray hair made a delightful shape, her large gray eyes were clear and lively, her mouth was painted dark red. " 'Love —may—come—to—anyone!' " she sang as she walked away. " 'The best —things in life—are free. . . .' "

Needless to say, my infatuation did not pass without comment from my family. For example, at supper out on the screened porch, one stormy evening when the candles flickered and guttered in their blue-and-white china candlesticks, Betsey said, "How's your crush, Lucy? Taught you how to make your fingernails look like claws dipped in blood, yet?"

I flushed. "That's disgusting!" I said. "You always take the most ignorant, stupid, *Boston* attitude to Mrs. Bogden. She's just above your comprehension, that's all."

"You can have her," Betsey said. "Joe Worthington says she was known
10 all over Europe as an adventuress."

"It's a lie!" I cried. I threw my napkin down on the table beside my plate. "She's wonderful, and beautiful, and understanding, and kind! Which is more than—more than—" But I could never express myself with the violence of the words that spoke in my head.

"Lucy! . . . Betsey!" Mother was like a moderator, calling the meeting to order. "Control yourselves. Betsey, even if a person in our midst seems neither what we should call wise nor distinguished, that is no excuse for repeating defamatory tales. Both of you! Be still!"

We sat, after our family custom of calling for a silence to put an end to
20 discord, while the salt air of evening slapped the backs of our necks and our bare arms; we saw the light on Badger's Island flash, at regular intervals, through the dusk. Mother, at the head of the table, sat erect as ever; Father sat at the other end, his long back hunched over, crumbling a roll between his fingers. Betsey had turned her gaze away from me onto her plate. Suddenly she cried, "Mother! How can you be so unfair? Mrs. Bogden is just the sort of person you disapprove of most, and yet you won't let me say anything against her!"

"You may express your disapproval if you like," Mother said. "Only you're not to condemn anyone. Or spread scandal. And if you should
30 ever find me taking an uncharitable attitude toward anyone, I hope very much that you will call my attention to it."

"I don't think Mrs. Bogden is *worthy* of charity," Betsey said. "She's a hard-boiled baby, if you ask me. You don't imagine she gives you all this famous understanding for your own sweet sake, do you, Luce? She's simply trying to get to know us."

"Mother! Do I have to listen?"

"Betsey, you're displaying an unwarranted vanity, it seems to me. The person in question *is* ordinary, but she may have sincere affection for Lucy. My hope is that Lucy is not so in need of affection that she will settle for
40 that brand of it for very long. But you are not to malign the person."

"Mother!" Betsey said, disgusted, "Why must you always be so Godlike?"

Mother smiled and shook her sandy head. Then, I remember, she expressed one of her most characteristic ideas—the sort of idea, I suspect,

Nancy Hale   247

upon which she meditated at the summits of those mountains she was always ascending. "None of us need to worry about being too much like God," she said. "But if you're talking about charity, it has always seemed to me that God is charitable not because people are in any way worthy of it, but because if he wasn't, he wouldn't be God."

It was in August—an unusually hot day—when the letter from Giles came, in the morning mail. I read it, and then hurried over to Mrs. Bogden's house.

She was sitting on the grass of the front lawn—none of our nineteenth-century cottages had modern terraces—on a big plaid steamer rug, doing her toenails in the sunshine. I knelt down on the rug beside her, sank back on my heels, and held my tongue while she finished the infinitely careful application of deep crimson varnish. Against the black knitted *maillot* she wore, Mrs. Bogden's legs and arms were beautifully brown and smooth.

At length, she put the brush back into the bottle of polish, twisted its cork tight, and smiled at me. "What troubles you, my sweet?" she said.

I thrust the letter at her, and at the same moment divulged its contents in a burst. "It's Giles! He wants to come *here!* He had some terrible row with his mother's husband. I think the Duke knocked him down. And he left, and wrote this from London. He wants to come and stay with *us*, before college opens, and what shall I *do?*"

Mrs. Bogden gazed at me earnestly, took the letter from my hand, and read it. She ran the ball of her thumb absent-mindedly over the address at the top of the first page, and put the letter slowly back into its envelope.

"What a beast Fallchester is," she remarked. "The boy really *is* in a jam, poor child. Life is so difficult, isn't it? I think it'd be good for him to come here. There are times when one does need utter, utter rest."

"But he *can't* stay at our house!" I cried. "Freezing to death at meals out on that horrible porch? Playing *beanbags?* With Betsey always snooping around? And Mother preaching at us all the time?" I swallowed hard. It was the first time I had ever criticized Mother outside the family, and my words sounded profane to me. I hurried past them. "Giles has never seen anything so absolutely awful as the way we live! He won't know what to make of it. He'll never want to see me again."

My idol smiled. "I'll put him up," she said, and as she spoke it was as if honey and bliss were dropping from her lips. "I'd love to have the poor child. I'll give a little party, for one of the nights he's here. Something a little amusing, p'raps? And plan an evening at the Magnolia Casino? Take lunch to Queen's Island, and a bit of champagne? And when there's nothing more diverting, dine down at the fisherman's dive in Clam Depot, just for fun, don't you think?"

"Oh, yes," I breathed, once more resurrected. "That would be *wonderful*. . . ."

We come now, in this string of old memories, to a scene which my mind always tends to avoid, but which I force myself to face. We are all on the beach at Clam Harbor. I am sitting on a huge, emerald-green Turkish towel, beside Mrs. Bogden, who has on one of her French *maillots;* pale blue, this time, against her radiant tan. I suppose I myself must have been wearing some dreadful Annette Kellerman. We are both looking up at my mother, who stands on the sand just at the rim of the emerald towel.

She is speaking about our plans for Giles's visit. She wears that baggy old gray bathing dress with its rows of rust-stained white braid; her hair
10 is inadequately tucked under a gray rubber cap. She must have paused to speak to us on her way down to the water's edge; perhaps I even called to her. Plain, austere, unmodified in any way by fashion, her appearance is simply overpowering.

"I don't feel that it is suitable," she is saying. "Since you say Mrs. Bogden has never seen Giles. It is not as if he were already her friend. He *is* a friend of ours. We have, Lucy, guest rooms and to spare. If he's asked to stay with us here before college opens, do by all means tell him to come. But he must stay at our house, and fall in with our normal occupations and amusements as any visitor might."
20 *I* realized that there was nothing more to be said. But Mrs. Bogden didn't. She said, "Simply, dear Mrs. Eliot, I've so much time on my hands, as I'm sure you've not. It would give me enormous pleasure to arrange little amusements for the children—*quelques petites divertisse-ments;*° something to accustom them to gaiety—"

"Lucy," Mother said, "is accustomed to simplicity."

"But don't you feel," Mrs. Bogden insisted, "that when one is young and, so to speak, on the verge of the great world, one needs the little help-ing nudge, the outstretched hand? In short, something a little *different* from this rather—simple—life? Life is so difficult, actually." But Mrs.
30 Bogden had made a fatal error.

"Very," my mother said. "And so there can be no question of having someone who is coming to pay us a visit staying with neighbors. How-ever kind their intentions," she added politely.

Above the burning yellow beach that ran for miles around the curve of Clam Harbor into Graniteport and so out again to Badger's Point, the sun seemed suddenly put out. Within a private night I got to my feet, shaking all over.

"Then I'll tell him not to come!" I cried, stone-blind, to the people still out in the sunshine. "I don't want him here! I won't *have* him come, that
40 way!"

There is no record in my memory of any answer to my words. That is the scene's end. But I remember well what came of it. I wrote to Giles that we were going to be driving around in the White Mountains after

24. *quelques petites divertissements,* some little diversions.

the middle of August, so we could not have him to stay beside the sea; but that I looked forward to seeing him at Beacon Street after college began. Nobody told me, or forbade me, to do this, or advised me how to go about doing it. It was my solution to my own problem, like a lid shutting on a particular time in my life.

I never saw Giles again. He never returned to Harvard, but stayed in England. A year or two later, after I had already moved to Arizona, I read in a Los Angeles paper that he had been married to a Lady Honor Wilkes; a cousin of his, the paper said. In the news photo she had one of those sharply chiseled British faces with short fair hair parted on the side. I have no idea whether they are still married.

Today I know nothing of the world in which people like that live, nothing; I left even the world of Boston when I came out here. I have only been back for Father's funeral. Every winter, of course, Mother pays me a visit on her way to stay with Betsey and the grandchildren in Seattle; it is odd how both Betsey and I have moved to the corners of the country farthest away from Boston. But distances don't faze Mother. She travels by jet, and arrives serene with a copy of the Upanishads in her hand. She is amazing.

She it was, for example, who after that year of my hopeless struggle to keep going, ending with my flunking my freshman exams at Radcliffe, found me this job of mine, to which—although I don't mean to sound boastful—everyone agrees I am so exactly suited. I have moved up over the years, and in spite of not possessing a degree, to being assistant director of this school for delicate children—children who are sent to us from all over the world—from Japan and Antibes and London, from New York and Middleburg. They are places, often, that are healthy enough in themselves; there has been only one lack in these children's fortunate lives to have made their eyes hollow and their coughs hacking.

The school is lodged in what was once a hospital, in the desert outside Tucson—a series of adobe blocks, constructed around small patios, each with a fountain in the middle and a colonnade, off which open eight to twelve rooms. I live in the one named Suguaro, with seven of the children and two of the younger teachers. In the daytime the sun is blazing, and the children take carefully supervised sunbaths, spaced into their schedules so that they will get them before eleven, when the sun becomes dangerous. In the evening the sun sets behind Tucson and T Mountain. Night in Arizona has a large, a sterile quality—clear black air and stars like arc-lights. It is then, after I have gone to sleep, that I am sometimes wakened by coyotes out in the desert, like a band of mad nightmare phantasms howling and laughing, and cannot go back to sleep, but lie here and remember the years of my own youth, which was such a sheltered one and passed among people who loved me.

My wholesome background had, of course, everything to do with my being allowed to try out at this job, untrained for it as I was. It is an axiom of the work that if you have never known emotional security in your childhood you cannot possibly impart it to others. I am one of those lucky ones who are able to say, My mother loved me, always, always. Mother produced the opportunity, in fact, that time when I was at my lowest ebb, just the way she always did produce whatever was needful— as though out of the air; as though by the Indian rope trick. She arranged for my interview with the then director, Miss Alden, who was in the East, through one of her myriad associations with worthwhile people in philanthropy, social betterment, and child welfare.

She saved me, at a time when Giles had disappeared forever from my life, and when I was ashamed to see Mrs. Bogden any more—embarrassed to; as if, by bungling the Giles business, I had let her down too badly. I was turned back on, reduced to, my own dreary, unappealing, unrewarding, lone self. Even then, I realized I was being saved from something, and that it was Mother who was saving me, after all, not Mrs. Bogden. Sometimes in the early days I used to feel that, by working at this job, I was helping the little boy whom Giles once was—the unloved, the forgotten, the suffering child of this century. It hadn't taken me long to realize, once it was too late, that Giles would have *loved* the life in our Clam Harbor house. It would have been the very life he had always been starved for. Any rebellion I'd ever felt toward it seemed to expire as though with a little sigh of relief as soon as I was settled in Arizona.

It had been Mrs. Bogden, it would appear, not me, who was building up a head of steam against Boston in the course of those long tête-à-têtes of ours. She never breathed a word to me about what must have been her rising fury, but less than three years after the summer of which I have been writing, she kicked over the traces, as people put it in the letters I got from Boston. Flew the coop. Bolted. She divorced Carola's father and married a Honolulu Hutchinson—immensely rich; as, indeed, Mr. Bogden had been. But, I realize now, Mrs. Bogden could not possibly have understood, when she married Mr. Bogden in London, about Bostonians and their attitudes to money. For them it is not something to lavish, or even to spend. It is something to nurture, like a plant. It is a sacred trust. In any case, it is nothing with which to have, as Mrs. Bogden would have said, f-u-n. I used to have a vision of how she must have looked as she boarded the Boston section of the Twentieth Century, Reno-bound. I saw her close the door of the compartment behind her, pull the little hat off her gray hair, take a handful of bills from her Hermès purse and throw them up into the air, stretch her arms out, throw back her lovely head—so like the powdered head of an eighteenth-century king's mistress—and exclaim, "God!"

But I had never actually seen Mrs. Bogden since I left Boston, until I went to San Francisco last week to meet the boat the Aylesworth child was sent to us by, from Hawaii. The Aylesworth child is typical of our pupils—stiff with tension from the violent emotions rich parents seem to spill around them like largesse: desire and hate and jealousy and malice and anger and more desire. If they could only see, if they could just grasp, that their conflicts are all their children have to use as nourishment! What can a child know of feeling but what it feels? The Aylesworth child was sent to us alone, which again is typical. The reasoning would be: Nothing could possibly happen to her on that nice, safe ship; if she's sick the stewardess can look after her, can't she? And, besides, the child's not a 10 baby, she's eight. . . . Not a baby, just a child who has begun obscurely to realize that it is facing life—*life*—with absolutely nothing to face it with. We here have come to feel that unloved children are often living out their parents' conflicts in a sort of pathetic attempt to offer some little solution. At school we rage against such parents.

I had gone on board to fetch her, and was walking up the promenade deck toward her stateroom—the Aylesworths would never spare expense, of course—when suddenly I saw Mrs. Bogden. She was coming along the deck very slowly, on the arm of, I suppose, her husband. I've said already that I know nothing of the world in which rich people navigate; nowa- 20 days, I know no world except the world of sick children; so it's possible that many rich people look the way this couple did, and that if I were more used to them I wouldn't have felt so shocked.

But the aging couple were as frightening to me as figures out of Hieronymus Bosch.° They came toward me, not seeing me—I am not a person anyone notices—he in white trousers with a pencil stripe and navy blue blazer, she in a cream-white, knitted costume and a white, broad-brimmed straw hat. Rich, they looked; rich, irritated, fussy, with eyes as bright as jewels; cynical, bored, unhappy. But it wasn't any of all that which shocked me, for I have often enough read such descriptions of 30 worldly people in the pages of novels. What I never read about in any book, what gives me the knot in the pit of my stomach, was the look in Mrs. Bogden's face; the look far behind it.

I'd thought for a moment of going up to her, holding out my hand, and saying, "Mrs. Bogden, it's Lucy Eliot." But the look in the still-beautiful, pleasure-loving, powdered old face stopped me while I peered, hesitating. The look I am talking about was a double look, really; it was two things at once. Part of it was fear, under the cream foundation—fear like a smart whip to brighten up the tired eyes; and part of it was the even deeper-hidden thing the fear was of: death, holding the whip and looking at me, 40 right there out of her face. I don't know what manner of death. Just death.

---

5. **Hieronymus Bosch,** a Dutch painter (*c.* 1460-1516), a satirist who devoted himself to the depiction of bizarre or grotesque (*diableries*) types.

I was too shaken to do anything but hurry on along the deck. But last night, back in Arizona again, I woke in the middle of the night and heard the coyotes howling and laughing crazily out in the sterile desert; and once more, as so many, many times before, my mind went back to Clam Harbor and the days when I was young. Once more I seemed to be sitting on the silvery splintered boards of the old dock in the morning cool, talking to Mrs. Bogden, who is dressed in her favorite dark red. Her face is turned away toward the sea, but—lying in the Western darkness—I could hear her voice asking me, as I have so often heard her ask, "The 10 way to be happy is always to be in love, isn't it? *Isn't it?*" She turns her lovely face toward me, and this time her face is full of death.

Suddenly, for the first time, I realized what it was I should have answered her. Within my narrow, schoolmistress's bed I felt my whole body strain as I imagined crying out, "No! No, it isn't! Feel what you ought to feel! Practice unity with all creation! Give yourself to the ocean!"

Because Mother was right, of course—about Mrs. Bogden as about everything else. Today, at the age of eighty-three, my mother's face has no death in it. Her face is filled with that life she has believed in all along; which always has existed and ever shall exist. For a while I lay there, 20 awake in Arizona, thinking with pride and absolute acceptance of my wonderful mother, but then—such is the unregenerate human ego—I had to turn my face to the pillow and begin to cry.

"What about me?" I kept blubbering as I squeezed the pillow around my head so that the children should not hear me, and smelled the curious scent that tears always have. "What about all those years? Where is my *life?*"

1909-
STEPHEN
SPENDER * Deus ex Machina

He was disappointed with himself, because, however hard he looked at it, the figure of the charioteer disappointed him. What he had admired in the photographs, the strict rigidity of the head, emphasised by the parallel, almost vertical lines of the tunic, the entire unaffectedness of the hands simply holding the broken reins, the darkness and staring singleness of the whole posture, was now spoiled for him by the discoloration of the metal, its jagged breaks, the ineptness of the museum wall behind, the presence of surrounding pieces of statuary all claiming his attention. He had travelled so many miles, but he could not live up to this moment anticipated since years. He stared at the figure, admitting that all he had expected was there, trying to concentrate, shutting everything else out from his mind. Now it became completely meaningless, riding away on unfocussed waves of space, wearing its archaic, slightly triumphant, almost ironic smile which withheld all significance.

He walked out into the blinding light, stumbling amongst the broken ruins of houses and temples. One temple stood four-squarely to the wind, its triangular roof and partly restored fluted columns facing the top of the valley where the road wound through olive groves into the bare, irregular mountains. Near to it some peasants, carrying spades and pickaxes, were hewing at the stony ground: a woman collected the stone and rubble in a basket. Behind the peasants, and larger than them, was the marble statue of a seated headless matron in flowing robes, a hole in the left shoulder where the socket of the arm had been inserted. The marble figure was not young or slender, but even in its mutilated form it had a certain fluid transparency, like a large white cloud in a sky full of such clouds, which made the kerchiefed working woman standing between him and it seem small, black, dirty, gawky.

The whole untidy mass of marble rubbish deposited on the hill, here the foundations of a house, here the beginnings of a road, here a pit full of broken fragments, everywhere a sense of upturned paving stones; the whole scene, he thought, turning away, had none of the slum-like intimacy, the wiry humanity, of modern untidiness and rubbish heaps; rather it was like a scattered evening sky, or blocks of shattered ice being carried down a river in spring sunlight.

But it all left him cold, as did the charioteer with his balanced, judging eyes quite unaware that the plunging horses which dragged him through another place and time had been broken off and he had been left floating in the rubbish heap of a museum of the sky.

On the sides of the mountain, the ruins of Delphi seemed small, and the German emigré who walked away from them wearing his shabby tourist's uniform of tweed, his rucksack, his spectacles, his short russet bristling beard, his camera, and carrying his stick, felt like a small ruin of a civilisation, too. He walked away up the road through the little modern village with its two hotels looking across the valley to Parnassus.

When he reached the last sentinel-like stone house, poised above the valley, he saw for the first time the eagles—four of them. They circled above the valley, like kites tugged at by the string of their magnifying eyes attached to some spot on the ground hundreds of feet below. There the valley deepened and grew greener and unfolded, a few creases still left in it, and divided by the river, until its ragged edge lay against the glass sea. Beyond the stretch of coast, the mountains receded and lay like a great curtain with rich folds drawn sideways above the dramatic plain, and the mouth of the river.

Where he walked now was a grassy upland, the road broad and comfortable, on either side of it fantastic cattle grazing, tufted coloured goats,
horned sheep, and highland cows with thick matted hair and great cork-
screw-shaped horns. All the cattle wore bells, and their tinkling produced
a sustained, transparent blur, like a sheet of colored flowers—say harebells.
But above this thin-drawn almost continuous note he heard the piping of
the shepherds and then above the tinkling and piping a whistling of other
shepherds, sharp and thin as whips, and occasionally, too, their brusque
flat shouting, as they called across to each other from side to side of this
10 hollowed upland, perhaps half a mile broad.

He seemed merely to have turned a corner and at once entered a landscape of music with four distinct concurrent themes, massed instruments
in an orchestra, the bells, the pipings, the whistling and the shouts. So
strong was this impression that on the road which, as it were, bisected the
symphony, he felt that the longer notes of bells and pipings formed a lower
clef beneath him, whilst the whistling and shouts formed an upper clef
above him. Just as in a visual landscape it is impossible to think of one-
self as not being part of that which is seen, so in this aural landscape he
had an aural vision of himself. He wondered what instrument he might
20 represent. Really though, his note only existed in his mind; it was the
lines of the clef running through the notes, or even, like the road, the
empty space between the clefs.

He reached a bend where the road swept away from the view along the
turn of the mountain side. The music stopped as instantly as it had begun,
for the road now emerged from the slight hollow of the upland which held
the sound as a shallow lake holds water, and the whole view of valley,
mountains and sea presented itself, with the eagles still circling above the
stream. He was tempted to go further, but the sky had clouded and a rumbling of thunder warned him to go back. He waited at the edge of the
30 road breathing the now agitated air and looking at the view here where
it was best.

At the edge of the road there was a shallow trench dug as an improvised
drain out of the loose, broken stones. The scratch of a faint shadow, the
suggestion of a minute rasping noise, made him look down at two beetles
which were scrambling amongst the stones, rolling between them a
rounded, oval-shaped pellet of dung. They worked with the inexhaustible, mechanical patience of their shut-in world, totally preoccupied with
manipulating a packing case considerably larger than themselves amongst
a valley of gigantic boulders. They did not attempt to consider any solution
40 of problems which presented themselves, they showed not the slightest
grasp of the realities of their situation, but like uncompromising idealists
simply proceeded along the direct line of an abstract idea which refused to
admit of any obstacles.

Again and again, not noticing that the way was flat and clear on either

Stephen Spender   255

side, they forced the pellet up the side of one particularly large stone. As soon as it had reached the top it rolled down again, bringing them with it; finally, it happened to roll rather further than before, with the result that in pushing it forward, quite by accident, they circumvented the stone and made some progress until they came to another similar obstacle.

The emigré watched the insects with something more than curiosity, with a certain passion of malice. Their concentration, their power of acting in abstraction, drew his attention like a magnet. Their patience and their impotence, the seeming futility of their efforts which were yet 10 crowned with a certain measure of success, made him smile ironically. He stood above their world and yet he felt himself to understand it. He was a god, he could easily perform a miracle which would astonish them utterly, he could sever their connubial bliss, he could rob them of the fruit of their labors, he could widow either of them or destroy them both.

With a curved smile, he prodded their little pellet with the ferrule of his stick. As he did so, touching their world, he felt a slight apprehension. Aware of his own power, he was aware, too, of the power of insects which crawl across the untouchable faces of the human dead, and whose militarised mechanical patterns of society survive, whilst civilisations per- 20 ish.

Robbed of their life's object, the beetles stayed perfectly still, a little raised on their back legs with their antennae lifted, like field wireless stations. A message seemed to arrive, for a moment later they were scrambling in their senseless, rickety way across stones to the ball, to which they attached themselves, waiting a moment before beginning their Sisyphus act again. Annoyed that his spite should have proved so ineffective, the German lifted his stick again and this time flicked the ball much further and watched it roll into a crevice. The beetles were thrown over on to their backs, where they lay perfectly still with their legs held downwards, pre- 30 tending to be dead. Then they suddenly came to life again; but this time they moved in hurried zigzags of clockwork agitation, and it was some seconds before they discovered the ball of dung. Now they seemed to crouch over it in a protective and threatening attitude, with a new awareness of danger.

The thunder groaned more loudly, there was an inhuman tension in the air, like the tiny stored up passion of the insects immensely magnified. The emigré looked down the road anxiously, aware that he was experiencing a momentary sensation like madness, in which he did not wish to be observed. No one was coming. He picked up some stones and threw them at 40 the beetles. The avalanche rocked them away from the ball and they immediately lay on their backs assuming the posture of death. He poked one of them with the ferrule of his stick; it did not move, but immediately he took the stick away, it turned over and started trying to escape. He took

a handful of earth and stones and threw them with all his force, burying the beetles. Then, with his stick, he carefully exhumed them; but
the bombardment which, on a human scale, would have destroyed an
army or a city had left them quite unharmed.

Trembling with a veiled indignation, this time he planted the ferrule of
his stick firmly against the centre of each of their bodies in turn and crushed
it against the ground. There was an enormous clap of thunder and he
started running back along the road to his hotel, guilty of an infinitesimal
murder, something, which in spite of his strained smile he knew had cut a
10 window into some darkness of his mind where he saw himself with the
powers of a god, using them, like all the gods, only to destroy.

1917-
J. F.
POWERS ✳ *Look How the Fish Live*

It had been a wonderful year in the yard, which was four city lots and
full of trees, a small forest and game preserve in the old part of town. Until that day, there hadn't been a single casualty, none at least that he
knew about, which was the same thing and more than enough where
there was so much life coming and going: squirrels, both red and gray,
robins, flickers, mourning doves, chipmunks, rabbits. These creatures,
and more, lived in the yard, and most of these he'd worried about in the
past. Some, of course, he'd been too late for, and perhaps that was best,
being able to bury what would have been his responsibility.
10 Obviously the children had been doing all they could for some time,
for when he happened on the scene the little bird was ensconced in grass
twisted into a nesting ring, soggy bread and fresh water had been set before it—the water in a tiny pie tin right under its bill—and a birdhouse
was only inches away, awaiting occupancy. Bird, food and drink, and
house were all in a plastic dishpan.

"Dove, isn't it?" said his wife, who had hoped to keep him off such a
case, he knew, and now was easing him into it.

"I don't know," he said, afraid that he did. It was a big little bird, several shades of gray, quills plainly visible because the feathers were only
20 beginning. Its bill was black and seemed too long for it. "A flicker maybe," he said, but he didn't think so. No, it was a dove, because where
were the bird's parents? Any bird but the dove would try to do some-

thing. Somewhere in the neighborhood this baby dove's mother was pos- ~
ing on a branch like peace itself, with no thought of anything in her head.

"Oh, God," he groaned.

"Where *are* the worms?" said his wife.

"We can't find any," said one of the children.

"Here," he said, taking the shovel from her. He went and dug near
some shrubbery with the shovel, which was probably meant for sand and
gravel. With this shovel he had buried many little things in the past. The
worms were deeper than he could go with such a shovel, or they were just
nowhere. He pried up two flagstones. Only ants and one many-legged 10
worm that he didn't care to touch.

He had found no worms, and when he came back to the bird, when he
saw it, he was conscious of returning empty-handed. His wife was going
into the house.

"That bird can't get into that house," he said. "It's for wrens."

"We know it," said the oldest child, quietly.

He realized then that he had pointed up an obvious difficulty that the
two girls had decently refrained from mentioning in front of the bird and
the two younger children, the boys. But he hadn't wanted them to *squeeze*
the dove into the wrenhouse. "Well, you might as well leave it where it is. 20
Keep the bird in the shade."

"That's what we're doing."

"We put him in the dishpan so we could move him around in the shade."

"Good. Does it eat or drink anything?"

"Of course."

He didn't like the sound of this. "Did you *see* it eat or drink anything?"

"No, she did."

"Did you see it eat or drink?"

"Drink."

"It didn't eat?"   30

"I didn't see him eat. He maybe did when we weren't watching."

"Did it drink like this?" He sipped the air and threw back his head,
swallowing.

"More like this." The child threw back her head only about half as far
as he had.

"Are you sure?"

"Of course."

He walked out into the yard to get away from them. He didn't know
whether the bird had taken any water. All he knew was that one of the
children had imitated a bird drinking—rather, had imitated him imitat- 40
ing a chicken. He didn't even know whether birds threw back their heads
in drinking. Was the dove a bird that had to have its mother feed it?

Probably so. And so probably, as he'd thought when he first saw the bird, there was no use. He was back again.

"How does it seem? Any different?"

"How do you mean?"

"Has it changed any since you found it?"

The little girls looked at each other. Then the younger one spoke: "He's not so afraid."

He was touched by this, in spite of himself. Now that they'd found the bird, she was saying, it would be all right. Was ever a bird in worse shape?
10 With food it couldn't eat, water it probably hadn't drunk and wouldn't, and with a house it couldn't get into—and *them!* Now they punished him with their faith in themselves and the universe, and later, when these failed and the bird began to sink, they would punish him some more, with their faith in him. He knew what was the best thing for the bird. When the children took their naps, then, maybe, he could do the job. He was not soft. He had flooded gophers out of their labyrinthine ways and beheaded them with the shovel; he had purged a generation of red squirrels from the walls and attic of the old house when he moved in, knowing it was them or him. But why did animals and birds do this to him? Why did
20 children?

"Why'd you pick this bird up? Why didn't you leave it where it was? The mother might've found it then."

"She couldn't lift him, could she?"

"Of course not."

"Well, he can't fly."

"No, but if you'd left it where it fell, the mother might see it. The mother bird has to feed a baby like this." Why couldn't she lift it? Why couldn't the two parents get together and just put it back in the nest? Why, down through the ages, hadn't birds worked out something for such
30 an emergency? As he understood it, they were descended from reptiles and had learned how to grow feathers and fly. The whale had gone to sea. But he didn't know whether he believed any of this. Here was a case that showed how incompetent nature really was. He was tired of such cases, of nature passing the buck to him. He hated to see spring and summer come to the yard, in a way. They meant death and mosquitoes to him.

It had been the worst year for mosquitoes that anyone could remember, and in Minnesota that was saying a lot. He had bought a spraying outfit, and DDT at $2.50 a quart, which, when you considered that there was no tax on it, made you think. A quart made two gallons, but he was
40 surprised how quickly it went. The words on the bottle, "Who enjoys your yard—you or the mosquitoes?," had stayed with him, however. He had engaged professionals, with a big machine mounted on a truck, to blow a gale of poison through the yard. (In other years, seeing such an

J. F. Powers   259

operation in other yards, he had worried about the bees.) The squirrels and rabbits in residence had evacuated the trees and lily beds while he stood by, hoping that they and the birds understood it was an emergency measure. He believed, however, that the birds received too much credit for eating annoying insects. Wasps, he knew, consumed great numbers of mosquitoes—but what about *them*? The mosquito hawk, a large, harmless insect, was a great killer of mosquitoes, but was itself killed by birds—by martins. That was the balance of nature for you. Balance for whom? You had to take steps yourself—drastic steps. Too drastic?

"Now I want you to show me exactly where you found this bird." 10

The little girls looked at each other.

"Don't say anything. Just take me to the exact spot."

They walked across the yard as if they really knew where they were going, and he and the little boys followed. The girls appeared to agree on a spot, but he supposed that one was under the influence of the other. The older one put out a foot and said "Here."

He hadn't realized they were being that exact. It was surprising how right they were. Fifty or sixty feet overhead, in a fork of a big white oak, he saw a nest, definitely a dove's nest, a jerry-built job if he ever saw one, the sky visible between the sticks, and something hanging down. He 20 moved away and gazed up again. It was only a large dead leaf, not what he'd feared, not a baby bird hanging by its foot. He felt better about having had the yard sprayed. The machine on the truck was very powerful, powerful enough to bend back the bushes and small trees, but he doubted that it had blown the baby dove out of the nest. This was just an unusually bad nest and the bird had fallen out. Nature had simply failed again.

"The nest! I see it! See?"

"Yes." He walked away from them, toward the garage. He hadn't called the nest to their attention because restoring the bird was out of the question for him—it was a job for the fire department or for God whose 30 eye is on the sparrow—but that didn't mean that the children might not expect him to do it.

"Just keep the bird in the shade," he called from the garage. He drove down to the office, which he hadn't planned to visit that day, and spent a few hours of peace there.

And came home to another calamity. In the kitchen, the little girls were waiting for him. Something, they said, had jumped out of the lilies and pushed one of the young bunnies that hadn't been doing anything, just eating grass near the playhouse. A weasel, they thought. Their mother hadn't seen it happen, had only heard the bunny crying, and had gone 40 up to bed. There was no use going to her. They were in possession of what information there was. He should ask them.

"Don't go out there!"

"Why not?"

"Mama says if the bunny has the rabies it might bite."

He stood still in thought. Most of his life had been spent in a more settled part of the country. There was a great deal he didn't know about wildlife, even about the red squirrel and the yellow-jacket wasp with which he had dealt firsthand, and he knew it. He could be wrong. But there was something ridiculous about what they were suggesting. "Did you see whatever it was that pushed the rabbit?"

"Of course!" said the child. It was this that distinguished her from all others in the house.

"What did it look like?"

"It went so fast."

This was ground they'd covered before, but he persevered, hoping to flush the fact that would explain everything. "What color was it?"

"Kind of—like the rabbit. But it went so fast."

This, too, was as before. "Maybe it was the mama rabbit," he said, adding something new. The more he thought about it, the more he liked it. "Maybe she didn't want the young one to come out in the open, in the daytime, I mean. Maybe she was just teaching it a lesson." He didn't know whether rabbits did that, but he did know that this particular mother was intelligent. He had first noticed her young ones, just babies then, in a shallow hole alongside a tiny evergreen which he had put a wire fence around, and over which he'd draped some "Shoo"—rope soaked with creosote, advertised as very effective against dogs, rabbits, and rodents of all kinds. And as for the punishment the young rabbit had taken from whatever it was, he had once seen a mother squirrel get tough with a little one that had strayed from the family tree.

"Would she hurt the young rabbit?" said the younger girl.

"She might. A little."

"This one was hurt a lot," said the eyewitness. She spoke with finality.

"Maybe it was a cat," he said, rallying. "You say it was about the same size."

The children didn't reply. It seemed to him that they did not trust him. His mama-rabbit theory was too good to be true. They believed in the weasel.

"A weasel would've killed it," he said.

"But if he saw *me*?"

"*Did* he see you?"

"Of course."

"Did you see *him*?"

"Of course!" cried the child, impatient with the question. She didn't appear to realize that she was cornered, that having seen the attacker she should be able to describe it. But she was under no obligation to be logical. He decided to wait a few years.

J. F. Powers 261

Out in the yard he scrutinized the ground around the playhouse for blood and fur, and saw none. He stepped to the edge of the lilies. Each year the lilies were thicker and less fruitful of flowers, and a gardener would have thinned them out. A gardener, though, would have spoiled this yard—for the fairies who, the children told him, played there. He didn't enter the lilies because he didn't want to encounter what he might. He was not forgetting the bird.

Passing through the kitchen, he noticed that the children were cutting up a catalogue, both pasting. Apparently the older one could no longer get the younger one to do all the scissor work. "How's the bird?"

"We don't know."

He stopped and got them in focus. "Why don't you know?"

"We haven't looked at it."

"Haven't looked at it! Why haven't you?"

"We've been doing this."

"This is why."

It was a mystery to him how, after crooning over the helpless creature, after entangling him in its fate, they could be this way. This was not the first time either. "Well, get out there and look at it!"

On the way out to look at it himself, he met them coming back. "He's all right," the older one said grumpily.

"Looks the same, huh?" He didn't catch what they said in reply, which wasn't much anyway. He found the bird where he'd last seen it, beside the back porch. He had expected it to be dying by now. Its rib showed clearly when it breathed, which was alarming, but he remembered that this had worried them when he first saw the bird. It did seem to be about the same.

He passed through the kitchen and, seeing the children all settled down again, he said, "Find a better place for it. It'll soon be in the sun."

A few moments later, he was intervening. They had the whole yard and yet they were arguing over two patches of shade, neither of which would be good for more than a few minutes. He carried the dishpan out into the yard, and was annoyed that they weren't following him, for he wanted them to see what he was doing and why. He put the dishpan down where the sun wouldn't appear again until morning. He picked it up again. He carried it across the yard to the foot of the white oak. On the ground, directly below the nest, there was and would be sun until evening, but near the trunk there would be shade until morning.

The bird was breathing heavily, as before, but it was in no distress—unless this was distress. He thought not. If the bird had a full coat of feathers, its breathing wouldn't be so noticeable.

He was pleasantly surprised to see a mature dove high above him. The dove wasn't near the nest, wasn't watching him—was just looking unconcerned in another part of the tree—but it was in the right tree. He tried to attract its attention, making what he considered a gentle bird noise. It flew away, greatly disappointing him.

He knelt and lifted the tin of water to the bird's mouth. This he did with no expectation that it would drink, but it did, it definitely did. The bird kept his bill in the water, waggling it once or twice, spilling some, and raised its head slightly—not as a chicken would. He tried a little bread, unsuccessfully. He tried the water again, and again the bird drank. The bread was refused again and also the water when it was offered the third time. This confirmed him in his belief that the bird had been drink-
10 ing before. This also proved that the bird was able to make decisions. After two drinks, the bird had said, in effect, no more. It hadn't eaten for some time, but it was evidently still sound in mind and body. It might need only a mother's care to live.

He went into the house. In the next two hours, he came to the window frequently. For a while he tried to believe that there might be maternal action at the foot of the oak while he wasn't watching. He knew better, though. All he could believe was that the mother might be staying away because she regarded the dishpan as a trap—assuming, of course, that she had spotted the baby, and assuming also that she gave a damn, which he
20 doubted.

Before dinner he went out and removed the birdhouse and then the bird from the dishpan, gently tipping it into the grass, not touching it. The nest the children had twined together slid with it, but the bird ended up more off than on the nest. There was plenty of good, growing grass under the dove, however. If, as the children claimed, the bird could move a little and if the mother did locate it, perhaps between them—he credited the baby with some intelligence—they might have enough sense to hide out in the lilies of the valley only a few feet away. There would be days ahead of feeding and growth before the little bird could fly, probably too
30 many days to pass on the ground in the open. Once the mother assumed her responsibility, however, everything would become easier—that is, possible. *He* might even build a nest nearby. (One year there had been a dove's nest in a chokecherry tree, only ten feet off the ground.) Within a few yards of the oak there were aged lilac bushes, almost trees, which would be suitable for a nest. At present, though, with the mother delinquent, the situation was impossible.

He looked up into the trees for her, in vain, and then down at the orphan. It had moved. It had taken up its former position precisely in the center of the little raft of grass the children had made for it, and this was
40 painful to see, this little display of order in a thing so small, so dumb, so sure.

It would not drink. He set the water closer, and the bread, just in case, and carried away the dishpan and the birdhouse. He saw the bowel movement in the bottom of the dishpan as a good omen, but was puzzled by the presence of a tiny dead bug of the beetle family. It could mean that the mother had been in attendance, or it could mean that the bug had simply dropped dead from the spraying, a late casualty.

After dinner, standing on the back porch, he heard a disturbance far out in the yard. Blue jays, and up to no good, he thought, and walked toward the noise. When he reached the farthest corner of the yard, the noise ceased, and began again. He looked into the trees across the alley. Then he saw two catbirds in the honeysuckle bushes only six feet away and realized that he had mistaken their rusty cries for those of blue jays at 10 some distance. The catbirds hopped, scolding, from branch to branch. They moved to the next bush, but not because of him, he thought. It was then that he saw the cat in the lilies. He stamped his foot. The cat, a black-and-white one marked like a Holstein cow, crashed through the lilies and out into the alley where the going was good, and was gone. The catbirds followed, flying low, belling the cat with their cries. In the distance he heard blue jays, themselves marauders, join in, doing their bit to make the cat's position known. High overhead he saw two dopey doves doing absolutely nothing about the cat, heard their little dithering noise, and was disgusted with them. It's a wonder you're not extinct, he thought, 20 gazing up at them. They chose that moment to show him the secret of their success.

He walked the far boundaries of the yard, stopping to gaze back at the old frame house, which was best seen at a distance. He had many pictures of it in his mind, for it changed with the seasons, gradually, and all during the day. The old house always looked good to him, in spring when the locust, plum, lilacs, honeysuckle, caragana, and mock orange bloomed around it; in summer, as it was now, almost buried in green; in autumn, when the yard was rolling with nuts, crashing with leaves, and the mountain ash berries turned red; and in winter, when, under snow and icicles, 30 with its tall mullioned windows sparkling, it reminded him of an old-fashioned Christmas card. For a hundred years it had been painted barn or Venetian red, with forest-green trim. In winter there were times when the old house, because of the light, seemed to be bleeding; the red then was profound and alive. Perhaps it knew something, after all, he thought. In January the yellow bulldozers would come for it and the trees. One of the old oaks, one which had appeared to be in excellent health, had recently thrown down half of itself in the night. "Herbal suicide," his wife had said.

Reaching the other far corner of the yard, he stood considering the 40 thick black walnut tree, which he had once, at about this time of year, thought of girdling with a tin shield to keep off the squirrels. But this would have taken a lot of tin, and equipment he didn't own to trim a neighboring maple and possibly an elm, and so he had decided to share the nuts with the squirrels. This year they could have them all. Few of the birds would be there when it happened, but the squirrels—there were at least a dozen in residence—were in for a terrible shock.

He moved toward the house, on the street side of the yard, on the lookout for beer cans and bottles which the teachers'-college students from
10 their parked cars tossed into the bushes. He knew, from several years of picking up after them, their favorite brand.

He came within twenty yards of the white oak, and stopped. He didn't want to venture too near in case the mother was engaged in feeding the baby, or was just about to make up her mind to do so. In order to see, however, he would have to be a little closer. He moved toward the white oak in an indirect line, and stopped again. The nest was empty. His first thought was that the bird, sensing the approach of darkness, had wisely retreated into the shelter of the lilies of the valley nearby, and then he remembered the recent disturbance on the other side of the yard. The cat
20 had last been seen at what had appeared a safe distance then. He was looking now for feathers, blood, bones. But he saw no such signs of the bird. Again he considered the possibility that it was hiding in the lilies of the valley. When he recalled the bird sitting in the very center of the nest, it did not seem likely that it would leave, ever—unless persuaded by the mother to do so. But he had no faith in the mother, and instead of searching the lilies, he stood where he was and studied the ground around him in a widening circle. The cat could've carried it off, of course, or—again— the bird could be safe among the lilies.

He hurried to the fallen oak. Seeing the little bird at such a distance
30 from the nest, and not seeing it as he'd expected he would, but entire, he had been deceived. The bird was not moving. It was on its back, not mangled but dead. He noted the slate-black feet. Its head was to one side on the grass. The one eye he could see was closed, and the blood all around it, enamel-bright, gave the impression, surprising to him, that it had poured out like paint. He wouldn't have thought such a little thing would even have blood.

He went for the shovel with which he'd turned up no worms for the bird earlier that day. He came back to the bird by a different route, having passed on the other side of a big tree, and saw the little ring of grass
40 that had been the bird's nest. It now looked like a wreath to him.

He dug a grave within a few feet of the bird. The ground was mossy there. He simply lifted up a piece of it, tucked in the bird, and dropped the sod down like a cover. He pounded it once with the back side of the shovel, thinking the bird would rest easier there than in most ground.

J. F. Powers   265

When he looked up from his work, he saw that he had company, Mr. and Mrs. Hahn, neighbors. He told them what had happened, and could see that Mr. Hahn considered him soft. He remembered that Mr. Hahn, who had an interest such as newspapers seemed to think everybody ought to have in explosions, didn't care to discuss the fallout.

The Hahns walked with him through the yard. They had heard there were no mosquitoes there now.

"Apparently it works," he said.

"The city should spray," said Mrs. Hahn.

"At least the swamps," said Mr. Hahn, who was more conservative. 10

He said nothing. They were perfectly familiar with his theory: that it was wet enough in the lily beds, in the weeds along the river, for mosquitoes to breed. When he explained that there just weren't enough swamps to breed that many mosquitoes, people smiled, and tried to refute his theory by talking about how little water it took, a bird bath, a tin can somewhere. "In my opinion, they breed right here, in this yard and yours."

"Anyway, they're not here now," said Mrs. Hahn.

He received this not as a compliment but as a polite denial of his theory. They were passing under the mulberry tree. In the bloody atmos- 20 phere prevailing in his mind that evening, he naturally thought of the purple grackle that had hung itself from a high branch with a string in the previous summer. "I'm sick of it all."

"Sick of *what*?" said Mrs. Hahn.

The Hahns regarded him as a head case, he knew, and probably wouldn't be surprised if he said that he was sick of them. He had stopped trying to adjust his few convictions and prejudices to company. He just let them fly. Life was too short. "Insects, birds, and animals of all kinds," he said. "Nature."

Mr. Hahn smiled. "There'd be too many of those doves if things like 30 that didn't happen."

"I suppose."

Mr. Hahn said: "Look how the fish live."

He looked at the man with interest. This was the most remarkable thing Mr. Hahn had ever said in his presence. But of course Mr. Hahn didn't appreciate the implications. Mr. Hahn didn't see himself in the picture at all.

"That includes children," he said, pursuing his original line. It was the children who were responsible for bringing the failures of nature to his attention. 40

Mrs. Hahn, who seemed to feel she was on familiar ground, gaily laughed. "Everybody who has them complains about them."

"*And* women," he added. He had almost left women out, and they belonged in. They were responsible for the children and the success of "Queen for a Day."

"And men," he added when he caught Mr. Hahn smiling at the mention of women. Men were at the bottom of it all.

"That doesn't leave much, does it?" said Mr. Hahn.

"No." Who *was* left? God. It wasn't surprising, for all problems were at bottom theological. He'd like to put a few questions to God. God, though, knowing his thoughts, knew his questions, and the world was already in possession of all the answers that would be forthcoming from God. Compassion for the Holy Family fleeing from Herod was laudable and meritorious, but it was wasted on soulless rabbits fleeing from soulless weasels. Nevertheless it was there just the same, or something very like it. As he'd said in the beginning, he was sick of it all.

"There he is now!" cried Mrs. Hahn.

He saw the black-and-white cat pause under the fallen oak.

"Should I get my gun?" said Mr. Hahn.

"No. It's his nature." He stamped his foot and hissed. The cat ran out of the yard. Where were the birds? They could be keeping an eye on the cat. Somewhere along the line they must have said the hell with it. He supposed there was a lesson in that for him. A man simply couldn't be compassionate with life to the full extent of his instincts and opportunities. A man had to accept his God-given limitations.

He accompanied the Hahns around to the front of the house, and there they met a middle-aged woman coming up the walk. He didn't know her, but the Hahns did, and introduced her. Mrs. Snyder.

"It's about civil defense," she said. Every occupant of every house was soon to be registered for purposes of identification in case of an emergency. Each block would have its warden, and Mrs. Snyder thought that he, since he lived on this property, which took up so much of the block . . .

"No."

"No?"

"No." He couldn't think of a job for which he was less suited, in view of his general outlook. He wouldn't be here anyway. Nor would this house, these trees.

While Mr. and Mrs. Hahn explained to Mrs. Snyder that the place was to become a parking lot for the teachers' college, he stood by in silence. He had never heard it explained so well. His friends had been shocked at the idea of doing away with the old house and trees — and for a parking lot! — and although he appreciated their concern, there was nothing to be done, and after a time he was unable to commiserate with them. This they didn't readily understand. It was as if some venerable figure in the community, only known to them but near and dear to him, had died or been murdered, and he failed to show proper sorrow and anger. The Hahns, however, were explaining how it was, turning this way and that, pointing to this building and that, to sites already taken, to those to be taken soon or in time. For them the words "the state" and "expansion" seemed sufficient. And the Hahns weren't employed by the teachers' college and they weren't old grads. It was impossible to account in such an easy way for their enthusiasm. They were scheduled for eviction themselves, they said, in a few years.

When they were all through explaining, it must have been annoying to them to hear Mrs. Snyder's comment. "Too bad," she said. She 10 glanced up at the old red house and then across the street at the new dormitory going up. There had been a parking lot there for a few years, but before that another big old house and trees. The new dormitory, apricot bricks and aluminum windows, was in the same style as the new library, a style known to him and his wife as Blank. "Too bad," Mrs. Snyder said again, with an uneasy look across the street, and then at him.

"There's no defense against that either," he said. If Mrs. Snyder understood what he meant, she didn't show it.

"Well," she said to Mr. Hahn, "how about you?"

They left him then, strolling down the walk together. Whether Mr. 20 Hahn became the block warden was a question in his mind that would have to be answered another time. He put the shovel away, and walked the boundaries of the yard for the last time that day, pausing twice to consider the house in the light of the moment. When he came to the grave, he stopped and looked around for a large stone. He took one from the mound where the hydrant rose up in the yard, the only place where the wild ginger grew, and set it on the grave, not as a marker but as an obstacle to the cat if it returned, as he imagined it would. It was getting dark in the yard, the night coming sooner there because of the great trees. Now the bats and owls would get to work, he thought, and went into the 30 doomed house.

1918-
GEORGE
P.
ELLIOTT ∗ Brother Quintillian and Dick the Chemist

I

Brother Quintillian Josephus at the age of thirty-five had achieved the station in life which he had desired from his earliest youth. In the days of

his sad, timid, solitary boyhood in the streets of East Oakland, surrounded by dinginess and brutal fellows, the College of the Most Blessed St. Anselm had gleamed in his imagination as the green tranquillity which only could requite his suffering years. St. Anselm's was a small college at the northeastern edge of the city, small and quiet and secluded among lawns and tall trees; he had seen it only three or four times when he was a boy with a very common name, Bob Johnson, for his family had had no car and he had not adventured about much on the streetcars by himself. But the green image of it glowed steadily in his mind like a vision of paradise.
10 When he grew older he realized that he could find a place in St. Anselm's, but only if he became a professor there. So he had studied very hard, and he had found that he liked studying hard; he had joined the Congregation and had put in his years of teaching at dingy, brutal parochial schools in Stockton and Chico and South San Francisco. And now he was securely set, an Assistant Professor of Logic and Medieval History at St. Anselm's. But after two years of living in these most blessed grounds, teaching and disputing as he had long desired, he discovered that he would have to face after all a trouble long deferred; there was nowhere in this life for him to go to avoid it any longer.

20 A mile or so above St. Anselm's, in the hills but still in Oakland, lived an atheist named Dick Carson. Every weekday morning Dick drove his old Dodge down to Emeryville where he worked as the chief research chemist for the Universal Metals Corporation. The final purpose of his researches was to increase the profits of Universal Metals. However, it's a stinking world as anyone can see, and Dick considered himself luckier than most to find only this one thing to hate about his job. He lived in a new, modern house for which he had undertaken to pay $125 a month for fifteen years; it was so placed in a recess of a wooded mountainside that not another house, at least as yet, was visible from any of its windows. The
30 house was designed to receive maximum benefit from the afternoon sun— Oakland is frequently overcast or foggy in the morning—and despite the surrounding trees it was both warm and bright on a good day. Dick had always wanted to be a scientist, and while he would have preferred it if he had been great he had settled down without much struggle to being good —"a sound man." He was an atheist because he saw no need for the hypothesis of a God at the basis of things in order to explain them; if he had seen the need he would have been perfectly willing to hypothesize the God, and he held no grudge against those who did. He could never have prayed to Him, however, and his acquaintance did not include many
40 people who could. Dick was thirty-five too, and he too had a trouble; as he saw it, it had been pushed upon him by chance and there was nothing to be done but bear it. His wife of eleven years whom he had loved, had been mashed to death in an automobile accident.

The doubt of Brother Quintillian could turn words into sounds and faces into vacant masks. For a long time he had not recognized what it was that was attacking him so, for it had not been subtle and intellectual as he had thought doubt would be. No, his doubt knew that he could syllogize it away if it came at him roundabout, so it jumped on him with bared teeth and tore at him through his senses. He would be standing in front of a classroomful of fresh and sullen faces, in the midst, say, of the Albigensian heresy in Languedoc or of a tight demonstration that some men are not all non-dogs, when suddenly he would be left standing there with not a notion in his head about what the next word was to be. "Dante's hatred for 10 Boniface VIII was a result of many factors, chief among which was—" Chief among which was what? What was the next word to be and which of these tilted-up faces cared? He was not even tempted to be facetious and say something like "—the horns of dilemma on the papal bulls" as he had done once successfully in a seminar. He simply, for a few seconds, had no idea what any of his words stood for any longer and no idea what these faces were doing in front of him. Then he would catch himself and go on. His attacks had not been frequent, and he had attributed them to dizziness or nerves or eyestrain. They would upset him for a few hours, and then he would forget about them. But one day his doubt, weary of these imperma- 20 nent sallies, assaulted him in his very fortress, where he was kneeling at Mass.

Dick was not sentimental, but he had loved his wife, loved her and needed her. She had fitted out their house with a taste that had become his own; she had persuaded him to go to parties and concerts and plays, where he had usually enjoyed himself; she had filled the house with a color and cheer which his rather saturnine turn of character had at once groused at and loved. The rugs and curtains were left, the bright chairs and the concerts and the wide acquaintance, but there was no cheer in any of it now that she was dead. He stayed at home most of the time after her 30 death, among the gay objects which with her absence became things only. Sometimes his friends, worried about him, would suggest that he ought to move out of this house which was full of associations for him, but he told them to shut up. He was not sentimental, and he knew that these objects of his were the things he liked best; to his taste they were functional and beautiful. To be sure he did not like them now, but he thought that he would again once he got out of his slump. She's dead and gone and that's an end to it; things are things and it's morbid to go on talking about the whole mess; for Christ's sake can't a man be left to get over his own un- happiness by himself? He took many vitamin pills and lost sleep. 40

It was a six o'clock Mass in late September, a cool morning after a mild night. Brother Quintillian found himself in the pew behind old Brother

Alphonsus, who spluttered and mumbled at his rosary. During the first part of the ritual he paid little attention to what was going on. It had happened so often before; his mood was sodden, the Eucharist exalted; like the seventy-seventh Hail Mary in a penance it seemed one more salaam to boredom. The acolyte who was swinging the censer was taken with a fit of annoying sneezes from the incense, and by the time he had lifted his eyes to glance at the sneezing boy the dreadful voiding had taken place. Father McElroy had become an old man in a silly costume, walking about, kneeling, bowing and bending, and bringing his hands together
10 before him in a way that could not have been more inscrutable. As Brother Quintillian looked, he saw the celebrant like a chef turn over some pages of a book, repeat as it were the recipe aloud in his silly cook's language, look into the tabernacle as it were into a little oven, then step aside to wait till the crackers should be ready to eat. He was so astonished that anyone should do these things that he did not even find it ludicrous, he even forgot to rise and sit and kneel and rise with the others about him. Not until the bell tinkled did he come to himself, and then he was so horrified at what he had done that he sat back in the pew in a cold tremble. He felt that he could not have desecrated the Eucharist more
20 profoundly had he blasphemed aloud at the moment of transubstantiation, and at the same time that it would be silly even in a ballet to dance around pretending to cook that flavorless, packaged fragment of God. When the rest of the community left he stayed behind as if in prayer; he was too weak to rise. He was wondering what he should do. Surely he was falling into a state of damnation.

For the psychosomatic theory of illness Dick had a physical chemist's scorn. When a high correlation between isolable personality traits and specific pathological symptoms could be demonstrated on a statistically sound basis he was quite willing to admit that there was some connection
30 between the two; what connection he refused to say. Himself, he leaned towards the endocrine view: that both symptoms and traits derived from some malfunction of the ductless glands. This unhappiness of his could hardly be called a character trait, yet he had plenty of symptoms beyond those called for by his grief: bad sleep and bad dreams, sour stomach, irascibility, constipation, lethargy. Vitamin-complex tablets didn't do it, his doctor could discover no infection in him, and four days in bed resting didn't do it. He was driven back upon his endocrines, and in particular he suspected his pituitary gland, the controller. But what it was secreting, which of its many chemicals (sixteen, was it?) was doing the damage
40 science could not yet tell him; there was nothing to be done. He could not bear to do nothing, so he fell back upon the remedy his mother had thought appropriate to any ill: diet. Sometimes he thought he benefited from cutting out all alcohol and fats, sometimes from eating only vegetables and

George P. Elliott   271

milk, sometimes from a very high protein diet; but the only permanent benefit he got from the dieting was the discovery that he was mildly allergic to okra. Meanwhile, his sleeping was troubled by the memory of the newspaper photograph of his wife's body half-sprawled out of the car in which she had been killed, and his waking was troubled by the irrational thought that if only he had gone with her on that ride instead of going to a movie he might have saved her.

The day on which Brother Quintillian was praying in the chapel despite classes and meals, Dick was putting in his eight hours analyzing an aluminum alloy made by a competitor of Universal Metals. At five o'clock 10 when Brother Quintillian emerged, half-staggering, Dick was buying yoghurt, wheat germ and canned glutenburger at a health food store.

Both of them were five feet ten inches tall, weighed about a hundred and fifty pounds, had ordinary brown hair, flecked blue eyes and rather fair complexion, and both of them were wondering how to get through the night.

II

Some of the brothers would be in the common room listening to the radio, reading the paper or talking; some would be out strolling, or pottering in some favorite part of the garden; some younger ones would be playing handball or working out in the gym. Brother Quintillian was 20 afraid that if he went directly to his room from the chapel he would be thought aloof and proud. He would have preferred to take a walk in the mellow air, nodding to whomever he met and meditating on the flowers, but his knees would not support him on such a venture. He went to the common room. It took all his strength for him to open the heavy door in a natural way and to step inside the room confidently, unhesitantly. There were four other brothers in the room. When he entered, they glanced at him. The two who were talking fell silent, and the one next to the radio turned it down. He was sure that they were ashamed of him, embarrassed for him, even revolted by him; by some little gesture, some mumbled 30 word he must have let them glimpse this morning at Mass his full impiety.

"Good afternoon, Brother," said Brother John. "Would you like to see the sporting page?"

Brother John's voice seemed altered a little, somewhat subdued, somewhat strained; he normally called Brother Quintillian by his nickname, Quin; he doted on baseball. Why then, Brother Quintillian wondered, did he behave like this? Surely he was being ironic in his offer? Surely he was being charitable to this leper?

"No thank you," said Brother Quintillian. He sank into a chair. "I think I will just rest here awhile." 40

He unbuttoned his collar in back and pulled his cassock up so that he could cross his legs.

"You look tired," said Brother Alphonsus, a strong old man.

"It's nothing, nothing. I'll rest awhile."

He was sorry he had not gone to his room to rest. He was making them very uncomfortable.

"It's Friday," said Brother Alphonsus.

"Yes, we're having fresh fish," said Brother Adrian.

"Do you know what kind?" asked Brother John.

10 "Halibut," said Brother Adrian. "I saw them unloading it."

"Do you like halibut?" asked Brother John.

None of the others answered, so Brother Quintillian knew that the question had been addressed to him. But he kept his eyes closed. His knees ached from the hours and hours of kneeling, and though he had not eaten or drunk all day he did not feel hungry. He was very tired, and he was sorry for the others, who were having to be nice to him. He would try to meet their charity by lightening them of the burden of courtesy, by pretending to doze.

"No," said Brother Gilbert from across the room, "he is not at all fond 20 of halibut."

"What does he like?" said Brother John eagerly.

"How does he like it prepared?" asked Brother Adrian.

"Well," said Brother Gilbert, who was the epicure of the community, "he prefers a bouillabaisse, as I remember."

"Oh Gilbert, we'll never be able to get that for him by dinner-time," said Brother John. "What can we do for him?"

"No, I suppose not," said Brother Gilbert. "He likes finnan haddie."

"Can you prepare it?" asked Brother John.

"He has fasted since last night," said Brother Adrian. "We must be 30 careful."

"If I had some," said Brother Gilbert, "I could prepare a mild sauce for it. And toast."

"Alphonse, you drive," said Brother John. "Go down right away to Spenger's and get a pound of finnan haddie. Anything else, Gilbert?"

"A jar of capers. But are you sure he wants to eat?"

"I'll go," said Brother Alphonsus, and left.

"He has not eaten for nearly twenty-four hours," said Brother Adrian. "He has been praying all day."

"A great humiliation," said Brother John.

40 They fell silent.

Brother Quintillian felt no hunger, least of all for finnan haddie. He wished only to be left alone. But he did not want to reject their kindness, so he said nothing.

"We should leave him to sleep a little," said Brother John.

George P. Elliott   273

"Yes," said Brother Adrian. "Gil, turn off the radio and come along."

"I must phone my sister before dinner," said Brother Gilbert.

"How is she getting along?" asked Brother Adrian.

"Very well. She's out of the cast now and her ribs are quite mended."

"I'm glad to hear that. Wasn't there a woman killed in that accident?"

"Yes, in the same car. A friend of hers."

"What was her name?"

"Sylvia Carson."

"Pity."

"A great humiliation," said Brother John mostly to himself as they 10 went out the door.

Like a sea anemone after the tidepool falls still he slowly began to unfold. Sylvia Carson, Sylvia Carson. The name had been floating around during the past month, since the accident. He had some other association to it. He spent several minutes uncovering his recollection—that good-looking fellow he'd seen at so many concerts and recitals, a chemist to whose house he had gone a few months before with a mutual friend. He had never met the wife, Sylvia. She had not been a lover of music. Duane? Dan? Duke? Dick, that was it, Dick Carson. Poor fellow, to have his wife killed like that. He was probably not a believer; he would need friends now. Poor 20 man.

Brother Quintillian made his way circuitously to the refrigerator, where he drank a glass of milk and put an apple in his pocket; went to his room to change into his black suit and select an album of records; and slipped out the side door. He did not feel weak any longer, and though he was sorry to disappoint the brothers who were getting and preparing the finnan haddie for him he could not have eaten it. He felt he should go immediately.

III

It took Brother Quintillian an hour to find Dick's place. The road was all uphill, and he got lost. His sore legs hardly obeyed him. 30

As he turned a corner among pines he saw the little house there below him. He sat on the bank to rest a bit and eat the apple—he did not want to be trembling with fatigue when he came to the door—and looked curiously at the house. There was a built-in ladder by the carport for the use of anyone who wanted to sun-bathe on the flat roof. The windows went from floor to ceiling; the wall that he could see was nearly solid with window. He was looking at the northern, back side of the house; he could see directly into the two bedrooms, one of which was tidy and perfect, the other rumpled and used. The only chair was a piece of yellow canvas art-

274 Stories

fully slung upon an iron frame, an angel-wing chair. The floor of the house was a slab of concrete only a few inches higher than the ground. The aim of all this, Brother Quintillian had read, was to be functional and to promote indoor-outdoor living. Brother Quintillian was an indoors man himself. He enjoyed the outdoors once in a while, on a beautiful day like this or in the well-ordered gardens of St. Anselm's, but the notion of mixing the two, of making little of the distinction between them, astonished him. He had no theory about this indoor-outdoor business except that it was very sophisticated; savages, he was sure, would never think of
10 doing it (nature is man's enemy and only a sophisticate would doubt it). He saw Dick come into the white, mechanized kitchen, take pans off the wall and spoons from a drawer, and open a can. He threw away his apple core, picked up the album he had laid beside him on the bank, and went down the road to this solitary house.

He saw Dick glance up at him and scowl; his heart sank within him. But Brother Quintillian made a great point of maintaining an outward appearance of confidence and good manners. He went directly to the kitchen door, smiling, and nodded to Dick. With elaborate reluctance Dick wiped his hands and opened the door.
20 "I am Brother Quintillian. You may not remember me."

"I remember you."

Brother Quintillian had intended to say something consoling to Dick, but this tone of his clearly made it impossible.

"I brought some records which I hoped you would find interesting."

"Okay. Go in front and sit down. I'll be along when I'm through eating."

Manners required Brother Quintillian to say something about how he hoped he wasn't intruding. But it was clear that he was intruding and that Dick, if asked, would say that he was; he felt it more important to stay
30 than to be polite. "Thank you, I will," he said, and went into the living room.

Not living room—living area. Dick was cooking in the kitchen area of the same room, on the other side of a partial wall. Behind a full-length green hanging, as Brother Quintillian saw through an opening in it, was one of the sleeping areas. The other sleeping area, he remembered having seen, had four walls and a door, and the bathroom of course did too, though the outer wall of the bathroom was a pane of frosted glass. Brother Quintillian took his seat on an odd but comfortable wooden chair, glad for a few minutes of freedom in which to look about him. There was not
40 even an atavistic fireplace in the room, just areas of white wall. There were three low bookshelves and a narrow one that reached to the ceiling. On the walls hung three abstract paintings and a primitive mask with corn husks for hair. In the center of the room stood a glass table on iron legs, low, large, free-form (that is to say, kidney-shaped); to his distress, on the

wall in the darkest corner just above the telephone, he saw an exquisite icon.

"Will you have something to eat?" Dick said around the corner, still in a churly voice.

"No, no thanks."

"It's not much of a dinner, but you're welcome."

"No, no, you just go ahead. I'll be happy to wait."

And he was happy to wait, for in trying to understand what view of things could produce this amazing house and what effect living in it would have on a man's soul he quite forgot his own concern. It was not that his doubt had been trivial or his experience that morning superficial; quite the contrary. But he had exhausted for the time his capacity for spontaneous remorse; wonder at this house quite made him feel happy, allowing him to forget what he could hardly bear to remember—his own great sin.

He heard Dick serving himself up his meal, the spoon angry in the saucepan. "How dreadful," thought Brother Quintillian, "to have no God to submit to. How angry he must be with nothing to do but blame chance, idiot chance. How afraid." Then Brother Quintillian did something that a man of his delicacy, his scruples could not have done in his situation without the strongest prompting, and he felt almost scandalized at himself for doing it: he tiptoed to the record player, adjusted it without Dick's permission or knowledge, and started playing the records he had brought. The records contained an ordinary of the Ambrosian Mass chanted by monks in a twelfth-century monastery. Technically the records were excellent, and the machine was superb. The thin voices, sepulchral and echoing and very pure, seemed to Brother Quintillian in some way not entirely foreign to this angular, stark house.

When the first side was played, Dick appeared at the end of the dividing wall, plate in hand, and stood listening attentively. He tossed his forelock back with a sweeping motion of the head and his body was not so slouched over as it had been. His fair eyes, dulled when Brother Quintillian had come in, were bright and quick.

"Hey," said Dick between bites, "that's terrific singing. That's an Ambrosian ordinary, isn't it?"

"Yes, yes, in what is believed to be its purest form." Brother Quintillian stuttered a little in his pleasure.

"You get that quaver?" said Dick. "Lord, what technique."

"Yes indeed. One has to write to Europe for the album."

"I think I'll get it. How much they stick you?"

"I'm ashamed to say. Three-and-a-half dollars a record. I can get the address for you if you like."

"Sure, do that. Let's cut it till I'm through eating. I want to really listen."

"Certainly, certainly." Brother Quintillian stopped the machine.

"Hey Brother," Dick called from back of his wall again, "tell me something about those records. That's the best singing I've heard in months."

Brother Quintillian went to the end of the cooking area. Dick was sitting at a leaf that dropped from the wall.

"Well, I've done a little work in the modes of the chants. I'm no expert, nothing like one, you understand, just an amateur.—Pardon me, what a convenient kitchen you have here. I've never seen one more compact. They're usually so crowded."

10 "It's all right. It doesn't make the glutenburger taste any better."

"Ah." There was a brief silence. "Would you tell me, what is glutenburger?"

"Ersatz meat. It's all right with enough ketchup. Have some."

"Just a bite."

"Here's a fork. Isn't it poor?"

"Not very good. Why do you eat it?"

"Some sort of nutritional trouble. The doctors haven't been able to isolate it. I thought I'd experiment around with diet."

"Any luck?" asked Brother Quintillian smiling.

20 "None. If a man hasn't got an appetite he might as well eat health food. Brother, you're sure you've had dinner?"

"No, thank you, no dinner. I fasted today."

"Is that so?" said Dick looking at him with interest. "Nothing to eat at all?"

"When I decided to come up to see you—it's quite a climb—I drank a glass of milk and ate an apple."

"Is that so? I haven't tried fasting yet. Just one day?"

"Usually. It depends."

"Do you find it does you good?"

30 "I think it does. I think so very sincerely. I believe I shall do it more often from now on."

"Is that so?" Dick was through with his meal. "I think I'll try it myself."

"Pardon me, but I am not sure you understand. It's not just doing without food."

"I know about fasting," said Dick rather heavily. "I think I'll try it all the same. Maybe it'll help me sleep. I sleep on something hard, you know."

"Indeed?"

But Dick was annoyed with himself for all these confidences he was making. "Let's go listen to those records."

40 In the passageway there was some confusion because neither of these fastidious men wanted to touch the other and neither wanted to go first. Finally Brother Quintillian, guestlike and mumbling apologetically, went ahead. He started to seat himself, but Dick told him to go put on the records.

George P. Elliott 277

They listened for forty-five minutes with complete attention. They did not speak, but looked at each other only once or twice, at some particularly impressive passage.

When it was over Brother Quintillian turned the machine off, and Dick leaned back in his chair shaking his head slowly.

"What musicianship," he said several times. "What musicianship."

"You liked it?" asked Brother Quintillian eagerly. "I am delighted."

"Perfection of technique. Is this the only recording they've made?"

"I'm afraid it is."

"What a pity it's all locked up in there." 10

"Maybe someday . . . ," Brother Quintillian said spreading his hands. "The monks were directed by Burckhardt, of course."

"Never heard of him."

"Oscar Burckhardt. He had a theory of phrasing which he developed from an annotated manuscript he found in Yugoslavia. He instructed this monastery in his method; they found it very difficult because it was so different from their own tradition. This is the result."

"A sound scholar," said Dick. "A damned sound man. The greatest pre-Baroque music I ever heard."

"Doesn't it suggest the arches of some of the Lombardy Romanesque 20 cathedrals? The same austere intensity?"

"No," said Dick brusquely. "I don't have anything to do with cathedrals."

"Just the lines," said Brother Quintillian fluttering his hands.

An uncomfortable silence settled upon them.

IV

"I'll keep him at arm's length," thought Dick to himself. "He's trying to creep up on me with these cathedrals and Masses. He's a pleasant enough guy, but he can take a hint. I wonder why he came up to see me. Well, maybe I can learn something from him."

"Pardon me," said Brother Quintillian, "perhaps I had better go now. 30 I really came just to play the records for you."

"Stick around," said Dick. "You've only been here an hour or so."

"We must have another musical evening soon."

"Sure, I've got a honey of a recording of Monteverdi; setting of a sestina by Petrarch. What form! It makes those lieder-writers look sick, for getting the most out of the words."

"I believe you," said Brother Quintillian. "I look forward to hearing it. Tell me, that icon over there? . . ."

"Sylvia's. She got it in Kodiak on a trip she took before the war. Sentimental, nineteenth-century stuff. Let's play chess." 40

278   Stories

"Oh yes. Still, it has its own charm. Chess? Oh dear, I'm not very good at it."

They set up the board and began an earnest game, the awkwardness between them gradually dissipating. In the midst of contemplating which of the three weak moves it would be best for him to make, Dick spoke in a musing voice, not raising his head. "What do you know about the history of fasting?"

"You mean in the Church?"

"No."

10 "It's mentioned frequently in the Old Testament."

"Anything else?"

"It is usually connected with purification."

"I guess I'll take your bishop," said Dick.

"You oblige me to take your knight," said Brother Quintillian.

"Now what?—There's often something to these old customs."

"Wisdom of the folk?"

"A sound physiochemical basis, like the use of bread-mold poultices generations before the discovery of penicillin. Of course, there's a lot of crap mixed up with it too. Superstition and that sort of stuff."

20 "As there is with science."

"For instance?" asked Dick still in a brooding voice.

"Some of the mental healers."

"All of them. There's no experimental basis for their theories. They're about as scientific as a Christian Science practitioner or a piece of the true Cross."

"Dianetics," said Brother Quintillian.

"It's a shame."

"Pardon me, if you take that pawn I'll be able to capture your queen in two moves."

30 "Thanks. I'll take it back if you don't mind."

"Not at all. It would be a pity to spoil a good game with a trivial error."

"A trivial error but I lose my queen," said Dick, and lapsed into silence.

After the game Brother Quintillian stood up energetically, thanked Dick for his hospitality, took up his records, and said good-bye.

"Wait a minute," said Dick, "I'll run you down the hill."

"I won't hear of it," said Brother Quintillian. "It's only a few minutes' walk."

"You haven't eaten today. Your blood sugar level is low. It wouldn't

40 be good for you."

"No, please, I beg you. It's a lovely night out."

"All the more reason for me to go out into it. I'm a safe driver."

"I had no thought. . . . Thank you very much."

As they were winding slowly down the hill toward St. Anselm's, Dick spoke. "You know, I'm enjoying this drive more than any I've taken for a long time."

"Why how extraordinary. What do you mean?"

"I'm not in a hurry," said Dick with uncalled-for energy. "I'm under no pressure. Sometimes I've thought that if I could just sit at home and never have to go out I'd be all right."

"Have you ever tested your theory, just stayed home for awhile?"

"Yes."

"Were you all right?"

"No. I could hardly wait to get back in my car again." 10

"I understand," said Brother Quintillian. "I understand very well."

At St. Anselm's, Dick parked and turned off the motor and the lights.

"Remember that three-voice Kyrie towards the end?"

"Like this?" said Brother Quintillian and hummed a few notes. "In unison?"

"Yes. I never heard anything so pure in my life."

"True, true."

For a few moments in the dark car side by side each was freed from his trouble, silently joined with the other in the memory of those thin and disciplined voices which celebrated by the very renunciation of overtone 20 and separateness, by a perfect weakness, their fearful mortality.

"Good night," they said to each other in the dark, "good-bye."

V

He drove back to his house feeling more nearly at peace with himself than he had for some time. As he walked from the carport toward the front door a sighing of wind in the trees drew his attention upward. It was a cloudless night, rare for Oakland; the stars were shining brightly. He could remember the names of only a few of them, of only, he discovered by counting, fifteen of them. He sighed as he thought of the great pleasure it had given him to study astronomy in college. What's the point of all that studying if you forget most of it? What use is it? Just a game. Still, learning 30 had been a great pleasure and always would be. Not the keenest pleasure he had known, but the most enduring. He turned off the lights in the main room and prepared for bed. On the stand beside the bed lay the current issue of a scientific journal; it contained a symposium on Einstein's unified field theory. He had read all the articles once and some he intended to read again, but though he picked it up he decided against reading it now. He turned off the light and lay on his back thinking.

The library lights were still burning, and from the student dormitories drifted radio music. He wanted to preserve intact the equanimity he had gained so recently and so tenuously; he would have to avoid any stray student or some Brother tardily walking in the garden at his offices. He got to his room safely enough, locked the door, and did not turn on the light. There were duties he knew he should be attending to, community duties, the daily duties of every Brother, the duties of a sinner. But he could not have performed any routine task well or profitably to himself, and he did not feel full of sin at this moment but rather full of wonder and joy. A holy wonder at the mysterious ways of God that had brought him thus to a deeper love for God by means of doubt and humiliation; joy in 10 the thought of God's mercy and God's perfection. He undressed and lay on his bed naked to God. His heart beat fast, his breath labored, and tears filled his eyes. There was pressed from his deepest feeling a prayer of thanksgiving.

The theory that would reconcile the great contradiction in physics, that would include in itself all the known data, that would harmonize in a few utter symbols all inferior theories—that he must try to understand. He knew it would be the crown of years of hard work, and he knew he might never achieve his high goal. But he remembered the labor he had performed to grasp the quantum theory in a seminar he had taken and the 20 final reward of it, and he knew, lying on his bed, that for him there could be no other full satisfaction in his life but to set out on that vague and perhaps unattainable and perhaps illusory quest for an understanding and an explanation of the limit of things. To be sure, he knew that even if he should attain this comprehension he would not be able to hold it long— that the arduous studies by which he would approach his goal would be too much for him to hold all at once in his mind, that the conclusion based on these studies would slip from him quickly. Quickly, but not completely, for though he would be able to reproduce the theory no better than he could now reproduce the quantum theory still he knew that once he had 30 grasped it he would feel a security and solidity that nothing could take from him, and that even if he failed finally to grasp it he yet would feel that he had been engaged in the highest enterprise of all.

The prayer that issued in a tumultuous whisper from his mouth was extravagant and ungrammatical at times, but true; it was his own and it meant his thanksgiving. The words were not, like the Hail Mary, accurately placed and polished by centuries of use; but neither were they, like the beads he had told in the chapel that day, words strung on a cord of fear. In half an hour he was empty, empty and weary. He was ready to sleep, but the bed was too soft. How could gratitude to God survive such 40 luxury as a warm, soft bed?

Even with a board between the mattress and the springs the bed was not hard enough. He did not quite see how lying on a hard surface could

George P. Elliott   281

promote sound sleep; there was some physiochemical basis to it, no doubt, possibly connected with the tonus of the striated muscles. But he was not interested in speculating on it now; he was sleepy, and content that he had made up his mind at last about his life, about his high and private quest. He spread out a blanket on the floor, on the side of the bed away from the window, stretched himself out on it without a pillow, and covered himself with another blanket. His feet stuck out, but he didn't care.

In his high and narrow cell, with the window blind pulled tight, on the concrete floor, he rolled himself up in a single blanket and lay on his side, glad of the cold and hardness, as happy as he would be.   10

1929-
DAN
JACOBSON * The Zulu and the Zeide

Old man Grossman was worse than a nuisance. He was a source of constant anxiety and irritation; he was a menace to himself and to the passing motorists into whose path he would step, to the children in the streets whose games he would break up, sending them flying, to the householders who at night would approach him with clubs in their hands, fearing him a burglar; he was a butt and a jest to the African servants, who would tease him on street corners.

It was impossible to keep him in the house. He would take any opportunity to slip out—a door left open meant that he was on the streets, a window unlatched was a challenge to his agility, a walk in the park was as 10 much a game of hide-and-seek as a walk. The old man's health was good, physically; he was quite spry, and he could walk far, and he could jump and duck if he had to. And all his physical activity was put to only one purpose: to running away. It was a passion for freedom that the old man might have been said to have, could anyone have seen what joy there could have been for him in wandering aimlessly about the streets, in sitting footsore on pavements, in entering other people's homes, in stumbling behind advertisement hoardings across undeveloped building plots, in toiling up the stairs of fifteen-story blocks of flats in which he had no business, in being brought home by large young policemen who winked at 20 Harry Grossman, the old man's son, as they gently hauled his father out of their flying-squad cars.

"He's always been like this," Harry would say, when people asked him about his father. And when they smiled and said, "Always?" Harry would say, "Always. I know what I'm talking about. He's my father, and I know what he's like. He gave my mother enough gray hairs before her time. All he knew was to run away."

Harry's reward would come when the visitors would say, "Well, at least you're being as dutiful to him as anyone can be."

It was a reward that Harry always refused. "Dutiful? What can you do? There's nothing else you can do." Harry Grossman knew that there was nothing else he could do. Dutifulness had been his habit of life; it had had to be, having the sort of father he had, and the strain of duty had made
10 him abrupt and begrudging. He even carried his thick, powerful shoulders curved inwards, to keep what he had to himself. He was a thick-set, bunch-faced man, with large bones, and short, jabbing gestures; he was in the prime of life, and he would point at the father from whom he had inherited his strength, and on whom the largeness of bone showed now only as so much extra leanness that the clothing had to cover, and say, "You see him? Do you know what he once did? My poor mother saved enough money to send him from the old country to South Africa; she bought clothes for him, and a ticket, and she sent him to her brother, who was already here. He was going to make enough money to bring me out, and
20 my mother and my brother, all of us. But on the boat from Bremen to London he met some other Jews who were going to South America, and they said to him, 'Why are you going to South Africa? It's a wild country, the savages will eat you. Come to South America and you'll make a fortune.' So in London he exchanges his ticket. And we don't hear from him for six months. Six months later he gets a friend to write to my mother asking her please to send him enough money to pay for his ticket back to the old country—he's dying in the Argentine, the Spaniards are killing him, he says, and he must come home. So my mother borrows from her brother to bring him back again. Instead of a fortune he brought her a
30 new debt, and that was all."

But Harry was dutiful, how dutiful his friends had reason to see again when they would urge him to try sending the old man to a home for the aged. "No," Harry would reply, his features moving heavily and reluctantly to a frown, a pout, as he showed how little the suggestion appealed to him. "I don't like the idea. Maybe one day when he needs medical attention all the time I'll feel differently about it, but not now, not now. He wouldn't like it, he'd be unhappy. We'll look after him as long as we can. It's a job. It's something you've got to do."

More eagerly Harry would go back to a recital of the old man's past.
40 "He couldn't even pay for his own passage out. I had to pay the loan back. We came out together—my mother wouldn't let him go by himself again, and I had to pay off her brother who advanced the money for us. I was a boy—what was I?—sixteen, seventeen, but I paid for his passage, and my own, and my mother's and then my brother's. It took me a long

Dan Jacobson 283

time, let me tell you. And then my troubles with him weren't over." Harry even reproached his father for his myopia; he could clearly enough remember his chagrin when shortly after their arrival in South Africa, after it had become clear that Harry would be able to make his way in the world and be a support to the whole family, the old man—who at that time had not really been so old—had suddenly, almost dramatically, grown so short-sighted that he had been almost blind without the glasses that Harry had had to buy for him. And Harry could remember too how he had then made a practice of losing the glasses or breaking them with the greatest frequency, until it had been made clear to him that he was no longer expected 10 to do any work. "He doesn't do that any more. When he wants to run away now he sees to it that he's wearing his glasses. That's how he's always been. Sometimes he recognizes me, at other times, when he doesn't want to, he just doesn't know who I am."

What Harry said about his father sometimes failing to recognize him was true. Sometimes the old man would call out to his son, when he would see him at the end of a passage, "Who are you?" Or he would come upon Harry in a room and demand of him, "What do you want in my house?"

"Your house?" Harry would say, when he felt like teasing the old man. "Your house?" 20

"Out of my house!" the old man would shout back.

"Your house? Do you call this your house?" Harry would reply, smiling at the old man's fury.

Harry was the only one in the house who talked to the old man, and then he did not so much talk to him, as talk of him to others. Harry's wife was a dim and silent woman, crowded out by her husband and the large-boned sons like himself that she had borne him, and she would gladly have seen the old man in an old-age home. But her husband had said no, so she put up with the old man, though for herself she could see no possible better end for him than a period of residence in a home for aged Jews 30 which she had once visited, and which had impressed her most favorably with its glass and yellow brick, and noiseless rubber tiles in its corridors, its secluded grassed grounds, and the uniforms worn by the attendants to the establishment. But she put up with the old man; she did not talk to him. The grandchildren had nothing to do with their grandfather—they were busy at school, playing rugby and cricket, they could hardly speak Yiddish, and they were embarrassed by him in front of their friends; and when the grandfather did take any notice of them it was only to call them Boers and *goyim* and *shkotzim*° in sudden quavering rages which did not disturb them at all. 40

The house itself was a big single-storied place of brick, with a corru-

---

39. *shkotzim,* a derogatory term for non-Jewish boys or youths; derived from the Hebrew word meaning blemish or abomination.

gated iron roof above and a wide stoep all round, Harry Grossman had bought years before, and in the continual rebuilding the suburb was undergoing it was beginning to look old-fashioned. But it was solid and prosperous, and within doors curiously masculine in appearance, like the house of a widower. The furniture was of the heaviest African woods, dark, and built to last, the passages were lined with bare linoleum, and the few pictures on the walls, big brown and gray mezzotints in heavy frames, had not been looked at for years. The servants were both men, large ignored Zulus who did their work and kept up the brown gleam of the furniture.

10 It was from this house that old man Grossman tried to escape. He fled through the doors and the windows and out into the wide sunlit streets of the town in Africa, where the blocks of flats were encroaching upon the single-storied houses behind their gardens. And in these streets he wandered.

It was Johannes, one of the Zulu servants, who suggested a way of dealing with old man Grossman. He brought to the house one afternoon Paulus, whom he described as his "brother." Harry Grossman knew enough to know that "brother" in this context could mean anything from the son of one's mother to a friend from a neighboring *kraal*, but by the 20 speech that Johannes made on Paulus's behalf he might indeed have been the latter's brother. Johannes had to speak for Paulus, for Paulus knew no English. Paulus was a "raw boy," as raw as a boy could possibly come. He was a muscular, mustached and bearded African, with pendulous earlobes showing the slits in which the tribal plugs had once hung; and on his feet he wore sandals the soles of which were cut from old motorcar tires, the thongs from red inner tubing. He wore neither hat nor socks, but he did have a pair of khaki shorts which were too small for him, and a shirt without any buttons. Buttons would in any case have been of no use, for the shirt could never have closed over his chest. He swelled magnificently out 30 of his clothing, and above, there was a head carried well back, so that his beard, which had been trained to grow in two sharp points from his chin, bristled ferociously forward under his melancholy and almost mandarin-like mustache. When he smiled, as he did once or twice during Johannes's speech, he showed his white, even teeth, but for the most part he stood looking rather shyly to the side of Harry Grossman's head, with his hands behind his back and his bare knees bent a little forward, as if to show how little he was asserting himself, no matter what his "brother" might have been saying about him.

His expression did not change when Harry said that it seemed hopeless, 40 that Paulus was too raw, and Johannes explained what the baas had just said. He nodded agreement when Johannes explained to him that the baas said that it was a pity that he knew no English. But whenever Harry looked at him, he smiled, not ingratiatingly, but simply smiling above his beard, as though saying, "Try me." Then he looked grave again as Johannes expatiated on his virtues. Johannes pleaded for his "brother." He said that the baas knew that he, Johannes, was a good boy. Would he, then, recommend to the baas a boy who was not a good boy too? The baas could see for himself, Johannes said, that Paulus was not one of these town boys, these street loafers; he was a good boy, come straight from the *kraal*. He was not a thief or a drinker. He was strong, he was a hard worker, he was clean, and he could be as gentle as a woman. If he, Johannes, were not telling the truth about all these things, then he deserved to be chased away. If Paulus failed in any single respect, then he, Johannes, would vol- untarily leave the service of the baas, because he had said untrue things to the baas. But if the baas believed him, and gave Paulus his chance, then he, Johannes, would teach Paulus all the things of the house and the garden, so that Paulus would be useful to the baas in ways other than the particular task for which he was asking the baas to hire him. And, rather daringly, Johannes said that it did not matter so much if Paulus knew no English, because the old baas, the *oubaas*, knew no English either.

It was as something in the nature of a joke—almost a joke against his father—that Harry Grossman gave Paulus his chance. For Paulus was given his chance. He was given a room in the servants' quarters in the back yard, into which he brought a tin trunk painted red and black, a roll of blankets, and a guitar with a picture of a cowboy on the back. He was given a houseboy's outfit of blue denim blouse and shorts, with red piping round the edges, into which he fitted, with his beard and his physique, like a king in exile in some pantomime. He was given his food three times a day, after the white people had eaten, a bar of soap every week, cast-off clothing at odd intervals, and the sum of one pound five shillings per week, five shillings of which he took, the rest being left at his request, with the baas, as savings. He had a free afternoon once a week, and he was allowed to entertain not more than two friends at any one time in his room. And in all the particulars that Johannes had enumerated, Johannes was proved reliable. Paulus was not one of these town boys, these street loafers. He did not steal or drink, he was clean and he was honest and hard-working. And he could be as gentle as a woman.

It took Paulus some time to settle down to his job; he had to conquer not only his own shyness and strangeness in the new house filled with strange people—let alone the city, which, since taking occupation of his room, he had hardly dared to enter—but also the hostility of old man Grossman, who took immediate fright at Paulus and redoubled his efforts to get away from the house upon Paulus's entry into it. As it happened, the first result of this persistence on the part of the old man was that Paulus was able to get the measure of the job, for he came to it with a willingness of spirit that the old man could not vanquish, but could only teach. Paulus had been given no instructions, he had merely been told to see that the old man did not get himself into trouble, and after a few days of bewilderment Paulus found his way. He simply went along with the old man.

At first he did so cautiously, following the old man at a distance, for he knew the other had no trust in him. But later he was able to follow the old man openly; still later he was able to walk side by side with him, and the old man did not try to escape from him. When old man Grossman went out, Paulus went too, and there was no longer any need for the doors and windows to be watched, or the police to be telephoned. The young bearded Zulu and the old bearded Jew from Lithuania walked together
10 in the streets of the town that was strange to them both; together they looked over the fences of the large gardens and into the shining foyers of the blocks of flats; together they stood on the pavements of the main arterial roads and watched the cars and trucks rush between the tall buildings; together they walked in the small, sandy parks, and when the old man was tired Paulus saw to it that he sat on a bench and rested. They could not sit on the bench together, for only whites were allowed to sit on the benches, but Paulus would squat on the ground at the old man's feet and wait until he judged the old man had rested long enough, before moving on again. Together they stared into the windows of the suburban shops, and
20 though neither of them could read the signs outside the shops, the advertisements on billboards, the traffic signs at the side of the road, Paulus learned to wait for the traffic lights to change from red to green before crossing a street, and together they stared at the Coca-Cola girls and the advertisements for beer and the cinema posters. On a piece of cardboard which Paulus carried in the pocket of his blouse Harry had had one of his sons print the old man's name and address, and whenever Paulus was uncertain of the way home, he would approach an African or a friendly-looking white man and show him the card, and try his best to follow the instructions, or at least the gesticulations which were all of the answers of
30 the white men that meant anything to him. But there were enough Africans to be found, usually, who were more sophisticated than himself, and though they teased him for his "rawness" and for holding the sort of job he had, they helped him too. And neither Paulus nor old man Grossman was aware that when they crossed a street hand-in-hand, as they sometimes did when the traffic was particularly heavy, there were white men who averted their eyes from the sight of this degradation, which could come upon a white man when he was old and senile and dependent.

Paulus knew only Zulu, the old man knew only Yiddish, so there was no language in which they could talk to one another. But they talked all
40 the same. They both explained, commented and complained to each other of the things they saw around them, and often they agreed with one another, smiling and nodding their heads and explaining again with their hands what each happened to be talking about. They both seemed to believe that they were talking about the same things, and often they un-

doubtedly were, when they lifted their heads sharply to see an aeroplane cross the blue sky between two buildings, or when they reached the top of a steep road and turned to look back the way they had come, and saw below them the clean impervious towers of the city thrust nakedly against the sky in brand-new piles of concrete and glass and brick facing. Then down they would go again, among the houses and the gardens where the beneficent climate encouraged both palms and oak trees to grow indiscriminately among each other—as they did in the garden of the house to which, in the evenings, Paulus and old man Grossman would eventually return. 10

In and about the house Paulus soon became as indispensable to the old man as he was on their expeditions out of it. Paulus dressed him and bathed him and trimmed his beard, and when the old man woke distressed in the middle of the night it would be for Paulus that he would call—"*Der schwarzer*," he would shout (for he never learned Paulus's name), "*vo's der schwarzer*"—and Paulus would change his sheets and pajamas and put him back to bed again. "Baas *Zeide*," Paulus called the old man, picking the Yiddish word for grandfather from the children of the house.

And that was something that Harry Grossman told everyone of. For 20 Harry persisted in regarding the arrangement as a kind of joke, and the more the arrangement succeeded the more determinedly did he try to spread the joke, so that it should be a joke not only against his father but a joke against Paulus too. It had been a joke that his father should be looked after by a raw Zulu; it was going to be a joke that the Zulu was successful at it. "Baas *Zeide*! That's what *der schwarzer* calls him—have you ever heard the like of it? And you should see the two of them, walking about in the streets hand-in-hand like two schoolgirls. Two clever ones, *der schwarzer* and my father going for a promenade, and between them, I tell you, you wouldn't be able to find out what day of the week or what 30 time of day it is."

And when people said, "Still that Paulus seems a very good boy," Harry would reply:

"Why shouldn't he be? With all his knowledge, are there so many better jobs that he'd be able to find? He keeps the old man happy—very good, very nice, but don't forget that that's what he's paid to do. What does he know any better to do, a simple Kaffir from the *kraal*? He knows he's got a good job, and he'd be a fool if he threw it away. Do you think," Harry would say, and this too would insistently be part of the joke, "if I had nothing else to do with my time I wouldn't be able to make the old 40 man happy?" Harry would look about his sitting room, where the floorboards bore the weight of his furniture, or when they sat on the stoep he would measure with his glance the spacious garden aloof from the street beyond the hedge. "I've got other things to do. And I had other things to do, plenty of them, all my life, and not only for myself." What these things were that he had had to do all his life would send him back to his joke. "No, I think the old man has just found his level in *der schwarzer*—and I don't think *der schwarzer* could cope with anything else."

Harry teased the old man to his face too, about his "black friend," and he would ask his father what he would do if Paulus went away; once he jokingly threatened to send the Zulu away. But the old man didn't believe the threat, for Paulus was in the house when the threat was made, and the old man simply left his son and went straight to Paulus's room,
10 and sat there with Paulus for security. Harry did not follow him; he would never have gone into any of his servants' rooms, least of all that of Paulus. For though he made a joke of him to others, to Paulus himself Harry always spoke gruffly, unjokingly, with no patience. On that day he had merely shouted after the old man, "Another time he won't be there."

Yet it was strange to see how Harry Grossman would always be drawn to the room in which he knew his father and Paulus to be. Night after night he came into the old man's bedroom when Paulus was dressing or undressing the old man; almost as often Harry stood in the steamy, untidy bathroom when the old man was being bathed. At these times he
20 hardly spoke, he offered no explanation of his presence. He stood dourly and silently in the room, in his customary powerful and begrudging stance, with one hand clasping the wrist of the other and both supporting his waist, and he watched Paulus at work. The backs of Paulus's hands were smooth and black and hairless, they were paler on the palms and at the fingernails, and they worked deftly about the body of the old man, who was submissive under the ministrations of the other. At first Paulus had sometimes smiled at Harry while he worked, with his straightforward, even smile in which there was no invitation to a complicity in patronage but rather an encouragement to Harry to draw forward. But after the
30 first few evenings of this work that Harry had watched, Paulus no longer smiled at his master. And while he worked Paulus could not restrain himself, even under Harry's stare, from talking a soft, continuous flow of Zulu, to encourage the old man and to exhort him to be helpful and to express his pleasure in how well the work was going. When Paulus would at last wipe the gleaming soap flakes from his dark hands he would sometimes, when the old man was tired, stoop low and with a laugh pick up the old man and carry him easily down the passage to his bedroom. Harry would follow; he would stand in the passage and watch the burdened, bare-footed Zulu until the door of his father's room closed behind
40 them both.

Only once did Harry wait on such an evening for Paulus to reappear from his father's room. Paulus had already come out, had passed him in the narrow passage, and had already subduedly said, "Good night, baas," before Harry called suddenly:

'Hey! Wait!"

"Baas," Paulus said, turning his head. Then he came quickly to Harry. "Baas," he said again, puzzled and anxious to know why his baas, who so rarely spoke to him, should suddenly have called him like this, at the end of the day, when his work was over.

Harry waited again before speaking, waited long enough for Paulus to say, "Baas?" once more, and to move a little closer, and to lift his head for a moment before letting it drop respectfully down.

"The *oubaas* was tired tonight," Harry said. "Where did you take him? What did you do with him?" 10

"Baas?" Paulus said quickly. Harry's tone was so brusque that the smile Paulus gave asked for no more than a moment's remission of the other's anger.

But Harry went on loudly, "You heard what I said. What did you do with him that he looked so tired?"

"Baas—I—" Paulus was flustered, and his hands beat in the air for a moment, but with care, so that he would not touch his baas. "Please, baas." He brought both hands to his mouth, closing it forcibly. He flung his hands away. "Johannes," he said with relief, and he had already taken the first step down the passage to call his interpreter. 20

"No!" Harry called. "You mean you don't understand what I say? I know you don't," Harry shouted, though in fact he had forgotten until Paulus had reminded him. The sight of Paulus's startled, puzzled, and guilty face before him filled him with a lust to see this man, this nurse with the face and the figure of a warrior, look more startled, puzzled, and guilty yet; and Harry knew that it could so easily be done, it could be done simply by talking to him in the language he could not understand. "You're a fool," Harry said. "You're like a child. You understand nothing, and it's just as well for you that you need nothing. You'll always be where you are, running to do what the white baas tells you to do. Look 30 how you stand! Do you think I understood English when I came here?" Harry said, and then with contempt, using one of the few Zulu words he knew, "*Hamba!* Go! Do you think I want to see you?"

"*Au*, baas!" Paulus exclaimed in distress. He could not remonstrate; he could only open his hands in a gesture to show that he knew neither the words Harry used, nor in what he had been remiss that Harry should have spoken in such angry tones to him. But Harry gestured him away, and had the satisfaction of seeing Paulus shuffle off like a schoolboy.

Harry was the only person who knew that he and his father had quarreled shortly before the accident that ended the old man's life took place; 40 this was something that Harry was to keep secret for the rest of his life.

Late in the afternoon they quarreled, after Harry had come back from the shop out of which he made his living. Harry came back to find his father wandering about the house, shouting for *der schwarzer*, and his wife complaining that she had already told the old man at least five times that *der schwarzer* was not in the house. It was Paulus's afternoon off.

Harry went to his father, and when his father came eagerly to him, he too told the old man, *"Der schwarzer's* not here." So the old man, with Harry following, turned away and continued going from room to room, peering in through the doors. *"Der schwarzer's* not here," Harry said. "What do you want him for?"

Still the old man ignored him. He went down the passage towards the
10 bedrooms. "What do you want him for?" Harry called after him.

The old man went into every bedroom, still shouting for *der schwarzer*. Only when he was in his own bare bedroom did he look at Harry. "Where's *der schwarzer?*" he asked.

"I've told you ten times I don't know where he is. What do you want him for?"

"I want *der schwarzer.*"

"I know you want him. But he isn't here."

"I want *der schwarzer.*"

"Do you think I haven't heard you? He isn't here."

20 "Bring him to me," the old man said.

"I can't bring him to you. I don't know where he is." Then Harry steadied himself against his own anger. He said quietly, "Tell me what you want. I'll do it for you. I'm here, I can do what *der schwarzer* can do for you."

"Where's *der schwarzer?*"

"I've told you he isn't here," Harry shouted, the angrier for his previous moment's patience. "Why don't you tell me what you want? What's the matter with me—can't you tell me what you want?"

"I want *der schwarzer.*"

30 "Please," Harry said. He threw out his arms towards his father, but the gesture was abrupt, almost as though he were thrusting his father away from him. "Why can't you ask it of me? You can ask me—haven't I done enough for you already? Do you want to go for a walk?—I'll take you for a walk. What do you want? Do you want—do you want—?" Harry could not think what his father might want. "I'll do it," he said. "You don't need *der schwarzer.*"

Then Harry saw that his father was weeping. The old man was standing up and weeping, with his eyes hidden behind the thick glasses that he had to wear; his glasses and his beard made his face a mask of age, as
40 though time had left him nothing but the frame of his body on which the clothing could hang, and this mask of his face above. But Harry knew when the old man was weeping—he had seen him crying too often before, when they had found him at the end of a street after he had wandered away, or even, years earlier, when he had lost another of the miser-

able jobs that seemed to be the only one he could find in a country in which his son had, later, been able to run a good business, drive a large car, own a big house.

"Father," Harry asked, "what have I done? Do you think I've sent *der schwarzer* away?" Harry saw his father turn away, between the narrow bed and the narrow wardrobe. "He's coming—" Harry said, but he could not look at his father's back, he could not look at his father's hollowed neck, on which the hairs that Paulus had clipped glistened above the pale brown discolorations of old age—Harry could not look at the neck turned stiffly away from him while he had to try to promise the re- 10 turn of the Zulu. Harry dropped his hands and walked out of the room.

No one knew how the old man managed to get out of the house and through the front gate without having been seen. But he did manage it, and in the road he was struck down. Only a man on a bicycle struck him down, but it was enough, and he died a few days later in the hospital.

Harry's wife wept, even the grandsons wept; Paulus wept. Harry himself was stony, and his bunched, protuberant features were immovable; they seemed locked upon the bones of his face. A few days after the funeral he called Paulus and Johannes into the kitchen and said to Johannes, "Tell him he must go. His work is finished."   20

Johannes translated for Paulus, and then, after Paulus had spoken, he turned to Harry. "He says, yes baas." Paulus kept his eyes on the ground; he did not look up even when Harry looked directly at him, and Harry knew that this was not out of fear or shyness, but out of courtesy for his master's grief—which was what they could not but be talking of, when they talked of his work.

"Here's his pay." Harry thrust a few notes towards Paulus, who took them in his cupped hands, and retreated.

Harry waited for them to go, but Paulus stayed in the room, and consulted with Johannes in a low voice. Johannes turned to his master. "He 30 says, baas, that the baas still has his savings."

Harry had forgotten about Paulus's savings. He told Johannes that he had forgotten, and that he did not have enough money at the moment, but would bring the money the next day. Johannes translated and Paulus nodded gratefully. Both he and Johannes were subdued by the death there had been in the house.

And Harry's dealings with Paulus were over. He took what was to have been his last look at Paulus, but this look stirred him again against the Zulu. As harshly as he told Paulus that he had to go, so now, implacably, seeing Paulus in the mockery and simplicity of his houseboy's clothing, to 40 feed his anger to the very end, Harry said, "Ask him what he's been saving for. What's he going to do with the fortune he's made?"

Johannes spoke to Paulus and came back with a reply. "He says, baas, that he is saving to bring his wife and children from Zululand to Johannesburg. He is saving, baas," Johannes said, for Harry had not seemed to understand, "to bring his family to this town also."

The two Zulus were bewildered to know why it should have been at that moment that Harry Grossman's clenched, fistlike features should suddenly seem to have fallen from one another, nor why he should have stared with such guilt and despair at Paulus, while he cried, "What else could I have done? I did my best," before the first tears came.

DRAMA

ca. 496-ca. 406 B.C.

SOPHOCLES * Antigone*

The Characters Represented

ANTIGONE
ISMENE
EURYDICE
CREON
HAIMON
TEIRESIAS
A SENTRY
A MESSENGER
CHORUS (*with a leader or* CHORAGOS)
SCENE: *Before the palace of Creon, King of Thebes. A central double door, and two lateral doors. A platform extends the length of the façade, and from this platform three steps lead down into the orchestra, or chorus-ground. Time: dawn of the day after the repulse of the Argive army from the assault on Thebes.*

Prologue

ANTIGONE *and* ISMENE *enter from the central door of the palace.*

ANTIG. Ismenê, dear sister,
You would think that we had already suffered enough
For the curse on Oedipus:
I cannot imagine any grief
That you and I have not gone through. And now—
Have they told you of the new decree of our King Creon?

ISM. I have heard nothing: I know
That two sisters lost two brothers, a double death
In a single hour; and I know that the Argive army
10 Fled in the night; but beyond this, nothing.

ANTIG. I thought so. And that is why I wanted you
To come out here with me. There is something we must do.

ISM. Why do you speak so strangely?

ANTIG. Listen, Ismenê:
Creon buried our brother Eteoclês
With military honours, gave him a soldier's funeral,
And it was right that he should; but Polyneicês,
Who fought as bravely and died as miserably,—
They say that Creon has sworn

---

*An English version by Dudley Fitts and Robert Fitzgerald.

No one shall bury him, no one mourn for him,   20
But his body must lie in the fields, a sweet treasure
For carrion birds to find as they search for food.
That is what they say, and our good Creon is coming here
To announce it publicly; and the penalty—
Stoning to death in the public square!
                              There it is,
And now you can prove what you are:
A true sister, or a traitor to your family.

    ISM.   Antigonê, you are mad! What could I possibly do?
    ANTIG.   You must decide whether you will help me or not.   30
    ISM.   I do not understand you. Help you in what?
    ANTIG.   Ismenê, I am going to bury him. Will you come?
    ISM.   Bury him! You have just said the new law forbids it.
    ANTIG.   He is my brother. And he is your brother, too.
    ISM.   But think of the danger! Think what Creon will do!
    ANTIG.   Creon is not strong enough to stand in my way.
    ISM.   Ah sister!

Oedipus died, everyone hating him
For what his own search brought to light, his eyes
Ripped out by his own hand; and Iocastê died,   40
His mother and wife at once: she twisted the cords
That strangled her life; and our two brothers died,
Each killed by the other's sword. And we are left:
But oh, Antigonê,
Think how much more terrible than these
Our own death would be if we should go against Creon
And do what he has forbidden! We are only women,
We cannot fight with men, Antigonê!
The law is strong, we must give in to the law
In this thing, and in worse. I beg the Dead   50
To forgive me, but I am helpless: I must yield
To those in authority. And I think it is dangerous business
To be always meddling.

    ANTIG.   If that is what you think,
I should not want you, even if you asked to come.
You have made your choice, you can be what you want to be.
But I will bury him; and if I must die,
I say that this crime is holy: I shall lie down
With him in death, and I shall be as dear
To him as he to me.   60
                It is the dead,
Not the living, who make the longest demands:
We die for ever . . .

296   Drama

You may do as you like,
Since apparently the laws of the gods mean nothing to you.
   ISM. They mean a great deal to me; but I have no strength
To break laws that were made for the public good.
   ANTIG. That must be your excuse, I suppose. But as for me,
I will bury the brother I love.
70   ISM.   Antigonê,
I am so afraid for you!
   ANTIG.   You need not be:
You have yourself to consider, after all.
   ISM. But no one must hear of this, you must tell no one!
I will keep it a secret, I promise!
   ANTIG.   Oh tell it! Tell everyone!
Think how they'll hate you when it all comes out
If they learn that you knew about it all the time!
   ISM. So fiery! You should be cold with fear.
80   ANTIG. Perhaps. But I am doing only what I must.
   ISM. But can you do it? I say that you cannot.
   ANTIG. Very well: when my strength gives out, I shall do no more.
   ISM. Impossible things should not be tried at all.
   ANTIG. Go away, Ismenê:
I shall be hating you soon, and the dead will too,
For your words are hateful. Leave me my foolish plan:
I am not afraid of the danger; if it means death,
It will not be the worst of deaths—death without honour.
   ISM. Go then, if you feel that you must.
90 You are unwise,
But a loyal friend indeed to those who love you.
Exit into the palace. ANTIGONE *goes off, left. Enter the* CHORUS.

Párodos
   CHOR. Now the long blade of the sun, lying   [STROPHE 1
Level east to west, touches with glory
Thebes of the Seven Gates. Open, unlidded
Eye of golden day! O marching light
Across the eddy and rush of Dircê's stream,°
Striking the white shields of the enemy
Thrown headlong backward from the blaze of morning!
   CHORAG. Polyneicês their commander
Roused them with windy phrases,
10 He the wild eagle screaming
Insults above our land,

---

   5. **Dircê's stream,** a spring named for Dircê, wife of a king of Thebes. Dircê was cruel to
Antiope, whose sons (sired by Zeus) killed Dircê and cast her body into the spring.

His wings their shields of snow,
His crest their marshalled helms.

    CHOR.   Against our seven gates in a yawning ring   [ANTISTROPHE 1
The famished spears came onward in the night;
But before his jaws were sated with our blood,
Or pinefire took the garland of our towers,
He was thrown back; and as he turned, great Thebes—
No tender victim for his noisy power—
Rose like a dragon behind him, shouting war.   20

    CHORAG.   For God hates utterly
The bray of bragging tongues;
And when he beheld their smiling,
Their swagger of golden helms,
The frown of his thunder blasted
Their first man from our walls.

    CHOR.   We heard his shout of triumph high in the air   [STROPHE 2
Turn to a scream; far out in a flaming arc
He fell with his windy torch, and the earth struck him.
And others storming in fury no less than his   30
Found shock of death in the dusty joy of battle.

    CHORAG.   Seven captains at seven gates
Yielded their clanging arms to the god
That bends the battle-line and breaks it.
These two only, brothers in blood,
Face to face in matchless rage,
Mirroring each the other's death,
Clashed in long combat.

    CHOR.   But now in the beautiful morning of victory   [ANTISTROPHE 2
Let Thebes of the many chariots sing for joy!   40
With hearts for dancing we'll take leave of war:
Our temples shall be sweet with hymns of praise,
And the long night shall echo with our chorus.

SCENE I

    CHORAG.   But now at last our new King is coming:
Creon of Thebes, Menoiceus' son.
In this auspicious dawn of his reign
What are the new complexities
That shifting Fate has woven for him?
What is his counsel? Why has he summoned
The old men to hear him?   50

Enter CREON *from the palace, center. He addresses the* CHORUS *from the top step.*

    CRE.   Gentlemen: I have the honour to inform you that our Ship of State, which recent storms have threatened to destroy, has come safely to harbour at last, guided by the merciful wisdom of Heaven. I have summoned you here this morning because I know that I can depend upon you: your devotion to King Laïos was absolute; you never hesitated in your duty to our late ruler Oedipus; and when Oedipus died, your loyalty was transferred to his children. Unfortunately, as you know, his two sons, the princes Eteoclês and Polyneicês, have killed each other in battle; and I, as the next in blood, have succeeded to the full power of the throne.

60   I am aware, of course, that no Ruler can expect complete loyalty from his subjects until he has been tested in office. Nevertheless, I say to you at the very outset that I have nothing but contempt for the kind of Governor who is afraid, for whatever reason, to follow the course that he knows is best for the State; and as for the man who sets private friendship above the public welfare, —I have no use for him, either. I call God to witness that if I saw my country headed for ruin, I should not be afraid to speak out plainly; and I need hardly remind you that I would never have any dealings with an enemy of the people. No one values friendship more highly than I; but we must remember that friends made at the risk of wrecking
70 our Ship are not real friends at all.

These are my principles, at any rate, and that is why I have made the following decision concerning the sons of Oedipus: Eteoclês, who died as a man should die, fighting for his country, is to be buried with full military honours, with all the ceremony that is usual when the greatest heroes die; but his brother Polyneicês, who broke his exile to come back with fire and sword against his native city and the shrines of his fathers' gods, whose one idea was to spill the blood of his blood and sell his own people into slavery—Polyneicês, I say, is to have no burial: no man is to touch him or say the least prayer for him; he shall lie on the plain, unburied; and
80 the birds and the scavenging dogs can do with him whatever they like.

This is my command, and you can see the wisdom behind it. As long as I am King, no traitor is going to be honoured with the loyal man. But whoever shows by word and deed that he is on the side of the State,—he shall have my respect while he is living, and my reverence when he is dead.

CHORAG.   If that is your will, Creon son of Menoiceus,
You have the right to enforce it: we are yours.

CRE.   That is my will. Take care that you do your part.

CHORAG.   We are old men: let the younger ones carry it out.

CRE.   I do not mean that: the sentries have been appointed.

90   CHORAG.   Then what is it that you would have us do?

CRE.   You will give no support to whoever breaks this law.

CHORAG.   Only a crazy man is in love with death!

CRE.   And death it is; yet money talks, and the wisest
Have sometimes been known to count a few coins too many.

Enter SENTRY *from left.*

SENT.   I'll not say that I'm out of breath from running, King, because every time I stopped to think about what I have to tell you, I felt like

going back. And all the time a voice kept saying, "You fool, don't you
know you're walking straight into trouble?"; and then another voice:
"Yes, but if you let somebody else get the news to Creon first, it will be
even worse than that for you!" But good sense won out, at least I hope it 100
was good sense, and here I am with a story that makes no sense at all; but
I'll tell it anyhow, because, as they say, what's going to happen's going to
happen, and—
    CRE. Come to the point. What have you to say?
    SENT. I did not do it. I did not see who did it. You must not punish
me for what someone else has done.
    CRE. A comprehensive defence! More effective, perhaps,
If I knew its purpose. Come: what is it?
    SENT. A dreadful thing . . . I don't know how to put it—
    CRE. Out with it!   110
    SENT.   Well, then;
The dead man—
                  Polyneicês—
Pause. The SENTRY *is overcome, fumbles for words.* CREON *waits impassively.*
                          out there—
                                  someone,—
New dust on the slimy flesh!
Pause. No sign from CREON.
Someone has given it burial that way, and
Gone . . .
Long pause. CREON *finally speaks with deadly control.*
    CRE. And the man who dared do this?
    SENT.   I swear I   120
Do not know! You must believe me!
                        Listen:
The ground was dry, not a sign of digging, no,
Not a wheeltrack in the dust, no trace of anyone.
It was when they relieved us this morning: and one of them,
The corporal, pointed to it.
                      There it was,
The strangest—
          Look:
The body, just mounded over with light dust: you see?   130
Not buried really, but as if they'd covered it
Just enough for the ghost's peace. And no sign
Of dogs or any wild animal that had been there.
And then what a scene there was! Every man of us
Accusing the other: we all proved the other man did it,
We all had proof that we could not have done it.
We were ready to take hot iron in our hands,

Walk through fire, swear by all the gods,
It was not I!
140 *I do not know who it was, but it was not I!*
[CREON'S *rage has been mounting steadily, but the* SENTRY *is too intent upon his story to notice it.*]
And then, when this came to nothing, someone said
A thing that silenced us and made us stare
Down at the ground: you had to be told the news,
And one of us had to do it! We threw the dice,
And the bad luck fell to me. So here I am,
No happier to be here than you are to have me:
Nobody likes the man who brings bad news.

> CHORAG.   I have been wondering, King: can it be that the gods have
> done this?

> CRE. [*Furiously*]   Stop!
150 Must you doddering wrecks
Go out of your heads entirely? "The gods!"
Intolerable!
The gods favour this corpse? Why? How had he served them?
Tried to loot their temples, burn their images,
Yes, and the whole State, and its laws with it!
Is it your senile opinion that the gods love to honour bad men?
A pious thought!—
　　　　　　　No, from the very beginning
There have been those who have whispered together,
160 Stiff-necked anarchists, putting their heads together,
Scheming against me in alleys. These are the men,
And they have bribed my own guard to do this thing.
Money!
[*Sententiously*] There's nothing in the world so demoralising as money.
Down go your cities,
Homes gone, men gone, honest hearts corrupted,
Crookedness of all kinds, and all for money!
　　　　　　　[*To Sentry*]　　　But you—!
I swear by God and by the throne of God,
170 The man who has done this thing shall pay for it!
Find that man, bring him here to me, or your death
Will be the least of your problems: I'll string you up
Alive, and there will be certain ways to make you
Discover your employer before you die;
And the process may teach you a lesson you seem to have missed:
The dearest profit is sometimes all too dear:
That depends on the source. Do you understand me?
A fortune won is often misfortune.

SENT. King, may I speak?
CRE.   Your very voice distresses me.   180
SENT. Are you sure that it is my voice, and not your conscience?
CRE. By God, he wants to analyze me now!
SENT. It is not what I say, but what has been done, that hurts you.
CRE. You talk too much.
SENT.   Maybe; but I've done nothing.
CRE. Sold your soul for some silver: that's all you've done.
SENT. How dreadful it is when the right judge judges wrong!
CRE. Your figures of speech
May entertain you now; but unless you bring me the man,
You will get little profit from them in the end.   190

                              [*Exit Creon into the palace.*

SENT. "Bring me the man"—!
I'd like nothing better than bringing him the man!
But bring him or not, you have seen the last of me here.
At any rate, I am safe!   [*Exit Sentry.*

Ode I

CHOR. Numberless are the world's wonders, but none   [STROPHE 1
More wonderful than man; the stormgrey sea
Yields to his prows, the huge crests bear him high;
Earth, holy and inexhaustible, is graven
With shining furrows where his plows have gone
Year after year, the timeless labour of stallions.
The lightboned birds and beasts that cling to cover,   [ANTISTROPHE 1
The lithe fish lighting their reaches of dim water,
All are taken, tamed in the net of his mind;
The lion on the hill, the wild horse windy-maned,   10
Resign to him; and his blunt yoke has broken
The sultry shoulders of the mountain bull.
Words also, and thought as rapid as air,   [STROPHE 2
He fashions to his good use; statecraft is his,
And his the skill that deflects the arrows of snow,
The spears of winter rain: from every wind
He has made himself secure—from all but one:
In the late wind of death he cannot stand.
O clear intelligence, force beyond all measure!   [ANTISTROPHE 2
O fate of man, working both good and evil!   20
When the laws are kept, how proudly his city stands!
When the laws are broken, what of his city then?
Never may the anárchic man find rest at my hearth,
Never be it said that my thoughts are his thoughts.

SCENE II

Re-enter SENTRY *leading* ANTIGONE.

CHORAG.   What does this mean? Surely this captive woman
Is the Princess, Antigonê. Why should she be taken?

SENT.   Here is the one who did it! We caught her
In the very act of burying him.—Where is Creon?

CHORAG.   Just coming from the house.

Enter CREON, *center.*

30   CRE.   What has happened?
Why have you come back so soon?

SENT. [*Expansively*]   O King,
A man should never be too sure of anything:
I would have sworn
That you'd not see me here again: your anger
Frightened me so, and the things you threatened me with;
But how could I tell then
That I'd be able to solve the case so soon?
No dice-throwing this time: I was only too glad to come!
40   Here is this woman. She is the guilty one:
We found her trying to bury him.
Take her, then; question her; judge her as you will.
I am through with the whole thing now, and glád óf it.

CRE.   But this is Antigonê! Why have you brought her here?

SENT.   She was burying him, I tell you!

CRE. [*Severely*]   Is this the truth?

SENT.   I saw her with my own eyes. Can I say more?

CRE.   The details: come, tell me quickly!

SENT.   It was like this:
50   After those terrible threats of yours, King,
We went back and brushed the dust away from the body.
The flesh was soft by now, and stinking,
So we sat on a hill to windward and kept guard.
No napping this time! We kept each other awake.
But nothing happened until the white round sun
Whirled in the centre of the round sky over us:
Then, suddenly,
A storm of dust roared up from the earth, and the sky
Went out, the plain vanished with all its trees
60   In the stinging dark. We closed our eyes and endured it.
The whirlwind lasted a long time, but it passed;
And then we looked, and there was Antigonê!
I have seen
A mother bird come back to a stripped nest, heard
Her crying bitterly a broken note or two

~ For the young ones stolen. Just so, when this girl
Found the bare corpse, and all her love's work wasted,
She wept, and cried on heaven to damn the hands
That had done this thing.

                              And then she brought more dust   70
And sprinkled wine three times for her brother's ghost.
We ran and took her at once. She was not afraid,
Not even when we charged her with what she had done.
She denied nothing.

                    And this was a comfort to me,
And some uneasiness: for it is a good thing
To escape from death, but it is no great pleasure
To bring death to a friend.

                              Yet I always say
There is nothing so comfortable as your own safe skin!   80
    CRE. [*Slowly, dangerously*]   And you, Antigonê,
You with your head hanging,—do you confess this thing?
    ANTIG.   I do. I deny nothing.
    CRE. [*To Sentry*]   You may go.

                                                 [*Exit Sentry.*

[*To Antigone*]   Tell me, tell me briefly:
Had you heard my proclamation touching this matter?
    ANTIG.   It was public. Could I help hearing it?
    CRE.   And yet you dared defy the law.
    ANTIG.   I dared.
It was not God's proclamation. That final Justice   90
That rules the world below makes no such laws.
Your edict, King, was strong,
But all your strength is weakness itself against
The immortal unrecorded laws of God.
They are not merely now: they were, and shall be,
Operative for ever, beyond man utterly.
I knew I must die, even without your decree:
I am only mortal. And if I must die
Now, before it is my time to die,
Surely this is no hardship: can anyone   100
Living, as I live, with evil all about me,
Think Death less than a friend? This death of mine
Is of no importance; but if I had left my brother
Lying in death unburied, I should have suffered.
Now I do not.

                    You smile at me. Ah Creon,
Think me a fool, if you like; but it may well be
That a fool convicts me of folly.

CHORAG.   Like father, like daughter: both headstrong, deaf to reason!
110 She has never learned to yield.
        CRE.   She has much to learn.
The inflexible heart breaks first, the toughest iron
Cracks first, and the wildest horses bend their necks
At the pull of the smallest curb.
                              Pride? In a slave?
This girl is guilty of a double insolence,
Breaking the given laws and boasting of it.
Who is the man here,
She or I, if this crime goes unpunished?
120 Sister's child, or more than sister's child,
Or closer yet in blood—she and her sister
Win bitter death for this!
                    [*To Servants*]   Go, some of you,
Arrest Ismenê. I accuse her equally.
Bring her: you will find her sniffling in the house there.
Her mind's a traitor: crimes kept in the dark
Cry for light, and the guardian brain shudders;
But how much worse than this
Is brazen boasting of barefaced anarchy!
130   ANTIG.   Creon, what more do you want than my death?
        CRE.   Nothing.
That gives me everything.
        ANTIG.   Then I beg you: kill me.
This talking is a great weariness: your words
Are distasteful to me, and I am sure that mine
Seem so to you. And yet they should not seem so:
I should have praise and honour for what I have done.
All these men here would praise me
Were their lips not frozen shut with fear of you.
140 [*Bitterly*]   Ah the good fortune of kings,
Licensed to say and do whatever they please!
        CRE.   You are alone here in that opinion.
        ANTIG.   No, they are with me. But they keep their tongues in leash.
        CRE.   Maybe. But you are guilty, and they are not.
        ANTIG.   There is no guilt in reverence for the dead.
        CRE.   But Eteoclês—was he not your brother too?
        ANTIG.   My brother too.
        CRE.   And you insult his memory?
        ANTIG. [*Softly*]   The dead man would not say that I insult it.
150   CRE.   He would: for you honour a traitor as much as him.
        ANTIG.   His own brother, traitor or not, and equal in blood.
        CRE.   He made war on his country. Eteoclês defended it.

ANTIG. Nevertheless, there are honours due all the dead.

CRE. But not the same for the wicked as for the just.

ANTIG. Ah Creon, Creon,
Which of us can say what the gods hold wicked?

CRE. An enemy is an enemy, even dead.

ANTIG. It is my nature to join in love, not hate.

CRE. [*Finally losing patience*] Go join them, then; if you must have
    your love,
Find it in hell!   160

CHORAG. But see, Ismenê comes:

Enter ISMENE, *guarded*.

Those tears are sisterly, the cloud
That shadows her eyes rains down gentle sorrow.

CRE. You too, Ismenê,
Snake in my ordered house, sucking my blood
Stealthily—and all the time I never knew
That these two sisters were aiming at my throne!

                                            Ismenê,
Do you confess your share in this crime, or deny it?
Answer me.   170

ISM. Yes, if she will let me say so. I am guilty.

ANTIG. [*Coldly*] No, Ismenê. You have no right to say so.   .
You would not help me, and I will not have you help me.

ISM. But now I know what you meant; and I am here
To join you, to take my share of punishment.

ANTIG. The dead man and the gods who rule the dead
Know whose act this was. Words are not friends.

ISM. Do you refuse me, Antigonê? I want to die with you:
I too have a duty that I must discharge to the dead.

ANTIG. You shall not lessen my death by sharing it.   180

ISM. What do I care for life when you are dead?

ANTIG. Ask Creon. You're always hanging on his opinions.

ISM. You are laughing at me. Why, Antigonê?

ANTIG. It's a joyless laughter, Ismene.

ISM.   But can I do nothing?

ANTIG. Yes. Save yourself. I shall not envy you.
There are those who will praise you; I shall have honour, too.

ISM. But we are equally guilty!

ANTIG.   No more, Ismenê.
You are alive, but I belong to Death.   190

CRE. [*To the Chorus*] Gentlemen, I beg you to observe these girls:
One has just now lost her mind; the other,
It seems, has never had a mind at all.

ISM. Grief teaches the steadiest minds to waver, King.

CRE.   Yours certainly did, when you assumed guilt with the guilty!

ISM.   But how could I go on living without her?

CRE.   You are.
She is already dead.

ISM.   But your own son's bride!

200   CRE.   There are places enough for him to push his plow.
I want no wicked women for my sons!

ISM.   O dearest Haimon, how your father wrongs you!

CRE.   I've had enough of your childish talk of marriage!

CHORAG.   Do you really intend to steal this girl from your son?

CRE.   No; Death will do that for me.

CHORAG.   Then she must die?

CRE. [*Ironically*]   You dazzle me.

                          —But enough of this talk!

[*To Guards*]   You, there, take them away and guard them well:

210 For they are but women, and even brave men run
When they see Death coming.   [*Exeunt Ismene, Antigone, and Guards.*

Ode II

[STROPHE 1]

CHOR.   Fortunate is the man who has never tasted God's vengeance!
Where once the anger of heaven has struck, that house is shaken
For ever: damnation rises behind each child
Like a wave cresting out of the black northeast,
When the long darkness under sea roars up
And bursts drumming death upon the windwhipped sand.

[ANTISTROPHE 1]

I have seen this gathering sorrow from time long past
Loom upon Oedipus' children: generation from generation
Takes the compulsive rage of the enemy god.

10 So lately this last flower of Oedipus' line
Drank the sunlight! but now a passionate word
And a handful of dust have closed up all its beauty.

What mortal arrogance   [STROPHE 2]
Transcends the wrath of Zeus?
Sleep cannot lull him, nor the effortless long months
Of the timeless gods: but he is young for ever,
And his house is the shining day of high Olympos.

All that is and shall be,
And all the past, is his.

20 No pride on earth is free of the curse of heaven.

The straying dreams of men   [ANTISTROPHE 2]
May bring them ghosts of joy:
But as they drowse, the waking embers burn them;

Sophocles   307

Or they walk with fixed éyes, as blind men walk.
But the ancient wisdom speaks for our own time:
   Fate works most for woe
   With Folly's fairest show.
Man's little pleasure is the spring of sorrow.
SCENE III
   CHORAG. But here is Haimon, King, the last of all your sons.
Is it grief for Antigonê that brings him here,   30
And bitterness at being robbed of his bride?
Enter HAIMON.
   CRE. We shall soon see, and no need of diviners.
                                    —Son,
You have heard my final judgment on that girl:
Have you come here hating me, or have you come
With deference and with love, whatever I do?
   HAI. I am your son, father. You are my guide.
You make things clear for me, and I obey you.
No marriage means more to me than your continuing wisdom.
   CRE. Good. That is the way to behave: subordinate   40
Everything else, my son, to your father's will.
This is what a man prays for, that he may get
Sons attentive and dutiful in his house,
Each one hating his father's enemies,
Honouring his father's friends. But if his sons
Fail him, if they turn out unprofitably,
What has he fathered but trouble for himself
And amusement for the malicious?
                          So you are right
Not to lose your head over this woman.   50
Your pleasure with her would soon grow cold, Haimon,
And then you'd have a hellcat in bed and elsewhere.
Let her find her husband in Hell!
Of all the people in this city, only she
Has had contempt for my law and broken it.
Do you want me to show myself weak before the people?
Or to break my sworn word? No, and I will not.
The woman dies.
I suppose she'll plead "family ties." Well, let her.
If I permit my own family to rebel,   60
How shall I earn the world's obedience?
Show me the man who keeps his house in hand,
He's fit for public authority.
                    I'll have no dealings
With law-breakers, critics of the government:

Whoever is chosen to govern should be obeyed—
Must be obeyed, in all things, great and small,
Just and unjust! O Haimon,
The man who knows how to obey, and that man only,
70 Knows how to give commands when the time comes.
You can depend on him, no matter how fast
The spears come: he's a good soldier, he'll stick it out.
Anarchy, anarchy! Show me a greater evil!
This is why cities tumble and the great houses rain down,
This is what scatters armies!
No, no: good lives are made so by discipline.
We keep the laws then, and the lawmakers,
And no woman shall seduce us. If we must lose,
Let's lose to a man, at least! Is a woman stronger than we?
80   CHORAG.   Unless time has rusted my wits,
What you say, King, is said with point and dignity.
      HAI. [*Boyishly earnest*]   Father:
Reason is God's crowning gift to man, and you are right
To warn me against losing mine. I cannot say—
I hope that I shall never want to say!—that you
Have reasoned badly. Yet there are other men
Who can reason, too; and their opinions might be helpful.
You are not in a position to know everything
That people say or do, or what they feel:
90 Your temper terrifies them—everyone
Will tell you only what you like to hear.
But I, at any rate, can listen; and I have heard them
Muttering and whispering in the dark about this girl.
They say no woman has ever, so unreasonably,
Died so shameful a death for a generous act:
"She covered her brother's body. Is this indecent?
"She kept him from dogs and vultures. Is this a crime?
"Death?—She should have all the honour that we can give her!"
This is the way thay talk out there in the city.
100 You must believe me:
Nothing is closer to me than your happiness.
What could be closer? Must not any son
Value his father's fortune as his father does his?
I beg you, do not be unchangeable:
Do not believe that you alone can be right.
The man who thinks that,
The man who maintains that only he has the power
To reason correctly, the gift to speak, the soul—
A man like that, when you know him, turns out empty.

Sophocles 309

It is not reason never to yield to reason! 110
In flood time you can see how some trees bend,
And because they bend, even their twigs are safe,
While stubborn trees are torn up, roots and all.
And the same thing happens in sailing:
Make your sheet fast, never slacken,—and over you go,
Head over heels and under: and there's your voyage.
Forget you are angry! Let yourself be moved!
I know I am young; but please let me say this:
The ideal condition
Would be, I admit, that men should be right by instinct; 120
But since we are all too likely to go astray,
The reasonable thing is to learn from those who can teach.
    CHORAG. You will do well to listen to him, King,
If what he says is sensible. And you, Haimon,
Must listen to your father.—Both speak well.
    CRE. You consider it right for a man of my years and experience
To go to school to a boy?
    HAI.   It is not right
If I am wrong. But if I am young, and right,
What does my age matter? 130
    CRE. You think it right to stand up for an anarchist?
    HAI. Not at all. I pay no respect to criminals.
    CRE. Then she is not a criminal?
    HAI. The City would deny it, to a man.
    CRE. And the City proposes to teach me how to rule?
    HAI. Ah. Who is it that's talking like a boy now?
    CRE. My voice is the one voice giving orders in this City!
    HAI. It is no City if it takes orders from one voice.
    CRE. The State is the King!
    HAI.   Yes, if the State is a desert. 140
                                              [*Pause.*
    CRE. This boy, it seems, has sold out to a woman.
    HAI. If you are a woman: my concern is only for you.
    CRE. So? Your "concern"! In a public brawl with your father!
    HAI. How about you, in a public brawl with justice?
    CRE. With justice, when all that I do is within my rights?
    HAI. You have no right to trample on God's right.
    CRE. [*Completely out of control*] Fool, adolescent fool! Taken in by a
      woman!
    HAI. You'll never see me taken in by anything vile.
    CRE. Every word you say is for her!
    HAI. [*Quietly, darkly*]   And for you. 150
And for me. And for the gods under the earth.

CRE. You'll never marry her while she lives.

HAI. Then she must die.—But her death will cause another.

CRE. Another?
Have you lost your senses? Is this an open threat?

HAI. There is no threat in speaking to emptiness.

CRE. I swear you'll regret this superior tone of yours!
You are the empty one!

HAI.   If you were not my father,
160 I'd say you were perverse.

CRE. You girlstruck fool, don't play at words with me!

HAI. I am sorry. You prefer silence.

CRE.   Now, by God—!
I swear, by all the gods in heaven above us,
You'll watch it, I swear you shall!
          [To the Servants] Bring her out!
Bring the woman out! Let her die before his eyes!
Here, this instant, with her bridegroom beside her!

HAI. Not here, no; she will not die here, King.
170 And you will never see my face again.
Go on raving as long as you've a friend to endure you.   [Exit Haimon.

CHORAG. Gone, gone.
Creon, a young man in a rage is dangerous!

CRE. Let him do, or dream to do, more than a man can.
He shall not save these girls from death.

CHORAG.   These girls?
You have sentenced them both?

CRE.   No, you are right.
I will not kill the one whose hands are clean.

180 CHORAG. But Antigonê?

CRE. [Somberly] I will carry her far away
Out there in the wilderness, and lock her
Living in a vault of stone, She shall have food,
As the custom is, to absolve the State of her death.
And there let her pray to the gods of hell:
They are her only gods:
Perhaps they will show her an escape from death,
Or she may learn,
                though late,
190 That piety shown the dead is pity in vain.   [Exit Creon.

Ode III

CHOR. Love, unconquerable   [STROPHE
Waster of rich men, keeper
Of warm lights and all-night vigil

Sophocles 311

In the soft face of a girl:
Sea-wanderer, forest-visitor!
Even the pure Immortals cannot escape you,
And mortal man, in his one day's dusk,
Trembles before your glory.
Surely you swerve upon ruin   [ANTISTROPHE
The just man's consenting heart,   10
As here you have made bright anger
Strike between father and son—
And none has conquered but Love!
A girl's glánce wórking the will of heaven:
Pleasure to her alone who mocks us,
Merciless Aphroditê.

SCENE IV

As ANTIGONE *enters guarded.*

    CHORAG. But I can no longer stand in awe of this,
Nor, seeing what I see, keep back my tears.
Here is Antigonê, passing to that chamber
Where all find sleep at last.   20
    ANTIG. Look upon me, friends, and pity me   [STROPHE 1
Turning back at the night's edge to say
Goodbye to the sun that shines for me no longer;
Now sleepy Death
Summons me down to Acheron, that cold shore:
There is no bridesong there, nor any music.
    CHOR. Yet not unpraised, not without a kind of honour,
You walk at last into the underworld;
Untouched by sickness, broken by no sword.
What woman has ever found your way to death?   30
    ANTIG. How often I have heard the story of Niobê, [ANTISTROPHE 1
Tantalos' wretched daughter, how the stone
Clung fast about her, ivy-close: and they say
The rain falls endlessly
And sifting soft snow; her tears are never done.
I feel the loneliness of her death in mine.
    CHOR. But she was born of heaven, and you
Are woman, woman-born. If her death is yours,
A mortal woman's, is this not for you
Glory in our world and in the world beyond?   40
    ANTIG. You laugh at me. Ah, friends, friends,   [STROPHE 2
Can you not wait until I am dead? O Thebes,
O men many-charioted, in love with Fortune,
Dear springs of Dircê, sacred Theban grove,
Be witnesses for me, denied all pity,

Unjustly judged! and think a word of love
For her whose path turns
Under dark earth, where there are no more tears.
    CHOR.   You have passed beyond human daring and come at last
50 Into a place of stone where Justice sits.
I cannot tell
What shape of your father's guilt appears in this.
    ANTIG.   You have touched it at last: that bridal bed [ANTISTROPHE 2
Unspeakable, horror of son and mother mingling:
Their crime, infection of all our family!
O Oedipus, father and brother!
Your marriage strikes from the grave to murder mine.
I have been a stranger here in my own land:
All my life
60 The blasphemy of my birth has followed me.
    CHOR.   Reverence is a virtue, but strength
Lives in established law: that must prevail.
You have made your choice,
Your death is the doing of your conscious hand.
    ANTIG.   Then let me go, since all your words are bitter,   [EPODE
And the very light of the sun is cold to me.
Lead me to my vigil, where I must have
Neither love nor lamentation; no song, but silence.
CREON *interrupts impatiently.*
    CRE.   If dirges and planned lamentations could put off death,
70 Men would be singing for ever.
    [*To the Servants*]   Take her, go!
You know your orders: take her to the vault
And leave her alone there. And if she lives or dies,
That's her affair, not ours: our hands are clean.
    ANTIG.   O tomb, vaulted bride-bed in eternal rock,
Soon I shall be with my own again
Where Persephonê welcomes the thin ghosts underground:
And I shall see my father again, and you, mother,
And dearest Polyneicês—
80   dearest indeed
To me, since it was my hand
That washed him clean and poured the ritual wine:
And my reward is death before my time!
And yet, as men's hearts know, I have done no wrong,
I have not sinned before God. Or if I have,
I shall know the truth in death. But if the guilt
Lies upon Creon who judged me, then, I pray,
May his punishment equal my own.

CHORAG.   O passionate heart,
Unyielding, tormented still by the same winds!   90
   CRE.   Her guards shall have good cause to regret their delaying.
   ANTIG.   Ah! That voice is like the voice of death!
   CRE.   I can give you no reason to think you are mistaken.
   ANTIG.   Thebes, and you my fathers' gods,
And rulers of Thebes, you see me now, the last
Unhappy daughter of a line of kings,
Your kings, led away to death. You will remember
What things I suffer, and at what men's hands,
Because I would not transgress the laws of heaven.
[To the Guards, simply]   Come: let us wait no longer.   100
                                        [Exit Antigone, left, guarded.

Ode IV

   CHOR.   All Danaê's beauty was locked away   [STROPHE 1
In a brazen cell where the sunlight could not come:
A small room, still as any grave, enclosed her.
Yet she was a princess too,
And Zeus in a rain of gold poured love upon her.
O child, child,
No power in wealth or war
Or tough sea-blackened ships
Can prevail against untiring Destiny!
And Dryas' son° also, that furious king,   [ANTISTROPHE 1 10
Bore the god's prisoning anger for his pride:
Sealed up by Dionysos in deaf stone,
His madness died among echoes.
So at the last he learned what dreadful power
His tongue had mocked:
For he had profaned the revels,
And fired the wrath of the nine
Implacable Sisters that love the sound of the flute.
And old men tell a half-remembered tale°   [STROPHE 2
Of horror done where a dark ledge splits the sea   20
And a double surf beats on the gréy shóres:
How a king's new woman, sick
With hatred for the queen he had imprisoned,

10. **Dryas' son,** Lykurgos, a king of Thrace who insulted Dionysos. Lykurgos was imprisoned in a rocky cave by Dionysos and later struck blind by Zeus. 19. **a half-remembered tale,** a reference to the story of Cleopatra, Phineus, and Eidothea (Idaea). Cleopatra, daughter of the North Wind, and Phineus, a king, had two sons. After Cleopatra's death, Phineus married Eidothea, who accused the sons of improper advances to her. Phineus imprisoned them in a cave and had their eyes blinded. In Sophocles' version, Eidothea rips out the sons' eyes.

Ripped out his two sons' eyes with her bloody hands
While grinning Arês watched the shuttle plunge
Four times: four blind wounds crying for revenge,
Crying, tears and blood mingled.—Piteously born,   [ANTISTROPHE 2
Those sons whose mother was of heavenly birth!
Her father was the god of the North Wind
30 And she was cradled by gales,
She raced with young colts on the glittering hills
And walked untrammeled in the open light:
But in her marriage deathless Fate found means
To build a tomb like yours for all her joy.

SCENE V

Enter blind TEIRESIAS, *led by a boy. The opening speeches of* TEIRESIAS *should
be in singsong contrast to the realistic lines of* CREON.

TEIRES.   This is the way the blind man comes, Princes, Princes,
Lock-step, two heads lit by the eyes of one.
CRE.   What new thing have you to tell us, old Teiresias?
TEIRES.   I have much to tell you: listen to the prophet, Creon.
CRE.   I am not aware that I have ever failed to listen.
40 TEIRES.   Then you have done wisely, King, and ruled well.
CRE.   I admit my debt to you. But what have you to say?
TEIRES.   This, Creon: you stand once more on the edge of fate.
CRE.   What do you mean? Your words are a kind of dread.
TEIRES.   Listen, Creon:
I was sitting in my chair of augury, at the place
Where the birds gather about me. They were all a-chatter,
As is their habit, when suddenly I heard
A strange note in their jangling, a scream, a
Whirring fury; I knew that they were fighting,
50 Tearing each other, dying
In a whirlwind of wings clashing. And I was afraid.
I began the rites of burnt-offering at the altar,
But Hephaistos failed me: instead of bright flame,
There was only the sputtering slime of the fat thigh-flesh
Melting: the entrails dissolved in grey smoke,
The bare bone burst from the welter. And no blaze!
This was a sign from heaven. My boy described it,
Seeing for me as I see for others.
I tell you, Creon, you yourself have brought
60 This new calamity upon us. Our hearths and altars
Are stained with the corruption of dogs and carrion birds
That glut themselves on the corpse of Oedipus' son.
The gods are deaf when we pray to them, their fire
Recoils from our offering, their birds of omen

Have no cry of comfort, for they are gorged
With the thick blood of the dead.

                             O my son,
These are no trifles! Think: all men make mistakes,
But a good man yields when he knows his course is wrong,
And repairs the evil. The only crime is pride.   70
Give in to the dead man, then: do not fight with a corpse—
What glory is it to kill a man who is dead?
Think, I beg you:
It is for your own good that I speak as I do.
You should be able to yield for your own good.
    CRE.   It seems that prophets have made me their especial province.
All my life long
I have been a kind of butt for the dull arrows
Of doddering fortune-tellers!

                      No, Teiresias: 80
If your birds—if the great eagles of God himself
Should carry him stinking bit by bit to heaven,
I would not yield. I am not afraid of pollution:
No man can defile the gods.

                     Do what you will,
Go into business, make money, speculate
In India gold or that synthetic gold from Sardis,
Get rich otherwise than by my consent to bury him.
Teiresias, it is a sorry thing when a wise man
Sells his wisdom, lets out his words for hire!   90
    TEIRES.   Ah Creon! Is there no man left in the world—
    CRE.   To do what?—Come, let's have the aphorism!
    TEIRES.   No man who knows that wisdom outweighs any wealth?
    CRE.   As surely as bribes are baser than any baseness.
    TEIRES.   You are sick, Creon! You are deathly sick!
    CRE.   As you say: it is not my place to challenge a prophet.
    TEIRES.   Yet you have said my prophecy is for sale.
    CRE.   The generation of prophets has always loved gold.
    TEIRES.   The generation of kings has always loved brass.
    CRE.   You forget yourself! You are speaking to your King.   100
    TEIRES.   I know it. You are a king because of me.
    CRE.   You have a certain skill; but you have sold out.
    TEIRES.   King, you will drive me to words that—
    CRE.   Say them, say them!
Only remember: I will not pay you for them.
    TEIRES.   No, you will find them too costly.
    CRE.   No doubt. Speak:

Whatever you say, you will not change my will.

TEIRES.   Then take this, and take it to heart!
110 The time is not far off when you shall pay back
Corpse for corpse, flesh of your own flesh.
You have thrust the child of this world into living night,
You have kept from the gods below the child that is theirs:
The one in a grave before her death, the other,
Dead, denied the grave. This is your crime:
And the Furies and the dark gods of Hell
Are swift with terrible punishment for you.
Do you want to buy me now, Creon?

                                        Not many days,
120 And your house will be full of men and women weeping,
And curses will be hurled at you from far
Cities grieving for sons unburied, left to rot
Before the walls of Thebes.
These are my arrows, Creon: they are all for you.
[*To Boy*]   But come, child: lead me home.
Let him waste his fine anger upon younger men.
Maybe he will learn at last
To control a wiser tongue in a better head.   [*Exit Teiresias.*

CHORAG.   The old man has gone, King, but his words
130 Remain to plague us. I am old, too,
But I cannot remember that he was ever false.

CRE.   That is true. . . . It troubles me.
Oh it is hard to give in! but it is worse
To risk everything for stubborn pride.

CHORAG.   Creon: take my advice.

CRE.   What shall I do?

CHORAG.   Go quickly: free Antigonê from her vault
And build a tomb for the body of Polyneicês.

CRE.   You would have me do this?
140   CHORAG.   Creon, yes!
And it must be done at once: God moves
Swiftly to cancel the folly of stubborn men.

CRE.   It is hard to deny the heart! But I
Will do it: I will not fight with destiny.

CHORAG.   You must go yourself, you cannot leave it to others.

CRE.   I will go.
                    —Bring axes, servants:
Come with me to the tomb. I buried her, I
Will set her free.
150   Oh quickly!

My mind misgives—
The laws of the gods are mighty, and a man must serve them
To the last day of his life!   [*Exit Creon.*

Pæan

CHORAG.   God of many names   [STROPHE 1
CHOR.   O Iacchos°
                                         son
of Cadmeian Sémelê
                         O born of the Thunder!
Guardian of the West
                         Regent
of Eleusis' plain
                 O Prince of mænad Thebes
and the Dragon Field by rippling Ismenos: 10
CHORAG.   God of many names   [ANTISTROPHE 1
CHOR.   the flame of torches
flares on our hills
                    the nymphs of Iacchos
dance at the spring of Castalia:
from the vine-close mountain
                            come ah come in ivy:
Evohé evohé! sings through the streets of Thebes.
CHORAG.   God of many names   [STROPHE 2
CHOR.   Iacchos of Thebes   20
heavenly Child
                of Sémelê bride of the Thunderer!
The shadow of plague is upon us:
                                come
with clement feet
                  oh come from Parnasos
down the long slopes
                     across the lamenting water.
CHORAG.   Iô Fire! Chorister of the throbbing stars! [ANTISTROPHE 2
O purest among the voices of the night!   30
Thou son of God, blaze for us!
    CHOR.   Come with choric rapture of circling Mænads
Who cry *Iô Iacche!*
                 God of many names!

---

2. **Iacchos,** another name for Dionysos; actually a minor deity associated with the Eleusinian mysteries and linked to Dionysos probably because the name sounds like Bacchus.

Éxodos

Enter MESSENGER, *left.*

MESS.   Men of the line of Cadmos, you who live
Near Amphion's citadel:
                              I cannot say
Of any condition of human life "This is fixed,
This is clearly good, or bad." Fate raises up,
And Fate casts down the happy and unhappy alike:
No man can foretell his Fate.
                              Take the case of Creon:
Creon was happy once, as I count happiness:
10 Victorious in battle, sole governor of the land,
Fortunate father of children nobly born.
And now it has all gone from him! Who can say
That a man is still alive when his life's joy fails?
He is a walking dead man. Grant him rich,
Let him live like a king in his great house: *
If his pleasure is gone, I would not give
So much as the shadow of smoke for all he owns.

CHORAG.   Your words hint at sorrow: what is your news for us?

MESS.   They are dead. The living are guilty of their death.

20 CHORAG.   Who is guilty? Who is dead? Speak!

MESS.   Haimon.
Haimon is dead; and the hand that killed him
Is his own hand.

CHORAG.   His father's? or his own?

MESS.   His own, driven mad by the murder his father had done.

CHORAG.   Teiresias, Teiresias, how clearly you saw it all!

MESS.   This is my news: you must draw what conclusions you can
from it.

CHORAG.   But look: Eurydicê, our Queen:
30 Has she overheard us?

Enter EURYDICE *from the palace, center.*

EURYD.   I have heard something, friends:
As I was unlocking the gate of Pallas' shrine,
For I needed her help today, I heard a voice
Telling of some new sorrow. And I fainted
There at the temple with all my maidens about me.
But speak again: whatever it is, I can bear it:
Grief and I are no strangers.

MESS.   Dearest Lady,
I will tell you plainly all that I have seen.
40 I shall not try to comfort you: what is the use,

Since comfort could lie only in what is not true?
The truth is always best.
                            I went with Creon
To the outer plain where Polyneicês was lying,
No friend to pity him, his body shredded by dogs.
We made our prayers in that place to Hecatê
And Pluto, that they would be merciful. And we bathed
The corpse with holy water, and we brought
Fresh-broken branches to burn what was left of it,
And upon the urn we heaped up a towering barrow   50
Of the earth of his own land.
                            When we were done, we ran
To the vault where Antigonê lay on her couch of stone.
One of the servants had gone ahead,
And while he was yet far off he heard a voice
Grieving within the chamber, and he came back
And told Creon. And as the King went closer,
The air was full of wailing, the words lost,
And he begged us to make all haste. "Am I a prophet?"
He said, weeping, "And must I walk this road,   60
"The saddest of all that I have gone before?
"My son's voice calls me on. Oh quickly, quickly!
"Look through the crevice there, and tell me
"If it is Haimon, or some deception of the gods!"
We obeyed; and in the cavern's farthest corner
We saw her lying:
She had made a noose of her fine linen veil
And hanged herself. Haimon lay beside her,
His arms about her waist, lamenting her,
His love lost under ground, crying out   70
That his father had stolen her away from him.
When Creon saw him the tears rushed to his eyes
And he called to him: "What have you done, child? Speak to me.
"What are you thinking that makes your eyes so strange?
"O my son, my son, I come to you on my knees!"
But Haimon spat in his face. He said not a word,
Staring—
            And suddenly drew his sword
And lunged. Creon shrank back, the blade missed; and the boy,
Desperate against himself, drove it half its length   80
Into his own side, and fell. And as he died
He gathered Antigonê close in his arms again,
Choking, his blood bright red on her white cheek.

And now he lies dead with the dead, and she is his
At last, his bride in the houses of the dead.

> [*Exit Eurydice into the palace.*

    CHORAG. She has left us without a word. What can this mean?
    MESS. It troubles me, too; yet she knows what is best,
Her grief is too great for public lamentation,
And doubtless she has gone to her chamber to weep
90 For her dead son, leading her maidens in his dirge.
    CHORAG. It may be so: but I fear this deep silence.

> [*Pause.*

    MESS. I will see what she is doing. I will go in.

> [*Exit Messenger into the palace.*

Enter CREON *with attendants, bearing* HAIMON's *body.*
    CHORAG. But here is the King himself: oh look at him,
Bearing his own damnation in his arms.
    CRE. Nothing you say can touch me any more.
My own blind heart has brought me
From darkness to final darkness. Here you see
The father murdering, the murdered son—
And all my civic wisdom!
100 Haimon my son, so young, so young to die,
I was the fool, not you; and you died for me.
    CHORAG. That is the truth; but you were late in learning it.
    CRE. This truth is hard to bear. Surely a god
Has crushed me beneath the hugest weight of heaven,
And driven me headlong a barbaric way
To trample out the thing I held most dear.
The pains that men will take to come to pain!
Enter MESSENGER *from the palace.*
    MESS. The burden you carry in your hands is heavy,
But it is not all: you will find more in your house.
110   CRE. What burden worse than this shall I find there?
    MESS. The Queen is dead.
    CRE. O port of death, deaf world,
Is there no pity for me? And you, Angel of evil,
I was dead, and your words are death again.
Is it true, boy? Can it be true?
Is my wife dead? Has death bred death?
    MESS. You can see for yourself.
The doors are opened, and the body of EURYDICE *is disclosed within.*
    CRE. Oh pity!
All true, all true, and more than I can bear!
120 O my wife, my son!

MESS. She stood before the altar, and her heart
Welcomed the knife her own hand guided,
And a great cry burst from her lips for Megareos dead,
And for Haimon dead, her sons; and her last breath
Was a curse for their father, the murderer of her sons.
And she fell, and the dark flowed in through her closing eyes.
　　CRE. O God, I am sick with fear.
Are there no swords here? Has no one a blow for me?
　　MESS. Her curse is upon you for the deaths of both.
　　CRE. It is right that it should be. I alone am guilty. 130
I know it, and I say it. Lead me in,
Quickly, friends.
I have neither life nor substance. Lead me in.
　　CHORAG. You are right, if there can be right in so much wrong.
The briefest way is best in a world of sorrow.
　　CRE. Let it come,
Let death come quickly, and be kind to me.
I would not ever see the sun again.
　　CHORAG. All that will come when it will; but we, meanwhile.
Have much to do. Leave the future to itself. 140
　　CRE. All my heart was in that prayer!
　　CHORAG. Then do not pray any more: the sky is deaf.
　　CRE. Lead me away. I have been rash and foolish.
I have killed my son and my wife.
I look for comfort; my comfort lies here dead.
Whatever my hands have touched has come to nothing.
Fate has brought all my pride to a thought of dust.
As CREON *is being led into the house, the* CHORAGOS *advances and speaks directly*
　　to the audience.
　　CHORAG. There is no happiness where there is no wisdom;
No wisdom but in submission to the gods.
Big words are always punished, 150
And proud men in old age learn to be wise.

1564-1616
WILLIAM
SHAKESPEARE * King Lear

Dramatis Personae

LEAR, king of Britain.
KING OF FRANCE.
DUKE OF BURGUNDY.
DUKE OF CORNWALL.
DUKE OF ALBANY.
EARL OF KENT.
EARL OF GLOUCESTER.
EDGAR, son to Gloucester.
EDMUND, bastard son to Gloucester.
CURAN, a courtier.
Old Man, tenant to Gloucester.
Doctor.
FOOL.
OSWALD, steward to Goneril.
A Captain employed by Edmund.
Gentleman attendant on Cordelia.
A Herald.
Servants to Cornwall.
GONERIL,
REGAN, } daughters to Lear.
CORDELIA,
Knights of Lear's train, Captains,
    Messengers, Soldiers, and Attendants.
SCENE: *Britain.*

Act I

SCENE I. *King Lear's palace.*
Enter KENT, GLOUCESTER, *and* EDMUND.
  KENT. I thought the king had more affected° the Duke of Albany
than Cornwall.
  GLOU. It did always seem so to us; but now, in the division of the
kingdom, it appears not which of the dukes he values most; for equalities°
are so weighed that curiosity° in neither can make choice of either's
moiety.

1. **affected,** been fond of, favored. 4. **equalities,** equivalences (in the lands assigned).
5. **curiosity,** nicety, close scrutiny.

KENT. Is not this your son, my lord?

GLOU. His breeding, sir, hath been at my charge. I have so often blushed to acknowledge him that now I am brazed° to it.

KENT. I cannot conceive you.   10

GLOU. Sir, this young fellow's mother could; whereupon she grew round-wombed, and had indeed, sir, a son for her cradle ere she had a husband for her bed. Do you smell a fault?

KENT. I cannot wish the fault undone, the issue of it being so proper.

GLOU. But I have a son, sir, by order of law, some year elder than this, who yet is no dearer in my account. Though this knave came something saucily into the world before he was sent for, yet was his mother fair; there was good sport at his making, and the whoreson must be acknowledged. Do you know this noble gentleman, Edmund?

EDM. No, my lord.   20

GLOU. My lord of Kent. Remember him hereafter as my honourable friend.

EDM. My services to your lordship.

KENT. I must love you, and sue to know you better.

EDM. Sir, I shall study deserving.°

GLOU. He hath been out nine years, and away he shall again. [Sennet] The king is coming.

Enter KING LEAR, CORNWALL, ALBANY, GONERIL, REGAN, CORDELIA, *and* Attendants.

LEAR. Attend the lords of France and Burgundy, Gloucester.

GLOU. I shall, my liege.   [*Exeunt Gloucester and Edmund.*

LEAR. Meantime we shall express our darker purpose.   30
Give me the map there. Know that we have divided
In three our kingdom; and 'tis our fast intent°
To shake all cares and business from our age,
Conferring them on younger strengths, while we
Unburthen'd crawl toward death. Our son of Cornwall,
And you, our no less loving son of Albany,
We have this hour a constant° will to publish
Our daughters' several dowers, that future strife
May be prevented now. The princes, France and Burgundy,
Great rivals in our youngest daughter's love,   40
Long in our court have made their amorous sojourn,
And here are to be answer'd. Tell me, my daughters,—
Since now we will divest us, both of rule,
Interest of territory, cares of state,—
Which of you shall we say doth love us most?

9. **brazed,** hardened. 25. **study deserving,** attempt to be worthy. 32. **fast intent,** firm intention. 37. **constant,** fixed.

That we our largest bounty may extend
Where nature doth with merit challenge.° Goneril,
Our eldest-born, speak first.
    Gon.   Sir, I love you more than words can wield the matter;°
50 Dearer than eye-sight, space, and liberty;
Beyond what can be valued, rich or rare;
No less than life, with grace, health, beauty, honour;
As much as child e'er loved, or father found;
A love that makes breath poor, and speech unable;
Beyond all manner of so much I love you.
    Cor. [Aside]   What shall Cordelia speak? Love, and be silent.
    Lear.   Of all these bounds, even from this line to this,
With shadowy forests and with champains° rich'd,
With plenteous rivers and wide-skirted meads,
60 We make thee lady. To thine and Albany's issue
Be this perpetual. What says our second daughter,
Our dearest Regan, wife to Cornwall?
    Reg.   I am made
Of that self metal as my sister,
And prize me at her worth. In my true heart
I find she names my very deed of love;°
Only she comes too short, that° I profess
Myself an enemy to all other joys
Which the most precious square of sense° possesses,
70 And find I am alone felicitate°
In your dear highness' love.
    Cor.   [Aside]   Then poor Cordelia!
And yet not so, since I am sure my love's
More ponderous than my tongue.
    Lear.   To thee and thine hereditary ever
Remain this ample third of our fair kingdom,
No less in space, validity,° and pleasure,
Than that conferr'd on Goneril. Now, our joy,
Although our last and least; to whose young love
80 The vines of France and milk of Burgundy
Strive to be interess'd;° what can you say to draw
A third more opulent° than your sisters? Speak.
    Cor.   Nothing, my lord.

47. Where . . . challenge, where both natural affection and merit claim it as due. 49. wield
the matter, avail in expressing. 58. champains, plains. 66. deed of love, precise quality of
my love. 67. that, in that. 69. square of sense, reference to the psychological diagram of the
mental powers in the form of a square whose sides are sense, appetite, motion and judgment.
70. felicitate, made happy. 77. validity, value. 81. to be interess'd, to a right in. 82. A
third more opulent. Lear perhaps refers to the crown which he intends for Cordelia, since
the parts of the kingdom are declared equal.

William Shakespeare   325

LEAR. Nothing?

COR. Nothing.

LEAR. Nothing will come of nothing. Speak again.

COR. Unhappy that I am, I cannot heave
My heart into my mouth. I love your majesty
According to my bond;° no more nor less.

LEAR. How, how, Cordelia? Mend your speech a little, 90
Lest you may mar your fortunes.

COR.   Good my lord,
You have begot me, bred me, loved me; I
Return those duties back as are right fit,
Obey you, love you, and most honour you.
Why have my sisters husbands, if they say
They love you all? Haply, when I shall wed,
That lord whose hand must take my plight° shall carry
Half my love with him, half my care and duty.
Sure, I shall never marry like my sisters, 100
To love my father all.

LEAR. But goes thy heart with this?

COR.   Ay, good my lord.

LEAR. So young, and so untender?

COR. So young, my lord, and true.

LEAR. Let it be so; thy truth then be thy dower!
For, by the sacred radiance of the sun,
The mysteries of Hecate, and the night;
By all the operation of the orbs
From whom we do exist and cease to be; 110
Here I disclaim all my paternal care,
Propinquity and property of blood,
And as a stranger to my heart and me
Hold thee from this° for ever. The barbarous Scythian,
Or he that makes his generation° messes
To gorge his appetite, shall to my bosom
Be as well neighbour'd, pitied, and relieved,
As thou my sometime daughter.

KENT.   Good my liege,—

LEAR. Peace, Kent! 120
Come not between the dragon and his wrath.
I loved her most, and thought to set my rest°
On her kind nursery.° Hence, and avoid my sight!
So be my grave my peace, as here I give

89. **bond,** duty, obligation. 98. **plight,** pledge. 114. **this,** this time forth. 115. **generation,** children. 122. **set my rest,** repose myself; a phrase from a game of cards, meaning "to stake all." 123. **nursery,** nursing.

Her father's heart from her! Call France. Who stirs?
Call Burgundy. Cornwall and Albany,
With my two daughters' dowers digest the third;
Let pride, which she calls plainness, marry her.
I do invest you jointly with my power,
130 Pre-eminence, and all the large effects°
That troop with majesty. Ourself, by monthly course,
With reservation of an hundred knights,
By you to be sustain'd, shall our abode
Make with you by due turn. Only we shall retain
The name and all the addition to a king;
The sway, revenue, execution of the rest,
Beloved sons, be yours; which to confirm,
This coronet° part between you.   [*Giving the crown.*
    KENT.   Royal Lear,
140 Whom I have ever honour'd as my king,
Loved as my father, as my master follow'd,
As my great patron thought on in my prayers,—
    LEAR. The bow is bent and drawn, make from° the shaft.
    KENT. Let it fall° rather, though the fork° invade
The region of my heart! Be Kent unmannerly,
When Lear is mad. What wouldst thou do, old man?
Think'st thou that duty shall have dread to speak,
When power to flattery bows? To plainness honour's bound,
When majesty stoops to folly.° Reverse thy doom;
150 And in thy best consideration check
This hideous rashness. Answer my life° my judgement,
Thy youngest daughter does not love thee least;
Nor are those empty-hearted whose low sounds
Reverb no hollowness.
    LEAR.   Kent, on thy life, no more!
    KENT. My life I never held but as a pawn°
To wage° against thy enemies; nor fear to lose it,
Thy safety being the motive.
    LEAR.   Out of my sight!
160 KENT. See better, Lear, and let me still remain
The true blank° of thine eye.
    LEAR. Now, by Apollo,—
    KENT.   Now, by Apollo, king,

130. **effects**, outward shows. 138. **coronet**, i.e., the crown intended for Cordelia. 143. **make from**, get out of the way of. 144. **fall**, fly, go. **fork**, barbed head of an arrow. 148-49. **To . . . folly.** Allegiance demands frankness when kingship stoops to folly. 151. **Answer my life**, let my life answer. 156. **pawn**, stake, wager. 157. **wage**, hazard, wager. 161. **blank**, white center of the target.

William Shakespeare 327

Thou swear'st thy gods in vain.

LEAR.   O, vassal! miscreant!

Laying his hand on his sword.

Alb. }
Corn. } Dear sir, forbear.

KENT.   Kill thy physician, and the fee bestow
Upon the foul disease. Revoke thy gift;
Or, whilst I can vent clamour from my throat,
I'll tell thee thou dost evil.   170

LEAR.   Hear me, recreant!
On thine allegiance, hear me!
That thou hast sought to make us break our vow,
Which we durst never yet, and with strain'd° pride
To come between our sentence and our power,
Which nor our nature nor our place can bear,
Our potency made good,° take thy reward.
Five days we do allot thee, for provision
To shield thee from disasters of the world,
And on the sixth to turn thy hated back   180
Upon our kingdom. If, on the tenth day following,
Thy banish'd trunk be found in our dominions,
The moment is thy death. Away! by Jupiter,
This shall not be revoked.

KENT.   Fare thee well, king; sith thus thou wilt appear,
Freedom lives hence, and banishment is here.
[*To Cordelia*] The gods to their dear shelter take thee, maid,
That justly think'st and hast most rightly said!
[*To Regan and Goneril*] And your large speeches may your deeds approve,
That good effects may spring from words of love.   190
Thus Kent, O princes, bids you all adieu;
He'll shape his old course in a country new.   [*Exit.*

Flourish. Re-enter GLOUCESTER, *with* FRANCE, BURGUNDY, *and* Attendants.

GLOU.   Here's France and Burgundy, my noble lord.

LEAR.   My lord of Burgundy,
We first address toward you, who with this king
Hath rivall'd for our daughter. What in the least
Will you require in present dower with her,
Or cease your quest of love?

BUR.   Most royal majesty,
I crave no more than what your highness offer'd,   200
Nor will you tender less.

LEAR.   Right noble Burgundy,

174. **strain'd,** excessive. 177. **Our potency made good,** our authority being maintained.

When she was dear to us, we did hold her so;
But now her price is fall'n. Sir, there she stands.
If aught within that little seeming° substance,
Or all of it, with our displeasure pieced,°
And nothing more, may fitly like° your grace,
She's there, and she is yours.
    BUR.   I know no answer.
210   LEAR. Will you, with those infirmities she owes,
Unfriended, new-adopted to our hate,
Dower'd with our curse, and stranger'd° with our oath,
Take her, or leave her?
    BUR.   Pardon me, royal sir;
Election makes not up° on such conditions.
    LEAR. Then leave her, sir; for, by the power that made me,
I tell you all her wealth.   [*To France*]   For you, great king,
I would not from your love make such a stray,°
To match you where I hate; therefore beseech you
220 To avert your liking a more worthier way
Than on a wretch whom nature is ashamed
Almost to acknowledge hers.
    FRANCE.   This is most strange,
That she whom even but now was your best object,
The argument of your praise, balm of your age,
The best, the dearest, should in this trice of time
Commit a thing so monstrous, to dismantle
So many folds of favour. Sure, her offence
Must be of such unnatural degree,
230 That monsters° it, or your fore-vouch'd° affection
Fall into taint;° which to believe of her,
Must be a faith that reason without miracle
Should never plant in me.
    COR.   I yet beseech your majesty,—
If for I want that glib and oily art,
To speak and purpose not, since what I well intend,
I'll do 't before I speak,—that you make known
It is no vicious blot, murder, or foulness,
No unchaste action, or dishonour'd step,
240 That hath deprived me of your grace and favour;
But even for want of that for which I am richer,

---

205. **seeming,** probably, specious, insincere; taken also with *little* to mean "seemingly small."
206. **pieced,** added. 207. **fitly like,** suitably please. 212. **stranger'd,** estranged. 215. **Election . . . up,** choice comes to no decision. 218. **make such a stray,** stray so far. 230. **monsters,** makes monstrous. **fore-vouch'd,** hitherto affirmed. 231. **taint,** decay.

A still-soliciting° eye, and such a tongue
As I am glad I have not, though not to have it
Hath lost me in your liking.
    LEAR.   Better thou
Hadst not been born than not to have pleased me better.
    FRANCE.   Is it but this,—a tardiness in nature
Which often leaves the history unspoke
That it intends to do? My lord of Burgundy,
What say you to the lady? Love 's not love   250
When it is mingled with regards° that stand
Aloof from the entire point. Will you have her?
She is herself a dowry.
    BUR.   Royal Lear,
Give but that portion which yourself proposed,
And here I take Cordelia by the hand,
Duchess of Burgundy.
    LEAR.   Nothing. I have sworn; I am firm.
    BUR.   I am sorry then you have so lost a father
That you must lose a husband.   260
    COR.   Peace be with Burgundy!
Since that respect and fortunes are his love,
I shall not be his wife.
    FRANCE.   Fairest Cordelia, that art most rich, being poor;
Most choice, forsaken; and most loved, despised!
Thee and thy virtues here I seize upon.
Be it lawful I take up what 's cast away.
Gods, gods! 'tis strange that from their cold'st neglect
My love should kindle to inflamed respect.
Thy dowerless daughter, king, thrown to my chance,   270
Is queen of us, of ours, and our fair France.
Not all the dukes of waterish° Burgundy
Can buy this unprized° precious maid of me.
Bid them farewell, Cordelia, though unkind;
Thou losest here, a better where° to find.
    LEAR.   Thou hast her, France; let her be thine; for we
Have no such daughter, nor shall ever see
That face of hers again. Therefore be gone
Without our grace, our love, our benison.
Come, noble Burgundy.   280
          [*Flourish. Exeunt all but France, Goneril, Regan, and Cordelia.*

---

242. **still-soliciting,** ever-begging. 251. **regards,** considerations. 272. **waterish,** well-watered (with rivers); used contemptuously, water being the symbol of fickleness. 273. **unprized,** not appreciated, or priceless. 275. **here ... where,** used as nouns.

FRANCE.   Bid farewell to your sisters.

COR.   The jewels of our father, with wash'd eyes
Cordelia leaves you. I know you what you are;
And like a sister am most loath to call
Your faults as they are named. Love well our father.
To your professed° bosoms I commit him;
But yet, alas, stood I within his grace,
I would prefer him to a better place.
So farewell to you both.

290   REG.   Prescribe not us our duty.

GON.   Let your study
Be to content your lord, who hath received you
At° fortune's alms. You have obedience scanted,
And well are worth the want that you have wanted.°

COR.   Time shall unfold what plighted° cunning hides,
Who cover faults, at last with shame derides.
Well may you prosper!

FRANCE.   Come, my fair Cordelia.

                    [*Exeunt France and Cordelia.*

GON.   Sister, it is not a little I have to say of what most nearly
300 appertains to us both. I think our father will hence to-night.

REG.   That 's most certain, and with you; next month with us.

GON.   You see how full of changes his age is; the observation we have
made of it hath not been little; he always loved our sister most; and with
what poor judgement he hath now cast her off appears too grossly.°

REG.   'Tis the infirmity of his age; yet he hath ever but slenderly
known himself.

GON.   The best and soundest of his time° hath been but rash; then
must we look from his age to receive, not alone the imperfections of
long-engraffed condition,° but therewithal the unruly waywardness that
310 infirm and choleric years bring with them.

REG.   Such unconstant starts are we like to have from him as this
of Kent's banishment.

GON.   There is further compliment of leave-taking between France
and him. Pray you, let 's hit° together. If our father carry authority with
such dispositions as he bears, this last surrender of his will but offend° us.

REG.   We shall further think of it.

GON.   We must do something, and i' the heat.°   [*Exeunt.*

---

286. **professed**, i.e., full of professions (avowals). 293. **At**, i.e., priced at. 294. **well . . .
wanted**, well deserve the lack of affection which you yourself have shown; *want* may, however,
refer to her dowry. 295. **plighted**, folded, insincere. 304. **grossly**, obviously. 307. **time**,
lifetime. 309. **long-engraffed condition**, long-implanted habit. 314. **hit**, agree. 315. **offend**,
harm, injure. 317. **i' the heat**, i.e., while the iron is hot.

SCENE II. *The Earl of Gloucester's castle.*
Enter EDMUND, *with a letter.*

EDM. Thou, Nature,° art my goddess; to thy law
My services are bound. Wherefore should I
Stand in the plague° of custom, and permit
The curiosity° of nations to deprive me,
For that I am some twelve or fourteen moonshines°
Lag of° a brother? Why bastard? wherefore base?
When my dimensions° are as well compact,°
My mind as generous, and my shape as true,
As honest madam's issue? Why brand they us
With base? with baseness? bastardy? base, base?   10
Who, in the lusty stealth of nature, take
More composition and fierce quality
Than doth, within a dull, stale, tired bed,
Go to the creating a whole tribe of fops,
Got 'tween asleep and wake? Well then,
Legitimate Edgar, I must have your land.
Our father's love is to the bastard Edmund
As to the legitimate. Fine word,—"legitimate"!
Well, my legitimate, if this letter speed,
And my invention thrive, Edmund the base   20
Shall top the legitimate. I grow; I prosper.
Now, gods, stand up for bastards!
Enter GLOUCESTER.

GLOU. Kent banish'd thus? and France in choler parted?
And the king gone to-night? Prescribed his power?
Confined to exhibition?° All this done
Upon the gad?° Edmund, how now? what news?
EDM. So please your lordship, none.   [*Putting up the letter.*
GLOU. Why so earnestly seek you to put up that letter?
EDM. I know no news, my lord.
GLOU. What paper were you reading?   30
EDM. Nothing, my lord.
GLOU. No? What needed then that terrible° dispatch of it into your
pocket? The quality of nothing hath not such need to hide itself. Let 's
see; come, if it be nothing, I shall not need spectacles.
EDM. I beseech you, sir, pardon me; it is a letter from my brother,

---

1. **Nature,** natural force; also, course of life undisciplined by culture. 3. **plague,** vexatious
injustice. 4. **curiosity,** nicety, fastidiousness. 5. **moonshines,** months. 6. **Lag of,** later than.
7. **dimensions,** bodily parts or proportions. **compact,** knit together. 25. **exhibition,** allowance. 26. **Upon the gad,** suddenly, as if pricked by a gad. 32. **terrible,** terrified.

that I have not all o'er-read; and for so much as I have perused, I find it not fit for your o'er-looking.

GLOU. Give me the letter, sir.

EDM. I shall offend, either to detain or give it. The contents, as in
40 part I understand them, are to blame.

GLOU. Let 's see, let 's see.

EDM. I hope, for my brother's justification, he wrote this but as an essay° or taste of my virtue.

GLOU. [*Reads*] "This policy and reverence of° age makes the world bitter to the best of our times; keeps our fortunes from us till our oldness cannot relish them. I begin to find an idle and fond bondage in the oppression of aged tyranny, who sways, not as it hath power, but as it is suffered. Come to me, that of this I may speak more. If our father would sleep till I waked him, you should enjoy half his revenue for ever,
50 and live the beloved of your brother,

EDGAR."

Hum! Conspiracy!—"Sleep till I waked him, you should enjoy half his revenue"—My son Edgar! Had he a hand to write this? a heart and brain to breed it in?—When came this to you? who brought it?

EDM. It was not brought me, my lord; there 's the cunning of it; I found it thrown in at the casement of my closet.°

GLOU. You know the character to be your brother's?

EDM. If the matter were good, my lord, I durst swear it were his; but, in respect of that, I would fain think it were not.
60 GLOU. It is his.

EDM. It is his hand, my lord; but I hope his heart is not in the contents.

GLOU. Has he never heretofore sounded you in this business?

EDM. Never, my lord; but I have heard him oft maintain it to be fit that, sons at perfect age, and fathers declined, the father should be as ward to the son, and the son manage his revenue.

GLOU. O villain, villain! His very opinion in the letter! Abhorred villain! Unnatural, detested,° brutish villain! worse than brutish! Go, sirrah, seek him; I'll apprehend him. Abominable villain! Where is he?

EDM. I do not well know, my lord. If it shall please you to suspend
70 your indignation against my brother till you can derive from him better testimony of his intent, you should run a certain course; where, if you violently proceed against him, mistaking his purpose, it would make a great gap in your own honour, and shake in pieces the heart of his obedience. I dare pawn down my life for him that he hath writ this to feel my affection to your honour, and to no further pretence° of danger.

GLOU. Think you so?

EDM. If your honour judge it meet, I will place you where you shall

43. **essay,** assay, trial. 44. **policy and reverence of,** i.e., policy of reverencing. 56. **closet,** private room. 67. **detested,** detestable. 75. **pretence,** intention, purpose.

William Shakespeare 333

hear us confer of this, and by an auricular assurance have your satisfaction, and that without any further delay than this very evening.

GLOU. He cannot be such a monster— 80

EDM. Nor is not, sure.

GLOU. To his father, that so tenderly and entirely loves him. Heaven and earth! Edmund, seek him out; wind me into him,° I pray you; frame the business after your own wisdom. I would unstate myself° to be in a due resolution.°

EDM. I will seek him, sir, presently; convey° the business as I shall find means, and acquaint you withal.

GLOU. These late eclipses in the sun and moon portend no good to us; though the wisdom of nature° can reason it thus and thus, yet nature finds itself scourged by the sequent° effects. Love cools, friendship falls 90 off, brothers divide. In cities, mutinies; in countries, discord; in palaces, treason; and the bond cracked 'twixt son and father. This villain of mine comes under the prediction; there 's son against father: the king falls from bias of nature; there 's father against child. We have seen the best of our time. Machinations, hollowness, treachery, and all ruinous disorders follow us disquietly to our graves. Find out this villain, Edmund; it shall lose thee nothing; do it carefully. And the noble and true-hearted Kent banished! his offence, honesty! 'Tis strange.   [*Exit.*

EDM. This is the excellent foppery° of the world, that, when we are sick in fortune,—often the surfeits of our own behaviour,—we make guilty 100 of our disasters° the sun, the moon, and the stars; as if we were villains on necessity; fools by heavenly compulsion; knaves, thieves, and treachers° by spherical predominance;° drunkards, liars, and adulterers by an enforced obedience of planetary influence; and all that we are evil in, by a divine thrusting on. An admirable evasion of whoremaster man, to lay his goatish disposition to the charge of a star! My father compounded with my mother under the dragon's tail, and my nativity was under Ursa major, so that it follows I am rough and lecherous. Fut, I should have been that I am, had the maidenliest star in the firmament twinkled on my bastardizing. Edgar— 110

Enter EDGAR.

and pat he comes like the catastrophe of the old comedy. My cue is villainous melancholy, with a sigh like Tom o' Bedlam.° O, these eclipses do portend these divisions! fa, sol, la, mi.

EDG. How now, brother Edmund? what serious contemplation are you in?

83. **wind me into him,** insinuate yourself into his confidence. 84. **unstate myself,** give up my position and dignity. 85. **due resolution,** actual certainty. 86. **convey,** manage with secrecy. 89. **wisdom of nature,** natural science. 90. **sequent,** consequent, following. 99. **foppery,** foolishness. 101. **disasters,** unfavorable aspects. 102. **treachers,** traitors. 103. **spherical predominance,** ascendancy of planets. 112. **Tom o' Bedlam.** See II, iii, 14, note below.

EDM. I am thinking, brother, of a prediction I read this other day, what should follow these eclipses.

EDG. Do you busy yourself with that?

EDM. I promise you, the effects he writes of succeed° unhappily; as of
120 unnaturalness between the child and the parent; death, dearth, dissolutions of ancient amities; divisions in state, menaces and maledictions against king and nobles; needless diffidences,° banishment of friends, dissipation of cohorts,° nuptial breaches, and I know not what.

EDG. How long have you been a sectary astronomical?°

EDM. When saw you my father last?

EDG. The night gone by.

EDM. Spake you with him?

EDG. Ay, two hours together.

EDM. Parted you in good terms? Found you no displeasure in him
130 by word nor countenance?

EDG. None at all.

EDM. Bethink yourself wherein you may have offended him; and at my entreaty forbear his presence until some little time hath qualified the heat of his displeasure, which at this instant so rageth in him, that with the mischief of° your person it would scarcely allay.°

EDG. Some villain hath done me wrong.

EDM. That 's my fear. I pray you have a continent° forbearance till the speed of his rage goes slower; and, as I say, retire with me to my lodging, from whence I will fitly bring you to hear my lord speak. Pray ye, go; there 's my key. If you do stir abroad, go armed.

EDG. Armed, brother?

EDM. Brother, I advise you to the best. I am no honest man if there be any good meaning toward you. I have told you what I have seen and heard; but faintly, nothing like the image and horror of it. Pray you, away!

EDG. Shall I hear from you anon?

EDM. I do serve you in this business.   [*Exit Edgar.*

A credulous father! and a brother noble,

Whose nature is so far from doing harms
150 That he suspects none; on whose foolish honesty

My practices ride easy! I see the business.

Let me, if not by birth, have lands by wit;

All with me 's meet that I can fashion fit.°   [*Exit.*

SCENE III.   *The Duke of Albany's palace.*

Enter GONERIL, *and* OSWALD, *her steward.*

---

119. **succeed,** come to pass. 122. **diffidences,** distrust of others. 122-123. **dissipation of cohorts,** breaking up of military organizations. 124. **sectary astronomical,** student of astrology. 135. **mischief of,** harm to. **allay,** be allayed. 137. **continent,** restraining. 153. **fashion fit,** fit to my purposes.

GON. Did my father strike my gentleman for chiding of his fool?
OSW. Yes, madam.
GON. By day and night he wrongs me; every hour
He flashes into one gross crime or other,
That sets us all at odds. I'll not endure it.
His knights grow riotous, and himself upbraids us
On every trifle. When he returns from hunting,
I will not speak with him; say I am sick.
If you come slack of former services,
You shall do well; the fault of it I'll answer.   [*Horns within.* 10
OSW. He 's coming, madam; I hear him.
GON. Put on what weary negligence you please,
You and your fellows; I'd have it come to question.
If he distaste it, let him to my sister,
Whose mind and mine, I know, in that are one,
Not to be over-ruled. Idle° old man,
That still would manage those authorities
That he hath given away! Now, by my life,
Old fools are babes again, and must be used
With checks as flatteries, when they are seen abused.°   20
Remember what I have said.
OSW.   Well, madam.
GON. And let his knights have colder looks among you;
What grows of it, no matter. Advise your fellows so.
I would breed from hence occasions,° and I shall,
That I may speak. I'll write straight to my sister
To hold my very course. Prepare for dinner.   [*Exeunt.*
SCENE IV. *A hall in the same.*
Enter KENT, *disguised.*
KENT. If but as well I other accents borrow,
That can my speech diffuse,° my good intent
May carry through itself to that full issue
For which I razed° my likeness. Now, banish'd Kent,
If thou canst serve where thou dost stand condemn'd,
So may it come, thy master, whom thou lovest,
Shall find thee full of labours.
Horns within. Enter LEAR, Knights, *and* Attendants.
LEAR. Let me not stay a jot for dinner; go get it ready. [*Exit an
Attendant*] How now? what art thou?
KENT. A man, sir.   10

16. **Idle**, foolish, silly. 20. **With . . . abused.** The line, probably corrupt, yields a sort of meaning if one understands *as* to mean "as well as," *they* to refer to *Old fools,* and *abused* to mean "deceived" or "misguided." 25. **breed from hence occasions,** find opportunities for opposition.
    2. **diffuse,** confuse; hence, disguise. 4. **razed,** erased.

LEAR. What dost thou profess?° what wouldst thou with us?

KENT. I do profess to be no less than I seem; to serve him truly that will put me in trust; to love him that is honest; to converse with him that is wise and says little; to fear judgement; to fight when I cannot choose; and to eat no fish.°

LEAR. What art thou?

KENT. A very honest-hearted fellow, and as poor as the king.

LEAR. If thou be as poor for a subject as he is for a king, thou art poor enough. What wouldst thou?

20 KENT. Service.

LEAR. Who wouldst thou serve?

KENT. You.

LEAR. Dost thou know me, fellow?

KENT. No, sir; but you have that in your countenance which I would fain call master.

LEAR. What's that?

KENT. Authority.

LEAR. What services canst thou do?

KENT. I can keep honest counsel, ride, run, mar a curious° tale in 30 telling it, and deliver a plain message bluntly; that which ordinary men are fit for, I am qualified in, and the best of me is diligence.

LEAR. How old art thou?

KENT. Not so young, sir, to love a woman for singing, nor so old to dote on her for any thing. I have years on my back forty eight.

LEAR. Follow me; thou shalt serve me. If I like thee no worse after dinner, I will not part from thee yet. Dinner, ho, dinner! Where 's my knave? my fool? Go you, and call my fool hither.   [*Exit an Attendant.* *Enter* OSWALD.

You, you, sirrah, where 's my daughter?

OSW. So please you,—   [*Exit.*

40 LEAR. What says the fellow there? Call the clotpoll° back. [*Exit a Knight*] Where 's my fool, ho? I think the world 's asleep.
Re-enter KNIGHT.

How now! where 's that mongrel?

KNIGHT. He says, my lord, your daughter is not well.

LEAR. Why came not the slave back to me when I called him?

KNIGHT. Sir, he answered me in the roundest° manner, he would not.

LEAR. He would not?

KNIGHT. My lord, I know not what the matter is; but, to my judgement, your highness is not entertained with that ceremonious affection as

---

11. **What . . . profess?** What is thy profession? 15. **eat no fish.** Roman Catholics, who observed the custom of eating fish on Fridays, were thought of as enemies of the government. 29. **curious,** elaborate. 40. **clotpoll,** blockhead. 45. **roundest,** plainest.

you were wont; there 's a great abatement of kindness appears as well in the general dependants° as in the duke himself also and your daughter. 50

LEAR. Ha! sayest thou so?

KNIGHT. I beseech you, pardon me, my lord, if I be mistaken; for my duty cannot be silent when I think your highness wronged.

LEAR. Thou but rememberest° me of mine own conception. I have perceived a most faint° neglect of late, which I have rather blamed as mine own jealous curiosity° than as a very pretence° and purpose of unkindness. I will look further into 't. But where 's my fool? I have not seen him this two days.

KNIGHT. Since my young lady 's going into France, sir, the fool hath much pined away. 60

LEAR. No more of that; I have noted it well. Go you, and tell my daughter I would speak with her. [*Exit an Attendant*] Go you, call hither my fool. [*Exit an Attendant.*

Re-enter OSWALD.

O, you sir, you, come you hither, sir. Who am I, sir?

OSW. My lady's father.

LEAR. 'My lady's father'! my lord's knave. You whoreson dog! you slave! you cur!

OSW. I am none of these, my lord; I beseech your pardon.

LEAR. Do you bandy° looks with me, you rascal? [*Striking him.*

OSW. I'll not be struck, my lord. 70

KENT. Nor tripped neither, you base foot-ball player.°

Tripping up his heels.

LEAR. I thank thee, fellow; thou servest me, and I'll love thee.

KENT. Come, sir, arise, away! I'll teach you differences. Away, away! If you will measure your lubber's length again, tarry; but away! Go to; have you wisdom? So. [*Pushes Oswald out.*

LEAR. Now, my friendly knave, I thank thee. There 's earnest of thy service. [*Giving Kent money.*

Enter FOOL.

FOOL. Let me hire him too. Here 's my coxcomb.°

Offering KENT *his cap.*

LEAR. How now, my pretty knave? how dost thou?

FOOL. Sirrah, you were best take my coxcomb. 80

---

50. **general dependants,** servants of the Duke of Albany. 54. **rememberest,** remindest. 55. **faint,** slight, or indifferent, half-hearted. 56. **jealous curiosity,** overscrupulous regard for his own dignity. **pretence,** intention, purpose. 69. **bandy,** strike a ball to and fro, as in tennis; here figurative, give and take. 71. **foot-ball player.** Football was a rough, dangerous, public sport without organization or officials, and under statutory ban; it was played in the streets by the worst element of the population. 78. **coxcomb,** fool's cap.

KENT. Why, fool?

FOOL. Why? For taking one's part that 's out of favour. Nay, an thou canst not smile as the wind sits, thou 'lt catch cold shortly. There, take my coxcomb. Why, this fellow has banished two on 's daughters, and did the third a blessing against his will; if thou follow him, thou must needs wear my coxcomb. How now, nuncle?° Would I had two coxcombs and two daughters!

LEAR. Why, my boy?

FOOL. If I gave them all my living,° I 'd keep my coxcombs myself.
90 There 's mine; beg another of thy daughters.

LEAR. Take heed, sirrah—the whip.

FOOL. Truth 's a dog must to kennel; he must be whipped out, when the Lady brach° may stand by the fire and stink.

LEAR. A pestilent gall to me!

FOOL. Sirrah, I'll teach thee a speech.

LEAR. Do.

FOOL. Mark it, nuncle:
Have more than thou showest,
Speak less than thou knowest,
100 Lend less than thou owest,°
Ride more than thou goest,°
Learn more than thou trowest,
Set less than thou throwest;°
Leave thy drink and thy whore,
And keep in-a-door,°
And thou shalt have more
Than two tens to a score.

KENT. This is nothing, fool.

FOOL. Then 'tis like the breath of an unfeed lawyer; you gave me
110 nothing for 't. Can you make no use of nothing, nuncle?

LEAR. Why, no, boy; nothing can be made out of nothing.

FOOL. [To Kent] Prithee, tell him, so much the rent of his land comes to. He will not believe a fool.

LEAR. A bitter fool!

FOOL. Dost thou know the difference, my boy, between a bitter fool and a sweet one?

LEAR. No, lad; teach me.

FOOL. That lord that counsell'd thee
To give away thy land,
120 Come place him here by me—

---

86. **nuncle**, contraction of "mine uncle," customary address of the licensed fool to his superior. 89. **living**, property. 93. **brach**, a female hound. 100. **owest**, ownest. 101. **goest**, i.e., on foot. 103. **Set ... throwest**, stake less at dice than you have a chance to throw, i.e., don't bet all you can. 105. **in-a-door**, at home.

    Do thou for him stand.
     The sweet and bitter fool
      Will presently appear;
      The one in motley° here,
       The other found out there.

LEAR. Dost thou call me fool, boy?

FOOL. All thy other titles thou hast given away; that thou wast born with.

KENT. This is not altogether fool, my lord.

FOOL. No, faith, lords and great men will not let me; if I had a 130 monopoly° out,° they would have part on 't; and ladies too, they will not let me have all fool to myself; they'll be snatching. Nuncle, give me an egg, and I'll give thee two crowns.

LEAR. What two crowns shall they be?

FOOL. Why, after I have cut the egg i' the middle and eat up the meat, the two crowns of the egg. When thou clovest thy crown i' the middle, and gavest away both parts, thou borest thine ass on thy back o'er the dirt. Thou hadst little wit in thy bald crown when thou gavest thy golden one away. If I speak like myself° in this, let him be whipped that first finds it so.   140

[*Singing*] Fools had ne'er less grace in a year;
   For wise men are grown foppish,°
  They know not how their wits to wear,
   Their manners are so apish.

LEAR. When were you wont to be so full of songs, sirrah?

FOOL. I have used it, nuncle, ever since thou madest thy daughters thy mother; for when thou gavest them the rod, and put'st down thine own breeches,

[*Singing*] Then they for sudden joy did weep,
   And I for sorrow sung,   150
  That such a king should play bo-peep,
   And go the fools among.°

Prithee, nuncle, keep a schoolmaster that can teach thy fool to lie. I would fain learn to lie.

LEAR. An you lie, sirrah, we'll have you whipped.

FOOL. I marvel what kin thou and thy daughters are. They'll have me whipped for speaking true, thou 'lt have me whipped for lying; and sometimes I am whipped for holding my peace. I had rather be any kind o' thing than a fool; and yet I would not be thee, nuncle; thou hast pared

---

124. **motley,** the particolored dress of the Fool. 131. **monopoly.** This allusion would be well understood, since the granting of monopolies by King James was a current abuse. **out,** taken out, granted. 139. **like myself,** like a fool. 142. **foppish,** foolish. 149-152. **Then . . . among.** These lines, and probably others below, are no doubt taken from old songs.

160 thy wit o' both sides and left nothing i' the middle. Here comes one o'
the parings.
Enter GONERIL.

LEAR.   How now, daughter! what makes that frontlet° on? Methinks
you are too much of late i' the frown.

FOOL.   Thou wast a pretty fellow when thou hadst no need to care for
her frowning; now thou art an O without a figure.° I am better than thou
art now; I am a fool, thou art nothing.   [*To Goneril*]   Yes, forsooth, I
will hold my tongue; so your face bids me, though you say nothing.
Mum, mum,
        He that keeps nor crust nor crum,
170   Weary of all, shall want some.
[*Pointing to Lear*]   That 's a shealed peascod.°

GON.   Not only, sir, this your all-licensed fool,
But other of your insolent retinue
Do hourly carp and quarrel, breaking forth
In rank and not-to-be-endured riots. Sir,
I had thought, by making this well known unto you,
To have found a safe redress; but now grow fearful,
By what yourself too late have spoke and done,
That you protect this course, and put it on°
180 By your allowance;° which if you should, the fault
Would not 'scape censure, nor the redresses sleep,°
Which, in the tender of a wholesome weal,°
Might in their working do you that offence,
Which else were shame, that then necessity
Will call discreet proceeding.°

FOOL.   For you know, nuncle,
        The hedge-sparrow fed the cuckoo so long,
        That it° had it head bit off by it young.
So out went the candle, and we were left darkling.°
190   LEAR.   Are you our daughter?

GON.   Come, sir,
I would you would make use of that good wisdom,
Whereof I know you are fraught,° and put away
These dispositions, that of late transport you
From what you rightly are.

---

162. **frontlet,** a band worn on the forehead; forehead; here, frowning visage. 165. **O without a figure,** cipher of no value unless joined to a figure. 171. **shealed peascod,** shelled pea
pod. 179. **put it on,** encourage it. 180. **allowance,** approval. 181. **nor the redresses sleep,**
punishment for the riotous conduct of Lear's attendants will be inflicted. 182. **tender . . . weal,**
preservation of the peace of the state. 184-185. **necessity . . . proceeding,** i.e., everyone will
justify her because of the necessity of the action. 188. **it.** The second and third *its* are pos-
sessives. 189. **darkling,** in the dark. 193. **fraught,** filled, endowed.

FOOL.   May not an ass know when the cart draws the horse? Whoop,
Jug! I love thee.°
LEAR.   Does any here know me? This is not Lear.
Doth Lear walk thus? speak thus? Where are his eyes?
Either his notion° weakens, his discernings   200
Are lethargied—Ha! waking? 'tis not so.
Who is it that can tell me who I am?
FOOL.   Lear's shadow.
LEAR.   I would learn that; for, by the marks of sovereignty, knowl-
edge, and reason, I should be false persuaded I had daughters.
FOOL.   Which they will make an obedient father.
LEAR.   Your name, fair gentlewoman?
GON.   This admiration,° sir, is much o' the savour
Of other your new pranks. I do beseech you
To understand my purposes aright.   210
As you are old and reverend, you should be wise.
Here do you keep a hundred knights and squires;
Men so disorder'd, so debauched and bold,
That this our court, infected with their manners,
Shows like a riotous inn. Epicurism° and lust
Make it more like a tavern or a brothel
Than a graced° palace. The shame itself doth speak
For instant remedy. Be then desired
By her that else will take the thing she begs,
A little to disquantity° your train;   220
And the remainder, that shall still depend,°
To be such men as may besort° your age,
And know themselves and you.
LEAR.   Darkness and devils!
Saddle my horses; call my train together.
Degenerate bastard! I'll not trouble thee.
Yet have I left a daughter.
GON.   You strike my people, and your disorder'd rabble
Make servants of their betters.
Enter ALBANY.
LEAR.   Woe that too late repents,—[*To Albany*]   O, sir, are you come? 230
Is it your will? Speak, sir. Prepare my horses.
Ingratitude, thou marble-hearted fiend,
More hideous when thou show'st thee in a child
Than the sea-monster!°

197-198. **Whoop, Jug! I love thee,** possibly a quotation from an old song; used by the Fool
to cover up his impertinence. *Jug*, probably, Joan. 200. **notion,** intellectual power. 208.
admiration, pretense of astonishment. 215. **Epicurism,** gluttony. 217. **graced,** honorable.
220. **disquantity,** diminish. 221. **depend,** be dependents. 222. **besort,** befit. 234. **sea-monster,**
possible allusion to the hippopotamus, said in Egyptian mythology to be a monster of ingratitude.

ALB.   Pray, sir, be patient.
    LEAR. [*To Goneril*]   Detested kite! thou liest:
My train are men of choice and rarest parts,°
That all particulars of duty know,
And in the most exact regard° support
240 The worships° of their name. O most small fault,
How ugly didst thou in Cordelia show!
Which, like an engine,° wrench'd my frame of nature
From the fix'd place; drew from my heart all love,
And added to the gall. O Lear, Lear, Lear!
Beat at this gate that let thy folly in,   [*Striking his head.*
And thy dear judgement out! Go, go, my people.
    ALB.   My lord, I am guiltless, as I am ignorant
Of what hath moved you.
    LEAR.   It may be so, my lord.
250 Hear, Nature, hear; dear goddess, hear!
Suspend thy purpose, if thou didst intend
To make this creature fruitful!
Into her womb convey sterility!
Dry up in her the organs of increase;
And from her derogate° body never spring
A babe to honour her! If she must teem,
Create her child of spleen, that it may live
And be a thwart° disnatured° torment to her!
Let it stamp wrinkles in her brow of youth;
260 With cadent° tears fret channels in her cheeks;
Turn all her mother's pains and benefits
To laughter and contempt, that she may feel
How sharper than a serpent's tooth it is
To have a thankless child! Away, away!   [*Exit.*
    ALB.   Now, gods that we adore, whereof comes this?
    GON.   Never afflict yourself to know more of it,
But let his disposition have that scope
As dotage gives it.
Re-enter LEAR.
    LEAR.   What, fifty of my followers at a clap?
270 Within a fortnight?
    ALB.   What 's the matter, sir?
    LEAR.   I'll tell thee. [*To Goneril*]   Life and death! I am ashamed

---

237. **parts,** qualities, accomplishments. 239. **in . . . regard,** with extreme care. 240. **worships,** honors. 242. **engine,** mechanical contrivance, perhaps a lever. 255. **derogate,** debased. 258. **thwart,** contrary. **disnatured,** without natural affection. 260. **cadent,** falling.

That thou hast power to shake my manhood thus;
That these hot tears, which break from me perforce,
Should make thee worth them. Blasts and fogs upon thee!
The untented° woundings of a father s curse
Pierce every sense about thee! Old fond eyes,
Beweep this cause again, I'll pluck ye out,
And cast you, with the waters that you lose,
To temper clay. Yea, is it come to this?   280
Ha! Let it be so. I have another daughter,
Who, I am sure, is kind and comfortable.°
When she shall hear this of thee, with her nails
She'll flay thy wolvish visage. Thou shalt find
That I'll resume the shape which thou dost think
I have cast off for ever. [*Exeunt Lear, Kent, and Attendants.*

 GON. Do you mark that, my lord?
 ALB. I cannot be so partial, Goneril,
To the great love I bear you,—
 GON. Pray you, content. What, Oswald, ho!   290
[*To the Fool*] You, sir, more knave than fool, after your master!
 FOOL. Nuncle Lear, nuncle Lear, tarry! Take the fool with thee.
   A fox, when one has caught her,
   And such a daughter,
   Should sure to the slaughter,
   If my cap would buy a halter.
   So the fool follows after.   [*Exit.*
 GON. This man hath had good counsel! A hundred knights!
'Tis politic and safe to let him keep
At point° a hundred knights; yes, that, on every dream, 300
Each buzz,° each fancy, each complaint, dislike,
He may enguard° his dotage with their powers,
And hold our lives in mercy. Oswald, I say!
 ALB. Well, you may fear too far.
 GON.   Safer than trust too far.
Let me still take away the harms I fear,
Not fear still to be taken.° I know his heart.
What he hath utter'd I have writ my sister.
If she sustain him and his hundred knights,
When I have show'd the unfitness,—   310
Re-enter OSWALD.

---

276. **untented,** not cleansed with lint, and therefore liable to fester. 282. **comfortable,** willing to comfort. 300. **At point,** under arms. 301. **buzz,** idle rumor. 302. **enguard,** surround with a guard. 307. **taken,** overtaken (by the *harms*).

344 Drama

How now, Oswald?
What, have you writ that letter to my sister?
Osw. Yes, madam.
Gon. Take you some company, and away to horse!
Inform her full of my particular fear,
And thereto add such reasons of your own
As may compact° it more. Get you gone;
And hasten your return. [*Exit Oswald*] No, no, my lord,
This milky gentleness and course of yours°
320 Though I condemn not, yet, under pardon,
You are much more at task° for want of wisdom
Than praised for harmful mildness.
Alb. How far your eyes may pierce I cannot tell:
Striving to better, oft we mar what 's well.
Gon. Nay, then—
Alb. Well, well; the event.°   [*Exeunt.*
Scene v. *Court before the same.*
Enter Lear, Kent, *and* Fool.
Lear. Go you before to Gloucester° with these letters. Acquaint my
daughter no further with any thing you know than comes from her
demand out of the letter. If your diligence be not speedy, I shall be there
afore you.
Kent. I will not sleep, my lord, till I have delivered your letter. [*Exit.*
Fool. If a man's brains were in 's heels, were 't not in danger of kibes?°
Lear. Ay, boy.
Fool. Then, I prithee, be merry; thy wit shall ne'er go slip-shod.°
Lear. Ha, ha, ha!
10 Fool. Shalt see thy other daughter will use thee kindly;° for though
she 's as like this as a crab 's like an apple,° yet I can tell what I can tell.
Lear. What canst tell, boy?
Fool. She will taste as like this as a crab does to a crab. Thou canst
tell why one's nose stands i' the middle on 's face?
Lear. No.
Fool. Why, to keep one's eyes of either side 's nose, that what a man
cannot smell out, he may spy into.
Lear. I did her° wrong—

---

317. **compact,** confirm. 319. **This . . . yours,** the cowardly weakness of your course. 321.
at task, taken to task, blamed. 326. **the event,** time will show.

1. **Gloucester,** not a reference to the Earl but to a place, possibly Cornwall. 6. **kibes,**
chilblains, or ulcerated sores on the heels. 8. **slip-shod,** in slippers. There are no brains, thinks
the Fool, in Lear's heels when they are on their way to visit Regan. 10. **kindly,** double sense:
according to filial nature and according to her own nature. 11. **a crab's . . . apple,** seems
proverbial for "a crab-apple's an apple." 18. **her.** Lear again thinks of Cordelia.

FOOL. Canst tell how an oyster makes his shell?

LEAR. No. 20

FOOL. Nor I neither; but I can tell why a snail has a house.

LEAR. Why?

FOOL. Why, to put his head in; not to give it away to his daughters, and leave his horns without a case.

LEAR. I will forget my nature. So kind a father! Be my horses ready?

FOOL. Thy asses are gone about 'em. The reason why the seven stars° are no more than seven is a pretty reason.

LEAR. Because they are not eight?

FOOL. Yes, indeed; thou wouldst make a good fool.

LEAR. To take 't again perforce! Monster ingratitude! 30

FOOL. If thou wert my fool, nuncle, I'd have thee beaten for being old before thy time.

LEAR. How 's that?

FOOL. Thou shouldst not have been old till thou hadst been wise.

LEAR. O, let me not be mad, not mad, sweet heaven! Keep me in temper;° I would not be mad!

Enter Gentleman.

How now! are the horses ready?

GENT. Ready, my lord.

LEAR. Come, boy.

FOOL. She that 's a maid now, and laughs at my departure, 40
Shall not be a maid long, unless things be cut shorter. [*Exeunt.*

Act II

SCENE I. *The Earl of Gloucester's castle.*
Enter EDMUND, *and* CURAN *meets him.*

EDM. Save thee,° Curan.

CUR. And you, sir. I have been with your father, and given him notice that the Duke of Cornwall and Regan his duchess will be here with him this night.

EDM. How comes that?

CUR. Nay, I know not. You have heard of the news abroad; I mean the whispered ones, for they are yet but ear-bussing° arguments?

EDM. Not I. Pray you, what are they?

CUR. Have you heard of no likely wars toward,° 'twixt the Dukes of Cornwall and Albany? 10

EDM. Not a word.

CUR. You may do, then, in time. Fare you well, sir. [*Exit.*

EDM. The duke be here to-night? The better! best!

26-27. **seven stars**, the Pleiades. 36. **temper**, sanity, mental balance.
1. **Save thee**, i.e., God save thee. 7. **ear-bussing**, lightly whispered. 9. **toward**, in prospect.

This weaves itself perforce into my business.
My father hath set guard to take my brother;
And I have one thing, of a queasy question,°
Which I must act. Briefness° and fortune, work!
Brother, a word! descend! Brother, I say!
Enter EDGAR.
My father watches. O sir, fly this place!
20 Intelligence is given where you are hid.
You have now the good advantage of the night.
Have you not spoken 'gainst the Duke of Cornwall?
He 's coming hither; now, i' the night, i' the haste,
And Regan with him. Have you nothing said
Upon his party° 'gainst the Duke of Albany?
Advise yourself.°
    EDG.   I am sure on 't, not a word.
    EDM.   I hear my father coming. Pardon me;
In cunning° I must draw my sword upon you.
30 Draw; seem to defend yourself; now quit you well.
Yield! Come before my father. Light, ho, here!
Fly, brother. Torches, torches! So, farewell.   [*Exit Edgar.*
Some blood drawn on me would beget° opinion
Of my more fierce endeavour. [*Wounds his arm*] I have seen drunkards
Do more than this in sport. Father, father!
Stop, stop! No help?
Enter GLOUCESTER, *and* Servants *with torches.*
    GLOU.   Now, Edmund, where 's the villain?
    EDM.   Here stood he in the dark, his sharp sword out,
Mumbling of wicked charms, conjuring the moon
40 To stand auspicious mistress.
    GLOU.   But where is he?
    EDM.   Look, sir, I bleed.
    GLOU.   Where is the villain, Edmund?
    EDM.   Fled this way, sir. When by no means he could—
    GLOU.   Pursue him, ho! Go after. [*Exeunt some Servants*] By no means
    what?
    EDM.   Persuade me to the murder of your lordship;
But that I told him the revenging gods
'Gainst parricides did all their thunders bend;
50 Spoke with how manifold and strong a bond

16. **queasy question,** hazardous, or ticklish, nature. 17. **Briefness,** promptitude. 25.
Upon his party, possibly, on his (i.e., Cornwall's) side. This would be confusing; Edmund is
credited with making it so in order to frighten Edgar. It may mean, "Have you said nothing
about the party Cornwall is forming against Albany?" 26. **Advise yourself,** probably, recollect, consider. 29. **cunning,** pretense. 33. **beget,** create (for me).

The child was bound to the father—sir, in fine,
Seeing how loathly opposite° I stood
To his unnatural purpose, in fell motion°
With his prepared sword he charges home
My unprovided body, lanced mine arm;
And when he saw my best alarum'd° spirits,
Bold in the quarrel's right, roused to the encounter,
Or whether gasted° by the noise I made,
Full suddenly he fled.
   GLOU.   Let him fly far: 60
Not in this land shall he remain uncaught;
And found—dispatch.° The noble duke my master,
My worthy arch° and patron, comes to-night.
By his authority I will proclaim it,
That he which finds him shall deserve our thanks,
Bringing the murderous coward to the stake;°
He that conceals him, death.
   EDM.   When I dissuaded him from his intent,
And found him pight° to do it, with curst speech
I threaten'd to discover him. He replied,   70
"Thou unpossessing° bastard! dost thou think,
If I would stand against thee, would the reposal
Of any trust, virtue, or worth in thee
Make thy words faith'd?° No; what I should deny,—
As this I would; ay, though thou didst produce
My very character,—I'd turn it all
To thy suggestion, plot, and damned practice;
And thou must make a dullard of the world,°
If they not thought the profits of my death
Were very pregnant and potential spurs   80
To make thee seek it."
   GLOU.   O strange and fasten'd° villain!
Would he deny his letter? I never got him.   [*Tucket within.*
Hark, the duke's trumpets! I know not why he comes.
All ports I'll bar; the villain shall not 'scape;
The duke must grant me that. Besides, his picture
I will send far and near, that all the kingdom
May have due note of him; and of my land,

---

52. **loathly opposite,** loathingly opposed. 53. **fell motion,** deadly thrust. 56. **best alarum'd,** thoroughly aroused to action as by a trumpet. 58. **gasted,** frightened. 62. **dispatch.** He will be killed immediately. 63. **arch,** chief. 66. **stake,** an allusion to tying prisoners to a stake, or a figure from bear-baiting. 69. **pight,** determined. 71. **unpossessing,** unable to inherit, beggarly. 74. **faith'd,** believed. 78. **make . . . world,** think the world an idiot. 82. **strange and fasten'd,** obdurate and confirmed.

Loyal and natural boy, I'll work the means
90 To make thee capable.°
Enter CORNWALL, REGAN, *and* Attendants.
    CORN.   How now, my noble friend! since I came hither,
Which I can call but now, I have heard strange news.
    REG.   If it be true, all vengeance comes too short
Which can pursue the offender. How dost, my lord?
    GLOU.   O madam, my old heart is crack'd, it 's crack'd!
    REG.   What, did my father's godson seek your life?
He whom my father named? your Edgar?
    GLOU.   O lady, lady, shame would have it hid!
    REG.   Was he not companion with the riotous knights
100 That tended upon my father?
    GLOU.   I know not, madam. 'Tis too bad, too bad.
    EDM.   Yes, madam, he was of that consort.°
    REG.   No marvel, then, though he were ill affected.
'Tis they have put him on° the old man's death,
To have the expense and waste of his revenues.
I have this present evening from my sister
Been well inform'd of them, and with such cautions,
That if they come to sojourn at my house,
I'll not be there.
110   CORN.   Nor I, assure thee, Regan.
Edmund, I hear that you have shown your father
A child-like office.
    EDM.   'Twas my duty, sir.
    GLOU.   He did bewray° his practice, and received
This hurt you see, striving to apprehend him.
    CORN.   Is he pursued?
    GLOU.   Ay, my good lord.
    CORN.   If he be taken, he shall never more
Be fear'd of doing harm. Make your own purpose,
120 How in my strength° you please. For you, Edmund,
Whose virtue and obedience doth this instant
So much commend itself, you shall be ours.
Natures of such deep trust we shall much need;
You we first seize on.
    EDM.   I shall serve you, sir,
Truly, however else.
    GLOU.   For him I thank your grace.
    CORN.   You know not why we came to visit you,—

90. **capable,** legitimate and hence able to become Gloucester's heir. 102. **consort,** set, company. 104. **put . . . on,** incited him to. 114. **bewray,** disclose. 120. **in my strength,** by my power and authority.

REG. Thus out of season, threading° dark-eyed night;
Occasions, noble Gloucester, of some prize,   130
Wherein we must have use of your advice.
Our father he hath writ, so hath our sister,
Of differences, which° I best thought it fit
To answer from our home; the several messengers
From hence attend dispatch.° Our good old friend,
Lay comforts to your bosom, and bestow
Your needful counsel to our businesses,
Which craves the instant use.
GLOU.   I serve you, madam.
Your graces are right welcome.   [*Exeunt.* 140
SCENE II. *Before Gloucester's castle.*
Enter KENT *and* OSWALD, *severally.*
OSW. Good dawning to thee, friend. Art of this house?
KENT. Ay.
OSW. Where may we set our horses?
KENT. I' the mire.
OSW. Prithee, if thou lovest me, tell me.
KENT. I love thee not.
OSW. Why then, I care not for thee.
KENT. If I had thee in Lipsbury pinfold,° I would make thee care
for me.
OSW. Why dost thou use me thus? I know thee not.   10
KENT. Fellow, I know thee.
OSW. What dost thou know me for?
KENT. A knave; a rascal; an eater of broken meats;° a base, proud,
shallow, beggarly, three-suited,° hundred-pound,° filthy, worsted-
stocking° knave; a lily-livered, action-taking,° whoreson, glass-gazing,°
superserviceable,° finical° rogue; one-trunk-inheriting° slave; one that
wouldst be a bawd in way of good service, and art nothing but the composition of a knave, beggar, coward, pander, and the son and heir of a
mongrel bitch—one whom I will beat into clamorous whining if thou
deniest the least syllable of thy addition.°   20

129. **threading,** passing through (as thread through the eye of a needle). 133. **which,** the
letter. 135. **attend dispatch,** wait to be dispatched.
8. **Lipsbury pinfold.** This phrase is unexplained. *Pinfold* means "pound for stray animals."
Critics have tried to see in it an allusion to the prize ring. 13. **broken meats,** leftovers for
servants. 14. **three-suited,** probable allusion to three suits a year allowed to servants. **hundred-pound,** possible allusion to the minimum property qualification for the status of a gentleman; sometimes seen as a reference to James I's wholesale creation of knights. 14-15. **worsted-
stocking,** too poor and menial to wear silk stockings. 15. **action-taking,** settling quarrels by
resort to law instead of arms, cowardly. **glass-gazing,** fond of looking in the mirror. 16.
superserviceable, officious. **finical,** excessively particular, probably, in dress. **one-trunk-
inheriting,** possessing effects sufficient for one trunk only. 20. **addition,** ironic reference to
titles of honor.

Osw. Why, what a monstrous fellow art thou, thus to rail on one that is neither known of thee nor knows thee!

Kent. What a brazen-faced varlet art thou, to deny thou knowest me! Is it two days ago since I tripped up thy heels, and beat thee before the king? Draw, you rogue; for, though it be night, yet the moon shines. I'll make a sop o' the moonshine° of you. You whoreson cullionly barber-monger,° draw!   [Drawing his sword.

Osw. Away! I have nothing to do with thee.

Kent. Draw, you rascal! You come with letters against the king, and
30 take vanity the puppet's part° against the royalty of her father. Draw, you rogue, or I'll so carbonado° your shanks. Draw, you rascal. Come your ways!

Osw. Help, ho! murder! help!

Kent. Strike, you slave! Stand, rogue! Stand, you neat° slave! Strike! Beating him.

Osw. Help, ho! murder! murder!

Enter EDMUND, with his rapier drawn.

Edm. How now! What 's the matter?°

Kent. With you, goodman boy,° if you please! Come, I'll flesh ye; come on, young master.

Enter CORNWALL, REGAN, GLOUCESTER, and Servants.

Glou. Weapons? arms? What 's the matter here?
40 Corn. Keep peace, upon your lives! He dies that strikes again. What is the matter?

Reg. The messengers from our sister and the king.

Corn. What is your difference? speak.

Osw. I am scarce in breath, my lord.

Kent. No marvel, you have so bestirred your valour. You cowardly rascal, nature disclaims in° thee; a tailor made thee.

Corn. Thou art a strange fellow: a tailor make a man?

Kent. A tailor, sir: a stone-cutter or a painter could not have made him so ill, though he had been but two hours at the trade.
50 Corn. Speak yet, how grew your quarrel?

Osw. This ancient ruffian, sir, whose life I have spared at suit of his gray beard,—

Kent. Thou whoreson zed!° thou unnecessary letter! My lord, if you

---

26. **sop o' the moonshine,** supposed punning allusion to a dish called "eggs in moonshine." 26-27. **cullionly barber-monger,** base frequenter of barber shops, fop. 30. **vanity the puppet's part.** Vanity was a character in the morality plays. 31. **carbonado,** cut you crosswise like meat for broiling. 34. **neat,** foppish. 36. **matter.** Kent takes the secondary meaning, "cause for quarrel." 37. **goodman boy,** contemptuously. 46. **disclaims in,** disowns. 53. **zed,** the letter Z, a Greek character; in the spelling of English words, known but unnecessary, and often not included in dictionaries.

will give me leave, I will tread this unbolted° villain into mortar and
daub the wall of a jakes with him. Spare my gray beard, you wagtail?°
CORN. Peace, sirrah!
You beastly knave, know you no reverence?
KENT. Yes, sir; but anger hath a privilege.
CORN. Why art thou angry?
KENT. That such a slave as this should wear a sword,   60
Who wears no honesty. Such smiling rogues as these,
Like rats, oft bite the holy cords° a-twain
Which are too intrinse° t' unloose; smooth° every passion
That in the natures of their lords rebel;
Bring oil to fire, snow to their colder moods;
Renege,° affirm, and turn their halcyon beaks°
With every gale and vary° of their masters,
Knowing nought, like dogs, but following.
A plague upon your epileptic° visage!
Smile you my speeches, as I were a fool?   70
Goose, if I had you upon Sarum plain,
I'd drive ye cackling home to Camelot.°
CORN. What, art thou mad, old fellow?
GLOU. How fell you out? say that.
KENT. No contraries hold more antipathy
Than I and such a knave.
CORN. Why dost thou call him knave? What is his fault?
KENT. His countenance likes me not.
CORN. No more perchance does mine, nor his, nor hers.
KENT. Sir, 'tis my occupation to be plain: 80
I have seen better faces in my time
Than stands on any shoulder that I see
Before me at this instant.
CORN.   This is some fellow,
Who, having been praised for bluntness, doth affect
A saucy roughness, and constrains the garb
Quite from his nature.° He cannot flatter, he,
An honest mind and plain, he must speak truth!

---

54. **unbolted,** unsifted; hence, coarse. 55. **wagtail,** name of a bird; epithet to denote
pertness. 62. **holy cords,** natural bonds of affection. 63. **intrinse,** defined as "entangled"
and as "very tightly drawn." **smooth,** flatter, humor. 66. **Renege,** deny. **halcyon beaks.**
The halcyon or kingfisher, if hung up, would turn his beak against the wind. 67. **vary,** variation.
69. **epileptic,** indication of Oswald's visage, pale with fright and distorted with a grin. 71-72.
Sarum ... Camelot. The allusion is to Sarum plain, the Salisbury plain (where large flocks of
geese were bred), and to Camelot, the seat of King Arthur and his Round Table, said to have
been at Cadbury and at Winchester. 86-87. **constrains ... nature,** assumes by an effort a
bearing or manner of speech which is wholly unnatural.

An they will take it, so; if not, he 's plain.
90 These kind of knaves I know which in this plainness
Harbour more craft and more corrupter ends
Than twenty silly ducking observants°
That stretch their duties nicely.°
    KENT. Sir, in good faith,° in sincere verity,
Under the allowance of your great aspect,
Whose influence, like the wreath of radiant fire
On flickering Phœbus̩' front,—
    CORN.   What mean'st by this?
    KENT. To go out of my dialect, which you discommend so much. I
100 know, sir, I am no flatterer. He that beguiled you in a plain accent was a
plain knave, which for my part I will not be, though I should win your
displeasure to entreat me to 't.
    CORN. What was the offence you gave him?
    Osw. I never gave him any.
It pleased the king his master very late
To strike at me, upon his misconstruction;°
When he, compact,° and flattering his displeasure,
Tripp'd me behind; being down, insulted, rail'd,
And put upon him such a deal of man,°
110 That worthied° him, got praises of the king
For him attempting° who was self-subdued;
And, in the fleshment° of this dread exploit,
Drew on me here again.
    KENT.   None of these rogues and cowards
But Ajax is their fool.°
    CORN.   Fetch forth the stocks!
You stubborn ancient knave, you reverend braggart,
We'll teach you—
    KENT.   Sir, I am too old to learn.
120 Call not your stocks for me. I serve the king,
On whose employment I was sent to you:
You shall do small respect, show too bold malice
Against the grace and person of my master,°
Stocking his messenger.
    CORN. Fetch forth the stocks! As I have life and honour,
There shall he sit till noon.

---

92. **ducking observants,** bowing, obsequious courtiers. 93. **nicely,** punctiliously. 94. **Sir, in good faith,** etc. Kent assumes the speech of courtly decorum. 106. **misconstruction,** misunderstanding (me). 107. **compact,** joined, united with Lear. 109. **put . . . man,** acted like such a hero. 110. **worthied,** won reputation. 111. **attempting,** assailing. 112. **fleshment,** excitement resulting from a first success. 115. **Ajax is their fool,** a scornful reference to Cornwall. Ajax, traditional braggart, is outdone by them in boasting. 123. **grace . . . master,** whom as a messenger Kent represented.

REG. Till noon! till night, my lord; and all night too.

KENT. Why, madam, if I were your father's dog,
You should not use me so.

REG.   Sir, being his knave, I will.   130

CORN. This is a fellow of the self-same colour
Our sister speaks of. Come, bring away the stocks!   [*Stocks brought out.*

GLOU. Let me beseech your grace not to do so.
His fault is much, and the good king his master
Will check him for 't. Your purposed low correction
Is such as basest and contemned'st wretches
For pilferings and most common trespasses
Are punish'd with. The king must take it ill,
That he 's so slightly valued in his messenger,
Should have him thus restrain'd.   140

CORN.   I'll answer that.

REG. My sister may receive it much more worse,
To have her gentleman abused, assaulted,
For following her affairs. Put in his legs.   [*Kent is put in the stocks.*
Come, my good lord, away.   [*Exeunt all but Gloucester and Kent.*

GLOU. I am sorry for thee, friend; 'tis the duke's pleasure,
Whose disposition, all the world well knows,
Will not be rubb'd° nor stopp'd. I'll entreat for thee.

KENT. Pray, do not, sir. I have watched and travell'd hard;
Some time I shall sleep out, the rest I'll whistle.   150
A good man's fortune may grow out at heels.
Give you° good morrow!

GLOU. The duke 's to blame in this; 'twill be ill taken.   [*Exit.*

KENT. Good king, that must approve° the common saw,°
Thou out of heaven's benediction comest
To the warm sun!
Approach, thou beacon to this under globe,
That by thy comfortable° beams I may
Peruse this letter! Nothing almost sees miracles
But misery. I know 'tis from Cordelia,   160
Who hath most fortunately been inform'd
Of my obscured course;° and shall find time
From this enormous state,° seeking to give
Losses their remedies.° All weary and o'er-watch'd,°

148. **rubb'd,** hindered, obstructed; term from bowls. 152. **Give you,** i.e., God give you. 154. **approve,** prove true. **saw,** proverb: "To run out of God's blessing into the warm sun," meaning "to go from better to worse." 158. **comfortable,** useful. 162. **obscured course,** Kent's disguised service to Lear. 163. **enormous state,** dislocated abnormal conditions. 162-64. **and . . . remedies,** an obscure passage. Daniel's conjecture of *she'll* for *shall* makes a sort of sense. 164. **o'er-watch'd,** exhausted with watching.

Take vantage, heavy eyes, not to behold
This shameful lodging.
Fortune, good night; smile once more; turn thy wheel!   [*Sleeps.*
SCENE III.   *A wood.*
Enter EDGAR.
        EDG.   I heard myself proclaim'd,
And by the happy hollow of a tree
Escaped the hunt. No port° is free; no place
That guard and most unusual vigilance
Does not attend° my taking. Whiles I may 'scape,
I will preserve myself; and am bethought°
To take the basest and most poorest shape
That ever penury, in contempt of man,
Brought near to beast. My face I'll grime with filth,
10 Blanket my loins, elf° all my hair in knots,
And with presented nakedness out-face
The winds and persecutions of the sky.
The country gives me proof and precedent
Of Bedlam beggars,° who, with roaring voices,
Strike in their numb'd and mortified° bare arms
Pins, wooden pricks,° nails, sprigs of rosemary;
And with this horrible object,° from low° farms,
Poor pelting° villages, sheep-cotes, and mills,
Sometime with lunatic bans,° sometime with prayers,
20 Enforce their charity. "Poor Turlygod!° poor Tom!"
That 's something yet! Edgar I nothing° am.   [*Exit.*
SCENE IV.   *Before Gloucester's castle. Kent in the stocks.*
Enter LEAR, FOOL, *and* Gentleman.
        LEAR.   'Tis strange that they should so depart from home,
And not send back my messenger.
        GENT.   As I learn'd,
The night before there was no purpose in them
Of this remove.°
        KENT.   Hail to thee, noble master!
        LEAR.   Ha!
Makest thou this shame thy pastime?
        KENT.   No, my lord.

---

    3. **port,** means of exit.   5. **attend,** watch, wait for.   6. **am bethought,** it has occurred to
me.   10. **elf,** tangle into elf-locks.   14. **Bedlam beggars,** called also "Tom o' Bedlams" and
"Abraham men"; they were lunatic patients of Bethlehem Hospital turned out to beg for their
bread.   15. **mortified,** numbed, insensible.   16. **wooden pricks,** skewers.   17. **object,** appearance. **low,** lowly.   18. **pelting,** paltry, petty.   19. **bans,** curses.   20. **Turlygod,** meaning
unknown; perhaps the name of a Bedlam beggar.   21. **nothing,** probably, not at all, in no
respect.
    5. **remove,** change of residence (of royalty).

FOOL. Ha, ha! he wears cruel° garters. Horses are tied by the heads, 10
dogs and bears by the neck, monkeys by the loins, and men by the legs.
When a man 's over-lusty at legs, then he wears wooden nether-stocks.°
LEAR.   What 's he that hath so much thy place mistook
To set thee here?
KENT.   It is both he and she—
Your son and daughter.
LEAR.   No.
KENT.   Yes.
LEAR.   No, I say.
KENT.   I say yea.   20
LEAR.   No, no, they would not.
KENT.   Yes, they have.
LEAR.   By Jupiter, I swear no!
KENT.   By Juno, I swear ay!
LEAR.   They durst not do 't;
They could not, would not do 't; 'tis worse than murder
To do upon respect° such violent outrage.
Resolve me with all modest haste which way
Thou mightest deserve or they impose this usage,
Coming from us.   30
KENT.   My lord, when at their home
I did commend° your highness' letters to them,
Ere I was risen from the place that show'd
My duty kneeling, came there a reeking post,
Stew'd in his haste, half breathless, panting forth
From Goneril his mistress salutations;
Deliver'd letters, spite of intermission,°
Which presently they read; on whose contents,
They summon'd up their meiny,° straight took horse,
Commanded me to follow and attend   40
The leisure of their answer, gave me cold looks,
And meeting here the other messenger,
Whose welcome I perceived had poison'd mine,—
Being the very fellow which of late
Display'd° so saucily against your highness,—
Having more man than wit about me, drew.°
He raised the house with loud and coward cries.

10. cruel, a double meaning: (1) "unkind," (2) "crewel," a thin yarn of which garters were
made. 12. nether-stocks, stockings. 27. upon respect, the respect due to Lear as king and
father. 32. commend, deliver, commit. 37. spite of intermission, in spite of interrupting me.
39. meiny, household. 45. Display'd, behaved ostentatiously. 46. drew, i.e., my sword.

Your son and daughter found this trespass worth
The shame which here it suffers.
50 FOOL.   Winter 's not gone yet, if the wild-geese fly that way.
          Fathers that wear rags
               Do make their children blind,
          But fathers that bear bags°
               Shall see their children kind.
          Fortune, that arrant whore,
               Ne'er turns the key to the poor.
But for all this, thou shalt have as many dolours° for thy daughters as thou
canst tell in a year.
     LEAR.   O, how this mother° swells up toward my heart!
60 Hysterica passio!° Down, thou climbing sorrow,
Thy element 's below! Where is this daughter?
     KENT.   With the earl, sir, here within.
     LEAR.   Follow me not;
Stay here.   [*Exit.*
     GENT.   Made you no more offence but what you speak of?
     KENT.   None.
How chance° the king comes with so small a number?
     FOOL.   An thou hadst been set i' the stocks for that question, thou
hadst well deserved it.
70   KENT.   Why, fool?
     FOOL.   We'll set thee to school to an ant, to teach thee there 's no
labouring i' the winter. All that follow their noses are led by their eyes
but blind men, and there 's not a nose among twenty but can smell him
that 's stinking. Let go thy hold when a great wheel runs down a hill, lest
it break thy neck with following it; but the great one that goes upward,
let him draw thee after. When a wise man gives thee better counsel, give
me mine again; I would have none but knaves follow it, since a fool
gives it.
          That sir° which serves and seeks for gain,
80   And follows but for form,
          Will pack° when it begins to rain,
               And leave thee in the storm.
          But I will tarry; the fool will stay,
               And let the wise man fly.
          The knave turns fool that runs away;
               The fool no knave, perdy.
     KENT.   Where learned you this, fool?

---

53. **bags,** moneybags.   57. **dolours,** griefs, with pun on "dollars."   59-60. **mother . . .
Hysterica passio,** a disease, apparently called by both these names, accompanied by a sense of
strangulation. Lear mistakes the epigastric discomfort of extreme grief for the disease.   67.
chance, chances it.   79. **sir,** great person.   81. **pack,** take himself off.

Fool.   Not i' the stocks, fool.

Re-enter Lear, *with* Gloucester.

Lear.   Deny to speak with me? They are sick? they are weary?
They have travell'd all the night? Mere fetches°—   90
The images of revolt and flying off.°
Fetch me a better answer.

Glou.   My dear lord,
You know the fiery quality of the duke,
How unremoveable and fix'd he is
In his own course.

Lear.   Vengeance! plague! death! confusion!
Fiery? what quality? Why, Gloucester, Gloucester,
I'd speak with the Duke of Cornwall and his wife.

Glou.   Well, my good lord, I have inform'd them so.   100

Lear.   Inform'd them! Dost thou understand me, man?

Glou.   Ay, my good lord.

Lear.   The king would speak with Cornwall; the dear father
Would with his daughter speak, commands her service.
Are they inform'd of this? My breath and blood!
Fiery? the fiery duke? Tell the hot duke that—
No, but not yet; may be he is not well.
Infirmity doth still neglect all office
Whereto our health is bound; we are not ourselves
When nature, being oppress'd, commands the mind   110
To suffer with the body. I'll forbear;
And am fall'n out with my more headier will,
To take° the indisposed and sickly fit
For the sound man. Death on my state! wherefore   [*Looking on* Kent.
Should he sit here? This act persuades me
That this remotion° of the duke and her
Is practice only. Give me my servant forth.
Go tell the duke and 's wife I'd speak with them,
Now, presently. Bid them come forth and hear me,
Or at their chamber-door I'll beat the drum   120
Till it cry sleep to death.°

Glou.   I would have all well betwixt you.   [*Exit.*

Lear.   O me, my heart, my rising heart! but, down!

Fool.   Cry to it, nuncle, as the cockney° did to the eels when she put
'em i' the paste alive; she knapped° 'em o' the coxcombs° with a stick

---

90. **fetches,** pretexts, dodges. 91. **flying off,** desertion. 112-113. **am . . . take,** am wrong
because of my more impetuous will in taking. 116. **remotion,** removal. 121. **cry sleep to
death,** i.e., put an end to sleep. 124. **cockney,** a word of disputed origin and meaning. It is
said to have meant a pampered, affected woman, a spoiled child, a milksop; the passage here
suggests the meaning "cook." 125. **knapped.** *Knap* means properly "to break asunder."
coxcombs, heads.

and cried, "Down, wantons, down!" 'Twas her brother that, in pure
kindness to his horse, buttered his hay.
Enter CORNWALL, REGAN, GLOUCESTER, *and* Servants.
    LEAR. Good morrow to you both.
    CORN.   Hail to your grace!   *[Kent is set at liberty.*
130 REG. I am glad to see your highness.
    LEAR. Regan, I think you are; I know what reason
I have to think so. If thou shouldst not be glad,
I would divorce me from thy mother's tomb,
Sepulchring an adultress. *[To Kent]* O, are you free?
Some other time for that. Beloved Regan,
Thy sister 's naught.° O Regan, she hath tied
Sharp-tooth'd unkindness, like a vulture, here!   *[Points to his heart.*
I can scarce speak to thee; thou 'lt not believe
With how depraved a quality—O Regan!
140 REG. I pray you, sir, take patience. I have hope
You less know how to value her desert
Than she to scant her duty.
    LEAR.   Say, how is that?
    REG. I cannot think my sister in the least
Would fail her obligation. If, sir, perchance
She have restrain'd the riots of your followers,
'Tis on such ground, and to such wholesome end,
As clears her from all blame.
    LEAR. My curses on her!
150 REG.   O, sir, you are old;
Nature in you stands on the very verge
Of her confine.° You should be ruled and led
By some discretion° that discerns your state
Better than you yourself. Therefore I pray you
That to our sister you do make return;
Say you have wrong'd her.
    LEAR.   Ask her forgiveness?
Do you but mark how this becomes the house:°
"Dear daughter, I confess that I am old;   *[Kneeling.*
160 Age is unnecessary. On my knees I beg
That you'll vouchsafe me raiment, bed, and food."
    REG. Good sir, no more; these are unsightly tricks.
Return you to my sister.
    LEAR.   *[Rising]* Never, Regan!
She hath abated me of half my train;
Look'd black upon me; struck me with her tongue,

136. **naught,** wicked. 152. **confine,** assigned boundary. 153. **discretion,** discreet person.
158. **how . . . house,** how this would be suited to our position.

Most serpent-like, upon the very heart.
All the stored vengeances of heaven fall
On her ingrateful top!° Strike her young bones,°
You taking airs, with lameness!   170
    CORN.   Fie, sir, fie!
    LEAR.   You nimble lightnings, dart your blinding flames
Into her scornful eyes! Infect her beauty,
You fen-suck'd° fogs, drawn by the powerful sun,
To fall and blister!
    REG.   O the blest gods! so will you wish on me
When the rash mood is on.
    LEAR.   No, Regan, thou shalt never have my curse;
Thy tender-hefted° nature shall not give
Thee o'er to harshness. Her eyes are fierce; but thine   180
Do comfort and not burn. 'Tis not in thee
To grudge my pleasures, to cut off my train,
To bandy hasty words, to scant my sizes,°
And in conclusion to oppose the bolt
Against my coming in. Thou better know'st
The offices of nature, bond of childhood,
Effects of courtesy, dues of gratitude;
Thy half o' the kingdom hast thou not forgot,
Wherein I thee endow'd.
    REG.   Good sir, to the purpose.   190
    LEAR.   Who put my man i' the stocks?   [Tucket within.
    CORN.   What trumpet 's that?
    REG.   I know 't—my sister's. This approves° her letter,
That she would soon be here.
Enter OSWALD.
                    Is your lady come?
    LEAR.   This is a slave, whose easy-borrow'd° pride
Dwells in the fickle grace of her he follows.
Out, varlet, from my sight!
    CORN.   What means your grace?
    LEAR.   Who stock'd° my servant? Regan, I have good hope   200
Thou didst not know on 't.
Enter GONERIL.
                    Who comes here? O heavens,
If you do love old men, if your sweet sway
Allow obedience, if yourselves are old,

---

169. **ingrateful top,** ungrateful head. **young bones,** i.e., unborn child. 174. **fen-suck'd.**
It was supposed that the sun sucked up poisons from fens or marshes. 179. **tender-hefted,** set
in a tender, delicate frame; gentle. 183. **sizes,** allowances. 193. **approves,** confirms. 196.
easy-borrow'd, put on without justification. 200. **stock'd,** put into the stocks.

Make it your cause;° send down, and take my part!
[*To Goneril*]   Art not ashamed to look upon this beard?
O Regan, will you take her by the hand?
    GON.   Why not by the hand, sir? How have I offended?
All 's not offence that indiscretion finds
210 And dotage terms so.
    LEAR.   O sides, you are too tough;°
Will you yet hold? How came my man i' the stocks?
    CORN.   I set him there, sir; but his own disorders
Deserved much less advancement.
    LEAR.   You! did you?
    REG.   I pray you, father, being weak, seem so.
If, till the expiration of your month,
You will return and sojourn with my sister,
Dismissing half your train, come then to me.
220 I am now from home, and out of that provision
Which shall be needful for your entertainment.
    LEAR.   Return to her, and fifty men dismiss'd?
No, rather I abjure all roofs, and choose
To wage° against the enmity o' the air,
To be a comrade with the wolf and owl,—
Necessity's sharp pinch! Return with her?
Why, the hot-blooded France, that dowerless took
Our youngest born, I could as well be brought
To knee° his throne, and, squire-like, pension beg
230 To keep base life afoot. Return with her?
Persuade me rather to be slave and sumpter°
To this detested groom.   [*Pointing at Oswald.*
    GON.   At your choice, sir.
    LEAR.   I prithee, daughter, do not make me mad.
I will not trouble thee, my child; farewell.
We'll no more meet, no more see one another.
But yet thou art my flesh, my blood, my daughter;
Or rather a disease that 's in my flesh,
Which I must needs call mine. Thou art a boil,
240 A plague-sore, or embossed° carbuncle,
In my corrupted blood. But I'll not chide thee;
Let shame come when it will, I do not call it.
I do not bid the thunder-bearer° shoot,
Nor tell tales of thee to high-judging Jove.

---

205. **Make . . . cause,** make my cause yours.   211. **sides . . . tough.** This is not figurative but indicates belief in an actual swelling of the heart so that it might break through the sides. 224. **wage,** wage war.   229. **knee,** fall on my knees before.   231. **sumpter,** pack horse; hence, drudge.   240. **embossed,** swollen, tumid.   243. **thunder-bearer,** Jupiter.

Mend when thou canst; be better at thy leisure;
I can be patient; I can stay with Regan,
I and my hundred knights.
REG.   Not altogether so.
I look'd not for you yet, nor am provided
For your fit welcome. Give ear, sir, to my sister;   250
For those that mingle reason with your passion
Must be content to think you old, and so—
But she knows what she does.
    LEAR.   Is this well spoken?
    REG.   I dare avouch° it, sir. What, fifty followers?
Is it not well? What should you need of more?
Yea, or so many, sith that both charge and danger
Speak 'gainst so great a number? How in one house
Should many people, under two commands,
Hold amity?° 'Tis hard; almost impossible.   260
    GON.   Why might not you, my lord, receive attendance
From those that she calls servants, or from mine?
    REG.   Why not, my lord? If then they chanced to slack° you,
We could control them. If you will come to me,—
For now I spy a danger,—I entreat you
To bring but five and twenty: to no more
Will I give place or notice.°
    LEAR.   I gave you all—
    REG.   And in good time you gave it.
    LEAR.   Made you my guardians, my depositaries;   270
But kept a reservation to be follow'd
With such a number. What, must I come to you
With five and twenty, Regan? said you so?
    REG.   And speak 't again, my lord; no more with me.
    LEAR.   Those wicked creatures yet do look well-favour'd
When others are more wicked;° not being the worst
Stands in some rank of praise.   [To Goneril]   I'll go with thee.
Thy fifty yet doth double five-and-twenty,
And thou art twice her love.
    GON.   Hear me, my lord: 280
What need you five and twenty, ten, or five,
To follow in a house where twice so many
Have a command to tend° you?
    REG.   What need one?
    LEAR.   O, reason not the need! Our basest beggars

---

255. **avouch,** acknowledge. 260. **Hold amity,** maintain friendship. 263. **slack,** be careless in their attendance on. 267. **notice,** countenance. 275-76. **Those . . . wicked.** Bad as Goneril is, there is a more exquisite quality of cruelty in Regan. 283. **tend,** wait on.

Are in the poorest thing superfluous.
Allow not nature more than nature needs,
Man's life is cheap as beast's. Thou art a lady;
If only to go warm were gorgeous,
290 Why, nature needs not what thou gorgeous wear'st,
Which scarcely keeps thee warm. But, for true need,—
You heavens, give me that patience,° patience I need!
You see me here, you gods, a poor old man,
As full of grief as age; wretched in both.
If it be you that stir these daughters' hearts
Against their father, fool me not so much
To bear it tamely; touch me with noble anger,
And let not women's weapons, water-drops,
Stain my man's cheeks! No, you unnatural hags,
300 I will have such revenges on you both
That all the world shall—I will do such things,—
What they are yet, I know not; but they shall be
The terrors of the earth. You think I'll weep;
No, I'll not weep.
I have full cause of weeping; but this heart
Shall break into a hundred thousand flaws,°
Or ere I'll weep. O fool, I shall go mad!
                [*Exeunt Lear, Gloucester, Kent, and Fool. Storm and tempest.*
    CORN. Let us withdraw; 'twill be a storm.
    REG. This house is little: the old man and his people
310 Cannot be well bestow'd.°
    GON. 'Tis his own blame;° hath put himself from rest,
And must needs taste his folly.
    REG. For his particular,° I'll receive him gladly,
But not one follower.
    GON.   So am I purposed.
Where is my lord of Gloucester?
    CORN. Follow'd the old man forth.
Re-enter GLOUCESTER.
                          He is return'd.
    GLOU. The king is in high rage.
320 CORN.   Whither is he going?
    GLOU. He calls to horse, but will I know not whither.
    CORN. 'Tis best to give him way; he leads himself.
    GON. My lord, entreat him by no means to stay.

292. **patience.** Patience seems to have been a term for the counterbalance which reason
might set up against the passions. 306. **flaws,** pieces; a flaw could also be a brief burst of
passion or a squall, which suits the rising storm. 310. **bestow'd,** lodged. 311. **blame,** fault.
313. **For his particular,** as for him individually.

Glou. Alack, the night comes on, and the bleak winds
Do sorely ruffle;° for many miles about
There 's scarce a bush.
    Reg.   O, sir, to wilful men
The injuries that they themselves procure
Must be their schoolmasters. Shut up your doors.
He is attended with a desperate train,°   330
And what they may incense him to,° being apt
To have his ear abused, wisdom bids fear.
    Corn. Shut up your doors, my lord; 'tis a wild night.
My Regan counsels well. Come out o' the storm.   [*Exeunt.*

Act III

Scene i. *A heath.*
Storm still. Enter Kent *and a* Gentleman, *meeting.*
    Kent. Who 's there, besides foul weather?
    Gent. One minded like the weather, most unquietly.
    Kent. I know you. Where 's the king?
    Gent. Contending with the fretful elements;
Bids the wind blow the earth into the sea,
Or swell the curled waters 'bove the main,°
That things might change or cease; tears his white hair,
Which the impetuous blasts, with eyeless rage,
Catch in their fury, and make nothing of;
Strives in his little world of man° to out-scorn   10
The to-and-fro-conflicting wind and rain.
This night, wherein the cub-drawn° bear would couch,°
The lion and the belly-pinched wolf
Keep their fur dry, unbonneted he runs,
And bids what will take all.
    Kent.   But who is with him?
    Gent. None but the fool, who labours to out-jest
His heart struck injuries.
    Kent.   Sir, I do know you,
And dare upon the warrant of my note°   20
Commend° a dear thing to you. There is division,
Although as yet the face of it is cover'd
With mutual cunning, 'twixt Albany and Cornwall;

---

325. **ruffle,** bluster. 330. **desperate train,** body of desperate followers. 331. **incense him
to,** incite him to undertake.
    6. **main,** mainland. 10. **little world of man,** the microcosm; allusion to the theory that
man is an epitome of the macrocosm, or universe, and moves in accordance with its laws and
influences. 12. **cub-drawn,** famished, with udders sucked dry. **couch,** lie close. 20. **upon
. . . note,** on the strength of what I know. 21. **Commend,** entrust.

Who have—as who have not, that their great stars
Throned and set high?—servants, who seem no less,
Which are to France the spies and speculations°
Intelligent of our state. What hath been seen,
Either in snuffs° and packings° of the dukes,
Or the hard rein which both of them have borne
30 Against the old kind king; or something deeper,
Whereof perchance these are but furnishings°—
But, true it is, from France there comes a power
Into this scatter'd° kingdom, who already,
Wise in our negligence, have secret feet
In some of our best ports, and are at point°
To show their open banner. Now to you:
If on my credit you dare build so far
To make your speed to Dover, you shall find
Some that will thank you, making just report
40 Of how unnatural and bemadding° sorrow
The king hath cause to plain.°
I am a gentleman of blood and breeding,
And from some knowledge and assurance offer
This office to you.
    GENT.   I will talk further with you.
    KENT.   No, do not.
For confirmation that I am much more
Than my out-wall,° open this purse and take
What it contains. If you shall see Cordelia,—
50 As fear not but you shall,—show her this ring;
And she will tell you who your fellow is
That yet you do not know. Fie on this storm!
I will go seek the king.
    GENT.   Give me your hand. Have you no more to say?
    KENT.   Few words, but, to effect,° more than all yet:
That, when we have found the king,—in which your pain
That way,° I'll this,—he that first lights on him
Holla the other.   *[Exeunt severally.*
SCENE II.   *Another part of the heath. Storm still.*
Enter LEAR *and* FOOL.
    LEAR.   Blow, winds, and crack your cheeks! rage! blow!
You cataracts and hurricanoes,° spout

26. **speculations,** scouts, spies. 28. **snuffs,** quarrels. **packings,** plottings. 31. **furnishings,**
outward shows. 33. **scatter'd,** divided. 35. **at point,** ready. 40. **bemadding,** distracting.
41. **plain,** complain of. 48. **out-wall,** exterior. 55. **to effect,** to the purpose. 56-57. **your
. . . way,** laborious quest (take you) that way.
    2. **hurricanoes,** waterspouts.

Till you have drench'd our steeples, drown'd the cocks!°
You sulphurous and thought-executing° fires,
Vaunt-couriers° to oak-cleaving thunderbolts,
Singe my white head! And thou, all-shaking thunder,
Smite flat the thick rotundity o' the world!
Crack nature's moulds, all germens° spill° at once,
That make ingrateful man!
    FOOL.   O nuncle, court holy-water° in a dry house is better than this 10
rain-water out o' door. Good nuncle, in; ask thy daughters' blessing!
Here 's a night pities neither wise man nor fools.
    LEAR.   Rumble thy bellyful! Spit, fire! spout, rain!
Nor rain, wind, thunder, fire are my daughters.
I tax not you, you elements, with unkindness;
I never gave you kingdom, call'd you children,
You owe me no subscription.° Then let fall
Your horrible pleasure. Here I stand your slave,
A poor, infirm, weak, and despised old man.
But yet I call you servile ministers,   20
That will with two pernicious daughters join
Your high-engender'd battles° 'gainst a head
So old and white as this. O! O! 'tis foul!
    FOOL.   He that has a house to put 's head in has a good head-piece.
      The cod-piece that will house
        Before the head has any,
      The head and he shall louse;
        So beggars marry many.
      The man that makes his toe
        What he his heart should make   30
      Shall of a corn cry woe,
        And turn his sleep to wake.°
For there was never yet fair woman but she made mouths in a glass.
    LEAR.   No, I will be the pattern of all patience;
I will say nothing.
Enter KENT.
    KENT.   Who 's there?
    FOOL.   Marry, here 's grace and a cod-piece; that 's a wise man and
a fool.
    KENT.   Alas, sir, are you here? Things that love night

---

3. **cocks,** weathercocks. 4. **thought-executing,** probably, acting with the quickness of
thought. 5. **Vaunt-couriers,** forerunners. 8. **germens,** germs, seeds. **spill,** destroy. 10.
court holy-water, flattery. 17. **subscription,** allegiance. 22. **high-engender'd battles,** bat-
talions levied in the heavens. 25-32. **The cod-piece . . . wake.** The man who illicitly has
children before he has a roof over his head will become a lice-ridden beggar. The man who
values his toe as much as his heart shall suffer severe pain from his corns while others have
only a twinge.

40 Love not such nights as these; the wrathful skies
Gallow° the very wanderers of the dark
And make them keep their caves. Since I was man,
Such sheets of fire, such bursts of horrid thunder,
Such groans of roaring wind and rain, I never
Remember to have heard. Man's nature cannot carry
The affliction nor the fear.
    LEAR.   Let the great gods,
That keep this dreadful pudder° o'er our heads,
Find out their enemies now. Tremble, thou wretch,
50 That hast within thee undivulged crimes,
Unwhipp'd of justice. Hide thee, thou bloody hand;
Thou perjured, and thou simular° of virtue
That art incestuous. Caitiff, to pieces shake,
That under covert and convenient seeming°
Hast practised on man's life. Close pent-up guilts,
Rive your concealing continents, and cry
These dreadful summoners grace.° I am a man
More sinn'd against than sinning.
    KENT.   Alack, bare-headed?
60 Gracious my lord, hard by° here is a hovel;
Some friendship will it lend you 'gainst the tempest.
Repose you there, while I to this hard house—
More harder than the stones whereof 'tis raised,
Which° even but now, demanding° after you,
Denied me to come in—return, and force
Their scanted courtesy.
    LEAR.   My wits begin to turn.
Come on, my boy. How dost, my boy? art cold?
I am cold myself. Where is this straw, my fellow?
70 The art of our necessities is strange,
And can make vile things precious. Come, your hovel.
Poor fool and knave, I have one part in my heart
That 's sorry yet for thee.
    FOOL. [*Singing*]   He that has and a little tiny wit,—
             With hey, ho, the wind and the rain,—
             Must make content with his fortunes fit,
             Though the rain it raineth every day.

---

41. **Gallow,** frighten, terrify. 48. **pudder,** turmoil. 52. **simular,** pretender. 54. **seeming,** hypocrisy. 56-57. **cry . . . grace,** pray for mercy at the hands of the officers of divine justice. A *summoner* was the police officer of an ecclesiastical court. 60. **hard by,** near by. 64. **Which,** i.e., the owners of the house. **demanding,** I inquiring.

LEAR. True, boy. Come, bring us to this hovel.

[*Exeunt. Lear and Kent*

FOOL. This is a brave night to cool a courtesan.
I'll speak a prophecy ere I go: 80
  When priests are more in word than matter;
  When brewers mar their malt with water;
  When nobles are their tailors' tutors;
  No heretics burn'd, but wenches' suitors;
  When every case in law is right;
  No squire in debt, nor no poor knight;
  When slanders do not live in tongues;
  Nor cutpurses come not to throngs;
  When usurers tell their gold i' the field;
  And bawds and whores do churches build;   90
  Then shall the realm of Albion
  Come to great confusion.
  Then comes the time, who lives to see 't,
  That going shall be used with feet.
This prophecy Merlin shall make, for I live before his time.°   [*Exit.*
SCENE III. *Gloucester's castle.*

Enter GLOUCESTER *and* EDMUND.

GLOU. Alack, alack, Edmund, I like not this unnatural dealing.
When I desired their leave that I might pity him, they took from me the
use of mine own house; charged me on pain of their perpetual displeasure
neither to speak of him, entreat for him, nor any way sustain him.

EDM. Most savage and unnatural!

GLOU. Go to; say you nothing. There 's a division between the dukes,
and a worse matter than that. I have received a letter this night—'tis
dangerous to be spoken—I have locked the letter in my closet. These injuries the king now bears will be revenged home;° there 's part of a power
already footed;° we must incline to the king. I will look him and privily 10
relieve him. Go you and maintain talk with the duke, that my charity be
not of him perceived; if he ask for me, I am ill and gone to bed. If I die
for it, as no less is threatened me, the king my old master must be
relieved. There is strange things toward, Edmund; pray you be
careful.   [*Exit.*

EDM. This courtesy, forbid thee,° shall the duke
Instantly know, and of that letter too.
This seems a fair deserving,° and must draw me

80-95. **I'll . . . time.** The Fool parodies prophetic riddles attributed to Merlin, a magician
of King Arthur's court.

9. **home,** thoroughly. 10. **footed,** landed. 16. **courtesy, forbid thee,** i.e., this kindness to
Lear you were forbidden to show. 18. **fair deserving,** meritorious action.

That which my father loses—no less than all,
20 The younger rises when the old doth fall.   [*Exit.*

SCENE IV.   *The heath. Before a hovel.*
Enter LEAR, KENT, *and* FOOL.

    KENT.   Here is the place, my lord; good my lord, enter.
The tyranny of the open night 's too rough
For nature to endure.   [*Storm still.*
    LEAR.   Let me alone.
    KENT.   Good my lord, enter here.
    LEAR.   Wilt break my heart?
    KENT.   I had rather break mine own. Good my lord, enter.
    LEAR.   Thou think'st 'tis much that this contentious storm
Invades us to the skin: so 'tis to thee;
10 But where the greater malady° is fix'd,
The lesser is scarce felt. Thou 'dst shun a bear;
But if thy flight lay toward the roaring sea,
Thou 'dst meet the bear i' the mouth. When the mind 's free,
The body 's delicate. The tempest in my mind
Doth from my senses take all feeling else
Save what beats there. Filial ingratitude!
Is it not as this mouth should tear this hand
For lifting food to 't? But I will punish home!
No, I will weep no more. In such a night
20 To shut me out! Pour on; I will endure.
In such a night as this! O Regan, Goneril!
Your old kind father, whose frank heart gave all,—
O, that way madness lies; let me shun that!
No more of that.
    KENT.   Good my lord, enter here.
    LEAR.   Prithee, go in thyself; seek thine own ease;
This tempest will not give me leave to ponder
On things would hurt me more. But I'll go in.
[*To the Fool*]   In, boy; go first. You houseless poverty,—
30 Nay, get thee in. I'll pray, and then I'll sleep.   [*Fool goes in.*
Poor naked wretches, wheresoe'er you are,
That bide° the pelting of this pitiless storm,
How shall your houseless heads and unfed sides,
Your loop'd and window'd° raggedness, defend you
From seasons such as these? O, I have ta'en
Too little care of this! Take physic, pomp;
Expose thyself to feel what wretches feel,

---

10. **greater malady.** There was a familiar belief that one passion might drive out or allay
another. 32. **bide,** endure. 34. **loop'd and window'd,** full of openings like windows and
loopholes.

That thou mayst shake the superflux° to them
And show the heavens more just.

EDG. [*Within*]   Fathom and half, fathom and half! Poor Tom!   40
The FOOL *runs out from the hovel.*

FOOL.   Come not in here, nuncle, here's a spirit. Help me, help me!

KENT.   Give me thy hand. Who 's there?

FOOL.   A spirit, a spirit! He says his name 's poor Tom.

KENT.   What art thou that dost grumble there i' the straw? Come
forth.
Enter EDGAR *disguised as a madman.*

EDG.   Away! the foul fiend follows me!
Through the sharp hawthorn blow the winds.
Hum! go to thy bed, and warm thee.

LEAR.   Didst thou give all to thy two daughters?
And art thou come to this?   50

EDG.   Who gives any thing to poor Tom? whom the foul fiend hath
led through fire and through flame, through ford and whirlpool, o'er
bog and quagmire; that hath laid knives under his pillow, and halters in
his pew; set ratsbane by his porridge; made him proud of heart, to ride
on a bay trotting-horse over four-inched bridges, to course his own shadow
for a traitor. Bless thy five wits!° Tom 's a-cold,—O, do de, do de, do de.
Bless thee from whirlwinds, star-blasting,° and taking! Do poor Tom some
charity, whom the foul fiend vexes. There could I have him now,—and
there,—and there again, and there!   [*Storm still.*

LEAR.   Have his daughters brought him to this pass?   60
Couldst thou save nothing? Wouldst thou give them all?

FOOL.   Nay, he reserved a blanket, else we had been all shamed.

LEAR.   Now all the plagues that in the pendulous° air
Hang fated o'er men's faults light on thy daughters!

KENT.   He hath no daughters, sir.

LEAR.   Death, traitor! nothing could have subdued nature
To such a lowness but his unkind daughters.
Is it the fashion that discarded fathers
Should have thus little mercy on their flesh?
Judicious punishment! 'twas this flesh begot   70
Those pelican° daughters.

EDG.   Pillicock° sat on Pillicock-hill.
Alow, alow, loo, loo!

---

38. **superflux,** superfluity, a word suggestive of the ethics of ownership in society.   56. **five
wits,** the five mental faculties: common wit, imagination, fantasy, judgment, memory.   57. **star-
blasting,** blighting by influence of the stars.   63. **pendulous,** suspended.   71. **pelican,** greedy;
a reference to the belief that young pelicans fed on the flesh of their mother's breasts.   72. **Pillicock,** from an old rhyme (suggested by *pelican*). *Pillicock* seems to have been used to mean
"darling."

FOOL. This cold night will turn us all to fools and madmen.

EDG. Take heed o' the foul fiend, obey thy parents; keep thy word justly; swear not; commit not with man's sworn spouse; set not thy sweet heart on proud array. Tom 's a-cold.

LEAR. What hast thou been?

EDG. A serving-man, proud in heart and mind; that curled my hair,
80 wore gloves° in my cap; served the lust of my mistress' heart, and did the act of darkness with her; swore as many oaths as I spake words, and broke them in the sweet face of heaven; one that slept in the contriving of lust, and waked to do it. Wine loved I deeply, dice dearly; and in woman out-paramoured the Turk. False of heart, light of ear,° bloody of hand; hog in sloth, fox in stealth, wolf in greediness, dog in madness, lion in prey. Let not the creaking of shoes nor the rustling of silks betray thy poor heart to woman. Keep thy foot out of brothels, thy hand out of plackets, thy pen from lenders' books, and defy the foul fiend.

Still through the hawthorn blow the winds,
90 Says suum, mun, hey, no, nonny.
Dolphin my boy, my boy, sessa!° let him trot by. *[Storm still.*

LEAR. Thou wert better in thy grave than to answer with thy un-covered body this extremity of the skies. Is man no more than this? Consider him well. Thou owest the worm no silk, the beast no hide, the sheep no wool, the cat° no perfume. Ha! here 's three on 's are sophisticated!° Thou art the thing itself; unaccommodated man° is no more but such a poor, bare, forked animal as thou art. Off, off, you lendings! come, unbutton here. *[Tearing off his clothes.*

FOOL. Prithee, nuncle, be contented; 'tis a naughty night to swim in.
100 Now a little fire in a wild field were like an old lecher's heart—a small spark, all the rest on 's body cold. Look, here comes a walking fire.
Enter GLOUCESTER, *with a torch.*

EDG. This is the foul fiend Flibbertigibbet.° He begins at curfew, and walks till the first cock; he gives the web and the pin,° squints the eye, and makes the hare-lip; mildews the white wheat,° and hurts the poor creature of earth.

Swithold° footed thrice the old;°
He met the night-mare, and her nine-fold;°
Bid her alight,

80. **gloves,** as his mistress' favors. 84. **light of ear,** foolishly credulous, frivolous. 90-91. **suum ... sessa,** part of Edgar's feigned insanity; the meaning of these lines cannot be derived. *Dolphin my boy,* a slang phrase, or bit of song. 95. **cat,** civet cat. **sophisticated,** clad in the trappings of civilized life. 96. **unaccommodated man,** man unprovided with clothes and necessaries, also man without social modification. 102. **Flibbertigibbet,** a fiend whose name Shakespeare borrowed from Harsnet's *Declaration* (1603). 103. **web and the pin,** cataract of the eye. 104. **white wheat,** approaching ripeness. 106. **Swithold,** understood as a corruption of St. Vitalis, who is said to have been invoked against nightmare. **footed thrice the old,** thrice traversed the wold (tract of hilly upland). 107. **nine-fold,** nine familiars; suggestive also certainly of nine foals.

And her troth plight,

And aroint thee,° witch, aroint thee!   110

KENT.   How fares your grace?

LEAR.   What 's he?

KENT.   Who 's there? What is 't you seek?

GLOU.   What are you there? Your names?

EDG.   Poor Tom, that eats the swimming frog, the toad, the tadpole, the wall-newt° and the water;° that in the fury of his heart, when the foul fiend rages, eats cow-dung for sallets,° swallows the old rat and the ditch-dog, drinks the green mantle of the standing pool; who is whipped from tithing to tithing,° and stock-punished° and imprisoned; who hath had three suits to his back, six shirts to his body, horse to ride, and weapon to 120 wear;

But mice and rats, and such small deer,°

Have been Tom's food for seven long year.

Beware my follower. Peace, Smulkin;° peace, thou fiend!

GLOU.   What, hath your grace no better company?

EDG.   The prince of darkness is a gentleman!

Modo he 's call'd, and Mahu.°

GLOU.   Our flesh and blood, my lord, is grown so vile,

That it doth hate what gets it.

EDG.   Poor Tom 's a-cold.   130

GLOU.   Go in with me; my duty cannot suffer

To obey in all your daughters' hard commands.

Though their injunction be to bar my doors

And let this tyrannous night take hold upon you,

Yet have I ventured to come seek you out

And bring you where both fire and food is ready.

LEAR.   First let me talk with this philosopher.

What is the cause of thunder?

KENT.   Good my lord, take his offer; go into the house.

LEAR.   I'll talk a word with this same learned Theban.°   140

What is your study?

EDG.   How to prevent the fiend and to kill vermin.

LEAR.   Let me ask you one word in private.

KENT.   Importune him once more to go, my lord;

His wits begin to unsettle.

GLOU.   Canst thou blame him?   [*Storm still.*

His daughters seek his death. Ah, that good Kent!

He said it would be thus, poor banish'd man!

---

110. **aroint thee,** begone.   116. **wall-newt,** lizard.   **water,** i.e., water newt.   117. **sallets,** salads.   119. **tithing to tithing,** i.e., from one ward or parish to another.   **stock-punished,** punished by being put into the stocks.   122. **deer,** probably, animals generally.   124. **Smulkin,** another name occuring in Harsnet.   127. **Modo ... Mahu,** two superior fiends in Harsnet. 140. **learned Theban,** possibly a current phrase to indicate a philosopher.

Thou say'st the king grows mad; I'll tell thee, friend,
150 I am almost mad myself. I had a son,
Now outlaw'd from my blood; he sought my life,
But lately, very late. I loved him, friend—
No father his son dearer. True to tell thee,
The grief hath crazed my wits. What a night 's this!
I do beseech your grace,—

LEAR.   O, cry you mercy, sir.
Noble philosopher, your company.

EDG. Tom 's a-cold.

GLOU. In, fellow, there, into the hovel; keep thee warm.

160 LEAR. Come, let 's in all.

KENT.   This way, my lord.

LEAR.   With him!
I will keep still with my philosopher.

KENT. Good my lord, soothe° him; let him take the fellow.

GLOU. Take him you on.

KENT. Sirrah, come on; go along with us.

LEAR. Come, good Athenian.

GLOU. No words, no words; hush!

EDG. Child Rowland° to the dark tower came.

170   His word was still, "Fie, foh, and fum,
I smell the blood of a British man."   [*Exeunt.*

SCENE V. *Gloucester's castle.*

Enter CORNWALL *and* EDMUND.

CORN. I will have my revenge ere I depart his house.

EDM. How, my lord, I may be censured, that nature thus gives way to
loyalty, something fears me to think of.

CORN. I now perceive it was not altogether your brother's evil disposition made him seek his death; but a provoking merit,° set a-work by
a reproveable badness in himself.

EDM. How malicious is my fortune, that I must repent to be just!
This is the letter he spoke of, which approves him° an intelligent party°
to the advantages of France. O heavens! that this treason were not, or not
10 I the detector!

CORN. Go with me to the duchess.

EDM. If the matter of this paper be certain, you have mighty business
in hand.

CORN. True or false, it hath made thee earl of Gloucester. Seek out
where they father is, that he may be ready for our apprehension.

164. soothe, humor, indulge. 169. Child Rowland, etc., fragments of the ballad *Child
Rowland and Burd Ellen.* The theme of Browning's *Childe Roland to the Dark Tower Came* is derived from these lines.
5. provoking merit, etc., i.e., a forward-looking merit (in Edgar) incited by the badness
of Gloucester. 8. approves him, proves him to be. intelligent party, spy or informer.

EDM. [*Aside*] If I find him comforting the king, it will stuff his suspicion more fully. [*Aloud*] I will persevere in my course of loyalty, though the conflict be sore between that and my blood.

CORN. I will lay trust upon thee; and thou shalt find a dearer father in my love. [*Exeunt.* 20

SCENE VI. *A chamber in a farmhouse adjoining the castle.*

Enter GLOUCESTER *and* KENT.

GLOU. Here is better than the open air; take it thankfully. I will piece out the comfort with what addition I can. I will not be long from you.

KENT. All the power of his wits have given way to his impatience. The gods reward your kindness! [*Exit Gloucester.*

Enter LEAR, EDGAR, *and* FOOL.

EDG. Fraeretto° calls me, and tells me Nero is an angler° in the lake of darkness. Pray, innocent,° and beware the foul fiend.

FOOL. Prithee, nuncle, tell me whether a madman be a gentleman or or a yeoman.

LEAR. A king, a king!

FOOL. No, he's a yeoman that has a gentleman to his son; for he's a 10 mad yeoman that sees his son a gentleman before him.

LEAR. To have a thousand with red burning spits
Come hissing in upon 'em,—

EDG. The foul fiend bites my back.

FOOL. He's mad that trusts in the tameness of a wolf, a horse's health, a boy's love, or a whore's oath.

LEAR. It shall be done; I will arraign them straight.
[*To Edgar*] Come, sit thou here, most learned justicer.°
[*To the Fool*] Thou, sapient sir, sit here. Now, you she foxes!

EDG. Look, where he stands and glares! 20
Wantest thou eyes at trial,° madam?
Come o'er the bourn, Bessy, to me.°

FOOL. Her boat hath a leak,
And she must not speak
Why she dares not come over to thee.

EDG. The foul fiend haunts poor Tom in the voice of a nightingale. Hoppedance° cries in Tom's belly for two white herring. Croak° not, black angel; I have no food for thee.

KENT. How do you, sir? Stand you not so amazed.
Will you lie down and rest upon the cushions? 30

LEAR. I'll see their trial first. Bring in the evidence.°

5. **Fraeretto,** another of the fiends from Harsnet. **Nero is an angler,** pointed out as an allusion to Rabelais, ii, 30, where Nero is described as a fiddler and Trajan as an angler. 6. **innocent,** simpleton, fool. 18. **justicer,** judge. 21. **Wantest ... trial,** meaning doubtful. Possibly Edgar alludes to the staring fiend. 22. **Come ... me,** first line of a ballad by William Birche (1558). 27. **Hoppedance,** a fiend. **Croak,** make a rumbling sound in the stomach to denote hunger. 31. **evidence,** witnesses.

[*To Edgar*] Thou robed man of justice, take thy place;
[*To the Fool*] And thou, his yoke-fellow° of equity,
Bench° by his side. [*To Kent*] You are o' the commission,°
Sit you too.
    EDG. Let us deal justly.
               Sleepest or wakest thou, jolly shepherd?
               Thy sheep be in the corn;
               And for one blast of thy minikin° mouth,
40   Thy sheep shall take no harm.
Pur!° the cat is gray.
    LEAR. Arraign her first; 'tis Goneril. I here take my oath before this
honourable assembly, she kicked the poor king her father.
    FOOL. Come hither, mistress. Is your name Goneril?
    LEAR. She cannot deny it.
    FOOL. Cry you mercy, I took you for a joint-stool.°
    LEAR. And here 's another, whose warp'd looks proclaim
What store° her heart is made on. Stop her there!
Arms, arms, sword, fire! Corruption in the place!
50 False justicer, why hast thou let her 'scape?
    EDG. Bless thy five wits!
    KENT. O pity! Sir, where is the patience now
That you so oft have boasted to retain?
    EDG. [*Aside*] My tears begin to take his part so much
They mar my counterfeiting.
    LEAR. The little dogs and all,
Tray, Blanch, and Sweet-heart, see, they bark at me.
    EDG. Tom will throw his head at them.
Avaunt, you curs!
60   Be thy mouth or black or white,
               Tooth that poisons if it bite;
               Mastiff, greyhound, mongrel grim,
               Hound or spaniel, brach or lym,°
               Or bobtail tike° or trundle-tail,°
               Tom will make them weep and wail;
               For, with throwing thus my head,
               Dogs leap the hatch,° and all are fled.

---

33. **yoke-fellow,** partner. 34. **Bench,** sit on the judgment seat. **o' the commission,** a justice of peace. 39. **minikin,** pretty, dainty. 41. **Pur,** perhaps the sound of a cat, or the name of a demon, or both. There is a fiend in Harsnet named Purre. 46. **joint-stool,** chair made by a joiner, possibly ornamented. The expression has a proverbial meaning not understood on which the Fool is punning in his reference to the stool Lear has placed before them to represent Goneril. 48. **store,** probably, material. 63. **lym,** lymmer, a species of bloodhound which runs by scent. 64. **tike,** small dog, cur. **trundle-tail,** curly tail. 67. **hatch,** lower half of a divided door.

Do de, de, de. Sessa! Come, march to wakes and fairs and market towns. Poor Tom, thy horn° is dry.

LEAR. Then let them anatomize Regan; see what breeds about her 70 heart. Is there any cause in nature that makes these hard hearts? [*To Edgar*] You, sir, I entertain for one of my hundred; only I do not like the fashion of your garments. You will say they are Persian attire;° but let them be changed.

KENT. Now, good my lord, lie here and rest awhile.

LEAR. Make no noise, make no noise; draw the curtains. So, so. We'll go to supper i' the morning.

FOOL. And I'll go to bed at noon.

Re-enter GLOUCESTER.

GLOU. Come hither, friend. Where is the king my master?

KENT. Here, sir; but trouble him not; his wits are gone. 80

GLOU. Good friend, I prithee, take him in thy arms;
I have o'erheard a plot of death upon° him.
There is a litter ready; lay him in 't
And drive towards Dover, friend, where thou shalt meet
Both welcome and protection. Take up thy master.
If thou shouldst dally half an hour, his life,
With thine, and all that offer to defend him,
Stand in assured loss.° Take up, take up!
And follow me, that will to some provision
Give thee quick conduct. 90

KENT.   Oppressed nature sleeps.
This rest might yet have balm'd° thy broken sinews,
Which, if convenience will not allow,
Stand in hard cure. [*To the Fool*] Come, help to bear thy master;
Thou must not stay behind.

GLOU.   Come, come, away!   [*Exeunt all but Edgar.*

EDG. When we our betters see bearing our woes,
We scarcely think our miseries our foes.
Who alone suffers suffers most i' the mind,
Leaving free things and happy shows behind. 100
But then the mind much sufferance° doth o'erskip
When grief hath mates, and bearing° fellowship.
How light and portable° my pain seems now,
When that which makes me bend makes the king bow,
He childed as I father'd!° Tom, away!
Mark the high noises, and thyself bewray°

69. **horn**, bottle carried by beggars. 73. **Persian attire**, rich, gorgeous attire (ironical). 82. **upon**, against. 88. **Stand in assured loss**, will assuredly be lost. 92. **balm'd**, cured, healed. 101. **sufferance**, suffering. 102. **bearing**, tribulation. 103. **portable**, endurable. 105. **He . . . father'd**, he has found the same cruelty in his children which I found in my father. 106. **bewray**, betray, reveal.

When false opinion, whose wrong thought defiles thee,
In thy just proof repeals° and reconciles thee.
What will hap more to-night, safe 'scape the king!°
110 Lurk, lurk.   [*Exit.*

SCENE VII. *Gloucester's castle.*
Enter CORNWALL, REGAN, GONERIL, EDMUND, *and* Servants.

CORN. Post speedily to my lord your husband; show him this letter:
the army of France is landed. Seek out the villain Gloucester.
                                    [*Exeunt some of the Servants.*
REG. Hang him instantly.
GON. Pluck out his eyes.
CORN. Leave him to my displeasure. Edmund, keep you our sister
company. The revenges we are bound to take upon your traitorous father
are not fit for your beholding. Advise the duke, where you are going, to°
a most festinate° preparation; we are bound° to the like. Our posts shall
be swift and intelligent° betwixt us. Farewell, dear sister; farewell, my
10 lord of Gloucester.°
Enter OSWALD.
How now? where 's the king?
OSW. My lord of Gloucester hath convey'd him hence.
Some five or six and thirty of his knights,
Hot questrists° after him, met him at gate;
Who, with some other of the lord's dependants,
Are gone with him towards Dover, where they boast
To have well-armed friends.
CORN.   Get horses for your mistress.
GON. Farewell, sweet lord, and sister.
20 CORN. Edmund, farewell.   [*Exeunt Goneril, Edmund, and Oswald.*
        Go seek the traitor Gloucester,
Pinion him like a thief, bring him before us.   [*Exeunt other Servants.*
Though well we may not pass upon° his life
Without the form of justice, yet our power
Shall do a courtesy to our wrath, which men
May blame, but not control.
Enter GLOUCESTER, *brought in by two or three.*
                  Who 's there? the traitor?
REG. Ingrateful fox! 'tis he.
CORN. Bind fast his corky° arms.

---

108. **repeals,** recalls, restores. 109. **What ... king!** Whatever else happens, may the
king escape!
7. **Advise ... to,** i.e., advise him to make. 8. **festinate,** hasty. **bound,** ready. 9. **intelligent,** serviceable in bearing intelligence. 9-10. **my ... Gloucester,** i.e., Edmund. In line 12
the reference is to Gloucester himself. 14. **questrists,** searchers. 23. **pass upon,** pass sentence
upon. 29. **corky,** withered with age.

William Shakespeare 377

GLOU. What mean your graces? Good my friends, consider   30
You are my guests. Do me no foul play, friends.
CORN. Bind him, I say.   [*Servants bind him.*
REG.   Hard, hard. O filthy traitor!
GLOU. Unmerciful lady as you are, I'm none.
CORN. To this chair bind him. Villain, thou shalt find—
REGAN *plucks his beard.*
GLOU. By the kind gods, 'tis most ignobly done
To pluck me by the beard.
REG. So white, and such a traitor!
GLOU.   Naughty lady,
These hairs which thou dost ravish from my chin   40
Will quicken° and accuse thee. I am your host;
With robbers' hands my hospitable favours°
You should not ruffle thus. What will you do?
CORN. Come, sir, what letters had you late from France?
REG. Be simple answered,° for we know the truth.
CORN. And what confederacy have you with the traitors
Late footed in the kingdom?
REG. To whose hands have you sent the lunatic king?
Speak.
GLOU.   I have a letter guessingly set down,   50
Which came from one that 's of a neutral heart,
And not from one opposed.
CORN.   Cunning.
REG.   And false.
CORN. Where hast thou sent the king?
GLOU. To Dover.
REG. Wherefore to Dover? Wast thou not charged at peril—
CORN. Wherefore to Dover? Let him answer that.
GLOU. I am tied to the stake,° and I must stand the course.
REG. Wherefore to Dover?   60
GLOU. Because I would not see thy cruel nails
Pluck out his poor old eyes; nor thy fierce sister
In his anointed flesh rash° boarish fangs.
The sea, with such a storm as his bare head
In hell-black night endured, would have buoy'd up,
And quench'd the stelled° fires;
Yet, poor old heart, he holp the heavens to rain.
If wolves had at thy gate howl'd that dern° time,

---

    41. **quicken,** come to life. 42. **hospitable favours.** The meaning is "the features of me, your host." 45. **simple answered,** straightforward in your answers. 59. **tied to the stake,** like a bear to be baited with dogs. 63. **rash,** slash. 66. **stelled,** fixed; sometimes defined as "starry." 68. **dern,** dreadful, dark.

Thou shouldst have said, "Good porter, turn the key,"
70 All cruels else subscribe:° but I shall see
The winged vengeance overtake such children.
    CORN. See 't shalt thou never. Fellows, hold the chair.
Upon these eyes of thine I'll set my foot.
    GLOU. He that will think to live till he be old,
Give me some help! O cruel! O you gods!
    REG. One side will mock another; the other too.
    CORN. If you see vengeance,—
    FIRST SERV.   Hold your hand, my lord!
I have served you ever since I was a child,
80 But better service have I never done you
Than now to bid you hold.
    REG.   How now, you dog!
    FIRST SERV. If you did wear a beard upon your chin,
I'd shake it on this quarrel.
    REG.   What do you mean?
    CORN. My villain!°   [*They draw and fight.*
    FIRST SERV. Nay, then, come on, and take the chance of anger.
    REG. Give me thy sword. A peasant stand up thus?
Takes a sword, and runs at him behind.
    FIRST SERV. O, I am slain! My lord, you have one eye left
90 To see some mischief on him. O!   [*Dies.*
    CORN. Lest it see more, prevent it. Out, vile jelly!
Where is thy lustre now?
    GLOU. All dark and comfortless. Where 's my son Edmund?
Edmund, enkindle all the sparks of nature
To quit° this horrid act.
    REG.   Out, treacherous villain!
Thou call'st on him that hates thee. It was he
That made the overture° of thy treasons to us,
Who is too good to pity thee.
100   GLOU. O my follies! then Edgar was abused.
Kind gods, forgive me that, and prosper him!
    REG. Go thrust him out at gates, and let him smell
His way to Dover. [*Exit one with Gloucester*] How is 't, my lord? how
    look you?
    CORN. I have received a hurt; follow me, lady.
Turn out that eyeless villain; throw this slave
Upon the dunghill. Regan, I bleed apace.
Untimely comes this hurt. Give me your arm.
                  [*Exit Cornwall, led by Regan.*

70. **All ... subscribe.** All other cruel creatures show forgiveness except you. 86. **villain,** servant, bondman. 95. **quit,** avenge. 98. **overture,** disclosure.

SEC. SERV.   I'll never care what wickedness I do,
If this man come to good.   110
    THIRD SERV.   If she live long,
And in the end meet the old° course of death,
Women will all turn monsters.
    SEC. SERV.   Let 's follow the old earl, and get the bedlam°
To lead him where he would. His roguish madness
Allows itself to any thing.
    THIRD SERV.   Go thou. I'll fetch some flax and whites of eggs
To apply to his bleeding face. Now, heaven help him!   [*Exeunt severally.*

Act IV

SCENE I.   *The heath.*
Enter EDGAR.
    EDG.   Yet better thus, and known to be contemn'd,
Than still contemn'd and flatter'd. To be worst,
The lowest and most dejected thing of° fortune,
Stands still in esperance,° lives not in fear.
The lamentable change is from the best;
The worst returns to laughter. Welcome, then,
Thou unsubstantial air that I embrace!
The wretch that thou hast blown unto the worst
Owes nothing to thy blasts.
Enter GLOUCESTER, *led by an* Old Man.
                        But who comes here?   10
My father, poorly led? World, world, O world!
But that thy strange mutations make us hate thee,
Life would not yield to age.
    OLD MAN.   O my good lord, I have been your tenant, and your
father's tenant, these fourscore years.
    GLOU.   Away, get thee away; good friend, be gone.
Thy comforts can do me no good at all;
Thee they may hurt.
    OLD MAN.   You cannot see your way.
    GLOU.   I have no way, and therefore want no eyes;   20
I stumbled when I saw. Full oft 'tis seen,
Our means secure us,° and our mere defects
Prove our commodities.° O dear son Edgar,
The food of thy abused father's wrath!
Might I but live to see thee in my touch,
I'd say I had eyes again!

---

112. **old,** customary, natural. 114. **bedlam,** Edgar.
    3. **dejected . . . of,** debased or humbled by. 4. **esperance,** hope. 22. **Our means secure us,** our resources make us overconfident. 23. **commodities,** benefits.

OLD MAN.   How now! Who 's there?

EDG. [*Aside*] O gods! Who is 't can say "I am at the worst"?
I am worse than e'er I was.

30   OLD MAN.   'Tis poor mad Tom.

EDG. [*Aside*] And worse I may be yet; the worst is not
So long as we can say "This is the worst."

OLD MAN.   Fellow, where goest?

GLOU.   Is it a beggar-man?

OLD MAN.   Madman and beggar too.

GLOU.   He has some reason, else he could not beg.
I' the last night's storm I such a fellow saw,
Which made me think a man a worm. My son
Came then into my mind, and yet my mind
40 Was then scarce friends with him. I have heard more since.
As flies to wanton boys, are we to the gods.
They kill us for their sport.

EDG.   [*Aside*] How should this be?
Bad is the trade that must play fool to sorrow,
Angering itself and others.—Bless thee, master!

GLOU.   Is that the naked fellow?

OLD MAN.   Ay, my lord.

GLOU.   Then, prithee, get thee away. If for my sake
Thou wilt o'ertake us hence a mile or twain,
50 I' the way toward Dover, do it for ancient love;
And bring some covering for this naked soul,
Who I'll entreat to lead me.

OLD MAN.   Alack, sir, he is mad!

GLOU.   'Tis the times' plague when madmen lead the blind.
Do as I bid thee, or rather do thy pleasure;
Above the rest, be gone.

OLD MAN.   I'll bring him the best 'parel° that I have,
Come on 't what will.   [*Exit.*

GLOU.   Sirrah, naked fellow,—

60   EDG.   Poor Tom 's a-cold. [*Aside*] I cannot daub it further.°

GLOU.   Come hither, fellow.

EDG. [*Aside*] And yet I must.—Bless thy sweet eyes, they bleed.

GLOU.   Know'st thou the way to Dover?

EDG.   Both stile and gate, horse-way and foot-path. Poor Tom hath
been scared out of his good wits. Bless thee, good man's son, from the foul
fiend! Five fiends have been in poor Tom at once: of lust, as Obidicut;
Hobbididence, prince of dumbness; Mahu, of stealing; Modo, of murder;

---

57. **'parel,** apparel. 60. **daub it further,** keep up the disguise.

Flibbertigibbet,° of mopping and mowing,° who since possesses chambermaids and waiting-women. So, bless thee, master!

Glou. Here, take this purse, thou whom the heavens' plagues 70
Have humbled to all strokes; that I am wretched
Makes thee the happier. Heavens, deal so still!
Let the superfluous° and lust-dieted° man,
That slaves your ordinance,° that will not see
Because he doth not feel, feel your power quickly;
So distribution° should undo excess,
And each man have enough. Dost thou know Dover?

Edg. Ay, master.

Glou. There is a cliff, whose high and bending head
Looks fearfully in the confined deep. 80
Bring me but to the very brim of it,
And I'll repair the misery thou dost bear
With something rich about me. From that place
I shall no leading need.

Edg.   Give me thy arm;
Poor Tom shall lead thee.   [*Exeunt.*

Scene ii. *Before the Duke of Albany's palace.*

Enter Goneril *and* Edmund.

Gon. Welcome, my lord. I marvel our mild husband
Not met us on the way.

Enter Oswald.

                Now, where 's your master?

Osw. Madam, within; but never man so changed.
I told him of the army that was landed;
He smiled at it. I told him you were coming;
His answer was "The worse." Of Gloucester's treachery
And of the loyal service of his son
When I inform'd him, then he call'd me sot°
And told me I had turn'd the wrong side out.° 10
What most he should dislike seems pleasant to him;
What like, offensive.

Gon.   [*To Edmund*] Then shall you go no further.
It is the cowish° terror of his spirit,
That dares not undertake; he'll not feel wrongs
Which tie him to an answer.° Our wishes on the way°

66-68. **Obidicut . . . Flibbertigibbet,** fiends borrowed, as before, from Harsnet. 68. **mopping and mowing,** making grimaces and mouths. 73. **superfluous,** having a superfluity. **lust-dieted,** probably, feeding luxuriously. 74. **slaves your ordinance,** i.e., makes the laws of heaven his slaves. 76. **distribution,** the principle of distributive justice in ethics.

9. **sot,** fool. 10. **turn'd the wrong side out,** put a wrong interpretation on the matter. 14. **cowish,** cowardly. 15-16. **he'll . . . answer,** i.e., in his cowardice he will ignore injuries he ought to resent. 16. **Our . . . way,** my wishes expressed to you on the way.

May prove effects.° Back, Edmund, to my brother;
Hasten his musters and conduct his powers.
I must change arms at home and give the distaff°
20 Into my husband's hands. This trusty servant
Shall pass between us. Ere long you are like to hear—
If you dare venture in your own behalf—
A mistress's command. Wear this; spare speech;   [*Giving a favour.*
Decline your head. This kiss, if it durst speak,
Would stretch thy spirits up into the air.
Conceive,° and fare thee well.
    EDM.   Yours in the ranks of death!
    GON.   My most dear Gloucester!   [*Exit Edmund.*
O, the difference of man and man!
30 To thee a woman's services are due;
My fool usurps my body.
    OSW.   Madam, here comes my lord.   [*Exit.*
Enter ALBANY.
    GON.   I have been worth the whistle.°
    ALB.   O Goneril,
You are not worth the dust which the rude wind
Blows in your face! I fear your disposition.
That nature which contemns it° origin
Cannot be border'd° certain in itself.
She that herself will sliver°and disbranch
40 From her material sap,° perforce must wither
And come to deadly use.
    GON.   No more! The text is foolish.
    ALB.   Wisdom and goodness to the vile seem vile;
Filths savour but° themselves. What have you done?
Tigers, not daughters, what have you perform'd?
A father, and a gracious aged man,
Whose reverence even the head-lugg'd° bear would lick,
Most barbarous, most degenerate! have you madded.°
Could my good brother suffer you to do it?
50 A man, a prince, by him so benefited!
If that the heavens do not their visible spirits
Send quickly down to tame these vile offences,°
It will come,

---

17. **prove effects,** come to pass. 19. **arms . . . distaff,** i.e., she must turn warrior and give
into Albany's hands the *arms,* or insignia, of housewifery. 26. **Conceive,** understand, take my
meaning. 33. **whistle.** She alludes to the proverb: "It is a poor dog that is not worth the
whistling." 37. **it,** its. 38. **border'd,** kept within bounds. 39. **sliver,** tear off. 40. **material
sap,** nourishing substance, that is, her father. 44. **savour but,** care only for. 47. **head-
lugg'd,** dragged by the head and infuriated. 48. **madded,** driven mad. 52. **offences,** offenders.

Humanity must perforce prey on itself,
Like monsters of the deep.

GON.   Milk-liver'd° man!
That bear'st a cheek for blows, a head for wrongs;
Who hast not in thy brows an eye discerning
Thine honour from thy suffering; that not know'st
Fools do those villains pity who are punish'd   60
Ere they have done their mischief. Where 's thy drum?
France spreads his banners in our noiseless° land,
With plumed helm thy state begins to threat,
Whiles thou, a moral° fool, sit'st still, and criest
"Alack, why does he so?"

ALB.   See thyself, devil!
Proper° deformity seems not in the fiend
So horrid as in woman.

GON.   O vain fool!

ALB.   Thou changed and self-cover'd° thing, for shame,   70
Be-monster not thy feature!° Were 't my fitness°
To let these hands obey my blood,
They are apt enough to dislocate and tear
Thy flesh and bones. Howe'er° thou art a fiend,
A woman's shape doth shield thee.

GON.   Marry, your manhood—mew!°
Enter a Messenger.

ALB.   What news?

MESS.   O, my good lord, the Duke of Cornwall 's dead,
Slain by his servant, going to put out
The other eye of Gloucester.   80

ALB.   Gloucester's eyes!

MESS.   A servant that he bred, thrill'd with remorse,°
Opposed against the act, bending his sword
To° his great master; who, thereat enraged,
Flew on him, and amongst them fell'd him dead;
But not without that harmful stroke which since
Hath pluck'd him after.

ALB.   This shows you are above,
You justicers, that these our nether crimes
So speedily can venge! But, O poor Gloucester!   90
Lost he his other eye?

56. **Milk-liver'd,** cowardly. 62. **noiseless,** peaceful, having none of the bustle of war.
64. **moral,** moralizing. 67. **Proper,** i.e., the deformity appropriate to the fiend. 70. **self-
cover'd,** having the true self concealed. 71. **Be-monster . . . feature,** do not, being fiend,
take on the outward form of woman. **my fitness,** suitable for me. 74. **Howe'er,** although.
76. **mew,** an exclamation of disgust. 82. **remorse,** pity. 83-84. **bending . . . /To,** directing
his sword against.

MESS.   Both, both, my lord.
This letter, madam, craves a speedy answer;
'Tis from your sister.
    GON. [*Aside*]   One way I like this well;
But being widow, and my Gloucester with her,
May all the building in my fancy pluck
Upon my hateful life. Another way,
The news is not so tart.°—I'll read, and answer.   [*Exit.*
100   ALB.   Where was his son when they did take his eyes?
    MESS.   Come with my lady hither.
    ALB.   He is not here.
    MESS.   No, my good lord; I met him back° again.
    ALB.   Knows he the wickedness?
    MESS.   Ay, my good lord; 'twas he inform'd against him,
And quit the house on purpose, that their punishment
Might have the freer course.
    ALB.   Gloucester, I live
To thank thee for the love thou show'dst the king,
110 And to revenge thine eyes. Come hither, friend;
Tell me what more thou know'st.   [*Exeunt.*
    SCENE III.   *The French camp near Dover.*
Enter KENT *and a* Gentleman.
    KENT.   Why the King of France is so suddenly gone back know you
the reason?
    GENT.   Something he left imperfect in the state, which since his
coming forth is thought of, which imports° to the kingdom so much fear
and danger that his personal return was most required and necessary.
    KENT.   Who hath he left behind him general?
    GENT.   The Marshal of France, Monsieur La Far.
    KENT.   Did your letters pierce the queen to any demonstration of grief?
    GENT.   Ay, sir; she took them, read them in my presence;
10 And now and then an ample tear trill'd° down
Her delicate cheek. It seem'd she was a queen
Over her passion, who, most rebel-like,
Sought to be king o'er her.
    KENT.   O, then it moved her.
    GENT.   Not to a rage; patience and sorrow strove
Who should express her goodliest. You have seen
Sunshine and rain at once: her smiles and tears
Were like. A better way:° those happy smilets
That play'd on her ripe lip seem'd not to know

99. **tart,** painful, grievous. 103. **back,** going back.
    4. **imports,** portends. 10. **trill'd,** trickled. 18. **A better way,** a better way to describe
Cordelia's response.

What guests were in her eyes, which parted thence　　　　20
As pearls from diamonds dropp'd. In brief,
Sorrow would be a rarity most beloved,
If all could so become it.
　　KENT.　　　　　　Made she no verbal question?
　　GENT.　Faith, once or twice she heaved° the name of "father"
Pantingly forth, as if it press'd her heart;
Cried "Sisters! sisters! Shame of ladies! sisters!
Kent! father! sisters! What, i' the storm? i' the night?
Let pity not be believed!" There she shook
The holy water from her heavenly eyes,　　　　　　　30
And clamour moisten'd;° then away she started
To deal with grief alone.
　　KENT.　　　　　　It is the stars,
The stars above us, govern our conditions;
Else one self° mate and mate could not beget
Such different issues. You spoke not with her since?
　　GENT.　No.
　　KENT.　Was this before the king return'd?
　　GENT.　　　　　　No, since.
　　KENT.　Well, sir, the poor distressed Lear 's i' the town,　　40
Who sometime, in his better tune,° remembers
What we are come about, and by no means
Will yield to see his daughter.
　　GENT.　　　　　　Why, good sir?
　　KENT.　A sovereign shame so elbows° him; his own unkindness,
That stripp'd her from his benediction, turn'd° her
To foreign casualties, gave her dear rights
To his dog-hearted daughters—these things sting
His mind so venomously that burning shame
Detains him from Cordelia.　　　　　　　　　　50
　　GENT.　　　　　　Alack, poor gentleman!
　　KENT.　Of Albany's and Cornwall's powers you heard not?
　　GENT.　'Tis so, they are afoot.
　　KENT.　Well, sir, I'll bring you to our master Lear
And leave you to attend him. Some dear cause
Will in concealment wrap me up awhile;
When I am known aright, you shall not grieve
Lending me this acquaintance. I pray you, go
Along with me.　　　　　　　　　　　　　　[Exeunt.

---

25. **heaved,** breathed out. 31. **clamour moisten'd,** moistened her cries of grief with tears.
35. **self,** same; that is, the same husband and the same wife. 41. **better tune,** saner moments.
45. **elbows,** thrusts away; possibly, vexes. 46. **turn'd,** expelled.

SCENE IV. *The same. A tent.*
Enter, with drum and colours, CORDELIA, Doctor, *and* Soldiers.
    COR.   Alack, 'tis he! Why, he was met even now
As mad as the vex'd sea, singing aloud,
Crown'd with rank fumiter° and furrow-weeds,°
With hardocks,° hemlock, nettles, cuckoo-flowers,°
Darnel,° and all the idle weeds that grow
In our sustaining° corn. A century° send forth;
Search every acre in the high-grown field,
And bring him to our eye. [*Exit an Officer*] What can man's wisdom°
In the restoring his bereaved° sense?
10 He that helps him take all my outward worth.
    DOCT.   There is means, madam.
Our foster-nurse of nature is repose,
The which he lacks; that to provoke in him,
Are many simples° operative,° whose power
Will close the eye of anguish.
    COR.   All blest secrets,
All you unpublish'd virtues of the earth,
Spring with my tears! Be aidant and remediate°
In the good man's distress! Seek, seek for him,
20 Lest his ungovern'd rage dissolve the life
That wants the means to lead it.
Enter a Messenger.
    MESS.   News, madam.
The British powers are marching hitherward.
    COR.   'Tis known before; our preparation stands
In expectation of them. O dear father,
It is thy business that I go about;
Therefore great France
My mourning and importun'd tears hath pitied.
No blown° ambition doth our arms incite,
30 But love, dear love, and our aged father's right.
Soon may I hear and see him!   [*Exeunt.*
SCENE V. *Gloucester's castle.*
Enter REGAN *and* OSWALD.
    REG.   But are my brother's powers set forth?

---

   3. **fumiter,** the weed "earth-smoke." **furrow-weeds,** weeds growing in the furrows of plowed lands. 4. **hardocks,** some kind of coarse weed. **cuckoo-flowers,** possibly, cowslips. 5. **Darnel,** a weed of the grass kind. The plants mentioned in this passage are probably selected because of their bitter and poisonous quality. 6. **sustaining,** giving sustenance. **century,** usually interpreted as a troop of 100 men, as in the Roman army; also taken to mean "sentry" or "scout." 8. **wisdom,** science. 9. **bereaved,** snatched away. 14. **simples,** medicinal plants. **operative,** effective. 18. **aidant and remediate,** helpful and remedial. 29. **blown,** puffed up with pride.

Osw.   Ay, madam.

Reg.   Himself in person there?

Osw.   Madam, with much ado.

Your sister is the better soldier.

Reg.   Lord Edmund spake not with your lord at home?

Osw.   No, madam.

Reg.   What might import my sister's letter to him?

Osw.   I know not, lady.

Reg.   'Faith, he is posted hence on serious matter.   10

It was great ignorance, Gloucester's eyes being out,

To let him live; where he arrives he moves

All hearts against us. Edmund, I think, is gone,

In pity of his misery, to dispatch

His nighted life; moreover, to descry

The strength o' the enemy.

Osw.   I must needs after him, madam, with my letter.

Reg.   Our troops set forth to-morrow. Stay with us;

The ways are dangerous.

Osw.   I may not, madam.   20

My lady charged my duty in this business.

Reg.   Why should she write to Edmund? Might not you

Transport her purposes by word?° Belike,°

Some things—I know not what. I'll love thee much—

Let me unseal the letter.

Osw.   Madam, I had rather—

Reg.   I know your lady does not love her husband;

I am sure of that, and at her late being here

She gave strange œillades° and most speaking looks

To noble Edmund. I know you are of her bosom.°   30

Osw.   I, madam?

Reg.   I speak in understanding; you are, I know 't.

Therefore I do advise you, take this note:°

My lord is dead; Edmund and I have talk'd,°

And more convenient is he for my hand

Than for your lady's. You may gather more.

If you do find him, pray you, give him this;

And when your mistress hears thus much from you,

I pray desire her call her wisdom to her.

So fare you well.   40

If you do chance to hear of that blind traitor,

Preferment falls on him that cuts him off.

---

23. **word,** word of mouth. **Belike,** it may be. 29. œillades, amorous glances. 30. **of her bosom,** in her confidence. 33. **take this note,** take note of this. 34. **have talk'd,** are affianced to one another (W. J. Craig).

Osw.   Would I could meet him, madam! I should show
What party I do follow.
REG.   Fare thee well.   [*Exeunt.*
SCENE VI.   *Fields near Dover.*
Enter GLOUCESTER, *and* EDGAR *dressed like a peasant.*
GLOU.   When shall we come to the top of that same hill?
EDG.   You do climb up it now. Look, how we labour.
GLOU.   Methinks the ground is even.
EDG.   Horrible steep.
Hark, do you hear the sea?
GLOU.   No, truly.
EDG.   Why, then, your other senses grow imperfect
By your eyes' anguish.
GLOU.   So may it be indeed.
10 Methinks thy voice is alter'd, and thou speak'st
In better phrase and matter than thou didst.
EDG.   You 're much deceived. In nothing am I changed
But in my garments.
GLOU.   Methinks you 're better spoken.
EDG.   Come on, sir; here 's the place. Stand still. How fearful
And dizzy 'tis to cast one's eyes so low!
The crows and choughs° that wing the midway air
Show scarce so gross as beetles. Half way down
Hangs one that gathers samphire°—dreadful trade!
20 Methinks he seems no bigger than his head.
The fishermen that walk upon the beach
Appear like mice; and yond tall anchoring bark,
Diminish'd to her cock;° her cock, a buoy
Almost too small for sight. The murmuring surge,
That on the unnumber'd idle pebbles chafes,
Cannot be heard so high. I'll look no more,
Lest my brain turn, and the deficient sight
Topple down headlong.
GLOU.   Set me where you stand.
30   EDG.   Give me your hand; you are now within a foot
Of the extreme verge. For all beneath the moon
Would I not leap upright.
GLOU.   Let go my hand.
Here, friend, 's another purse; in it a jewel
Well worth a poor man's taking. Fairies and gods
Prosper it with thee! Go thou farther off;
Bid me farewell, and let me hear thee going.

17. **choughs,** jackdaws. 19. **samphire,** an herb called sea-fennel and the herb of St. Pierre,
used for pickles. 23. **cock,** cock-boat.

EDG. Now fare you well, good sir.

GLOU.   With all my heart.

EDG. [*Aside*] Why I do trifle thus with his despair   40
Is done to cure it.

GLOU.   [*Kneeling*] O you mighty gods!
This world I do renounce, and, in your sights,
Shake patiently my great affliction off.
If I could bear it longer, and not fall
To quarrel with your great opposeless° wills,
My snuff° and loathed part of nature should
Burn itself out. If Edgar live, O, bless him!
Now, fellow, fare thee well.   [*He falls forward and faints.*]

EDG.   Gone, sir; farewell.   50
And yet I know not how conceit° may rob
The treasury of life when life itself
Yields to the theft. Had he been where he thought,
By this, had thought been past. Alive or dead?
Ho, you sir! friend! Hear you, sir! speak!
Thus might he pass° indeed; yet he revives.
What are you, sir?

GLOU.   Away, and let me die.

EDG. Hadst thou been aught but gossamer, feathers, air,
So many fathom down precipitating,   60
Thou 'dst shiver'd like an egg; but thou dost breathe;
Hast heavy substance; bleed'st not; speak'st; art sound.
Ten masts at each° make not the altitude
Which thou hast perpendicularly fell;
Thy life 's a miracle. Speak yet again.

GLOU. But have I fall'n, or no?

EDG. From the dread summit of this chalky bourn.°
Look up a-height;° the shrill-gorged° lark so far
Cannot be seen or heard. Do but look up.

GLOU. Alack, I have no eyes.   70
Is wretchedness deprived that benefit,
To end itself by death? 'Twas yet some comfort
When misery could beguile the tyrant's rage
And frustrate his proud will.

EDG.   Give me your arm.
Up: so. How is 't? Feel you your legs? You stand.

GLOU. Too well, too well.

EDG.   This is above all strangeness.

---

46. **opposeless,** irresistible.　47. **snuff,** useless residue; the metaphor is taken from the smoking wick of a candle.　51. **conceit,** imagination.　56. **pass,** die.　63. **at each,** end to end. 67. **bourn,** limit, boundary.　68. **a-height,** on high.　**shrill-gorged,** shrill-throated.

Upon the crown o' the cliff what thing was that
80 Which parted from you?
  GLOU.   A poor unfortunate beggar.
  EDG.   As I stood here below, methought his eyes
Were two full moons; he had a thousand noses,
Horns whelk'd° and waved like the enridged° sea.
It was some fiend; therefore, thou happy father,
Think that the clearest° gods, who make them honours
Of men's impossibilities,° have preserved thee.
  GLOU.   I do remember now. Henceforth I'll bear
Affliction till it do cry out itself
90 "Enough, enough," and die. That thing you speak of,
I took it for a man; often 'twould say
"The fiend, the fiend"—he led me to that place.
  EDG.   Bear free° and patient thoughts.
[Enter Lear, fantastically dressed with wild flowers] But who comes here?
The safer° sense will ne'er accommodate°
His master thus.
  LEAR.   No, they cannot touch° me for coining;
I am the king himself.
  EDG.   O thou side-piercing sight!
100   LEAR.   Nature's above art in that respect. There's your press-money.°
That fellow handles his bow like a crow-keeper.° Draw me a clothier's
yard.° Look, look, a mouse! Peace, peace; this piece of toasted cheese will
do 't. There's my gauntlet; I'll prove it on a giant. Bring up the brown
bills.° O, well flown, bird!° i' the clout,° i' the clout! hewgh! Give the
word.°
  EDG.   Sweet marjoram.
  LEAR.   Pass.
  GLOU.   I know that voice.
  LEAR.   Ha! Goneril with a white beard! They flattered me like a dog,
110 and told me I had white hairs in my beard ere the black ones were there.
To say "ay" and "no" to every thing that I said—!"Ay" and "no" too
was no good divinity.° When the rain came to wet me once, and the wind
to make me chatter; when the thunder would not peace° at my bidding;

84. whelk'd, explained as "twisted"; also as "swollen, as with whelks or knobs." enridged,
furrowed. 86. clearest, most glorious. 87. men's impossibilities, things impossible to men.
93. free, probably, free from fear. 95. safer, saner. accommodate, furnish, equip. 97. touch,
arrest, prosecute. 100. press-money, bonus given soldiers when they were pressed into service.
101. crow-keeper, boy employed as a crow-frightener. 101-02. clothier's yard, arrow the
length of a cloth yard. 103-04. brown bills, soldiers carrying pikes, or the pikes themselves.
104. well flown, bird. Lear may think he is hawking, or he may be speaking of the flight of
an arrow. clout, target. 105. word, password. 111-12. "Ay" ... divinity. Refers to the
Biblical condemnation of hypocrisy and false statements. See Jas. 5:12. 113. peace, hold its
peace.

there I found 'em, there I smelt 'em out. Go to, they are not men o' their
words! They told me I was every thing; 'tis a lie, I am not ague-proof.

GLOU.   The trick° of that voice I do well remember.
Is 't not the king?

LEAR.   Ay, every inch a king!
When I do stare, see how the subject quakes.
I pardon that man's life. What was thy cause?   120
Adultery?
Thou shalt not die. Die for adultery? No!
The wren goes to 't, and the small gilded fly
Does lecher in my sight.
Let copulation thrive; for Gloucester's bastard son
Was kinder to his father than my daughters
Got 'tween the lawful sheets.
To 't, luxury,° pell-mell! for I lack soldiers.
Behold yond simpering dame,
Whose face between her forks° presages snow,   130
That minces virtue, and does shake the head
To hear of pleasure's name;
The fitchew° nor the soiled horse° goes to 't
With a more riotous appetite.
Down from the waist they are Centaurs,
Though women all above.
But° to the girdle do the gods inherit,°
Beneath is all the fiends'.
There 's hell, there 's darkness, there 's the sulphurous pit,
Burning, scalding, stench, consumption; fie, fie, fie! pah, pah! Give me an 140
ounce of civet; good apothecary, sweeten my imagination. There 's money
for thee.

GLOU.   O, let me kiss that hand!

LEAR.   Let me wipe it first; it smells of mortality.

GLOU.   O ruin'd piece° of nature! This great world
Shall so wear out to nought. Dost thou know me?

LEAR.   I remember thine eyes well enough. Dost thou squiny° at me?
No, do thy worst, blind Cupid; I'll not love. Read thou this challenge;
mark but the penning of it.

GLOU.   Were all the letters suns, I could not see one.   150

EDG. [Aside]   I would not take this from report; it is,
And my heart breaks at it.

LEAR.   Read.

---

116. **trick,** peculiar characteristic. 128. **luxury,** lust. 130. **forks,** legs; possibly ornaments
which hold up hair. 133. **fitchew,** polecat. **soiled horse,** horse turned out to grass. 137. **But,**
only. **inherit,** possess. 145. **piece,** masterpiece. 147. **squiny,** squint, look askance.

GLOU. What, with the case° of eyes?

LEAR. O, ho, are you there with me?° No eyes in your head, nor no money in your purse? Your eyes are in a heavy case, your purse in a light; yet you see how this world goes.

GLOU. I see it feelingly.

LEAR. What, art mad? A man may see how this world goes with no
160 eyes. Look with thine ears; see how yond justice rails upon yond simple thief. Hark in thine ear; change places and, handy-dandy,° which is the justice, which is the thief? Thou hast seen a farmer's dog bark at a beggar?

GLOU. Ay, sir.

LEAR. And the creature run from the cur? There thou mightst behold the great image of authority: a dog 's obeyed in office.
Thou rascal beadle, hold thy bloody hand!
Why dost thou lash that whore? Strip thine own back;
Thou hotly lust'st to use her in that kind
For which thou whipp'st her. The usurer hangs the cozener.°
170 Through tatter'd clothes small vices do appear;
Robes and furr'd gowns hide all. Plate sin with gold,
And the strong lance of justice hurtless breaks;
Arm it in rags, a pigmy's straw does pierce it.
None does offend, none, I say, none; I'll able° 'em:
Take that of me, my friend, who have the power
To seal the accuser's lips. Get thee glass eyes
And, like a scurvy politician,° seem
To see the things thou dost not. Now, now, now, now!
Pull off my boots. Harder, harder! so.
180 EDG. [Aside] O, matter and impertinency mix'd!
Reason in madness!

LEAR. If thou wilt weep my fortunes, take my eyes.
I know thee well enough; thy name is Gloucester.
Thou must be patient. We came crying hither;
Thou know'st, the first time that we smell the air
We wawl and cry. I will preach to thee: mark.

GLOU. Alack, alack the day!

LEAR. When we are born, we cry that we are come
To this great stage of fools. This'° a good block.°
190 It were a delicate stratagem to shoe
A troop of horse with felt. I'll put 't in proof,
And when I have stol'n upon these sons-in-law,
Then kill, kill, kill, kill, kill, kill!

154. **case,** mere sockets. 155. **are . . . me?** Is that what you refer to? 161. **handy-dandy,** take your choice of hands, as in a well-known child's game. 169. **cozener,** cheater. 174. **able,** give warrant to. 177. **politician,** trickster. 189. **This',** this is. **block,** probably, hat, from the form on which it was molded.

Enter a Gentleman, *with* Attendants.

GENT.   O, here he is; lay hand upon him. Sir,
Your most dear daughter—
   LEAR.   No rescue? What, a prisoner? I am even
The natural fool of fortune. Use me well;
You shall have ransom. Let me have surgeons;
I am cut to the brains.
   GENT.   You shall have any thing.   200
   LEAR.   No seconds? all myself?
Why, this would make a man a man of salt,°
To use his eyes for garden water-pots,
Ay, and laying autumn's dust. I will die bravely,
Like a smug° bridegroom. What! I will be jovial.
Come, come, I am a king; masters, know you that?
   GENT.   You are a royal one, and we obey you.
   LEAR.   Then there 's life in 't. Come, an you get it, you shall get it by
running. Sa, sa, sa, sa.°   [*Exit running; Attendants follow.*
   GENT.   A sight most pitiful in the meanest wretch,   210
Past speaking of in a king! Thou hast one daughter
Who redeems nature from the general curse
Which twain have brought her to.
   EDG.   Hail, gentle sir.
   GENT.   Sir, speed you.° What 's your will?
   EDG.   Do you hear aught, sir, of a battle toward?°
   GENT.   Most sure and vulgar;° every one hears that,
Which° can distinguish sound.
   EDG.   But, by your favour,
How near 's the other army?   220
   GENT.   Near and on speedy foot; the main descry
Stands on the hourly thought.°
   EDG.   I thank you, sir; that 's all.
   GENT.   Though that the queen on special cause is here,
Her army is moved on.
   EDG.   I thank you, sir.   [*Exit Gentleman.*
   GLOU.   You ever-gentle gods, take my breath from me;
Let not my worser spirit tempt me again
To die before you please!
   EDG.   Well pray you, father.   230
   GLOU.   Now, good sir, what are you?
   EDG.   A most poor man, made tame to fortune's blows,

---

202. **man of salt,** of salt tears. 205. **smug,** original meaning of trim or spruce. 209. **Sa...
sa.** French Ça, ça—a hunting cry to urge on dogs. 215. **speed you,** God speed you. 216. **toward,** impending, at hand. 217. **vulgar,** in everyone's mouth, generally known. 218. **Which,**
who. 221-22. **the main ... thought,** the full view of the main body is expected any hour.

Who, by the art of known and feeling° sorrows,
Am pregnant to good pity. Give me your hand,
I'll lead you to some biding.°
    GLOU.   Hearty thanks.
The bounty and the benison of heaven
To boot, and boot!°
Enter OSWALD.
    OSW.   A proclaim'd prize! Most happy!
240 That eyeless head of thine was first framed flesh
To raise my fortunes. Thou old unhappy traitor,
Briefly thyself remember;° the sword is out
That must destroy thee.
    GLOU.   Now let thy friendly hand
Put strength enough to 't.   [*Edgar interposes.*
    OSW.   Wherefore, bold peasant,
Darest thou support a publish'd traitor? Hence!
Lest that the infection of his fortune take
Like hold on thee. Let go his arm.
250   EDG.   Chill° not let go, zir, without vurther 'casion.
    OSW.   Let go, slave, or thou diest!
    EDG.   Good gentleman, go your gait,° and let poor volk pass. An
chud° ha' bin zwaggered out of my life, 'twould not ha' bin zo long as 'tis
by a vortnight. Nay, come not near th' old man; keep out, che vor ye,° or
ise° try whether your costard° or my ballow° be the harder; chill be
plain with you.
    OSW.   Out, dunghill!°
    EDG.   Chill pick your teeth, zir. Come; no matter vor your foins.°
They fight, and EDGAR *knocks him down.*
    OSW.   Slave, thou hast slain me. Villain, take my purse.
260 If ever thou wilt thrive, bury my body,
And give the letters which thou find'st about me
To Edmund earl of Gloucester; seek him out
Upon the British party! O, untimely death! Death!   [*Dies.*
    EDG.   I know thee well—a serviceable villain,
As duteous to the vices of thy mistress
As badness would desire.
    GLOU.   What, is he dead?
    EDG.   Sit you down, father; rest you.
Let 's see these pockets; the letters that he speaks of

233. **feeling**, heartfelt, deep. 235. **biding**, abiding place. 238. **To boot, and boot,** i.e., in addition (to my thanks), I wish you the bounty of heaven. 242. **thyself remember**, confess thy sins. 250. **Chill**, I will. Edgar adopts a dialect, apparently of the south country. 252. **go your gait**, go your own way. 252-53. **An/chud**, if I could. 254. **che vor ye**, I warn you. 255. **ise**, I shall. **costard**, an apple, slang for "head." **ballow**, cudgel. 257. **dunghill**, person of the lowest extraction. 258. **foins**, thrusts in fencing.

May be my friends. He 's dead; I am only sorry 270
He had no other death's-man.° Let us see.
Leave,° gentle wax; and, manners, blame us not:
To know our enemies' minds, we rip their hearts;
Their papers is more lawful.
    [*Reads*] "Let our reciprocal vows be remembered. You have many
opportunities to cut him off. If your will want not, time and place will be
fruitfully° offered. There is nothing done, if he return the conqueror; then
am I the prisoner, and his bed my gaol; from the loathed warmth whereof
deliver me, and supply the place for your labour.
    "Your—wife, so I would say— 280
            "Affectionate servant,°   "GONERIL."
O indistinguish'd space of woman's will!°
A plot upon her virtuous husband's life,
And the exchange my brother! Here in the sands
Thee I'll rake up,° the post unsanctified
Of murderous lechers; and in the mature time
With this ungracious° paper strike the sight
Of the death-practised° duke. For him 'tis well
That of thy death and business I can tell.
    GLOU.   The king is mad. How stiff is my vile sense, 290
That I stand up, and have ingenious° feeling
Of my huge sorrows! Better I were distract;°
So should my thoughts be sever'd from my griefs,
And woes by wrong imaginations lose
The knowledge of themselves.   [*Drum afar off.*
    EDG.   Give me your hand.
Far off, methinks, I hear the beaten drum.
Come, father, I'll bestow you with a friend.   [*Exeunt.*
SCENE VII.   *A tent in the French camp.* LEAR *on a bed asleep, soft music
playing;* Gentleman, *and others attending.*
Enter CORDELIA, KENT, *and* Doctor.
    COR.   O thou good Kent, how shall I live and work
To match thy goodness? My life will be too short,
And every measure fail me.
    KENT.   To be acknowledged, madam, is o'er-paid.
All my reports go with the modest truth;
Nor more nor clipp'd,° but so.
    COR.   Be better suited;°
These weeds are memories° of those worser hours.

271. **death's-man,** executioner. 272. **Leave,** by your leave. 277. **fruitfully,** amply, fully.
281. **servant,** lover. 282. **indistinguish'd ... will,** incalculable range of woman's appetite.
285. **rake up,** cover up. 287. **ungracious,** wicked. 288. **death-practised,** whose death is
plotted. 291. **ingenious,** conscious, perceptive. 292. **distract,** distracted, crazy.
  6. **clipp'd,** curtailed. 7. **suited,** dressed. 8. **memories,** remembrances.

I prithee put them off.

10 KENT.   Pardon me, dear madam;
Yet to be known shortens my made intent;°
My boon I make it, that you know me not
Till time and I think meet.

COR.   Then be 't so, my good lord.   [*To the Doctor*]   How does the
king?

DOCT.   Madam, sleeps still.

COR.   O you kind gods,
Cure this great breach in his abused nature!
The untuned and jarring senses, O, wind up°
20 Of this child-changed° father!

DOCT.   So please your majesty
That we may wake the king? He hath slept long.

COR.   Be govern'd by your knowledge, and proceed
I' the sway of your own will. Is he array'd?

GENT.   Ay, madam; in the heaviness of sleep
We put fresh garments on him.

DOCT.   Be by, good madam, when we do awake him;
I doubt not of his temperance.°

COR.   Very well.

30 DOCT.   Please you, draw near. Louder the music there!

COR.   O my dear father, restoration hang
Thy medicine on my lips, and let this kiss
Repair those violent harms that my two sisters
Have in thy reverence made!

KENT.   Kind and dear princess!

COR.   Had you not been their father, these white flakes°
Had challenged pity of them. Was this a face
To be opposed against the warring winds?
To stand against the deep dread-bolted° thunder?
40 In the most terrible and nimble stroke
Of quick, cross lightning? to watch—poor perdu!°—
With this thin helm? Mine enemy's dog,
Though he had bit me, should have stood that night
Against my fire; and wast thou fain, poor father,
To hovel thee with swine and rogues forlorn,
In short and musty straw? Alack, alack!
'Tis wonder that thy life and wits at once
Had not concluded all.° He wakes; speak to him.

11. **made intent,** carefully thought-out purpose. 19. **wind up,** tightening of strings of a musical instrument for tuning. 20. **child-changed,** changed (in mind) by children's cruelty. 28. **temperance,** sanity. 36. **flakes,** locks of hair. 39. **dread-bolted,** furnished with the dreadful thunderstone. 41. **perdu,** soldier placed in a position of peculiar danger. 48. **concluded all,** come to an end all together.

DOCT. Madam, do you; 'tis fittest.

COR. How does my royal lord? How fares your majesty? 50

LEAR. You do me wrong to take me out o' the grave.
Thou art a soul in bliss; but I am bound
Upon a wheel of fire, that mine own tears
Do scald like molten lead.

COR.   Sir, do you know me?

LEAR. You are a spirit, I know; when did you die?

COR. Still, still, far wide!

DOCT. He 's scarce awake; let him alone awhile.

LEAR. Where have I been? Where am I? Fair daylight?
I am mightily abused. I should e'en die with pity, 60
To see another thus. I know not what to say.
I will not swear these are my hands. Let 's see;
I feel this pin prick. Would I were assured
Of my condition!

COR.   O, look upon me, sir,
And hold your hands in benediction o'er me.
No, sir, you must not kneel.

LEAR.   Pray, do not mock me.
I am a very foolish fond old man,
Fourscore and upward, not an hour more nor less; 70
And, to deal plainly,
I fear I am not in my perfect mind.
Methinks I should know you, and know this man;
Yet I am doubtful; for I am mainly° ignorant
What place this is; and all the skill I have
Remembers not these garments; nor I know not
Where I did lodge last night. Do not laugh at me;
For, as I am a man, I think this lady
To be my child Cordelia.

COR.   And so I am, I am. 80

LEAR. Be your tears wet? yes, 'faith. I pray weep not.
If you have poison for me, I will drink it.
I know you do not love me; for your sisters
Have, as I do remember, done me wrong.
You have some cause, they have not.

COR.   No cause, no cause.

LEAR. Am I in France?

KENT.   In your own kingdom, sir.

LEAR. Do not abuse me.

DOCT. Be comforted, good madam. The great rage 90

74. **mainly,** perfectly.

You see is kill'd in him; and yet it is danger
To make him even o'er° the time he has lost.
Desire him to go in; trouble him no more
Till further settling.°

Cor. Will 't please your highness walk?

Lear.   You must bear with me.
Pray you now, forget and forgive; I am old and foolish.

                                [Exeunt all but Kent and Gentleman.

Gent. Holds it true, sir, that the Duke of Cornwall was so slain?

Kent. Most certain, sir.

100   Gent. Who is conductor of his people?

Kent. As 'tis said, the bastard son of Gloucester.

Gent. They say Edgar, his banished son, is with the Earl of Kent in
Germany.

Kent. Report is changeable. 'Tis time to look about; the powers of
the kingdom approach apace.

Gent. The arbitrement° is like to be bloody. Fare you well, sir.

                                                [Exit.

Kent. My point and period° will be throughly wrought,
Or well or ill, as this day's battle 's fought.   *[Exit.*

Act V

Scene i. *The British camp, near Dover.*

Enter, with drum and colours, Edmund, Regan, Gentlemen, *and* Soldiers.

Edm. Know of the duke if his last purpose hold,
Or whether since he is advised by aught
To change the course. He 's full of alteration
And self-reproving. Bring his constant pleasure.°

                              [To a Gentleman, who goes out.

Reg. Our sister's man is certainly miscarried.°

Edm. 'Tis to be doubted, madam.

Reg.   Now, sweet lord,
You know the goodness I intend upon you.
Tell me—but truly—but then speak the truth,
10 Do you not love my sister?

Edm.   In honour'd° love.

Reg. But have you never found my brother's way
To the forfended° place?

Edm.   That thought abuses you.

Reg. I am doubtful that you have been conjunct°

---

92. **even o'er,** give an account of, go over in his mind. 94. **settling,** composing of his mind.
106. **arbitrement,** decision by arms. 107. **period,** end aimed at.
   4. **constant pleasure,** settled decision. 5. **miscarried,** lost, perished. 11. **honour'd,** honorable. 13. **forfended,** forbidden. 15. **conjunct,** joined.

And bosom'd with her,° as far as we call hers.

EDM. No, by mine honour, madam.

REG. I never shall endure her. Dear my lord,
Be not familiar with her.

EDM.   Fear me not.   20
She and the duke her husband!

Enter, with drum and colours, ALBANY, GONERIL, *and* Soldiers.

GON. [*Aside*] I had rather lose the battle than that sister
Should loosen him and me.

ALB. Our very loving sister, well be-met.
Sir, this I hear; the king is come to his daughter,
With others whom the rigour of our state
Forced to cry out. Where I could not be honest,
I never yet was valiant; for this business,
It toucheth us as France invades our land,
Not bolds the king, with others,° whom, I fear,   30
Most just and heavy causes° make oppose.°

EDM. Sir, you speak nobly.

REG.   Why is this reason'd?

GON. Combine together 'gainst the enemy;
For these domestic and particular broils
Are not the question here.

ALB.   Let 's then determine
With the ancient of war° on our proceeding.

EDM. I shall attend you presently at your tent.

REG. Sister, you'll go with us?   40

GON. No.

REG. 'Tis most convenient;° pray go with us.

GON. [*Aside*] O, ho, I know the riddle.—I will go.

As they are going out, enter EDGAR *disguised.*

EDG. If e'er your grace had speech with man so poor,
Hear me one word.

ALB.   I'll overtake you.   [*Exeunt all but Albany and Edgar.*
                               Speak.

EDG. Before you fight the battle, ope this letter.
If you have victory, let the trumpet sound
For him that brought it. Wretched though I seem,   50
I can produce a champion that will prove
What is avouched° there. If you miscarry,°

16. **bosom'd with her,** in her confidence; suggesting also her embraces. 30. **Not . . . others,** not because France encourages the king and others. 31. **heavy causes,** weighty reasons. **make oppose,** compel to fight (against us). 38. **ancient of war,** veteran soldiers. 42. **convenient,** proper, befitting. 52. **avouched,** formally asserted. **miscarry,** perish, come to destruction.

Your business of the world hath so an end,
And machination ceases. Fortune love you!
    ALB. Stay till I have read the letter.
    EDG.   I was forbid it.
When time shall serve, let but the herald cry,
And I'll appear again.
    ALB. Why, fare thee well. I will o'erlook° thy paper.   [*Exit Edgar.*
Re-enter EDMUND.
60   EDM. The enemy 's in view; draw up your powers.
Here is the guess of their true strength and forces
By diligent discovery;° but your haste
Is now urged on you.
    ALB.   We will greet the time.°   [*Exit.*
    EDM. To both these sisters have I sworn my love;
Each jealous° of the other, as the stung
Are of the adder. Which of them shall I take?
Both? one? or neither? Neither can be enjoy'd
If both remain alive. To take the widow
70 Exasperates, makes mad her sister Goneril;
And hardly shall I carry out my side,°
Her husband being alive. Now then we'll use
His countenance° for the battle, which being done,
Let her who would be rid of him devise
His speedy taking off. As for the mercy
Which he intends to Lear and to Cordelia,
The battle done, and they within our power,
Shall never see his pardon; for my state
Stands on me to defend, not to debate.°   [*Exit.*
SCENE II.   *A field between the two camps.*
Alarum within. Enter, with drum and colours, LEAR, CORDELIA, *and* Soldiers,
over the stage; and exeunt.
Enter EDGAR *and* GLOUCESTER.
    EDG. Here, father, take the shadow of this tree
For your good host; pray that the right may thrive.
If ever I return to you again,
I'll bring you comfort.
    GLOU.   Grace go with you, sir!   [*Exit Edgar.*
Alarum and retreat within. Re-enter EDGAR.
    EDG. Away, old man; give me thy hand; away!

---

   59. **o'erlook,** peruse. 62. **discovery,** reconnoitering. 64. **greet the time,** face the situation.
66. **jealous,** suspicious. 71. **carry out my side,** win my game; possibly a figure from cards.
73. **countenance,** authority. 78-79. **my state ... debate,** my position depends upon maintenance by force, not on debate.

King Lear hath lost, he and his daughter ta'en.
Give me thy hand; come on.
    Glou.   No farther, sir; a man may rot even here.
    Edg.   What, in ill thoughts again? Men must endure   10
Their going hence, even as their coming hither;
Ripeness° is all. Come on.
    Glou.   And that 's true too.   [*Exeunt.*
Scene iii.   *The British camp near Dover.*
Enter, in conquest, with drum and colours, Edmund; Lear *and* Cordelia,
prisoners; Captain, Soldiers, & c.
    Edm.   Some officers take them away. Good guard,
Until their greater pleasures first be known
That are to censure them.
    Cor.   We are not the first
Who with best meaning have incurr'd the worst.
For thee, oppressed king, I am cast down;
Myself could else out-frown false fortune's frown.
Shall we not see these daughters and these sisters?
    Lear.   No, no, no, no! Come, let 's away to prison.
We two alone will sing like birds i' the cage.   10
When thou dost ask me blessing, I'll kneel down
And ask of thee forgiveness. So we'll live,
And pray, and sing, and tell old tales, and laugh
At gilded butterflies,° and hear poor rogues
Talk of court news; and we'll talk with them too,
Who loses and who wins; who 's in, who 's out;
And take upon 's the mystery of things,
As if we were God's spies; and we'll wear out,°
In a wall'd prison, packs and sects° of great ones
That ebb and flow by the moon.   20
    Edm.   Take them away.
    Lear.   Upon such sacrifices, my Cordelia,
The gods themselves throw incense. Have I caught thee?
He that parts us shall bring a brand from heaven
And fire us hence like foxes.° Wipe thine eyes;
The good-years° shall devour them, flesh and fell,°
Ere they shall make us weep! We'll see 'em starve first.
Come.   [*Exeunt Lear and Cordelia, guarded.*
    Edm.   Come hither, captain; hark.

---

   12. **Ripeness,** readiness.
   14. **gilded butterflies,** courtiers. 18. **wear out,** forget, efface from memory; possibly, outlive. 19. **sects,** parties. 25. **fire ... foxes,** i.e., as foxes are driven out of their holes by fire and smoke. 26. **good-years,** apparently a general word for evil; thought sometimes to be the name of a disease. **flesh and fell,** flesh and skin.

30 Take thou this note [*Giving a paper*]; go follow them to prison.
One step I have advanced thee; if thou dost
As this instructs thee, thou dost make thy way
To noble fortunes. Know thou this, that men
Are as the time is; to be tender-minded
Does not become a sword. Thy great employment
Will not bear question;° either say thou 'lt do 't,
Or thrive by other means.
    CAPT.   I'll do 't, my lord.
    EDM.   About it; and write happy° when thou hast done.
40 Mark, I say, instantly; and carry it so
As I have set it down.
    CAPT.   I cannot draw a cart, nor eat dried oats;
If it be man's work, I'll do it.   [*Exit.*
Flourish. Enter ALBANY, GONERIL, REGAN, *another* Captain, *and* Soldiers.
    ALB.   Sir, you have shown to-day your valiant strain,
And fortune led you well. You have the captives
That were the opposites of this day's strife;
I do require them of you, so to use them
As we shall find their merits and our safety
May equally determine.
50   EDM.   Sir, I thought it fit
To send the old and miserable king
To some retention° and appointed guard;
Whose age has charms in it, whose title more,
To pluck the common bosom° on his side
And turn our impress'd lances° in our eyes
Which do command them. With him I sent the queen,
My reason all the same; and they are ready
To-morrow, or at further space, to appear
Where you shall hold your session. At this time
60 We sweat and bleed: the friend hath lost his friend;
And the best quarrels, in the heat, are cursed
By those that feel their sharpness.
The question° of Cordelia and her father
Requires a fitter place.
    ALB.   Sir, by your patience,
I hold you but a subject of this war,
Not as a brother.
    REG.   That 's as we list° to grace him.
Methinks our pleasure might have been demanded

36. **bear question,** be argued about. 39. **write happy,** call yourself happy. 52. **retention,** custody. 54. **common bosom,** the affection of the mob. 55. **impress'd lances,** weapons of troops impressed into service. 63. **question,** cause. 68. **list,** please.

Ere you had spoke so far. He led our powers, 70
Bore the commission° of my place and person,
The which immediacy° may well stand up
And call itself your brother.
    GON.   Not so hot!
In his own grace he doth exalt himself,
More than in your addition.
    REG.   In my rights
By me invested, he compeers° the best.
    GON.   That were the most if he should husband you.
    REG.   Jesters do oft prove prophets. 80
    GON.   Holla, holla!
That eye that told you so look'd but a-squint.°
    REG.   Lady, I am not well; else I should answer
From a full-flowing stomach.° General,
Take thou my soldiers, prisoners, patrimony;
Dispose of them, of me; the walls are thine.°
Witness the world that I create thee here
My lord and master.
    GON.   Mean you to enjoy him?
    ALB.   The let-alone lies not in your good will. 90
    EDM.   Nor in thine, lord.
    ALB.   Half-blooded° fellow, yes.
    REG.   [*To Edmund*] Let the drum strike, and prove my title thine.
    ALB.   Stay yet; hear reason. Edmund, I arrest thee
On capital treason; and, in thine attaint,°
This gilded serpent [*Pointing to Goneril*]. For your claim, fair sister,
I bar it in the interest of my wife;
'Tis she is sub-contracted to this lord,
And I, her husband, contradict your bans.
If you will marry, make your loves to me; 100
My lady is bespoke.
    GON.   An interlude!°
    ALB.   Thou art arm'd, Gloucester. Let the trumpet sound.
If none appear to prove upon thy person
Thy heinous, manifest, and many treasons,
There is my pledge [*Throwing down a glove*]! I'll make it on thy heart,
Ere I taste bread, thou art in nothing less
Than I have here proclaim'd thee.

71. **commission,** warrant as representative. 72. **immediacy,** next in authority, or nearness
of his being my agent. 78. **compeers,** is equal with. 82. **That . . . a-squint,** reference to a
proverb: Love being jealous makes a good eye look asquint. 84. **full-flowing stomach,** full
tide of angry rejoinder. 86. **the walls are thine,** probably a phrase signifying complete surrender. 92. **Half-blooded,** partly of mean blood. 95. **attaint,** impeachment, accused of
treason with you. 102. **interlude,** play-acting, i.e., you are melodramatic.

REG.   Sick, O, sick!
110 GON. [*Aside*] If not, I'll ne'er trust medicine.
EDM.   There 's my exchange.   [*Throwing down a glove.*
What in the world he is
That names me traitor, villain-like he lies.
Call by thy trumpet; he that dares approach,
On him, on you, who not? I will maintain
My truth and honour firmly.
ALB.   A herald, ho!
EDM.   A herald, ho, a herald!
ALB.   Trust to thy single virtue; for thy soldiers,
120 All levied in my name, have in my name
Took their discharge.
REG.   My sickness grows upon me.
ALB.   She is not well; convey her to my tent.   [*Exit Regan, led.*
Enter a Herald.
Come hither, herald,—Let the trumpet sound,—
And read out this.
CAPT.   Sound, trumpet!   [*A trumpet sounds.*
HER. [*Reads*] "If any man of quality or degree within the lists of the
army will maintain upon Edmund, supposed Earl of Gloucester, that he
is a manifold traitor, let him appear by the third sound of the trumpet.
130 He is bold in his defence."   [*First trumpet.*
HER.   Again!   [*Second trumpet.*
HER.   Again!   [*Third trumpet.*
Trumpet answers within.
Enter EDGAR, *at the third sound, armed, with a trumpet before him.*
ALB.   Ask him his purposes, why he appears
Upon this call o' the trumpet.
HER.   What are you?
Your name, your quality? and why you answer
This present summons?
EDG.   Know my name is lost;
By treason's tooth bare-gnawn and canker-bit;°
140 Yet am I noble as the adversary
I come to cope.
ALB.   Which is that adversary?
EDG.   What 's he that speaks for Edmund Earl of Gloucester?
EDM.   Himself. What say'st thou to him?
EDG.   Draw thy sword,
That, if my speech offend a noble heart,
Thy arm may do thee justice. Here is mine.

---

139. **canker-bit,** withered, i.e., bitten by the caterpillar.

Behold, it is the privilege of mine honours,
My oath, and my profession. I protest,
Maugre° thy strength, place, youth, and eminence,   150
Despite thy victor sword and fire-new° fortune,
Thy valour and thy heart, thou art a traitor,
False to thy gods, thy brother, and thy father;
Conspirant 'gainst this high-illustrious prince;
And, from the extremest upward° of thy head
To the descent and dust below thy foot,
A most toad-spotted° traitor. Say thou "No,"
This sword, this arm, and my best spirits, are bent
To prove upon thy heart, whereto I speak,
Thou liest.   160
        EDM.   In wisdom° I should ask thy name;
But since thy outside looks so fair and warlike,
And that thy tongue some say° of breeding breathes,
What safe and nicely I might well delay
By rule of knighthood, I disdain and spurn.
Back do I toss these treasons to thy head,°
With the hell-hated° lie o'erwhelm thy heart,
Which, for they yet glance by and scarcely bruise,
This sword of mine shall give them instant way,
Where they shall rest for ever. Trumpets, speak!   170
Alarums. They fight. EDMUND *falls.*
        ALB.   Save him, save him!
        GON.   This is practice, Gloucester.
By the law of arms thou wast not bound to answer
An unknown opposite; thou art not vanquish'd,
But cozen'd and beguiled.
        ALB.   Shut your mouth, dame,
Or with this paper shall I stop it. Hold, sir;
Thou worse than any name, read thine own evil.
No tearing, lady! I perceive you know it.   [*Gives the letter to Edmund.*
        GON.   Say if I do—the laws are mine, not thine.   180
Who can arraign me for 't?
        ALB.   Most monstrous! oh!
Know'st thou this paper?
        GON.   Ask me not what I know.   [*Exit.*
        ALB.   Go after her; she 's desperate; govern her.

---

150. **Maugre,** in spite of. 151. **fire-new,** freshly gained. 155. **upward,** top. 157. **toad-spotted,** venomous, or having spots of infamy. 161. **wisdom,** prudence, i.e., Edmund might have demanded that his adversary be his equal in rank. 163. **say,** flavor, indication; possibly for "assay," proof. 166. **head,** i.e., to thy teeth. 167. **hell-hated,** hated as hell is hated.

EDM. What you have charged me with, that have I done;
And more, much more; the time will bring it out.
'Tis past, and so am I. But what art thou
That hast this fortune° on me? If thou 'rt noble,
190 I do forgive thee.
          EDG.   Let 's exchange charity.
I am no less in blood than thou art, Edmund;
If more, the more thou hast wrong'd me.
My name is Edgar, and thy father's son.
The gods are just, and of our pleasant vices
Make instruments to plague us.
The dark and vicious place where thee he got
Cost him his eyes.
          EDM.   Thou hast spoken right, 'tis true;
200 The wheel° is come full circle; I am here.
          ALB. Methought thy very gait did prophesy
A royal nobleness. I must embrace thee;
Let sorrow split my heart if ever I
Did hate thee or thy father!
          EDG.   Worthy prince, I know 't.
          ALB. Where have you hid yourself?
How have you known the miseries of your father?
          EDG. By nursing them, my lord. List a brief tale;
And when 'tis told, O that my heart would burst!
210 The bloody proclamation to escape,
That follow'd me so near,—O, our lives' sweetness!
That we the pain of death would hourly die
Rather than die at once!— taught me to shift
Into a madman's rags, to assume a semblance
That very dogs disdain'd; and in this habit
Met I my father with his bleeding rings,°
Their precious stones new lost; became his guide,
Led him, begg'd for him, saved him from despair;
Never,—O fault!—reveal'd myself unto him
220 Until some half-hour past, when I was arm'd.
Not sure, though hoping, of this good success,
I ask'd his blessing, and from first to last
Told him my pilgrimage. But his flaw'd heart—
Alack, too weak the conflict to support!—
'Twixt two extremes of passion, joy and grief,
Burst smilingly.
          EDM.   This speech of yours hath moved me,

189. **fortune,** victory, success. 200. **wheel,** wheel of fortune. 216. **rings,** sockets.

William Shakespeare   407

And shall perchance do good; but speak you on;
You look as you had something more to say.

    ALB. If there be more, more woeful, hold it in;   230
For I am almost ready to dissolve,
Hearing of this.

    EDG.   This would have seem'd a period
To such as love not sorrow; but another,
To amplify too much, would make much more,
And top extremity. Whilst I was big in clamour, came there in a man,
Who, having seen me in my worst estate,
Shunn'd my abhorr'd society; but then, finding
Who 'twas that so endured, with his strong arms   240
He fasten'd on my neck and bellow'd out
As he'd burst heaven; threw him on my father;
Told the most piteous tale of Lear and him
That ever ear received; which in recounting
His grief grew puissant, and the strings of life
Began to crack. Twice then the trumpets sounded,
And there I left him tranced.

    ALB.   But who was this?

    EDG. Kent, sir, the banish'd Kent, who in disguise
Follow'd his enemy king and did him service   250
Improper for a slave.

Enter a Gentleman, *with a bloody knife.*

    GENT. Help, help! O, help!

    EDG.   What kind of help?

    ALB.   Speak, man.

    EDG. What means this bloody knife?

    GENT.   'Tis hot, it smokes;
It came even from the heart of—O, she 's dead!

    ALB. Who dead? speak, man.

    GENT. Your lady, sir, your lady! and her sister
By her is poisoned; she hath confess'd it.   260

    EDM. I was contracted to them both; all three
Now marry in an instant.

    EDG.   Here comes Kent.

Enter KENT.

    ALB. Produce the bodies, be they alive or dead.
This judgement of the heavens, that makes us tremble,
Touches us not with pity.   *[Exit Gentleman.*
        [To Kent] O, is this he?
The time will not allow the compliment
Which very manners urges.

KENT.   I am come
270 To bid my king and master aye good night.
Is he not here?
ALB.   Great thing of us forgot!
Speak, Edmund, where 's the king? and where 's Cordelia?
[*The bodies of Goneril and Regan are brought in*] See'st thou this object, Kent?
KENT.   Alack, why thus?
EDM.   Yet Edmund was beloved;
The one the other poison'd for my sake,
And after slew herself.
280 ALB.   Even so. Cover their faces.
EDM.   I pant for life. Some good I mean to do,
Despite of mine own nature. Quickly send—
Be brief in it—to the castle; for my writ
Is on the life of Lear and on Cordelia.
Nay, send in time!
ALB.   Run, run, O, run!
EDG.   To who, my lord? Who has the office? send
Thy token of reprieve.
EDM.   Well thought on. Take my sword,
290 Give it the captain.
ALB.   Haste thee, for thy life.   [*Exit Edgar.*
EDM.   He hath commission from thy wife and me
To hang Cordelia in the prison and
To lay the blame upon her own despair,
That she fordid° herself.
ALB.   The gods defend her! Bear him hence awhile.
                              [*Edmund is borne off.*
Re-enter LEAR, *with* CORDELIA *dead in his arms;* EDGAR, Captain, *and others*
following.
LEAR.   Howl, howl, howl! O, you are men of stones!
Had I your tongues and eyes, I'd use them so
That heaven's vault should crack. She 's gone for ever!
300 I know when one is dead, and when one lives.
She 's dead as earth. Lend me a looking-glass;
If that her breath will mist or stain the stone,°
Why, then she lives.
KENT.   Is this the promised end?°
EDG.   Or image of that horror?
ALB.   Fall and cease!°
LEAR.   This feather stirs; she lives! if it be so,

---

295. **fordid,** destroyed.   302. **stone,** crystal (of which the mirror is made).   304. **end,** Last Judgment.   306. **Fall and cease.** Possibly, let the heavens fall and all things cease.

William Shakespeare   409

It is a chance which does redeem all sorrows
That ever I have felt.
 KENT.   [*Kneeling*] O my good master!   310
 LEAR. Prithee away.
 EDG.   'Tis noble Kent, your friend.
 LEAR. A plague upon you, murderers, traitors all!
I might have saved her; now she 's gone for ever!
Cordelia, Cordelia! stay a little. Ha!
What is 't thou say'st? Her voice was ever soft,
Gentle, and low, an excellent thing in woman.
I kill'd the slave that was a-hanging thee.
 CAPT. 'Tis true, my lords, he did.
 LEAR.   Did I not, fellow?   320
I have seen the day, with my good biting falchion°
I would have made them skip. I am old now,
And these same crosses° spoil me. Who are you?
Mine eyes are not o' the best; I'll tell you straight.
 KENT. If fortune brag of two she loved and hated,
One of them we behold.
 LEAR. This is a dull sight. Are you not Kent?
 KENT.   The same,
Your servant Kent. Where is your servant Caius?
 LEAR. He 's a good fellow, I can tell you that; 330
He'll strike, and quickly too. He 's dead and rotten.
 KENT. No, my good lord; I am the very man,—
 LEAR. I'll see that straight.
 KENT. That from your first of difference° and decay
Have follow'd your sad steps.
 LEAR.   You are welcome hither.
 KENT. Nor no man else. All 's cheerless, dark, and deadly.
Your eldest daughters have fordone themselves,
And desperately° are dead.
 LEAR.   Ay, so I think.   340
 ALB. He knows not what he says: and vain is it
That we present us to him.
 EDG.   Very bootless.
Enter a Captain.
 CAPT. Edmund is dead, my lord.
 ALB.   That 's but a trifle here.
You lords and noble friends, know our intent.
What comfort to this great decay may come

---

321. **falchion,** sword; properly, a sword curved at the point with the edge on the convex side. 323. **crosses,** troubles. 334. **first of difference,** beginning of your change of fortune for the worst. 339. **desperately,** in despair.

Shall be applied. For us, we will resign,
During the life of this old majesty,
350 To him our absolute power; [*To Edgar and Kent*]   you to your rights;
With boot, and such addition as your honours
Have more than merited. All friends shall taste
The wages of their virtue, and all foes
The cup of their deservings. O, see, see!
   LEAR.   And my poor fool° is hang'd! No, no, no life!
Why should a dog, a horse, a rat, have life,
And thou no breath at all? Thou 'lt come no more,
Never, never, never, never, never!
Pray you, undo this button. Thank you, sir.
360 Do you see this? Look on her! look! her lips!
Look there, look there!   [*Dies.*
   EDG.   He faints! My lord, my lord!
   KENT.   Break, heart; I prithee break!
   EDG.   Look up, my lord.
   KENT.   Vex not his ghost. O, let him pass! he hates him
That would upon the rack of this tough world
Stretch him out longer.
   EDG.   He is gone indeed.
   KENT.   The wonder is, he hath endured so long.
370 He but usurp'd his life.
   ALB.   Bear them from hence. Our present business
Is general woe. [*To Kent and Edgar*]   Friends of my soul, you twain
Rule in this realm, and the gored state sustain.
   KENT.   I have a journey, sir, shortly to go;
My master calls me, I must not say no.
   EDG.   The weight of this sad time we must obey,
Speak what we feel, not what we ought to say.
The oldest hath borne most. We that are young
Shall never see so much, nor live so long.

                                   [*Exeunt, with a dead march.*

---

355. **my poor fool,** i.e., Cordelia. It has sometimes been wrongly thought that this refers
to the Fool, but *fool*, as here used, is a term of endearment.

1828-1906
HENRIK IBSEN * Hedda Gabler*

CHARACTERS

JØRGEN TESMAN, University Research Fellow in the History of Civilization
HEDDA, his wife
MISS JULIANE TESMAN, his aunt
MRS. ELVSTED
JUDGE BRACK
EILERT LØVBORG
BERTE, the Tesmans' maid

A NOTE ON THE PRONUNCIATION: The approximate Norwegian pronunciation of names likely to be difficult to a speaker of English is suggested below (the syllable in capitals is accented; the unaccented *e* is close to English *e* in *quiet*).

> JØRGEN   YUR-gen (*g* as in *bargain*)
> JULLE   YOOL-le (short *oo*)
> EILERT LØVBORG   AY-lert LUV-borg°
> BERTE   BAIR-te

SCENE: *The* Tesmans' *villa in a fashionable residential section of the town.*

Act I

A spacious, handsome, tastefully furnished room. Dark décor. In the rear, a wide doorway with open portieres. Beyond is a smaller room, furnished in the same style as the front room. A door, right, leads to the front hall. Left, French doors, with portieres drawn aside, through which can be seen a part of a roofed verandah and trees with autumn foliage. Front center, an oval table covered with a cloth. Chairs around it. Front right, a wide, dark, porcelain stove, a high-backed easy chair, a footstool with a pillow, and two ottomans. In the corner far right, a sofa and a small, round table. Front left, a sofa, set out from the wall. Far left, beyond the French doors, an upright piano. On both sides of the doorway, rear center, whatnots with knickknacks. Against the rear wall of the inner room, a sofa, and in front of it a table and two chairs. Above the sofa, a portrait of a handsome, elderly man in general's uniform. Over the table hangs a lamp with milky, white glass. There are several bouquets of flowers, in vases and glasses, in various places in the front room. Others are lying on the tables. Thick carpets on the floors of both rooms. The morning sun is shining through the French doors.

MISS JULIANE TESMAN, *with hat and parasol, enters right, followed by* BERTE, *who carries a bouquet of flowers wrapped in paper.* MISS TESMAN *is a nice-looking*

---

*Translated by Otto Reinert. °Løvborg means, literally, "leaf-castle"—a fact of possible bearing on the play's symbolism.

woman of 65, of pleasant mien, neatly but not expensively dressed in a gray suit. BERTE *is a middle-aged servant girl, of rather plain and countrified appearance.*

MISS TES. [*Stops inside the door, listens, says in a low voice*]   On my word— I don't think they are even up yet!

BER. [*Also softly*]   That's what I told you, miss. When you think how late the steamer got in last night. And afterwards—! Goodness!—all the stuff she wanted unpacked before she turned in.

MISS TES.   Well—just let them sleep. But fresh morning air—*that* we can give them when they come in here.

Goes and opens the French doors wide.

BER. [*By the table, lost, still holding the flowers*]   Please, miss—I just don't see a bit of space anywhere! I think I'd better put these over here.

Puts the flowers down on the piano.

10   MISS TES.   Well, well, my dear Berte. So you've got yourself a new mistress now. The good Lord knows it was hard for me to let you go.

BER. [*Near tears*]   What about me, then, miss! What shall *I* say? I who have served you and Miss Rina all these blessed years.

MISS TES.   We shall just have to make the best of it, Berte. There's nothing else to do. Jørgen can't do without you, you know. He just can't. You've looked after him ever since he was a little boy.

BER.   Yes, but miss—I'm ever so worried about leaving Miss Rina. The poor dear lying there all helpless. With that new girl and all! She'll never learn how to make things nice and comfortable for an invalid.

20   MISS TES.   Oh yes, you'll see. I'll teach her. And of course, you know, I'll do most of it myself. So don't you worry yourself about my poor sister, Berte.

BER.   Yes, but there's another thing, too, miss. I'm scared I won't be able to suit young Mrs. Tesman.

MISS TES.   Oh, well. Good heavens. So there is a thing or two— Right at first—

BER.   For I believe she's ever so particular.

MISS TES.   Can you wonder? General Gabler's daughter? Just think of the kind of life she was used to when the General was alive. Do you 30 remember when she rode by with her father? That long black riding habit she wore? And the feather in her hat?

BER.   Oh, I remember, all right. But I'll be blessed if I ever thought she and the young master would make a pair of it.

MISS TES.   Nor did I. By the way, while I think of it, Berte. Jørgen has a new title now. From now on you must refer to him as "the Doctor."

BER.   Yes, the young mistress said something about that, too, last night. Soon as they were inside the door. Then it's really so, miss?

MISS TES.   It certainly is. Just think, Berte—they have made him a doctor abroad. During the trip, you know. I hadn't heard a thing about 40 it till last night on the pier.

BER. Well, I daresay he could be anything he put his mind to, *he* could—smart as *he* is. But I must say I'd never thought he'd turn to doctoring people, too.

MISS TES. Oh, that's not the kind of doctor he is. [*Nods significantly*] And as far as that is concerned, there is no telling but pretty soon you may have to call him something grander yet.

BER. You don't say! What might that be, miss?

MISS TES. [*Smiles*] Wouldn't you like to know! [*Moved*] Ah yes, indeed—! If only dear Jochum could see from his grave what has become of his little boy! [*Looking around*] But look, Berte—what's this for? Why 50 have you taken off all the slip covers?

BER. She told me to. Said she can't stand slip covers on chairs.

MISS TES. Do you think they mean to make this their everyday living room, then?

BER. It sure sounded that way. Mrs. Tesman did, I mean. For he— the doctor—he didn't say anything.

JØRGEN TESMAN *enters from the right side of the inner room. He is humming to himself. He carries an open, empty suitcase. He is of medium height, youthful-looking, thirty-three years old, somewhat stoutish. Round, open, cheerful face. Blond hair and beard. He wears glasses and is dressed in a comfortable, rather casual suit.*

MISS TES. Good morning, good morning, Jørgen!

TES. [*In the doorway*] Auntie! Dearest Aunt Julle! [*Comes forward and shakes her hand*] All the way out here—as early as this! Hm?

MISS TES. Well—I just had to drop in for a moment. To see how you 60 are getting along, you know.

TES. Even though you haven't had a good night's sleep.

MISS TES. Oh, that doesn't matter at all.

TES. But you did get home from the pier all right, I hope. Hm?

MISS TES. Oh yes, certainly I did, thank you. The Judge was kind enough to see me all the way to my door.

TES. We were so sorry we couldn't give you a ride in our carriage. But you saw for yourself—all the boxes Hedda had.

MISS TES. Yes, she certainly brought quite a collection.

BER. [*To Tesman*] Should I go and ask Mrs. Tesman if there's any- 70 thing I can help her with?

TES. No, thank you, Berte—you'd better not. She said she'll ring if she wants you.

BER. [*Going right*] Well, all right.

TES. But, look—you might take this suitcase with you.

BER. [*Takes it*] I'll put it in the attic. [*Exits right.*

TES. Just think, Auntie—that whole suitcase was brimful of copies of old documents. You wouldn't believe me if I told you all the things I

have collected from libraries and archives all over. Quaint old items
80 nobody has known anything about.

MISS TES. Well, no, Jørgen. I'm sure you haven't wasted your time
on your honeymoon.

TES. No, I think I may say I have not. But take your hat off, Auntie
—for goodness' sake. Here! Let me untie the ribbon for you. Hm?

MISS TES. [*While he does so*] Ah, God forgive me, if this isn't just as
if you were still at home with us!

TES. [*Inspecting the hat*] My, what a fine-looking hat you've got
yourself!

MISS TES. I bought it for Hedda's sake.

90 TES. For Hedda's sake? Hm?

MISS TES. So she won't need to feel ashamed of me if we ever go out
together.

TES. [*Patting her cheek*] If you don't think of everything, Auntie!
[*Puts the hat down on a chair by the table*] And now—over here to the sofa
—we'll just sit and chat for a while till Hedda comes.

They seat themselves. She places her parasol in the corner by the sofa.

MISS TES. [*Takes both his hands in hers and gazes at him*] What a blessing
it is to have you back again, Jørgen, big as life! You—Jochum's little boy!

TES. For me, too, Aunt Julle. To see you again. For you have been
both father and mother to me.

100 MISS TES. Ah, yes—don't you think I know you'll always keep a spot
in your heart for these two old aunts of yours!

TES. So Aunt Rina isn't any better, hm?

MISS TES. Oh no. We mustn't look for improvement in her case, poor
dear. She is lying there just as she has been all these years. Just the same,
may the good Lord keep her for me a long time yet! For else I just
wouldn't know what to do with myself, Jørgen. Especially now, when
I don't have you to look after any more.

TES. [*Pats her back*] There, there, now!

MISS TES. [*Changing tone*] And to think that you are a married man,
110 Jørgen! And that you were the one to walk off with Hedda Gabler. The
lovely Hedda Gabler. Just think! As many admirers as she had!

TES. [*Hums a little, smiles contentedly*] Yes, I daresay I have quite a few
good friends here in town who'd gladly be in my shoes, hm?

MISS TES. And such a lovely, long honeymoon you had! More than
five—almost six months!

TES. Well, you know—for me it has been a kind of study tour as well.
All the collections I had to go through. And the books I had to read!

MISS TES. Yes, I suppose. [*More confidentially, her voice lowered a little*]
But listen, Jørgen—haven't you got something—something special to tell
120 me?

TES.   About the trip?

MISS TES.   Yes.

TES.   No—I don't know of anything besides what I wrote in my letters. They gave me a doctor's degree down there—but I told you that last night; I'm sure I did.

MISS TES.   Well, yes, that sort of thing—What I mean is—don't you have certain—certain—expectations?

TES.   Expectations?

MISS TES.   Ah for goodness' sake, Jørgen! I am your old Auntie, after all!   130

TES.   Certainly I have expectations.

MISS TES.   Well!!

TES.   I fully expect to be made a professor one of these days.

MISS TES.   Professor—oh yes—

TES.   I may even say I am quite certain of it. But dear Aunt Julle— you know this just as well as I do!

MISS TES. [*Laughing a little*]   Of course I do. You're quite right. [*Changing topic*]   But we were talking about the trip. It must have cost a great deal of money—hm, Jørgen?

TES.   Well, now; you know that large stipend went quite a long way. 140

MISS TES.   I just don't see how you made it do for both of you, though.

TES.   No, I suppose that's not so easy to understand, hm?

MISS TES.   Particularly with a lady along. For I have always heard that is ever so much more expensive.

TES.   Well, yes, naturally. That *is* rather more expensive. But Hedda had to have this trip, Auntie! She really had to. Nothing less would do.

MISS TES.   No, I daresay. For a wedding journey is quite the thing these days. But now tell me—have you had a chance to look around here yet?

TES.   I certainly have. I have been up and about ever since dawn. 150

MISS TES.   And what do you think of it all?

TES.   Delightful! Perfectly delightful! The only thing is I don't see what we are going to do with the two empty rooms between the second sitting room in there and Hedda's bedroom.

MISS TES. [*With a chuckle*]   Oh my dear Jørgen—you may find them useful enough—when the time comes!

TES.   Of course, you're right, Auntie! As my library expands, hm?

MISS TES.   Quite so, my dear boy. It was your library I was thinking of.

TES.   But I'm really most happy on Hedda's behalf. For you know, be- 160 fore we were engaged she used to say she wouldn't care to live anywhere but in Secretary Falk's house.

MISS TES.   Yes, just think—wasn't that a lucky coincidence, that it was up for sale right after you had left?

TES. Yes, Aunt Julle. We've certainly been lucky. Hm?

MISS TES. But it will be expensive, my dear Jørgen. Terribly expensive—all this.

TES. [*Looks at her, a bit crestfallen*] Yes, I daresay it will, Auntie.

MISS TES. Heavens, yes!

170 TES. How much, do you think? Roughly. Hm?

MISS TES. No, I couldn't possibly say till all the bills arrive.

TES. Well, anyway, Judge Brack managed to get very reasonable terms for us. He said so himself in a letter to Hedda.

MISS TES. Yes, and I won't have you uneasy on that account, Jørgen. Besides, I have given security for the furniture and the carpets.

TES. Security? You? But dear Aunt Julle—what kind of security could you give?

MISS TES. The annuity.

TES. [*Jumps up*] What! Your and Aunt Rina's annuity?

180 MISS TES. Yes. I didn't know what else to do, you see.

TES. [*Standing before her*] But are you clear out of your mind, Auntie! That annuity—that's all the two of you have to live on!

MISS TES. Oh well, there's nothing to get so excited about, I'm sure. It's all just a matter of form, you know. That's what the Judge said, too. For he was kind enough to arrange the whole thing for me. Just a matter of form—those were his words.

TES. That's all very well. Still—

MISS TES. For now you'll have your own salary, you know. And, goodness—what if we do have a few expenses—Help out a bit right at first—? That would only be a joy for us—

190 TES. Oh, Auntie! When will you ever stop making sacrifices for my sake!

MISS TES. [*Gets up, puts her hands on his shoulders*] But what other happiness do I have in this world than being able to smooth your way a little, my own dear boy? You, who haven't had either father or mother to lean on? And now the goal is in sight, Jørgen. Things may have looked black at times. But heaven be praised; you're on top now!

TES. Yes, it's really quite remarkable the way things have worked out.

MISS TES. Yes—and those who were against you—who tried to block your way—now they are tasting defeat. They are down, Jørgen! He, the most dangerous of them all, his fall was the greatest! He made his bed, and now he is lying in it—poor, lost wretch that he is!

TES. Have you had any news about Eilert? Since I went away, I mean?

MISS TES. Just that he is supposed to have published a new book.

TES. What? Eilert Løvborg? Recently? Hm?

MISS TES. That's what they say. But I wonder if there can be much to it. What do you think? Ah—but when *your* new book comes, that will be something quite different, Jørgen! What is it going to be about?

TES. It will deal with the domestic industries of Brabant during the
Middle Ages.

MISS TES. Just think—being able to write about something like that!

TES. But as far as that is concerned, it may be quite some time before
it is ready. I have all these collections to put in order first, you see.

MISS TES. Yes, collecting and putting things in order—you certainly
know how to do that. In that you are your father's son.

TES. Well, I must say I am looking forward to getting started. Particularly now, that I've got my own delightful home to work in.

MISS TES. And most of all now that you have the one your heart
desired, dear Jørgen.

TES. [*Embracing her*] Oh yes, yes, Aunt Julle! Hedda—she is the most 220
wonderful part of it all! [*Looks toward the doorway*] There—I think she
is coming now, hm?

HEDDA *enters from the left side of the inner room. She is twenty-nine years old.
Both features and figure are noble and elegant. Pale, ivory complexion. Steel-gray
eyes, expressive of cold, clear calm. Beautiful brown hair, though not particularly
ample. She is dressed in a tasteful, rather loose-fitting morning costume.*

MISS TES. [*Going toward her*] Good morning, my dear Hedda! A very
happy morning to you!

HED. |*Giving her hand*] Good morning, dear Miss Tesman! So early
a call? That is most kind.

MISS TES. [*Seems slightly embarrassed*] And—has the little lady of the
house slept well the first night in her new home?

HED. Passably, thank you.

TES. [*Laughs*] Passably! You are a good one, Hedda! You were sleep- 230
ing like a log when I got up.

HED. Fortunately. And then, of course, Miss Tesman, it always takes
time to get used to new surroundings. That has to come gradually.
[*Looks left*] Oh dear. The maid has left the verandah doors wide open.
There's a veritable flood of sunlight in here.

MISS TES. [*Toward the doors*] Well, then, we'll just close them.

HED. No, no, not that. Tesman, dear, please pull the curtains. That
will give a softer light.

TES. [*Over by the French doors*] Yes, dear. There, now! Now you have
both shade and fresh air, Hedda. 240

HED. We certainly can use some air in here. Such loads of flowers—
But, Miss Tesman, please—won't you be seated?

MISS TES. No thanks. I just wanted to see if everything was all right
—and so it is, thank goodness. I had better get back to Rina. I know she
is waiting for me, poor thing.

TES. Be sure to give her my love, Auntie. And tell her I'll be around
to see her later today.

Miss Tes. I'll certainly do that!— Oh my! I almost forgot! [*Searches the pocket of her dress*] I have something for you, Jørgen. Here.

Tes. What's that, Auntie? Hm?

250   Miss Tes. [*Pulls out a flat parcel wrapped in newspaper and gives it to him*] Here you are, dear.

Tes. [*Opens the parcel*] Well, well, well! So you took care of them for me, Aunt Julle! Hedda! Now, isn't that sweet, hm?

Hed. [*By the whatnot, right*] If you'd tell me what it is—

Tes. My old slippers! *You* know!

Hed. Oh really? I remember you often talked about them on the trip.

Tes. Yes, for I missed them so. [*Walks over to her*] Here—now you can see what they're like, Hedda.

Hed. [*Crosses toward stove*] Thanks. I don't know that I really care.

260   Tes. [*Following*] Just think—Aunt Rina embroidered these slippers for me. Ill as she was. You can't imagine how many memories they hold for me!

Hed. [*By the table*] Hardly for me.

Miss Tes. That's true, you know, Jørgen.

Tes. Yes, but—I just thought that now that she's one of the family—

Hed. [*Interrupting*] I don't think we'll get on with that maid, Tesman.

Miss Tes. Not get on with Berte?

Tes. Whatever makes you say that, dear? Hm?

270   Hed. [*Points*] Look—she has left her old hat on the chair over there.

Tes. [*Appalled, drops the slippers*] But Hedda—!

Hed. What if somebody were to come and see it!

Tes. No, no, Hedda—that's Aunt Julle's hat!

Hed. Oh?

Miss Tes. [*Picking up the hat*] Yes, indeed it is. And it isn't old either, my dear young lady.

Hed. I really didn't look that closely—

Miss Tes. [*Tying the ribbons*] I want you to know that this is the first time I have had it on my head. On my word it is!

280   Tes. And very handsome it is, too. Really a splendid-looking hat!

Miss Tes. Oh, I don't know that it is anything so special, Jørgen. [*Looks around*] My parasol—? Ah, here it is. [*Picks it up*] For that is mine, too. [*Mutters*] Not Berte's.

Tes. New hat and new parasol! What do you think of that, Hedda!

Hed. Very nice indeed.

Tes. Yes, don't you think so? Hm? But, Auntie, take a good look at Hedda before you leave. See how pretty and blooming she looks.

Miss Tes. Dear me, Jørgen; that's nothing new. Hedda has been lovely all her days.   [*She nods and walks right.*]

TES. [*Following*]   Yes, but have you noticed how full-figured and 290 healthy she looks after the trip? How she has filled out?

HED. [*Crossing*]   Oh—stop it!

MISS TES. [*Halts, turns around*]   Filled out?

TES.   Yes, Aunt Julle. You can't see it so well now when she wears that dress. But, I who have the opportunity—

HED. [*By the French doors, impatiently*]   Oh, you have no opportunity at all!

TES.   It must be the mountain air in Tyrol.

HED. [*Curtly interrupting*]   I am just as I was when I left.

TES.   Yes, so you say. I just don't think you're right. What do you 300 think, Auntie?

MISS TES. [*Has folded her hands, gazes at Hedda*]   Lovely—lovely—lovely; that is what Hedda is.   [*Goes over to her, inclines her head forward with both her hands, and kisses her hair*]   God bless and keep Hedda Tesman. For Jørgen's sake.

HED. [*Gently freeing herself*]   There, there. Now let me go.

MISS TES. [*In quiet emotion*]   Every single day I'll be over and see you two.

TES.   Yes, please do, Auntie. Hm?

MISS TES.   Goodbye, goodbye!   310

She leaves through door, right. TESMAN *sees her out. The door remains ajar.* TESMAN *is heard repeating his greetings for* AUNT RINA *and his thanks for the slippers. In the meantime,* HEDDA *paces up and down, raises her arms, clenching her fists, as in quiet rage. Opens the curtains by the French doors and stands looking out. In a few moments,* TESMAN *re-enters and closes the door behind him.*

TES. [*Picking up the slippers*]   What are you looking at, Hedda?

HED. [*Once again calm and controlled*]   Just the leaves. They are so yellow. And so withered.

TES. [*Wrapping the slippers in their paper, putting the parcel down on the table*]   Well, you know—we're in September now.

HED. [*Again restless*]   Yes—just think. We are already in—September.

TES.   Don't you think Aunt Julle acted strange, Hedda? Almost solemn. I wonder why. Hm?

HED.   I hardly know her, you see. Isn't she often like that?

TES.   Not the way she was today.

HED. [*Turning away from the French doors*]   Do you think she minded 320 that business with the hat?

TES.   Oh, I don't think so. Not much. Perhaps a little bit right at the moment—

HED.   Well, I'm sorry, but I must say it strikes me as very odd— putting her hat down here in the living room. One just doesn't do that.

TES.   Well, you may be sure Aunt Julle won't ever do it again.

HED.   Anyway, I'll make it up to her, somehow.

Tes. Oh yes, Hedda; if only you would!

Hed. When you go over there today, why don't you ask her over for tonight?

Tes. I'll certainly do that. And then there is one other thing you could do that she'd appreciate ever so much.

Hed. What?

Tes. If you could just bring yourself to call her Auntie. For my sake, Hedda, hm?

Hed. No, Tesman, no. You really mustn't ask me to do that. I have already told you I won't. I'll try to call her Aunt Juliane. That will have to do.

Tes. All right, if you say so. I just thought that now that you're in the family—

Hed. Hmmm—I don't know about that—

She walks toward the doorway.

Tes. [*After a brief pause*] Anything the matter, Hedda? Hm?

Hed. I'm just looking at my old piano. It doesn't quite go with the other furniture in here.

Tes. As soon as I get my first pay check we'll have it traded in.

Hed. No—I don't want to do that. I want to keep it. But let's put it in this inner room and get another one for out here. Whenever it's convenient, I mean.

Tes. [*A little taken back*] Well—yes—we could do that—

Hed. [*Picks up the bouquet from the piano*] These flowers weren't here last night.

Tes. I suppose Aunt Julle brought them for you.

Hed. [*Looking at the flowers*] There's a card here. [*Takes it out and reads*] "Will be back later." Can you guess who it's from?

Tes. No. Who? Hm?

Hed. Thea Elvsted.

Tes. No, really? Mrs. Elvsted! Miss Rysing that was.

Hed. That's right. The one with that irritating head of hair she used to show off with. An old flame of yours, I understand.

Tes. [*Laughs*] Well, now—that didn't last long! Anyway, that was before I knew you, Hedda. Just think—her being in town.

Hed. Strange, that she'd call on us. I have hardly seen her since we went to school together.

Tes. As far as that goes, I haven't seen her either for—God knows how long. I don't see how she can stand living in that out-of-the-way place. Hm?

Hed. [*Suddenly struck by a thought*] Listen, Tesman—isn't it some place near there that he lives—what's his name—Eilert Løvborg?

Tes. Yes, that's right. He is up there, too.

Berte *enters right.*

BER. Ma'am, she's here again, that lady who brought those flowers a while back. [*Pointing*] The flowers you're holding in your hand, ma'am.

HED. Ah, she is? Well, show her in, please.

BERTE *opens the door for* MRS. ELVSTED *and exits.* MRS. ELVSTED *is of slight build, with a pretty, soft face. Her eyes are light blue, large, round, rather prominent, of a timid and querying expression. Her hair is strikingly light in color, almost whitish, and unusually rich and wavy. She is a couple of years younger than* HEDDA. *She is dressed in a dark visiting dress, tasteful, but not quite in the most recent fashion.*

HED. [*Walks toward her. Friendly*] Good morning, my dear Mrs. Elvsted. How very nice to see you again.

MRS. ELV. [*Nervous, trying not to show it*] Well, yes, it is quite some time since we met.

TES. [*Shaking hands*] And we, too. Hm?   380

HED. Thank you for your lovely flowers—

MRS. ELV. Please, don't—I would have come here yesterday afternoon. But I was told you were still traveling—

TES. You've just arrived in town, hm?

MRS. ELV. I got here yesterday, at noon. Oh, I was quite desperate when I learned you weren't home.

HED. Desperate? But why?

TES. But my dear Mrs. Rysing—I mean Mrs. Elvsted—

HED. There is nothing wrong, I hope?

MRS. ELV. Yes there is. And I don't know a single soul other than 390 you that I can turn to here.

HED. [*Putting the flowers down on the table*] Come—let's sit down here on the sofa.

MRS. ELV. Oh, I'm in no mood to sit!

HED. Of course you are. Come on.

She pulls MRS. ELVSTED *over to the sofa and sits down next to her.*

TES. Well, now, Mrs.—? Exactly what—?

HED. Has something—special happened at home?

MRS. ELV. Well, yes—and no. Oh, but I am so afraid you are going to misunderstand!

HED. In that case, it seems to me you ought to tell us exactly what 400 has happened, Mrs. Elvsted.

TES. After all, that's why you are here. Hm?

MRS. ELV. Yes, yes, of course. Well, then, maybe you already know —Eilert Løvborg is in town.

HED. Is Løvborg—!

TES. No! You don't say! Just think, Hedda—Løvborg's back!

HED. All right. I can hear.

MRS. ELV. He has been here a week already. Imagine—a whole week! In this dangerous place. Alone! With all that bad company around.

410 HED. But my dear Mrs. Elvsted—why is he a concern of yours?

MRS. ELV. [*With an apprehensive look at her, says quickly*] He tutored the children.

HED. Your children?

MRS. ELV. My husband's. I don't have any.

HED. In other words, your stepchildren.

MRS. ELV. Yes.

TES. [*With some hesitation*] But was he—I don't quite know how to put this—was he sufficiently—regular—in his way of life to be thus employed? Hm?

420 MRS. ELV. For the last two years, there hasn't been a thing to object to in his conduct.

TES. No, really? Just think, Hedda!

HED. I hear.

MRS. ELV. Not the least little bit, I assure you! Not in any respect. And yet—knowing he's here—in the big city—And with all that money, too! I'm scared to death!

TES. But in that case, why didn't he remain with you and your husband? Hm?

MRS. ELV. After his book came out, he was too restless to stay.

430 TES. Ah yes, that's right. Aunt Julle said he has published a new book.

MRS. ELV. Yes, a big new book, about the course of civilization in general. It came out about two weeks ago. And since it has had such big sales and been discussed so much and made such a big splash—

TES. It has, has it? I suppose this is something he has had lying around from better days?

MRS. ELV. You mean from earlier?

TES. Yes.

MRS. ELV. No; it's all been written since he came to stay with us. During this last year.

440 TES. Well, now! That's very good news, Hedda! Just think!

MRS. ELV. Yes, if it only would last!

HED. Have you seen him since you came to town?

MRS. ELV. No, not yet. I had a great deal of trouble finding his address. But this morning I finally tracked him down.

HED. [*Looks searchingly at her*] Isn't it rather odd that your husband—hm—

MRS. ELV. [*With a nervous start*] My husband! What about him?

HED. That he sends you to town on such an errand? That he doesn't go and look after his friend himself?

Mrs. Elv. Oh, no, no—my husband doesn't have time for things 450 like that. Besides, I have some—some shopping to do, anyway.

Hed. [*With a slight smile*] Well, in that case, of course—

Mrs. Elv. [*Getting up, restlessly*] And now I beg of you, Mr. Tesman —won't you please receive Eilert Løvborg nicely if he calls on you? And I am sure he will. After all— Such good friends as you two used to be. And then you both do the same kind of work—the same studies, as far as I know.

Tes. We used to, at any rate.

Mrs. Elv. Yes. And that's why I implore you to please, please, try to keep an eye on him—you too. You'll do that, Mr. Tesman, won't you? 460 Promise?

Tes. With the greatest pleasure, Mrs. Rysing.

Hed. Elvsted.

Tes. I'll gladly do as much for Eilert as I possibly can. You may certainly count on that.

Mrs. Elv. Oh, how good and kind you are! [*Clasps his hands*] Thank you, thank you, thank you! [*Nervously*] You see, my husband is so very fond of him.

Hed. [*Getting up*] You ought to write him a note, Tesman. Maybe he won't come without an invitation. 470

Tes. Yes, I suppose that would be the right thing to do, Hedda. Hm?

Hed. The sooner the better. Right away, *I* think.

Mrs. Elv. [*Pleadingly*] If only you would!

Tes. I'll write this minute. Do you have his address, Mrs.—Mrs. Elvsted?

Mrs. Elv. Yes. [*Pulls a slip of paper from her bag and gives it to him*] Here it is.

Tes. Very good. Well, then, if you'll excuse me— [*Looks around*] By the way—the slippers? Ah, here we are. [*Leaving with the parcel.*]

Hed. Be sure you write a nice, warm, friendly letter, Tesman. And 480 a long one, too.

Tes. Certainly, certainly.

Mrs. Elv. But not a word that it is I who—!

Tes. No, that goes without saying, I should think. Hm?

[*Goes out right through inner room.*]

Hed. [*Goes over to Mrs. Elvsted, smiles, says in a low voice*] There! We just killed two birds with one stone.

Mrs. Elv. What do you mean?

Hed. Didn't you see I wanted him out of the room?

Mrs. Elv. Yes, to write that letter—

Hed. And to speak to you alone. 490

Mrs. Elv. [*Flustered*] About this same thing?

Hed. Exactly.

MRS. ELV. [*Anxious*] But there *is* nothing more, Mrs. Tesman! Really, there isn't!

HED. Oh yes, there is. There is considerably more. I can see that much. Over here— We are going to have a real, nice, confidential talk, you and I.

She forces MRS. ELVSTED *down in the easy chair and seats herself on one of the ottomans.*

MRS. ELV. [*Worried, looks at her watch*] But my dear Mrs. Tesman—I had really thought I would be on my way now.

500 HED. Oh I am sure there is no rush. Now, then. Tell me about yourself. How are things at home?

MRS. ELV. That is just what I don't want to talk about.

HED. But to me—! After all, we are old schoolmates.

MRS. ELV. But you were a year ahead of me. And I used to be so scared of you!

HED. Scared of me?

MRS. ELV. Terribly. For when we met on the stairs, you always ruffled my hair.

HED. Did I really?

510 MRS. ELV. Yes. And once you said you were going to burn it off.

HED. Oh, but you know—I wasn't serious!

MRS. ELV. No, but I was such a silly, then. Anyway, afterwards we drifted far apart. Our circles are so very different, you know.

HED. All the more reason for getting close again. Listen. In school we called each other by our first names.

MRS. ELV. Oh I'm sure you're wrong—

HED. I'm sure I'm not! I remember it quite clearly. And now we want to be open with one another, just the way we used to. [*Moves the ottoman closer*] There, now! [*Kisses her cheek*] You call me Hedda.

520 MRS. ELV. [*Seizes her hands*] Oh, you are so good and kind! I'm not used to that.

HED. There, there! And I'll call you my dear Thora, just as in the old days.

MRS. ELV. My name is Thea.

HED. So it is. Of course. I meant Thea. [*Looks at her with compassion*] So you're not much used to goodness and kindness, Thea? Not in your own home?

MRS. ELV. If I even had a home! But I don't. I never have had one.

530 HED. [*Looks at her for a moment*] I thought there might be something like this.

MRS. ELV. [*Helplessly, looking straight ahead*] Yes—yes—yes—

HED. I am not sure if I quite remember— Didn't you first come to your husband as his housekeeper?

MRS. ELV. I was really hired as governess. But his wife—his first wife

—was ailing already then and was practically bedridden. So I had to take charge of the household as well.

Hed. But in the end you became his wife.

Mrs. Elv. [*Dully*] So I did.

Hed. Let's see. How long ago is that?   540

Mrs. Elv. Since my marriage?

Hed. Yes.

Mrs. Elv. About five years.

Hed. Right. It must be that long.

Mrs. Elv. Oh, those five years! Or mostly the last two or three! Oh, Mrs. Tesman—if you could just imagine!

Hed. [*Slaps her hand lightly*] Mrs. Tesman? Shame on you!

Mrs. Elv. Oh yes; all right, I'll try. Yes—if you could just—conceive —understand—

Hed. [*Casually*] And Eilert Løvborg has been living near you for some 550 three years or so, hasn't he?

Mrs. Elv. [*Looks at her uncertainly*] Eilert Løvborg? Yes—he has.

Hed. Did you know him before? Here in town?

Mrs. Elv. Hardly at all. That is, of course I did in a way. I mean, I knew *of* him.

Hed. But up there— You saw a good deal of him; did you?

Mrs. Elv. Yes, he came over to us every day. He was supposed to tutor the children, you see. For I just couldn't do it all by myself.

Hed. Of course not. And your husband—? I suppose he travels quite a bit.   560

Mrs. Elv. Well, yes, Mrs. Tes—Hedda—as a public magistrate, you know, he very often has to travel all over his district.

Hed. [*Leaning against the armrest on the easy chair*] Thea—poor, sweet Thea—now you have to tell me everything—just as it is.

Mrs. Elv. You'd better ask me, then.

Hed. How *is* your husband, Thea? I mean—you know—*really*? To be with. What kind of person is he? Is he good to you?

Mrs. Elv. [*Evasively*] I believe he thinks he does everything for the best.

Hed. But isn't he altogether too old for you? He is more than 570 twenty years older, isn't he?

Mrs. Elv. [*With irritation*] Yes, there is that, too. But there isn't just one thing. Every single little thing about him repels me! We don't have a thought in common, he and I. Not a thing in the world!

Hed. But isn't he fond of you all the same? I mean in his own way?

Mrs. Elv. I don't know. I think I am just useful to him. And I don't use much money. I am inexpensive.

Hed. That is foolish of you.

Mrs. Elv. [*Shakes her head*] Can't be changed. Not with him. I

580 don't think he cares for anybody much except himself. Perhaps the children a little.

HED. And Eilert Løvborg, Thea.

MRS. ELV. [Looks at her] Eilert Løvborg? What makes you think that?

HED. Well, it seems to me that when he sends you all the way to town to look after him— [With an almost imperceptible smile] Besides, you said so yourself. To Tesman.

MRS. ELV. [With a nervous twitch] Did I? I suppose I did. [With a muted outburst] No! I might as well tell you now as later. For it's bound to come out, anyway.

590 HED. But my dear Thea—?

MRS. ELV. All right. My husband doesn't know I've gone!

HED. What! He doesn't know?

MRS. ELV. He wasn't even home. He's away again. Oh, I just couldn't take it any longer, Hedda! It had become utterly impossible. All alone as I was.

HED. So what did you do?

MRS. ELV. I packed some of my things. Just the most necessary. Without telling anybody. And left.

HED. Just like that?

600 MRS. ELV. Yes. And took the next train to town.

HED. But dearest Thea—how did you dare to do a thing like that!

MRS. ELV. [Rises, walks] What else could I do?

HED. But what do you think your husband will say when you go back?

MRS. ELV. [By the table; looks at her] Go back to him?

HED. Yes!

MRS. ELV. I'll never go back.

HED. [Rises, approaches her slowly] So you have really, seriously— left everything?

MRS. ELV. Yes. It seemed to me there was nothing else I could do.

610 HED. And quite openly, too.

MRS. ELV. You can't keep a thing like that secret, anyway.

HED. But what do you think people will say, Thea?

MRS. ELV. In God's name, let them say whatever they like. [Sits down on the sofa, dully, tired] For I have only done what I had to do.

HED. [After a brief silence] And what do you plan to do with yourself? What sort of work will you do?

MRS. ELV. I don't know yet. I only know I have to live where Eilert Løvborg is. If I am to live at all.

HED. [Moves a chair from the table closer to Mrs. Elvsted, sits down, strokes her hands] Thea—tell me. How did this—this friendship between you 620 and Eilert Løvborg—how did it begin?

MRS. ELV. Oh, it grew little by little. I got some sort of power over him.

HED. Oh?

MRS. ELV. He dropped his old ways. Not because I asked him to. I never dared to do that. But I think he must have noticed how I felt about that kind of life. So he changed.

HED. [*Quickly suppresses a cynical smile*] So you have—rehabilitated him, as they say. Haven't you, Thea?

MRS. ELV. At least, that's what *he* says. On the other hand, he has turned me into a real human being. Taught me to think—and understand 630 —all sorts of things.

HED. Maybe he tutored you, too?

MRS. ELV. No, not tutored exactly. But he talked to me. About so many, many things. And then came that lovely, lovely time when I could share his work with him. He let me help him!

HED. He did?

MRS. ELV. Yes! Whatever he wrote, he wanted us to be together about it.

HED. Just like two good comrades.

MRS. ELV. [*With animation*] Comrades!—that's it! Imagine, Hedda 640 —that's just what he called it, too. Oh, I really ought to feel so happy. But I can't. For you see, I don't know if it will last.

HED. You don't trust him any more than that?

MRS. ELV. [*Heavily*] The shadow of a woman stands between Eilert Løvborg and me.

HED. [*Tensely, looks at her*] Who?

MRS. ELV. I don't know. Somebody or other from—his past. I don't think he has ever really forgotten her.

HED. What has he told you about it?

MRS. ELV. He has mentioned it only once—just casually.   650

HED. And what did he say?

MRS. ELV. He said that when they parted she was going to kill him with a gun.

HED. [*Cold, controlled*] Oh, nonsense. People don't do that sort of thing here.

MRS. ELV. No, I know. And that is why I think it must be that red-headed singer he used to—

HED. Yes, I suppose so.

MRS. ELV. For I remember people said she carried a loaded gun.

HED. Well, then I'm sure it's she.   660

MRS. ELV. [*Wringing her hands*] Yes, but just think, Hedda—now I hear that she—that singer—that she's here in town again, too! Oh, I'm just desperate—!

HED. [*With a glance toward the inner room*] Shhh! Here's Tesman. [*Rises and whispers*] Not a word about all this to anybody, Thea!

MRS. ELV. [*Jumps up*] No, no. For God's sake—!

TESMAN, *carrying a letter, enters from the right side of the inner room.*

TES. There, now—here's the missive, all ready to go!

HED. Good. But I believe Mrs. Elvsted wants to be on her way. Wait a moment. I'll see you to the garden gate.

670 TES. Say, Hedda—do you think Berte could take care of this?

HED. [*Takes the letter*] I'll tell her.

BERTE *enters right.*

BER. Judge Brack is here and wants to know if you're receiving.

HED. Yes, ask the Judge please to come in. And—here—drop this in a mailbox, will you?

BER. [*Takes the letter*] Yes, ma'am.

She opens the door for JUDGE BRACK *and exits. The* JUDGE *is forty-five years of age. Rather thickset, but well-built and with brisk, athletic movements. Roundish face, aristocratic profile. His hair is short, still almost completely black, very neatly dressed. Lively, sparkling eyes. Thick eyebrows and mustache with cut-off points. He is dressed in an elegant suit, a trifle youthful for his age. He wears pince-nez glasses, attached to a string, and lets them drop from time to time.*

JUDGE BRACK. [*Hat in hand, salutes*] May one pay one's respects as early as this?

HED. One certainly may.

TES. [*Shaking his hand*] You are always welcome. [*Introducing*]
680 Judge Brack—Miss Rysing—   [*Hedda groans.*

BRACK. [*Bowing*] Delighted!

HED. [*Looks at him, laughs*] How nice it is to see you in daylight, Judge!

BRACK. You find me changed, perhaps?

HED. A bit younger, I think.

BRACK. Much obliged.

TES. But what do you think of Hedda? Hm? Did you ever see her in such bloom? She positively—

HED. Will you please leave me out of this? You had better thank the Judge for all the trouble he has taken.

690 BRACK. Oh, nonsense. It's been a pleasure.

HED. Yes, you are indeed a faithful soul. But my friend here is dying to be off. Don't leave, Judge. I'll be back in a minute.

[*Mutual goodbyes. Mrs. Elvsted and Hedda exit, right.*

BRACK. Well, now—your wife—is she tolerably satisfied?

TES. Yes, indeed, and we really can't thank you enough. That is, I understand there will have to be some slight changes made here and there. And there are still a few things—just a few trifles—we'll have to get.

BRACK. Oh? Really?

TES. But we certainly don't want to bother you with that. Hedda said she's going to take care of it herself. But do sit down, hm?

700 BRACK. Thanks. Maybe just for a moment— [*Sits down by the table*] There's one thing I'd like to talk to you about, my dear Tesman.

TES. Oh? Ah, I see! [*Sits down*] I suppose it's the serious part of the festivities that's beginning now. Hm?

BRACK. Oh—there's no great rush as far as the money is concerned. Though I must say I wish we could have established ourselves a trifle more economically.

TES. Out of the question, my dear fellow! Remember, it's all for Hedda! You, who know her so well—! After all, I couldn't put her up like any little middle-class housewife—

BRACK. No, I suppose— That's just it.   710

TES. Besides—fortunately—it can't be long now before I receive my appointment.

BRACK. Well, you know—things like that have a way of hanging fire.

TES. Perhaps you have heard something? Something definite? Hm?

BRACK. No, nothing certain— [*Interrupting himself*] But that reminds me. I have some news for you.

TES. Oh?

BRACK. Your old friend Eilert Løvborg is back in town.

TES. I know that already.

BRACK. So? Who told you?   720

TES. The lady who just left.

BRACK. I see. What did you say her name was again? I didn't quite catch—

TES. Mrs. Elvsted.

BRACK. Ah yes—the Commissioner's wife. Yes, it's up in her part of the country that Løvborg has been staying, too.

TES. And just think. I am so glad to hear it. He is quite respectable again.

BRACK. Yes, so they say.

TES. And he has published a new book, hm?   730

BRACK. Oh yes.

TES. Which is making quite a stir.

BRACK. Quite an unusual stir.

TES. Just think! Isn't that just wonderful! He—with his remarkable gifts. And I was so sure he'd gone under for good.

BRACK. That seems to have been the general opinion.

TES. What I don't understand, though, is what he is going to do with himself. What sort of living can he make? Hm?

During the last remark HEDDA *re-enters, right.*

HED. [*To Brack, with a scornful little laugh*] Tesman is forever worrying about how people are going to make a living.   740

TES. Well, you see, we are talking about poor Eilert Løvborg, Hedda.

HED. [*With a quick look at him*] You are? [*Sits down in the easy chair by the stove and asks casually*] What is the matter with him?

TES. Well, you see, I believe he's run through his inheritance a long time ago. And I don't suppose he can write a new book every year. Hm? So I really must ask how he is going to make out.

BRACK. Maybe I could help you answer that.

TES. Yes?

BRACK. Remember, he has relatives with considerable influence.

750 TES. Ah—unfortunately, those relatives have washed their hands of him long ago.

BRACK. Just the same, they used to call him the hope of the family.

TES. Yes, before! But he has ruined all that.

HED. Who knows? [*With a little smile*] I hear the Elvsteds have rehabilitated him.

BRACK. And then this book—

TES. Well, I certainly hope they will help him to find something or other. I just wrote him a letter. Hedda, dear, I asked him to come out here tonight.

760 BRACK. Oh dear, I am sorry. Don't you remember—you're supposed to come to my little stag dinner tonight? You accepted last night on the pier, you know.

HED. Had you forgotten, Tesman?

TES. So I had.

BRACK. Oh well. I'm sure he won't come, so it doesn't really make any difference.

TES. Why is that? Hm?

BRACK. [*Gets up somewhat hesitantly, rests his hands on the back of the chair*] Dear Tesman—and you, too, Mrs. Tesman—I cannot in good conscience let you remain in ignorance of something, which—which—

770 TES. Something to do with Eilert?

BRACK. With both you and him.

TES. But my dear Judge, do speak!

BRACK. You must be prepared to find that your appointment will not come through as soon as you hope and expect.

TES. [*Jumps up, nervously*] Something's happened? Hm?

BRACK. It may conceivably be made contingent upon the result of a competition.

TES. Competition! Just think, Hedda!

HED. [*Leaning farther back in her chair*] Ah—I see, I see—!

780 TES. But with whom? Don't tell me with—?

BRACK. Precisely. With Eilert Løvborg.

TES. [*Claps his hands together*] No, no! This can't be! It is unthinkable! Quite impossible! Hm?

BRACK. All the same, that's the way it may turn out.

TES. No, but Judge, this would amount to the most incredible callousness toward me! [*Waving his arms*] For just think—I'm a married man! We married on the strength of these prospects, Hedda and I. Got our-

selves deep in debt. Borrowed money from Aunt Julle, too. After all, I
had practically been promised the post, you know. Hm?

BRACK. Well, well. I daresay you'll get it in the end. If only after a 790
competition.

HED. [*Motionless in her chair*] Just think, Tesman. It will be like a kind
of contest.

TES. But dearest Hedda, how can you be so unconcerned!

HED. [*Still without moving*] I'm not at all unconcerned. I'm dying to
see who wins.

BRACK. In any case, Mrs. Tesman, I'm glad you know the situation
for what it is. I mean—before you proceed to make the little additional
purchases I understand you threaten us with.

HED. This makes no difference as far as that is concerned. 800

BRACK. Really? Well, in that case, of course—Goodbye! [*To Tesman*]
I'll pick you up on my afternoon walk.

TES. What? Oh yes, yes, of course. I'm sorry; I'm just all confused.

HED. [*Without getting up, gives her hand*] Goodbye, Judge. Come back
soon.

BRACK. Thanks. Goodbye, goodbye.

TES. [*Sees him to the door*] Goodbye, my dear Judge. You really must
excuse me— [*Judge Brack exits, right.*

TES. [*Pacing the floor*] Oh, Hedda, Hedda! One should never venture
into fairyland. Hm? 810

HED. [*Looks at him, smiles*] Do *you* do that?

TES. Well, yes—it can't be denied—it was most venturesome of me
to rush into marriage and set up a home on the strength of mere prospects.

HED. Well, maybe you're right.

TES. Anyway—we do have our own nice, comfortable home, now.
Just think, Hedda—the very home both of us dreamed about. Set our
hearts on, I may almost say. Hm?

HED. [*Rises, slowly, tired*] The agreement was that we were to maintain a certain position—entertain—

TES. Don't I know it! Dearest Hedda—I have been so looking for- 820
ward to seeing you as hostess in a select circle! Hm? Well, well, well! In
the meantime, we'll just have to be content with one another. See Aunt
Julle once in a while. Nothing more. And you were meant for such a
different kind of life, altogether!

HED. I suppose a footman is completely out of the question.

TES. I'm afraid so. Under the circumstances, you see—we couldn't
possibly—

HED. And as for getting my own riding horse—

TES. [*Aghast*] Riding horse!

HED. I suppose I musn't even think of that. 830

TES. Good heavens, no! That goes without saying, I hope!

HED. [*Walking*]   Well—at least I have one thing to amuse myself with in the meantime.

TES. [*Overjoyed*]   Oh thank goodness for that! And what *is* that, Hedda, hm?

HED. [*In the doorway, looks at him with suppressed scorn*]   My guns—Jørgen!

TES. [*In fear*]   Your guns!

HED. [*With cold eyes*]   General Gabler's guns.

[*She exits left, through the inner room.*

TES. [*Runs up to the doorway, calls after her*]   But Hedda! Good gracious! Hedda, dear! Please don't touch those dangerous things! For my sake, Hedda! Hm?

Act II

The same room at the TESMANS'. *The piano has been moved out and replaced by an elegant little writing desk. A small table has been placed near the sofa, left. Most of the flowers have been removed.* MRS. ELVSTED'S *bouquet is on the big table front center. Afternoon.*

HEDDA, *dressed to receive callers, is alone. She is standing near the open French doors, loading a revolver. Its mate is lying in an open case on the desk.*

HED. [*Looking down into the garden, calls*]   Hello there, Judge! Welcome back!

JUDGE BRACK [*Off stage*]   Thanks, Mrs. Tesman!

HED. [*Raises the gun, sights*]   Now I am going to shoot you, Judge Brack!

BRACK. [*Calls off stage*]   No—no—no! Don't point the gun at me like that!

HED.   That's what you get for sneaking in the back door!   [*Fires.*

BRACK. [*Closer*]   Are you out of your mind—!

HED.   Oh dear—did I hit you?

10   BRACK. [*Still off stage*]   Stop that nonsense!

HED.   Come on in, then.

JUDGE BRACK, *dressed for dinner, enters, left. He carries a light overcoat over his arm.*

BRACK.   Dammit! Do you still fool around with that thing? What are you shooting at, anyway?

HED.   Oh—just firing off into blue air.

BRACK. [*Gently but firmly taking the gun away from her*]   With your permission, Mrs. Tesman. [*Looks at it*]   Ah yes, I remember this gun very well.   [*Looks around*]   Where is the case? Ah, here we are.   [*Puts the gun in the case and closes it*]   That's enough of that silliness for today.

HED.   But in the name of heaven, what do you expect me to do with 20 myself?

BRACK.   No callers?

HED. [*Closing the French doors*]   Not a soul. All my close friends are still out of town, it seems.

Henrik Ibsen   433

BRACK. And Tesman is out, too, perhaps?

HED. [*By the desk, puts the gun case in a drawer*] Yes. He took off for the aunts' right after lunch. He didn't expect you so early.

BRACK. I should have thought of that. That was stupid of me.

HED. [*Turns her head, looks at him*] Why stupid?

BRACK. I would have come a little—sooner.

HED. [*Crossing*] If you had, you wouldn't have found anybody home. 30
For I have been in my room ever since lunch, changing my clothes.

BRACK. And isn't there the tiniest little opening in the door for negotiations?

HED. You forgot to provide one.

BRACK. Another stupidity.

HED. So we'll have to stay in here. And wait. For I don't think Tesman will be back for some time.

BRACK. By all means. I'll be very patient.

HEDDA *sits on the sofa in the corner.* BRACK *puts his overcoat over the back of the nearest chair and sits down, keeping his hat in his hand. Brief silence. They look at one another.*

HED. Well?

BRACK. [*In the same tone*] Well? 40

HED. I said it first.

BRACK. [*Leans forward a little*] All right. Let's have a nice little chat, Mrs. Tesman.

HED. [*Leans back*] Don't you think it's an eternity since last time we talked? I don't count last night and this morning. That was nothing.

BRACK. You mean—just the two of us?

HED. Something like that.

BRACK. There hasn't been a day I haven't wished you were back again.

HED. My feelings, exactly. 50

BRACK. Yours? Really, Mrs. Tesman? And I have been assuming you were having such a wonderful time.

HED. I'd say!

BRACK. All Tesman's letters said so.

HED. Oh yes, he! He's happy just poking through old collections of books. And copying old parchments—or whatever they are.

BRACK. [*With a touch of malice*] Well, that's his calling, you know. Partly, anyway.

HED. Yes, so it is. And in that case I suppose— But I! Oh, Judge! You've no idea how bored I've been. 60

BRACK. [*With sympathy*] Really? You're serious?

HED. Surely you can understand that? For a whole half year never to see anyone who knows even a little bit about our circle? And talks our language?

434 Drama

BRACK. Yes, I think I would find that trying, too.

HED. And then the most unbearable thing of all—

BRACK. Well?

HED. —everlastingly to be in the company of the same person—

BRACK. [*Nods in agreement*] Both early and late—yes. I can imagine—
70 at all possible times—

HED. I said everlastingly.

BRACK. All right. Still, it seems to me that with as excellent a person as our Tesman, it ought to be possible—

HED. My dear Judge—Tesman is a specialist.

BRACK. Granted.

HED. And specialists are not at all entertaining travel companions. Not in the long run, at any rate.

BRACK. Not even—the specialist—one happens to love?

HED. Bah! That nauseating word!

80 BRACK. [*Puzzled*] Really, now, Mrs. Tesman—?

HED. [*Half laughing, half annoyed*] *You* ought to try it some time! Listening to talk about the history of civilization, early and late—

BRACK. Everlastingly—

HED. All right. And then this business about the domestic industry in the Middle Ages—! That's the ghastliest part of it all!

BRACK. [*Looking searchingly at her*] But in that case—tell me—how am I to explain—?

HED. That Jørgen Tesman and I made a pair of it, you mean?

BRACK. If you want to put it that way—yes.

90 HED. Come now. Do you really find that so strange?

BRACK. Both yes and no—Mrs. Tesman.

HED. I had danced myself tired, my dear Judge. My season was over— [*Gives a slight start*] No, no—I don't really mean that. Won't think it, either!

BRACK. Nor do you have the slightest reason to, I am sure.

HED. Oh—as far as reasons are concerned— [*Looks at him as if trying to read his mind*] And, after all, Jørgen Tesman must be said to be a most proper young man in all respects.

BRACK. Both proper and substantial. Most certainly.

100 HED. And one can't say there is anything exactly comical about him. Do you think there is?

BRACK. Comical? No—o. I wouldn't say that—

HED. All right, then. And he is a most assiduous collector. Nobody can deny that. I think it is perfectly possible he may go quite far, after all.

BRACK. [*Looks at her rather uncertainly*] I assumed that you, like everybody else, were convinced that he will in time become an exceptionally eminent man?

HED. [*With a weary expression*] Yes, I was. And then, you see—there

he was, wanting so desperately to be allowed to provide for me—I don't
know why I shouldn't have accepted?   110

BRACK. No, certainly. From that point of view—

HED. For you know, Judge, that was considerably more than my
other admirers were willing to do.

BRACK. [*Laughs*] Well! Of course I can't answer for all the others. But
as far as I am concerned, I have always had a certain degree of—respect
for the bonds of matrimony. You know—as a general proposition, Mrs.
Tesman.

HED. [*Lightly*] Well, I never really counted very heavily on *you*—

BRACK. All I want is a nice, confidential circle, in which I can be of
service, both in deed and in counsel. Be allowed to come and go like a 120
true and trusted friend—

HED. You mean, of the master of the house—?

BRACK. [*With a slight bow*] To be perfectly frank—rather of the mistress. But by all means—the master, too, of course. Do you know, that
kind of—shall I say, triangular?—relationship can really be a great comfort to all parties involved.

HED. Yes, many were the times I missed a second travel companion.
To be twosome in the compartment—brrr!

BRACK. Fortunately, the wedding trip is over.

HED. [*Shakes her head*] There's a long journey ahead. I've just arrived 130
at a station on the way.

BRACK. Well, at the station one gets out and moves around a bit,
Mrs. Tesman.

HED. I never get out.

BRACK. Really?

HED. No. For there's always someone around, who—

BRACK. [*Laughs*]—looks at one's legs; is that it?

HED. Exactly.

BRACK. Oh well, really now—

HED. [*With a silencing gesture*] I won't have it! Rather stay in my seat 140
—once I'm seated. Twosome and all.

BRACK. I see. But what if a third party were to join the couple?

HED. Well, now—*that* would be something altogether different!

BRACK. A proven, understanding friend—

HED. —entertaining in all sorts of lively ways—

BRACK. —and not at all a specialist!

HED. [*With audible breath*] Yes, that would indeed be a comfort.

BRACK. [*Hearing the front door open, looking at her*] The triangle is
complete.

HED. [*Half aloud*] And the train goes on.

TESMAN, *in gray walking suit and soft hat, enters, right. He carries a pile of* 150
paperbound books under his arm. Others are stuffed in his pockets.

TES. [*As he walks up to the table in front of the corner sofa*] Puuhh—! Quite some load to carry, all this—and in this heat, too. [*Puts the books down*] I am positively perspiring, Hedda. Well, well. So you're here already, my dear Judge. Hm? And Berte didn't tell me.

BRACK. [*Rises*] I came through the garden.

HED.   What are all those books?

TES. [*Leafing through some of them*] Just some new publications in my special field.

HED.   Special field, hm?

160   BRACK.   Ah yes—professional publications, Mrs. Tesman.

BRACK *and* HEDDA *exchange knowing smiles.*

HED.   Do you still need more books?

TES.   Yes, my dear. There is no such thing as having too many books in one's special field. One has to keep up with what is being written and published, you know.

HED.   I suppose.

TES. [*Searching among the books*] And look. Here is Eilert Løvborg's new book, too. [*Offers it to her*] Want to take a look at it, Hedda? Hm?

HED.   No—thanks just the same. Or perhaps later.

TES.   I glanced at it on my way home.

170   BRACK.   And what do you think of it? As a specialist yourself?

TES.   It is remarkable for its sobriety. He never wrote like that before. [*Gathers up all the books*] I just want to take these into my study. I am so much looking forward to cutting them open! And then I'll change. [*To Brack*] I assume there's no rush to be off, is there?

BRACK.   Not at all. We have plenty of time.

TES.   In that case, I think I'll indulge myself a little. [*On his way out with the books he halts in the doorway and turns*] That's right, Hedda—Aunt Julle won't be out to see you tonight, after all.

HED.   No? Is it that business with the hat, do you think?

180   TES.   Oh, no—not at all. How can you believe a thing like that about Aunt Julle! Just think! No, it's Aunt Rina. She's feeling very poorly.

HED.   Isn't she always?

TES.   Yes, but it's especially bad today, poor thing.

HED.   Well, in that case I suppose she ought to stay home. I shall have to put up with it; that's all.

TES.   And you have no idea how perfectly delighted Aunt Julle was, even so. Because of how splendid you look after the trip, Hedda!

HED. [*Half aloud, rising*] Oh, these everlasting aunts!

TES.   Hm?

190   HED. [*Walks over to the French doors*] Nothing.

TES.   No? All right. Well, excuse me. [*Exits right, through inner room.*]

BRACK.   What is this about a hat?

HED.   Oh, something with Miss Tesman this morning. She had put her hat down on the chair over there. [*Looks at him, smiles*] So I pretended to think it was the maid's.

BRACK. [*Shakes his head*] But my dear Mrs. Tesman—how could you do a thing like that! And to that excellent old lady, too!

HED. [*Nervously pacing the floor*] Well, you see—something just takes hold of me at times. And then I can't help myself—[*Throws herself down in the easy chair near the stove*] Oh I can't explain it even to myself. 200

BRACK. [*Behind her chair*] You aren't really happy—that's the trouble.

HED. [*Staring into space*] I don't know any reason why I should be. Do you?

BRACK. Well, yes—partly because you've got the home you've always wanted.

HED. [*Looks up at him and laughs*] So you too believe that story about my great desire?

BRACK. You mean, there is nothing to it?

HED. Well, yes; there is *something* to it.

BRACK. Well? 210

HED. There is this much to it, that last summer I used Tesman to see me home from evening parties.

BRACK. Unfortunately—my route was in quite a different direction.

HED. True. You walked other roads last summer.

BRACK. [*Laughs*] Shame on you, Mrs. Tesman! So, all right—you and Tesman—?

HED. One evening we passed by here. And Tesman, poor thing, was practically turning himself into knots trying to find something to talk about. So I felt sorry for all that erudition—

BRACK. [*With a doubting smile*] You did? Hm— 220

HED. I really did. So, just to help him out of his misery, I happened to say that I'd like to live in this house.

BRACK. Just that?

HED. That was all—*that* evening.

BRACK. But afterwards—?

HED. Yes, my frivolity had consequences, Judge.

BRACK. Unfortunately—that's often the way with frivolities. It happens to all of us, Mrs. Tesman.

HED. Thanks! So in our common enthusiasm for Mr. Secretary Falk's villa Tesman and I found each other, you see! The result was en- 230 gagement and wedding and honeymoon abroad and all the rest of it. Well, yes, my dear Judge—I've made my bed—I almost said.

BRACK. But this is priceless! And you didn't really care for the house at all?

HED. Certainly not.

BRACK. Not even now? After all, we've set up quite a comfortable home for you here, haven't we?

HED. Oh—it seems to me I smell lavender and rose sachets in all the rooms. But maybe that's a smell Aunt Julle brought with her.

240 BRACK. [*Laughs*] My guess is rather the late lamented Secretary's wife.

HED. It smells of mortality, whoever it is. Like corsages—the next day. [*Clasps her hands behind her neck, leans back, looks at him*] Judge, you have no idea how dreadfully bored I'll be—out here.

BRACK. But don't you think life may hold some task for you, too, Mrs. Tesman?

HED. A task? With any kind of appeal?

BRACK. Preferably that, of course.

HED. Heaven knows what kind of task that might be. There are times when I wonder if— [*Interrupts herself*] No; I'm sure that wouldn't 250 work, either.

BRACK. Who knows? Tell me.

HED. It has occurred to me that maybe I could get Tesman to enter politics.

BRACK. [*Laughs*] Tesman! No, really—I must confess that—politics doesn't strike me as being exactly Tesman's line.

HED. I agree. But suppose I were to prevail on him, all the same?

BRACK. What satisfaction could you possibly find in that? If he can't succeed—why do you want him even to try?

HED. Because I am bored, I tell you! [*After a brief pause*] So you 260 think it's quite out of the question that Tesman could ever become prime minister?

BRACK. Well, you see, Mrs. Tesman—to do that he'd first of all have to be a fairly wealthy man.

HED. [*Getting up, impatiently*] Yes! There we are! These shabby circumstances I've married into! [*Crosses the floor*] That's what makes life so mean. So outright ludicrous! For that's what it is, you know.

BRACK. Personally I believe something else is to blame.

HED. What?

BRACK. You've never been through anything that's really stirred you.

270 HED. Something serious, you mean?

BRACK. If you like. But maybe it's coming now.

HED. [*With a toss of her head*] You are thinking of that silly old professorship! That's Tesman's business. I refuse to give it a thought.

BRACK. As you wish. But now—to put it in the grand style—now when a solemn challenge of responsibility will be posed? Demands made on you? [*Smiles*] New demands, Mrs. Tesman.

HED. [*Angry*] Quiet! You'll never see anything of the kind.

BRACK. [*Cautiously*] We'll talk about this a year from now—on the outside.

280 HED. [*Curtly*] I'm not made for that sort of thing, Judge! No demands for me!

BRACK. But surely you, like most women, are made for a duty, which—

HED. [*Over by the French doors*] Oh, do be quiet! Often it seems to me there's only one thing in the world that I am made for.

BRACK. [*Coming close*] And may I ask what that is?

HED. [*Looking out*] To be bored to death. Now you know. [*Turns, looks toward the inner room, laughs*] Just as I thought. Here comes the professor.

BRACK. [*Warningly, in a low voice*] Steady, now, Mrs. Tesman!   290

TESMAN, *dressed for a party, carrying his hat and gloves, enters from the right side of the inner room.*

TES. Hedda, any word yet from Eilert Løvborg that he isn't coming, hm?

HED. No.

TES. In that case, I wouldn't be a bit surprised if we have him here in a few minutes.

BRACK. You really think he'll come?

TES. I am almost certain he will. For I'm sure it's only idle gossip what you told me this morning.

BRACK. Oh?

TES. Anyway, that's what Aunt Julle said. She doesn't for a moment 300 believe he'll stand in my way. Just think!

BRACK. I'm very glad to hear that.

TES. [*Puts his hat and his gloves down on a chair, right*] But you must let me wait for him as long as possible.

BRACK. By all means. We have plenty of time. Nobody will arrive at my place before seven—seven-thirty, or so.

TES. And in the meantime we can keep Hedda company. Take our time. Hm?

HED. [*Carrying Brack's hat and coat over to the sofa in the corner*] And if worst comes to worst, Mr. Løvborg can stay here with me.   310

BRACK. [*Trying to take the things away from her*] Let me, Mrs. Tesman— What do you mean—"if worst comes to worst"?

HED. If he doesn't want to go with you and Tesman.

TES. [*Looks dubiously at her*] But, dearest Hedda—do you think that will quite do? He staying here with you? Hm? Remember, Aunt Julle won't be here.

HED. No, but Mrs. Elvsted will. The three of us will have a cup of tea together.

TES. Oh yes; *that* will be perfectly all right!

BRACK. [*With a smile*] And perhaps the wiser course of action for him. 320

HED. What do you mean?

BRACK. Begging your pardon, Mrs. Tesman—you've often enough

looked askance at my little stag dinners. It's been your opinion that only men of the firmest principles ought to attend.

Hed. I should think Mr. Løvborg is firm-principled enough now. A reformed sinner—

Berte *appears in door, right.*

Ber. Ma'am—there's a gentleman here who asks if—

Hed. Show him in, please.

Tes. [*Softly*] I'm sure it's he! Just think!

Eilert løvborg *enters, right. He is slim, gaunt. Of* Tesman's *age, but he looks older and somewhat dissipated. Brown hair and beard. Pale, longish face, reddish spots on the cheekbones. Dressed for visiting in elegant, black, brand-new suit. He carries a silk hat and dark gloves in his hand. He remains near the door, makes a quick bow. He appears a little embarrassed.*

330 Tes. [*Goes over to him, shakes his hand*] My dear Eilert—at last we meet again!

Løv. [*Subdued voice*] Thanks for your note, Jørgen! [*Approaching Hedda*] Am I allowed to shake your hand, too, Mrs. Tesman?

Hed. [*Accepting his proffered hand*] I am very glad to see you, Mr. Løvborg. [*With a gesture*] I don't know if you two gentlemen—

Løv. [*With a slight bow*] Judge Brack, I believe.

Brack. [*Also bowing lightly*] Certainly. Some years ago—

Tes. [*To Løvborg, both hands on his shoulders*] And now I want you to feel quite at home here, Eilert! Isn't that right, Hedda? For you plan to
340 stay here in town, I understand. Hm?

Løv. Yes, I do.

Tes. Perfectly reasonable. Listen—I just got hold of your new book, but I haven't had a chance to read it yet.

Løv. You may save yourself the trouble.

Tes. Why do you say that?

Løv. There's not much to it.

Tes. Just think—you saying that!

Brack. Nevertheless, people seem to have very good things to say about it.

350 Løv. That's exactly why I wrote it—so everybody would like it.

Brack. Very wise of you.

Tes. Yes, but Eilert—!

Løv. For I am trying to rebuild my position. Start all over again.

Tes. [*With some embarrassment*] Yes, I suppose you are, aren't you? Hm?

Løv. [*Smiles, puts his hat down, pulls a parcel out of his pocket*] When *this* appears—Jørgen Tesman—this you must read. For this is the real thing. This is me.

Tes. Oh really? And what is it?

Løv. The continuation.

Tes. Continuation? Of what? 360

Løv. Of the book.

Tes. Of the new book?

Løv. Of course.

Tes. But Eilert—you've carried the story all the way up to the present!

Løv. So I have. And this is about the future.

Tes. The future! But, heavens—we don't know a thing about the future!

Løv. No, we don't. But there are a couple of things to be said about it all the same. [*Unwraps the parcel*] Here, let me show you— 370

Tes. But that's not your handwriting.

Løv. I have dictated it. [*Leafs through portions of the manuscript*] It's in two parts. The first is about the forces that will shape the civilization of the future. And the second [*Riffling through more pages*]—about the course which that future civilization will take.

Tes. How remarkable! It would never occur to me to write anything like that.

Hed. [*Over by the French doors, her fingers drumming the pane*] Hmm—No—

Løv. [*Replacing the manuscript in its wrappings and putting it down on the table*] I brought it along, for I thought maybe I'd read parts of it aloud 380 to you this evening.

Tes. That's very good of you, Eilert. But this evening—? [*Looks at Brack*] I'm not quite sure how to arrange that—

Løv. Some other time, then. There's no hurry.

Brack. You see, Mr. Løvborg, there's a little get-together over at my house tonight. Mainly for Tesman, you know—

Løv. [*Looking for his hat*] In that case, I certainly won't—

Brack. No, listen. Won't you do me the pleasure to join us?

Løv. [*Firmly*] No, I won't. But thanks all the same.

Brack. Oh come on! Why don't you do that? We'll be a small, select 390 circle. And I think I can promise you a fairly lively evening, as Hed—as Mrs. Tesman would say.

Løv. I don't doubt that. Nevertheless—

Brack. And you may bring your manuscript along and read aloud to Tesman over at my house. I have plenty of room.

Tes. Just think, Eilert! Wouldn't that be nice, hm?

Hed. [*Intervening*] But can't you see that Mr. Løvborg doesn't want to? I'm sure he would rather stay here and have supper with me.

Løv. [*Looks at her*] With you, Mrs. Tesman?

Hed. And with Mrs. Elvsted. 400

Løv. Ah—! [*Casually*] I ran into her at noon today.

Hed.   Oh? Well, she'll be here tonight. So you see your presence is really required, Mr. Løvborg. Otherwise she won't have anybody to see her home.

Løv.   True. All right, then, Mrs. Tesman—I'll stay, thank you.

Hed.   Good. I'll just tell the maid.

She rings for Berte *over by the door, right.* Berte *appears just off stage.* Hedda *talks with her in a low voice, points toward the inner room.* Berte *nods and exits.*

Tes.   [*While Hedda and Berte are talking, to Løvborg*]   Tell me, Eilert—is it this new subject—about the future—is that what you plan to lecture on?

410   Løv.   Yes.

Tes.   For the bookseller told me you have announced a lecture series for this fall.

Løv.   Yes, I have. I hope you won't mind too much.

Tes.   Of course not! But—

Løv.   For of course I realize it is rather awkward for you.

Tes.   [*Unhappily*]   Oh well—I certainly can't expect—that just for my sake—

Løv.   But I will wait till you receive your appointment.

Tes.   Wait? But—but—but—you mean you aren't going to compete
420   with me? Hm?

Løv.   No. Just triumph over you. In people's opinion.

Tes.   Oh, for goodness' sake! Then Aunt Julle was right, after all! I knew it all the time. Hedda! Do you hear that! Just think—Eilert Løvborg isn't going to stand in our way after all.

Hed.   [*Tersely*]   Our? I have nothing to do with this.

Hedda *walks into the inner room, where* Berte *is bringing in a tray with decanters and glasses.* Hedda *nods her approval and comes forward again.*

Tes.   [*During the foregoing business*]   How about that, Judge? What do you say to this? Hm?

Brack.   I say that moral victory and all that—hm—may be glorious enough and beautiful enough—
430   Tes.   Oh, I agree. All the same—

Hed.   [*Looks at Tesman with a cold smile*]   You look thunderstruck.

Tes.   Well, I am—pretty much—I really believe—

Brack.   After all, Mrs. Tesman, that was quite a thunderstorm that just passed over.

Hed.   [*Points to the inner room*]   How about a glass of cold punch, gentlemen?

Brack.   [*Looks at his watch*]   A stirrup cup. Not a bad idea.

Tes.   Splendid, Hedda. Perfectly splendid. In such a light-hearted mood as I am now—
440   Hed.   Please. You, too, Mr. Løvborg.

LØV. [*With a gesture of refusal*]   No, thanks. Really. Nothing for me.
BRACK.   Good heavens, man! Cold punch isn't poison, you know!
LØV.   Perhaps not for everybody.
HED.   I'll keep Mr. Løvborg company in the meantime.
TES.   All right, Hedda. You do that.
He and BRACK *go into the inner room, sit down, drink punch, smoke cigarettes, and engage in lively conversation during the next scene.* EILERT LØVBORG *remains standing near the stove.* HEDDA *walks over to the desk.*
HED.   [*her voice a little louder than usual*]   I'll show you some pictures, if you like. You see—Tesman and I, we took a trip through Tyrol on our way back.
She brings an album over to the table by the sofa. She sits down in the far corner of the sofa. LØVBORG *approaches, stops, looks at her. He takes a chair and sits down at her left, his back toward the inner room.*
HED. [*Opens the album*]   Do you see these mountains, Mr. Løvborg? They are the Ortler group. Tesman has written their name below. Here 450 it is: "The Ortler group near Meran."
LØV. [*Has looked steadily at her all this time. Says slowly*]   Hedda—Gabler!
HED. [*With a quick glance sideways*]   Not that! Shhh!
LØV. [*Again*]   Hedda Gabler!
HED. [*Looking at the album*]   Yes, that used to be my name. When— when we two knew each other.
LØV.   And so from now on—for the whole rest of my life—I must get used to never again saying Hedda Gabler.
HED. [*Still occupied with the album*]   Yes, you must. And you might as well start right now. The sooner the better, I think.   460
LØV. [*With indignation*]   Hedda Gabler married? And married to— Jørgen Tesman!
HED.   Yes—that's the way it goes.
LØV.   Oh, Hedda, Hedda—how could you throw yourself away like that!
HED. [*With a fierce glance at him*]   What's this? I won't have any of that!
LØV.   What do you mean?
TESMAN *enters from the inner room.*
HED. [*Hears him coming and remarks casually*]   And this here, Mr. Løvborg, this is from somewhere in the Ampezzo valley. Just look at those peaks over there.   [*With a kindly look at Tesman*]   What did you say 470 those peaks were called, dear?
TES.   Let me see. Oh, they—they are the Dolomites.
HED.   Right. Those are the Dolomites, Mr. Løvborg.
TES.   Hedda, I thought I'd just ask you if you don't want me to bring you some punch, after all? For you, anyway? Hm?
HED.   Well, yes; thanks. And a couple of cookies, maybe.
TES.   No cigarettes?

HED.   No.

TES.   All right.

He returns to the inner room, then turns right. BRACK *is in there, keeping an eye on* HEDDA *and* LØVBORG *from time to time.*

480   LØV. [*Still in a low voice*]   Answer me, Hedda. How could you do a thing like that?

HED. [*Apparently engrossed in the album*]   If you keep on using my first name I won't talk to you.

LØV.   Not even when we're alone?

HED.   No. You may think it, but you must not say it.

LØV.   I see. It offends your love for—Jørgen Tesman.

HED. [*Glances at him, smiles*]   Love? That's a good one!

LØV.   Not love, then.

HED.   But no infidelities, either! I won't have it.

490   LØV.   Hedda—answer me just this one thing—

HED.   Shhh!

TESMAN *enters with a tray from the inner room.*

TES.   Here! Here are the goodies.   [*Puts the tray down.*

HED.   Why don't you get Berte to do it?

TES. [*Pouring punch*]   Because I think it's so much fun waiting on you, Hedda.

HED.   But you've filled both glasses. And Mr. Løvborg didn't want any—

TES.   I know, but Mrs. Elvsted will soon be here, won't she?

HED.   That's right. So she will.

500   TES.   Had you forgotten about her? Hm?

HED.   We've been so busy looking at this.   [*Shows him a picture*] Remember this little village?

TES.   That's the one just below the Brenner Pass, isn't it? We spent the night there—

HED.   —and ran into that lively crowd of summer guests.

TES.   Right! Just think—if we only could have had you with us, Eilert! Oh well.

Returns to the inner room, sits down, and resumes his conversation with BRACK.

LØV.   Just tell me this, Hedda—

HED.   What?

510   LØV.   Wasn't there love in your feelings for me, either? Not a touch— not a shimmer of love? Wasn't there?

HED.   I wonder. To me, we seemed to be simply two good comrades. Two close friends.   [*Smiles*]   You, particularly, were very frank.

LØV.   You wanted it that way.

HED.   And yet—when I think back upon it now, there was something beautiful, something thrilling, something brave, I think, about the secret frankness—that comradeship that not a single soul so much as suspected.

Henrik Ibsen   445

Løv.   Yes, wasn't there, Hedda? Wasn't there? When I called on your father in the afternoons— And the General sat by the window with his newspapers—his back turned—   520

Hed.   And we two in the sofa in the corner—

Løv.   —always with the same illustrated magazine—

Hed.   —for want of an album, yes—

Løv.   Yes, Hedda—and then when I confessed to you—! Told you all about myself, things the others didn't know. Sat and told you about all my orgies by day and night. Dissipation day in and day out! Oh, Hedda—what sort of power in you was it that forced me to tell you things like that?

Hed.   You think there was some power in me?

Løv.   How else can I explain it? And all those veiled questions you   530 asked—

Hed.   —which you understood so perfectly well—

Løv.   That you could ask such questions! With such complete frankness!

Hed.   *Veiled*, if you please.

Løv.   But frankly all the same. All about—that!

Hed.   And to think that you answered, Mr. Løvborg!

Løv.   Yes, that's just what I can't understand—now, afterwards. But tell me, Hedda; wasn't love at the bottom of our whole relationship? Didn't you feel some kind of urge to—purify me—when I came to you   540 in confession? Wasn't that it?

Hed.   No, not quite.

Løv.   Then what made you do it?

Hed.   Do you find it so very strange that a young girl—when she can do so, without anyone knowing—

Løv.   Yes—?

Hed.   —that she wants to take a peek into a world which—

Løv.   —which—?

Hed.   —she is not supposed to know anything about?

Løv.   So that was it!   550

Hed.   That, too. That, too—I think—

Løv.   Companionship in the lust for life. But why couldn't *that* at least have continued?

Hed.   That was your own fault.

Løv.   You were the one who broke off.

Hed.   Yes, when reality threatened to enter our relationship. Shame on you, Eilert Løvborg! How could you want to do a thing like that to your frank and trusting comrade!

Løv.   [*Clenching his hands*] Oh, why didn't you do it! Why didn't you shoot me down, as you said you would!   560

HED. Because I'm scared of scandal.

LØV. Yes, Hedda. You are really a coward.

HED. A terrible coward. [*Changing her tone*] But that was your good luck, wasn't it? And now the Elvsteds have healed your broken heart very nicely.

LØV. I know what Thea has told you.

HED. Perhaps you have told her about us?

LØV. Not a word. She is too stupid to understand.

HED. Stupid?

570 LØV. In things like that.

HED. And I'm a coward. [*Leans forward, without looking in his eyes, whispers*] But now *I* am going to confess something to *you*.

LØV. [*Tense*] What?

HED. That I didn't dare to shoot—

LØV. Yes—?

HED. —that was not the worst of my cowardice that night.

LØV. [*Looks at her a moment, understands, whispers passionately*] Oh, Hedda! Hedda Gabler! Now I begin to see what was behind the companionship! You and I! So it *was* your lust for life—!

580 HED. [*In a low voice, with an angry glance*] Take care! Don't you believe that!

Darkness is falling. The door, right, is opened, and BERTE *enters.*

HED. [*Closing the album, calls out, smiling*] At last! So there you are, dearest Thea! Come in!

MRS. ELVSTED *enters. She is dressed for a party.* BERTE *exits, closing the door behind her.*

HED. [*In the sofa, reaching out for Mrs. Elvsted*] Sweetest Thea, you have no idea how I've waited for you.

In passing, MRS. ELVSTED *exchanges quick greetings with* TESMAN *and* BRACK *in the inner room. She walks up to the table and shakes* HEDDA'S *hand.* EILERT LØVBORG *rises. He and* MRS. ELVSTED *greet one another with a silent nod.*

MRS. ELV. Maybe I ought to go in and say hello to your husband?

HED. No, never mind that. Let them be. They're soon leaving, anyway.

MRS. ELV. Leaving?

590 HED. They're off to a spree.

MRS. ELV. [*Quickly, to Løvborg*] Not you?

LØV. No.

HED. Mr. Løvborg stays here with us.

MRS. ELV. [*Pulls up a chair, is about to sit down next to Løvborg*] Oh, how wonderful it is to be here!

HED. Oh no, little Thea. Not that. Not there. Over here by me, please. I want to be in the middle.

MRS. ELV. Just as you like.

She walks in front of the table and seats herself on the sofa, on HEDDA's *right.*
LØVBORG *sits down again on his chair.*

LØV. [*After a brief pause, to Hedda*] Isn't she lovely to look at?

HED. [*Gently stroking her hair*] Just to look at?

LØV. Yes. For you see—she and I—we are real comrades. We have 600
absolute faith in one another. And we can talk together in full freedom.

HED. Unveiled, Mr. Løvborg?

LØV. Well—

MRS. ELV. [*In a low voice, clinging to Hedda*] Oh, I am so happy, Hedda!
For just think—he says I have inspired him, too!

HED. [*Looks at her with a smile*] No, really! He says that?

LØV. And she has such courage, Mrs. Tesman! Such courage of
action.

MRS. ELV. Oh, my God—courage—! I!

LØV. Infinite courage—when it concerns the comrade. 610

HED. Yes, courage—if one only had that.

LØV. What then?

HED. Then maybe life would be tolerable, after all. [*Changing her
tone*] But now, dearest Thea, you want a glass of nice, cold punch.

MRS. ELV. No, thanks. I never drink things like that.

HED. Then what about you, Mr. Løvborg?

LØV. Thanks. Nothing for me, either.

MRS. ELV. No, nothing for him, either.

HED. [*Looks firmly at him*] If I say so?

LØV. Makes no difference. 620

HED. [*Laughs*] Poor me! So I have no power over you at all. Is that
it?

LØV. Not in that respect.

HED. Seriously, though; I really think you should. For your own sake.

MRS. ELV. No, but Hedda—!

LØV. Why so?

HED. Or rather for people's sake.

LØV. Oh?

HED. For else they might think you don't really trust yourself—
That you lack self-confidence— 630

MRS. ELV. [*Softly*] Don't, Hedda!

LØV. People may think whatever they like for all I care—for the
time being.

MRS. ELV. [*Happy*] Exactly!

HED. I could easily tell from watching Judge Brack just now.

LØV. Tell what?

HED. He smiled so contemptuously when you didn't dare to join
them in there.

Løv. Didn't I dare to! It's just that I'd much rather stay here and
640 talk with you!

Mrs. Elv. But that's only natural, Hedda.

Hed. The Judge had no way of knowing that. And I also noticed he smiled and looked at Tesman when you didn't dare to go to his silly old party.

Løv. Didn't dare! Are you saying I didn't dare?

Hed. *I* am not. But that's how Judge Brack understood it.

Løv. Let him.

Hed. So you're not going?

Løv. I'm staying here with you and Thea.

650 Mrs. Elv. Of course, he is, Hedda!

Hed. [*Smiles, nods approvingly*] That's what I call firm foundations. Principled forever; that's the way a man ought to be! [*Turning to Mrs. Elvsted, stroking her cheek*] What did I tell you this morning—when you came here, quite beside yourself—?

Løv. [*Puzzled*] Beside herself?

Mrs. Elv. [*In terror*] Hedda—Hedda—don't!

Hed. Now do you see? There was no need at all for that mortal fear of yours—[*Interrupting herself*] There, now! Now we can all three relax and enjoy ourselves.

660 Løv. [*Startled*] What's all this, Mrs. Tesman?

Mrs. Elv. Oh, God, Hedda—what are you saying? What are you doing?

Hed. Please be quiet. That horrible Judge is looking at you.

Løv. In mortal fear? So that's it. For my sake.

Mrs. Elv. [*Softly, wailing*] Oh, Hedda—if you only knew how utterly miserable you have made me!

Løv. [*Stares at her for a moment. His face is distorted.*] So that was the comrade's happy confidence in me!

Mrs. Elv. Oh, my dearest friend—listen to me first—!

670 Løv. [*Picks up one of the glasses of punch, raises it, says hoarsely*] Here's to you, Thea! [*Empties the glass, puts it down, picks up the other one.*

Mrs. Elv. [*Softly*] Hedda, Hedda—why did you want to do this?

Hed. Want to! I! Are you mad?

Løv. And here's to you, too, Mrs. Tesman! Thanks for telling me the truth. Long live the truth! [*He drains the glass and is about to fill it again.*

Hed. [*Restrains him*] That's enough for now. Remember you are going to a party.

Mrs. Elv. No, no, no!

Hed. Shhh! They are looking at you.

680 Løv. [*Puts his glass down*] Listen, Thea—tell me the truth—

Mrs. Elv. I will, I will!

Løv. Did your husband know you were coming after me?

MRS. ELV. [*Wringing her hands*] Oh, Hedda—do you hear what he's asking?

LØV. Did the two of you agree that you were to come here and look after me? Maybe it was his idea, even? Did he send you? Ah, I know what it was—he missed me in the office, didn't he? Or was it at the card table?

MRS. ELV. [*Softly, in agony*] Oh, Løvborg, Løvborg!

LØV. [*Grabs a glass and is about to fill it*] Here's to the old Commissioner, 690 too!

HED. [*Stops him*] No more now. You're supposed to read aloud for Tesman tonight—remember?

LØV. [*Calm again, puts the glass down*] This was silly of me, Thea. I'm sorry. To take it this way. Please, don't be angry with me. You'll see—both you and all those others—that even if I have been down—! With your help, Thea—dear comrade.

MRS. ELV. [*Beaming*] Oh, thank God—!

In the meantime, BRACK *has looked at his watch. He and* TESMAN *get up and come forward.*

BRACK. [*Picking up his coat and hat*] Well, Mrs. Tesman; our time is up.   700

HED. I suppose it is.

LØV. [*Rising*] Mine, too, Judge.

MRS. ELV. [*Softly, pleadingly*] Oh, Løvborg—don't do it!

HED. [*Pinches her arm*] They can hear you!

MRS. ELV. [*With a soft exclamation*] Ouch!

LØV. [*To Brack*] You were good enough to ask me—

BRACK. So you're coming, after all?

LØV. If I may.

BRACK. I'm delighted.

LØV. [*Picks up his manuscript and says to Tesman*] For there are a couple 710 of things here I'd like to show you before I send it off.

TES. Just think! Isn't that nice! But—dearest Hedda—? In that case, how are you going to get Mrs. Elvsted home? Hm?

HED. We'll manage somehow.

LØV. [*Looking at the two women*] Mrs. Elvsted? I'll be back to pick her up, of course. [*Coming closer*] About ten o'clock, Mrs. Tesman? Is that convenient?

HED. Certainly. That will be fine.

TES. Then everything is nice and settled. But don't expect me that early, Hedda.   720

HED. You just stay as long as—as long as you want, dear.

MRS. ELV. [*In secret fear*] I'll be waiting for you here, then, Mr. Løvborg.

Løv. [*Hat in hand*]   Of course, Mrs. Elvsted.

Brack.   All aboard the pleasure train, gentlemen! I hope we'll have a lively evening—as a certain fair lady would say.

Hed.   Ah—if only the fair lady could be present. Invisible.

Brack.   Why invisible?

Hed.   To listen to some of your unadulterated liveliness, Judge.

730   Brack. [*Laughs*]   I shouldn't advise the fair lady to do that!

Tes. [*Also laughing*]   You're a good one, Hedda! Just think!

Brack.   Well—good night, ladies!

Løv. [*With a bow*]   Till about ten, then.

Brack, Løvborg, *and* Tesman *go out, right. At the same time* Berte *enters from the inner room with a lighted lamp, which she places on the table, front center. She goes out the same way.*

Mrs. Elv. [*Has risen and paces restlessly up and down*]   Hedda, Hedda—how do you think all this will end?

Hed.   At ten o'clock he'll be here. I see him already. With vine leaves in his hair. Flushed and confident.

Mrs. Elv.   I only hope you're right.

Hed.   For then, you see, he'll have mastered himself. And be a free
740 man for all the days of his life.

Mrs. Elv.   Dear God—how I hope you are right! That he comes back like that.

Hed.   That is the way he will come. No other way.   [*She rises and goes closer to Mrs. Elvsted.*] *You* may doubt as long as you like. I believe in him. And now we'll see—

Mrs. Elv.   There is something behind all this, Hedda. Some hidden purpose.

Hed.   Yes, there is! For once in my life I want to have power over a human destiny.

Mrs. Elv.   But don't you already?

Hed.   I don't and I never have.

750   Mrs. Elv.   But your husband—?

Hed.   You think that's worth the trouble? Oh, if you knew how poor I am! And you got to be so rich!   [*Embraces her passionately*]   I think I'll have to burn your hair off, after all!

Mrs. Elv.   Let me go! Let me go! You scare me, Hedda!

Ber. [*In the doorway*]   Supper is served, ma'am.

Hed.   Good. We're coming.

Mrs. Elv.   No, no, no! I'd rather go home by myself! Right now!

760   Hed.   Nonsense! You'll have your cup of tea first, you little silly. And then—at ten o'clock—Eilert Løvborg comes—with vine leaves in his hair!

[*She almost pulls Mrs. Elvsted toward the doorway.*

Act III

The same room at the TESMANS'. *The doorway and the French windows both have their portieres closed. The lamp, turned half down, is still on the table. The stove is open. Some dying embers can be seen.*

MRS. ELVSTED, *wrapped in a big shawl, is in the easy chair near the stove, her feet on a footstool.* HEDDA, *also dressed, is lying on the sofa, covered by a blanket.*

MRS. ELV. [*After a while suddenly sits up, listens anxiously; then she wearily sinks back in her chair, whimpers softly*] Oh my God, my God—not yet!

BERTE *enters cautiously, right, carrying a letter.*

MRS. ELV. [*Turns and whispers tensely*] Well—has anybody been here?

BER. [*In a low voice*] Yes. Just now there was a girl with this letter.

MRS. ELV. [*Quickly, reaches for it*] A letter! Give it to me!

BER. No, ma'am. It's for the Doctor.

MRS. ELV. I see.

BER. Miss Tesman's maid brought it. I'll leave it here on the table.

MRS. ELV. All right.

BER. [*Puts the letter down*] I'd better put out the lamp. It just reeks.

MRS. ELV. Yes, do that. It must be daylight soon, anyway.   10

BER. [*Putting out the lamp*] It's light already, ma'am.

MRS. ELV. Light already! And still not back!

BER. No, so help us. Not that I didn't expect as much—

MRS. ELV. You did?

BER. Yes, when I saw a certain character was back in town. Taking off with them. We sure heard enough about him in the old days!

MRS. ELV. Not so loud. You are waking up Mrs. Tesman.

BER. [*Looks toward the sofa, sighs*] God forbid—! Let her sleep, poor thing. Do you want me to get the fire going again?

MRS. ELV. Not on my account, thank you.   20

BER. All right; I won't, then.   [*Exits quietly, right.*

HED. [*Awakened by the closing door*] What's that?

MRS. ELV. Just the maid.

HED. [*Looks around*] Why in here—? Oh, I remember! [*Sits up, rubs her eyes, stretches*] What time is it, Thea?

MRS. ELV. [*Looks at her watch*] Past seven.

HED. When did Tesman get home?

MRS. ELV. He didn't.

HED. Not home yet!

MRS. ELV. [*Getting up*] Nobody's come.   30

HED. And we who waited till four!

MRS. ELV. [*Wringing her hands*] And *how* we waited!

HED. [*Her hand covering a yawn*] We—ll. We could have saved ourselves that trouble.

MRS. ELV. Did you get any sleep at all?

452 Drama

HED. Yes, I slept pretty well, I think. Didn't you?

MRS. ELV. Not a wink. I just couldn't, Hedda! It was just impossible.

HED. [*Rises, walks over to her*] Well, now! There's nothing to worry about, for heaven's sake. I know exactly what's happened.

40 MRS. ELV. Then tell me please. Where do you think they are?

HED. Well, first of all, I'm sure they were terribly late leaving the Judge's—

MRS. ELV. Dear, yes. I'm sure you're right. Still—

HED. —and so Tesman didn't want to wake us up in the middle of the night. [*Laughs*] Maybe he didn't want us to see him, either—after a party like that.

MRS. ELV. But where do you think he has gone?

HED. To the aunts', of course. His old room is still there, all ready for him.

50 MRS. ELV. No, he can't be there. Just a few minutes ago there came a letter for him from Miss Tesman. It's over there.

HED. Oh? [*Looks at the envelope*] So it is—Auntie Julle herself. In that case, I suppose he's still at Brack's. And there's Eilert Løvborg, too— reading aloud, with vine leaves in his hair.

MRS. ELV. Oh Hedda—you're only saying things you don't believe yourself.

HED. My, what a little imbecile you really are, Thea!

MRS. ELV. Yes, I suppose I am.

HED. And you look dead tired, too.

60 MRS. ELV. I *am* dead tired.

HED. Why don't you do as I say. Go into my room and lie down.

MRS. ELV. No, no—I wouldn't be able to go to sleep, anyway.

HED. Of course, you would.

MRS. ELV. And your husband is bound to be home any minute now. And I have to know right away.

HED. I'll let you know as soon as he gets here.

MRS. ELV. You promise me that, Hedda?

HED. I do. You just go to sleep.

MRS. ELV. Thanks. At least I'll try. [*Exits through inner room.*

HEDDA *goes to the French doors, opens the portieres. The room is now in full daylight. She picks up a little hand mirror from the desk, looks at herself, smooths her hair. Walks over to door, right, rings the bell for the maid.* BERTE *presently appears.*

70 BER. You want something, ma'am?

HED. Yes. You'll have to start the fire again. I'm cold.

BER. Yes, ma'am! I'll get it warm in no time. [*Rakes the embers together and puts in another piece of wood. Then she suddenly listens.*] There's the doorbell, ma'am.

HED. All right. See who it is. I'll take care of the stove myself.

BER. You'll have a nice blaze going in a minute. [*Exits right.*

HEDDA *kneels on the footstool and puts in more pieces of wood. Presently* TESMAN
*enters, right. He looks tired and somber. He tiptoes toward the doorway and is
about to disappear between the portieres.*

HED. [*By the stove, without looking up*] Good morning.

TES. [*Turning*] Hedda! [*Comes closer*] For heaven's sake—you up 80
already? Hm?

HED. Yes, I got up very early this morning.

TES. And I was so sure you'd still be sound asleep! Just think!

HED. Not so loud. Mrs. Elvsted is asleep in my room.

TES. Mrs. Elvsted stayed here all night?

HED. Yes. Nobody came for her, you know.

TES. No, I suppose—

HED. [*Closes the stove, rises*] Well, did you have a good time at the
Judge's?

TES. Were you worried about me? Hm? 90

HED. I'd never dream of worrying about you. I asked if you had a
good time.

TES. Yes, indeed. Nice for a change, anyway. But I think I liked it
best early in the evening. For then Eilert read to me. Just think—we
were more than an hour early! And Brack, of course, had things to see to.
So Eilert read.

HED. [*Sits down at the right side of the table*] So? Tell me all about it.

TES. [*Sits down on an ottoman near the stove*] Oh Hedda, you'll never
believe what a book that will be! It must be just the most remarkable
thing ever written! Just think! 100

HED. Yes, but I don't really care about that—

TES. I must tell you, Hedda—I have a confession to make. As he was
reading—something ugly came over me—

HED. Ugly?

TES. I sat there envying Eilert for being able to write like that!
Just think, Hedda!

HED. All right. I'm thinking!

TES. And yet, with all his gifts—he's incorrigible, after all.

HED. I suppose you mean he has more courage for life than the rest
of you? 110

TES. No, no—I don't mean that. I mean that he's incapable of exercising moderation in his pleasures.

HED. What happened—in the end?

TES. Well—*I* would call it a bacchanal, Hedda.

HED. Did he have vine leaves in his hair?

TES. Vine leaves? No, I didn't notice any vine leaves. But he gave
a long, muddled speech in honor of the woman who had inspired him
in his work. Those were his words.

HED. Did he mention her name?

120 TES. No, he didn't. But I'm sure it must be Mrs. Elvsted. You just wait and see if I'm not right!

HED. And where did you and he part company?

TES. On the way back to town. We left—the last of us did—at the same time. And Brack came along, too, to get some fresh air. Then we decided we'd better see Eilert home. You see, he had had altogether too much to drink!

HED. I can imagine.

TES. But then the strangest thing of all happened, Hedda! Or maybe I should say the saddest. I'm almost ashamed—on Eilert's behalf—even 130 talking about it.

HED. Well—?

TES. You see, on the way back I happened to be behind the others a little. Just for a minute or two—you know—

HED. All right, all right—!

TES. And when I hurried to catch up with them, can you guess what I found by the roadside? Hm?

HED. How can I possibly—?

TES. You mustn't tell this to a living soul, Hedda! Do you hear! Promise me that, for Eilert's sake. [*Pulls a parcel out of his coat pocket*] 140 Just think—I found this!

HED. Isn't that what he had with him here yesterday?

TES. Yes! It's his whole, precious, irreplaceable manuscript! And he had dropped it—just like that! Without even noticing! Just think, Hedda! Isn't that awfully sad?

HED. But why didn't you give it back to him?

TES. In the condition he was in! Dear—I just didn't dare to.

HED. And you didn't tell any of the others that you had found it, either?

150 TES. Of course not. I didn't want to, for Eilert's sake—don't you see?

HED. So nobody knows that you have Eilert Løvborg's papers?

TES. Nobody. And nobody must know, either.

HED. And what did you and he talk about afterwards?

TES. I didn't have a chance to talk to him at all after that. For when we came into town, he and a couple of the others simply vanished. Just think!

HED. Oh? I expect they took him home.

TES. I suppose that must be it. And Brack took off on his own, too.

HED. And what have you been doing with yourself since then?

160 TES. Well, you see, I and some of the others went home with one of the younger fellows and had a cup of early morning coffee. Or night coffee maybe, rather. Hm? And now, after I've rested a bit and poor Eilert's had some sleep, I'll take this back to him.

HED. [*Reaches for the parcel*] No—don't do that! Not right away, I mean. Let me look at it first.

TES. Dearest Hedda—honestly, I just don't dare to.

HED. Don't you dare to?

TES. No, for I'm sure you realize how utterly desperate he'll be when he wakes up and finds that the manuscript is gone. For he hasn't got a copy, you know. He said so himself. 170

HED. [*Looks searchingly at him*] But can't a thing like that be written over again?

TES. Hardly. I really don't think so. For, you see—the inspiration—

HED. Yes, I daresay that's the main thing. [*Casually*] By the way, here's a letter for you.

TES. Imagine!

HED. [*Gives it to him*] It came early this morning.

TES. It's from Aunt Julle, Hedda! I wonder what it can be. [*Puts the manuscript down on the other ottoman, opens the letter, skims the content, jumps up*] Oh Hedda! She says here that poor Aunt Rina is dying!

HED. You know we had to expect that. 180

TES. And if I want to see her again I had better hurry. I'll rush over right away.

HED. [*Suppressing a smile*] You'll rush?

TES. Dearest Hedda of mine—if only you could bring yourself to come along! Hm?

HED. [*Rises, weary, with an air of refusal*] No, no. You musn't ask me that. I don't want to look at death and disease. I want to be free from all that's ugly.

TES. Well, all right— [*Rushing around*] My hat? My coat? Oh—out here in the hall. I just hope I won't be too late, Hedda. Hm? 190

HED. Oh I'm sure that if you rush—

BERTE *appears in the door, right.*

BER. Judge Brack is here and wants to know if he may see you.

TES. At this hour! No, no. I can't possibly see him now!

HED. But I can. [*To Berte*] Tell the Judge please to come in.

[*Berte exits.*

HED. [*With a quick whisper*] Tesman! The package!

She grabs it from the ottoman.

TES. Yes! Give it to me!

HED. No, no. I'll hide it for you till later.

She walks over to the desk and sticks the parcel in among the books on the shelf. In his hurry TESMAN *is having difficulties getting his gloves on.* JUDGE BRACK *enters, right.*

HED. [*Nods to him*] If *you* aren't an early bird— 200

BRACK. Yes, don't you think so? [*To Tesman*] You're going out, too?

TES.   Yes, I must go and see the aunts. Just think, the invalid—she's dying!

BRACK.   Oh, I'm terribly sorry! In that case, don't let me keep you. At such a moment—

TES.   Yes, I really must run. Goodbye, goodbye! [*Hurries out, right.*

HED.   [*Approaching Brack*]   It appears that things were quite lively last night over at your house.

210   BRACK.   Indeed, Mrs. Tesman—I didn't get to bed at all.

HED.   You didn't either?

BRACK.   As you see. But tell me—what has Tesman told you about the night's adventures?

HED.   Just some tiresome story about having coffee with somebody someplace—

BRACK.   I believe I know all about that coffee. Eilert Løvborg wasn't one of them, was he?

HED.   No, they had taken him home first.

BRACK.   Tesman, too?

220   HED.   No. Some of the others, he said.

BRACK.   [*Smiles*]   Jørgen Tesman is really an ingenuous soul, you know.

HED.   He certainly is. But why do you say that? Is there something more to all this?

BRACK.   Yes, there is.

HED.   Well! In that case, why don't we make ourselves comfortable, Judge. You'll tell your story better, too.

She sits down at the left side of the table, BRACK *near her at the adjacent side.*

HED.   All right?

BRACK.   For reasons of my own I wanted to keep track of my guests' movements last night. Or, rather—some of my guests.

230   HED.   Eilert Løvborg was one of them, perhaps?

BRACK.   As a matter of fact—he was.

HED.   Now you are really making me curious.

BRACK.   Do you know where he and a couple of the others spent the rest of the night, Mrs. Tesman?

HED.   No—tell me. If it is at all tellable.

BRACK.   Oh, certainly it can be told. They turned up at an exceptionally gay early morning gathering.

HED.   Of the lively kind?

BRACK.   The very liveliest.

240   HED.   A little more about this, Judge.

BRACK.   Løvborg had been invited beforehand. I knew all about that. But he had declined. He is a reformed character, you know.

HED.   As of his stay with the Elvsteds—yes. But he went after all?

BRACK.   Well, yes, you see, Mrs. Tesman—unfortunately, the spirit moved him over at my house last evening.

Henrik Ibsen   457

HED. Yes, I understand he became inspired.

BRACK. Quite violently inspired. And that, I gather, must have changed his mind. You know, we men don't always have as much integrity as we ought to have.

HED. Oh I'm sure you're an exception, Judge Brack. But about 250 Løvborg—?

BRACK. To make a long story short—he ended up at Miss Diana's establishment.

HED. Miss Diana's?

BRACK. She was the hostess at this gathering—a select circle of intimate friends, male and female.

HED. Is she a redhead, by any chance?

BRACK. That's correct.

HED. And a singer—of sorts?

BRACK. Yes—that, too. And a mighty huntress—of men, Mrs. Tes- 260 man. You seem to have heard of her. Eilert Løvborg used to be one of her most devoted protectors in his more affluent days.

HED. And how did it all end?

BRACK. Not in a very friendly fashion, apparently. It seems that after the tenderest reception Miss Diana resorted to brute force—

HED. Against Løvborg?

BRACK. Yes. He accused her or her woman friends of having stolen something of his. Said his wallet was gone. And other things, too. In brief, he's supposed to have started a pretty wicked row.

HED. And—? 270

BRACK. Well—there was a general free-for-all—men and women both. Fortunately, the police stepped in—

HED. The police—!

BRACK. Yes. But I'm afraid this will be an expensive escapade for Eilert Løvborg, crazy fool that he is.

HED. Well!

BRACK. It appears that he made quite violent objection—struck an officer in the ear and tore his coat. So they had to take him along.

HED. How do you know all this?

BRACK. From the police. 280

HED. [Staring straight ahead] So that's how it was. No vine leaves in his hair.

BRACK. Vine leaves, Mrs. Tesman?

HED. [Changing her tone] But tell me, Judge Brack—why did you keep such a close watch on Eilert Løvborg?

BRACK. Well—for one thing, it is obviously of some concern to me if he testifies that he came straight from my party.

HED. So you think there will be an investigation?

BRACK. Naturally. But I suppose that doesn't really matter too much.

₂₉₀ However, as a friend of the house I considered it my duty to give you and Tesman a full account of his night-time exploits.

HED. Yes, but why?

BRACK. Because I very strongly suspect that he intends to use you as a kind of screen.

HED. Really! Why do you think that?

BRACK. Oh, come now, Mrs. Tesman! We can use our eyes, can't we? This Mrs. Elvsted—she isn't leaving town right away, you know.

HED. Well, even if there should be something going on between those two, I'd think there would be plenty of other places they could meet.

₃₀₀ BRACK. But no home. After last night, every respectable house will once again be closed to Eilert Løvborg.

HED. And so should mine, you mean?

BRACK. Yes. I admit I would find it more than embarrassing if the gentleman were to become a daily guest here, Mrs. Tesman. If he, as an outsider—a highly dispensable outsider—if he were to intrude himself—

HED. —into the triangle?

BRACK. Precisely. It would amount to homelessness for me.

HED. [*Smiling*] Sole cock-o'-the-walk—so, that's your goal, is it, Judge?

₃₁₀ BRACK. [*Nods slowly, lowers his voice*] Yes. That is my goal. And for that I will fight with every means at my disposal.

HED. [*Her smile fading*] You're really a dangerous person, you know—when you come right down to it.

BRACK. You think so?

HED. Yes. I am beginning to think so now. And I must say I am exceedingly glad you don't have any kind of hold on me.

BRACK. [*With a noncommittal laugh*] Well, well, Mrs. Tesman! Maybe there is something to what you are saying, at that. Who knows what I might do if I did.

₃₂₀ HED. Really, now, Judge Brack! Are you threatening me?

BRACK. [*Rising*] —Nonsense! For the triangle, you see—is best maintained on a voluntary basis.

HED. My sentiments, exactly.

BRACK. Well, I have said what I came to say. And now I should get back to town. Goodbye, Mrs. Tesman! [*Walks toward the French doors.*

HED. [*Rises*] You're going through the garden?

BRACK. Yes. For me that's a short cut.

HED. Yes, and then it's a back way.

BRACK. Quite true. I have nothing against back ways. There are ₃₃₀ times when they are most intriguing.

HED. You mean when real ammunition is used?

BRACK. [*In the doorway, laughs back at her*] Oh good heavens! I don't suppose one shoots one's tame roosters!

Henrik Ibsen 459

HED. [*Laughs also*] No—not if one has only one—!
They nod to each other, both still laughing. He leaves. She closes the door behind him. For a few moments she remains by the door, quite serious now, looking into the garden. Then she walks over to the doorway and opens the portieres wide enough to look into the inner room. Walks to the desk, pulls LØVBORG'S *manuscript from the bookshelf and is about to read in it when* BERTE'S *voice, very loud, is heard from the hall, right.* HEDDA *turns around, listens. She hurriedly puts the manuscript into the drawer of the desk and puts the key down on its top.* EILERT LØVBORG, *wearing his coat and with his hat in his hand, flings open the door, right. He looks somewhat confused and excited.*

LØV. [*Turned toward the invisible Berte in the hall*] —And I say I must! You can't stop me!
He closes the door, turns, sees HEDDA, *immediately controls himself, greets her.*

HED. [*By the desk*] Well, well, Mr. Løvborg—aren't you a trifle late coming for Thea?

LØV. Or a trifle early for calling on you. I apologize.

HED. How do you know she is still here?   340

LØV. The people she is staying with told me she's been gone all night.

HED. [*Walks over to the table*] Did they seem—strange—when they told you that?

LØV. [*Puzzled*] Strange?

HED. I mean, did they seem to find it a little—unusual?

LØV. [*Suddenly understands*] Ah, I see what you mean! Of course! I'm dragging her down with me. No, as a matter of fact, I didn't notice anything. I suppose Tesman isn't up yet?

HED. I—I don't think so—

LØV. When did he get home?   350

HED. Very late.

LØV. Did he tell you anything?

HED. Yes, he said you'd all had quite a time over at Brack's.

LØV. Just that?

HED. I think so. But I was so awfully sleepy—
MRS. ELVSTED *enters through portieres in the rear.*

MRS. ELV. [*Toward him*] Oh, Løvborg! At last!

LØV. Yes, at last. And too late.

MRS. ELV. [*In fear*] What is too late?

LØV. Everything is too late now. It's all over with me.

MRS. ELV. Oh no, no! Don't say things like that!   360

LØV. You'll say the same yourself when you hear—

MRS. ELV. I don't want to hear—!

HED. Maybe you'd rather talk with her alone? I'll leave.

LØV. No, stay—you, too. I beg you to.

MRS. ELV. But I don't want to listen, do you hear?

LØV. It isn't last night I want to talk about.

Mrs. Elv.   What about, then?

Løv.   We'll have to part, Thea.

Mrs. Elv.   Part!

370   Hed.   [*Involuntarily*]   I knew it!

Løv.   For I don't need you any more.

Mrs. Elv.   And you can stand there and tell me a thing like that! Don't need me! Why can't I help you the way I did before? Aren't we going to keep on working together?

Løv.   I don't intend to work any more.

Mrs. Elv.   [*Desperately*]   What am I going to do with my life, then?

Løv.   You'll have to try to live your life as if you'd never known me.

Mrs. Elv.   But I can't do that!

Løv.   Try, Thea. Go back home.

380   Mrs. Elv.   [*Agitated*]   Never again! Where you are I want to be! And you can't chase me away just like that. I want to stay right here! Be with you when the book appears.

Hed.   [*In a tense whisper*]   Ah—yes—the book!

Løv.   [*Looks at her*]   My book—and Thea's. For that's what it is.

Mrs. Elv.   That's what I feel, too. And that's why I have the right to be with you when it comes out. I want to see all the honor and all the fame you'll get. And the joy—I want to share the joy, too.

Løv.   Thea, our book is never going to come out.

Hed.   Ah!

390   Mrs. Elv.   It won't!

Løv.   *Can't* ever appear.

Mrs. Elv.   [*With fearful suspicion*]   Løvborg, what have you done with the manuscript?

Hed.   [*Watching him tensely*]   Yes—what about the manuscript?

Mrs. Elv.   Where is it?

Løv.   Oh Thea—please, don't ask me about that!

Mrs. Elv.   Yes, yes—I want to be told! I have the right to know—right now!

Løv.   All right. I've torn it to pieces.

400   Mrs. Elv.   [*Screams*]   Oh, no! No!

Hed.   [*Involuntarily*]   But that's not—!

Løv.   [*Looks at her*]   Not true, you think?

Hed.   [*Composing herself*]   Well, of course, if you say so. You should know. It just sounds so—so unbelievable.

Løv.   All the same, it's true.

Mrs. Elv.   [*Hands clenched*]   Oh God—oh God, Hedda. He has torn his own work to pieces!

Løv.   I have torn my whole life to pieces, so why not my life's work as well?

410   Mrs. Elv.   And that's what you did last night?

Løv. Yes, I tell you! In a thousand pieces. And scattered them in the fjord. Far out—where the water is clean and salty. Let them drift there, with wind and current. Then they'll sink. Deep, deep down. Like me, Thea.

Mrs. Elv. Do you know, Løvborg—this thing you've done to the book—all the rest of my life I'll think of it as killing a little child.

Løv. You are right. It is like murdering a child.

Mrs. Elv. But then, how could you? For the child was mine, too!

Hed. [*Almost soundlessly*] The child—

Mrs. Elv. [*With a deep sigh*] So it's all over. I'll go now, Hedda.   420

Hed. But you aren't leaving town?

Mrs. Elv. Oh, I don't know myself what I'll do. There's only darkness before me.   [*Exits, right.*

Hed. [*Waits for a moment*] Aren't you going to see her home, Mr. Løvborg?

Løv. I? Through the streets? Letting people see her with me?

Hed. Of course, I don't know what else may have happened last night. But is it really so absolutely irreparable—?

Løv. Last night is not the end of it. That I know. And yet, I don't really care for that kind of life any more. Not again. She has broken all 430 the courage for life and all the defiance that was in me.

Hed. [*Staring ahead*] So that sweet little goose has had her hand in a human destiny. [*Looks at him*] But that you could be so heartless, even so!

Løv. Don't tell me I was heartless!

Hed. To ruin everything that's given her soul and mind meaning for such a long, long time! You don't call that heartless!

Løv. Hedda—to you I can tell the truth.

Hed. The truth?

Løv. But first promise me—give me your word you'll never let Thea 440 know what I'm going to tell you now.

Hed. You have it.

Løv. All right. It isn't true what I just told her.

Hed. About the manuscript?

Løv. Yes. I have not torn it up. Not thrown it in the sea, either.

Hed. But then—where is it?

Løv. I've destroyed it just the same. Really, I have, Hedda!

Hed. I don't understand.

Løv. Thea said that what I had done seemed to her like murdering a child.   450

Hed. Yes—she did.

Løv. But killing a child, that's not the worst thing a father can do to it.

Hed. No?

Løv.　No. And the worst is what I don't want Thea to know.

Hed.　What *is* the worst?

Løv.　Hedda—suppose a man, say, early in the morning, after a stupid, drunken night—suppose he comes home to his child's mother and says: Listen, I've been in such and such a place. I've been here—and I've been there. And I had our child with me. In all those places. And the
460 child is lost. Gone. Vanished. I'll be damned if I know where it is. Who's got hold of it—

Hed.　Yes—but when all is said and done—it is only a book, you know.

Løv.　Thea's pure soul was in that book.

Hed.　I realize that.

Løv.　Then you surely also realize that she and I can have no future together.

Hed.　Where do you go from here?

Løv.　Nowhere. Just finish everything off. The sooner the better.

470 Hed.　[*A step closer*] Listen—Eilert Løvborg— Couldn't you make sure it's done beautifully?

Løv.　Beautifully? [*Smiles*] With vine leaves in the hair, as you used to say.

Hed.　Oh no. I don't believe in vine leaves any more. But still beautifully! For once. Goodbye. Go now. And don't come back.

Løv.　Goodbye, Mrs. Tesman. Give my regards to Jørgen Tesman. *He is about to leave.*

Hed.　Wait! I want to give you something—a remembrance. *Goes to the desk, opens the drawer, takes out the gun case. Returns to* Løvborg *with one of the revolvers.*

Løv.　The gun? That's the remembrance?

Hed.　[*Nods slowly*] Do you recognize it? It was pointed at you once.

480 Løv.　You should have used it then.

Hed.　Take it! *You* use it.

Løv.　[*Pockets the gun*] Thanks!

Hed.　And beautifully, Eilert Løvborg! That's all I ask!

Løv.　Goodbye, Hedda Gabler.　　　　　　　　　　　[*Exits, right.*

Hedda *listens by the door for a moment. Then she crosses to the desk, takes out the manuscript, glances inside the cover, pulls some of the pages halfway out and looks at them. Carries the whole manuscript over to the chair by the stove. She sits down with the parcel in her lap. After a moment she opens the stove and then the manuscript.*

Hed.　[*Throws a bundle of sheets into the fire, whispers*]　Now I'm burning your child, Thea. You—curlyhead! [*Throws more sheets in*]　Your and Eilert Løvborg's child.　[*Throws all the rest of the manuscript into the stove*] I am burning—I am burning your child.

Act IV

The same rooms at the Tesmans'. *Evening. The front room is dark. The inner room is lighted by the ceiling lamp over the table. Portieres cover the French doors.*

Hedda, *in black, is walking up and down in the dark of the front room. She goes into the inner room, turning left in the doorway. She is heard playing a few bars on the piano. She reappears and comes forward again.* Berte *enters from the right side of the inner room. She carries a lighted lamp, which she puts down on the table in front of the corner sofa. Her eyes show signs of weeping; she wears black ribbons on her uniform. She exits quietly, right.* Hedda *goes over to the French windows, looks between the portieres into the dark. Presently* Miss Tesman, *in mourning, with hat and veil, enters, right.* Hedda *walks over to meet her, gives her her hand.*

Miss Tes. Yes, my dearest Hedda—here you see me in my garb of grief. For now at last my poor sister has fought her fight to the end.

Hed. I already know—as you see. Tesman sent word.

Miss Tes. Yes, he promised he'd do that. But I thought that to you, Hedda—here in the house of life—I really ought to bring the tidings of death myself.

Hed. That is very kind of you.

Miss Tes. Ah, but Rina shouldn't have died just now. There should be no mourning in Hedda's house at this time.

Hed. [*Changing the topic*] I understand she had a very quiet end. 10

Miss Tes. Oh so beautiful, so peaceful! She left us so quietly! And then the unspeakable happiness of seeing Jørgen one more time! To say goodbye to him to her heart's content! Isn't he back yet?

Hed. No. He wrote I mustn't expect him back very soon. But do sit down.

Miss Tes. No—no, thanks, my dear, blessed Hedda. Not that I wouldn't like to. But I don't have much time. I must go back and prepare her as best I can. I want her to look right pretty when she goes into her grave.

Hed. Is there anything I can help you with? 20

Miss Tes. I won't have you as much as think of it! That's not for Hedda Tesman to lend a hand to. Or lend thoughts to, either. Not now, of all times!

Hed. Oh—thoughts! We can't always control our thoughts—

Miss Tes. [*Still preoccupied*] Ah yes—such is life. At home we're making a shroud for Rina. And here, too, there'll be sewing to do soon, I expect. But of quite a different kind, thank God!

Tesman *enters, right.*

Hed. So finally you're back!

Tes. You here, Aunt Julle? With Hedda? Just think!

Miss Tes. I am just about to leave, Jørgen dear. Well—did you do all 30 the things you promised me you'd do?

Tes.   No, I'm afraid I forgot half of them, Auntie. I'd better run in again tomorrow. I'm all confused today. I can't seem to keep my thoughts together.

Miss Tes.   But dearest Jørgen—you mustn't take it this way!

Tes.   Oh, I mustn't? How do you mean?

Miss Tes.   You ought to be joyful in the midst of your sorrow. Glad for what's happened. The way I am.

Tes.   Oh yes, of course. You're thinking of Aunt Rina.

40   Hed.   You're going to feel lonely now, Miss Tesman.

Miss Tes.   The first few days, yes. But I hope that won't last long. Dear Rina's little parlor won't be empty for long, if I can help it!

Tes.   Oh? And who do you want to move in there. Hm?

Miss Tes.   Ah—it's not very hard to find some poor soul who needs nursing and comfort.

Hed.   And you really want to take on such a burden all over again?

Miss Tes.   Heavens! God forgive you, child—burden? It has not been a burden to me.

Hed.   Still—a stranger, who—

50   Miss Tes.   Oh, it's easy to make friends with sick people. And I sorely need something to live for, I, too. Well, the Lord be praised, maybe soon there'll be a thing or two an old aunt can turn her hand to here.

Hed.   Please, don't let our affairs worry you—

Tes.   Yes, just think—how lovely it would be for the three of us, if only—

Hed.   If only—?

Tes.   [Uneasy]   Oh, nothing. I daresay it will all work out. Let's hope it will, hm?

Miss Tes.   Well, well. I can see that you two have something to talk
60   about.   [With a smile]   And perhaps Hedda has something to tell you, Jørgen! Goodbye! I'm going home to Rina, now.   [Turns around in the door]   Dear, dear—how strange to think—! Now Rina is both with me and with Jochum!

Tes.   Yes, just think, Aunt Julle! Hm?   [Miss Tesman exits, right.

Hed.   [Coldly scrutinizing Tesman]   I wouldn't be at all surprised if you aren't more affected by this death than she is.

Tes.   Oh, it isn't just Aunt Rina's death, Hedda. It's Eilert I worry about.

Hed.   [Quickly]   Any news about him?

70   Tes.   I went over to his room this afternoon to tell him the manuscript is safe.

Hed.   Well? And didn't you see him?

Tes.   No. He wasn't home. But I ran into Mrs. Elvsted and she told me he'd been here early this morning.

Hed.   Yes, right after you'd left.

Tes.   And he said he'd torn up the manuscript? Did he really say that?

Hed.   Yes. So he claimed.

Tes.   But dear God—in that case he really must have been out of his mind! So I assume you didn't give it to him either, hm, Hedda?

Hed.   No. He didn't get it.   80

Tes.   But you told him we had it, of course?

Hed.   No. [*Quickly*] Did you tell Mrs. Elvsted?

Tes.   No, I didn't want to. But you ought to have told him, Hedda. Just think—what if he does something rash—something to hurt himself! Give me the manuscript, Hedda! I want to rush down to him with it right this minute. Where is it?

Hed.   [*Cold, motionless, one arm resting on the chair*]   I haven't got it any more.

Tes.   You haven't got it! What do you mean by that?

Hed.   I burned it—the whole thing.   90

Tes.   [*Jumps up*]   Burned it! Burned Eilert's book!

Hed.   Don't shout. The maid might hear you.

Tes.   Burned it? But good God—no, no, no—! This can't be—!

Hed.   It is all the same.

Tes.   But do you realize what you've done, Hedda? It's illegal! Willful destruction of lost property! You just ask Judge Brack! He'll tell you!

Hed.   You'd better not talk about this to anyone—the Judge or anybody else.

Tes.   But how could you do a thing like that! I never heard anything like it! What came over you? What can possibly have been going on in   100 your head? Answer me! Hm?

Hed.   [*Suppresses an almost imperceptible smile*]   I did it for your sake, Jørgen.

Tes.   For my sake!

Hed.   When you came back this morning and told me he had read aloud to you—

Tes.   Yes, yes! What then?

Hed.   You confessed you were jealous of him for having written such a book.

Tes.   But good gracious—! I didn't mean it as seriously as all that! 110

Hed.   All the same. I couldn't stand the thought that somebody else was to overshadow you.

Tes.   [*In an outburst of mingled doubt and joy*]   Hedda—oh Hedda! Is it true what you're saying! But—but—but—I never knew you loved me like that! Just think!

Hed.   In that case, I might as well tell you—that—just at this time— [*Breaks off, vehemently*]   No, no! You can ask Aunt Julle. She'll tell you.

TES.   I almost think I know what you mean, Hedda!   [*Claps his hands*]
120 For goodness sake! Can that really be so! Hm?

HED.   Don't shout so! The maid can hear you.

TES. [*Laughing with exuberant joy*]   The maid! Well, if you don't take
the prize, Hedda! The maid—but that's Berte! I'm going to tell Berte
myself this very minute!

HED. [*Her hands clenched in despair*]   Oh I'll die—I'll die, in all this!

TES.   In what, Hedda? Hm?

HED. [*Cold and composed*]   In all this—ludicrousness, Jørgen.

TES.   Ludicrous? That I'm so happy? Still—maybe I oughtn't to tell
Berte, after all.

130 HED.   Oh, go ahead. What difference does it make?

TES.   No, not yet. But on my word—Aunt Julle must be told. And
that you've started to call me "Jørgen," too! Just think! She'll be ever so
happy—Aunt Julle will!

HED.   Even when you tell her that I have burned Eilert Løvborg's
papers?

TES.   No, oh no! That's true! That about the manuscript—nobody
must know about that. But to think that you'd burn for me, Hedda—
I certainly want to tell *that* to Aunt Julle! I wonder now—is that sort of
thing usual with young wives, hm?

140 HED.   Why don't you ask Aunt Julle about that, too?

TES.   I shall—I certainly shall, when I get the chance.   [*Looks uneasy
and disturbed again*]   But the manuscript! Good God—I don't dare to
think what this is going to do to poor Eilert!

MRS. ELVSTED, *dressed as on her first visit, wearing hat and coat, enters, right.*

MRS. ELV. [*Gives a hurried greeting, is obviously upset*]   Oh Hedda, you
must forgive me for coming here again!

HED.   What has happened, Thea?

TES.   Something to do with Eilert Løvborg again? Hm?

MRS. ELV.   Yes, yes—I'm so terribly afraid something's happened to
him.

150 HED. [*Seizing her arm*]   Ah—you think so?

TES.   Oh dear—why do you think that, Mrs. Elvsted?

MRS. ELV.   I heard them talking about him in the boarding house,
just as I came in. And people are saying the most incredible things about
him today.

TES.   Yes, imagine! I heard that, too! And I can testify that he went
straight home to bed! Just think!

HED.   And what did they say in the boarding house?

MRS. ELV.   Oh, I didn't find out anything. Either they didn't know
any details or— They all became silent when they saw me. And I didn't
dare to ask.

TES. [*Pacing the floor uneasily*] We'll just have to hope—to hope that 160 you heard wrong, Mrs. Elvsted!

MRS. ELV. No, no. I'm sure it was he they were talking about. And somebody said something about the hospital or—

TES. The hospital—!

HED. Surely, that can't be so!

MRS. ELV. I got so terribly frightened! So I went up to his room and asked for him there.

HED. Could you bring yourself to do that, Thea?

MRS. ELV. What else could I do? For I felt I just couldn't stand the 170 uncertainty any longer.

TES. But I suppose you didn't find him in, either, did you? Hm?

MRS. ELV. No. And the people there didn't know anything about him. He hadn't been home since yesterday afternoon, they said.

TES. Yesterday! Just think! How could they say that!

MRS. ELV. I don't know what else *to* think—something bad must have happened to him!

TES. Hedda, dear—? What if I were to walk downtown and ask around for him—?

HED. No, no—don't you go and get mixed up in all this.

JUDGE BRACK, *hat in hand, enters through the door, right, which* BERTE *opens and closes for him. He looks serious and greets the others in silence.* 180

TES. So here you are, Judge, hm?

BRACK. Yes. I had to see you this evening.

TES. I can see you have got Aunt Julle's message.

BRACK. That, too—yes.

TES. Isn't it sad, though?

BRACK. Well, my dear Tesman—that depends on how you look at it.

TES. [*Looks at him uncertainly*] Has something else happened?

BRACK. Yes.

HED. [*Tense*] Something sad, Judge Brack?

BRACK. That, too, depends on how you look at it, Mrs. Tesman. 190

MRS. ELV. [*Bursting out*] Oh, I'm sure it has something to do with Eilert Løvborg!

BRACK. [*Looks at her for a moment*] Why do you think that, Mrs. Elvsted? Maybe you already know something—?

MRS. ELV. [*Confused*] No, no; not at all. It's just—

TES. For heaven's sake, Brack, out with it!

BRACK. [*Shrugging his shoulders*] Well—unfortunately, Eilert Løvborg's in the hospital. Dying.

MRS. ELV. [*Screams*] Oh God, oh God!

TES. In the hospital! And dying! 200

HED. [*Without thinking*] So soon—!

MRS. ELV. [*Wailing*] And we didn't even part as friends, Hedda!

HED. [*Whispers*] Thea, Thea—for heaven's sake—!

MRS. ELV. [*Paying no attention to her*] I want to see him! I want to see him alive!

BRACK. Won't do you any good, Mrs. Elvsted. Nobody can see him.

MRS. ELV. Then tell me what's happened to him! What?

TES. For, surely, he hasn't himself—!

HED. I'm sure he has.

210 TES. Hedda! How can you—!

BRACK. [*Observing her all this time*] I am sorry to say that your guess is absolutely correct, Mrs. Tesman.

MRS. ELV. Oh, how awful!

TES. Did it himself! Just think!

HED. Shot himself!

BRACK. Right again, Mrs. Tesman.

MRS. ELV. [*Trying to pull herself together*] When did this happen, Judge?

BRACK. This afternoon. Between three and four.

TES. But dear me—where can he have done a thing like that? Hm?

220 BRACK. [*A little uncertain*] Where? Well—I suppose in his room. I don't really know—

MRS. ELV. No, it can't have been there. For I was up there sometime between six and seven.

BRACK. Well, then, some other place. I really can't say. All I know is that he was found. He had shot himself—in the chest.

MRS. ELV. Oh, how horrible to think! That he was to end like that!

HED. [*To Brack*] In the chest?

BRACK. Yes—as I just told you.

HED. Not in the temple?

230 BRACK. In the chest, Mrs. Tesman.

HED. Well, well—the chest is a good place, too.

BRACK. How is that, Mrs. Tesman?

HED. [*Turning him aside*] Oh—nothing.

TES. And you say the wound is fatal? Hm?

BRACK. No doubt about it—absolutely fatal. He's probably dead already.

MRS. ELV. Yes, yes! I feel you're right! It's over! It's all over! Oh, Hedda!

TES. But tell me—how do *you* know all this?

240 BRACK. [*Tersely*] A man on the force told me. One I had some business with.

HED. [*Loudly*] At last a deed!

TES. [*Appalled*] Oh dear—what are you saying, Hedda!

HED. I am saying there is beauty in this.

BRACK. Well, now—Mrs. Tesman—

TES. Beauty—! Just think!

Mrs. Elv.   Oh, Hedda—how can you talk about beauty in a thing like this!

Hed.   Eilert Løvborg has settled his account with himself. He has had the courage to do—what had to be done.   250

Mrs. Elv.   But you mustn't believe it happened that way! He did it when he was not himself!

Tes.   In despair! That's how!

Hed.   He did not. I am certain of that.

Mrs. Elv.   Yes he did! He was not himself! That's the way he tore up the book, too!

Brack.   [*Puzzled*]   The book? You mean the manuscript? Has he torn it up?

Mrs. Elv.   Yes, last night.

Tes.   [*Whispers*]   Oh, Hedda—we'll never get clear of all this!   260

Brack.   That is strange.

Tes.   [*Walking the floor*]   To think that this was to be the end of Eilert! Not to leave behind him anything that would have preserved his name—

Mrs. Elv.   Oh, if only it could be put together again!

Tes.   Yes, if only it could. I don't know what I wouldn't give—

Mrs. Elv.   Maybe it can, Mr. Tesman.

Tes.   What do you mean?

Mrs. Elv.   [*Searching her dress pocket*]   Look. I have kept these little slips he dictated from.

Hed.   [*A step closer*]   Ah—!   270

Tes.   You've kept them, Mrs. Elvsted? Hm?

Mrs. Elv.   Yes. Here they are. I took them with me when I left. And I've had them in my pocket ever since—

Tes.   Please, let me see—

Mrs. Elv.   [*Gives him a pile of small paper slips*]   But it's such a mess. Without any kind of system or order—!

Tes.   But just think if we could make sense out of them, all the same! Perhaps if we helped each other—

Mrs. Elv.   Oh yes! Let's try, anyway!

Tes.   It will work! It *has* to work! I'll stake my whole life on this!   280

Hed.   You, Jørgen? Your life?

Tes.   Yes, or at any rate all the time I can set aside. My own collections can wait. Hedda, you understand—don't you? Hm? This is something I owe Eilert's memory.

Hed.   Maybe so.

Tes.   And now, my dear Mrs. Elvsted, we want to get to work. Good heavens, there's no point brooding over what's happened. Hm? We'll just have to acquire sufficient peace of mind to—

Mrs. Elv.   All right, Mr. Tesman. I'll try to do my best.

Tes.   Very well, then. Come over here. Let's look at these slips right   290 away. Where can we sit? Here? No, it's better in the other room. If you'll excuse us, Judge! Come along, Mrs. Elvsted.

MRS. ELV.   Oh dear God—if only it were possible—

TESMAN *and* MRS. ELVSTED *go into the inner room. She takes off her hat and coat. Both sit down at the table under the hanging lamp and absorb themselves in eager study of the slips.* HEDDA *walks over toward the stove and sits down in the easy chair. After a while,* BRACK *walks over to her.*

HED.   [*In a low voice*]   Ah, Judge—what a liberation there is in this thing with Eilert Løvborg!

BRACK.   Liberation, Mrs. Tesman? Well, yes, for him perhaps one may say there was liberation of a kind—

HED.   I mean for me. There is liberation in knowing that there is such a thing in the world as an act of free courage. Something which becomes
300 beautiful by its very nature.

BRACK.   [*Smiles*]   Well—dear Mrs. Tesman—

HED.   Oh I know what you're going to say! For you see—you really are a kind of specialist, too!

BRACK.   [*Looks at her fixedly*]   Eilert Løvborg has meant more to you than perhaps you're willing to admit, even to yourself. Or am I wrong?

HED.   I won't answer such questions. All I know is that Eilert Løvborg had the courage to live his own life. And then now—this—magnificence! The beauty of it! Having the strength and the will to get up and leave life's feast—so early—
310 BRACK.   Believe me, Mrs. Tesman, this pains me, but I see it is necessary that I destroy a pretty illusion—

HED.   An illusion?

BRACK.   Which could not have been maintained very long, anyway.

HED.   And what is that?

BRACK.   He didn't shoot himself—of his own free will.

HED.   Not of his own—!

BRACK.   No. To tell the truth, the circumstances of Eilert Løvborg's death aren't exactly what I said they were.

HED.   [*Tense*]   You've held something back? What?
320 BRACK.   For the sake of poor Mrs. Elvsted I used a few euphemisms.

HED.   What?

BRACK.   First—he is already dead.

HED.   In the hospital.

BRACK.   Yes. And without regaining consciousness.

HED.   What else haven't you told?

BRACK.   The fact that it didn't happen in his room.

HED.   Well, does that really make much difference?

BRACK.   Some. You see—Eilert Løvborg was found shot in Miss Diana's bedroom.

HED. [*Is about to jump up, but sinks back*] That's impossible, Judge 330
Brack! He can't have been there again today!

BRACK. He was there this afternoon. He came to claim something he said they had taken from him. Spoke some gibberish about a lost child—

HED. So that's why—!

BRACK. I thought maybe he meant his manuscript. But now I hear he has destroyed that himself. So I suppose it must have been something else.

HED. I suppose. So it was there—so they found him there?

BRACK. Yes. With a fired gun in his pocket. Mortally wounded.

HED. Yes—in the chest. 340

BRACK. No—in the guts.

HED. [*Looks at him with an expression of disgust*] That, too! What is this curse that turns everything I touch into something ludicrous and low!

BRACK. There is something else, Mrs. Tesman. Something I'd call— nasty.

HED. And what is that?

BRACK. The gun they found—

HED. [*Breathless*] What about it?

BRACK. He must have stolen it.

HED. [*Jumps up*] Stolen! That's not true! He didn't! 350

BRACK. Anything else is impossible. He *must* have stolen it. —Shhh!

TESMAN *and* MRS. ELVSTED *have risen from the table and come forward into the front room.*

TES. [*With papers in both hands*] D'you know, Hedda—you can hardly see in there with that lamp! Just think!

HED. I am thinking.

TES. I wonder if you'd let us use your desk, hm?

HED. Certainly, if you like. [*Adds quickly*] Wait a minute, though! Let me clear it off a bit first.

TES. Ah, there's no need for that, Hedda. There's plenty of room.

HED. No, no. I want to straighten it up. Carry all this in here. I'll put it on top of the piano for the time being.

She has pulled an object, covered by note paper, out of the bookcase. She puts several other sheets of paper on top of it and carries the whole pile into the left part of the inner room. TESMAN puts the papers down on the desk and moves the lamp from the corner table over to the desk. He and MRS. ELVSTED sit down and resume their work. HEDDA returns. 360

HED. [*Behind Mrs. Elvsted's chair, softly ruffling her hair*] Well, little Thea—how is Eilert Løvborg's memorial coming along?

MRS. ELV. [*Looks up at her, discouraged*] Oh God—I'm sure it's going to be terribly hard to make anything out of all this.

TES. But we have to. We just don't have a choice. And putting other people's papers in order—that's just the thing for me.

HEDDA *walks over to the stove and sits down on one of the ottomans.* BRACK *stands over her, leaning on the easy chair.*

HED. [*Whispers*] What were you saying about the gun?

BRACK. [*Also softly*] That he must have stolen it.

HED. Why, necessarily?

370 BRACK. Because any other explanation ought to be out of the question, Mrs. Tesman.

HED. Oh?

BRACK. [*Looks at her for a moment*] Eilert Løvborg was here this morning, of course. Isn't that so?

HED. Yes.

BRACK. Were you alone with him?

HED. Yes, for a while.

BRACK. You didn't leave the room while he was here?

HED. No.

380 BRACK. Think. Not at all? Not even for a moment?

HED. Well—maybe just for a moment—out in the hall.

BRACK. And where was the gun case?

HED. In the—

BRACK. Mrs. Tesman?

HED. On the desk.

BRACK. Have you looked to see if both guns are still there?

HED. No.

BRACK. You needn't bother. I saw the gun they found on Løvborg, and I knew it immediately. From yesterday—and from earlier occasions,
390 too.

HED. Perhaps you have it?

BRACK. No, the police do.

HED. What are the police going to do with it?

BRACK. Try to find the owner.

HED. Do you think they will?

BRACK. [*Leans over her, whispers*] No, Hedda Gabler—not as long as I keep quiet.

HED. [*With a hunted look*] And if you don't?

BRACK. [*Shrugs his shoulders*] Of course, there's always the chance that
400 the gun was stolen.

HED. [*Firmly*] Rather die!

BRACK. [*Smiles*] People *say* things like that. They don't *do* them.

HED. [*Without answering*] And if the gun was not stolen—and if they find the owner—then what happens?

BRACK. Well, Hedda—then comes the scandal!

HED. The scandal!

BRACK. Yes—the scandal. That you are so afraid of. You will of course be required to testify. Both you and Miss Diana. Obviously, she'll

Henrik Ibsen   473

have to explain how the whole thing happened. Whether it was accident or homicide. Did he try to pull the gun out of his pocket to threaten her? 410 And did it fire accidentally? Or did she grab the gun away from him, shoot him, and put it back in his pocket? She might just possibly have done that. She's a pretty tough girl—Miss Diana.

HED. But this whole disgusting affair has nothing to do with me.

BRACK. Quite so. But you'll have to answer the question: Why did you give Eilert Løvborg the gun? And what inferences will be drawn from the fact that you did?

HED. [*Lowers her head*] That's true. I hadn't thought of that.

BRACK. Well—luckily, there's nothing to worry about as long as I don't say anything. 420

HED. [*Looks up at him*] So then I'm in your power, Judge. From now on you can do anything you like with me.

BRACK. [*In an even softer whisper*] Dearest Hedda—believe me, I'll not misuse my position.

HED. In your power, all the same. Dependent on your will. Servant to your demands. Not free. Not free! [*Rises suddenly*] No—I can't stand that thought! Never!

BRACK. [*Looks at her, half mockingly*] Most people submit to the inevitable.

HED. [*Returning his glance*] Perhaps. [*Walks over to the desk. Suppresses* 430 *a smile and mimics Tesman's way of speaking*] Well? Do you think you can do it, Jørgen? Hm?

TES. Lord knows, Hedda. Anyway, I can already see it will take months.

HED. [*Still mimicking*] Just think! [*Runs her hands lightly through Mrs. Elvsted's hair*] Doesn't this seem strange to you, Thea? Sitting here with Tesman—just the way you used to with Eilert Løvborg?

MRS. ELV. Oh dear—if only I could inspire your husband, too!

HED. Oh, I'm sure that will come—in time.

TES. Well, yes—do you know, Hedda? I really think I begin to feel 440 something of the kind. But why don't you go and talk to the Judge again.

HED. Isn't there anything you two can use me for?

TES. No, not a thing, dear. [*Turns around*] From now on, you must be good enough to keep Hedda company, my dear Judge!

BRACK. [*Glancing at Hedda*] I'll be only too delighted.

HED. Thank you. But I'm tired tonight. I think I'll go and lie down for a while on the sofa in there.

TES. Yes, you do that, dear; why don't you? Hm?

HEDDA *goes into the inner room, closes the portieres behind her. Brief pause. Suddenly, she is heard playing a frenzied dance tune on the piano.*

MRS. ELV. [*Jumps up*] Oh God! What's that!

TES. [*Running to the doorway*] But dearest Hedda—you mustn't play 450 dance music tonight, for goodness' sake! Think of Aunt Rina! And Eilert, too!

HED. [*Peeks in from between the portieres*] And Aunt Julle. And everybody. I'll be quiet. [*She pulls the portieres shut again.*]

TES. [*Back at the desk*] I don't think it's good for her to see us at such a melancholy task. I'll tell you what, Mrs. Elvsted. You move in with Aunt Julle, and then I'll come over in the evenings. Then we can sit and work over there. Hm?

MRS. ELV. Maybe that would be better—

460 HED. [*From the inner room*] I hear every word you're saying, Tesman. And how am I going to spend my evenings?

TES. [*Busy with the papers*] Oh, I'm sure Judge Brack will be good enough to come out and see you, anyway.

BRACK. [*In the easy chair, calls out gaily*] Every single night, as far as I'm concerned, Mrs. Tesman! I'm sure we're going to have a lovely time, you and I!

HED. [*Loud and clear*] Yes, don't you think that would be nice, Judge Brack? You—sole cock-o'-the walk—

A shot is heard from the inner room. TESMAN, *Mrs.* ELVSTED, *and* JUDGE BRACK *all jump up.*

TES. There she is, fooling with those guns again.

He pulls the portieres apart and runs inside. MRS. ELVSTED *also.* HEDDA, *lifeless, is lying on the sofa. Cries and confusion.* BERTE, *flustered, enters, right.*

470 TES. [*Shouts to Brack*] She's shot herself! In the temple! Just think!

BRACK. [*Half stunned in the easy chair*] But, merciful God—! People don't *do* things like that!

1897-
THORNTON
WILDER * *The Skin of Our Teeth*

CHARACTERS

ANNOUNCER
SABINA (*or* MISS SOMERSET)
MR. FITZPATRICK (*or* VOICE *or* STAGE MANAGER)
MRS. ANTROBUS
DINOSAUR
TELEGRAPH BOY
MAMMOTH
GLADYS
HENRY
MR. ANTROBUS
REFUGEES ⎫
DOCTOR ⎪
PROFESSOR ⎪
JUDGE (*or* MOSES) ⎬ Guests
HOMER ⎪
MISS E. MUSE ⎪
MISS T. MUSE ⎪
MISS M. MUSE ⎭
USHERS
NEGROES (*or* CHAIR PUSHERS)
CONVEENERS
FORTUNE TELLER
BINGO CALLER (*or* VOICE FROM THE BINGO PARLOR)
· CHORUS
BROADCAST OFFICIAL
ACTORS
MR. TREMAYNE
HESTER
IVY
FRED BAILEY
BABY

Act I

SCENE. *Home, Excelsior, New Jersey.*

A projection screen in the middle of the curtain. The first lantern slide: the name of the theatre, and the words: NEWS EVENTS OF THE WORLD. An ANNOUNCER'S *voice is heard.*

ANN. The management takes pleasure in bringing to you—The News Events of the World:

Slide of the sun appearing above the horizon.

Freeport, Long Island:

The sun rose this morning at 6:32 a.m. This gratifying event was first reported by Mrs. Dorothy Stetson of Freeport, Long Island, who promptly telephoned the Mayor.

The Society for Affirming the End of the World at once went into a special session and postponed the arrival of that event for TWENTY-FOUR HOURS. All honor to Mrs. Stetson for her public spirit.

10 New York City:

Slide of the front doors of the theatre in which this play is playing; three cleaning WOMEN *with mops and pails.*

The X Theatre. During the daily cleaning of this theatre a number of lost objects were collected as usual by Mesdames Simpson, Pateslewski, and Moriarty.

Among these objects found today was a wedding ring, inscribed: To Eva from Adam. Genesis II: 18. The ring will be restored to the owner or owners, if their credentials are satisfactory.

Tippehatchee, Vermont:

Slide representing a glacier.

The unprecedented cold weather of this summer has produced a condition that has not yet been satisfactorily explained. There is a report that
20 a wall of ice is moving southward across these counties. The disruption of communications by the cold wave now crossing the country has rendered exact information difficult, but little credence is given to the rumor that the ice had pushed the Cathedral of Montreal as far as St. Albans, Vermont.

For further information see your daily papers.

Excelsior, New Jersey:

Slide of a modest suburban home.

The home of Mr. George Antrobus, the inventor of the wheel. The discovery of the wheel, following so closely on the discovery of the lever, has centered the attention of the country on Mr. Antrobus of this attractive
30 suburban residence district. This is his home, a commodious seven-room house, conveniently situated near a public school, a Methodist church, and a firehouse; it is right handy to an A. and P.

Slide of MR. ANTROBUS *on his front steps, smiling and lifting his straw hat. He holds a wheel.*

Mr. Antrobus, himself. He comes of very old stock and has made his way up from next to nothing.

It is reported that he was once a gardener, but left that situation under circumstances that have been variously reported.

Mr. Antrobus is a veteran of foreign wars, and bears a number of scars, front and back.

Slide of Mrs. ANTROBUS, *holding some roses.*

This is Mrs. Antrobus, the charming and gracious president of the Excelsior Mothers' Club. 40

Mrs. Antrobus is an excellent needlewoman; it is she who invented the apron on which so many interesting changes have been rung since.

Slide of the FAMILY *and* SABINA.

Here we see the Antrobuses with their two children, Henry and Gladys, and friend. The friend in the rear, is Lily Sabina, the maid.

I know we all want to congratulate this typical American family on its enterprise. We all wish Mr. Antrobus a successful future. Now the management takes you to the interior of this home for a brief visit.

Curtain rises. Living room of a commuter's home. SABINA—*straw-blonde, over-rouged—is standing by the window back center, a feather duster under her elbow.*

SAB. Oh, oh, oh! Six o'clock and the master not home yet.

Pray God nothing serious has happened to him crossing the Hudson River. If anything happened to him, we would certainly be inconsolable 50 and have to move into a less desirable residence district.

The fact is I don't know what'll become of us. Here it is the middle of August and the coldest day of the year. It's simply freezing; the dogs are sticking to the sidewalks; can anybody explain that? No.

But I'm not surprised. The whole world's at sixes and sevens, and why the house hasn't fallen down about our ears long ago is a miracle to me.

A fragment of the right wall leans precariously over the stage. SABINA *looks at it nervously and it slowly rights itself.*

Every night this same anxiety as to whether the master will get home safely: whether he'll bring home anything to eat. In the midst of life we are in the midst of death, a truer word was never said.

The fragment of scenery flies up into the lofts. SABINA *is struck dumb with surprise, shrugs her shoulders and starts dusting* MR. ANTROBUS' *chair, including the under side.*

Of course, Mr. Antrobus is a very fine man, an excellent husband and 60 father, a pillar of the church, and has all the best interests of the community at heart. Of course, every muscle goes tight every time he passes a policeman; but what I think is that there are certain charges that ought not to be made, and I think I may add, ought not to be allowed to be made; we're all human; who isn't?

She dusts MRS. ANTROBUS' *rocking chair.*

Mrs. Antrobus is as fine a woman as you could hope to see. She lives only

for her children; and if it would be any benefit to her children she'd see the rest of us stretched out dead at her feet without turning a hair,— that's the truth. If you want to know anything more about Mrs. Antro-
70 bus, just go and look at a tigress, and look hard.

As to the children—

Well, Henry Antrobus is a real, clean-cut American boy. He'll graduate from High School one of these days, if they make the alphabet any easier.

—Henry, when he has a stone in his hand, has a perfect aim; he can hit anything from a bird to an older brother—Oh! I didn't mean to say that! —but it certainly was an unfortunate accident, and it was very hard getting the police out of the house.

Mr. and Mrs. Antrobus' daughter is named Gladys. She'll make some good man a good wife some day, if he'll just come down off the movie
80 screen and ask her.

So here we are!

We've managed to survive for some time now, catch as catch can, the fat and the lean, and if the dinosaurs don't trample us to death, and if the grasshoppers don't eat up our garden, we'll all live to see better days, knock on wood.

Each new child that's born to the Antrobuses seems to them to be suffi-cient reason for the whole universe's being set in motion; and each new child that dies seems to them to have been spared a whole world of sor-row, and what the end of it will be is still very much an open question.
90 We've rattled along, hot and cold, for some time now—

A portion of the wall above the door, right, flies up into the air and disappears.

—and my advice to you is not to inquire into why or whither, but just enjoy your ice cream while it's on your plate,—that's my philosophy. Don't forget that a few years ago we came through the depression by the skin of our teeth! One more tight squeeze like that and where will we be?

This is a cue line. Sabina *looks angrily at the kitchen door and repeats.*

. . . we came through the depression by the skin of our teeth; one more tight squeeze like that and where will we be?

Flustered, she looks through the opening in the right wall; then goes to the window and reopens the Act.

Oh, oh, oh! Six o'clock and the master not home yet. Pray God nothing has happened to him crossing the Hudson. Here it is the middle of August and the coldest day of the year. It's simply freezing; the dogs are sticking.
100 One more tight squeeze like that and where will we be?

Voice. [*Off stage*] Make up something! Invent something!

Sab. Well . . . uh . . . this certainly is a fine American home . . . and— uh . . . everybody's very happy . . . and—uh . . .

Suddenly flings pretense to the winds and coming downstage says with indignation:

I can't invent any words for this play, and I'm glad I can't. I hate this play and every word in it.

Thornton Wilder 479

As for me, I don't understand a single word of it, anyway,—all about the troubles the human race has gone through, there's a subject for you. Besides the author hasn't made up his silly mind as to whether we're all living back in caves or in New Jersey today, and that's the way it is all the way through. 110

Oh—why can't we have plays like we used to have—*Peg o' My Heart*, and *Smilin' Thru*, and *The Bat*, good entertainment with a message you can take home with you?

I took this hateful job because I had to. For two years I've sat up in my room living on a sandwich and a cup of tea a day, waiting for better times in the theatre. And look at me now: I—I who've played *Rain* and the *Barretts of Wimpole Street* and *First Lady*—God in Heaven!

The STAGE MANAGER puts his head out from the hole in the scenery.

MR. FITZ.   Miss Somerset!! Miss Somerset!

SAB.   Oh! Anyway!—nothing matters! It'll all be the same in a hundred years. 120

[*Loudly*] We came through the depression by the skin of our teeth,—that's true!—one more tight squeeze like that and where will we be?

Enter MRS. ANTROBUS, a mother.

MRS. A.   Sabina, you've let the fire go out.

SAB.   [*In a lather*]   One-thing-and-another; don't-know-whether-my-wits-are-upside-or-down; might-as-well-be-dead-as-alive-in-a-house-all-sixes-and-sevens. . . .

MRS. A.   You've let the fire go out. Here it is the coldest day of the year right in the middle of August, and you've let the fire go out.

SAB.   Mrs. Antrobus, I'd like to give my two weeks' notice, Mrs. Antrobus. A girl like I can get a situation in a home where they're rich 130 enough to have a fire in every room, Mrs. Antrobus, and a girl don't have to carry the responsibility of the whole house on her two shoulders. And a home without children, Mrs. Antrobus, because children are a thing only a parent can stand, and a truer word was never said; and a home, Mrs. Antrobus, where the master of the house don't pinch decent, self-respecting girls when he meets them in a dark corridor. I mention no names and make no charges. So you have my notice, Mrs. Antrobus. I hope that's perfectly clear.

MRS. A.   You've let the fire go out!—Have you milked the mammoth?

SAB.   I don't understand a word of this play.—Yes, I've milked the 140 mammoth.

MRS. A.   Until Mr. Antrobus comes home we have no food and we have no fire. You'd better go over to the neighbors and borrow some fire.

SAB.   Mrs. Antrobus! I can't! I'd die on the way, you know I would. It's worse than January. The dogs are sticking to the sidewalks. I'd die.

MRS. A.   Very well, I'll go.

SAB.   [*Even more distraught, coming forward and sinking on her knees*]   You'd

never come back alive; we'd all perish; if you weren't here, we'd just perish. How do we know Mr. Antrobus'll be back? We don't know. If you
150 go out, I'll just kill myself.

MRS. A.   Get up, Sabina.

SAB.   Every night it's the same thing. Will he come back safe, or won't he? Will we starve to death, or freeze to death, or boil to death or will we be killed by burglars? I don't know why we go on living. I don't know why we go on living at all. It's easier being dead.

She flings her arms on the table and buries her head in them. In each of the succeeding speeches she flings her head up—and sometimes her hands—then quickly buries her head again.

MRS. A.   The same thing! Always throwing up the sponge, Sabina. Always announcing your own death. But give you a new hat—or a plate of ice cream—or a ticket to the movies, and you want to live forever.

SAB.   You don't care whether we live or die; all you care about is those
160 children. If it would be any benefit to them you'd be glad to see us all stretched out dead.

MRS. A.   Well, maybe I would.

SAB.   And what do they care about? Themselves—that's all they care about.

[Shrilly] They make fun of you behind your back. Don't tell me: they're ashamed of you. Half the time, they pretend they're someone else's children. Little thanks you get from them.

MRS. A.   I'm not asking for any thanks.

SAB.   And Mr. Antrobus—you don't understand *him*. All that work
170 he does—trying to discover the alphabet and the multiplication table. Whenever he tries to learn anything you fight against it.

MRS. A.   Oh, Sabina, I know you.

When Mr. Antrobus raped you home from your Sabine hills, he did it to insult me.

He did it for your pretty face, and to insult me.

You were the new wife, weren't you?

For a year or two you lay on your bed all day and polished the nails on your hands and feet:

You made puff-balls of the combings of your hair and you blew them up
180 to the ceiling.

And I washed your underclothes and I made you chicken broths.

I bore children and between my very groans I stirred the cream that you'd put on your face.

But I knew you wouldn't last.

You didn't last.

SAB.   But it was I who encouraged Mr. Antrobus to make the alphabet. I'm sorry to say it, Mrs. Antrobus, but you're not a beautiful woman, and you can never know what a man could do if he tried. It's girls like

Thornton Wilder   481

I who inspire the multiplication table.
I'm sorry to say it, but you're not a beautiful woman, Mrs. Antrobus, 190
and that's the God's truth.

Mrs. A. And you didn't last—you sank to the kitchen. And what
do you do there? *You let the fire go out!*
No wonder to you it seems easier being dead.
Reading and writing and counting on your fingers is all very well in their
way,—but I keep the home going.

Mrs. A. —There's that dinosaur on the front lawn again. —Shoo!
Go away. Go away.
The baby Dinosaur *puts his head in the window.*

Din. It's cold.

Mrs. A. You go around to the back of the house where you belong. 200

Din. It's cold.

The Dinosaur *disappears.* Mrs. Antrobus *goes calmly out.* Sabina *slowly
raises her head and speaks to the audience. The central portion of the center wall
rises, pauses, and disappears into the loft.*

Sab. Now that you audience are listening to this, too, I understand
it a little better.
I wish eleven o'clock were here; I don't want to be dragged through this
whole play again.
The Telegraph Boy *is seen entering along the back wall of the stage from the
right. She catches sight of him and calls:*
Mrs. Antrobus! Mrs. Antrobus! Help! There's a strange man coming to
the house. He's coming up the walk, help!
Enter Mrs. Antrobus *in alarm, but efficient.*

Mrs. A. Help me quick!
They barricade the door by piling the furniture against it.
Who is it? What do you want?

T. Boy. A telegram for Mrs. Antrobus from Mr. Antrobus in the city. 210

Sab. Are you sure, are you sure? Maybe it's just a trap!

Mrs. A. I know his voice, Sabina. We can open the door.
Enter the Telegraph Boy, *12 years old, in uniform. The* Dinosaur *and* Mam-
moth *slip by him into the room and settle down front right.*
I'm sorry we kept you waiting. We have to be careful, you know.
[*To the Animals*] Hm! . . . Will you be quiet? [*They nod.*
Have you had your supper? [*They nod.*
Are you *ready* to come in? [*They nod.*
Young man, have you any fire with you? Then light the grate, will you?
*He nods, produces something like a briquet; and kneels by the imagined fireplace,
footlights center. Pause.*
What are people saying about this cold weather?
He makes a doubtful shrug with his shoulders.
Sabina, take this stick and go and light the stove.

220 SAB. Like I told you, Mrs. Antrobus; two weeks. That's the law. I hope that's perfectly clear. [Exit.

MRS. A. What about this cold weather?

T. BOY. [Lowered eyes] Of course, I don't know anything . . . but they say there's a wall of ice moving down from the North, that's what they say. We can't get Boston by telegraph, and they're burning pianos in Hartford.

. . . It moves everything in front of it, churches and post offices and city halls.

I live in Brooklyn myself.

230 MRS. A. What are people doing about it?

T. BOY. Well . . . uh . . . Talking, mostly.

Or just what you'd do a day in February.

There are some that are trying to go South and the roads are crowded; but you can't take old people and children very far in a cold like this.

MRS. A. —What's this telegram you have for me?

T. BOY. [Fingertips to his forehead] If you wait just a minute; I've got to remember it.

The ANIMALS *have left their corner and are nosing him. Presently they take places on either side of him, leaning against his hips, like heraldic beasts.*

This telegram was flashed from Murray Hill to University Heights! And then by puffs of smoke from University Heights to Staten Island.

240 And then by lantern from Staten Island to Plainfield, New Jersey. What hath God wrought! [He clears his throat.

"To Mrs. Antrobus, Excelsior, New Jersey:

My dear wife, will be an hour late. Busy day at the office.

Don't worry the children about the cold just keep them warm burn everything except Shakespeare." [Pause.

MRS. A. Men! —He knows I'd burn ten Shakespeares to prevent a child of mine from having one cold in the head. What does it say next? *Enter* SABINA.

T. BOY. "Have made great discoveries today have separated em from en."

250 SAB. I know what that is, that's the alphabet, yes it is. Mr. Antrobus is just the cleverest man. Why, when the alphabet's finished, we'll be able to tell the future and everything.

T. BOY. Then listen to this: "Ten tens make a hundred semi-colon consequences far-reaching." [Watches for effect.

MRS. A. The earth's turning to ice, and all he can do is to make up new numbers.

T. BOY. Well, Mrs. Antrobus, like the head man at our office said: a few more discoveries like that and we'll be worth freezing.

MRS. A. What does he say next?

260 T. BOY. I . . . I can't do this last part very well.

Thornton Wilder   483

He clears his throat and sings.
"Happy w'dding ann'vers'ry to you, Happy ann'vers'ry to you—"
The ANIMALS *begin to howl soulfully;* SABINA *screams with pleasure.*

MRS. A.   Dolly! Frederick! Be quiet.

T. BOY.   [*Above the din*]   "Happy w'dding ann'vers'ry, dear Eva; happy w'dding ann'vers'ry to you."

MRS. A.   Is that in the telegram? Are they singing telegrams now?
He nods.
The earth's getting so silly no wonder the sun turns cold.

SAB.   Mrs. Antrobus, I want to take back the notice I gave you. Mrs. Antrobus, I don't want to leave a house that gets such interesting telegrams and I'm sorry for anything I said. I really am.

MRS. A.   Young man, I'd like to give you something for all this 270 trouble; Mr. Antrobus isn't home yet and I have no money and no food in the house—

T. BOY.   Mrs. Antrobus . . . I don't like to . . . appear to . . . ask for anything, but . . .

MRS. A.   What is it you'd like?

T. BOY.   Do you happen to have an old needle you could spare? My wife just sits home all day thinking about needles.

SAB.   [*Shrilly*]   We only got two in the house. Mrs. Antrobus, you know we only got two in the house.

MRS. A.   [*After a look at Sabina, taking a needle from her collar*]   Why yes, 280 I can spare this.

T. BOY.   [*Lowered eyes*]   Thank you, Mrs. Antrobus. Mrs. Antrobus, can I ask you something else? I have two sons of my own; if the cold gets worse, what should I do?

SAB.   I think we'll all perish, that's what I think. Cold like this in August is just the end of the whole world.   [*Silence.*

MRS. A.   I don't know. After all, what does one do about anything? Just keep as warm as you can. And don't let your wife and children see that you're worried.

T. BOY.   Yes. . . . Thank you, Mrs. Antrobus. Well, I'd better be 290 going. —Oh, I forgot! There's one more sentence in the telegram. "Three cheers have invented the wheel."

MRS. A.   A wheel? What's a wheel?

T. BOY.   I don't know. That's what it said. The sign for it is like this. Well, goodbye.

The WOMEN *see him to the door, with goodbyes and injunctions to keep warm.*

SAB.   [*Apron to her eyes, wailing*]   Mrs. Antrobus, it looks to me like all the nice men in the world are already married; I don't know why that is.
   [*Exit.*

MRS. A.   [*Thoughtful; to the Animals*]   Do you ever remember hearing

tell of any cold like this in August? [*The Animals shake their heads.*
300 From your grandmothers or anyone? [*They shake their heads.*
Have you any suggestions? [*They shake their heads.*
She pulls her shawl around, goes to the front door and opening it an inch calls:
HENRY. GLADYS. CHILDREN. Come right in and get warm.
No, no, when mama says a thing she means it.
Henry! HENRY. Put down that stone. You know what happened last
time.
[*Shriek*] HENRY! Put down that stone!
Gladys! Put down your dress!! Try and be a lady.
The CHILDREN *bound in and dash to the fire. They take off their winter things and
leave them in heaps on the floor.*
GLAD. Mama, I'm hungry. Mama, why is it so cold?
HEN. [*At the same time*] Mama, why doesn't it snow? Mama, when's
310 supper ready? Maybe, it'll snow and we can make snowballs.
GLAD. Mama, it's so cold that in one more minute I just couldn't of
stood it.
MRS. A. Settle down, both of you, I want to talk to you.
*She draws up a hassock and sits front center over the orchestra pit before the im-
aginary fire. The* CHILDREN *stretch out on the floor, leaning against her lap.
Tableau by Raphael. The* ANIMALS *edge up and complete the triangle.*
It's just a cold spell of some kind. Now listen to what I'm saying:
When your father comes home I want you to be extra quiet. He's had a
hard day at the office and I don't know but what he may have one of his
moods.
I just got a telegram from him very happy and excited, and you know
what that means. Your father's temper's uneven; I guess you know that.
Shriek.
320 Henry! Henry!
Why—why can't you remember to keep your hair down over your forehead? You must keep that scar covered up. Don't you know that when
your father sees it he loses all control over himself? He goes crazy. He
wants to die.
*After a moment's despair she collects herself decisively, wets the hem of her apron
in her mouth and starts polishing his forehead vigorously.*
Lift your head up. Stop squirming. Blessed me, sometimes I think that
it's going away—and then there it is: just as red as ever.
HEN. Mama, today at school two teachers forgot and called me by
my old name. They forgot, Mama. You'd better write another letter to
the principal, so that he'll tell them I've changed my name. Right out
330 in class they called me: Cain.
MRS. A. [*Putting her hand on his mouth, too late; hoarsely*] Don't say it.
[*Polishing feverishly*] If you're good they'll forget it. Henry, you didn't
hit anyone . . . today, did you?

Thornton Wilder 485

Hen. Oh . . . no-o-o!

Mrs. A. [*Still working, not looking at Gladys*] And, Gladys, I want you to be especially nice to your father tonight. You know what he calls you when you're good—his little angel, his little star. Keep your dress down like a little lady. And keep your voice nice and low. Gladys Antrobus!! What's that red stuff you have on your face?

[*Slaps her*] You're a filthy detestable child!

Rises in real, though temporary, repudiation and despair.

Get away from me, both of you! I wish I'd never seen sight or sound of you. Let the cold come! I can't stand it. I don't want to go on.

She walks away.

Glad. [*Weeping*] All the girls at school do, Mama.

Mrs. A. [*Shrieking*] I'm through with you, that's all!—Sabina! Sabina!—Don't you know your father'd go crazy if he saw that paint on your face? Don't you know your father thinks you're perfect? Don't you know he couldn't live if he didn't think you were perfect?—Sabina!

Enter Sabina.

Sab. Yes, Mrs. Antrobus!

Mrs. A. Take this girl out into the kitchen and wash her face with the scrubbing brush.

Mr. A. [*Outside, roaring*] "I've been working on the railroad, all the livelong day . . . etc."

The Animals *start running around in circles, bellowing.* Sabina *rushes to the window.*

Mrs. A. Sabina, what's that noise outside?

Sab. Oh, it's a drunken tramp. It's a giant, Mrs. Antrobus. We'll all be killed in our beds, I know it!

Mrs. A. Help me quick. Quick. Everybody.

Again they stack all the furniture against the door. Mr. Antrobus *pounds and bellows.*

Who is it? What do you want?—Sabina, have you any boiling water ready?—Who is it?

Mr. A. Broken-down camel of a pig's snout, open this door.

Mrs. A. God be praised! It's your father.—Just a minute, George! —Sabina, clear the door, quick. Gladys, come here while I clean your nasty face!

Mr. A. She-bitch of a goat's gizzard, I'll break every bone in your body. Let me in or I'll tear the whole house down.

Mrs. A. Just a minute, George, something's the matter with the lock.

Mr. A. Open the door or I'll tear your livers out. I'll smash your brains on the ceiling, and Devil take the hindmost.

Mrs. A. Now, you can open the door, Sabina. I'm ready.

The door is flung open. Silence. Mr. Antrobus—*face of a Keystone Comedy Cop—stands there in fur cap and blanket. His arms are full of parcels, including a large stone wheel with a center in it. One hand carries a railroad man's lantern. Suddenly he bursts into joyous roar.*

MR. A. Well, how's the whole crooked family?

Relief. Laughter. Tears. Jumping up and down. ANIMALS *cavorting.* ANTROBUS *throws the parcels on the ground. Hurls his cap and blanket after them. Heroic embraces. Melee of* HUMANS *and* ANIMALS, SABINA *included.*

370 I'll be scalded and tárred if a man can't get a little welcome when he comes home. Well, Maggie, you old gunny-sack, how's the broken down old weather hen?—Sabina, old fishbait, old skunkpot.—And the children, —how've the little smellers been?

GLAD. Papa, Papa, Papa, Papa, Papa.

MR. A. How've they been, Maggie?

MRS. A. Well, I must say, they've been as good as gold. I haven't had to raise my voice once. I don't know what's the matter with them.

MR. A. [*Kneeling before Gladys*] Papa's little weasel, eh?—Sabina, there's some food for you.—Papa's little gopher?

380 GLAD. [*Her arm around his neck*] Papa, you're always teasing me.

MR. A. And Henry? Nothing rash today, I hope. Nothing rash?

HEN. No, Papa.

MR. A. [*Roaring*] Well that's good, that's good—I'll bet Sabina let the fire go out.

SAB. Mr. Antrobus, I've given my notice. I'm leaving two weeks from today. I'm sorry, but I'm leaving.

MR. A. [*Roar*] Well, if you leave now you'll freeze to death, so go and cook the dinner.

SAB. Two weeks, that's the law.   [*Exit.*

390 MR. A. Did you get my telegram?

MRS. A. Yes.—What's a wheel?

He indicates the wheel with a glance. HENRY *is rolling it around the floor. Rapid, hoarse interchange:* MRS. ANTROBUS: *What does this cold weather mean? It's below freezing.* ANTROBUS: *Not before the children!* MRS. ANTROBUS: *Shouldn't we do something about it?—start off, move?* ANTROBUS: *Not before the children!!!*
He gives HENRY *a sharp slap.*

HEN. Papa, you hit me!

MR. A. Well, remember it. That's to make you remember today. Today. The day the alphabet's finished; and the day that we *saw* the hundred—the hundred, the hundred, the hundred, the hundred, the hundred—there's no end to 'em.

I've had a day at the office!

Take a look at that wheel, Maggie—when I've got that to rights: you'll see a sight.

400 There's a reward there for all the walking you've done.

MRS. A. How do you mean?

MR. A. [*On the hassock looking into the fire; with awe*] Maggie, we've reached the top of the wave. There's not much more to be done. We're there!

MRS. A. [*Cutting across his mood sharply*]   And the ice?

MR. A.   The ice!

HEN. [*Playing with the wheel*]   Papa, you could put a chair on this.

MR. A. [*Broodingly*].   Ye-e-s, any booby can fool with it now,—but I thought of it first.

MRS. A.   Children, go out in the kitchen. I want to talk to your father 410 alone.

The CHILDREN *go out.* ANTROBUS *has moved to his chair up left. He takes the goldfish bowl on his lap; pulls the canary cage down to the level of his face. Both the* ANIMALS *put their paws up on the arm of his chair.* MRS. ANTROBUS *faces him across the room, like a judge.*

MRS. A.   Well?

MR. A. [*Shortly*]   It's cold.—How things been, eh? Keck, keck, keck.— And you, Millicent?

MRS. A.   I know it's cold.

MR. A. [*To the canary*]   No spilling of sunflower seed, eh? No singing after lights-out, y'know what I mean?

MRS. A.   You can try and prevent us freezing to death, can't you? You can do something? We can start moving. Or we can go on the animals' backs?   420

MR. A.   The best thing about animals is that they don't talk much.

MAMMOTH.   It's cold.

MR. A.   Eh, eh, eh! Watch that!—

—By midnight we'd turn to ice. The roads are full of people now who can scarcely lift a foot from the ground. The grass out in front is like iron,— which reminds me, I have another needle for you.—The people up north —where are they? Frozen . . . crushed. . . .

MRS. A.   Is that what's going to happen to us?—Will you answer me?

MR. A.   I don't know. I don't know anything. Some say that the ice is going slower. Some say that it's stopped. The sun's growing cold. What 430 can I do about that? Nothing we can do but burn everything in the house, and the fenceposts and the barn. Keep the fire going. When we have no more fire, we die.

MRS. A.   Well, why didn't you say so in the first place?

MRS. ANTROBUS *is about to march off when she catches sight of two* REFUGEES, *men, who have appeared against the back wall of the theatre and who are soon joined by others.*

REFS.   Mr. Antrobus! Mr. Antrobus! Mr. An-nn-tro-bus!

MRS. A.   Who's that? Who's that calling you?

MR. A. [*Clearing his throat guiltily*]   Hm—let me see.

Two REFUGEES *come up to the window.*

REF.   Could we warm our hands for a moment, Mr. Antrobus? It's very cold, Mr. Antrobus.

440   ANOTHER REF.   Mr. Antrobus, I wonder if you have a piece of bread or something that you could spare.

Silence. They wait humbly. MRS. ANTROBUS *stands rooted to the spot. Suddenly a knock at the door, then another hand knocking in short rapid blows.*

MRS. A.   Who are these people? Why, they're all over the front yard. What have they come *here* for?

Enter SABINA.

SAB.   Mrs. Antrobus! There are some tramps knocking at the back door.

MRS. A.   George, tell these people to go away. Tell them to move right along. I'll go and send them away from the back door. Sabina, come with me.   [*She goes out energetically.*

MR. A.   Sabina! Stay here! I have something to say to you.

He goes to the door and opens it a crack and talks through it.

450 Ladies and gentlemen! I'll have to ask you to wait a few minutes longer. It'll be all right . . . while you're waiting you might each one pull up a stake of the fence. We'll need them all for the fireplace. There'll be coffee and sandwiches in a moment.

SABINA *looks out door over his shoulder and suddenly extends her arm pointing, with a scream.*

SAB.   Mr. Antrobus, what's that??—that big white thing? Mr. Antrobus, it's ICE. It's ICE!!

MR. A.   Sabina, I want you to go in the kitchen and make a lot of coffee. Make a whole pail full.

SAB.   Pail full!!

MR. A.   [*With gesture*]   And sandwiches . . . piles of them . . . like this.

460   SAB.   Mr. An . . . !!

Suddenly she drops the play, and says in her own person as MISS SOMERSET, *with surprise.*

Oh, *I* see what this part of the play means now! This means refugees.

She starts to cross to the proscenium.

Oh, I don't like it. I don't like it.

She leans against the proscenium and bursts into tears.

MR. A.   Miss Somerset!

STG. MGR.   [*Off stage*]   Miss Somerset!

SAB.   [*Energetically, to the audience*]   Ladies and gentlemen! Don't take this play serious. The world's not coming to an end. You know it's not. People exaggerate! Most people really have enough to eat and a roof over their heads. Nobody actually starves—you can always eat grass or something. That ice-business—why, it was a long, long time ago. Besides

470 they were only savages. Savages don't love their families—not like we do.

Mr. A. *and* Stg. Mgr.   Miss Somerset!!
There is renewed knocking at the door.
Sab.   All right. I'll say the lines, but I won't think about the play.
Enter Mrs. Antrobus.
Sab. [*Parting thrust at the audience*]   And I advise *you* not to think about
the play, either.   [*Exit Sabina.*
Mrs. A.   George, these tramps say that you asked them to come to the
house. What does this mean?   [*Knocking at the door.*
Mr. A.   Just . . . uh. . . . There are a few friends, Maggie, I met on the
road. Real nice, real useful people. . . .
Mrs. A. [*Back to the door*]   Now, don't you ask them in!
George Antrobus, not another soul comes in here over my dead body.   480
Mr. A.   Maggie, there's a doctor there. Never hurts to have a good
doctor in the house. We've lost a peck of children, one way and another.
You can never tell when a child's throat will get stopped up. What you
and I have seen—!!!   [*He puts his fingers on his throat, and imitates diphtheria.*
Mrs. A.   Well, just one person then, the Doctor. The others can go
right along the road.
Mr. A.   Maggie, there's an old man, particular friend of mine—
Mrs. A.   I won't listen to you—
Mr. A.   It was he that really started off the A.B.C.'s.
Mrs. A.   I don't care if he perishes. We can do without reading or   490
writing. We can't do without food.
Mr. A.   Then let the ice come!! Drink your coffee!! I don't want any
coffee if I can't drink it with some good people.
Mrs. A.   Stop shouting. Who else is there trying to push us off the
cliff?
Mr. A.   Well, there's the man . . . who makes all the laws. Judge
Moses!
Mrs. A.   Judges can't help us now.
Mr. A.   And if the ice melts? . . . and if we pull through? Have you
and I been able to bring up Henry? What have we done?   500
Mrs. A.   Who are those old women?
Mr. A. [*Coughs*]   Up in town there are nine sisters. There are three or
four of them here. They're sort of music teachers . . . and one of them re-
cites and one of them—
Mrs. A.   That's the end. A singing troupe! Well, take your choice,
live or die. Starve your own children before your face.
Mr. A. [*Gently*]   These people don't take much. They're used to starving.
They'll sleep on the floor.
Besides, Maggie, listen: no, listen:
Who've we got in the house, but Sabina? Sabina's always afraid the worst   510
will happen. Whose spirits can she keep up? Maggie, these people never
give up. They think they'll live and work forever.

MRS. A. [*Walks slowly to the middle of the room*] All right, let them in. Let them in. You're master here.

[*Softly*]—But these animals must go. Enough's enough. They'll soon be big enough to push the walls down, anyway. Take them away.

MR. A. [*Sadly*] All right. The dinosaur and mammoth—! Come on, baby, come on Frederick. Come for a walk. That's a good little fellow.

DIN. It's cold.

520 MR. A. Yes, nice cold fresh air. Bracing.

He holds the door open and the ANIMALS *go out. He beckons to his friends. The* REFUGEES *are typical elderly out-of-works from the streets of New York today.* JUDGE MOSES *wears a skull cap.* HOMER *is a blind beggar with a guitar. The seedy crowd shuffles in and waits humbly and expectantly.* ANTROBUS *introduces them to his wife who bows to each with a stately bend of her head.*

Make yourself at home, Maggie, this the doctor . . . m . . . Coffee'll be here in a minute. . . . Professor, this is my wife. . . . And . . . Judge . . . Maggie, you know the Judge.

[*An old blind man with a guitar*] Maggie, you know . . . you know Homer? —Come right in, Judge.—Miss Muse—are some of your sisters here? Come right in. . . . Miss E. Muse, Miss T. Muse, Miss M. Muse.

MRS. A. Pleased to meet you.

Just . . . make yourself comfortable. Supper'll be ready in a minute.

[*She goes out, abruptly.*

MR. A. Make yourself at home, friends. I'll be right back. [*He goes out.* *The* REFUGEES *stare about them in awe. Presently several voices start whispering "Homer! Homer!" All take it up.* HOMER *strikes a chord or two on his guitar, then starts to speak.*

530 HOM. Μῆνιν ἄειδε, θεά, Πηληϊάδεω Ἀχιλῆος, οὐλομένην, ἥ μυρί' Ἀχαιοῖς ἄλγε' ἔθηκεν, πολλὰς δ' ἰφθίμους ψυχὰς —°

HOMER'S *face shows he is lost in thought and memory and the words die away on his lips. The* REFUGEES *likewise nod in dreamy recollection. Soon the whisper "Moses, Moses!" goes around. An aged Jew parts his beard and recites dramatically.*

MOS. ܀ܩܡ ܠܫܡ ܐܪܝܕ ܝܢܨ ܠܡܨ ܐܩܝܡܣ ܥܠܝܗܪ ܐܪܝܕ ܩܝܨ܀ ܩܝܪܣܠܘ ܠܨ ܐܩܝܨ ܨܘ ܠܩܥܝܨ ܠܝܨ ܠܨܝܠ܀ ܠܘܠܠ ܩܝܨ ܩܡܒ

The same dying away of the words takes place, and on the part of the REFUGEES *the same retreat into recollection. Some of them murmur, "Yes, yes." The mood is broken by the abrupt entrance of* MR. *and* MRS. ANTROBUS *and* SABINA *bearing platters of sandwiches and a pail of coffee.* SABINA *stops and stares at the guests.*

MR. A. Sabina, pass the sandwiches.

SAB. I thought I was working in a respectable house that had respectable guests. I'm giving my notice, Mr. Antrobus: two weeks, that's the law.

530. "Sing, muse of song, of the wrath of Achilles, Peleus' son, accursed (wrath), which caused countless woes for the Achaeans, and many brave souls...." Iliad, Book I. 532. "In the beginning, God created the Heavens and the earth; And the Earth was waste and void; And the darkness was upon the face of the deep. And the Lord said let there be light and there was light." Gen. 1: 1-3.

Mr. A.   Sabina! Pass the sandwiches.

Sab.   Two weeks, that's the law.

Mr. A.   There's the law. That's Moses.

Sab. [*Stares*]   The Ten Commandments—FAUGH!!—[*To Audience*]   540
That's the worst line I've ever had to say on any stage.

Mr. A.   I think the best thing to do is just not to stand on ceremony,
but pass the sandwiches around from left to right.—Judge, help yourself
to one of these.

Mrs. A.   The roads are crowded, I hear?

Guests. [*All talking at once*]   Oh, ma'am, you can't imagine ... You
can hardly put one foot before you . . . people are trampling one another.
Sudden silence.

Mrs. A.   Well, you know what I think it is,—I think it's sun-spots!

Guests. [*Discreet hubbub*]   Oh, you're right, Mrs. Antrobus . . . that's
what it is. . . . That's what I was saying the other day.   [*Sudden silence.*   550

Mr. A.   Well, I don't believe the whole world's going to turn to ice.
All eyes are fixed on him, waiting.
I can't believe it. Judge! Have we worked for nothing? Professor! Have
we just failed in the whole thing?

Mrs. A.   It is certainly very strange—well fortunately on both sides
of the family we come of very hearty stock.—Doctor, I want you to meet
my children. They're eating their supper now. And of course I want them
to meet you.

Miss M. Muse.   How many children have you, Mrs. Antrobus?

Mrs. A.   I have two,—a boy and a girl.

Mos. [*Softly*]   I understood you had two sons, Mrs. Antrobus.   560
Mrs. Antrobus *in blind suffering; she walks toward the footlights.*

Mrs. A. [*In a low voice*]   Abel, Abel, my son, my son, Abel, my son,
Abel, Abel, my son.
The Refugees *move with few steps toward her as though in comfort murmuring
words in Greek, Hebrew, German, et cetera. A piercing shriek from the kitchen—*
Sabina's *voice. All heads turn.*

Mr. A.   What's that?

Sabina *enters, bursting with indignation, pulling on her gloves.*

Sab.   Mr. Antrobus—that son of yours, that boy Henry Antrobus—
I don't stay in this house another moment!—He's not fit to live among
respectable folks and that's a fact.

Mrs. A.   Don't say another word, Sabina. I'll be right back.
Without waiting for an answer she goes past her into the kitchen.

Sab.   Mr. Antrobus, Henry has thrown a stone again and if he hasn't
killed the boy that lives next door, I'm very much mistaken. He finished
his supper and went out to play; and I heard such a fight; and then I saw   570
it. I saw it with my own eyes. And it looked to me like stark murder.

Mrs. Antrobus *appears at the kitchen door, shielding* Henry *who follows her.*

When she steps aside, we see on HENRY's *forehead a large ochre and scarlet scar in the shape of a C.* MR. ANTROBUS *starts toward him. A pause.* HENRY *is heard saying under his breath:*

HEN.   He was going to take the wheel away from me. He started to throw a stone at me first.

MRS. A.   George, it was just a boyish impulse. Remember how young he is.

[*Louder, in an urgent wail*]   George, he's only four thousand years old.

SAB.   And everything was going along so nicely!

Silence. ANTROBUS *goes back to the fireplace.*

MR. A.   Put out the fire! Put out all the fires.

[*Violently*]   No wonder the sun grows cold.

He starts stamping on the fireplace.

MRS. A.   Doctor! Judge! Help me!—George, have you lost your mind?

580   MR. A.   There is no mind. We'll not try to live.

[*To the guests*]   Give it up. Give up trying.   [*Mrs. Antrobus seizes him.*

SAB.   Mr. Antrobus! I'm downright ashamed of you.

MRS. A.   George, have some more coffee.—Gladys! Where's Gladys gone?

GLADYS *steps in, frightened.*

GLAD.   Here I am, mama.

MRS. A.   Go upstairs and bring your father's slippers. How could you forget a thing like that, when you know how tired he is?

ANTROBUS *sits in his chair. He covers his face with his hands.* MRS. ANTROBUS *turns to the* REFUGEES.

Can't some of you sing? It's your business in life to sing, isn't it? Sabina! *Several of the women clear their throats tentatively, and with frightened faces gather around* HOMER's *guitar. He establishes a few chords. Almost inaudibly they start singing, led by* SABINA: "*Jingle Bells.*" MRS. ANTROBUS *continues to* ANTROBUS *in a low voice, while taking off his shoes:*

George, remember all the other times. When the volcanoes came right up

590 in the front yard.

And the time the grasshoppers ate every single leaf and blade of grass, and all the grain and spinach you'd grown with your own hands. And the summer there were earthquakes every night.

MR. A.   Henry! Henry!   [*Puts his hand on his forehead.*

Myself. All of us, we're covered with blood.

MRS. A.   Then remember all the times you were pleased with him and when you were proud of yourself.—Henry! Henry! Come here and recite to your father the multiplication table that you do so nicely.

HENRY *kneels on one knee beside his father and starts whispering the multiplication table.*

HEN. [*Finally*]   Two times six is twelve; three times six is eighteen—I

600 don't think I know the sixes.

Enter GLADYS *with the slippers.* MRS. ANTROBUS *makes stern gestures to her: Go in there and do your best. The* GUESTS *are now singing "Tenting Tonight."*

GLAD. [*Putting slippers on his feet*] Papa . . . papa . . . I was very good in school today. Miss Conover said right out in class that if all the girls had as good manners as Gladys Antrobus, that the world would be a very different place to live in.

MRS. A. You recited a piece at assembly, didn't you? Recite it to your father.

GLAD. Papa, do you want to hear what I recited in class?
Fierce directorial glance from her mother.
"THE STAR" by Henry Wadsworth LONGFELLOW.

MRS. A. Wait!!! The fire's going out. There isn't enough wood! Henry, go upstairs and bring down the chairs and start breaking up the 610 beds.   [*Exit Henry. The singers return to "Jingle Bells," still very softly.*

GLAD. Look, Papa, here's my report card. Lookit. Conduct A! Look, Papa. Papa, do you want to hear the Star, by Henry Wadsworth Long-fellow? Papa, you're not mad at me, are you?—I know it'll get warmer. Soon it'll be just like spring, and we can go to a picnic at the Hibernian Picnic Grounds like you always like to do, don't you remember? Papa, just look at me once.

Enter HENRY *with some chairs.*

MR. A. You recited in assembly, did you?   [*She nods eagerly.*
You didn't forget it?

GLAD. No!!! I was perfect.   620

Pause. Then ANTROBUS *rises, goes to the front door and opens it. The* REFUGEES *draw back timidly; the song stops; he peers out of the door, then closes it.*

MR. A. [*With decision, suddenly*] Build up the fire. It's cold. Build up the fire. We'll do what we can. Sabina, get some more wood. Come around the fire, everybody. At least the young ones may pull through. Henry, have you eaten something?

HEN. Yes, papa.

MR. A. Gladys, have you had some supper?

GLAD. I ate in the kitchen, papa.

MR. A. If you do come through this—what'll you be able to do? What do you know? Henry, did you take a good look at that wheel?

HEN. Yes, papa.   630

MR. A. [*Sitting down in his chair*] Six times two are—

HEN. —twelve; six times three are eighteen; six times four are—Papa, it's hot and cold. It makes my head all funny. It makes me sleepy.

MR. A. [*Gives him a cuff*] Wake up. I don't care if your head is sleepy. Six times four are twenty-four. Six times five are—

HEN. Thirty. Papa!

MR. A. Maggie, put something into Gladys' head on the chance she can use it.

MRS. A.   What do you mean, George?

640   MR. A.   Six times six are thirty-six.
Teach her the beginning of the Bible.

GLAD.   But, Mama, it's so cold and close.

HENRY *has all but drowsed off. His father slaps him sharply and the lesson goes on.*

MRS. A.   "In the beginning God created the heavens and the earth, and the earth was waste and void; and the darkness was upon the face of the deep—"

The singing starts up again louder. SABINA *has returned with wood.*

SAB.   [*After placing wood on the fireplace, comes down to the footlights and addresses the audience.*]   Will you please start handing up your chairs? We'll need everything for this fire. Save the human race.—Ushers, will you pass the chairs up here? Thank you.

HEN.   Six times nine are fifty-four; six times ten are sixty,

In the back of the auditorium the sound of chairs being ripped up can be heard.
USHERS *rush down the aisles with chairs and hand them over.*

650   GLAD.   "And God called the light Day and the darkness he called Night."

SAB.   Pass up your chairs, everybody. Save the human race.

Act II

SCENE.   *Atlantic City Boardwalk.*

Toward the end of the intermission, though with the house-lights still up, lantern slide projections begin to appear on the curtain. Timetables for trains leaving Pennsylvania Station for Atlantic City. Advertisements of Atlantic City hotels, drugstores, churches, rug merchants; fortune tellers, Bingo parlors.

When the house-lights go down, the voice of an ANNOUNCER *is heard.*

ANN.   The Management now brings you the News Events of the World. Atlantic City, New Jersey:

Projection of a chrome postcard of the waterfront, trimmed in mica with the legend:

FUN AT THE BEACH.

This great convention city is playing host this week to the anniversary convocation of that great fraternal order—the Ancient and Honorable Order of Mammals, Subdivision Humans. This great fraternal, militant and burial society is celebrating on the Boardwalk, ladies and gentlemen, its six hundred thousandth Annual Convention.

It has just elected its president for the ensuing term—

Projection of MR. *and* MRS. ANTROBUS *posed as they will be shown a few moments later.*

Mr. George Antrobus of Excelsior, New Jersey. We show you President
10   Antrobus and his gracious and charming wife, every inch a mammal. Mr. Antrobus has had a long and chequered career. Credit has been paid to him for many useful enterprises including the introduction of the lever, of the wheel and the brewing of beer. Credit has been also extended to Pres-

Thornton Wilder   495

ident Antrobus's gracious and charming wife for many practical suggestions, including the hem, the gore, and the gusset; and the novelty of the year,—frying in oil. Before we show you Mr. Antrobus accepting the nomination, we have an important announcement to make. As many of you know, this great celebration of the Order of the Mammals has received delegations from the other rival Orders,—or shall we say: esteemed concurrent Orders: the WINGS, the FINS, the SHELLS, and so on. 20 These Orders are holding their conventions also, in various parts of the world, and have sent representatives to our own, two of a kind.

Later in the day we will show you President Antrobus broadcasting his words of greeting and congratulation to the collected assemblies of the whole natural world.

Ladies and Gentlemen! We give you President Antrobus!

The screen becomes a Transparency. MR. ANTROBUS *stands beside a pedestal;* MRS. ANTROBUS *is seated wearing a corsage of orchids.* ANTROBUS *wears an untidy Prince Albert; spats; from a red rosette in his buttonhole hangs a fine long purple ribbon of honor. He wears a gay lodge hat,—something between a fez and a legionnaire's cap.*

MR. A. Fellow-mammals, fellow-vertebrates, fellow-humans, I thank you. Little did my dear parents think,—when they told me to stand on my own two feet,—that I'd arrive at this place.

My friends, we have come a long way. 30

During this week of happy celebration it is perhaps not fitting that we dwell on some of the difficult times we have been through. The dinosaur is extinct— [*Applause.*

—the ice has retreated; and the common cold is being pursued by every means within our power.

MRS. ANTROBUS *sneezes, laughs prettily, and murmurs: "I beg your pardon."*

In our memorial service yesterday we did honor to all our friends and relatives who are no longer with us, by reason of cold, earthquakes, plagues and . . . and . . . [*Coughs*] differences of opinion.

As our Bishop so ably said . . . uh . . . so ably said. . . .

MRS. A. [*Closed lips*] Gone, but not forgotten. 40

MR. A. "They are gone, but not forgotten."

I think I can say, I think I can prophesy with complete . . . uh . . . with complete. . . .

MRS. A. Confidence.

MR. A. Thank you, my dear,—With complete lack of confidence, that a new day of security is about to dawn.

The watchword of the closing year was: Work. I give you the watchword for the future: Enjoy Yourselves.

MRS. A. George, sit down!

MR. A. Before I close, however, I wish to answer one of those unjust 50

TUNE TELLER *rises, puts her pipe down on the stool, unfurls her voluminous*
s, gives a sharp wrench to her bodice and strolls towards the audience, swinging
ips like a young woman.

OR. TEL.   I tell the future. Keck. Nothing easier. Everybody's future   150
 their face. Nothing easier.
 who can tell your past, —eh? Nobody!
 r youth,—where did it go? It slipped away while you weren't looking.
 le you were asleep. While you were drunk? Puh! You're like our
 ds, Mr. and Mrs. Antrobus; you lie awake nights trying to know
 r past. What did it mean? What was it trying to say to you?
 nk! Think! Split your heads. I can't tell the past and neither can you.
 iybody tries to tell you the past, take my word for it, they're charla-
 ! Charlatans! But I can tell the future.
 suddenly barks at a passing chair-pusher]   Apoplexy!
 returns to the audience]   Nobody listens.—Keck! I see a face among   160
 now—I won't embarrass him by pointing him out, but, listen, it may
 ou: Next year the watchsprings inside you will crumple up. Death by
 et,—Type Y. It's in the corners of your mouth. You'll decide that
 should have lived for pleasure, but that you missed it. Death by
 et,—Type Y. . . . Avoid mirrors. You'll try to be angry,—but no!
 o anger.
 forward, confidentially]   And now what's the immediate future of our
 ds, the Antrobuses? Oh, you've seen it as well as I have, keck,—that
 iness of the head; that Great Man dizziness? The inventor of beer and
 owder. The sudden fits of temper and then the long stretches of   170
 ia? "I'm a sultan; let my slave-girls fan me?" You know as well as I
 's coming. Rain. Rain. Rain in floods. The deluge. But first you'll see
 ieful things—shameful things. Some of you will be saying: "Let him
 n. He's not worth saving. Give the whole thing up." I can see it
 ur faces. But you're wrong. Keep your doubts and despairs to your-
 s.
 n there'll be the narrow escape. The survival of a handful. From
 uction,—total destruction.
 ints sweeping with her hand to the stage.
 of the animals, a few will be saved: two of a kind, male and female,
 of a kind.   18
 eads of CONVEENERS *appear about the stage and in the orchestra pit, jeering*

 NV.   Charlatan! Madam Kill-joy! Mrs. Jeremiah! Charlatan!
 R. TEL.   And *you!* Mark my words before it's too late. Where'll *you*

 NV.   The croaking raven. Old dust and ashes. Rags, bottles, sacks.
 R. TEL.   Yes, stick out your tongues. You can't stick your tongues
 r enough to lick the death-sweat from your foreheads. It's too late to

and malicious accusations that were brought against me during this last
electoral campaign.

Ladies and gentlemen, the charge was made that at various points in my
career I leaned toward joining some of the rival orders,—that's a lie.

As I told reporters of the *Atlantic City Herald*, I do not deny that a few
months before my birth I hesitated between . . . uh . . . between pin-
feathers and gill-breathing,—and so did many of us here,—but for the
last million years I have been viviparous, hairy and diaphragmatic.

Applause. Cries of "Good old Antrobus," "The Prince chap!" "Georgie," etc.

ANN.   Thank you. Thank you very much, Mr. Antrobus.

60 Now I know that our visitors will wish to hear a word from that gracious
and charming mammal, Mrs. Antrobus, wife and mother,—Mrs.
Antrobus!

MRS. ANTROBUS *rises, lays her program on her chair, bows and says:*

MRS. A.   Dear friends, I don't really think I should say anything.
After all, it was my husband who was elected and not I.

Perhaps, as president of the Woman's Auxiliary Bed and Board Society,
—I had some notes here, oh, yes, here they are:—I should give a short
report from some of our committees that have been meeting in this
beautiful city.

Perhaps it may interest you to know that it has at last been decided that
70 the tomato is edible. Can you hear me? The tomato *is* edible.

A delegate from across the sea reports that the thread woven by the
silkworm gives a cloth . . . I have a sample of it here . . . can you see it?
smooth, elastic. I should say that it's rather attractive,—though personally I prefer less shiny surfaces. Should the windows of a sleeping apartment be open or shut? I know all mothers will follow our debates on this
matter with close interest. I am sorry to say that the most expert authorities have not yet decided. It does seem to me that the night air would be
bound to be unhealthy for our children, but there are many distinguished
authorities on both sides. Well, I could go on talking forever,—as Shake-
80 speare says: a woman's work is seldom done; but I think I'd better join
my husband in saying thank you, and sit down. Thank you. [*She sits down.*

ANN.   Oh, Mrs. Antrobus!

MRS. A.   Yes?

ANN.   We understand that you are about to celebrate a wedding
anniversary. I know our listeners would like to extend their felicitations
and hear a few words from you on that subject.

MRS. A.   I have been asked by this kind gentleman . . . yes, my friends
this spring Mr. Antrobus and I will be celebrating our five thousandth
wedding anniversary.

90 I don't know if I speak for my husband, but I can say that, as for me, I
regret every moment of it.   [*Laughter of confusion.*

I beg your pardon. What I *mean* to say is that I do not regret one moment of it. I hope none of you catch my cold. We have two children. We've always had two children, though it hasn't always been the same two. But as I say, we have two fine children, and we're very grateful for that. Yes, Mr. Antrobus and I have been married five thousand years. Each wedding anniversary reminds me of the times when there were no weddings. We had to crusade for marriage. Perhaps there are some women within the sound of my voice who remember that crusade and those struggles; we fought for it, didn't we? We chained ourselves to lampposts and we 100 made disturbances in the Senate,—anyway, at last we women got the ring.

A few men helped us, but I must say that most men blocked our way at every step: they said we were unfeminine.

I only bring up these unpleasant memories, because I see some signs of backsliding from that great victory.

Oh, my fellow mammals, keep hold of that.

My husband says that the watchword for the year is Enjoy Yourselves. I think that's very open to misunderstanding. My watchword for the year is: Save the Family. It's held together for over five thousand years: Save 110 it! Thank you.

ANN.   Thank you, Mrs. Antrobus.   [*The transparency disappears.*] We had hoped to show you the Beauty Contest that took place here today. President Antrobus, an experienced judge of pretty girls, gave the title of Miss Atlantic City 1942, to Miss Lily-Sabina Fairweather, charming hostess of our Boardwalk Bingo Parlor.

Unfortunately, however, our time is up, and I must take you to some views of the Convention City and conveeners,—enjoying themselves.

A burst of music; the curtain rises.

The Boardwalk. The audience is sitting in the ocean. A handrail of scarlet cord stretches across the front of the stage. A ramp—also with scarlet hand rail—descends to the right corner of the orchestra pit where a great scarlet beach umbrella or a cabana stands. Front and right stage left are benches facing the sea; attached to each bench is a street-lamp.

The only scenery is two cardboard cut-outs six feet high, representing shops at the back of the stage. Reading from left to right they are: SALT WATER TAFFY: FORTUNE TELLER; then the blank space; BINGO PARLOR; TURKISH BATH. They have practical doors, that of the Fortune Teller's being hung with bright gypsy curtains.

By the left proscenium and rising from the orchestra pit is the weather signal; it is like the mast of a ship with cross bars. From time to time black disks are hung on it to indicate the storm and hurricane warnings. Three roller chairs, pushed by melancholy NEGROES file by empty. Throughout the act they traverse the stage in both directions.

From time to time, CONVEENERS, dressed like MR. ANTROBUS, cross the stage.

work now—bail out the flood with your soup spoons. You've had your chance and you've lost.

CONV. Enjoy yourselves!!!

They disappear. The FORTUNE TELLER *looks off left and puts her finger on her lip.*

190 FOR. TEL. They're coming—the Antrobuses. Keck. Your hope. Your despair. Your selves.

Enter from the left, MR. *and* MRS. ANTROBUS *and* GLADYS.

MRS. A. Gladys Antrobus, stick your stummick in.

GLAD. But it's easier this way.

MRS. A. Well, it's too bad the new president has such a clumsy daughter, that's all I can say. Try and be a lady.

FOR. TEL. Aijah! That's been said a hundred billion times.

MRS. A. Goodness! Where's Henry? He was here just a minute ago. Henry!

Sudden violent stir. A roller-chair appears from the left. About it are dancing in great excitement HENRY *and a* NEGRO CHAIR-PUSHER.

HEN. [*Slingshot in hand*] I'll put your eye out. I'll make you yell, like

200 you never yelled before.

NEG. [*At the same time*] Now, I warns you. I warns you. If you make me mad, you'll get hurt.

MR. A. Henry! What is this? Put down that slingshot.

MRS. A. [*At the same time*] Henry! HENRY! Behave yourself.

FOR. TEL. That's right, young man. There are too many people in the world as it is. Everybody's in the way, except one's self.

HEN. All I wanted to do was—have some fun.

NEG. Nobody can't touch my chair, nobody, without I allow 'em to. You get clean away from me and you get away fast.

[*He pushes his chair off, muttering.*

210 MR. A. What were you doing, Henry?

HEN. Everybody's always getting mad. Everybody's always trying to push you around. I'll make him sorry for this; I'll make him sorry.

MR. A. Give me that slingshot.

HEN. I won't. I'm sorry I came to this place. I wish I weren't here. I wish I weren't anywhere.

MRS. A. Now, Henry, don't get so excited about nothing. I declare I don't know what we're going to do with you. Put your slingshot in your pocket, and don't try to take hold of things that don't belong to you.

MR. A. After this you can stay home. I wash my hands of you.

220 MRS. A. Come now, let's forget all about it. Everybody take a good breath of that sea air and calm down.

A passing CONVEENER *bows to* ANTROBUS *who nods to him.*

Who was that you spoke to, George?

MR. A. Nobody, Maggie. Just the candidate who ran against me in the election.

Mrs. A. The man who ran against you in the election!!

She turns and waves her umbrella after the disappearing Conveener.

My husband didn't speak to you and he never will speak to you.

Mr. A. Now, Maggie.

Mrs. A. After those lies you told about him in your speeches! Lies, that's what they were.

Glad. *and* Hen. Mama, everybody's looking at you. Everybody's 230 laughing at you.

Mrs. A. If you must know, my husband's a SAINT, a downright SAINT, and you're not fit to speak to him on the street.

Mr. A. Now, Maggie, now, Maggie, that's enough of that.

Mrs. A. George Antrobus, you're a perfect worm. If you won't stand up for yourself, I will.

Glad. Mama, you just act awful in public.

Mrs. A. [*Laughing*] Well, I must say I enjoyed it. I feel better. Wish his wife had been there to hear it. Children, what do you want to do?

Glad. Papa, can we ride in one of those chairs? Mama, I want to ride 240 in one of those chairs.

Mrs. A. No, sir. If you're tired you just sit where you are. We have no money to spend on foolishness.

Mr. A. I guess we have money enough for a thing like that. It's one of the things you do at Atlantic City.

Mrs. A. Oh, we have? I tell you it's a miracle my children have shoes to stand up in. I didn't think I'd ever live to see them pushed around in chairs.

Mr. A. We're on a vacation, aren't we? We have a right to some treats, I guess. Maggie, some day you're going to drive me crazy. 250

Mrs. A. All right, go. I'll just sit here and laugh at you. And you can give me my dollar right in my hand. Mark my words, a rainy day is coming. There's a rainy day ahead of us. I feel it in my bones. Go on, throw your money around. I can starve. I've starved before. I know how.

A Conveener *puts his head through Turkish Bath window, and says with raised eyebrows:*

Con. Hello, George. How are ya? I see where you brought the WHOLE family along.

Mrs. A. And what do you mean by that?

Conveener *withdraws head and closes window.*

Mr. A. Maggie, I tell you there's a limit to what I can stand. God's Heaven, haven't I worked *enough?* Don't I get *any* vacation? Can't I even give my children so much as a ride in a roller-chair? 260

Mrs. A. [*Putting out her hand for raindrops*] Anyway, it's going to rain very soon and you have your broadcast to make.

Mr. A. Now, Maggie, I warn you. A man can stand a family only just so long. I'm warning you.

Enter SABINA *from the Bingo Parlor. She wears a flounced red silk bathing suit, 1905. Red stockings, shoes, parasol. She bows demurely to* ANTROBUS *and starts down the ramp.* ANTROBUS *and the* CHILDREN *stare at her.* ANTROBUS *bows gallantly.*

MRS. A. Why, George Antrobus, how can you say such a thing! You have the best family in the world.

MR. A. Good morning, Miss Fairweather.

SABINA *finally disappears behind the beach umbrella or in a cabana in the orchestra pit.*

MRS. A. Who on earth was that you spoke to, George?

MR. A. [*Complacent; mock-modest*] Hm . . . m . . . just a . . . solambaka
270 keray.

MRS. A. What? I can't understand you.

GLAD. Mama, wasn't she beautiful?

HEN. Papa, introduce her to me.

MRS. A. Children, will you be quiet while I ask your father a simple question?—Who did you say it was, George?

MR. A. Why-uh . . . a friend of mine. Very nice refined girl.

MRS. A. I'm waiting.

MR. A. Maggie, that's the girl I gave the prize to in the beauty contest,—that's Miss Atlantic City 1942.

280 MRS. A. Hm! She looked like Sabina to me.

HEN. [*At the railing*] Mama, the life-guard knows her, too. Mama, he knows her well.

MR. A. Henry, come here.—She's a very nice girl in every way and the sole support of her aged mother.

MRS. A. So was Sabina, so was Sabina; and it took a wall of ice to open your eyes about Sabina.—Henry, come over and sit down on this bench.

MR. A. She's a very different matter from Sabina. Miss Fairweather is a college graduate, Phi Beta Kappa.

290 MRS. A. Henry, you sit here by mama. Gladys—

MR. A. [*Sitting*] Reduced circumstances have required her taking a position as hostess in a Bingo Parlor; but there isn't a girl with higher principles in the country.

MRS. A. Well, let's not talk about it.—Henry, I haven't seen a whale yet.

MR. A. She speaks seven languages and has more culture in her little finger than you've acquired in a lifetime.

MRS. A. [*Assumed amiability*] All right, all right, George. I'm glad to know there are such superior girls in the Bingo Parlors.—Henry, what's
300 that?   [*Pointing at the storm signal, which has one black disk.*]

HEN. What is it, Papa?

MR. A. What? Oh, that's the storm signal. One of those black disks means bad weather; two means storm; three means hurricane; and four means the end of the world.

As they watch it a second black disk rolls into place.

MRS. A.   Goodness! I'm going this very minute to buy you all some raincoats.

GLAD.   [*Putting her cheek against her father's shoulder*]   Mama, don't go yet. I like sitting this way. And the ocean coming in and coming in. Papa, don't you like it?

MRS. A.   Well, there's only one thing I lack to make me a perfectly 310 happy woman: I'd like to see a whale.

HEN.   Mama, we saw two. Right out there. They're delegates to the convention. I'll find you one.

GLAD.   Papa, ask me something. Ask me a question.

MR. A.   Well . . . how big's the ocean?

GLAD.   Papa, you're teasing me. It's—three-hundred and sixty million square-miles—and—it—covers—three-fourths—of—the—earth's—surface—and—its—deepest-place—is—five—and—a—half—miles—deep—and—its—average—depth—is—twelve-thousand—feet. No, Papa, ask me something hard, real hard.   320

MRS. A. [*Rising*]   Now I'm going off to buy those raincoats. I think that bad weather's going to get worse and worse. I hope it doesn't come before your broadcast. I should think we have about an hour or so.

HEN.   I hope it comes and zzzzzz everything before it. I hope it—

MRS. A.   Henry!—George, I think . . . maybe, it's one of those storms that are just as bad on land as on the sea. When you're just as safe and safer in a good stout boat.

HEN.   There's a boat out at the end of the pier.

MRS. A.   Well, keep your eye on it. George, you shut your eyes and get a good rest before the broadcast.   330

MR. A.   Thundering Judas, do I have to be told when to open and shut my eyes? Go and buy your raincoats.

MRS. A.   Now, children, you have ten minutes to walk around. Ten minutes. And, Henry: control yourself. Gladys, stick by your brother and don't get lost.   [*They run off.*

MRS. A.   Will you be all right, George?

CONVEENERS *suddenly stick their heads out of the Bingo Parlor and Salt Water Taffy store, and voices rise from the orchestra pit.*

CONV.   George. Geo-r-r-rge! George! Leave the old hen-coop at home, George. Do-mes-ticated Georgie!

MRS. A. [*Shaking her umbrella*]   Low common oafs! That's what they are. Guess a man has a right to bring his wife to a convention, if he wants 340 to.   [*She starts off.*

What's the matter with a family, I'd like to know. What else have they got to offer?

Exit. ANTROBUS *has closed his eyes. The* FORTUNE TELLER *comes out of her shop and goes over to the left proscenium. She leans against it watching* SABINA *quizzically.*

FOR. TEL.   Heh! Here she comes!

SAB.   [*Loud whisper*]   What's he doing?

FOR. TEL.   Oh, he's ready for you. Bite your lips, dear, take a long breath and come on up.

SAB.   I'm nervous. My whole future depends on this. I'm nervous.

350   FOR. TEL.   Don't be a fool. What more could you want? He's forty-five. His head's a little dizzy. He's just been elected president. He's never known any other woman than his wife. Whenever he looks at her he realizes that she knows every foolish thing he's ever done.

SAB.   [*Still whispering*]   I don't know why it is, but every time I start one of these I'm nervous.

The FORTUNE TELLER *stands in the center of the stage watching the following:*

FOR. TEL.   You make me tired.

SAB.   First tell me my fortune.

The FORTUNE TELLER *laughs dryly and makes the gesture of brushing away a nonsensical question.* SABINA *coughs and says:*

Oh, Mr. Antrobus,—dare I speak to you for a moment?

MR. A.   What?—Oh, certainly, certainly, Miss Fairweather.

360   SAB.   Mr. Antrobus . . . I've been so unhappy. I've wanted . . . I've wanted to make sure that you don't think that I'm the kind of girl who goes out for beauty contests.

FOR. TEL.   That's the way!

MR. A.   Oh, I understand. I understand perfectly.

FOR. TEL.   Give it a little more. Lean on it.

SAB.   I knew you would. My mother said to me this morning: Lily, she said, that fine Mr. Antrobus gave you the prize because he saw at once that you weren't the kind of girl who'd go in for a thing like that. But, honestly, Mr. Antrobus, in this world, honestly, a good girl doesn't

370   know where to turn.

FOR. TEL.   Now you've gone too far.

MR. A.   My dear Miss Fairweather!

SAB.   You wouldn't know how hard it is. With that lovely wife and daughter you have. Oh, I think Mrs. Antrobus is the finest woman I ever saw. I wish I were like her.

MR. A.   There, there. There's . . . uh . . . room for all kinds of people in the world, Miss Fairweather.

SAB.   How wonderful of you to say that. How generous!—Mr. Antrobus, have you a moment free? . . . I'm afraid I may be a little con-

380   spicuous here . . . could you come down, for just a moment, to my beach cabana . . . ?

Thornton Wilder   505

MR. A. Why-uh . . . yes, certainly . . . for a moment . . . just for a moment.

SAB. There's a deck chair there. Because: you know you *do* look tired. Just this morning my mother said to me: Lily, she said, I hope Mr. Antrobus is getting a good rest. His fine strong face has deep deep lines in it. Now isn't it true, Mr. Antrobus: you work too hard?

FOR. TEL. Bingo!   [*She goes into her shop.*

SAB. Now you will just stretch out. No, I shan't say a word, not a word. I shall just sit there,—privileged. That's what I am.   390

MR. A. [*Taking her hand*] Miss Fairweather . . . you'll . . . spoil me.

SAB. Just a moment. I have something I wish to say to the audience. —Ladies and gentlemen. I'm not going to play this particular scene tonight. It's just a short scene and we're going to skip it. But I'll tell you what takes place and then we can continue the play from there on. Now in this scene—

MR. A. [*Between his teeth*] But, Miss Somerset!

SAB. I'm sorry. I'm sorry. But I have to skip it. In this scene, I talk to Mr. Antrobus, and at the end of it he decides to leave his wife, get a divorce at Reno and marry me. That's all.   400

MR. A. Fitz!—Fitz!

SAB. So that now I've told you we can jump to the end of it,—where you say:

Enter in fury MR. FITZPATRICK, *the stage manager.*

FITZ. Miss Somerset, we insist on your playing this scene.

SAB. I'm sorry, Mr. Fitzpatrick, but I can't and I won't. I've told the audience all they need to know and now we can go on.

Other ACTORS *begin to appear on the stage, listening.*

FITZ. And *why* can't you play it?

SAB. Because there are some lines in that scene that would hurt some people's feelings and I don't think the theatre is a place where people's feelings ought to be hurt.   410

FITZ. Miss Somerset, you can pack up your things and go home. I shall call the understudy and I shall report you to Equity.

SAB. I sent the understudy up to the corner for a cup of coffee and if Equity tries to penalize me I'll drag the case right up to the Supreme Court. Now listen, everybody, there's no need to get excited.

FITZ. *and* MR. A. Why can't you play it . . . what's the matter with the scene?

SAB. Well, if you must know, I have a personal guest in the audience tonight. Her life hasn't been exactly a happy one. I wouldn't have my friend hear some of these lines for the whole world. I don't suppose it 420 occurred to the author that some other women might have gone through the experience of losing their husbands like this. Wild horses wouldn't drag from me the details of my friend's life, but . . . well, they'd been married twenty years, and before he got rich, why, she'd done the washing and everything.

FITZ. Miss Somerset, your friend will forgive you. We must play this scene.

SAB. Nothing, nothing will make me say some of those lines . . . about "a man outgrows a wife every seven years" and . . . and that one
430 about "the Mohammedans being the only people who looked the subject square in the face." Nothing.

FITZ. Miss Somerset! Go to your dressing room. I'll *read* your lines.

SAB. Now everybody's nerves are on edge.

MR. A. Skip the scene.   [*Mr. Fitzpatrick and the other Actors go off.*

SAB. Thank you. I knew you'd understand. We'll do just what I said. So Mr. Antrobus is going to divorce his wife and marry me. Mr. Antrobus, you say: "It won't be easy to lay all this before my wife."

The ACTORS *withdraw.* ANTROBUS *walks about, his hand to his forehead muttering:*

MR. A. Wait a minute. I can't get back into it as easily as all that. "My wife is a very obstinate woman." Hm . . . then you say . . . hm . . .
440 Miss Fairweather, I mean Lily, it won't be easy to lay all this before my wife. It'll hurt her feelings a little.

SAB. Listen, George: *other* people haven't got feelings. Not in the same way that we have,—we who are presidents like you and prize-winners like me. Listen, other people haven't got feelings; they just imagine they have. Within two weeks they go back to playing bridge and going to the movies.

Listen, dear: everybody in the world except a few people like you and me are just people of straw. Most people have no insides at all. Now that you're president you'll see that. Listen, darling, there's a kind of secret
450 society at the top of the world,—like you and me,—that know this. The world was made for us. What's life anyway? Except for two things, pleasure and power, what is life? Boredom! Foolishness. You know it is. Except for those two things, life's nau-se-at-ing. So,—come here!

She moves close. They kiss.

So.

Now when your wife comes, it's really very simple; just tell her.

MR. A. Lily, Lily: you're a wonderful woman.

SAB. Of course I am.

They enter the cabana and it hides them from view. Distant roll of thunder. A third black disk appears on the weather signal. Distant thunder is heard. MRS. ANTROBUS *appears carrying parcels. She looks about, seats herself on the bench left, and fans herself with her handkerchief. Enter* GLADYS *right, followed by two* CONVEENERS. *She is wearing red stockings.*

Mrs. A. Gladys!

Glad. Mama, here I am.

Mrs. A. Gladys Antrobus!!! Where did you get those dreadful 460 things?

Glad. Wha-a-t? Papa liked the color.

Mrs. A. You go back to the hotel this minute!

Glad. I won't. I won't. Papa liked the color.

Mrs. A. All right. All right. You stay here. I've a good mind to let your father see you that way. You stay right here.

Glad. I . . . I don't want to stay if . . . if you don't think he'd like it.

Mrs. A. Oh . . . it's all one to me. I don't care what happens. I don't care if the biggest storm in the whole world comes. Let it come. [*She folds her hands.*] Where's your brother? 470

Glad. [*In a small voice*] He'll be here.

Mrs. A. Will he? Well, let him get into trouble. I don't care. I don't know where your father is, I'm sure. [*Laughter from the cabana.*

Glad. [*Leaning over the rail*] I think he's . . . Mama, he's talking to the lady in the red dress.

Mrs. A. Is that so? [*Pause.*
We'll wait till he's through. Sit down here beside me and stop fidgeting . . . what are you crying about?

Distant thunder. She covers Gladys's *stockings with a raincoat.*

Glad. You don't like my stockings.

Two Conveeners *rush in with a microphone on a standard and various paraphernalia. The* Fortune Teller *appears at the door of her shop. Other characters gradually gather.*

Broadcast Official. Mrs. Antrobus! Thank God we've found you 480 at last. Where's Mr. Antrobus? We've been hunting everywhere for him. It's about time for the broadcast to the conventions of the world.

Mrs. A. [*Calm*] I expect he'll be here in a minute.

B. Off. Mrs. Antrobus, if he doesn't show up in time, I hope you will consent to broadcast in his place. It's the most important broadcast of the year.

Sabina *enters from cabana followed by* Antrobus.

Mrs. A. No, I shan't. I haven't one single thing to say.

B. Off. Then won't you help us find him, Mrs. Antrobus? A storm's coming up. A hurricane. A deluge!

2nd Conv. [*Who has sighted Antrobus over the rail*] Joe! Joe! Here he is. 490

B. Off. In the name of God, Mr. Antrobus, you're on the air in five minutes. Will you kindly please come and test the instrument? That's all we ask. If you just please begin the alphabet slowly.

Antrobus, *with set face, comes ponderously up the ramp. He stops at the point where his waist is level with the stage and speaks authoritatively to the* Officials.

Mr. A. I'll be ready when the time comes. Until then move away. Go away. I have something I wish to say to my wife.

B. Off. [*Whimpering*] Mr. Antrobus! This is the most important broadcast of the year.

The Officials *withdraw to the edge of the stage.* Sabina *glides up the ramp behind* Antrobus.

Sab. [*Whispering*] Don't let her argue. Remember arguments have nothing to do with it.

500 Mr. A. Maggie, I'm moving out of the hotel. In fact, I'm moving out of everything. For good. I'm going to marry Miss Fairweather. I shall provide generously for you and the children. In a few years you'll be able to see that it's all for the best. That's all I have to say.

B. Off. Mr. Antrobus! I hope you'll be ready. This is the most important broadcast of the year.

Bingo Announcer. A—nine; A—nine. D—forty-two; D—forty-two. C thiity; C—thirty. B—seventeen; B—seventeen. C—forty; C—forty.

Glad. What did Papa say, 510 Mama? I didn't hear what papa said.

Chorus. Bingo!!

B. Off. Mr. Antrobus. All we want to do is test your voice with the alphabet.

Mr. A. Go away. Clear out.

Mrs. A. [*Composedly with lowered eyes*] George, I can't talk to you until you wipe those silly red marks off your face.

Mr. A. I think there's nothing to talk about. I've said what I have to say.

520 Sab. Splendid!!

Mr. A. You're a fine woman, Maggie, but . . . but a man has his own life to lead in the world.

Mrs. A. Well, after living with you for five thousand years I guess I have a right to a word or two, haven't I?

Mr. A. [*To Sabina*] What can I answer to that?

Sab. Tell her that conversation would only hurt her feelings. It's-kinder-in-the-long-run-to-do-it-short-and-quick.

Mr. A. I want to spare your feelings in every way I can, Maggie.

B. Off. Mr. Antrobus, the hurricane signal's gone up. We could 530 begin right now.

Mrs. A. [*Calmly, almost dreamily*] I didn't marry you because you were perfect. I didn't even marry you because I loved you. I married you because you gave me a promise.

She takes off her ring and looks at it.

That promise made up for your faults. And the promise I gave you made up for mine. Two imperfect people got married and it was the promise that made the marriage.

MR. A.   Maggie, . . . I was only nineteen.

MRS. A.   [*She puts her ring back on her finger*]   And when our children were growing up, it wasn't a house that protected them; and it wasn't our love, that protected them—it was that promise.   540
And when that promise is broken—this can happen!

With a sweep of the hand she removes the raincoat from GLADYS' *stockings.*

MR. A.   [*Stretches out his arm, apoplectic*]   Gladys!! Have you gone crazy? Has everyone gone crazy?
[*Turning on Sabina*]   You did this. You gave them to her.

SAB.   I never said a word to her.

MR. A.   [*To Gladys*]   You go back to the hotel and take those horrible things off.

GLAD.   [*Pert*]   Before I go, I've got something to tell you,—it's about Henry.

MRS. A.   [*Claps her hands peremptorily*]   Stop your noise,—I'm taking 550 her back to the hotel, George. Before I go I have a letter. . . . I have a message to throw into the ocean.   [*Fumbling in her handbag.*
Where is the plagued thing? Here it is.

She flings something—invisible to us—far over the heads of the audience to the back of the auditorium.

It's a bottle. And in the bottle's a letter. And in the letter is written all the things that a woman knows.
It's never been told to any man and it's never been told to any woman, and if it finds its destination, a new time will come. We're not what books and plays say we are. We're not what advertisements say we are. We're not in the movies and we're not on the radio.
We're not what you're all told and what you think we are: We're our- 560 selves. And if any man can find one of us he'll learn why the whole universe was set in motion. And if any man harm any one of us, his soul—the only soul he's got—had better be at the bottom of that ocean,—and that's the only way to put it. Gladys, come here. We're going back to the hotel.

She drags GLADYS *firmly off by the hand, but* GLADYS *breaks away and comes down to speak to her father.*

SAB.   Such goings-on. Don't give it a minute's thought.

GLAD.   Anyway, I think you ought to know that Henry hit a man with a stone. He hit one of those colored men that push the chairs and the man's very sick. Henry ran away and hid and some policemen are looking for him very hard. And I don't care a bit if you don't want to have anything to do with mama and me, because I'll never like you again and I 570 hope nobody ever likes you again,—so there!

[*She runs off. Antrobus starts after her.*

MR. A.   I . . . I have to go and see what I can do about this.

SAB. You stay right here. Don't you go now while you're excited. Gracious sakes, all these things will be forgotten in a hundred years. Come, now, you're on the air. Just say anything,—it doesn't matter what. Just a lot of birds and fishes and things.

B. OFF. Thank you, Miss Fairweather. Thank you very much. Ready, Mr. Antrobus.

MR. A. [*Touching the microphone*] What is it, what is it? Who am I 580 talking to?

B. OFF. Why, Mr. Antrobus! To our order and to all the other orders.

MR. A. [*Raising his head*] What are all those birds doing?

B. OFF. Those are just a few of the birds. Those are the delegates to our convention,—two of a kind.

MR. A. [*Pointing into the audience*] Look at the water. Look at them all. Those fishes jumping. The children should see this!—There's Maggie's whales!! Here are your whales, Maggie!!

B. OFF. I hope you're ready, Mr. Antrobus.

MR. A. And look on the beach! You didn't tell me these would be 590 here!

SAB. Yes, George. Those are the animals.

B. OFF. [*Busy with the apparatus*] Yes, Mr. Antrobus, those are the vertebrates. We hope the lion will have a word to say when you're through. Step right up, Mr. Antrobus, we're ready. We'll just have time before the storm.

[*Pause. In a hoarse whisper*] They're wait-ing.

It has grown dark. Soon after he speaks a high whistling noise begins. Strange veering lights start whirling about the stage. The other characters disappear from the stage.

MR. A. Friends. Cousins. Four score and ten billion years ago our forefather brought forth upon this planet the spark of life,—

He is drowned out by thunder. When the thunder stops the FORTUNE TELLER *is seen standing beside him.*

FOR. TEL. Antrobus, there's not a minute to be lost. Don't you see the 600 four disks on the weather signal? Take your family into that boat at the end of the pier.

MR. A. My family? I have no family. Maggie! Maggie! They won't come.

FOR. TEL. They'll come.—Antrobus! Take these animals into that boat with you. All of them,—two of each kind.

SAB. George, what's the matter with you? This is just a storm like any other storm.

MR. A. Maggie!

SAB. Stay with me, we'll go . . .

610 [*Losing conviction*] This is just another thunderstorm,—isn't it! Isn't it?

MR. A. Maggie!!!

Mrs. Antrobus *appears beside him with* Gladys.

Mrs. A. [*Matter-of-fact*] Here I am and here's Gladys.

Mr. A. Where've you been? Where have you been? Quick, we're going into that boat out there.

Mrs. A. I know we are. But I haven't found Henry.

[*She wanders off into the darkness calling "Henry!"*

Sab. [*Low urgent babbling, only occasionally raising her voice*] I don't believe it. I don't believe it's anything at all. I've seen hundreds of storms like this.

For. Tel. There's no time to lose. Go. Push the animals along before 620 you. Start a new world. Begin again.

Sab. Esmeralda! George! Tell me,—is it really serious?

Mr. A. [*Suddenly very busy*] Elephants first. Gently, gently.—Look where you're going.

Glad. [*Leaning over the ramp and striking an animal on the back*] Stop it or you'll be left behind!

Mr. A. Is the Kangaroo there? *There* you are! Take those turtles in your pouch, will you?

[*To some other animals, pointing to his shoulder*] Here! You jump up here. You'll be trampled on.

Glad. [*To her father, pointing below*] Papa, look—the snakes! 630

Mrs. A. I can't find Henry. Hen-ry!

Mr. A. Go along. Go along. Climb on their backs.—Wolves! Jackals, —whatever you are,—tend to your own business!

Glad. [*Pointing, tenderly*] Papa,—look.

Sab. Mr. Antrobus—take me with you. Don't leave me here. I'll work. I'll help. I'll do anything.

Three Conveeners *cross the stage, marching with a banner.*

Conv. George! What are you scared of?—George! Fellas, it looks like rain.—"Maggie, where's my umbrella?"—George, setting up for Barnum and Bailey.

Mr. A. [*Again catching his wife's hand*] Come on now, Maggie,—the 640 pier's going to break any minute.

Mrs. A. I'm not going a step without Henry. Henry!

Glad. [*On the ramp*] Mama! Papa! Hurry. The pier's cracking, Mama. It's going to break.

Mrs. A. Henry! Cain! CAIN!

Henry *dashes into the stage and joins his mother.*

Hen. Here I am, Mama.

Mrs. A. Thank God!—now come quick.

Hen. I didn't think you wanted me.

Mrs. A. Quick!

She pushes him down before her into the aisle.

Sab. [*All the Antrobuses are now in the theatre aisle. Sabina stands at the*

650 *top of the ramp.*]   Mrs. Antrobus, take me. Don't you remember me? I'll work. I'll help. Don't leave me here!

MRS. A. [*Impatiently, but as though it were of no importance*]   Yes, yes. There's a lot of work to be done. Only hurry.

FOR. TEL. [*Now dominating the stage. To Sabina with a grim smile*]   Yes, go—back to the kitchen with you.

SAB. [*Half-down the ramp. To Fortune Teller*]   I don't know why my life's always being interrupted—just when everything's going fine!!

She dashes up the aisle. Now the CONVEENERS *emerge doing a serpentine dance on the stage. They jeer at the* FORTUNE TELLER.

CONV.   Get a canoe—there's not a minute to be lost! Tell me my future, Mrs. Croaker.

660 FOR. TEL.   Paddle in the water, boys—enjoy yourselves.

VOICE FROM THE BINGO PARLOR.   A—nine; A—nine. C—twenty-four; C—twenty-four.

CONV.   Rags, bottles, and sacks.

FOR. TEL.   Go back and climb on your roofs. Put rags in the cracks under your doors.—Nothing will keep out the flood. You've had your chance. You've had your day. You've failed. You've lost.

VOICE FROM THE BINGO PARLOR.   B—fifteen; B—fifteen.

FOR. TEL. [*Shading her eyes and looking out to sea*]   They're safe. George Antrobus! Think it over! A new world to make.—Think it over!

Act III

SCENE.   *Home, Excelsior, New Jersey.*

Just before the curtain rises, two sounds are heard from the stage: a cracked bugle call.

The curtain rises on almost total darkness. Almost all the flats composing the walls of MR. ANTROBUS'S *house, as of Act I, are up, but they lean helter-skelter against one another, leaving irregular gaps. Among the flats missing are two in the back wall, leaving the frames of the window and door crazily out of line. Off stage, back right, some red Roman fire is burning. The bugle call is repeated. Enter* SABINA *through the tilted door. She is dressed as a Napoleonic camp follower, "la fille du regiment," in begrimed reds and blues.*

SAB.   Mrs. Antrobus! Gladys! Where are you?

The war's over. The war's over. You can come out. The peace treaty's been signed.

Where are they?—Hmpf! Are they dead, too? Mrs. Annnntrobus! Glaaaadus! Mr. Antrobus'll be here this afternoon. I just saw him down-town. Huuuurry and put things in order. He says that now that the war's over we'll all have to settle down and be perfect.

Enter MR. FITZPATRICK, *the stage manager, followed by the whole company, who stand waiting at the edges of the stage.* MR. FITZPATRICK *tries to interrupt* SABINA.

FITZ.   Miss Somerset, we have to stop a moment.

SAB.   They may be hiding out in the back—

FITZ.   Miss Somerset! We have to stop a moment.   10

SAB.   What's the matter?

FITZ.   There's an explanation we have to make to the audience.—
Lights, please.

[*To the actor who plays Mr. Antrobus*]   Will you explain the matter to
the audience?

*The lights go up. We now see that a balcony or elevated runway has been erected at
the back of the stage, back of the wall of the Antrobus house. From its extreme
right and left ends ladder-like steps descend to the floor of the stage.*

MR. A.   Ladies and gentlemen, an unfortunate accident has taken
place back stage. Perhaps I should say *another* unfortunate accident.

SAB.   I'm sorry. I'm sorry.

MR. A.   The management feels, in fact, we all feel that you are due
an apology. And now we have to ask your indulgence for the most serious 20
mishap of all. Seven of our actors have . . . have been taken ill. Apparently, it was something they ate. I'm not exactly clear what happened.

All the ACTORS *start to talk at once.* ANTROBUS *raises his hand.*

Now, now—not all at once. Fitz, do you know what it was?

FITZ.   Why, it's perfectly clear. These seven actors had dinner together, and they ate something that disagreed with them.

SAB.   Disagreed with them!!! They have ptomaine poisoning. They're
in Bellevue Hospital this very minute in agony. They're having their
stomachs pumped out this very minute, in perfect agony.

MR. A.   Fortunately, we've just heard they'll all recover.

SAB.   It'll be a miracle if they do, a downright miracle. It was the 30
lemon meringue pie.

ACTORS.   It was the fish . . . it was the canned tomatoes . . . it was the
fish.

SAB.   It was the lemon meringue pie. I saw it with my own eyes; it
had blue mould all over the bottom of it.

MR. A.   Whatever it was, they're in no condition to take part in this
performance. Naturally, we haven't enough understudies to fill all those
roles; but we do have a number of splendid volunteers who have kindly
consented to help us out. These friends have watched our rehearsals, and
they assure me that they know the lines and the business very well. Let me 40
introduce them to you—my dresser, Mr. Tremayne,—himself a distinguished Shakespearean actor for many years; our wardrobe mistress,
Hester; Miss Somerset's maid, Ivy; and Fred Bailey, captain of the ushers
in this theatre.

These persons bow modestly. IVY *and* HESTER *are colored girls.*

Now this scene takes place near the end of the act. And I'm sorry to say

we'll need a short rehearsal, just a short run-through. And as some of it takes place in the auditorium, we'll have to keep the curtain up. Those of you who wish can go out in the lobby and smoke some more. The rest of you can listen to us, or . . . or just talk quietly among yourselves, as you
50 choose. Thank you. Now will you take it over, Mr. Fitzpatrick?

FITZ. Thank you.—Now for those of you who are listening perhaps I should explain that at the end of this act, the men have come back from the War and the family's settled down in the house. And the author wants to show the hours of the night passing by over their heads, and the planets crossing the sky . . . uh . . . over their heads. And he says—this is hard to explain—that each of the hours of the night is a philosopher, or a great thinker. Eleven o'clock, for instance, is Aristotle. And nine o'clock is Spinoza. Like that. I don't suppose it means anything. It's just a kind of poetic effect.

60 SAB. Not mean anything! Why, it certainly does. Twelve o'clock goes by saying those wonderful things. I think it means that when people are asleep they have all those lovely thoughts, much better than when they're awake.

IVY. Excuse me, I think it means,—excuse me, Mr. Fitzpatrick—

SAB. What were you going to say, Ivy?

IVY. Mr. Fitzpatrick, you let my father come to a rehearsal; and my father's a Baptist minister, and he said that the author meant that—just like the hours and stars go by over our heads at night, in the same way the ideas and thoughts of the great men are in the air around us all the
70 time and they're working on us, even when we don't know it.

FITZ. Well, well, maybe that's it. Thank you, Ivy. Anyway,—the hours of the night are philosophers. My friends, are you ready? Ivy, can you be eleven o'clock? "This good estate of the mind possessing its object in energy we call divine." Aristotle.

IVY. Yes, sir. I know that and I know twelve o'clock and I know nine o'clock.

FITZ. Twelve o'clock? Mr. Tremayne, the Bible.

TRE. Yes.

FITZ. Ten o'clock? Hester,—Plato? [She nods eagerly.
80 Nine o'clock, Spinoza,—Fred?

BAIL. Yes, sir.

FRED BAILEY picks up a great gilded cardboard numeral IX and starts up the steps to the platform. MR. FITZPATRICK strikes his forehead.

FITZ. The planets!! We forgot all about the planets.

SAB. O my God! The planets! Are they sick too? [Actors nod.

FITZ. Ladies and gentlemen, the planets are singers. Of course, we can't replace them, so you'll have to imagine them singing in this scene. Saturn sings from the orchestra pit down here. The Moon is way up there.

And Mars with a red lantern in his hand, stands in the aisle over there—
Tz-tz-tz. It's too bad; it all makes a very fine effect. However! Ready—
nine o'clock: Spinoza.

BAIL. [*Walking slowly across the balcony, left to right*] "After experience 90
had taught me that the common occurrences of daily life are vain and
futile—"

FITZ. Louder, Fred. "And I saw that all the objects of my desire and
fear—"

BAIL. "And I saw that all the objects of my desire and fear were in
themselves nothing good nor bad save insofar as the mind was affected by
them—"

FITZ. Do you know the rest? All right. Ten o'clock. Hester. Plato.

HES. "Then tell me, O Critias, how will a man choose the ruler that
shall rule over him? Will he not—"   100

FITZ. Thank you. Skip to the end, Hester.

HES. ". . . can be multiplied a thousand fold in its effects among the
citizens."

FITZ. Thank you.—Aristotle, Ivy?

IVY. "This good estate of the mind possessing its object in energy we
call divine. This we mortals have occasionally and it is this energy which
is pleasantest and best. But God has it always. It is wonderful in us; but
in Him how much more wonderful."

FITZ. Midnight. Midnight, Mr. Tremayne. That's right,—you've
done it before.—All right, everybody. You know what you have to do.— 110
Lower the curtain. House lights up. Act Three of THE SKIN OF OUR
TEETH.

As the curtain descends he is heard saying:
You volunteers, just wear what you have on. Don't try to put on the
costumes today.

House lights go down. The Act begins again. The Bugle call. Curtain rises.
Enter SABINA.

SAB. Mrs. Antrobus! Gladys! Where are you?
The war's over.—You've heard all this—   [*She gabbles the main points.*
Where—are—they? Are—they—dead, too, et cetera.
I—just—saw—Mr.—Antrobus—downtown, et cetera.   [*Slowing up.*
He says that now that the war's over we'll all have to settle down and be
perfect. They may be hiding out in the back somewhere. Mrs. An-tro-bus. 120
                              [*She wanders off. It has grown lighter.*
A trapdoor is cautiously raised and MRS. ANTROBUS *emerges waist-high and*
listens. She is disheveled and worn; she wears a tattered dress and a shawl half
covers her head. She talks down through the trapdoor.

MRS. A. It's getting light. There's still something burning over there
—Newark, or Jersey City. What? Yes, I could swear I heard someone
moving about up here. But I can't see anybody. I say: I can't see anybody.

She starts to move about the stage. GLADYS' *head appears at the trapdoor. She is holding a* BABY.

GLAD. Oh, Mama. Be careful.

MRS. A. Now, Gladys, you stay out of sight.

GLAD. Well, let me stay here just a minute. I want the baby to get some of this fresh air.

MRS. A. All right, but keep your eyes open. I'll see what I can find. I'll have a good hot plate of soup for you before you can say Jack Robin-
130 son. Gladys Antrobus! Do you know what I think I see? There's old Mr. Hawkins sweeping the sidewalk in front of his A. and P. store. Sweeping it with a broom. Why, he must have gone crazy, like the others! I see some other people moving about, too.

GLAD. Mama, come back, come back.

MRS. ANTROBUS *returns to the trapdoor and listens.*

MRS. A. Gladys, there's something in the air. Everybody's move ment's sort of different. I see some women walking right out in the middle of the street.

140 SABINA'S VOICE. Mrs. An-tro-bus!

MRS. A. *and* GLAD. What's that?!!

SABINA'S VOICE. Glaaaadys! Mrs. An-tro-bus!

Enter SABINA.

MRS. A. Gladys, that's Sabina's voice as sure as I live.—Sabina! Sabina!—Are you *alive?!!*

SAB. Of course, I'm alive. How've you girls been?—*Don't* try and kiss me. I never want to kiss another human being as long as I live. Sh-sh, there's nothing to get emotional about. Pull yourself together, the war's over. Take a deep breath,—the war's over.

MRS. A. The war's over!! I don't believe you. I don't believe you. I can't believe you.

GLAD. Mama!

150 SAB. Who's that?

MRS. A. That's Gladys and her baby. I don't believe you. Gladys, Sabina says the war's over. Oh, Sabina.

SAB. [*Leaning over the Baby*] Goodness! Are there any babies left in the world! Can it *see?* And can it cry and everything?

GLAD. Yes, he can. He notices everything very well.

SAB. Where on earth did you get it? Oh, I won't ask.—Lord, I've lived all these seven years around camp and I've forgotten how to behave. —Now we've got to think about the men coming home.—Mrs. Antrobus, go and wash your face, I'm ashamed of you. Put your best clothes on.
160 Mr. Antrobus'll be here this afternoon. I just saw him downtown.

MRS. A. *and* GLAD. He's alive!! He'll be here!! Sabina, you're not joking?

MRS. A. And Henry?

Thornton Wilder 517

SAB. [*Dryly*] Yes, Henry's alive, too, that's what they say. Now don't stop to talk. Get yourselves fixed up. Gladys, you look terrible. Have you any decent clothes? [*Sabina has pushed them toward the trapdoor.*

MRS. A. [*Half down*] Yes, I've something to wear just for this very day. But, Sabina,—who won the war?

SAB. Don't stop now,—just wash your face.

A whistle sounds in the distance.

Oh, my God, what's that silly little noise? 170

MRS. A. Why, it sounds like . . . it sounds like what used to be the noon whistle at the shoe-polish factory. [*Exit.*

SAB. That's what it is. Seems to me like peacetime's coming along pretty fast—shoe polish!

GLAD. [*Half down*] Sabina, how soon after peacetime begins does the milkman start coming to the door?

SAB. As soon as he catches a cow. Give him time to catch a cow, dear.

[*Exit Gladys. Sabina walks about a moment, thinking.*

Shoe polish! My, I'd forgotten what peacetime was like.

She shakes her head, then sits down by the trapdoor and starts talking down the hole.

Mrs. Antrobus, guess what I saw Mr. Antrobus doing this morning at dawn. He was tacking up a piece of paper on the door of the Town Hall. 180 You'll die when you hear: it was a recipe for grass soup, for a grass soup that doesn't give you the diarrhea. Mr. Antrobus is still thinking up new things.—He told me to give you his love. He's got all sorts of ideas for peacetime, he says. No more laziness and idiocy, he says. And oh, yes! Where are his books? What? Well, pass them up. The first thing he wants to see are his books. He says if you've burnt those books, or if the rats have eaten them, he says it isn't worthwhile starting over again. Everybody's going to be beautiful, he says, and diligent, and very intelligent.

A hand reaches up with two volumes.

What language is that? Pu-u-gh,—mold! And he's got such plans for you, Mrs. Antrobus. You're going to study history and algebra—and so are 190 Gladys and I—and philosophy. You should hear him talk:

Taking two more volumes.

Well, these are in English, anyway.—To hear him talk, seems like he expects you to be a combination, Mrs. Antrobus, of a saint and a college professor, and a dancehall hostess, if you know what I mean.

Two more volumes.

Ugh. German!

She is lying on the floor; one elbow bent, her cheek on her hand, meditatively.

Yes, peace will be here before we know it. In a week or two we'll be asking the Perkinses in for a quiet evening of bridge. We'll turn on the radio and hear how to be big successes with a new toothpaste. We'll trot down to the movies and see how girls with wax faces live—all *that* will begin again. Oh, Mrs. Antrobus, God forgive me but I enjoyed the war. Every- 200

518 Drama

body's at their best in wartime. I'm sorry it's over. And, oh, I forgot! Mr. Antrobus sent you another message—can you hear me?—

Enter HENRY, *blackened and sullen. He is wearing torn overalls, but has one gaudy admiral's epaulette hanging by a thread from his right shoulder, and there are vestiges of gold and scarlet braid running down his left trouser leg. He stands listening.* Listen! Henry's never to put foot in this house again, he says. He'll kill Henry on sight, if he sees him.

You don't know about Henry??? Well, where have you been? What? Well Henry rose right to the top. Top of *what?* Listen, I'm telling you. Henry rose from corporal to captain, to major, to general.—I don't know how to say it, but the enemy is *Henry;* Henry *is* the enemy. Everybody knows that.

210   HEN.   He'll kill me, will he?

      SAB.   Who are *you?* I'm not afraid of you. The war's over.

      HEN.   I'll kill him so fast. I've spent seven years trying to find him; the others I killed were just substitutes.

      SAB.   Goodness! It's Henry!—   *[He makes an angry gesture.* Oh, I'm not afraid of you. The war's over, Henry Antrobus, and you're not any more important than any other unemployed. You go away and hide yourself, until we calm your father down.

      HEN.   The first thing to do is to burn up those old books; it's the ideas he gets out of those old books that . . . that makes the whole world so you
220 can't live in it.

He reels forward and starts kicking the books about, but suddenly falls down in a sitting position.

      SAB.   You leave those books alone!! Mr. Antrobus is looking forward to them a-special.—Gracious sakes, Henry, you're so tired you can't stand up. Your mother and sister'll be here in a minute and we'll think what to do about you.

      HEN.   What did they ever care about me?

      SAB.   There's that old whine again. All you people think you're not loved enough, nobody loves you. Well, you start being lovable and we'll love you.

      HEN. *[Outraged]*   I don't want anybody to love me.

230   SAB.   Then stop talking about it all the time.

      HEN.   I *never* talk about it. The last thing I want is anybody to pay any attention to me.

      SAB.   I can hear it behind every word you say.

      HEN.   I want everybody to hate me.

      SAB.   Yes, you've decided that's second best, but it's still the same thing.—Mrs. Antrobus! Henry's here. He's so tired he can't stand up.

MRS. ANTROBUS *and* GLADYS, *with her* BABY, *emerge. They are dressed as in Act I.* MRS. ANTROBUS *carries some objects in her apron, and* GLADYS *has a blanket over her shoulder.*

Mrs. A. *and* Glad.   Henry! Henry! Henry!

Hen. [*Glaring at them*]   Have you anything to eat?

Mrs. A.   Yes, I have, Henry. I've been saving it for this very day,— two good baked potatoes. No! Henry! one of them's for your father. 240 Henry!! Give me that other potato back this minute.

Sabina *sidles up behind him and snatches the other potato away.*

Sab.   He's so dog-tired he doesn't know what he's doing.

Mrs. A.   Now you just rest there, Henry, until I can get your room ready. Eat that potato good and slow, so you can get all the nourishment out of it.

Hen.   You all might as well know right now that I haven't come back here to live.

Mrs. A.   Sh. . . . I'll put this coat over you. Your room's hardly damaged at all. Your football trophies are a little tarnished, but Sabina and I will polish them up tomorrow.   250

Hen.   Did you hear me? I don't live here. I don't belong to anybody.

Mrs. A.   Why, how can you say a thing like that! You certainly do belong right here. Where else would you want to go? Your forehead's feverish, Henry, seems to me. You'd better give me that gun, Henry. You won't need that any more.

Glad. [*Whispering*]   Look, he's fallen asleep already, with his potato half-chewed.

Sab.   Puh! The terror of the world.

Mrs. A.   Sabina, you mind your own business, and start putting the room to rights.   260

Henry *has turned his face to the back of the sofa.* Mrs. Antrobus *gingerly puts the revolver in her apron pocket, then helps* Sabina. Sabina *has found a rope hanging from the ceiling. Grunting, she hangs all her weight on it, and as she pulls the walls begin to move into their right places.* Mrs. Antrobus *brings the overturned tables, chairs and hassock into the positions of Act I.*

Sab.   That's all we do—always beginning again! Over and over again. Always beginning again.

She pulls on the rope and a part of the wall moves into place. She stops. Meditatively. How do we know that it'll be any better than before? Why do we go on pretending? Some day the whole earth's going to have to turn cold anyway, and until that time all these other things'll be happening again: it will be more wars and more walls of ice and floods and earthquakes.

Mrs. A.   Sabina!! Stop arguing and go on with your work.

Sab.   All right. I'll go on just out of *habit*, but I won't believe in it.

Mrs. A. [*Aroused*]   Now, Sabina. I've let you talk long enough. I don't want to hear any more of it. Do I have to explain to you what everybody 270 knows,—everybody who keeps a home going? Do I have to say to you what nobody should ever *have* to say, because they can read it in each other's eyes?

Now listen to me: [*Mrs. Antrobus takes hold of the rope.*
I could live for seventy years in a cellar and make soup out of grass and
bark, without ever doubting that this world has a work to do and will
do it.
Do you hear me?

SAB. [*Frightened*]   Yes, Mrs. Antrobus.

280   MRS. A.   Sabina, do you see this house,—216 Cedar Street,—do you
see it?

SAB.   Yes, Mrs. Antrobus.

MRS. A.   Well, just to have known this house is to have seen the idea
of what we can do someday if we keep our wits about us. Too many
people have suffered and died for my children for us to start reneging
now. So we'll start putting this house to rights. Now, Sabina, go and see
what you can do in the kitchen.

SAB.   Kitchen! Why is it that however far I go away, I always find
myself back in the kitchen?   [*Exit.*

MRS. A. [*Still thinking over her last speech, relaxes and says with a reminiscent
290 smile*]   Goodness gracious, wouldn't you know that my father was a par-
son? It was just like I heard his own voice speaking and he's been dead
five thousand years. There! I've gone and almost waked Henry up.

HEN. [*Talking in his sleep, indistinctly*]   Fellows . . . what have they done
for us? . . . Blocked our way at every step. Kept everything in their own
hands. And you've stood it. When are you going to wake up?

MRS. A.   Sh, Henry. Go to sleep. Go to sleep. Go to sleep.—Well,
that looks better. Now let's go and help Sabina.

GLAD.   Mama, I'm going out into the backyard and hold the baby
right up in the air. And show him that we don't have to be afraid any more.
Exit GLADYS *to the kitchen.* MRS. ANTROBUS *glances at* HENRY, *exits into
kitchen.* HENRY *thrashes about in his sleep. Enter* ANTROBUS, *his arms full of
bundles, chewing the end of a carrot. He has a slight limp. Over the suit of Act I he
is wearing an overcoat too long for him, its skirts trailing on the ground. He lets his
bundles fall and stands looking about. Presently his attention is fixed on* HENRY,
whose words grow clearer.

300   HEN.   All right! What have you got to lose? What have they done for
us? That's right—nothing. Tear everything down. I don't care what you
smash. We'll begin again and we'll show 'em.

ANTROBUS *takes out his revolver and holds it pointing downwards. With his back
towards the audience he moves toward the footlights.* HENRY'S *voice grows louder
and he wakes with a start. They stare at one another. Then* HENRY *sits up quickly.
Throughout the following scene* HENRY *is played, not as a misunderstood or misguided young man, but as a representation of strong unreconciled evil.*
All right! Do something.   [*Pause.*
Don't think I'm afraid of you, either. All right, do what you were going
to do. Do it.   [*Furiously.*

Thornton Wilder   521

Shoot me, I tell you. You don't have to think I'm any relation of yours. I haven't got any father or any mother, or brothers or sisters. And I don't want any. And what's more I haven't got anybody over me; and I never will have. I'm alone, and that's all I want to be: alone. So you can shoot me.   310

MR. A.   You're the last person I wanted to see. The sight of you dries up all my plans and hopes. I wish I were back at war still, because it's easier to fight you than to live with you. War's a pleasure—do you hear me?—War's a pleasure compared to what faces us now: trying to build up a peacetime with you in the middle of it.

ANTROBUS *walks up to the window.*

HEN.   I'm not going to be a part of any peacetime of yours. I'm going a long way from here and make my own world that's fit for a man to live in. Where a man can be free, and have a chance, and do what he wants to do in his own way.

MR. A.   [*His attention arrested; thoughtfully. He throws the gun out of the window and turns with hope*]   . . . Henry, let's try again.   320

HEN.   Try what? Living *here?*—Speaking polite downtown to all the old men like you? Standing like a sheep at the street corner until the red light turns to green? Being a good boy and a good sheep, like all the stinking ideas you get out of your books? Oh, no. I'll make a world, and I'll show you.

MR. A.   [*Hard*]   How can you make a world for people to live in, unless you've first put order in yourself? Mark my words: I shall continue fighting you until my last breath as long as you mix up your idea of liberty with your idea of hogging everything for yourself. I shall have no pity on you. I shall pursue you to the far corners of the earth. You and I want the 330 same thing; but until you think of it as something that everyone has a right to, you are my deadly enemy and I will destroy you.—I hear your mother's voice in the kitchen. Have you seen her?

HEN.   I have no mother. Get it into your head. I don't belong here. I have nothing to do here. I have no home.

MR. A.   Then why did you come here? With the whole world to choose from, why did you come to this one place: 216 Cedar Street, Excelsior, New Jersey. . . . Well?

HEN.   What if I did? What if I wanted to look at it once more, to see if—   340

MR. A.   Oh, you're related, all right—When your mother comes in you must behave yourself. Do you hear me?

HEN. [*Wildly*]   What is this?—*must behave* yourself. Don't you say *must* to me.

MR. A.   Quiet!

Enter MRS. ANTROBUS *and* SABINA.

HEN.   Nobody can say *must* to me. All my life everybody's been crossing me,—everybody, everything, all of you. I'm going to be free, even if I have to kill half the world for it. Right now, too. Let me get my hands on his throat. I'll show him.

He advances toward ANTROBUS. *Suddenly,* SABINA *jumps between them and calls out in her own person.*

350 SAB. Stop! Stop! Don't play this scene. You know what happened last night. Stop the play.

The men fall back, panting. HENRY *covers his face with his hands.*

Last night you almost strangled him. You became a regular savage. Stop it!

HEN. It's true. I'm sorry. I don't know what comes over me. I have nothing against him personally. I respect him very much . . . I . . . I admire him. But something comes over me. It's like I become fifteen years old again. I . . . I . . . listen: my own father used to whip me and lock me up every Saturday night. I never had enough to eat. He never let me have enough money to buy decent clothes. I was ashamed to go downtown. I never could go to the dances. My father and my uncle put rules 360 in the way of everything I wanted to do. They tried to prevent my living at all.—I'm sorry. I'm sorry.

MRS. A. [*Quickly*] No, go on. Finish what you were saying. Say it all.

HEN. In this scene it's as though I were back in High School again. It's like I had some big emptiness inside me,—the emptiness of being hated and blocked at every turn. And the emptiness fills up with the one thought that you have to strike and fight and kill. Listen, it's as though you have to kill somebody else so as not to end up killing yourself.

SAB. That's not true. I knew your father and your uncle and your mother. You imagined all that. Why, they did everything they could for 370 you. How can you say things like that? They didn't lock you up.

HEN. They did. They did. They wished I hadn't been born.

SAB. That's not true.

MR. A. [*In his own person, with self-condemnation, but cold and proud*] Wait a minute. I have something to say, too. It's not wholly his fault that he wants to strangle me in this scene. It's my fault, too. He wouldn't feel that way unless there were something in me that reminded him of all that. He talks about an emptiness. Well, there's an emptiness in me, too. Yes,—work, work, work,—that's all I do. I've ceased to *live*. No wonder he feels that anger coming over him.

380 MRS. A. There! At least you've said it.

SAB. We're all just as wicked as we can be, and that's the God's truth.

MRS. A. [*Nods a moment, then comes forward; quietly*] Come. Come and put your head under some cold water.

SAB. [*In a whisper*] I'll go with him. I've known him a long while. You have to go on with the play. Come with me.

HENRY *starts out with* SABINA, *but turns at the exit and says to* ANTROBUS:

HEN. Thanks. Thanks for what you said. I'll be all right tomorrow.

Thornton Wilder   523

I won't lose control in that place. I promise.

Exeunt HENRY *and* SABINA. ANTROBUS *starts toward the front door, fastens it.* MRS. ANTROBUS *goes up stage and places the chair close to table.*

MRS. A.   George, do I see you limping?

MR. A.   Yes, a little. My old wound from the other war started smarting again. I can manage.   390

MRS. A.   [*Looking out of the window*]   Some lights are coming on,—the first in seven years. People are walking up and down looking at them. Over in Hawkins' open lot they've built a bonfire to celebrate the peace. They're dancing around it like scarecrows.

MR. A.   A bonfire! As though they hadn't seen enough things burning—Maggie,—the dog died?

MRS. A.   Oh, yes. Long ago. There are no dogs left in Excelsior.—You're back again! All these years. I gave up counting on letters. The few that arrived were anywhere from six months to a year late.

MR. A.   Yes, the ocean's full of letters, along with the other things.   400

MRS. A.   George, sit down, you're tired.

MR. A.   No, you sit down. I'm tired but I'm restless.

Suddenly, as she comes forward:

Maggie! I've lost it. I've lost it.

MRS. A.   What, George? What have you lost?

MR. A.   The most important thing of all: The desire to begin again, to start building.

MRS. A.   [*Sitting in the chair right of the table*]   Well, it will come back.

MR. A.   [*At the window*]   I've lost it. This minute I feel like all those people dancing around the bonfire—just relief. Just the desire to settle down; to slip into the old grooves and keep the neighbors from walking 410 over my lawn.—Hm. But during the war,—in the middle of all that blood and dirt and hot and cold—every day and night, I'd have moments, Maggie, when I *saw* the things that we could do when it was over. When you're at war you think about a better life; when you're at peace you think about a more comfortable one. I've lost it. I feel sick and tired.

MRS. A.   Listen! The baby's crying.

I hear Gladys talking. Probably she's quieting Henry again. George, while Gladys and I were living here—like moles, like rats, and when we were at our wits' end to save the baby's life—the only thought we clung to was that you were going to bring something good out of this suffering. 420 In the night, in the dark, we'd whisper about it, starving and sick.—Oh, George, you'll have to get it back again. Think! What else kept us alive all these years? Even now, it's not comfort we want. We can suffer whatever's necessary; only give us back that promise.

Enter SABINA *with a lighted lamp. She is dressed as in Act I.*

SAB.   Mrs. Antrobus . . .

MRS. A.   Yes, Sabina?

SAB. Will you need me?

MRS. A. No, Sabina, you can go to bed.

SAB. Mrs. Antrobus, if it's all right with you, I'd like to go to the bon-
430 fire and celebrate seeing the war's over. And, Mrs. Antrobus, they've
opened the Gem Movie Theater and they're giving away a hand-painted
soup tureen to every lady, and I thought one of us ought to go.

MR. A. Well, Sabina, I haven't any money. I haven't seen any money
for quite a while.

SAB. Oh, you don't need money. They're taking anything you can
give them. And I have some . . . some . . . Mrs. Antrobus, promise you
won't tell anyone. It's a little against the law. But I'll give you some, too.

MR. A. What is it?

SAB. I'll give you some, too. Yesterday I picked up a lot of . . . of
440 beef-cubes!

MRS. ANTROBUS *turns and says calmly:*

MRS. A. But, Sabina, you know you ought to give that in to the
Center downtown. They know who needs them most.

SAB. [*Outburst*] Mrs. Antrobus, I didn't make this war. I didn't ask for
it. And, in my opinion, after anybody's gone through what we've gone
through, they have a right to grab what they can find. You're a very nice
man, Mr. Antrobus, but you'd have got on better in the world if you'd
realized that dog-eat-dog was the rule in the beginning and always will
be. And most of all now.

[*In tears*] Oh, the world's an awful place, and you know it is. I used to
450 think something could be done about it; but I know better now. I hate it.
I hate it.

She comes forward slowly and brings six cubes from the bag.

All right. All right. You can have them.

MR. A. Thank you, Sabina.

SAB. Can I have . . . can I have one to go to the movies?

[*Antrobus in silence gives her one*] Thank you.

MR. A. Good night, Sabina.

SAB. Mr. Antrobus, don't mind what I say. I'm just an ordinary girl,
you know what I mean, I'm just an ordinary girl. But you're a bright
man, you're a very bright man, and of course you invented the alphabet
460 and the wheel, and, my God, a lot of things . . . and if you've got any
other plans, my God, don't let me upset them. Only every now and then
I've got to go to the movies. I mean my nerves can't stand it. But if you
have any ideas about improving the crazy old world, I'm really with you.
I really am. Because it's . . . it's . . . Good night.

She goes out. ANTROBUS *starts laughing softly with exhilaration.*

MR. A. Now I remember what three things always went together
when I was able to see things most clearly: three things. Three things:

He points to where SABINA *has gone out.*

The voice of the people in their confusion and their need. And the thought of you and the children and this house. . . . And . . . Maggie! I didn't dare ask you: my books! They haven't been lost, have they?

MRS. A.   No. There are some of them right here. Kind of tattered.   470

MR. A.   Yes.—Remember, Maggie, we almost lost them once before? And when we finally did collect a few torn copies out of old cellars they ran in everyone's head like a fever. They as good as rebuilt the world. *Pauses, book in hand, and looks up.*

Oh, I've never forgotten for long at a time that living is struggle. I know that every good and excellent thing in the world stands moment by moment on the razor-edge of danger and must be fought for—whether it's a field, or a home, or a country. All I ask is the chance to build new worlds and God has always given us that. And has given us [*Opening the book*] voices to guide us; and the memory of our mistakes to warn us. Maggie, you and I will remember in peacetime all the resolves that were   480 so clear to us in the days of war. We've come a long ways. We've learned. We're learning. And the steps of our journey are marked for us here.

He stands by the table turning the leaves of a book.

Sometimes out there in the war,—standing all night on a hill—I'd try and remember some of the words in these books. Parts of them and phrases would come back to me. And after a while I used to give names to the hours of the night.   [*He sits, hunting for a passage in the book.*

Nine o'clock I used to call Spinoza. Where is it: "After experience had taught me—"

The back wall has disappeared, revealing the platform. FRED BAILEY *carrying his numeral has started from left to right.* MRS. ANTROBUS *sits by the table sewing.*

BAIL.   "After experience had taught me that the common occurrences of daily life are vain and futile; and I saw that all the objects of my desire   490 and fear were in themselves nothing good nor bad save insofar as the mind was affected by them; I at length determined to search out whether there was something truly good and communicable to man."

Almost without break HESTER, *carrying a large Roman numeral ten, starts crossing the platform.* GLADYS *appears at the kitchen door and moves towards her mother's chair.*

HES.   "Then tell me, O Critias, how will a man choose the ruler that shall rule over him? Will he not choose a man who has first established order in himself, knowing that any decision that has its spring from anger or pride or vanity can be multiplied a thousand fold in its effects upon the citizens?"

HESTER *disappears and* IVY, *as eleven o'clock, starts speaking.*

IVY.   "This good estate of the mind possessing its object in energy we call divine. This we mortals have occasionally and it is this energy which   500 is pleasantest and best. But God has it always. It is wonderful in us; but in Him how much more wonderful."

As Mr. Tremayne *starts to speak,* Henry *appears at the edge of the scene, brooding and unreconciled, but present.*

Tre. "In the beginning, God created the Heavens and the earth; And the Earth was waste and void; And the darkness was upon the face of the deep. And the Lord said let there be light and there was light."
Sudden black-out and silence, except for the last strokes of the midnight bell. Then just as suddenly the lights go up, and Sabina *is standing at the window, as at the opening of the play.*

Sab. Oh, oh, oh. Six o'clock and the master not home yet. Pray God nothing serious has happened to him crossing the Hudson River. But I wouldn't be surprised. The whole world's at sixes and sevens, and why the house hasn't fallen down about our ears long ago is a miracle to me.
She comes down to the footlights.
510 This is where you came in. We have to go on for ages and ages yet.
You go home.
The end of this play isn't written yet.
Mr. and Mrs. Antrobus! Their heads are full of plans and they're as confident as the first day they began,—and they told me to tell you: good night.

1 2 3 4 5 6 7 8 9 10 11 12 13 14 15 16 17 18 19 20 21 22 23 24 25   B   75 74 73 72 71 70 69 68 67 66 65

THE UNITED NATIONS
Background, Organization, Functions, Activities

THE UNITED NATIONS
Background, Organization, Functions, Activities

AMRY VANDENBOSCH
Professor of Political Science
University of Kentucky
Lexington, Kentucky

WILLARD N. HOGAN
Professor of Political Science
State University Teachers College
New Paltz, New York

GREENWOOD PRESS, PUBLISHERS
WESTPORT, CONNECTICUT

To SERGEANT ROBERT LESLIE JONES, JR.
and his comrades
of many nations

INTRODUCTION

In this book Professors Vandenbosch and Hogan have presented a lucid picture of the complex factors involved in the processes and practices of international organization. Their approach to the multiple facets of this activity appears to be quite objective and sufficiently comprehensive to furnish an over-all evaluation of the progress already achieved.

It is almost impossible, indeed, for any author dealing with the dynamic problems of international relations ever to give a completely up-to-date report. Events flow swiftly, and frequently a decision on mere procedure does affect basically the course of action on a fundamental substantive matter. Professors Vandenbosch and Hogan have come close to that desirable goal and do not fail to indicate where students can find follow-up information concerning items of particular interest.

The literature on the United Nations and the Specialized Agencies already embraces hundreds of titles, outside the publications of the intergovernmental bodies themselves; yet, not all phases of their evolution have been fully surveyed nor submitted to the fire of critical appraisal.

One point that this book brings forth with particular emphasis is that all activities of the United Nations system are part of an indivisible aim: collective security. This collective security, as the authors point out, is the hope of all men, and the human being thus again becomes the principal subject of international action.

Opinions may differ as to the actual degree of world community achieved from the political standpoint, but there seems to be a general agreement on the geophysical and geodemographic unity of the world emphasized and made more evident by scientific and technological progress.

There may also be different evaluations of the prospects of building supranational as distinguished from international bodies through which the world can strive for higher forms of organization.

But there can be no controversy over the fact that all peoples, whatever may be their individual philosophy, even those now under the temporary sway of nationalism, wish to be a part in the broader picture of the world as their best insurance against being by-passed by the process of advancement towards a better and more peaceful life.

And, as the authors show, they are all playing a role, through the development of national foreign policies, based upon the expressions of public opinion and their contributions to a worldwide supranational public opinion.

Public opinion always acts reasonably when well informed. This book of Professors Vandenbosch and Hogan will contribute to its enlightenment.

B. COHEN
Assistant Secretary-General
for Public Information
The United Nations

NEW YORK, N.Y.
March, 1952

PREFACE

The purpose of this book is to give an explanation of the United Nations—its background, organization, functions, and activities. This volume has been prepared primarily for introductory college classes studying the United Nations system or contemporary international organization. It is hoped, however, that the book will also be useful in connection with discussion groups and as a source of information for those who wish to go beyond the daily paper or the weekly news digest.

The United Nations is as broad in scope as the whole field of international relations, and it is involved in a tremendous variety of important activities. The Charter provides for an extensive organization, which has become more ramified in the course of the few years of the institution's development. The authors have attempted to present a systematic treatment of both the complex structure and the varied activities in a single, convenient volume. This is no small task, and we shall be gratified if the performance is moderately successful.

Footnotes have been kept to the minimum, in the feeling that they are more bothersome than helpful to the less advanced student as well as to the general reader. Neither have we considered it wise, for two reasons, to include a comprehensive bibliography. First, a complete list of all the documents and other publications by and about the United Nations would by itself fill a small volume. Second, such a bibliography is unnecessary for our purposes. A student or reader who wishes to engage in further pursuit of any particular point may consult the bibliographic note on page 331. The sources indicated there will give him additional information, and many of them include bibliographies which can be used for still further investigation.

Many of the chapters were used in preliminary form in classes at the University of Kentucky, Berea College, and the State University Teachers College at New Paltz. The comments and questions of our students were very helpful, and we are grateful for this opportunity of a "trial run." We wish to express our thanks to William Agar, Acting Director, Special Services Division, U.N. Department of Public Information, who was always willing to answer questions and to assist us in locating materials concerning the United Nations. Mrs. Glennalou Ryan provided an invaluable service in typing, checking details, and helping with preparation of the manuscript. There is strong reason for us to include the conventional recognition of the encouragement and assistance of our wives, Mary Belle Vandenbosch and Hildur C. Hogan.   All statements, interpretations, and possible errors, however, are the responsibility of the authors alone.

The period covered by this book runs to September 1, 1951. It has been possible to consider developments after that date to only a slight degree.

AMRY VANDENBOSCH
WILLARD N. HOGAN

LEXINGTON, KY.
NEW PALTZ, N.Y.
April, 1952

CONTENTS

LIST OF TABLES

xiii

PART I

BACKGROUND

Chapter 1

WORLD COMMUNITY

When Wendell Willkie made his famous flight around the world in 1942, he returned with the conviction that "our thinking in the future must be world-wide." [1] The experience of traveling 31,000 miles in forty-nine days impressed Mr. Willkie with the fact that moving from one continent to another had become quick and easy. In terms of travel time there are no longer any distant points in the world. The peoples of the Far East are as close to America as California is to New York by the fastest trains. The establishment of close contacts among the peoples of the world means that their activities affect one another and that their problems have become matters of mutual concern.

Human society has been revolutionized by modern technology, especially in the fields of transportation and communication. At the beginning of the nineteenth century it took eight to ten days for a passenger to go by stage from New York City to Boston, a distance of about 250 miles. When the American federal government was being established in 1789 it took two weeks to notify George Washington that he had been elected President and to bring him from Mount Vernon to New York. Today the same trip could be made in four hours by train or in one hour by airplane. The difficulties of travel to the southern and western parts of the United States were even greater, and at some seasons of the year communication practically ceased over large parts of the country. When the colonial settlers first came to North America a perilous ocean voyage of weeks or months was involved. Now overnight flights to Europe are a matter of routine.

Less than 150 years ago, inventors who attempted to build steam railways were considered to be demented. A school board in Ohio probably reflected the popular attitude when it refused the use of its schoolhouse for a discussion of railroads in these words: [2]

You are welcome to use the schoolhouse to debate all proper questions in, but such things as railroads are impossibilities and rank infidelity. There is nothing in the

[1] Wendell Willkie, *One World,* Simon and Schuster, New York, 1943, p. 2.

[2] Quoted in Avery Craven and Walter Johnson, *The United States: Experiment in Democracy,* Ginn, Boston, 1947, p. 339.

word of God about them. If God had designed that His intelligent creatures should travel at the frightful speed of fifteen miles an hour, by steam, He would have clearly foretold it through His holy prophets. It is a device of Satan to lead Immortal souls down to Hell.

Henry Clay, in his speech [3] attacking President Andrew Jackson for vetoing the bill to improve the Maysville (Kentucky) road, said that it took his family four days to reach Lexington from Maysville in April, 1829. This is a distance of about 68 miles, and the trip now takes about an hour and a half by automobile.

There has been a tremendous acceleration in the speed of contacts between peoples living at distances from each other. In the span of two lifetimes the attitude toward speed of travel has changed from considering 15 miles an hour a frightful speed, to debates over whether a human being could travel 60 miles an hour and live, to nonchalant acceptance of a jet airplane pilot's report that he "loafed along" at 500 miles an hour.

Communication developed even more rapidly in terms of speed. Before the telegraph, telephone, radio, and television, messages could be transmitted over long distances only as fast as the most rapid form of transportation. [4] Now messages travel around the world at about 186,000 miles a second, the speed of light. A man making a speech in a large auditorium can be heard thousands of miles away before the sound waves of his voice reach the rear rows of the audience before him. The famous case of the Battle of New Orleans has often been cited to illustrate the differences in human affairs occasioned by the rate of communication. That battle was fought on January 8, 1815, when the War of 1812 had been over for fifteen days. The Treaty of Ghent ending the war had been signed on December 24, 1814. It was not until February 19, six weeks after the battle and almost two months after the war was over, that General Jackson heard the news! In contrast, the Security Council of the United Nations passed its first resolution in the Korean case less than twenty-four hours after the outbreak of the fighting. Without the modern technology of communication, the war might have been over before the Security Council learned that it had started.

Rapid transportation and instantaneous communication have made possible a network of world-wide contacts and interests. The most distant parts of the globe are no longer the personal concern merely of an occasional traveler. Millions of people, including the fictional but all-important "average citizen," find woven into their daily lives the consequences of modern technology, which has shrunk the barriers of time and distance to a small fraction of their former significance. There is quick, easy, and frequent contact by large numbers of people between countries and continents. The news from all over the world

[3] This was Clay's speech on the American System given at Cincinnati, Ohio, Aug. 3, 1830.

[4] Except for a few localized exceptions like smoke signals, flashing lights, etc.

can be known everywhere the same day it happens. The social pattern of small, isolated communities has given way to a large and complicated system, no part of which can be insulated from the impact of events vital to distant parts of the world.

Development of the new pattern of human society has been accompanied by a fundamental change in the impact and implications of warfare. It is no longer possible to restrict the fighting to the actual battle area and to make a sharp distinction between combatants and noncombatants. Modern war is industrialized war. The worker in a munitions factory is as important as the soldier at the front. The transportation system and the food supply become the object of enemy attacks. The purpose is to break the resistance of the enemy by destroying his capacity for waging war. Any technique that tends to destroy or undermine the ability to resist is brought into use. Air power, high explosives, atomic bombs, guided missiles, and other devices make it possible to strike the enemy far behind the lines. This means "total war," involving mass destruction of lives and property and threatening the very survival of civilization. Under these circumstances a resort to war anywhere is of concern everywhere, simply because the forces inherent in modern technology create a situation in which no country can hope to remain immune from the spreading effects of war. The most powerful country cannot, by itself, assure its own security. Protection from the ravages of war can be found only in cooperative action for the prevention of war. Recognition of this fact lies at the heart of the belief that "our thinking in the future must be world-wide."

Modern society is also characterized by a condition of economic interdependence. Because of the uneven distribution of important mineral resources, the differences in climate, and the diversity of soils, no one country can produce all the commodities which are necessary for its economic life. Moreover, the advantages of geographic specialization make it profitable for countries to exchange products rather than try to be self-sufficient. This situation naturally affects some countries more than others. Great Britain, for example, is dependent upon imports for a large part of its food supply, and half its people would starve if they were cut off from the rest of the world. The vital importance of this fact may be appreciated by recalling that at the beginning of World War II the British government boasted of an increase in food stocks which would make it possible to hold out against blockade for four months.

The United States and the Soviet Union, because of their large size and varied resources, are not as economically dependent as smaller countries. Yet they, too, are highly dependent upon other countries. The United States consumes about 50 per cent of the world's output of tin, but that important metal is not mined in this country. The United States produces practically no nickel, while Canada alone accounts for about 90 per cent of total world production. The United States is the greatest consumer of rubber; until recently, most of the supply was imported, but the dependence on overseas areas in this respect has been reduced by the ability to produce synthetic rubber. The "American standard of living" owes much to American resources and productivity, but without imports it would lack coffee, tea, bananas, cola drinks, chocolate, spices, high-quality steel, telephones, most cosmetics and pharmaceuticals, and many other familiar products. Vastly inferior and more expensive substitutes would have to be found for materials which now go into the making of automobiles, newspapers, electrical appliances, soap, paint, insulation materials, machinery of all types, and large numbers of other articles. It is somewhat ironical that a country as powerful as the United States is deficient in some thirty materials which are essential to the prosecution of war.

The condition of economic interdependence also applies to exports. Much of the industrial and agricultural production of the United States is tied to the availability of export markets. Even before World War II, the United States sold abroad about 10 per cent of its annual production. In the case of certain staple industries this ran as high as 20 or even 50 per cent. The foreign market is important to many industries, such as automobile and machinery manufacturers. This situation also applies to agriculture, since the United States exports great quantities of wheat, tobacco, hog products, and cotton. When measures to combat the depression were being considered by Franklin D. Roosevelt's first administration, Secretary of Agriculture Wallace pointed out [5] that a self-contained United States

must be prepared to make permanent the retirement of from 40 to 100 million acres of crop-land. Forty million if we take out good land; 100 million if we take out the worst. Furthermore, if we continue year after year with only 25 or 30 million acres of cotton in the South instead of 40 or 45 million acres, it may be necessary after a time to shift part of the southern population, and there is a question as to just what kind of activity these southern farm laborers should engage in. We will find exactly the same dilemma, although not on quite such a great scale, in the corn and wheat belts.

It has been estimated that in 1937 some 2,400,000 Americans made their living by producing industrial and agricultural goods for export, not counting transport workers and others whose jobs depended indirectly on the export trade.[6]

The great importance of world trade for the domestic prosperity was well stated by Secretary of State Cordell Hull in a speech before the American section of the International Chamber of Commerce on May 2, 1933, in these words: [7]

[5] H. A. Wallace, *America Must Choose*, World Affairs Pamphlets, No. 3, Boston, 1934.

[6] Horace Taylor and Harold Barger, *The American Economy in Operation*, Harcourt, Brace, New York, 1949, p. 679.

[7] U.S. Department of State, *Press Releases*, May 6, 1933, p. 315.

The far-reaching effect of international trade is further understood when we recall that South American countries must export and sell abroad from 30 to 50 percent of their total production; England must sell 25 percent; New Zealand, 40 percent; and Japan 45 to 60 percent. America must look mainly to those countries to purchase her surplus foodstuffs, raw materials and finished manufactures. A slump on the international market, from any cause, with a serious drop of export prices and values, can cause a breakdown of the entire economic and financial life of these large exporting countries, and this in turn paralyzes our own foreign trade and, as has been demonstrated during this panic, cuts in half our production and trade among ourselves here at home, and throws millions of wage-earners out of employment. . . . The view is eternally sound that our home market must be supplemented by a growing foreign trade for the purpose of stable and desirable domestic prosperity.

The technological and economic factors are by no means the only ones which involve a substantial degree of interdependence among the peoples of the world. All aspects of human culture transcend national boundaries and reflect cosmopolitan tendencies in human activities, interests, and loyalties. There is a common heritage of law, philosophy, literature, art, religion, and ethical ideas throughout Western civilization. Latin America has a common heritage from Latin Europe. If any American is tempted to think of a self-sufficient United States, let him reflect that the very language in which he expresses himself is a borrowed product. If any Soviet citizen is similarly tempted, let him remember that Karl Marx was a German who worked in England. The truth is that the culture of every country is strongly, if not predominantly, affected by conditions and movements in other parts of the world. Furthermore, such influences are not limited to the fact of historical derivation. Each country is a part of the world. Hermit kingdoms and iron curtains may distort that fact, but they cannot eliminate it.

The great religions of the world claim adherents in many lands. Christianity, Judaism, Mohammedanism, Hinduism, Confucianism, and the others have a world-wide influence. They represent forces which must be taken into account by the policies of national governments. Roman Catholics in Eastern Europe and Zionists in the United States are only two examples of this fact. Science also is international in its scope and outlook. It has produced its wonders by a process of cross-fertilization between the ideas and work of men and women from many countries. To wrap science in the trappings of nationalism is to suffocate it.

Every important social and economic group is to some extent opposed to another group within the same country and sympathetic to a similar group in other countries. Employers' associations share with labor unions the tendency to organize across national frontiers. A scientist, a chess player, or a vegetarian may have more in common with fellow enthusiasts in distant lands than he does with many people in his own home town. The ideological conflict of the modern world is in itself evidence of the fact that social groups and interests are not organized exclusively along national lines. The idea of completely independent, self-sufficient, and homogeneous countries is a legal fiction which receives some psychological encouragement from the abstractions of maps with their boundaries and separate blocks of color. The legal fiction and the map, however, do not encompass the whole of the social reality.

Recognition of contemporary technological, economic, and cultural conditions and forces leads to the question, "Is there a world community?" It is not easy to give a simple and definitive answer to this question. If "community" is taken in the biological sense of a population in a habitat, the earth can be viewed as one habitat and the human race is certainly one species. If, on the other hand, one considers the idea of locality and relative smallness of area as the test, the world as a matter of definition could not be one community. If communication is the essential factor, as it would seem to be by etymology, then the existence of modern technology means that there is a world community. However, the psychological or subjective criterion, that a community exists when its members feel that they "belong together," is not satisfied. Nor can a world community be said to exist if emphasis is placed on the idea of group likeness and homogeneity in contrast to other groups which show greater cultural divergencies.

The question, "Is there a world community?" is partly one of fact and partly one of terminology. There is a substantial degree of interdependence, and the processes of social interaction operate on a world-wide scale. Quick and easy communication has linked many countries, and its universal extension is technically feasible.

The sense of world community exists, but only in an embryonic stage since it is the dominant loyalty of a very small fraction of the world's population. Narrow nationalism remains a powerful force, and attitudes based on feelings of antagonism are prevalent and ominous. In this situation, the best answer to the question posed above is to consider community as a matter of degree,[8] and to say that a world community does exist. It is, however, much more advanced in its technological phases than in its psychological and governmental aspects. Man's capacity to organize the developing world community lags behind the forces which are creating that community. It becomes necessary, therefore, to consider the problem of world political organization in terms of the state system and the development of international cooperation.

[8] This is consistent with the historical development of the term in the social sciences. See the article on "Community" in the *Encyclopedia of the Social Sciences*, Vol. 4, Macmillan, New York, 1931.

Chapter 2

THE STATE SYSTEM

The state is the basic unit of international society. There have been several different kinds of states in the course of history, and the one most commonly prevailing today is the nation-state. There is a strong tendency to assume that the peoples of the world have always grouped themselves together in nation-states, but nothing could be further from the truth. Indeed, the present state system is hardly three centuries old. The state, it must be remembered, is not an end in itself, but an instrument in meeting man's social needs. Thus the form and character of the state have changed with man's shifting economic conditions and social needs.

Ancient State Systems

Two forms of the state were found in ancient times: the city-state and the empire. The first was found in a very high degree of development among the ancient Greeks.[1] The modern city is a trading, manufacturing, and residential community, and its political boundaries do not extend beyond this community. It is highly dependent economically and does not enjoy political autonomy. The Greek city-state, however, was not exclusively an urban or trading center; it also included within its political boundaries a considerable area of the surrounding territory. From the point of view of this discussion the most important characteristic of the city-state was its political independence. The Greek city-states, large and small, were regarded as independent sovereign bodies, each the equal of the other. They were to a large degree economically self-sufficient. An important characteristic of the Greek city-state was the amazing vigor of its political life. The whole of the individual's life was identified with the city; he was bound to it by religious, cultural, and economic as well as political ties. This many-sided intimate relationship of the citizen to his city produced an intense patriotism for his small but independent political community.

A number of independent political units living in such proximity must in-

---

[1] City-states were also found in Italy in antiquity and in Italy and northwestern Europe in the Middle Ages.

evitably develop some form of interstate relations. In fact, the Greek city-states developed an incipient interstate order not unlike that of our modern international system. They were united by a large network of treaties regulating their commercial and other relations. Diplomatic representatives were exchanged, and the principles and practices governing such exchange reached a high degree of development. Certain practices, like the immunity granted to diplomatic agents, were remarkably like those found in modern international law. There were laws regulating the rights of aliens, the right of asylum was recognized, and on occasion aliens were naturalized.

Two important fundamental ideas in the field of international relations have come down to us from the Greek city-states, namely, those of arbitration and of confederation. While often resorting to arbitration as a means of settling disputes with one another, they failed to utilize this method in times of great crisis. The devastating Peloponnesian War, which left both parties exhausted and Greece an easy prey to the foreign conqueror, might not have been fought had Sparta accepted the offer of Pericles to submit the dispute to arbitration. The numerous leagues and confederations of Greek history indicate that the Greeks also had the idea of confederation on the basis of equality. The Greeks were apparently the first in the history of Europe to establish an interstate council. The amphictyonic council, though primarily a religious body, is of great significance in the history of international relations, for it attempted to limit the cruelties of war by laying down certain rules of warfare. Among the measures prohibited under the rules were the cutting off of a city's water supply and the annihilation of populations.

Another striking similarity between the ancient and medieval city-state and the modern national state is the strong tendency toward imperialism exhibited by both. Like the modern national state the Greek city-state sought to attain a high degree of economic self-sufficiency. But with the increase of population, resulting from the growth of commerce and industry, self-sufficiency became steadily more difficult, if not impossible, of attainment. Large quantities of necessities had to be imported. This economic condition soon reflected itself in the foreign policy of the city-states, as indicated by the desire to open foreign markets, the efforts to establish fortified trading posts in foreign lands, the multiplication of colonies, the attempt to levy tribute on foreign cities, and the frequent reduction of leagues to empires. Athens under Pericles was reproached for having changed the Delian Confederation into a despotic empire, "enslaving her cities contrary to treaty." [2]

In spite of the fact that the Greeks were united by the bonds of race, religion, language, and customs, they failed to solve the problem of their inter-city relations. Though they made truly remarkable progress in the rudimentary development of an international law and organization, they failed to impress their interstate system with unity and stability. In this respect they forecast

[2] F. Melian Stawell, *Growth of International Thought*, Holt, New York, 1930, p. 22.

the same fatal inability of the nation-states centuries later. They failed to develop their interstate institutions far enough. The separate political entities were unwilling to subordinate their particular interests to the larger interests of all Greece. They exhausted themselves fighting each other and in the end were overcome by foreign foes.

The second form of political organization known to the ancient world was the empire, which had its origin in the conquest of a large number of principalities, small kingdoms, and city-states. While a few of the empires developed rather elaborate systems of imperial administration, most of them rested upon military despotism and quickly suffered disintegration. The Babylonian, the Persian, the Assyrian, the Egyptian, and the Macedonian were among the larger of the empires of the ancient Near East. Even among these states, whose underlying principle was dominance and not the free association of equals, some forms of interstate relations were present. Treaty relations were not uncommon among the units of the empire and between them and lesser states.

With Rome we have the development of a city-state into an empire that covered nearly all the Mediterranean region and extended its rule even as far as England. During the period of the empire, Rome dealt with other peoples on the basis not of equality but of subordination. The Roman Empire impressed order upon the world but at the expense of the liberty of the peoples it conquered. But even Rome made a contribution to the modern system of international law and organization. The development of international law in its formative period was greatly influenced by the Roman institution of the *jus gentium*. Since the traditional Roman law was applicable only to Romans, aliens were at first tried under their own laws. But when the magistrate had to apply laws to cases between Romans and non-Romans, or when there was no Roman law applicable in cases involving Roman citizens, he would seek a rule already common in the practice of most nations. This law, *jus gentium*, came to be understood as "the law which all men everywhere obey." At this stage it dealt with subject matter now known as private international law, or conflict of laws. Later *jus gentium* came to be identified with natural law, and later still, in the early Middle Ages, its use as a term became limited to that part of natural law which deals with *jus inter gentes*, that is, the law governing the relations between peoples, or international law. Aside from this the contribution of the Romans to international law and relations was slight.

THE RISE OF THE NATIONAL STATE

The fall of the Roman Empire was not immediately followed by the rise of the modern state. There was a long transition period of nearly a thousand years, during which the "state" actually disappeared from Western Europe. When the nomadic hordes from the north and northeast swarmed over the

Roman Empire a period of rapid disintegration set in. The state had once more to be built up within a primitive society. This long historical process can be only briefly described here.

Though the political unity of the Western world had been shattered, the spell of the former political universalism long continued to sway the medieval mind. The theory had ultimately, however, to yield before the facts. In the welter of barbarian disorder the primary need of the people was for protection, and to obtain it they turned to the strong man of the immediate neighborhood rather than to a distant shadow emperor. The strong man became the lord of the district. Imperial unity disappeared, and in its place came a hierarchy of knights, barons, counts, marquises, dukes, and kings. Each received his lands from the one next above him in the hierarchy, and in return was required to render military service and economic dues. At the base was the peasant, bound to the soil in serfdom. The distinction between public office and private property was lost; political power became identified with land ownership. The general result was the fragmentation of political power. Though the king was generally able to exact tribute, he was unable to enforce order in every district of his dominions. The local lords carried on war and diplomacy very much as if they were the sovereigns of independent states.

While Europe thus underwent a long period of economic and political disintegration, a strong cultural unifying agency remained in the Church. Christianity had been for a long time proscribed, but Rome finally had been compelled to come to terms with the new religion. Although the state had earlier been hostile to Christianity, it now gave it a favored position. The changed position of the Church had far-reaching effects on its character. Its rapid growth and preferred position soon enabled it to contest with the empire itself for supremacy. Since the people of the Middle Ages regarded themselves as Christians first, under the spiritual authority of the Papacy, they felt only a secondary loyalty to the temporal princes. As long as that attitude prevailed the Church had a powerful advantage over the secular authorities, for no ruler could long remain in power after he had been excommunicated by the Pope and his people enjoined from obeying him. Through the acquisition of vast areas of land the Church also enjoyed a large measure of temporal power. An institution of such universal influence necessarily exerted a strong cohesive force in an age of disintegration. It is not surprising therefore that the medieval Church rendered valuable services in the interest of internationalism. It sought to restrict the ravages of incessant warfare. By its declaration of the "truce of God" the Church forbade fighting on certain days of the week and in certain seasons of the year, and it endeavored constantly to extend the number of days of truce. Moreover, the Church forbade fighting in the vicinity of church buildings and against certain classes of the population, such as clerics, pilgrims, merchants, women, and peasants. The Church thus tried to abate the rigors of war and to alter its character, changing it from a private to a public affair. The Papacy also encouraged arbitration by serving as an arbitrator in the settlement of several important disputes. For example, the Pope acted as arbitrator in the famous dispute between Portugal and Spain concerning the boundaries of the areas in the New World which they claimed on the grounds of discovery.

From the chaos of feudal society the nation-state of modern times gradually emerged. The thousands of loosely associated petty lordships of which feudal society was composed were finally consolidated under the king to make the monarchical, national state. To this movement of unification the growth of commerce and the consequent development of towns gave a tremendous impetus. The towns with their compact populations, their vigor and greater economic and political strength became more than a match for the feudal barons. The chief interest of the burghers was in extending trade over a constantly wider area, but the fragmentation of political power and the incessant warfare which accompanied it obstructed and depressed trade. The townsmen, therefore, joined forces with the king to break the political power of the barons. At this stage of historical evolution the new middle class was the ally of the king in establishing the absolute monarchy, for a strong central government able to keep law and order over the whole country was clearly in its interest. At a later date it led the movement for a limited, constitutional monarchy. Centralized control having been established, it demanded such share in political power as its steadily mounting economic power seemed to justify.

The passing of feudalism and the emergence of the modern state is vividly reflected in the writings of Machiavelli, an Italian statesman and diplomat who lived from 1469 to 1527. Machiavelli marks the close of one epoch and the beginning of another. The idea of a united Europe under an imperial ruler did not interest him, and he was frankly and thoroughly nonreligious or secular in his outlook. He was passionately interested in the national unification of his native Italy. He saw other countries unified under strong kings, and since he believed that Italy could be unified only under a strong monarch, he wished to advise the Italian prince on how to maintain and extend his authority. Machiavelli was a man of the world and based his advice on observation and experience. The prince who would be successful, he concluded, must stop at nothing. He must be prepared to use not only physical force and craft but, if the circumstances demanded it, even fraud and treachery. The state was an end in itself and was not bound by the rules which govern private morality.

The term "national state" has been used to describe the separate independent states which emerged from feudal society. But what is the national state, as contrasted with other forms of the state? It is the union of nationality, or nation, with the state. What is the nation and how did it develop? The Middle Ages gave birth to the great peoples of Europe as we now know them

—the French, the Germans, the Italians, the Spanish, and the English. Some centuries later, as a continuation of this movement, nationalities developed in the remainder of Europe, the Americas, and more recently in Asia and limited parts of Africa. Each of these peoples emerged with a common language and a fairly definite national culture and became identified with certain geographic areas. In the course of time a very strong feeling of community interests developed. Just what the common qualities or definite interests are which produce this strong feeling of unity it is difficult to say. One may point to certain common elements, such as language, religion, territory, custom, race, and the tradition of a common political life, but no one of these is inseparable from nationality. The Swiss, Belgians, and Canadians have no common language, the Jews until recently had no common territory, the Indians have separated into two states, and it is highly doubtful whether there are any nations with a racial stock of a high degree of purity. In the last analysis a people are a nation if they believe that they constitute a nation, and that belief is the most important element in the situation or movement.

Though nationalism may be difficult to define or explain, there can be no doubt of the tremendous influence it exerts in the life of the modern world. Carlton J. H. Hayes, a leading American historian and student of the movement, calls it the "most significant factor in public life today." [3]   The force of nationalism is illustrated first of all in the irresistible drive toward making state lines coincide with those of nationality, of establishing nationalities as political units. When a state is based upon nationality it is called a "national state." The movement to make the nation and the state one was of long duration, and the forces behind the movement are not yet spent. Two of the great nations of Europe, the German and the Italian, did not achieve political unification until the latter half of the nineteenth century. The present force of the movement can be seen in South Asia, where peoples are vigorously striving to achieve national unity. Nearly all the young nations of that region have since World War II won the struggle for political independence.

The movement did not, however, operate everywhere to enlarge the state. In multinational states, like those of Austria-Hungary, Turkey, and the British Empire, it operated to break up the larger units. When the movement tends to dissolve larger states into numerous small states, it is clearly operating counter to the economic forces and the technological developments of modern society, which are integrating constantly larger areas.

More significant even than the historical process set in motion by nationalism is the state of mind that generally accompanies it. The nationalist mentality exalts loyalty to the nation or the national state, making it superior to every other loyalty. In the Middle Ages, men were primarily loyal to their religion and their spiritual authorities; later, everything yielded before loyalty to the national state. A powerful American metropolitan daily journal for a

[3] *Essay on Nationalism,* Macmillan, New York, 1926, p. 1.

long time carried as its slogan at the top of the editorial column the words of the American patriot, Stephen Decatur, "Our country, in her intercourse with nations may she be right, but our country right or wrong." Men have been filled with a holy zeal for furthering their country's "sacred mission" or realizing her "manifest destiny" and have unquestioningly and cheerfully laid down their lives for their country. Because of these characteristics nationalism has been compared to religion.[4]

THE NATIONAL STATE AND IMPERIALISM

The national state had hardly emerged before it set out on a policy of colonial expansion. Commerce was instrumental in the formation of the nation-state; thereafter, it strongly influenced, if it did not dominate, its policies. The Dutch were still fighting for their independence when their government chartered the East India Company to stake out a vast trade area in the Far East. The movement of expansion which began in the early modern period has continued intermittently, reaching its climax in the period just preceding World War I. As a result of this movement nearly one-half of the world's area came into a relationship of political subordination to a small group of advanced powers. It becomes necessary briefly to examine the economic and political forces behind this extraordinary movement.

With the growth of commerce a money economy arose and with it a scarcity of gold and silver. Moreover, the rising national kings were rapidly increasing their expenditures, both in maintaining costly courts and in carrying on wars or preparing for future ones. Under these conditions it was easy for the king and his ministers to be misled into believing that the precious metals constituted a form of wealth more desirable than other forms. They, therefore, bent every effort toward building up a large supply of gold in the national treasury. One way of acquiring gold and silver was by mining it, either at home or by the discovery and the exploitation of rich new mines in distant lands. Spain became rich through the latter method. Most of the other rising European national states had to content themselves with the indirect method, the method of acquiring the precious metals through a large, profitable foreign trade. By stimulating exports and depressing imports a large surplus trade balance was built up, which so-called "favorable" balance of international trade could be paid in gold and silver. This policy of stimulating exports and depressing imports and of forcing the balance to be paid in gold is called "mercantilism." In practice, it led to the application of the principle of monopoly to all phases of colonial trade. Only the nationals of the mother country were permitted to sell in the market of the colony or to purchase raw materials or commercial luxuries there, and the carrying trade between the mother country and the colony was likewise reserved for them.

[4] *Ibid.*, Chap. 4, "Nationalism as a Religion."

This monopoly of trade and shipping was enforced by very severe penalties —the confiscation of cargo and vessel, and sometimes even death.

In the beginning, the governments and the chartered trading companies had no desire for political control over the backward areas. They desired only trading monopolies, but they discovered that they could not safeguard these monopolies and obtain a lucrative trade unless they also governed, and so against their wishes even the trading companies became rulers over vast areas. The shift from a commercial to a territorial and political basis did not solve all the problems of the profit-minded companies. The more important ones steadily declined or got into difficulties, and in the end their governments had to take over their interests, assuming both liabilities and assets. Thus the powers of the Dutch East India Company were transferred to the Dutch government in 1798, while the British East India Company continued sixty years more before being taken over by the Crown.

Following the Napoleonic Wars there was a period of about a century during which the general interest in colonies declined. This waning interest was the result of several influences. France had lost an enormous colonial empire to Great Britain, and the latter in turn had lost her richest colonies by revolution. Spain likewise had lost almost a whole continent through independence movements. Of what profit were colonies if they could be retained only by costly wars and if their ultimate destiny was independence anyway? The free-trade doctrines of Adam Smith had gained wide popularity, and under their influence governments were steadily relaxing the restrictions on their colonial trade. With the growth of the industrial revolution domestic markets expanded enormously and the relative importance of colonial trade declined correspondingly. The French Revolution had also popularized certain liberal and humanitarian ideas which had a bearing on colonialism. All these forces had a share in producing a strong anticolonial movement from 1815 to about 1875.

A combination of forces caused imperialism to break out with renewed force in the third quarter of the nineteenth century. The industrial revolution led to a steady acceleration of production, with the result that the home market of most of the industrial countries seemed to have become saturated. The less advanced industrial countries began to raise their tariff walls to save the home market for their own less developed industries. As a result, pressure was brought to bear upon the governments of industrial countries to find an outlet for the ever-increasing volume of machine products. Improved means of transportation had lowered shipping costs so that goods could successfully be shipped over long distances. New inventions and the production of new goods led to an increased demand for tropical products such as cotton, rubber, and copra, while higher standards of living brought about a demand for other products like sugar, coffee, cocoa, tea, and bananas. Markets and raw products did not exhaust the needs of the industrialized countries. Machine production under a system of *laissez faire* led to great accumulations of capital which could no longer find a sufficiently profitable outlet at home to satisfy the hunger of the investors for dividends. Undeveloped countries offered higher returns on investments, but the owners of surplus capital were loath to invest their money in backward areas unless their investments were safeguarded by the existence of political control, preferably by the home government but at any rate by one of the advanced powers. Thus the chief economic forces operating almost unbridled in the industrial and capitalist society of the day pushed the governments in the direction of imperialism.

There were still other forces impelling toward imperialism. The new medical science, improved methods of sanitation, and hygiene steadily cut down the death rate. Though increased productivity of the machine enabled a given territory to support a larger population than before, there nevertheless developed an anxiety about the future. This fear of population pressure reinforced the economic forces making for imperialism. Psychological factors likewise played a part. While imperialism netted the average citizen nothing but an increased tax burden, he was nevertheless an ardent supporter of the aggressive imperialist policies of his government. Often the humbler the citizen the more eagerly he grasped at the expansion of his ego through the exploits and enhanced prestige of the state of which he was a citizen. As a result of these various forces, governments had the support of nearly every class in the state for their imperialist policies.

During this last recrudescence of imperialism, Africa, the islands in the Pacific Ocean, and large parts of Asia fell under some form of Western political control. Imperialism did not everywhere take the same outward form. Here it resulted in outright annexation, as in the case of the Philippines, Korea, and large areas of Africa; there, in the establishment of protectorates, as in the case of Egypt; elsewhere, in unequal treaties and extraterritorial rights, as in China; and still elsewhere, in temporary occupations and the control of customs, as in the Caribbean and Central America. Sometimes it took such vague and indefinite forms as spheres of influence and interests. Frequently there was a progression, a ripening of one form into another until the stage of complete annexation was reached.

The peak of colonial expansion was reached at about the first decade of this century. At that time nearly half the earth's surface and over a third of its population were under colonial rule. In terms of population Great Britain had the largest empire, followed by France, the Netherlands, Japan, Germany, the United States, Portugal, Belgium, Italy, and Spain.

The imperialism of the last years was self-destructive; it sowed the seeds of its own disintegration. The earlier imperialism sought primarily trade in the backward areas; the chief economic characteristic of the latter imperialism was the export of capital to these regions and the introduction there of the capitalistic system of production. This involved the construction of good roads and railroads, the development of rapid means of communication, and the introduction of a money economy where only barter within numerous small areas had existed before. Western standards of administration were introduced at the behest of the new enterprises and education at the demand of the middle-class liberals in the mother country. In brief, the introduction of the capitalistic system of production led to the growth of towns and an indigenous middle class, and brought about the same economic, social, intellectual, and political transformation which was the basic cause underlying the development of nationalism in the West.[5]

The penetration of Western influences developed a cultural defense reaction in the colony. Since World War I the colonial world has been rocked from end to end by movements for national independence. Because the movement in India was under the leadership of an unusual personality employing startling methods, the nationalist movement in that country for years engrossed world attention, but similar movements of varying intensity developed in Burma, Indochina, China, Korea, the Philippines, and Indonesia and is now developing in Africa. The result has been a period of decolonization, beginning about the time of World War I. The British Dominions first became equal partners of the Commonwealth with the United Kingdom; shortly after World War II, India, Burma, Ceylon, the Philippines, and Indonesia became independent.

The conclusion of World War I also saw the establishment of international supervision of the administration of former enemy territories. This was a recognition of the principle that the government of undeveloped areas was a matter of international concern requiring some sort of international regulation, in so far as certain peoples were not yet ready for self-government. The mandates system, as this arrangement was called, was converted into the trusteeship system under the United Nations. In addition all members of the United Nations have, in ratifying the Charter, accepted very comprehensive obligations with respect to their dependencies. They undertake to ensure the political, economic, social, and educational advancement of the people in their dependent areas and to prepare them for self-government.

Characteristics of the Modern State System

We have seen how the political fragmentation of the Middle Ages finally yielded to a political reintegration, resulting in the formation of a new political unit, the country-state, which was to develop a century or two later into the nation-state. After a century or more of struggle the king had acquired mastery over the cities and barons within his territory and freedom from Pope and emperor externally. The king did not have long to wait for a justification and rationalization of the new state of affairs by a learned jurist. In 1576

[5] N. J. Spykman, "The Social Background of Asiatic Nationalism," *American Journal of Sociology*, Vol. 32, pp. 396–411.

there appeared a book [6] by a French writer, Jean Bodin, in which the legal theory of the new state was expounded. This theory is noteworthy for the exposition of the doctrine of sovereignty. Bodin defined sovereignty as the "supreme power over citizens and subjects, unrestrained by the laws." The chief function of sovereignty is law-making, and since the sovereign is the source of law, he is not bound by it. While the sovereign is thus above the law he is not free from moral restraint; he is limited by obligations arising from natural and divine law. Moreover, the sovereign is morally bound to observe treaties with other sovereigns and contracts with his own subjects. While Bodin favored an absolute monarchy, he distinguished carefully between the state and the government or ruler and held that the possession of sovereignty was the characteristic of the state, regardless of the form of government.

The new states existed for a considerable time before they were actually recognized in a formal document. In the Treaty of Westphalia of 1648 the new states were for the first time recognized as the component units of the world's political organization. This treaty in effect gave the new society of national states a fundamental law. In this fundamental law the individual states were recognized as having certain characteristics, the two most important of which were sovereignty and equality.

Since Bodin the doctrine of national sovereignty has been restated and elaborated innumerable times. The doctrine received classic formulation in a much-quoted passage in one of Chief Justice Marshall's opinions.[7]

The jurisdiction of the nation within its own territory is necessarily exclusive and absolute. It is susceptible of no limitation not imposed by itself. Any restriction upon it, deriving validity from an external source, would imply a diminution of its sovereignty to the extent of the restriction, and an investment of that sovereignty to the same extent in that power which could impose such restriction. All exceptions, therefore, to the full and complete power of a nation within its own territories, must be traced up to the consent of the nation itself. They can flow from no other legitimate source.

It would be quite impossible to build a system of international law on the basis of a doctrine of sovereignty like that outlined above. Only chaos can obtain in a world of states each without responsibility to the other and none recognizing a higher law than that flowing from its own consent. Indeed, the first fruits of the doctrine of a world of separate states "unrestrained by law" was a long period of savage warfare and chaos. A brilliant Dutch jurist, Huig de Groot, who later became known as the father of international law, was shocked at the licentious conduct of the new states. "Throughout Christendom," he wrote, "I saw a license of which savages would be ashamed. Men rushed to arms on the most frivolous pretexts, and once war was declared there

---

[6] *The Republic.*
[7] *The Schooner Exchange v. M'Fadden,* 7 Cranch 116, 136 (1812).

was no respect for the laws of God or men, nothing but a riot of fury as though authorization had been given for every sort of crime."

Horrified by the license of the period, Grotius, the Latinized name by which de Groot is generally known, set out to prove "that there does exist a common law between nations," binding alike in war and peace. His great book, *The Law of War and Peace* [8] appeared in 1625, while Europe was being ravaged by the Thirty Years' War. Grotius insisted that there exists a universal standard of justice applicable to states as well as individuals, and he appealed to the statesmen of his day to make state practices conform to this higher law. The need of some restraint upon the licentious conduct of states was so generally felt that Grotius's appeal at once met with a vigorous response. Thus, before the new system of separate and sovereign states had been recognized in an international treaty, the forces for a new legal integration of the world had been set in motion.

The second characteristic of the modern state system is the equality of all its members. "No principle of general law is more universally acknowledged," said Chief Justice Marshall in an opinion over a hundred years ago, "than the perfect equality of nations. Russia and Geneva have equal rights." States are not, however, equal in population, area, economic strength, or any other of a number of practical tests that may be applied. In population they vary from a few hundred thousands to several hundred millions; in area the Soviet Union with a territory of more than eight million square miles stands out in sharp contrast to Luxembourg with about a thousand square miles. A system which ignored such actual inequalities by giving all states equal rights would not long endure. As a matter of fact, the modern state system does not accord all states equal rights. Reference may be made to two of the most outstanding examples of legal inequalities in international constitutional law. Under the Covenant of the League of Nations the large powers were granted permanent seats on the Council, while the small states had to be content with elective, rotating seats. The same system has been continued in the Charter of the United Nations. The International Labor Organization Convention likewise gives a favored position to the large powers. The exigencies of world politics naturally give the large powers a much greater influence in world politics than the smaller ones can hope to exercise. The only sense in which states can be said to be equal is in the protection of such rights as international law gives to all states. The weakest state is entitled to have its rights respected by the strongest.

The most striking characteristic of the modern state system is just this great inequality of states in practical world politics. This is so universally recognized that states are spoken of as first-, second-, or third-, and even fourth-class powers. A state's rank in world politics is dependent upon a combination of factors, among which population, geographical position, area, natural resources,

[8] The book was written in Latin under the title of *De jure belli ac pacis*.

economic development, social cohesion, tradition, and military strength may be listed. The cynic may say that it is only the last which counts in this rating of states, but it must be remembered that military strength is largely determined by the other factors named. The United States and the Soviet Union are today the two strongest states. They are frequently called superstates, while Great Britain and France are regarded as Great Powers. China was granted a Great Power position in the United Nations primarily because of its enormous population and its strategic position in Eastern Asia, especially in World War II. China has the area and population of a Great Power, but it is undeveloped industrially and lacks social cohesion and political unity. India now probably has a better claim to a Great Power position than China. Italy and Japan, both weak in natural resources, held a position among the Great Powers because of their population, geographical position, and military prestige. Their military expenditures, however, placed a terrific strain on their economic systems, and their position among the Great Powers was therefore a bit precarious.

The task of naming the states which rank as second-class powers becomes even more difficult, and to fix the rank of lesser states is practically impossible. Australia, Brazil, Canada, Poland, Spain, Rumania, Mexico, Czechoslovakia, Yugoslavia, Turkey, Argentina, Sweden, Belgium, and the Netherlands are among the states which may be listed as of secondary rank. Belgium and the Netherlands, though both small in area and population, are both very productive. Belgium administers a large and important colonial territory, and the Netherlands did so until recently.

The role which states play in international politics varies from time to time. Changes in technology, the exhaustion of certain key resources, a disastrous war, the loss of colonial empire, and political unification movements may affect the ranking of states in world politics. The unification of Germany and of Italy; the westernization of Japan in the last half of the nineteenth century; the defeat of Germany and the dissolution of the Austro-Hungarian Empire in World War I; the defeat of Italy, Germany, and Japan in World War II—all these brought about marked shifts in the power relationships of the states. Such shifts are always accompanied by a strain in world politics, as it destroys such balance of forces as exists at the moment.

The number of sovereign or independent states in the world at present is about seventy. There are a few small states, like San Marino, Liechtenstein, Andorra, and the Vatican City, whose position in the family of nations is so anomalous that they can hardly be included in the number of fully sovereign states. Liechtenstein, for example, was, in 1920, denied membership in the League of Nations on the ground that it was not in a position to meet all the international obligations which would rest upon it by virtue of the Covenant. Likewise difficult to classify are the trust areas under the United Nations. At present they play an important though passive role in world politics.

It should not be forgotten that nationalism is not the only force which sweeps across world politics. Panracial movements, such as Pan-Germanism, Pan-Slavism, Pan-Latinism, Pan-Hispanism, Pan-Africanism, and the Pan-Asiatic movement have upon occasion exerted a considerable influence in world politics. Again, other movements, such as Pan-Islamism, have sought concerted action not upon the basis of nationality or race but upon the basis of a common religion. At times Pan-Islamic movements have caused France, Great Britain, and the Netherlands, which had large Mohammedan populations in the colonial territories, much concern. Mohammedans, however, are divided religiously. Moreover, their first loyalty is to the nationalist movements of the countries in which they live rather than to Pan-Islamism. The Soviet Union, and Communists throughout the world, would like to force the reorganization of the world upon a horizontal rather than a vertical basis. They emphasize class interests and differences rather than national ones.

Chapter 3

THE DEVELOPMENT OF INTERNATIONAL COOPERATION

Consideration of world community and the state system reveals that modern life is inextricably international and interdependent, but that its political organization is based fundamentally upon the conception of separate and independent nation-states. Therefore, the area of effective government action does not conform to the conditions and requirements of the time. International organization, which may be defined as the agencies and methods of international cooperation,[1] has been developed in answer to this situation and in an attempt to meet this need. It has to do with the structure and procedure of cooperative relations between or among the nation-states of the world. International organization would not exist if the entire world were organized as one superstate. Nor would there be a place for it if the various nation-states were completely self-contained and separate from each other. International organization presupposes a situation of legally independent nation-states, in contact with each other and affected by activities transcending their boundaries.

The remainder of this chapter will be concerned with the agencies and methods of international cooperation as they developed from early modern times. Consideration will be given to the diplomatic and consular services, treaties, international conferences, international administrative organization, and methods for the pacific settlement of disputes.

DIPLOMATIC AND CONSULAR SERVICES

Diplomacy has been defined as "the application of intelligence and tact to the conduct of official relations between the governments of independent states."[2] It is the science and the art of representation of states and of negotiations between them. It is a method of communication between the governments of independent states through individuals appointed for the purpose.

---

[1] See the article on "International Organization" in the *Encyclopedia of the Social Sciences*, Vol. 8, Macmillan, New York, 1932.

[2] Sir Ernest Satow, *A Guide to Diplomatic Practice*, Vol. 1, Longmans, New York, 1917, p. 1.

Diplomats are expected to "win friends and influence people" for their country and its policies. Envoys and other special representatives from one government to another were known in the ancient world. Diplomacy in its modern form began, however, with the city-states of Renaissance Italy. The diplomat was an agent and personal representative of the sovereign. The dignity and prestige of his prince was considered to be vested in him. He was entitled to be treated with due respect, and any affront or slight shown to him was received as an insult to his sovereign.

Great stress was placed upon formal honors and prestige, and there was often an unseemly scramble for precedence. The negotiations leading up to the Peace of Westphalia in 1648 were impeded for some six years because of controversies over meeting places, titles, and rank of envoys. In 1661, there was a street fight between retainers of the French and Spanish ambassadors in London over which of their coaches should be next to the royal coach in the reception of the Swedish ambassador. Another such incident took place at a court ball in London, in the winter of 1768: [3]

The Russian ambassador, Ivan Czernichew, arriving first, took his place immediately next to the Count von Seilern, ambassador of the Emperor, who was on the first of two benches arranged in the diplomatic box. The French ambassador, Comte du Chatelet-Lomon, came in late, and climbing on to the second bench, managed to sit down between his two colleagues. A lively interchange of words followed, and in the duel which arose out of the incident the Russian was wounded.

At the Congress of Vienna in 1815, and at Aix-la-Chapelle in 1818, rules of precedence were worked out in order to put an end to this type of bickering. Four grades of diplomats were recognized—ambassadors and papal legates or nuncios, envoys extraordinary and ministers plenipotentiary, ministers resident, and chargés d'affaires. The first three groups are accredited to the sovereign or chief of state; the last, to the minister of foreign affairs. Precedence within these grades is based upon length of service. Thus, the "dean" of the diplomatic corps in Washington, D.C., at any given time is the ambassador who has been at that post the longest. The present rules of diplomatic precedence are based upon the idea of the equality of states. However, they were adopted primarily for the practical purpose of finding an acceptable and automatic solution for the problem, and are of very little importance except in a ceremonial way.

Because diplomats represent the dignity of their government, and in order to expedite their work, certain privileges and immunities have been recognized for them. The official residence [4] of an ambassador or minister is inviolable. The chief of mission, his family, and servants are immune from the local juris-

[3] *Ibid.*, p. 19.
[4] The official residence of an ambassador is known as an "embassy"; that of a minister as a "legation."

diction.   Diplomatic privileges and immunities include freedom from arrest, relief from customs duties and other taxes, and exemption for witness duty. The right of extending asylum to fugitives was formerly claimed on the basis that an embassy or legation had extraterritorial status.   The recent trend has been to restrict the right of asylum on the ground that it is not permissible for a diplomat to harbor fugitives from justice.   In this matter, as in other questions of diplomatic privileges and immunities, the problem is to accord sufficient freedom from local jurisdiction for the status and functions of foreign diplomatic missions, but to guard against their possible abuse or unnecessary extension.

Diplomatic representatives are appointed and sent by their governments, and they are formally received by the head of government (or foreign minister) to which they are accredited.   They enter upon their work after being chosen by their own governments and accepted for the purpose by the other government concerned.   An exchange of ambassadors between two countries is based upon custom and agreement, rather than upon any presumed right of legation under international law.   Diplomatic representation is worked out between governments on a mutual and reciprocal basis.   For example, the United States government would not send an ambassador to a foreign government which refused to return the compliment.   The idea of reciprocity extends even to the rank of the officials concerned.   The United States exchanges ambassadors, or exchanges ministers, with another country; it does not send an ambassador and accept a minister.   The higher rank has ordinarily been reserved for the more important foreign posts, but the United States now maintains embassies in all the Latin-American republics and in some of the other smaller countries.   Before an ambassador or minister is appointed, it is customary to inquire whether he is acceptable to the other government.   Any indication that an individual is *persona non grata* means that he will not be appointed.   Likewise, if a diplomatic official, after his appointment, becomes *persona non grata* he will be recalled or transferred immediately.

The modern means of rapid communication have had an important effect on the conduct of diplomacy.   Before the days of telegraph, telephone, and radio, an ambassador in a distant country had to act on his own initiative in applying his instructions and in dealing with new situations as they arose.   Today an ambassador anywhere in the world can be in almost instantaneous contact with his foreign office, and he can receive fresh instructions day by day.   Not only that, but heads of governments frequently enter into direct communication with each other.   For example, Prime Minister Winston Churchill and President Franklin D. Roosevelt exchanged over seventeen hundred messages and met in nine meetings, "comprising in all 120 days of close personal contact." [5] The relations between President Roosevelt and Prime Minister Churchill were unusual, of course, but in times of crisis responsible heads of state are certain

[5] Speech by Winston Churchill before House of Commons on Apr. 17, 1945.

to seek direct contact with each other. This might appear at first thought to reduce an ambassador from a position of initiative and judgment to that of a mere messenger. The diplomat himself has retained a substantial degree of importance for two reasons. For one thing, there is no substitute for the tact and skill with which instructions are interpreted to foreign governments, and the telegraph has not abolished the need for this personal touch. For another thing, the technological developments of the modern world have vastly increased the areas of human life which come within the scope of international diplomatic relations. When all is said and done, however, the centralized control of foreign policy has tended to increase. The ambassador's job is still important, but he is now a member of a team directed from the capital of his country.

The consular service is designed to expedite foreign trade and commerce, and to assist the citizens of a nation in various other ways. As Potter says, "The essential cause which has produced the modern consular system is the need for some official governmental assistance to, and supervision over, the conduct of international intercourse by the private citizens of the various nations. To this is to be added the need for protection against illegal treatment." [6] Thus, while the diplomat is concerned with the public policy of his government, the consul provides assistance to individual citizens by furnishing information on trade opportunities, keeping and certifying records, extending assistance to travelers, protecting property interests entrusted to him, and performing many other duties of a similar nature.

The consul is an official of the government which appoints him, and he receives a commission as evidence of his authority to act. While he is not accredited to a chief of state, like an ambassador, he is authorized to perform his duties in the territory of a foreign government by the issuance of a document called an "exequatur." He is a national official commissioned and authorized to act abroad for specified purposes. While diplomats are usually stationed only in foreign capitals, consular offices are to be found in all cities of commercial importance.

Consular officers are not entitled to all the privileges and immunities of diplomats, but they do receive certain rights and immunities needed for the efficient performance of their duties. These include unrestricted communication with the home government, access to fellow nationals especially when they are under arrest, maintenance of an inviolable archives, and freedom from local control in all matters pertaining to consular duties. Inviolability of premises and immunity from civil and criminal jurisdiction are not consular rights under international law but may be recognized by treaties. [7]

[6] Pitman B. Potter, *An Introduction to the Study of International Organization*, Appleton-Century-Crofts, New York, 1948, 5th ed., p. 67.

[7] For a recent case, see Lawrence Preuss, "Consular Immunities: The Kasenkina Case (U.S.–U.S.S.R.)," *American Journal of International Law*, January, 1949, pp. 36–56.

The status and functions of diplomats and consuls are defined by customary international law and by treaties. Each nation determines the organization of its diplomatic and consular services. Diplomats are without exception made responsible to the foreign office or its equivalent. Consular officers are sometimes supervised by the department of commerce of their government. Since 1924, the United States has had an integrated foreign service including both diplomatic and consular officers.[8] Each government defines the duties of, and issues its own instructions to, its diplomatic and consular services. The functions of the foreign service tend to be substantially similar among the various nations, and the following description will serve as an illustration of diplomatic and consular duties and activities throughout the world: [9]

The Foreign Service represents the United States abroad, interprets for its information and guidance events, situations, and opinions in the country to which the personnel is assigned, and endeavors to promote goodwill and common understanding.

The officers and employees of the Foreign Service protect the interests of the United States in accordance with treaties and international law, and advise, protect, and assist American citizens resident, traveling, or having interests abroad. They seek to prevent or to correct practices which might discriminate against the United States or its citizens.

They negotiate treaties, conventions, and protocols regarding international intercourse, tariffs, shipping, commerce, and the preservation of the peace in conformity and in accordance with the instruction of the Secretary of State and the President. They observe, analyze, and report on political, social, and economic conditions and trends of significance in the country in which they are assigned. Some major subjects of these reports are legislative programs, public opinion, market conditions, trade statistics, finance, production, labor, agriculture, forestry, fishing, mining, natural resources, shipping, freights, charters, legislation, tariffs, and laws.

One of the important functions of the Foreign Service is the promotion and protection of the foreign trade of the United States. Trade inquiries, trade disputes, and market conditions are the subject of numerous communications. Miscellaneous inquiries on a wide variety of subjects are answered.

Other Foreign Service functions include:

a. Issuance of passports to American citizens, registration of American citizens within the consular district of their residence abroad;

b. Issuance of bills of health to American and foreign vessels proceeding to the ports of the United States or its possessions; submission of reports on health conditions;

c. Issuance of visas to foreigners wishing to visit or immigrate into the United States;

d. Dissemination of information pertaining to the United States, its policies, and its way of life;

[8] Graham H. Stuart, *American Diplomatic and Consular Service,* Appleton-Century-Crofts, New York, 1936, pp. 185–187.

[9] *The Foreign Service of the United States,* U.S. Department of State Publication 3612, Aug. 15, 1949, pp. 4–6.

e. Promotion and protection of American shipping generally and reporting on shipping conditions; entry and clearance of American ships and aircraft; relief of seamen; shipment and discharge of seamen; settlement of disputes;

f. Certification of invoices of goods shipped to the United States; investigation of and reporting on foreign market values and undervaluations of merchandise for the protection of revenues; assistance in preventing the importation of prohibited articles; administration of regulations relating to plant and animal quarantine; supervision of disinfection of merchandise intended for export to the United States;

g. Custody, administration, and settlement of estates of American citizens and seamen who have died abroad;

h. Extradition cases.

Foreign Service officers perform notarial services in accordance with United States Federal, State, and local laws, and are frequently commissioned to take testimony.

TREATIES

A treaty is a formal international agreement.[10] If states are considered to be sovereign and legally independent, it follows that affairs of concern to two or more of them can be regulated only by mutual consent. This consent can be based on the acceptance of customary rules and practices, or it can be given by definite acts of agreement for the settlement of specific issues or the establishment of new rules and practices.

Treaties have made an important contribution to the development of international cooperation. Modern technology, especially in the fields of transportation and communication, has made possible a tremendous increase in the number and scope of the contacts and activities which transcend national boundaries. A consequence has been a corresponding growth in the need for devices of agreement and cooperation. The United States, for example, had entered into approximately three hundred treaties by 1898, but during the past fifty years it has become a party to well over twice that number. Other countries have experienced a comparable trend. There have also been a change and an expansion in the subjects covered by treaties. Most treaties prior to the nineteenth century were concerned with such subjects as alliances, truces, terms of peace, and royal marriages. The majority of modern treaties deal with social, economic, and governmental affairs, including agreements on navigation and commerce, copyright and patent law, settlement of claims, citizenship, extradition, and postal facilities.

Most early treaties were bilateral, creating obligations between two states with respect to each other. At present, a large percentage of the treaties con-

[10] Many other terms are used. "Convention" has been used both for some of the great international agreements like the Hague Conventions, and also for some of secondary importance. "Protocol" is used to describe records of discussion, articles of explanation, annexes, or even a multilateral treaty itself. Other terms are "arrangement," "declaration," "exchange of notes," *"modus vivendi,"* "procès-verbal," *"compromis,"* "covenant," and "charter." There is great confusion in the use of these terms.

cluded are multilateral. This tendency is to be expected with the increase in matters of common international concern. If, for example, sixty states are interested in rules of navigation on the high seas, or postal communications, or some other matter, agreement could be reached through bilateral treaties only if each state concluded fifty-nine treaties. Obviously this would be an impossibly complex procedure. A multilateral treaty with sixty signatories is the logical solution, since in this way one agreement establishes a common arrangement or standard which each accepts as an obligation with respect to all the others.

CONFERENCES

An international conference involves the consideration and discussion, with a view to agreement, of matters of common interest by the representatives of two or more states. Thus, conference in its simplest form is a technique of diplomacy, and the practice of international conferences has grown out of an extension of diplomatic negotiation. The distinguishing features of a conference are that it is arranged in advance for the consideration of designated questions and that it is attended by representatives specially appointed for the purpose. International conferences have been held on a great variety of subjects, from peace treaties to the control of opium, from the establishment of national boundaries to the prohibition of the use of white phosphorus in matches. From the Peace of Westphalia in 1648 to the third quarter of the nineteenth century, most of the international conferences [11] were concerned with the terms of peace to conclude a war. Conferences were also held to deal with important political issues of common concern. An outstanding example of this type was the concert of Europe, which attempted to maintain the European Settlement of 1815 through a series of conferences at Aix-la-Chapelle in 1818, Troppau in 1820, Laibach in 1821, and Verona in 1822.

About one hundred years ago, the use of conferences to deal with needed services and administrative questions of common international concern became increasingly frequent. Some early examples are the International Sanitary Conference at Paris in 1851, the general conference on statistics at Brussels in 1853, the Conference of Hanover to deal with navigation of the Elbe in 1861, two conferences as to marine signaling in 1864, and so on. The conference method was also used in connection with the establishment and operation of the various international administrative organizations.

Three types of international conferences may be distinguished: the *ad hoc*, the periodic, and the recurrent or continuing. The first of these is specially arranged, deals with its agenda, and at the conclusion of its meetings goes out of existence. An *ad hoc* conference is convened upon the initiative of one state (or a group of states), by addressing invitations to other states whose coopera-

[11] Or "congresses." The two terms are now used interchangeably.

tion for the purpose is sought. The agenda is proposed by the initiating state and must have the concurrence of the other participants. The conference usually meets on the territory of the initiating state, and it is customary to select the chief delegate of that country as presiding officer. An illustration of the *ad hoc* conference is the Washington Conference of 1922, which was convened on the initiative of the United States. The chief advantage of the *ad hoc* conference is that it furnishes a more expeditious method than ordinary diplomatic negotiations to deal with special issues or problems. Its disadvantages are the special effort required to initiate the conference, the suspicion of ulterior motives often directed against the initiating state, the problem of obtaining advance agreement on the agenda, the difficulty of arranging for adequate preparatory work, and the lack of continuity.

The Hague Conferences of 1899 and 1907 and the system of inter-American conferences are examples of the periodic type. Such conferences are designed to meet from time to time, and each arranges for the convening of its successor. Thus the special initiative of one state is not required, but there is still a lack of continuity and an inadequacy of preparatory work between the conferences.

A great improvement in the system occurred with the advent of the League of Nations, and later the United Nations. Recurrent meetings are automatically provided for. General international conferences are in practically continuous session. There is no problem of inertia to be overcome; no one state has to assume the burden of the initiative; continuity is maintained; and there is a secretariat to handle the preparatory and interim work. The various organs of the United Nations provide a method for continuing consideration and discussion, with a view to agreement, of the problems and affairs within their jurisdiction. Also, special conferences may be called to deal with individual questions as, for example, the problem of trade and employment.

International conferences have developed from a device used on special occasions, in a quite sporadic and haphazard manner, to an institutionalized arrangement of fundamental importance in the current system of international organization. Like the multilateral treaty, the conference technique can be used as a device of international legislation. The states of the world, or most of them, may agree to certain rules and regulations in a general conference, and thus give their consent to designated provisions governing a matter of common concern. In fact, it is usually by an international conference that the terms of such a treaty are agreed upon.

With all its advantages and possibilities, the device of international conferences cannot be used indiscriminately as a sort of panacea. It is wise to adopt a somewhat critical view toward the apparent instinct to "hold a conference" at the slightest provocation. Certain conditions must obtain if a conference is to be successful. The question with which the conference is to deal must be fairly definite and one on which there is already a considerable area of agreement.   There must also be adequate preparation of agenda and data.   Very important, of course, are the personal qualities of the delegates.[12]

INTERNATIONAL ADMINISTRATIVE ORGANIZATIONS

One result of modern technology has been a great increase in the number, variety, and importance of activities transcending the limits of national boundaries.   These are needs and problems which cannot be met merely by international agreements and conferences, as indispensable as these devices are.   A machinery for collective action on matters of common concern is also necessary.   For this reason, administrative agencies to perform services beyond the scope of separate national action have been established.

When large numbers of people become interested in a given activity or problem, they tend to create an organization to further their joint purposes and objectives.   The area of international affairs is no exception to this rule, and many different groups have organized on a basis transcending the jurisdiction of any one nation-state.   One type is the business concern, such as Standard Oil or the Ford Motor Company, operating in more than one country.   Another type is the international humanitarian organization, of which the outstanding example is the Red Cross.   A third type is the international organization of an economic or professional interest group, such as the World Federation of Trade Unions, the International Chamber of Commerce, or the Inter-Parliamentary Union.   As Eagleton says, "There is an International Wine Office to encourage the use of wine, and an International Bureau against Alcoholism to discourage it." [13]   A recent publication [14] listed fourteen international organizations concerned with textbook revision as an aid to international understanding.   These agencies are known as "private international organizations" to indicate their nongovernmental status.   There are literally hundreds, perhaps thousands, of them in existence, ranging from large and well-known organizations of great importance to small and ephemeral groups.

The development described in the preceding paragraph was followed by the formation of "public international organizations" or, as they are sometimes called, "public international unions."   Such agencies have an official governmental status, are established by treaties, have a permanent or continuing organization, are normally open to the membership of all qualified states, and function to administer activities of interest to all the participating states.

The Universal Postal Union furnishes an instructive example of a public international organization.   A brief survey of its origin and work will give an

---

[12] Potter, *op. cit.*, p. 121.

[13] Clyde Eagleton, *International Government*, Ronald, New York, 1948, rev. ed., p. 159.

[14] UNESCO, *A Handbook for the Improvement of Textbooks and Teaching Materials as Aids to International Understanding*, Paris, 1949, pp. 24–32.

insight into the significance of this particular method of international cooperation.   Under the original system of completely separate national postal administrations, correspondence with other parts of the world was slow, unre-
liable, and expensive, as the following description indicates: [15]

> Not only were the rates of postage very high, but the tariffs were confused by the
> fact that the charges varied according to the respective route of transit.   Thus, for
> instance, there were three different rates between Germany and Austria, five different
> rates between Germany and Australia, four different rates between Germany and
> Italy according to the particular route taken by the letter. . . .   A letter from the
> United States to Australia would pay either five, thirty-three, forty-five, or sixty
> cents, or $1.02 per half ounce, according to the route by which it was sent.   Mail
> service was by no means frequent, but the fact that a letter was prepaid for a certain
> route often prevented it from taking advantage of a quicker means of communica-
> tion. . . .   Charges in general were very high. . . .   In making up a through rate,
> the transit charges of every country whose administration handled the letter would
> be included.   The accounts of such mutual charges were exceedingly complicated
> and it took a vast amount of clerical work to keep them balanced.   Further difficulty
> was introduced through the difference in weights and in currency, all of which had to
> be taken into account in computing rates.   It will be apparent . . . that the service
> lacked the rapidity and cheapness which alone could make it a real influence in the
> development of world-wide business relations.

During the first half of the nineteenth century, attempts were made to improve this situation through bilateral treaties, but with little success.   It became apparent that a solution could be reached only by general international
action.   The first postal conference was called in 1863, upon the initiative of
the United States, for a discussion of the principles involved.   The General
Postal Union was formally established in 1875, and three years later its name
was changed to the Universal Postal Union.[16]   The basic purpose of this
Union is to unite its members in a single postal territory for the reciprocal exchange of correspondence.   Freedom of transit for the mail is guaranteed
throughout the world postal territory.   A uniform rate is established for foreign correspondence, and transit charges are fixed on the basis of weight and
mileage.   There is a Universal Postal Congress, which usually meets at five-
year intervals.   It reviews the basic Convention of the Union and the subsidiary agreements.   Proposals involving important changes must receive a
two-thirds vote, and lesser changes a simple majority.   The proposed modifications are subject to ratification by the members, but in practice this has
become a mere formality.

[15] Paul S. Reinsch, *Public International Unions,* World Peace Foundation, Boston, 1916,
2d ed., pp. 21–22.

[16] This was the second public international union to be established.   The first was the
International Telegraphic Union, formed in 1865.   A few international agencies with
regional or local functions were established even earlier.   Apparently the first of these was
the Rhine River Commission of 1804.

The Universal Postal Union maintains an international bureau, which operates under the supervision of the Swiss postal system. It serves as an organ of liaison, information, and consultation; gives opinions on questions in dispute; acts as a clearinghouse for the settlement of postal accounts; and performs other functions of a similar nature. In 1948, a permanent executive and liaison committee was established, composed of nineteen members elected on a geographical basis. It meets once a year and has the functions of the maintenance of close relations with members of the Union to improve the international postal service, the study of technical questions, relations with other international organizations, and control of the activities of the international bureau.

As of September, 1948, there were eighty-eight members of the Universal Postal Union. The members are divided into seven classes for purposes of apportioning expenses (set at an annual maximum of about $190,000 at the present time). Each member has one vote in the Universal Postal Congress. However, the Great Powers have special influence because of the admission of colonies to voting membership, and because in practice representation on committees is limited for the less important states. In 1948, the Universal Postal Union became one of the specialized agencies of the United Nations.[17]

By the time of World War I, there were in existence thirty public international unions with administrative bureaus or commissions.[18] The more important problems with which they dealt were transportation and communication facilities, disease and sanitation, economic problems, and labor legislation. These organizations included the International Bureau of Weights and Measures, the European Danube Commission, the Wireless Telegraph Union, the International Sugar Union, the International Institute of Agriculture, the Union for the Publication of Customs Tariffs, the International Office of Public Health, the Union for the Suppression of the African Slave Trade, the International Opium Commission, the Central Bureau for the International Map of the World, and so on. After World War I, new needs led to the creation of additional international organizations, such as the International Commission for Air Navigation, in addition to the administrative machinery of the League of Nations.

There has been great variety among the public international organizations in size and organization, but some common features are discernible. They are established by an agreement made in an international conference, and there is nearly always provision for a periodic conference. There is usually some kind of council or commission to act between conferences, to supervise the work carried on, and to revise the administrative regulations. Also, there is a bureau or secretariat to perform the routine work involved in the function of the agency. Expenses are met by contributions from the members,

[17] See p. 160.
[18] Reinsch, *op. cit.*, p. 4.

except for a few cases like the Danube Commission or the Sanitary Councils, which were self-supporting. Contributions may be allocated by dividing the members into different classes or categories, or by population, amount of commerce, length of railways, or some other factors. Inequality of voting may or may not be correlated with unequal financial contributions. The principle of unanimous consent has not been directly violated, but business has been conducted by majority vote in practice. This is accomplished by providing for consent to the basic agreements and allowing the international organization to carry out routine work and to make changes in subsidiary regulations by majority vote. A state which opposes such a change may withdraw from the organization. As a practical matter, however, the inconvenience of losing the advantages of membership is usually too strong an influence to make withdrawal a real alternative. No country can afford, for example, not to belong to the Universal Postal Union, even though it may not favor some of the regulations.

For the most part, the work of these organizations consists of research, publication, recommendation, reporting, and routine administrative tasks. Sometimes they have a limited control over individuals or over a specified activity in a given locality (the Danube Commission, for example). Basically, the control remains in the hands of the member states. The international administrative organizations are devices of cooperation, not agencies of governmental power or jurisdiction in the true sense. They offer a means of providing essential services which the member states acting separately could not provide for themselves. Their force rises from their practical indispensability. States retain power and control, but they cannot afford to do without international organization because of the compulsion of conditions and circumstances. It should be noted, also, that the international administrative organizations have furnished a valuable precedent for reconciling the legal fiction of independent sovereignty with the dynamics of modern world interdependence and with the pressing need of effective cooperative action.

Pacific Settlement of Disputes

Contacts between nation-states and the many activities transcending national boundaries sometimes give rise to disputes and conflicts. For this reason, methods of peaceful settlement are needed if the arbitrary use of force is to be avoided. Judicial settlement in international relations is developing in a way not unlike the development of the judicial process within the state. Among primitive peoples self-help is the only form of redress for the violation of customary law. Gradually self-help gives way to arbitration, and arbitration in turn develops into the judicial process. Instead of the parties' fighting out the dispute, they began the practice of voluntarily submitting the dispute to neutral third parties. Later still the settlement of dis-

putes was brought under the authority of the state, which assumed the prerogative of appointing the judges and of executing their judgments. With this, the
settlement of the dispute became judicial proceeding in the modern sense of
the term.

The handling of disputes by government agencies on the basis of law thus
became a normal feature of national political organization. A development
very similar to this took place with respect to the settlement of disputes between states. The process was, however, much slower and never became quite
as complete. Principal reliance continued to be placed on the method of
self-help. If a dispute could not be settled through diplomatic channels or
by international conferences, rights could be secured only by the unilateral
action of claimant states through self-help or, as it is called in international
law, self-redress. This often meant a resort to some kind of coercion, ranging
all the way from the threat of force, tariff discrimination, economic boycott,
etc., to full-scale war. Methods of pacific settlement are intended to provide
an alternative means for settling disputes. They represent a very important
part of modern international organization.

Good Offices and Mediation. Though good offices and mediation are essentially negotiation, they are discussed here to illustrate the shift from self-help
to arbitration and judicial settlement. After two states have gone to war or are
drifting toward war, a third state may offer its good offices in bringing them
together again so that their differences may be peacefully adjusted. Third
states are always free to tender their good offices, and the disputant states may
take no offense at the action. It involves no actual interference in the dispute,
for the state tendering its good offices makes no suggestions touching the substance of the disagreement. The moment a third state comes with suggestions for conciliating the differences and bringing about a settlement of
the dispute it assumes the role of a mediator.[19] Mediation is a delicate function and not lightly undertaken by governments. When mediation occurs it
most generally follows upon a successful tender of good offices. States may
sometimes find themselves eager to end a war in which they are engaged, but
political expediency and national pride prevent them from opening direct
conversations for that purpose. In such cases a tender of good offices is welcome and may be instrumental in bringing hostilities to a close. It was under
such conditions that President Theodore Roosevelt was able to induce Japan
and Russia to accept his good offices for bringing about a peace conference between the two countries on American soil. Roosevelt's activities during the

---

[19] The Hague Convention for the Pacific Settlement of International Disputes defines
mediation as "reconciling the opposing claims and appeasing the feelings of resentment
which may have arisen between the States at variance." The Hague Conferences sought
to encourage the use of good offices and mediation by making it a friendly right of third
states to offer good offices or mediation without offense to the disputant states and by
regularizing the procedure.

negotiations would indicate that his services did not stop with good offices but developed into mediation.

Commissions of Inquiry. Another step forward in the use of impartial third parties in the settlement of disputes between states was made in the Hague Convention for the Pacific Settlement of International Disputes. If settlement by diplomacy fails, the parties are urged to institute an International Commission of Inquiry, with the object of facilitating "a solution of these differences by elucidating the facts by means of an impartial and conscientious investigation." It must be carefully noted that the Commission's report is limited to a statement of the facts and that the parties reserve entire freedom as to the effect to be given to the statement. Even this mild arrangement was not acceptable to most states until disagreements involving honor and vital interests had been excluded from its scope. This method of settling disputes has some notable successes to its credit, chief among which is the Dogger Bank case of 1904. In the Russo-Japanese War, a Russian squadron of warships had made a sudden attack upon an English fishing fleet, as a result of which considerable damage was done and two lives were lost. British feeling ran high, and there was considerable danger of war breaking out between the two countries. The matter was settled by the appointment of a Commission of Inquiry, three of whose members were of neutral nationality, to inquire into and report upon the facts and circumstances of the incident. As a result of the report Russia recognized its responsibility and paid the British fishermen an indemnity.

The general principle of the Commission of Inquiry was adopted and extended by Secretary of State Bryan in some thirty treaties negotiated between the United States and other countries in the years 1913 and 1914. The provisions of the Bryan treaties differ from those of the Hague Convention in several respects. The Commission is appointed in advance and is made permanent, no disagreements are excluded from its scope, and hostilities are prohibited until the Commission has made its report. The great value of the Bryan treaties lay in the fact that they provided for a "cooling-off" period in which hostilities were prohibited and for the ascertainment of facts which might become the basis of an acceptable solution.

Arbitration. The method of arbitration in the settlement of interstate disputes is almost as old as history. It had an honorable record in the history of the Greek city-states and was resorted to extensively during the Middle Ages. It is often stated that the practice lapsed throughout the early modern period and that the Jay Treaty between the United States and Great Britain in 1794 marks the beginning of the modern period of international arbitration. This is not strictly correct, for there were many cases of international arbitration throughout the seventeenth and eighteenth centuries.[20]

[20] E. O. Van Boetzelaer, *Les Arbitrages Internationaux Néerlandais de 1581 à 1794,* Drukkerij H. Buurman, Leiden, 1929.

The Hague Convention for the Pacific Settlement of International Disputes defines arbitration as "the settlement of international disputes between states by judges of their own choice, and on the basis of respect for law," with an obligation to accept the award in good faith. Arbitration, in summary, involves the settlement of interstate disputes (1) by voluntary action, (2) by judges chosen by the parties to the dispute, (3) on the basis of respect for law, and (4) with an obligation to accept the award as binding.

It is often asserted that arbitration is identical with the process of adjudication. It is pointed out that in practice the vast majority of arbitral decisions have been decided squarely on the basis of legal rules and that compromise and political expediency have seldom played a role. While this is undoubtedly true, it must nevertheless be remembered that the process of arbitration does reserve a large area for the play of equity, compromise, and expediency. The arbitrators are not always highly trained jurists; often they are diplomats and statesmen without legal training or judicial experience. Moreover, it should be remembered that the parties to the dispute agree upon, or select, those principles which shall guide the arbitral tribunal in reaching its conclusions. For these reasons arbitration may be regarded as a combination of legislative and judicial functions. While arbitration does not make changes in general international law, it often does make a change in the existing legal rights of the parties. So we may conclude that arbitration differs from judicial procedure in the strict sense of the word by (1) the selection of the arbitrators, which is made by the disputant parties themselves, for the settlement of a particular dispute, (2) the selection by the disputants of the principles upon which the tribunal shall base its award, and (3) the submission of the dispute to arbitration, which is purely voluntary.

Arbitration as a means of settling international disputes steadily gained in favor throughout the nineteenth century. One of the most notable cases of arbitration of this century was the Alabama Claims case settled in 1872. The United States charged Great Britain with not having fully lived up to its neutral duties in the Civil War. The British government had allowed confederate cruisers to be fitted out in British ports and to go out from them to prey upon American shipping, as a consequence of which the war had been prolonged and American military expenditures greatly increased. The United States government demanded an indemnity for the injuries which it had sustained. It was not until after several years of diplomatic discussion that Great Britain finally agreed by the Treaty of Washington to submit the differences between the two governments to arbitration. The court of arbitration was composed of five members; one appointed by each of the parties and one each by the King of Italy, the President of the Swiss Confederation, and the Emperor of Brazil. The tribunal awarded the American government the sum of $15,500,000 as the amount of damages due it for the injuries sustained through the failure of the British government to fulfill its neutral duties. The settlement of this serious international dispute by means of arbitration made a profound impression upon world opinion and stimulated the movement for arbitration everywhere.

While resort to arbitration became more frequent as the century wore on, an attempt to institutionalize arbitration and to remove some of the defects which practice had revealed was not made until the close of the century. There were at least three serious defects in the procedure. In the first place, recourse to arbitration was entirely a voluntary matter; there was no obligation to use this method of settlement even in cases generally regarded as most suitable for it. In the second place, there was no permanent and readily accessible court of arbitration to which cases could be submitted. For every case submitted arbitrators had to be chosen anew, and often the parties to the dispute found it difficult to agree upon them. Lastly, since there was no general code of arbitral procedure for the guidance of the tribunal, the disputant states had to agree upon such a code after the dispute arose. Negotiations to arrive at this agreement, called a *compromis,* often proved difficult and occasionally led to delay and further friction.

The First Hague Conference sought to remove these defects by setting up permanent machinery and improving the processes of arbitration. These efforts were incorporated in an elaborate convention, called the Convention for the Pacific Settlement of International Disputes,[21] drafted and adopted at the First Hague Conference and amended at the Second. An attempt was made to secure a provision for compulsory arbitration, if only for certain limited classes of disputes. This effort was unsuccessful. The best that could be obtained from the conference was the declaration of a *voeu,* a "wish," stating that the conference was unanimous "in admitting the principle of compulsory arbitration" and "in declaring that certain disputes, in particular those relating to the interpretation and application of the provisions of international agreements may be submitted to compulsory arbitration without restriction." This declaration was, of course, meaningless so far as any legal effect was concerned. States remained free to arbitrate or not as they saw fit and as interests and expediency might dictate.[22]

The Hague Conferences also sought to set up a continuous arbitral body, but the so-called Permanent Court of Arbitration for which the Convention provides is hardly worthy of the name. It provides for a panel of judges and a bureau, which serves as a registrar for the Court and which is housed

[21] Also commonly called the First Hague Convention.

[22] Article 38 of the Convention, which dealt with the jurisdiction of arbitration, was of the same tenor: "In questions of a legal nature, and especially in the interpretation or application of International Conventions, arbitration is recognized by the Contracting Powers as the most effective, and at the same time the most equitable, means of settling disputes which diplomacy has failed to settle. Consequently, it would be desirable that, in disputes about the above-mentioned questions, the Contracting Powers should, if the case arose, have recourse to arbitration, in so far as circumstances permit."

at The Hague.   States which are members of the Court must keep on file with the Bureau the names of not more than four persons "of known competency in questions of international law, of the highest moral reputation, and disposed to accept the duties of arbitrators."   The same person may be selected by different powers.   The members of the Court are appointed for a term of six years, subject to renewal.   From this panel of names arbitrators must be selected whenever states care to have recourse to the Court of Arbitration for the settlement of their differences.   The number of names on the panel varies somewhat but is generally around 135.   The bureau of the Court is under the direction and control of the Permanent Administrative Council, composed of the diplomatic corps at The Hague and the Minister for Foreign Affairs, who acts as the presiding officer.

The Hague Conferences further sought to facilitate arbitration by laying down in advance, for the adoption of disputants who desired to resort to arbitration, methods of selecting the arbitrators and the rule of procedure which should govern the court.   When the parties to a dispute agree to submit it to arbitration, the question at issue, the names of the arbitrators or the method of their selection, the principles of law or equity upon which the Court is to base its judgment, and the rules to govern the procedure of the Court are all laid down in a treaty, generally called a *compromis*.   By incorporating as many of these items as possible in a general convention, ready for the use of disputants at all times, the difficulty of drawing up a *compromis* is lessened. The First Hague Convention provides a method of selecting the judges and a model code of procedure for the use of the Court.   If the disputants cannot agree on the composition of the tribunal, the Convention provides that each party shall appoint two arbitrators, of whom only one may be its own national or chosen from the persons selected by it as members of the Court.   These arbitrators together are then to choose an umpire.   Should the votes be equally divided, the choice of the umpire is entrusted to a third power, selected by agreement of the parties.   If still no agreement is reached, each party shall select a different power, and the choice of the umpire is made in concert by the powers thus selected.   If after the exhaustion of all these methods, no agreement has been reached, an umpire is chosen by lot.

It should be borne in mind that these rules of procedure thus carefully elaborated were no more than suggestions; they are in no sense binding.

This so-called Hague Permanent Court of Arbitration, which is neither a "court" nor "permanent," came into existence in 1907.   Some twenty cases were disposed of by tribunals whose membership was selected either in whole or in part from the panel of names which constitutes the Court.   At present its chief significance is as a step in the procedure for nominating judges to be elected to the International Court of Justice.[23]

The great unsolved problem of international relations is to induce states to

[23] See p. 191.

submit their disputes to arbitration or adjudication. The world is covered by a network of treaties, mostly bilateral, providing for the settlement of international disputes by arbitration, but in so far as they provide for obligatory arbitration they are almost invariably accompanied by exceptions so sweeping as to rob the commitment of all meaning. When the effort to make arbitration obligatory failed at the Hague Conference, it was hoped that practically the same end would be reached by the encouragement of the negotiation of a large number of bilateral treaties after the model of the Franco-British Treaty of 1903. Under this treaty the parties agreed to submit differences of a legal nature or involving the interpretation of treaties, provided, nevertheless, that they do not affect the vital interests, the independence, or the honor of the two contracting states and do not concern the interests of third parties.

American administrations have at various times sought to take an active part in the general movement for compulsory arbitration. The United States government negotiated and signed a number of general treaties providing for the obligatory arbitration of disputes involving legal questions, but likewise subject to the usual exception of differences involving national honor, independence, vital interests, or the interests of third states. As if this breach in the commitment to obligatory arbitration were not large enough, the Senate widened it even more. It was assumed that after the general arbitration treaty came into effect, each *compromis* or agreement for the subsequent submission of particular disputes to arbitration would be concluded by executive agreement rather than by formal treaty, for under the American Constitution a formal treaty requires the consent of the Senate for ratification, and that by a two-thirds vote. The Senate amended the arbitration treaties so as to provide that the submission of each dispute to arbitration could take place only by formal treaty. President Roosevelt objected to this and at first declined to present the amended treaties to the foreign governments for their approval, but in 1908 they were submitted and ratified. These arbitration treaties actually represent a backward step from earlier American practice, for the United States had often arbitrated differences without the conclusion of a formal treaty which had to be submitted to the Senate for prior consent. It must be remembered that it will not always be easy to get two-thirds of the Senate to favor the submission of a dispute after it arises.

The effort to relate the United States to other countries in a network of arbitration treaties more binding in their provisions was renewed by President Taft's administration. In 1911 Secretary Knox negotiated treaties with France and Great Britain respectively, in which the exceptions of national honor and vital interest were dropped and provision was made for the submission to arbitration of all "justiciable" disputes, that is, disputes involving questions of a legal nature. A joint commission was to be set up under each of these treaties for the purpose of determining in each case whether or not the particular difference was justiciable.   The Senate struck out the provision for the joint commission and inserted reservations prohibiting the submission to arbitration of a number of questions, such as the admission of aliens, debts owed by foreign states, and the Monroe Doctrine.   This mutilation of his arbitration treaties so disgusted President Taft that he withdrew them from the Senate and abandoned the whole project.

A new attack upon the problem was made by Secretary of State Kellogg. It was his idea that if the former vague exceptions of national honor, vital interests, or independence were replaced by new exceptions more precise in character, their scope would be greatly narrowed.   Secretary Kellogg therefore began the negotiation of a new series of arbitration treaties, of which the treaty of 1928 with France was the model.   While the treaty provides for the submission to arbitration of all justiciable disputes, it excepts any dispute which

(a) is within the domestic jurisdiction of either of the High Contracting Parties, (b) involves the interests of third parties, (c) depends upon or involves the maintenance of the traditional attitude of the United States concerning American questions, commonly described as the Monroe Doctrine, (d) depends upon or involves the observance of the obligations of France in accordance with the Covenant of the League of Nations.

It must be seriously doubted whether these exceptions are any narrower than the older ones they replaced, especially when we keep in mind that the parties are themselves the judge of whether a given dispute falls within these exceptions.

The high-water mark in international arbitration before World War II was reached in the Covenant of the League of Nations, which represents a collective agreement containing a broad commitment for the arbitration of disputes as an alternative to other methods.   Under Article 12 the members of the League agreed to submit either to arbitration or to inquiry by the Council any dispute arising between them likely to lead to a rupture.   Under the terms of Article 13 the members further agreed to submit to arbitration any dispute which they deemed suitable for arbitration and which could not be satisfactorily settled by diplomacy.   Furthermore, the Covenant listed certain classes of cases which are declared to be among those generally suitable for submission to arbitration.   The classes named were disputes involving the interpretation of a treaty, a question of international law, a breach of an international obligation, and the nature and extent of such breach.   After World War I there were other treaties of considerable scope providing for arbitration, among which the treaties of the Locarno Pact of 1925 were probably the most important.   A Central American Court of Arbitration after the manner of the Hague Court of Arbitration was created by agreement of the Central American states in 1923. Excluded from the jurisdiction of the tribunal were disputes involving the old vague exceptions—sovereignty, national honor, vital interests, and independence.

The defects of arbitration as a means of settling international disputes are obvious. Yet its defects are also the sources of its strength. The fact that for each particular case submitted the parties to the dispute should be free to select their own judges and include their own nationals as members of the arbitral tribunal indicated how little inclined states are to submit their disputes to the decision of impartial judges. This reluctance is further reflected in the wide reservations which are generally made in the agreements providing only for optional jurisdiction. It is not an exaggeration to say that states are willing to submit to arbitration only such unimportant disputes as the expediency and interests of the hour may dictate. It should be remembered that the decisions which proceed from arbitral tribunals are often based wholly or in part on compromise and not on strict legal rules or principles. Yet it is just these features which also constitute the merits of arbitration, for the chief problem in the maintenance of peace is that of inducing states to settle their disputes by pacific means. States can in many instances be induced to accept arbitration when they would not be willing to accept another method more nearly approaching true judicial settlement. While it is true that the most dangerous disputes, those most likely to lead to war, are seldom submitted, arbitration does nevertheless provide a method whereby a large number of irritating disputes can be removed from the field of controversy.

Judicial Settlement. This is the most highly developed form of pacific settlement. As its name implies, it involves decision by an impartial court upon the basis of law. The differences between arbitration and judicial settlement and the superiority of the latter over the former are clearly stated in Secretary Root's instructions to the American delegates to the Second Hague Conference: [24]

> It has been a very general practice for arbitrators to act, not as judges deciding questions of fact and law upon the record before them under a sense of judicial responsibility, but as negotiators effecting settlements of the questions brought before them in accordance with the traditions and usages subject to all the considerations and influences which affect diplomatic agents. The two methods are radically different, proceed upon different standards of honorable obligation, and frequently lead to widely differing results. It very frequently happens that a nation which would be very willing to submit its differences to an impartial judicial determination is unwilling to subject them to this kind of diplomatic process. . . . It should be your effort to bring about in the Second Conference a development of the Hague Tribunal into a permanent tribunal composed of judges who are judicial officers and nothing else, who are paid adequate salaries, who have no other occupation, and who will de-

---

[24] Quoted in J. W. Garner, *Recent Developments in International Law*, Calcutta University, Calcutta, 1925, p. 667.

vote their entire time to the trial and decision of international causes by judicial methods and under a sense of judicial responsibility. These judges should be so selected from different countries that the different systems of law and procedure and the principal languages shall be fairly represented. The court shall be made of such dignity, consideration, and rank that the best and ablest jurists will accept appointment to it, and that the whole world will have absolute confidence in its judgments.

At the Second Hague Conference efforts were made to set up an International Prize Court and a Court of Arbitral Justice, but with little success in either case. Prize courts, which deal with the title to property seized on the high seas during time of war, form a part of the national governmental machinery and therefore their impartiality may be under some suspicion. There was not any great difficulty in the organization of the Court, but the convention providing for it was never ratified because there was no general international agreement with respect to prize law. The project for the Court of Arbitral Justice failed because of inability to agree on a method for the selection of judges. The small powers, led by Brazil, insisted upon the right of each state, large or small, to designate a judge. Since there were forty-one states represented at the Conference, this method would have meant a court of forty-one judges!

In connection with judicial settlement, reference should be made to the short-lived Central American Court of Justice. This Court was organized in 1907, with the active encouragement of the United States. It was opened in the following year, and in the course of its nine years of existence it adjudicated nine cases. Unfortunately the United States government, which had been instrumental in helping to create the court, also helped to destroy it. Under the terms of the Bryan-Chamorro Treaty between the United States and Nicaragua, the former was ceded not only the exclusive right to construct a canal across Nicaraguan territory, but also a naval base in the Gulf of Fonseca and two small islands in the Caribbean Sea. Costa Rica protested this treaty as violating its right to be consulted in a matter which so closely affected its interests, and it brought suit against Nicaragua before the Court. The Court sustained the claim of Costa Rica and declared the treaty void. When the United States government tacitly supported the position of Nicaragua in claiming that the Court had exceeded its competence, the other Central American states had no desire to renew the ten-year period for which the Court originally had been created.

After World War I, the Permanent Court of International Justice was established and made some very useful contributions to the judicial settlement of international disputes. The judicial organ of the United Nations is the International Court of Justice.[25]

[25] See Chap. 13.

Chapter 4

INTERNATIONAL LAW

To avoid anarchy is as essential for states as it is for individuals; hence regulation of interstate relations becomes as necessary as the regulation of the relations between man and man within states. Now it is obvious that the purpose of law has not been achieved if it prevents anarchy within the state only to create greater anarchy among states. The function of municipal and international law is the same, namely, to reduce human relations to order on principles of justice. Moreover, chaos in the international sphere will in the end cause a breakdown of many of the relations within the state. Postwar periods with their numerous political upheavals give abundant evidence of this truth.

NATURE OF INTERNATIONAL LAW

A leading English jurist defines international law as "the body of rules and principles of action which are binding upon civilized states in their relations with one another." [1] For the purpose of completeness there should probably be added to this definition the clause, "or with the nationals of other states." Now we shall have to admit frankly that at the present moment there exists a great divergence of viewpoints with respect to the nature of international law. One school of writers maintains that international law is not law at all, but merely international morality or ethics. On the other hand, there are an increasing number of scholars who hold not only that international law is law, but that considering the facts and practices of international life the term "supranational law" should replace the term "international law," as more accurately describing its true character. [2] It is a law not merely between states but above or superior to states.

---

[1] J. L. Brierly, *The Law of Nations,* Oxford, New York, 1942, 3d ed., p. 1. Westlake, another distinguished English student of international law, simply defines international law as "the law of the society of states." *International Law,* Vol. I, Cambridge, New York, 1910, p. 1.

[2] J. P. A. Francois, *Handboek van het Volkenrecht,* Vol. I, Tjeenk Willink, Zwolle, 1931, pp. 19*ff;* J. W. Garner, "Limitations on National Sovereignty in International Relations," *American Political Science Review,* Vol. XIX, pp. 1*ff.*

The reason some people find it difficult to accept international law as law is largely that it is very different from national law in several respects. International law differs from national, or municipal, law [3] in the way it is enacted, interpreted, and enforced. Law had its origin in custom; among primitive people custom is the only source of law. A custom becomes law, generally called "customary law," when the community feels that this particular custom ought to be enforced by the application of penalties. The idea that man can consciously make law is found only in societies more or less advanced. While customary law remains an element in the law of most countries, as, for instance, the common law of the English-speaking countries, the great bulk of national law now is statute law; it has its origin in decree or legislation. International law, since it is less developed, is still largely customary law, and in so far as it has been consciously made it has come into existence by the treaty-making process and not by the decree of a sovereign or the act of a legislative body. There is neither a world sovereign nor a world legislature to enact international law.

A second important difference between national and international law is to be noted. When individuals within a state clash as to their respective rights under the law, any one of the individuals concerned may bring the case before the proper courts to have his rights defined and enforced. For centuries each state was the final arbiter of its claims under international law. If direct negotiations between two states over conflicting claims failed, the two might agree to submit the question to arbitration, but the parties to the dispute were under no obligation to do so. If negotiations between the disputant states broke down and resort was had to war, the other states in the family of nations, unless their direct interests led them to participate in the war, merely declared their "neutrality." This has all been greatly changed. By numerous bipartite treaties states have agreed to submit disputes to arbitration or judicial settlement; the members of the United Nations are under obligation to compose their differences by arbitration, judicial settlement, or conciliation. There is now an International Court of Justice, whose compulsory jurisdiction has been accepted by a large number of states.[4] States have lost a great deal of their right to be the sole and final interpreters of their rights under international law.

International law also lacks legal character, so it is frequently contended, because there is neither international executive nor police for its enforcement. It is not necessary that the agency which enforces a law should be a part of the organization or body which enacts it. England was without an effective national enforcement machinery long after the itinerant judges had firmly established a national "common law." The Catholic Church in the Middle

[3] The student should be careful not to confuse municipal law with city law. By "municipal law" is meant national law, as contrasted with international law.
[4] See Chap. 13.

Ages originated much law but did not itself enforce it. Even in the United States today the power which enacts law and the power which enforces it are not always organs of the same unit of government. In a few instances cases arising under Federal laws are tried in state courts, while the laws of our states are often dependent upon local courts and local administrative officials for enforcement. Thus international society still relies almost wholly upon the states themselves for the enforcement of the rules of international law.

The sanctions of international law do not differ greatly from those of national law. Municipal law must rely chiefly upon such sanctions as public opinion, habit, self-interest, and expediency, and good faith for its observance. Physical coercion is not an essential characteristic of law. John Bassett Moore points out that a large part of constitutional law is not enforced by means of specific penalties.[5] Force is at best only one means of enforcing law and its importance as a sanction is much overrated. As Laski correctly pointed out, "The will of the State obtains preeminence over the wills of the other groups exactly to the point where it is interpreted with sufficient wisdom to obtain general acceptance and no further. Should it venture into dangerous places it pays the penalty of its audacity. It finds its sovereignty by consent transformed into impotence by agreement."[6] The mere addition of penalties will not make an unpopular law enforceable. Far more important is the general recognition of law as binding and habitual obedience to it, and in this respect international law suffers little in comparison with municipal law. Though unnoticed by the public, scores of cases are daily being adjusted before national courts and in offices of foreign affairs on the basis of international law. Most treaties are faithfully executed, and it is only rarely that an arbitral decision is not carried out. The Permanent Court of International Justice under the League of Nations and its successor, the International Court of Justice, have not found their judgments flouted, even though they have had no international sheriff at their disposal. The judgments of international tribunals have almost invariably been carried out, and in many of the cases adjudicated by them national feeling ran high. Decisions of international courts are as uniformly obeyed as decisions of municipal courts. No state openly defies international law, though it may contest what the rule of law is in a particular case.

The Jay Treaty affords an interesting example of the operation of self-interest as a sanction in international law. Under this treaty the United States agreed to submit to arbitration British claims for the loss of vessels captured by French ships which had been armed in the ports of the United States. The arbitration tribunal held that the United States had failed to perform its neutral duties and awarded Great Britain $143,428. The payment of this award by the United States established the principle that a government is liable in

[5] *International Law and Some Current Illusions,* Macmillan, New York, 1924, p. 292.

[6] Harold J. Laski, *The Problem of Sovereignty,* Yale University Press, New Haven, 1917, p. 14.

damages for failure to enforce strictly its neutral duties and laid the basis for a similar claim (the Alabama Claims case) against England over half a century later. Unfortunately, statesmen and the public do not always take a long-range view of matters and hence are not sufficiently moved by the advantages of reciprocity based upon law to make this sanction as effective as it ought to be.

Some writers profess to see in war the highest and ultimate sanction of international law and even speak of intervention as the vicarious enforcement of international law. Whatever practical justification there may have been for such action under previous conditions, self-help can never be recognized as a legal sanction. It is only when used by the international community or upon its authorization that intervention or war can be regarded as possessed of legal character. We cannot speak of a sanction as having legal character in cases where the state is plaintiff, judge, and sheriff in its own cause. Self-help is essentially a mark of lawlessness. When the international community is more fully developed, self-redress will give way to collective enforcement.

Relation of International Law to National Law

In view of what has been said above about the nature of international law, some explanation of the relation between municipal law—probably better called national law—and international law is in order. Because international law is most generally enforced through municipal law and by national agents, the impression is conveyed that national law is superior to international law. A brief examination of the facts will show that this impression is erroneous. Some modern constitutions specifically state that international law is part of the national law. American courts and less unequivocally so the British courts have held in many decisions that international law is part of the law of the land. American courts have never deviated from the principle laid down by Chief Justice Jay in a decision in 1792 that "the United States had, by taking a place among the nations of the earth, become amenable to the law of nations" and that "it was to their interest as well as their duty to provide that those laws should be respected and obeyed." [7] In a leading English case the court held "that the law of nations, wherever any question arises, which is properly the object of its jurisdiction, is adopted in its fullest extent by the common law of England, and held to be part of the law of the land." [8]

[7] *Chisholm v. Georgia*, 2 Dallas 419 (1793). See also *The "Nereide,"* 9 Cranch 423 (1815), and *The "Paquete Habana,"* 175 U.S. 700 (1900). See article by Harold Sprout, "Theories as to the Applicability of International Law in the Federal Courts of the United States," *American Journal of International Law*, Vol. XVI, pp. 288ff.

[8] *Emperor of Austria v. Day and Kossuth*, 2 Giffard 628 (1861). In a more recent case, that of the West Rand Central Gold Mining Company, the court accepted this principle rather cautiously, stating that "the international law sought to be applied must, like anything else, be proved by satisfactory evidence, which must show either that the particular

48 BACKGROUND

A second principle observed by American and British courts is that a legislative act is assumed to be in harmony with international law unless clearly in conflict with it. In an early decision Chief Justice Marshall said, "An act of Congress ought never to be construed to violate the law of nations if any other possible construction remains."[9] Thus courts will strain a point to avoid a conflict between the two laws. Moreover, there is in all countries a large body of legislation whose direct object is the enforcement of the obligations of international law. As examples of such laws the United States statutes for the protection of diplomatic agents may be cited.

But what happens in case of a clear conflict between municipal and international law? In this event the national courts apply the statute. They cannot well do otherwise, since they are the immediate agents of their governments and receive their instructions from them. From this it must not be concluded that municipal law is superior to international law, that it can set aside a rule of international law in favor of a statute. The executive may reverse the decision of the courts, and often does. The President or the Secretry of State, either upon his own initiative or upon the demand of foreign countries invoking a rule of international law, will generally order an immediate suspension of the enforcement of the law and at once seek either the repeal of the law or the negotiation of a treaty with the state involved so as to iron out the difficulty. This was done, for example, in the case of the United States prohibition laws, which called for the arrest of rumrunners beyond the three-mile maritime belt. In this case the President, through the Secretary of the Treasury, ordered the customs officials to refrain from seizing foreign liquor smugglers beyond the three-mile limit. In the meanwhile, the State Department negotiated a series of treaties with foreign countries, under which the United States was given jurisdiction over vessels of the nations of these states beyond the three-mile limit for the purpose of enforcing its prohibition laws.

A similar conflict may arise between treaties and statutes. In a badly considered case the United States Supreme Court laid down the rule that the latest expression of the national will prevails.[10] This is the rule in nearly all countries, though there seems to be some uncertainty about the rule in Switzerland.[11] Thus Congress may nullify by unilateral action an earlier treaty as

proposition put forward has been recognized and acted upon by our country, or that it is of such a nature, and has been so widely and generally accepted, that it can hardly be supposed that any civilized state would repudiate it." L.R. 2 K.B. 391 (1905).

[9] The "Charming Betsy," 2 Cranch 64, 118 (1804). For an English decision of similar import see The "Annapolis," 30 L.J. P. & M. 201 (1861).

[10] Pitman Potter, "International Law and National Law in the United States," American Journal of International Law, Vol. XIX (1925), pp. 315ff.

[11] See Ruth D. Masters, International Law in National Courts: A Study of the Enforcement of International Law in German, Swiss, French and Belgian Courts, Columbia University Press, New York, 1932.

American national law, but the treaty remains binding as an international obligation. Here, too, the treaty may be saved by Executive order, as when President Wilson ordered the release of aliens drafted into the army under the provisions of the conscription act. In case there is no redress for the alien in municipal law, his government may make diplomatic presentation in his behalf. If the United States does not admit that a rule of international law has been violated or the terms of a treaty broken, the matter may be submitted to arbitration or judicial settlement. If the case is submitted to an international tribunal, the latter will apply international law, in which case international law triumphs in the end. As a matter of fact, the United States Supreme Court has several times been reversed by an international tribunal. Should the United States refuse to submit the case to arbitration or judicial settlement it would be guilty of a violation of international law or, in the case of a breach of a treaty, of failure to carry out its international obligations.

INDIVIDUALS UNDER INTERNATIONAL LAW

The forerunners of Grotius recognized the individual as the subject of international law; they recognized the state as such a subject only by exception. Grotius, who is almost universally accorded the title of the father of international law, took the position that international law regulated not only the relations between one state and the subjects of another but even the relations between subjects of different states. Beginning with Hobbes, and followed by Pufendorf, the view that international law regulated only the relations between states became generally accepted. This development is very largely accounted for by the manner in which international society has developed. The growth of the doctrine of an uncontrolled absolute state sovereignty led to the exclusion of individuals and all public-law communities other than the state as subjects of international law. New juridical bodies, such as international administrative unions, the League of Nations and the United Nations, and new juridical communities, such as the mandates and trust territories, came into existence, and these became the subjects of rights and obligations under international law. The individual is again gradually emerging as a subject of international law.

The question of whether the individual is already a subject of international law has engendered much theoretical discussion, but need not detain us long. The individual is the basic unit of society and the real object of all law, and an increasing number of jurists throughout the world are taking the position that a democratic international law must place individuals in the first rank of subjects.[12] The Institute of International Law at its meeting in New York

[12] Philip C. Jessup, "The Subjects of a Modern Law of Nations," *A Modern Law of Nations*, Macmillan, New York, 1948; Nicolas S. Politis, *New Aspects of International Law*,

in 1929 adopted a Declaration of the International Rights of Man, proclaiming that it is the duty of every state to ensure each individual an equal right to life, liberty, property, freedom of religion, free choice of language, and education in this language.[13] The opponents of this view hold that while individuals are the objects of international law, states are its sole subjects. Oppenheim gives expression to this point of view when he states that "all duties which necessarily have to be imposed upon individual human beings according to the Law of Nations are not international duties, but duties imposed by municipal law in accordance with a right granted to or a duty imposed upon the state concerned by International Law." [14] A commission of the Economic and Social Council of the United Nations has drafted a Universal Declaration of Human Rights and is now at work on drafting an International Covenant of Human Rights.[15]

It is a well-known fact that theory generally runs ahead of practice, and for that reason it may be more profitable to survey actual international practice. In a number of cases, such as piracy, blockade running, and the carriage of contraband, individuals have long been directly subject to the rules of international law and punishable under it. Whereas the state enforces the rule, the authority to do so is derived not from national but from international law. The courts of England and the United States have held that counterfeiting the money of other states is an offense against international law.[16] In addition to the rights to which the individual is subject under customary international law, the individual has also become the bearer of rights and duties under numerous treaties. This is especially true in the case of treaties setting up international tribunals. The extinct Central American Court of Justice had authority under certain conditions to take jurisdiction over cases of individuals against states and actually heard several such cases. The International Prize Court, which was to have been established under the Twelfth Convention of the Second Hague Conference, was to be clothed with authority to hear cases on appeal by individuals from the national prize courts.

Carnegie Endowment, New York, 1928, pp. 18ff; Clyde Eagleton, *International Government*, Ronald, New York, 1932, pp. 177–185; J. B. Scott, "The Individual, the State, the International Community," *American Society of International Law Proceedings*, Vol. 24, 1930, pp. 15–32; and Quincy Wright, *Research in International Law since the War*, Carnegie Endowment, New York, 1930, p. 23.

[13] Sir Thomas Barclay, "New Declaration of Rights of Man," *Contemporary Review*, Vol. 140, pp. 331–336, September, 1931.

[14] L. Oppenheim, *International Law*, edited by A. McNair, Longmans, Roberts and Green, London, 1928, 4th ed., p. 21.   See also Charles Fenwick, *International Law*, Appleton-Century-Crofts, New York, 2d ed., 1924–1934, p. 85; and Amos S. Hershey, *Essentials of International Public Law and Organization*, Macmillan, New York, 1927, rev. ed., p. 157.

[15] *These Rights and Freedoms*, Department of Public Information, United Nations, 1950.

[16] *Emperor of Austria v. Day and Kossuth*, 2 Giffard 628 (1861), and *United States v. Arjona*, 120 U.S. 479 (1887).

Likewise, under the mixed arbitration tribunals set up under the Treaty of Versailles and the other peace treaties concluding World War I, individuals are given the right to present their claims without the interposition of their governments. The individual in these cases is pressing his own personal claims, not those of his government. The individual likewise has become the subject of legal obligations under a large number of treaties by which governments confer upon international bodies power to lay down regulations directly binding upon their nationals, without the specific approval of the governments in each case or the transformation of these regulations into national law. A number of commissions with such powers are found in international river law.[17] There is a growing demand that aliens by international treaty be given the privilege of suing states before an international court.

There is also the reverse side of the practice just described which needs to be presented for a balanced picture. Only states can be parties in cases before the International Court of Justice. Normally individuals can get their cases before claims commissions only if they are adopted as its own by the state. Of two equally good claims the government may accept one and reject the other for presentation before the commission, though it is not often likely to do so. Moreover, the government may sacrifice an individual's claim for political or other reasons. Since claims must be presented through a government, stateless persons, *i.e.*, persons who are citizens of no state, cannot get their claims brought before the commissions. Generally, too, the damage awarded the claimant is paid to his government and not to him directly. As a result, the individual may not always get the award after all. Thus while the individual may be a subject of international law, it should be remembered that in general he becomes the bearer of rights and duties under international law only through the intermediary of the state and in his quality as a subject of it, and that these rights will be his only so long as he remains a national of the state concerned, and only for so long as the states signatory to the treaty by which these rights and obligations are created wish to keep the treaty in force.

Sources of International Law

The sources of international law are custom, agreement, and general principles of law. In the manner of its growth, international law resembles the common law. Its chief source is custom, but not every custom in the field of international relations falls within the sphere of law. Only those practices with respect to which there has developed a general conviction that their application has become obligatory have legal character. As Article 38 of the Statute of the International Court of Justice has it, "The Court shall ap-

[17] Pitman Potter, *Introduction to the Study of International Organization*, Appleton-Century-Crofts, New York, 3d ed., 1928, pp. 176–177.

ply . . . international custom, as evidence of a general practice accepted as law." The difficulty of determining whether a particular custom has developed into a rule of law constitutes a major problem with respect to this source. Often this can be determined only by submission of the issue to judicial settlement. A classic example of a court decision based upon customary international law is the case of the *Paquete Habana*, which arose in the Spanish-American War. One of the most firmly established rules of international law is the right of a belligerent to capture enemy vessels on the high seas. But when an American warship brought in a couple of small fishing smacks belonging to enemy nationals the court refused to condemn them, for the reason that "by an ancient usage among civilized nations, beginning centuries ago and gradually ripening into a rule of international law, coast fishing vessels, pursuing their vocation of catching and bringing in fresh fish have been recognized as exempt, with their cargoes and crews, from capture as prize of war." [18]

Agreement, as expressed in treaties and conventions, constitutes a second source of international law. An analogy is sometimes drawn between the rule of treaties in international law and that of statutes in national law, but the analogy, while useful, is a very imperfect one, for the ordinary treaty between two or more states cannot be regarded as an independent source of law. Very frequently the object of a treaty is to create an obligation which does not exist in general international law, and of course such a treaty is binding only upon the parties to it. In other cases the object of a treaty may be to set aside an existing rule of law. In neither of these cases can a treaty be said to be a source of law, though binding upon the parties to it. Only a treaty setting up an international institution or creating a new general rule governing future conduct, ratified by a large number of states, can be regarded as a "law-making" treaty. In a strictly technical sense even such a general treaty cannot be said to be a "law-making" treaty unless ratified by all the states of the world, but the ratification of such treaties in a large number of states, including all the leading ones, has the practical effect of world legislation.

In addition to custom and agreement there is a third source of international law, a source which has aptly been described as "original." The Statute of the International Court of Justice refers to this source as "the general principles of law recognized by civilized nations." Williams calls this element of international law "original law" for the reason that it has its "direct origin in morality and the common recognition of mankind, and is the law for the nations without the support of treaty, convention, or agreement—however desirable for practical reasons such support may be." [19] Because so much of international law has its source in the general principles of law or, as some

---

[18] *The "Paquete Habana,"* 175 U.S. 677 (1900).

[19] Sir John Fischer Williams, *Chapters on Current International Law and the League of Nations,* Longmans, Roberts and Green, London, 1929, p. 23.

contend, in the moral feelings of mankind, it has been exposed to the reproach of vagueness and uncertainty. The justice of this reproach cannot altogether be denied, but it should be remembered that international law is still in the early days of its development. With improvement in the process of international legislation an ever-increasing percentage of international law will become embodied in conventions, and its rules will thus take on greater precision. The common law of Anglo-Saxon countries has experienced a similar development.

Authority, while often listed as a fourth source of international law, is more generally regarded as an evidence of existing rules. Under this category come "judicial decisions and the teachings of the most highly qualified publicists of the various nations," as the Statute of the International Court of Justice phrases it. However, the Statute qualifies this source as "a subsidiary means for the determination of the rules of law." Moreover, the Statute expressly prohibits the Court from adopting the Anglo-American rule of *stare decisis,* that is, of using its decisions as binding precedents.[20] Jurists do not, of course, make law. Their writings furnish evidence of the general attitude toward rules of international law, the weight of their authority in each case being dependent upon the standing of the authors. For this reason the resolutions of the Institute of International Law have great weight as evidence of a rule of law.

Evidences of the rules of international law are also found in public documents such as the opinions of attorneys general, diplomatic correspondence, instructions for diplomatic and consular officers, the decisions of municipal courts, municipal statutes and decrees, and the records of international conferences.

THE WEAKNESSES OF INTERNATIONAL LAW

Not even the most ardent internationalist will deny that international law has grave weaknesses. While these defects have, no doubt, been overemphasized by critics they are nevertheless real and cannot be ignored. Nor is it in the interest of the promotion of the rule of law in international relations to close our eyes to these defects, for the more open-eyed the world becomes to their existence, the more quickly may we expect to see them remedied.

The inadequacy of international law, and also much of its strength, flows from the fact that so large a part of its rules are derived from custom and reason. Custom develops in answer to social needs; gradually some of these customs become recognized as obligatory, as rules of law. Customary law is thus a phenomenon of living society, a product of social needs. But customary law has at least two serious defects. In the first place many of its rules lack precision and objectivity. The rules of municipal law are much more definite, for by far the larger part of these rules have their source in statutes, codes, and

[20] Article 59. The decision of the court has no binding force except between the parties and in respect of that particular case.

a vast body of judicial decisions. The national lawyer can go to the statute books, codes, or court reports and obtain a fairly definite answer to the question of what the rule of law is on a specific point, though of course he cannot always be sure how the courts will apply the rule in every specific case. The international lawyer lacks these definite sources. It is difficult to know when a custom has ripened into a rule of law or to obtain a common agreement as to what are general principles of law or to determine the specific rules which flow from them. While the law derived from general principles is not entirely subjective, it does leave much to be desired in the way of objectivity.

A second grave defect of customary law is the slowness with which it develops. In primitive society, where social and economic conditions change imperceptibly, this is not a serious matter, but in modern society with its vast and rapid changes customary law soon lags behind the new legal needs born of fundamental social transformations. How great this lag is, can be seen from the narrowness of the scope of international law. Some of the most vital relations between states in an interdependent world have not yet been subjected to the control of law. States are very loath to admit law into just those spheres of their activities in which dangerous conflicts arise. Armaments, tariffs, migrations, the relation of advanced to backward peoples, and the distribution of raw materials are some of the highly important subjects which have thus far escaped the regulation of international law.

The root of these defects in international law may be traced to the lack of a well-developed process of international legislation and the inability to compel states to submit disputes with each other to judicial settlement.

TREATY MAKING AND INTERNATIONAL LEGISLATION

We have seen that municipal law originated in custom, that customary law later became in large part judge-made law, as the judge wove the changing sentiment of the community into the law. Customary law and judge-made law change very slowly, much too slowly in a rapidly developing society. We now look to legislative bodies to make changes in the law and make new law to meet the ever-changing needs of modern society. Indeed, we have become so accustomed to look to the legislative method for the enactment of law that we forget that even today not all municipal laws are so made. Some laws reach the statute books by means of the initiative and referendum, and constitutional law, in the form of new constitutions and amendments, is generally made in a manner quite different from ordinary legislation. But none of these forms of lawmaking are found in the international community. A central international legislative body is still lacking. This is not surprising, since the international community is still primitively organized. The international community, however, is making a conscious effort to make changes in its law and to widen its scope. The term "international legislation" has been used to describe both the process and the product of this effort.

The conscious formulation of legal rules in the international sphere originally took place by means of bipartite agreements or treaties, generally negotiated through the regular diplomatic channels. Because the rules of the law of nations were often vague and uncertain, many inconveniences and difficulties beset the intercourse between states. These bipartite treaties served in part to facilitate this intercourse by laying down these rules in explicit terms. But these treaties served also to call into being a special legal relationship between the parties, whose provisions went beyond the recognized rules of international law. By inclusion in an ever larger number of treaties between other states and by extended application, these regulations gradually become incorporated in international law.

Soon collective or multilateral treaties began to be made, increasing in number with the increasing development of international society.[21] Multilateral treaties may be limited to the original signatory states, but treaties general in nature and legislative in character increasingly are left open for the adherence of all the states of the world. For example, the Briand-Kellogg Pact for the renunciation of war was negotiated through the regular diplomatic channels, signed at Paris by the representatives of fifteen countries, and came into effect as soon as it was ratified by all the signatory states, but it remains open as long as may be necessary for adherence by all the other powers of the world. Multilateral treaties are generally negotiated at conferences of representatives of the states concerned. In the beginning these conferences were called at the initiative of one of the states, but gradually the practice of holding periodic conferences developed, since the regulations governing a subject cannot be laid down once and for all but must be periodically revised to meet changed conditions. In some cases the state upon whose territory the conference meets is charged with the task of making the necessary preparations for the conferences; in other cases a permanent bureau is established to perform this work. Thus have the organs of international legislation evolved over the course of the last century or more.

New international law was first made by a collective treaty at the Congress of Vienna in 1815. This Congress laid down the ranks of diplomatic representatives, legislated against the slave traffic, and attempted to secure the free navigation of the important international rivers. After a period of inactivity, the work of consciously developing international law was again taken in hand

---

[21] In terms such as "bipartite" and "multilateral," "-partite" refers to the number of parties to the treaty and "-lateral" to the nature of the obligation incurred. Thus a bilateral treaty carries a two-sided obligation, though it may be a multipartite treaty, as for instance in the case of two or more states dealing with another state. A treaty in which the number of signatories is more than two and the obligation runs from each to each is a multilateral treaty.

with the Congress of Paris in 1856. From this time on the movement takes
on two directions, one toward the mitigation of the brutalities of war and the
other toward the building of an international legal order and the creation of
international organs of government. From conferences seeking to cope with
the problem of mitigating the brutalities of war have emerged a series of conventions: the Declaration of Paris (1856), regulating belligerent rights of
capture at sea; the Geneva Convention for the Amelioration of the Condition of
the Wounded in War (1864); the Hague Conventions (1899, 1907), regulating
the conduct of war and the rights and duties of belligerents and neutrals; the
Declaration of London (1909), which represents an attempt to codify the laws
of war at sea; and the Washington Conference resolutions (1922), seeking to
regulate the use of submarines. Not all the above conventions have come
into force.

Of greater significance were the advances made in the more fruitful direction
of constructing an international legal order. During the past seventy-five
years conferences have been held dealing with a wide variety of subjects. The
Berlin Congo Conference of 1884–1885 laid down important regulations with
respect to the acquisition and government of backward areas, while the two
Hague Peace Conferences were successful in drawing up rules for the pacific
settlement of international disputes. A series of important conferences took
place from 1865 on, culminating in the formation of a number of international
public unions. The first of these, the Conference on Telegraphic Correspondence which met at Paris in 1865, formed the Universal Telegraph Union, which
in 1908 took the name of Telegraphic Union. Other conferences resulted in
the founding of the Universal Postal Union (1874), the Union for the Protection of Industrial Property (1883), the Union for the Protection of Works
of Art and Literature (1886), the Pan American Union (1890), the European
Union of Railway Freight Transportation (1890), and the International
Labor Organization (1919). One of the fruits of these organizatizons is the development of an international administrative law.

With the founding of the League of Nations an important advance was made
in the direction of a more rapid and uniform development of international law.
Though the Assembly and Council did not purport to legislate, they did have
the power within a narrow sphere to pass legislative regulations, in the form of
resolutions, which were binding upon the governments without their ratification. The Assembly on occasion served as a diplomatic conference for the
drafting of general treaties. The chief function of the League of Nations in
the work of international legislation was to direct, to stimulate, and to prepare
the way for a systematic development of international law. The League instituted a number of committees of experts charged with the task of preparing
treaties on special subjects. Furthermore, there were a number of technical
organizations within the League, such as the Health Organization and the
Communication and Transit Organization, which were continually busy with

the development of international regulations within these special spheres. The work of the codification of international law was also undertaken under the auspices of the League of Nations. All these activities gave impetus, unity, and continuity to the work of international legislation. The United Nations has built upon and expanded this work.

Entitled to more than casual mention in this connection is the work of the International Labor Organization, which, though it had an organization separate from that of the League of Nations and worked independently of it, was still essentially an integral part of it. In 1946, it became a "specialized agency of the United Nations." [22] The object of the International Labor Organization is to establish an international code of labor standards and law. As a result of its work a large number of conventions and recommendations have been adopted.

The shift in treaty making from bipartite treaties negotiated through diplomatic channels to collective treaties drafted at international conferences has greatly speeded up the process of international legislation. A single multipartite treaty is the equivalent of many bipartite treaties. For example, the Briand-Kellogg Pact, to which there were sixty-two parties, would have required 1,891 bipartite treaties.

THE PROCESS OF TREATY MAKING

The first step in the process of treaty making is that of negotiation. The proposals of the various interested parties are made and discussed, views are harmonized, preliminary or tentative agreement is reached, and the treaty is drafted. Treaties may be negotiated by regular diplomatic representatives, by commissioners or delegates especially appointed for the purpose, or in special cases by a foreign minister or even a chief of state.[23] Negotiations are, of course, always conducted under the authority of the executive official responsible for the foreign relations of a state. The individual negotiators are supplied with "full powers" (or credentials) which define the scope of their instructions and authority, and which make it possible for all parties to ascertain that they are dealing with duly constituted representatives of the interested states.

The second step is signature of the treaty. This means only that the negotiators have agreed upon a draft which they undertake to refer to the consideration of the appropriate constitutional authorities of their governments. It follows that signature of a treaty does not put it into effect or give rise to a binding obligation on the states which have been parties to the negotiations. This limited significance of signing a treaty should be carefully noted because there is a rather common misconception on this point. For example, American

[22] See p. 158.
[23] For example, negotiation of the Treaty of Versailles by President Wilson and the foreign ministers of the Allied Powers.

foreign policy is sometimes criticized on the basis that a treaty has been signed before the text is publicly known.   The implication of such a criticism often is that international commitments have been made by secret diplomacy.   An understanding of the true significance of signing a treaty should contribute to a more accurate appraisal of the methods used in American foreign policy.

The third step in the treaty-making process is ratification, which involves acceptance of the treaty terms by the appropriate constitutional authorities of the state.   Originally, the rule of ratification was designed to protect the sovereign from errors or deceit by the negotiators.   Its primary importance at the present time is to provide a democratic element in foreign policy by requiring that binding international obligations cannot arise without formal concurrence of a constitutional authority representing all the people.   The process for ratifying a treaty is a domestic matter, to be determined by each state for itself.   In modern democracies it is quite common for treaties to be referred to the national legislative body.   The United States Constitution requires that consent of two-thirds of the Senate be obtained before a treaty is ratified by the President.[24]

The fourth step is an exchange of ratifications.   This gives notice of formal acceptance by the respective parties to a treaty and serves to put it into effect as between them.   It is customary to take the additional fifth step of proclamation or promulgation of the treaty.   This is a requirement in the United States so far as putting a treaty into effect is concerned.   Treaties are a part of the supreme law of the land.   Therefore, they must be formally published in order that their terms may be known.

Requirements for the Legal Validity of Treaties

Which agency in the state is empowered to make treaties is a constitutional question and not a question of international law.   This power is generally vested in the head of the state, subject usually to some control of the representative body.

Treaties may be written in any language.   Originally, treaties were concluded in Latin; later, French was so universally used that it came to be regarded as the "official and authentic" language of diplomacy.   In recent years French has lost the primacy it once enjoyed, having been compelled to share honors with English.   The Covenant of the League of Nations was drawn up in French and English, and the two texts were equally authentic.   The Treaty of Versailles was concluded in both French and English, but in case of doubt as to meaning the French text was decisive.   There now seems to be a growing practice for states to conclude bipartite treaties in the languages of the two

---

[24] It should be noted that the Senate does not ratify a treaty, but merely gives its "advice and consent."   After favorable Senate action, the President is free to ratify or to withhold ratification.

parties. In case both texts are regarded as equally authentic, difficulties may arise, as the two texts may not always be in perfect accord. The Charter of the United Nations was adopted in five equally authentic texts, namely, Chinese, French, Russian, English, and Spanish (Article 3).

A treaty is invalid if coercion has been used against the negotiators or against the agencies or organs of the state having to do with treaty making, but coercion applied against the state does not invalidate a treaty. Nearly all peace treaties have been signed under coercion, though, of course, the negotiators were left free to sign or not to sign. Obviously, this anomaly will continue so long as war in all its forms is not made illegal.

A new condition for the validity of treaties came into existence with the Covenant of the League of Nations. Article 18 of the Covenant prescribed that "every treaty or international engagement entered into hereafter by any Member of the League shall be forthwith registered with the Secretariat and shall as soon as possible be published by it. No such treaty or international engagement shall be binding until so registered." It was hoped that this provision would combat secret diplomacy, remove causes for distrust and conflict, promote public control, and awaken public interest. The provision on this subject in the United Nations Charter differs slightly from that in the Covenant. Instead of declaring that no treaty is binding until so registered, Article 102 of the Charter states that no party to any such treaty which has not been registered with the Secretariat "may invoke that treaty or agreement before any organ of the United Nations." The international engagements registered with the United Nations are published by it in its United Nations Treaty Series. Texts are published in the languages of negotiation, and in French and English, if either of these official United Nations languages were not used for the original texts.

REVISION AND TERMINATION OF TREATIES

Not the least important of the problems connected with international legislation is that of the revision of treaties. Burdensome and outworn treaties constitute a dangerous source of friction and may even lead to war. Some provision for their peaceful termination or revision must be provided. Even if a treaty is entirely acceptable to both parties at the time of negotiation, changed conditions may make its continuance intolerable. In the past, revision and even termination, when diplomacy failed, were obtained by going to war. If war as an instrument of national policy is to be removed from the international order, pacific means of making changes become all the more necessary. The framers of the League Covenant were not blind to this need and sought to meet it by the inclusion of the provision found in Article 19, which provides that "the Assembly may from time to time advise the reconsideration by members of the League of treaties which have become inapplicable and the consideration of international conditions whose continuance might endanger the peace of the world." This provision, one of the most important in the Covenant, remained a dead letter.

The United Nations Charter contains no specific provision with respect to the revision of treaties. It was feared that any provision of this sort, however mild, would lead to a weakening of the sanctity of treaties, as states dissatisfied with their treaty obligations would seek to invoke the aid of the United Nations to obtain release from them. The Great Powers wished to avoid including a provision in the Charter which could serve as an invitation to the former enemy states of World War II to clamor for revision of the peace treaties, as did the Central Powers between the wars. As a result of these considerations the General Assembly was not specifically authorized to recommend the revision of treaties, but it does have this power under the very broad terms of Article 14 which states it "may recommend measures for the peaceful adjustment of any situation, regardless of origin, which it deems likely to impair the general welfare or friendly relations among nations . . ." Under Chapter VI of the Charter, "The Pacific Settlement of Disputes," and Chapter VII, "Action with Respect to Threats to the Peace, Breaches of the Peace and Acts of Aggression," the Council may do the same and, in effect, go much beyond that.

Treaties may be terminated in various ways. Fulfillment of terms completes a treaty obligation. For example, a treaty for the cession of territory is "executed" or carried out when this one transaction has been completed. A treaty may expire by a time limit provided for in its text. Sometimes a treaty is made with a stipulation that it will be in effect for a certain number of years, often with some form of optional renewal for an additional period. A treaty may be replaced or superseded by a new agreement. One party to a treaty may renounce its rights; it is not to be expected, however, that a state will give up any of its rights without receiving some alternative concessions.

Another way to terminate a treaty is for one of the parties to denounce it. This is usually a controversial matter. The doctrine of *rebus sic stantibus* is sometimes invoked. This means that a treaty was concluded under a certain set of conditions, and that a material change in the relevant circumstances furnishes a legitimate reason for terminating it. However, unilateral denunciation at the option of one party is inconsistent with a stable system of dependable international agreements. Terminating a treaty without consent of the other parties is therefore considered a violation of the obligation involved. Finally, a treaty may be terminated by the extinction of one of the parties as a state.

CODIFICATION OF INTERNATIONAL LAW

The term "codification of international law" is used in several different senses. Strictly speaking, the object of codification is to make international law clearer, more precise, and more unified—to systematize an already existing body of law. "Codification" is also used to mean the work of reducing to a unified whole a body of law in which there is as yet no unity. In order to reduce many of its conflicting rules to unity it may be necessary to make changes not only of a formal but also of a material nature. When used in this sense "codification" involves not only a restatement of the law; it involves some legislation as well. Finally, the term "codification" is used to mean the creation of a uniform law by filling in gaps and correcting defects. In this sense it is used by people who desire to incorporate important reforms in the law, such as making war illegal. But this is really no longer codification; it is essentially legislation.

Several sporadic efforts to codify international law were made before the creation of the League of Nations. Aside from the field of international administrative law, where considerable progress in codification was made, the successful efforts nearly all dealt with the laws of war and neutrality. Over a dozen such conventions came out of the two Hague Conferences of 1899 and 1907. However, one of the Hague Conventions deals with the pacific settlement of international disputes. The Pan-American conferences have also been engaged in the work of furthering the codification of international law for the American continents.

During the first few years of its existence the League of Nations confined its activities in this field to promoting the codification of law in a number of special and technical subjects. Thus, the Barcelona Conference, called under its aegis, laid down the principles of international law on communication and transit. Also the League played an important part in the formation of other conventions, such as the Convention for the Simplification of Customs Formalities and the Convention on Traffic in Women and Children. In 1924 the League of Nations began actively to undertake the work of the codification of general international law. A Committee of Experts for the Progressive Codification of International Law was appointed, and the work of narrowing down the subjects considered ripe for codification was begun. Of the numerous subjects investigated three were considered to be in this category, namely, nationality, the territorial seas, and the responsibility of states. After much preparation the Council summoned the first codification conference, which met at The Hague in the early part of 1930. The conference was anything but a success, as very little agreement was reached on the statement of the law on any of the subjects before the conference. In spite of this initial failure the work is being continued.

Under the provisions of the Charter of the United Nations, "the General Assembly shall initiate studies and make recommendations for the purpose of promoting international cooperation in the political field and encouraging the progressive development of international law and its codification" (Article 13).

In pursuance of this provision the General Assembly on November 21, 1947, voted to establish an International Law Commission for the purpose of promoting the progressive development of international law and its "eventual" codification. This Commission is composed of fifteen experts on international law, representing the chief forms of civilization and the basic legal systems of the world. It has selected three topics deemed by it as ready for attempted codification, namely, the law of treaties, arbitral procedure, and the regime of the high seas.

OBSTACLES TO INTERNATIONAL LEGISLATION

While legislation is the most important problem in international relations, it is also the most difficult. States want the benefits of law but are unwilling to make the sacrifices necessary to secure these benefits. They wish to remain as free as before the act of legislation. This is an utter impossibility, of course. That kind of attitude within the state would lead to confusion worse confounded. States are still too much impressed with their surface conflict of interests and too little by their underlying common interests.

The chief obstacle to international legislation is the principle of the sovereignty of states and the concomitant rule that no state is bound by a new rule of law unless it has expressly or impliedly given assent to it. Because of this principle many writers reject the term "international legislation," for the essence of legislation is that "it binds all persons subject to the jurisdiction of the body legislating, whether they assent to it or not, whether their duly appointed representatives have assented to it or not." [25] While this is giving the term too restricted a meaning, it does nevertheless point out a great impediment in the treaty-making process. Very often the refusal of a leading or key state to ratify a treaty may cause all other states likewise to refuse ratification.

The doctrine of the equality of states likewise brings its difficulties. The smallest of states claim an equal right with large states in the formation of new law. This is, of course, an anomaly, which in time will have to disappear. While small states should be given the equal enjoyment and protection of such rights as international law may create, they cannot always expect to share equally with the great powers in the formation of that law.

What about the future development of international law? An American scholar predicts that "more and more there will be a shifting of emphasis from the rights of states to duties, from individual to collective responsibility, from national sovereignty to international control, from independence to interdependence, and ultimately the law governing the relations of states will tend to become less and less international and more and more supernational." [26]

---

[25] Arnold D. McNair, "International Legislation," *Iowa Law Review*, Vol. 19, 1934, p. 178.

[26] J. W. Garner, *Recent Developments in International Law*, Calcutta University, Calcutta, 1925, p. 818.

Chapter 5

THE LEAGUE OF NATIONS

No institution, and least of all a world organization, springs suddenly into existence, full-blown.   The League of Nations was no exception to this rule. Violence is as old as mankind and war as old as political association, but reaction against war and plans for preventing it likewise have a long history.

EARLY PLANS

Plans for organizing peace have had their advocates over the centuries. Dante, in his *De monarchia,* which was published early in the fourteenth century, pleaded for the organization of the Christian world on an imperial basis, in the interest of unity and peace.   At about the same time, Pierre Dubois, a French lawyer, suggested a kind of permanent confederation of the various countries of Christendom as a means of maintaining peace by the application of sanctions against aggressors.   Henry IV of France in his Grand Design (1603) proposed a general council for Europe, on which each of the large states would be represented by four commissioners and the smaller ones by two. Decisions by the general council were to be binding and, if necessary, to be enforced by the collective forces of the member states.   Other noteworthy projects for organizing peace were advanced by Emeric Crucé, a Frenchman (*The New Cyneas,* 1623), William Penn (*Essay towards the Present and Future Peace of Europe,* 1694), the Abbé de Saint-Pierre (*A Project for Making Peace Perpetual in Europe,* 1714), and the German philosopher Immanuel Kant (*Essay on Eternal Peace,* 1795).

HISTORICAL PRECEDENTS

At the heart of nearly all the above plans was the international conference. This could hardly be otherwise, as consultation and conference must be at the center of all cooperation.   Moreover, there were historical precedents in abundance for associating conferences with peace, as nearly every war ended with a conference to restore peace.   From the use of conferences to restore peace to the idea of conferences to keep the peace is not a long step.   The powers which emerged victorious from the Napoleonic Wars—Austria, Prussia, Russia, and Great Britain—gave this idea formal expression in the Quadruple Alliance. The basic idea behind this alliance was that the Great Powers whose coopera- tion had won the victory should also ensure the peace by consulting each other in case of a threat to the peace and by common or authorized action against the disturber. France, under the clever diplomacy of Talleyrand, was ad- mitted to this group in 1818, and the method worked quite well for a while. Four conferences were held from 1818 to 1822; revolutions in Italy and Spain, which it was feared might lead to war, were suppressed. Largely because of coolness of Britain toward the system, the practice of regular conferences was dropped, but the idea was not wholly abandoned. Known as the "concert of Europe," it continued, in the form of intermittent conferences, to regulate in- ternational affairs at critical moments, from 1822 until the outbreak of World War I.

The concert of Europe operated quite successfully in the Berlin Congress of 1878, which dealt with the situation in the Near East; the Berlin Conference of 1884–1885, which sought to regulate imperialistic competition in Central Africa; the Algeciras Conference of 1912–1913, which dealt with the dangerous situation which had developed in Morocco; and the London Conference of 1912–1913, which probably kept the Balkan War from exploding into a general conflagration. While the concert may be credited with preventing war in numerous cases, it by no means prevented all wars, and it failed to meet the crisis in 1914. The concert had many weaknesses. Peace was often preserved among the Great Powers at the expense of the smaller, weaker countries. The concert functioned only intermittently and was wholly without regular or con- tinuous administration and conference organs, and it did nothing to cope with economic nationalism and militarism or to promote the things which made for peace.

A second strand which went into the formation of the League of Nations was the movement for limitation of armaments and the systematization of arbitration which culminated in the Hague Peace Conferences of 1899 and 1907. The development and successful functioning of a number of public international unions constituted a third element. Some of these organizations were set up to deal with an administrative problem, as in the case of the Uni- versal Postal Union; others had considerable power to deal with local situa- tions, such as the Rhine Commission and the European Danube Commission. Though limited in their jurisdiction, they served to suggest the possibility of international cooperation in a more integrated fashion and on a wider scale. Added to these elements and reinforcing them was the peace movement, which had many supporters in all countries. The various national associations had begun to link up in an international movement which was exerting a deep and widespread influence.

Looked at historically, the League of Nations was not a new and marvelous invention so far as its structure and methods were concerned, since ample precedents for these may be found in preceding international institutions. The League did provide for the first time a comprehensive system, with the union in one institution of a number of separate elements which had previously existed in a piecemeal fashion. The most radical departure lay in the emphasis on the principle of collective security, in contrast to the traditional nineteenth-century principle of neutrality of third states toward belligerents engaged in an international conflict.

DRAFTING OF THE COVENANT

The idea of an over-all international organization made much progress during World War I. In the midst of a sanguinary struggle men's minds naturally turned to schemes for preventing a recurrence of the tragedy. During these years, a large number of drafts of plans for the maintenance of peace were made by various individuals and peace groups. One of the most influential of these plans was that outlined by General J. C. Smuts of South Africa in an essay published on the eve of the peace conference. The movement for the creation of an international organization to prevent war and to promote peace received tremendous impetus when President Woodrow Wilson became its eloquent leader and placed behind it the backing of his government. Though it was the last of his famous Fourteen Points for the peace settlement, issued in January, 1918, it was easily the most important and most discussed item of his peace program.[1] It ran as follows: "A general association of nations must be formed under specific covenants for the purpose of affording mutual guarantees of political independence and territorial integrity to great and small states alike."

President Wilson insisted that the proposed League of Nations be created as an integral part of the general treaty of peace. He probably feared that unless this were done there might be no League of Nations, as governments might fail to ratify the constitution for the international organization if it were separated from the peace treaties. It is noteworthy that the Covenant was drafted by a relatively small number of people. The commission responsible for this task had in the beginning only ten members, two representatives from each of the five Great Powers; later, after protest from the small states, it was enlarged by nine additional members. President Wilson served as chairman of this committee.

The Covenant [2] was an unusually well drafted document. The chief explanation for this is that it was drawn up by a small group, which also happened to contain men of exceptional ability for this type of work. However, from the point of view of democratic procedure, this method has little to recommend it.

As Part I of the Treaty of Versailles, the Covenant was signed on June 28;

[1] See Appendix 3.
[2] See Appendix 4.

it likewise became Part I of the other peace treaties made in 1919–1920. After obtaining the required number of ratifications it went into effect on January 10, 1920.

STRUCTURE AND FUNCTIONS

The original members of the League of Nations were divided into two groups: (1) signatories of the Covenant which also ratified it, and (2) invited states, thirteen in number, which were also named in the Annex of the Covenant. Other states could be admitted to the League by a two-thirds vote of the Assembly. Any member could withdraw after two years' notice of its intention to do so, provided all its international obligations, both in general and under the Covenant, had been fulfilled at the time of withdrawal. Altogether sixty-two states were members of the League at one time or another; the largest number of members at any time was fifty-eight during 1937–1938.

The League of Nations had three main organs, the Assembly, the Council, and the Secretariat. Closely affiliated with it, in some respects a part of the League, were the Permanent Court of International Justice and the International Labor Organization. The judges of the Permanent Court were elected by the Assembly and the Council; its budget was part of the League's budget. The Court was also authorized to give advisory opinions upon "any dispute or question referred to it by the Council or by the Assembly."

The International Labor Organization was less closely tied up with the League than was the Permanent Court, but its budget was likewise a part of the League's budget. These two organs were sometimes called autonomous parts of the League of Nations. This is not altogether an accurate description of the relations between these two bodies to the League, as an institution which is dependent upon another for its budget is not wholly autonomous.

Each member could have as many as three representatives in the Assembly, but regardless of the number of representatives a state chose to send, it had only one vote. The Assembly most closely resembled a diplomatic conference; it certainly was not an international legislative body. As a general rule, substantive decisions could be made only by the unanimous agreement of the members represented at the meeting. Normally, the Assembly met annually and each Assembly chose its own president, generally from among the small states not at the time represented on the Council.

The Covenant provided that the Council was to be composed of representatives of the "Principal Allied and Associated Powers"—the United States of America, the British Empire, France, Italy, and Japan—together with four other members of the League "selected by the Assembly from time to time in its discretion." The Council could be enlarged, however, by the addition of either or both permanent and nonpermanent members. This could be done in each case by the Council with the approval of the majority of the Assembly.

As originally planned, the Great Powers were to have a very slight majority in the Council, but this they never had in fact. When the United States failed to join the League, a small state was chosen to fill the vacant seat. The ratio of Great Powers to small states in the Council membership became steadily more favorable to the latter. In the election of members to the nonpermanent seats, bloc voting developed, and since there were always smaller groups of states or isolated states which as a result had little chance of being elected, there was constant pressure for the enlargement of the Council. The number of nonpermanent members was increased from four to six in 1922, to nine in 1926, to ten in 1933, and finally to eleven in 1936. At first, there was no regulation as to the term of office of nonpermanent members, but in 1926 it was set at three years. The number of permanent members has also varied, increasing from four in 1920, to six in 1934–1935, and then declining to two at the end of 1939. The number was increased from four to five in 1926, when Germany was admitted to membership in the League and was given a permanent seat in the Council. When the Soviet Union was admitted in 1934, the number reached the peak of six, but it was to stand at this figure for only a few months. Japan's withdrawal from the League became effective in March, 1935, and the number of permanent seats was back to five. When, in October of the same year, Germany ceased to be a member of the League, the number was again reduced by one. Italy's notice of withdrawal became effective in December, 1939, the same month in which the Soviet Union was expelled from the League for its attack on Finland, and as a result only two permanent members remained, namely, France and Great Britain. The small states were now in overwhelming control of the League, but all power had departed from it.

There was no clear line of demarcation between the functions of the Assembly and the Council. The Covenant defined the powers of each in identical language; each could "deal at its meetings with any matter within the sphere of the League or affecting the peace of the world." However, the Covenant conferred on each body a number of special or exclusive functions. Among the exclusive functions of the Assembly were the admission of new members, election of the nonpermanent members of the Council, apportioning the expenses of the League among the members, and advising "the reconsideration by Members of the League of treaties which have become inapplicable and the consideration of international conditions whose continuance might endanger the peace of the world." The Council likewise had a number of exclusive functions, among which were the nomination of additional permanent members of the Council, formulating plans for the reduction of armaments, advising upon the means by which the members of the League were to preserve, as against external aggression, the territorial integrity and existing political independence of their fellow members, and supervision of the mandates system. Because of some of the special powers conferred upon it by the Covenant and because of its smaller size and its more frequent meetings, the Council did develop into something like an executive body, while the role of the Assembly was more restricted to primary action and the determination of principles.

The basic functions of the League were four in number. One of these was the formulation of plans for "the reduction of national armaments to the lowest point consistent with national safety" (Article 8). Another basic function was to "preserve as against external aggression the territorial integrity and existing political independence of all Members of the League." This was the famous Article 10 whose provisions became the predominant issue in the controversy which arose when President Wilson sought Senate approval for United States membership. Together with Article 11, laying down the principle of collective security, it constituted the core of the Covenant. The settlement of international disputes constituted the third important function (Articles 12 to 16). The fourth major function may be characterized as providing a means for peaceful change. It was incorporated in Article 19. Its provisions were weak. Under it the Assembly was authorized to "advise" the reconsideration of treaties which had become an obstacle to peaceful relations and the consideration of international conditions which were dangerous to peace. The selection of these four as the most important functions of the League is not to minimize others, such as the supervision of mandates, and the other work of the League in promoting human welfare. In the long run, these functions might have been far more important than those listed above, but unfortunately the League was not to have many decades of development. In the short run it would, and did, stand or fall with its ability to handle the four functions named.

Brief History of the League

The history of the League of Nations may be divided into three periods, as follows: 1920–1927, growth; 1927–1932, uncertainty; 1932–1939, decline and collapse.

1920–1927, *Growth*. During the first period the foundations had to be laid and the superstructure erected. Because of the failure of the United States to become a member, the League could not become what the framers of the Covenant had designed. The British, who had not been very happy about guaranteeing the territorial integrity and political independence of all members of the League, now lost all enthusiasm for it. They had hoped that the League might be the means of bringing the British and American peoples into close association and cooperation in world politics, but with the United States out of the League and the American people reverting to their former isolationist ideas, the League threatened to serve as a wedge to drive the two countries apart, and even into increasing hostility. If the British navy should be called upon to apply sanctions against an aggressor and if the United States government should assert the same neutral rights that it did before it became a belligerent in the late war, the possibility of an open clash between the two countries was not a remote one. This no sane Britisher cared to contemplate. British policy in the League of Nations, therefore, was to dilute the guarantee function.

The absence of the United States from the League also tended to drive Britain and France apart. What France desired most of all in the peace settlement was a guarantee against future attack and invasion by Germany. Clemenceau had at first demanded the detachment of the left bank of the Rhine from Germany, either by annexation to France or by the creation of a demilitarized buffer state of this area. President Wilson would not yield to this demand. As a substitute, France accepted a tripartite alliance which pledged Britain and the United States to go to the aid of France in case of attack by Germany. Great Britain and France ratified the treaty, but the United States Senate refused to give its consent to the President for ratification, and since the treaty specifically stipulated that it would be binding only if ratified by all three parties, the treaty of alliance did not become a fact. France now felt itself aggrieved. It had surrendered what it regarded as vital national interests without receiving anything in exchange. France, therefore, became very insistent that the security provisions of the Covenant be faithfully and fully enforced. Because the British would not go along with its League policy, France adopted a policy toward Germany which the British thought unreasonable and which provoked considerable British sympathy for Germany. The contrasting views of France and Britain on the League of Nations have been epitomized as follows: France regarded it as an "incomplete superstate," while Great Britain looked upon it as "a cooperative association of independent states" and "a center of influence." [3]

The absence of the United States from the new organization was also largely responsible for the failure of the plan to place all international bureaus, those already established as well as those which might be created in the future, under the direction of the League. Existing bureaus could be placed under the League only with the consent of all parties to the treaties under which they were established, but since some important countries were not members of the League, this was not possible in every case. Prewar international bureaus, like the Telegraphic Union and the Universal Postal Union, were not brought under the League. The League established a Health Organization in 1920, but the old International Office of Public Health was not abolished, because of the unwillingness of some of its members who were not members of the League to give their consent. The result was the parallel operation of two organizations with very similar functions and, in large part, with overlapping memberships.

During these early years, the League did develop a system of international administrative cooperation. Three so-called "technical organizations" were formed, namely, the Economic and Financial Organization, the Communica-

[3] Sir Alfred Zimmern, *The League of Nations and the Rule of Law, 1918–1935*, Macmillan, London, 1936, p. 339.

tions and Transit Organization, and the Health Organization. There were
also created a number of permanent advisory commissions, whose functions did
not differ greatly from the technical organizations. These commissions dealt
with such problems as intellectual cooperation, protection of children and
young people, and slavery.

During this period, the League also enjoyed a minor success in stopping a
Greek invasion of Bulgaria, which occurred in the autumn of 1925. The
Council, whose chairman at the moment happened to be Briand of France,
acted vigorously on the basis of Article 11 and was able to restore peaceful
relations between the two small states.

It was also during this period that the Locarno treaties were signed, as a
result of which Germany in 1926 became a member of the League. The
Locarno Pact was regarded as a long step forward in organizing the peace of
Europe, and the admission of Germany to the League made the latter more of
a universal organization and less of an alliance of victorious powers. However, the admission of Germany to the League, with a permanent seat on the
Council, provoked a constitutional crisis, as three middle-class powers—Poland,
Spain, and Brazil—likewise demanded permanent Council seats. This claim
was denied them, but a significant concession was made to these states. Article
4 was amended so as to give the Assembly the power to fix by a two-thirds
majority the rules dealing with the election of nonpermanent members of the
Council. Under this authorization the Assembly passed a regulation whereby
this body could, by a two-thirds vote, declare a member eligible for reelection.
By this method these states were granted what amounted to a semipermanent
seat on the Council. Upon their failure to obtain permanent seats, Brazil and
Spain gave notice of their intention to withdraw from the League; however,
Spain withdrew its resignation before the required two years' notice had ex-
pired. Brazil ceased to be a member in June, 1928.

1927–1932, *Uncertainty.* This period of the League's history began with
a fairly hopeful movement. During 1927 and 1928, the Briand-Kellogg Pact
was negotiated. It was signed August 27, 1928, by fifteen governments; it
came into force on July 24, 1929. Other states were invited to adhere, and
within a few years it had more adherents than the League had members. It
was hoped that the Briand-Kellogg Pact, the adherents of which renounced
war as an instrument of national policy, might serve as a bridge between the
United States and the League. No state could go to war in violation of the
Covenant without also violating the Pact, and though the latter contained no
provisions for implementation, it was hoped that in case of the application of
sanctions against an aggressor by the League, the United States would do nothing to hinder such action and possibly might give it some passive support.
These hopes do not seem to have been wholly unfounded when it is remembered
that the isolationist Senator William E. Borah, who was chairman of the important Senate Foreign Relations Committee during these years, declared that

it was inconceivable that the United States would be indifferent to a violation of the Briand-Kellogg Pact.

An important factor in the troubles and uncertainties of these years was the world economic depression of 1929 and the years following. Though the World Economic Conference, convened by the League in 1927, issued what amounted to a Magna Charta for international commercial cooperation, nothing came of it in practice. With the deepening of the depression, economic nationalism became more rampant than ever. The *rapprochement* between Germany and France also came to an abrupt end in 1929, with the death of Stresemann and the election of a considerable number of National Socialists to the German parliament. In September of 1931 occurred the "incident" in Manchuria, which soon developed into a flagrant case of aggression. This clear violation of the Covenant, the Nine Power Treaty, and the Briand-Kellogg Pact was met with little coordination of action or policy between Washington and Geneva. None of the powers upon whom the enforcement of sanctions would fall were prepared to join in any form of collective action which might involve military action. On January 7, 1932, the United States government announced that it would not "recognize any situation, treaty or agreement which may be brought about by means contrary to the covenants and obligations of the Pact of Paris of August 27, 1928." In March, the Assembly adopted the Stimson nonrecognition doctrine for application by League members with respect to the Japanese violation of the Covenant. In 1932, after many years of preparation, the Disarmament Conference assembled, but by this time the world situation had so deteriorated as to doom from the start any efforts for the limitation of armaments.

1932–1939, *Decline and Collapse.* On March 27, 1933, Japan gave notice of its intention to withdraw from the League, and Germany followed by a similar action on October 24 of the same year; in conformity with the requirement of two years' notice, these two countries ceased to be members in 1935. This loss of two Great Powers was somewhat offset by the admission of the Soviet Union in September, 1934, but it had entered the League only out of fear of the rise of Hitler, who rose to power on a platform of bitter anticommunism. Encouraged by the successful defiance of the League by Japan, Germany took one step after another in setting aside provisions of the Treaty of Versailles, and in March, 1936, denounced the Treaty of Locarno. In 1935, Italy invaded Ethiopia and on May 9 of the following year declared that country annexed. League sanctions, halfheartedly applied and never extended to include military measures, failed to stop the aggression. There now began a flight from the Covenant and the League. Some members made interpretative declarations diluting their obligations under the Covenant. Others withdrew from the League altogether. Notice of withdrawal was given by Paraguay in February, 1935; by Nicaragua in June, 1935; by Guatemala in May, 1936; by Honduras in July, 1936; by El Salvador in July, 1937; by Italy in

December, 1937; by Venezuela in July, 1938; by Hungary in April, 1939; and by Spain in May, 1939.

As a result of these events there developed a movement for the reform of the League. On July 4, 1936, the Assembly of the League, in an extraordinary session, passed a resolution requesting the Council to invite governments to send in proposals to improve "the application of the principles of the Covenant," and three months later it set up a committee of inquiry to examine these proposals. The committee recommended that the Covenant should be amended so as to eliminate from it all expressions which recalled the divisions of the Great War or, in other words, to separate the Covenant from the peace treaties. There was a widespread feeling that it had been a mistake to tie the Covenant to the peace treaties and that the League was breaking down under the burden of these treaties. The committee also recommended the coordination of the various peace pacts—the Briand-Kellogg Pact and the Treaty of Rio de Janeiro of 1933—and the Covenant in order to facilitate cooperation between member and nonmember states in the maintenance of peace. There was also a strong demand for universality of membership, but this demand ran into the difficulty that anything like a general membership could be obtained only by watering down the obligations which membership would impose. However that may be, the movement for reform came to nought.

It was evident long before World War II broke out that the League would be powerless to do anything about it. Such efforts as were made to prevent the war were made outside the League. Too weak to do anything to prevent or to suppress armed hostilities, the League performed a courageous but quixotic act in expelling the Soviet Union, on December 14, 1939, for attacking Finland. After this the League became dormant. The Assembly, which had not met in several years, convened for its last session on April 8, 1946, when it took the necessary steps legally to terminate its existence and to transfer its assets to the newly created United Nations.

WHY THE LEAGUE OF NATIONS FAILED

Quite naturally, the question of why the League failed has been repeatedly raised. A multitude of answers have been given, but unfortunately there is no simple or easy answer to this query. It has been asserted frequently that the failure of the United States to join was the primary reason for the League's weakness. Few will deny that the absence of the United States was a severe blow to the League's strength and prestige, but there is no guarantee that the United States government would have continued to give the League hearty support. With the first real difficulties, the American people might easily have lapsed into isolationism again. It may be that the bitter experience of a second world war was necessary to convince them that there is no security apart from collective security. By a lukewarm or reluctant participation in the League, the United States might have been a greater detriment to the successful development of the League inside it than outside it. The League badly needed the membership of all the Great Powers, but this it would not have had even if the United States had joined. More was needed, however, than the membership of all the Great Powers. What was needed in addition was the solidarity of the Great Powers, and that was sadly lacking, especially in the 1930's. There is little to justify the belief that the mere presence of the United States at the Council table would have profoundly altered this fundamental lack of agreement.

Some critics hold that the League suffered from a grave constitutional weakness in that it permitted states to resort to war under certain conditions.[4] By permitting exceptions to the prohibition of war, the Covenant seemed to assume that war remained the normal solution of international conflicts. The rule requiring unanimity of all the members of the Council, other than parties to the dispute, in making decisions with respect to disputes has been widely criticized as unworkable. This criticism also applies, of course, to the general rule that decisions of the Assembly or of the Council required the agreement of all the members present.

From the point of view of organizing peace, the League of Nations rested upon three or four main pillars. These were the provision for the reduction of armaments (Article 8), the guarantees against aggression (Articles 10 and 16), the settlement of disputes (Articles 12 to 15 and 17), and the provision for peaceful change (Article 19). The last two dovetailed into each other somewhat, as the settlement of a dispute may involve a considerable revision of existing treaties. Because these pillars were not of equal strength, the League suffered from imbalance. The drafters of the Covenant attempted to make the guarantees against aggression very strong, while the provisions for the reduction of armaments and for peaceful change were made relatively weak. Not only was the provision for peaceful change weak, but it seems to be tacked on as an afterthought. Now it is true that order is the first condition of all civilized society and that without it justice is hardly possible, but on the other hand no amount of force can maintain a *status quo* which large numbers of peoples have come to regard as grossly unjust. Order and change must be linked together as siamese twins; the one is impossible without the other. The League Covenant probably placed too much emphasis upon order and too little upon change.

However, the failure of the League was fundamentally not due to weaknesses of constitution or structure, serious as these may have been. The basic difficulty was the absence of the will to make it work. Good machinery for

---

[4] Hans J. Morgenthau, *Politics among Nations*, Knopf, New York, 1948, pp. 374–375.

international cooperation can be very helpful if the will to cooperate exists, and it can make common action more effective, but without that will the best organization will be useless.

Because the League failed to provide security, which is the necessary condition for nearly everything else, the excellent work of the League and its agencies in many fields failed to receive the attention it deserved. Both the International Labor Organization and the Permanent Court of International Justice were highly successful institutions, and both survived the League in fact if not in each case in name. The League demonstrated that the difficulties of creating an international secretariat can be overcome. The Secretariat apparently was an effective and loyal body of international civil servants; at least there was very little criticism of it. The mandates system may be judged moderately successful. The League was very successful in its activities in promoting human welfare, even while it was failing dismally in its security function.

When the League of Nations is adjudged a failure, these achievements must not be forgotten.

PART II
ORIGIN, STRUCTURE, AND PROCEDURE

Chapter 6

DRAFTING THE CHARTER

Though the League of Nations had failed to provide security, the idea of an international organization to prevent war and to promote peace was not abandoned. In fact, the failure to prevent World War II strengthened rather than weakened popular demand throughout the world for an effective system of collective security. Evidence soon began to appear that at long last even the people of the United States were undergoing a change of attitude. On August 14, 1941, thus several months before the United States formally entered the war, President Roosevelt and Prime Minister Churchill met at sea and drafted the Atlantic Charter,[1] a statement of war aims somewhat like the famous Fourteen Points of President Wilson in World War I. The eighth and last point of the Charter, in speaking of a "permanent system of general security" indicated that the United States, which only a few years before had enacted neutrality legislation far more rigid than that which was on the statute books in 1914, in the vain hope of keeping out of the impending war, was now prepared to enter a system of collective security. However, one can also see in this statement the doom of the League of Nations, since it contains no reference to the League.

What were the reasons for the decision to start all over again? There was first of all the important psychological reason that it would be better to found a new organization than to try to revive one to which was attached the stigma of failure. The Covenant would in any case have to be revised; it might be less difficult to draft a new document than to modify the old. President Roosevelt probably also believed that the American people would more freely and more enthusiastically join a new world organization than they would the League, about which there had centered one of the most bitter political campaigns in American history. Moreover, the experience with the League had indicated that no security organization could be effective unless all the Great Powers were members of it. But it was highly unlikely that the Soviet Union could be induced to rejoin the League, from which it had been expelled in 1939 for attacking Finland. Thus a new security organization would have to be established if for no other reason than Soviet hostility to the League.

[1] See Appendix 6.

If the Atlantic Charter was the first step in the creation of the United Nations Organization, the United Nations Declaration of January 1, 1942, was the second.[2]   In this important document, which was signed on New Year's Day by Roosevelt, Churchill, Litvinov, and Soong for their respective governments and by the representatives of twenty-two other states on the following day, the signatories pledged all their resources in the common struggle against their enemies until complete victory was won.   They subscribed to the "program of purposes and principles" embodied in the Atlantic Charter. As other states subsequently entered the war on the side of the United Nations, they too signed the Declaration.   There next followed the Moscow Declaration of October 30, 1943, signed by Molotov for the Soviet Union, Eden for Great Britain, Hull for the United States, and Foo Ping-Sheung for China.[3]   From the point of view of forming a new international organization, this document was very important, since its statements on this subject were more specific than those of the Atlantic Charter, and it also definitely committed the Soviet Union to active cooperation in establishing a security organization.   The four Great Power signatories declared that "they recognize the necessity of establishing at the earliest practical date a general international organization, based on the principle of the sovereign equality of all peace-loving states, and open to membership by all such states, large and small, for the maintenance of international peace and security."   They agreed that they would "consult with one another and as occasion required with other Members of the United Nations with a view to joint action on behalf of the community of nations" for "the purpose of maintaining international peace and security pending the re-establishment of law and order and the inauguration of a system of general security."   They also agreed to "confer and cooperate with one another and with other Members of the United Nations to bring about a practicable general agreement with respect to the regulation of armaments in the postwar period."

Shortly after the Moscow Conference, President Roosevelt, Prime Minister Churchill, and Premier Stalin met at Tehran and on December 1, 1943, issued a joint statement [4] in which they declared that the three Great Powers were determined "to work together in war and in the peace that shall follow," and that this concord would win an enduring peace.   They recognized "fully the supreme responsibility resting upon us and all the United Nations to make a peace which will command the goodwill of the overwhelming mass of the peoples of the world and banish the scourge and terror of war for many generations."   They further declared that they would seek "the cooperation and active participation of all nations, large and small, whose peoples in heart

[2] See Appendix 7.
[3] See Appendix 8.
[4] See Appendix 9.

and mind are dedicated, as are our own peoples, to the elimination of tyranny and slavery, oppression and intolerance," and that they would "welcome them, as they may choose to come, into a world family of Democratic Nations."

In these several solemn declarations all the members of the United Nations had pledged themselves to cooperate in establishing a new international organization for the maintenance of peace. The Great Powers—China, Great Britain, the Soviet Union, and the United States—had very definitely gone on record as determined to establish such an international organization. France, primarily because there was no legitimate, representative government to speak for it, was the only important country on the Allied side which was not definitely committed long before hostilities ceased. But before the conference to draft the Charter was convened, France, by becoming an adherent of the United Nations Declaration (December 26, 1944), had pledged itself in a general way to cooperate in the creation of a new security organization.

The Dumbarton Oaks Proposals

The United Nations Conference on International Organization—the official name of the remarkable gathering of representatives of many states which gave final form to the Charter—was preceded by long and careful preparation, especially on the part of the United States government. As early as 1941, there was set up in the Department of State a group of specialists for the study of postwar problems. It was at first composed of only regular members of the Department's staff, but later a number of economists, historians, geographers, political scientists, and country and regional specialists were brought in from the outside to aid in research and the formulation of policy proposals for the peace settlement.[5] Members of Congress were frequently called in for consultation. The British government had a similar group, called the Post-Hostilities Planning Committee.

A major step in the development of the United Nations Charter was the so-called Dumbarton Oaks Conversations held at Washington from August 21 to October 7, 1944. These conversations were held in two phases. In the first phase, representatives of the United States, the United Kingdom, and the Soviet Union conferred for six weeks on the main outlines of the proposed international organization; in the second the representatives of the Soviet Union dropped out and those of China entered. The Soviet Union was then not at war with Japan, and hence felt that its neutral status as far as the war in the Pacific was concerned made it improper for its representatives to sit in a conference of this kind with China which was active only in the war in the Pacific.

[5] *Postwar Foreign Policy Preparation,* U.S. Department of State Publication 3580, General Foreign Policy Series 15, 1950.

With the American tentative proposals as a base, joint proposals were drafted. These became known as the Dumbarton Oaks Proposals.[6] In the drafting of these proposals a large number of difficult questions needed to be answered. A Department of State account of the Conversations summarizes the leading questions before the group in the early stages as follows: [7]

Should economic and social as well as security matters be included within the scope of the projected organization? Should provision be made for withdrawal from membership, for suspension of the rights of a member, and for expulsion of a member? What should be the composition of the body to give military advice to the Council? By what vote should the Council reach decisions? Should members of the Council that were parties to the dispute—including parties that were major nations with permanent membership on the Council—have the right to vote or be required to abstain from voting in decisions by the Council on the dispute? The latter was fundamental to the rights and obligations of members in the organization, to the relation of large and small nations, and to the basic principles on which the organization would function. The British came with the view that the votes of any parties to a dispute should not be taken into account. The American position, presented at this stage, was that a permanent member, like a non-permanent member, should not vote in connection with a dispute to which it was a party. The Soviet representatives held the contrary view. There was, however, no question concerning the general requirement of unanimity of the permanent members in reaching decisions on nonprocedural matters of peace and security, since from the outset there was no disagreement among the three Governments on this provision.

A number of questions remained unsolved. A bomb was thrown into the Conversations when Ambassador Gromyko demanded that "the sixteen Soviet Republics" should be included among the original members of the organization. No agreement was reached on this issue, nor on that of voting in the Security Council. Nor was anything included in the Proposals on the question of colonies and of the future of the mandates system in particular. It was decided to reserve these questions for later decision.

The conversations with the Chinese representatives apparently led to no additions to or modifications of the joint proposals which had been agreed upon in the "Soviet phase." The Chinese pressed three points for adoption: [8]

1. The Charter should stipulate that, in the settlement of disputes under the United Nations, due regard should be paid to "principles of justice and international law."

2. The Assembly should promote the development and revision of the rules and principles of international law.

3. The Charter should specifically provide for the promotion of educational and other forms of cultural cooperation.

[6] Called "Dumbarton Oaks" after the name of the estate in Washington at which the meetings were held. For the text, see Appendix 10.

[7] *Postwar Foreign Policy Preparation, op. cit.,* p. 317.

[8] *Ibid.,* p. 333.

It was agreed to leave these questions open and to discuss these proposals later with the Soviet government with a view to seeking their incorporation in the charter at the coming general United Nations Conference on International Organization.

The (Dumbarton Oaks) Proposals for the Establishment of a General International Organization were published on October 9, 1944, two days after the close of the Conversations, and were sent to all the other United Nations governments for their views. In the meanwhile, the United States government was making efforts to find acceptable solutions to the more important of the unsolved questions. The Department of State worked out a formula for voting in the Security Council which was accepted by the British but rejected by the Soviet government. Agreements on the more knotty of the open questions were finally reached at a meeting of President Roosevelt, Prime Minister Churchill, and Marshal Stalin at Yalta on the Crimean Peninsula, February 4 to 11, 1945.[9]

At this conference it was decided that a United Nations conference on the proposed world organization would be convened in the United States in April, that all the United Nations and such of the Associated Nations as had declared war on the common enemy by March 1 would be invited to attend, and that the United States and British delegations to the conference would support the Soviet proposal to admit to original membership the two Soviet Socialist Republics of the Ukraine and Byelorussia. The Soviet Union now accepted the American formula for voting in the Security Council, which was that decisions on procedural matters would be made by affirmative votes of seven members but that decisions on all other matters would require the affirmative votes of seven members including the concurring votes of the permanent members, *i.e.*, the Great Powers, except that in decisions in the pacific settlement of controversies a party to a dispute should abstain from voting.

At the Dumbarton Oaks Conversations the Chinese, Soviet, and British representatives had pressed for a discussion of proposals for a trusteeship system to replace the League of Nations mandates system, but because of a lack of agreement within the government on this matter the United States representatives were not prepared to proceed with this question. This problem had not yet been wholly solved at the time of Yalta, but sufficient progress had been made to permit the United States government to join in a preliminary agreement on territorial trusteeship. This agreement covered the following points: the Great Powers would consult each other on the question before the United Nations conference; the proposed trusteeship system would apply only to three specified categories of territories; there would be no discussion of actual territories at the conference; and the question of which territories within

[9] *A Decade of American Foreign Policy, Basic Documents, 1941–1949*, Senate Document No. 123, 81st Congress, 1st Session, pp. 27–28. For the text, see Appendix 11.

the specified categories would be placed under trusteeship would be a matter for subsequent agreements.

A final step in preparation for the United Nations Conference, at least for the American states, was the discussion of the Dumbarton Oaks Proposals at the Inter-American Conference on Problems of War and Peace held at Mexico City, February 21 to March 8, 1945. This Conference adopted a resolution which endorsed the Dumbarton Oaks Proposals as a basis for establishing international organization for promoting peace and welfare among nations, but which also expressed the desire that certain points be taken into consideration at the San Francisco Conference for incorporation in the Charter. Among these points were: [10]

the aspiration of universality as an ideal toward which the Organization should tend in the future;
the desirability of amplifying and making more specific the powers of the General Assembly in order that its action, as the fully representative organ of the international community may be rendered effective . . . ;
the desirability of extending the jurisdiction and competence of the International Tribunal or International Court of Justice;
the desirability of creating an international agency specially charged with promoting intellectual and moral cooperation among nations; and
the desirability of giving an adequate representation to Latin-America on the Security Council.

These points are of special interest and significance, as they represented the views not only of Latin-American countries but also of many other small states, and forecast the position they would take in the drafting of the Charter at the San Francisco Conference.

THE SAN FRANCISCO CONFERENCE

It had been agreed at Yalta that invitations to the Conference should be issued by the government of the United States on behalf of the governments of Great Britain, the Soviet Union, and China and of the Provisional French government. The last-named, however, would serve as a sponsor only under conditions which the United States government regarded as inconsistent with the Yalta decisions; thus the invitations to the Conference were issued in the name of the other four governments.

The United Nations Conference on International Organization convened in opening session at San Francisco on April 25, 1945, with delegations from forty-six states present. In pursuance of the Yalta Agreement, Britain and the United States sponsored the admission of the Ukraine and Byelorussia, and this proposal obtained the approval of the Conference. This was made easier

[10] *Postwar Foreign Policy Preparation, op. cit.,* pp. 405–406.

by the fact that their admission was tacitly bracketed with that of Argentina. The Latin-American delegations had no enthusiasm for admitting the first two, and the Soviet Union was opposed to the admission of the last. When Denmark was liberated, it was invited to send a delegation, which it did on June 5. The Soviet delegation demanded that an invitation be sent to the Provisional Government of Poland to send delegates, but Britain and the United States were opposed to the admission of Poland until a new representative Polish government had been formed in accordance with the agreement on this subject made at Yalta. Poland was not invited to participate in the Conference, but a place was reserved for Poland's signature of the Charter, thus making it an original member of the United Nations.

At this point it may be well to draw some comparisons between the Paris Conference which drafted the Covenant of the League of Nations and the San Francisco Conference which wrote the Charter of the United Nations. The Paris Conference met at the end of a war, while the San Francisco Conference convened at the climax of a war. President Roosevelt was convinced that it would be highly desirable to draft the Charter at a time of maximum cooperation among the United Nations. It was his idea that the Charter would extend the cooperation which had been developed in the desperate war against the Axis Powers into the peace and give it a permanent basis and organization.

President Wilson had insisted upon tying the Covenant and the peace treaties together, so that the one could not easily be taken without the other. He did this chiefly to make sure of the adoption of the Covenant, but also because he felt that serious mistakes in the peace treaties might be corrected by the League of Nations. However, between the wars many attacks were made on the League on the ground that it was the bulwark of unfair treaties. Others, less severe in their criticism, argued that the League suffered from the burden of unpopular treaties. The San Francisco Conference was not a peace conference; it had only one function, namely, to draft the Charter. In contrast with his predecessor, President Roosevelt thought it wise rigidly to separate the Charter and the new organization from the peace treaties or their enforcement. Only the future can tell which was the wiser course. After all, the international climate in which the United Nations will have to operate will be largely determined by the kind of peace treaties which are concluded among the belligerents, and the United Nations cannot but be affected by them.

The fact that the Conference was held in the United States, and on the west coast in particular, is indicative of the profound changes which had taken place in world politics in the years since 1919. It is true that because of war conditions the Conference could not have been held in Europe, or even very well in England. But the shift to San Francisco is, nevertheless, symbolic. Asia had become about as important, if not wholly as important, in world politics as Europe, and North America had become the chief center of diplomatic influence.

It is customary for the foreign minister of the host government to be chosen as the presiding officer of an international conference. This is a practice so rigidly adhered to that any departure from it is regarded as a blow to the prestige of the host country. Yet the practice was departed from at San Francisco with very little feeling. Eden for Britain and Molotov for the Soviet Union asked that the chairmanship of the public meetings be rotated among the four sponsoring governments. Eden pleaded that it was essential that the Conference make clear that the four governments were acting in unity and that this unity would continue throughout the Conference, while Molotov made co-chairmanship a matter of principle—the principle of equality. The Conference accepted the proposal for the four co-chairmen for the plenary sessions. The chief of the American delegation was made the sole chairman of the Steering Committee and the Executive Committee.

The Conference brought together a large number of very able men. Most governments sent their best. Present were Molotov of the Soviet Union; Eden, Attlee, Halifax, Cranborne, Clark Kerr, and Cadogan of England; Paul-Boncour and Basdevant of France; Spaak and Rolin of Belgium; Van Kleffens and Van Mook of the Netherlands; Koo and Soong of China; King and St. Laurent of Canada; Fraser of New Zealand; Evatt of Australia; Padilla of Mexico; Belt of Cuba; Lie of Norway; Masaryk of Czechoslovakia; Pasha Badawi of Egypt; Mudaliar of India; Romulo of the Philippines; Smuts of South Africa; and Vandenberg of the United States—to name only a few of the outstanding delegates. While there were many able men among the delegations, there was no one of the stature of Wilson or Clemenceau or Lloyd George at Paris. Neither Stalin nor Churchill was there. President Roosevelt, who had planned to attend to give the opening address, had been removed by death on the eve of the Conference. The fresh memory of his great leadership had a pervasive influence on the Conference; in the debates his name was often mentioned and his ideals were frequently pleaded. There was no one present to give the Conference great moral and dynamic leadership.

Field Marshal Jan C. Smuts, who had played a leading role in drafting the Covenant at Paris twenty-five years before, graced the Conference with his presence but his influence was not great. It is difficult to understand why this extraordinary personality played so minor a role at San Francisco. He was deeply concerned, almost obsessed, with the idea of security, and his great fear was that the Conference might prove abortive. Convinced that peace could be maintained only by the concentration of great authority in the Great Powers, he did little more than support the positions of the Big Five. His age, his illness, and his active participation in three wars probably account for this attitude. So far as the text of the Charter is concerned his chief influence was on the drafting of the preamble, which bears the impress of his idealism, but much of his felicity of expression was lost through amendments and reediting.

The Conference was divided into four commissions, and the commissions were again divided into committees, as follows:

Commission I. General Provisions
    Committee 1. Preamble, Purposes, Principles
    Commitee 2. Membership, Amendment, Secretariat
Commission II. General Assembly
    Committee 1. Structure and Procedures
    Committee 2. Political and Security Functions
    Committee 3. Economic and Security Functions
    Committee 4. Trusteeship System
Commission III. Security Council
    Committee 1. Structure and Procedures
    Committee 2. Peaceful Settlement
    Committee 3. Enforcement Arrangements
    Committee 4. Regional Arrangements
Commission IV. Judicial Organization
    Committee 1. International Court of Justice
    Committee 2. Legal Problems

The commissions served little if any purpose. The real work was done in the committees, including the Coordination Committee and the Advisory Committee of Jurists. In the closing days of the Conference these two committees had the arduous task of harmonizing the work of the "technical" committees and of ironing out defects in phraseology. The plenary sessions of the Conference and also the meetings of the commissions were open to the public, but the committee meetings were not. The United States government had prepared a slate for commission and committee chairmen, which was adopted by the Conference. Since this slate was drawn up chiefly with geographic distribution and other similar factors in mind, it was only accidentally that it produced efficient presiding officers. A few of the chairmen were excellent; some were indifferent.

Language at international conferences always constitutes a problem. It was expected that English and French would be the language of the Conference, but there was pressure for the adoption of other languages as well. Soong of China suggested that, in the interest of saving time, only English be the working language of the Conference, but his proposal received little support. In the end, English and French were made the "working" languages and English, French, Spanish, Chinese, and Russian the official languages. Speeches made in either English or French were interpreted into the other language, and speeches given in any other language were reproduced in both of the first two. All documents were produced in each of the five official languages, which made for a tremendous amount of work.

CHIEF ISSUES

The Dumbarton Oaks Proposals had been drafted by representatives of the United States, Great Britain, and Russia, with China little more than a consultant. Conscious of the burden which they were carrying in the war against the Axis, and convinced that the burdens of maintaining the peace would likewise fall on them, the Great Powers had reserved for themselves a special, if not a privileged, position in the Proposals which they had drafted at Dumbarton Oaks and Yalta and which became the "working paper" of the Conference. Though France had not participated in drafting the Proposals and had refused to serve as a sponsor for the Conference, it had been given the position of a big power in the Proposals. While the Big Five in general stood firmly together against the onslaught of the small states, there was not complete unity among them. There was a marked solidarity between the United States and the United Kingdom; China walked a tightrope between the United States and the United Kingdom on the one hand and the Soviet Union on the other; while France exercised little force in any direction. France had not found itself after the national disaster and was uncertain. It was also a bit peevish, suffering from hurt pride. The Soviet Union sometimes took positions which the Anglo-American delegations found it difficult to defend, but the Big Five succeeded in keeping a very nearly solid front.

Nor were the small states altogether homogeneous. Some, like Canada, Brazil, the Netherlands, and Australia regarded themselves as "middle powers," entitled in some respects to a special position among the non-Great Powers. It was to fit their special position that the provision was written into the Charter that in electing the nonpermanent members of the Security Council "due regard" should be "specially paid, in the first instance to the contribution of Members of the United Nations to the maintenance of international peace and security and to the other purposes of the Organization." A few small states voted regularly with the Big Five, either out of conviction or because they were satellite states.

In some circles in the United States there has persisted the myth of London's controlling the votes of the Dominions in international conferences. During the 1920 presidential campaign, when the League of Nations was an issue, it was frequently charged that Britain had six votes in the Assembly while the United States, if it were to join, would have only one. This was never more than a myth, but it was one which events at the San Francisco Conference thoroughly dispelled. The Australian, New Zealand, and Canadian delegations were among the most active in the attack on the privileged position given to the Big Five in the Proposals. Indeed, Evatt of Australia, ably supported by Fraser of New Zealand, became the leader of the small states in this struggle.

The Latin-American states occupied a peculiar position in the Conference. They are so numerous that they controlled a large bloc of votes—two-fifths of the total—and when they united on a position, as they frequently did, they could exert great influence. It is one of the anomalies of an international conference that voting power has frequently so little relation to population. The Latin-American countries have a combined population only equal to that of the United States, yet because it is divided into many states, they have twenty times the voting power of their northern neighbor.

The so-called Arab states had joined in a League not long before the Conference convened. On some questions, notably trusteeship matters, they voted regularly as a bloc.

To understand what the chief issues were, it is necessary to note briefly how the principle of great-power supremacy had been built into the structure and procedure of the Organization in the Dumbarton Oaks Proposals and the voting formula agreed upon at Yalta. The Security Council would be invested with very great power; its members would have power to take decisions binding upon all members of the United Nations. The Security Council would be composed of eleven members: the Big Five as permanent members, plus six members elected by the General Assembly for a term of two years, three retiring each year. All decisions would be made by a vote of seven, but in nonprocedural matters the seven votes would have to include the concurring votes of the permanent members, except that in the pacific settlement of disputes the parties to the dispute should abstain from voting. A permanent member could veto decisions of the Security Council to resort to enforcement measures or sanctions for breach of the peace, measures for regulating armaments, and the like. Moreover, each of the five permanent members could prevent the admission of new members and the suspension or expulsion of members and could block the appointment of a Secretary-General. Moreover, each permanent member of the Security Council would have the power to veto any amendment of the Charter.

The small states sought to whittle down the special powers which were accorded the Big Five in the Dumbarton Oaks Proposals and to improve their own relative position. Specifically, they fought for an increase of the powers of the General Assembly, where they would enjoy an overwhelming majority, for an increase in the number of nonpermanent members of the Security Council, for a decrease in the power of the Security Council, for automatic or compulsory jurisdiction for the International Court of Justice, for giving the General Assembly or the International Court power to interpret the Charter, and for an easy amending process. And, above all, they wished to make more precise and to restrict the veto power of the Big Five. It was over the voting formula in the Security Council that the most intense controversy developed.

The attack on the veto took many forms, some of them ingenious. There was an attempt made to define acts of aggression in the Charter and to make the action of the Security Council automatic in such cases. If the Council were deprived of discretionary power in a number of cases, the veto would to that extent be restricted. Another line of attack was to increase the size of the vote necessary to make all decisions, and to reduce the required number of concurring votes of permanent members from five to four or three.

It became evident during the debates on the Yalta voting formula that the sponsoring powers were not themselves wholly clear as to how far the veto extended. To obtain clarification the representatives of the small states submitted a questionnaire of twenty-three points. The statement [11] of the sponsoring states in reply was not specific on every question, but it did clarify the atmosphere on one important point. The Soviet Union, which previously had insisted that the veto also apply to the consideration of disputes by the Council, now yielded on this point and joined in a statement with the other sponsoring states that the rule of unanimity did not apply to the discussion and consideration of disputes.

Many of the delegates were unhappy about the extension of the veto to amendments. They argued that they could more easily acquiesce in some of the features they had had to accept if, in due time, these could be modified by amendments. They pleaded that they could go home and ask for ratification of a Charter with many unpopular features provided it contained a fairly liberal amending procedure. Australia was especially insistent in this matter. The Great Power answer was that unless the veto did extend to amendments the predominant position which the Charter gave them would mean nothing, for it might soon be taken away from them. The Great Powers stood adamant and there was nothing for the small states to do but to accept their stand. The provision adopted is that amendments may be added to the Charter when proposed by a two-thirds vote of the members of the General Assembly and ratified by two-thirds of the members of the United Nations, including all the permanent members of the Security Council (Article 108). The only concession made to the wishes of the small states was that a general reviewing conference may be held when desired by two-thirds of the members of the General Assembly and any seven members of the Security Council. As one of its last efforts to liberalize the amending procedure, Australia successfully proposed that the question of a review conference be placed on the agenda of the General Assembly after ten years. However, any proposal for revision must obtain a two-thirds vote of the conference and the ratification of two-thirds of the members of the United Nations, including all the permanent

[11] See Appendix 12.

members of the Security Council. Thus the predominant position of the five Great Powers is secure behind this formidable barrier against amendments or revision of the Charter without their consent.

In this contest between the Great Powers and the small states, nearly all the advantages were on the side of the former, for the reason that a United Nations organization could function effectively only with all the Great Powers as members; with one or two of the Great Powers absent it would have little, if any, value. Before this inexorable fact the small states had to bow. They were able to effect many changes, most of them improvements, in the Dumbarton Oaks Proposals, but they were unable to dislodge the Great Powers from the predominant position the latter had created for themselves in that document.

Another issue which presented considerable difficulty was that of regional arrangements. The Dumbarton Oaks Proposals not only had recognized that there should be room for them within the framework of the Charter but had provided that the "Security Council should encourage settlement of local disputes through such regional arrangements or by such regional agencies." There was the feeling in several quarters that these provisions were inadequate. The Latin-American countries and the United States wished to safeguard the traditional American policy of nonintervention from the outside in the affairs of the Western Hemisphere. Some European countries wished to make sure that treaties of mutual assistance would be legal under the Charter. Others still were concerned about creating a second line of security in case the Security Council should be unable to act because of the veto.

Article 52 gives the solution to this problem. Clause 1 of the article runs as follows:

Nothing in the present Charter precludes the existence of regional arrangements or agencies for dealing with such matters relating to the maintenance of international peace and security as are appropriate for regional action, provided that such arrangements or agencies and their activities are consistent with the Purposes and Principles of the United Nations.

This clause, together with the provision in Article 53 that where the Security Council utilizes regional arrangements or agencies for enforcement action under its authority no such action shall be taken by the regional agency (with certain exceptions) without the authorization of the Security Council, was the solution agreed upon to harmonize regionalism with universalism.

There was still another problem to which an answer had to be found. The veto in a sense creates an anomaly. According to Article 1, the first purpose of the United Nations is "to maintain international peace and security, and to that end: to take effective collective measures for the prevention and removal of threats to the peace, and for the suppression of acts of aggression or other breaches of the peace," yet the veto may prevent the Security Council from functioning. What is the effect of the veto? Does the veto free members of the duty, and even deprive them of the right, of acting against an aggressor? If it did, what a strange international security organization the United Nations would be! Article 51 gives the answer: "Nothing in the present Charter shall impair the inherent right of individual or collective self-defense if an armed attack occurs against a Member of the United Nations, until the Security Council has taken the measures necessary to maintain international peace and security."

By these provisions it was thought to harmonize the veto with collective security and regionalism with universalism.

CHARTER AND COVENANT COMPARED

The Charter is a much longer document than the Covenant and is not nearly so well drafted. The Charter is composed of 111 articles; the Covenant had only 26. The Charter is involved and repetitious; the Covenant was simple and direct. The Covenant has only a short preamble, but the Charter has, in addition to a long preamble, a chapter entitled "Purposes and Principles." The Charter has a large vestibule.

The Charter reflects far greater concern for the solution of economic and social problems, and it provides for an organ—the Economic and Social Council—whose sole function is to promote international cooperation for this purpose. The Covenant provided for no such organ.

From the point of view of general structure, the League and the United Nations were rather similar. The Council was not greatly different from the Security Council in composition, nor was the Assembly basically different from the General Assembly. Provisions in the Covenant for the Secretariat were much the same as those in the Charter. The constitution of the Mandates Commission was quite different from the complicated manner in which the Trusteeship Council is set up. The International Court of Justice is more nearly an integral part of the United Nations than was the Permanent Court of International Justice, but in structure—and in jurisdiction and procedure, as well—the new court is almost identical with the old.

While there are many similarities between the two organizations, there are also many important differences. In the League, the functions of the Council and the Assembly were not clearly differentiated; in the United Nations the functions and powers of the Security Council and the General Assembly are rather sharply divided. The maintenance of international peace and security is the primary function of the Security Council, and it has power to act and to bind all the members of the United Nations, always provided there is Great Power unanimity.

Under the League, unanimity was required (with a few exceptions) for decisions in both Council and Assembly, but only unanimity of those present. In the United Nations, the Council can make decisions by a vote of seven members, but in nonprocedural, or substantive, matters these seven votes must include the concurring votes of the five Great Powers. In the General Assembly decisions on important questions require a two-thirds vote, decisions on other matters only a simple majority. The provisions on voting in the two most important organs are thus far more liberal under the Charter than under the League. Amendments to the Covenant required the ratification of all the members of the League whose representatives composed the Council and of a majority of the members of the League whose representatives composed the Assembly. Thus, not only the permanent members of the Council, but every member had the power of vetoing amendments to the Covenant. As has already been noted, only the permanent members of the Security Council have the power to veto amendments to the Charter. With respect to voting procedure, the Charter clearly represents a considerable advance over the Covenant.

The Charter contains more comprehensive provisions with respect to dependent peoples than did the Covenant. The Charter contains a Declaration Regarding Non-Self-Governing Territories which is binding on all members of the United Nations which administer such territories. Under it they recognize an obligation to promote the social, economic, and cultural welfare of the inhabitants and to prepare them for self-government as rapidly as possible. The trusteeship system of the Charter is in many respects a continuation of the mandates system of the Covenant, but with essential differences. The territories under the trusteeship system are classified quite differently from those of the mandates system, and the Trusteeship Council has far greater power than did the Mandates Commission.

The Charter gives greater recognition to regional arrangements for the maintenance of peace and security. The Covenant (Article 21) stated, "Nothing in this Covenant shall be deemed to affect the validity of international engagements, such as treaties of arbitration or regional understandings like the Monroe Doctrine, for securing the maintenance of peace." Some of the Latin-American countries asked for clarification of this ambiguous statement but never received much enlightenment. In any case, nothing was done to implement the provision.

THE UNITED NATIONS NOT STATIC

However important the Charter may be in determining the character of the Organization, especially in its early stages, it must be remembered that the United Nations is a living institution, and no living institution can be impounded within the precise terms of a text. The determination of its members to make it work, practices which are developed in meeting new situations, interpretations of the Charter, resolutions and decisions which fill in its broad provisions—all these will have a tremendous influence in determining the future development of the United Nations. Indeed, the remarkable constitutional development the United Nations has already undergone in the few years of its existence is encouraging proof of a remarkable vitality.

Chapter 7

BASIC CHARACTERISTICS OF THE UNITED NATIONS

The United Nations cannot be understood in its proper perspective unless its basic characteristics as an international organization are kept clearly in mind. It cannot be classified in any ready-made category, because it is not one of a large number of similar institutions or agencies. In some ways, it is unique, and therefore the possibilities of significant comparison and contrast are quite limited. In other ways, it reveals a fundamental similarity to many devices and institutions which have existed in the history of the world. We cannot assign to it a technical label, compounded from the Greek and Latin, and feel that we have it adequately placed in the labyrinth of descriptive classification. We can, however, maintain perspective and order in our study by determining the principal characteristics of the United Nations as a device of political organization.

An analysis from this point of view discloses six characteristics which can be identified as significant and basic: The United Nations is a system of international organization. Its chief purpose and function lie in the field of collective security. It developed as an extension of a wartime alliance. It gives special recognition to the principle of joint action by the Great Powers. It is primarily an association of member states. The United Nations has a legal status and international personality of its own.

A System of International Organization

Modern international organization began as a piecemeal and unsystematic affair.[1] During the nineteenth century, for example, national states were not subject to any external or superior legal control or regulation. Yet they were in contact with each other, and there were many activities which transcended national boundaries. The answer to this situation was a limited amount of voluntary cooperation. Special measures were used to meet immediate pressing needs. There were diplomats, treaties, conferences, *ad hoc* agencies, and other devices, but the agencies and methods of international

[1] See Chap. 3.

cooperation remained sporadic, mostly bilateral in form and scope, and restricted to specific needs and areas. There was no over-all system, such as now exists in connection with the United Nations.

What are the criteria by which a general system of international organization may be identified? A minimum of four tests must be applied. A system, in contrast to an unrelated and piecemeal set of devices, exists when there is a definitely constituted agency, an established continuity, generality of membership, and a broad scope of functions.

The Charter of the United Nations is a constitution for international organization. It establishes an agency with specified powers to carry out certain designated functions. This is in contrast to such methods as voluntary cooperation through bilateral diplomatic arrangements, or the convening of international conferences from time to time. A system of political organization exists when there is an interrelated pattern for the distribution of governmental functions and powers. Even when the powers delegated to a more inclusive organization are very slight, a pattern of distribution still exists. The United Nations is entrusted with certain functions, and by the Charter it is endowed with the corresponding degree of authority. This fact should not be confused with the question of the extent to which it has been able to perform its functions and to use its authority. Sometimes, for one reason or another, an organization cannot in fact use powers which have previously been granted to it. That is a matter of how it works in practice, and it will be appropriate to consider this problem later.[2] The point here is that an agency of international cooperation has been established by constitutional provision.

The matter of continuity is also important. Transitory activities and methods which come and go with great frequency do not provide the basis of stability required for a genuine system of international organization. The element of long-term duration is necessary. For example, one of the great disadvantages of the international conferences during the nineteenth century was that they adjourned *sine die* when their immediate job was done. A new conference could be convened only with great difficulty. The devices of international cooperation were temporary and discontinuous. There was usually no staff work between conferences, and there was very little carry over or accumulation of effort. The provision that meetings shall regularly take place at frequent intervals has removed great obstacles from the common discussion of matters of international concern. The United Nations includes an institutionalized system of regularly recurring conferences.

Geographic inclusiveness is a third test of a system of international organization. Universality of membership, although desirable, is not essential, provided the support and participation are sufficiently widespread to enable the agency to function on a global basis. From this point of view, the United Nations is in a stronger position than was the League of Nations. Although a number of countries have not yet become members for one reason or an-

[2] See Chaps. 14–19.

other, it does include all the Great Powers and a very large percentage of all the other countries of the world. As is well known, the United States was never a member of the League, nor did the Soviet Union join until 1934. It was anticipated, of course, that the United Nations would become a world organization in the complete sense. Therefore the Charter provided for the later admission of "peace-loving states" not numbered among the original signatories. Nine countries have been admitted under this procedure, but quite a few others remain outside. In terms of the purposes and objectives of the United Nations, this situation may be viewed as a temporary one. If the Organization is successful and if the tensions of the "cold war" are resolved, substantial universality of membership should follow as a matter of course.

The fourth criterion for a general system of international organization is that of a relatively broad scope of functions. An agency to handle one service (such as postal communications) or one technical problem (such as standard measurements) would hardly come within this definition. The scope of the United Nations, however, is as broad as the activities and possibilities of international political, economic, and social cooperation. Its purposes are to maintain international peace and security; to develop friendly relations among nations and to take appropriate measures to strengthen universal peace; and to achieve international cooperation in the social, economic, and related fields and in encouraging respect for human rights and fundamental freedoms. The only restriction on the scope of the United Nations is the provision that it shall not intervene in matters which are "essentially within the domestic jurisdiction of any state." Thus, it is potentially able to function across the whole field of modern international relations.

The United Nations, then, may be characterized as a general system of international organization because it is a definitely constituted agency, with an established continuity, generality of membership, and broad functional scope. Its six principal organs, with the subsidiary organs and affiliated specialized agencies, cover a very large proportion of contemporary international organization. The major exceptions, so far as governmental organizations are concerned, are certain regional agencies like the Pan American Union. These, however, are recognized by the Charter as being compatible with the United Nations, and in the broad sense, there is very little distinction to be made at the present time between the United Nations systems and public international organization as a whole.[8]

ORGANIZATION FOR COLLECTIVE SECURITY

"Collective security" characterizes the United Nations in terms of its chief purpose. Certainly the peoples of the world will judge it on the basis of its contribution to the prevention of war. This is consistent with the

[8] For a definition of "private international organization," see p. 31.

background of the Organization and the provisions of the Charter. The key idea in establishing the United Nations was that victory in World War II must be followed by "winning the peace." The first clause in the Preamble to the Charter speaks of the determination "to save succeeding generations from the scourge of war." The first purpose stated in Article 1 is "to maintain international peace and security." Admission to membership is open only to "peace-loving states." The General Assembly is to consider and make recommendations for the settlement of international disputes and on "the general principles of cooperation in the maintenance of international peace and security." The Security Council has the "primary responsibility for the maintenance of international peace and security." The provisions of the Charter on international economic and social cooperation are introduced with the stated purpose of creating "conditions of stability and well-being which are necessary for peaceful and friendly relations among nations."

Even a cursory reading of the Charter is sufficient to indicate that considerations of international peace and security are paramount. Disputes and situations which threaten the peace are to be handled by the General Assembly and the Security Council.[4] It is not enough, however, to deal with disputes as they arise. The conditions of lasting peace must be established in the world, if the United Nations is to succeed. In the long run, prevention is much more important than cure. For this reason, emphasis is placed upon international economic and social cooperation, upon human rights and fundamental freedoms, and upon the welfare of non-self-governing peoples. Thus, international peace and security are to be maintained by both direct and indirect methods—the former to handle emergencies and the latter to establish the basis of a lasting peace.

The United Nations represents an attempt to maintain peace through the principle of collective security. During the nineteenth century, international law and organization incorporated the principle of self-help. War was a fact outside the realm of law. When war occurred between two countries, others had a choice of joining in as belligerents or of remaining outside the conflict as impartial "neutrals." This conception of the legal status of war was abandoned by the Covenant of the League of Nations. The idea was that any nation which started a war would be opposed by the rest of the world. All third parties would come to the assistance of a victim of aggression. A potential aggressor, knowing this, would never dare launch an attack. Thus, wars would be prevented and the peace made secure. Although the League was unable to prevent World War II, the principle of concern (that an attack against one nation is an attack against all) remains valid.[5]

---

[4] See Chaps. 8 and 9.

[5] Article 11 of the Covenant provided that "any war or threat of war, whether immediately affecting any of the Members of the League or not, is hereby declared a matter of concern to the whole League, and the League shall take any action that may be deemed wise and effectual to safeguard the peace of nations."

Every organized community and every political society is based upon the principle of collective security. An attack upon one member cannot remain a matter of indifference to the entire group. If the rights of one are violated, an offense against the community has taken place and the agencies of the group take the appropriate action. A murder, a burglary, an assault are not considered as affairs merely for the victim or for his family and friends. They violate the public peace, and the entire group is affected. This concept, as applied through the United Nations, means that joint action is to be taken by the members against any nation which commits a breach of the peace. This, if it is carried out in practice, means defeat to an aggressor and protection for the victim. Under the United Nations system, international peace is to be maintained by a system of collective security.

EXTENSION OF A WARTIME ALLIANCE

Historically speaking, the United Nations developed from the great alliance against the Axis Powers during World War II. The nations which united to destroy the aggressors were to cooperate in maintaining the peace after the military victory was won. Evolution from the stage of idea and aspiration to that of institutional embodiment may be traced through a series of declarations and conferences, beginning with the Atlantic Charter and proceeding to the United Nations Declaration, the Moscow Conference, the Dumbarton Oaks Conference, the Yalta Conference, and the San Francisco Conference.[6] Original membership was open only to states which participated in the San Francisco Conference or had previously signed the United Nations Declaration. Enemy states and wartime neutrals were excluded from this group, and may become members only by being voted in through the usual admissions procedure.

The characteristic of the United Nations as the extension of a wartime alliance is of more than merely historical interest. It continues to have significance in some of the situations and problems with which the United Nations must deal. For example, the Franco government in Spain is the only remaining survivor among the collaborators with Nazi Germany and Fascist Italy. The policy to be adopted toward Spain on this account has been the subject of one of the disagreements among members of the United Nations. The Soviet Union has contended that the mere existence of the Franco regime is a "threat to the peace" and that therefore the Security Council should undertake to bring about its removal from power. On the other hand, the internal governmental administration of a state is usually considered an "essentially domestic question." The United States government took the position, in 1946, that the Franco regime was a "potential menace" to the peace but not an immediate "threat" within the meaning of the Charter. The

[6] See Chap. 6.

majority on the Security Council were willing to go only as far as keeping Spain from membership in the United Nations and its affiliated agencies, and in recommending the withdrawal of ambassadors from Madrid. This was not sufficient to remove Franco as head of the Spanish government, and it is questionable whether the policy of suspending full diplomatic relations can be logically maintained when the policy toward other countries is on the basis that recognition does not imply approval of a government. In 1950, the General Assembly modified its position on this question.[7]

Neither Italy nor the former Axis satellites have been admitted to membership because of a difference of opinion between the Soviet Union and other members of the Security Council.[8] The Soviet Union has vetoed the applications of Ireland and Portugal on the basis of their alleged close relations and sympathies with the Axis. It has not been willing to accept Austria as a member, despite the understanding that Austria should be treated as a liberated country rather than an ex-enemy state.

The position of Switzerland is of some interest. That small European neutral has had a special relation to the development of modern international organization, and Geneva was the seat of the League of Nations. Yet Switzerland was not eligible for original membership under the policy adopted and has not applied for admission, although it has adhered to the Statute of the International Court of Justice under a special arrangement.[9]

Although the United Nations originated as the extension of a wartime alliance, it was not tied to or given responsibility for the peace treaties after World War II. The idea was that the new organization should not be shouldered with this difficult task, but should be responsible only for maintaining the peace after its basis was established. At the time the Charter was drafted, it was expected that the peace treaties would be concluded fairly soon after the end of hostilities. This has not proved to be the case. Therefore the United Nations has operated thus far in a different type of situation from the one for which it was designed. As time passes, it becomes difficult and then impossible to keep the issues of the peace settlement separate from the disputes which now threaten and disrupt international peace. Obviously, for example, the United Nations cannot ignore, or function independently of, conflicting policies in the occupation and rehabilitation of Germany.

At the present time, the efforts of the United Nations are hampered and its activities impeded by the disintegration of the partnership of nations by which it was established. Cooperation in defeating the Axis has been replaced by the "cold war," and in this fact lies the crucial problem for the eventual success or failure of the United Nations.

[7] See pp. 209–210.

[8] See pp. 141–143.

[9] For a typical Swiss view of this situation, see William E. Rappard, "The United Nations as Viewed from Geneva," *American Political Science Review*, June, 1946, pp. 545–551.

JOINT ACTION BY THE GREAT POWERS

"It was taken as axiomatic . . . that the cornerstone of world security is the unity of those nations which formed the core of the grand alliance against the Axis." [10] This axiom is reflected in the so-called principle of unanimity of the Great Powers. It is obvious that international peace and security in the modern world largely depend upon the capacity of the major powers to cooperate. Global warfare can be waged only by the leading industrial nations. Factories have become the arsenals not only of democracies, but of all fighting nations. Large-scale warfare is impossible without a huge industrial system requiring advanced scientific technology and tremendous resources of manpower and raw materials.

With the defeat of the Axis, the Great Powers among the victors had in fact almost a monopoly of the means for waging a modern global war. To reduce it to the simplest terms, as of 1945: If the United States, Great Britain, the Soviet Union, France, and China remained united and in basic agreement, how could a third world war occur? If, on the other hand, they disagreed to the point of fighting among themselves, what could the result be except a third world war? Upon this line of reasoning, the conclusion was reached that the prerequisite of a successful United Nations was unity among these five Great Powers. The Charter was drafted and the plans made in accordance with this basic assumption.

A special position was recognized for those nations which had the power to wage a modern war and which would have to accept predominant responsibility for maintaining peace. This principle was implemented by the status and functions assigned to the Security Council, which is the "enforcement arm" of the United Nations and the only constituent organ given the authority to arrive at decisions binding upon the member states.[11] It is made an agent of the entire Organization with the "primary responsibility for the maintenance of international peace and security." In the Security Council, the Great Powers are in a special category as to both membership and decision making. China, France, the Soviet Union, Great Britain, and the United States are named in the Charter as permanent members, while the other members are elected by the General Assembly for terms of two years. Decisions of the Security Council, except on matters of procedure, can be made only with the concurrence of the permanent members. In other words, the Security Council is set up in such a way that it can enforce international peace and security only to the extent that unity and agreement exist among the Great Powers. It should be noted that the permanent members cannot

[10] *Report to the President on the Results of the San Francisco Conference*, U.S. Department of State Publication No. 2349, Conference Series 71, June 26, 1945, p. 68.
[11] See Chap. 9.

be deprived of their special position without their own consent, since the concurrence of each is required for any amendment to the Charter.[12]

Unity of the Great Powers is necessary if the United Nations is to function successfully, but it is not sufficient to guarantee this objective. The permanent members of the Security Council cannot by themselves make affirmative decisions under the Charter. Seven votes are required, and they have only five. At least two of the nonpermanent members must agree with them if action is to be taken. Stated another way, any five of the six nonpermanent members acting as a bloc could exercise a collective veto. Actual issues, however, usually do not find states in opposition to each other on the basis of size. The basic division, thus far, has been the split within the ranks of the Great Powers, with each side attracting followers among the smaller countries.

Prior to 1945 the principle of unanimity in arriving at decisions was a basic postulate of international organization. With limited exceptions, a unanimous vote of all members was required. Even under the League of Nations, unanimity was the rule except for a few matters specifically stated in the Covenant.[13] The reason, of course, was an argument from the concept of sovereignty. If a state could be bound without its own consent, it was not considered sovereign. If it were obligated to accept the results of a majority vote contrary to its own wishes, it would be bound without its own consent. In the United Nations, all the members except the Great Powers gave up this privilege. The latter did not receive a new prerogative. They merely retained one which was normally vested in all members of previous international organizations. Relative to the others, they have a special position; but it should be recognized that decisions can be made in all organs of the United Nations by a less-than-unanimous vote. A simple or a two-thirds majority is sufficient, with the sole exception of substantive decisions of the Security Council. Here unanimity is required, not of all members as was the case for the Council of the League of Nations, but only of the permanent members. Thus, in terms of the development of modern international organization, the United Nations represents a rather sharp, but incomplete, departure from the previous rule of unanimity.

AN ASSOCIATION OF MEMBER STATES

The United Nations is primarily an association of its member states. It is a device or instrument of cooperation for the achievement of certain common ends by joint international action. It is not a superstate or a world

---

[12] Also, the permanent members of the Security Council are automatically entitled to representation on the Trusteeship Council.

[13] For example, in 1923, an important resolution concerning an amendment to Article 10 of the Covenant was defeated in the Assembly of the League by the sole adverse vote of Persia.

government.   As a "fourth level of government" (in addition to local, state, and national) it remains in a rudimentary stage.   A clear understanding of this point will enable the student to deal more constructively with the frequent questions born of frustration and impatience: Why doesn't the United Nations do thus and so?   Why does it permit a few to block the majority will with impunity?   The answer is, of course, that the United Nations operates by joint action based upon agreement, not by force imposed from above.   Where the necessary agreement does not exist, the means for making and implementing decisions are not available.

A fundamental consideration in any system of political organization is that of the distribution of power.   There are three, and only three, basic patterns, although many modifications and variations are possible.   A *unitary* system places the power in a central government.   Subdivisions exist, but they operate under supervision and legal control, and on the basis of authority delegated to them.   A *conjederation* places the power in the constituent units.   Any central agencies which are established for convenience in operation obtain their authority from and remain legally subject to the component members of the confederation.   Legal authority and governmental powers are decentralized, whereas under the unitary form they are centralized.   The third type is the *federal* system under which power is divided by constitutional arrangement between the central government and the constituent members of the federation.

The United States is a leading example of the federal principle.   The Articles of Confederation left the real powers of government with the individual states.   The Constitution adopted at Philadelphia in 1787 divided these powers between the national government and the states.   On the basis of the constitutional theory held in the South before the Civil War, and not entirely forgotten today, the seceding states in 1861 organized the Confederacy.   Their argument was that the central government was no more than a creature of the states acting jointly, and that the attempt to make it more would enable the North unjustly to control the Union at the expense of the South.

France and Great Britain have unitary forms of government.   Subdivisions exist for historic reasons and for administrative convenience, and there are issues based on localism and sectionalism, but those countries could not have a "states' rights" question in the American sense.   The Soviet Union is a federation in constitutional form, but operates as a unitary system under the practice of a one-party dictatorship.   Germany ran the gamut, in less than one hundred fifty years, from confederation to federal state and then to a unitary system.   One of the main issues now is how much power shall be given to a central government and how much to the component states.

The United Nations would be classified as a confederation, since most of the powers of government are retained by the member states.   This is obvious from the slightest knowledge of the United Nations.   However, three other tests for identifying the confederal form may be mentioned.   They are legislation, taxation, and enforcement directly upon individual citizens.   In either a federal or a unitary system, the central government has substantial powers of legislation and taxation, and deals with individual citizens on its own account without having another level of government as a necessary intermediary.   The United Nations does not have legislative authority.   It does not have the power of taxation, although the members could not refuse to pay the assessments voted by the General Assembly without violating their obligations under the Charter.   The United Nations does not have the authority to enforce its decisions directly upon individuals.[14]   That must be done by the governments of the member states.

In addition to these general considerations, there are two principles stated in Article 2 of the Charter which are important in connection with the question of distribution of power.   The "sovereign equality" of all the members is asserted, and the United Nations is prohibited from intervening in matters "which are essentially within the jurisdiction of any state."   The powers of government and the status of independence from external legal control have been expressly retained by the member states.   By adopting the Charter they have delegated power and accepted obligations by their explicit voluntary consent, and only to a limited degree for a specified purpose.

The term "equality" should be understood in the juridical or legal sense. No one intended to assert an obvious absurdity by any claims of equality in size, population, power, or any other material sense, just as the authors of the Declaration of Independence were aware of human differences when they wrote that "all men are created equal."   Under the Charter of the United Nations, "sovereign equality" means equal legal status, equal representation, and equal voting power.   Each member has one vote regardless of its size, population, wealth, influence, or any other factor.   This is one of the important characteristics of a confederation or association, as contrasted with the federal type of organization.   It is customary for the members of a federation to be equal in some respects.   For example, in the American system of government all the states have exactly the same constitutional and legal status, and they have a guarantee of equal representation in the Senate.   There is no theoretical reason that a federation could not be established with complete equality of all its members.   This does not happen in practice, however, because the larger members will not agree to enter a federation on terms of complete equality of votes and influence.   Thus, in the United States, the more populous states have greater representation in one House of Congress and in the electoral votes for the Presidency.   It is safe to assume, therefore, that the amount of power transferred to an international organization will be comparatively slight until the principle of unequal representation is introduced in some way.

One question of interpretation of the Charter is the relation of the principle

---

[14] The United Nations does, of course, exercise direct supervision over its own staff.

of sovereign equality to the special position of the Great Powers. Is the latter an exception to the former? Is there an inconsistency in the Charter? It seems difficult to reconcile the concepts of "sovereign equality" and of "predominant responsibility." One should be careful not to exaggerate the discrepancy, however. All the members of the United Nations are juridical equals. They are equal in representation and voting, except that in the Security Council one permanent member can prevent the reaching of an affirmative decision but no one nonpermanent member has this power. The best interpretation seems to be that the special position of the Great Powers is an exception to the general rule of sovereign equality. Potentially, this is very important. Since the Security Council is the agent of all the members, and can make decisions binding upon them in the enforcement of international peace and security, a full utilization of all the powers granted by the Charter might destroy some of the attributes of sovereignty for all except the permanent members. For example, if a state can be obligated to use its armed forces, possibly against its own wishes, in order to help enforce a Security Council decision, what has happened to the traditional conception of sovereignty?

The reservation of "domestic jurisdiction" applies to all the organs and activities of the United Nations, with the sole exception that it cannot be used to prevent action of the Security Council in carrying out its responsibility of maintaining international peace and security. This principle of the Charter confines the scope of the United Nations to the area of the relations among the nation-states of the world. Its field is *international* cooperation. At the San Francisco Conference, the adoption of this principle in its present form was severely criticized on the ground that it would tend to weaken the new Organization unduly. However, the Great Powers insisted on it since otherwise the broad scope of the Charter might enable unwelcome interference in the domestic society and economy of the member states. Some of the smaller countries also supported the same principle because of the fear that the Security Council in the exercise of its functions might make recommendations involving essentially domestic measures and then use pressure to secure their acceptance.

In actual practice, several important problems of interpretation have arisen. In the Spanish and Czechoslovak cases, questions were raised as to whether the internal regime of a state or a change in government is essentially a matter of domestic jurisdiction. In the former case the Security Council, although it did not adopt a resolution, proceeded on the assumption that it did have the right to take action, and the General Assembly adopted a resolution containing specific recommendations. During discussion of the Czechoslovak case, the United States took the position that the matter was one of domestic jurisdiction only if there had been no interference, direct or indirect, from a foreign power. The Soviet Union, which had urged stronger action against

Franco, insisted that a change in government is exclusively within the domestic jurisdiction of a state.

The relation of governmental systems to international peace was considered in the Greek question. Also, attention has been given to this factor in voting on application for admission to the United Nations. The domestic-jurisdiction principle has been invoked in questions involving non-self-governing territories. During the Indonesian dispute, the Netherlands government claimed initially that, under international law, colonial administration is a matter of domestic concern. The Security Council did not accept this protest. The same type of problem arises under Article 73(e) of the Charter, which provides for the submission of information concerning dependent territories. The extent to which specific information can be required and reviewed has been a heated point of discussion in the General Assembly.

The application of the domestic-jurisdiction principle to questions of human rights was debated when the government of India complained to the General Assembly about the treatment of the Indian minority in the Union of South Africa. India contended that discriminatory treatment violated bilateral agreements and the United Nations Charter and that it threatened peaceful relations among nations. The Union of South Africa claimed that no international agreements were applicable and that the treatment of nationals within a country is a matter of domestic jurisdiction. This question was not explicitly decided, but the General Assembly proceeded with discussion and the adoption of a resolution which implied its authority to act. The Soviet Union has consistently held the position that any attempt to protect individual human rights by international action constitutes interference in domestic questions. That government has used its interpretation of the same principle against the proposal to establish a system of inspection in connection with the international control of atomic energy.[15]

The reservation of domestic jurisdiction is a crucial question for the future of the United Nations. Important problems and issues are no longer sharply divisible into domestic and international categories, if indeed they ever were. The great questions of our day have both aspects. Foreign and national problems are inextricably interwoven. One needs only to think of the relations between foreign aid and taxation, the "cold war" and civil liberties, export markets and full employment, and many others, to see this point. Whether the United Nations achieves a broad or a narrow scope depends largely upon the interpretation given to the domestic-jurisdiction principle, just as the scope of Federal activity in the United States depends to an important degree upon an interpretation of the balance between the implied powers delegated to the national government and the reserved powers of the states. The principle is stated in general terms, and the situation to which it applies is complex. Decisions often will depend upon viewpoints

[15] See Chap. 15.

of the Charter, so that "its interpretation will become a decisive factor in determining whether the United Nations will be an organization of large and expanding responsibilities or be kept within relatively narrow limits dictated by a strict interpretation of the provisions of the Charter." [16]

An International Personality

We have seen that the United Nations follows the confederal form of political organization and that it is *primarily* an association of member states. It must be emphasized at once, however, that the United Nations is not a *mere* association of members. In many ways it is definitely more than that. It is a distinct entity on its own account. It may well be described as an international legal personality. It has the power to enter into treaties, and it has a headquarters, a legal status, a staff, and even a flag of its own.

An instance of the treaty-making capacity [17] is found in Article 43 of the Charter, which provides that agreements for the provision of armed forces shall be concluded between the Security Council and members of the United Nations. The capacity of an international organization to enter into commitments apart from its members is a new practice which has interesting possibilities for future development. It establishes a precedent which might be used to enlarge the scope of international action. Another type of agreement which the United Nations can make has reference to the international trusteeship system. The Charter, in this case, specifies that the terms of trusteeship arrangements must be approved by the General Assembly or the Security Council. The result is clearly to establish a relation of agreement as to the trusteeship territory between the administering authority and an organ of the United Nations. It is interesting to note also that the Charter makes it possible for international organizations to make agreements with each other. For example, under Article 63 the Economic and Social Council may enter into agreements with the specialized agencies defining the terms on which they shall be brought into relationship with the United Nations. These agreements are subject to the approval of the General Assembly.

One of the first questions in establishing the United Nations was the location of its headquarters. First it met in London, next at Hunter College in the Bronx and at other places in New York City, and then on Long Island in a reconverted gyroscope factory at Lake Success and a building at Flushing Meadows left over from the 1939 World's Fair. All these locations were temporary or interim headquarters. The selection of a permanent seat of the Organization was given careful consideration from the beginning. President

---

[16] Leland M. Goodrich and Edvard Hambro, *Charter of the United Nations: Commentary and Documents,* World Peace Foundation, Boston, 1949, 2d ed., p. 113.

[17] The use of the term "agreement" instead of "treaty" in the Charter has no special significance.

Roosevelt had once favored the Azores for the meeting place of the General Assembly.[18]   Here the delegates would be free from undue pressure, yet air transportation would make the location easily accessible to the delegates.   Another suggestion was the Black Hills of South Dakota, so that the delegates could gaze upon the dinosaurs and realize that their own job was to prevent the extinction of man.   Geneva, which had been the seat of the League of Nations, did not seem a wise choice for several reasons: Switzerland was not eligible for original membership in the United Nations, public opinion might identify the new organization too closely with the League failure, and the Soviet Union was opposed to the selection of Geneva.

It was finally decided that the permanent headquarters would be established in the United States.   Three different groups representing the United Nations traveled thousands of miles at an expense of over $300,000 to investigate personally a number of sites.   The choice had narrowed down to Philadelphia or San Francisco, neither considered entirely satisfactory, when John D. Rockefeller, Jr., offered the United Nations a gift of a 17-acre plot of land, worth $8,500,000, along the East River in New York City.   This offer was quickly accepted, and the permanent headquarters of the United Nations became a metropolitan skyscraper development.   The Secretariat building, which was the first unit to be constructed, was ready for occupancy by the latter part of 1950.   The specialized agencies chose to establish headquarters of their own, instead of becoming a part of United Nations headquarters.[19]   The seat of the International Court of Justice is at The Hague.

Location of the headquarters of an international organization within the territory of one of its members raises some difficult problems of relationships and jurisdiction.   From the international viewpoint, all the members are equally interested and have equal rights and authority.   Subjection to the legal control of one national government would be unacceptable to the other members and completely inconsistent with the very idea of international organization.   On the other hand, the host government has rights and duties arising from territorial jurisdiction, and it is concerned with protecting its national interests from possible harmful influences within the country but immune from legal control.   Even if the status of the headquarters site itself is satisfactorily adjusted, there remain many problems of access and transit across national territory, especially as concerns the staff of the organization, fire protection, postal and other communications, taxation, administration of customs, policing of adjacent areas, and so forth.

A mutually acceptable arrangement was worked out in the form of an Agreement between the United Nations and the United States of America

[18] Sumner Welles, *Where Are We Heading?* Harper, New York, 1946, pp. 31–32. See also pp. 48–50 for Welles's opinion that the selection of New York City was a serious mistake.

[19] See Appendix 15.

regarding the Headquarters of the United Nations. The basis for this agreement was substantially the application to this special case of the principles applying to the status of foreign embassies. The headquarters district is under the control and authority of the United Nations, and it has power to make regulations operative there for the full execution of its functions. The Federal, state, and local laws of the United States apply except to the extent to which they are inconsistent with regulations made by the United Nations pursuant to its authority. The United States is not to impose any impediment to the transit to or from the headquarters district of persons attached to or doing business with the United Nations, permanent representatives are to have the same privileges and immunities as diplomatic envoys, and facilitative arrangements are agreed on for public services and protection. Any dispute between the United Nations and the United States concerning an interpretation or application of the agreement is to be settled by arbitration.

Arrangements for the interim headquarters at Lake Success and the General Assembly sessions at Flushing Meadows follow in principle the concepts of the agreement for the permanent headquarters. On November 8, 1949, an interesting incident occurred when the bar in the delegates' lounge at Lake Success was closed under a New York State law providing that alcoholic beverages shall not be sold on Election Day while the polls are open. The question was raised as to why an international organization should be subject to legislation of this character. The answer obviously is that the state law could have been made inapplicable in this case if the General Assembly had wished to pass a resolution on the grounds of necessity for the "full execution of its functions." This was not done, but a representative of the United Nations conferred with the State Liquor Authority and the exempt status of the international bar was recognized.

The United Nations has a legal status. Article 104 of the Charter provides that "the Organization shall enjoy in the territory of each of its Members such legal capacity as may be necessary for the exercise of its functions and the fulfillment of its purposes." This means that the United Nations is a juridical personality with capacity to contract, to acquire and dispose of property, and to institute legal proceedings—all in its own name. Under American law, the United Nations has in some respects the status of a corporation. It holds title to real estate in this country, where property law is a state rather than a national affair. In the acquisition of the headquarters site, special precautions were taken to be sure that there would be no cloud on the title or adverse claims against United Nations ownership. The history of various parcels of land composing the site was such that this was a very complicated task indeed. The headquarters agreement provides, in effect, that the United States has a first option in case the United Nations ever disposes of the site or any part of it.

The United Nations has a staff of its own, composed of officials and employees. This is another indication of a distinctive organizational entity. It

involves three major questions: (1) an international civil service; (2) privileges and immunities of the staff; and (3) claims by the United Nations arising from injuries to its agents.   The status and problems of an international
civil service are discussed below.[20]

The question of privileges and immunities of personnel associated with the
United Nations is analogous to the headquarters problem, in the sense that
the status of an international organization within the territorial jurisdiction
of one nation is involved.   The United States does not admit that officials and
employees of international organizations are entitled to diplomatic privileges
and immunities under customary international law.   So far as this country
is concerned, such privileges and immunities must arise from treaties or from
municipal legislation.   In 1945, Congress passed the International Organizations Immunities Act which gives to public international organizations, recognized as such by the Secretary of State, about the same privileges and immunities as those accorded to foreign embassies and diplomatic officers.   This
measure is applicable to United Nations representatives and officials, but from
the international viewpoint it has certain drawbacks.   It is based on national
comity, and not on a right under international law.   The status of international organizations is compromised by certain of its provisions.   For example,
the Secretary of State is authorized to withhold the privileges and immunities
concerned if an officer of an international organization is found unacceptable
for entry into the United States.

The General Assembly approved, in February, 1946, a Convention on the
Privileges and Immunities of the United Nations.[21]   This Convention definitely recognizes the international status of persons associated with the United
Nations in any important capacity.   By the end of 1949, a total of thirty-six
countries had accepted its provisions.   However, the United States government has not done so.   One of the stumbling blocks has been the question of
United States citizens employed by the United Nations.   Would not the
granting of privileges and immunities to this group, including exemption
from taxation [22] on their salaries, create a special class and be contrary to
the idea of equal treatment of all citizens?   Another problem is the interest
of the United States in the activities of resident aliens within the country.
From time to time, the fear is expressed in newspaper editorials and on
the floor of Congress that an unsupervised entry of aliens makes an international organization an opportunity for spies.[23]   Can the host government
assure that its hospitality will not be abused without infringing on inter-

---

[20] See Chap. 12.

[21] For the text, see Appendix 13.

[22] See p. 189.

[23] On the other hand, in the Gubitchev case the Soviet Union accused the FBI of having
access to inside information from the Secretariat.

national prerogatives, or claiming a supervisory position in relation to an organization including other national states?

No satisfactory answer to such dilemmas has been found, but the problem is an acute one. The headquarters agreement assumes the acceptance by the United States of the Convention on Privileges and Immunities. The status of the United Nations within the United States will not be definitely established until a mutually satisfactory arrangement on privileges and immunities is reached.

The assassination of Count Bernadotte in September, 1948, while he was acting as United Nations Mediator in Palestine, brought to sharp focus the question of whether the United Nations is competent to bring a claim against the responsible government for injury done to one of its agents. This question was referred to the International Court of Justice for an advisory opinion, and the Court unanimously gave an affirmative answer, saying that: [24]

In the opinion of the Court, the Organization was intended to exercise and enjoy, and is in fact exercising and enjoying, functions and rights which can only be explained on the basis of the possession of a large measure of international personality and the capacity to operate upon an international plane. It is at present the supreme type of international organization, and it could not carry out the intentions of its founders if it was devoid of international personality. It must be acknowledged that its Members, by entrusting certain functions to it, with the attendant duties and responsibilities, have clothed it with the competence required to enable those functions to be effectively discharged.

An injury to an agent is an injury to the principal. The United Nations has the competence to claim reparation, on its own account, for such an injury. In this respect it constitutes an international personality distinct from the member states which compose it.

We have seen that the United Nations has treaty-making capacity, headquarters, legal status, and a staff. It also has an official flag, a seal, and an emblem. The official emblem was designed as a circular map of the world between two olive branches. The flag consists of the emblem centered on a field of light blue. There is a flag code, stating its dimensions and proportions, and restricting its sale and use to purposes closely connected with the aims and ideals of the United Nations. It must always be treated with respect and must never be subordinated to any other flag in either size or position. Thus the symbolism of a distinctive organizational entity has begun to develop. When commercial advertising has exploited the name "United Nations," the emblem, and the flag, the Secretary-General has protested and has sought

[24] *I.C.J. Reports of Judgments, Advisory Opinions and Orders,* 1949, p. 179. See also Quincy Wright, "The Jural Personality of the United Nations," *American Journal of International Law,* July, 1949, pp. 509–516. Israel paid an indemnity of $54,628 to the United Nations in the Bernadotte case.

Federal and state legislation (unsuccessfully thus far) against such practices.

The principal organs and the specialized agencies of the United Nations have definite and important functions delegated to them. The Organization as a whole has the attributes of an international personality, as we have seen. There is also the fact that units of social organization tend to develop a life of their own. The very existence of the United Nations introduces a new factor and a new dimension into the formulation and execution of national policies. There is a strong segment of public opinion in the United States, for example, which will be critical of any policy which appears to ignore or by-pass the United Nations. The President and the State Department are under the necessity of recognizing this fact in advocating measures of foreign policy which will be supported by the American people. Although the United Nations is primarily an association of member states, it is definitely more than that. It is an international personality with real influence and as such must be taken seriously in connection with contemporary international relations and foreign policy.

Chapter 8

THE GENERAL ASSEMBLY

The General Assembly consists of all the members of the United Nations. Since this is the only one of the principal organs of which this is true, and because of some of the functions given to it, the General Assembly may be considered the central body of the United Nations. It has been called the "town meeting of the world," because it is the one place where all the members, large and small, may be heard in debate and discussion.

Each member of the General Assembly has one vote, and is entitled to a maximum of five representatives. The latter provision was the subject of considerable discussion at the San Francisco Conference. There was a desire to see that the General Assembly did not become too large for efficient operation. Also, some of the smaller countries were afraid that they would be placed at a disadvantage in relation to the larger and wealthier members. On the other hand, the broad scope of the agenda and the heavy demands of committee work indicate a need for a relatively large number of representatives. In practice, the size of delegations may be greatly increased by the appointment of alternates, advisers, and experts. The rules of procedure state that a member may have not more than five representatives and five alternates, and that the delegation may include as many advisers and experts as needed. Only the representatives and alternates, however, may sit in the General Assembly or serve as chairmen of committees.

The representatives are appointed by the respective member governments. Their qualifications are determined entirely by those governments, and in general are the same as the requirements established in each case for the foreign service. Article 8 of the Charter provides that "the United Nations shall place no restrictions on the eligibility of men and women to participate in any capacity and under conditions of equality in its principal and subsidiary organs." This, of course, merely prohibits the United Nations from discrimination on the basis of sex and does not place any restriction on the members in appointing their delegations. The representatives serve at the pleasure of their governments and may be recalled at any time. They act upon instructions and are responsible directly to their governments. In this respect the General Assembly resembles a diplomatic conference rather than a legislative body.

FUNCTIONS AND POWERS

The functions of the General Assembly are very broad in scope and of a varied nature. For convenience in discussion, they may be classified under the five headings of deliberative, supervisory, financial, elective, and constituent functions.[1]

Deliberation refers to the important provisions for discussion, study, and recommendation. The General Assembly may discuss any questions or any matters within the scope of the Charter or relating to the powers and functions of any organs of the United Nations (Article 10). It may make recommendations to the members or to the Security Council, or both, on any such questions or matters, with the sole exception that it shall not make any recommendation with regard to a dispute being handled by the Security Council unless the latter so requests. This exception is one provision of the Charter which reflects the feeling that the functions of the General Assembly and the Security Council should be more distinctly separated than was the case with the Assembly and Council of the League of Nations.

Matters for discussion by the General Assembly include the "general principles of cooperation in the maintenance of international peace and security" and principles governing the regulation of armaments. The specific reference to these matters is meant to illustrate, and not to restrict, the scope of the broad powers of discussion and recommendation conferred by the Charter. The General Assembly may call the attention of the Security Council to situations which are likely to endanger international peace and security. It has the obligation of initiating studies and making recommendations for the purposes of promoting international cooperation and assisting in the realization of human rights and fundamental freedoms. Subject to the exception of a dispute being handled by the Security Council, the General Assembly may recommend measures for the peaceful adjustment of any situation, regardless of origin, which it deems likely to impair the general welfare or friendly relations among nations.

In practice, the General Assembly has made broad use of its powers of discussion. It is a forum for the consideration of disputes or situations affecting international peace, and of matters involving the activities of the United Nations. It is only necessary to examine the agenda for one of the regular sessions of the General Assembly to confirm this. For example, the fifth session, which convened in September, 1950, first took care of the organizational details and then proceeded to a general debate, in which the heads of delegations made general policy statements. Items for discussion included, among others,

[1] This is the classification used by Goodrich and Hambro p. 25. This is in turn based on the description used in the report to the President by the chairman of the United States delegation to the San Francisco Conference. The terms used in this report were "to deliberate, to administer, to elect, to approve budgets and to initiate amendments."

the questions of Palestine, the former Italian colonies, Greece, China and the Far East, Korea, human rights in the Balkans, international control of atomic energy, technical assistance for underdeveloped countries, freedom of information, refugees and stateless persons, South-West Africa and other trusteeship problems, and relations with Spain.

The discussions in the General Assembly are not restricted to the debating of questions and they are not "mere talk." The term "deliberation" means discussion or consideration with a view to choice or decision, and this function of the General Assembly is in accordance with this connotation. The scope of deliberation extends beyond the actual discussion itself in two ways. First, the power of discussion implies the authorization to obtain the facts and information needed for purposes of discussion. Article 13 of the Charter requires the General Assembly to initiate studies for the purpose of promoting international cooperation in various fields. Reports and information may be requested from other organs of the United Nations and legal opinions may be sought from the International Court of Justice.

In specific disputes and questions considered by the General Assembly, there has never been any doubt of the competence to obtain relevant facts and information. The commissions appointed pursuant to resolutions in the cases of Palestine, Greece, and Korea had among their functions the making of investigations in the field and the observance of the situations on the spot. Thus, in practice, the implied power of fact finding and investigation has been broadly construed. There is no doubt that the General Assembly may authorize any study, investigation, or fact-finding procedure which is relevant to any question which it has under consideration. It is not restricted to ivory towers and cloistered walls.

Second, deliberation goes beyond "mere" discussion by arriving at recommendations. This function is specifically authorized in the Charter for the entire range of subjects which the General Assembly may discuss, with the sole exception of a dispute or situation being handled by the Security Council. The General Assembly is directed to make recommendations, as well as to initiate studies, for the promotion of international cooperation. Such recommendations have been an important factor in such questions as those of Palestine, Spain, Greece, Korea, and the Security Council voting procedure. It should be noted that "recommendations" have not been construed as referring only to formal resolutions passed by the General Assembly and addressed to other organs of the United Nations or members of the Organization. Activities undertaken under the authority of General Assembly resolutions in the cases of Palestine, Greece, and Korea included consultation, conciliation, and mediation. The commissions established in connection with these cases had among their responsibilities the function of assisting in negotiations toward an agreed settlement, both by acting as intermediaries for the parties and by making suggestions to facilitate an acceptable solution in each case.

Recommendations, of course, do not constitute legally binding decisions. They reflect the opinion and advice of the General Assembly. Their effect depends upon the force with which they commend themselves to acceptance. It is here that the separation of functions between the General Assembly and the Security Council becomes apparent. The former goes as far as it can through fact finding, discussion, persuasion, and recommendation. Enforcement action is a matter for the Security Council. This division of responsibilities is well illustrated by the Palestine case. It was generally felt that the plan of partition with economic union adopted as the recommendation of the General Assembly was *the* United Nations solution. But when this was not accepted by the parties, the Security Council did not proceed upon the basis that this plan was automatically binding and enforceable. The delegation of the United States argued that the Security Council could not take action merely to enforce a recommendation of the General Assembly against unwilling parties to the dispute, but only in the event of a finding of a threat to or breach of international peace under Article 39. This interpretation was followed, in effect, by the Security Council. The General Assembly has broad powers of study, discussion, and recommendation. It has no powers under the Charter of reaching decisions which are legally binding upon the members, or of taking enforcement action.

Although the General Assembly's powers of discussion and recommendation are very extensive, there is one important limitation. Article 2, paragraph 7, of the Charter prohibits intervention in matters which are "essentially within the domestic jurisdiction of any state." This is one of the "Purposes and Principles" of the Organization and applies to all the organs, agencies, and activities of the United Nations. Therefore, the General Assembly must observe this restriction when it undertakes to "discuss any questions or any matters within the scope of the present Charter." The growing interdependence of domestic and foreign affairs makes the interpretation of Article 2, paragraph 7, a difficult, somewhat artificial, and certainly a crucial matter.

When the question of Franco Spain was considered by the General Assembly in 1946, some delegations contended that the governmental regime of a state is "essentially a domestic matter" and therefore any attempt to deal with this case would amount to intervention contrary to Article 2(7). This argument did not convince the General Assembly, which proceeded to take action in this matter.[2]

The domestic-jurisdiction limitation has also been involved in the discussions of the treatment of non-self-governing territories. It was argued, for example, that the creation by the General Assembly of an *ad hoc* committee to examine information transmitted by members concerning the territories for which they

---

[2] See pp. 209–210.

are responsible was a violation of this limitation. Again, this type of opposition was unsuccessful and the General Assembly did establish such a committee.

A very interesting case involving the same question is that of the Indian minority in the Union of South Africa. In 1946, the government of India submitted a complaint regarding the treatment of this group. South Africa, supported by some other delegations, denied the right of the General Assembly to consider the case on the ground that it was a matter "essentially of domestic jurisdiction." However, the great majority supported the competence of the General Assembly, since friendly relations between two member states had been impaired. In December, 1946, a resolution was adopted stating this conclusion and affirming that the treatment of the group concerned should be in accordance with international obligations, including the provisions of the Charter. The Union of South Africa denied the General Assembly jurisdiction and did not put the resolution into effect. The next year an attempt at reaffirmation of the resolution failed of passage, and no further attempt at putting it into effect was made by the General Assembly.[3]

The United States delegation argued in this case that it would be a sign of weakness to restate a decision which had not produced the results intended. Would a firm stand against South Africa in this case have created a possible precedent for injecting the United Nations into the question of civil rights in the United States? There is an obligation under Article 1(3) of the Charter to respect the purpose of achieving international cooperation "in promoting and encouraging respect for human rights and for fundamental freedoms for all without distinction as to race, sex, language, or religion." Would it be possible for another member of the United Nations to complain that the treatment of a minority group in the United States jeopardized friendly relations among nations, and thus give the United Nations a basis for reviewing the situation?

When an internal matter becomes the subject of an international dispute, is it a question "essentially of domestic jurisdiction"? Obviously, one of the most important factors in the evolution of the United Nations will be the trend in the interpretation of this provision. If a broad and flexible construction is placed on the powers to deal with international disputes, the road is open to the establishment of a stronger international agency. A tendency to withhold from the General Assembly all matters having important domestic implications would indicate a narrow and restrictive range of international action through the United Nations.

It has been noted that, under the provisions of the Charter, recommendations of the General Assembly are not legally binding. However, there is nothing to prevent members from *agreeing in advance* to accept a particular recom-

[3] See pp. 210–211.

mendation as binding.   This occurred in connection with the question of the former Italian colonies.   The United States, Great Britain, France, and the Soviet Union were unable to agree on the disposition of these colonies when the Italian peace treaty was drafted.   They decided, however, to allow this treaty to enter into force and agreed that, if the Council of Foreign Ministers did not reach a settlement within a year, the question would be referred to the General Assembly and its recommendation accepted as binding upon the parties.

This case points to a possible method for strengthening the position and influence of the General Assembly.   It also furnishes a precedent for the exercise of a limited international legislative function.   The Charter does not confer any legislative powers.   Nevertheless, to the extent that advance agreements are made to accept as the final determination the results of a vote in the General Assembly in specific cases, an embryonic legislative function results.   If this first precedent is followed by a trend, the next step might be for the members, or some of them, to agree in advance to accept the recommendation of the General Assembly on specified types of questions.   This would be a technique analogous to the use of the "optional clause" for accepting the compulsory jurisdiction of an international court for questions capable of judicial settlement.[4]

Any proposal to give the General Assembly authority to make binding decisions must reexamine the question of voting representation.   The system of one vote for each member, large and small, is grossly unequal in terms of population.   In the General Assembly as now constituted it would be theoretically possible to get a majority (31 out of 60 votes), which would represent only 5.5 per cent of the total population of the members.[5]   A two-thirds majority could be obtained by votes representing only 11.0 per cent of the population.   On the other hand, the votes of the 21 smallest members, with 2.3 per cent of the total population, could prevent the formation of a two-thirds majority.   It seems fantastic to contemplate an arrangement under which one-eighth of the people concerned could legislate for the entire group and bind the other seven-eighths against their will, or in which 97 per cent of the people might be unable to form a two-thirds majority.

These theoretical extremes probably would not be reached in practice, but there is a real and substantial possibility that a small minority of the population would often control the decisive votes.   There is an observable tendency toward bloc voting on many issues.   This is especially important in connection with the Latin-American group.   With twenty members, they have one-third

[4] See pp. 194–195, below.   The Acheson plan, adopted in 1950, contemplates action on the basis of General Assembly recommendations in the event of an act of aggression and the failure of the Security Council to act.   See Appendix 21.

[5] These calculations are based upon the population figures given in Table 2 at the end of this chapter.

of the votes in the General Assembly but only 8.1 per cent of the population of all the members. The American countries north of the Rio Grande have two votes, while those to the south, with a smaller total population, have twenty votes. The Latin-American bloc, by picking up one additional vote, could exercise a veto over any General Assembly decision requiring a two-thirds majority.

Another reflection of the extreme disparity among the members is the fact that three of them (China, India, and the Soviet Union) have more than half the total population represented in the United Nations. Representation in the General Assembly in proportion to population obviously is not the solution to the problem. Clearly, any system of voting based solely upon population would be inacceptable to the United States and other technologically advanced countries which have to bear the financial and other burdens of carrying out United Nations decisions. This whole question also is deeply involved in the East-West conflict. Formulas based on a combination of population with industrial production or with educational levels have attracted some interest, but no proposal for amendment of the Charter in this respect has been made by any government. One possibility might be to establish a double system for voting, in which a majority of all members and a majority of the population represented would be required for a decision. Such an arrangement would make it impossible for either a group of small countries or a few large ones to bind the others without their consent, but either group would be in a position to block action. This might lead to deadlock in the General Assembly under certain circumstances. For example, if the Communist regime in China is admitted, that country plus the present Soviet bloc would have about 40 per cent of the vote as weighted according to population but only six out of sixty on the present basis. India, by voting with the minority on a given issue, would create a majority of the weighted vote for a group having only seven votes out of sixty. A comparable result could also be created by a small group of the more populous members other than India.

It might be possible to work out a compromise formula by which the larger countries would be given additional votes, but not strictly in proportion to population. The dilemma then arises that the weighted representation would seem inadequate to the countries with the largest population, while the small countries (whose votes are needed to amend the Charter) would resist the idea of surrendering the principle of voting equality for all members. This is a difficult and perplexing problem, but a solution is necessary if the authority of the General Assembly is to be materially strengthened.

The *supervisory* function of the General Assembly refers to its powers of control and regulation of other organs and agencies of the United Nations. As the central body, it receives and considers reports from the other organs. While the Security Council is coordinate with the General Assembly, its annual and special reports are to include an account of measures which it has decided upon or taken to maintain international peace and security. These reports are discussed by the General Assembly, and recommendations to the Security Council or to the members may result. The annual report of the Secretary-General is important as the basis of general discussion at the opening of the regular sessions of the General Assembly.

Responsibility for the discharge of functions in the field of international economic and social cooperation is vested in the General Assembly and, under its authority, in the Economic and Social Council. Approval by the General Assembly is required for the Economic and Social Council to call international conferences, to make agreements with the specialized agencies, or to request an advisory opinion of the International Court of Justice. All the functions of the United Nations with regard to trusteeship agreements for nonstrategic areas are vested in the General Assembly, and the Trusteeship Council operates under its authority in regard to such areas. Thus, the General Assembly has definite supervisory powers over two of the other principal organs of the United Nations. It also establishes regulations for the appointment of the staff of the Secretariat, and it may make recommendations for the coordination of the various specialized agencies.

The *financial* function of the General Assembly includes its responsibility for budgetary arrangements of the United Nations and the apportionment of expenses among the members. Article 17(1) states that "the General Assembly shall consider and approve the budget of the Organization." This is an important provision because it involves the power to review the work of the other organs when their expenditure estimates are presented, and to exercise a degree of control by deciding which activities will receive financial support, and to what extent.

The General Assembly apportions the expenses of the United Nations among the members, and the resulting assessments constitute binding obligations in each case. There has been considerable debate over this apportionment. The Charter does not lay down any criteria in this connection, and the General Assembly is free to determine the criteria to be used. The basic principle has been that of ability to pay. However, there have been three major deviations from an automatic application of this concept. First, a ceiling on the maximum contribution of any one member has been recognized. In the estimates submitted by the Committee on Contributions in 1946, the United States was slated to pay almost 50 per cent of the total. It was argued by the United States delegation, however, that no one member should pay more than one-third in order that it would not have an overwhelming financial interest in the Organization. The United States finally agreed to pay 39.89 per cent temporarily. This assessment was reduced to 39.79 per cent for 1950, and to 38.92 per cent for 1951. The United States continues to support the maximum of one-third as a goal to be reached as soon as possible. For the scale of assessments recommended in 1951, see Table 1.

One of the complications in this connection arises from the location of the United Nations Headquarters in the United States. Most of the expenditures must be made in this country, but the dollar shortage in the international balance of payments creates a difficulty for many members, over and above the question of their actual financial capacity. To help alleviate this situation, some contributions have been accepted in Swiss francs and the question of extending this practice to other currencies has been investigated. This appears feasible to the extent that the United Nations spends funds in other parts of the world, as in the case of its European office and its various activities and missions elsewhere.

A second qualification on the principle of ability lies in the question of a per capita ceiling. The General Assembly has given some consideration to the argument that the per capita contribution of any member should not exceed the per capita contribution of the member bearing the highest assessment. Iceland and Sweden, for example, pay more *per capita* than does the United States. Application of a per capita limitation means, of course, that a country with a small population but a comparatively high national income would receive a reduction in its assessment. Consequently, a greater burden would fall on the poorer countries. As between two members with equal national incomes, the one with less population (and therefore more income per capita) would pay a smaller total assessment. A formula based upon national income per capita as a measure of ability to pay cannot be used at the present time without conflicting with the principle of a maximum of one-third for any one member.

A third factor which stands in the way of an automatic application of an ability-to-pay formula is the inadequacy of statistical information. Complete and comparable figures on financial capacity, national income per capita, etc., do not exist. Also the information available is subject to differing interpretations. In the actual determination of the assessments, the standard of ability to pay has been the starting point, but it has been modified by the other factors discussed above and by a process of negotiation. The present tendency is to take the figures for preceding years as a point of departure. Then the members who think their assessments are too high press for a reduction. It is for the General Assembly itself to make the final determination.

The importance of the financial and budgetary functions of the General Assembly should not be underestimated. Control of the purse strings is a potent power. This, along with the supervisory functions, provides a key position in the internal administration of the entire Organization and has a significant influence on the scope of the activities undertaken by it. Whenever the merits of an undertaking are debated, the ace of trumps is held by those with power to decide whether money shall be spent on it.

In addition to the control and apportionment of funds, the size of the United Nations budget is an important question. The General Assembly approved

TABLE 1. MEMBERS OF THE UNITED NATIONS, DATES OF ADMISSION, AND
SCALE OF ASSESSMENTS

Member	Date of ratification	Scale of assessment for 1951,[1] per cent
Original members		
Argentina	Sept. 24, 1945	1.85
Australia	Nov. 1, 1945	1.92
Belgium	Dec. 27, 1945	1.35
Bolivia	Nov. 14, 1945	0.08
Brazil	Sept. 21, 1945	1.85
Byelorussian S.S.R.	Oct. 24, 1945	0.24
Canada	Nov. 9, 1945	3.30
Chile	Oct. 11, 1945	0.41
China	Sept. 28, 1945	6.00
Colombia	Nov. 5, 1945	0.37
Costa Rica	Nov. 2, 1945	0.04
Cuba	Oct. 15, 1945	0.31
Czechoslovakia	Oct. 19, 1945	0.99
Denmark	Oct. 9, 1945	0.79
Dominican Republic	Sept. 4, 1945	0.05
Ecuador	Dec. 21, 1945	0.05
Egypt	Oct. 22, 1945	0.71
El Salvador	Sept. 26, 1945	0.05
Ethiopia	Nov. 13, 1945	0.08
France	Aug. 31, 1945	6.00
Greece	Oct. 25, 1945	0.18
Guatemala	Nov. 21, 1945	0.06
Haiti	Sept. 27, 1945	0.04
Honduras	Dec. 17, 1945	0.04
India	Oct. 30, 1945	3.41
Iran	Oct. 16, 1945	0.45
Iraq	Dec. 21, 1945	0.17
Lebanon	Oct. 15, 1945	0.06
Liberia	Nov. 2, 1945	0.04
Luxembourg	Oct. 17, 1945	0.05
Mexico	Nov. 7, 1945	0.63
Netherlands	Dec. 10, 1945	1.35
New Zealand	Sept. 19, 1945	0.50
Nicaragua	Sept. 6, 1945	0.04
Norway	Nov. 27, 1945	0.50
Panama	Nov. 13, 1945	0.05
Paraguay	Oct. 12, 1945	0.04

TABLE 1. MEMBERS OF THE UNITED NATIONS, DATES OF ADMISSION, AND SCALE OF ASSESSMENTS (*Continued*)

Member	Date of ratification	Scale of assessment for 1951,[1] per cent
Original members		
Peru	Oct. 31, 1945	0.20
Philippine Republic	Oct. 11, 1945	0.29
Poland	Oct. 24, 1945	1.05
Saudi Arabia	Oct. 18, 1945	0.08
Syria	Oct. 19, 1945	0.11
Turkey	Sept. 28, 1945	0.91
Ukrainian S.S.R.	Oct. 24, 1945	0.92
Union of South Africa	Nov. 7, 1945	1.04
U.S.S.R.	Oct. 24, 1945	6.98
United Kingdom	Oct. 20, 1945	11.37
United States	Aug. 8, 1945	38.92
Uruguay	Dec. 18, 1945	0.18
Venezuela	Nov. 15, 1945	0.30
Yugoslavia	Oct. 19, 1945	0.36
Elected members		
Afghanistan	Nov. 19, 1946	0.06
Iceland	Nov. 19, 1946	0.04
Sweden	Nov. 19, 1946	1.85
Siam	Dec. 16, 1946	0.24
Pakistan	Sept. 30, 1947	0.74
Yemen	Sept. 30, 1947	0.04
Burma	Apr. 19, 1948	0.15
Israel	May 11, 1949	0.12
Indonesia	Sept. 28, 1950	

[1] From "Record of the General Assembly's Fifth Session," *United Nations Bulletin*, Vol. X, No. 1, Jan. 1, 1951, p. 76.

budgetary appropriations of $47,798,600 for 1951.[6]   On this basis, the United States assessment would be about $18,603,215 or 12.4 cents per capita for an entire year.   The corresponding figure would be 13.6 cents for Iceland, 12.7 cents for Sweden, 11.6 cents for Canada, 10.8 cents for Great Britain, 1.7 cents

[6] *United Nations Bulletin*, Vol. X, No. 1, Jan. 1, 1951, p. 75.   Since some miscellaneous income is available, the assessments are actually a little lower than would be expected on the basis of total expenditures of the Organization.

for the Soviet Union, and less than a penny for China.   These examples represent a wide variation, but the range in per capita national income is also very great.   The figures just quoted include only the general operating budget of the United Nations, and therefore do not account for the entire financial support being given to the activities of the Organization.   Construction of the permanent headquarters was facilitated by a $65,000,000 interest-free loan from the United States.   Each specialized agency has its own budget and scale of assessments.   With the inclusion of these amounts, the contributions of the United States reached a total of $107,268,000, or about 71 cents per capita, for the fiscal year ending June 30, 1951.

The United Nations has been completely dependent on contributions from members.   Undoubtedly its influence and activities could be strengthened if supplementary sources of income were developed.   One step in this direction is the creation of a United Nations Postal Administration under a resolution passed by the General Assembly in November, 1950.   Stamps are issued for use on official United Nations mail and for sale to philatelists, and revenues have been estimated at $300,000 for the first year of operation alone.

The budgetary function of the General Assembly also includes the responsibility of considering and approving any financial and budgetary arrangements with specialized agencies.   It also examines the administrative budgets of such agencies with a view to making recommendations to them.   It is a principle of the United Nations that the technical agencies established to meet specialized needs should be relatively autonomous, yet "brought into relation" with the Organization.   The application of this principle in budgetary terms has raised the question of the degree of control which the General Assembly may exercise over the expenditure items proposed by the specialized agencies.   During negotiations over this matter, the representatives of these agencies argued that there existed only the right to examine the budgets and to make recommendations concerning their form, but not to control their content.   The opposing view supported the principle of budgetary consolidation.

In the compromise finally reached, the specialized agencies agreed to consult concerning appropriate arrangements for the inclusion of their budgets within a general budget of the United Nations with the exact nature of such arrangements to be specified in supplementary agreements.   The pattern of these agreements varies.   Some of the specialized agencies have agreed to certain common financial practices and have submitted their budgets for discussion and recommendation, while others merely transmit copies of their reports. However, it remains possible for the General Assembly to give publicity to the various budgetary practices and to make constructive suggestions for their improvement.

The *elective* function of the General Assembly is of two distinct types.   One has to do with the admission of new members into the United Nations.   While the Charter uses the term "admission" in this connection, it seems appropriate to think of it as an election to membership. This process is accomplished by the General Assembly upon the recommendation of the Security Council. While the Charter does not so specify, the practice has been for a prospective member to file an application addressed to the Secretary-General. It is then transmitted to the Security Council and, after its action, to the General Assembly. To the end of 1950, all applicants so recommended have been admitted, but a number of applicants have not been recommended by the Security Council. It has sometimes been argued that a *favorable* recommendation is not essential under the Charter, that the General Assembly can use its own judgment after formal consideration before the Security Council, but this point of view has not been accepted in practice.[7] It is clear that no new member can be admitted without favorable affirmative action by the General Assembly.

Another question of membership is that of the basis for losing it. A member with its contribution in arrears may lose its voting rights. A member against which preventive or enforcement action is being taken may be suspended by the General Assembly upon the recommendation of the Security Council, but the latter acting alone may restore it to the exercise of the rights and privileges of membership. A member may be expelled, by the same procedure as in the case of suspension, if it persistently violates the principles of the Charter. The right of withdrawal is not mentioned in the Charter. It does exist, however, on the basis of an agreed interpretation at the San Francisco Conference, but emphasis is placed on the "highest duty" of each member to continue its cooperation with the United Nations.

The other phase of the elective function vested in the General Assembly has to do with the choice of members for other organs. Thus the General Assembly elects the six nonpermanent members of the Security Council, all the eighteen members of the Economic and Social Council, and some of the members of the Trusteeship Council. Acting as a coordinate body with the Security Council, it participates in the election of judges to the International Court of Justice. The Secretary-General is "appointed" by the General Assembly upon the recommendation of the Security Council.

The *constituent* function of the General Assembly refers to the provision (Article 108) that amendments to the Charter are proposed, or "adopted," by that body prior to their referral to members for ratification. Also, the General Assembly participates with the Security Council in calling a general conference of members to review the Charter. If such a conference has not been held before the tenth annual session of the General Assembly (which will occur in 1955), the proposal to do so is to be placed on the agenda of that session. By the end of 1951, no amendments had been proposed and no general conference had been called.

[7] See pp. 141–143.

ORGANIZATION AND STRUCTURE

The General Assembly is required by Article 20 of the Charter to meet in regular annual sessions "and in such special sessions as occasion may require." The opening date for the annual session has been set by the General Assembly as the third Tuesday in September. Sessions are held at the headquarters of the United Nations unless the General Assembly decides otherwise. The practice of meeting occasionally elsewhere than New York City seems to be favored, although it increases the expenses of holding a session. The first part of the third session was held in Paris in the autumn of 1948, and there is considerable interest in holding a session in some other part of the world, possibly Moscow.

The General Assembly has held two special sessions (in 1947 and 1948), both on the Palestine question. Such sessions are convoked by the Secretary-General at the request of the Security Council or of a majority of the members of the United Nations.

The General Assembly elects its own President for each session. It has been the practice to choose the presiding officer from the small or middle powers, and to cover the major geographic areas of the world in succession. The Presidents for the first five regular sessions were Spaak of Belgium, Aranha of Brazil, Evatt of Australia, Romulo of the Philippines, and Entezam of Iran.

According to rules which have been adopted, no representative may address the General Assembly without having previously obtained permission of the President. This is a procedural requirement, and it does not give the President authority to use the power of recognition in order to control the viewpoints which may obtain a hearing. The President is required by the rules to call upon representatives in the order in which they signify their desire to speak. The General Assembly itself decides such questions as a time limit on speeches, closing the list of speakers, and appeals from rulings on points of order. However, the position of President of the General Assembly is an influential one. He directs the discussion and ensures observance of the rules, he may call a speaker to order if his remarks are not relevant to the subject under discussion, he makes the initial decision on a point of order, he may accord the right of reply to a member after the list of speakers is closed if this seems desirable, and of course the prestige and dignity of the position is of some consequence. His influence as a spokesman for the United Nations as a whole rivals in some ways that of the Secretary-General.

The General Assembly also elects seven Vice-Presidents for each session. If the President finds it necessary to be absent during a meeting, he appoints one of the Vice-Presidents to take his place. However, if the President becomes unable to perform his functions, a new President is to be elected for the remainder of the term.

The staff required by the General Assembly is provided and directed by the Secretary-General. Thus, although the General Assembly has general supervision over the internal administration of the entire Organization, it does not directly supervise the staff needed for its own functions. However, it does establish regulations for the staff of the Secretariat as a whole and it retains the supervisory and financial functions. The General Assembly has ultimate control but not immediate responsibility in relation to the staff which it uses. It is too early to say whether this fact will have any significant influence on the trend of development in the relationships between the General Assembly and the Secretary-General, but quite possibly it will. It is safe to assume that he who controls routine administration has the opportunity to influence the making of policy.

A very important part of the organization of the General Assembly is the committee system. Detailed discussion and debate on a wide variety of questions would be impossible without this device. As might be expected, therefore, most of the actual work is done by committees, of which the General Assembly has established four types. These are the main committees, to consider substantive matters referred to them; the procedural committees, needed for the organization and conduct of business; the standing committees, with continuing functions; and the *ad hoc* committees, required from time to time for special purposes.

Six main committees are constituted at each session. All members of the General Assembly have the right to be represented on each of them. They consider items referred to them by the General Assembly and prepare draft recommendations and resolutions for submission to the plenary meetings. They are established on the basis of subject matter, as follows:

The First (Political and Security) Committee considers such items as admission, suspension, and expulsion of members; political and security matters within the scope of the Charter; the general principles of cooperation in the maintenance of international peace and security; the principles governing the regulation of armaments; the promotion of international cooperation in the political field; and the peaceful adjustment of situations likely to impair the general welfare and friendly relations among nations.

The Second (Economic and Financial) Committee is concerned with the economic and financial matters within the scope of the Charter, including those phases of the program of the Economic and Social Council and of the specialized agencies. Promotion of international economic cooperation, including questions of higher standards of living, full employment, and conditions of economic progress, comes within the province of this committee.

The Third (Social, Humanitarian and Cultural) Committee considers any social, humanitarian, cultural, educational, health, and related matters within the scope of the Charter and corresponding aspects of the program of the Economic and Social Council and of the specialized agencies. Matters of international cooperation in these fields, assistance in the realization of human rights and fundamental freedoms, and conditions of social progress are referred to it.

The Fourth (Trusteeship) Committee is concerned with the functions of the General Assembly relating to the international trusteeship system and to the Declaration Regarding Non-Self-Governing Territories.

The Fifth (Administrative and Budgetary) Committee considers matters pertaining to the budget; apportionment of expenses among the members; financial and budgetary arrangements with the specialized agencies; and staff regulations for the Secretariat.

The Sixth (Legal) Committee considers the legal and constitutional aspects of items assigned to it, matters relating to the International Court of Justice, legal questions referred by other committees, and the progressive development and eventual codification of international law.

There are two procedural committees. The General Committee consists of the President of the General Assembly, the seven Vice-Presidents, and the Chairmen of the main committees.[8] It considers the provisional agenda and applications for the inclusion of additional items. It assists the President in drawing up the agenda for each plenary meeting, in determining the priority of items, in coordinating the proceedings of all committees, and in the general conduct of his work. The Credentials Committee examines the credentials of the representatives of members, and reports on them to the General Assembly.

The standing committees have continuing functions which must be dealt with not only during the sessions of the General Assembly but also in the intervals between them. There are two committees of this type. The Advisory Committee for Administrative and Budgetary Questions consists of nine members, two of whom are financial experts. The members are selected for three-year terms on the basis of broad geographic representation, personal qualifications, and experience. This committee makes an expert examination of the budget of the United Nations, and advises the Fifth Committee. The Committee on Contributions considers the apportionment of expenses and related questions. It consists of seven members who serve for three years on a staggered basis.

The *ad hoc* committees are set up either by the plenary Assembly or by any of its Committees to handle specific problems. Thirteen such bodies, including a Permanent Headquarters Committee, Board of Auditors, Committee on Negotiations with the United States, etc., were established during the first regular session of the General Assembly. The Special Committee on Palestine, set up during the first special session, is another illustration. It is now the practice to establish an *ad hoc* (special) political committee to share the work

[8] It is customary for five of the Vice-Presidents to be chosen from representatives of the Great Powers, and for the chairmen of the main committees to come from the smaller countries.

involved in the political and security matters facing the First Committee.

The "Little Assembly," or Interim Committee of the General Assembly, represents a special question of organization. In September, 1947, the United States delegation proposed that a standing committee of the whole be established to assist the General Assembly by handling preliminary and continuing work between the regular and special sessions. It was felt that the Assembly could not adequately discharge its wide responsibilities during the sessions. The Soviet Union objected to this step on the grounds that it was unauthorized by the Charter, exceeded the power of the General Assembly to establish subsidiary organs, and represented an attempt to circumvent the Security Council by setting up another body to handle some of the same functions.

After thorough discussion, it was decided to form such a committee on a temporary basis.[9] Its jurisdiction was carefully restricted to matters expressly referred to it by the General Assembly, important disputes or situations proposed for inclusion on the agenda of the General Assembly, and methods of implementing the general principles of international cooperation in the political field. To enable the Interim Committee to discharge its functions as an advisory body to the General Assembly, it was given the power to conduct investigations and to advise on the matter of summoning a special session of the Assembly. The Interim Committee was prohibited from trespassing on the functions of any of the other United Nations organs, and from discussing any matter being handled by the Security Council. Some of the matters referred to this Committee were consultation with the United Nations Temporary Commission on Korea, the problem of voting in the Security Council, and promotion of international cooperation in the political field.

At the end of 1950, the Interim Committee remained on a temporary basis. The Soviet bloc has maintained its original objections and has not participated in the work of the "Little Assembly" in any way. The Soviet argument of illegality under the Charter does not seem to be well taken as long as the Committee remains in a subordinate and advisory position to the General Assembly. It is true, of course, that continuing deadlocks in the Security Council tend to give a greater practical importance to the discussions and recommendations in the General Assembly and its subsidiary organs.

In connection with questions of organization and structure, it is necessary to make a comment on the "unofficial" aspects, such as would be represented by the party leaders and the caucus in a legislative body. There are no political parties in the General Assembly. However, some tendency toward bloc voting is discernible. The Soviet, Arab, and Latin-American members, for example, form distinct groups and must be reckoned with as such. On particular issues, such as that of colonial administration, rather definite groupings of members are apparent. There is, too, the practice of advance consultation which is often employed. Information gained and attitudes expressed in this

[9] See Appendix 16.

way may influence to some degree the positions taken by members in formal debate.   The contacts among delegations are a factor in the work of the General Assembly.   The unofficial and informal elements of organization have evolved only to a slight extent, but the operating structure cannot be fully explained without reference to them.

PROCEDURE

The Charter provides that the General Assembly shall adopt its own rules of procedure.   At the beginning of each session [10] the necessary organizational measures are taken, including the election of officers, constitution of the committees, and adoption of the agenda.   General debate is opened and reports from other organs are received.   Matters requiring direct action by the entire Assembly, such as the election of members to other organs, are handled in the plenary meetings held from time to time during the sessions.   Other items are referred to the committees.

As a normal practice, the General Assembly does not make a final decision on any matter until it has received the report of the committee concerned. The committees perform the usual function of such devices by making a detailed study of the items referred to them, thus saving the time of the full Assembly.   Since all members of the parent body are entitled to representation on each of the important committees, this division of labor is not among the members, as in a legislative body, but among different representatives of the same members.   In effect, the system is one of a series of committees of the whole, which can function simultaneously because each member may have several representatives.   The committees follow the European practice in having both a chairman and a *rapporteur* in each case.   It is the function of the latter to report for the committee and to be its spokesman when its proposals are under consideration in a plenary meeting.

The General Assembly usually accepts the recommendations of its committees, but not always.   In December, 1948, Spanish was made a third "working language" despite a committee report to the effect that it was inadvisable to impose the additional financial burden involved.   In November, 1949, the plenary Assembly rejected a resolution proposed by its Trusteeship Committee which would have required members administering trust territories to submit detailed plans for leading natives to the stage of independence.

Decisions in the General Assembly are made by a two-thirds majority of those present and voting for "important" questions, and a simple majority for other matters.   "Important" questions include recommendations with respect to the maintenance of international peace and security, election of members to

---

[10] A minute of silence is observed at the beginning of the first plenary meeting of each session.   Despite many suggestions, it would not be possible to have a public prayer which would satisfy all beliefs.

other organs,[11] the admission of new members to the United Nations, suspension and expulsion of members, questions relating to the operation of the trusteeship system, and budgetary questions.   This is a sharp departure from the former unanimity rule in international organizations.

It is notable that the basis of those *present and voting* is the least restrictive provision which is possible.   When the requirement is based upon *all the members*, each absentee and each abstention amounts in effect to a negative vote.   When it is based upon *all those present*, each abstention amounts to a negative vote.   For example, in a body having 100 members with 10 absent and 10 present but not voting, a simple majority of all the members would mean 51 votes, as compared with 46 on the basis of those present, and 41 for those present and voting.   Furthermore, in the General Assembly, any doubt as to whether a particular question requires a two-thirds majority is determined by a simple majority.   Thus a bare majority of those present and voting may decide any issue except those either listed in the Charter or recognized by the majority itself to be one of the "important" questions.[12]   All committees make their decisions by a simple majority vote.

A quorum in the General Assembly, under a rule effective January 1, 1950, is one-third of the members so far as the opening of a meeting is concerned, but no question can be put to a vote unless a majority of the members are present.   Votes are normally taken by a show of hands or by standing, but any representative may request a roll call.   When this is done, the roll is called in the English alphabetical order of the names of the members, beginning with one drawn by lot.   All elections are held by secret ballot.   There are no nominations except in connection with the election of judges to the International Court of Justice.

One special problem of procedure relates to the use of several official languages—English, French, Spanish, Chinese, and Russian.   The first three of these are designated as "working languages."   Verbatim records are drawn up and the *Journal* of the General Assembly is issued in the working languages. Summary records, and all resolutions and other important documents, are made available in all five official languages.   For the speeches, a system of simultaneous translations is used.   Headphones are provided and, with a switch of a dial, a representative or observer may follow the proceedings in any of the languages.   The story is told of one visitor, not aware of this system, who was puzzled at the ease with which everyone else seemed to understand Chinese.

The meetings of the General Assembly and of its committees are held in public unless it decides otherwise in exceptional circumstances.   Any decisions taken in closed meetings are to be promptly announced.   The press, radio,

---

[11] Except for the election of judges to the International Court of Justice, which requires an absolute majority in the General Assembly.

[12] An exception to this general rule is found in Article 108 of the Charter, which provides that proposed amendments shall receive a two-thirds majority of all the members.

TABLE 2. SELECTED STATISTICS FOR MEMBERS OF THE UNITED NATIONS

Member	Area, thousands of square miles [1]	Population, thousands [2]	Birth rate [3]	Death rate [4]	Infant mortality rate [5]	Illiteracy rate [6]	Per capita income, 1949, U.S. dollars [7]
Afghanistan	251	12,000	*	*	*	*	50
Argentina	1,074	16,818	24.4	9.4	79.0	*	346
Australia	2,975	7,912	22.9	9.5	25.3	*	679
Belgium	12	8,614	17.2	12.9	57.2	5.6	582
Bolivia	413	3,990	30.7	12.7	113.1	*	55
Brazil	3,288	49,340	*	*	*	56.7	112
Burma	261	18,304	32.4	23.0	203.8	*	36
Byelorussian S.S.R.	80	5,568	*	*	*	*	(a)
Canada	3,843	13,549	26.9	9.2	42.8	3.8	870
Chile	286	5,709	33.2	18.1	169.1	28.2	188
China	3,759	463,493	*	*	*	*	27
Colombia	440	11,015	35.1	14.3	136.6	44.2	132
Costa Rica	20	838	41.0	11.8	97.4	*	125
Cuba	44	5,199	25.2	11.1	83.0	22.1	296
Czechoslovakia	49	12,463	23.3	11.5	83.2	4.1	371
Denmark	17	4,230	18.9	8.9	35.3	*	689
Dominican Republic	19	2,277	38.7	9.3	77.3	*	75
Ecuador	106	3,404	*	*	122.0	*	40
Egypt	386	20,045	43.5	21.3	152.8	85.2	100
El Salvador	13	2,150	39.5	13.2	100.4	72.8	92
Ethiopia	350	16,700	*	*	*	*	38
France	213	41,550	21.0	13.8	56.0	3.8	482
Greece	51	7,856	27.0	12.4	100.7	40.8	128

Guatemala	42	2,787	*	*	*	65.4	77
Haiti	11	3,750	*	*	*	*	40
Honduras	59	1,326	40.3	14.4	22.4	66.3	83
Iceland	40	140	27.8	8.6	130.1	*	476
India	1,197	346,000	25.5	17.2	28.8	90.9	57
Indonesia	576	72,000	28.5	20.3	*	*	25
Iran	618	18,387	*	*	*	*	85
Iraq	168	4,800	*	*	50.9	*	85
Israel	*	1,058	29.4	6.9	*	*	389
Lebanon	3	1,238	18.3	5.4	*	*	125
Liberia	43	1,648	*	*	74.9	*	38
Luxembourg	1	295	14.4	12.6	102.3	*	553
Mexico	760	24,448	44.6	16.8	26.8	51.6	121
Netherlands	16	9,956	23.7	8.1	23.8	*	502
New Zealand	103	1,881	24.9	9.1	95.1	*	856
Nicaragua	57	1,184	35.4	10.1	29.6	*	89
Norway	125	3,233	19.6	8.8	*	*	587
Pakistan	367	74,437	18.0	12.3	50.1	*	51
Panama	29	764	33.0	7.1	52.0	35.3	183
Paraguay	157	1,304	31.7	8.9	110.8	*	84
Peru	482	8,204	25.9	10.8	96.0	56.6	100
Philippines	116	19,498	32.4	16.5	139.8	*	44
Poland	120	24,448	24.3	13.7	*	23.1	300
Saudi Arabia	*	6,000	*	*	23.2	*	40
Sweden	173	6,956	17.4	10.0	*	0.1	780
Syria	72	3,135	*	*	68.1	*	100
Thailand	198	17,987	27.1	10.2	*	*	36
Turkey	296	19,623	*	*	79.1	*	125

TABLE 2. SELECTED STATISTICS FOR MEMBERS OF THE UNITED NATIONS (Continued)

Member	Area, thousands of square miles [1]	Population, thousands [2]	Birth rate [3]	Death rate [4]	Infant mortality rate [5]	Illiteracy rate [6]	Per capita income, 1949, U.S. dollars [7]
Ukrainian S.S.R.	223	30,960	*	*	*	*	(a)
Union of South Africa	472	12,112	26.7	9.1	40.1	*	264
U.S.S.R.	8,599	193,000	*	*	*	*	308
United Kingdom	94	50,363	17.0	11.7	34.1	*	773
United States	3,022	149,215	24.0	9.7	31.1	4.3	1,453
Uruguay	72	2,353	20.7	8.9	65.7	*	331
Venezuela	352	4,595	43.3	12.5	97.8	56.6	322
Yemen	75	4,500	*	*	*	*	40
Yugoslavia	99	16,040	28.3	13.6	132.3	45.2	146

* Information not given.

[1] Based upon information in the *Yearbook of the United Nations, 1947–1948*, pp. 1119, 1122. The *Statistical Yearbook* and the *Demographic Yearbook* (both published by the United Nations) give the area of each country and territory of the world in square kilometers. The figure for Indonesia has been converted from the latter source.

[2] Based upon information in the *Demographic Yearbook, 1949–1950*, pp. 71–83. Later figures, to the extent available, may be found by consulting the latest issue of the *Monthly Bulletin of Statistics*, published by the Statistical Office of the United Nations.

[3] The "crude birth rate," that is, the number of live births per 1,000 population. The information is taken from the *Demographic Yearbook, 1949–1950*, pp. 288–295. The figures are given for 1949 or the latest available year. Many of the figures are estimates, sometimes based upon incomplete information. Notes and comments in the *Yearbook* explain the significance of the data.

132

TABLE 2. SELECTED STATISTICS FOR MEMBERS OF THE UNITED NATIONS (*Continued*)

[4] The "crude death rate," that is, the number of deaths exclusive of stillbirths, per 1,000 population. The information is taken from the *Demographic Yearbook, 1949–1950*, pp. 380–387. The figures represent reports or estimates for 1949 or the latest available year.

[5] The number of deaths of infants under one year of age per 1,000 live births. The information is taken from the *Demographic Yearbook, 1949–1950*, pp. 410–415. The figures represent reports or estimates for 1949 or the latest available year. The data used in calculating these rates are not always comparable with the data used in other columns of this table. For example, in the case of Indonesia, the *Demographic Yearbook* gives birth and death rates for the Indonesian population and infant mortality rates for Europeans only.

[6] The percentage of illiterate population at the latest census for each country. The dates range from 1928 to 1945. The United States figure is for 1930; the question on illiteracy was not asked in the 1940 census. The information is taken from *Statistical Yearbook, 1949–1950*, pp. 486–494. The percentages are given in most cases for illiterate population ten years of age or over. The lower age limit varies for a few countries. The figure 15 in this column, for example, would mean that 15 per cent of the population old enough to read and write could not do so.

[7] From *National and Per Capita Incomes of Seventy Countries in 1949 Expressed in United States Dollars*, Statistical Office of the United Nations, October, 1950. See also *United Nations Bulletin*, Dec. 15, 1950, p. 720.

(*a*) Included in figure for the U.S.S.R.

films, and even television are used to report its proceedings to the world.   Hundreds of visitors come to the United Nations Headquarters when important meetings are to be held.   There they can observe the sessions and see famous statesmen in the flesh.   Groups from civic organizations, and high school and college students, usually make up a large proportion of the visitors but they are by no means the only ones.   The United Nations has become quite a tourist attraction.   This, in America, is certainly a mark of success.   One has only to see the swarming lobby and the rush for tickets on a busy day to wonder what the old-school diplomats would make of it.

The General Assembly, in an attempt to improve and speed up its work, appointed early in 1949 a Committee on Methods and Procedures.   This Committee made a careful study of the factors affecting the duration of sessions and presented some recommendations.   These were considered by the Sixth (Legal) Committee and presented to the Assembly itself in November, 1949.   This study resulted in some modifications of the rules.   However, it was clear the primary factor in the length of sessions was due not to defective rules of procedure but to the number and complexity of the questions submitted and to the political problems raised by them.

Chapter 9

THE SECURITY COUNCIL

The Security Council is composed of eleven members of the United Nations. China, France, the Soviet Union, Great Britain, and the United States are named in the Charter as permanent members. Thus, the five states that were Great Powers at the close of World War II occupy a special position. These five were the leaders of the wartime alliance against the Axis nations, and they bore the brunt of the fighting and losses by which the victory was won. Also, a definite relationship between power and responsibility was sought. The members with the greatest resources of industry, technology, and manpower would necessarily take a leading part in keeping the peace of the world. It followed that they should have a leading role in making the decisions involved.

This arrangement is obviously a rigid and inflexible one, yet the list of Great Powers of the world does not remain static. Some on that list in 1945 may not belong in that classification in 2045, or 1995, or even 1965. Other countries may rise to the top in the scale of power. If this should happen, the permanent members of the Security Council would not coincide with the actual Great Powers and the argument in favor of designating permanent members would be lost. The only way to add to or substract from this category is by amendment of the Charter, and this cannot be done without the concurrence of all the permanent members. Thus, each of the five can block its removal from this group, as long as it exists as a state and remains a member of the United Nations, and no new permanent member can be added without the agreement of all five now in that category. The designation of permanent members follows the precedent of the Covenant of the League of Nations, but that arrangement was more flexible since the Council with the approval of the Assembly could create new permanent members.

The six nonpermanent members of the Security Council are elected for two-year terms by the General Assembly. These elections are staggered, so that three members complete their terms and three new ones are elected each year. The elections are held each fall during the regular annual session of the General Assembly, and the new terms begin on the following January 1. The nonpermanent members are ineligible for immediate reelection. The Charter provides two criteria for election to the Security Council. Due regard is to be paid "in the first instance to the contributions of Members of the United Nations to the maintenance of international peace and security and other purposes of the Organization." The General Assembly is the sole judge of the relevance of this qualification to the election of any particular member to a nonpermanent seat on the Security Council.

The other criterion is that of "equitable geographical distribution." Since the beginning, the actual distribution of the six elective seats has been one each for Eastern and Western Europe, two for Latin America, one for the Arab states, and one for the British Dominions.[1] Disputes concerning this matter have arisen on three occasions. In 1947, there was a heated contest between the Ukraine and India. For the former, it was argued that it had made an important contribution to winning the war, and that if it were not elected Eastern Europe would be unrepresented. Moreover, the Soviet Union was insistent that the Ukraine be elected. On behalf of India, there was the objection that the Ukraine was not an independent state and to elect it would give the Soviet Union two votes on the Security Council. Also, it was argued that India was fully qualified on the basis of ability to contribute to the purposes of the United Nations, and with Australia no longer a member of the Security Council, a geographic area with more than a half billion population would not be represented if the Ukraine were elected. After eleven ballots, India withdrew as a candidate in order to break the deadlock.

In 1949, the election of Yugoslavia (in preference to Czechoslovakia) to take the place of the Ukraine was bitterly contested by the Soviet Union. Mr. Vishinsky insisted that there was a gentlemen's agreement permitting the United Nations members in each geographic area to select the candidate for that group. This, in effect, would allow the Soviet Union to name the nonpermanent member for Eastern Europe. It was argued, on the other hand, that Yugoslavia is both a Slav and a Communist country and, as the Yugoslavs said, they had not changed their geographical position. The United States supported the Yugoslav candidacy, on the grounds that a Great Power should not be permitted to dictate the General Assembly's election of any particular country, that the geographical criterion was met, and that a Communist country independent of the Kremlin was to be preferred to one controlled from Moscow. Great Britain voted for Czechoslovakia, presumably on the grounds that it was premature to place Tito's Yugoslavia on the Security Council, and that the resulting increase in East-West tension would do more harm than good. Yugoslavia was elected by a narrow margin, but agreement on the basic issue involved was not reached.

In 1950, there was protracted balloting over the contest between Lebanon and Turkey to succeed Egypt as a member of the Security Council. On behalf of Lebanon it was argued that the seat should go to an Arab state. Those supporting Turkey contended that, under the principle of geographical representation, the Middle East and not just the Arab bloc should provide the suc-

[1] See Table 3, at the end of this chapter.

cessor to Egypt. There was also a feeling that Turkey was under special scrutiny by the Soviet Union and that, if trouble developed in that part of the world, it might be a good idea to have Turkey represented on the Security Council. A further argument against the candidacy of Lebanon was that none of the Arab countries should be selected while their differences with Israel remained unsolved. Turkey was finally elected on the fifteenth ballot.

The size of the Security Council is a problem. Because of the nature of its functions, it should be small enough to operate quickly and with a minimum of organizational complexity. On the other hand, there is considerable pressure for membership on it. A maximum of opportunity for different countries to be elected is provided by the short term of two years and by the prohibition of two successive terms for any one member. Still, six nonpermanent seats are not enough to provide continuous representation for all the major areas of the world. There is also the problem of the "middle powers." The present arrangement lumps together all countries except the Big Five. However, there is a greater disparity between Canada and Panama, for example, than between Canada and France. The League of Nations met this problem by declaring members eligible for reelection provided they obtained a two-thirds vote in the Assembly, instead of the simple majority ordinarily required. This cannot be done for the Security Council of the United Nations without an amendment of the Charter. In view of the number of small states, it is not likely that a two-thirds majority would approve such a step. And if it were done, the problem would become even more acute for all the countries not placed in the intermediate category.

Each member of the Security Council has one representative, instead of the maximum of five allowed for the General Assembly. This is another example of the emphasis on a small compact group designed to reach decisions expeditiously. The representatives to the Security Council are appointed by their respective governments and act on instructions from them.

Functions and Powers

The Security Council has the "primary responsibility for the maintenance of international peace and security." In carrying out its duties under this responsibility, the Security Council acts on behalf of all the members of the United Nations. It is an agent of the entire Organization in this respect. The main functions of the Security Council may be classified under the headings of deliberation, enforcement, and election.

Deliberation includes such activities as discussion, investigation, and recommendation. The Charter contemplates a certain logical progression of steps by which international disputes would be handled, beginning with the existence of a dispute or situation "the continuance of which is likely to endanger the maintenance of international peace and security." There is, first of all, an obligation on the parties to seek a solution by peaceful means of their own choice. The Security Council may call upon the parties to settle their disputes by such means, and it is specifically authorized to "investigate any dispute, or any situation which might lead to international friction or give rise to a dispute, in order to determine whether the continuance of the dispute or situation is likely to endanger the maintenance of international peace and security." It may recommend appropriate procedures or methods of adjustment at any stage of such a dispute or situation. If the parties do not achieve a settlement by peaceful means, they are obligated to refer the matter to the Security Council.

Article 39 of the Charter provides that "the Security Council shall determine the existence of any threat to the peace, breach of the peace, or act of aggression and shall make recommendations, or decide what measures shall be taken in accordance with Articles 41 and 42, to maintain or restore international peace and security." This, in the event that pacific settlement fails, introduces a course of action which may lead to actual enforcement measures. In practice, the Security Council has been reluctant to make a formal finding of the existence of a "threat to the peace, breach of the peace, or act of aggression," and has done so only as a last resort.

The process of deliberation, both in pacific settlement and in the preliminary stages of enforcement action, is much broader than mere debate and resolution passing in the meetings at the United Nations headquarters. As in the case of the analogous function in the General Assembly, field investigations may be made. This was done, for example, in connection with the Greek, Indonesian, and Palestine disputes. Also, continuing efforts may be made under Security Council auspices to settle a dispute as between the parties. Examples of this are the establishment of the Committee of Good Offices in the Indonesian dispute, the Truce Commission and the United Nations Mediator in Palestine, and the continuing efforts of the Security Council in the Korean case.

The activities of study, discussion, and recommendation are not confined to the handling of individual disputes, but are also exercised by the Security Council in the consideration of other questions related to the maintenance of international peace and security. By Article 26 of the Charter, the Security Council is made responsible for formulating plans for the establishment of a system for the regulation of armaments. This question has been discussed, especially in the Commission for Conventional Armaments created as a subsidiary organ of the Security Council, but no basic agreement has been reached among the Great Powers. The problem of the international control of atomic energy arose after the Charter was written at San Francisco, but its relation to the major function of the Security Council is obvious. The United Nations Atomic Energy Commission was established by a resolution of the General Assembly. However, it is responsible to and operates under the supervision of the Security Council.[2]

[2] See pp. 240–244.

The *enforcement* function of the Security Council refers to the power to decide what measures shall be taken to maintain or restore international peace and security, if both peaceful settlement among the parties and recommendations of the Security Council fail in this objective.   For this reason, it is often called the "enforcement arm" of the United Nations.   The first step in this connection would be the application of measures not involving the use of armed force.   Such measures "may include complete or partial interruption of economic relations and of rail, sea, postal, telegraphic, radio, and other means of communication, and the severance of diplomatic relations" (Article 41 of the Charter).   If this is inadequate, the Security Council is authorized to take such military action as may be necessary (Article 42).   Decisions made by the Security Council in the exercise of this responsibility are binding upon the members of the United Nations.   This is in contrast to the League of Nations, under which it was for each member to decide for itself whether an occasion had arisen for the application of sanctions.

The armed forces and facilities necessary for the maintenance of international peace and security were to be contributed by members of the United Nations, in accordance with special agreements to be concluded with the Security Council.   No agreement of this type has been reached as yet, because of the differences between the Soviet Union and the Western Powers.   The size of the contribution of each permanent member has been a basic issue.   The Soviet delegation has insisted on the principle of equality, as regards both strength and composition of the armed forces.   The other delegations have upheld the principle of comparability, by which the contributions might differ widely as to the strength of the separate land, sea, and air components.   The emphasis would be on the provision of a balanced and effective force for the Security Council, and differences in the size and composition of existing national forces would be taken into account.[3]

Obviously, if the Soviet position were accepted, each component of the United Nations armed forces would be limited initially to a strength five times the smallest contribution of that component.   For example, if China were able to furnish only a nominal naval force for the Security Council, then an effective international naval force would be automatically impossible.   On the other hand, if the Soviet Union should accept the principle of comparable contributions, it would be confronted with the possibility of an international armed force in which the naval and air components might be predominantly Anglo-American.

There is specific recognition, in Article 45 of the Charter, that it might become necessary for the United Nations to take urgent military action.   Members are to hold national air-force contingents immediately available for

[3] For a summary of the opposing viewpoints concerning the armed forces to be provided, see Leland M. Goodrich and Edvard Hambro, *Charter of the United Nations: Commentary and Documents*, World Peace Foundation, Boston, 1949, 2d ed., pp. 281–286.

combined international enforcement action. However, the strength and degree of readiness of these contingents, as well as plans for their combined action, are to be determined within the limits of the special agreements mentioned above. It follows that this provision of the Charter has not been implemented as yet.

A Military Staff Committee was established "to advise and assist the Security Council on all questions relating to the Security Council's military requirements for the maintenance of international peace and security, the employment and command of forces placed at its disposal, the regulation of armaments, and possible disarmament" (Article 47 of the Charter). The Military Staff Committee consists of the Chiefs of Staff of the permanent members of the Security Council or their representatives. In addition to its duties of giving advice and assistance, it is also responsible for the strategic direction of any armed forces which may be placed at the disposal of the Security Council.

So far as the Charter of the United Nations is concerned, the problem of an international police force would be met by a system of national contingents placed under international direction for a specified purpose. This goes further than a mere combined or coordinated use of separate national forces, which was essentially the system contemplated by the Covenant of the League of Nations. However, it definitely does not represent an attempt to establish a permanent international military force.

It should be noted that the provision for national contingents to be made available to the Security Council by special agreements does not preclude the possibility of establishing an independent international armed police force, at least on a small scale. The idea of a United Nations "guard force" was suggested by the Secretary-General in 1948, and has been accepted in a modified form by the General Assembly.[4]

The Security Council's enforcement function is carefully safeguarded in the Charter. Article 51, which explicitly recognizes the inherent right of individual or collective self-defense in the event of an armed attack against a member, provides for the exercise of that right only "until the Security Council has taken the measures necessary to maintain international peace and security." Action by members under Article 51 is to be reported to the Security Council and in no way affects the authority and responsibility of the latter. Regional arrangements or agencies may be utilized for enforcement action. But no such action is to be taken by regional arrangement or agencies without the authorization of the Security Council, except for measures against the enemy states of World War II. In connection with the international trusteeship system, Article 83 of the Charter provides that "all functions of the United Nations relating to strategic areas, including the approval of the terms of the trusteeship agreements and of their alteration or amendment, shall be exercised by the Security Council."

4 See p. 189.

The enforcement functions and powers of the Security Council are directed to its responsibility for the maintenance of international peace and security, rather than to the laying down of specific terms for the settlement of individual disputes. If a condition of agreement and mutual confidence existed among the Great Powers, there would be a danger that they might use the Security Council in such a way as to promote their own interest in the maintenance of peace, but they are also concerned for their freedom and independence. They do not want the type of peace which results from merely forcing the weak to bow to the strong. They want the Security Council to be capable of enforcing peace, but not capable of dictating unjust terms of settlement. Of course, the current disagreement among the Great Powers results in a situation in which the proper function of the Security Council is likely to suffer more from deadlock than from abuse of power. Nevertheless, from a long-term point of view, the other danger must be recognized as a possibility.

The *elective* function of the Security Council includes its responsibilities relating to the admission of new members and to the constitution of certain other organs.

As indicated above,[5] new members of the United Nations are admitted by vote of the General Assembly upon recommendation of the Security Council. As of Jan. 1, 1952, nine members had been admitted in this way.[6] However five applicants—Albania, Bulgaria, Hungary, Rumania, and the Mongolian People's Republic—had not received the necessary seven affirmative votes to be recommended for admission. Seven applicants—Austria, Italy, Ireland, Portugal, Finland, Transjordan, and Ceylon—failed to receive the votes of all the permanent members of the Security Council because of the opposition of the Soviet Union.[7]

Albania was not recommended for admission because of its conduct in connection with the Corfu Channel incident and the Greek case, and also because of its failure to reaffirm its pre-1939 bilateral treaties. The Soviet government supported this application on the basis of the war record of the Albanian people. The applications of Bulgaria, Hungary, and Rumania were not supported by most members of the Security Council because of their alleged violations of human rights contrary to treaty commitments. Also, Bulgaria was accused of giving aid to the guerrillas in northern Greece. The application of the Mongolian People's Republic was not approved because of doubts as to its international status.

The application of Austria was opposed by the Soviet Union on the grounds that an ex-enemy state should not be admitted until the treaty of peace with it had entered into force. The United States took the position that commitments had been made to treat Austria as a liberated, rather than an enemy, country.

[5] P. 122.

[6] For a list of original and admitted members, see Table 1, pp. 120–121.

[7] See pp. 145–150 for a discussion of the voting procedure in the Security Council.

The British government thought that the Austrian application was premature in view of the military occupation. A resolution was proposed by Australia to recommend Austria for admission at a time and under conditions to be determined by the General Assembly. This resolution was defeated by the opposition of the Soviet Union.

The applications of Ireland, Portugal, and Transjordan were initially opposed by the Soviet Union on the basis that they did not have diplomatic relations with that government. It was also contended that Ireland was neutral, or even sympathetic with the enemy, during the war, that Portugal had special ties with Franco Spain, and that the independent status of Transjordan was questionable.

The Soviet Union supported the admission of Italy and Finland on condition that Bulgaria, Hungary, and Rumania also be admitted. That condition was not accepted by other members of the Security Council. When Ceylon applied for admission, the Soviet Union expressed doubts concerning its degree of independence and asked for a postponement of the decision. When this proposal was defeated, a favorable recommendation was prevented by an adverse Soviet vote.

These deadlocks in the Security Council led to much criticism and repeated discussions in the General Assembly. When the latter, on several occasions, passed resolutions requesting reconsideration, the members of the Security Council maintained their initial positions. Because of the widespread feeling that some members of the Security Council were not basing their votes in this matter upon the provisions of the Charter, the General Assembly also decided to request an advisory opinion from the International Court of Justice. The majority of the judges, in an opinion handed down in May, 1948,[8] reached the conclusion that a member of the United Nations "is not juridically entitled" to make its consent to admission of an applicant subject to conditions not expressly provided in Article 4, paragraph 1, of the Charter.[9]

Thus, in the opinion of the Court, there could be only five valid qualifications for membership in the United Nations. An applicant must (1) be a state; (2) be peace-loving; (3) accept the obligations of the Charter; (4) be able to carry out these obligations; and (5) be willing to do so. This would rule out the imposition of such conditions as the establishment of diplomatic relations with particular states and making the admission of one applicant depend upon the admission of another one. Six of the fifteen judges wrote dissenting opinions, in which they held that the admission of a new member was essentially a political and not merely a procedural act. The enumerated conditions are essential according to the minority view, but there is no specific

[8] See Appendix 17.

[9] "Membership in the United Nations is open to all other peace-loving states which accept the obligations contained in the present Charter and, in the judgment of the Organization, are able and willing to carry out these obligations."

statement in the Charter indicating that they are sufficient. They did not find a legal obligation upon the United Nations to admit applicant states. It is interesting to note that the decision of the Court did not divide entirely along East-West lines. Three of the minority judges, who believed that the Soviet position in this matter was legally sound, were nationals of Canada, Great Britain, and France.

After the advisory opinion of the Court, the various members of the Security Council continued to maintain their initial positions. This, of course, constitutes a refusal by the Soviet Union to accept the opinion of the majority on the Court. Even aside from this fact, it is clear that the Charter provides no automatic test of qualifications in concrete cases. Whether or not a state is "peace-loving" and "able and willing to carry out its international obligations" are matters which each member of the Security Council and of the General Assembly must determine for itself when voting upon an application.

The Security Council has an important responsibility with reference to questions of suspension and expulsion. A member of the United Nations against which preventive or enforcement action has been taken may be suspended from the exercise of the rights and privileges of membership by the General Assembly upon the recommendation of the Security Council. However, the latter may restore these rights and privileges upon its own determination. Expulsion of a member which has persistently violated the principles of the Charter is accomplished by the same procedure as in the case of suspension.

The other type of elective function possessed by the Security Council has reference to the composition of other organs. It participates in the election of judges to the International Court of Justice, and its recommendation is necessary for the appointment of a Secretary-General. Thus the responsibilities of the Security Council in this connection, while important, are not nearly so extensive as those of the General Assembly.[10]

ORGANIZATION AND PROCEDURE

The organization of the Security Council is quite simple. This might be expected from the facts that it has only eleven members and that each member has only one representative at the meetings. In a body of this size, elaborate organization is scarcely possible and obviously unnecessary.

The Charter provides that the Security Council shall be so organized as to be able to function continuously, and that each member shall be represented

[10] For the situation which arose at the expiration of the first term of the Secretary-General, when the Security Council was unable to agree on any recommendation, see p. 177. In addition to its main functions of deliberation, enforcement, and election, the Security Council also participates concurrently with the General Assembly in any proposal to call a General Conference to review the Charter, and it recommends the basis on which a state not a member of the United Nations may become a party to the Statute of the International Court of Justice.

at all times at the seat of the Organization.   This is intended to give assurance that the Security Council will be able to function promptly whenever necessary to maintain peace and security.   If assistance is to be given to a victim of aggression, any delay may have very serious consequences.   Therefore it is intended to avoid any delays involved in convening a session of the Security Council, and in the time which it would take for the representatives to assemble. Under the rules which have been adopted, the interval between meetings shall not be longer than fourteen days.

The Charter provides that the Security Council shall decide on the method of selecting its President.   A system of automatic rotation was adopted, under which the office is held by each member in turn for one calendar month according to alphabetical order in English.   .This method puts all the members on a basis of complete equality so far as the opportunity to preside is concerned, and it eliminates the problems and possible frictions involved in making a choice or indicating a preference.   Such a system of rotation means, of course, that the Presidency of the Council cannot be an office with important functions on its own account and that there cannot be much continuity of leadership at this point.   This method may also lead to a rather bizarre situation upon occasion; thus in January, 1950, when the question of China was facing the Security Council, it was the turn of the representative of China to preside.   In August, 1950, it was the turn of the Soviet Union, which had been boycotting the meetings since the preceding January.   The Soviet representative returned to assume the presidency of the Council and to tie it up in procedural knots for a month.

A body as small as the Security Council does not need a large number of committees.   However, there have been some organizational developments of this type.   The Military Staff Committee was created by provisions of the Charter as a subsidiary body of the Security Council.   The United Nations Atomic Energy Commission was created by a resolution of the General Assembly, but was made responsible to the Security Council.   The Commission on Conventional Armaments was established by the Security Council itself to consider the problem of the regulation of armaments other than atomic energy and weapons of mass destruction.   The Committee of Experts was created at the first meeting of the Security Council in January, 1946, for the purpose of examining the Provisional Rules of Procedure and such other matters as might be entrusted to it.   The Committee on the Admission of New Members has the responsibility of examining applications for membership in the United Nations.   It is the usual practice for subsidiary bodies created by the Security Council for matters of general and continuing interest to be constituted as committees of the whole.   In addition various *ad hoc* or special bodies have been established from time to time.   Examples of these are the Committee of Good Offices on the Indonesian Question, the United Nations Commission for India and Pakistan, the United Nations Truce Commission for Palestine, and the Sub-Committee of Three to Collect Information on Candidates for Governor-ship of Trieste.

The staff for the Security Council is provided by the Secretariat. This includes clerks, translators, and other necessary personnel. The Secretary-General, or a deputy, attends the meetings.

The Charter provides that the Security Council shall determine its own rules of procedure. The first order of business is the adoption of an agenda. The rules provide that a provisional agenda shall be drawn up by the Secretary-General and approved by the President of the Security Council. In the conduct of business, the President is to call upon the representatives in the order in which they signify a desire to speak. The President decides points of order, but may be overruled by vote of the members.

There are five official languages: English, French, Spanish, Russian, and Chinese. The first two of these are working languages. A speech in one of the working languages is translated into the other. A speech in another language is translated into both working languages. Ordinarily, the Security Council uses a system of consecutive, rather than simultaneous, translation. This slows up the proceedings, and physical facilities for simultaneous translation are available. The principal reason for the slower method is probably a desire for more time to reflect upon the implications of statements made before the Council. Because of the great interest in the proceedings, both simultaneous and consecutive translations have been provided since August 1, 1950.

Verbatim records are maintained in the working languages. Resolutions, records of public meetings, and all important documents are reproduced in all five official languages. The meetings are held in public, unless it is decided otherwise for special reasons in a given case. An example of a matter dealt with in a closed meeting is the consideration of recommendations to the General Assembly for the appointment of a Secretary-General. After each private meeting, the Security Council issues a communiqué through the Secretary-General.

UNANIMITY AND THE VETO

The question of the voting procedure in the Security Council has attained such a crucial importance that it is necessary to give careful attention to this problem and its implications.

The relevant Charter provisions are found in Article 27, which provides that each member of the Security Council shall have one vote; that decisions on procedural matters shall be made by an affirmative vote of seven members; and that decisions on all other matters shall be made by seven affirmative votes, including the concurring votes of the permanent members. On matters of pacific settlement, a party to a dispute is to abstain from voting.

The requirement of concurring votes of the permanent members for decisions on important or substantive matters is based on the principle of unanimity of the Great Powers.   It was a basic assumption at the San Francisco Conference that the United Nations could not succeed without agreement and unity among its leading members.   In particular, it was believed that decisions to use force for the maintenance of international peace and security could not successfully be carried out against the opposition of one or more of the Great Powers.   Nor could the governments of these Powers be expected to participate in an arrangement by which their armed forces could be used without their consent.

The principle that unanimity among the permanent members is a prerequisite to enforcement action finds support in practical considerations.   The leading industrial nations have almost a monopoly of the means of waging a modern global war.   If a reasonable degree of cooperation exists among them, it is difficult to see how a large-scale war could occur.   If, however, they disagree to the point of fighting each other, the obvious result would be a third world war.   Cooperation among the permanent members is essential if the Security Council is to perform its function.   Since its decisions are to be taken by a procedure of voting, the outcome of the voting on a resolution indicates whether or not the necessary agreement exists.   If all the members vote the same way, this shows that they agree on the measures to be taken.   If some vote for and some against a proposal, this shows that they disagree and therefore are not prepared to cooperate in the suggested course of action.   If four of the permanent members vote in the affirmative, and one in the negative, the proposal is thereby blocked because all of them do not concur.   This is said to be a "veto."   In other words, unanimity does not exist in such a case.

Some of the smaller countries at the San Francisco Conference objected to this voting procedure on the grounds that it violated the principle of "sovereign equality" of all members, and that it would weaken the Security Council by creating the likelihood that it might not be able to reach decisions necessary to the discharge of its functions.   The Great Powers, however, emphasized the importance of the principle of unanimity and insisted that they were not prepared to abandon their position on this point.[11]

In the actual operation of the Security Council, the veto became almost entirely an issue between the Soviet Union and the other permanent members. By January, 1951, there had been more than forty instances in which resolutions before the Security Council had received at least seven affirmative votes but had not been carried as the result of the negative vote of one permanent member.   The only veto by a member other than the Soviet Union was one by France in August, 1947, in opposing a proposal in connection with consideration of the Indonesian question.   The Soviet score of vetoes includes, however, a number of negative votes on each of several issues.   For example, seven

[11] See pp. 87–89.

applications for membership have been opposed by the Soviet Union, and some of these have been brought to a vote more than once.[12]

The Security Council uses two different voting procedures, depending on whether the vote is being taken on a procedural or a substantive question. However, these terms are not defined in the Charter and some difficult questions of interpretation have arisen.   The governments of the permanent members made a statement on this subject at the San Francisco Conference, but this neither settles all the questions nor has any necessary binding effect on the countries which did not subscribe to it or on the Security Council itself. It is agreed that procedural matters include the internal organization and rules of the Security Council, election of its President, decisions on the time and place of meetings, adoption of the agenda, establishment of subsidiary organs, and the question of whether a particular dispute or situation is to be discussed. Decisions to take enforcement action, or to make recommendations, are clearly substantive in character.

A proposal to conduct an investigation has been considered a substantive question, on the basis that such a step may inaugurate a "chain of events" with major political consequences, in the course of which the Security Council might have to make decisions as to enforcement measures.   The Soviet Union has argued that the decision to discuss a dispute or situation may start a "chain of events" leading to the necessity for substantive decisions.   The Iranian dispute was the first test case of this point, and the Soviet government tacitly accepted the majority view that discussion within the Security Council, not involving an investigation, is a procedural matter.

In a doubtful case, the question of whether a proposal requires the unanimous vote of the Great Powers assumes great importance.   This fact can easily be illustrated by reference to the Soviet challenge to the right of the representative of the Nationalist Government of China to continue as a member of and to preside over the Security Council.   If this were considered a procedural matter involving a decision of credentials, the affirmative votes of any seven members would be controlling.   If it were considered a substantive decision, any resolution would be subject to the veto of one permanent member.   This would raise the further question of whether the representative of China could veto his own removal.   In practice, the Security Council has made its own determination, without requesting an opinion from the International Court of Justice or any other body.   Its interpretation has been guided by the principle that any doubt as to the applicable voting procedure is to be settled by a substantive vote. Thus, any question which is not clearly and admittedly procedural becomes subject to veto.   The possibility of vetoing a proposal to decide a resolution by any seven affirmative votes, and then of vetoing the substance of the resolution, is sometimes called the "double veto."   A precedent for mitigating the

[12] For the disputes in connection with which the veto has been used, see pp. 205–219.

effects of this procedure was established in September, 1950, when the Security Council upheld by a procedural vote a ruling of its President to the effect that the representative of China could not use the "double veto" to prevent an invitation to the Communist regime in China to participate in a discussion of the status of Formosa.

A special question relates to the effect of an abstention from voting. A party to a dispute is required to refrain from voting in connection with the process of pacific settlement. It is quite clear that this does not prevent the Security Council from reaching a valid decision without the concurring vote of a permanent member. The result of any other interpretation would be the ridiculous conclusion that the Charter requires a procedure which automatically makes the Security Council unable to fulfil one of its major functions.

But there is another aspect to the question of abstention. The Charter requires the "concurring votes of the permanent members" for a decision on a substantive matter. Suppose a permanent member is absent, or does not vote? Contrary to what one might expect from the language used, the interpretation in practice has been that an abstention from voting does not constitute a veto. Even in the most important decisions, if seven affirmative votes are cast and no permanent member casts a negative vote, the proposal is considered as adopted. This interpretation, it should be noted, makes possible some flexibility in the voting procedure, since it is possible for a permanent member to refrain from endorsing a proposal and still to allow the others to go ahead with it if they desire. In this respect, the language of the Charter has not been interpreted in as restrictive a fashion as might have been possible. This interpretation was of the greatest importance in the Korean case, since it permitted the resolutions of June 25 and June 27 to be adopted in the absence of the Soviet Union.

Dissatisfaction with the Security Council voting procedure, frequent use of the veto by the Soviet Union, and the problems of interpretation have resulted in much discussion and a number of suggestions. The General Assembly undertook the consideration of this matter as early as 1946, and this was one of the questions which the Interim Committee was instructed to place on its agenda. In April, 1949, the General Assembly passed a resolution recommending that the members of the Security Council should consider as procedural certain designated types of decisions; that the permanent members should consult among themselves whenever feasible with a view to avoiding use of the veto, and to exercise it only on questions of vital importance; and that members of the United Nations should exclude the principle of unanimity to the greatest extent feasible in agreements conferring functions upon the Security Council. On October 18, 1949, it was announced that the permanent members had agreed upon the principle and practice of consultation before important decisions are made. There was no other change in the position of these governments on the question.

The veto has become a crucial issue in the work of the United Nations, and in attitudes toward it and its prospects of success.   More than any other issue connected with the United Nations, it has acquired emotional overtones and, in the United States at least, has high headline value.   It is especially important, therefore, to consider some of the implications of this problem for the United Nations and for the practice of international cooperation in general. Since the veto is a type of negative vote, it becomes necessary to examine the question of *voting* in relation to the Security Council.

Voting is one method which is used in the process of decision making.   But there are other possible methods, of which force, diplomacy, persuasion, and informal agreement are examples.   It is often assumed that some kind of simple or qualified majority voting is the democratic way to settle all issues, but this assumption is unwarranted.   Democracy involves the protection of the minority as well as the rule of the majority.   Overwhelming majority votes do not necessarily indicate government by a democratic process, as Hitler's Germany so clearly demonstrated.   Conversely, a requirement of unanimity may exist in a democratic system.   One example of this is trial by jury, a cherished right in Anglo-Saxon jurisprudence.   It takes a unanimous vote of the jury to convict a person of a crime; not even an eleven-to-one majority can accomplish this.   Another example in the United States is the constitutional provision that no state can be deprived of equal representation in the Senate without its own consent.

There is another consideration which should not be forgotten.   Decisions can be made by voting only within the context of an agreement and a willingness to accept the results of the vote, even if it is contrary to one's interests and desires.   First principles cannot be compromised, nor can they be yielded to the expressed wishes of a majority.   Questions of honor and of vital interest cannot be settled this way.   The Civil War in the United States occurred when the opposition between the sections reached the point at which the conflicting views over states' rights and slavery were too deeply held to be settled by a process of voting.   As Lincoln said in his second inaugural, "Both parties deprecated war, but one of them would *make* war rather than let the nation survive, and the other would *accept* war rather than let it perish, and the war came."

When a powerful group refuses to subject itself to the verdict of the polls, voting ceases to be a device for arriving at decisions and for settling issues. The question, then, to be raised with respect to the Security Council is whether voting is an appropriate and useful procedure by which basic disagreements between East and West may be resolved.   Vetoes do not occur until these disagreements are brought to a vote.   To some extent, therefore, it is possible to say that the trouble with the veto is the vote.[13]

[13] For a stimulating discussion of this problem, see James B. Reston, "Votes and Vetoes," *Foreign Affairs*, October, 1946, pp. 13–22.

Decisions by voting require agreement to accept the results, even though adverse. They also require a mutually satisfactory basis of representation in the voting body. The present arrangement in the Security Council is that of one vote for each member, although there are great discrepancies among them in population, wealth, and influence. Among the permanent members, China has more than ten times the population of France. If all the members are considered, the disparity is much greater. Ecuador, for example, has a population of 3,400,000. It therefore has, in proportion to population, 136 times the voting representation of China, 57 times that of the Soviet Union, and 44 times that of the United States. Should Ecuador have equal weight with the United States, Great Britain, and the Soviet Union in arriving at decisions to take enforcement action, in view not only of the population disparity but also of the difference in the contributions which would be made in carrying out the decisions? It seems obvious that the device of voting for decision making in international organizations will be of limited usefulness until a better solution for the problem of representation is found.[14]

Another basic question in connection with the veto is that of the relation of the voting procedure in the Security Council to the whole process of cooperation through the United Nations. Defeat of a proposal in that body by one negative vote is labeled a "veto," but often other types of refusals to accept the majority opinion do not strike the public consciousness in the same fashion. For example, the Union of South Africa has refused to place the former mandate of South-West Africa under the international trusteeship despite several resolutions of the General Assembly stating that this should be done. Israel refused to accept the General Assembly recommendation that Jerusalem be internationalized. Great Britain and France served notice that they would resist any attempt to extend international supervision of colonies and that they would refuse to comply with resolutions calling for political information and plans. The United States Senate, in consenting to ratification of the Statute of the International Court of Justice, attached the reservation that virtually gives the United States government a veto over submission of cases to the Court when it is a party and alleges that the dispute is essentially a matter of domestic jurisdiction. The United States also claimed the right of veto over the status of the former Japanese mandated islands in the Pacific.

The real problem of the United Nations is the development of a sufficient degree of cooperation among its members, and especially the Great Powers. Agreement on the basis and methods for the maintenance of international peace and security is the objective. The result of a vote on a given proposal merely indicates whether or not agreement exists in that case. A veto is a reflection of disunity, rather than its cause. No solution of the problem of the veto is adequate unless it contributes to a solution of the conflict and tension among the permanent members of the Security Council.

[14] See pp. 116–117.

TABLE 3. NONPERMANENT MEMBERS OF THE SECURITY COUNCIL,
GEOGRAPHICAL DISTRIBUTION [1]

1946	1947	1948	1949	1950	1951 [2]
Australia	....	Canada	....	India	....
Brazil	....	Argentina	....	Ecuador	....
Poland	....	Ukrainian S.S.R.	....	Yugoslavia	....
Egypt	Syria	....	Egypt	....	Turkey
Mexico	Colombia	....	Cuba	....	Brazil
Netherlands	Belgium	....	Norway	....	Netherlands

[1] Leaders indicate retention of membership for the following year.

[2] In 1952 new members were Pakistan, Chile, and Greece, with Turkey, Brazil, and the Netherlands retaining their membership.

Chapter 10

THE ECONOMIC AND SOCIAL COUNCIL

It was recognized, in framing the Charter of the United Nations, that economic and social conditions have an important relation to the maintenance of international peace. Economic misery and social unrest involve frustrations and tensions which destroy order, stability, and security. Under such conditions, peace can be preserved only by the maintenance of a *status quo* backed by overwhelming force. This type of situation certainly will be a temporary and explosive one.

It was felt that the improvement of world economic and social conditions would alleviate international tensions and thus assist in the maintenance of peace and security. The United Nations, through the General Assembly and the Security Council, would deal with such disputes as might arise. But a large number of major disputes would put an intolerable strain upon these organs, and in the long run an enduring peace could be established only by preventing the rise of serious international conflicts. The Charter, in Article 55, provides that the United Nations shall assist in creating "conditions of stability and well-being which are necessary for peaceful and friendly relations among nations" by promoting:

(a) higher standards of living, full employment, and conditions of economic and social progress and development;

(b) solutions of international economic, social, health, and related problems; and international cultural and educational cooperation; and

(c) universal respect for, and observance of, human rights and fundamental freedoms for all without distinction as to race, sex, language, or religion.

Recognition of the relation of economic and social cooperation to the maintenance of international peace is very important. In the long run, the greatest opportunities of the United Nations probably lie in this field. However, it is necessary to interject a warning against a too facile acceptance of this assumption in an exaggerated form. A recent United Nations booklet, for example, opens with this sentence: "It has long been recognized that to ensure peace, it is necessary to solve the world's economic and social problems." [1]

[1] *The Economic and Social Council,* Reference Pamphlet No. 2, United Nations, 1949, p. 1.

Without detracting from the importance or relevance of this idea, one may point out that it is neither that simple nor that automatic. What is the exact relation of economic and social conditions to group conflict? The social sciences are not able, in their present stage of development, to give a definite answer. It is known, however, that there is a relationship and that the whole problem is a complex one with a number of variables.

The peoples who are economically most advanced, and who have relatively high standards of social welfare, are not always the least warlike. Napoleon's France probably had a higher "level of living" than any other country on the continent of Europe at the time. Germany in 1939 had "full employment" and was better off economically than India and many other countries. Dozens of similar examples can readily be drawn from the slightest knowledge of history. As a matter of fact, a measure of economic advancement is necessary for large-scale warfare. It is only the great industrial nations, with their huge resources and productivity, which have the capacity to fight a global war. If all the peoples of the world were poverty-stricken, small and localized wars might occur but the shadow of atomic annihilation would not hang over the entire world. Nor is the standard (or level) of living, "American" or otherwise, any guarantee of peace because of the simple psychological fact that human wants are insatiable. Sometimes those who have the most are the most dissatisfied with what they have. The extent of dissatisfaction and frustration does not bear an exact inverse correlation to the abundance of goods.

On the other hand, it is equally obvious that some tensions are associated with economic and social deprivation. The real question is the extent and incidence of the dissatisfaction with the *status quo,* and the point at which it becomes inflammable. Some insight into the nature of this complex problem will enable a more solid foundation to be laid for the important work of international economic and social cooperation. And it will forestall the frustration which would be produced in a reaction to the results of an uncritical reliance upon this type of activity as a panacea. One important consideration which presents a real opportunity at the present time is that frustration within a group seems to be at a minimum when conditions are improving and when there is a hopeful attitude concerning the attainment of significant goals by peaceful means.

Without putting all our peace-and-security eggs in the one basket of economic and social cooperation, we can recognize its special importance at the present time. Modern technology has made the nations of the world interdependent in fact. The practice of international cooperation is essential if the economic, social, and political conditions and activities are to be geared to the technological facts of life. This must be done if the evolution of modern society is to take place in an orderly fashion. The task in this connection is the fundamental one of creating the economic and social conditions of peace and security in the modern world. The foundation is not the whole house, but without it the house cannot be built.

Under the League of Nations, activities in the field of international economic and social cooperation were extensively developed.[2] The Covenant of the League provided (in Article 23) for "social and other activities," including the attempt to secure fair and humane conditions of labor; just treatment of native inhabitants of colonial territories; supervision of agreements with regard to traffic in women and children, and in opium and other dangerous drugs; supervision of trade in arms and ammunition with the countries in which the control of this traffic was necessary; maintenance of freedom of communications and transit; and steps for the prevention and control of disease. In addition to these specific provisions, both the Assembly and the Council were authorized to deal with any matter "within the sphere of action of the League or affecting the peace of the world." The work of the League of Nations in international economic and social cooperation became increasingly important and successful, but this development was overshadowed by the political crisis of the 1930's. The experience was not entirely lost, however. In addition to the concrete results obtained at the time, there was a definite influence on the recognition given to this type of international cooperation in the organization of the United Nations.

The Charter of the United Nations provides for an Economic and Social Council, which is designated as one of the six principal organs and which operates under the authority of the General Assembly. This is in contrast to the League arrangement, under which the responsibility for this type of work was vested in the political organs (Council and Assembly) and carried out by subsidiary commissions and committees. The result was to give the economic and social activities a subordinate emphasis and to allow them to be unduly influenced by political considerations.

The Economic and Social Council is composed of eighteen members of the United Nations elected by the General Assembly for terms of three years. There is a staggered arrangement, so that the terms of office of six members expire each year. There are no permanent members designated in the Charter, as in the case of the Security Council, and no criteria are specified to guide the General Assembly in electing members to the Economic and Social Council. At the San Francisco Conference, the Canadian and French delegations proposed that the countries of chief industrial importance be assured of places on the Council. The majority was opposed to making any such formal distinction, and election remains open to all members of the United Nations equally. However, since states represented on the Economic and Social Council are eligible for immediate reelection, somewhat the same result has been achieved in practice.[3] The Great Powers and the other countries of chief

[2] See p. 168.

[3] For members of the Economic and Social Council, 1946–1951, see Table 4, p. 168.

industrial importance have repeatedly been elected, and also an attempt has been made to give representation to different economic systems and a variety of interests.

FUNCTIONS AND POWERS

The functions of the Economic and Social Council lie in the areas of studies and reports, discussion and recommendations, and coordination.

Studies and reports are specifically authorized by Article 62, paragraph 1, of the Charter which states that "the Economic and Social Council may make or initiate studies and reports with respect to international economic, social, cultural, educational, health, and related matters. . . ." No one can really come to grips with the problems in these fields without the basic facts. There is a lamentable dearth of adequate statistical and other information about economic and social conditions throughout the world. There has never been an accurate census of the population in many areas, and it is difficult to make even a reasonably reliable estimate in some cases. The same difficulty applies to our knowledge of resources, productivity, and other basic factors.

Only an international agency can hope to compile factual information and to collect comparable statistics on a world-wide basis. The United Nations picked up where the League left off and has broadened its activities to a significant extent. The Economic and Social Council has made studies dealing with such subjects as the problems of refugees, the world shortage of housing, the reconstruction of devastated areas, and the economic status of women. In cooperation with the Secretariat, the Council has initiated the preparation of a statistical yearbook, a demographic yearbook, and a survey of world economic conditions. A compilation of relevant information has been a first step in the accomplishments of the Economic and Social Council and its subordinate agencies, such as the Commission on Human Rights.[4] To mention one example at this point, the Draft Declaration on the Death of Missing Persons was prepared in order to provide a common standard for declaring a missing person as legally dead. Millions had disappeared during the war. A number of practical problems hinged on the question of whether they were to be considered as dead or merely missing. In many cases, estates could not be inherited, insurance payments claimed, or other property settlements made. The remaining spouse who might wish to remarry would have a legal problem. This question involved many different countries, each with its own laws and procedures. The need for a common standard was obvious. Compilation of the relevant factual information was essential before recommendations for a common standard could be made. A by-product of this process, as happens in so many cases, is a body of information useful to scholars

4 See pp. 131–133.

and practitioners concerned with the legal, administrative, and other phases of this particular question.

Cooperation in studying and reporting on international economic and social conditions leads in the direction of a definition of areas of agreement on important factual information and on the identification of the problems of general concern.   It is an important phase of the practice of international cooperation.   The difficulties are great, and the achievement is still very incomplete, for both technical and political reasons.   But the reports and studies prepared under the auspices of the Economic and Social Council already are very useful in a number of ways, and much greater possibilities will be realized to the extent that secrecy of basic economic and social information ceases to become a weapon in the cold war.

Another important function of the Economic and Social Council is that of *discussion and recommendations*.   The Charter authorizes the Council, in Article 62, paragraph 1, to make "recommendations with respect to any such matters to the General Assembly, to the Members of the United Nations, and to the specialized agencies concerned."   This is the form taken by any decisions which the Economic and Social Council may reach.   This organ of the United Nations has no authority to make decisions binding upon the members or the other organs.   Its influence in this connection is measured by the extent to which its recommendations are accepted.   Its method is persuasion, not force.

It is clear that the authority to make recommendations extends to international cooperation in economic, social, cultural, educational, health, and related matters.   Some question has arisen concerning the competence of the Economic and Social Council in specific international disputes involving an economic or financial aspect.   In 1946, the Council received proposals of the Czechoslovak and Yugoslav governments for the restoration of Danube vessels which had belonged to them, had been taken away by the German army, and were then under the control of the United States.   Several delegates argued that the Council had no jurisdiction over a political dispute between interested parties, but there was general agreement that the Council had a legitimate concern with the economic situation involving the restoration of traffic on the Danube.   The chairman, Mr. Sampar of Yugoslavia, stated that it was within the competence of the Council to make appropriate recommendations, since the question involved international economic issues and there was doubt as to ownership of the property.   The Council finally passed a resolution recommending that a conference be held in Vienna to resolve the basic problems obstructing international traffic on the Danube.

Early in 1948, the Yugoslav government asked the Economic and Social Council to pass a resolution calling upon the United States to "cease causing damage to Yugoslavia" by further retention of gold transferred from that country and deposited with the Federal Reserve Board of New York during the war. After discussion, the Council concluded that it was not competent to deal with this question (1) because it was a particular dispute between two states, and (2) because of the juridical issues involved.

In addition to the general powers of discussion and recommendation, two specific techniques are recognized in the Charter. First, the Economic and Social Council "may prepare draft conventions for submission to the General Assembly, with respect to matters falling within its competence." The draft convention has proved to be a very useful device. Every salesman knows the value of having his papers ready, complete with dotted line, and his pen unsheathed. A draft convention furnishes the text of a proposed agreement. If a country is willing to accept the terms, all it need do is sign and ratify. The tedious work of negotiation is already done. Also, it is much easier to approach agreement on a common standard since the same draft, or model, is offered to all parties.

The other technique of discussion and recommendation stated in the Charter is found in the provision that the Economic and Social Council "may call, in accordance with the rules prescribed by the United Nations, international conferences on matters falling within its competence." The conference, as a method of international cooperation, has been discussed earlier.[5] It is an important device for discussion and recommendation. The General Assembly, at its first session, adopted this rule:

Pending the adoption, under paragraph 4 of Article 62 of the Charter, of definitive rules for the calling of international conferences, the Economic and Social Council may, after due consultation with Members of the United Nations, call international conferences in conformity with the spirit of Article 62 on any matter within the competence of the Council, including the following: international trade and employment; the equitable adjustment of prices on the international market; and health.

Later the General Assembly invited the Secretary-General to prepare, in consultation with the Council, draft rules to govern the calling of international conferences.

From the beginning the Economic and Social Council has called international conferences, some upon instructions from the General Assembly [6] and some upon its own initiative.[7] Although the criteria are not stated in the Charter and the General Assembly had not adopted definitive rules, it has been the practice that the Council may call only intergovernmental conferences and may not call them on matters "essentially within the domestic jurisdiction of any state" on account of the provisions of Article 2, paragraph 7.

The Economic and Social Council's most important function of *coordination*

---

[5] See pp. 29–31.

[6] For example, the Conference on Freedom of Information, Geneva, 1948.

[7] For example, the International Health Conference, New York, 1946; World Statistical Congress, Washington, 1947; United Nations Conference on Trade and Employment, Havana, 1947.

relates to the "specialized agencies" of the United Nations. Article 57, paragraph 1, of the Charter provides that "the various specialized agencies, established by intergovernmental agreement and having wide international responsibilities, as defined in their basic instruments, in economic, social, cultural, educational, health, and related fields, shall be brought into relationship with the United Nations. . . ." Thus, the term "specialized agencies" has a particular meaning in the United Nations system. It includes international organizations created by intergovernmental agreement and having "wide international responsibilities." The latter term, in practice, has been given both a geographic and a functional connotation. No strictly regional agencies have been included in this category. Technical or service organizations have been designated as "specialized agencies" only if they perform a function of major importance and general interest. The nature of such agencies may be indicated by a brief summary of those which have been established or initiated.[8]

The International Labor Organization (ILO) was established after World War I as an autonomous associate of the League of Nations. It seeks by international action to improve labor conditions, raise living standards, and promote economic and social stability. In December, 1946, arrangements were completed for the ILO to become a specialized agency of the United Nations. One feature of the ILO which requires special mention is its arrangement for representation of member countries. The Conference, as the highest authority of the ILO, is composed of national delegations including two government delegates and one delegate each of management and labor. Thus, one-half the representatives to the Conference are nongovernmental delegates. This is an interesting departure from the usual pattern of representation in international organizations.

The Food and Agriculture Organization of the United Nations (FAO) grew out of a conference held at Hot Springs, Virginia, in 1943. The purpose and scope of this agency is indicated by these words in the preamble to its constitution:

The Nations accepting this Constitution, being determined to promote the common welfare by furthering separate and collective action on their part for the purposes of: raising levels of nutrition and standards of living of the peoples under their respective jurisdictions, securing improvements in the efficiency of the production and distribution of all food and agricultural products, bettering the condition of rural populations, and thus contributing toward an expanding world economy. . . .

The United Nations Educational, Scientific and Cultural Organization (UNESCO) assumes that lasting peace cannot be built exclusively on political and economic arrangements, but must be founded on the intellectual

---

[8] For a description of the functions and organization of each specialized agency, see *Yearbook of the United Nations, 1948–1949*, pp. 981–1118.

and moral solidarity of mankind. The preamble to its constitution states that "since wars begin in the minds of men, it is in the minds of men that the defences of peace must be constructed." It is the purpose of UNESCO to collaborate in the work of advancing the mutual knowledge and understanding of peoples; to give fresh impulse to popular education and the spread of culture; and to maintain, increase, and diffuse knowledge. These goals are sought to be realized by a wide variety of projects for international cooperation in the fields of education, science, and culture.

The International Civil Aviation Organization (ICAO) originated in a conference held in Chicago in 1944, for the purpose of laying down principles and arrangements for the development of international civil aviation in a safe and orderly manner. The aims and objectives of ICAO, as stated in Article 44 of the Convention on International Civil Aviation, are as follows:

. . . to develop the principles and techniques of international air navigation and to foster the planning and development of international air transport so as to: (a) Insure the safe and orderly growth of international civil aviation throughout the world; (b) Encourage the arts of aircraft design and operation for peaceful purposes; (c) Encourage the development of airways, airports, and air navigation facilities for international civil aviation; (d) Meet the needs of the peoples of the world for safe, regular, efficient and economical air transport; (e) Prevent economic waste caused by unreasonable competition; (f) Insure that the rights of contracting States are fully respected and that every contracting State has a fair opportunity to operate international airlines; (g) Avoid discrimination between contracting States; (h) Promote safety of flight in international air navigation; (i) Promote generally the development of all aspects of international civil aeronautics.

The International Bank for Reconstruction and Development (called simply "the Bank") grew out of the Bretton Woods Conference of 1944 and was designed to promote the international flow of capital for productive purposes and to assist in financing the rebuilding of devastated areas and the development of resources of member nations. The objectives were to help raise the levels of production, to assist member nations in attaining balanced economies in which exports could pay for essential imports, and thus to contribute to a healthy expansion of international trade. In its lending operations, the Bank may make, guarantee, or participate in loans to its member countries directly, to any of their political subdivisions, or to private business enterprises in the territories of members. First emphasis was placed on reconstruction, where there was an urgent need and also opportunity for rapid improvement in the level of productivity, but it was expected that development loans would assume a major role in the operation of the Bank. The Bank's capital is derived from shares subscribed by member nations, in proportion to their relative economic resources. Total subscribed capital is more than $8 billion, of which 20 per cent is paid-in capital and the remainder is in the form of a guarantee fund.

The International Monetary Fund ("the Fund") also grew out of the Bretton Woods Conference. Its purpose is to promote stability in international currency matters and to encourage the expansion of world trade. This is to be done by (1) working toward the eventual removal of restrictions on foreign exchange transactions; (2) setting up a schedule of exchange rates in terms of gold and United States dollars, so that traders who wish to buy in foreign countries can obtain the currencies they require at known and stable rates; and (3) ensuring that any major changes in foreign exchange practices will be submitted to international consultation before being put into effect. The Fund is also authorized to engage in foreign exchange and gold transactions with members, in order to provide a secondary line of monetary reserves. As the source of capital funds, a subscription quota was set for each member. This is payable partly in gold and partly in the member's own currency. These quotas vary from $500,000 for Honduras and Panama to $1,300,000,000 for the United Kingdom and $2,750,000,000 for the United States. Voting power and the amounts which may be drawn from the Fund are both related to the size of these quotas.

The Universal Postal Union (UPU) originated with the heavy increase in international mail during the nineteenth century.[9] It became a specialized agency of the United Nations on July 1, 1948. Virtually all independent nations, non-self-governing territories, and United Nations trust territories are now members of UPU, which forms a "single postal territory for the reciprocal exchange of correspondence." The basic purpose is "to secure the organization and improvement of the various international postal services, and to promote the development of international collaboration in this field." Maximum and minimum rates, weight limits, and dimensions are fixed for "ordinary mail," which is defined to include letters, postcards, commercial papers, printed matter, raised print for the blind, samples of merchandise, small packets, and phonopost articles (such as phonograph records). Supplemental agreements include provisions for other services, such as insured mail, parcel post, money orders, cash-on-delivery packages, postal checks, collection orders, and subscriptions to periodicals. Certain articles are prohibited. These include opium and other narcotics, explosive substances, immoral articles, and most live animals.

The International Telecommunication Union (ITU) is another international organization dating from the nineteenth century. Electrical telegraphy came into use in Europe about 1838, and shortly thereafter the governments concerned began to conclude agreements on standardized operation, types of conductors and apparatus, and the collection of telegraph rates. In 1865, a general treaty was signed at Paris by twenty countries, and the International Telegraph Union came into existence. Radio telegraphy was first put to use in 1899, to increase the security of maritime navigation. An International

[9] See pp. 31–33.

Radio-telegraph Union was established in 1906, since this new device could not be used effectively without international regulations. In 1932, arrangements were made to merge these two organizations into the International Telecommunication Union. The objectives of the ITU are to maintain and extend international cooperation for the improvement and rational use of telecommunication, to promote the development and most efficient operation of technical facilities, to harmonize the actions of nations in the attainment of these ends. In order to accomplish these objectives, the ITU (1) is instrumental in allocating the radio frequency spectrum and registering radio frequency assignments; (2) seeks to establish the lowest rates possible, taking into account efficient service and sound financial administration; (3) promotes measures for ensuring the safety of life through the cooperation of telecommunication service; and (4) makes studies and recommendations, and collects and publishes information for the benefit of its members. The ITU became a specialized agency of the United Nations on January 1, 1949.

The World Health Organization (WHO) is one of the new international organizations, having officially come into existence in April, 1948. This new agency was, of course, preceded by a long history of international cooperation in the field of public health. Quarantine measures have existed for centuries, and for many years international health agreements have been in force. The Health Organization of the League of Nations did much to extend this type of work. The WHO thus builds upon a long experience. Its objective is "the attainment by all peoples of the highest possible level of health," with "health" being defined as "a state of complete physical, mental and social well-being and not merely the absence of disease or infirmity." WHO is to serve as the coordinating authority on international health work, to maintain certain necessary international services, to promote and conduct research in the field of health, and to promote improved standards of teaching in the health, medical, and related professions.

The International Refugee Organization (IRO) is a nonpermanent specialized agency created to deal with the problem of refugees and displaced persons resulting from World War II. By definition, IRO is concerned with persons who were victims of Nazi, Fascist, or Falangist regimes, or were deported for forced labor, or became refugees or displaced persons for reasons of race, religion, nationality, or political opinion. It was estimated that there were about a million in these groups, in addition to the much larger number repatriated by the armies of occupation. With respect to such persons, IRO performs the functions of repatriation; identification, registration, and classification; care and assistance; legal and political protection; transport; and resettlement. Repatriation is encouraged and assisted, with due regard to the principle that no one shall be repatriated against his will. The IRO was scheduled to end operations by the end of 1951, with other organizational arrangements to be made for the refugee problem after that time.

The World Meteorological Organization (WMO) has as its objectives world-wide cooperation in the establishment of observing stations and other meteorological services; systems for the rapid exchange of weather information; standardization of meteorological observations and statistics; further application of meteorology to aviation, shipping, agriculture, and other activities; and encouragement of research and training in the field. International cooperation in meteorology was undertaken by a conference held in Brussels in 1853, primarily for the purpose of dealing with the weather and climate of the oceans, and by an organization of meteorological institutions established in 1878. The establishment of WMO converted this into an intergovernmental organization, for the purpose of strengthening the meteorological services with their respective governments and in their relations with other international organizations.

In addition to the eleven specialized agencies described above, there are two which have been initiated but not yet established: the Inter-Governmental Maritime Consultative Organization (IMCO) and the International Trade Organization (ITO).

IMCO would function in an advisory capacity to promote international co-operation in matters concerning safety at sea, shipping, removal of discriminatory action and unnecessary restrictions, and exchange of information. There are a great number of international conventions and agreements on many subjects related to shipping. There have been several international organizations dealing with some aspect of shipping. However, the need was felt for a central maritime organization to promote the objectives indicated above and to deal on behalf of shipping with agencies in such related fields as telecommunication and aviation.

ITO was planned under the auspices of the Economic and Social Council. After considerable preparatory work, a Charter was drafted at a United Nations Conference on Trade and Employment which met in Havana from November, 1947, to March, 1948. Its purposes and objectives are a balanced and expanding world economy; promotion of the economic development of underdeveloped countries, access on equal terms to needed markets and productive facilities; reduction of tariffs and other trade barriers; elimination of measures disrupting economic progress; and promotion of cooperation in fields relating to international trade.

Each of the "specialized agencies" of the United Nations has its own charter or constitution, sphere of action, structure,[10] budget, and staff, in accordance with the principle of functional organization. Although each of these agencies

---

[10] Although there are variations in details and terminology, the specialized agencies follow the same general pattern of international organization. There is an over-all conference or assembly, which meets periodically and is the highest authority of the agency; an executive board or its equivalent, which is responsible for directing the agency between meetings of its conference; and a secretariat, which performs the staff administrative functions assigned to the agency.

has a separate and distinct identity, they are not completely autonomous and unrelated to each other. They are "brought into relationship" with the United Nations, by means of agreements which are negotiated by the Economic and Social Council and approved by the General Assembly. This is necessary because of the obvious relation between their various activities and the objectives of the United Nations in the general field of international economic and social cooperation. Also, it is necessary because their various activities are not mutually exclusive but involve a considerable degree of overlapping and concern for different phases of essentially the same problems. Health, food, and refugees; aviation and meteorology; finances, currency, and international trade; labor, food, and education represent only a few of the more obvious interconnections between the work of the various specialized agencies. The principle of functional organization applied to related activities has the advantages of concentrating effort on specific areas of interest, but it does create the problem of coordination. It is a very difficult administrative task to achieve an effective working arrangement, which is neither thwarted by resistance from specialized interests nor allowed to evaporate into lip service to the general principle of coordination.

The agreements which have been concluded fall into three general patterns, with some minor variations within each group. The most detailed agreements, and the most effective from the viewpoint of coordination, are those concluded with ILO, FAO, ICAO, UNESCO, WHO, and IRO. Each of these agreements provides for reciprocal representation without vote at meetings of organs where matters of concern to the organization in question are being considered. Reciprocal proposal of agenda items is provided for. The specialized agency agrees to transmit a regular report on its activities, and provision is made for the exchange of information and documents. There are detailed provisions for cooperation in administrative matters, especially personnel, budgetary, and financial procedures. It was not possible to reach agreement on a common headquarters for the specialized agencies. The desirability of the eventual development of a unified civil service was recognized. With respect to budgetary and financial relationships, each agreement provides for consultation on appropriate arrangements for including the budget of the specialized agency within the general budget of the United Nations. Pending the conclusion of supplementary arrangements, there is consultation at the top administrative level on the preparation and transmission of the budgets and on the consideration of financial matters of common concern.

The second pattern is found in the agreements with UPU and ITU, both highly technical and long-established agencies. The provisions in these cases are more general. With respect to budgetary and financial matters, these two specialized agencies merely agree that they will transmit their annual budgets to the United Nations and that the General Assembly may make recommendations on them. They do not promise to abide by these recommendations.

The third pattern, providing even more autonomy for the specialized agencies, is found in the agreements with the Bank and the Fund. These two are recognized as "independent" international organizations. The right of reciprocal representation is limited, as representatives of the United Nations are permitted to attend only meetings of the Board of Governors. The United Nations recognizes that "it would be sound policy to refrain from making recommendations to the Bank," and there are limitations to safeguard confidential information. The full autonomy of the Bank and the Fund in deciding the form and content of their budgets is recognized. This position of relative autonomy and independence was justified on the basis of the special nature and responsibility of these two agencies.

It will be evident from the above discussion that the Economic and Social Council's function of coordination with respect to the specialized agencies is a very important and complex one. Its responsibilities in this connection, together with the coordination and supervision of its own subsidiary bodies, are as broad as the wide and expanding field of intergovernmental economic and social cooperation among members of the United Nations. Thus, the Economic and Social Council has a key role in developing the prerequisites of a stable and orderly world. Its functions of coordination, however, are not limited to intergovernmental cooperation. Article 71 of the Charter provides that the Council "may make suitable arrangements for consultation with non-governmental organizations which are concerned with matters within its competence."

The rapid growth of activities transcending national boundaries during the second half of the nineteenth century led to the organization of a large number of agencies concerned with a variety of interests and problems. These were usually described as "private international organizations" to distinguish them from the public, or intergovernmental, organizations such as UPU and ITU.[11] The term "nongovernmental organization" is more descriptive, however, and it is questionable as to whether the word "private" carries accurate connotations for such organizations as the International Federation of Agricultural Producers, the International Chamber of Commerce, or the American Federation of Labor.

Two categories of nongovernmental organizations (NGO's) have consultative status with the Economic and Social Council. Category A includes those which have a basic interest in most of the activities of the Council and are closely linked with the economic and social life of the area which they represent. They may submit items for inclusion on the provisional agenda of the Council. They are permitted to present written statements limited to 2,000 words in length and, with the permission of the Council, to make ex-

[11] See p. 31.

planatory oral statements. They may also send observers to all the public meetings of the Council. Category B includes organizations which have a special competence but are concerned specifically with only a few of the fields of activity covered by the Council. They do not have the authority to submit items for the provisional agenda, but they are permitted to observe the public meetings and to present written statements limited to 500 words in length; they may also be invited to consult with committees of the Council.

By June, 1951, a total of ninety-five nongovernmental organizations had been brought into consultative arrangement with the Economic and Social Council. Nine of these [12] were in category A and the remaining eighty-six in category B.[13] The language of Article 71 of the Charter uses the term "nongovernmental organization" without the qualifying adjective "international." It was felt, however, that national organizations should normally present their views through their governments or through international organizations to which they might belong. National organizations may be included in the list after consultation with the member state concerned if they represent a field not covered by any international organization or have special experience upon which the Economic and Social Council wishes to draw. Of the ninety-five organizations with consultative status, eighty-eight are international and seven (all in category B) are national organizations.

At a meeting of the Council on February 27, 1950, unanimous approval was given to certain revisions in the procedure for consultative arrangements, on the basis of recommendations by the Council Committee on Non-Governmental Organizations (Council NGO Committee). The principal change was to emphasize the importance of consultation at the working level, in order that items coming from the NGO's would reach the Council itself only after careful preliminary consideration. It was felt that this would make possible a more effective use of the consultative arrangements and would discourage the practice of submitting items and statements for merely propagandistic purposes.

ORGANIZATION AND PROCEDURE

The Economic and Social Council has developed a rather complex organizational structure, as might be expected from its broad terms of reference and

[12] International Confederation of Trade Unions, International Chamber of Commerce, International Co-operative Alliance, International Federation of Agricultural Producers, International Federation of Christian Trade Unions, International Organization of Employers, Inter-Parliamentary Union, World Federation of Trade Unions, and World Federation of United Nations Associations.

[13] With an alphabetical range from Agudas Israel World Organization to World's Young Women's Christian Association, and with an amazing variety of interest groups. For a list, see *The Economic and Social Council, op. cit.,* pp. 97–100. The former category C was merged with category B in 1950.

the great variety of economic and social matters which come within its area of concern.   There are five types of subsidiary organs reporting to the Council: functional commissions, regional commissions, standing committees, *ad hoc* committees, and special bodies.

The functional commissions are small expert bodies designed to advise the Council on specific aspects of its work.   They vary in size from twelve to eighteen members.   States are elected as members of the commissions. They in turn nominate individuals, after consultation with the Secretary-General, in order to secure balanced representation in the various fields. These nominations must be confirmed by the Council.   Functional commissions have been set up for the following subjects: economic and employment, transport and communications, statistical, human rights, social, status of women, narcotic drugs, fiscal, and population.   In some cases, subcommissions have been established.

There are three regional commissions, one for Europe, one for Asia and the Far East, and one for Latin America.   Each consists of the members of the United Nations in its area and certain other interested states.   Each commission has the functions, for the area concerned, of facilitating concerted action for economic reconstruction and raising the level of economic activity; investigating and studying economic and technological problems and developments; and collecting, evaluating, and disseminating economic, technological, and statistical information.

The names of the standing committees are self-explanatory.   They are the Committee on Negotiations with Inter-Governmental Agencies; Committee on Arrangements for Consultation with Non-Governmental Organizations; Agenda Committee; and Interim Committee on Programme of Meetings.

Examples of *ad hoc* committees, established from time to time to deal with particular problems, are those on Genocide, Appeal for Children, and Procedure.

One of the special bodies is the Permanent Central Opium Board, composed of eight persons appointed for five years by the Economic and Social Council. Members are to be connected with and have a knowledge of the situation in drug-manufacturing and drug-consuming countries, but they are not to hold any office which puts them in a position of direct dependence upon their governments.   This Board is concerned with the general international supervision of the narcotics trade.   The supervisory body consists of four experts who make an estimate of needs for narcotic drugs for medical and scientific purposes, and publish an annual statement fixing the limits for imports and manufacture.   The United Nations International Children's Emergency Fund (UNICEF) uses contributions from governments, voluntary agencies, and individuals for the benefit of children and adolescents of countries which were the victims of aggression, for child-health purposes generally, and to safeguard the health of expectant and nursing mothers. The Administrative Committee on Co-ordination is composed of the Secretary-General of the United Nations, as chairman, and the corresponding officers of the specialized agencies. Its purpose is to implement the coordination of activities and to prevent duplication of work. The Interim Co-ordinating Committee for International Commodity Arrangements keeps informed of and facilitates consultation or action with respect to commodity problems.

In 1951, an *ad hoc* committee set up to review the organization and operation of the Council recommended that three regular sessions be held each year; that there be an annual program of work with related groups of subjects; and that items on the agenda be discussed in plenary sessions in so far as possible. Recommendations were also made for streamlining the organization of the functional commissions and subcommissions in order to reduce the organizational complexity.

Subject to the general provisions of the Charter, the Economic and Social Council determines its own rules of procedure. At least two regular sessions are held each year, one of which takes place shortly before the opening of the regular session of the General Assembly. Special sessions may be held if necessary. Each session is held at the seat of the United Nations, unless the Council decides otherwise.[14] Each year at the beginning of its first meeting the Council elects a President and two Vice-Presidents. They are eligible for reelection, but none of them may hold office after the country which he represents has ceased to be a member of the Council. The President declares the opening and closing of each meeting, directs the discussion, ensures observance of the rules of procedure, accords the right to speak, puts questions to a vote, and announces decisions.

Each member of the Economic and Social Council is permitted to have one representative at its meetings. Decisions are made by a majority of those present and voting. The meetings are held in public sessions unless the Council decides otherwise. The provisional agenda for each session is drawn up by the Secretary-General in consultation with the President of the Council. The official languages are English, French, Chinese, Russian, and Spanish. The first two of these are working languages. The system of simultaneous translation is the same as that used by the General Assembly.[15] Summary records of the public meetings of the Council, its committees and subsidiary bodies, are prepared by the Secretariat and made available to the public. The records of private meetings are made available as the Council may decide.

[14] The first regular session, early in 1946, was held in London. Beginning in 1948, one session each year has been held in Geneva.

[15] See p. 129.

TABLE 4. MEMBERSHIP IN ECONOMIC AND SOCIAL COUNCIL
1946–1951 [1]

1946	1947	1948	1949	1950	1951
Belgium			....
Canada	....		....
Chile	.........................../....................................
China	.........................../....................................
France	.........................../....................................
Peru	.........................../....................................
Cuba	....
Czechoslovakia	....			....
India	....		....
Norway	....
Soviet Union	............/.................................../............
United Kingdom	............/.................................../............
Colombia						
Greece						
Lebanon	/................................
Ukraine						
United States	/..................................../........................
Yugoslavia						
	Netherlands	....
	Venezuela	....
	Turkey	....
	Byelorussia	....
	New Zealand	....
		Brazil	....
		Poland	........................./............
		Australia	....
		Denmark	....
				Mexico	....
				Iran	....
				Pakistan	....
					Philippines
					Sweden
					Uruguay

[1] The first six countries above were originally elected for three years each, the next six for two years each, and the next six for one year each. A vertical line indicates immediate reelection. Belgium resigned at the end of 1946 and was elected to a regular term beginning in 1949. Canada, Czechoslovakia and India were elected a second time after intervals of nonmembership. It is suggested that the student, on the basis of the above chart, list the expiring terms and the new members for each year to determine the extent of regional or bloc representation. Note especially how Belgium and the Netherlands have exchanged places on the Economic and Social Council and on the Security Council (see p. 151).

Chapter 11

THE TRUSTEESHIP COUNCIL

The Charter (Article 7) includes the Trusteeship Council among the six principal organs of the United Nations. It is given a position of dignity in the structure of the United Nations, but it is nevertheless a subordinate body. It functions as an auxiliary organ to the General Assembly in supervising the administration of nonstrategic trust territories, and to the Security Council in the case of strategic areas.

The Trusteeship Council is constituted quite differently from the Mandates Commission under the League of Nations. It is composed of member states, while the members of the Mandates Commission were experts appointed by the League of Nations Council and were not representatives of their governments. Undoubtedly in large measure because of this difference in character, the Trusteeship Council is a more vigorous body than was the Mandates Commission, but it is also more political. Despite the requirement of the Charter that the interests of the inhabitants of the trust territories be the first consideration in the deliberations of the Council, this is by no means always the case. It is sometimes used, as are all other bodies of the United Nations, as a forum for ideological propaganda. It may be argued that while the Charter does not set up a council of independent experts (like the Mandates Commission) it does expect the representatives of the members to be specialists on colonial problems, for Article 86, clause 2, provides that "each Member of the Trusteeship Council shall designate one specially qualified person to represent it therein." It is not clear that this was meant to be an enforceable qualification, since no one is expressly empowered to determine whether the representatives are "specially qualified." So far, no attempt has been made to disqualify a representative, and it is very doubtful whether any member would admit the authority of the Council to do so.

The Trusteeship Council is constituted in a complicated manner, because of certain basic considerations which underlie its organization. First, it was considered necessary to give automatic membership to all states administering trust territories. Secondly, it was felt that these states should be balanced by an equal number of nonadministering states. Thirdly, since all the Great Powers had a keen interest in the colonial problem and it was improbable that all of them would become administering states, provision had to be made to ensure the membership of each on the Council. This is done by giving all the permanent members of the Security Council membership in the Trusteeship Council. In summary, the Council is composed of (1) members administering trust territories; (2) such of the permanent members of the Security Council, *i.e.*, the Five Great Powers, as are not administering trust territories; and (3) as many other members elected for three-year terms by the General Assembly as may be necessary to equalize the number of members who administer and those who do not administer trust territories.

The language of Article 86 is not wholly clear as to the composition of the Trusteeship Council in case the number of members administering trust territories is less than or only equal to the number of permanent members not administering trust territories. There would then be no occasion to call on the third, or elective category, since the number of nonadministering states would equal or outnumber the administering states without the election of additional nonadministering states. Would the Council be legally constituted in this case? Presumably it would, for obviously the third category was added primarily to prevent the administering states from having a majority of votes in the Council, and secondarily to give small states representation. The drafters of this article assumed, however, that at least three of the five Great Powers would become administering states and that the above contingency was not likely to occur.

Because of the peculiar provisions governing its constitution, the Trusteeship Council could not be set up until some trust agreements had been approved and some territories thereby placed under the trusteeship system. This involved some delay, as the procedure laid down by Article 79 for approval of the agreements involved difficulties of interpretation. The procedure envisages two separate steps: (1) an agreement by "the states directly concerned," and (2) approval of the agreement by the General Assembly or the Security Council, depending upon whether the territory concerned was to be a nonstrategic or a strategic trust area. Beyond the statement that in case of territories held under mandate by a member of the United Nations the mandatory power must be a party to the agreement, the term "states directly concerned" is nowhere defined. In effect, "the states directly concerned" became the state which was in control of the territory, which in all cases but one also happened to be the mandatory power. The Soviet Union contended that all the Great Powers were included in the meaning of the disputed phrase, and that for this reason they had been made permanent members of the Trusteeship Council. However, once an agreement has been approved by the General Assembly or the Security Council, the validity of the agreement can no longer be questioned.

On December 13, 1946, the General Assembly approved agreements for eight of the former mandates, with the former mandatories named as administering states. The Trusteeship Council could now be set up. Australia, Belgium, France, New Zealand, and the United Kingdom became members of the Council as administering states, while China, the Soviet Union, and the United States became members by virtue of being permanent members of the Security Council. Since the administering states numbered five and the nonadministering members only three, two members had to be elected by the General Assembly in order to make the membership of the Trusteeship Council complete. The General Assembly elected Mexico and Iraq as members for a term of three years. The Trusteeship Council met in opening session on March 26, 1947. On the ground that it regarded the trust agreements as not in conformity with the Charter, the Soviet Union refused to participate in the elections and did not designate a representative until April 21, 1948.

As a result of the approval by the Security Council on April 2, 1947, of the strategic-area trusteeship agreement for the former Japanese mandated islands submitted by the United States, the Trusteeship Council had to be enlarged. By the change of status of the United States, the number of administering states had increased to six, while the number of nonadministering states had declined to four. Thus two additional members had to be elected to the Council. The General Assembly elected Costa Rica and the Philippines for three-year terms. When the terms of Iraq and Mexico expired in 1949, Iraq was reelected for three years and Argentina was elected to replace Mexico. To complete the unexpired term of Costa Rica, which had resigned, the General Assembly elected the Dominican Republic. The General Assembly, in 1950, reelected the Dominican Republic for a term of three years and elected Thailand to replace the Philippines.

The present (1952) members of the Trusteeship Council are as follows:

A. Administering states
   Australia
   Belgium
   France
   New Zealand
   United Kingdom
   United States of America

B. Permanent members of the Security Council not administering territories:
   China
   Soviet Union

C. Elected nonadministering states:
   Iraq (1947–1949; 1950–1952)
   Argentina (1950–1952)
   Dominican Republic (1951–1953)
   Thailand (1951–1953)

A pattern of "bloc" representation has emerged in the elections to the Trusteeship Council. Of the four elected states members, two are from

Latin America, one from the Arab League, and one from Asia. When there are so few seats to distribute, "bloc" representation becomes difficult, though the fact that several of the usual groups are assured representation as administering states or as permanent members of the Security Council simplifies the problem considerably. South Asia, the Arab countries, and Latin America are the three regions which do not have automatic representation on the Trusteeship Council; hence there is much justification for adhering to the pattern which seems to be consciously followed.

An anomalous situation arose when the 1950 General Assembly approved the trusteeship agreement for Somaliland, with Italy as the administering state. As an administering state, Italy would automatically become a member of the Trusteeship Council, if Italy were a member of the United Nations, which it is not. Its application for membership has been vetoed by the Soviet Union. To meet this difficulty, the Trusteeship Council has, in effect, accorded Italy a limited membership. It adopted twelve new rules of procedure, which gave Italy the right to participate without vote in the Council's deliberations on Somaliland and on general questions concerning the trusteeship system. Members of the Advisory Council for Somaliland, which was created by the General Assembly to assist and advise Italy in its administration of the territory, may also participate in discussions on that territory. On February 23, 1951, the Trusteeship Council passed a resolution requesting the General Assembly to include in the agenda of the sixth regular session "the question of the full participation of Italy in the work of the Trusteeship Council."

ORGANIZATION, VOTING, AND PROCEDURE

The Charter (Article 90) speaks only of a President, but the Council under its own rules has also a Vice-President. They are elected "by secret and separate ballots" at the beginning of the regular session in June from among the representatives of the members of the Council. The Council seems to have adopted the practice of alternating these positions between administering and nonadministering members; that is, when the President is a representative of a member of the first group, the Vice-President is chosen from among the representatives of the second, and vice versa. The President may appoint one of his alternates or advisers to participate in the proceedings and to vote in the Council, but in this case the President may not exercise his right to vote.

Each member of the Council has one vote. Though the permanent members of the Security Council are also permanent members of the Trusteeship Council, they do not have a veto. Decisions are made by a majority vote of the members present and voting. The Council meets in regular sessions but may be convened at any time on the request of a majority of its members.

The Trusteeship Council is authorized by the Charter to adopt its own rules of procedure.

POWERS AND ACTIVITIES

The Trusteeship Council assists the General Assembly in supervising the administration of nonstrategic trust areas and operates under its authority. It also assists the Security Council in performing "those functions of the United Nations under the trusteeship system relating to political, economic, social and educational matters in the strategic areas."

The Trusteeship Council carries out its functions chiefly in the three ways authorized by Article 87: (1) considering reports submitted by the administering authority, (2) accepting and examining petitions, and (3) sending missions to investigate conditions in the trust territories. Each administering authority must submit an annual report for each of its trust territories. In preparing this report it must follow a detailed questionnaire of nearly 250 questions prepared by the Trusteeship Council on the political, economic, social, and educational advancement of the inhabitants of the territories entrusted to its administration. Specialized agencies are invited to study these annual reports and make observations and suggestions. When the annual written report is examined by the Council, a special representative of the administering authority is given a temporary seat in order that he may give a further oral explanation and answer technical questions. Following this examination and general debate, the Council drafts a report of its own, which is incorporated in its annual report to the General Assembly, in the case of nonstrategic territories and areas, and to the Security Council in the case of strategic areas. Each report contains, in addition to a statement on conditions in the territory, the conclusions and recommendations of the Council, and also the individual views of its members.

The Trusteeship Council is also authorized by the Charter to "accept petitions and examine them in consultation with the administering authority." According to the Council's rules of procedure, petitions must, as a general rule, be presented in writing, though in certain circumstances they may be presented orally. Petitions are always presented to the administering authority for comment before the Council examines and acts on them. Petitions may be presented not only by individuals and organizations in the territories but also by others if they concern the affairs of one or more trust territories or the operation of the trusteeship system generally.

The number of petitions submitted to the Council is very large. During its first five sessions the Council considered 124 petitions and had a backlog of hundreds more. The 1949 General Assembly asked the Council to take measures to expedite their examination and disposal. Nearly a hundred petitions awaited the consideration of the eighth session (February, 1951) of the Council. The petitions cover a wide range of subjects, such as "property claims, land titles, denial of civil and human rights, racial discrimination, pooɪ educational services, and appeals for greater participation in local adminis tration. Many of the petitioners present personal grievances. For instance, Mr. H. O. Kallaghe, of Sumbawanga-Ulika in Tanganyika, claims the return of a dowry from his wife. He was forced to divorce her, he says, 'without any specific reason.' " [1]

Some of the petitions, however, deal with very important problems and issues. For example, the people of Western Samoa, through their representa-tives, petitioned for the right of self-government. The administering author-ity, New Zealand, asked the Council to send a mission to examine the problem on the spot. As a result, the Council sent a special mission to Western Samoa, under the chairmanship of Francis B. Sayre, the United States representative on the Council. After spending most of July and August, 1947, in Samoa, the mission recommended some far-reaching changes in policy which were adopted by the government of New Zealand. Other petitions have raised such questions as administrative unions of trust with nontrust territories and the unification of Ewe peoples—questions which became major issues.

The petition from the All Ewe Conference, which came before the Trustee-ship Council at its second session, raised an important but difficult problem. The Ewes are a West African tribe whose people are distributed over three territories: French Togo; Togoland, under British administration; and the Gold Coast Colony, also British. The Ewes desire to be united under a single administration. The consideration of this problem has taken up much time of the Trusteeship Council, and considerable time of the General As-sembly as well. The British and French governments have set up a Con-sultative Commission elected by the Ewes and have taken other measures to satisfy the natural desire of this tribe for administrative and ultimately po-litical unification, but the Ewes do not regard them as adequate.

Lastly, the Trusteeship Council may provide for periodic visits to the trust territories, subject only to the condition that these visits must be "at times agreed upon with the administering authority." This is a power which the Mandates Commission frequently wished it had, but which was never granted it, because of the opposition of the colonial powers in the Council of the League of Nations. The Trusteeship Council is making regular and effective use of this means of acquiring firsthand information about the conditions and problems of the trust territories and the spirit and quality of their ad-ministration. The first regular mission visited Tanganyika and Ruanda-Urundi in July, August, and September of 1948. Tanganyika is a British-administered trust territory, and Ruanda-Urundi a Belgian-administered one, both in East Africa. The second regular visiting mission went to West

[1] "Important Issues before the Eighth Session of the Trusteeship Council," *United Nations Bulletin*, Vol. X, No. 3, Feb. 1, 1951.

Africa, spending the last two months of 1949, in the four trust territories of British and French Cameroons and British and French Togoland. The third mission, in the spring of 1950, visited the trust territories in the Pacific— New Guinea, Western Samoa, Nauru, and the Trust Territory of the Pacific Islands. A fourth regular visiting mission, in 1951, visited the trust territories in East Africa. This was the second mission to Tanganyika and Ruanda-Urundi and the first to Somaliland under Italian administration. It is planned to send out one regular visiting mission each year, with the hope that each of the territories may be visited every three or four years.

Periodic visiting missions play a very significant role in the work of the Trusteeship Council in supervising the administration of the various trust territories, though apparently their organization and methods are not beyond improvement. A resolution adopted by the General Assembly in November, 1950, contains a number of suggestions for improving their organization and functional methods. The General Assembly was of the opinion that the work of the missions would be more effective if they visited fewer territories on any one trip and remained longer in each territory.

To serve as a reminder to both inhabitants and the administering authority of the special status of the territory, and as a symbol of the ideals and aspirations of the trusteeship system, the 1949 General Assembly recommended that the blue and white flag of the United Nations be flown in each trust territory, alongside the flag of the administering country.

Chapter 12

THE SECRETARIAT

The Secretariat consists of the Secretary-General and the staff of the United Nations.

It is the Secretariat, more than any other organ, which transforms the United Nations from a series of periodic meetings of Assembly and Councils into a permanent and cohesive organization. It is the main centripetal force in the international system. Without the Secretariat, the United Nations would be deprived of its center of communication and coordination, its *international* core as distinct from the national character of the delegations, which make up the Assembly and the Councils.[1]

The Secretary-General is appointed by the General Assembly upon the recommendation of the Security Council. When a candidate is being considered for recommendation, the Security Council meets in private session. The General Assembly may reject a name submitted to it. In that case, however, it cannot proceed to make its own choice but must wait until another recommendation is made. Voting on this question is by secret ballot.

The appointment of a candidate requires only a simple majority of those present and voting in the General Assembly, as contrasted with a two-thirds majority for election of states to membership on the Security Council, the Economic and Social Council, and the Trusteeship Council. The recommendation of a candidate by the Security Council, however, requires at least seven votes including the concurring votes of all the permanent members. Thus, the choice of a Secretary-General is in effect subject to the veto. This means that China, France, Great Britain, the Soviet Union, and the United States must be in agreement on a candidate if the office is to be filled. Considerable negotiation is involved, and it is to be expected that each Secretary-General will come from a small country and will not be too closely affiliated with the policies of any one of the Great Powers.

The first Secretary-General, Mr. Trygve Lie, is a Norwegian. When he was appointed on February 1, 1946, he was the unanimous choice of the Security Council and there were only three adverse votes in the General Assembly. On several occasions since then, Mr. Lie has been "in the middle" of the East-West conflict. No one could please both sides at all times, and

[1] *The United Nations Secretariat,* Carnegie Endowment, New York, 1950, pp. 8–9.

Mr. Lie has been called both a "Soviet spy" and a "running-dog of the imperialists." The present Secretary-General, fortunately, has not considered it his job to please one side or the other but has taken an international point of view and has tried to strengthen the United Nations as a true world organization.

The term of office for a Secretary-General is not specified in the Charter. A period of three years was considered at the San Francisco Conference, but this proposal was dropped when it appeared that the veto would apply to a recommendation by the Security Council. If the permanent members had to agree unanimously, a three-year term would be too short. Frequent reelection might either deprive a Secretary-General of his independence or force him to leave office as soon as he gained experience in the position. The General Assembly decided, in January, 1946, that (1) the term of appointment should be such as to enable a man of eminence and high attainment to take the position; (2) the first Secretary-General should be appointed for five years, with eligibility for reappointment; (3) the length of term might be modified later in the light of experience; and (4) it was desirable that no member should offer a retiring Secretary-General any governmental position in which the confidential information he had obtained might be a source of embarrassment to other members.

The original five-year term expired on February 1, 1951. When this question was taken up during the fall of 1950, the Security Council was unable to agree on a recommendation. The Soviet Union opposed a new term for Mr. Lie, on the grounds that he was incapable of being an objective and unbiased person. The United States indicated that it would not support any other candidate, since it would view any attempt to remove him from office as punishment for doing his duty in the Korean case. When this deadlock was not broken by a series of meetings and negotiations, the General Assembly adopted a resolution by a vote of 46 to 5, with 8 abstentions, to continue Mr. Lie in office for three more years. Only the Soviet bloc voted in the negative. The representative of China abstained from supporting Mr. Lie because he "went out of his way to circulate a memorandum which amounted to a plea" to admit the Chinese Communists to the Security Council. The Arab states abstained because they thought that Mr. Lie had not been entirely impartial in the Palestine case.

The position of Secretary-General is stronger in the United Nations than it was in the League of Nations. There are two reasons for this. One is that the Charter grants this office more important powers and functions than did the Covenant of the League. The other reason has to do with the incumbent of the office. Sir Eric Drummond, the Secretary-General of the League of Nations for the first thirteen years of its existence, did not assume responsibilities of direction and leadership. Under him, the office was a rather colorless and routine one. Mr. Lie, however, has used the powers given him in the Charter and has exercised a rather forceful leadership in behalf of the United Nations.

FUNCTIONS OF THE SECRETARY-GENERAL

Article 97 of the Charter provides that the Secretary-General shall be the "chief administrative officer" of the United Nations, and it is this title which describes his position and essential functions.   The responsibilites of this office are by no means restricted to administrative duties in the routine managerial sense.   It should be noted, on the other hand, that the Charter does not designate the Secretary-General as a chief executive, although he has exercised some functions which may be described as executive in type.   Examples of this are his responsibilities for implementing decisions of the other organs in cooperation with the members and his capacity of spokesman for the United Nations as a whole.   It would be quite misleading, however, to think of the Secretary-General's position as analogous to that of the chief executive of a national government.   There are some indications of an embryonic executive authority, and as the United Nations becomes stronger, these trends may develop in a manner which it is difficult to foresee.   At present, the principle of "sovereign equality" of members means that any real executive authority for the Secretary-General must exist by sufferance and be restricted to a narrow range.   Conversely, all the wide variety of functions exercised by that office can be classified as "executive" in the traditional sense only in a very arbitrary way.   In short, the "chief administrative officer" of the United Nations holds a unique position which can be understood to best advantage by reference to the actual duties and responsibilities involved.

The functions of the Secretary-General may be grouped under three headings—administrative and service, political, and representational.

The *administrative and service* function includes the responsibility for organizing and directing the complex and varied activities which are necessary for the operation of the Organization.   The staffs of the other organs, with the exception of the International Court of Justice,[2] form a part of the Secretariat. The Secretary-General, therefore, is responsible for the performance of the essential staff work required if the General Assembly, the Security Council, the Economic and Social Council, and the Trusteeship Council are to function efficiently.   The provision of space, utilities, supplies, and equipment; the recruitment of clerks, stenographers, translators, janitors, and guards; the operation of a transportation service and a cafeteria; the compilation of information and the preparation of reports; the maintenance of records and the distribution of documents—these are a sample of the elements in the complex machinery of an international secretariat.

---

[2] The Court has its headquarters at The Hague and has its own staff, under the direction of the Registrar.

A large number of resolutions passed by the General Assembly provide for some action on the part of the Secretary-General. This may involve, for example, communication with member governments, ascertaining the steps to be taken to give effect to the Assembly's recommendations, or the provision of information needed for consideration of a matter. He may be asked to facilitate consultation among members on a given subject, as in the case of relief plans and programs in 1947. He has been asked to prepare recommendations on the operation of a United Nations telecommunication system, the organization of a United Nations postal service, and other matters. The Secretary-General also has been given definite administrative assignments—for example, the organization of the United Nations Appeal for Children (UNAC).

The administrative and service staff work involves certain technical functions. Studies are undertaken and expert advice given to the other organs upon their request. A statistical unit has been established to examine, evaluate, and analyze statistics from governments, specialized agencies, and other sources. This unit publishes useful statistical information and coordinates the statistical activities of the specialized agencies. Some of the assignments given to the Secretariat in the field of reports and studies include analysis of information submitted on the economic, social, and educational conditions in non-self-governing territories; surveys of world economic conditions and trends; preparatory work for the International Law Commission; and preparation of suggestions concerning the form and character of reports of commissions and other subsidiary organs of the Economic and Social Council. Another technical function is the preparation of draft conventions, as in the case of the draft convention on genocide.

Important financial responsibilities also are involved in the administrative and service functions of the Secretary-General. Subject to the authority and regulations of the General Assembly, he prepares the budget of the United Nations, allocates funds, controls expenditures, collects the contributions from members, and has the custody of all funds. The Secretary-General has also been delegated the task of consulting with the specialized agencies and undertaking to develop arrangements for common fiscal controls and for common budgetary, administrative, and financial practices.[3]

A special case of an administrative responsibility imposed on the Secretary-General by terms of the Charter is found in Article 102, which provides that every treaty and international agreement entered into by any member of the United Nations must be registered with the Secretariat and published by it.

The problem of administrative coordination is a difficult one in an agency like the United Nations, with its sixty member states, six principal organs, various subsidiary organs and specialized agencies, and broad scope of functions. The centrifugal tendencies are very great, but the Organization will

[3] The work resulting from these responsibilities is, of course, carried out by appropriate staff assistance under the direction of the Secretary-General.

ORIGIN, STRUCTURE, AND PROCEDURE

be relatively ineffective unless it can operate as an integrated system with a coherent over-all program embodying generally recognized priorities. With the natural divisions of opinion as to what should be done and how, with the inevitable vested interests in this or that activity, and with the great diversity of cultural backgrounds found among the personnel, strong leadership is needed to see that the United Nations is a real *system* and not a loose aggregation of separate blocs.

The General Assembly has certain supervisory functions, and the Economic and Social Council has coordinating responsibilities in its fields of effort.[4] It remains for the Secretary-General, however, to supply administrative coordination through staff activities and daily operations. For example, the agreements bringing the specialized agencies into relationship with the United Nations require continuous positive effort for their implementation. The Secretary-General meets with the directors of these organizations, provides personnel for liaison purposes, arranges for an exchange of documents and information, consults on the division of work, and performs other tasks in this connection.[5] Furthermore, the preparation of the various annual reports in the Secretariat offers an opportunity to describe the activities and programs in perspective and in relation to each other. This is an invaluable assistance to the General Assembly and to the Economic and Social Council in the establishment of priorities. The Secretary-General, of course, has an important task of administrative coordination in securing proper organization and teamwork of the Secretariat itself.

The Secretary-General has important functions which may be described as *political,* meaning that they require the capacity to exercise discretion and influence in the formulation of policy. The chief source of authority in this connection is found in Article 99 of the Charter, which provides that "the Secretary-General may bring to the attention of the Security Council any matter which in his opinion may threaten the maintenance of international peace and security." This goes beyond any right conferred upon the Secretary-General of the League of Nations, who could call a meeting of the Council only when asked to do so by a member.

The provisions of Article 99 make it possible for the Secretary-General to secure consideration by the Security Council of a dispute, situation, or other matter which might not be raised by a member of the Council. It also affords even greater opportunities for leadership and the exercise of influence in the United Nations. The fact that the Secretary-General may call attention to "any matter" means that he can present information or state opinions in connection with a dispute or situation already under discussion. Several

---

[4] See Chaps. 8 and 10.

[5] To formalize this arrangement, there has been created an Administrative Committee on Coordination, composed of the Secretary-General as chairman and the corresponding official of each specialized agency.

instances of this have occurred. When the question of Iran was before the Security Council, the Secretary-General submitted a memorandum setting forth his own views on the legal aspects. When the Greek question was being considered in 1946, he reserved the right to make his own inquiries or investigations to determine whether he should consider making any statement to the Council. More recent examples may be found in the very active efforts of Mr. Lie to find some basis for settling the question of the representation of China in the United Nations, in his proposals for a twenty-year program of peace,[6] and in his attempts to find some basis for negotiation among the Great Powers.

Another way in which the Secretary-General exercises a political influence is through the annual report on the work of the Organization. This is prepared each year prior to the opening of the regular session of the General Assembly, and it serves as one basis for the opening debates and statements of policy. The report is much more than a routine summary. It states the main issues, with the Secretary-General's own opinions and recommendations. It has a real influence and, incidentally, is an excellent source of information on the accomplishments and problems of the United Nations from year to year. In addition to presenting his annual report, the Secretary-General may propose items for the agenda of the General Assembly, the Security Council, and the Trusteeship Council. He prepares the provisional agenda for these organs and for the Economic and Social Council, and may make written or oral statements to them. Thus, he is in a position to exercise initiative and influence by making proposals, effecting the establishment of priorities, and advocating the viewpoints which he considers appropriate.

The *representational* function of the Secretary-General arises from the fact that he is the only person who stands for the United Nations as a whole. All the other organs are composed of a number of members and each has a special area of responsibility. The delegations, of course, speak only for individual countries. There is only one Secretary-General, however, and he is concerned with the entire Organization. The Secretary-General represents the United Nations in negotiations with other agencies and with governments, and his office is the normal channel of communication with the United Nations. On occasion he has been empowered by the General Assembly to enter into agreements with states, as in the case of the headquarters agreement.

The Charter provision (Article 98) that the Secretary-General shall act in that capacity in all meetings of the General Assembly and the three Councils is an assurance that there will not be a tendency for each organ to develop its own little secretary-general. In addition, the fact that the staffs serving these organs are a part of the Secretariat underscores the intention and practice of giving the Secretary-General an important central place in the work of the United Nations.

6 See Appendix 20.

The position of the Secretary-General as chief administrative officer, with the functions indicated above, gives both an opportunity and a responsibility for leadership. The powers granted by the Charter are stated in broad terms and are not unduly restrictive on the development of this office. The force of circumstances and the personal qualities of international statesmanship combine to produce a line of development which has interesting and important potentialities. No one can say exactly what the role and status of the Secretary-General will be after a few decades, any more than the later trends in the office of President of the United States could have been predicted in 1789.

ORGANIZATION OF THE SECRETARIAT

The best method for organizing the Secretariat raised some difficult questions of public administration. One view, held by the minority, was that the staff should be organized on the basis of the bodies to be served. There would be a division of the Secretariat to serve the Security Council, one for the General Assembly, and so on. The objections to this were that it might give rise to divided loyalties, and that duplication and waste of time would be difficult to avoid. For example, the regular meetings of the General Assembly and of the Economic and Social Council are held at different times of the year. There is no reason that an economist, or any expert, might not serve one in July and the other in November. This is particularly true since many of the items on which the Economic and Social Council makes recommendations then go to the General Assembly for consideration. If different departments of the Secretariat were maintained for the two organs, separate staffs would be working on the same subject at various stages of progress. Obviously this would be very inefficient.

The majority view was that the organization should be set up on a functional basis. Each department of the Secretariat has distinctive functions but it can serve any organ as occasion requires. The Department of Economic Affairs, for example, serves primarily the Economic and Social Council, but it also is used by the General Assembly, the Trusteeship Council, and other organs as appropriate. As another example, legal experts may be needed in connection with the work of any of the organs. It is better to have one Legal Department than to have a separate legal section for the General Assembly and each of the three Councils.

Although the functional principle was adopted as the basis for organization of the Secretariat, some deviations were introduced for practical reasons. Since the Security Council has exclusive power to deal with military and enforcement measures, there are special units in the Department of Security Council Affairs to serve that organ alone. Also, there are many cases of specialization at subordinate levels; for example, one organizational unit will prepare the provisional agenda for the General Assembly and another will do the same work for the Economic and Social Council. There is no attempt to maintain absolute adherence to any one abstract principle. The conception is rather one of having the organization based on functional needs and, within this general framework, establishing a pattern which will serve the practical needs most effectively. It should also be noted that some departments of the Secretariat are more closely tied to organizational counterparts than others. For example, the Department of Economic Affairs serves primarily the Economic and Social Council, the Second (Economic and Financial) Committee of the General Assembly, and the various advisory commissions in that field; the Legal Department advises or maintains liaison with all the other organs; while the Department of Public Information serves the entire Organization and the general public.

The regional basis of staff organization remains to be mentioned. This is found in the United Nations in connection with the branch office in Geneva, the regional economic commissions, and the various visiting missions. How to secure the most efficient staffing of these groups and maintain an integrated Secretariat is a real problem of administrative management.

A brief description of each major division of the Secretariat will indicate the organizational arrangement and the principal duties of the United Nations staff:

The Department of Security Council Affairs provides such services as notification of meetings and preparation of agenda, reports, and documentation for the Security Council and for the First (Political) Committee of the General Assembly. It obtains information and prepares reports with reference to threats to peace, the pacific settlement of disputes, and the general principles of cooperation; advises the Security Council on rules of procedure; prepares studies on the political aspects of military agreements, and assists in negotiations of such agreements; makes studies on the size of armaments and traffic in arms; participates in investigations and advises on the security aspects of strategic trusteeship areas; and helps to formulate plans related to the application of enforcement measures.

The Department of Economic Affairs provides services and assistance required in connection with economic and statistical problems. It undertakes the publication of economic studies and reports; services international conferences on subjects in this field; and furnishes expert assistance, particularly for underdeveloped countries. It maintains close relations with the various specialized agencies dealing with labor, food and agriculture, trade transport and communications, banking, and finance.

The Department of Social Affairs is responsible for staffing the Third (Social, Humanitarian and Cultural) Committee of the General Assembly; the Economic and Social Council when it deals with problems of human rights, status of women, narcotic drugs, health, refugees, education, and cultural activities; and the subsidiary organs such as the Commission on Human Rights. It prepares the meetings and work programs of these bodies; carries out, according to instructions, any studies or other technical assignments in the social field; issues publications; assists in the preparation of draft conventions; and services international conferences. It keeps in touch, through documentation and reciprocal representation, with specialized agencies and other organizations concerned with labor, health, education, science and culture, and refugees.

The Department of Trusteeship and Information from Non-Self-Governing Territories carries this long and awkward title as an accurate reflection of the two different types of responsibilities for peoples who have not yet reached the stage of self-government.[7] This Department serves the Trusteeship Council, the Fourth (Trusteeship) Committee of the General Assembly, and other organs of the United Nations. It provides assistance on studies and documentation; the drafting and consideration of trusteeship agreements; formulation of questionnaires; examination of reports from the administering authorities; acceptance and examination of petitions; and periodic official visits and surveys.

The Legal Department of the Secretariat advises on legal and constitutional questions, encourages the progressive development and codification of international law, and maintains liaison with the International Court of Justice. This work involves legal assistance and opinions on interpretations of the Charter, draft treaties, resolutions, contracts, claims, and national laws of interest to the United Nations. The staff of this Department negotiates agreements such as those relating to privileges and immunities and it carries out the Secretariat's responsibility for the registration, classification, and publication of treaties.

Conference and General Services is the name of the department which makes arrangements and provides services for the meetings and conferences held under the auspices of the United Nations. It cooperates in scheduling the meetings; provides translation, interpretation, reproduction, and graphic presentation services; edits and publishes the journals and official records; provides general services such as purchasing, transportation arrangements, hotel accommodations, and buildings management; handles mail, cables, telephone, and telegraph services; and supervises the files. This, in an organization the size and complexity of the United Nations, is a tremendous managerial task. This department has about one-half the total number of employees in the Secretariat.

Administrative and Financial Services is the department which plans and executes the personnel, budgetary, and fiscal programs of the United Nations. It provides data and maintains relationships with the other organs and the specialized agencies on these questions; advises the Secretary-General on pro-

[7] See Chap. 11.

posed programs of organization prior to their adoption with respect to their personnel, budgetary, and financial implications; and it is responsible for arranging with member governments for the payment of their contributions.

The Department of Public Information advises the Secretary-General on information policy, and, working with the specialized agencies, it supervises and maintains facilities at headquarters for representatives of all information media; maintains information centers in various parts of the world; provides services for press coverage of United Nations activities and issues informative publications; organizes sales and distribution throughout the world of informative material issued by the United Nations; broadcasts accounts of United Nations activities and provides facilities for commercial and governmental broadcasting services; maintains film and photographic coverage, and encourages the production of films; provides informative material and related services to educational agencies, lecturers, and nongovernmental organizations; prepares surveys of press and radio opinion; and maintains the library and reference services of the United Nations.

Since public opinion is a crucial factor in the success of the United Nations, the information activities are of the greatest importance. A wide variety of media is used, as may be judged from the preceding paragraph. Further mention of a few selected activities is appropriate, however. A service for visitors to headquarters is maintained. They may observe any of the public meetings, subject to the availability of space. A "briefing" program explains the setup, and questions about the Organization will be answered. Experience has shown that permitting visitors to see the United Nations in action is one of the best ways to arouse interest in it. By 1950, visitors to Lake Success and Flushing Meadows were averaging over one thousand a day. When the head of the Soviet delegation, Mr. Malik, returned to assume the Presidency of the Security Council in August, 1950, as many as 23,000 visitors had to be turned away in a single day. Most of the visitors seem to take a sincere interest in the United Nations, and few are so naïve as to make the famous, and perhaps apocryphal, remark that "it's all right, but there are so many foreigners around."

One important project is known as United Nations Radio, broadcasting daily from headquarters in many different languages. When the Security Council took action in the Korean case, United Nations Radio went on the air twenty-four hours a day, seven days a week, broadcasting the news in twenty-seven different languages. In August, 1950, the Security Council became a popular television feature with a villain to hiss and a hero to cheer.

Another example of information work is the designation of various colleges and schools as volunteer educational centers. Materials are furnished and other assistance is given by the Department of Public Information in order to spread knowledge about the United Nations among teachers and through them to the general public.

Each department of the Secretariat is headed by an Assistant Secretary-General. These officials were appointed by the Secretary-General for terms of five years. At the San Francisco Conference, a proposal to have an Assistant Secretary-General of the nationality of each of the Great Powers was defeated because of the opposition of the small countries. The same result, however, has been achieved in practice. The nationalities of the department heads, as of January, 1951, were as follows: Security Council Affairs, the Soviet Union; Economic Affairs, Great Britain; Social Affairs, France; Trusteeship and Information from Non-Self-Governing Territories, China; Public Information, Chile; Legal, Czechoslovakia; Conference and General Services, India; and Administrative and Financial Services, United States.

The Assistant Secretaries-General serve almost entirely as heads of the individual departments. The development has not been in the direction of a general policy group or cabinet which would collaborate on the over-all program. There is a small Executive Office which assists the Secretary-General on those functions which he does not delegate to departments but retains as his personal responsibility. The head of this office is the Executive Assistant to the Secretary-General. If the Secretary-General is absent or unable to perform his functions, he deputizes one of the Assistant Secretaries-General to act for him.

THE STAFF

The staff is appointed by the Secretary-General under regulations made by the General Assembly. Members of the Secretariat are prohibited from seeking or receiving instructions from any government or from any other authority external to the United Nations. They constitute an international civil service. Upon appointment, all members of the staff must subscribe to the following oath or declaration:

I solemnly swear (undertake, affirm, promise) to exercise in all loyalty, discretion and conscience the functions entrusted to me as a member of the international civil service of the United Nations, to discharge those functions and regulate my conduct with the interests of the United Nations only in view, and not to seek or accept instructions in regard to the performance of my duties from any government or other authority external to the Organization.

A person does not lose his national citizenship by accepting employment with the Secretariat, but he serves the entire membership and his first loyalty in connection with his work belongs to the United Nations. There is, accordingly, a sharp distinction between the status of a member of the Secretariat and that of a member of a national delegation. The former performs an international function, while the latter serves the interests of his own country. Member states have an obligation not to seek influence over employees of the Secretariat. Once a staff member has been appointed, his tenure is subject solely to determination by the Secretary-General. This principle was successfully asserted in connection with Czechoslovak nationals on the staff in 1948. If delegates from Communist China are admitted as representatives of that country, the question may arise in a more complex form. It is likely that the Chinese at United Nations headquarters would be divided, at least for a time, between Nationalists functioning as international civil servants and Communists as members and employees of the delegation.

A very interesting situation arose during the Soviet absence from meetings of the Security Council between January and August, 1950. The Assistant Secretary-General for Security Council Affairs is a Russian. It became his duty to make arrangements and provide staff services for the sessions which the Soviet delegation was denouncing as "illegal." While the Soviet representatives stayed away from the meetings, the Russian Assistant Secretary-General continued to perform his duties as an international civil servant. During August two Russians sat side by side at meetings of the Security Council, Mr. Malik as President and Mr. Zinchenko as Assistant Secretary-General. On one occasion, Mr. Malik said that he had a communication to place before the Council, but since the Russian text was not available, he would ask the Assistant Secretary-General to read it. There was some grim humor in this situation: Mr. Malik's English is completely adequate, but the Soviet representative could not in any way imply that the Russian language is in a secondary position; Mr. Zinchenko is also a Russian, and it is the job of the Secretariat to see that all the required translations are available!

One of the most remarkable accomplishments of the United Nations is the success with which several thousand employees from over sixty countries [8] have been molded into an effective working staff. This is especially notable in view of the fact that the job had to be done with great speed and under very difficult world conditions. People of different languages, customs, cultural backgrounds, and administrative practices had to learn to work together effectively. Many problems remain, but the staff has functioned quite well and solid foundations have been laid for a developing international civil service.

An adequate supply of competent and efficient personnel is essential to the growth and success of the United Nations. This means more than technical expertness. An "international outlook" is indispensable. The viewpoint needed has been well described in the following words: [9]

A lack of attachment to any one country does not constitute an international outlook. A superior indifference to the emotions and prejudices of those whose world is bounded by the frontiers of a single state does not constitute an international outlook. A blurred indistinctness of attitude towards all questions, proceeding from a

---

[8] Nationals of nonmember states are eligible for employment.

[9] C. Wilfred Jenks, "Some Problems of an International Civil Service," *Public Administration Review*, Spring, 1943, p. 105.

freedom of prejudice born of lack of vitality, does not constitute an international outlook. The international outlook required of the international civil servant is an awareness made instinctive by habit of the needs, emotions, and prejudices of the peoples of differently-circumstanced countries, as they are felt and expressed by the peoples concerned, accompanied by a capacity for weighing these frequently imponderable elements in a judicial manner before reaching any decision to which they are relevant.

The Charter provides that the paramount consideration in the employment of staff shall be the necessity of securing the highest standards of efficiency, competence, and integrity. Some regard is to be paid to recruitment on as wide a geographical basis as possible. Yet it would be fatal to the development of a real international civil service if positions should be regarded as "spoils" allocated to the disposal of member states. The international outlook would be overshadowed, efficiency might become a secondary consideration, and the authority of the Secretary-General would be difficult to maintain. The geographic distribution of employees remains a difficult problem, especially since the trained and available personnel tends to be concentrated in a few countries. It is to be expected that the lower paid jobs must be filled for the most part by local employees. It follows that American citizens will have a very high proportion of these jobs. Of about 2,900 permanent positions at headquarters in 1950, almost 1,900 were designated as "locally recruited" and slightly more than 1,000 as "internationally recruited." [10] United States nationals held about one-third of these "international" positions. Ten members held three-fourths of them. All the Latin-American countries combined held about 8 per cent of the total, and the Soviet Union, apparently from its own desire, had only twelve positions.

Some countries whose nationals have comparatively small representation among the employees have expressed dissatisfaction with the situation. At the General Assembly session of 1947, a resolution to require allocation of positions in the same ratio as budgetary contributions was defeated by the narrowest margin. The actual distribution of jobs, however, happens to be quite close to the distribution of financial assessments. It is encouraging to note that after great efforts there has been some improvement in the geographic distribution of employees.

The salary classification plan adopted in 1946 was based on a scheme of nineteen grades with three to seven salary steps within each grade. The base salary ranged from $1,580 a year for the first step in Grade 1 to $11,000 for the position of top-ranking director.[11] The recent trend has been toward a

---

[10] The seven lowest salary grades and all linguistic positions were designated as "locally recruited." In addition to the permanent positions, there were at the time several hundred temporary positions at headquarters and about a thousand employees in other locations.

[11] The Secretary-General receives $20,000 plus a representation allowance of the same

grouping of positions in a smaller number of broad categories. A perplexing problem of equitable compensation arises from the fact that some countries exempt salaries paid to their nationals by the United Nations from income taxes, while others do not.[12] The same gross salary becomes a widely variable net salary if uniform treatment as to tax exemption does not exist. Pending the ratification by all members of the Convention on the Privileges and Immunities of the United Nations,[13] employees are in effect reimbursed for the national income taxes which they pay.

UNITED NATIONS FIELD SERVICE

In November, 1949, the General Assembly approved a proposal by the Secretary-General that a United Nations Field Service be established as a part of the staff. It is designed to provide technical and protective services for United Nations missions in the field. Guards have been regularly employed for duty at United Nations headquarters. It was felt by the advocates of the new plan that the staff service to field missions would be strengthened if the guard system were extended and the missions accompanied by aides wearing a United Nations uniform. The Field Service is not to exceed 300 persons. It is not a military force and will not carry weapons, except that side arms may be authorized on special occasions. Despite its small size and nonmilitary character, however, it is an international police force and it creates a precedent for further strengthening of the United Nations along similar lines. In addition to its protective duties, the Field Service has such tasks as handling radio communications and driving trucks.

Training of recruits includes a course in police methods, first-aid instruction, shorthand, and typewriting. Because the jeep is such an essential element in connection with field missions, the recruits are sent to a plant at Toledo, Ohio, for some concentrated instruction on how to keep a jeep in condition under all circumstances.

In addition to the Field Service itself, the General Assembly approved the establishment of a Panel of Field Observers. This consists of a list of names which can be drawn upon for observation duties in connection with truce enforcement, plebiscites, and similar matters.

---

amount, and he is provided with a furnished residence. Each Assistant Secretary-General receives $13,500 plus an allowance which has been fixed at $8,500.

[12] The United States does not exempt an American citizen employed by the United Nations from paying a Federal income tax on his salary.

[13] See Appendix 13.

Chapter 13

THE INTERNATIONAL COURT OF JUSTICE

The International Court of Justice is the principal judicial organ of the United Nations. Provision is made for the Court by Articles 92 to 96 of the Charter, and a detailed Statute to govern its functioning is made an integral part of the Charter by reference. There was some question at the San Francisco Conference as to whether the Permanent Court of International Justice, which had served as a "world court" during the period of the League of Nations,[1] should be continued or replaced by a new organization. Some delegates felt that the continuity of international judicial institutions should be preserved, that the Permanent Court of International Justice represented a great forward step and should not be scrapped, that there were references to it in a large number of treaties, and that its record was a very good one.

On the other hand, the majority thought that it was better to start with a clean slate. The former Court had lapsed so far as election of judges was concerned, and it was not feasible to reinstate the procedure. It was argued that the new Court would be intimately connected with the United Nations and should be created as a part of that system. On any other basis there would be difficulties in membership. Some countries which were not to be initial members of the United Nations had been parties to the Statute of the Permanent Court of International Justice. Conversely, some members of the United Nations (for example, the United States) had never been such parties. On the whole, it seemed better to create a new organizational entity but to preserve the continuity of concept and function. No attempt was made to revive the Permanent Court of International Justice as such, and the International Court of Justice was created as one of the six principal organs of the United Nations. However, the Statute of the present Court is specifically based upon that of the former one. The two instruments are substantially identical, with only the necessary changes in terminology. This identity is even carried to the numbering of the articles of the new Statute, to facilitate reference. For example, Article 38 of the new Statute parallels Article 38 of the earlier one. Emphasis is placed upon the fact that the principal judicial organ of the United

---

[1] See p. 90.

Nations is the successor and heir of the Permanent Court of International Justice.[2]

By provision of the Charter (Article 93), all members of the United Nations are parties to the Statute of the Court. In addition, other countries may be parties to the Statute by accepting conditions determined in each case by the General Assembly upon the recommendation of the Security Council. The conditions which have been laid down are the acceptance of the Statute and of the same obligations as United Nations members with respect to the Court, and an undertaking to contribute to the expenses an amount assessed by the General Assembly after consultation with the government concerned. By July, 1950, Switzerland and the Principality of Liechtenstein had taken advantage of this opportunity. The Court is also open to states not parties to the Statute on conditions laid down by the Security Council. The principal condition which has been established is the acceptance in advance of all the obligations of a party to the Statute for a particular dispute or a general class of disputes.

ELECTION OF JUDGES

One of the major difficulties in creating a world court has been that of a method for selecting the judges. As international organization developed, it was the practice for national governments to appoint personnel, who acted upon instructions and who represented the viewpoints and policies of their respective countries. A genuine judicial proceeding, however, requires impartial judges who do not take orders from the parties to disputes brought before the court. It was necessary, on this account, to find some acceptable method for selecting judges who could function independently of the various governments constituting a world court. But the states of the world have been reluctant to make this type of concession to the needs of international organization. The idea of sovereignty furnished theoretical grounds for insisting that "no state can be bound without its own consent." From a practical point of view, national governments have been slow to surrender the power to settle disputes into the hands of an impartial third party or agency over which they would have no control.

The method of selecting judges [3] for the International Court of Justice is based upon an ingenious and complicated compromise between the prerequisites of a world court and the demands of nationalism. First of all, it is provided that "the Court shall be composed of a body of independent judges,

---

[2] It is of interest to note that articles by Manley O. Hudson, published periodically in the *American Journal of International Law*, refer to both institutions as "the Court." Thus, an article in the *Journal* for January, 1950, is entitled "The Twenty-eighth Year of the World Court."

[3] The judges are known as "members" of the Court, and states are spoken of as "parties to the Statute." It is the states which are "members" of the United Nations.

elected regardless of their nationality from among persons of high moral character, who possess the qualifications required in their respective countries for appointment to the highest judicial offices, or are juriconsults of recognized competence in international law" (Article 2 of the Statute). Although the judges are to be elected "regardless of their nationality," no two of them may be nationals of the same state. Further, to assure that no one country or group will dominate the Court, it is provided that the main forms of civilization and of the principal legal systems of the world shall be represented.

In the actual procedure of selecting the judges, the first step is that of nominations by the national groups in the Permanent Court of Arbitration.[4] No group may nominate more than four persons, not more than two of whom may be of their own nationality. (In case only one vacancy is to be filled, not more than two candidates may be nominated by each group.) Before making these nominations, each national group is supposed to consult its highest court of justice, its legal faculties and schools of law, and its academies devoted to the study of law. When the candidates have been duly nominated, the Secretary-General of the United Nations prepares a list of the persons in alphabetical order. The General Assembly and the Security Council then proceed independently of one another to elect fifteen of these candidates to become the members of the Court. The candidates who receive an absolute majority of votes in both the General Assembly and the Security Council are considered as elected. This provision is an interesting exception to the voting procedure on all other matters. An "absolute majority" means more than 50 per cent of the total number of members, while other decisions in the General Assembly are taken by either a simple or a two-thirds majority of those present and voting. In the Security Council, an absolute majority would be six and all other decisions require at least seven affirmative votes. In electing the judges, no distinction is made between permanent and nonpermanent members, and therefore the "veto" does not apply.

The filling of vacancies and other problems of electing the judges are spelled out in the Statute in precise detail. One example may be of some interest here. Article 10, paragraph 3, of the Statute provides, "In the event of more than one national of the same state obtaining an absolute majority of the votes both of the General Assembly and of the Security Council, the eldest of these only shall be considered as elected."

The judges are elected for terms of nine years, and are eligible for reelection. The terms are staggered, so that the tenure of five judges expires every three years. Vacancies are filled in the same manner as the regular elections, and a judge elected to replace another member holds office for the remainder of his predecessor's term.

[4] See p. 39. In the case of members of the United Nations not represented in the Permanent Court of Arbitration, candidates are nominated by national groups appointed for this purpose by their governments.

By the procedure outlined above, it has been possible to constitute a broadly representative world court [5] composed of a body of independent judges. Although national governments take part in the procedure of nomination and election, the judges are not appointed as representatives of their countries and do not act upon instructions. They are officials of an international judiciary, and as such enjoy diplomatic privileges and immunities.

FUNCTIONS AND POWERS

The International Court of Justice, as the principal judicial organ of the United Nations, has two types of responsibilities. It decides cases brought before it and gives advisory opinions on legal questions.

Only states may be parties in cases before the Court. Jurisdiction extends to all cases which the parties refer to it and all matters provided for in the Charter of the United Nations or in other international agreements. The Charter, however, does not provide for automatic referral of any disputes or cases to the Court.[6] Article 33, which imposes an obligation to seek pacific settlement of international disputes, refers to various methods including "judicial settlement." Under this provision, the parties might use the Court or they might resort to some other judicial procedure. Article 95, which is included in the section of the Charter dealing with the International Court of Justice, expressly provides that "nothing in the present Charter shall prevent Members of the United Nations from entrusting the solution of their differences to other tribunals by virtue of agreements already in existence or which may be concluded in the future." In this connection, it should also be noted that the Security Council in making recommendations as to methods of pacific settlement "should also take into consideration that legal disputes should as a general rule be referred by the parties to the International Court of Justice . . ." (Article 36). In short, for a case to reach the Court it must (1) involve a dispute or contending claims between states; (2) be justiciable, or subject to settlement on that basis of law; (3) be referred to the Court.

The first case brought before the International Court of Justice was the dispute between Great Britain and Albania over the mining of the Corfu Channel.[7] This referral was made by Great Britain upon the recommendation of the Security Council. The Court took jurisdiction of the case over the protest of Albania, and handed down a decision that the latter was responsible under international law for the damage and loss of human life. The amount of compensation to be paid by Albania was fixed at £843,947. Other cases sub-

[5] In 1952, the fifteen judges were nationals of Belgium, Brazil, Canada, Chile, China, Egypt, France, Mexico, Norway, Poland, El Salvador, the Soviet Union, Great Britain, the United States, and Yugoslavia.

[6] However, such an obligation might exist in a separate treaty, or because of an acceptance of the Court's compulsory jurisdiction. See pp. 194–195.

[7] See pp. 211–212.

mitted to the Court by the end of 1949 included a dispute between Great Britain and Norway over fishing rights in certain areas off the Norwegian coast, a complaint by France concerning the treatment of French nationals in Egypt, and a dispute between Colombia and Peru over the granting of asylum by the Colombian Ambassador to a Peruvian citizen.

COMPULSORY OR AUTOMATIC JURISDICTION

The question of compulsory jurisdiction has been a stumbling block in the development of international judicial institutions. One characteristic of the judicial process in every national legal system is the capacity of the courts to assert jurisdiction independently of the desires of parties to disputes. In a criminal case, the accused has no choice as to whether he will appear for trial. He is compelled to do so. In civil actions, once a court takes cognizance of a complaint the defendant must appear for the proceedings as directed. If he fails to do so, he is in contempt of court and can be summarily punished. It would be fantastic to imagine a national legal system in which the parties to a dispute could decide for themselves as to whether they would accept the jurisdiction of the courts. In international affairs, however, the situation is different. We are dealing with states, not individual citizens. We find that the idea of sovereignty and the practice of nationalism militate against an acceptance of compulsory jurisdiction in this field. Governments have been unwilling to take the step of establishing a genuine supranational legal authority.

How can the deadlock be broken between national legal independence and compulsory jurisdiction as an essential condition of international judicial settlement? A partial solution has been found in the "optional clause" device. Article 36, paragraph 2, provides:

The states parties to the present Statute may at any time declare that they recognize as compulsory *ipso facto* and without special agreement, in relation to any other state accepting the same obligation, the jurisdiction of the Court in all legal disputes concerning:

    a. the interpretation of a treaty;

    b. any question of international law;

    c. the existence of any fact which, if established, would constitute a breach of an international obligation;

    d. the nature or extent of the reparation to be made for the breach of an international obligation.

Under this provision, any state willing to do so may voluntarily accept for certain types of disputes the compulsory jurisdiction of the Court. The fiction of sovereignty is preserved by the act of state consent, and in practice the road is open for the maximum of international legal authority that national governments are willing to tolerate. Declarations under the "optional clause" may be made either conditionally or unconditionally, and may be made for a specified period of time. By July, 1949, a total of thirty-four states had signed declarations accepting compulsory jurisdiction in accordance with the "optional clause." Most of these made reciprocity a condition. That is, they would not be bound to accept the compulsory jurisdiction of the Court in connection with a given dispute unless the other party also accepted it. As to the period of time, most of the declarations were made for five or ten years, or until notice of termination.

Some states have accepted the "optional clause" with reservations. For example, members of the British Commonwealth [8] make an exception of disputes with each other, which are to be settled in such manner as the parties agree. Guatemala reserved its dispute with Great Britain concerning the territory of Belize, unless the Court would decide it *ex aequo et bono!* [9] The United States Senate, in consenting to ratification, attached a reservation making an exception of "disputes with regard to matters which are essentially within the domestic jurisdiction of the United States of America as determined by the United States of America." The first part of this clause is of no great significance because the Charter itself (in Article 7, paragraph 2) definitely excludes from the scope of the United Nations "matters which are essentially within the domestic jurisdiction of any state." The last part of the clause, however, gives the United States a sort of veto in the international judicial process, because it has a basis for nullifying the acceptance of compulsory jurisdiction for any dispute to which it may be a party. This does not necessarily lead to the conclusion that American acceptance of the Court's compulsory jurisdiction is meaningless, since an invocation of the reservation would be a very grave matter unless the dispute was clearly within the category of "domestic jurisdiction." France, Mexico, and Pakistan have made similar reservations, and the British Dominions had previously reserved matters which were in the domestic jurisdiction according to international law.

The law to be applied by the International Court of Justice includes international conventions establishing rules recognized by the contesting parties; international custom, as evidence of a general practice accepted as law; and the general principles of law recognized by civilized nations. Judicial decisions and the teachings of qualified publicists may be used as subsidiary means for the determination of rules of law. However, it is expressly provided that each decision has no binding force except between the parties and in respect of that particular case. The rule of *stare decisis*, that previous decisions constitute binding precedents for future cases involving the same issue, is not followed. The Statute of the Court in this particular case follows the practice

[8] These countries accepted the "optional clause" of the Permanent Court of International Justice. Such obligations carry over to the new Court.

[9] On considerations of right and justice, rather than solely on strict legal rules.

on the continent of Europe rather than the Anglo-American conception. Equity jurisprudence is recognized in the capacity of the Court to decide a case *ex aequo et bono* if the parties agree.

ENFORCEMENT OF DECISIONS

For the enforcement of its decisions the Court must rely upon two considerations. First is the fact that each member of the United Nations has an obligation under the Charter to comply with its decisions together with the prestige and moral weight of the Court itself. Once a case is submitted to the process of judicial settlement, the decision is likely to be accepted even by the losing party. This assumption is borne out by experience of the Permanent Court of International Justice, which handled a substantial number of cases without the development of any tendency to flout its decisions. The record here seems to be analogous to that of arbitration proceedings. The real difficulty is not with refusal to accept the results when the method is used, but with getting states to agree to use the method.

The second consideration is that if any party to a case fails to perform obligations arising from a decision of the Court, the other party may have recourse to the Security Council, which may make recommendations or decide upon measures to be taken. Presumably this authorization falls within the general framework of the enforcement powers of the Security Council and would be limited to measures necessary for the maintenance or restoration of international peace and security. It was not intended that the Security Council should act as a sort of sheriff for the Court, but that it should be able to deal with threats to the peace arising from failure to carry out a judgment of the Court.

ADVISORY OPINIONS

In addition to deciding cases referred to it, the International Court of Justice has the responsibility of giving advisory opinions on legal questions when requested by the General Assembly or the Security Council.[10] The International Court does not, of course, give advisory opinions on its own initiative. Use of the courts for legal advice to other departments of government is customary in many countries, but it is not practiced in the United States. In this country, the President relies on the Attorney-General for legal advice, and Congress on its own legal staff. Neither the executive nor the legislative branch ever requests an advisory opinion on a legal question from the Supreme Court. Conversely, the Supreme Court does not give legal advice or answer hypotheti-

---

[10] The General Assembly also may authorize other organs of the United Nations and the specialized agencies to request advisory opinions on legal questions arising within the scope of their activities.

cal questions but only entertains cases in which actual contending claims have already arisen. The International Court of Justice, however, follows normal European practice, and it is competent to give legal advice to the other organs and agencies of the United Nations.

Although advisory opinions from the Court have great prestige and moral force, the General Assembly and the Security Council have no obligation to accept them as binding. They represent advice, rather than decisions. Each organ makes its own decisions on matters within its competence. The Court is not the final authority on matters of interpretation of the Charter, in the sense that the Supreme Court exercises that function with respect to the Constitution of the United States. The first advisory opinion,[11] on conditions of admission to membership, supported the position of the majority in the Security Council and the General Assembly, but it did not result in a change in the practice of the minority nor was it considered to have any automatic effect. The advisory opinion on reparation for injuries suffered in the service of the United Nations served to clarify and emphasize the fact that the United Nations is an international personality with legal capacity to bring claims appropriate to the discharge of its functions.[12] Advisory opinions were also requested in connection with the dispute over the peace treaties with Bulgaria, Hungary, and Rumania, and concerning the international status of South-West Africa.[13]

It is too early to say how important advisory opinions will be in the work of the United Nations. Definite possibilities are indicated by previous experience. Advisory opinions definitely were useful to the League of Nations in settling international disputes.[14] Many times disputant states consented to have the Council or Assembly ask for an advisory opinion when they were unwilling to submit a dispute to the Court for a binding judgment. By separating the legal from the political issues and thus narrowing the controversial aspects of a dispute, advisory opinions are a great help in the work of conciliation.

ORGANIZATION AND PROCEDURE

The seat of the International Court of Justice is at The Hague. It may, however, exercise its functions elsewhere if desirable. The Court is required to remain permanently in session, except during judicial vacations. The judges are entitled to periodic leave, as determined by the Court. They are bound, unless on leave or prevented from attending by illness or other serious reason, to hold themselves permanently at the disposal of the Court. The full Court

[11] See pp. 142–143.
[12] See p. 109.
[13] See pp. 218–219; 290–291.
[14] The Permanent Court of International Justice gave twenty-seven advisory opinions.

sits in each case, except that it may form chambers composed of three or more judges to deal with particular categories of cases; for example, labor cases or those relating to transit and communications. A quorum of nine judges is sufficient to constitute the Court.

The Court elects its own President and Vice-President for terms of three years, and they are eligible for reelection. The Registrar is appointed by the Court, which also provides for the appointment of such other officers as may be necessary. This arrangement is different from that for the other organs of the United Nations, in which cases the Secretary-General furnishes the needed staff. The official languages of the Court are French and English. Cases are initiated by a notification or application addressed to the Registrar. Provision is made for due notice to all parties concerned, representation by agents and counsel, written and oral proceedings, public hearings (unless decided otherwise), official minutes, and a judgment which states the reasons on which it is based. Within the framework of these basic requirements, the Court determines its own rules of procedure.

Decisions are made by a majority vote of the judges present. The President of the Court does not vote except in case of a tie. This is an interesting departure from the old rule of unanimity in international organization. In the first place, as we have seen, the judges do not represent the national governments, and there are only fifteen judges and not one for each party to the Statute of the Court. It is true that some concession is made to the idea of national representation by allowing each party to a dispute to have on the Court one judge of its nationality or choice (Article 31 of the Statute), but with majority rather than unanimous voting, no one party is in the position to "veto" a decision of the Court. Any judge may deliver a separate opinion if he does not agree with the majority, and rather liberal use has been made of this right of dissent during the early years of the International Court of Justice.

The expenses of the Court are borne by the parties to the Statute in a manner determined by the General Assembly. The annual expenses have been running between $600,000 and $650,000 a year. Each judge receives an annual salary, which may not be decreased during a term of office. In February, 1946, the General Assembly fixed the annual salary at 54,000 Netherlands florins, although the budget of the United Nations is voted in United States dollars. When the florin was devaluated in September, 1949, a peculiar problem was created. There was no decrease in the number of florins paid to each judge, but there was a reduction of about 30 per cent in purchasing power in terms of dollars. Many of the judges were adversely affected. For example, the American national on the Court, in so far as he returns to the United States or has expenses there, would suffer a serious disadvantage. Does this violate the stipulation against decreasing a judge's salary during his term of office?

The General Assembly was asked to direct the payment of these salaries in dollars, but no action was taken for the 1950 budget.

Something of the flavor of the Court's proceeding may be gained from the following description: [15]

Cases referred to the Court are entered on the General List, a scroll of hand-made Dutch paper, under the direction of the Registrar, Dr. Edvard Hambro. Notifications are sent at once to all concerned and to states and parties entitled to appear during the proceedings. If written statements are submitted, they are considered by the judges in private sessions. These usually are held in the Bol Room, so-called because its walls are hung with canvases by the 17th-century Dutch painter, Ferdinand Bol.

On the day announced for public hearings, the judges gather in two small council chambers decorated with portraits of Presidents and judges of previous Courts. In long black robes, with lace jabots emerging from under their stiff white collars, the members of the Court, preceded by the Registrar, file into the Great Hall of Justice, a high oak-panelled room. An usher, dressed in a black uniform, a silver chain around his shoulders, announces: "La Cour," and all present rise.

The judges proceed slowly toward a dais which occupies almost the entire length of the Great Hall. Behind it three lofty stained-glass windows show, in allegory, the development of mankind from primitive days to a time when war has been banished as an instrument of international politics.

The members of the Court take their places behind a long table, with the President in the centre, the Vice-President to his right, and the other judges seated on either side in order of seniority. The Registrar sits at a right angle to them, at one of the far ends of the table. In the first row of seats facing the Court are the agents, counsel, and advocates. Behind them is a row of seats for distinguished visitors, with the press and public occupying the remaining places on the floor and in the galleries.

After an opening address by the President, the representatives of parties concerned make their oral statements from a platform opposite the President. Official languages of the Court are English and French, although other languages may be used. In the Corfu Channel case heard in 1949, for example, Albanian and Russian were heard. Interpretation is from the floor, usually by the Court's own interpreters.

At the close of the public hearing—which may vary from the one day of the advisory opinion concerning new Members to the several weeks of the Corfu Channel dispute—the Court withdraws. Decisions are reached as soon as possible after private and secret deliberations and by majority vote of the judges present. They are announced, together with the Court's reasons, in public session, either as judgments, in cases of litigation, or as advisory opinions. The Court's judgments are final and without appeal.

[15] *United Nations Bulletin,* Vol. VIII, No. 7, Apr. 1, 1950, pp. 308–310.

PART III
WORK AND ACCOMPLISHMENTS

Chapter 14

INTERNATIONAL PEACE AND SECURITY

The most important aspect of the work of the United Nations has to do with the maintenance of international peace and security. Its chief purpose and responsibility lie in this field, and it will be judged by the degree of success achieved in this connection. Therefore it is necessary to "look at the record" of the United Nations in dealing with international disputes and to raise the question of its effectiveness.

The United Nations system for the pacific settlement of international disputes begins with the duty of members to seek a solution by peaceful means of their own choice. Article 33, paragraph 1, of the Charter provides that "the parties to any dispute, the continuance of which is likely to endanger the maintenance of international peace and security, shall, first of all, seek a solution by negotiation, enquiry, mediation, conciliation, arbitration, judicial settlement, resort to regional agencies or arrangements, or other peaceful means of their own choice." Thus, it will be seen that the United Nations Charter incorporates and builds upon the methods and procedures which had developed in an earlier stage of international organization.[1]

The obligation stated in Article 33 does not necessarily apply to all international disputes. A minor dispute unlikely to endanger peace and security might go unsettled until forgotten. The emphasis in drafting the Charter was to see that such disputes as might occur would not disrupt the peace and security of the world. The United Nations is concerned with serious disputes, and not with every little difference and disagreement which may arise in the daily conduct of international affairs. The test lies in the question of whether or not there is any real danger to peace.

In the event that the parties to a dispute do not fulfill their obligations under Article 33, provisions are made for the United Nations to assume responsibilities suited to the circumstances of the case. The Security Council, when necessary, is to call upon the parties to settle their disputes by peaceful means. The Security Council may investigate any dispute, or any situation which might lead to international friction or give rise to a dispute. In practice, this power of investigation has been broadly interpreted and has been used in such a way

[1] See pp. 34–43.

as to make it a very important step in the process of peaceful settlement.

Any member of the United Nations may bring any dispute or threatening situation to the attention of the Security Council or the General Assembly. The former is obligated to maintain international peace and security by measures ranging from recommendations to actual enforcement action. The General Assembly may, of course, discuss any matter within the scope of the Charter and, with one restriction, may make appropriate recommendations.[2] A state which is not a member of the United Nations may also bring to the attention of the Security Council or the General Assembly any dispute to which it is a party if it accepts in advance the Charter obligations of pacific settlement. At any stage of a dispute or threatening situation, the Security Council may recommend procedures or methods of adjustment. This would seem to exclude recommendations as to the terms, as contrasted with methods, of settlement. In practice, however, the Security Council, in view of its broad responsibilities under the Charter, has not considered its authority to be limited in this respect. If the parties to a dispute fail to settle it by pacific means, they have an obligation to refer it to the Security Council, which, in this event, may recommend appropriate terms of settlement. Also, if the parties to a dispute so request, the Security Council may make recommendations with a view to pacific settlement.

Thus, it will be seen that the Charter is based upon the idea of a series of steps in handling serious international disputes or situations which threaten to disrupt the peace. The parties have, in the first place, an obligation to use peaceful means of settlement. If this is insufficient, the Security Council or the General Assembly may undertake investigations and recommendations, either upon their own authority or upon referral by the disputants themselves or by some third party. This series of steps should not be thought of as a rigid sequence, but as a range of possibilities to be utilized as appears appropriate and feasible. The Security Council, for example, is not obligated to wait until each technique listed in Article 33 has been attempted and has failed, but may intervene whenever it seems that the parties to a dispute are not accomplishing the objective of peaceful settlement.

If a dispute is not settled by peaceful means, the Security Council is to determine "the existence of any threat to the peace, breach of the peace, or act of aggression" and shall make recommendations or decide what measures shall be taken to maintain or restore international peace and security. In the first instance, enforcement action is to be based upon measures not involving the use of armed force. These may include "complete or partial interruption of economic relations and of rail, sea, air, postal, telegraphic, radio, and other means of communication, and the severance of diplomatic relations."[3] If

[2] See pp. 139–140.

[3] Also, provisional measures may be applied pending a Security Council decision, in order to prevent "an aggravation of the situation."

Iran. On January 19, 1946, the government of Iran stated that interference by the Soviet Union in the internal affairs of Iran had brought about a situation which might lead to international friction, and it requested that the matter be brought before the Security Council. This request was considered, and the Security Council decided unanimously to refer the question back to the parties for further negotiation and asked that it be kept informed of the results achieved. On March 18, 1946, the government of Iran alleged that there was a dispute with the Soviet Union, the continuance of which was likely to endanger international peace and security. Specifically, the Soviet Union was charged with maintaining troops in Iranian territory contrary to treaty provisions that they would be withdrawn by March 2, 1946. The Security Council undertook a discussion of this matter, although the representative of the Soviet Union objected and refused to participate. A resolution was passed deferring action for several weeks but retaining the Iranian complaint on the agenda. After it became clear that Soviet troops had been withdrawn, further discussion was adjourned.

Greece. The Greek question was first brought before the United Nations by the Soviet Union, just two days after the Iranian complaint of January, 1946. The Security Council was requested to discuss the situation in Greece on the grounds that the presence of British troops after the termination of the war constituted interference with internal affairs and caused extraordinary tension. It appears that the complaint of the Soviet Union was really a counterpoise to the charges brought against that country by Iran. Various statements were presented, and on February 6, 1946, a resolution was passed declaring the matter closed. In August, 1946, the Ukraine brought up this matter again, declaring that a situation had arisen in the Balkans which presented a grave danger to peace. The Security Council again discussed the matter, but with no conclusive results since none of the resolutions presented received a sufficient affirmative vote to be adopted.

In December, 1946, the government of Greece requested the Security Council to give early consideration to a situation which was leading to friction between Greece and its neighbors. The Security Council discussed this matter and decided to appoint a Commission of Investigation, composed of a representative of each of the members of the Council as constituted in 1947. The Commission held a total of seventy-three meetings in the Balkans between January and April, 1947, compiled extensive evidence, and devoted sixteen meetings in Geneva to the preparation of its report. The majority of the Commission concluded that Yugoslavia and, to a lesser extent, Albania and Bulgaria had supported the guerrilla warfare in Greece, although the general condition of unrest in Greece helped to explain the situation. It was recommended that the countries concerned should attempt to reestablish normal relations and should abstain from any action likely to maintain or increase tension and unrest. Continued support to armed guerrilla bands in Greece would be considered "as a threat to the peace within the meaning of the Charter." The Soviet Union and Poland considered the evidence cited by the majority of the Commission as contradictory and inconclusive, and they challenged the reliability of witnesses who had testified on behalf of Greece. The recommendations based on the majority report were unacceptable to the Soviet Union, and the minority report was not acceptable to the other permanent members of the Security Council. Therefore, no agreement could be reached, and on September 15, 1947, a resolution was passed removing the Greek question from the agenda, so that it could be considered by the General Assembly.

The discussion in the General Assembly resulted in a resolution, adopted October 21, 1947, which "took account" of the report by the Committee of Investigation; called upon Albania, Bulgaria, and Yugoslavia to do nothing to aid the guerrillas; called upon these three countries and Greece to cooperate in settling their disputes by peaceful means; and established a Special Committee to observe and assist in implementing the recommendations. This action was strongly opposed by the Soviet bloc, which has steadfastly refused to cooperate with the United Nations Special Committee on the Balkans. The Committee has attempted to carry out its assignments by keeping the developments under observation and by preparing reports from time to time. The scope and intensity of the fighting were reduced, especially when Yugoslavia ceased its help to the guerrillas operating across the border. Conditions in Greece became somewhat more stabilized, but no real solution was reached and the situation remains a potentially explosive and dangerous one.

Indonesia. The Indonesian question was first brought before the Security Council by the Ukraine on January 21, 1946, the same day that the Soviet Union made the first complaint in the Greek case. It was alleged that the situation which had arisen in Indonesia after World War II constituted a threat to the maintenance of international peace and security. After a long discussion, proposals to establish a commission of inquiry failed of adoption.

In July, 1947, the government of Australia brought to the attention of the Security Council the hostilities in progress in Java and Sumatra between armed forces of the Netherlands and the Republic of Indonesia and urged that immediate action be taken. At the same time, the government of India called the attention of the Security Council to the situation in Indonesia. The Netherlands argued that control of colonial territory was a matter within domestic jurisdiction under international law and that therefore the United Nations had no authority to intervene. The Netherlands, however, was ready to invite a number of other governments to send representatives to report on the situation and was willing to accept a United States tender of "good offices" in the matter. On August 1, 1947, the Security Council passed a resolution calling upon the parties to cease hostilities forthwith, to settle their disputes by arbitration or other peaceful means, and to keep the Council informed of the progress of the settlement. Later the same month, the Security Council passed two additional resolutions, one requesting the members having career consuls in Batavia to instruct them to prepare a joint report on observance of the cease-fire order and the conditions in areas under military occupation. The other resolution established a Committee of Good Offices.[7]

During the latter part of 1947, the chief endeavor was to implement the cease-fire order, to arrange for the withdrawal of armed forces, and to secure the commencement of political negotiations. In January, 1948, the *Renville* settlement was signed. This agreement, concluded on board the United States auxiliary warship *Renville*, provided for a truce in military operations and acceptance of a basis of discussion for settlement of the dispute. During 1948, little significant progress was made in implementing the *Renville* agreement. There were charges and countercharges concerning an alleged economic blockade by the Netherlands, the line of demarcation for observance of a military truce was disputed, and there was a deadlock in the negotiations for a political settlement. The Security Council and its Committee of Good Offices continued their efforts, but in December, 1948, the Netherlands government, for a second time, resorted to what it called "police action." It charged the Indonesians with violating the truce and with the instigation of sabotage and reprisals. The representative of the Republic of Indonesia denied this and accused the Netherlands of a policy of economic and political warfare. The Security Council held several emergency meetings during Christmas week and called for a cessation of hostilities and the release of certain political prisoners (including the President of the Republic of Indonesia) held by the Netherlands.

A new effort was made in January, 1949, when the Security Council continued its discussions and, on the twenty-eighth of the month, adopted a resolution calling for the discontinuance of military operations and guerrilla warfare, release of political prisoners, facilities for the effective functioning of the Republican government, cooperation in the restoration of peace and order, and resumption of negotiations. Also, the Committee of Good Offices was reconstituted as the United Nations Commission for Indonesia and given additional functions, such as recommending the extent to which areas controlled by the Republic under the *Renville* agreement should be progressively returned to its administration, of supervising such transfers, and of recommending whether Netherlands forces should be retained temporarily in any area to assist in maintaining law and order and in observing elections.

In March, 1949, the Commission reported that the resolution of January 28 had not been followed, and that the Netherlands government proposed to convene a round-table conference at The Hague on the Indonesian question. The Security Council, on March 23, instructed the Commission to assist the parties in reaching an agreement as to implementation of the January resolution and the time and conditions for holding the proposed conference. The

[7] Indonesia selected Australia as a member of this Committee; the Netherlands selected Belgium; and these two members selected the United States as the third member.

Indonesian question was also brought up and discussed in the General Assembly during the spring of 1949. By July, 1949, arrangements had been made for the cessation of military operations, political prisoners had been released, and Netherlands troops were evacuated from Republican territory under the observation of United Nations military observers. Dutch and Indonesian representatives met in a round-table conference at The Hague in September and October of 1949, at which an agreement was reached for an independent United States of Indonesia, associated with the Netherlands in a Union on the basis of sovereign equality. This solution was accepted by the Security Council and the General Assembly. Sovereignty was transferred to the new state on December 27, 1949, and in September of the following year, the Republic of Indonesia became the sixtieth member of the United Nations.

Syria and Lebanon. In February, 1946, the governments of Syria and Lebanon brought to the attention of the Security Council the continued presence of British and French troops in those countries, claiming that this constituted a violation of sovereignty which might give rise to serious disputes. The question was discussed and several suggestions made. The United States offered a proposal expressing confidence that the foreign troops would be withdrawn as soon as practicable. The Soviet Union proposed amendments to have the Security Council make a recommendation of immediate withdrawal. These amendments were not accepted. The United States draft resolution then received seven affirmative votes but was not adopted because of Soviet opposition. However, Great Britain and France proceeded to comply with the sentiments of the majority by withdrawing their troops from Syria and Lebanon, to the satisfaction of those countries.

Spain. The Spanish question was first discussed by the General Assembly in February, 1946, as the result of a complaint by the government of Panama. A resolution was passed recalling the decisions of the San Francisco and Potsdam Conferences that the admission of Franco Spain to the United Nations would not be supported, endorsing those decisions, and asking that members of the United Nations act in accordance with them. In April, 1946, the government of Poland brought the Spanish question before the Security Council, charging that the activities of the Franco government had caused international friction and endangered international peace and security. A subcommittee was appointed to investigate and report. The subcommittee found that, although the Franco government did not constitute a threat to the peace within the meaning of Article 39 of the Charter, it was a potential menace to international peace and security. This position was accepted by the majority, but the Soviet Union felt that definite measures should be taken to ensure the overthrow of the Franco regime, since it had been closely identified with the Axis aggressors. Most of the other members of the Security Council were unwilling to embark on such a drastic course of action.

Accordingly, no decision could be reached and the question was removed from the agenda of the Security Council on November 4, 1946, in order that the General Assembly might be free to act.

On December 12, 1946, the General Assembly passed a resolution recommending that the Franco government be debarred from membership in international agencies and conferences connected with the United Nations; that the Security Council consider the measures to be taken if a new and acceptable government were not formed in Spain within a reasonable time; and that all members of the United Nations immediately recall their ambassadors from Madrid. This recommendation was adopted despite strong opposition by some delegations. One argument was that it would constitute interference in the internal affairs of Spain contrary to Article 2, paragraph 7, of the Charter, since the internal governmental regime of a country is a matter of domestic jurisdiction. However, the majority of the General Assembly concluded that the situation in Spain was of international concern and a potential menace to peace. The other chief objection was that the recommendations calling for recall of ambassadors, and for action if a more democratic regime were not established, were matters within the province of the Security Council.

In November, 1947, the General Assembly reviewed the situation and adopted a resolution expressing its confidence that the Security Council would "exercise its responsibilities under the Charter as soon as it considers that the situation in regard to Spain so requires." Stronger proposals, including one to ask the Security Council to take enforcement measures, did not receive the necessary two-thirds vote, and the Franco regime maintained its position in Spain.

The General Assembly, in November, 1950, voted to revoke those parts of the 1946 resolution which debarred Spain from membership in the specialized agencies and which recommended that ambassadors be withdrawn from Madrid. This left each specialized agency and each member state to make its own decisions concerning Franco Spain. The arguments in favor of this action were that the specialized agencies are technical rather than political organizations, and that the maintenance of diplomatic relations does not imply approval of a regime. It was pointed out that the General Assembly condemnation of Franco remained in effect, and that the work of such agencies as the World Health Organization and the Universal Postal Union was intended to serve the peoples of the world regardless of political considerations. There was opposition from several delegations which felt that Franco Spain should not "come in by the back door." Others charged that the United States was interested in building up Spain as a strategic base against the Soviet Union. The final vote was 38 in favor of the resolution, 10 against,[8] and 12 abstentions.

Indians in South Africa. In June, 1946, the government of India requested that the General Assembly place on its agenda the question of the treatment

[8] All the eastern European members, and Guatemala, Mexico, Uruguay, and Israel.

of Indians in the Union of South Africa. The latter government was charged with enacting discriminatory measures, especially the Asiatic Land Tenure and Indian Representation Act of 1946 which restricted rights of Indians in regard to trade and residence. These measures, it was alleged, violated the Capetown Agreements of 1927 and 1932 between India and South Africa and were contrary to the principles of the United Nations Charter concerning human rights and freedoms. The Union of South Africa denied the General Assembly's competence to deal with the Indian complaint, on the grounds that it concerned a matter essentially within its domestic jurisdiction.

After lengthy debate, the General Assembly adopted a resolution on December 8, 1946, which stated that friendly relations between the two member states had been impaired, and that the treatment of Indians in the Union of South Africa should be in conformity with international obligations. The two governments were requested to report the measures adopted to this effect at the next session of the General Assembly. During the following year, India reported that South Africa had taken no steps to put the resolution into effect, that the situation had grown worse, and that it had been impossible to reach a common basis of discussion. South Africa still denied the General Assembly's jurisdiction and did not consider itself bound by the resolution. In particular, that government refused to accept as a basis of discussion a resolution which contained or implied a condemnation of it. Although the question was discussed at the 1947 session of the General Assembly, no new resolutions were passed. A reaffirmation of the earlier resolution was opposed by some delegations because of the feeling, expressed by the representative of the United States, that it would be a mistake and a sign of weakness to restate a decision which had not produced the expected results. The delegate of India argued, on the other hand, that failure to confirm the 1946 resolution, in face of a violation of it, meant a departure from the position taken previously and that such practices would undermine the authority of the General Assembly.

The question was again considered during the third regular session of the General Assembly. On May 14, 1949, a resolution was adopted inviting the governments of India and the Union of South Africa to enter into a discussion (with Pakistan also invited to participate) at a round-table conference, taking into consideration the purposes and principles of the Charter and the Declaration of Human Rights. The Union of South Africa, however, has maintained its original position and no generally acceptable solution has been reached.

Corfu Channel. In January, 1947, the British government brought before the Security Council a complaint against Albania, alleging that an unnotified minefield had been laid in the Corfu Channel by the Albanian government, or with its connivance, resulting in damage to two British warships with attendant loss of life. The Security Council decided to invite Albania (a nonmember of the United Nations) to participate, without vote, in the discussion, on condition that it accept for this case the obligations of membership. The Albanian government accepted this invitation. A subcommittee was appointed to examine the available evidence, and after its report the discussion was continued in the Security Council. A British draft resolution to settle the case on the basis of a finding that Albania was at fault as charged was lost by the negative vote of the Soviet Union. Thereupon, on April 3, 1947, a resolution was passed recommending that the case be referred to the International Court of Justice.[9]

Palestine. Of all the disputes referred to the United Nations, the Palestine question was one of the most complex and difficult, and it is the only situation which has resulted in the convening of a special session of the General Assembly. After World War I, Palestine had become a British mandate under the League of Nations. The question of its status after World War II was complicated by the changed position of Great Britain in world affairs, by the strategic and political importance of the Near East, and by the historic and seemingly irreconcilable rivalries between the Jews and the Arabs. In April, 1947, the British government requested that the question of Palestine be placed on the agenda of the General Assembly at its next regular session and that a special session be called to initiate a consideration of this situation. A majority of the members of the United Nations concurred in this request, and the first special session of the General Assembly opened on April 28, 1947. As a result of its deliberations a Special Committee on Palestine (UNSCOP) was set up to ascertain and record relevant facts, to examine the questions and issues involved, to conduct investigations in Palestine and elsewhere, to receive oral and written testimony, to consider the various religious interests, to prepare a report, and to submit proposals for a solution of the problem.

The work of the Special Committee resulted in two proposals. The majority recommended a plan of partition into independent Arab and Jewish states, with economic union for Palestine as a whole. The city of Jerusalem would be a separate entity, to be placed under the international trusteeship system with the United Nations designated as the administering authority. The minority proposal contemplated an independent federal state with Jerusalem as its capital. The General Assembly, after lengthy deliberations, adopted on November 29, 1947, the plan of partition with economic union, requested the Security Council to take the necessary measures to implement the plan, and established a United Nations Palestine Commission to supervise the transitional period.

The recommendation of the General Assembly was completely unacceptable to both the Jews and the Arabs. When the Palestine Commission reported to the Security Council in February, 1948, that it would be unable to maintain law and order after termination of the British mandate unless adequate mili-

[9] See pp. 193–194 below.

tary forces were made available, it became necessary for the Security Council to consider what action it should take.   The situation in Palestine was critical, and Great Britain as the mandatory power was not willing to use military measures or to cooperate with the United Nations Palestine Commission in implementing the plan of partition with economic union adopted by the General Assembly.   Under these circumstances, the Security Council was not in a position to use force to impose the plan, especially since some members, particularly the United States, argued that the proper function of the Council was to maintain international peace and security rather than to enforce any specific terms of settlement.   The efforts in the spring of 1948, therefore, turned in the direction, first, of bringing about a truce to prevent the spread of fighting and, second, of convening a second special session of the General Assembly to consider further the question of the future government of Palestine.

Repeated efforts to secure a truce during the spring of 1948 were unsuccessful.   On May 14, 1948 (the day before the termination of the British mandate), the General Assembly decided to appoint a United Nations Mediator in Palestine to use his good offices with the local authorities, to arrange for the operation of necessary public services, to assure protection of the holy places, to promote a peaceful adjustment of the situation, and to cooperate with the Truce Commission previously established by the Security Council. By the same resolution, the United Nations Palestine Commission was relieved of further responsibilities.   Count Folke Bernadotte of Sweden, Vice-President of the International Red Cross, was chosen as the United Nations Mediator.

The situation entered a new phase with the termination of the mandate, the proclamation of the state of Israel, its immediate recognition by the United States and several other countries, and the entrance of Arab armed forces into Palestine.   The Security Council was finally able to arrange a temporary truce, which went into effect on June 11 for a period of four weeks.   However, the Mediator was unable to secure a negotiated settlement during this time. An appeal to prolong the truce was rejected by the Arabs, and hostilities were resumed.   On July 15, 1948, the Security Council passed another resolution ordering the authorities concerned to issue cease-fire orders and stating that in the event of noncompliance further action would be considered.   The Mediator was instructed to bring about the demilitarization of Jerusalem and to supervise the truce, which was to last until a peaceful adjustment was reached.   Many violations of the truce were reported, however, and on September 17, the United Nations Mediator was assassinated, probably by a band of Jewish terrorists.   Mr. Ralph J. Bunche, of the Secretariat, was designated as Acting Mediator.

The General Assembly, at its third regular session, proceeded to a consideration of the progress report which Count Bernadotte had submitted just prior to his death.   On December 11, 1948, a United Nations Conciliation

Commission for Palestine was established by the General Assembly to assist in a final settlement. During the winter and spring of 1949, the Acting Mediator was on the island of Rhodes conducting negotiations for a general armistice between Israel and the various Arab states, while the Conciliation Commission established headquarters at Lausanne to facilitate an exchange of views in relation to its general task of conciliation, the problems of territorial adjustments, the status of Jerusalem, and refugees.

Armistice agreements had been concluded for all the fighting fronts by July, 1949. The peace treaties and the definitive settlement, however, remained as unsettled issues. As of June, 1951, it had not been possible to delimit the final boundaries to the satisfaction of both Jews and Arabs, while charges and countercharges of violations of the armistice frontiers continued to be brought before the Mixed Armistice Commission and the Security Council itself. As to the status of Jerusalem, the General Assembly recommended at its fourth regular session in 1949, that the city be established as a *corpus separatum* under a special international regime administered by the United Nations. This plan could not be implemented because of its unacceptability to both parties, with the result that Israel remained in control of the new city and Jordan of the old city.

The Arab refugees presented an especially difficult problem, and one whose solution is essential to the establishment of a stable peace in Palestine. In the fall of 1950, the number of refugees was estimated at 800,000. Two-thirds of them were housed in temporary improvised quarters and the remainder in tents. This huge number is a drain on the economy of the area, and the refugees are resentful of their condition. The United Nations Relief and Works Agency for Palestine Refugees in the Near East, which was established in October, 1949, provided for rations to refugees on relief and attempted to institute a works program for employment purposes. The work projects were confined at first to the construction of roads and to forestry, since these activities involve a high percentage of hand labor. Later the scope was broadened to include archeological excavations, garment making, and handicrafts; however, the works program remained very limited in terms of the total need, because of lack of opportunities for constructive work projects, the expense in relation to the cost of direct relief, and the shortage of funds for the purpose.

Egypt. In July, 1947, the government of Egypt brought to the Security Council its dispute with Great Britain concerning the evacuation of British troops from Egypt and termination of the existing administrative regime in the Sudan. The representative of Egypt asserted that the treaty of 1936, defining relations between the two countries, had been completed under special circumstances which, with the defeat of the Axis Powers, were no longer relevant. Restrictions on Egyptian sovereignty and the stationing of British troops in that country could not be justified. The representative of Great

Britain claimed that no evidence had been offered that international peace and security were endangered by the situation and that therefore the Charter was not applicable. Moreover, negotiations for revision of the treaty in question had been conducted between the two parties and agreement had been reached on all points except that relating to the right of the Sudanese to choose their own future status. The Security Council heard these statements and discussed several draft proposals, but no resolution received a sufficient affirmative vote to be adopted and no action was taken.

India and Pakistan. The conflict between India and Pakistan was brought before the Security Council by the representative of India in January, 1948, largely on the basis that the situation in Kashmir threatened to endanger international peace and security. The Council heard the statements of the parties and, on January 17, passed a resolution calling upon them to take all measures within their power to improve the situation. The President of the Security Council conferred with representatives of the two governments in an attempt to find some common ground of agreement. The next step was the formation of a United Nations Commission for India and Pakistan, which was to investigate the situation on the spot, keep the Security Council informed, and exercise a mediatory influence. It was generally recognized that the first objective was a cessation of the fighting and that the future status of Kashmir should be determined by a fair plebiscite. The difficulty was in getting the parties concerned to agree on the terms for ending hostilities and on the basis for conducting the plebiscite.

The work of the Commission during 1948 was devoted to obtaining a cease-fire and truce agreement and to developing proposals for the organization of a plebiscite. A cease-fire order finally became effective on January 1, 1949, exactly one year after the dispute was first referred to the Security Council. Unconditional acceptance of detailed truce proposals still was not obtained, and the efforts to reconcile the opposing points of view continued. In March, 1949, Admiral Chester Nimitz was nominated as Plebiscite Administrator, but over a year later he was still waiting at United Nations Headquarters for negotiation of a truce agreement to be completed.

By a resolution adopted on March 14, 1950, the Security Council decided to appoint a United Nations Representative to replace the Commission for India and Pakistan. The chief duties of the Representative were to assist in the preparation and supervise the implementation of a plan of progressive demilitarization agreed on by the parties; to be at the disposal of the two governments for consultation and suggestions; to exercise all the powers and responsibilities formerly vested in the Commission; and to arrange at the appropriate stage of demilitarization for the Plebiscite Administrator to assume his assigned functions.

Sir Owen Dixon of Australia was appointed as United Nations representative for India and Pakistan. He spent about three months in these countries and held several conferences with their prime ministers. On September 15, 1950, he reported to the Security Council that he had been unable to achieve any agreement between India and Pakistan for implementing either demilitarization or the holding of a plebiscite. Partition of the entire disputed area might be a solution except for the Valley of Kashmir itself, which is claimed by both sides. The government of India, which had the advantage of possession, did not agree to the restrictions on her power and administration which the United Nations representative felt were essential to an independent and free expression of the will of the people concerned. A new effort was made in 1951, with the appointment of Mr. Frank P. Graham to help achieve demilitarization preparatory to a plebiscite.

Czechoslovakia. In March, 1948, the government of Chile brought to the attention of the Security Council allegations that the political independence of Czechoslovakia had been violated by interference of the Soviet Union. The question was placed on the agenda of the Security Council despite the protest of the Soviet representative, who declared that discussion of this situation would constitute gross interference in the internal affairs of Czechoslovakia and would be a violation of Article 2, paragraph 7, of the Charter. The complaints concerning Soviet interference or threats of force were categorically denied. The Security Council proceeded to discuss this matter and to hear statements from Mr. Jan Papanek, the permanent representative of Czechoslovakia to the United Nations prior to the assumption of control in that country by the Communists. The Security Council also invited the existing government of Czechoslovakia to take part in the discussion. This invitation was declined, on the grounds that the change in governmental regime was entirely a matter of domestic jurisdiction and that the complaint was a pretext for hostile maneuvering by the Western Powers. A proposal to appoint a subcommittee to investigate the situation was lost by the adverse vote of the Soviet Union,[10] and nothing further could be done by the Security Council.

Trieste. The government of Yugoslavia complained to the Security Council in July, 1948, that the United States and Great Britain, through the Allied Military Command in Trieste, were violating clauses of the peace treaty with Italy and were jeopardizing the independence of the Free Territory of Trieste. The complaint especially referred to matters of money and foreign trade, and of alleged plans to incorporate Trieste into Italy. This question was discussed by the Security Council. A proposal to condemn the measures concerned was initiated by Yugoslavia and supported by the Soviet Union and the Ukraine. However, it received only two affirmative votes, and no further action was taken by the Security Council.

Hyderabad. In August, 1948, the government of Hyderabad asked that

---

[10] Discussion is considered a procedural matter, but a proposal to investigate is treated as a substantive question requiring the concurrence of all the permanent members. See p. 148.

its dispute with India be brought to the attention of the Security Council. The communication charged that the Princely State had been exposed to violent intimidation, threats of invasion, frontier violations, and a crippling economic blockade. The following month, Hyderabad reported first a threat of invasion and then an actual invasion. The representative of India contended that Hyderabad was not competent to bring a question before the Security Council, since it was not a state and not independent. India had been compelled to take action because of the reign of terror by private armies in Hyderabad. All resistance to the forces of India collapsed, and while the Security Council was discussing the case, a message was received from the Nizam of Hyderabad withdrawing the complaint. The representative of India stated that order had been restored, that the Nizam was cooperating with Indian officials, and that allegations to the contrary came from extremist agitators. The Hyderabad delegation to the United Nations claimed that the Nizam had been coerced into cooperation with India. The government of Pakistan, which had been invited to participate in the discussion, asked that the situation be rectified. The discussion of this question was continued by the Security Council in the spring of 1949, but no further developments took place.

Berlin. The dispute over the Berlin blockade was placed on the provisional agenda of the Security Council on October 4, 1948, as a result of identical notifications from the governments of France, Great Britain, and the United States, calling attention to the serious situation which had arisen from the unilateral imposition by the Soviet Union of restrictions on transport and communications between the Western zones of occupation in Germany and Berlin. The notifications stated that the Soviet action was contrary to Article 2 of the Charter and constituted a threat to peace. Further recourse to negotiation among the parties seemed to be useless, and the Security Council was asked to consider the question at the earliest opportunity. The Soviet Union stated that this question did not come within the competence of the Security Council, since the solution of problems relating to Germany was a matter for the governments responsible for the military occupation and since the Council of Foreign Ministers had been set up to deal with the peaceful settlement of all issues related to ex-enemy countries. Also, the Soviet Union blamed the Western Powers, and specifically the currency reforms initiated by them, for the difficulties; the restrictions imposed by the Soviet authorities were "defensive countermeasures." The representative of the United States asserted that the instant question did not deal with Germany as an ex-enemy country but with the threat to international peace and security growing out of the relations among the victors over Germany.

The Security Council decided to hear the question, and it was discussed at some length, although the Soviet Union refused to take part in the discussions on the basis that they were taking place illegally in violation of Article 107 of the Charter. On October 22, 1948, the six neutral members of the Security Council offered a joint draft resolution which, among other things, called upon the four governments to remove the restrictions constituting the "Berlin blockade" and to hold an immediate meeting of the four military governors to deal with the currency issue. This resolution was defeated by the adverse vote of the Soviet Union. Subsequently, a series of informal negotiations held between Mr. Jessup of the United States and Mr. Malik of the Soviet Union led to an agreement by the four governments and the lifting of the blockade in May, 1949.

Human Rights in the Balkans. In March, 1949, the governments of Australia and Bolivia raised in the General Assembly "the question of the observance in Bulgaria and Hungary of human rights and fundamental freedoms including questions of religious and civil liberties, with special reference to recent trials of church leaders." Later the question was extended to include Rumania. This item was placed on the agenda, although the Soviet Union and Poland argued that a matter of domestic jurisdiction was involved and that the application of terms and procedures of the peace treaties was not within the competence of the General Assembly. On April 30, 1949, a resolution was adopted expressing deep concern at the grave accusations made, noting with satisfaction the steps already taken by several states signatories to the peace treaties, drawing the attention of the governments concerned to their obligations, and retaining the question on the agenda.

At the fourth regular session of the General Assembly, this question was discussed again. The United States and Great Britain had attempted to follow the procedure stipulated in the peace treaties by sending notes to Bulgaria, Hungary, and Rumania accusing them of violating the clauses dealing with respect for human rights and fundamental freedoms. These governments rejected the accusations and refused to appoint their representatives on the commissions provided for in the treaties as a procedure to settle disputes arising under their terms. In these circumstances, a proposal was adopted to request an advisory opinion from the International Court of Justice on the legal issues involved. In opposition to this proposal, the Soviet Union contended that the treaty procedure was inapplicable unless the three powers (Great Britain, the United States, and the Soviet Union) jointly recognized the existence of a dispute between themselves on the one hand and the defeated countries on the other, and that this was not the case. The argument seemed to be that a dispute does not exist unless the opposing parties agree that there is a dispute. The three Balkan countries took the position, defended by the Soviet Union in the General Assembly, that the treaty procedure relating to the settlement of disputes was not applicable because they did not admit that a dispute existed.

The International Court of Justice gave as its opinion that (1) a dispute did exist within the meaning of the relevant treaty provisions; (2) Bulgaria,

Hungary, and Rumania had an obligation to carry out the measures relating to the settlement of disputes, including the appointment of representatives to the treaty commission; and (3) in the event of their failure to do so, the Secretary-General was not authorized to appoint the thi: 1 member of a commission upon the request of the other party to the dispute.   In practical terms, this meant that a dispute existed but the treaty procedure for handling it could not be put into effect.   In November, 1950, the General Assembly adopted, by 40 votes to 3 with 12 abstentions, a resolution condemning Bulgaria, Hungary, and Rumania for willful refusal to fulfil their treaty obligations in this matter.

EFFECTIVENESS

The crucial question, of course, is whether or not the United Nations is effective in helping to maintain international peace and security.   During the first five years of its existence, seventeen disputes or situations dangerous to peace were handled by the General Assembly and the Security Council. Some of them were settled, as in the cases of the withdrawal of Soviet troops from Iran and of British and French troops from Syria and Lebanon.   Some of the questions, like the question of Hyderabad and the change of government in Czechoslovakia, have lapsed so far as active consideration by the United Nations is concerned.   Some, like Indonesia and Palestine, have resulted in major political changes by peaceful means.   Still others, notably the Korean case and the Communist Chinese intervention, have resulted in widespread hostilities.   There is no doubt that the work of the United Nations has been constructive and helpful in many respects.   It has provided a method and exerted an influence toward the control of international violence in the postwar world.   Yet at the same time, the basic difficulties have not been solved. The divisive forces remain strong, and the "cold war" is a compelling reality. The United Nations, in this situation, is useful and helpful, but at the present time it is not a complete answer and it is certainly not a panacea.

It is apparent that a consideration of the disputes and situations referred to the General Assembly and the Security Council does not reveal the full story of the threats to international peace and security.   Some questions are formulated and placed on the agenda.   Others, equally important or more so, are not put forward in that way.   Yet they cannot be ignored.   Such problems as the drafting of the major peace treaties, the future role of Germany, the regulation of armaments, the control of atomic energy, and the East-West conflict itself are not among the seventeen dangerous disputes and situations referred to above.   Beyond the achievements of the United Nations in the settlement of this or that specific dispute, there lies the question of its effect on the general international atmosphere.   Is the net result to weaken dangerous tensions and to strengthen the forces of cooperation and mutual understanding?   On the basis of a "calculated risk," does it increase the odds against a third world war in this generation?

Paradoxically, the United Nations may create disputes as well as settle them.   The town meeting of the world can be a forum for insult and vilification as well as for compromise and pacification.   Continuous conference diplomacy may lead to frustration and anger as well as to better understanding. Many of the most serious disagreements among members have occurred over questions relating to the functioning of the United Nations itself.   The problem of the veto had to do with the voting procedure in the Security Council. If there were no international organization reaching decisions by a voting process, one occasion for argument might be eliminated.   The questions of admitting new members, of electing nonpermanent members of the Security Council, and of establishing an Interim Committee of the General Assembly have involved bitter disputes from time to time.   The deadlock in the United Nations over the Chinese case, with the Soviet walkout, was based on a dispute concerning whether the Nationalist or the Communist delegation was entitled to represent China in the Security Council and other organs.

To argue, however, on the basis of the paradox stated in the preceding paragraph that the number of international disputes could be reduced by abolishing the United Nations would be like throwing out the baby to get rid of the dirty bath water.   The existence of the United Nations means that international disputes are handled at a new level and in a changed context.   The real question is that of the net effect.   On balance, does it have a helpful influence and constructive potentialities?   Its establishment grew out of the mutual interest in having an institutionalized means of settling disputes.   This signifies that international organization has developed to the stage where there is general recognition of a vital need for a system of collective security. There are disputes over the scope, interpretation, and implementation of such a system.   But when men quarrel over the methods by which disputes should be settled they are paying tribute to their tacit agreement that the methods are necessary and must be developed.   The problem of the veto and other conflicts over the functioning of the United Nations are often disheartening, but at least they show that the Organization is being taken seriously.   It is submitted that a close study of the background and work of the United Nations will lead to the conclusion that it is a big step on a long journey, as yet far from adequate but nonetheless useful, and that without giving any guarantees it does improve the chances of preventing a third world war.

The United Nations, in its work of attempting to maintain international peace and security, must rely largely on persuasion rather than force.   In connection with the disputes and situations discussed above, use has been made of the techniques of negotiation, "good offices," fact finding, conciliation, mediation, cooling-off periods, cease-fire agreements and truces, and recommendations for judicial settlement.   Only as a result of overt aggression in the

Korean case did the Security Council resort to enforcement measures. Emphasis has been on finding a solution, acceptable to the parties, which would be consistent with the maintenance of international peace and security. There are two fundamental reasons for this, in addition to the general objective of avoiding the use of armed force for the settlement of international disputes. First, only the Security Council is authorized to take enforcement measures, and it cannot decide to do so if one of the permanent members is opposed to such action. The exception in the Korean case was made possible only by the fortuitous absence of the Soviet Union over another issue. All the Great Powers plus at least two other members must agree in order to reach a decision to take action. This alone would serve to place the emphasis on attempts to work out an agreed solution. Second, the United Nations as such has no force at its disposal. The Charter provides for armed forces to be made available to the Security Council, by agreement with members of the United Nations, and for a Military Staff Committee. However, no such agreements have been concluded, and the United Nations is necessarily limited to persuasion, augmented by whatever opinion becomes mobilized behind its efforts and the pressure which member states may apply in a direction consistent with the aims of the Organization. In the Korean case the military forces were supplied by members acting under a resolution of the Security Council. This might be called an international force by designation.

Essentially, the United Nations provides an instrument of peaceful change —of real but limited usefulness under present world conditions. It attempts to rule out change by aggression, threats, and breaches of the peace, and to facilitate the use of pacific methods. In two of the questions referred to the United Nations, important changes were brought about and a major war was avoided each time. Both Israel and Indonesia became independent states and were admitted as members of the United Nations. These were certainly major accomplishments of peaceful change. But reaching an agreement, acceptable to the parties, which prevents a breach of the peace is not the whole question of peaceful change. There are also considerations of justice. The first emphasis, of course, must be placed on peace and security, since without some degree of stability and order the voice of justice has no chance to be heard. Nevertheless, a policy and a system which does not look beyond peace for its own sake will soon prove sterile. Peaceful adjustment is to be sought "in conformity with the principles of justice and international law." A dispute settled without actual fighting but, for example, by the sacrifice of the rights of small nations would not conform to the principles laid down in the Charter.

The question of treaty revision is a thorny one. Stability and order require a respect for international contractual obligations. Yet if treaty rights are as rigid as the laws of the Medes and Persians were said to be, they will eventually be neither respected nor observed. A procedure of peaceful revision is necessary. Usually, however, when the question comes up one party wants the treaty changed and the other does not, and states have been very reluctant to surrender the right to determine these matters for themselves. The Covenant of the League of Nations provided, by Article 19, that "the Assembly may from time to time advise the reconsideration by Members of the League of treaties which have become inapplicable, and the consideration of international conditions whose continuance might endanger the peace of the world." The United Nations Charter has a similar, but less definite, provision in Article 14, which authorizes the General Assembly to make recommendations for the peaceful adjustment of any situation likely to impair the general welfare or friendly relations among nations.[11] At the second session of the General Assembly, Argentina proposed that a revision of the peace treaty with Italy be considered. However, this proposal was later withdrawn and no action was taken. Egypt, in its complaint against Great Britain in 1947, relied in part on the argument that changed circumstances had made the Anglo-Egyptian Treaty of 1936 inapplicable. Article 14 has been invoked, alone or in conjunction with the more comprehensive terms of Article 10, as a basis for consideration of the cases of Spain, South Africa, Palestine, and Korea by the General Assembly. It is not to be expected, however, that revision of treaties would be the chief emphasis during the first few years of the United Nations, when the main peace treaties after World War II cannot be written because of the "cold war." Pacific methods have been utilized by the General Assembly and the Security Council largely in an attempt to bring about a situation of international peace and security in which an orderly and just revision of obsolete treaties will be possible.

[11] One reason for not mentioning treaty revision specifically in the Charter was the fear that such a mention might be construed as an invitation to the ex-enemy states to seek a revision of the peace treaties.

Chapter 15

THE KOREAN CRISIS

The events in Korea since the surrender of Japan, and especially the invasion of the territory south of the thirty-eighth parallel by armed forces from the north, confronted the United Nations with an acute test of its ability to stop aggression and to maintain world peace. The invasion of the Republic of Korea was in a real sense aggression against the United Nations itself, for the Republic was its ward, if not its child. The military invasion constituted a bold and direct challenge to the purposes and authority of the United Nations. The League of Nations failed to meet a similar test, after which its prestige and influence waned. While the survival of the United Nations may not be at stake by what is happening in Korea, its future development will undoubtedly be greatly affected by the outcome.

Korea's geographic position in East Asia is somewhat similar to that of the Low Countries in Western Europe. It is surrounded by large countries, none of which has been willing to see it fall under the control of the others. Korea borders on China and Russia and is separated from Japan by only 120 miles of water. Assuming a world in which each state must look to its own security, Korea is of the utmost strategic importance to its three large neighbors. For centuries China regarded the peninsular kingdom, as it did nearly all neighboring states, as a vassal, but during much of this time Korea sent tribute to both Japan and China. Japan invaded Korea with large forces in the years 1592–1598, as a preliminary to the conquest of China, but the expedition failed. In 1894, the two countries went to war over the control of Korea, and in 1904, Russia and Japan clashed over the same issue. Japan succeeded in reducing Korea to a protectorate in 1905 and in 1910 formally annexed the country.

The question of the provision that should be made for Korea immediately after World War II presented the United States and its allies with no small problem. It was generally agreed that the country should have its independence, but unfortunately Koreans had had no experience with democratic political methods or modern public administration. They had had no government of their own for thirty-five years and a poor one before that. In view of all the circumstances, it seemed best to preface Korean independence with a short period of trusteeship.

At the conclusion of a conference at Cairo in November, 1943, President Roosevelt, Prime Minister Churchill, and Generalissimo Chiang Kai-shek issued (December 1) a joint statement outlining the war aims of their governments in the Far East. It contained the following declaration with respect to Korea: "The aforesaid three great powers, mindful of the enslavement of the people of Korea, are determined that in due course Korea shall become free and independent." At this time the Soviet Union was still neutral in the war against Japan and hence was not a signatory of this declaration, but at the Yalta Conference it agreed to enter the war in the Pacific two or three months after the conclusion of hostilities in Europe. The Soviet Union declared war on Japan on August 8, and on August 14 Japan surrendered. Rarely has a state through so little military effort acquired so much diplomatic advantage. Soviet armed forces almost immediately marched south to occupy Korean territory down to the thirty-eighth parallel, while some time later American forces established military government south of that line. The origin of this line of demarcation is shrouded in military secrecy, but presumably it was quickly decided upon by staff officers when Japan suddenly collapsed. The decision was probably made chiefly for the purpose of facilitating the disarmament and repatriation of the Japanese. But, whatever its origin and purpose, the thirty-eighth parallel became in effect the frontier between two separate and mutually hostile regimes.

Moscow Agreement

This division of Korea into two occupational zones, governed by opposing ideologies, created all manner of difficulties. It strangled the economic life of the country and prevented any manner of political unification. An effort was made to remedy the situation at the Moscow Conference of December, 1945, at which the foreign ministers of the Soviet Union, the United Kingdom, and the United States agreed that there should be set up "a provisional Korean government," "with a view to the re-establishment of Korea as an independent state" and the "creation of conditions for developing the country on democratic principles. . . ." To assist the formation of a provisional Korean government there was to be established a Joint Commission composed of representatives of the two occupational commands. It was to consult with Korean "democratic parties and social organizations" in preparing proposals for submission to the governments of China, the Soviet Union, Great Britain, and the United States. The proposals were not, however, to envisage immediate independence but "a four-power trusteeship . . . for a period of up to five years."

The Joint Commission met in Seoul in March, 1946, but was unable to get beyond discussing the first step in the procedure. The Soviet Union demanded that all Korean groups which opposed the Moscow agreement for a trusteeship should be excluded from consultations and from the future provisional government. This would have excluded all but the Communists, as all other groups bitterly resented both the phrase "in due course" of the Cairo declaration and the five-year trusteeship directive laid down in the Moscow agreement. Indeed, the Communists were as vehement in denunciation of the trusteeship announcement as other political groups until they received the cue that they were to support it. Unable to reach an agreement on this issue of party consultation, the Joint Commission adjourned. After an appeal by Secretary Marshall to Foreign Minister Molotov, meetings were resumed in May, 1947, but all to no avail. The Soviet representatives finally proposed the creation of a "provisional assembly" of those parties which "fully support the Moscow Agreement," on the basis of equal representation of the two zones. This proposal the United States delegation rejected as inconsistent with the fact that the American zone contained approximately two-thirds of the country's twenty-nine million people. An American proposal for a four-power conference to plan a speedy implementation of the Moscow agreement, with suggestions that election be held shortly in both zones with a view to establishing zonal legislatures, representatives from which would join to compose a national provisional legislature, was accepted by China and the United Kingdom but rejected by the Soviet Union. In acknowledging this rejection the United States government expressed the view that the situation with respect to Korea could not be continued indefinitely, and that since bilateral negotiations were stalemated it would refer the problem of Korean independence to the forthcoming session of the General Assembly of the United Nations. However, at the insistence of the chief of the Soviet delegation the Joint Commission was reconvened. The Soviet Union now proposed that both governments withdraw their troops at the beginning of 1948. In the General Assembly, the Soviet delegate, Mr. Gromyko, protested that the Korean question was not within the competence of the United Nations and repeated the proposal which the Soviet representative had made to the Joint Commission, namely, that both states simultaneously withdraw their forces from Korea.

QUESTION BEFORE THE UNITED NATIONS

In the meanwhile the General Assembly had placed the Korean question on its agenda. On November 14, 1947, it adopted a modified American resolution calling for elections for a national assembly and for the establishment of a United Nations Temporary Commission on Korea, under whose "observation" the elections were to take place. The National Assembly was to form a national government, which, in consultation with the Commission, would (1) constitute its own national security forces and dissolve all other military or semimilitary formations, (2) take over the functions of government from the military commands and civilian authorities of the northern and southern zones, and (3) arrange with the occupying powers for the complete withdrawal of their armed forces as early as practicable and if possible within ninety days.

The United Nations Temporary Commission on Korea (UNTCOK) was unable to carry out its mandate for the whole of Korea because of the refusal of the Soviet commander to cooperate or even to permit it to enter North Korea. UNTCOK thereupon turned to the Interim Committee ("Little Assembly") of the General Assembly for further directives. The Interim Committee declared that in its view it was incumbent upon the Commission to implement the program outlined by the resolution of the General Assembly of November 14, 1947, in such parts of Korea as were accessible to it. The UNTCOK thereupon proceeded with plans for the elections for the National Assembly, which were held on May 30, 1948. In view of the necessarily immature character of Korean political life, the elections may be regarded as fairly successful. There was a movement, instigated from the north, to boycott the election, but this failed. About 80 per cent of the electorate registered, and of these 90 per cent voted. Because of the many parties in the field and the large number of independent candidates, the election results did not form a stable basis for government. No party won a majority of the seats; in fact, the independents constituted the largest group.

Steps to organize the new government were now taken in rapid succession. The Assembly drafted a constitution which was promulgated on July 17, 1948. Dr. Syngman Rhee was elected President by a very large majority, but his first choice for prime minister was rejected by the Assembly. On August 15, the new government took over the administration from the American occupational authorities. After receiving a report from UNTCOK on the discharge of its mandate, the General Assembly of the United Nations on December 12 declared (by a vote of 48 to 6) that the government of the Republic of Korea was "a lawful government . . . based on elections which were a valid expression of the free will of the electorate of that part of Korea . . . and that this is the only such government in Korea." A new Commission on Korea was set up to follow developments and to lend its good offices to bring about the union of south and north under one government. The United States recognized the new government on August 12. The Chinese government extended "provisional" recognition on the same day, and the Philippine government followed some days later.

The United Nations had thus helped to establish the government of the Republic of Korea, which claimed but could not exercise jurisdiction over the whole country. Almost simultaneously there was being created in the north a government which called itself the Democratic People's Republic of Korea, fashioned after the political institutions of the Soviet Union, with its capital at Pyongyang. This government, recognized by the Soviet Union and its satellites, likewise claimed jurisdiction over all Korea. Neither government was able to establish national control by peaceful means; in the end, one of them attempted to impose political unity on the country by force.

On September 18, 1948, the Soviet government notified the American government that, in response to an appeal of the Supreme National Assembly of Korea, it would withdraw its troops from North Korea before the end of the year, and it expressed the hope that the United States government would also agree to evacuate its troops from South Korea within this period. To this suggestion the United States government replied that it regarded the question of troop withdrawal as part of the larger question of Korean unity and independence. Soviet forces, with the exception of a military training mission, supposedly were withdrawn from North Korea before the end of 1948. American withdrawal took place some six months later. On June 29, 1949, the United Nations Commission for Korea (UNCOK),[1] which by a General Assembly resolution of December 12, 1948, replaced the temporary commission (UNTCOK), reported the final departure of United States occupation forces from Korea. At the request of the Korean government about five hundred officers and men remained to help train its security forces.

The United Nations Commission on Korea was no more successful than its predecessor in winning the cooperation of the northern regime in unifying the country. On February 18, 1949, it sent the Soviet Union a telegram, through the Secretary-General, requesting its good offices in establishing contact with the northern government. Some time later it sent a letter to the Premier of the Democratic People's Republic. The Commission did not receive a reply to either communication. In the meantime the northern regime was carrying on its own campaign for unification by such methods as undermining the southern government by infiltration tactics, radio appeals, manifestoes, and calls for conferences and elections looking toward political unification—under the aegis of the northern regime, of course.

Both the Republic of Korea and the Democratic People's Republic of Korea applied for membership in the United Nations. The application of the latter was not considered, while that of the former was defeated in the Security Council by a Soviet veto (April 8, 1949).

The Commission on June 29, 1949, reported that it had verified the withdrawal of United States forces from South Korea, leaving only a military advisory group of five hundred men. The Commission sent word to the Soviet Union that it was prepared to extend the same offices of observance and verification of the withdrawal of Soviet forces, but no reply was received to this offer.

That the relations between North and South Korea were getting worse and taking on a hostile character is evidenced from the resolution of the General

---

[1] The new Commission was composed of representatives of India (chairman), Australia, China, El Salvador, France, the Philippines, and Turkey.

Assembly of October 21, 1949, extending the life of the Commission on Korea, which was now charged with the additional function of observing and reporting developments "which might lead to or otherwise involve military conflict." This new function became the first task of the Commission. At an Independence Day celebration on March 1, 1950, President Rhee indicated that he would strive to reunite the country, by peaceful means if possible but by military measures if necessary. On the same occasion the chairman of the Commission on Korea reminded the audience that the United Nations was created to facilitate the peaceful settlement of disputes, while the United States Ambassador, John J. Muccio, warned against combating communism by other than democratic methods.

The North Korean propaganda campaign for political unification of the whole country was stepped up in June. For successive days Radio Pyongyang repeatedly broadcast an appeal for unification. In response to this appeal the Commission on Korea, on June 10, sent a representative across the thirty-eighth parallel to meet with three representatives of North Korea. They met at a point just across the parallel, but the meeting came to nought, as the northern representatives stated that they were only agents and had no authority to enter into discussion or accept documents.

INVASION OF SOUTH KOREA

The crossing of the thirty-eighth parallel by the armed forces of North Korea in the early morning of June 25, 1950, precipitated a crisis of the utmost gravity for the United Nations. In defiance of the attempt of the United Nations to unify Korea by peaceful means, the Soviet-created government now sought to achieve the same object by imposing its own regime by force. So direct a challenge to the authority and purposes of the United Nations could be ignored only at great cost to its prestige and future development. This aggression likewise confronted the United States with a most difficult decision. It was the only country which was in a position to give any real immediate aid to the South Koreans in repelling the aggression. The decision of the United States to support strong United Nations action involved tremendous military risks. Few of the American troops stationed in nearby Japan had had much combat training.

At the request of the United States the Security Council met the same day the invasion was launched. When the Council met on the afternoon of June 25, it had before it a report from UNCOK to the Secretary-General drawing attention to the "serious situation which is developing which is assuming character of full-scale war and may endanger the maintenance of international peace and security." The Council passed an amended and revised American resolution requesting the immediate cessation of hostilities and calling upon the authorities of North Korea to withdraw their armed forces to the thirty-eighth parallel. UNCOK was directed to communicate its fully considered recommendations on the situation, to observe the withdrawal of the North Korean forces to the thirty-eighth parallel, and to keep the Security Council informed on the execution of this resolution. Lastly, the resolution called upon all members of the United Nations "to render every assistance to the United Nations in the execution of this resolution and to refrain from giving assistance to the North Korean authorities." The resolution was adopted by nine votes—those of China, Cuba, Ecuador, Egypt, France, India, Norway, the United Kingdom, and the United States. The Soviet Union was absent, and Yugoslavia did not vote.

On June 26, President Truman announced that, in accordance with the resolution of the Security Council, American personnel in Korea was actively cooperating in the defense of the Republic and that steps were being taken "to expedite and augment assistance of the type being furnished under the Mutual Defense Assistance Program." On June 27, the President announced that he had ordered "United States air and sea forces to give Korean government troops cover and support." The President also stated that he had ordered a unit of the U.S. Navy to prevent any attack on Formosa and had called upon the Nationalist Chinese government to cease all air and sea operations against the mainland. "The determination of the future status of Formosa," he declared, "must await the restoration of security in the Pacific, a peace settlement with Japan, or consideration by the United Nations." The President justified these measures on the ground that the attack upon Korea had made "plain beyond all doubt that communism had passed beyond the use of subversion to conquer independent nations and will now use armed invasion and war." Communism had defied the orders of the United Nations issued to preserve peace and security. "In these circumstances the occupation of Formosa by Communist forces would be a direct threat to the security of the Pacific area and to the United States forces performing their lawful and necessary functions in that area." The measures taken by the United States with respect to China failed to receive the endorsement of many governments which supported the United Nations resolution.

The President at this time also announced that he had ordered the strengthening of American forces in the Philippines and the acceleration of military assistance to the Philippine government and similarly "to the forces of France and the Associated States in Indo-China and the despatch of a military mission to provide close working relations with those forces."

The Security Council met again on June 27. Again it had before it a resolution introduced by the United States representative. The resolution took note of the fact that its call for a cessation of hostilities had not been heeded, nor had the North Korean troops withdrawn to the thirty-eighth parallel. It also noted that the Republic of Korea had appealed to the United Nations for immediate and effective steps to secure peace and security. In view of these facts it recommended "that the Members of the United Nations furnish such assistance to the Republic of Korea as may be necessary to repel the armed attack and to restore international peace and security in the area." The resolution was adopted by a vote of seven in favor to one against. Yugoslavia cast the lone vote against it. The representatives of India and Egypt, since they had no instructions from their governments, did not participate.

The Security Council met for the third time in six days on June 30. At this meeting the representative of India reported that his government "accepted" the resolution adopted at the previous meeting, while the representative of Egypt stated that he would have abstained had he been able to participate in the voting. He explained that he would have abstained from voting for the reason, first, that the Korean conflict was but a new phase of the "deep-rooted divergencies between the Western and Eastern blocs" and secondly that the United Nations had ignored several cases of aggression in the past and could not consistently take action as it was now doing in the case of Korea. Mr. Austin, the United States representative, informed the Security Council that President Truman had that morning authorized the U.S. Air Force to conduct missions on specific military targets in North Korea wherever militarily necessary, had ordered a naval blockade of the entire Korean coast, and had authorized General MacArthur to use certain supporting ground forces.

On July 7, the Security Council met for a fourth time to consider the crisis in Korea. The Council at this meeting adopted a resolution, proposed jointly by the United Kingdom and France, recommending that all members providing military forces and other assistance, pursuant to the resolutions of June 25 and 27, make such forces and assistance available to a unified command under the United States, requesting the United States to designate the commander of such forces, authorizing the unified command at its discretion to use the United Nations flag in the course of operations against North Korean forces concurrently with the flags of the various participating nations, and requesting the United States to provide the Security Council with reports on the course of action taken under the unified command. The resolution was adopted by a vote of 7 to 0. The Soviet Union was still absent, and Egypt, India, and Yugoslavia abstained. On the next day, July 8, President Truman announced that in response to the request of the Security Council he had designated General Douglas MacArthur as the Commander of the United Nations Forces in Korea.

Nearly all the members of the United Nations responded favorably to the resolution of June 27. Secretary-General Trygve Lie was able to report on July 14 that, aside from the United States, fifty-two governments had replied favorably. All offered moral support, many material assistance, and a few military aid. Only the Chinese Nationalist government offered to make available a significant number of troops. It agreed to make available for use in Korea some 33,000 seasoned men. This embarrassing offer was turned aside

by the United States government with the suggestion that, in view of the
threat of invasion of Taiwan by Communist forces from the mainland, it would
be desirable for the Chinese military authorities to hold discussions with representatives of General MacArthur's headquarters before any final decisions
were made to reduce the defense forces on the island.

COMMUNIST VIEWS

In its report of June 26 to the Secretary-General, UNCOK stated that "all
the evidence continues to point to a calculated co-ordinated attack prepared
and launched with secrecy," that "South Korean forces were deployed on
wholly defensive basis" and were taken "completely by surprise."   The Korean
Communist version as given by General Kim Usung and reported by UNCOK
was that "South Korea, having rejected every Northern proposal for peaceful
unification, had crowned its iniquity by launching an invasion force across the
parallel, . . . thus precipitating North Korean counter attacks for which it
would have to assume the consequences."   This was also the view adopted by
Poland, which in addition protested against "aggression of the United States
on Korea, and on the territory of China, and against the announced intervention in the Philippines and in Viet Nam."   The Soviet government likewise
accepted the view that the events in Korea were provoked by an attack from
the south, and in addition it challenged the validity of the action of the
Security Council on the ground that the resolution did not have the concurring
votes of all the permanent members as required by Article 27 of the Charter.
The Soviet government justified its absence from the Security Council with the
argument that so long as China was excluded from representation (meaning
Communist China, of course) it was impossible for that body to take decisions
having legal force.   The United States was accused of armed intervention in
Korea and of "aggression, simultaneously in a whole number of the countries
of Asia."

To the Soviet allegation that the action of the Security Council with respect
to Korea was illegal, the United States government replied at considerable
length in a statement of June 30.   It pointed out that by a long series of
precedents the practice had been established whereby abstention by permanent
members of the Security Council did not constitute a veto.   Every member
of the United Nations, including the Soviet Union, had acquiesced in this
practice.   It cited ten resolutions of the Council on substantive matters on
which the Soviet Union had abstained but the legality of which it had never
challenged.   The United States statement further pointed out that the Soviet
government had not questioned the legality of action taken by the Security
Council in at least three instances in which it had voted with the majority
but on which other permanent members of the Council had abstained.   "The
voluntary absence of a permanent member from the Security Council," so

the United States contended, "is clearly analogous to abstention." It further drew attention to the provision of Article 28 of the Charter that the Security Council shall be so organized as to be able to function continuously and that this injunction would be defeated if the absence of a representative of a permanent member were construed to have the effect of preventing all substantive action by the Council. The United States statement also disposed of the Soviet claim about the absence of Chinese representation. The representative of the Nationalist government had been seated as the representative of China in accordance with the Rules of Procedure of the Council, and this accreditation had never been withdrawn. Therefore, the vote of the Nationalist representative on the resolutions of June 25 and 27 was the official vote of China.

A most effective refutation of the Russian arguments was made by Mr. Chauvel, the representative of France in the Security Council. He reminded the Soviet government that it always claimed to be the champion of democracy, and as such it could not consistently challenge the credentials of the Chinese representative, for that was a matter for the decision of the Council and not for any single member. With respect to the Soviet argument that the action of the Council was illegal because it had been taken without its concurring vote, Mr. Chauvel stressed the view that membership in the Council had a dual character and carried a dual responsibility. The representatives were on the one hand representatives of their governments, but on the other they were members of a body whose primary function was the maintenance of international peace and security. The latter was a collective and joint responsibility, a mandate conferred by all the members of the United Nations. This responsibility could not be shirked merely because the Council had failed to accept a member's point of view on a given matter. It was a maxim of Roman law that no one had the right to invoke his own mistakes to his own advantage. By abandoning the Council, the Soviet Union had abandoned the Charter. "When it returned to both, it would recover its right of speech, of criticism, of vote, and of veto. Until then the USSR had no moral or legal basis for contesting United Nations action."

The Soviet Union did not stop with declaring the action of the Security Council illegal. It decided to obstruct action from within by returning to the Council. Mr. Yakov A. Malik, permanent representative of the Soviet Union to the United Nations, returned to the Council on August 1 and, in accordance with established procedures, assumed its presidency for the month. He had not attended its meetings since January. Throughout the month of his chairmanship he put on a masterful exhibition of obstructionism. With the Soviet representative back in the Security Council, that body again became the international sounding board for Soviet Communist propaganda. He sought to divide the countries of the free world by driving a wedge between the United States and those countries which, though they supported the United Nations action on Korea, were not happy about American Far Eastern policy.

CHINESE COMMUNIST INTERVENTION

The first twelve weeks of military operations were very discouraging for the United Nations forces. They were pressed back behind a perimeter around Pusan, a vital seaport on the southern tip of the peninsula. They were able to hold this perimeter, however, while they were steadily building up their strength through reinforcements. In mid-September the military picture dramatically changed by the bold maneuver of General MacArthur in effecting a successful amphibious landing at Inchon near Seoul. In not many days the government of Korea was back in its capital city and the North Korean troops rapidly withdrew northward with heavy loss of men and supplies.

The northward march of the victorious armies precipitated the question of the military objectives of the United Nations forces. Were they to stop at the thirty-eighth parallel or were they to press on to the Manchurian border? It was a military question with very important political implications. India, which had recognized the Communist regime in China and had entered into diplomatic relations with it, warned that crossing the parallel might bring the Chinese Communists into the war. Moreover, India's Prime Minister was of the opinion that it would be unwise for the United Nations to attempt more than the restoration of conditions as they were before the aggression. Others were of the view that to stop at the parallel would leave everything unsettled and give the forces of aggression the opportunity to prepare for a new attack. The matter was brought before the General Assembly, which was in session. On October 7, it adopted a resolution which by implication authorized advance beyond the parallel. The General Assembly in its resolution recalled the essential objectives of its actions of 1947, 1948, and 1949 as "the establishment of a unified, independent and democratic Government of Korea," and it therefore recommended that "all appropriate steps be taken to ensure conditions of stability throughout Korea," and that "all constituent acts be taken, including the holding of elections, under the auspices of the United Nations, for the establishment of a unified, independent and democratic Government in the sovereign State of Korea." This resolution also looked toward the reconstruction of this sorely stricken land by calling upon the Economic and Social Council "to develop plans for relief and rehabilitation on the termination of hostilities" and "to expedite the study of long-term measures to promote the economic development and social progress of Korea." A United Nations Commission for the Unification and Rehabilitation of Korea (UNCURK), composed of Australia, Chile, Netherlands, Pakistan, Philippines, Thailand, and Turkey, was created to replace the United Nations Commission on Korea (UNCOK).[2]

As the United Nations forces approached the Manchurian border late in October they encountered Chinese forces, small at first but steadily increasing in number. On November 5, General MacArthur reported the fact of Chinese Communist intervention. The United Nations were now confronted with what amounted to an "entirely new war."

The United States immediately requested the Security Council to consider the new development. The Council considered a resolution sponsored by six members calling upon all "states and authorities, and in particular those responsible for the action voted above, to refrain from assisting or encouraging the North Korean authorities, to prevent their nationals or individuals or units of their armed forces from giving assistance to North Korean forces and to cause the immediate withdrawal of any such nationals, individuals, or units which may presently be in Korea." The resolution also affirmed that it was the intention of the United Nations to respect the Chinese frontier with Korea and fully to protect legitimate Chinese and Korean interests in the frontier zone. The resolution came up for a vote on November 30. It was vetoed by the Soviet Union. The United States now requested that the matter of Chinese aggression be placed upon the agenda of the General Assembly. After the failure of an attempt to bring about a cease-fire agreement, the General Assembly on February 1, 1951, by a vote of 51 to 5, adopted a resolution finding the People's Republic of China guilty of aggression in Korea and affirming that it continued to be the policy of the United Nations to bring about a cessation of hostilities in Korea and the achievement of its objectives in Korea by peaceful means.

On May 18, 1951, the General Assembly followed up this resolution with another recommending that all states apply an embargo on the shipment of arms and implements of war to Communist China and North Korea.

EFFORTS AT MEDIATION

Attempts at mediation began almost immediately upon the outbreak of hostilities in Korea. Prime Minister Nehru of India on July 13, 1950, sent personal messages to Premier Stalin and Secretary Acheson proposing a solution of the Korean problem by giving Communist China a seat on the Security Council as a first step, to be followed by negotiations among the United States, the Soviet Union, and China for the permanent solution of the Korean problem. The move was rejected by the United States on the ground that yielding now to Communist demands would be tantamount to rewarding aggression.

A concession was made to Communist China when the Security Council on

[2] The resolution was passed by 47 votes in favor, with 5 opposed and 8 abstentions.

November 8 voted to invite a representative of the People's Republic of China to be present during discussion by the Council of the special report of the United Nations Command in Korea. A little later the Political and Security Committee of the General Assembly voted to invite the Peiping government to take part in general discussions of the Korean problem, including American "aggression" in Korea. A delegation shortly arrived from Peiping, but its only activity was bitter incrimination of American "imperialism" in the Far East. Under the leadership of an Asia-Arab group of states, the General Assembly on December 14 passed a resolution requesting the President of the Assembly to appoint two persons to be associated with himself in constituting a team to determine the basis on which a satisfactory cease-fire could be arranged. The President, Mr. N. Entezam of Iran, appointed Sir Benegal Rau of India and Mr. L. B. Pearson of Canada to serve with him. The group met with no cooperation from the Chinese Communists and had to report that its efforts had ended in failure. The Communist government in a statement to Mr. Entezam on December 22, repeated in a message of January 17 to the First Committee of the General Assembly, stated its conditions for a truce as follows: (1) the withdrawal of all foreign troops from Korea and the settlement of "Korean domestic affairs by the Koreans themselves," (2) the withdrawal of United States forces from Formosa, and (3) Chinese Communist representation in the United Nations.

The United Nations in spite of this rebuff in effect invited a continuation of efforts to reach a truce agreement. The General Assembly resolution of February 1, which branded Red China as an aggressor, contained a request to the President of the Assembly to designate two persons who would meet with him at any suitable opportunity to use their good offices to bring about a cessation of hostilities in Korea and the achievement of United Nations objectives by peaceful means.

The United Nations forces after the intervention by the Chinese Communists were forced to withdraw from North Korea to a line south of Seoul. After a few months, however, they were again able to move forward against the enemy. Their steady progress probably had something to do with the suggestion made by Mr. Malik, the chief Soviet delegate to the United Nations, in a radio broadcast on June 23, 1951, proposing that the time had come to settle the problem of the armed conflict in Korea and indicating that the Soviet Union would encourage discussions for a cease-fire agreement. On June 29, General M. B. Ridgway, who some time before had succeeded General MacArthur as Chief of United Nations forces in Korea, acted on the Soviet suggestion by communicating to the Commander-in-chief of the Communist forces in Korea that he was prepared to appoint a representative if such a meeting was indeed desired. The contact thus made resulted in the beginning of negotiations at Kaesong on July 10. But it soon became clear that the Communists were in no hurry to reach an agreement. Negotiations were broken off several times. Many weary months were spent in negotiations, but no agreement had been reached in November, 1951 (time of writing).

CONCLUSIONS

The first reaction to the decision of the United Nations to resist the aggression in Korea with vigor and determination was, in general, one of hearty approval. Some, disturbed by the steadily declining prestige of the United Nations, spoke of it as a new birth for that institution. The more enthusiastic declared that the decision had electrified the free world, heartened the half-hearted in Europe and Asia, encouraged the fence sitters to climb down on the right side, and dispelled defeatism. The decisive action of the United Nations in meeting aggression would in the future discourage satellites from being used by the Soviet Union and then left in the lurch. It would unite the free world. The lessons learned and the confidence gained from successfully repelling aggression would make it easier to meet succeeding ones.

The great gains that would come from the successful application of sanctions against an aggressor were easily discernible, and it was also easy to see what dire consequences would have come from a failure to meet the crisis squarely. It was more difficult, however, especially in the early stages, to envisage all the problems which would have to be met and what would be the situation if the action failed or ended in a stalemate. As the campaign to repel aggression lengthened into months and threatened to continue for years, the tensions within the free world became more and more evident. This development was due to several factors. A number of Asiatic countries had only just acquired their independence, and there lingered throughout Asia considerable suspicion of the large Western Powers. The sentiment of neutralism was widely prevalent. There was a feeling among the peoples of these new states that because of their grave internal problems and weakness they ought not to allow themselves to be drawn into either power bloc.

There was also the problem created by the fact that American policy in the Far East could not be wholly extricated from United Nations policy with respect to Korea, and later China. American national policy in Asia by no means enjoyed universal endorsement. India, whose moral influence in all Asia is very great, was at odds with American policy with respect to Indochina and China. India and the United Kingdom had recognized the Communist government of China. India disliked American support of the French in Indochina, which it regarded as intervention in support of colonialism. It was necessary, of course, to have a unified command for the United Nations forces in Korea, and it was also clear that the commander-in-chief would have to be an American and that the only logical choice was General MacArthur. But General MacArthur was known for his positive political views on Far Eastern policy. All this complicated the problem and sometimes dampened enthusiasms. The Soviet Union quickly seized upon this situation and directed all of its powerful propaganda activities toward deepening this rift and sowing doubt and suspicion.

The difference became most evident in the matter of branding Communist China an aggressor and of applying some sort of sanctions against it. Many states voted for this measure with great reluctance. Some European governments feared that it might lead to a war with China, which would almost certainly draw many American divisions to Asia and away from Europe, where the real test with the Soviet Union might be precipitated just when the United States had become inextricably involved in the East. There was also a feeling that marking China an aggressor would only make a settlement more difficult without any compensating gains. To the United States it was a relatively simple moral problem. Aggression is aggression, no matter by whom it is committed. To abandon principle for expediency was only to invite disaster. Moreover, it would put the United Nations in an absurd position. If the Communist Chinese in Korea were not aggressors, then surely North Koreans, fighting in their own country, were not aggressors. If the Chinese in Korea were not aggressors, then the United Nations forces were.

One aspect of the problem is difficult to evaluate. The South Koreans had put up a heroic defense against aggression and had received much aid from the members of the United Nations; nevertheless, the war had left the Koreans impoverished and their country devastated. Even if in the end the United Nations were successful in repelling the aggression, would Korea's example inspire other small countries in a strategic position to stand firmly against aggression. or would it rather lead them to seek appeasement? The free world was not indifferent to the plight of the stricken Koreans. Measures for the relief of Korea were undertaken by the United Nations almost immediately after the invasion began, and on December 1, 1950, the General Assembly established the Korean Reconstruction Agency (UNKRA) for the relief and reconstruction of Korea. Unless outside help became available in large measure communism would still stand an excellent chance of winning all of Korea, even though it had lost on the field of battle.

The Korean experience demonstrated that the United Nations Charter had far more flexibility than even many liberal constructionists had thought possible. The absence of the Soviet Union had not blocked action by the Security Council, and when the Soviet representative returned to the Council to paralyze it, the case was shifted to the General Assembly. All in all, much was learned in every way about international cooperation in maintaining collective security. But not all the lessons were positive. Some were negative. While there were many advantages in moving the Korean issue from the Security Council to the vetoless General Assembly, it did not solve all the problems and it created some new ones. A body of sixty members is a bit unwieldy for serving as a supervisor, if not the director, of a military cam-

238 WORK AND ACCOMPLISHMENTS

paign. It has also brought into bold relief the problem that is created by the fact that under conditions of modern, mechanized warfare only a few states can contribute any real military aid. Not over a fourth of the members of the United Nations made any contribution to the military forces in Korea, and most of these, aside from the United States, made only token contributions. As months of hostilities followed each other the American people became restive and even resentful of the meager aid it had received, and a recrudescence of old isolationist sentiments were noticeable in American public opinion. The large number of small states in the General Assembly who make no contribution to the United Nations cause in Korea have the controlling vote in deciding the basic policies. This cannot be regarded as an ideal situation. It touches the whole problem of the proper basis for representation in the United Nations organs, and especially in the General Assembly.

As the days of the United Nations police action went on interminably and the American casualty list lengthened, many Americans became frightened. There arose the nightmare of the possibility that the Korean campaign could not be brought to a successful conclusion. Suppose the aggressors were driven out of the country, would not a huge army have to be kept at the border indefinitely? Strict logic would require carrying the military campaign to the Korean hinterland of Manchuria, North China, and even Siberia, but this might precipitate World War III. General MacArthur had chafed under the directives to limit the war to Korea even though the enemy forces were supported by bases in China and were operating from this sheltered zone. A leading candidate for the presidency of the United States was clearly appealing to a strong latent sentiment of many of his fellow countrymen by declaring the military operations in Korea "useless."

What must not be forgotten is that the situation in Korea is only a phase or a part of the whole world situation. Can the basic issues which divide the free world from the Communist-dominated world be resolved? If they can, the solution in Korea will be a simple matter. As yet, however, neither force nor diplomacy has brought peace to the world.

Chapter 16

ARMAMENTS AND ATOMIC ENERGY

The regulation and control of armaments is a central problem for a system of collective security. When a nation relies on its own armed strength for protection, it has security only so long as it is stronger than any potential enemy or group of enemies. If, however, it is this strong, other nations will be too weak to protect themselves on the same basis. One Great Power, with its allies, might become so strong that no enemy dare attack it. But it is impossible for two Great Powers, or two alliances, to be that much stronger than each other. When each attempts to become stronger relative to the other, the result is an armaments race which in itself is a grave threat to international peace and security. Under the expectation of violence, each party views the other's defensive preparations as evidence of aggressive intent and speeds up the tempo of its own armament as a counterdefense. This is in turn construed as a threat, to be answered by additional measures which continue to feed the vicious spiral. One nation might possibly guarantee its security by its armed strength, but by the same token all others would be insecure and from an international viewpoint the problem would not be solved. When circumstances are such that no one nation can be overwhelmingly successful in an armaments race, all nations are insecure. Security and aggression cannot be clearly and objectively separated, with all nations strong enough to defend themselves but too weak to attack others, because the same weapons and the same bases may be used for defense or attack. The government of a Great Power does not assume that a potential enemy will never use its strength aggressively.

The Covenant of the League of Nations emphasized the idea of *reduction* of national armaments. When the attempt was made to implement this concept, it became obvious that nations would not voluntarily give up their armed forces until they had obtained security. But collective security cannot become a reality until the reliance upon competitive national armaments is ended. This is the fundamental and as yet unsolved dilemma of the armaments question. The Charter of the United Nations approaches the problem with the emphasis on regulation of armaments, with the idea that force may have to be utilized to maintain security and that minimum as well as maximum limits may have to be set. The United Nations, however, has faced the same dilemma in regulating national armaments as the League of Nations did in reducing them.

CONTROL OF ATOMIC ENERGY

A few weeks after the Charter was signed at San Francisco, an atomic bomb was dropped on Hiroshima. Consequently the United Nations began its work confronted with an overshadowing problem that had not been known to the delegates who planned the Organization. One of the first undertakings was to seek a means for dealing with this situation. The General Assembly, on January 24, 1946, unanimously adopted a resolution to establish a United Nations Atomic Energy Commission to deal with the problems raised by the discovery of atomic energy and other related matters. This Commission is composed of one representative from each of the states represented on the Security Council and also includes a representative of Canada when the latter is not a member of the Security Council. The Commission was directed to study all phases of the problem with the utmost dispatch, and to submit its reports and recommendations to the Security Council. The following terms of reference were prescribed: (1) extending between all nations the exchange of basic scientific information for peaceful ends; (2) control of atomic energy to the extent necessary to ensure its use only for peaceful purposes; (3) elimination from national armaments of atomic weapons and of all other major weapons adaptable to mass destruction; (4) effective safeguards by way of inspection and other means to protect complying states against the hazards of violations and evasions.

At the first meeting of the Commission, on June 14, 1946, the government of the United States submitted a proposed plan based upon the creation of an International Atomic Development Authority entrusted with all phases of the development and use of atomic energy.[1] The fundamental importance of immediate punishment for infringements of the rights of this Authority was stressed, and the American representative, Mr. Bernard Baruch, declared that "there must be no veto to protect those who violate their solemn agreements not to develop or use atomic energy for destructive purposes." The United States plan contained the following specific proposals:

1. The International Atomic Development Authority should conduct continuous surveys of world supplies of uranium and thorium and bring the raw materials under its control.

2. The Authority should control and operate all the primary plants producing fissionable products in dangerous quantities and all plants dealing with uranium or thorium after it had once reached the potential of dangerous use.

3. The Authority should possess the exclusive right to conduct research in

[1] This was the so-called Baruch plan. In its main outlines, it followed the recommendations of the Acheson-Lilienthal report which was published in March, 1946. The Baruch plan, however, placed more emphasis on the swift, sure, and vetoless punishment of a violator of an atomic energy agreement, and it placed less reliance on "denaturing" fissionable materials as a part of the control plan.

the field of atomic explosives, and all other atomic research should be open only to nations under license of the Authority, which would furnish them with denatured materials.

4. Dangerous activities of the Authority, and its stock piles, should be decentralized and strategically distributed.

5. Freedom for any inspection deemed necessary by the Authority should be granted by nations.

The United States proposed that, once renunciation of the bomb as a weapon had been agreed on and an adequate system of control put into effective operation with punishments set up for any violations, manufacture of atomic bombs should stop, existing bombs should be disposed of under treaty, and the Authority should be given full information as to the know-how for atomic energy production. Subject to constitutional processes, the United States government would make available to the Authority, at successive stages, the information necessary for its effective functioning at each of these stages in its progressive assumption of control.

At the second meeting of the Commission, five days later, the Soviet Union presented its plan,[2] which was based on proposals for the conclusion of an international agreement to forbid the production and use of atomic weapons. The essentials of such an agreement would be:

1. The production and use of atomic weapons would be forbidden.

2. Within three months from the entry into force of the agreement, all stocks of atomic weapons would be destroyed.

3. Any violation of the agreement would be regarded as a serious threat against humanity.

4. Violation of the agreement would be severely punished under the domestic legislation of the contracting parties.

5. The agreement would be of indefinite duration, coming into force after approval by the Security Council and ratification by all its permanent members.

6. All states, whether members of the United Nations or not, would be obliged to fulfil all the provisions of the agreement.

The representative of the Soviet Union also proposed the creation of two committees of the whole, one to develop the exchange of scientific information and the other to prepare recommendations for outlawing and preventing the use of atomic energy for the harm of humanity.

The American and Soviet proposals of June, 1946, presented the opposing viewpoints which have persisted, with the major issues unchanged, in all the attempts to find some formula by which atomic energy might be brought under international control. For purposes of a convenient summary, four specific points of fundamental disagreement may be recognized in the oceans of words that have poured forth on this subject. First, there was the question of the

[2] This was the so-called Gromyko plan.

order in which the essential steps would be taken. The United States insisted that the establishment of an adequate system of international control and inspection was a prerequisite to the effective prohibition of atomic weapons, and refused to share its "know-how" concerning atomic energy until there was agreement on this prior point. The Soviet Union wanted to outlaw and destroy all atomic weapons as a first step, and then establish a system of international control. This would, of course, put the two countries on an equality in this matter before serious negotiations on the control system were started. The United States government did not intend to surrender the new weapon until effective safeguards were in operation and wanted to be sure that atomic disarmament would not, in effect, leave it helpless against an evader of the plan. The Soviet government, on the contrary, was unwilling to submit to a substantial degree of international control and inspection while the Americans retained a supply of atomic bombs.

The proposal that a plan of international control go into effect by successive stages was not sufficient to break this deadlock. The problem of agreement on the first step remained. So far as the United States was concerned, the stage of destroying its bombs and giving up its "secrets" would not be reached until an adequate system of international control and inspection had been established. In the Soviet view, this meant that the United States would retain its advantage in the earlier stages and would be in a position to decide at what point its atomic weapons could safely be destroyed. Therefore, the Soviet Union might consider itself as making present concessions in return for promises as to the future. It should be noted that redemption of these promises depended in part on action by Congress, which cannot constitutionally be bound as to future action. The American proposal on making information available to the International Atomic Development Authority contained the phrase "subject to constitutional processes." Any agreement on atomic energy would take the form of a treaty, requiring the consent of the Senate by a two-thirds majority. Also, the Atomic Energy Act signed by the President in August, 1946, provided that there should be no international exchange of information with respect to the use of atomic energy for industrial purposes "until Congress declares by joint resolution that effective and enforceable international safeguards against the use of atomic energy for destructive purposes have been established."

At first thought, it may seem strange that the Soviet government regarded itself as being asked to make concessions in return for insubstantial promises. After all, it was the United States which had the atomic bomb and was offering to surrender its exclusive control. The answer lies to a considerable extent in the second point of fundamental disagreement, the question of inspection. The Baruch proposals included the stipulation that the international control authority must have unlimited rights of access for inspection purposes. Otherwise there would be no assurance against undetected violations or evasions of an agreement on atomic weapons. The Soviet government insisted on periodic and limited inspection, feeling that greater reliance must be placed on the national governments, that continuous and unlimited rights of inspection were unnecessary and in fact would amount to supervision, and that an international agency with a majority composition of "capitalist" representatives might develop harmful policies and activities. For example, a thorough inspection would give the International Authority comprehensive information on the Soviet industrial complex and would provide data by which a potential enemy could pinpoint vital targets in the Soviet Union. This possibility was unacceptable to the Soviet government.

The third major point of disagreement involved the question of the authority to be given to an international control agency. The United States considered that complete ownership and operation of all plants producing fissionable materials was essential. The Soviet government thought in terms of an international commission which would have designated supervisory powers but which would not own and operate any plants, at least in that country. It seemed obvious that the Soviet Union would be in a minority position on the International Atomic Development Authority. The decisions would be made by a majority of "capitalist" members under the leadership of the United States. In this connection, Soviet suspicion was aroused not only by potential threats to national security, but also by fears of discrimination in the development of atomic energy for peaceful purposes. For example, a major Soviet goal is to increase industrial productivity, and its available energy per capita is quite low. Could the International Authority be expected to make decisions on the location and ownership of atomic plants in such a way as to decrease the gap in energy resources between the Soviet Union and the leading "capitalist" countries? Whatever the Soviet leaders thought at the time on this point, the maximum of international control which they would permit was far below the minimum that the American government considered essential.

In the fourth place, the question of the veto was an issue. The United States insisted that after an international agreement on atomic energy was reached the control agency must operate outside the voting procedure prescribed by Article 27 of the Charter. Suppose a plan of international control were agreed to, the United States destroyed its atomic bombs and released its information concerning atomic energy to the world, and then one of the permanent members of the Security Council violated the plan and used the veto to prevent any enforcement action to be taken against it. This was the sort of situation which the United States representative had in mind when he insisted so strongly that the veto must be eliminated for atomic matters. The Soviet Union, however, remained unwilling to sacrifice its sovereignty to this extent and stood pat on the letter of the Charter as it had so recently been written at San Francisco. The Soviet government was not going to put itself at the mercy of a voting majority of "capitalist" countries. The only concession on this point was first made in the course of General Assembly debates on disarmament during the fall of 1946, when Mr. Molotov said that the unanimity rule of the Charter had nothing to do with the day-to-day operation of the proposed international control commission. But the question still remained of whether a Great Power might violate the agreement, or be suspected of doing so, and prevent any enforcement measures against itself.

It is entirely possible that the importance of the veto question has been overemphasized in the discussions. To a large extent, it is a symbolic rather than an actual problem. If a Great Power took the drastic step of violating the international agreement, would it then acquiesce in enforcement action directed against it because of a previous commitment to be bound by a majority vote? Obviously not. It is safe to assume that attempts at enforcement would be resisted in such a case, whatever the voting procedure might be. To carry them out would mean atomic warfare, and a government which would precipitate such a situation certainly would not hesitate to break its pledge respecting a voting procedure in an international agency. Moreover, Article 51 of the Charter explicitly recognizes the inherent right in individual or collective self-defense if an armed attack occurs and the Security Council does not deal with it effectively. Therefore, a veto in the Security Council would not impede enforcement measures if the atomic violation were considered to be equivalent to an armed attack. Since a serious violation of an international agreement on atomic weapons could hardly have any other purpose than an armed attack, it is likely that measures of preventive defense could be taken by the other members of the United Nations within the framework of the Charter. Of course, there is some doubt and supposition on this point. If a violation of an atomic control plan did not constitute an "armed attack" within the meaning of Article 51, and did not result in immediate war on considerations of national security or power politics, a real difficulty in connection with the voting procedure would be involved. Since the veto question is near the crux of the whole matter symbolically, but of a much more limited importance actually, the question arises of whether it would be safe to make any concessions, in return for a satisfactory *quid pro quo* on other points, to the Soviet view that international control of atomic energy should be subordinated to the regular procedures of the Security Council.

The United Nations Atomic Energy Commission submitted its first report to the Security Council on December 31, 1946. Agreement had been reached that international control of atomic energy was technically feasible. The political basis for international control was a different matter, with all the members of the Commission, except the Soviet Union and Poland, agreeing with the substance of the Baruch proposals.

The report [3] of the Commission described the results of the work which had

[3] This report was adopted by a vote of 10 to 0 in the Commission. The Soviet Union and Poland abstained from being parties to any decision on the substance of the proposals.

been done during the year. In its general findings it stated that scientifically, technically, and practically it was feasible (1) to extend among all nations the exchange of basic scientific information on atomic energy for peaceful ends; (2) to control atomic energy to the extent necessary to ensure its use only for peaceful purposes; (3) to accomplish the elimination from national armaments of atomic weapons; and (4) to provide effective safeguards by way of inspection and other means to protect complying states against the hazards of violations and evasions. The report stated that an effective control system must be international and must be established by an enforceable multilateral treaty or convention, administered by an international agency within the United Nations. An agreement to outlaw national production, possession, or use of atomic weapons was considered essential but would not be sufficient to guarantee peaceful use or to provide effective safeguards against violations or evasions.

On the basis of these findings, the Commission recommended the creation of a strong and comprehensive system of control and inspection. An international authority possessing the power and responsibility necessary for the prompt and effective discharge of its duties would be established. The rule of unanimity of the permanent members which governed all the substantive decisions of the Security Council would have no relation to the work of this Authority. The exchange of basic scientific information should be promoted, with safeguards against dangerous uses of atomic energy itself. There would be a minimum of interference with the operations of national agencies. Representatives of the Authority would have unimpeded rights of access for the performance of their inspections. The manufacture, possession, and use of atomic weapons would be prohibited, and there would be provision for the disposal of existing stocks and for the proper use of fissionable materials. The methods for determining violations would be specified in the treaty. Enforcement measures and the punishment of violators would not be subject to veto. Finally, the treaty would provide a schedule for the completion of the transitional process leading step by step to the full and effective establishment of international control of atomic energy.

The Security Council considered the Commission's report during February and March, 1947, and adopted a resolution urging a continuation of the inquiry into all phases of the problem and the preparation of a draft convention. The Commission was also asked to submit a second report before the next regular session of the General Assembly. At a meeting on March 19, 1947, the Atomic Energy Commission instructed its committees to study particularly those questions on which agreements among its members had not been reached. A thorough consideration of the amendments and additions which the Soviet Union had proposed before the Security Council did not, however, lead the Commission to revise the findings and recommendations which it had reached in its first report.

At the Commission's meeting of June 11, 1947, the representative of the Soviet Union presented for consideration a set of "provisions on which an international agreement or convention on atomic energy control should be based." These proposals were a restatement and elaboration of the previous Soviet position, and it was decided that there was no reason to alter the program of work already laid out for the preparation of the Commission's second report [4] to the Security Council.   In the course of discussion, however, several delegations expressed a desire to have certain points clarified.   Accordingly, the representative of Great Britain addressed a letter containing eleven questions to the Soviet representative and these were answered by the latter.   In January, 1948, a detailed study of the Soviet proposals, as elaborated by this set of questions and answers, was begun.   On March 29, the British representative presented, on behalf of his own delegation and those of Canada, China, and France, a joint report analyzing these proposals.

The report stated that any effective plan for international control of atomic energy must provide against the danger of misuse of atomic materials through their diversion from legitimate uses and secret manufacture.   The Soviet proposals did not face these basic problems, as the powers and functions of the proposed international control commission were to be limited to "periodic inspection" and "special investigations," the latter to be undertaken only in case of suspicion of clandestine activities.   This would be an inadequate safeguard. Only management of the plant by an international agency would enable it to keep check on the nuclear fuels involved.   In regard to the "special investigations," the scope of inspection was to be so restricted that in practice there would be no opportunity for the international control commission to become suspicious.

Even if violations should be detected, the report continued, the international control commission would not have any powers to prevent or correct them, since it could only make recommendations to the Security Council and would not possess any independent powers of enforcing its decisions.   At best this would result in delays during which illegal activities could continue unchecked. With reference to the Soviet position that destruction of atomic weapons should take place before the conclusion of an international agreement to enforce that prohibition, the report asserted that this would give no assurance (1) that nations which were known to possess atomic weapons would in fact destroy them; (2) that nations which were not known to have atomic weapons, but which might have them, would carry out their obligations; or (3) that nations would be prevented from manufacturing atomic weapons in the future.

The joint report came to this conclusion: [5]

The Soviet Union proposals are not an acceptable basis for the international control of atomic energy.   The United Nations Atomic Energy Commission cannot

[4] Presented in September, 1947.
[5] *Yearbook of the United Nations, 1947–1948*, p. 470.

endorse any scheme which would not prevent the diversion of atomic material, which provides no effective means for the detection of clandestine activities and which has no provision for prompt and effective enforcement action. The Soviet Union Government has not only proposed a scheme that is fundamentally inadequate for the control of atomic energy, but at the same time has made the overriding stipulation that they will not agree to establish even such a feeble scheme of control until all atomic weapons have been prohibited and destroyed. It is completely unrealistic to expect any nation to renounce atomic weapons without any assurance that all nations will be prevented from producing them.

On April 5, 1948, the representative of the Soviet Union replied [6] to the arguments contained in the joint report. Concerning the question of "periodic inspection," he stated that there could not be any other kind. Any measures which had to be applied continuously in respect of productive facilities and raw materials could not be regarded as inspection but would constitute management or supervision. However, the majority proposals for management, supervision, and licensing of atomic facilities were not acceptable to the Soviet Union. There was no basis for any "special investigation" in the absence of suspicion in regard to violations. Personnel selected for this function should not be regarded as tourists who could go any place freely with or without reason. A convention prohibiting atomic weapons should be regarded as a first step in the system of establishing international control, to be followed by other important steps. International control of atomic energy as such would be useless in the absence of a convention prohibiting atomic weapons. With regard to the criticism as to the lack of enforcement powers on the part of the international control agency, it was maintained that the question of sanctions was entirely within the jurisdiction and scope of the Security Council. To place such powers elsewhere would be contrary to the letter and spirit of the Charter of the United Nations.

The Atomic Energy Commission, in May, 1948, reported that it had reached an impasse. In almost two years of work, it had succeeded in making clear the essentials of a plan for the control of atomic energy. However, the divergency of views on major principles was so great and so persistent that a draft convention on the subject could not be prepared. The Commission concluded that no useful purpose could be served by continuing its negotiations. It therefore recommended that, until such time as the General Assembly found that this situation no longer existed or the permanent members of the Atomic Energy Commission found some basis of agreement by prior consultation, negotiations in the Commission be suspended.

The Security Council discussed this report but was unable to reach any substantive decision because the same impasse prevailed there as in the Atomic Energy Commission. It did adopt a resolution, by a procedural vote, direct-

[6] At a meeting of the Working Committtee of the United Nations Atomic Energy Commission.

ing the Secretary-General to transmit to the General Assembly and the members of the United Nations, as a matter of general concern, the three reports of the Atomic Energy Commission and the record of the Security Council deliberations on the subject. The suspension of work suggested by the Commission was not accepted by the Security Council. The General Assembly considered the reports and records at its next regular meeting. As a result, it adopted a resolution on November 4, 1948, approving the majority proposals [7] as constituting the necessary basis for establishing an effective system of international control; expressing its deep concern at the impasse in the Atomic Energy Commission; and regretting that unanimous agreement had not been reached. It requested the six permanent members of the Commission to consult in order to determine if there existed a basis for agreement, and to report to the General Assembly. Also, it called upon the Atomic Energy Commission to resume its sessions, to survey its program of work, and to proceed to the further study of such subjects as it considered to be practicable and useful.

As a result of this resolution, the Commission resumed its work early in 1949. It continued its study, compilation of materials, and discussion, but the same basic impasse continued along the lines of the fundamental disagreement which had existed from the beginning. The verification of a successful atomic explosion in the Soviet Union and the publicity about a possible "hydrogen" bomb did not alter the opposing viewpoints with respect to proposals for establishing a system of international control. These new developments would seem to make an effective inspection all the more necessary in the opinion of the majority. Conversely, they did nothing to alter the Soviet insistence that prohibition of atomic weapons must come first, and that the powers of an international control agency must be strictly limited.

The General Assembly, at its fourth regular session in the fall of 1949, again discussed this question and passed a resolution essentially reaffirming its former position concerning the urgent necessity of continuing the effort to reach agreement. The President of the General Assembly, Carlos Romulo of the Philippines, addressed a special appeal to the permanent members of the Atomic Energy Commission to make every effort "to explore even the remotest possibility of an effective agreement." He suggested that attention be directed to the possibility of (1) a short-term atomic armistice accompanied by an inspection system; (2) an interim prohibition on the use of atomic weapons, with adequate safeguards; (3) further compromises between the majority and minority plans; and (4) a new approach to the fundamental problem of control.

On December 3, Mr. Romulo said that the replies which he had received were encouraging. Unfortunately, the consultations among the six permanent

[7] Essentially the Baruch plan, as accepted and developed by the majority on the United Nations Atomic Energy Commission. Its main features are summarized above.

members of the Atomic Energy Commission were suspended early in 1950 as
a result of the Soviet refusal to participate in any meetings with the Nationalist
delegation of China, nor was any progress made after the Soviet boycott of
United Nations meetings ended in August.

CONVENTIONAL ARMAMENTS

The international control of atomic energy is only a part of the question of
disarmament, or regulation of armaments. Even if atomic weapons were completely and effectively prohibited, other highly destructive means of warfare
would remain available unless they, too, were eliminated or brought under
effective international control.   During the second part of its first regular session, in the fall of 1946, the General Assembly considered the general principles
governing the regulation and reduction of national armaments. The discussion included a number of related topics, such as the international control of
atomic energy, information on national armaments, a system of inspection,
and the implementation of Article 43 of the Charter.   A resolution, representing a compromise between the various viewpoints, was adopted on December
14, 1946. It recognized the "necessity of an early general regulation and
reduction of armaments and armed forces," and recommended that the Security
Council give prompt consideration to formulating practical measures; that the
effective prohibition of atomic weapons be facilitated to the greatest possible
extent; that an arrangement for this purpose be established within the framework of the Security Council; that the placing of armed forces at the disposal
of the Security Council be accelerated; and that the armed forces of members
outside their own territories be withdrawn as rapidly as possible.

This resolution was adopted while the United Nations Atomic Energy Commission was considering its first report to the Security Council, and there was
an important connection between these two developments.   It was the position
of the Soviet Union that the international control of atomic energy could be
considered as only one aspect of the broader question of general disarmament.
This position reinforced that government's contention that prohibition of
atomic weapons should be the first step and also was consistent with its insistence that the whole matter be kept within the framework of the Security
Council.   The United States, however, feared that the question of atomic
energy, as a unique and overwhelming problem, might be submerged in the
consideration of general disarmament.   It also was obvious that the veto could
not be eliminated with respect to this problem except by a recognition that the
usual voting procedure in the Security Council would not be applicable in enforcing an atomic-energy agreement.

The United States government at first asked that the Security Council consider the question of atomic energy before it dealt with general disarmament
at all.   This proposal was not acceptable, and it was agreed that there would

be simultaneous but separate discussions of atomic energy and other types of armament. A Commission for Conventional Armaments was therefore created as a subsidiary organ of the Security Council in February, 1947. This Commission proceeded to its discussions on the basis that it was to consider all armaments and armed forces except "weapons of mass destruction," which were defined to include atomic explosive weapons, radioactive-material weapons, lethal chemical and biological weapons, and any weapons developed in the future which have characteristics comparable in destructive effect to those listed. The Soviet Union continued to oppose separation of the two questions, on the basis that it was artificial and would divert the Commission from practical proposals for the general regulation and reduction of armaments.

The central issues in the deliberations of the Commission for Conventional Armaments and its Working Committee were (1) the terms of reference of the Commission in relation to atomic weapons and other weapons of mass destruction; and (2) the relationship between the general regulation of armaments and factors affecting the state of international relations. The majority on the Commission went on the assumption that a system of armament regulation and reduction could be put into effect only in an atmosphere of international confidence and security. Examples of conditions essential to such confidence were the establishment of an adequate series of agreements for forces pledged to the Security Council under Article 43 of the Charter, an adequate system for the international control of atomic energy, and the conclusion of peace settlements with Germany and Japan. The Soviet representative thought that this amounted to a refusal to implement the General Assembly's resolution of December 14, 1946, which had contained no conditions or prerequisites. Security, in the view of his government, was dependent upon the speedy formulation and implementation of practical measures for the regulation and reduction of armaments, including the prohibition of atomic weapons. The stand taken by the majority, he said, could give rise only to a new armaments race.

In September, 1948, the Soviet Union introduced in the General Assembly a draft resolution proposing that, as a first step, the permanent members of the Security Council should reduce by one-third during one year all existing land, naval, and air forces; and that atomic weapons should be prohibited as intended for purposes of aggression. This proposal was not adopted, but the General Assembly did, on November 19, 1948, pass a resolution containing (1) a recommendation that the Security Council pursue the study of the question through the Commission for Conventional Armaments in order to obtain concrete results as soon as possible; (2) a proposal that the Commission devote its first attention to obtaining and checking information from member states with regard to their armed forces and conventional armaments; and (3) an invitation to the Security Council to report to the General Assembly on the effect given to these recommendations.

The plan of work to obtain information on conventional armaments was not approved by the Security Council on account of an adverse vote by the Soviet Union. During the discussion in the fourth session of the General Assembly (fall of 1949), the representative of the Soviet Union charged that the "Anglo-American bloc had refused any reduction in armaments; was maintaining an artificial division between atomic and other weapons; and had begun an armaments race and extended their system of strategic bases and military alliances." In reply, France, Norway, Great Britain, and the United States pointed out that it was necessary to have all relevant information, and that it would be useless if not verified. No reduction of conventional armaments was conceivable unless the international control of atomic energy was achieved. This was a single question with two aspects, being handled by two separate bodies which the Security Council could coordinate. If the Western European countries were rearming with American aid, it was, they said, because they feared the intentions of the Soviet Union and not because they were opposed to disarmament.

President Truman, in his speech of October 24, 1950, before the General Assembly suggested that the work on atomic energy and conventional armaments might be more closely brought together, possibly by a new and consolidated disarmament commission. This was a change in the United States position that the two questions should be handled by separate bodies. Aggression with any weapons, and not merely the existence of the atomic bomb, had come to be the chief problem. This shift in the American approach did not imply any change in the belief that an international atomic-energy control agency must operate without the restriction of the veto. Agreement on a control plan does require unanimity; after that, the control agency would operate by majority vote. In other words, the commission which develops the agreement could follow a procedure different from that of the agency which carries out the agreement once it is made.

Although the Soviet government had insisted all along that the question of atomic energy and conventional armaments could not be separated, Mr. Vishinsky took President Truman's suggestion for a coordinated approach as a piece of "skulduggery" designed to prevent any real work on atomic control. At the time, the strategy of the Soviet government was to insist that a nation refusing to outlaw atomic bombs was automatically an aggressor.

As of this writing, no real progress has been made in resolving the substantive difficulties for international regulation of armaments, on account of the unsatisfactory relations among some of the permanent members of the Security Council. In other words, Great Powers do not agree to limit their armaments under circumstances of a "cold war."

Chapter 17

ECONOMIC AND SOCIAL COOPERATION

It is difficult to describe in a limited space the work and accomplishments of the United Nations in the field of international economic and social cooperation. There are two reasons for this difficulty. In the first place these activities cover a very broad range. Administration of postal services, lowering of trade barriers, economic reconstruction, development of rinderpest vaccine, halting of a cholera epidemic in Egypt, resettlement of refugees, facilitating international exchange of books, improvement of statistics, control of opium traffic, and steps to stabilize currency exchange rates are only a few random samples from a long and varied list of activities. Some idea of the scope and variety of this work may be gained from the fact that a catalogue of United Nations economic and social projects in 1950 listed 723 different items.[1]

The other reason for the difficulty of giving adequate treatment to this type of work in a brief space is that its results are often indirect or intangible. In some cases, the United Nations operates a definite program, and it is relatively easy to describe the specific accomplishments. One can say, for example, that during a stated period of time a given number of refugees were repatriated or resettled, and their geographic location can be indicated. Or, as another example, statistics are available as to the number of pieces of mail handled in a year through arrangements administered by the Universal Postal Union. In some cases, the work carried on under the auspices of the United Nations is one factor among many others. If one says that the International Monetary Fund approved the devaluation of the British pound from $4.03 to $2.80, the statement is true enough but what is the exact "accomplishment" of the United Nations? There is no doubt that the existence and operation of the Fund contribute to the stability of international currency exchange, but any attempt to measure the extent of this effect soon gets into a zone of uncertainty.

Much of the work of the United Nations through its various organs and specialized agencies takes the form of recommendations to states. The International Labor Organization is credited with a very definite influence in raising the standard of labor in various parts of the world. However, its work

---

[1] *Catalogue of Economic and Social Projects*, 1950 (UN Doc. E/1670).

has been persuasive, cooperative, and educational, and it is impossible to say that on a given date the ILO reduced the number of hours in a workday by so much. Its influence is important and obvious but not subject to exact quantitative measurement.

Because of these considerations, the economic and social work of the United Nations will be indicated in this chapter by giving brief descriptions of typical work of importance in various fields. The problems which have been attacked fall into two categories: those resulting from World War II, and those of a continuing and long-range nature. The emphasis for the first group has been on the operation of programs to deal with immediate emergencies and needs as in the cases, among others, of UNRRA [2] and the IRO. The first task for the long-range problems was that of preparation and organization. This preliminary stage has been largely completed, and attention has been turned to carrying out responsibilities assigned in the various economic and social fields. This work has involved four types of activities. First, considerable progress has been made in the collection, analysis, presentation, and dissemination of information. Studies, reports, bulletins, yearbooks, and other publications are increasing in number and variety. Second, conferences arranged under the auspices of agencies in the economic and social field have been a means of preparing international agreements and facilitating the cooperation of governments and experts in dealing with problems of economic development, transport, statistics, housing and town planning, cartography, child welfare, conservation of resources, and others. Third, draft conventions have been prepared to serve as recommendations for common international standards and to remove barriers to the solution of problems of mutual concern. This type of work has been done in such fields as human rights, genocide, freedom of information, synthetic drugs, declaration of death of missing persons, suppression of prostitution, and economic statistics. Finally, there is the extensive field of technical assistance, in which the specialized agencies are closely associated with the work of the United Nations.

The remainder of this chapter will be devoted to the work and accomplishments of the United Nations and its specialized agencies in the fields of labor standards; transport and communications; food and agriculture; finance; economic development; health; refugees; social welfare; and education, science and culture.[3]

---

[2] The United Nations Relief and Rehabilitation Administration, an emergency agency which is no longer in existence.

[3] The specialized agencies prepare annual reports on their programs and activities. Records and reports of the six principal organs are published. Useful summaries may be found in the *Yearbook of the United Nations* and, upon occasion, in the *United Nations Bulletin.* The U.S. Department of State publishes a *Current Review of Economic and Social Problems in the United Nations.* For the members of the various specialized agencies, see Table 5.

TABLE 5. MEMBERS OF THE UNITED NATIONS AND THE SPECIALIZED AGENCIES
(As of August 1, 1951)

Member	UN	ILO	UPU	ITU	FAO	UNESCO	ICAO	WHO	Bank	Fund	IRO	WMO	(ITO)[1]	(IMCO)[1]
Afghanistan	x	x	x	x	x	x	x	x					x	
Albania		x	x	x				x						
Argentina	x	x	x	x	x	x	x	x						
Australia	x	x	x	x	x	x	x	x	x	x	x	x	x	x
Austria		x	x	x	x	x	x	x	x	x		x	x	x
Belgium	x	x	x	x	x	x	x	x	x	x	x	x	x	x
Bolivia	x	x	x	x	x	x	x	x	x	x			x	
Brazil	x	x	x	x	x	x	x	x	x	x			x	
Bulgaria		x	x	x				x				x		
Burma	x		x	x	x	x	x	x	x	x			x	
Byelorussian S.S.R.	x		x	x				x				x		
Canada	x	x	x	x	x	x	x	x	x	x	x		x	
Ceylon		x	x	x	x	x	x	x	x	x		x	x	
Chile	x	x	x	x	x	x	x	x	x	x		x	x	x
China	x	x	x	x	x	x	x	x	x	x	x	x	x	
Colombia	x	x	x	x	x	x	x	x	x	x			x	
Costa Rica	x	x	x	x	x	x	x	x	x	x			x	
Cuba	x	x	x	x	x	x	x	x	x	x		x	x	
Czechoslovakia	x	x	x	x	x	x	x	x	x	x		x	x	
Denmark	x	x	x	x	x	x	x	x	x	x	x	x	x	
Dominican Republic	x	x	x	x	x	x	x	x	x	x	x	x	x	
Ecuador	x	x	x	x	x	x	x	x	x	x		x	x	
Egypt	x	x	x	x	x	x	x	x	x	x		x	x	
El Salvador	x	x	x	x	x	x	x	x	x	x			x	

Ethiopia · · · · · · · · · · · ·
Finland · · · · · · · · · · · ·
France · · · · · · · · · · · ·
German Federal Republic
Greece · · · · · · · · · · · ·
Guatemala · · · · · · · ·
Haiti · · · · · · · · · · · · · ·
Honduras · · · · · · · · · ·
Hungary · · · · · · · · · · ·
Iceland · · · · · · · · · · ·
India · · · · · · · · · · · · ·
Indonesia · · · · · · · · · ·
Iran · · · · · · · · · · · · · ·
Iraq · · · · · · · · · · · · · ·
Ireland · · · · · · · · · · ·
Israel · · · · · · · · · · · ·
Italy · · · · · · · · · · · · · ·
Japan · · · · · · · · · · · · ·
Jordan · · · · · · · · · · · ·
Korea · · · · · · · · · · · · ·
Lebanon · · · · · · · · · · ·
Liberia · · · · · · · · · · ·
Luxembourg · · · · · · · ·
Mexico · · · · · · · · · · · ·
Netherlands · · · · · · · ·
New Zealand · · · · · · ·
Nicaragua · · · · · · · · · ·
Norway · · · · · · · · · · · ·

TABLE 5. MEMBERS OF THE UNITED NATIONS AND THE SPECIALIZED AGENCIES
(As of August 1, 1951) (Continued)

Member	UN	ILO	UPU	ITU	FAO	UNESCO	ICAO	WHO	Bank	Fund	IRO	WMO	(ITO)[1]	(IMCO)[1]
Pakistan	x	x	x	x	x	x	x	x	x	x		x	x	
Panama	x	x	x	x	x	x		x	x	x			x	
Paraguay	x		x	x	x		x	x	x			x		
Peru	x	x	x	x	x	x	x	x	x	x		x	x	
Philippines	x	x	x	x	x	x	x	x	x	x		x	x	
Poland	x	x	x	x		x	x	x				x		
Portugal		x	x	x	x			x				x		
Rumania			x	x				x						
Saudi Arabia	x		x	x				x						
Spain				x	x	x		x				x		
Sweden	x	x	x	x	x	x	x	x	x	x		x	x	x
Switzerland		x	x	x	x	x	x	x			x	x	x	
Syria	x	x	x	x	x	x		x	x	x		x	x	
Thailand	x	x	x	x	x	x	x	x	x	x		x	x	
Turkey	x	x	x	x	x	x	x	x	x	x		x	x	
Ukrainian S.S.R.	x		x	x				x				x		
Union of South Africa	x	x	x	x	x	x	x	x	x			x	x	
U.S.S.R.	x		x	x				x				x		
United Kingdom	x	x	x	x	x	x	x	x	x	x	x	x	x	x
United States	x	x	x	x	x	x	x	x	x	x	x	x	x	x
Uruguay	x	x	x	x	x	x		x	x	x	x	x	x	
Venezuela	x	x	x	x	x	x		x	x	x	x	x	x	
Yemen	x		x	x				x						
Yugoslavia	x	x	x	x	x	x	x	x	x	x		x	x	
Total[2]	60	64	86	84	66	64	57	78	49	49	18	66	52	12

¹ Not yet formally established. The information given is for the Interim Commission of the International Trade Organization and the Preparatory Committee of the Intergovernmental Maritime Consultative Organization.

² The totals include, in addition to the members given, the following:

ILO: Viet-Nam. Japan has been admitted, but must still ratify the ILO Constitution.

UPU: Belgian Congo; French Morocco; French overseas territories; Indochina; Netherlands Antilles and Surinam; Portuguese Colonies of West Africa; Portuguese Colonies of East Africa, Asia, and Oceania; San Marino; Tunisia; United Kingdom overseas colonies, protectorates and territories under trusteeship; United States possessions; Vatican City.

ITU: Belgian Congo and territory of Ruanda Urundi; French protectorates of Morocco and Tunisia; overseas territories of the French Republic and territories administered as such; Monaco; Portuguese colonies; Southern Rhodesia; colonies, protectorates, overseas territories and territories under Mandate or Trusteeship of the United Kingdom; territories of the United States; Vatican City; Spanish zone of Morocco and the totality of Spanish possessions. Yemen has yet to accede to the ITU Convention. Korea has been approved for membership but an instrument of accession must be deposited before Korea can become a member. A few of the signatories of the ITU Convention have not yet ratified it.

FAO: Cambodia; Viet-Nam. Hungary has given notice of withdrawal, effective January 25, 1952.

UNESCO: Cambodia; Laos; Monaco; Viet-Nam.

WHO: Cambodia; Laos; Monaco; Viet-Nam. Southern Rhodesia is an associate member. Ten members have notified WHO of their withdrawal, and the World Health Assembly has resolved that their resumption of active membership would be welcomed at any time. They are: Albania, Bulgaria, Byelorussian S.S.R., China, Czechoslovakia, Hungary, Poland, Rumania, Ukrainian S.S.R., and the Soviet Union.

WMO: Belgian Congo; Bermuda; British central African territories; British east African territories; British Malayan territories; British west African territories; French Cameroons; French Equatorial Africa; French Morocco; French Oceania; French Somaliland; French Togo; French West Africa; Hong Kong; Indochina; Madagascar; New Caledonia; Portuguese East Africa; Portuguese West Africa; Tunisia. Bulgaria and Ceylon have been admitted as members, but have not yet deposited their instruments of accession to the WMO Convention.

ITO: Southern Rhodesia.

LABOR STANDARDS

Social justice to the working peoples of the world is recognized as a basic condition of a durable peace. The International Labor Organization was established in 1919 to promote the improvement of economic and social conditions among working people everywhere. Between the two world wars, the ILO completed thousands of studies, held hundreds of conferences, and sent scores of missions to give expert assistance. Some of its conventions which were adopted called for an eight-hour day and a forty-eight-hour week, holidays with pay, improved working conditions on ships, freedom of association and the right to organize, and sickness and old-age insurance. Other conventions were designed to forbid forced labor, nightwork of women, employment of women in underground mines, employment of children under fifteen years of age, and the use of white lead in paint.

At a conference in 1944, the ILO adopted the Declaration of Philadelphia which reaffirmed the principles that labor is not a commodity, that poverty anywhere constitutes a danger to prosperity everywhere, and that freedom of expression and of association are essential to sustained progress. The Declaration went on to recognize that it is a solemn obligation of the ILO to promote objectives including full employment and a living wage; extension of social security and medical care; maternity protection and child welfare; adequate food, housing, and recreation; the right to bargain collectively; equality of educational and vocational opportunity; and adequate health and safety measures.

In 1946 the ILO became a specialized agency of the United Nations. It has continued its basic program and objectives, with some change in emphasis to meet the special problems and opportunities which have existed in recent years. Manpower problems continue to have high priority in the work of the Organization. Exchanges of views and of technical experience are given by discussions in conferences and committees, the establishment of regional manpower offices to furnish technical assistance, the sending of advisory commissions upon request, and the distribution of information. The subjects of major concern in this connection include the adjustment of labor supply and demand, vocational guidance and training, and international migration. In 1949 a field office for Asia and the Far East was established, and a regional conference on technical and vocational training was held at Singapore. Later, a similar office for Latin America was opened. Advisory missions have been sent to Italy, Turkey, Egypt, and other countries in the Near East. A vitally important method for adjusting labor supply and demand is the employment service, by which workers and employers are brought into touch with each other. The ILO has encouraged the expansion of such services in various ways, and has prepared a draft convention on the subject.

The prevention of unemployment has always been one of the major objectives of the ILO.   This question, which had been very prominent during the 1930's, required new attention as a substantial amount of unemployment developed in several countries in 1948 and 1949.   The ILO has emphasized the importance of effective institutional arrangements for implementing full employment policy.   Complete and reliable statistics also are essential for the framing and administration of full employment policies, and the ILO has attempted to obtain improvements in this connection.   Comprehensive studies have been made of various technical factors relating to the maintenance of full employment.   One example may be cited here: during 1949, a committee of the ILO considered the problem of instability in the construction industry and formulated several conclusions as to timing of public works and the coordination of financial resources.

Conventions adopted by the ILO in the field of social security cover employees in industry, commerce, and agriculture.   They provide for compulsory insurance against sickness, old age, and death and for payment of compensation for industrial accidents and occupational diseases.   New and broader social security plans have been produced by a number of governments during the past few years, and the ILO has been working toward the formulation of recommendations based on the concepts of comprehensive coverage and of social adequacy as the main criterion of benefits to be paid.   A Committee of Social Security Experts met in New Zealand early in 1950 to lay the basis for this development.   A questionnaire was drafted for the purpose of obtaining the views of governments on the objectives and minimum standards of social security for discussion at the thirty-fourth session of the International Labor Conference in 1951.

An example of a special problem handled with ILO assistance is the coordination of the application of national social security systems to boatmen navigating the Rhine.   Since World War II, the countries bordering on the Rhine have made their social security systems more complete and more nearly equal. As the result of a conference convened by ILO in 1949, it was possible to secure uniformity of treatment for all boatmen engaged in commercial navigation on the Rhine.   This is based on equality for the nationals of all participating states and the determination of social security legislation applicable to the crew of a vessel by reference to the country in which the owner of the vessel has his principal place of business.   The same conference also dealt with uniform conditions of work for boatmen on the Rhine.

Freedom of association and the right to organize have always been of vital concern to the labor movement.   In 1949 the ILO adopted a draft convention which would establish the right of both workers and employers to join organizations of their own choice.   Ratification of this convention would place one of the fundamental rights of man in an international treaty.   The most appropriate method for international examination of alleged infringements of trade-union rights has been discussed.   It was decided to establish a fact-finding and conciliation commission for this purpose.

The broad field of industrial safety has been attacked from several angles throughout the history of the ILO.   Conventions and recommendations have been made on such matters as inspection, prevention of industrial accidents, marking of weight on heavy vessels in sea transport, and protection of building workers.   During 1949 a model code of safety regulations for underground work in coal mines was adopted, and work was begun on similar codes for civil engineering and the chemical industry.   The magnitude and value of this type of work may be indicated by the fact that the revised model code of safety regulations for industrial establishments includes several thousand provisions and runs to nearly 500 pages of print.   It is hoped that this model code will be especially helpful to the underdeveloped countries in building up their own codes of industrial safety regulations.

Maritime labor is another subject of special concern to the ILO.   A conference held in Seattle, Washington, in 1946 resulted in the most comprehensive set of provisions governing life at sea ever drafted.   Under these provisions, a seaman must have a preemployment medical examination and subsequent periodic examinations.   To qualify as an able seaman, he must have three years' experience and must pass a practical test of seamanship.   One convention is devoted to such matters as location of crew quarters, sleeping space, size and construction of berths, number of washrooms, lighting, ventilation, heating, the mess, and recreational facilities.   Others deal with food supplies and the qualification of cooks.

The ILO constitution states as urgent requirements the provision of an adequate living wage and recognition of the principle of equal remuneration for work of equal value.   In order to implement these principles, the ILO has adopted a number of conventions and recommendations and has initiated discussions and studies.   These deal with such questions as the machinery for establishing minimum wages, the rate of wages adequate for a reasonable standard of living, guaranteed wages, protection against unjustified deductions, fair-wage clauses in public contracts, and equal pay for men and women. Attention is being given to questions connected with agricultural wages.

The problems of women and children have received special consideration. These include nightwork and heavy labor, minimum age limits in particular occupations, employment of women before and after childbirth, maternity benefits, provision of day nurseries, and standards for domestic work.

The ILO works by the indirect methods of discussion, fact finding, and recommendation.   Therefore, its accomplishments are rather difficult to measure.   It cannot reduce the hours of labor or provide an increase in wages by fiat.   One cannot say that it achieved this or that tangible result on such and such a day.   It is impossible, however, to make even a cursory examination of the work of the ILO without coming to the conclusion that it has had, and continues to have, an important cumulative effect upon working conditions. Its accomplishments, although incapable of precise measurement, are quite real.

One of the outstanding trends in ILO work during the past few years has been the increasing emphasis on technical assistance, which is being used to supplement the traditional methods of conference, discussion, fact finding, draft conventions, etc., in various fields of activity. Since 1948, advisory missions have made studies and recommendations on social policy and labor legislation in Turkey; facilities for vocational and technical training in ten Latin-American countries; problems of migration and land settlement in seven Latin-American countries; manpower facilities and needs in the Middle East; training within industry in eight European countries; manpower problems and vocational training in Egypt, Greece, India, and Pakistan; social security in the Philippines, Czechoslovakia, Iran, Egypt, and India; labor statistics in Venezuela; social conditions in the petroleum industry in Iran and Iraq; conditions of work on plantations in Ceylon and India; and others. Written technical advice, in contrast to visiting missions, is provided frequently on a wide variety of questions. A fellowships program has been established to encourage and provide financial assistance for study in such fields as employment organization, vocational training and guidance, social security administration, industrial relations, labor inspection, and industrial health, safety, and welfare. Also, the ILO participates in the expanded cooperative program of technical assistance set up under the auspices of the Economic and Social Council.

One effect of the technical-assistance program is to place more emphasis on agricultural questions in the underdeveloped areas, in contrast to the problems of the highly industrialized countries. The ILO has always been concerned with the welfare of agricultural labor, but work was not pursued so intensively in this field because of the urgency of industrial problems in the leading member states, the complexity of the agricultural situation, and the fact that farm workers were not as highly organized as their industrial brothers. A marked tendency to shift this emphasis has occurred as interest has grown in the idea of international cooperation for technical assistance to the underdeveloped countries.

TRANSPORT AND COMMUNICATIONS

Technological improvements in transport and communications were among the leading influences in the development of modern international organization. Of the thirteen specialized agencies in operation or being constituted, five are concerned with work in these fields.[4]

[4] Universal Postal Union, International Telecommunication Union, International Civil Aviation Organization, International Maritime Consultative Organization, and World Meteorological Organization. The first two of these are the only specialized agencies which were originally established in the nineteenth century.

The Universal Postal Union has continued its task of administering the services necessary for uniting the world in a single postal territory for the reciprocal exchange of correspondence. The importance of this work may be gauged from the fact that the number of pieces of correspondence moving internationally increased from less than 144,000,000 in 1875 to more than 3,256,000,000 in 1930. There was a sharp drop during the war, but by 1947 the figure had risen to approximately 2,000,000,000 pieces.

The twelfth Universal Postal Congress, which met in 1947, agreed on a number of revisions in its basic provisions and regulations. These included such matters as more efficient arrangements for international money order and cash-on-delivery services; and changes in the weight limits and mailing cost of printed papers and periodicals. Suggestions were made on limitations of payments to air transport companies. Minor revisions were made in the agreement concerning insured letters, parcel post, and collection of bills. The agreement on subscriptions to newspapers and periodicals remained unchanged.

The international bureau, or permanent secretariat, of UPU compiles information and issues publications of great usefulness to postal authorities. These include such reference materials as a list of air-mail services, a list of airports, maps of air-mail lines, a world map of surface communication routes, and a directory of post offices. As a means of keeping all members informed of new developments, the bureau issues a monthly journal, *L'Union Postale*, in Arabic, Chinese, English, French, Russian, and Spanish. The bureau is also a godsend to philatelists, since it receives postage stamps of all types used in the territory of each member and is required to distribute them to all other members. In 1948, for example, 2,542 different kinds of stamps were received and distributed. In addition to these and other traditional services, the bureau is developing an exchange of technical information among the various postal administrations.

The major task of the International Telecommunication Union in recent years has been concerned with the rapid developments and technical complexities of radio transmission. The Administrative Radio Conference, meeting in Atlantic City in 1947, revised the radio regulations of 1938 which had been made obsolete by scientific advances. A new world-wide frequency allocation table extending up to 10,500,000 kilocycles was set up. The recent importance of the higher frequencies is shown by the fact that in 1938 the spectrum had been charted only up to 200,000 kilocycles. Revised frequency bands were allocated, and practical machinery for putting the new allocations into effect was created. The revised regulations also cover the details of reservation of "distress frequencies" for lifesaving and rescue work; station identification signals; frequencies for air and marine navigational aids such as radar stations and for meteorological messages; and other matters relating to the efficient use of radio. The World Frequency Assignment List is a document of some 1,250 pages covering all frequencies in the radio spectrum from 15 kilocycles to 12,500 megacycles and recording the priorities of every nation for their use. This list is used in registering claims for frequencies and all negotiations between governments concerning alleged interferences are based upon the ITU records.

There is a great deal of international competition in the field of high-frequency broadcasting. The ITU is attempting to work out an equitable system for allocating space and time in each broadcasting band. The answer to this problem will not be found, however, in technical considerations alone, since strong political forces seek outlets for propaganda through international broadcasting.

The ITU also issues technical publications, including the periodical *Telecommunications Journal.*

The development of aviation has become one of the strongest influences in the field of international transport and communication. The first international commercial air service began between London and Paris a little over thirty years ago. In 1948 nearly a quarter of a million people were carried across the North Atlantic alone by air. Seventy different airlines, representing all major nations, have more than two thousand aircraft providing international service. In this situation there was obvious need to establish the International Civil Aviation Organization, in order to promote cooperation on the technical, economic, and legal aspects of international flying.

One of the most important duties of ICAO is to develop uniform standards of safety on international air routes. Traffic regulations for other types of vehicles are commonplace. Each nation has created its own rules of the road, but there are no radical differences within the confines of any one country. It is taken for granted that there must be traffic laws to prevent accidents, and that these laws must be about the same in all cities through which a motorist passes. Otherwise, travel by automobile would be impossibly dangerous. Flying is more swift and complex, and an airplane may cross several countries within a very short time. Lack of uniformity in flight rules and regulations would result in confusion and a large number of accidents.

ICAO attempts to achieve technical uniformity at a high level of quality. For example, an airplane must be structurally sound, and must carry enough fuel; the crew must have certain experience, knowledge, and skill; they must be physically fit; and adequate weather reports must be available for the planned route. The standards which have already gone into effect include those on personnel licensing; aeronautical maps and charts; rules of the air; meteorological codes; dimensional practices, to be used in air-ground communications; operation of aircraft on international scheduled services; aircraft nationality and registration marks; airworthiness; and facilitation of international air transport.

Another accomplishment of ICAO is the creation of a network of ocean weather stations in the North Atlantic, which has the greatest volume of transoceanic traffic and some of the most unpredictable weather in the world. The vessels operating this network cruise at designated locations. They send helium-filled balloons to a height of 60,000 feet, with mechanisms attached to give readings of the humidity, temperature, and pressure of the air. The upper-air observations are made every six hours, and surface weather conditions are recorded every three hours. These ships provide the current weather data which air transport requires, they are communications relay points for aircraft, and they serve as rescue posts for planes in distress. As a result of this service, a dramatic rescue took place in October, 1947, when sixty-nine passengers were saved from the *Bermuda Sky Queen*. About a year later, four crew members were saved from a sinking U.S. Air Force plane. In addition, passengers of sinking ships have been rescued and at least one ship saved from the ice.

Another ICAO project is the Icelandic joint-support agreement. Iceland is the logical location for weather observations, radio aids, and an area traffic center. These services are very costly, however, and residents of Iceland would not derive much direct benefit from them. Should each Icelander be expected to pay $4 a year to maintain them for airlines of other countries? The result is that ten nations share in the cost of providing area traffic control, meteorological stations, and communications services in Iceland.

The development of aviation has brought many legal problems. A typical task undertaken by ICAO is the conclusion of a convention on the international recognition of rights in aircraft. The chief importance of this convention lies in the fact that the very mobility of the airplane makes for difficulty in taking out mortgages. If a person loans money and takes a mortgage on aircraft, the property might be seized in another country for debt, and the investor would lose his money. The new convention makes it possible for mortgages and other property rights contracted in one country to be generally recognized. It will be much easier, therefore, for operators to borrow money for the purchase of new equipment.

The ICAO issues a periodic bulletin and other publications.

The Inter-Governmental Maritime Consultative Organization (IMCO) will parallel ICAO in the field of ocean shipping. The need for one central organization to perform administrative services under the numerous maritime conventions has been evident for a long time. The immediate impetus for the new organization, however, came from Allied experience during and after World War II in a series of intergovernmental shipping organizations.

The World Meteorological Organization was established to take over the work of an older nongovernmental organization in this field.[5] Millions of dollars depend upon taking advantage of favorable weather and upon adequate warning of bad weather. Such industries as aviation, shipping and trucking, agriculture, outdoor movies, resorts, sports, and building trades require ac-

[5] See p. 33.

curate information daily. Ships and planes need detailed information on weather conditions over wide areas. The international exchange of weather information is essential to permit accurate forecasting within national borders and to facilitate international travel. Under the procedures used by the WMO, meteorological information is made available from all parts of the world to experts who make the forecasts. As a result of this work, the vocabulary of meteorology has become an international language. In conjunction with the International Telecommunication Union, special frequencies have been set aside for transmitting weather information and warnings by radio. International standards for flight weather reporting have been worked out with the International Civil Aviation Organization.

The Transport and Communications Commission of the Economic and Social Council has considered and made recommendations on such international problems as inland transport; movement of persons and goods; transport statistics; standardized highway marking systems; and the coordination of activities in the fields of aviation, shipping, and telecommunications with respect to safety of life at sea and in the air. Passports and frontier formalities have been considered by experts on the subject, and the Economic and Social Council has expressed the view that it is desirable for these formalities to be reduced and simplified to the extent consistent with national security.

Food and Agriculture

The production and distribution of food is one of the most important problems of international cooperation in the economic and social field. A large proportion, probably two-thirds, of the world's population is perpetually undernourished, and millions of people are constantly subject to the threat of famine. The Food and Agriculture Organization of the United Nations was created in the recognition that hunger is a breeding ground for social unrest and conflict, and in the belief that ways could be found to develop and maintain an adequate food supply. The FAO encourages the use of modern tools and methods to increase crop yields. It promotes conservation of existing food supplies and searches for new sources. It studies problems of maldistribution and provides a forum for review of national policies. This agency does not operate a huge program of its own, but cooperates with governmental and other agencies in studies, reports, technical assistance, demonstration projects, conferences, and similar methods. A wide variety of projects has been undertaken. It is possible here only to indicate the nature of this work by brief descriptions of some of these activities.

The first thing done after the organization had been established was to make a survey of the world's food supplies in relation to needs. The World Food Survey, made by a group of experts and published in 1946, covered seventy countries and about 90 per cent of the world's population. This constituted a fundamental document on food supplies and estimates of the needs. This revealed that food supplies would have to be increased by more than 100 per cent in twenty-five years to bring the diets of the ill-fed up to a reasonably good level and to allow for population growth. Therefore, the world food problem is one of expansion and distribution, not one of overproduction and surpluses.

The FAO was established to deal with work of a long-term nature. However, it soon appeared that more immediate functions would have to be assumed because of the critical postwar food shortage. Starving people were not interested in long-term programs. The FAO assumed some of the agricultural rehabilitation work begun by the United Nations Relief and Rehabilitation Administration, a temporary agency. Another emergency job was the initiation of the International Emergency Food Council to recommend the allocation of scarce foodstuffs and some other products among importing countries. If this had not been done, the food situation in many countries would have been even worse. This work was later absorbed by the FAO. Although the allocated authority consisted only in the power to make recommendations, the extent to which the latter were carried out showed that international cooperation was a real factor in this important matter.

Rice is a staple food for half the world's population. In 1949, the FAO organized an International Rice Commission, which is the first international body to be concerned expressly with problems of the production and use of one food. Its projects include the scientific cataloguing of rice varieties and the launching of work on rice breeding.

Rinderpest is a deadly virus disease of bovine animals that is especially widespread in the Far East, Asia, and Africa. It kills close to a million cattle a year in China alone. FAO veterinarians, with the cooperation of the Chinese Ministry of Agriculture, developed an improved vaccine and assisted in working out an annual program of vaccination for fifteen million animals. With use of the vaccine developed in China, similar programs have been set up in a number of other countries in Africa and Asia. Considerable work also has been done on other animal diseases, such as hog cholera, erysipelas, foot-and-mouth disease, tuberculosis of cattle, and poultry diseases.

One very interesting project has to do with rotenone, the insecticide which places the gardener on somewhat equal terms with the insects. In China before World War II, modern insecticides were used by only a few of the richest farmers. However, native plants had been used for centuries to kill insects. One plant, derris, was known as "fish poison." It had been discovered long ago that if the roots of the derris vine were thrown into a pond, the fish would be killed and rise to the top. The fish killed in this manner could be eaten without ill effects to human beings. Derris root, in short, has the characteristic of being poisonous to cold-blooded animals and harmless to warm-blooded ones. The insecticide manufactured from it is called "rotenone."

Derris grows in China in both a wild and a cultivated state, but methods of applying it were limited and provincial. Some farmers, for example, make their own insecticides by grinding derris root and mixing it with clay. An FAO team in China found a boarded-up war plant in Shanghai and undertook the manufacture of rotenone. They made an extractor from kerosene drums, pipe, and junk, and took other technical short cuts. Simple sprayers and dusters were also made. As a result, rice production increased by four or five bushels per acre.

Other FAO projects include, among others, a fight on predatory locusts; hybrid-maize breeding; soil-fertility practices; improvement of forestry programs and fisheries resources; and control of infestation of food in storage by rats, molds, and fungi. A catalogue of genetic stocks has been undertaken. This will include data on all varieties of food plants wherever they may be found. A plant breeder, needing some particular quality for a strain which he hopes to produce, will have the world's total varieties of that plant under his survey through the FAO catalogue. Another service which has been started is a seed stock of outstanding varieties of cereals, grasses, legumes, oil seeds, and vegetables. This stock is maintained at Rome, Italy, and samples are distributed for experimental purposes to plant breeders around the world. Some excellent studies and statistical reports have been made. These range from the surveys of world food and agriculture to such specialized subjects as salted cod.

FINANCE

The flow of investment capital and the stability of exchange rates are of great importance for the promotion of international trade, and therefore for international cooperation in the economic field. Countries with surplus funds need foreign investment outlets, and other countries need to borrow capital to develop their economies. The International Bank for Reconstruction and Development is the first international organization for long-term foreign lending. Creditor as well as debtor countries are represented on its board; thus it affords the unique opportunity for both lenders and borrowers to participate in drafting its policies.

Immediately after World War II the attention of the Bank was directed to Europe, where the need was urgent and the best opportunity existed to raise levels of productivity quickly. Loans for reconstruction purposes included $250 million to France, $195 million to the Netherlands, $40 million to Denmark, and $12 million to Luxembourg. The agreements provided for the purchase of specific commodities which the borrowing countries needed to step up production and to contribute to the reconstruction of Europe. The funds were used mainly for industrial and agricultural machinery, transportation equipment, and basic raw materials. Other loans made by the Bank to the European area included $12 million to four Dutch shipping companies for the purchase of six merchant vessels, and $16 million to Belgium for reequipment of its steel and power industries.

As time went on the major attention of the Bank was shifted in two ways. When the Marshall Plan went into operation, reconstruction loans for Western Europe were available through the Economic Cooperation Administration. The Bank, accordingly, used its funds to serve other parts of the world. The other change was a shift in emphasis from reconstruction to development. The more recent loans have been made for developing productive facilities and resources rather than for repairing wartime damage.

Loans of a development type include $16 million to instrumentalities of the Chilean government for the development of hydroelectric power and water resources, and the importation of modern agricultural machinery; $34.1 million to agencies of the Mexican government for electric-power development; and $75 million [6] to a Brazilian corporation for the expansion of hydroelectric-power facilities and telephone installations. India was the first country in Asia to receive a loan from the Bank. Transportation is a critical problem there, and $34 million was made available for the reconstruction and development of state-owned railways. Proceeds will be used to finance part of the purchase price of locomotives, boilers, and spare parts.

An interesting project in India arose from the fact that much good agricultural land had gone out of cultivation because of the inroads of a weed known as "kans grass." This is a stubborn plant with deep roots. The Indian government had made experiments to eradicate it by deep ploughing, using tractors left by the U.S. Army. The experiments were successful, and the government proposed to tackle the job in many parts of central India over a total area as large as the state of Connecticut. Since this plan offered a cheap means for a very urgent increase in food production, a loan of $10 million was made for the importation of tractors and other equipment to clear the land.

Loans have been made for the development of timber resources in Finland and Yugoslavia, and for the construction of a hydroelectric plant in El Salvador. In July, 1950, two loans were made to Turkey, where inadequate harbor facilities had resulted in overcrowding and excessive port charges, thereby limiting both foreign trade and essential coastwise traffic. A loan of $12.5 million was made for the development of Turkey's major ports over a period of twenty-five years. In addition, a loan of $3.9 million was made to finance the construction of grain-storage facilities. These should play an important role in agricultural development. Grain is Turkey's largest crop, but present storage facilities are inadequate and poorly equipped. In 1950, loans for development projects were also made to Australia, Colombia, Ethiopia, Thailand, and Uruguay. By 1951, the total amount of loans had passed the billion-dollar mark.

[6] Later increased to $90 million.

Before a loan is made, the Bank satisfies itself that the borrower would be unable to obtain the loan in the private-capital market under reasonable conditions, that the project is soundly conceived, and that the borrower will be able to repay. The process of assuring itself that these conditions have been met has led the Bank into providing a useful service of surveys and advice to governments. Some twenty countries have been visited, advice and assistance have been made available, and loan negotiations are in progress.

The accomplishments of the International Monetary Fund are difficult to state, because of the highly technical and confidential nature of its work and because so many different factors enter into the international financial situation. The Fund was designed to provide machinery for consultation on international monetary problems, and to facilitate the expansion and balanced growth of international trade; to promote stability of currency exchange, and to avoid competitive depreciation; to eliminate foreign-exchange restrictions on current transactions; and to make available short-term financial assistance, so that temporary maladjustments in the balance of payments could be corrected without resort to restrictive measures.

The Fund has provided the machinery of consultation, and it has worked toward the other objectives. By 1950, par values of more than forty national currencies had been established by international agreement. During its first two years of operation, the Fund extended credits to seventeen of its members in a total amount of $725,500,000. Although this type of activity was intended to eliminate short-term maladjustments, a substantial portion of the credits went to countries in which far-reaching economic adjustments would be necessary to establish a genuine equilibrium in the balance of payments. The major underlying problem is that of a dollar shortage. The countries which need goods from the United States have been unable to earn the dollars to pay for them. Greatly increased production in those countries and a basic realignment of export-import transactions are necessary to change this situation. In the meantime, the Fund has made a significant contribution, but its assistance represents only a small percentage of the total dollar aid which has been made available through the Economic Recovery Administration (Marshall Plan) and in other ways. The Fund is in a position to correct temporary balance-of-payment maladjustments in a genuine multilateral trading system, but it cannot cure the world's deep-seated economic ills.

The most dramatic test of the Fund came with the devaluation of the British pound and a number of other currencies in 1949. The measures were taken in cooperation and consultation with the Fund, which played a useful role in securing a proper range of currency relationships. These devaluations were not followed by a cycle of competitive depreciations, such as occurred in the 1930's, but how much of this was due to the International Monetary Fund and how much to basic economic factors is a moot point.

The financial work of the United Nations is not limited to that of the Bank and the Fund. The Economic and Social Council is interested in financial questions and has established a fiscal commission as a subsidiary organ. In 1947 the Council requested the Secretary-General to build up a fiscal information service. Information has been compiled and various studies made in this field. Publications have been issued on such subjects as public debt and international tax agreements.

ECONOMIC DEVELOPMENT

The specialized agencies of the United Nations deal with the major phases of international economic and social cooperation. There is, however, a need for coordination, and there are certain over-all problems of economic development which cannot be handled adequately on the basis of separate functional agencies. The Economic and Social Council is responsible for the general coordination of programs in this field, and it has undertaken to promote world economic development by the establishment of regional economic commissions, the promotion of international trade, conferences on certain basic problems of general interest, and a program of technical assistance.

The Economic Commission for Europe, created by a resolution of the Economic and Social Council in March, 1947, was the first regional agency of the United Nations. Later, two other regional economic commissions were established, one for Latin America and one for Asia and the Far East. Their functions are to initiate and participate in measures for concerted action; to make or sponsor studies of economic and technological problems and developments; and to undertake or sponsor the collection, evaluation, and dissemination of economic, technological, and statistical information. These regional economic commissions operate on very small budgets, and they can take no action without agreement of the countries concerned. They provide a forum for discussion and a clearinghouse for information. Arrangements are made for representatives of various countries to meet and to talk over the common problems of the area. The result is collective, rather than individual, examination of economic questions of mutual interest.

The type of work done by the regional economic commissions can best be explained by a few illustrations. One of the greatest recovery needs in postwar Europe was an increase in coal production. The United States seemed the most likely source for machinery to modernize the mines, but through a list and detailed description of mining machinery needs it was found that a large proportion of the items could be supplied by manufacturing resources in Europe. Another difficult problem was the shortage of wood to reinforce the coal pits. The deficit in 1948 amounted to twenty-five million pit props. The Coal Committee of ECE provided a forum through which the various countries could see how much pitwood was available and decide how it should be shared. The allocations arrived at in this way were only recommendations, not binding decisions, but nonetheless a helpful service was provided. Another example was the shortage of refractories to reline steel furnaces needed for economic recovery in Italy. Silica bricks could be made in the British and American zones of occupied Germany if the necessary quartzite could be obtained from the French zone. Labor was not available at the quartzite mines, and the Italians offered to send the manpower and accept the material produced in payment. The Americans helped by supplying information on methods of mining quartzite in Alaska, thus making it possible for work to proceed during the winter months. Action followed, the French government gave priority to the job, including extra cigarettes to the miners, and the silica brick crisis was met. The regional economic commissions cannot finance or operate huge projects, but they can be very helpful in ironing out difficulties and providing a cooperative method for eliminating bottlenecks which could not be removed by individual countries acting separately.

The expansion of international trade is essential to the development of a sound world economic order. Three major conferences to negotiate on tariff reductions have been held since 1946: one in Geneva; one at Annecy, France; and one at Torquay, England. A fifty-six-nation conference on trade and employment met in Havana during the winter of 1947–1948. A charter was drafted, by which the countries ratifying it would agree to negotiate for the reduction of tariffs, to observe certain detailed rules for the reduction or elimination of other trade barriers, to refrain from the use of quotas except under carefully defined circumstances, to refrain from certain restrictive business practices, and to comply with equitable principles in concluding commodity agreements. When this charter is accepted by enough governments, the International Trade Organization (ITO) will come into existence as a specialized agency of the United Nations. Its function will be to provide a forum for discussion and a mechanism for settling disputes in this field. In the meantime, an Interim Commission is doing preparatory work. The United States, which took a leading part in initiating the proposed ITO, has not ratified the agreement. Until this is done, there seems to be very little hope for its establishment or effectiveness.

There have been important developments with respect to commodity problems. In August, 1949, the International Wheat Agreement entered into force between four exporting and thirty-two importing countries. By June, 1950, sales totaling 14,551,000 metric tons of wheat annually had been guaranteed under the terms of this agreement. Other commodities which have been under study and discussion include tin, cotton, and sugar.

As an example of a conference on an important subject of general concern, the United Nations Conference on the Conservation and Utilization of Resources may be mentioned. This Conference was held at Lake Success in 1949, and was the first occasion on which scientists and other experts from all over the world met at the invitation of the United Nations to exchange information and discuss common problems. A total of 706 experts from more than fifty countries attended. In addition, 22 nongovernmental organizations and 152 learned scientific societies sent representatives. The topics of chief concern were minerals, forests, fuels and energy, water, land, and fish and wildlife. It was decided to publish the full records and documentation of the Conference. There was general agreement that many of the ideas and suggestions should be followed up in connection with various programs with which the United Nations is concerned.

The program of technical assistance to underdeveloped areas [7] has become one of greatest importance in the field of international cooperation. The rate of technological progress in different geographic areas has been very unequal, and many parts of the world do not share in the advantages of modern techniques. It was estimated that in 1949 more than half the world's population received annual incomes averaging less than $100 per capita, as compared with better than $1,400 for the United States. The economy of the underdeveloped areas is typically agrarian, but the average output per person in agriculture is less than one-tenth that in the more advanced countries. Average life expectancy is low, illiteracy is widespread, communicable diseases are prevalent, malnutrition is the rule, and starvation often occurs.

The gap between the most and the least highly developed countries has been increasing, in spite of the growing interdependence of the modern world. Higher levels of output and better economic organization make it easier to produce capital for further development. Technological progress has a cumulative effect, so that the less developed countries fall farther behind, relatively speaking. The people in these areas, however, are becoming more aware of and dissatisfied with their situation, and they are anxious to increase productivity and raise their living standards. It is also obvious that the wide gap between great wealth and grinding poverty constitutes a source of unrest and instability. Added to these considerations is the recognition that prosperity is indivisible or, to put it another way, that prosperous customers are good for business. Here, then, is a program which appeals to internationalist idealism by proposing to help the world's underprivileged peoples, and which offers the hard-boiled realist bigger and better markets. It also seems to provide an opportunity to allay some of the unrest and dissatisfaction which tend to erupt in open violence and which are a continual menace to international peace.

The United Nations had been providing technical assistance for economic development in various ways. In December, 1948, the General Assembly passed a resolution calling for an expansion of this program. The next month President Truman, in his inaugural address, proposed "a bold new program for making the benefits of our scientific advances and industrial progress

---

[7] The term "underdeveloped" is now used instead of the more patronizing and resented word "backward."

available for the improvement and growth of under-developed areas." He
said, in part, that [8]

Our aim should be to help the free peoples of the world, through their own efforts
to produce more food, more clothing, more materials for housing, and more mechanical power to lighten their burdens.

We invite other countries to pool their technological resources in this undertaking.
Their contributions will be warmly welcomed. This should be a cooperative enterprise in which all nations work together through the United Nations and its specialized agencies wherever practicable. It must be a world-wide effort for the achievement of peace, plenty, and freedom.

Early in 1949 the Economic and Social Council passed a resolution requesting the Secretary-General, in consultation with the interested specialized
agencies, to prepare a plan for an expanded cooperative plan of technical assistance for economic development. At its session in the fall of 1949, the General
Assembly unanimously endorsed this program. In extending technical assistance, the participating organizations are instructed to observe certain general
principles, including the following: (1) assistance shall be given only on request in agreement with the government concerned; (2) the assistance furnished shall not be a means of foreign economic and political interference; (3)
distinctions arising from the political structure of the country requiring assistance, or from the race or religion of its population, shall be avoided;
and (4) in establishing priorities, due regard shall be paid to the urgency of
needs and the geographical distribution of applicants.

The amount of $288,000 for technical assistance had been included in the
United Nations budget for 1949. This was increased to $508,420 for 1950,
and the same amount for 1951. Under the regular 1950 program, sixteen
countries requested expert advice, and approximately fifty experts of some
twenty different nationalities were made available. The forms of the proposed assistance are technical advisory services, training, demonstration
projects, pilot plants, and dissemination of technical information. At a conference in June, 1950, representatives of fifty governments pledged contributions of about $20 million, over and above the regular United Nations budget.
Under the expanded program, 265 requests were received from fifty-five governments by the end of 1950.

One of the advantages of this program is that it can achieve substantial results with a very small expenditure of funds. The export of know-how does
not need to be a costly operation. Slight technical improvements, which
may be quickly suggested by an expert, can make a real difference in food
production per acre, for example. All this is valuable and useful work, and
should not be underestimated. The problem of economic development on a
large scale, however, raises the question of capital investments in many times

[8] This was the famous "Point Four" proposal.

the amounts yet made available.   Private investors are not likely to be interested unless the loans are made in areas with stable social and political conditions, or unless they receive government guarantees against loss.   The only
alternative, so far as private investment is concerned, is the type of speculative
capital which asks for enormous profits as compensations for unusual risks.
This is obviously an undesirable method in the circumstances.   Direct government financing raises the specter of economic imperialism, unless a genuine
internationalized system of capital investment can be worked out through
the United Nations.   In the meantime, the program of technical assistance for
economic development goes ahead in a modest way.   This is potentially one
of the most significant trends in the field of international economic and social
cooperation.[9]

HEALTH

It has been recognized for a long time that the protection of health requires
international cooperation.   Germs do not respect international boundaries,
and they enter a country without the sanction of passport or visa.   At the
San Francisco Conference in 1945, health was considered a field of United
Nations concern.   One of the first acts of the Economic and Social Council
was the creation of a technical preparatory committee to prepare for an international health conference.   This conference, which was held in June, 1946,
drafted the constitution of the World Health Organization (WHO).   The
interim preparatory commission for WHO was granted unusual operating powers in view of the acute postwar health problems.   Thus activities could be
undertaken before the formal establishment of WHO itself.

One of the first projects was a malaria-control program in Greece, where
this disease attacked one to three million persons annually and resulted in
thousands of deaths.   A nationwide campaign was started by the Greek government in 1946 with the assistance first of UNRRA and later of a WHO mission.   Some 96,000 acres of malarious swamps were sprayed from airplanes
with DDT, and several hundred thousand houses were sprayed by hand.
After two years the death rate had dropped sharply, and in some regions the
incidence had fallen from 85 to 5 per cent.   The control of malarial mosquitoes and the Dacas fly also made possible a substantial increase in rice and
olive production.   In 1949, antimalarial operations were carried on in twenty
different countries.

For the first time in history, tuberculosis is being fought on an international
scale by the coordinated efforts of medical and health personnel, with laboratory and other technical facilities.   This program calls for tuberculin testing
of 50,000,000 children in Europe alone.   Tuberculosis centers were established

[9] For a description of this program, see *United Nations Work and Programs for Technical Assistance,* UN Department of Public Information, April, 1951.

and studies begun in countries of Asia, Africa, and Latin America. In India, WHO installed the first BCG (vaccine) laboratory in that country. By December, 1949, tests for tuberculosis had been given to 18,000,000 children and young adults, and 8,400,000 had been immunized against infection.

A dramatic success for international cooperation in the field of health was scored in connection with the outbreak of a serious cholera epidemic in Egypt in the autumn of 1947. Cholera has always been a dread disease, and strict quarantines have been enforced against its spread. Modern transportation, however, creates new problems. The incubation period for cholera is about five days. Formerly a traveler who contracted the disease would fall sick before his ship could reach a distant point, and quarantine regulations could be enforced. With air travel, an American tourist might pick up the germ in Cairo, for example, spend a day or two in Paris and London, and be back in New York or Washington before he showed any symptoms. Under these conditions a serious cholera epidemic could spread far and rapidly.

In the Egyptian epidemic, 20,877 cases with a mortality rate of almost 50 per cent were reported within eight weeks. The interim commission of WHO was consulted by cable and immediately went into action. Thirty-six countries connected with Egypt by land, sea, or air routes, as well as the WHO epidemiological station at Singapore and the Pan American Sanitary Bureau at Washington, were kept informed on the situation, thus enabling them to take the necessary quarantine measures. WHO collected information on the potential production of cholera vaccine; supplied the vaccine promptly at greatly reduced cost; served as a procurement agency and sent large quantities of essential drugs and medical supplies to Egypt by chartered plane; and provided the Egyptian government with information on current methods of cholera control. That government, with WHO advice and assistance, undertook to inoculate every person in Egypt. As a result of these measures, an all-time world's record for halting a major epidemic was established.

The WHO has provided the assistance of experts and demonstration teams to help member countries to organize or expand programs in the six priority fields of malaria, tuberculosis, venereal diseases, nutrition, maternal and child health, and environmental sanitation. The international disease-reporting services have been expanded, so that quarantine officers may receive faster and more complete information. Assistance is given to governments for the organization of public health services, and about two hundred fellowships a year are awarded for the training of public health personnel. The technical services of WHO include the fields of biological standardization, international pharmacopoeia, health statistics, and revision of international sanitary conventions.

The WHO has a strong interest in the program of technical assistance for economic development, on the thesis that the world cannot rise to economic health on the backs of unhealthy people. Throughout the underdeveloped areas of the world, there is much suffering and countless human lives are wasted on account of diseases which could be prevented by relatively simple procedures. Other diseases in the same areas could be controlled only by techniques requiring much greater professional training and an organized large-scale effort. In any case, economic development cannot progress very far without adequate measures for the protection of public health.

REFUGEES

At the end of World War II there were about eight million refugees and displaced persons in Central Europe. About seven million were repatriated by the allied armies and by UNRRA, but most of the remaining million would not voluntarily return to their countries of origin. The great majority of these were from areas to which the Soviet system had been extended, and they either were opposed to communism or feared punishment. Many, however, did not want to return to communities where memories of Nazi persecution would haunt them, and there were some who could not return immediately to distant homes because of practical difficulties. In addition to these one million persons, there were smaller groups stranded in Asia and Africa.

In 1947 the International Refugee Organization inherited the task of protecting and resettling the refugees and displaced persons. The IRO is an outstanding example of international administration. It has been an operating agency, rather than a forum for study and discussion. The magnitude of the task carried out by IRO is indicated by a few statistics. It assumed initially the responsibility for complete maintenance of about 720,000 persons in the displaced-persons camps of central Europe. (The remainder of the million had some assets of their own, or were able to work in the local economies or for the occupation forces.) This meant the provision of food, shelter, and medical care for a group of people as large as the population of Cincinnati or Buffalo. In this connection, for example, IRO had one of the largest housing programs ever operated by a single authority.

By May 31, 1951, about a million refugees and displaced persons had been reestablished. About 930,000 chose to settle in new homes, and the remainder were assisted in returning to their countries of origin. Repatriation has been the primary objective, but IRO has followed the principle that no individual should be repatriated against his will. The Soviet Union was strongly opposed to this position, insisting that the decision in each case should be made by the government of the person's nationality or place of origin, and none of the Soviet countries assisted in this work.

At the peak of its operations, IRO was one of the largest mass transportation agencies in the world. During the summer of 1949 it had a fleet of thirty to thirty-five chartered ships and was using an average of twenty-seven trains a month for movements within Europe. The cost of maintenance and transportation largely explains the fact that IRO has spent more money than all the rest of the United Nations and the specialized agencies combined. Its largest annual budget was $155 million, but the simple arithmetical process of dividing this figure by the number of refugees will show that no great extravagance was lavished upon them. It may be taken as an axiom of government that the assumption of major operating responsibility involves the expenditure of money in large amounts.

The IRO operated an International Tracing Service for three years, seeking to establish the fate of persons who disappeared during the war. In 1948, for example, 48,121 requests about missing persons were received. It was possible to give some information in response to 18,113 of these inquiries, and in 16,367 cases either the missing person was found or proof of death established. One of the most tragic situations was that about 19,000 unsolved inquiries about missing children were still on file at the end of 1949.

The IRO is a temporary agency. It was originally scheduled to terminate at the end of June, 1950, but this term was extended to the end of 1951. The General Assembly has made provision for a High Commissioner's Office for Refugees, to exercise continuing responsibility for the protection of refugees and stateless persons. One of the big remaining problems is that of the so-called "hard core." This includes persons who are chronically ill, the aged, and others debarred by the various national immigration laws. Some, who would be eligible themselves, have relatives with severe handicaps and are not willing to break up their families. A special problem is that of the "forgotten elite"—professional persons such as doctors, artists, and teachers whom no country seems to want as immigrants. Every effort, however, is being made to resettle this group before the termination of IRO. It is slow work, but some countries like Norway, Israel, and France have undertaken to help with the "hard core" in one way or another.

A new problem arose in 1948, as a result of the hostilities in Palestine, with about 750,000 Arabs becoming refugees. The General Assembly created an emergency relief program and appealed for voluntary contributions. The Palestine Conciliation Commission established an economic survey mission to study the situation and make recommendations. The report, submitted in November, 1949, proposed a combined relief and works program under which direct relief would be gradually replaced by useful projects furnishing employment to the refugees. The mission determined that useful work could be found in view of the opportunities to improve and reclaim land, increase the supply of water, extend road systems, and improve sanitation and shelter. On the basis of this report, the General Assembly established a new agency, the United Nations Relief and Works Agency for Palestine Refugees in the Near East, to carry out a relief and works program over an eighteen-month period. The estimated cost of $54,900,000 was to be financed by voluntary governmental contributions. The question of Palestine refugees is of the greatest importance, not only from the social and humanitarian point of view but also because it is a major problem in arriving at a definitive settlement between the Jews and the Arabs.

SOCIAL WELFARE

Various activities in the field of social welfare have been undertaken by the United Nations. The international control of narcotic drugs began before World War I on the initiative of the United States, which was concerned with the problem of drug addiction in the Philippines. Later the League of Nations did much useful work in this field. In 1946 the United Nations assumed the responsibility for international cooperation to prevent or restrict the abuse of narcotics. A Commission on Narcotic Drugs was established as a direct successor to the League's Advisory Committee on this subject. The first task of the Commission was to deal with problems of organization and to reestablish the controls which had lapsed during the war. Attention was then directed to limits on the production of raw materials and to those narcotics now covered by existing international agreements. The discovery of new synthetic drugs has created an urgent situation. Amidone, for example, has the same effects as morphine, is possibly more dangerous, and can be easily produced. A protocol approved by the General Assembly in 1948 places new drugs under international control and provides that the World Health Organization shall decide whether a particular drug is habit-forming. The decision of WHO is automatically binding.

One problem to which the Commission has devoted considerable attention is the coca leaf, from which cocaine is made. This leaf is chewed in many parts of South America. In 1949, a commission of inquiry was sent at the request of the governments of Bolivia and Peru to study the effects of coca chewing in the Andes, and to investigate the possibilities of limiting the production and distribution of coca leaves.

Another welfare activity of the greatest importance has been the work of the United Nations International Children's Emergency Fund (UNICEF). Millions of children in Europe and Asia were in a desperate plight as a result of the war. By 1950, assistance had been given through UNICEF in providing a daily supplementary meal for over five million children and nursing or pregnant mothers in thirteen different countries. UNICEF contributed to the meal, which was ordinarily a school lunch, the protective foods such as milk, meat, fish, fats, and fish-liver oil. The government of the assisted country provided bread or cereals, potatoes, sugar, or whatever other foods were available locally. The supplementary meal amounted to 400 to 600 calories daily, a small but important part of a child's nutritional needs. UNICEF has also attacked the problem of building up the local production of milk. Its activities are not restricted to food supply, however, and it has helped to supply clothing and to cooperate with other organizations in the protection of child health. In 1950 the emphasis shifted from emergency relief to long-term projects for child welfare throughout the world. Funds for UNICEF were raised through voluntary contributions from governmental and private sources. By January, 1951, a total of $152 million had been received for this program. About half this amount came from the United States.

Other social-welfare activities of concern to the United Nations include supervision of the various international conventions for the suppression of traffic in women and children and of obscene publications, and discussion, studies, and dissemination of information in such fields as crime prevention, family life, and administration of social-welfare services. A test of whether relief could be made available in a particular emergency came with the earthquake in Ecuador on August 5, 1949. A special representative of the Secretary-General and experts from the specialized agencies were sent to the scene to help in any way possible. More concretely, $340,000 was made available from UNICEF funds. At the peak, this provided food, blankets, and soap for over 53,000 children.

EDUCATION, SCIENCE, AND CULTURE

One of the best known of the specialized agencies is the United Nations Educational, Scientific and Cultural Organization (UNESCO). In its constitution occurs the oft-quoted statement, "since wars begin in the minds of men, it is in the minds of men that the defences of peace must be constructed." As its name implies, UNESCO is concerned with a broad range of programs and activities in the fields of education, science, and culture. The task of UNESCO was conceived as collaboration to advance mutual knowledge and understanding of peoples through all means of mass communications; to give fresh impulse to popular education and to the spread of culture; and to maintain, increase, and diffuse knowledge. This, on a budget averaging between $8 million and $9 million a year, is a large order, and one of the perplexing problems has been the definition of concrete objectives within such a broad field.

The situation arising from wartime destruction of thousands of schools, museums, and libraries gave UNESCO one of its first tasks. A balance sheet of needs and resources was established, direct assistance was given where the need was greatest, and a world-wide campaign to obtain voluntary contributions was organized. A Temporary International Council for Educational Reconstruction was set up to plan relief campaigns and to coordinate the work of the separate national voluntary agencies.[10] National bodies, especially in the United States, contributed many million dollars' worth of aid in the form of educational materials, books, fellowships and study grants, and technical advisory commissions for war-devastated countries. Direct UNESCO grants were made, on a much smaller scale, for books and periodicals, sound projectors

10 In UNESCO circles, this was known as Operation TICER.

and radios for schools, microfilm equipment, and museum and laboratory supplies. Token grants have been made for various types of emergency aid to war-devastated areas and for such cooperative activities as voluntary international work camps. These token grants represent a small drop in a large bucket, so far as the total need is concerned, but their main purpose is to stimulate voluntary contributions and action on a much larger scale.

One of the major concerns of UNESCO has been the problem of fundamental education, especially in relation to the adjustment of peoples at various stages of development to modern industrial civilization. A quarterly journal and an annotated monthly bibliography of relevant literature in fundamental education are published as a technical information service. Conferences and educational missions have been organized on such subjects as illiteracy and adult education. Basic studies designed to assist in improving the quality of textbooks and teaching materials have been undertaken. Teaching about the United Nations and the specialized agencies has been encouraged by such methods as international essay and poster competition, and the issuance of pamphlets with suggestions and bibliography.

Another type of attack on the problem of fundamental education was the initiation of a pilot project in the Marbial Valley in Haiti, to show how to attack poverty, disease, and ignorance in an underdeveloped area with 97 per cent illiteracy. A sociological survey was completed and steps were taken to standardize Creole spelling and grammar, preliminary to the preparation of schoolbooks in the local language. A small clinic and a school were opened, and plans for agricultural development were made. The success of the project was limited, however, in the sense that accomplishments represented a very small beginning on a very big job. For example, the patients at the clinic responded to the treatment for yaws, but the problem of malnutrition remained. The scope of the project may be indicated by the fact that in 1949 the government of Haiti and UNESCO each contributed $13,500. In 1950, the UNESCO contribution was increased to $20,000.

In the area of the natural sciences, one of the principal projects has been the establishment of field science cooperation offices in Asia, the Middle East, and Latin America to act as liaison agents between the more scientifically advanced countries and the less highly developed areas. UNESCO has cooperated with international scientific organizations by means of grants-in-aid and conferences on abstracting of scientific literature and other problems. As a project in the popularization of science, discussions were initiated in 1949 on the theme "Food and People." Excellent background material was prepared in collaboration with FAO, WHO, and the United Nations Secretariat. The subject of "Energy in the Service of Man" was decided on as the topic for 1950.

One of the important projects in the social sciences is a study of international prejudices and tensions and possible techniques of correction. This includes a comprehensive analysis of forces that influence understanding among peoples and shape their social attitudes. The principal forces being considered are nationalism, technology, population trends, cultural heritages, and ideological conflicts. A scientific study of international organization has been initiated, a limited documentation service is provided, and a quarterly journal (*International Bulletin of the Social Sciences*) is being published.

UNESCO has an extensive cultural program in the arts, literature, and philosophy. It helped to establish the International Theatre Institute. A long-range project has been launched to promote the translation of the most important works of literature of every country. A system of book coupons has been developed to enable soft-currency countries to purchase books in hard-currency countries. In effect, UNESCO acts as a banker, exchanging the currency of one country for that of another and thus eliminating, within the limits of available funds, the foreign-exchange problem in the purchase of books. In the field of philosophy, UNESCO has laid special emphasis on the philosophic bases of human rights.

In connection with the international exchange of persons, UNESCO has given priority to the collection and publication of information about the availability and conditions of fellowships and scholarships; the analysis of obstacles to the free movement of persons between countries, with recommendations for their elimination; and the administration of a limited number of fellowships, and the stimulation of others from both governmental and private funds.

Another important part of UNESCO's program is concerned with mass communication. Surveys of the technical facilities of press, radio, and films in forty-five countries have been completed and published. An international agreement to facilitate the circulation of visual and auditory materials has been opened to signature. A study is being made of the current variations in the Braille system throughout the world, with a view to reaching agreement on principles of uniformity and rationalization. UNESCO has been active in disseminating the Universal Declaration of Human Rights and in the preparation of exhibits and other materials on this subject.

A unique clause in UNESCO's constitution provides for an element of direct participation by the peoples of the member states. National cooperating bodies exist in some thirty countries. The United States National Commission for UNESCO comprises 100 persons, of whom not more than 60 may be representatives of national voluntary organizations interested in educational, scientific, and cultural matters. Not more than 10 may be officials of the Federal government, and not more than 15 of state and local governments. The remaining 15 are chosen at large. This organizational feature, as well as the objectives and program, emphasizes the fact that the main purpose of UNESCO is to aid in creating a climate of intellectual cooperation among the peoples of the world.

Chapter 18

NON-SELF-GOVERNING
TERRITORIES AND TRUSTEESHIP

As a result of the imperialist movement in the centuries following the period of exploration, a large part of the non-European world was brought under the control of Western European states. These territories were called "colonies," though strictly speaking only territories settled by peoples of the so-called mother country are colonies. Noncontinguous territories inhabited by a relatively dense indigenous population are more properly called "dependent territories" or "dependencies."

Thus the British territories in North America, Australia, and New Zealand were properly called colonies. In these colonies, institutions of self-government were established almost immediately upon the arrival of the colonists and the demand for independence developed rapidly. The thirteen British colonies in North America, which subsequently became the United States of America, took up arms and won their independence before the end of the eighteenth century.

The territories, dependent on the other hand, were nearly all found in the Tropical Zone and had climates which did not attract Europeans as permanent settlers. During the first centuries of the imperialist movement, the native peoples of these conquered territories received harsh treatment and frequently were ruthlessly exploited. Gradually other ideas began to penetrate the thinking of the West and in course of time the administration of the colonies became more enlightened. A number of factors contributed to this development. Though belatedly, an increasing number of people began to demand the application of Christian principles to all phases of social life. The slogan of the French Revolution, "Liberty, Equality, and Fraternity," had its influence, as also the humanitarian movement of the nineteenth century. The rapid advance of democracy and democratic ideas not only helped to improve colonial administration, it undermined the whole institution of colonialism and brought it into ill repute. An ever-growing number of people found it difficult to harmonize imperialism with democratic principles. So long as people in the colonies remained passive, the issue did not become acute, but with the development of nationalism in these territories the democratic peoples of the West found themselves in a position which steadily became more distasteful and costly to them. There also developed among peoples of states which had no colonies a feeling that the power over dependencies was used to favor commercially the nationals of the metropolitan country.[1] There developed a widespread conviction that imperialism was an important cause of war.

Imperialism was a lively issue in the early decades of this century. An American scholar characterized imperialism as "the most impressive achievement and the most momentous world problem of our age."[2] On the eve of World War I nearly a third of the world's population lived in non-self-governing territories. In the fifth of his Fourteen Points, President Wilson in January, 1918, gave expression to the feeling which at the time generally prevailed with respect to the colonial issue and the peace settlement. He declared:

A free, open-minded, and absolutely impartial adjustment of all colonial claims, based upon a strict observance of the principle that in determining all such questions of sovereignty the interests of the population concerned must have equal weight with the equitable claims of the government whose title is to be determined.

It is interesting to note that President Wilson placed the interests of the indigenous population only on a level with the "equitable claims" of the states seeking authority to govern them. He did not propose that the Peace Conference make arrangement for colonies in general. No colonial power would have accepted that. However, a mild provision applicable to all non-self-governing territories of states members of the League of Nations was inserted in the Covenant. Under Article 23(b), the members of the League "undertake to secure just treatment of the native inhabitants of territories under their control."

The Peace Conference could deal in an effective manner only with the colonies of the former enemy countries. It was generally agreed on the one hand that the former German colonies and Turkish territories should not be restored to their former rulers and on the other that they were not ready for independence. President Wilson was unalterably opposed to annexation, and in this position he was backed by a strong world opinion. There remained, thus, only two solutions: (1) direct administration by the proposed new international organization, and (2) administration by a designated country subject to supervision of the League of Nations. The first was not feasible be-

[1] The term "metropolitan country" instead of "mother country" is now generally used to designate the dominant state. The latter expression is clearly inappropriate when the people in the dependency are of a different race from the inhabitants of the controlling state. Since "metropolis" means "mother city," it is really no more appropriate than "mother country" for these dependencies. Sometimes, following the French, the term "metropole" is used.

[2] Parker Thomas Moon, *Imperialism and World Politics*, Macmillan, New York, 1926, p. 1.

cause it was unacceptable to the chief Allied Powers which had conquered these territories. Furthermore, it was thought to be unwise to burden the League of Nations with an experiment in the international administration of colonies. National administration subject to international supervision remained as the only feasible solution. The mandates system, as the arrangement was called, can therefore be regarded as a compromise between the views of those who were hostile to territorial annexation and colonialism on the one hand, and the desires of the chief Allied Powers which had conquered these territories and wanted to annex them, on the other. Secondly, it was an attempt to solve the problem of securing administration in the interests of the native population and of the world rather than in the interests of the administering country in such territories as, in the euphemistic language of Article 22 of the Covenant, "are inhabited by peoples not yet able to stand by themselves under the strenuous conditions of the modern world."

THE LEAGUE MANDATE SYSTEM

The outlines of the mandates system were laid down in Article 22 of the Covenant. It stated as the basic principle to be applied to the mandated territories that "the well-being and development of such peoples form a sacred trust of civilization" and that "the best method of giving practical effect to this principle is that the tutelage of such peoples should be entrusted to advanced nations who by reason of their resources, their experience or their geographical position can best undertake this responsibility, and who are willing to accept it, and that this tutelage should be exercised by them as Mandatories on behalf of the League."

It provided for three types of mandates, which later were designated as A, B, and C. The former Turkish territories were regarded as having "reached a stage of development where their existence as independent nations can be provisionally recognized subject to the rendering of administrative advice and assistance by a Mandatory until such time as they are able to stand alone." These mandates, classed as A mandates, were intended to be of relatively short duration, but only one of these territories, Iraq, had acquired its independence before World War II. It became independent in 1932, and at the same time it became a member of the League of Nations. Only Great Britain and France held A mandates. The former was the mandatory for Iraq and Palestine (including Transjordan), and the latter for Syria and Lebanon.

The former German territories in Africa were described as being "at such a stage that the Mandatory must be responsible for the administration of the territory" under conditions which would guarantee freedom of conscience and religion, and prohibition of certain abuses such as slave trade and arms and liquor traffic, and would secure "equal opportunities of trade and commerce of other Members of the League." These territories were designated as B mandates. The mandatory power for Tanganyika, West Togo, and the western Cameroons was Great Britain; for East Togo and the eastern Cameroons, France; and for Ruanda-Urundi, Belgium.

The remaining former German territories were classified as C mandates. The Covenant stated that these, "owing to the sparseness of their population, or their small size, or their remoteness from the centers of civilization, or their geographical contiguity to the territory of the Mandatory, and other circumstances," could be best administered under the laws of the Mandatory "as integral portions of its territory." The large but sparsely settled South-West Africa was assigned to the Union of South Africa as a mandatory; the former German islands in the Central Pacific, north of the equator, became the mandated territory of Japan; Western Samoa was placed under the administration of New Zealand; and North-East New Guinea was entrusted to Australia as mandatory. The small island of Nauru was placed under the joint administration of Great Britain, Australia, and New Zealand.

It will be noted that the chief difference between the three types of mandates consisted in the amount of administrative authority conferred upon the mandatory. The authority of the mandatory power was restricted to rendering "administrative advice and assistance" in case of the A mandates, while in the case of B mandates the administering state had complete governmental power, subject to a few express restrictions. The C mandated territories could be administered "under the laws of the Mandatory as integral portions of its territory."

The degree of authority, control, or administration to be exercised by the mandatory was determined in each case by an agreement between the Council of the League of Nations and the mandatory, but in every case the mandatory was under the obligation of rendering an annual report of its administration to the Council. The Covenant further provided for the institution of a permanent commission "to receive and examine" the annual reports and "to advise the Council on all matters relating to the observance of the mandates."

Such in brief outline was the mandates system. The system was not without weaknesses and inconsistencies, but in general it may be said to have been successful. It made for high standards of administration in the interests of the native population and it also served to stimulate the administrations of other dependencies to achieve higher levels of native welfare.

THE CHARTER AND NON-SELF-GOVERNING TERRITORIES

The Dumbarton Oaks Proposals did not contain a single reference to colonial questions. At the time of the Dumbarton Oaks Conversations, the participating governments were not yet prepared to discuss this subject. The United States government, which was expected to take the lead in this matter, found itself in a peculiar position. Americans, largely because of their historical background, have always been strongly anticolonial, and now that many colonial territories in the Pacific were being freed of the enemy by American armed forces, many argued that the American government had a special responsibility to ensure their freedom. However, events in the war had also aroused other sentiments, especially in the armed forces. Japan had fortified the islands in the Pacific over which it exercised a mandate under the League of Nations. This was done in violation of the Covenant and of the terms of the mandate. These islands, athwart the sea lanes from Hawaii to the Philippines, were conquered by American armed forces at great cost. Regarding these islands primarily from the point of view of American defense, the Army and Navy quite naturally desired their annexation in outright sovereignty.

Had the United States government yielded to this demand of the defense departments, its moral influence in the movement for some sort of international regulation of the colonial problem would have been destroyed. The Department of State, therefore, adamantly resisted the demands for outright annexation. It was not until this internal conflict had been solved that the American government could exercise any vital leadership in this matter. The difficulty was solved by a compromise. It was agreed that the United States government would press for a special kind of trusteeship for the former Japanese mandated islands which would give it the right to fortify them and to close all or parts of them for reasons of security.

At Yalta, President Roosevelt, Prime Minister Churchill, and Marshal Stalin reached agreement on the basic principles of an international trusteeship system which would apply to (1) existing mandates of the League of Nations, (2) territories detached from the enemy as a result of the present war, and (3) any other territory which might voluntarily be placed under trusteeship. It was to apply to no other territories. It was further agreed that the five powers which were to have permanent seats on the Security Council would consult each other on this question before the San Francisco Conference. These consultations did not take place before the Conference, but were held while the trusteeship provisions of the Charter were being drafted.

The articles finally hammered out at the Conference are grouped in three chapters and deal with two types of dependencies. Chapter XI deals with all non-self-governing territories except those which are under trusteeship, whereas Chapters XII and XIII outline the position of territories which have been placed under the international trusteeship system. Most of the dependent territories in the world fall under the first group. It was not to be expected that states would accept much United Nations interference in the administration of territories over which they had acquired jurisdiction decades ago. What they accepted in Chapter XI was a general declaration of principles governing the administration of their non-self-governing territories. Thus the United States as a member of the United Nations has agreed to be guided by these principles in governing Alaska, the Hawaiian Islands, Puerto Rico, and its other dependencies. The second group of dependencies falling within the scope of the Charter provisions are the territories placed under the international trusteeship system. It may be argued that Chapter XI applies to all dependencies, trust territories as well as others, for it lays down the goals of administration of "territories whose peoples have not yet attained a full measure of self-government." However that may be, it is a matter of little significance, since the basic objectives of the trusteeship system are stated at length in Article 76, and these objectives include practically all, if not actually all, of those listed in Article 73 for the administration of non-self-governing territories.

DEPENDENCIES NOT UNDER TRUSTEESHIP

As has already been indicated, Chapter XI constitutes a general declaration of principles governing the administration of territories "whose peoples have not yet attained a full measure of self-government." Under Article 73 all members of the United Nations "which have or assume responsibilities" for the administration of non-self-governing territories accept a number of far-reaching obligations. They "recognize the principle that the interests of the inhabitants of these territories are paramount, and accept as a sacred trust the obligation to promote to the utmost . . . the well-being of the inhabitants of this territory." To this end administering states are to ensure their political, economic, social, and educational advancement, to develop self-government, "to assist them in the progressive development of their free political institutions," "to further international peace and security," and "to promote constructive measures of development." They also agree to "transmit regularly to the Secretary-General for information purposes, subject to such limitation as security and constitutional considerations may require, statistical and other information of a technical nature relating to economic, social, and educational conditions in the territories for which they are respectively responsible. . . ."

Article 74 stipulates that the policy of the members of the United Nations in administering non-self-governing territories "must be based on the general principle of good-neighborliness." This provision seems quite superfluous, since the obligation to pursue a policy of "good-neighborliness" is assumed throughout the Charter and is explicitly stated in many articles.

Chapter XI of the Charter is an extension and an elaboration of Article 23(e) of the Covenant of the League. It starts from the basic principle that all questions of colonial policy and administration are international in character and therefore subject to a measure of world accountability. Unfortunately, its provisions are frequently vague and repetitious and occasionally inconsistent. The language of Chapter XI gives no answer to the question of what constitutes a non-self-governing territory or who is to determine what territories fall within the scope of the Declaration. The District of Columbia is not self-governing, yet it is quite clearly not the intention of the Charter to include such territories within the scope of Article XI. Since the General Assembly may "discuss any questions or any matters within the scope" of the Charter and make recommendations to the members "on any such questions or matters" (Article 10), it may presumably also specify in recommendatory form the territories which fall within the scope of the Declaration. In practice it is left to the members to determine which of their territories are non-self-governing. Very much the same is true of other vague clauses of the chapter. It is the administering government which in first instance decides what these clauses mean, subject always to such pressure as the General Assembly can exert through discussion and recommendation.

Administering states are "to promote to the utmost . . . the well-being of the inhabitants of these territories," but "within the system of international peace and security established by the present Charter." It does not seem possible that a policy of promoting the well-being of dependent peoples could endanger international peace and security, except in a negative way. Moreover, the last clause is an unfortunate qualification of the sound general principle stated in the first. In a seriously disturbed world this qualification may easily be used to annul the general principle. The question may also be raised as to whether it is wise or fair to require of peoples which are regarded as not yet ready to govern themselves that they make positive contributions to international peace and security.

The heart of the Declaration is found in Article 73(e), which requires the administering states to transmit information regularly to the Secretary-General on conditions in their non-self-governing territories. However, this obligation is qualified by a number of restrictions. Only information of a technical nature need be transmitted, the term "political" having been purposely omitted from the clause; the obligation to transmit information is "subject to such limitation as security and constitutional considerations may require"; and the transmission of the reports to the Secretary-General is "for information purposes." It must not be forgotten, however, that this information can be used by the General Assembly as the basis for discussion and recommendation, and this is being done increasingly.

The great majority of the members of the United Nations are states which have no colonies, and many of them have memories of a former colonial status. It is natural that these countries should press for the largest measure of international accountability possible under the terms of Chapter XI. Some sought to require administering states to submit political information. This movement was bitterly opposed by the states with colonial responsibilities and was defeated. A resolution of the General Assembly (November 3, 1947) states that the voluntary transmission of information on the development of self-governing institutions in non-self-governing territories and its summarizing by the Secretary-General "are entirely in conformity with the spirit of Article 73 of the Charter, and should be . . . encouraged."   Some governments supply political information; others refuse to do so.

Somewhat similar differences arose over the use to be made of the information transmitted to the Secretary-General.   By a resolution of December 14, 1946, the General Assembly recommended that the information transmitted in the course of 1947 should be "summarized, analyzed and classified by the Secretary-General and included in his report to the second session of the General Assembly," and that the Secretary-General communicate to the specialized agencies the information transmitted, with a view to making all relevant data available to their expert and deliberative bodies.   The resolution provided further that the Secretary-General convene an *ad hoc* committee composed in equal numbers of representatives of members transmitting information and of representatives elected by the General Assembly, and that the *ad hoc* committee examine the Secretary-General's summary and analysis of the information transmitted "with a view to making recommendations to the General Assembly regarding the procedures to be followed in the future. . . ."   The basic procedures of the above resolution were extended indefinitely by a series of resolutions adopted by the General Assembly on November 3, 1947.

A third controversy arose over the question of whether the Secretary-General may receive or collect information from sources other than the governments of the administering states.   The colonial powers insist that only information furnished by their governments be considered.

There is a strong inclination on the part of the noncolonial states to minimize the differences in status under the Charter of non-self-governing and trust territories and to assimilate the former to the latter.   There was, for example, the drive to make of the *ad hoc* examining committee a duplicate of the Trusteeship Council.   The representative of China actually proposed to confer upon the Trusteeship Council this examining function.   The colonial powers resent the sharp criticisms of their administration frequently made by the representatives of countries whose standards of social welfare are not above those of the dependencies concerned and whose progressive development in democratic government leaves much to be desired.   They frequently remind the General Assembly of the differences between Chapter XI on the one hand and Chapters XII and XIII on the other, and point out that the competence of the United Nations under the first is much less than under the other two.

In conclusion it should be noted that the problem of dependent territories has greatly diminished, at least quantitatively, since World War II.   Lebanon, Syria, Palestine, and Transjordan, the former A mandates in the Near East, became full-fledged members of the family of nations.   The 450 million people on the subcontinent of India have acquired national independence, as have also the Philippines with 19 million population; Indonesia, with 80 million people; and Burma with a population of 17 million. Ceylon with over 7 million people, attained dominion status in the Commonwealth of Nations. The peoples of Indochina have been granted self-government within the French Union. Korea is no longer a Japanese dependency, although it is not yet a happy land. The combined population of non-self-governing territories is now reduced to something like 150 million.

The original list of territories (1946) under Chapter XI contained seventy-four dependencies, but this number has been considerably reduced. Because of protests of the Republic of Panama, the United States no longer reports on the Panama Canal Zone. The United Kingdom has ceased to report on Malta, and France has ceased sending in reports on a number of territories, presumably because of change in their constitutional status.

THE TRUSTEESHIP SYSTEM

The basic objectives of the trusteeship system are laid down in Article 76. They are practically the same as those outlined in Article 73 for the administration of non-self-governing territories. Superficially there seems to be at least one important difference. In the case of non-self-governing territories the administering states are under obligation "to develop self-government," whereas in the case of trust territories the basic political objective is declared to be the progressive development of the inhabitants "towards self-government or independence as may be appropriate to the particular circumstances of each territory and its peoples and the freely expressed wishes of the peoples concerned, and as may be provided by the terms of each trusteeship agreement." The representatives of some of the noncolonial countries at the San Francisco Conference wished to have independence stated as the goal for the administration of both kinds of territories, but this proposal was bitterly opposed by the delegates of the colonial powers. As a compromise it was included for the one and not the other. It was argued that self-government included the possibility of independence but that it was unwise to emphasize the latter as a goal, since independence might not be feasible for all territories, as for example small or isolated territories. Moreover, when a people attains a certain level of social and economic development it cannot be denied its independence if it really desires it. The emphasis should therefore be placed upon social and economic development. If that is done the political development will largely take care of itself.

The trusteeship system applies to three types of territories, namely, former League of Nations mandates, territories detached from the enemy as a result of World War II, and territories voluntarily placed under the system.[3] Because the Union of South Africa has refused to place South-West Africa under the system, the question of whether members of the United Nations are under

[3] For the territories under the trusteeship system, see Table 6.

legal obligation to place former mandated territories under the trusteeship system has been much discussed. Article 77 states that "the trusteeship system shall apply to such territories in the following categories as may be placed thereunder by means of trusteeship agreements." It is obvious that a state cannot be compelled to enter into an agreement against its wishes, but it has been argued that the word "may" must be interpreted to mean that the administering state has the choice of either placing the territory under trusteeship or of giving it independence. The administering state need not propose an agreement, but in that case it loses the right to govern the territory. The General Assembly in 1946, 1947, and 1948 urged the Union to propose a trusteeship agreement, and finally, in 1949, it asked the International Court of Justice for an advisory opinion on the question of the Union's international obligations with respect to the territory.

The International Court of Justice gave its advisory opinion July 11, 1950. The Court declared as its opinion that South-West Africa is a territory under international mandate assumed by the Union of South Africa on December 17, 1920, that the General Assembly is legally qualified to exercise the supervisory functions previously exercised by the League of Nations with regard to the administration of the territory, and that the Union of South Africa is under an obligation to submit to supervision and control of the General Assembly and to render annual reports to it. The Court was further of the opinion that the competence to determine and modify the international status of the territory did not rest with the Union acting alone, but with the Union acting with the consent of the United Nations. However, the Court was further of the opinion that the provisions of the Charter do not impose on the Union of South Africa a legal obligation to place the territory under the trusteeship system. While the advisory opinion of the International Court of Justice offers no support for United Nations action to compel South Africa to place the territory under trusteeship, it would seem to block rather effectively any plans of the Union to incorporate the territory within its own domain.

Of the second category of territories named in Article 77, Italian Somaliland was placed under the trusteeship system in 1950. Unable to reach an agreement among themselves on the disposition of the former Italian colonies, the United States, Great Britain, France, and the Soviet Union finally placed the matter before the General Assembly for decision. In accordance with resolutions of this body, Libya obtained its independence on December 24, 1951; Somaliland was placed under Italian administration within the United Nations trusteeship system for ten years, after which it is to be independent; and Eritrea was federated with Ethiopia as an autonomous unit under the Ethiopian Crown.

Under the terms of the Treaty of Peace with Japan signed at San Francisco on September 8, 1951, Japan must concur in any proposal of the United States to the United Nations to place under the trusteeship system, with the United

States as the sole administering authority, the Ryukyu, Bonin, Rosario, Volcano, Parece Vela, and Marcus Islands.

Not many people believe that any dependencies will voluntarily be placed under the trusteeship system. Certainly there has been no rush by colonial powers to place their dependencies under the system. Yet the possibility of this happening should not be wholly discounted. The pressure of world public opinion, especially as it expresses itself through the United Nations, for extensive educational facilities and social services makes colonial administration very expensive and bars any significant economic advantage to the administering country. Under these conditions states may not always wish to retain the expensive luxury of administering colonies, though national pride makes them reluctant to withdraw. But in this case the state would wish to free itself completely from the responsibility of administering the dependency, and would therefore be inclined to grant it independence.

The system set up by the Charter is very much like the mandates system of the League of Nations, with some important differences. As in the case of mandates, a territory comes under the system only by an agreement, called the "trusteeship agreement," which states "the terms under which the trust territory will be administered," and designates "the authority which will exercise the administration of the trust territory." The administering authority may be one or more states or the Organization itself. Only in the case of one trust territory does the administering authority consist of more than one state. Australia, New Zealand, and the United Kingdom are named as the joint administrators of Nauru, but in fact the island is administered by Australia alone. Condominiums have not been very successful, as witness the Anglo-Egyptian Sudan and the New Hebrides, and it is not likely that this form will be used. Administration by the Organization itself is somewhat of an anomaly in a trusteeship system, since the function of the United Nations in this case would not be supervisory but administrative. To date no territory has been placed under the administration of the Organization. The General Assembly by a resolution of November 29, 1947, recommended that "the city of Jerusalem shall be established as a *corpus separatum* under a special international regime and shall be administered by the United Nations." This resolution, reinforced by another one of December 9, 1949, which would have placed Jerusalem under the administration of the Trusteeship Council, could not be implemented because of the opposition of Israel and Jordan.

STRATEGIC AREAS

As has already been indicated, the United States insisted upon a special kind of trusteeship to meet what is regarded as its military requirements in the former Japanese mandated islands in the Pacific. This was provided for in Article 82 of the Charter which stipulates "that there may be designated, in any trusteeship agreement, a strategic area or areas which include part or all of the trust territory to which the agreement applies, without prejudice to any special agreement or agreements under Article 43." Whereas the functions of the United Nations with regard to trusteeship agreements for nonstrategic territories "including the approval of the terms of the agreements, and of their alteration or amendment" are exercised by the General Assembly, assisted by the Trusteeship Council, in the case of strategic areas, these same functions are exercised by the Security Council, where each of the permanent members—the five Great Powers—has the power of veto. The basic objectives of the system are equally applicable to the people of all trust territories. Moreover, the Security Council must, "subject to the provisions of the trusteeship agreements and without prejudice to security considerations," make use of the assistance of the Trusteeship Council in performing the functions of the United Nations under the trusteeship system relating to political, economic, social, and educational matters in strategic areas.

There is only one trust territory of the strategic type, and that is the Trust Territory of the Pacific Islands, which are the former Japanese mandated islands, and which before World War I had been colonies of Germany. The agreement,[4] approved by the Security Council on April 2, 1947, designates the United States of America as the administering authority. The right of the administering state to close any areas of the territory is recognized in Article 13 of the agreement.

This trust territory was first administered by the United States Department of the Navy, but in 1951 it was placed under civilian rule, and the Security Council has turned over to the Trusteeship Council its functions regarding political, economic, social, and educational matters. Since security matters remain under the jurisdiction of the Security Council, the United States can prohibit inspection of its military bases on the islands by representatives of any of the United Nations organs.

The United States demanded the inclusion in the agreement of the provision that "the administering authority may determine the extent of their applicability to any areas which may from time to time be specified by it as closed for security reasons" (Article 13). There was objection to this as establishing a dangerous principle, but it was nevertheless accepted. In spite of objections, the United States practically acquired the right to administer the islands as a part of the United States (Article 3). The draft which the United States submitted did not contain a provision for independence as a goal of the administration. To meet Soviet objections, a compromise on this issue was reached. Independence was accepted as an aim, but subject to the qualifying clause, "as may be appropriate to the particular circumstances of the trust territory and its peoples and the freely expressed wishes of the peoples concerned" (Article 6).

[4] See Appendix 14 for text of the agreement.

The trusteeship system, in contrast with the mandates system, not only expects the trust territories to contribute to the maintenance of peace but emphasizes their obligation to do so. The Covenant (Article 22, clause 5) stipulated that in the B mandates the administering states were to prohibit traffic in arms and to prevent "the establishment of fortifications or military and naval bases and of military training of the natives for other than police purposes and the defence of territory." The first basic objective of the trusteeship system, according to Article 76 of the Charter, is "to further international peace and security," and Article 84 specifically lays upon the administering authority the duty to ensure that the trust territory play its part in the maintenance of international peace and security, and to this end it may "make use of volunteer forces, facilities, and assistance from the trust territory in carrying out the obligations toward the Security Council undertaken in this regard by the administering authority. . . ." This provision applies to both strategic and nonstrategic areas.

REGIONAL COMMISSIONS

An effect of colonial expansion and rivalry has sometimes been the fragmentation into a number of small, unnatural administrative units of regions which could be governed much more effectively as one. The Caribbean is such a region. During the early days of World War II, the islands of the Caribbean became isolated, as a result of the German submarine campaign, and economic and social conditions, which already were bad, became worse. To meet the emergency the British and American governments created the Anglo-American Caribbean Commission. The Commission proved so successful that it was put on a permanent basis by an agreement of 1946, with the governments of France and the Netherlands also as members, and renamed the Caribbean Commission. The object of the Commission is to encourage and strengthen cooperation among the members and their territories "with a view toward improving the economic and social well-being of the peoples of those territories." This is to be done by "promoting scientific, technological, and economic development in the Caribbean area and facilitating the use of resources and concerted treatment of mutual problems, avoiding duplication in the work of existing research agencies, surveying needs, ascertaining what research has been done, facilitating research on cooperative basis, and recommending further research."

A similar commission was set up for the islands of the South Pacific by an agreement of 1947, with the governments of Australia, France, New Zealand, Great Britain, and the United States as signatories. The South Pacific Commission, like the Caribbean Commission, is a consultative and advisory body to the participating governments "in matters affecting the economic and social development of the non-self-governing territories within the scope of the Commission and the welfare and advancement of their peoples."

This kind of cooperation is in pursuance of the pledge made by members of the United Nations in Article 73 of the Charter, "to cooperate with one another and, when and where appropriate, with specialized international bodies with a view to the practical achievement of the social, economic, and scientific purposes set forth in this Article."

CONCLUSIONS

It is fortunate that the colonial problem as such has greatly declined in magnitude in recent years, for the United Nations has not demonstrated its suitability for dealing with it. The Big Four struggled over the disposition of the former Italian colonies for several years, took one position and then another on what should be done with them, and finally left it to the General Assembly to decide. In the meanwhile there was uncertainty and stagnation in the territories. Moreover, no one who knows anything about conditions in the former Italian colonies believes that they are ready for independence. A Big Four commission which visited the territories for the purpose of making an investigation of this problem in 1948 declared that an overwhelming majority of Libyans are illiterate and the degree of political understanding is low. Libya has nevertheless been made a sovereign state and is now on its own. It is inconceivable that Somaliland can be prepared for independence in ten years. The interests of the inhabitants had very little to do with the decisions for the disposition of these territories. Confusion, dictatorship, or domination from the outside may well be the lot of these two territories unless some special regime is set up under the United Nations to prevent their collapse.

In the modern world, good government and self-government are closely related. Self-government is never secure where there is bad government, and in any case it is not of very great value there. On the other hand, colonial powers have been prone to set the standards unnecessarily high and to use them as an excuse for delaying the grant of independence.

There was much criticism of the demand of the United States for a "strategic" type of trusteeship in the Charter and for its "take it or leave it" attitude with respect to the trust agreement it submitted to the Security Council for the former Japanese mandated islands. It looked like a thinly veiled scheme of annexation. By placing the territory under civilian administration and by requesting the shift of the nonmilitary supervisory functions to the Trusteeship Council, the United States government has done much to allay criticism. In viewing the American position certain factors should be kept in mind, such as the special geographic position of these islands, their strategic importance for the defense of the United States, and their minor economic value and small population. There is no danger that the inhabitants are going to be exploited; it is more likely that they will be pampered. The American costs of administration (exclusive of military expenditures) run to several million dollars a year for the 60,000 inhabitants. It is not probable that the islands will ever be wholly self-supporting. Nevertheless, by demanding a highly special regime for the territory, which already had an international status, the United States did lose considerable moral authority in the matter of dependent areas.

The colonial question has entered a strange stage. The overwhelming majority of the members of the United Nations are underdeveloped countries, many of them with memories of former colonial status. Their representatives in the General Assembly and in the Trusteeship Council reflect a strong feeling against colonialism. The Soviet Union and its satellites are opposed on principle to all dependencies—that is, non-Communist ones—hence no administration of non-self-governing territories has ever a good feature in their eyes. Administering states are thus held up to standards of civil and political rights and social welfare which few of the critics have attained at home. In effect, the international community will no longer tolerate the political domination of one people by another unless the latter are wholly unprepared for independence, the standards of administration are high, and the interests of the inhabitants are made paramount. It is not surprising that the administering states have regarded some of the demands and criticisms as irresponsible and have reacted sharply. The atmosphere has become so embittered that fruitful cooperation is difficult.

The inhabitants of most non-self-governing territories, and especially of trust territories, are more fortunate than the citizens of many independent underdeveloped countries. They have moral claims upon technologically advanced metropolitan countries for help in raising their standards of living. Puerto Rico is making perceptible progress by means of generous help from the United States. Her less fortunate neighbors may have to wait for aid. The Philippine Republic still benefits from its former position as a dependency of the United States. In addition to huge sums of money poured, directly and indirectly, into the country (nearly $2 billion between 1945 and 1949) the American government has agreed to aid its former dependency to the extent of $50 million annually for five years (1950–1955). The hard-pressed British already before the war had their colonial development and welfare fund.

The colonial problem has moved into a new phase. The many countries with their large populations which won their independence in recent years are faced with grave economic problems. Political independence did not solve any of the basic social and economic problems of these underdeveloped countries; it merely shifted the responsibility for solving them to the inhabitants of these territories, but unfortunately most of these peoples are without adequate financial resources, technology, or administrative experience. President Truman's fourth point of his inaugural address (1949)—his bold new program for extending technological assistance to underdeveloped countries—as well as the United Nations program of technical assistance are aimed at filling this void. So long as these countries remain economically weak they will remain politically and militarily weak and an easy prey to communism. This is an urgent problem of vast magnitude, and one beset by very great difficulties.

TABLE 6. TERRITORIES UNDER THE TRUSTEESHIP SYSTEM

Trust territory	Administering authority	Population	Area, square miles
New Guinea	Australia	1,006,200	93,000
Ruanda-Urundi	Belgium	3,718,646	20,916
Cameroons	France	2,702,500	166,797
Togoland	France	944,446	21,236
Western Samoa	New Zealand	72,936	1,133
Tanganyika	United Kingdom	7,079,557	392,688
Cameroons	United Kingdom	991,000	34,081
Togoland	United Kingdom	382,200	13,040
Nauru	Australia	3,162	82
Trust Territory of Pacific Islands	United States of America	60,000	687
Somaliland	Italy	1,300,000	194,000
Total		18,260,647	937,660

Chapter 19

HUMAN RIGHTS AND FUNDAMENTAL
FREEDOMS

One of the principal functions of the United Nations is to promote universal respect for and observance of human rights. This is considered one of the most important aspects of the fundamental task of establishing the conditions of a lasting peace. Handling dangerous international disputes and preventing a resort to aggression do not by any means constitute the full responsibility of the United Nations. It is important to do these things when and if necessary, but in the long run the major objective is the attainment of an international order in which disputes will always be settled by pacific means.

The Charter of the United Nations makes seven definite references to the matter of human rights. The drafters of the Charter did not merely pay it lip service, but made it a really important foundation stone. The preamble refers to the determination "to reaffirm faith in fundamental human rights, in the dignity and worth of the human person, in the equal rights of men and women and of nations large and small. . . ." Article 1 of the Charter mentions, as one of the purposes of the United Nations, "to achieve international co-operation in . . . promoting and encouraging respect for human rights and for fundamental freedoms for all without distinction as to race, sex, language, or religion." Article 13 makes it the responsibility of the General Assembly to initiate studies and make recommendations for the purpose, among others, of assisting in the realization of human rights and fundamental freedoms. The provisions of the Charter dealing with international economic and social cooperation, as necessary for peaceful and friendly relations among nations, include an obligation to promote "universal respect for, and observance of, human rights and fundamental freedoms for all without distinction as to race, sex, language, or religion" (Article 55). The Economic and Social Council is authorized to make recommendations for this purpose (Article 62) and is instructed to set up commissions in economic and social fields and for the promotion of human rights (Article 68). Finally, one of the basic objectives of the trusteeship system, as stated in Article 76 of the Charter, is "to encourage respect for human rights and for fundamental freedoms for all without distinction as to race, sex, language, or religion, and to encourage recognition of the interdependence of the peoples of the world."

It is of the greatest importance that the Charter of the United Nations, as the constitution of modern international organization, incorporates a democratic ideology. The repeated emphasis on "human rights and fundamental freedoms" puts organized international cooperation in the attainment of world peace and security on a basis springing from a cultural and political heritage friendly to the ideals of American democracy. Moreover, it is quite clear that peace is not conceived as the mere absence of war and aggression, but as an affirmative condition with the positive qualities of welfare for the human race. As the world became more interdependent and life more complicated, the problem of human rights became universal and more directly related to the conditions for maintaining international peace and security. Violations of elementary human rights had been a major contributing cause of World War II, and it became apparent after the publication of the Dumbarton Oaks proposals that the peoples of the world were determined to create strong international machinery to prevent a recurrence of that experience. Inspiration for this movement was also derived from the "four freedoms" as stated by President Roosevelt,[1] the Atlantic Charter of August, 1941, and the Declaration by the United Nations of January 1, 1942.

The Charter of the United Nations does not contain a bill of rights. The content and scope of "human rights and fundamental freedoms" were left for later elaboration. Americans are accustomed to thinking of a bill of rights as an essential part of a constitution, in order to protect the individual against excessive or arbitrary governmental power. The original draft of the Federal constitution, however, did not contain a bill of rights, but this portion of the Constitution came into existence as a series of ten amendments ratified in 1791. Very limited powers were granted to the United Nations, so that a bill of rights was not needed in order to prevent it from abusing its authority. The problem is not to protect individuals against the United Nations as American citizens are protected against arbitrary action by governmental agencies and officials. The problem is to achieve a greater degree of international cooperation in promoting human rights among and within the member states. In the United States, certain restrictions on the states are found in the Federal constitution and its amendments. In the United Nations system the only restrictions on the members are those found in the general obligations of the Charter itself and in the subsidiary commitments which may be accepted. As yet, the United Nations acts through its members and has no direct way of assuring rights and freedoms to individual citizens.

---

[1] In his state of the Union message of January, 1941. The "four freedoms" are freedom of religion and of speech, and freedom from fear and from want. See Appendix 5.

THE COMMISSION ON HUMAN RIGHTS

The Economic and Social Council in February, 1946, established a preliminary Commission on Human Rights and on June 21, 1946, adopted the terms of reference of the permanent Commission and determined its membership. This Commission consists of representatives of eighteen members of the United Nations.   Thus, it was decided that the Commission on Human Rights would consist of representatives of governments, rather than of experts serving in their individual capacities.   The Economic and Social Council selects the eighteen members of the United Nations to be represented.   Each member then selects its representative for the Commission.   With a view to securing balanced representation in various fields, however, the Economic and Social Council directed the Secretary-General to "consult with the governments of the members so selected before the representatives are finally nominated by these governments and confirmed by the Council."   The term of office is three years, on a staggered basis, and members are eligible for reelection.

The Commission on Human Rights was directed to submit proposals, recommendations, and reports concerning an international bill of human rights; international declarations or conventions on civil liberties, the status of women, freedom of information and similar matters; the protection of minorities; the prevention of discrimination on grounds of race, sex, language, or religion; and any other matter concerning human rights.   It does not have the authority to take action in individual cases involving human rights.   For basic documentation, the Secretary-General was requested to make arrangements for the compilation of a yearbook on human rights; collection and publication of information on the activities relating to human rights of all organs of the United Nations; collection and publication of information concerning human rights arising from trials of war criminals, quislings, and traitors; preparation of a survey of the development of human rights; and the collection of plans and declarations on human rights by specialized agencies and nongovernmental organizations.

When the Commission met, it soon became apparent that the drafting of an international bill of human rights would have to be done in several stages. The first task was to elaborate a Declaration defining the fundamental human rights and freedoms.   This was conceived "as a common standard of achievement for all peoples."   It would be a statement of principles, rather than a binding and enforceable legal obligation, and its influence would be moral and educational.   The next step was to be an international convention or treaty, setting forth in precise terms the provisions which governments are willing to accept as legally binding.   Finally, it was obvious that there would be a need for machinery to ensure the observance of human rights and to deal with violations.   This required the development of "measures of implementation."

In accordance with this conception of its threefold task, the Commission first undertook the writing of a Declaration on Human Rights. This work was done in a very careful and meticulous way. Using documentation furnished by the Secretariat, a drafting committee prepared a first draft. In the light of comments from member governments, the Commission as a whole revised it. Then the revised draft was circulated, the drafting committee met again, and the Commission prepared its final proposal. This went to the Economic and Social Council, and then to the General Assembly which referred the proposal to its Third Committee. This Committee made a very detailed examination, going over the draft almost word by word. The resulting document went to the General Assembly, which adopted the Universal Declaration of Human Rights [2] on December 10, 1948, by a vote of 48 to 0, with 8 abstentions and 2 members absent.

All this careful, detailed work was necessary because of the great differences in cultural, philosophic, and legal views. If the Declaration were to command respect and allegiance, and if it were to be more than a string of maxims, it was essential to reach the fullest possible understanding about every word and clause. In the drafting of the Declaration, three basic issues could be discerned. The first had to do with the relation between the individual and the state. Most of the members believed that the fundamental individual freedoms should be expressed, and that human and not state rights should be emphasized. The representatives of the Soviet members, however, stressed the duty of man to the state and the community, and urged the inclusion of more explicit safeguards of the sovereign rights of the "democratic state." The discussion of the meaning, and ambiguity, of this phrase was one of the most important debates in the Commission. Traditional bills of rights in the Western world, notably those of France and the United States, have been concerned with protections of the individual against arbitrary governmental action. The bill of rights in the Soviet constitution is written in terms of guarantees to the individual by the state. In the former, individual rights are to be preserved by directing governments not to take forbidden action. In the latter, the concern is with governmental responsibility for taking affirmative action.

The second basic issue related to the emphasis to be given the traditional individual-personal rights, as compared with the so-called economic-social rights. All members wanted to see both types of rights confirmed, and the Universal Declaration as adopted actually does this. The Soviet representatives interpreted the problem as being essentially one of the duty of the state to guarantee economic and social rights to "the broad masses of the people." They considered the traditional rights formal and empty without the guarantee of the new economic, social, and educational rights. A declaration of rights, without provisions for their guarantee by the state and society, reminded the

[2] For text, see Appendix 19.

Soviet representative of a saying from the Russian fairy tales, "Only the toes are left, the body is gone." The British and American representatives laid greater stress on the personal, civil, and political liberties, and held the view that governments are in a position only to promote, not guarantee, economic, social, and educational rights. The representative of France took an intermediate position. He did not want to overlook the traditional values, but to him "social security" belonged to the essence of human rights, and he thought that it required special emphasis because it was not well established.

The third issue was the underlying one of the nature and origin of human rights. On what basis does man possess them? If they are "natural" rights, every person possesses them because he is a human being; they are "inalienable." The state does not have, and cannot have, any legal right or authority to abrogate them, but is obligated to recognize and respect them. If, on the other hand, human rights are conferred by society or the state, they may also be withdrawn by the authority which grants them. The Universal Declaration accepts the natural-rights philosophy. The first clause in the preamble is: "Whereas recognition of the inherent dignity and of the equal and inalienable rights of all members of the human family is the foundation of freedom, justice and peace in the world." Article 1 of the Declaration reads: "All human beings are born free and equal in dignity and rights. They are endowed with reason and conscience and should act towards one another in a spirit of brotherhood."

In addition to these basic issues, there was some disagreement as to the kind of document the Declaration should be. All the members agreed that it should be short and concise, so as to be readily understandable. However, the approach of the United States, Great Britain, and China was to emphasize the positive side of rights and freedoms, and whenever possible to leave the restrictions to the Covenant to be drafted later. The representative of France wanted the Declaration to be more explicit, and thought it should go further than any previous declarations of human rights. The Soviet states thought that, in addition to an enumeration of rights and freedoms, there should be provisions indicating the action to be taken to realize them. They also wanted certain limitations stated: for example, freedom of speech, etc., should be denied to Nazis, Fascists, and others who work against democratic interests. Furthermore, they wanted it made clear that the realization of rights and freedoms is subject to the laws of the countries concerned.

The work of the Commission was further complicated by the existence of five official languages and by different connotations of key terms. Great care had to be taken to see that the same meaning was understood by all the representatives. The value of the Declaration would be considerably lessened if there were too many ambiguities and uncertainties as to the precise scope of the various provisions. A few examples will illustrate the type of questions which came up in the discussions.

To an American, the statement "All men are created equal" may seem perfectly obvious in meaning. But there were two objections to it. First, in some countries, where the emancipation of women is recent or still in progress, the term "men" might not be understood in the generic sense. It had to be made clear that women were included too. The other objection came from those who did not wish to endorse the idea of a divine creator. Therefore, the statement became, "All human beings are born free and equal in dignity and rights." This also, it will be noted, gives some content or explanation to the term "equal."

Article 2 states that everyone is entitled to rights and freedoms "without distinction of any kind, such as race, colour, sex, language, religion, political or other opinion, national or social origin, property, birth or other status." The word "birth" was added to an earlier draft after a long discussion as to whether "class" or some other word would better convey the idea sought for.

A proposal was made for inclusion of the statement, "Everyone is entitled to a good social and international order." The Soviet representative, Professor Pavlov, argued that an order which permitted private ownership of the means of production, and the resulting exploitation of one group by another, could not possibly be "good." The statement was revised and finally became, "Everyone is entitled to a social and international order in which the rights and freedoms set forth in this Declaration can be fully realized" (Article 28).

The Universal Declaration of Human Rights, as adopted, contains a preamble and thirty articles. The first two articles constitute an affirmation of human rights and freedoms, and they are meant to apply to everyone, everywhere. Articles 3 through 15 state the traditional rights as they have been known in the Western world. These include the right to life, liberty, and security,[3] to recognition as a person before the law, and to a fair trial. Slavery, torture, cruel and inhuman punishment, arbitrary arrest, and arbitrary interference with home, family, or correspondence are prohibited. All persons are entitled to equal protection of the laws. Ex post facto laws are forbidden. There is recognition of the right to a nationality, to freedom of movement, and to seek asylum from persecution in another state. Article 16 states the equal right of men and women to marry and to found a family. Article 17 deals with the right to own property. The next two articles affirm the basic freedoms of thought, conscience, religion, opinion, and expression. Articles 20 and 21 state the rights of peaceful assembly and association, and to a share in the government of one's country.

The next six articles proclaim the economic, social, and educational rights. Article 22 is of special interest as a concise statement of the philosophy underlying this conception of human rights. It states that "everyone, as a member of society, has the right to social security, and is entitled to realization, through

[3] Is it a commentary on the modern world that "security" replaces "pursuit of happiness" in the classic American trinity of human rights?

national effort and international cooperation and in accordance with the organization and resources of each State, of the economic, social and cultural rights indispensable for his dignity and the free development of his personality." Specific rights in this area include work, protection against unemployment, just remuneration, trade unions, rest and leisure, periodic holidays with pay, an adequate standard of living, education, and participation in the cultural life of the community. The branding of children as "illegitimate" is prohibited by the statement that "all children, whether born in or out of wedlock, shall enjoy the same social protection." To counteract such activities as the Nazi youth movement, it was provided that "parents have a prior right to choose the kind of education that shall be given to their children."

Article 28 refers to the social and international order. Article 29 is a statement of duties, rather than rights. It says that everyone has duties to the community "in which alone the free and full development of his personality is possible." Exercise of rights and freedoms is subject only to limitations determined by law for the purpose of securing recognition of the rights of others and meeting the "just requirements of morality, public order and the general welfare in a democratic society." The rights and freedoms may in no case be exercised contrary to the purposes and principles of the United Nations. The final article reflects a precaution against the technique of using freedoms to destroy a democratic order by providing that nothing in the Declaration shall be interpreted to give any state, group, or individual a basis for destroying any of the rights and freedoms which it defines.

The Universal Declaration of Human Rights was adopted by the General Assembly without a dissenting vote. Two countries, El Salvador and Yemen, were absent when the vote was taken. There were eight abstentions. Saudi Arabia refused to approve the Declaration on account of Article 18 which recognizes the right to change one's religion. The delegate from Saudi Arabia thought this was contrary to the Koran, but other Mohammedan countries did not follow this interpretation. The Union of South Africa abstained because of the opinion that the Declaration "went too far" in being progressive. The remaining six abstentions were accounted for by the Soviet Union and the other Communist countries. They considered it as an unprogressive eighteenth-century document, with no guarantees that the stated rights would be achieved. They also objected to the idea of inalienable rights of the individual, on the grounds that the concept of an isolated individual is contrary to social reality.

After the adoption of the Universal Declaration of Human Rights by the General Assembly, the Commission on Human Rights undertook the next stage of its work. The principal task in this connection is to prepare a draft covenant, which will be an international convention or treaty legally binding upon all the states which ratify it. The signatory states will be responsible for seeing to it that their internal regimes conform to the obligations of the

Covenant, and thus the agreements reached in the area of human rights will pass from the realm of principle to that of enforceable law. Measures of implementation have also been considered in connection with this state of the Commission's work, since it is necessary to lay down some basis for enforcement machinery in the proposed Covenant on Human Rights.

A draft was prepared in 1949 and circulated to member governments for their comments. The Commission on Human Rights revised this document at its meeting during March, April, and May, 1950, and referred it to the Economic and Social Council. It then went to the General Assembly, which adopted a series of resolutions [4] concerning it after extensive debate in the Third (Social, Humanitarian and Cultural) Committee. Several features in the Covenant as drafted were declared unacceptable, and it was decided that the Commission on Human Rights should rewrite the draft and submit it to the next regular session of the General Assembly.

The first question which arose in connection with the draft covenant was that of its scope in relation to the Universal Declaration of Human Rights. The definition of precise legal obligations which governments are willing to accept at the present time is quite a different matter from statements of principles or of aspirations. For example, what is the legal counterpart of the principle that everyone has a right to "life, liberty and security"? The right to live is of course the most important of all. Without it, all the others are entirely meaningless. This right was asserted in the Declaration. For the Covenant, however, a number of possible exceptions or limitations were put forward, most of them by the United States. These included circumstances in which it would be considered lawful to deprive a person of life, such as suppression of rebellion or riot, self-defense, accident, killing for violation of honor, to prevent an escape, by the military in time of war, medical operation in the absence of gross negligence or malpractice, through a voluntary medical experiment, or by officers of the law to prevent a crime. The British approach was to emphasize that no one should be deprived of his life "intentionally," and to list the limitations.

In the traditional bills of rights in the Western world, the "right to life" has really consisted of constitutional and legal protection against illegal deprivation of life by the state. It is manifestly absurd to think of a governmental guarantee against death. The right to life may be inalienable, but it is not absolute. The most that can be done by a positive approach is to combine the traditional protections with the responsibility of the state to maintain adequate conditions of human living. The latter might include jobs, social security, healthful environment, and so forth. In 1950 the Commission on Human Rights decided to take the position that the right to life must be protected by law, and drafted the statement that "to take life shall be a crime, save in the execution of a sentence of a court, or in self-defense, or in the case

4 On Dec. 4, 1950.

of enforcement measures authorized by the Charter." Limits were also placed on capital punishment.

The problem of freedom of the press offers another example. To Americans, this "right" usually means absence of censorship, that Congress and the state legislatures may pass no laws "abridging the freedom of the press." To the Soviets, it means access to supplies such as ink and newsprint. To them, unless the state assures this access to supplies by "democratic" interests and denies the privilege to Fascists, the "freedom of the press" is only a camouflage by which the exploiters of the people maintain their monopolistic position. The provision of the draft covenant on this point is based on the idea that states shall not interfere illegally or arbitrarily with the right recognized in Article 19 of the Universal Declaration that "everyone has the right to freedom of opinion and expression; this right includes freedom to hold opinions without interference and to seek, receive and impart information and ideas through any media and regardless of frontiers."

As one more example of the problem of specific legal definition of a human right, Article 5 of the Declaration says that "no one shall be subjected to torture or to cruel, inhuman or degrading treatment or punishment." In this connection, some of the inhuman Nazi medical experiments come to mind. But how can such things be categorically outlawed without at the same time prohibiting, for example, compulsory sterilization of mental incompetents as practiced in some countries? After thorough consideration, and consultation with the World Health Organization, the Commission arrived at this statement: "In particular, no one shall be subjected against his will to medical or scientific experimentation involving risk, where such is not required by his state of physical or mental health."

The nature of the permissible limitations on human rights posed an important issue. To what extent, and by what justification, may states place restrictions upon the rights and freedoms of individuals within their jurisdiction? It is established constitutional doctrine in the United States, for example, that the guarantees of the Federal bill of rights are subject to limitations of public policy and the rights of other individuals. Freedom of religion does not include the right to practice polygamy or human sacrifice, or to handle poisonous snakes in public. The freedoms of speech and of the press do not extend to libel, obscenity, incitement to riot, or yelling "fire" in a crowded theater. Maintenance of a balance between individual rights, social obligation, and the public welfare is a matter of interpretation and practice. The problem is that the specific recognition of limitations may give governments a pretext for nullifying the individual rights. If restrictions can be justified where the public welfare requires, how can governments be prevented from abusing the scope of this limitation? If individual rights can be restricted when this is necessary and reasonable in the public interest, what then is the meaning of "necessary and reasonable"? If only arbitrary limitations are allowed, who decides what is "arbitrary"? The difficulty is compounded by the suspicion that the countries in which individual rights are most in need of protection would be the first to whittle down the rights by broad interpretations of the allowable limitations.

The issue of limitations also raised the question of whether they should be stated in one all-embracing article, as the United States suggested, or whether the precise limitations should be stated in each article, as Great Britain wished. The draft covenant as it came from the Commission on Human Rights was a compromise between the American and British views. It attempts to state the limitations as concisely and definitely as possible, and to restrict them to a justifiable range. The basic freedoms, for example, are subject only to such limitations as are pursuant to law and are necessary for the protection of public safety (and national security), public order, health or morals, or the rights and freedoms of others. It will readily be seen that a great deal will still depend upon interpretation and practice.

The question of derogation is a special aspect of the problem of limitations. This referred to the modification or withdrawal of rights and freedoms because of war or other national emergency. The governmental right of derogation is recognized in the countries with the most advanced conception of civil liberties, but in such countries it is also limited to the strict necessities of the occasion. During war, censorship is established to the extent necessary to protect national security, and martial law may be invoked when, for example, an invasion makes it impossible for the civil courts to function. Other examples of derogation will occur to the reader. However, if the draft covenant should state that individual rights and freedoms may be annulled in case of public emergency, an avenue of arbitrary and unreasonable restriction would be left open. This problem is handled by strictly limiting the right of derogation to an emergency or disaster, and by providing that in any case there may be no derogation from certain rights such as those against torture and unlawful deprivation of life.

Another important problem of transforming a declaration of principles into legally binding obligations lay in the question of provisions on applicability to federal states and non-self-governing territories. The federal question is especially important for the United States, in which much of the legal authority concerning human rights lies in the states, while the national government has the responsibility for enforcing treaty obligations. It can be foreseen that a treaty increasing the power of the national government at the expense of "states' rights" would meet great difficulties in the Senate. The United States urged a text which would recognize its constitutional division of powers, while many other delegations protested that the result would be an unfair disparity of obligations as between federal and unitary states.

The majority in the Third Committee were in favor of a stipulation that the covenant would apply automatically to all the non-self-governing territories

administered by a signatory country.   The British and several other delegations argued that this would deprive the non-self-governing peoples of the right
to decide for themselves.

Another question of the scope of the covenant was how many of the rights
and freedoms it should codify.   One viewpoint was that it should comprise
the basic individual, civil, and political rights, while some delegations wanted
to extend it to include the economic and social rights as well.   It became
obvious that the complexity and controversial nature of the latter area would
make it impossible to draft a covenant expeditiously if an attempt should be
made to put into legal form all the rights mentioned in the Universal Declaration.   The Commission on Human Rights decided, therefore, that the traditional field would be covered as an initial step and that the resulting draft would
be a *first* covenant of human rights.   Work could then proceed on the drafting
of a *second* covenant embodying the economic and social rights.   However,
this decision was rejected by the General Assembly, which affirmed that both
categories should be included in the draft covenant.

The problem of implementation was another fundamental issue which had
to be considered in connection with the draft covenant.   There were two
different conceptions of this problem.   The Soviet Union conceived implementation as the realization by each state in its own way of the rights and
freedoms concerned.   Under this view, there would be no international machinery to supervise or assure the observance of the declaration and the covenant.   Human rights and freedoms, according to the Soviet Union, involve
the relation between the individual and the state.   This is held to be a matter
of domestic jurisdiction, and international machinery would be a violation of
Article 2, paragraph 2, of the Charter.

Others had a conception of implementation which would allow for some
supervision or review of the condition of human rights within the states ratifying the covenant.   They did not consider that human rights were the exclusive domestic concern of each state and, even if they were, the situation
would be changed by the ratification of the proposed international covenant.
The non-Soviet delegates wished to devise some measures by which the United
Nations could do something about human rights when and if they were violated.   There was a variety of opinions on what these measures should be.
Some thought of the Commission on Human Rights as the proper agency for
this task.   Others would set up separate organs, perhaps a special commission
or even an international court of human rights.   The representative of China
stressed the importance of a more positive view.   He would emphasize the
realization of human rights by education and cooperation, rather than the
punishment of delinquencies in this field.

Still another issue related to the question of petitions.   There was agreement that signatory states should have the right of initiating complaints
concerning violations of the covenant.   When it came to the question of

whether individuals, groups and organizations could submit petitions, there was sharp difference of opinion.   The Soviet Union was opposed to such a right in principle, arguing that it would introduce a disruptive element into the "natural relationship" between the state and its citizens.   Later, this position was modified to admit the possibility that organizations of a "wide demo-cratic basis" might submit petitions.   The second attitude was held by the United States, Great Britain, and China.   They were not opposed in principle but wanted to exercise caution, lest false hopes might be aroused as to the actual force of international guarantees in the near future.   The third school of thought, led by Australia and India, wanted an immediate recognition of the right of petition for individuals and groups.   Among other arguments, they urged that granting the right need involve no commitment as to how the peti-tions would be handled, and that it would be a mockery to tell people they had certain rights and then refuse to listen to complaints that these rights had been violated.

The machinery for implementation, as recommended in the first draft cove-nant, would consist of a Human Rights Committee, composed of seven mem-bers elected by the parties to the covenant for five-year terms on a staggered basis.   Any party to the covenant could complain to another party alleged to be violating any of its provisions.   If satisfaction were not obtained, a complaint could then be made to the Committee, whose function would be to investigate the facts, offer its "good offices," and make a report on the situation.   Thus, it will be seen that the cautious approach was adopted for purpose of the draft covenant.   Only signatory states would be represented on the Hu-man Rights Committee.   A country unwilling to ratify and place its own situation under scrutiny would not have an opportunity to file complaints con-cerning other countries.   Individuals and groups would not as yet be given the right of petition.   No international court of human rights was to be estab-lished, and the international machinery to be instituted was to have no co-ercive or enforcement powers.

These draft provisions were severely criticized during the debate in the General Assembly's Third Committee during November, 1950.   On the one hand, the representative of the Soviet Union stated that all articles dealing with measures of implementation were unacceptable as infringing on the domestic jurisdiction of signatory states.   On the other hand, the majority of the Committee felt that there should be provisions for consideration of petitions from individuals and organizations on alleged violations of human rights.   These provisions might be inserted in the covenant itself or in sepa-rate protocols.   There was also a widespread feeling that the economic, so-cial, and cultural rights should be included in the first draft covenant.   As a result of this dissatisfaction, the Commission on Human Rights was requested to submit a revised draft.

Anyone who wishes to study the ideological struggle of the modern world would do well to make a careful examination of the proceedings of the Commission on Human Rights. The place of the individual in the social order, the authority of government, all the fundamental issues of rights and freedoms have been exhaustively stated and reviewed there by representatives of all the major cultures, philosophies, and legal systems. It has furnished a forum without parallel in history for the most searching comparative analysis of ideas and views on the crucial problems of liberty and authority.

It must be recognized that the question of human rights and freedoms has far-reaching implications. Their effective international guarantees would mean a fundamental change in the relation between the individual and the state. As was indicated above,[5] the object is not to limit the power of the United Nations but to protect individual rights and freedoms against abuse by their respective governments. It is well to remember that, under the Constitution of the United States, there was for many years very little basis for Federal protection of the rights of citizens against their respective state governments. The first ten amendments, or Bill of Rights, consisted of restrictions on the Federal government. The only *Federal* restrictions on the freedom of a state to treat its own citizens as it pleased were those enumerated in Article 1, Section 10, of the Constitution. Of these, the only ones which dealt directly with human rights were the prohibitions against bills of attainder and ex post facto laws. The adoption of the Fourteenth Amendment after the Civil War first opened up a wide area for Federal action to secure individual rights against the state governments. This power was used in a limited way for many years, and Federal action still does not occupy this whole field of governmental authority.

Even though the draft covenant has not been submitted for ratification, some jurisprudence is beginning to develop on the subject of human rights. There is, first of all, a possibility that the Universal Declaration may of itself have some significance for the development of international law. It is possible to argue that the Declaration constitutes an authoritative definition and interpretation of the provisions of the Charter on this subject, and that it is a contribution to "the general principles of law recognized by civilized nations." In a Canadian case (*In re Drummond Wren*), the Supreme Court of Ontario ruled restrictive covenants illegal as in conflict with the United Nations Charter. Mr. Justice Black, of the United States Supreme Court, asked in a concurring opinion (*In re Oyama v. Calif.*), "How can this nation be faithful to this international pledge if state laws which bar land ownership and occupancy by aliens on account of race are permitted?" In April, 1950, the California appellate court ruled that a state law restricting land ownership by aliens was invalid as in conflict with the Charter of the United Nations. There has been considerable criticism of this decision on the ground that the provisions of the Charter on human rights are not self-executing, that

⁵ See p. 299.

is, they have no specific content and legal force in this country until Congress legislates on the subject.[6]   The point remains open to question for the present, since the case has not been reviewed by the United States Supreme Court.

It is easy to see, however, that ratification of the proposed covenant by the United States might have some interesting and important constitutional and legal consequences, even though an international court in this field is not contemplated at this time.   The Federal government doubtless would gain authority in the field of civil rights, and the scope of "states' rights" would be correspondingly narrowed.   It is possible that governmental power would be increased in another way if the Federal government were considered internationally responsible for violations of human rights by individuals or groups within its territory.

Obviously, the question of an international covenant on human rights is a very real and practical one.   It is a mistake to think of this matter as some abstract proposition with no relevance to actual conditions.   In this connection, it is of interest to take note of some of the criticism of the proposed Covenant.. The American Bar Association has been especially prominent in this connection and seems to have four major reasons for its position.   One of its criticisms, that the source of human rights is placed in legislative fiat, does not seem to be supported by the language of the Declaration and draft Covenant itself.   Second, the Association objects to the so-called economic, social, and educational rights on the ground that they embody a collectivist philosophy. In the third place, some of the passages are considered vague and ambiguous. Finally, the American Bar Association points to alleged implications as to changes in the American form of government, especially if jurisdiction is given to an international court, and considers that ratification of the draft covenant by the United States would constitute an improper use of the treaty power.[7]

The suggestion has been made that the present work of the Commission on Human Rights might be based on the rights and freedoms essential to the functioning of the United Nations itself.[8]   These might include, for example, freedom to travel to the headquarters of the Organization, the right to be informed about meetings and decisions of the United Nations, the right to express an opinion on the policy of one's government in the United Nations, and other rights applicable in this connection.   The Commission, however, continues to work on the basis of securing a maximum area of agreement among governments on international cooperation in the protection of human rights and fundamental freedoms for everyone, everywhere.

[6] Manley O. Hudson, "Charter Provisions on Human Rights in American Law," *American Journal of International Law*, July, 1950, pp. 543–548. Another viewpoint is expressed by Quincy Wright in "National Courts and Human Rights—The Fujii Case," *American Journal of International Law*, January, 1951, pp. 62–82.

[7] "International Human Rights," *Law and Contemporary Problems*, 1949, pp. 451–478.

[8] *Ibid.*, pp. 428–429.

OTHER WORK ON HUMAN RIGHTS

Activities of the United Nations in the field of human rights and fundamental freedoms have not been confined to the work of the Commission on Human Rights. Selected problems have been handled as separate items under the auspices of the Economic and Social Council and the General Assembly. Among the most important of these have been freedom of information and of the press, genocide, and the status of women.

Freedom of Information and the Press. It has been recognized from the beginning that freedom of information is closely linked with the maintenance of international peace and security. The General Assembly pointed out in a resolution of February 13, 1946, that "the United Nations cannot achieve the purposes for which it has been created unless the peoples of the world are fully informed of its aims and activities." The General Assembly further stated in a resolution of December 14, 1946, that "freedom of information is a fundamental human right and is the touchstone of all the freedoms to which the United Nations is consecrated," and that "understanding and cooperation among nations are impossible without an alert and sound world opinion which, in turn, is wholly dependent upon freedom of information."

To help define this concept and to determine the attendant responsibilities, a United Nations Conference on Freedom of Information was convened in Geneva during the spring of 1948. All members of the United Nations and several nonmember states were invited to participate in this Conference, and the specialized agencies and a number of nongovernmental organizations were invited to attend. Delegates representing fifty-four governments were present, and three others sent observers. The concept and problems of freedom of information were thoroughly discussed and debated for about four weeks. The results of the conference took the form of a series of resolutions and three draft conventions—on the gathering and international transmission of news, on the institution of an international right of correction,[9] and on freedom of information.

A Sub-Commission on Freedom of Information and of the Press was established as a subsidiary organ of the Commission on Human Rights.[10] This Sub-Commission consists of twelve experts who serve in their personal capacities, not as official representatives. They are elected by the Commission on

---

[9] By this right a state which feels that news reports, which are likely to injure its international relations and which have been disseminated abroad, are false or distorted may submit its version of the facts to the state in whose territory the reports were published. The latter then has the obligation to make the statement of "correction" available to news enterprises.

[10] The Commission also had a Sub-Commission on Prevention of Discrimination and Protection of Minorities.

Human Rights for three-year terms subject to the consent of their governments. The Sub-Commission has undertaken studies and made recommendations in connection with the provisions on freedom of information and of the press in the Universal Declaration of Human Rights and in the draft covenant. It has also held several conferences for the purpose of discussion and arriving at recommendations. Throughout these sessions, the fundamental difference between the Western and Soviet concepts of a "free press" has been maintained rather than resolved. The Soviet representatives have repeatedly made the argument that information should be used in the interests of the people and not of big capitalist newspaper monopolies. They have emphasized that an international convention on the subject should be an instrument in the struggle for peace and against war propaganda. Censorship in the Soviet Union is allegedly directed not against freedom of information, but against the spreading of false and distorted information. They contend that the whole field of mass information in the United States and Great Britain is controlled by "big business." The Polish representative said on one occasion that the assertion that all in the United States are equally free to influence public opinion is just as true as the assertion that the Waldorf-Astoria is open to millionaires and beggars.

Members from the Western countries, on the other hand, continue to stress the concept of a free press, which is familiar in the American tradition. They readily admit that distorted or malicious information may be disseminated, but they feel that the best corrective is in the competition of ideas and the healthy lash of public criticism. Repressive government censorship would create more evils than it could possibly eliminate. They believe that people should be allowed access to news from all sources and to all kinds of different opinions. According to this conception, the effort to control ideas and information by an authoritarian regime is the most dangerous of all governmental controls and the very negation of a free press.

It can be readily understood how difficult it is to reconcile such divergent points of view as those held by the Communist countries on the one hand and the Western European and English-speaking countries on the other. The Soviet bloc received considerable support from Latin-American and Middle Eastern countries. A proposed Mexican amendment, for example, would have authorized censorship on the basis of "national dignity," "national prestige" and "national security"! Such "permissible restrictions" would justify practically any curb on the transmission of news, and the convention in which such provisions were incorporated would afford not protection but legal justification for suppressing freedom of information.

Genocide. "Genocide" is a new name for an old crime. It means the destruction of groups of human beings. The destruction may take the form of massacres, executions, or deprival of food and housing. The birth rate may be restricted by the forced segregation of the sexes, or the special characteristics of the group may be destroyed by such means as the forced transfer of its children to other groups. Massacres, pogroms, and mass killings were an old story in human history long before Cato's slogan *Carthago delenda est,* and this sorry record by no means stopped with the sacking of Carthage. In Nazi Germany, genocide was practiced on a large scale as a deliberate policy of state carried out with scientific ingenuity. The punishment of these crimes became one of the war aims of the Allied nations. The Nuremberg trials included, as one part of the indictment, crimes against humanity, namely murder, extermination, enslavement, deportation, and other inhuman acts committed against any civilian population before or during the war, or persecutions on political, racial, or religious grounds committed in connection with the war. The trial and conviction of the Nazi leaders by the International Military Tribunal were endorsed by a resolution of the General Assembly. However, there was a feeling that penal repression of this kind should not be limited to acts connected with war, but should be of universal application.

The convention on genocide seeks to make this offense an international crime. There is some precedent for this in the treatment of piracy, traffic in women and children, and the slave trade, which are now recognized as offenses against humanity and the law of nations. The purpose is to secure general agreement to placing genocide in the same category as an international crime. The convention was drafted by an *ad hoc* committee established by the Economic and Social Council, and was approved by the General Assembly on December 9, 1948, after consideration by the Sixth (Legal) Committee. Genocide is defined in the draft convention as any of the following acts committed with intent to destroy, in whole or in part, a national, ethnic, racial, or religious group as such: (1) killing members of the group; (2) causing serious bodily or mental harm to members of the group; (3) deliberately inflicting on the group conditions of life calculated to bring about its physical destruction in whole or in part; (4) imposing measures intended to prevent births within the group; and (5) forcibly transferring the children of the group to another group.

The Soviet representative wanted to extend the definition to include "cultural genocide," meaning any deliberate act committed with the intention of destroying any language, religion, or culture or any national, racial, or religious beliefs. The majority agreed that crimes like the destruction of churches, schools, and libraries, or other measures of cultural extermination, were barbarous, but that this question belonged to the field of human rights. To extend the genocide convention to cover this field would make it too broad and general, even vague, and would weaken the purpose of preventing and punishing the physical destruction of entire human groups.

The United States representative wished to include "political" groups among those to be protected against genocide, but the majority decided against this. Some held that such groups are not sufficiently defined to be included, and some thought that to include them might lead to interference in the internal affairs of countries.

Violations are to be tried by "a competent tribunal of the State in the territory of which the act was committed." An international jurisdiction is not established by the convention, although the way is left open for its possible future development by providing the alternative of "such an international penal tribunal as may have jurisdiction with respect to those Contracting Parties which shall have accepted its jurisdiction."

The question naturally arises of the value of the genocide convention. In the discussions in the Sixth Committee of the General Assembly the greatest pessimism was expressed by the British delegate. He argued that individual genocide is already punishable by the laws of all countries, whereas genocide committed by states is punishable only by war. A regime committing such a crime would not hold back on account of a convention or surrender itself for trial by an international tribunal. No steps should be taken, he thought, to lead people to believe that some great forward step had been taken when nothing had really been changed. The representative of Czechoslovakia said that although the existence of a convention on genocide might not have deterred Hitler, it would have at least precluded a spirit of toleration toward him and would have made it difficult to conclude agreements such as the one at Munich.

The feeling prevailed that it was important to give a precise definition of genocide and to make a solemn international affirmation of its outlawry. There would then be a legal basis for collective international safeguards. Despite the fact that some representatives retained a degree of skepticism and that many were not fully satisfied by all the provisions, the convention on genocide was adopted by a unanimous vote of the General Assembly. It went into effect in January, 1951, three months after it had been ratified by twenty countries.[11]

Status of Women. The status of women has been recognized by the United Nations as a special problem. One of the prohibited discriminations in the field of human rights and fundamental freedoms is that on account of sex, and Article 8 of the Charter provides that "the United Nations shall place no restrictions on the eligibility of men and women to participate in any capacity and under conditions of equality in its principal and subsidiary organs."

In June, 1946, the Economic and Social Council established a Commission on the Status of Women, to serve as an expert body on matters pertaining to this question. Its functions are to prepare recommendations and reports on the promotion of women's rights in political, economic, social, and educa-

---

[11] Not including the United States. For an elucidation of the arguments pro and con, see *Hearings before a Subcommittee of the Committee on Foreign Relations on Executive O, The International Convention on the Prevention and Punishment of the Crime of Genocide,* United States Senate, 81st Congress, 2d Session (Government Printing Office, 1950).

tional affairs. It was also instructed to watch for, study, and make recommendations on urgent matters requiring immediate attention. The Commission is composed of fifteen members. The representatives are nominated by the governments of the elected countries after consultation with the Secretary-General. The nominations then go to the Economic and Social Council for confirmation. By this procedure it is possible to get members with expert knowledge on all aspects of women's status. It has been the practice for all fifteen representatives to be women.

The Commission has advocated political rights for women, to include universal adult suffrage; equal rights to vote, to be elected, and to hold office; and equal participation in government. In civil matters, the aim is full equality. With respect to marriage, the Commission seeks freedom of choice, dignity of the wife, monogamy, equal rights to dissolution of marriage, equal rights to guardianship of children, and the right of a married woman to retain her own nationality if she wishes. As to legal capacity, the Commission declared that women, single or married, should have equal rights to enter into contracts, and to acquire and dispose of inherited property. In order to prevent economic and social discrimination against women, equal rights with men are sought in regard to such matters as labor, wages, and holidays.

The Commission has taken the position that women are entitled to special protection in certain circumstances, such as before and after childbirth. Also, an effective system of health and social insurance legislation is advocated. Some of the subjects which have been emphasized in the studies, conferences, and recommendations of the Commission are political rights, especially the suffrage and office holding; nationality of married women; property rights of married women; application of penal law to women; and educational opportunities for women.

PART IV
FUTURE

Chapter 20

STRENGTHENING THE UNITED NATIONS

The United Nations is a going concern. Its record of activities and accomplishments during its first six years is an impressive one, considering the difficulties which have existed. Yet a secure world peace has not been established, and even the optimist will agree that the road ahead is long, difficult, and dangerous. It is in relation to these facts that the necessity and possibilities of strengthening the United Nations must be judged.

MAKING EFFECTIVE DECISIONS

It is essential to the success of the United Nations that it be capable of making effective decisions. If a stalemate develops between opposing groups, the Organization will be unable to accomplish its purposes and it will lose the support and respect of governments and peoples. If agreement is limited to formal resolutions which pay tribute to the principles of the United Nations but do not affect the actual course of events, the label of hypocrisy will be added to that of impotence. The basic question is, "What steps can be taken so that the organs of the United Nations can reach decisions more expeditiously and implement them more effectively?"

At the San Francisco Conference, the Charter was drafted on the basis that decisions could be made in the General Assembly by a simple or two-thirds majority, and in the Security Council by seven votes out of eleven with the concurrence of all the permanent members. Agreement and joint action by the Great Powers were considered indispensable to the maintenance of international peace and security. Decisions would be reached if the Big Five and a sufficient number of other members were in agreement. The decisions would be practically effective if the same countries supported them and put them into operation. Of course, no one expected that the Great Powers would see eye to eye on every question; rather, the hope was that there would be a sufficient degree of cooperation to permit a mutually acceptable solution for disputes and situations dangerous to peace and security.

The development of the "cold war" placed emphasis on security *against* an opposing bloc rather than on security *with* other members of a general world organization. East-West antagonism presents a cleavage too wide to be bridged by mutual confidence and agreed cooperation. This unfortunate fact alters the situation in which the United Nations functions, and it radically changes the problem of reaching effective decisions. Under the "rule of unanimity" the Great Powers must be in agreement; in a time of "cold war" they are in fundamental disagreement. It is difficult for them to cooperate in the achievement of collective security when they are thinking in terms of security from each other. This means that there is constant danger of a stalemate on questions of critical importance. Consequently, a need is felt for some alternative means of arriving at significant decisions.

The small countries at the San Francisco Conference had opposed the Great Power veto, but the Big Five, and especially the United States and the Soviet Union, had insisted on it. After the frightful possibilities of atomic bombs became apparent, there was considerable discussion in many countries about the establishment of some form of world government in place of the United Nations. The idea of "eliminating the veto" became a slogan and rallying point for many who were convinced of an urgent necessity for a much stronger world organization than the United Nations as it existed. The veto question also became a symbol of high emotional value to the American public as the Soviet Union played its role of a minority of one among the permanent members of the Security Council.

The campaign to "eliminate the veto," however, tended to confuse cause with effect. One negative vote, blocking unanimity of agreement, was merely a reflection of the power and inclination of the Soviet Union to pursue policies not acceptable to the other Great Powers. It does no good to reach decisions by a majority vote if the minority has the power to prevent the decisions from being carried out. In such cases, the majority can prevail only by inducing the minority to cooperate or by finding some means to make its opposition ineffective. Reaffirmation by balloting that the majority is the majority certainly does not reach the heart of this problem.

A more practical and promising approach was to seek a basis for eliminating the so-called "abuse of the veto." This would recognize the propriety of refusing to be bound by majority voting in matters considered vital to national security or involving actual enforcement measures. On the other hand, frivolous and obstructive use of the unanimity rule would be precluded. There is a wide latitude for interpretation and negotiation on this point, since the Charter is far from definitive on the question of vetoable items. Some, like the adoption of the agenda and the election of a presiding officer, are clearly procedural. Others, like the use of enforcement measures, are obviously substantive and therefore subjective to the rule of unanimity. But there is much doubtful ground between these clear-cut extremes. Does the proposal to discuss a matter involve a substantive decision? How about a proposal to establish a commission of inquiry? These are only two of the many questions which could be raised concerning the elusive and controversial distinction between "procedural" and "substantive" matters.

In 1948 the General Assembly, upon the proposal of the United States, gave an extensive consideration to this subject. A list of various types of questions which appeared appropriate for decision by a procedural vote was discussed. As a result, recommendations were made to the Security Council that the permanent members agree not to exercise the privilege of the veto on questions of pacific settlement, the admission of new members, and other matters not involving decisions on enforcement measures. These recommendations have not been accepted by the Soviet Union, which has continued to exercise its prerogatives of a negative vote on much the same basis as before. However, the permanent members of the Security Council did announce their acceptance of the General Assembly's recommendation that they resort to consultation in order to hold the number of vetoes to a minimum. This technique has some promise. Informal discussion may provide an opportunity for exploring areas of agreement and thus promote a "meeting of the minds." Also, it may help to ease the situation in the respect that there are no vetoes when questions are not brought to a formal vote. Forcing a vote on a proposition known to be unacceptable to the minority invites a veto and may increase rather than alleviate tension, especially in terms of public opinion.

One result of stalemate in the Security Council has been an increased emphasis on the General Assembly. In the latter organ, "important" decisions may be made by a two-thirds majority of the members present and voting. There is no veto. Although the decisions of the General Assembly are recommendations rather than binding obligations, there are ways of making its influence felt in dispute concerning which the permanent members of the Security Council are not able to agree. The Greek case, for example, was removed from the agenda of the Security Council, and the General Assembly proceeded to consider the matter and to appoint the United Nations Special Committee on the Balkans. The situation in Korea was not referred to the Security Council prior to June, 1950. The General Assembly had undertaken to find a solution and, among other things, had appointed the United Nations Commission which was in Korea when the war broke out. The prompt report of an impartial international body was an important factor in making possible the swift and decisive action of the Security Council.

One obvious way to strengthen the General Assembly is to enable it to function continuously. The Charter provides for regular annual sessions and for special sessions which may be called upon the request of the Security Council or a majority of the members of the United Nations. Most of the regular sessions have lasted about three months or a little less, although the third Assembly reconvened in the spring of 1949, because its business was not completed the preceding December. Two special sessions have been held, both to deal with the situation in Palestine. The Interim Committee of the

General Assembly (or "Little Assembly") was established in 1947 as a committee of the whole to function between sessions. This provided a means for continuous study and discussion of matters related to the work of the General Assembly, and for the preparation of recommendations to the parent body. It could also exercise a limited amount of delegated authority, as when it authorized the United Nations Temporary Commission on Korea to proceed with the supervision of elections in the southern part of the country in 1948. The Soviet Union objected to the creation of the Interim Committee and has never participated in its work, on the grounds than an illegal attempt was being made to undermine the Security Council and transfer its functions to a subsidiary organ of the General Assembly.

At the fifth Assembly in 1950, the United States delegation presented four recommendations "designed to increase the effectiveness of United Nations action against aggression." [1] After some modification, these proposals were introduced as a joint resolution by Canada, France, the Philippines, Turkey, Great Britain, the United States, and Uruguay. The purpose was to strengthen the General Assembly in the event of the Security Council's inability to deal with an act of aggression because of the veto. The proposals were (1) a provision for calling the General Assembly into emergency session upon twenty-four hours' notice; (2) the establishment of a "peace patrol" to observe situations dangerous to world peace and report upon them; (3) a plan for the designation of units within national armed forces to be ready for prompt service on behalf of the United Nations; and (4) the establishment of a committee to study and report on means which might be used to carry out the purposes and principles of the Charter.

The "Uniting for Peace" resolution [2] was adopted by the General Assembly on November 2, 1950, by a vote of 52 to 5, with 2 abstentions. This makes possible prompt consideration by the General Assembly if the Security Council is prevented from acting in case of an act of aggression. An emergency session could be convened within twenty-four hours, instead of two weeks as required under the previous rules. The General Assembly may discuss the situation and adopt a recommendation by a two-thirds majority. This would not constitute action nor would it represent a binding obligation under the Charter. Nevertheless, as Mr. John Foster Dulles said in his speech of October 9, recommendations can be equally effective if made to a responsive membership. [3]

[1] See address of Secretary of State Acheson before the General Assembly, Sept. 20, 1950; speech by John Foster Dulles before the Political and Security Committee on Oct. 9; speech by Andrei Vishinsky before the same Committee the next day; and subsequent debates.

[2] This resolution incorporated the four points of the joint resolution and also the main principles of a Chilean draft resolution on the strengthening of democratic principles as a means of contributing to the maintenance of peace. For the text, see Appendix 21.

[3] It may be noted in this connection that the Security Council resolutions of June 25 and 27, 1950, on the Korea case took the form of "requests," not directives.

The adoption of these proposals provides a method for making decisions without the requirement of unanimity among the permanent members of the Security Council. The effectiveness of any such decisions will depend entirely upon the extent to which they were accepted and carried out by member states. The Soviet Union objected to the proposals on the basis that they were intended to destroy the basic principle of joint responsibility of the Great Powers and that they violated the Charter by attempting to deprive the Security Council of its legitimate powers. This was not an unnatural opposition, since the practical effect of the plan is to enlarge the area of decisions which can be taken without the consent of the Soviet Union.

In gauging the probable effectiveness of the proposals in question, it must be kept in mind that, under the Charter, the General Assembly cannot take over the functions and prerogatives of the Security Council, and that neither Soviet power nor Soviet intransigence can merely be voted out of existence. But it may be possible to create a situation in which the majority take action sanctioned by the United Nations without the prerequisite of an affirmative vote of all the permanent members of the Security Council. There may be occasions when the Soviet Union, for example, will oppose and vote against a resolution but not interfere with measures taken by others to carry it out. The Korean case, in fact, already furnishes an example of this. The Soviet Union certainly opposed United Nations armed assistance to the Republic of Korea, and a veto of the Security Council resolutions was not interposed only because of a boycott of the meetings over another issue. Nevertheless, at this writing the Soviet Union has not taken up arms in support of the North Korea regime which it sponsored. The very existence of a capacity to make effective decisions without unanimity among the Great Powers will tend toward acceptance of such decisions and will reduce the significance of the veto. This fact will have profound consequences for the future development of the United Nations. The advance knowledge that one member can block the wishes of the majority puts a premium on obstruction by a determined minority. When this obstacle is removed, the minority is more likely to seek maximum concessions to its point of view through negotiations.

Article 51 of the Charter refers to the inherent right of individual and collective self-defense in the event of an armed attack and the failure of the Security Council to maintain international peace and security. No machinery was established, however, for reaching decisions to invoke the right of collective self-defense under Article 51. One interesting suggestion [4] is that members be invited to conclude a multilateral treaty agreeing that they would accept a two-thirds vote of the General Assembly, including at least three of the Great Powers. A formal treaty to this effect is not necessarily involved in the proposals under discussion, but it is anticipated that in an emergency the

[4] Advocated, for example, by the American Association for the United Nations. This is the idea of the Thomas-Douglas resolution (Senate Concurrent Resolution No. 52, 81st Congress, 2d Session).

members would vote responsibly in the General Assembly and be responsive to a resolution adopted by a two-thirds majority.

A second point in the proposals was the establishment of a "peace observation commission," or "peace patrol," preferably not to include any of the Great Powers. Such a commission could go or send observers to areas of friction, with the consent of the countries whose territories would be visited. It might draw upon the panel of field observers already established by the General Assembly. The very presence of a United Nations Commission should operate to discourage aggression, and in the event it did occur, the Security Council and the General Assembly would have prompt and reliable information. When fighting breaks out between countries, each side takes great pains to prove that the other was the aggressor. The position of a United Nations commission is likely, therefore, to have considerable practical value, especially in determining the position of peoples with no direct interest in the particular controversy itself. This conclusion does not depend upon speculation, however, since commissions created by the General Assembly have already proved their value in Greece and Korea.

A consideration of the distinction between effective decisions and "mere resolutions" cannot overlook the question of an international police force. Article 43 of the Charter provides for armed forces to be made available by agreement between the members and the Security Council. This provision has not been implemented because of the basic disagreements among the Great Powers. The United Nations Guard has been established in the Secretariat under the authorization of the General Assembly. This, of course, is a very small nonmilitary armed force by designation. The members were requested to furnish the necessary assistance to protect the Republic of Korea from aggression and to restore peace. The United States carried a large share of the burden, but it should be noted that within three months after the initial attack sixteen different countries had committed military forces for use under the United Nations flag.[5]

The resolution adopted by the fifth Assembly included a plan by which each member would designate within its national armed forces one or more United Nations units. They would be specially trained and equipped and continuously maintained in readiness for prompt service on behalf of the United Nations. This does not involve a specific earmarking of forces, or the establishment of an international army as such. It merely means that the members should be ready to use armed force on behalf of the United Nations if the necessity should arise and if the appropriate decisions are made. Technical advice on organization, training, and equipment of such units might be made available by means of attaching to the Secretariat a panel of military experts. This proposal contemplates the same type of international armed force as does

[5] *United Nations Bulletin,* Vol. IX, No. 7, Oct. 1, 1950, pp. 305–307. Many more offered economic assistance, medical supplies, etc.

Article 43 of the Charter, namely, a system of national contingents to be placed under international command for specified purposes. Since, however, the necessary agreements with the Security Council have not been concluded, the members would establish the national contingents upon the recommendation of the General Assembly.

How Strengthen the United Nations?

The necessity and desire to strengthen the United Nations raise the question of method. Three main approaches may be identified. They are (1) amendment of the Charter; (2) interpretation of the Charter and of the powers of the United Nations; and (3) actual use of the Organization.

About six weeks after the Charter was signed at San Francisco, an atomic bomb was dropped on Hiroshima. Many who knew what a future atomic war might mean began to ask whether a Charter written in the preatomic age were not obsolete before it was ratified. Some of the nuclear physicists and various other people talked about a world government strong enough to administer world law and to ensure world peace. Books like *An Anatomy of Peace* by Emery Reves, *Modern Man Is Obsolete* by Norman Cousins, and *Peace or Anarchy* by Cord Meyer, Jr., commanded a wide attention. New interest was aroused by the idea, advocated by Clarence Streit since 1938, of a federal union of democracies to strengthen the forces of freedom and to serve as a nucleus for an eventual world government. Ely Culbertson, the bridge expert, publicized a pet plan of his own. A group of scholars centered at the University of Chicago drafted a constitution to show what a federal republic of the world "might look like." For a while there was an epidemic of plans and movements, practically all of them on the theme that the United Nations would be too weak and must be replaced (or greatly altered) by some kind of stronger world government.

When questions were raised as to how this would be brought about, the tendency was to insist that it could be done because it must be done. Unspeakable catastrophe was the only alternative, and time was short. In fact, however, none of these plans had an answer for the basic dilemma of world government—that of effectiveness and acceptability. Obviously a plan is useless unless it would be effective in practice. No plan has a chance to be tried out in practice unless it is widely acceptable, especially to those who control the governments of the leading nations. Any proposal which had a chance of being widely accepted, in fact as well as in theory, was likely not to be sufficiently effective to control the policies of governments.

The procedure for amending the Charter (Article 108) requires the concurrence of all the permanent members of the Security Council. Thus, amendatory proposals are themselves subject to the veto. It does not seem logical to suppose that a Great Power ready to veto resolutions offered within the scope of the Charter would be willing to accept amendments giving greater powers to an international organization and taking away the right of veto. The real problem has not been one of constitution making. There was nothing in the Charter which prohibited or restricted the maximum amount of international cooperation which was obtainable in practice. On the contrary, there were scope and authorization under it for vastly more cooperation than was being attained. The world-government advocates were well-intentioned, but their efforts were misdirected because of a misapprehension as to the nature of the problem at issue. The function of a constitutional document is to record a consensus which has been reached. It can even influence the extent to which a consensus is achieved, and it can be an important element in the maintenance of a subsequent unity. All this can be illustrated from the development and history of the United States Constitution. One thing a constitutional document cannot do, however, is to create a consensus and a unity in the absence of the essential social, economic, political, and psychological factors.

Another method for strengthening the United Nations is by interpretation of the Charter. There are enough general terms, and ambiguous provisions, to offer many opportunities for a broad construction of the functions and powers of the United Nations. This field would expand tremendously if the Great Powers had more confidence in each other, but already important precedents have been established. The Security Council intervened in the Indonesian case despite the contention of the Netherlands government that the dispute was between a state and one of its colonies and therefore a matter within domestic jurisdiction. In several instances, the Security Council has handled a dispute without making a formal finding under Article 39. It has not shown a tendency to evade its responsibilities by hiding behind legal technicalities or a narrow literalism. The General Assembly has been inclined to give a broad interpretation to its mandate to discuss, and make recommendations on any matters within the scope of the Charter.

Even in connection with the veto there are some liberalizing precedents. The most notable of these is concerned with the significance of an abstention from voting. The Charter, Article 27, refers to the "concurring votes" of the permanent members of the Security Council. If one of the Big Five abstains from voting, does it show its concurrence? Or is an affirmative vote necessary? The interpretation in practice has been that a resolution is adopted when there are at least seven affirmative votes and when no permanent member casts a negative vote. In other words, the veto has been modified by interpretation even at the expense of straining the language of the Charter. This has had the most important consequences. The Security Council could pass the resolution on Korea in June, 1950, in the absence of the Soviet Union because of the ruling that nonvoting is not a veto. If the precedents had been that "concurrence" requires a definite affirmative vote, the resolutions could have been vetoed by the absence of the Soviet Union.   If it is true that the Korean case represents the real turning point in the United Nations, the interpretation that an abstention is not a veto will rank in historic significance with the case of *Marbury v. Madison* in the constitutional development of the United States.

At the San Francisco Conference it was assumed that the United Nations could not use force to maintain peace without the unanimity of the Great Powers.   In the Korean case it did use force without the concurrence of all the Great Powers.   The significance of this fact is the destruction of the veto to the extent that the overwhelming majority show a united determination in a crisis.   It has been established that no one member, no matter how powerful, can block action by the United Nations.   This has been done by interpretation and practical action, not by amendment of the Charter.

Basically, the way to strengthen the United Nations is to use it.   All methods and actions which are appropriate to the purpose and not prohibited by the Charter may be utilized.   Accomplishments [6] have a cumulative effect upon subsequent developments, since success feeds on success and failure leads to failure.   The United Nations, in six years of operation, has become a reality which cannot be ignored.   The member states, however, remain the depositories of power.   The United Nations, although an international personality and an influential institution in its own right, is still primarily an association of members.   The confederation has become stronger, but it has not been transposed into a federation.

Under these circumstances, a prime requisite is genuine and constant support in terms of national policies.   This does not imply an admonition to altruism on the part of the nations.   There is room for enlightened selfishness in two respects.   First, most governments, and certainly their peoples, have a vested interest in peace and security.   The statesman and the citizen can be interested in the success of the United Nations on the same basis as that on which they want their community to have adequate police and fire departments.   Second, the United Nations presents an opportunity for the mobilization of support for national policies.   For example, let us assume that it is in the strategic interest of the United States to resist a conquest of South Korea by a Communist regime.   How, except for the United Nations, could the backing of fifty-two other countries be obtained for international action against the aggressor?   Conversely, the Soviet Union has opportunity to benefit from the fact that many important countries (India is an outstanding example) have not written a blank check in favor of the United States, but show themselves capable of picking and choosing among various aspects of American policy.

The concept of regionalism offers one approach to the coordination of national policies with general collective action.   Articles 52 and 53 of the

[6] For a descripiton of accomplishments, see Chaps. 14–19.

Charter specifically recognize the validity of regional arrangements within the over-all pattern of the Organization. The elements of geography, historic tradition, and immediacy of interest unite to give force to this concept. It is impossible to escape the conclusion, however, that regionalism offers a technique of limited value rather than a solution to the problem. There are many reasons for this. Regions are not mutually exclusive. Boundaries cannot be drawn to eliminate overlapping security zones. Germany, Iran, Korea, and many other places are of interest to both East and West. Often there is a gradation of interests as between close neighbors and more distant areas, but a remote geographic area may be considered of vital importance, as for example in the case of American policy toward Korea. Even if regional boundaries could be objectively determined, there would remain the question of outposts and advance bases needed to defend one's region against attack. These outposts and bases would be in someone else's region. With the interdependence of the modern world, and in view of the far-flung security zones of the Great Powers, the problem of world peace must be solved on a global scale if it is to be solved at all.

The breakdown of the principle of unanimity changed the significance of regionalism within the United Nations. The compelling problem shifted from subsidiary arrangements within a general system to methods for security against another member of that system. The more notable organizational results are found in the Soviet bloc, on the one hand, and the North Atlantic Pact, on the other. The latter was devised as a means for collective self-defense under Article 51 of the Charter, rather than as a regional arrangement under Article 52. The situation which produced it was not contemplated at the time of the San Francisco Conference, and it seems fair to conclude that the North Atlantic Pact is neither expressly sanctioned nor prohibited by the Charter. If it helps to stabilize the world political situation by forestalling a potential armed attack on Western Europe, it will eventually contribute to the strengthening of the United Nations. If, as the Soviets claim, it is designed as a basis for aggression, or even if it contributes unnecessarily to international tension, it is of course inconsistent with the principles and purposes of the United Nations. At present, any judgment on that question has to do with the integrity and wisdom of national policies.

The question of what the peoples of the world can do to strengthen the United Nations involves the problem of public opinion. It is easy to speak glibly of "world public opinion," but upon analysis this term may represent little more than a figure of speech or a sentimental abstraction. It is true, however, that the United Nations has begun to capture popular imagination in the United States and many other countries. Foreign offices feel impelled to defend their policies in terms of United Nations principles and decisions. Support of the United Nations is avowedly a cornerstone of American foreign policy, and any Secretary of State who proposed to go in the contrary direction would have a lot of explaining to do. It may be premature to talk about world public opinion, but certainly there is a parallel development in many countries. Out of this there begin to emerge a common international institution and symbolism.

Conclusion

Strengthening the United Nations is a process involved in the development of international society. One of the most notable facts about the United Nations is that it has been strengthened during the past six years. In terms of an effective organization for the maintenance of international peace and security, however, it is an infant requiring a long period of growth to reach maturity.

The United Nations has placed foreign affairs and international relations in a new context. Decisions of national policy must now be made from a different perspective. The United Nations has demonstrated that it can prevent or stop small wars. It cannot, of course, prevent a Great Power from making war if it is determined to do so. It has created a situation, however, in which even the Great Powers are impelled to justify their policies, in terms of the principles of the United Nations. More than that, it provides a broader range of methods for preventing a resort to hostilities. When there seems no other way out of an impasse, it may possibly reach some solution or adjustment through the United Nations. The possibilities of the United Nations are along lines which were stated as follows in connection with the Berlin blockade: [7]

So long as the Great Powers are deadlocked, the Security Council cannot coerce one or the other into a settlement; when the possibility of agreement exists, the United Nations machinery can focus the attention of the world and provide the way to work out the settlement; above all, the constant application of the principles of conciliation embodied in the Charter can operate to prevent the irreparable and disastrous rupture of negotiations.

The very existence of the United Nations presents increased opportunities for peaceful settlement and encourages the use of pacific methods.

One of the most significant developments in the United Nations is the emergence of what might be called a "third force." There are great dangers in a bipolar world, with all countries lined up on opposing sides in the East-West conflict. Such a situation involves two gigantic blocs, mutually hostile to each other and with little room for the operation of conciliating influences. If, however, there are members of the United Nations which will throw their weight against any aggressor, a better balance will be achieved. The role

[7] A. H. Feller, *Annual Review of United Nations Affairs, 1949*, edited by Clyde Eagleton, New York University Press, New York, 1950, p. 8.

of India in relation to the Korean conflict is a leading example in point. The government of India endorsed the use of force to stop the attack from North Korea, but did not approve all proposals made by the United States. The need for support from other countries tends to modify policies of both the United States and the Soviet Union. Moreover, the United Nations provides a forum in which small countries collectively can exert a real influence.

From the viewpoint of practical international politics, a "third force" is taking shape within the general organization rather than on a regional or geographic basis. This fact points to the basic fallacy in all proposals to attempt a reorganization of the United Nations so as to exclude the Soviet Union. Certainly many important nations would resent and resist an ultimatum to line up on one side. Such a step would increase the tension between East and West, at precisely the place where an alleviation of tension is most needed. Moreover, the emerging "third force" would be destroyed and one of the most hopeful trends in the present situation would be brought to an abrupt end.

The United Nations presents a method, an institution, and an opportunity. Its influence and prestige have increased as it has dealt with succeeding crises in the postwar world. The problem of strengthening the United Nations in the future is essentially one of contributing to the achievement and maintenance of international peace and security. This is no simple and easy task, nor is it one which can be done in sheltered isolation from the social, economic, and political problems of the modern world. The challenge is as broad, and as important, as the building of a stable and peaceful world order. The success of the United Nations is linked with the future of modern civilization.

BIBLIOGRAPHIC NOTE

The purpose of this bibliographic note is to provide an introductory guide to the literature concerning the United Nations. In a volume of this scope, a definitive bibliography on the United Nations and related topics is not feasible because a mere listing of items would require a considerable monograph verging on the encyclopedic. For example, a catalogue of the titles of the publications issued by the United Nations itself during 1949 alone constituted a booklet of forty-eight printed pages. More important, however, is the fact that an inclusive bibliography is not necessary for an introduction to the United Nations. Accordingly, this bibliographic note is designed to provide a reference to the publications of greatest value to the student and interested citizen, and to mark a point of departure for further study.

The United Nations publishes the official records of the various organs. These are, of course, a basic source for reference work. The *Yearbook of the United Nations* gives a detailed account of the structure and activities of the Organization. This publication contains a wealth of information and includes such items as the texts of the more important resolutions, verbatim rules of procedure of the various organs, membership of all the organizational units and delegations, and a summary record of activities with citations to the basic documents. *Everyman's United Nations* (3d ed., 1952) is published as a ready reference guide to the organization, functions, activities, and accomplishments of the United Nations.

The *Annual Report of the Secretary-General* provides a very useful summary and interpretation of the work of the Organization each year. The specialized agencies also publish reports concerning their activities. The *United Nations Bulletin* is an official periodical prepared by the Department of Public Information. It is issued on a semimonthly basis and is indispensable for following the current proceedings.

Many reports, bulletins, and pamphlets on a variety of topics are published by the United Nations. A list of *Current United Nations Publications* is issued from time to time by the Sales and Circulation Section of the Department of Public Information. The *United Nations Study Kit* contains a selection of pamphlets and booklets of general interest; it is especially useful for discussion groups and for persons who wish a brief over-all introduction to the United Nations and its activities. The sales agent in the United States for all United Nations publications is the International Documents Service, Columbia University Press.

The United States government publishes annually a report of the President to Congress on *United States Participation in the United Nations*. The material in these reports is based on drafts made by officers of the Department of State who have taken part in the work described. The result is a useful summary of the work of the United Nations from the American viewpoint. The Department of State

Bulletin and *Documents and State Papers* contain many articles on topics related to the United Nations, and the Department issues various pamphlets on individual questions.

Most recent books on world affairs and international relations devote attention to the United Nations. Some of the more useful books with that Organization as their major focus of attention are:

Eugene P. Chase, *The United Nations in Action,* McGraw-Hill, New York, 1950. A textbook giving a nontechnical but fairly comprehensive explanation of the origin, development, and work of the United Nations.

Vera Micheles Dean, *The Four Cornerstones of Peace,* McGraw-Hill, New York, 1946. A "primer" of four international conferences leading to the establishment of the United Nations. There is also a chapter entitled "The American Voter and International Organization."

Clyde Eagleton (ed.), *Annual Review of United Nations Affairs,* New York University Press, New York, 1950, 1951. The proceedings of the first and second New York University Institutes for Annual Review of the United Nations.

Herbert Vere Evatt, *The United Nations,* Harvard University Press, Cambridge, Mass., 1948. A small book based on lectures at Harvard University; reflects the "small power" viewpoint of which Mr. Evatt has been a leading spokesman.

Herbert Vere Evatt, *The Task of Nations,* Duell, Sloan & Pearce, New York, 1949. A discussion and interpretation of the third General Assembly.

Leland M. Goodrich and Edvard Hambro, *Charter of the United Nations: Commentary and Documents,* World Peace Foundation, Boston, 1949. A systematic account of the constitutional development of the United Nations. Contains a useful bibliography.

L. Larry Leonard, *International Organization,* McGraw-Hill, New York, 1951.

Trygve Lie and others, *Peace on Earth,* Hermitage House, New York, 1949. A discussion by various United Nations officials.

Useful books for further exploration of the development and significance of international organization are:

Clyde Eagleton, *International Government,* Ronald, New York, 1948.

Pitman B. Potter, *An Introduction to the Study of International Organization,* Appleton-Century-Crofts, New York, 1948. Contains a valuable bibliography of the standard works on international organization, politics, and law; diplomacy and treaties; the conference system; international administration, methods of peaceful settlement; and the League of Nations.

Harold M. Vinacke, *International Organization,* Appleton-Century-Crofts, New York, 1934.

There is a considerable body of periodical literature on the United Nations and related subjects. The *Bulletin* has been mentioned above. The *United Nations World* is a monthly publication of general interest. It contains interpretative articles and special features.

International Organization, a quarterly publication of the World Peace Foundation, is concerned largely with information and articles on the work of the United Nations and the specialized agencies. It is supplemented by the quarterly *Documents of International Organizations.*

Other periodicals which devote a substantial amount of space to the United Nations include *International Conciliation, Foreign Policy Reports, The American Journal of International Law, The American Political Science Review,* and *Foreign Affairs.* This is by no means an exhaustive list. Consultation of an index to periodical literature, or even a cursory examination of the periodical collection of any library, will show that all publications concerned with contemporary affairs necessarily devote some attention to the United Nations.

The United Nations does not function in a vacuum. The student of international organization will do well, therefore, to consult some books on general world politics for background. Among the many good books in this field the following will be found useful:

Hans Morgenthau, *Politics among Nations,* Knopf, New York, 1948. An analysis of international politics within reasonable compass, with a power-politics point of view.

Walter R. Sharp and Grayson Kirk, *Contemporary International Politics,* Rinehart, New York, 1940. An excellent, comprehensive survey as of the eve of World War II.

Robert Strausz-Hupé and Stefan T. Possony, *International Relations: In the Age of the Conflict between Democracy and Dictatorship,* McGraw-Hill, New York, 1950. A comprehensive survey and keen analysis of current forces in world politics. Useful and significant documents are dispersed throughout the text. The authors adhere rather strongly to the power-politics school.

APPENDIXES

APPENDIXES

Appendix 1

CHARTER OF THE UNITED NATIONS

WE THE PEOPLES OF THE UNITED NATIONS
DETERMINED

to save succeeding generations from the scourge of war, which twice in our lifetime has brought untold sorrow to mankind, and to reaffirm faith in fundamental human rights, in the dignity and worth of the human person, in the equal rights of men and women and of nations large and small, and
to establish conditions under which justice and respect for the obligations arising from treaties and other sources of international law can be maintained, and
to promote social progress and better standards of life in larger freedom,

AND FOR THESE ENDS

to practice tolerance and live together in peace with one another as good neighbors, and
to unite our strength to maintain international peace and security, and
to ensure, by the acceptance of principles and the institution of methods, that armed force shall not be used, save in the common interest, and
to employ international machinery for the promotion of the economic and social advancement of all peoples,

HAVE RESOLVED TO COMBINE OUR EFFORTS
TO ACCOMPLISH THESE AIMS.

Accordingly, our respective Governments, through representatives assembled in the city of San Francisco, who have exhibited their full powers found to be in good and due form, have agreed to the present Charter of the United Nations and do hereby establish an international organization to be known as the United Nations.

CHAPTER I

PURPOSES AND PRINCIPLES

Article 1

The Purposes of the United Nations are:'
1. To maintain international peace and security, and to that end: to take effective collective measures for the prevention and removal of threats to the peace, and for the suppression of acts of aggression or other breaches of the peace, and to bring about by peaceful means, and in conformity with the principles of justice and inter-

national law, adjustment or settlement of international disputes or situations which might lead to a breach of the peace;

2. To develop friendly relations among nations based on respect for the principle of equal rights and self-determination of peoples, and to take other appropriate measures to strengthen universal peace;

3. To achieve international cooperation in solving international problems of an economic, social, cultural, or humanitarian character, and in promoting and encouraging respect for human rights and for fundamental freedoms for all without distinction as to race, sex, language, or religion; and

To be a center for harmonizing the actions of nations in the attainment of these common ends.

Article 2

The Organization and its Members, in pursuit of the Purposes stated in Article 1, shall act in accordance with the following Principles.

1. The Organization is based on the principle of the sovereign equality of all its Members.

2. All Members, in order to ensure to all of them the rights and benefits resulting from membership, shall fulfill in good faith the obligations assumed by them in accordance with the present Charter.

3. All Members shall settle their international disputes by peaceful means in such a manner that international peace and security, and justice, are not endangered.

4. All Members shall refrain in their international relations from the threat or use of force against the territorial integrity or political independence of any state, or in any other manner inconsistent with the Purposes of the United Nations.

5. All Members shall give the United Nations every assistance in any action it takes in accordance with the present Charter, and shall refrain from giving assistance to any state against which the United Nations is taking preventive or enforcement action.

6. The Organization shall ensure that states which are not Members of the United Nations act in accordance with these Principles so far as may be necessary for the maintenance of international peace and security.

7. Nothing contained in the present Charter shall authorize the United Nations to intervene in matters which are essentially within the domestic jurisdiction of any state or shall require the Members to submit such matters to settlement under the present Charter; but this principle shall not prejudice the application of enforcement measures under Chapter VII.

CHAPTER II

MEMBERSHIP

Article 3

The original Members of the United Nations shall be the states which, having participated in the United Nations Conference on International Organization at San Francisco, or having previously signed the Declaration by United Nations of January 1, 1942, sign the present Charter and ratify it in accordance with Article 110.

Article 4

1. Membership in the United Nations is open to all other peace-loving states which accept the obligations contained in the present Charter and, in the judgment of the Organization are able and willing to carry out these obligations.

2. The admission of any such state to membership in the United Nations will be effected by a decision of the General Assembly upon the recommendation of the Security Council.

Article 5

A member of the United Nations against which preventive or enforcement action has been taken by the Security Council may be suspended from the exercise of the rights and privileges of membership by the General Assembly upon the recommendation of the Security Council. The exercise of these rights and privileges may be restored by the Security Council.

Article 6

A Member of the United Nations which has persistently violated the Principles contained in the present Charter may be expelled from the Organization by the General Assembly upon the recommendation of the Security Council.

CHAPTER III

ORGANS

Article 7

1. There are established as the principal organs of the United Nations: A General Assembly, a Security Council, an Economic and Social Council, a Trusteeship Council, an International Court of Justice, and a Secretariat.
2. Such subsidiary organs as may be found necessary may be established in accordance with the present Charter.

Article 8

The United Nations shall place no restrictions on the eligibility of men and women to participate in any capacity and under conditions of equality in its principal and subsidiary organs.

CHAPTER IV

THE GENERAL ASSEMBLY

Composition

Article 9

1. The General Assembly shall consist of all the Members of the United Nations.
2. Each Member shall have not more than five representatives in the General Assembly.

Functions and Powers

Article 10

The General Assembly may discuss any questions or matters within the scope of the present Charter or relating to the powers and functions of any organs provided for in the present Charter, and except as provided in Article 12, may make recommendations to the Members of the United Nations or to the Security Council or to both on any such questions or matters.

Article 11

1. The General Assembly may consider the general principles of cooperation in the maintenance of international peace and security, including the principles govern-

ing disarmament and the regulation of armaments, and may make recommendations with regard to such principles to the Members or to the Security Council or to both.

2. The General Assembly may discuss any questions relating to the maintenance of international peace and security brought before it by any Member of the United Nations, or by the Security Council, or by a state which is not a Member of the United Nations in accordance with Article 35, paragraph 2, and, except as provided in Article 12, may make recommendations with regard to any such questions to the state or states concerned or to the Security Council or to both. Any such question on which action is necessary shall be referred to the Security Council by the General Assembly either before or after discussion.

3. The General Assembly may call the attention of the Security Council to situations which are likely to endanger international peace and security.

4. The powers of the General Assembly set forth in this Article shall not limit the general scope of Article 10.

Article 12

1. While the Security Council is exercising in respect of any dispute or situation the functions assigned to it in the present Charter, the General Assembly shall not make any recommendation with regard to that dispute or situation unless the Security Council so requests.

2. The Secretary-General, with the consent of the Security Council, shall notify the General Assembly at each session of any matters relative to the maintenance of international peace and security which are being dealt with by the Security Council and shall similarly notify the General Assembly, or the Members of the United Nations if the General Assembly is not in session, immediately the Security Council ceases to deal with such matters.

Article 13

1. The General Assembly shall initiate studies and make recommendations for the purpose of:

a. promoting international cooperation in the political field and encouraging the progressive development of international law and its codification;

b. promoting international cooperation in the economic, social, cultural, educational, and health fields, and assisting in the realization of human rights and fundamental freedoms for all without distinction as to race, sex, language, or religion.

2. The further responsibilities, functions, and powers of the General Assembly with respect to matters mentioned in paragraph 1(b) above are set forth in Chapters IX and X.

Article 14

Subject to the provisions of Article 12, the General Assembly may recommend measures for the peaceful adjustment of any situation, regardless of origin, which it deems likely to impair the general welfare or friendly relations among nations, including situations resulting from a violation of the provisions of the present Charter setting forth the Purposes and Principles of the United Nations.

Article 15

1. The General Assembly shall receive and consider annual and special reports from the Security Council; these reports shall include an account of the measures

that the Security Council has decided upon or taken to maintain international peace and security.

2. The General Assembly shall receive and consider reports from the other organs of the United Nations.

Article 16

The General Assembly shall perform such functions with respect to the international trusteeship system as are assigned to it under Chapters XII and XIII, including the approval of the trusteeship agreements for areas not designated as strategic.

Article 17

1. The General Assembly shall consider and approve the budget of the Organization.

2. The expenses of the Organization shall be borne by the Members as appor tioned by the General Assembly.

3. The General Assembly shall consider and approve any financial and budgetary arrangements with specialized agencies referred to in Article 57 and shall examine the administrative budgets of such specialized agencies with a view to making recommendations to the agencies concerned.

Voting

Article 18

1. Each member of the General Assembly shall have one vote.

2. Decisions of the General Assembly on important questions shall be made by a two-thirds majority of the members present and voting. These questions shall include: recommendations with respect to the maintenance of international peace and security, the election of the non-permanent members of the Security Council, the election of the members of the Economic and Social Council, the election of members of the Trusteeship Council in accordance with paragraph 1(c) of Article 86, the admission of new Members to the United Nations, the suspension of the rights and privileges of membership, the expulsion of Members, questions relating to the operation of the trusteeship system, and budgetary questions.

3. Decisions on other questions, including the determination of additional categories of questions to be decided by a two-thirds majority, shall be made by a majority of the members present and voting.

Article 19

A Member of the United Nations which is in arrears in the payment of its financial contributions to the Organization shall have no vote in the General Assembly if the amount of its arrears equals or exceeds the amount of the contributions due from it for the preceding two full years. The General Assembly may, nevertheless, permit such a Member to vote if it is satisfied that the failure to pay is due to conditions beyond the control of the Member.

Procedure

Article 20

The General Assembly shall meet in regular annual sessions and in such special sessions as occasion may require. Special sessions shall be convoked by the Secretary-

General at the request of the Security Council or of a majority of the Members of the United Nations.

Article 21

The General Assembly shall adopt its own rules of procedure. It shall elect its President for each session.

Article 22

The General Assembly may establish such subsidiary organs as it deems necessary for the performance of its functions.

CHAPTER V

THE SECURITY COUNCIL

Composition

Article 23

1. The Security Council shall consist of eleven Members of the United Nations. The Republic of China, France, the Union of Soviet Socialist Republics, the United Kingdom of Great Britain and Northern Ireland, and the United States of America shall be permanent members of the Security Council. The General Assembly shall elect six other Members of the United Nations to be non-permanent members of the Security Council, due regard being specially paid, in the first instance to the contribution of Members of the United Nations to the maintenance of international peace and security and to the other purposes of the Organization, and also to equitable geographical distribution.

2. The non-permanent members of the Security Council shall be elected for a term of two years. In the first election of the non-permanent members, however, three shall be chosen for a term of one year. A retiring member shall not be eligible for immediate re-election.

3. Each member of the Security Council shall have one representative.

Functions and Powers

Article 24

1. In order to ensure prompt and effective action by the United Nations, its Members confer on the Security Council primary responsibility for the maintenance of international peace and security, and agree that in carrying out its duties under this responsibility the Security Council acts on their behalf.

2. In discharging these duties the Security Council shall act in accordance with the Purposes and Principles of the United Nations. The specific powers granted to the Security Council for the discharge of these duties are laid down in Chapters VI, VII, VIII, and XII.

3. The Security Council shall submit annual and, when necessary, special reports to the General Assembly for its consideration.

Article 25

The Members of the United Nations agree to accept and carry out the decisions of the Security Council in accordance with the present Charter.

Article 26

In order to promote the establishment and maintenance of international peace and security with the least diversion for armaments of the world's human and economic resources, the Security Council shall be responsible for formulating, with the assistance of the Military Staff Committee referred to in Article 47, plans to be submitted to the Members of the United Nations for the establishment of a system for the regulation of armaments.

Voting

Article 27

1. Each member of the Security Council shall have one vote.
2. Decisions of the Security Council on procedural matters shall be made by an affirmative vote of seven members.
3. Decisions of the Security Council on all other matters shall be made by an affirmative vote of seven members including the concurring votes of the permanent members; provided that, in decisions under Chapter VI, and under paragraph 3 of Article 52, a party to a dispute shall abstain from voting.

Procedure

Article 28

1. The Security Council shall be so organized as to be able to function contin-uously. Each member of the Security Council shall for this purpose be represented at all times at the seat of the Organization.
2. The Security Council shall hold periodic meetings at which each of its members may, if it so desires, be represented by a member of the government or by some other specially designated representative.
3. The Security Council may hold meetings at such places other than the seat of the Organization as in its judgment will best facilitate its work.

Article 29

The Security Council may establish such subsidiary organs as it deems necessary for the performance of its functions.

Article 30

The Security Council shall adopt its own rules of procedure, including the method of selecting its President.

Article 31

Any Member of the United Nations which is not a member of the Security Council may participate, without vote, in the discussion of any question brought before the Security Council whenever the latter considers that the interests of that Member are specially affected.

Article 32

Any Member of the United Nations which is not a member of the Security Coun-cil or any state which is not a Member of the United Nations, if it is a party to a dispute under consideration by the Security Council, shall be invited to participate, without vote, in the discussion relating to the dispute. The Security Council shall lay down such conditions as it deems just for the participation of a state which is not a Member of the United Nations.

CHAPTER VI

PACIFIC SETTLEMENT OF DISPUTES

Article 33

1. The parties to any disputes, the continuance of which is likely to endanger the maintenance of international peace and security, shall, first of all, seek a solution by negotiation, enquiry, mediation, conciliation, arbitration, judicial settlement, resort to regional agencies or arrangements, or other peaceful means of their own choice.

2. The Security Council shall, when it deems necessary, call upon the parties to settle their dispute by such means.

Article 34

The Security Council may investigate any dispute, or any situation which might lead to international friction or give rise to a dispute, in order to determine whether the continuance of the dispute or situation is likely to endanger the maintenance of international peace and security.

Article 35

1. Any Member of the United Nations may bring any dispute, or any situation of the nature referred to in Article 34, to the attention of the Security Council or of the General Assembly.

2. A state which is not a Member of the United Nations may bring to the attention of the Security Council or of the General Assembly any dispute to which it is a party if it accepts in advance, for the purposes of the dispute, the obligations of pacific settlement provided in the present Charter.

3. The proceedings of the General Assembly in respect of matters brought to its attention under this Article will be subject to the provisions of Articles 11 and 12.

Article 36

1. The Security Council may, at any stage of a dispute of the nature referred to in Article 33 or of a situation of like nature, recommend appropriate procedures or methods of adjustment.

2. The Security Council should take into consideration any procedures for the settlement of the dispute which have already been adopted by the parties.

3. In making recommendations under this Article the Security Council should also take into consideration that legal disputes should as a general rule be referred by the parties to the International Court of Justice in accordance with the provisions of the Statute of the Court.

Article 37

1. Should the parties to a dispute of the nature referred to in Article 33 fail to settle it by the means indicated in that Article, they shall refer it to the Security Council.

2. If the Security Council deems that the continuance of the dispute is in fact likely to endanger the maintenance of international peace and security, it shall

decide whether to take action under Article 36 or to recommend such terms of settlement as it may consider appropriate.

Article 38

Without prejudice to the provisions of Articles 33 to 37, the Security Council may, if all the parties to any dispute so request, make recommendations to the parties with a view to a pacific settlement of the dispute.

CHAPTER VII

ACTION WITH RESPECT TO THREATS TO THE PEACE, BREACHES OF THE PEACE, AND ACTS OF AGGRESSION

Article 39

The Security Council shall determine the existence of any threat to the peace, breach of the peace, or act of aggression and shall make recommendations, or decide what measures shall be taken in accordance with Articles 41 and 42, to maintain or restore international peace and security.

Article 40

In order to prevent an aggravation of the situation, the Security Council may, before making the recommendations or deciding upon the measures provided for in Article 39, call upon the parties concerned to comply with such provisional measures as it deems necessary or desirable. Such provisional measures shall be without prejudice to the rights, claims, or position of the parties concerned. The Security Council shall duly take account of failure to comply with such provisional measures.

Article 41

The Security Council may decide what measures not involving the use of armed force are to be employed to give effect to its decisions, and it may call upon the Members of the United Nations to apply such measures. These may include complete or partial interruption of economic relations and of rail, sea, air, postal, telegraphic, radio, and other means of communication, and the severence of diplomatic relations.

Article 42

Should the Security Council consider that measures provided for in Article 41 would be inadequate or have proved to be inadequate, it may take such action by air, sea, or land forces as may be necessary to maintain or restore international peace and security. Such action may include demonstrations, blockade, and other operations by air, sea, or land forces of Members of the United Nations.

Article 43

1. All Members of the United Nations, in order to contribute to the maintenance of international peace and security, undertake to make available to the Security Council, on its call and in accordance with a special agreement or agreements, armed forces, assistance, and facilities, including rights of passage, necessary for the purpose of maintaining international peace and security.

2. Such agreement or agreements shall govern the numbers and types of forces, their degree of readiness and general location, and the nature of the facilities and assistance to be provided.

3. The agreement or agreements shall be negotiated as soon as possible on the initiative of the Security Council. They shall be concluded between the Security Council and Members or between the Security Council and groups of Members and shall be subject to ratification by the signatory states in accordance with their respective constitutional processes.

Article 44

When the Security Council has decided to use force it shall, before calling upon a Member not represented on it to provide armed forces in fulfillment of the obligations assumed under Article 43, invite that Member, if the Member so desires, to participate in the decisions of the Security Council concerning the employment of contingents of that Member's armed forces.

Article 45

In order to enable the United Nations to take urgent military measures, Members shall hold immediately available national air-force contingents for combined international enforcement action. The strength and degree of readiness of these contingents and plans for their combined action shall be determined, within the limits laid down in the special agreement or agreements referred to in Article 43, by the Security Council with the assistance of the Military Staff Committee.

Article 46

Plans for the application of armed force shall be made by the Security Council with the assistance of the Military Staff Committee.

Article 47

1. There shall be established a Military Staff Committee to advise and assist the Security Council on all questions relating to the Security Council's military requirements for the maintenance of international peace and security, the employment and command of forces placed at its disposal, the regulation of armaments, and possible disarmament.

2. The Military Staff Committee shall consist of the Chiefs of Staff of the permanent members of the Security Council or their representatives. Any Member of the United Nations not permanently represented on the Committee shall be invited by the Committee to be associated with it when the efficient discharge of the Committee's responsibilities requires the participation of that Member in its work.

3. The Military Staff Committee shall be responsible under the Security Council for the strategic direction of any armed force placed at the disposal of the Security Council. Questions relating to the command of such forces shall be worked out subsequently.

4. The Military Staff Committee, with the authorization of the Security Council and after consultation with appropriate regional agencies, may establish regional subcommittees.

Article 48

1. The action required to carry out the decisions of the Security Council for the maintenance of international peace and security shall be taken by all the Members of the United Nations or by some of them, as the Security Council may determine.

2. Such decisions shall be carried out by the Members of the United Nations directly and through their action in the appropriate international agencies of which they are members.

Article 49

The Members of the United Nations shall join in affording mutual assistance in carrying out the measures decided upon by the Security Council.

Article 50

If preventive or enforcement measures against any state are taken by the Security Council, any other state, whether a Member of the United Nations or not, which finds itself confronted with special economic problems arising from the carrying out of those measures shall have the right to consult the Security Council with regard to a solution of those problems.

Article 51

Nothing in the present Charter shall impair the inherent right of individual or collective self-defense if an armed attack occurs against a Member of the United Nations, until the Security Council has taken the measures necessary to maintain international peace and security. Measures taken by Members in the exercise of this right of self-defense shall be immediately reported to the Security Council and shall not in any way affect the authority and responsibility of the Security Council under the present Charter to take at any time such action as it deems necessary in order to maintain or restore international peace and security.

CHAPTER VIII

REGIONAL ARRANGEMENTS

Article 52

1. Nothing in the present Charter precludes the existence of regional arrangements or agencies for dealing with such matters relating to the maintenance of international peace and security as are appropriate for regional action, provided that such arrangements or agencies and their activities are consistent with the Purposes and Principles of the United Nations.

2. The Members of the United Nations entering into such arrangements or constituting such agencies shall make every effort to achieve pacific settlement of local disputes through such regional arrangements or by such regional agencies before referring them to the Security Council.

3. The Security Council shall encourage the development of pacific settlement of local disputes through such regional arrangements or by such regional agencies either on the initiative of the states concerned or by reference from the Security Council.

4. This Article in no way impairs the application of Articles 34 and 35.

Article 53

1. The Security Council shall, where appropriate, utilize such regional arrangements or agencies for enforcement action under its authority. But no enforcement action shall be taken under regional arrangements or by regional agencies without the authorization of the Security Council, with the exception of measures against any enemy state, as defined in paragraph 2 of this Article, provided for pursuant to Article 107 or in regional arrangements directed against renewal of aggressive policy on the part of any such state, until such time as the Organization may, on request of the Governments concerned, be charged with the responsibility for preventing further aggression by such a state.

2. The term enemy state as used in paragraph 1 of this Article applies to any state which during the Second World War has been an enemy of any signatory of the present Charter.

Article 54

The Security Council shall at all times be kept fully informed of activities undertaken or in contemplation under regional arrangements or by regional agencies for the maintenance of international peace and security.

CHAPTER IX

INTERNATIONAL ECONOMIC AND SOCIAL COOPERATION

Article 55

With a view to the creation of conditions of stability and well-being which are necessary for peaceful and friendly relations among nations based on respect for the principles of equal rights and self-determination of peoples, the United Nations shall promote:

a. higher standards of living, full employment, and conditions of economic and social progress and development;

b. solutions of international economic, social, health, and related problems; and international cultural and educational cooperation; and

c. universal respect for, and observance of, human rights and fundamental freedoms for all without distinction as to race, sex, language, or religion.

Article 56

All Members pledge themselves to take joint and separate action in cooperation with the Organization for the achievement of the purposes set forth in Article 55.

Article 57

1. The various specialized agencies, established by intergovernmental agreement and having wide international responsibilities, as defined in their basic instruments, in economic, social, cultural, educational, health, and related fields, shall be brought into relationship with the United Nations in accordance with the provisions of Article 63.

2. Such agencies thus brought into relationship with the United Nations are hereinafter referred to as specialized agencies.

Article 58

The Organization shall make recommendations for the coordination of the policies and activities of the specialized agencies.

Article 59

The Organization shall, where appropriate, initiate negotiations among the states concerned for the creation of any new specialized agencies required for the accomplishment of the purposes set forth in Article 55.

Article 60

Responsibility for the discharge of the functions of the Organization set forth in this Chapter shall be vested in the General Assembly and, under the authority of the

General Assembly, in the Economic and Social Council, which shall have for this purpose the powers set forth in Chapter X.

CHAPTER X

THE ECONOMIC AND SOCIAL COUNCIL

Composition

Article 61

1. The Economic and Social Council shall consist of eighteen Members of the United Nations elected by the General Assembly.
2. Subject to the provisions of paragraph 3, six members of the Economic and Social Council shall be elected each year for a term of three years. A retiring member shall be eligible for immediate re-election.
3. At the first election, eighteen members of the Economic and Social Council shall be chosen. The term of office of six members so chosen shall expire at the end of one year, and of six other members at the end of two years, in accordance with arrangements made by the General Assembly.
4. Each member of the Economic and Social Council shall have one representative.

Functions and Powers

Article 62

1. The Economic and Social Council may make or initiate studies and reports with respect to international economic, social, cultural, educational, health, and related matters to the General Assembly, to the Members of the United Nations, and to the specialized agencies concerned.
2. It may make recommendations for the purpose of promoting respect for, and observance of, human rights and fundamental freedoms for all.
3. It may prepare draft conventions for submission to the General Assembly, with respect to matters falling within its competence.
4. It may call, in accordance with the rules prescribed by the United Nations, international conferences on matters falling within its competence.

Article 63

1. The Economic and Social Council may enter into agreements with any of the agencies referred to in Article 57, defining the terms on which the agency concerned shall be brought into relationship with the United Nations. Such agreements shall be subject to approval by the General Assembly.
2. It may coordinate the activities of the specialized agencies through consultation with and recommendations to such agencies and through recommendations to the General Assembly and to the Members of the United Nations.

Article 64

1. The Economic and Social Council may take appropriate steps to obtain regular reports from the specialized agencies. It may make arrangements with the Members of the United Nations and with the specialized agencies to obtain reports on the steps taken to give effect to its own recommendations and to recommendations on matters falling within its competence made by the General Assembly.
2. It may communicate its observations on these reports to the General Assembly.

Article 65

The Economic and Social Council may furnish information to the Security Council and shall assist the Security Council upon its request.

Article 66

1. The Economic and Social Council shall perform such functions as fall within its competence in connection with the carrying out of the recommendations of the General Assembly.

2. It may, with the approval of the General Assembly, perform services at the request of Members of the United Nations and at the request of specialized agencies.

3. It shall perform such other functions as are specified elsewhere in the present Charter or as may be assigned to it by the General Assembly.

Voting

Article 67

1. Each member of the Economic and Social Council shall have one vote.

2. Decisions of the Economic and Social Council shall be made by a majority of the members present and voting.

Procedure

Article 68

The Economic and Social Council shall set up commissions in economic and social fields and for the promotion of human rights, and such other commissions as may be required for the performance of its functions.

Article 69

The Economic and Social Council shall invite any Member of the United Nations to participate, without vote, in its deliberations on any matter of particular concern to that Member.

Article 70

The Economic and Social Council may make arrangements for representatives of the specialized agencies to participate, without vote, in its deliberations and in those of the commissions established by it, and for its representatives to participate in the deliberations of the specialized agencies.

Article 71

The Economic and Social Council may make suitable arrangements for consultation with non-governmental organizations which are concerned with matters within its competence. Such arrangements may be made with international organizations and, where appropriate, with national organizations after consultation with the Member of the United Nations concerned.

Article 72

1. The Economic and Social Council shall adopt its own rules of procedure, including the method of selecting its President.

2. The Economic and Social Council shall meet as required in accordance with its

rules, which shall include provision for the convening of meetings on the request of a majority of its members.

CHAPTER XI

DECLARATION REGARDING NON-SELF-GOVERNING TERRITORIES

Article 73

Members of the United Nations which have or assume responsibilities for the administration of territories whose peoples have not yet attained a full measure of self-government recognize the principle that the interests of the inhabitants of these territories are paramount, and accept as a sacred trust the obligation to promote to the utmost, within the system of international peace and security established by the present Charter, the well-being of the inhabitants of these territories, and, to this end:

   a. to ensure, with due respect for the culture of the peoples concerned, their political, economic, social, and educational advancement, their just treatment, and their protection against abuses;

   b. to develop self-government, to take due account of the political aspirations of the peoples, and to assist them in the progressive development of their free political institutions, according to the particular circumstances of each territory and its peoples and their varying stages of advancement;

   c. to further international peace and security;

   d. to promote constructive measures of development, to encourage research, and to cooperate with one another and, when and where appropriate, with specialized international bodies with a view to the practical achievement of the social, economic, and scientific purposes set forth in this Article; and

   e. to transmit regularly to the Secretary-General for information purposes, subject to such limitations as security and constitutional considerations may require, statistical and other information of a technical nature relating to economic, social, and educational conditions in the territories for which they are respectively responsible other than those territories to which Chapters XII and XIII apply.

Article 74

Members of the United Nations also agree that their policy in respect of the territories to which this Chapter applies, no less than in respect of their metropolitan areas, must be based on the general principle of good-neighborliness, due account being taken of the interests and well-being of the rest of the world, in social, economic, and commercial matters.

CHAPTER XII

INTERNATIONAL TRUSTEESHIP SYSTEM

Article 75

The United Nations shall establish under its authority an international trusteeship system for the administration and supervision of such territories as may be placed thereunder by subsequent individual agreements. These territories are hereinafter referred to as trust territories.

Article 76

The basic objectives of the trusteeship system, in accordance with the Purposes of the United Nations laid down in Article 1 of the present Charter, shall be:

a. to further international peace and security;

b. to promote the political, economic, social, and educational advancement of the inhabitants of the trust territories, and their progressive development towards self-government or independence as may be appropriate to the particular circumstances of each territory and its peoples and the freely expressed wishes of the peoples concerned, and as may be provided by the terms of each trusteeship agreement;

c. to encourage respect for human rights and for fundamental freedoms for all without distinction as to race, sex, language, or religion, and to encourage recognition of the interdependence of the peoples of the world; and

d. to ensure equal treatment in social, economic, and commercial matters for all Members of the United Nations and their nationals, and also equal treatment for the latter in the administration of justice, without prejudice to the attainment of the foregoing objectives and subject to the provisions of Article 80.

Article 77

1. The trusteeship system shall apply to such territories in the following categories as may be placed thereunder by means of trusteeship agreements:

a. territories now held under mandate;

b. territories which may be detached from enemy states as a result of the Second World War; and

c. territories voluntarily placed under the system by states responsible for their administration.

2. It will be a matter for subsequent agreement as to which territories in the foregoing categories will be brought under the trusteeship system and upon what terms.

Article 78

The trusteeship system shall not apply to territories which have become Members of the United Nations, relationship among which shall be based on respect for the principle of sovereign equality.

Article 79

The terms of trusteeship for each territory to be placed under the trusteeship system, including any alteration or amendment, shall be agreed upon by the states directly concerned, including the mandatory power in the case of territories held under mandate by a Member of the United Nations, and shall be approved as provided for in Articles 83 and 85.

Article 80

1. Except as may be agreed upon in individual trusteeship agreements, made under Articles 77, 79, and 81, placing each territory under the trusteeship system, and until such agreements have been concluded, nothing in this Chapter shall be construed in or of itself to alter in any manner the rights whatsoever of any states or any peoples or the terms of existing international instruments to which Members of the United Nations may respectively be parties.

2. Paragraph 1 of this Article shall not be interpreted as giving grounds for delay or postponement of the negotiation and conclusion of agreements for placing mandated and other territories under the trusteeship system as provided for in Article 77.

Article 81

The trusteeship agreement shall in each case include the terms under which the trust territory will be administered and designate the authority which will exercise the administration of the trust territory. Such authority, hereinafter called the administering authority, may be one or more states or the Organization itself.

Article 82

There may be designated, in any trusteeship agreement, a strategic area or areas which may include part or all of the trust territory to which the agreement applies, without prejudice to any special agreement or agreements made under Article 43.

Article 83

1. All functions of the United Nations relating to strategic areas, including the approval of the terms of the trusteeship agreements and of their alteration or amendment, shall be exercised by the Security Council.

2. The basic objectives set forth in Article 76 shall be applicable to the people of each strategic area.

3. The Security Council shall, subject to the provisions of the trusteeship agreements and without prejudice to security considerations, avail itself of the assistance of the Trusteeship Council to perform those functions of the United Nations under the trusteeship system relating to political, economic, social, and educational matters in the strategic areas.

Article 84

It shall be the duty of the administering authority to ensure that the trust territory shall play its part in the maintenance of international peace and security. To this end the administering authority may make use of volunteer forces, facilities, and assistance from the trust territory in carrying out the obligations towards the Security Council undertaken in this regard by the administering authority, as well as for local defense and the maintenance of law and order within the trust territory.

Article 85

1. The functions of the United Nations with regard to trusteeship agreements for all areas not designated as strategic, including the approval of the terms of the trusteeship agreements and of their alteration or amendment, shall be exercised by the General Assembly.

2. The Trusteeship Council, operating under the authority of the General Assembly, shall assist the General Assembly in carrying out these functions.

CHAPTER XIII

THE TRUSTEESHIP COUNCIL

Composition

Article 86

1. The Trusteeship Council shall consist of the following Members of the United Nations:

    a. those Members administering trust territories;

    b. such of those Members mentioned by name in Article 23 as are not administering trust territories; and

c. as many other Members elected for three-year terms by the General Assembly as may be necessary to ensure that the total number of members of the Trusteeship Council is equally divided between those Members of the United Nations which administer trust territories and those which do not.

2. Each member of the Trusteeship Council shall designate one specially qualified person to represent it therein.

Functions and Powers

Article 87

The General Assembly and, under its authority, the Trusteeship Council, in carrying out their functions, may:

a. consider reports submitted by the administering authority;
b. accept petitions and examine them in consultation with the administering authority;
c. provide for periodic visits to the respective trust territories at times agreed upon with the administering authority; and
d. take these and other actions in conformity with the terms of the trusteeship agreements.

Article 88

The Trusteeship Council shall formulate a questionnaire on the political, economic, social, and educational advancement of the inhabitants of each trust territory, and the administering authority for each trust territory within the competence of the General Assembly shall make an annual report to the General Assembly upon the basis of such questionnaire.

Voting

Article 89

1. Each member of the Trusteeship Council shall have one vote.
2. Decisions of the Trusteeship Council shall be made by a majority of the members present and voting.

Procedure

Article 90

1. The Trusteeship Council shall adopt its own rules of procedures, including the method of selecting its President.
2. The Trusteeship Council shall meet as required in accordance with its rules, which shall include provision for the convening of meetings on the request of a majority of its members.

Article 91

The Trusteeship Council shall, when appropriate, avail itself of the assistance of the Economic and Social Council and of the specialized agencies in regard to matters with which they are respectively concerned.

CHAPTER XIV

THE INTERNATIONAL COURT OF JUSTICE

Article 92

The International Court of Justice shall be the principal judicial organ of the United Nations. It shall function in accordance with the annexed Statute, which is based upon the Statute of the Permanent Court of International Justice and forms an integral part of the present Charter.

Article 93

1. All Members of the United Nations are *ipso facto* parties to the Statute of the International Court of Justice.

2. A state which is not a Member of the United Nations may become a party to the Statute of the International Court of Justice on conditions to be determined in each case by the General Assembly upon the recommendation of the Security Council.

Article 94

1. Each Member of the United Nations undertakes to comply with the decision of the International Court of Justice in any case to which it is a party.

2. If any party to a case fails to perform the obligations incumbent upon it under a judgment rendered by the Court, the other party may have recourse to the Security Council, which may, if it deems necessary, make recommendations or decide upon measures to be taken to give effect to the judgment.

Article 95

Nothing in the present Charter shall prevent Members of the United Nations from entrusting the solution of their differences to other tribunals by virtue of agreements already in existence or which may be concluded in the future.

Article 96

1. The General Assembly or the Security Council may request the International Court of Justice to give an advisory opinion on any legal question.

2. Other organs of the United Nations and specialized agencies, which may at any time be so authorized by the General Assembly, may also request advisory opinions of the Court on legal questions arising within the scope of their activities.

CHAPTER XV

THE SECRETARIAT

Article 97

The Secretariat shall comprise a Secretary-General and such staff as the Organization may require. The Secretary-General shall be appointed by the General Assembly upon the recommendation of the Security Council. He shall be the chief administrative officer of the Organization.

Article 98

The Secretary-General shall act in that capacity in all meetings of the General Assembly, of the Security Council, of the Economic and Social Council, and of the

Trusteeship Council, and shall perform such other functions as are entrusted to him by these organs. The Secretary-General shall make an annual report to the General Assembly on the work of the Organization.

Article 99

The Secretary-General may bring to the attention of the Security Council any matter which in his opinion may threaten the maintenance of international peace and security.

Article 100

1. In the performance of their duties the Secretary-General and the staff shall not seek or receive instructions from any government or from any other authority external to the Organization. They shall refrain from any action which might reflect on their position as international officials responsible only to the Organization.

2. Each Member of the United Nations undertakes to respect the exclusively international character of the responsibilities of the Secretary-General and the staff and not to seek to influence them in the discharge of their responsibilities.

Article 101

1. The staff shall be appointed by the Secretary-General under regulations established by the General Assembly.

2. Appropriate staffs shall be permanently assigned to the Economic and Social Council, the Trusteeship Council, and, as required, to other organs of the United Nations. These staffs shall form a part of the Secretariat.

3. The paramount consideration in the employment of the staff and in the determination of the conditions of service shall be the necessity of securing the highest standards of efficiency, competence, and integrity. Due regard shall be paid to the importance of recruiting the staff on as wide a geographical basis as possible.

CHAPTER XVI

MISCELLANEOUS PROVISIONS

Article 102

1. Every treaty and every international agreement entered into by any Member of the United Nations after the present Charter comes into force shall as soon as possible be registered with the Secretariat and published by it.

2. No party to any such treaty or international agreement which has not been registered in accordance with the provisions of paragraph 1 of this Article may invoke that treaty or agreement before any organ of the United Nations.

Article 103

In the event of a conflict between the obligations of the Members of the United Nations under the present Charter and their obligations under any other international agreement, their obligations under the present Charter shall prevail.

Article 104

The Organization shall enjoy in the territory of each of its Members such legal capacity as may be necessary for the exercise of its functions and the fulfillment of its purposes.

Article 105

1. The Organization shall enjoy in the territory of each of its Members such privileges and immunities as are necessary for the fulfillment of its purposes.

2. Representatives of the Members of the United Nations and officials of the Organization shall similarly enjoy such privileges and immunities as are necessary for the independent exercise of their functions in connection with the Organization.

3. The General Assembly may make recommendations with a view to determining the details of the application of paragraphs 1 and 2 of this Article or may propose conventions to the Members of the United Nations for this purpose.

CHAPTER XVII

TRANSITIONAL SECURITY ARRANGEMENTS

Article 106

Pending the coming into force of such special agreements referred to in Article 43 as in the opinion of the Security Council enable it to begin the exercise of its responsibilities under Article 42, the parties to the Four-Nation Declaration, signed at Moscow, October 30, 1943, and France, shall, in accordance with the provisions of paragraph 5 of that Declaration, consult with one another and as occasion requires with other Members of the United Nations with a view to such joint action on behalf of the Organization as may be necessary for the purpose of maintaining international peace and security.

Article 107

Nothing in the present Charter shall invalidate or preclude action, in relation to any state which during the Second World War has been an enemy of any signatory to the present Charter, taken or authorized as a result of that war by the Governments having responsibility for such action.

CHAPTER XVIII

AMENDMENTS

Article 108

Amendments to the present Charter shall come into force for all Members of the United Nations when they have been adopted by a vote of two thirds of the members of the General Assembly and ratified in accordance with their respective constitutional processes by two thirds of the Members of the United Nations, including all the permanent members of the Security Council.

Article 109

1. A General Conference of the Members of the United Nations for the purpose of reviewing the present Charter may be held at a date and place to be fixed by a two-thirds vote of the members of the General Assembly and by a vote of any seven members of the Security Council. Each Member of the United Nations shall have one vote in the conference.

2. Any alteration of the present Charter recommended by a two-thirds vote of the conference shall take effect when ratified in accordance with their respective constitutional processes by two thirds of the Members of the United Nations including all the permanent members of the Security Council.

3. If such a conference has not been held before the tenth annual session of the General Assembly following the coming into force of the present Charter, the proposal to call such a conference shall be placed on the agenda of that session of the General Assembly, and the conference shall be held if so decided by a majority vote of the members of the General Assembly and by a vote of any seven members of the Security Council.

CHAPTER XIX

RATIFICATION AND SIGNATURE

Article 110

1. The present Charter shall be ratified by the signatory states in accordance with their respective constitutional processes.

2. The ratifications shall be deposited with the Government of the United States of America, which shall notify all the signatory states of each deposit as well as the Secretary-General of the Organization when he has been appointed.

3. The present Charter shall come into force upon the deposit of ratifications by the Republic of China, France, the Union of Soviet Socialist Republics, the United Kingdom of Great Britain and Northern Ireland, and the United States of America, and by a majority of the other signatory states. A protocol of the ratifications deposited shall thereupon be drawn up by the Government of the United States of America which shall communicate copies thereof to all the signatory states.

4. The states signatory to the present Charter which ratify it after it has come into force will become original Members of the United Nations on the date of the deposit of their respective ratifications.

Article 111

The present Charter, of which the Chinese, French, Russian, English, and Spanish texts are equally authentic, shall remain deposited in the archives of the Government of the United States of America. Duly certified copies thereof shall be transmitted by that Government to the Governments of the other signatory states.

IN FAITH WHEREOF the representatives of the Governments of the United Nations have signed the present Charter.

DONE at the city of San Francisco the twenty-sixth day of June, one thousand nine hundred and forty-five.

Appendix 2

STATUTE OF THE INTERNATIONAL
COURT OF JUSTICE

Article 1

The International Court of Justice established by the Charter of
the United Nations as the principal judicial organ of the United
Nations shall be constituted and shall function in accordance with the
provisions of the present Statute.

CHAPTER I

ORGANIZATION OF THE COURT

Article 2

The Court shall be composed of a body of independent judges,
elected regardless of their nationality from among persons of high
moral character, who possess the qualifications required in their respective countries for appointment to the highest judicial offices, or
are jurisconsults of recognized competence in international law.

Article 3

1. The Court shall consist of fifteen members, no two of whom may
be nationals of the same state.

2. A person who for the purposes of membership in the Court could
be regarded as a national of more than one state shall be deemed to
be a national of the one in which he ordinarily exercises civil and
political rights.

Article 4

1. The members of the Court shall be elected by the General Assembly and by the Security Council from a list of persons nominated by

the national groups in the Permanent Court of Arbitration, in accordance with the following provisions.

2. In the case of Members of the United Nations not represented in the Permanent Court of Arbitration, candidates shall be nominated by national groups appointed for this purpose by their governments under the same conditions as those prescribed for members of the Permanent Court of Arbitration by Article 44 of the Convention of The Hague of 1907 for the pacific settlement of international disputes.

3. The conditions under which a state which is a party to the present Statute but is not a Member of the United Nations may participate in electing the members of the Court shall, in the absence of a special agreement, be laid down by the General Assembly upon recommendation of the Security Council.

Article 5

1. At least three months before the date of the election, the Secretary-General of the United Nations shall address a written request to the members of the Permanent Court of Arbitration belonging to the states which are parties to the present Statute, and to the members of the national groups appointed under Article 4, paragraph 2, inviting them to undertake, within a given time, by national groups, the nomination of persons in a position to accept the duties of a member of the Court.

2. No group may nominate more than four persons, not more than two of whom shall be of their own nationality. In no case may the number of candidates nominated by a group be more than double the number of seats to be filled.

Article 6

Before making these nominations, each national group is recommended to consult its highest court of justice, its legal faculties and schools of law, and its national academies and national sections of international academies devoted to the study of law.

Article 7

1. The Secretary-General shall prepare a list in alphabetical order of all the persons thus nominated. Save as provided in Article 12, paragraph 2, these shall be the only persons eligible.

2. The Secretary-General shall submit this list to the General Assembly and to the Security Council.

Article 8

The General Assembly and the Security Council shall proceed independently of one another to elect the members of the Court.

Article 9

At every election, the electors shall bear in mind not only that the persons to be elected should individually possess the qualifications required, but also that in the body as a whole the representation of the main forms of civilization and of the principal legal systems of the world should be assured.

Article 10

1. Those candidates who obtain an absolute majority of votes in the General Assembly and in the Security Council shall be considered as elected.

2. Any vote of the Security Council, whether for the election of judges or for the appointment of members of the conference envisaged in Article 12, shall be taken without any distinction between permanent and non-permanent members of the Security Council.

3. In the event of more than one national of the same state obtaining an absolute majority of the votes both of the General Assembly and of the Security Council, the eldest of these only shall be considered as elected.

Article 11

If, after the first meeting held for the purpose of the election, one or more seats remain to be filled, a second and, if necessary, a third meeting shall take place.

Article 12

1. If, after the third meeting, one or more seats still remain unfilled, a joint conference consisting of six members, three appointed by the General Assembly and three by the Security Council, may be formed at any time at the request of either the General Assembly or the Security Council, for the purpose of choosing by the vote of an absolute

majority one name for each seat still vacant, to submit to the General Assembly and the Security Council for their respective acceptance.

2. If the joint conference is unanimously agreed upon any person who fulfils the required conditions, he may be included in its list, even though he was not included in the list of nominations referred to in Article 7.

3. If the joint conference is satisfied that it will not be successful in procuring an election, those members of the Court who have already been elected shall, within a period to be fixed by the Security Council, proceed to fill the vacant seats by selection from among those candidates who have obtained votes either in the General Assembly or in the Security Council.

4. In the event of an equality of votes among the judges, the eldest judge shall have a casting vote.

Article 13

1. The members of the Court shall be elected for nine years and may be re-elected; provided, however, that of the judges elected at the first election, the terms of five judges shall expire at the end of three years and the terms of five more judges shall expire at the end of six years.

2. The judges whose terms are to expire at the end of the above-mentioned initial periods of three and six years shall be chosen by lot to be drawn by the Secretary-General immediately after the first election has been completed.

3. The members of the Court shall continue to discharge their duties until their places have been filled. Though replaced, they shall finish any cases which they may have begun.

4. In the case of the resignation of a member of the Court, the resignation shall be addressed to the President of the Court for transmission to the Secretary-General. This last notification makes the place vacant.

Article 14

Vacancies shall be filled by the same method as that laid down for the first election, subject to the following provision: the Secretary-General shall, within one month of the occurrence of the vacancy, proceed to issue the invitations provided for in Article 5, and the date of the election shall be fixed by the Security Council.

Article 15

A member of the Court elected to replace a member whose term of office has not expired shall hold office for the remainder of his predecessor's term.

Article 16

1. No member of the Court may exercise any political or administrative function, or engage in any other occupation of a professional nature.

2. Any doubt on this point shall be settled by the decision of the Court.

Article 17

1. No member of the Court may act as agent, counsel, or advocate in any case.

2. No member may participate in the decision of any case in which he has previously taken part as agent, counsel, or advocate for one of the parties, or as a member of a national or international court, or of a commission of enquiry, or in any other capacity.

3. Any doubt on this point shall be settled by the decision of the Court.

Article 18

1. No member of the Court can be dismissed unless, in the unanimous opinion of the other members, he has ceased to fulfil the required conditions.

2. Formal notification thereof shall be made to the Secretary-General by the Registrar.

3. This notification makes the place vacant.

Article 19

The members of the Court, when engaged on the business of the Court, shall enjoy diplomatic privileges and immunities.

Article 20

Every member of the Court shall, before taking up his duties, make a solemn declaration in open court that he will exercise his powers impartially and conscientiously.

Article 21

1. The Court shall elect its President and Vice-President for three years; they may be re-elected.

2. The Court shall appoint its Registrar and may provide for the appointment of such other officers as may be necessary.

Article 22

1. The seat of the Court shall be established at The Hague. This, however, shall not prevent the Court from sitting and exercising its functions elsewhere whenever the Court considers it desirable.

2. The President and the Registrar shall reside at the seat of the Court.

Article 23

1. The Court shall remain permanently in session, except during the judicial vacations, the dates and duration of which shall be fixed by the Court.

2. Members of the Court are entitled to periodic leave, the dates and duration of which shall be fixed by the Court, having in mind the distance between The Hague and the home of each judge.

3. Members of the Court shall be bound, unless they are on leave or prevented from attending by illness or other serious reasons duly explained to the President, to hold themselves permanently at the disposal of the Court.

Article 24

1. If, for some special reason, a member of the Court considers that he should not take part in the decision of a particular case, he shall so inform the President.

2. If the President considers that for some special reason one of the members of the Court should not sit in a particular case, he shall give him notice accordingly.

3. If in any such case the member of the Court and the President disagree, the matter shall be settled by the decision of the Court.

Article 25

1. The full Court shall sit except when it is expressly provided otherwise in the present Statute.

2. Subject to the condition that the number of judges available to constitute the Court is not thereby reduced below eleven, the Rules of the Court may provide for allowing one or more judges, according to circumstances and in rotation, to be dispensed from sitting.

3. A quorum of nine judges shall suffice to constitute the Court.

Article 26

1. The Court may from time to time form one or more chambers, composed of three or more judges as the Court may determine, for dealing with particular categories of cases; for example, labor cases and cases relating to transit and communications.

2. The Court may at any time form a chamber for dealing with a particular case. The number of judges to constitute such a chamber shall be determined by the Court with the approval of the parties.

3. Cases shall be heard and determined by the chambers provided for in this Article if the parties so request.

Article 27

A judgment given by any of the chambers provided for in Articles 26 and 29 shall be considered as rendered by the Court.

Article 28

The chambers provided for in Articles 26 and 29 may, with the consent of the parties, sit and exercise their functions elsewhere than at The Hague.

Article 29

With a view to the speedy despatch of business, the Court shall form annually a chamber composed of five judges which, at the request of the parties, may hear and determine cases by summary procedure. In addition, two judges shall be selected for the purpose of replacing judges who find it impossible to sit.

Article 30

1. The Court shall frame rules for carrying out its functions. In particular, it shall lay down rules of procedure.

2. The Rules of the Court may provide for assessors to sit with the Court or with any of its chambers, without the right to vote.

Article 31

1. Judges of the nationality of each of the parties shall retain their right to sit in the case before the Court.

2. If the Court includes upon the Bench a judge of the nationality of one of the parties, any other party may choose a person to sit as judge. Such person shall be chosen preferably from among those persons who have been nominated as candidates as provided in Articles 4 and 5.

3. If the Court includes upon the Bench no judge of the nationality of the parties, each of these parties may proceed to choose a judge as provided in paragraph 2 of this Article.

4. The provisions of this Article shall apply to the case of Articles 26 and 29. In such cases, the President shall request one or, if necessary, two of the members of the Court forming the chamber to give place to the members of the Court of the nationality of the parties concerned, and, failing such, or if they are unable to be present, to the judges specially chosen by the parties.

5. Should there be several parties in the same interest, they shall, for the purpose of the preceding provisions, be reckoned as one party only. Any doubt upon this point shall be settled by the decision of the Court.

6. Judges chosen as laid down in paragraphs 2, 3, and 4 of this Article shall fulfil the conditions required by Articles 2, 17 (paragraph 2), 20, and 24 of the present Statute. They shall take part in the decision on terms of complete equality with their colleagues.

Article 32

1. Each member of the Court shall receive an annual salary.

2. The President shall receive a special annual allowance.

3. The Vice-President shall receive a special allowance for every day on which he acts as President.

4. The judges chosen under Article 31, other than members of the Court, shall receive compensation for each day on which they exercise their functions.

5. These salaries, allowances, and compensation shall be fixed by the General Assembly. They may not be decreased during the term of office.

6. The salary of the Registrar shall be fixed by the General Assembly on the proposal of the Court.

7. Regulations made by the General Assembly shall fix the conditions under which retirement pensions may be given to members of the Court and to the Registrar, and the conditions under which members of the Court and the Registrar shall have their traveling expenses refunded.

8. The above salaries, allowances, and compensation shall be free of all taxation.

Article 33

The expenses of the Court shall be borne by the United Nations in such a manner as shall be decided by the General Assembly.

CHAPTER II

COMPETENCE OF THE COURT

Article 34

1. Only states may be parties in cases before the Court.

2. The Court, subject to and in conformity with its Rules, may request of public international organizations information relevant to cases before it, and shall receive such information presented by such organizations on their own initiative.

3. Whenever the construction of the constituent instrument of a public international organization or of an international convention adopted thereunder is in question in a case before the Court, the Registrar shall so notify the public international organization concerned and shall communicate to it copies of all the written proceedings.

Article 35

1. The Court shall be open to the states parties to the present Statute.

2. The conditions under which the Court shall be open to other states shall, subject to the special provisions contained in treaties in force, be laid down by the Security Council, but in no case shall such conditions place the parties in a position of inequality before the Court.

3. When a state which is not a Member of the United Nations is a party to a case, the Court shall fix the amount which that party is to contribute towards the expenses of the Court. This provision shall not apply if such state is bearing a share of the expenses of the Court.

Article 36

1. The jurisdiction of the Court comprises all cases which the parties refer to it and all matters specially provided for in the Charter of the United Nations or in treaties and conventions in force.

2. The states parties to the present Statute may at any time declare that they recognize as compulsory *ipso facto* and without special agreement, in relation to any other state accepting the same obligation, the jurisdiction of the Court in all legal disputes concerning:

    a. the interpretation of a treaty;

    b. any question of international law;

    c. the existence of any fact which, if established, would constitute a breach of an international obligation;

    d. the nature or extent of the reparation to be made for the breach of an international obligation.

3. The declarations referred to above may be made unconditionally or on condition of reciprocity on the part of several or certain states, or for a certain time.

4. Such declarations shall be deposited with the Secretary-General of the United Nations, who shall transmit copies thereof to the parties to the Statute and to the Registrar of the Court.

5. Declarations made under Article 36 of the Statute of the Permanent Court of International Justice and which are still in force shall be deemed, as between the parties to the present Statute, to be acceptances of the compulsory jurisdiction of the International Court of Justice for the period which they still have to run and in accordance with their terms.

6. In the event of a dispute as to whether the Court has jurisdiction, the matter shall be settled by the decision of the Court.

Article 37

Whenever a treaty or convention in force provides for reference of a matter to a tribunal to have been instituted by the League of Nations, or to the Permanent Court of International Justice, the matter shall, as between the parties to the present Statute, be referred to the International Court of Justice.

Article 38

1. The Court, whose function is to decide in accordance with international law such disputes as are submitted to it, shall apply:

a. international conventions, whether general or particular, establishing rules expressly recognized by the contesting states;

b. international custom, as evidence of a general practice accepted as law;

c. the general principles of law recognized by civilized nations;

d. subject to the provisions of Article 59, judicial decisions and the teachings of the most highly qualified publicists of the various nations, as subsidiary means for the determination of rules of law.

2. This provision shall not prejudice the power of the Court to decide a case *ex aequo et bono,* if the parties agree thereto.

CHAPTER III

PROCEDURE

Article 39

1. The official languages of the Court shall be French and English. If the parties agree that the case shall be conducted in French, the judgment shall be delivered in French. If the parties agree that the case shall be conducted in English, the judgment shall be delivered in English.

2. In the absence of an agreement as to which language shall be employed, each party may, in the pleadings, use the language which it prefers; the decision of the Court shall be given in French and English. In this case the Court shall at the same time determine which of the two texts shall be considered as authoritative.

3. The Court shall, at the request of any party, authorize a language other than French or English to be used by that party.

Article 40

1. Cases are brought before the Court, as the case may be, either by the notification of the special agreement or by a written application addressed to the Registrar. In either case the subject of the dispute and the parties shall be indicated.

2. The Registrar shall forthwith communicate the application to all concerned.

3. He shall also notify the Members of the United Nations through the Secretary-General, and also any other states entitled to appear before the Court.

Article 41

1. The Court shall have the power to indicate, if it considers that circumstances so require, any provisional measures which ought to be taken to preserve the respective rights of either party.

2. Pending the final decision, notice of the measures suggested shall forthwith be given to the parties and to the Security Council.

Article 42

1. The parties shall be represented by agents.

2. They may have the assistance of counsel or advocates before the Court.

3. The agents, counsel, and advocates of parties before the Court shall enjoy the privileges and immunities necessary to the independent exercise of their duties.

Article 43

1. The procedure shall consist of two parts: written and oral.

2. The written proceedings shall consist of the communication to the Court and to the parties of memorials, counter-memorials and, if necessary, replies; also all papers and documents in support.

3. These communications shall be made through the Registrar, in the order and within the time fixed by the Court.

4. A certified copy of every document produced by one party shall be communicated to the other party.

5. The oral proceedings shall consist of the hearing by the Court of witnesses, experts, agents, counsel, and advocates.

Article 44

1. For the service of all notices upon persons other than the agents, counsel, and advocates, the Court shall apply direct to the government of the state upon whose territory the notice has to be served.

2. The same provision shall apply whenever steps are to be taken to procure evidence on the spot.

Article 45

The hearing shall be under the control of the President or, if he is unable to preside, of the Vice-President; if neither is able to preside, the senior judge present shall preside.

Article 46

The hearing in Court shall be public, unless the Court shall decide otherwise, or unless the parties demand that the public be not admitted.

Article 47

1. Minutes shall be made at each hearing and signed by the Registrar and the President.
2. These minutes alone shall be authentic.

Article 48

The Court shall make orders for the conduct of the case, shall decide the form and time in which each party must conclude its arguments, and make all arrangements connected with the taking of evidence.

Article 49

The Court may, even before the hearing begins, call upon the agents to produce any document or to supply any explanations. Formal note shall be taken of any refusal.

Article 50

The Court may, at any time, entrust any individual, body, bureau, commission, or other organization that it may select, with the task of carrying out an enquiry or giving an expert opinion.

Article 51

During the hearing any relevant questions are to be put to the witnesses and experts under the conditions laid down by the Court in the rules of procedure referred to in Article 30.

Article 52

After the Court has received the proofs and evidence within the time specified for the purpose, it may refuse to accept any further oral or written evidence that one party may desire to present unless the other side consents.

Article 53

1. Whenever one of the parties does not appear before the Court, or fails to defend its case, the other party may call upon the Court to decide in favor of its claim.

2. The Court must, before doing so, satisfy itself, not only that it has jurisdiction in accordance with Articles 36 and 37, but also that the claim is well founded in fact and law.

Article 54

1. When, subject to the control of the Court, the agents, counsel, and advocates have completed their presentation of the case, the President shall declare the hearing closed.

2. The Court shall withdraw to consider the judgment.

3. The deliberations of the Court shall take place in private and remain secret.

Article 55

1. All questions shall be decided by a majority of the judges present.

2. In the event of an equality of votes, the President or the judge who acts in his place shall have a casting vote.

Article 56

1. The judgment shall state the reasons on which it is based.

2. It shall contain the names of the judges who have taken part in the decision.

Article 57

If the judgment does not represent in whole or in part the unanimous opinion of the judges, any judge shall be entitled to deliver a separate opinion.

Article 58

The judgment shall be signed by the President and by the Registrar. It shall be read in open court, due notice having been given to the agents.

Article 59

The decision of the Court has no binding force except between the parties and in respect of that particular case.

Article 60

The judgment is final and without appeal. In the event of dispute as to the meaning or scope of the judgment. the Court shall construe it upon the request of any party.

Article 61

1. An application for revision of a judgment may be made only when it is based upon the discovery of some fact of such a nature as to be a decisive factor, which fact was, when the judgment was given, unknown to the Court and also to the party claiming revision, always provided that such ignorance was not due to negligence.

2. The proceedings for revision shall be opened by a judgment of the Court expressly recording the existence of the new fact, recognizing that it has such a character as to lay the case open to revision, and declaring the application admissible on this ground.

3. The Court may require previous compliance with the terms of the judgment before it admits proceedings in revision.

4. The application for revision must be made at latest within six months of the discovery of the new fact.

5. No application for revision may be made after the lapse of ten years from the date of the judgment.

Article 62

1. Should a state consider that it has an interest of a legal nature which may be affected by the decision in the case, it may submit a request to the Court to be permitted to intervene.

2. It shall be for the Court to decide upon this request.

Article 63

1. Whenever the construction of a convention to which states other than those concerned in the case are parties is in question, the Registrar shall notify all such states forthwith.

2. Every state so notified has the right to intervene in the proceedings; but if it uses this right, the construction given by the judgment will be equally binding upon it.

Article 64

Unless otherwise decided by the Court, each party shall bear its own costs.

Article 67

The Court shall deliver its advisory opinions in open court, notice having been given to the Secretary-General and to the representatives of Members of the United Nations, of other states and of international organizations immediately concerned.

Article 68

In the exercise of its advisory functions the Court shall further be guided by the provisions of the present Statute which apply in contentious cases to the extent to which it recognizes them to be applicable.

CHAPTER V

AMENDMENT

Article 69

Amendments to the present Statute shall be effected by the same procedure as is provided by the Charter of the United Nations for amendments to that Charter, subject however to any provisions which the General Assembly upon recommendation of the Security Council may adopt concerning the participation of states which are parties to the present Statute but are not Members of the United Nations.

Article 70

The Court shall have power to propose such amendments to the present Statute as it may deem necessary, through written communications to the Secretary-General, for consideration in conformity with the provisions of Article 69.

Appendix 3

THE FOURTEEN POINTS OF PRESIDENT WOODROW WILSON [1]

I. Open covenants of peace, openly arrived at, after which there shall be no private international understandings of any kind but diplomacy shall proceed always frankly and in the public view.

II. Absolute freedom of navigation upon the seas, outside territorial waters, alike in peace and in war, except as the seas may be closed in whole or in part by international action for the enforcement of international covenants.

III. The removal, so far as possible, of all economic barriers and the establishment of an equality of trade conditions among all the nations consenting to the peace and associating themselves for its maintenance.

IV. Adequate guarantees given and taken that national armaments will be reduced to the lowest point consistent with domestic safety.

V. A free, open-minded, and absolutely impartial adjustment of all colonial claims, based upon a strict observance of the principle that in determining all such questions of sovereignty the interests of the populations concerned must have equal weight with the equitable claims of the government whose title is to be determined.

. . . .

XIV. A general association of nations must be formed under specific covenants for the purpose of affording mutual guarantees of political independence and territorial integrity to great and small states alike.

[1] Address delivered at a joint session of the two houses of Congress, Jan. 8, 1918 (*Excerpt*), Ray Stannard Baker and William E. Dodd, *The Public Papers of Woodrow Wilson, War and Peace*, Vol. I, Harper, New York, 1926, pp. 159–161.

Appendix 4

COVENANT OF THE LEAGUE OF NATIONS
(Selected Provisions)

Article 2

The action of the League under this Covenant shall be effected through the instrumentality of an Assembly and of a Council, with a permanent Secretariat.

Article 4

4. The Council may deal at its meetings with any matter within the sphere of action of the League or affecting the peace of the world.

Article 8

1. The Members of the League recognize that the maintenance of peace requires the reduction of national armaments to the lowest point consistent with national safety and the enforcement by common action of international obligations.

2. The Council, taking account of the geographical situation and circumstances of each State, shall formulate plans for such reduction for the consideration and action of the several Governments.

3. Such plans shall be subject to reconsideration and revision at least every ten years.

4. After these plans shall have been adopted by the several Governments, the limits of armaments therein fixed shall not be exceeded without the concurrence of the Council.

5. The Members of the League agree that the manufacture by private enterprise of munitions and implements of war is open to grave objections. The Council shall advise how the evil effects attendant upon such manufacture can be prevented, due regard being had to the necessities of those Members of the League which are not able to manufacture the munitions and implements of war necessary for their safety.

6. The Members of the League undertake to interchange full and frank information as to the scale of their armaments, their military, naval and air programs and the condition of such of their industries as are adaptable to warlike purposes.

Article 9

A permanent Commission shall be constituted to advise the Council on the execution of the provisions of Articles 1 and 8 and on military, naval and air questions generally.

Article 10

The Members of the League undertake to respect and preserve as against external aggression the territorial integrity and existing political independence of all Members of the League. In case of any such aggression or in case of any threat or danger of such aggression the Council shall advise upon the means by which this obligation shall be fulfilled.

Article 11

1. Any war or threat of war, whether immediately affecting any of the Members of the League or not, is hereby declared a matter of concern to the whole League, and the League shall take any action that may be deemed wise and effectual to safeguard the peace of nations. In case any such emergency should arise the Secretary-General shall on the request of any Member of the League forthwith summon a meeting of the Council.

2. It is also declared to be the friendly right of each Member of the League to bring to the attention of the Assembly or of the Council any circumstance whatever affecting international relations which threatens to disturb international peace or the good understanding between nations upon which peace depends.

Article 12

1. The Members of the League agree that, if there should arise between them any dispute likely to lead to a rupture, they will submit the matter either to arbitration *or judicial settlement* or to inquiry by the Council, and they agree in no case to resort to war until three months after the award by the arbitrators *or the judicial decision,* or the report by the Council.

2. In any case under this Article the award of the arbitrators *or the judicial decision* shall be made within a reasonable time, and the report of the Council shall be made within six months after the submission of the dispute.

Article 13

1. The Members of the League agree that, whenever any dispute shall arise between them which they recognize to be suitable for submission to arbitration *or judicial settlement,* and which can not be satisfactorily settled by diplomacy, they will submit the whole subject-matter to arbitration *or judicial settlement.*

2. Disputes as to the interpretation of a treaty, as to any question of international law, as to the existence of any fact which, if established, would constitute a breach of any international obligation, or as to the extent and nature of the reparation to be made for any such breach, are declared to be among those which are generally suitable for submission to arbitration *or judicial settlement.*

3. *For the consideration of any such dispute, the court to which the case is referred shall be the Permanent Court of International Justice, established in accordance with Article 14, or any tribunal agreed on by the parties to the dispute or stipulated in any convention existing between them.*

4. The Members of the League agree that they will carry out in full good faith any award *or decision* that may be rendered, and that they will not resort to war against a Member of the League which complies therewith. In the event of any failure to carry out such an award *or decision,* the Council shall propose what steps should be taken to give effect thereto.

Article 14

The Council shall formulate and submit to the Members of the League for adoption plans for the establishment of a Permanent Court of International Justice. The Court shall be competent to hear and determine any dispute of an international character which the parties thereto submit to it. The Court may also give an advisory opinion upon any dispute or question referred to it by the Council or by the Assembly.

Article 15

1. If there should arise between Members of the League any dispute likely to lead to a rupture, which is not submitted to arbitration *or judicial settlement* in accordance with Article 13, the Members of the League agree that they will submit the matter to the Council. Any party to the dispute may effect such submission by giving notice of the existence of the dispute to the Secretary-General, who will make all necessary arrangements for a full investigation and consideration thereof.

2. For this purpose the parties to the dispute will communicate to the Secretary-General, as promptly as possible, statements of their case with all the relevant facts and papers, and the Council may forthwith direct the publication thereof.

3. The Council shall endeavor to effect a settlement of the dispute, and, if such efforts are successful, a statement shall be made public giving such facts and explanations regarding the dispute and the terms of settlement thereof as the Council may deem appropriate.

4. If the dispute is not thus settled, the Council either unanimously or by a majority vote shall make and publish a report containing a statement of the facts of the dispute and the recommendations which are deemed just and proper in regard thereto.

5. Any member of the League represented on the Council may make a public statement of the facts of the dispute and of its conclusions regarding the same.

6. If a report by the Council is unanimously agreed to by the Members thereof other than the Representatives of one or more of the parties to the dispute, the Members of the League agree that they will not go to war with any party to the dispute which complies with the recommendation of the report.

7. If the Council fails to reach a report which is unanimously agreed to by the members thereof, other than the Representatives of one or more of the parties to the dispute, the Members of the League reserve to themselves the right to take such action as they shall consider necessary for the maintenance of right and justice.

8. If the dispute between the parties is claimed by one of them, and is found by the Council, to arise out of a matter which by international law is solely within the domestic jurisdiction of that party, the Council shall so report, and shall make no recommendation as to its settlement.

9. The Council may in any case under this Article refer the dispute to the Assembly. The dispute shall be so referred at the request of either party to the dispute, provided that such request be made within fourteen days after the submission of the dispute to the Council.

10. In any case referred to the Assembly, all the provisions of this Article and of Article 12 relating to the action and powers of the Council shall apply to the action and powers of the Assembly, provided that a report made by the Assembly, if concurred in by the Representatives of those Members of the League represented on the Council and of a majority of the other Members of the League, exclusive in each

case of the Representatives of the parties to the dispute, shall have the same force as a report by the Council concurred in by all the members thereof other than the Representatives of one or more of the parties to the dispute.

Article 16

1. Should any Member of the League resort to war in disregard of its covenants under Articles 12, 13 or 15, it shall *ipso facto* be deemed to have committed an act of war against all other Members of the League, which hereby undertake immediately to subject it to the severance of all trade or financial relations, the prohibition of all intercourse between their nationals and the nationals of the covenant-breaking State, and the prevention of all financial, commercial or personal intercourse between the nationals of the covenant-breaking State and the nationals of any other State, whether a Member of the League or not.

2. It shall be the duty of the Council in such case to recommend to the several Governments concerned what effective military, naval or air force the Members of the League shall severally contribute to the armed forces to be used to protect the covenants of the League.

3. The Members of the League agree, further, that they will mutually support one another in the financial and economic measures which are taken under this Article, in order to minimize the loss and inconvenience resulting from the above measures, and that they will mutually support one another in resisting any special measures aimed at one of their number by the covenant-breaking State, and that they will take the necessary steps to afford passage through their territory to the forces of any of the Members of the League which are cooperating to protect the covenants of the League.

4. Any Member of the League which has violated any covenant of the League may be declared to be no longer a Member of the League by a vote of the Council concurred in by the Representatives of all the other members of the League represented thereon.

Article 22

1. To those colonies and territories which as a consequence of the late war have ceased to be under the sovereignty of the States which formerly governed them and which are inhabited by peoples not yet able to stand by themselves under the strenuous conditions of the modern world, there should be applied the principle that the well-being and development of such peoples form a sacred trust of civilization and that securities for the performance of this trust should be embodied in this Covenant.

2. The best method of giving practical effect to this principle is that the tutelage of such peoples should be intrusted to advanced nations who by reason of their resources, their experience or their geographical position can best undertake this responsibility, and who are willing to accept it, and that this tutelage should be exercised by them as Mandatories on behalf of the League.

3. The character of the mandate must differ according to the stage of the development of the people, the geographical situation of the territory, its economic conditions and other similar circumstances.

4. Certain communities formerly belonging to the Turkish Empire have reached a stage of development where their existence as independent nations can be provisionally recognized subject to the rendering of administrative advice and assistance by a Mandatory until such time as they are able to stand alone. The wishes of these communities must be a principal consideration in the selection of the Mandatory.

5. Other peoples, especially those of Central Africa, are at such a stage that the Mandatory must be responsible for the administration of the territory under conditions which will guarantee freedom of conscience and religion, subject only to the maintenance of public order and morals, the prohibition of abuses such as the slave trade, the arms traffic and the liquor traffic, and the prevention of the establishment of fortifications of military and naval bases and of military training of the natives for other than police purposes and the defense of territory, and will also secure equal opportunities for the trade and commerce of other Members of the League.

6. There are territories, such as Southwest Africa and certain of the South Pacific islands, which, owing to the sparseness of their population, or their small size, or their remoteness from the centers of civilization, or their geographical contiguity to the territory of the Mandatory, and other circumstances, can be best administered under the laws of the Mandatory as integral portions of its territory, subject to the safeguards above mentioned in the interests of the indigenous population.

7. In every case of mandate, the Mandatory shall render to the Council an annual report in reference to the territory committed to its charge.

8. The degree of authority, control or administration to be exercised by the Mandatory shall, if not previously agreed upon by the Members of the League, be explicitly defined in each case by the Council.

9. A permanent Commission shall be constituted to receive and examine the annual reports of the Mandatories and to advise the Council on all matters relating to the observance of the mandates.

Article 23

Subject to and in accordance with the provisions of international conventions existing or hereafter to be agreed upon, the Members of the League:

a. will endeavor to secure and maintain fair and humane conditions of labor for men, women and children, both in their own countries and in all countries to which their commercial and industrial relations extend, and for that purpose will establish and maintain the necessary international organizations;

b. undertake to secure just treatment of the native inhabitants of territories under their control;

c. will entrust the League with the general supervision over the execution of agreements with regard to traffic in women and children, and the traffic in opium and other dangerous drugs;

d. will entrust the League with the general supervision of the trade in arms and ammunition with the countries in which the control of this traffic is necessary in the common interest;

e. will make provision to secure and maintain freedom of communications and of transit and equitable treatment for the commerce of all Members of the League. In this connection, the special necessities of the regions devastated during the war of 1914–1918 shall be borne in mind;

f. will endeavor to take steps in matters of international concern for the prevention and control of disease.

Appendix 5

THE FOUR FREEDOMS [1]

In the future days, which we seek to make secure, we look forward to a world founded upon four essential human freedoms.

The first is freedom of speech and expression—everywhere in the world.

The second is freedom of every person to worship God in his way—everywhere in the world.

The third is freedom from want—which, translated into world terms, means economic understandings which will secure to every nation a healthy peacetime life for its inhabitants—everywhere in the world.

The fourth is freedom from fear—which translated into world terms, means a world-wide reduction of armaments to such a point and in such a thorough fashion that no nation will be in a position to commit an act of physical aggression against any neighbor—anywhere in the world.

[1] *Annual Message of the President to the Congress,* Jan. 6, 1941 (*Excerpt*), Senate Document No. 188, 77th Congress, 2d Session, pp. 86–87.

Appendix 7

THE UNITED NATIONS DECLARATION, JANUARY 1, 1942 [1]

A joint declaration by the United States of America, the United Kingdom of Great Britain and Northern Ireland, the Union of Soviet Socialist Republics, China, Australia, Belgium, Canada, Costa Rica, Cuba, Czechoslovakia, Dominican Republic, El Salvador, Greece, Guatemala, Haiti, Honduras, India, Luxembourg, Netherlands, New Zealand, Nicaragua, Norway, Panama, Poland, South Africa, Yugoslavia.

The Governments signatory hereto,

Having subscribed to a common program of purposes and principles embodied in the Joint Declaration of the President of the United States of America and the Prime Minister of the United Kingdom of Great Britain and Northern Ireland dated August 14, 1941, known as the Atlantic Charter,

Being convinced that complete victory over their enemies is essential to defend life, liberty, independence and religious freedom, and to preserve human rights and justice in their own lands as well as in other lands, and that they are now engaged in a common struggle against savage and brutal forces seeking to subjugate the world, declare:

(1) Each Government pledges itself to employ its full resources, military or economic, against those members of the Tripartite Pact and its adherents with which such government is at war.

(2) Each Government pledges itself to cooperate with the Governments signatory hereto and not to make a separate armistice or peace with the enemies.

The foregoing declaration may be adhered to by other nations which are, or which may be, rendering material assistance and contributions in the struggle for victory over Hitlerism.

[1] U.S. Department of State Publication 1732, United States Executive Agreement Series 236, Washington, D.C., 1942.

Appendix 8

THE MOSCOW DECLARATION ON GENERAL SECURITY, NOVEMBER 1, 1943 [1]

The Governments of the United States of America, the United Kingdom, the Soviet Union and China: united in their determination, in accordance with the Declaration by the United Nations of January 1, 1942, and subsequent declarations, to continue hostilities against those Axis powers with which they respectively are at war until such powers have laid down their arms on the basis of unconditional surrender; conscious of their responsibility to secure the liberation of themselves and the peoples allied with them from the menace of aggression; recognizing the necessity of ensuring a rapid and orderly transition from war to peace and of establishing and maintaining international peace and security with the least diversion of the world's human and economic resources for armaments; jointly declare:

1. That their united action, pledged for the prosecution of the war against their respective enemies, will be continued for the organization and maintenance of peace and security.

2. That those of them at war with a common enemy will act together in all matters relating to the surrender and disarmament of that enemy.

3. That they will take all measures deemed by them to be necessary to provide against any violation of the terms imposed upon the enemy.

4. That they recognize the necessity of establishing at the earliest practicable date a general international organization, based on the principle of the sovereign equality of all peace-loving states, and open to membership by all such states, large and small, for the maintenance of international peace and security.

5. That for the purpose of maintaining international peace and security pending the reestablishment of law and order and the inauguration of a system of general security, they will consult with one another and as occasion requires with other members of the United Nations with a view to joint action on behalf of the community of nations.

6. That after the termination of hostilities they will not employ their military forces within the territories of other states except for the purposes envisaged in this declaration and after joint consultation.

7. That they will confer and co-operate with one another and with other members of the United Nations to bring about a practicable general agreement with respect to the regulation of armaments in the post-war period.

[1] *Department of State Bulletin*, Vol. IX, pp. 307 *ff*.

Appendix 9

THE TEHRAN DECLARATION OF THE THREE POWERS, DECEMBER 1, 1943 [1]

We—the President of the United States, the Prime Minister of Great Britain, and the Premier of the Soviet Union, have met these four days past, in this, the Capital of our Ally, Iran, and have shaped and confirmed our common policy.

We express our determination that our nations shall work together in war and in the peace that will follow.

As to war—our military staffs have joined in our round table discussions, and we have concerted our plans for the destruction of the German forces. We have reached complete agreement as to the scope and timing of the operations to be undertaken from the east, west and south.

The common understanding which we have here reached guarantees that victory will be ours.

And as to peace—we are sure that our concord will win an enduring Peace. We recognize fully the supreme responsibility resting upon us and all the United Nations to make a peace which will command the goodwill of the overwhelming mass of the peoples of the world and banish the scourge and terror of war for many generations.

With our Diplomatic advisors we have surveyed the problems of the future. We shall seek the cooperation and active participation of all nations, large and small, whose peoples in heart and mind are dedicated, as are our own peoples, to the elimination of tyranny and slavery, oppression and intolerance. We will welcome them, as they may choose to come, into a world family of Democratic Nations.

No power on earth can prevent our destroying the German armies by land, their U Boats by sea, and their war plants from the air.

Our attack will be relentless and increasing.

Emerging from these cordial conferences we look with confidence to the day when all peoples of the world may live free lives, untouched by tyranny, and according to their varying desires and their own consciences.

We came here with hope and determination. We leave here, friends in fact, in spirit and in purpose.

ROOSEVELT, CHURCHILL AND STALIN

[1] *Toward the Peace—Documents,* U.S. Department of State Publication 2298, pp. 15-16.

Appendix 10

(DUMBARTON OAKS) PROPOSALS FOR THE ESTABLISHMENT OF A GENERAL INTERNATIONAL ORGANIZATION [1]

There should be established an international organization under the title of The United Nations, the Charter of which should contain provisions necessary to give effect to the proposals which follow.

CHAPTER I. PURPOSES

The purpose of the Organization should be:

1. To maintain international peace and security; and to that end to take effective collective measures for the prevention and removal of threats to the peace and the suppression of acts of aggression or other breaches of the peace, and to bring about by peaceful means adjustment or settlement of international disputes which may lead to a breach of the peace;

2. To develop friendly relations among nations and to take other appropriate measures to strengthen universal peace;

3. To achieve international cooperation in the solution of international economic, social and other humanitarian problems; and

4. To afford a center for harmonizing the actions of nations in the achievement of these common ends.

CHAPTER II. PRINCIPLES

In pursuit of the purposes mentioned in Chapter I the Organization and its members should act in accordance with the following principles:

1. The Organization is based on the principle of the sovereign equality of all peace-loving states.

2. All members of the Organization undertake, in order to ensure to all of them the rights and benefits resulting from membership in the Organization, to fulfill the obligations assumed by them in accordance with the Charter.

3. All members of the Organization shall settle their disputes by peaceful means in such a manner that international peace and security are not endangered.

4. All members of the Organization shall refrain in their international relations

[1] The United Nations Conference on International Organization. *Selected Documents,* U.S. Department of State Publication 2490, Conference Series, 83, pp. 87*ff.*

from the threat or use of force in any manner inconsistent with the purposes of the Organization.

5. All members of the Organization shall give every assistance to the Organization in any action undertaken by it in accordance with the provisions of the Charter.

6. All members of the Organization shall refrain from giving assistance to any state against which preventive or enforcement action is being undertaken by the Organization.

The Organization should ensure that states not members of the Organization act in accordance with these principles so far as may be necessary for the maintenance of international peace and security.

CHAPTER III. MEMBERSHIP

1. Membership of the Organization should be open to all peace-loving states.

CHAPTER IV. PRINCIPAL ORGANS

1. The Organization should have as its principal organs:
   a. A General Assembly;
   b. A Security Council;
   c. An international court of justice; and
   d. A Secretariat

2. The Organization should have such subsidiary agencies as may be found necessary.

CHAPTER V. THE GENERAL ASSEMBLY

Section A. Composition

All members of the Organization should be members of the General Assembly and should have a number of representatives to be specified in the Charter.

Section B. Functions and Powers

1. The General Assembly should have the right to consider the general principles of cooperation in the maintenance of international peace and security, including the principles governing disarmament and the regulation of armaments; to discuss any questions relating to the maintenance of international peace and security brought before it by any member or members of the Organization or by the Security Council; and to make recommendations with regard to any such principles or questions. Any such questions on which action is necessary should be referred to the Security Council by the General Assembly either before or after discussion. The General Assembly should not on its own initiative make recommendations on any matter relating to the maintenance of international peace and security which is being dealt with by the Security Council.

2. The General Assembly should be empowered to admit new members to the organization upon recommendation of the Security Council.

3. The General Assembly should, upon recommendation of the Security Council, be empowered to suspend from the exercise of any rights or privileges of membership any member of the Organization against which preventive or enforcement action shall have been taken by the Security Council. The exercise of the rights and

privileges thus suspended may be restored by decision of the Security Council. The General Assembly should be empowered, upon recommendation of the Security Council, to expel from the Organization any member of the Organization which persistently violates the principles contained in the Charter.

4. The General Assembly should elect the non-permanent members of the Security Council and the members of the Economic and Social Council provided for in Chapter IX. It should be empowered to elect, upon recommendation of the Security Council, the Secretary-General of the Organization. It should perform such functions in relation to the election of the judges of the international court of justice as may be conferred upon it by the statute of the court.

5. The General Assembly should apportion the expenses among the members of the Organization and should be empowered to approve the budgets of the Organization.

6. The General Assembly should initiate studies and make recommendations for the purpose of promoting international cooperation in political, economic and social fields and of adjusting situations likely to impair the general welfare.

7. The General Assembly should make recommendations for the coordination of the policies of international economic, social and other specialized agencies brought into relation with the Organization in accordance with agreements between such agencies and the Organization.

8. The General Assembly should receive and consider annual and special reports from the Security Council and reports from other bodies of the Organization.

Section C. Voting

1. Each member of the Organization should have one vote in the General Assembly.

2. Important decisions of the General Assembly, including recommendations with respect to the maintenance of international peace and security; election of members of the Security Council; election of members of the Economic and Social Council; admission of members, suspension of the exercise of the rights and privileges of members, and expulsion of members; and budgetary questions, should be made by a two-thirds majority of those present and voting. On other questions, including the determination of additional categories of questions to be decided by a two-thirds majority, the decisions of the General Assembly should be made by a simple majority vote.

Section D. Procedure

1. The General Assembly should meet in regular annual sessions and in such special sessions as occasion may require.

2. The General Assembly should adopt its own rules of procedure and elect its President for each session.

3. The General Assembly should be empowered to set up such bodies and agencies as it may deem necessary for the performance of its functions.

CHAPTER VI. THE SECURITY COUNCIL

Section A. Composition

The Security Council should consist of one representative of each of eleven members of the Organization. Representatives of the United States of America, the

United Kingdom of Great Britain and Northern Ireland, the Union of Soviet Socialist Republics, the Republic of China, and, in due course, France, should have permanent seats. The General Assembly should elect six states to fill the non-permanent seats. These six states should be elected for a term of two years, three retiring each year. They should not be immediately eligible for reelection. In the first election of the non-permanent members three should be chosen by the General Assembly for one-year terms and three for two-year terms.

Section B. Principal Functions and Powers

1. In order to ensure prompt and effective action by the Organization, members of the Organization should by the Charter confer on the Security Council primary responsibility for the maintenance of international peace and security and should agree that in carrying out these duties under this responsibility it should act on their behalf.

2. In discharging these duties the Security Council should act in accordance with the purposes and principles of the Organization.

3. The specific powers conferred on the Security Council in order to carry out these duties are laid down in Chapter VIII.

4. All members of the Organization should obligate themselves to accept the decisions of the Security Council and to carry them out in accordance with the provisions of the Charter.

5. In order to promote the establishment and maintenance of international peace and security with the least diversion of the world's human and economic resources for armaments, the Security Council, with the assistance of the Military Staff Committee referred to in Chapter VIII, Section B, paragraph 9, should have the responsibility for formulating plans for the establishment of a system of regulation of armaments for submission to the members of the Organization.

Section C. Voting

(Note.—The question of voting procedure in the Security Council is still under consideration.) [Agreed upon at the Yalta Conference. See Appendix 11 for text.]

Section D. Procedure

1. The Security Council should be so organized as to be able to function continuously and each state member of the Security Council should be permanently represented at the headquarters of the Organization. It may hold meetings at such other places as in its judgment may best facilitate its work. There should be periodic meetings at which each state member of the Security Council could if it so desired be represented by a member of the government or some other special representative.

2. The Security Council should be empowered to set up such bodies or agencies as it may deem necessary for the performance of its functions including regional sub-committees of the Military Staff Committee.

3. The Security Council should adopt its own rules of procedure, including the method of selecting its President.

4. Any member of the Organization should participate in the discussion of any question brought before the Security Council whenever the Security Council considers that the interests of that member of the Organization are specially affected.

5. Any member of the Organization not having a seat on the Security Council and any state not a member of the Organization, if it is a party to a dispute under con-

sideration by the Security Council, should be invited to participate in the discussion relating to the dispute.

CHAPTER VII. AN INTERNATIONAL COURT OF JUSTICE

1. There should be an international court of justice which should constitute the principal judicial organ of the Organization.

2. The court should be constituted and should function in accordance with a statute which should be annexed to and be a part of the Charter of the Organization.

3. The statute of the court of international justice should be either (a) the Statute of the Permanent Court of International Justice, continued in force with such modifications as may be desirable or (b) a new statute in the preparation of which the Statute of the Permanent Court of International Justice should be used as a basis.

4. All members of the Organization should *ipso facto* be parties to the statute of the international court of justice.

5. Conditions under which states not members of the Organization may become parties to the statute of the international court of justice should be determined in each case by the General Assembly upon recommendation of the Security Council.

CHAPTER VIII. ARRANGEMENTS FOR THE MAINTENANCE OF INTERNATIONAL PEACE AND SECURITY INCLUDING PREVENTION AND SUPPRESSION OF AGGRESSION

Section A.   Pacific Settlement of Disputes

1. The Security Council should be empowered to investigate any dispute, or any situation which may lead to international friction or give rise to a dispute, in order to determine whether its continuance is likely to endanger the maintenance of international peace and security.

2. Any state, whether member of the Organization or not, may bring any such dispute or situation to the attention of the General Assembly or of the Security Council

3. The parties to any dispute the continuance of which is likely to endanger the maintenance of international peace and security should obligate themselves, first of all, to seek a solution by negotiation, mediation, conciliation, arbitration, or judicial settlement, or other peaceful means of their own choice. The Security Council should call upon the parties to settle their dispute by such means.

4. If, nevertheless, parties to a dispute of the nature referred to in paragraph 3 above fail to settle it by the means indicated in that paragraph, they should obligate themselves to refer it to the Security Council. The Security Council should in each case decide whether or not the continuance of the particular dispute is in fact likely to endanger the maintenance of international peace and security, and, accordingly, whether the Security Council should deal with the dispute, and, if so, whether it should take action under paragraph 5.

5. The Security Council should be empowered, at any stage of a dispute of the nature referred to in paragraph 3 above, to recommend appropriate procedures or methods of adjustment.

6. Justiciable disputes should normally be referred to the international court of justice. The Security Council should be empowered to refer to the court, for advice, legal questions connected with other disputes.

7. The provisions of paragraphs 1 to 6 of Section A should not apply to situations

or disputes arising out of matters which by international law are solely within the domestic jurisdiction of the state concerned.

Section B.   Determination of Threats to the Peace or Acts of Aggression and Action with Respect Thereto

1. Should the Security Council deem that a failure to settle a dispute in accordance with procedures indicated in paragraph 3 of Section A, or in accordance with its recommendations made under paragraph 5 of Section A, constitutes a threat to the maintenance of international peace and security, it should take any measures necessary for the maintenance of international peace and security in accordance with the purposes and principles of the Organization.

2. In general the Security Council should determine the existence of any threat to the peace, breach of the peace or act of aggression and should make recommendations or decide upon the measures to be taken to maintain or restore peace and security.

3. The Security Council should be empowered to determine what diplomatic, economic, or other measures not involving the use of armed force should be employed to give effect to its decisions, and to call upon members of the Organization to apply such measures.   Such measures may include complete or partial interruption of rail, sea, air, postal, telegraphic, radio and other means of communication and the severance of diplomatic and economic relations.

4. Should the Security Council consider such measures to be inadequate, it should be empowered to take such action by air, naval or land forces as may be necessary to maintain or restore international peace and security.   Such action may include demonstrations, blockade and other operations by air, sea or land forces of members of the Organization.

5. In order that all members of the Organization should contribute to the maintenance of international peace and security, they should undertake to make available to the Security Council, on its call and in accordance with a special agreement or agreements concluded among themselves, armed forces, facilities and assistance necessary for the purpose of maintaining international peace and security.   Such agreement or agreements should govern the numbers and types of forces and the nature of the facilities and assistance to be provided.   The special agreement or agreements should be negotiated as soon as possible and should in each case be subject to approval by the Security Council and to ratification by the signatory states in accordance with their constitutional processes.

6. In order to enable urgent military measures to be taken by the Organization there should be held immediately available by the members of the Organization national air force contingents for combined international enforcement action.   The strength and degree of readiness of these contingents and plans for their combined action should be determined by the Security Council with the assistance of the Military Staff Committee within the limits laid down in the special agreement or agreements referred to in paragraph 5 above.

7. The action required to carry out the decisions of the Security Council for the maintenance of international peace and security should be taken by all the members of the Organization in cooperation or by some of them as the Security Council may determine.   This undertaking should be carried out by the members of the Or-

ganization by their own action and through action of the appropriate specialized organizations and agencies of which they are members.

8. Plans for the application of armed force should be made by the Security Council with the assistance of the Military Staff Committee referred to in paragraph 9 below.

9. There should be established a Military Staff Committee the functions of which should be to advise and assist the Security Council on all questions relating to the Security Council's military requirements for the maintenance of international peace and security, to the employment and command of forces placed at its disposal, to the regulation of armaments, and to possible disarmament. It should be responsible under the Security Council for the strategic direction of any armed forces placed at the disposal of the Security Council. The Committee should be composed of the Chiefs of Staff of the permanent members of the Security Council or their representatives. Any member of the Organization not permanently represented on the Committee should be invited by the Committee to be associated with it when the efficient discharge of the Committee's responsibilities requires that such a state should participate in its work. Questions of command of forces should be worked out subsequently.

10. The members of the Organization should join in affording mutual assistance in carrying out the measures decided upon by the Security Council.

11. Any state, whether a member of the Organization or not, which finds itself confronted with special economic problems arising from the carrying out of measures which have been decided upon by the Security Council should have the right to consult the Security Council in regard to a solution of those problems.

Section C. Regional Arrangements

1. Nothing in the Charter should preclude the existence of regional arrangements or agencies for dealing with such matters relating to the maintenance of international peace and security as are appropriate for regional action, provided such arrangements or agencies and their activities are consistent with the purposes and principles of the Organization. The Security Council should encourage settlement of local disputes through such regional arrangements or by such regional agencies, either on the initiative of the states concerned or by reference from the Security Council.

2. The Security Council should, where appropriate, utilize such arrangements or agencies for enforcement action under its authority, but no enforcement action should be taken under regional arrangements or by regional agencies without the authorization of the Security Council.

3. The Security Council should at all times be kept fully informed of activities undertaken or in contemplation under regional arrangements or by regional agencies for the maintenance of international peace and security.

CHAPTER IX. ARRANGEMENTS FOR INTERNATIONAL
ECONOMIC AND SOCIAL COOPERATION

Section A. Purpose and Relationships

1. With a view to the creation of conditions of stability and well-being which are necessary for peaceful and friendly relations among nations, the Organization should facilitate solutions of international economic, social and other humanitarian problems and promote respect for human rights and fundamental freedoms. Responsi-

bility for the discharge of this function should be vested in the General Assembly, and, under the authority of the General Assembly, in an Economic and Social Council.

2. The various specialized economic, social and other organizations and agencies would have responsibilities in their respective fields as defined in their statutes. Each such organization or agency should be brought into relationship with the Organization on terms to be determined by agreement between the Economic and Social Council and the appropriate authorities of the specialized organization or agency, subject to approval by the General Assembly.

Section B. Composition and Voting

The Economic and Social Council should consist of representatives of eighteen members of the Organization. The states to be represented for this purpose should be elected by the General Assembly for terms of three years. Each such state should have one representative, who should have one vote. Decisions of the Economic and Social Council should be taken by simple majority vote of those present and voting.

Section C. Functions and Powers of the Economic and Social Council

1. The Economic and Social Council should be empowered:
   a. to carry out, within the scope of its functions, recommendations of the General Assembly;
   b. to make recommendations, on its own initiative, with respect to international economic, social and other humanitarian matters;
   c. to receive and consider reports from the economic, social and other organizations or agencies brought into relationship with the Organization, and to coordinate their activities through consultations with, and recommendations to, such organizations or agencies;
   d. to examine the administrative budgets of such specialized organizations or agencies with a view to making recommendations to the organizations or agencies concerned;
   e. to enable the Secretary-General to provide information to the Security Council;
   f. to assist the Security Council upon its request; and
   g. to perform such other functions within the general scope of its competence as may be assigned to it by the General Assembly.

Section D. Organization and Procedure

1. The Economic and Social Council should set up an economic commission, a social commission, and such other commissions as may be required. These commissions should consist of experts. There should be a permanent staff which should constitute a part of the Secretariat of the Organization.

2. The Economic and Social Council should make suitable arrangements for representatives of the specialized organizations or agencies to participate without vote in its deliberations and in those of the commissions established by it.

3. The Economic and Social Council should adopt its own rules of procedure and the method of selecting its President.

Chapter X. The Secretariat

1. There should be a Secretariat comprising a Secretary-General and such staff as may be required. The Secretary-General should be the chief administrative officer of the Organization. He should be elected by the General Assembly, on recommendation of the Security Council, for such term and under such conditions as are specified in the Charter.

2. The Secretary-General should act in that capacity in all meetings of the General Assembly, of the Security Council, and of the Economic and Social Council and should make an annual report to the General Assembly on the work of the Organization.

3. The Secretary-General should have the right to bring to the attention of the Security Council any matter which in his opinion may threaten international peace and security.

Chapter XI. Amendments

Amendments should come into force for all members of the Organization, when they have been adopted by a vote of two-thirds of the members of the General Assembly and ratified in accordance with their respective constitutional processes by the members of the Organization having permanent membership on the Security Council and by a majority of the other members of the Organization.

Chapter XII. Transitional Arrangements

1. Pending the coming into force of the special agreement or agreements referred to in Chapter VIII, Section B, paragraph 5, and in accordance with the provisions of paragraph 5 of the Four-Nation Declaration, signed at Moscow, October 30, 1943, the states parties to that Declaration should consult with one another and as occasion arises with other members of the Organization with a view to such joint action on behalf of the Organization as may be necessary for the purpose of maintaining international peace and security.

2. No provision of the Charter should preclude action taken or authorized in relation to enemy states as a result of the present war by the Governments having responsibility for such action.

Note

In addition to the question of voting procedure in the Security Council referred to in Chapter VI, several other questions are still under consideration.

Washington, D.C.
October 7, 1944

Appendix 11

YALTA AGREEMENTS ON WORLD ORGANIZATION, FEBRUARY 11, 1945 [1]

The Crimea Conference of the Heads of the Governments of the United States of America, the United Kingdom, and the Union of Soviet Socialist Republics which took place from February 4th to 11th came to the following conclusions:

I. World Organisation

It was decided:

(1) that a United Nations Conference on the proposed world organisation should be summoned for Wednesday, 25th April, 1945, and should be held in the United States of America.

(2) the Nations to be invited to this Conference should be:

(a) the United Nations as they existed on the 8th February, 1945; and

(b) such of the Associated Nations as have declared war on the common enemy by 1st March, 1945. (For this purpose by the term "Associated Nation" was meant the eight Associated Nations and Turkey). When the Conference on World Organization is held, the delegates of the United Kingdom and United States of America will support a proposal to admit to original membership two Soviet Socialist Republics, i.e. the Ukraine and White Russia.

(3) that the United States Government on behalf of the Three Powers should consult the Government of China and the French Provisional Government in regard to decisions taken at the present Conference concerning the proposed World Organisation.

(4) that the text of the invitation to be issued to all the nations which would take part in the United Nations Conference should be as follows:

Invitation

"The Government of the United States of America, on behalf of itself and of the Governments of the United Kingdom, the Union of Soviet Socialist Republics, and the Republic of China and of the Provisional Government of the French Republic, invite the Government of —— to send representatives to a Conference of the United Nations to be held on 25th April, 1945, or soon thereafter, at San Francisco in the United States of America to prepare a Charter for a General International Organisation for the maintenance of international peace and security.

[1] U.S. Department of State Press Release 239, Mar. 24, 1947.

"The above named governments suggest that the Conference consider as affording a basis for such a Charter the Proposals for the Establishment of a General International Organisation, which were made public last October as a result of the Dumbarton Oaks Conference, and which have now been supplemented by the following provisions for Section C of Chapter VI:

" 'C. Voting

" '1. Each member of the Security Council should have one vote.

" '2. Decisions of the Security Council on procedural matters should be made by an affirmative vote of seven members.

" '3. Decisions of the Security Council on all other matters should be made by an affirmative vote of seven members including the concurring votes of the permanent members; provided that, in decisions under Chapter VIII, Section A and under the second sentence of paragraph 1 of Chapter VIII, Section C, a party to a dispute should abstain from voting.'

"Further information as to arrangements will be transmitted subsequently.

"In the event that the Government of —— desires in advance of the Conference to present views or comments concerning the proposals, the Government of the United States of America will be pleased to transmit such views and comments to the other participating Governments."

TERRITORIAL TRUSTEESHIP

It was agreed that the five Nations which will have permanent seats on the Security Council should consult each other prior to the United Nations Conference on the question of territorial trusteeship.

The acceptance of this recommendation is subject to its being made clear that territorial trusteeship will only apply to (a) existing mandates of the League of Nations; (b) territories detached from the enemy as a result of the present war; (c) any other territory which might voluntarily be placed under trusteeship; and (d) no discussion of actual territories is contemplated at the forthcoming United Nations Conference or in the preliminary consultations, and it will be a matter for subsequent agreement which territories within the above categories will be placed under trusteeship.

Appendix 12

STATEMENT BY THE DELEGATIONS OF THE FOUR SPONSORING GOVERNMENTS ON VOTING PROCEDURE IN THE SECURITY COUNCIL, JUNE 7, 1945 [1]

Specific questions covering the voting procedure in the Security Council have been submitted by a Sub-Committee of the Conference Committee on Structure and Procedures of the Security Council to the Delegations of the four Governments sponsoring the Conference—the United States of America, the United Kingdom of Great Britain and Northern Ireland, the Union of Soviet Socialist Republics, and the Republic of China. In dealing with these questions, the four Delegations desire to make the following statement of their general attitude towards the whole question of unanimity of permanent members in the decisions of the Security Council.

Part I

1. The Yalta voting formula recognizes that the Security Council, in discharging its responsibilities for the maintenance of international peace and security, will have two broad groups of functions. Under Chapter VIII, the Council will have to make decisions which involve its taking direct measures in connection with settlement of disputes, adjustment of situations likely to lead to disputes, determination of threats to the peace, removal of threats to the peace, and suppression of breaches of the peace. It will also have to make decisions which do not involve the taking of such measures. The Yalta formula provides that the second of these two groups of decisions will be governed by a procedural vote—that is, the vote of any seven members. The first group of decisions will be governed by a qualified vote—that is, the vote of seven members, including the concurring votes of the five permanent members, subject to the proviso that in decisions under Section A and a part of Section C of Chapter VIII parties to a dispute shall abstain from voting.

2. For example, under the Yalta formula a procedural vote will govern the decisions made under the entire Section D of Chapter VI. This means that the Council will, by a vote of any seven of its members, adopt or alter its rules of procedure;

[1] *A Decade of American Foreign Policy*, Senate Document No. 123, 81st Congress, 1st Session, pp. 1057–1060.

determine the method of selecting its President; organize itself in such a way as to be able to function continuously; select the times and places of its regular and special meetings; establish such bodies or agencies as it may deem necessary for the performance of its functions; invite a member of the Organization not represented on the Council to participate in its discussions when that member's interests are specially affected; and invite any state when it is a party to a dispute being considered by the Council to participate in the discussion relating to that dispute.

3. Further, no individual member of the Council can alone prevent consideration and discussion by the Council of a dispute or situation brought to its attention under paragraph 2, Section A, Chapter VIII. Nor can parties to such dispute be prevented by these means from being heard by the Council. Likewise, the requirement for unanimity of the permanent members cannot prevent any member of the Council from reminding the members of the Organization of their general obligations assumed under the Charter as regards peaceful settlement of international disputes.

4. Beyond this point, decisions and actions by the Security Council may well have major political consequences and may even initiate a chain of events which might, in the end, require the Council under its responsibilities to invoke measures of enforcement under Section B, Chapter VIII. This chain of events begins when the Council decides to make an investigation, or determines that the time has come to call upon states to settle their differences, or makes recommendations to the parties. It is to such decisions and actions that unanimity of the permanent members applies, with the important proviso, referred to above, for abstention from voting by parties to a dispute.

5. To illustrate: in ordering an investigation, the Council has to consider whether the investigation—which may involve calling for reports, hearing witnesses, dispatching a commission of inquiry, or other means—might not further aggravate the situation. After investigation, the Council must determine whether the continuance of the situation or dispute would be likely to endanger international peace and security. If it so determines, the Council would be under obligation to take further steps. Similarly, the decision to make recommendations, even when all parties request it to do so, or to call upon parties to a dispute to fulfill their obligations under the Charter, might be the first step on a course of action from which the Security Council could withdraw only at the risk of failing to discharge its responsibilities.

6. In appraising the significance of the vote required to take such decisions or actions, it is useful to make comparison with the requirements of the League Covenant with reference to decisions of the League Council. Substantive decisions of the League of Nations Council could be taken only by the unanimous vote of all its members, whether permanent or not, with the exception of parties to a dispute under Article XV of the League Covenant. Under Article XI, under which most of the disputes brought before the League were dealt with and decisions to make investigations taken, the unanimity rule was invariably interpreted to include even the votes of the parties to a dispute.

7. The Yalta voting formula substitutes for the rule of complete unanimity of the League Council a system of qualified majority voting in the Security Council. Under this system nonpermanent members of the Security Council individually would have no veto. As regards the permanent members, there is no question

under the Yalta formula of investing them with a new right, namely, the right to veto, a right which the permanent members of the League Council always had. The formula proposed for the taking of action in the Security Council by a majority of seven would make the operation of the Council less subject to obstruction than was the case under the League of Nations rule of complete unanimity.

8. It should also be remembered that under the Yalta formula the five major powers could not act by themselves, since even under the unanimity requirement any decisions of the Council would have to include the concurring votes of at least two of the non-permanent members. In other words, it would be possible for five non-permanent members as a group to exercise a "veto." It is not to be assumed, however, that the permanent members, any more than the non-permanent members, would use their veto power willfully to obstruct the operation of the Council.

9. In view of the primary responsibilities of the permanent members, they could not be expected, in the present condition of the world, to assume the obligation to act in so serious a matter as the maintenance of international peace and security in consequence of a decision in which they had not concurred. Therefore, if a majority voting in the Security Council is to be made possible, the only practicable method is to provide, in respect of non-procedural decisions, for unanimity of the permanent members plus the concurring votes of at least two of the non-permanent members.

10. For all these reasons, the four Sponsoring Governments agreed on the Yalta formula and have presented it to this Conference as essential if an international organization is to be created through which all peace-loving nations can effectively discharge their common responsibilities for the maintenance of international peace and security.

PART II

In the light of the considerations set forth in Part I of this statement, it is clear what the answers to the questions submitted by the Sub-committee should be, with the exception of Question 19. The answer to that question is as follows:

1. In the opinion of the Delegations of the Sponsoring Governments, the Draft Charter itself contains an indication of the application of the voting procedures to the various functions of the Council.

2. In this case, it will be unlikely that there will arise in the future any matters of great importance on which a decision will have to be made as to whether a procedural vote would apply. Should, however, such a matter arise, the decision regarding the preliminary question as to whether or not such a matter is procedural must be taken by a vote of seven members of the Security Council, including the concurring votes of the permanent members.

Appendix 13

CONVENTION ON THE PRIVILEGES AND IMMUNITIES OF THE UNITED NATIONS, APPROVED BY GENERAL ASSEMBLY, FEBRUARY 13, 1946 [1]

Whereas Article 104 of the Charter of the United Nations provides that the Organization shall enjoy in the territory of each of its Members such legal capacity as may be necessary for the exercise of its functions and the fulfillment of its purposes and

Whereas Article 105 of the Charter of the United Nations provides that the Organization shall enjoy in the territory of each of its Members such privileges and immunities as are necessary for the fulfillment of its purposes and that representatives of the Members of the United Nations and officials of the Organization shall similarly enjoy such privileges and immunities as are necessary for the independent exercise of the functions in connection with the Organization:

Consequently the General Assembly by a resolution adopted on 13 February 1946, approved the following convention and proposes it for accession by each Member of the United Nations.

ARTICLE I. JURIDICAL PERSONALITY

Section 1. The United Nations shall possess juridical personality. It shall have the capacity:
(a) to contract;
(b) to acquire and dispose of immovable and movable property;
(c) to institute legal proceedings.

ARTICLE II. PROPERTY, FUNDS AND ASSETS

Section 2. The United Nations, its property and assets wherever located and by whomsoever held, shall enjoy immunity from every form of legal process except in so far as in any particular case it has expressly waived its immunity. It is, however, understood that no waiver of immunity shall extend to any measure of execution.

Section 3. The premises of the United Nations shall be inviolable. The property and assets of the United Nations, wherever located and by whomsoever held, shall be immune from search, requisition, confiscation, expropriation and any other form of interference, whether by executive, administrative, judicial or legislative action.

[1] UN Doc. A/64, pp. 25–27.

401

Section 4. The archives of the United Nations, and in general all documents belonging to it or held by it, shall be inviolable wherever located.

Section 5. Without being restricted by financial controls, regulations or moratoria of any kind,

(a) The United Nations may hold funds, gold or currency of any kind and operate accounts in any currency;

(b) The United Nations shall be free to transfer its funds, gold or currency from one country to another or within any country and to convert any currency held by it into any other currency.

Section 6. In exercising its rights under section 5 above, the United Nations shall pay due·regard to any representations made by the Government of any Member in so far as it is considered that effect can be given to such representations without detriment to the interests of the United Nations.

Section 7. The United Nations, its assets, income and other property shall be:

(a) exempt from all direct taxes; it is understood, however, that the United Nations will not claim exemption from taxes which are, in fact, no more than charges for public utility services;

(b) exempt from customs duties and prohibitions and restrictions on imports and exports in respect of articles imported or exported by the United Nations for its official use. It is understood, however, that articles imported under such exemption will not be sold in the country into which they were imported except under conditions agreed with the Government of that country;

(c) exempt from customs duties and prohibitions and restrictions on imports and exports in respect of its publications.

Section 8. While the United Nations will not, as a general rule, claim exemption from excise duties and from taxes on the sale of movable and immovable property which form part of the price to be paid, nevertheless when the United Nations is making important purchases for official use of property on which such duties and taxes have been charged or are chargeable, Members will, whenever possible, make appropriate administrative arrangements for the remission or return of the amount of duty or tax.

ARTICLE III. FACILITIES IN RESPECT OF COMMUNICATIONS

Section 9. The United Nations shall enjoy in the territory of each Member for its official communications treatment not less favourable than that accorded by the Government of that Member to any other Government, including its diplomatic mission, including the matter of priorities, rates and taxes on mails, cables, telegrams, radiograms, telephotos, telephone and other communications; and press rates for information to the press and radio. No censorship shall be applied to the official correspondence and other official communications of the United Nations.

Section 10. The United Nations shall have the right to use codes and to dispatch and receive its correspondence by courier or in bags, which shall have the same immunities and privileges as diplomatic couriers and bags.

ARTICLE IV. THE REPRESENTATIVES OF MEMBERS

Section 11. Representatives of Members to the principal and subsidiary organs of the United Nations and to conferences convened by the United Nations, shall, while exercising their functions and during their journey to and from the place of meeting, enjoy the following privileges and immunities:

(a) immunity from personal arrest or detention and from seizure of their personal baggage, and, in respect of words spoken or written and all acts done by them in their capacity as representatives, immunity from legal process of every kind;

(b) inviolability for all papers and documents;

(c) the right to use codes and to receive papers or correspondence by courier or in sealed bags;

(d) exemption in respect of themselves and their spouses from immigration restrictions, alien registration or national service obligations in the State they are visiting or through which they are passing in the exercise of their functions;

(e) the same facilities in respect of currency or exchange restrictions as are accorded to representatives of foreign governments on temporary official missions;

(f) the same immunities and facilities in respect of their personal baggage as are accorded to diplomatic envoys, and also;

(g) such other privileges, immunities and facilities, not inconsistent with the foregoing, as diplomatic envoys enjoy, except that they shall have no right to claim exemption from customs duties on goods imported (otherwise than as part of their personal baggage) or from excise duties or sales taxes.

Section 12.   In order to secure, for the representatives of Members to the principal and subsidiary organs of the United Nations and to conferences convened by the United Nations, complete freedom of speech and independence in the discharge of their duties, the immunity from legal process in respect of words spoken or written and all acts done by them in discharging their duties shall continue to be accorded, notwithstanding that the persons concerned are no longer the representatives of Members.

Section 13.   Where the incidence of any form of taxation depends upon residence, periods during which the representatives of Members to the principal and subsidiary organs of the United Nations and to conferences convened by the United Nations are present in a State for the discharge of their duties shall not be considered as periods of residence.

Section 14. Privileges and immunities are accorded to the representatives of Members not for the personal benefit of the individuals themselves, but in order to safeguard the independent exercise of their functions in connection with the United Nations.   Consequently a Member not only has the right but is under a duty to waive the immunity of its representative in any case where in the opinion of the Member the immunity would impede the course of justice, and it can be waived without prejudice to the purpose for which the immunity is accorded.

Section 15.   The provisions of sections 11, 12 and 13 are not applicable as between a representative and the authorities of the State of which he is a national or of which he is or has been the representative.

Section 16.   In this article the expression "representatives" shall be deemed to include all delegates, deputy delegates, advisers, technical experts and secretaries of delegations.

ARTICLE V. OFFICIALS

Section 17.   The Secretary-General will specify the categories of officials to which the provisions of this article and article VII shall apply.   He shall submit these categories to the General Assembly. Thereafter these categories shall be communicated to the Governments of all Members. The names of the officials included in these categories shall from time to time be made known to the Governments of Members.

Section 18. Officials of the United Nations shall:

(a) be immune from legal process in respect of words spoken or written and all acts performed by them in their official capacity;

(b) be exempt from taxation on the salaries and emoluments paid to them by the United Nations;

(c) be immune from national service obligations;

(d) be immune, together with their spouses and relatives dependent on them, from immigration restrictions and alien registration;

(e) be accorded the same privileges in respect of exchange facilities as are accorded to the officials of comparable ranks forming part of diplomatic missions to the government concerned;

(f) be given, together with their spouses and relatives dependent on them, the same repatriation facilities in time of international crisis as diplomatic envoys;

(g) have the right to import free of duty their furniture and effects at the time of first taking up their post in the country in question.

Section 19. In addition to the immunities and privileges specified in section 18, the Secretary-General and all Assistant Secretaries-General shall be accorded in respect of themselves, their spouses and minor children, the privileges and immunities, exemptions and facilities accorded to diplomatic envoys, in accordance with international law.

Section 20. Privileges and immunities are granted to officials in the interests of the United Nations and not for the personal benefit of the individuals themselves. The Secretary-General shall have the right and the duty to waive the immunity of any official in any case where, in his opinion, the immunity would impede the course of justice and can be waived without prejudice to the interests of the United Nations. In the case of the Secretary-General, the Security Council shall have the right to waive immunity.

Section 21. The United Nations shall co-operate at all times with the appropriate authorities of Members to facilitate the proper administration of justice, secure the observance of police regulations, and prevent the occurrence of any abuse in connection with the privileges, immunities and facilities mentioned in this article.

ARTICLE VI. EXPERTS ON MISSIONS FOR THE UNITED NATIONS

Section 22. Experts (other than officials coming within the scope of article V) performing missions for the United Nations shall be accorded such privileges and immunities as are necessary for the independent exercise of their functions during the period of their missions, including the time spent on journeys in connection with their missions. In particular they shall be accorded:

(a) immunity from personal arrest or detention and from seizure of their personal baggage;

(b) in respect of words spoken or written and acts done by them in the course of the performance of their mission, immunity from legal process of every kind. This immunity from legal process shall continue to be accorded notwithstanding that the persons concerned are no longer employed on missions for the United Nations.

(c) inviolability for all papers and documents;

(d) for the purpose of their communications with the United Nations, the right to use codes and to receive papers or correspondence by courier or in sealed bags;

(e) the same facilities in respect of currency or exchange restrictions as are accorded to representatives of foreign governments on temporary official missions;

(f) the same immunities and facilities in respect of their personal baggage as are accorded to diplomatic envoys.

Section 23. Privileges and immunities are granted to experts in the interests of the United Nations and not for the personal benefit of the individuals themselves. The Secretary-General shall have the right and the duty to waive the immunity of any expert in any case where, in his opinion, the immunity would impede the course of justice and it can be waived without prejudice to the interests of the United Nations.

ARTICLE VII. UNITED NATIONS LAISSEZ-PASSER

Section 24. The United Nations may issue United Nations *laissez-passer* to its officials. These *laissez-passer* shall be recognized and accepted as valid travel documents, by the authorities of Members, taking into account the provisions of section 25.

Section 25. Applications for visas (where required) from the holders of United Nations *laissez-passer*, when accompanied by a certificate that they are travelling on the business of the United Nations, shall be dealt with as speedily as possible. In addition, such persons shall be granted facilities for speedy travel.

Section 26. Similar facilities to those specified in section 25 shall be accorded to experts and other persons who, though not holders of United Nations *laissez-passer*, have a certificate that they are travelling on the business of the United Nations.

Section 27. The Secretary-General, Assistant Secretaries-General and Directors travelling on United Nations *laissez-passer* on the business of the United Nations shall be granted the same facilities as are accorded to diplomatic envoys.

Section 28. The provisions of this article may be applied to the comparable officials of specialized agencies if the agreements for relationship made under Article 63 of the Charter so provide.

ARTICLE VIII. SETTLEMENT OF DISPUTES

Section 29. The United Nations shall make provisions for appropriate modes of settlement of:

(a) disputes arising out of contracts or other disputes of a private law character, to which the United Nations is a party;

(b) disputes involving any official of the United Nations who by reason of his official position enjoys immunity, if immunity has not been waived by the Secretary-General.

Section 30. All differences arising out of the interpretation or application of the present convention shall be referred to the International Court of Justice, unless in any case it is agreed by the parties to have recourse to another mode of settlement. If a difference arises between the United Nations on the one hand and a Member on the other hand, a request shall be made for an advisory opinion on any legal question involved in accordance with Article 96 of the Charter and Article 65 of the Statute of the Court. The opinion given by the Court shall be accepted as decisive by the parties.

FINAL ARTICLE

Section 31. This convention is submitted to every Member of the United Nations for accession.

Section 32. Accession shall be effected by deposit of an instrument with the Secretary-General of the United Nations and the convention shall come into force as regards each Member on the date of deposit of each instrument of accession.

Section 33. The Secretary-General shall inform all Members of the United Nations of the deposit of each accession.

Section 34. It is understood that, when an instrument of accession is deposited on behalf of any Member, the Member will be in a position under its own law to give effect to the terms of this convention.

Section 35. This convention shall continue in force as between the United Nations and every Member which has deposited an instrument of accession for so long as that Member remains a Member of the United Nations, or until a revised general convention has been approved by the General Assembly and that Member has become a party to this revised convention.

Section 36. The Secretary-General may conclude with any Member or Members supplementary agreements adjusting the provisions of this convention so far as that Member or those Members are concerned. These supplementary agreements shall in each case be subject to the approval of the General Assembly.

Appendix 14

TRUSTEESHIP AGREEMENT FOR THE FORMER JAPANESE MANDATED ISLANDS— RESOLUTION OF THE SECURITY COUNCIL, APRIL 2, 1947 [1]

PREAMBLE

Whereas Article 75 of the Charter of the United Nations provides for the establishment of an international trusteeship system for the administration and supervision of such territories as may be placed thereunder by subsequent agreements; and

Whereas under Article 77 of the said Charter the trusteeship system may be applied to territories now held under mandate; and

Whereas on 17 December 1920 the Council of the League of Nations confirmed a mandate for the former German islands north of the equator to Japan, to be administered in accordance with Article 22 of the Covenant of the League of Nations; and

Whereas Japan, as a result of the Second World War, has ceased to exercise any authority in these islands;

Now, therefore, the Security Council of the United Nations, having satisfied itself that the relevant articles of the Charter have been complied with, hereby resolves to approve the following terms of trusteeship for the Pacific Islands formerly under mandate to Japan.

ARTICLE 1

The Territory of the Pacific Islands, consisting of the islands formerly held by Japan under mandate in accordance with Article 22 of the Covenant of the League of Nations, is hereby designated as a strategic area and placed under the trusteeship system established in the Charter of the United Nations. The Territory of the Pacific Islands is hereinafter referred to as the trust territory.

ARTICLE 2

The United States of America is designated as the administering authority of the trust territory.

[1] U.S. Deparment of State Publication 2992, Treaties and Other International Acts Series 1665.

ARTICLE 3

The administering authority shall have full powers of administration, legislation, and jurisdiction over the territory subject to the provisions of this agreement, and may apply to the trust territory, subject to any modifications which the administering authority may consider desirable, such of the laws of the United States as it may deem appropriate to local conditions and requirements.

ARTICLE 4

The administering authority, in discharging the obligations of trusteeship in the trust territory, shall act in accordance with the Charter of the United Nations, and the provisions of this agreement, and shall, as specified in Article 83(2) of the Charter, apply the objectives of the international trusteeship system, as set forth in Article 76 of the Charter, to the people of the trust territory.

ARTICLE 5

In discharging its obligations under Article 76(a) and Article 84, of the Charter, the administering authority shall ensure that the trust territory shall play its part, in accordance with the Charter of the United Nations, in the maintenance of international peace and security. To this end the administering authority shall be entitled:

1. to establish naval, military and air bases and to erect fortifications in the trust territory;

2. to station and employ armed forces in the territory; and

3. to make use of volunteer forces, facilities and assistance from the trust territory in carrying out the obligations toward the Security Council undertaken in this regard by the administering authority, as well as for the local defense and the maintenance of law and order within the trust territory.

ARTICLE 6

In discharging its obligations under Article 76(b) of the Charter, the administering authority shall:

1. foster the development of such political institutions as are suited to the trust territory and shall promote the development of the inhabitants of the trust territory toward self-government or independence, as may be appropriate to the particular circumstances of the trust territory and its peoples and the freely expressed wishes of the peoples concerned; and to this end shall give to the inhabitants of the trust territory a progressively increasing share in the administrative services in the territory; shall develop their participation in government; shall give due recognition to the customs of the inhabitants in providing a system of law for the territory; and shall take other appropriate measures toward these ends;

2. promote the economic advancement and self-sufficiency of the inhabitants, and to this end shall regulate the use of natural resources; encourage the development of fisheries, agriculture, and industries; protect the inhabitants against the loss of their lands and resources; and improve the means of transportation and communication;

3. promote the social advancement of the inhabitants, and to this end shall protect the rights and fundamental freedoms of all elements of the population without discrimination; protect the health of the inhabitants; control the traffic in arms and ammunition, opium and other dangerous drugs, and alcohol and other spirituous beverages; and institute such other regulations as may be necessary to protect the inhabitants against social abuses; and

4. promote the educational advancement of the inhabitants, and to this end shall take steps toward the establishment of a general system of elementary education; facilitate the vocational and cultural advancement of the population; and shall encourage qualified students to pursue higher education, including training on the professional level.

ARTICLE 7

In discharging its obligations under Article 76(c), of the Charter, the administering authority shall guarantee to the inhabitants of the trust territory freedom of conscience, and, subject only to the requirements of public order and security, freedom of speech, of the press, and of assembly; freedom of worship, and of religious teaching; and freedom of migration and movement.

ARTICLE 8

1. In discharging its obligations under Article 76(d) of the Charter, as defined by Article 83(2) of the Charter, the administering authority, subject to the requirements of security, and the obligation to promote the advancement of the inhabitants, shall accord to nationals of each Member of the United Nations and to companies and associations organized in conformity with the laws of such Member, treatment in the trust territory no less favorable than that accorded therein to nationals, companies and associations of any other United Nation except the administering authority.

2. The administering authority shall ensure equal treatment to the Members of the United Nations and their nationals in the administration of justice.

3. Nothing in this Article shall be so construed as to accord traffic rights to aircraft flying into and out of the trust territory. Such rights shall be subject to agreement between the administering authority and the state whose nationality such aircraft possesses.

4. The administering authority may negotiate and conclude commercial and other treaties and agreements with Members of the United Nations and other states, designed to attain for the inhabitants of the trust territory treament by the Members of the United Nations and other states no less favorable than that granted by them to the nationals of other states. The Security Council may recommend, or invite other organs of the United Nations to consider and recommend, what rights the inhabitants of the trust territory should acquire in consideration of the rights obtained by Members of the United Nations in the trust territory.

ARTICLE 9

The administering authority shall be entitled to constitute the trust territory into a customs, fiscal, or administrative union or federation with other territories under United States jurisdiction and to establish common services between such territories and the trust territory where such measures are not inconsistent with the basic objectives of the International Trusteeship System and with the terms of this agreement.

ARTICLE 10

The administering authority, acting under the provisions of Article 3 of this agreement, may accept membership in any regional advisory commission, regional authority, or technical organization, or other voluntary association of states, may cooperate with specialized international bodies, public or private, and may engage in other forms of international co-operation.

ARTICLE 11

1. The administering authority shall take the necessary steps to provide the status of citizenship of the trust territory for the inhabitants of the trust territory.

2. The administering authority shall afford diplomatic and consular protection to inhabitants of the trust territory when outside the territorial limits of the trust territory or of the territory of the administering authority.

ARTICLE 12

The administering authority shall enact such legislation as may be necessary to place the provisions of this agreement in effect in the trust territory.

ARTICLE 13

The provisions of Articles 87 and 88 of the Charter shall be applicable to the trust territory, provided that the administering authority may determine the extent of their applicability to any areas which may from time to time be specified by it as closed for security reasons.

ARTICLE 14

The administering authority undertakes to apply in the trust territory the provisions of any international conventions and recommendations which may be appropriate to the particular circumstances of the trust territory and which would be conducive to the achievement of the basic objectives of Article 6 of this agreement.

ARTICLE 15

The terms of the present agreement shall not be altered, amended or terminated without the consent of the administering authority.

ARTICLE 16

The present agreement shall come into force when approved by the Security Council of the United Nations and by the Government of the United States after due constitutional process.

Appendix 15

AGREEMENT BETWEEN THE UNITED NATIONS AND THE UNITED STATES OF AMERICA REGARDING THE HEADQUARTERS OF THE UNITED NATIONS, SIGNED JUNE 26, 1947 [1]

THE UNITED NATIONS AND THE UNITED STATES OF AMERICA:

Desiring to conclude an agreement for the purpose of carrying out the resolution adopted by the General Assembly on 14 December 1946 to establish the seat of the United Nations in the City of New York and to regulate questions arising as a result thereof;

Have appointed as their representatives for this purpose:

The United Nations:

Trygve Lie, Secretary-General, and

The United States of America:

George C. Marshall, Secretary of State,

Who have agreed as follows:

ARTICLE I. DEFINITIONS

Section 1

In this agreement:

(a) The expression "headquarters district" means:

(1) the area defined as such in Annex 1;

(2) any other lands or buildings which from time to time may be included therein by supplemental agreement with the appropriate American authorities;

(b) the expression "appropriate American authorities" means such federal, state, or local authorities in the United States as may be appropriate in the context and in accordance with the laws and customs of the United States, including the laws and customs of the state and local government involved;

(c) the expression "General Convention" means the Convention on the Privileges and Immunities of the United Nations approved by the General Assembly of the United Nations on 13 February 1946, as acceded to by the United States;

[1] UN Doc. A/427, Oct. 27, 1947, p. 9–18.

(d) the expression "United Nations" means the international organization established by the Charter of the United Nations, hereinafter referred to as the "Charter";

(e) the expression "Secretary-General" means the Secretary-General of the United Nations.

ARTICLE II. THE HEADQUARTERS DISTRICT

Section 2

The seat of the United Nations shall be the headquarters district.

Section 3

The appropriate American authorities shall take whatever action may be necessary to assure that the United Nations shall not be dispossessed of its property in the headquarters district, except as provided in Section 22 in the event that the United Nations ceases to use the same, provided that the United Nations shall reimburse the appropriate American authorities for any costs incurred, after consultation with the United Nations, in liquidating by eminent domain proceedings or otherwise any adverse claims.

Section 4

(a) The United Nations may establish and operate in the headquarters district:

(1) its own short-wave sending and receiving radio broadcasting facilities, including emergency link equipment, which may be used on the same frequencies (within the tolerances prescribed for the broadcasting service by applicable United States regulations) for radio-telegraph, radio-teletype, radio-telephone, radio-telephoto, and similar services;

(2) one point-to-point circuit between the headquarters district and the office of the United Nations in Geneva (using single side-band equipment) to be used exclusively for the exchange of broadcasting programmes and inter-office communications;

(3) low power, micro wave, low or medium frequencies, facilities for communication within headquarters buildings only, or such other buildings as may temporarily be used by the United Nations;

(4) facilities for point-to-point communications to the same extent and subject to the same conditions as committed under applicable rules and regulations for amateur operation in the United States, except that such rules and regulations shall not be applied in a manner inconsistent with the inviolability of the headquarters district provided by Section 9(a);

(5) such other radio facilities as may be specified by supplemental agreement between the United Nations and the appropriate American authorities.

(b) The United Nations shall make arrangements for the operation of the services referred to in this section with the International Telecommunication Union, the appropriate agencies of the Government of the United States and the appropriate agencies of other affected Governments with regard to all frequencies and similar matters.

(c) The facilities provided for in this section may, to the extent necessary for efficient operation, be established and operated outside the headquarters district. The appropriate American authorities will, on request of the United Nations, make arrangements, on such terms and in such manner as may be agreed upon by supplemental agreement, for the acquisition or use by the United Nations of appropriate premises for such purposes and the inclusion of such premises in the headquarters district.

Section 5

In the event that the United Nations should find it necessary and desirable to establish and operate an aerodrome, the conditions for the location, use and operation of such an aerodrome and the conditions under which there shall be entry into and exit therefrom shall be the subject of a supplemental agreement.

Section 6

In the event that the United Nations should propose to organize its own postal service, the conditions under which such service shall be set up shall be the subject of a supplemental agreement.

ARTICLE III. LAW AND AUTHORITY IN THE HEADQUARTERS DISTRICT

Section 7

(a) The headquarters district shall be under the control and authority of the United Nations as provided in this agreement.

(b) Except as otherwise provided in this agreement or in the General Convention, the federal, state and local law of the United States shall apply within the headquarters district.

(c) Except as otherwise provided in this agreement or in the General Convention, the federal, state and local courts of the United States shall have jurisdiction over acts done and transactions taking place in the headquarters district as provided in applicable federal, state and local laws.

(d) The federal, state and local courts of the United States, when dealing with cases arising out of or relating to acts done or transactions taking place in the headquarters district, shall take into account the regulations enacted by the United Nations under Section 8.

Section 8

The United Nations shall have the power to make regulations, operative within the headquarters district, for the purpose of establishing therein conditions in all respects necessary for the full execution of its functions. No federal, state or local law or regulation of the United States which is inconsistent with a regulation of the United Nations authorized by this section shall, to the extent of such inconsistency, be applicable within the headquarters district. Any dispute, between the United Nations and the United States, as to whether a regulation of the United Nations is authorized by this section or as to whether a federal, state or local law or regulation is inconsistent with any regulation of the United Nations authorized by this section, shall be promptly settled as provided in Section 21. Pending such settlement, the regulation of the United Nations shall apply, and the federal, state or local law or regulation shall be inapplicable in the headquarters district to the extent that the United Nations claims it to be inconsistent with the regulation of the United Nations. This section shall not prevent the reasonable application of fire protection regulations of the appropriate American authorities.

Section 9

(a) The headquarters district shall be inviolable. Federal, state or local officers or officials of the United States, whether administrative, judicial, military or police, shall not enter the headquarters district to perform any official duties therein except with the consent of and under conditions agreed to by the Secretary-General. The service of legal process, including the seizure of private property, may take place within the headquarters district only with the consent of and under conditions approved by the Secretary-General.

(b) Without prejudice to the provisions of the General Convention or Article IV of this agreement, the United Nations shall prevent the headquarters district from becoming a refuge either for persons who are avoiding arrest under the federal, state, or local law of the United States or are required by the Government of the United States for extradition to another country, or for persons who are endeavoring to avoid service of legal process.

Section 10

The United Nations may expel or exclude persons from the headquarters district for violation of its regulations adopted under Section 8 or for other cause. Persons who violate such regulations shall be subject to other penalties or to detention under arrest only in accordance with the provisions of such laws or regulations as may be adopted by the appropriate American authorities.

ARTICLE IV.   COMMUNICATIONS AND TRANSIT

Section 11

The federal, state or local authorities of the United States shall not impose any impediments to transit to or from the headquarters district of (1) representatives of Members of officials of the United Nations, or of specialized agencies as defined in Article 57, paragraph 2, of the Charter, of the families of such representatives or officials; (2) experts performing missions for the United Nations or for such specialized agencies; (3) representatives of the press, or of radio, film, or other information agencies, who have been accredited by the United Nations (or by such a specialized agency) in its discretion after consultation with the United States; (4) representatives of non-governmental organizations recognized by the United Nations for the purpose of consultation under Article 71 of the Charter; or (5) other persons invited to the headquarters district by the United Nations or by such specialized agency on official business. The appropriate American authorities shall afford any necessary protection to such persons while in transit to or from the headquarters district. This section does not apply to general interruptions of transportation which are to be dealt with as provided in Section 17, and does not impair the effectiveness of generally applicable laws and regulations as to the operation of means of transportation.

Section 12

The provisions of Section 11 shall be applicable irrespective of the relations existing between the Governments of the persons referred to in that section and the Government of the United States.

Section 13

(a) Laws and regulations in force in the United States regarding the entry of aliens shall not be applied in such manner as to interfere with the privileges referred to in Section 11. When visas are required for persons referred to in that Section, they shall be granted without charge and as promptly as possible.

(b) Laws and regulations in force in the United States regarding the residence of aliens shall not be applied in such manner as to interfere with the privileges referred to in Section 11 and, specifically, shall not be applied in such manner as to require any such person to leave the United States on account of any activities performed by him in his official capacity. In case of abuse of such privileges of residence by any such person in activities in the United States outside his official capacity, it is understood that the privileges referred to in Section 11 shall not be construed to grant him exemption from the laws and regulations of the United States regarding the continued residence of aliens, provided that:

(1) No proceedings shall be instituted under such laws or regulations to require any such person to leave the United States except with the prior approval of the Secretary of State of the United States. Such approval shall be given only after consultation with the appropriate Member in the case of a representative of a Member (or a member of his family) or with the Secretary-General or the principal executive officer of the appropriate specialized agency in the case of any other person referred to in Section 11;

(2) A representative of the Member concerned, the Secretary-General or the principal Executive Officer of the appropriate specialized agency, as the case may be, shall have the right to appear in any such proceedings on behalf of the person against whom they are instituted;

(3) Persons who are entitled to diplomatic privileges and immunities under Section 15 or under the General Convention shall not be required to leave the United States otherwise than in accordance with the customary procedure applicable to diplomatic envoys accredited to the United States.

(c) This section does not prevent the requirement of reasonable evidence to establish that persons claiming the rights granted by Section 11 come within the classes described in that section, or the reasonable application of quarantine and health regulations.

(d) Except as provided above in this section and in the General Convention, the United States retains full control and authority over the entry of persons or property into the territory of the United States and the conditions under which persons may remain or reside there.

(e) The Secretary-General shall, at the request of the appropriate American authorities, enter into discussions with such authorities, with a view to making arrangements for registering the arrival and departure of persons who have been granted visas valid only for transit to and from the headquarters district and sojourn therein and in its immediate vicinity.

(f) The United Nations shall, subject to the foregoing provisions of this section, have the exclusive right to authorize or prohibit entry of persons or property into the headquarters district and to prescribe the conditions under which persons may remain or reside there.

Section 14

The Secretary-General and the appropriate American authorities shall, at the request of either of them, consult as to methods of facilitating entrance into the

United States, and the use of available means of transportation, by persons coming from abroad who wish to visit the headquarters district and do not enjoy the rights referred to in this Article.

ARTICLE V. RESIDENT REPRESENTATIVES TO THE UNITED NATIONS

Section 15

(1) Every person designated by a Member as the principal resident representative to the United Nations of such Member or as a resident representative with the rank of ambassador or minister plenipotentiary,

(2) Such resident members of their staffs as may be agreed upon between the Secretary-General, the Government of the United States and the Government of the Member concerned,

(3) Every person designated by a Member of a specialized agency, as defined in Article 57, paragraph 2, of the Charter, as its principal resident representative, with the rank of ambassador or minister plenipotentiary at the headquarters of such agency in the United States, and

(4) Such other principal resident representatives of members of a specialized agency and such resident members of the staffs of representatives of a specialized agency as may be agreed upon between the principal executive officer of the specialized agency, the Government of the United States and the Government of the Member concerned, shall whether residing inside or outside the headquarters district, be entitled in the territory of the United States to the same privileges and immunities, subject to corresponding conditions and obligations, as it accords to diplomatic envoys accredited to it. In the case of Members whose governments are not recognized by the United States, such privileges and immunities need be extended to such representatives, or persons on the staffs of such representatives, only within the headquarters district, at their residences and offices outside the district, in transit between the district and such residences and offices, and in transit on official business to or from foreign countries.

ARTICLE VI. POLICE PROTECTION OF THE HEADQUARTERS DISTRICT

Section 16

(a) The appropriate American authorities shall exercise due diligence to ensure that the tranquility of the headquarters district is not disturbed by the unauthorized entry of groups of persons from outside or by disturbances in its immediate vicinity and shall cause to be provided on the boundaries of the headquarters district such police protection as is required for these purposes.

(b) If so requested by the Secretary-General, the appropriate American authorities shall provide a sufficient number of police for the preservation of law and order in the headquarters district, and for the removal therefrom of persons requested under the authority of the United Nations. The United Nations shall, if requested, enter into arrangements with the appropriate American authorities to reimburse them for the reasonable cost of such services.

ARTICLE VII. PUBLIC SERVICES AND PROTECTION OF THE HEADQUARTERS DISTRICT

Section 17

(a) The appropriate American authorities will exercise to the extent requested by the Secretary-General the powers which they possess with respect to the supplying of public services to ensure that the headquarters district shall be supplied on equitable terms with the necessary public services, including electricity, water, gas, post, telephone, telegraph, transportation, drainage, collection of refuse, fire protection, snow removal, et cetera. In case of any interruption or threatened interruption of any such services, the appropriate American authorities will consider the needs of the United Nations as being of equal importance with the similar needs of essential agencies of the Government of the United States, and will take steps accordingly, to ensure that the work of the United Nations is not prejudiced.

(b) Special provisions with reference to maintenance of utilities and underground construction are contained in Annex 2.

Section 18

The appropriate American authorities shall take all reasonable steps to ensure that the amenities of the headquarters district are not prejudiced and the purposes for which the district is required are not obstructed by any use made of the land in the vicinity of the district. The United Nations shall on its part take all reasonable steps to ensure that the amenities of the land in the vicinity of the headquarters district are not prejudiced by any use made of the land in the headquarters district by the United Nations.

Section 19

It is agreed that no form of racial or religious discrimination shall be permitted within the headquarters district.

ARTICLE VIII.   MATTERS RELATING TO THE OPERATION OF THIS AGREEMENT

Section 20

The Secretary-General and the appropriate American authorities shall settle by agreement the channels through which they will communicate regarding the application of the provisions of this agreement and other questions affecting the headquarters district, and may enter into such supplemental agreements as may be necessary to fulfill the purposes of this agreement. In making supplemental agreements with the Secretary-General, the United States shall consult with the appropriate state and local authorities. If the Secretary-General so requests, the Secretary of State of the United States shall appoint a special representative for the purpose of liaison with the Secretary-General.

Section 21

(a) Any dispute between the United Nations and the United States concerning the interpretation or application of this agreement or of any supplemental agreement, which is not settled by negotiation or other agreed mode of settlement, shall be referred for final decision to a tribunal of three arbitrators, one to be named by the Secretary-General, one to be named by the Secretary of State of the United States, and the third to be chosen by the two, or, if they should fail to agree upon a third, then by the President of the International Court of Justice.

(b) The Secretary-General or the United States may ask the General Assembly to request of the International Court of Justice an advisory opinion on any legal question arising in the course of such proceedings. Pending the receipt of the opinion of the Court, an interim decision of the arbitral tribunal shall be observed by both parties. Thereafter, the arbitral tribunal shall render a final decision, having regard to the opinion of the Court.

ARTICLE IX. MISCELLANEOUS PROVISIONS

Section 22

(a) The United Nations shall not dispose of all or any part of the land owned by it in the headquarters district without the consent of the United States. If the United States is unwilling to consent to a disposition which the United Nations wishes to make of all or any part of such land, the United States shall buy the same from the United Nations at a price to be determined as provided in paragraph (d) of this section.

(b) If the seat of the United Nations is removed from the headquarters district, all right, title and interest of the United Nations in and to real property in the headquarters district or any part of it shall, on request of either the United Nations or the United States be assigned and conveyed to the sub-division of a state in which it is located or, if such sub-division shall not desire it, then to the state in which it is located. If none of the foregoing desire the same, it may be disposed of as provided in paragraph (a) of this Section.

(c) If the United Nations disposes of all or any part of the headquarters district, the provisions of other sections of this agreement which apply to the headquarters district shall immediately cease to apply to the land and buildings so disposed of.

(d) The price to be paid for any conveyance under this section shall, in default of agreement, be the then fair value of the land, buildings and installations, to be determined under the procedure provided in Section 21.

Section 23

The seat of the United Nations shall not be removed from the headquarters district unless the United Nations should so decide.

Section 24

This agreement shall cease to be in force if the seat of the United Nations is removed from the territory of the United States, except for such provisions as may be applicable in connection with the orderly termination of the operations of the United Nations at its seat in the United States and the disposition of its property therein.

Section 25

Wherever this agreement imposes obligations on the appropriate American authorities, the Government of the United States shall have the ultimate responsibility for the fulfillment of such obligations by the appropriate American authorities.

Section 26

The provisions of this agreement shall be complementary to the provisions of the General Convention. In so far as any provision of this agreement and any provisions of the General Convention relate to the same subject matter, the two provisions shall, wherever possible, be treated as complementary, so that both provisions shall be applicable and neither shall narrow the effect of the other; but in any case of absolute conflict, the provisions of this agreement shall prevail.

Section 27

This agreement shall be construed in the light of its primary purpose to enable the United Nations at its headquarters in the United States, fully and efficiently to discharge its responsibilities and fulfill its purposes.

Section 28

This agreement shall be brought into effect by an exchange of notes between the Secretary-General, duly authorized pursuant to a resolution of the General Assembly of the United Nations, and the appropriate executive officer of the United States, duly authorized pursuant to appropriate action of the Congress.

In witness thereof the respective representatives have signed this Agreement and have affixed their seals hereto.

Done in duplicate, in the English and French languages, both authentic, at Lake Success, this twenty-sixth day of June, 1947.

ANNEX 1

The area referred to in Section 1(a)(1) consists of:

(a) the premises bounded on the East by the westerly side of Franklin D. Roosevelt Drive, on the West by the easterly side of First Avenue, on the North by the southerly side of East Forty-Eighth Street, and on the South by the northerly side of East Forty-Second Street, all as proposed to be widened, in the Borough of Manhattan, City and State of New York, and

(b) an easement over Franklin D. Roosevelt Drive, above a lower limiting plane to be fixed for the construction and maintenance of an esplanade, together with the structures thereon and the foundations and columns to support the same in locations below such limiting plane, the entire area to be more definitely defined by supplemental agreement between the United Nations and the United States of America.

ANNEX 2. MAINTENANCE OF UTILITIES AND UNDERGROUND CONSTRUCTION

Section 1

The Secretary-General agrees to provide passes to duly authorized employees of the City of New York, the State of New York, or any of their agencies or sub-divisions, for the purpose of enabling them to inspect, repair, maintain, reconstruct and relocate utilities, conduits, mains and sewers within the headquarters district.

Section 2

Underground constructions may be undertaken by the City of New York, or the State of New York, or any of their agencies or sub-divisions, within the headquarters district only after consultation with the Secretary-General, and under conditions which shall not disturb the carrying out of the functions of the United Nations.

Appendix 16

RESOLUTION OF THE GENERAL ASSEMBLY ESTABLISHING AN INTERIM COMMITTEE, NOVEMBER 13, 1947 [1]

THE GENERAL ASSEMBLY,

Conscious of the responsibility specifically conferred upon it by the Charter in relation to matters concerning the maintenance of international peace and security (Articles 11 and 35), the promotion of international co-operation in the political field (Article 13) and the peaceful adjustment of any situations likely to impair the general welfare or friendly relations among nations (Article 14);

Deeming it necessary for the effective performance of these duties to establish an interim committee to consider such matters during the period between the closing of the present session and the opening of the next regular session of the General Assembly, and report with its conclusions to the General Assembly;

Recognizing fully the primary responsibility of the Security Council for prompt and effective action for the maintenance of international peace and security (Article 24),

Resolves, that

1. There shall be established, for the period between the closing of the present session and the opening of the next regular session of the General Assembly, an Interim Committee on which each Member of the General Assembly shall have the right to appoint one representative;

2. The Interim Committee, as a subsidiary organ of the General Assembly established in accordance with Article 22 of the Charter, shall assist the General Assembly in the performance of its functions by discharging the following duties:

(a) To consider and report, with its conclusions, to the General Assembly on such matters as have been referred to it by the General Assembly;

(b) To consider and report with its conclusions to the General Assembly on any dispute or any situation which, in virtue of Articles 11 (paragraph 2), 14 or 35 of the Charter, has been proposed for inclusion in the agenda of the General Assembly by any Member of the United Nations or brought before the General Assembly by the Security Council, provided the Committee previously determines the matter to be both important and requiring preliminary study. Such determina-

[1] *The United States and the United Nations: Report by the President to the Congress for the Year* 1947, U.S. Department of State Publication 3024, International Organization and Conference Series III, 1, pp. 159–162.

tion shall be made by a majority of two-thirds of the members present and voting, unless the matter is one referred by the Security Council under Article 11 (paragraph 2), in which case a simple majority will suffice;

(c) To consider, as it deems useful and advisable, and report with its conclusions to the General Assembly on methods to be adopted to give effect to that part of Article 11 (paragraph 1), which deals with the general principles of co-operation in the maintenance of international peace and security, and to that part of Article 13 (paragraph 1a), which deals with the promotion of international co-operation in the political field;

(d) To consider, in connexion with any matter under discussion by the Interim Committee, whether occasion may require the summoning of a special session of the General Assembly and, if it deems that such session is required, so to advise the Secretary-General in order that he may obtain the views of the Members of the United Nations thereon;

(e) To conduct investigations and appoint commissions of enquiry within the scope of its duties, as it may deem useful and necessary, provided that decisions to conduct such investigations or enquiries shall be made by a two-thirds majority of the members present and voting. An investigation or enquiry elsewhere than at the headquarters of the United Nations shall not be conducted without the consent of the State or States in whose territory it is to take place;

(f) To report to the next regular session of the General Assembly on the advisability of establishing a permanent committee of the General Assembly to perform the duties of the Interim Committee as stated above with any changes considered desirable in the light of experience;

3. In discharging its duties the Interim Committee shall at all times take into account the responsibilities of the Security Council under the Charter for the maintenance of international peace and security as well as the duties assigned by the Charter or by the General Assembly or by the Security Council to other Councils or to any committee or commission. The Interim Committee shall not consider any matter of which the Security Council is seized;

4. Subject to paragraphs 2(b) and 2(e) above, the rules of procedure of the General Assembly shall, so far as they are applicable, govern the proceedings of the Interim Committee and such sub-committees and commissions as it may set up. The Interim Committee shall, however, have authority to adopt such additional rules as it may deem necessary provided that they are not inconsistent with any of the rules of procedure of the General Assembly. The Interim Committee shall be convened by the Secretary-General not later than six weeks following the close of the second regular session of the General Assembly. It shall meet as and when it deems necessary for the conduct of its business;

5. The Secretary-General shall provide the necessary facilities and assign appropriate staff as required for the work of the Interim Committee, its sub-committees and commissions.

Appendix 17

ADVISORY OPINION OF THE INTERNATIONAL COURT OF JUSTICE ON CONDITIONS OF ADMISSION OF A STATE TO MEMBERSHIP IN THE UNITED NATIONS, MAY 28, 1948 [1]

On November 17th, 1947, the General Assembly of the United Nations adopted the following Resolution:

THE GENERAL ASSEMBLY,

"Considering Article 4 of the Charter of the United Nations,

"Considering the exchange of views which has taken place in the Security Council at its Two hundred and fourth, Two hundred and fifth, and Two hundred and sixth Meetings, relating to the admission of certain States to membership in the United Nations,

"Considering Article 96 of the Charter,

"Requests the International Court of Justice to give an advisory opinion on the following question:

" 'Is a Member of the United Nations which is called upon, in virtue of Article 4 of the Charter, to pronounce itself by its vote, either in the Security Council or in the General Assembly, on the admission of a State to membership in the United Nations, juridically entitled to make its consent to the admission dependent on conditions not expressly provided by paragraph 1 of the said Article? In particular, can such a Member, while it recognizes the conditions set forth in that provision to be fulfilled by the State concerned, subject its affirmative vote to the additional condition that other States be admitted to membership in the United Nations together with that State?' . . ."

. . . .

Before examining the request for an opinion, the Court considers it necessary to make the following preliminary remarks:

The question put to the Court is divided into two parts, of which the second begins with the words "In particular," and is presented as an application of a more general idea implicit in the first.

[1] Advisory Opinion of the International Court of Justice, May 28, 1948. *I.C.J. Reports of Judgments, Advisory Opinions and Orders,* 1948, pp. 57–115.

The request for an opinion does not refer to the actual vote. Although the Members are bound to conform to the requirements of Article 4 in giving their votes, the General Assembly can hardly be supposed to have intended to ask the Court's opinion as to the reasons which, in the mind of a Member, may prompt its vote. Such reasons, which enter into a mental process, are obviously subject to no control. Nor does the request concern a Member's freedom of expressing its opinion. Since it concerns a condition or conditions on which a Member "makes its consent dependent," the question can only relate to the statements made by a Member concerning the vote it proposes to give.

It is clear from the General Assembly's Resolution of November 17th, 1947, that the Court is not called upon either to define the meaning and scope of the conditions on which admission is made dependent, or to specify the elements which may serve in a concrete case to verify the existence of the requisite conditions.

The clause of the General Assembly's Resolution, referring to "the exchange of views which has taken place . . . ," is not understood as an invitation to the Court to say whether the views thus referred to are well founded or otherwise. The abstract form in which the question is stated precludes such an interpretation.

The question put is in effect confined to the following point only: are the conditions stated in paragraph 1 of Article 4 exhaustive in character in the sense that an affirmative reply would lead to the conclusion that a Member is not legally entitled to make admission dependent on conditions not expressly provided for in that Article, while a negative reply would, on the contrary, authorize a Member to make admission dependent also on other conditions.

* * *

Understood in this light, the question, in its two parts, is and can only be a purely legal one. To determine the meaning of a treaty provision—to determine, as in this case, the character (exhaustive or otherwise) of the conditions for admission stated therein—is a problem of interpretation and consequently a legal question.

It has nevertheless been contended that the question put must be regarded as a political one and that, for this reason, it falls outside the jurisdiction of the Court. The Court cannot attribute a political character to a request which, framed in abstract terms, invites it to undertake an essentially judicial task, the interpretation of a treaty provision. It is not concerned with the motives which may have inspired this request, nor with the considerations which, in the concrete cases submitted for examination to the Security Council, formed the subject of the exchange of views which took place in that body. It is the duty of the Court to envisage the question submitted to it only in the abstract form which has been given to it; nothing which is said in the present opinion refers, either directly or indirectly, to concrete cases or to particular circumstances.

It has also been contended that the Court should not deal with a question couched in abstract terms. That is a mere affirmation devoid of any justification. According to Article 96 of the Charter and Article 65 of the Statute, the Court may give an advisory opinion on any legal question, abstract or otherwise.

Lastly, it has also been maintained that the Court cannot reply to the question put because it involves an interpretation of the Charter. Nowhere is any provision to be found forbidding the Court, "the principal judicial organ of the United Nations," to exercise in regard to Article 4 of the Charter, a multilateral treaty, an interpretative function which falls within the normal exercise of its judicial powers.

Accôrdingly, the Court holds that it is competent, on the basis of Article 96 of the Charter and Article 65 of the Statute, and considers that there are no reasons why it should decline to answer the question put to it.

In framing this answer, it is necessary first to recall the "conditions" required, under paragraph 1 of Article 4, of an applicant for admission. This provision reads as follows:

"Membership in the United Nations is open to all other peace-loving States which accept the obligations contained in the present Charter and, in the judgment of the Organisation, are able and willing to carry out these obligations." The requisite conditions are five in number: to be admitted to membership in the United Nations, an applicant must (1) be a State; (2) be peace-loving; (3) accept the obligations of the Charter; (4) be able to carry out these obligations; and (5) be willing to do so.

All these conditions are subject to the judgment of the Organization. The judgment of the Organization means the judgment of the two organs mentioned in paragraph 2 of Article 4, and, in the last analysis, that of its Members. The question put is concerned with the individual attitude of each Member called upon to pronounce itself on the question of admission.

Having been asked to determine the character, exhaustive or otherwise, of the conditions stated in Article 4, the Court must in the first place consider the text of that Article. The English and French texts of paragraph 1 of Article 4 have the same meaning, and it is impossible to find any conflict between them. The text of this paragraph, by the enumeration which it contains and the choice of its terms, clearly demonstrates the intention of its authors to establish a legal rule which, while it fixes the conditions of admission, determines also the reasons for which admission may be refused; for the text does not differentiate between these two cases and any attempt to restrict it to one of them would be purely arbitrary.

The terms "Membership in the United Nations is open to all other peace-loving States which . . ." and "Peuvent devenir Membres des Nations unies tous autres États pacifiques," indicate that States which fulfil the conditions stated have the qualifications requisite for admission. The natural meaning of the words used leads to the conclusion that these conditions constitute an exhaustive enumeration and are not merely stated by way of guidance or example. The provision would lose its significance and weight, if other conditions, unconnected with those laid down, could be demanded. The conditions stated in paragraph 1 of Article 4 must therefore be regarded not merely as the necessary conditions, but also as the conditions which suffice.

Nor can it be argued that the conditions enumerated represent only an indispensable minimum, in the sense that political considerations could be superimposed upon them, and prevent the admission of an applicant which fulfils them. Such an interpretation would be inconsistent with the terms of paragraph 2 of Article 4, which provide for the admission of "tout État remplissant ces conditions"—"any such State." It would lead to conferring upon Members an indefinite and practically unlimited power of discretion in the imposition of new conditions. Such a power would be inconsistent with the very character of paragraph 1 of Article 4 which, by reason of the close connexion which it establishes between membership and the observance of the principles and obligations of the Charter, clearly constitutes a legal regulation of the question of the admission of new States. To warrant an interpretation other than that which ensues from the natural meaning of the words, a decisive reason would be required which has not been established.

Moreover, the spirit as well as the terms of the paragraph preclude the idea that considerations extraneous to these principles and obligations can prevent the admission of a State which complies with them. If the authors of the Charter had meant to leave Members free to import into the application of this provision considerations extraneous to the conditions laid down therein, they would undoubtedly have adopted a different wording.

The Court considers that the text is sufficiently clear; consequently, it does not feel that it should deviate from the consistent practice of the Permanent Court of International Justice, according to which there is no occasion to resort to preparatory work if the text of a convention is sufficiently clear in itself.

The Court furthermore observes that Rule 60 of the Provisional Rules of Procedure of the Security Council is based on this interpretation. The first paragraph of this Rule reads as follows:

"The Security Council shall decide whether in its judgment the applicant is a peace-loving State and is able and willing to carry out the obligations contained in the Charter, and accordingly whether to recommend the applicant State for membership."

It does not, however, follow from the exhaustive character of paragraph 1 of Article 4 that an appreciation is precluded of such circumstances of fact as would enable the existence of the requisite conditions to be verified.

Article 4 does not forbid the taking into account of any factor which it is possible reasonably and in good faith to connect with the conditions laid down in that Article. The taking into account of such factors is implied in the very wide and very elastic nature of the prescribed conditions; no relevant political factor—that is to say, none connected with the conditions of admission—is excluded.

It has been sought to deduce either from the second paragraph of Article 4, or from the political character of the organ recommending or deciding upon admission, arguments in favor of an interpretation of paragraph 1 of Article 4, to the effect that the fulfilment of the conditions provided for in that Article is necessary before the admission of a State can be recommended or decided upon, but that it does not preclude the Members of the Organization from advancing considerations of political expediency, extraneous to the conditions of Article 4.

But paragraph 2 is concerned only with the procedure for admission, while the preceding paragraph lays down the substantive law. This procedural character is clearly indicated by the words "will be effected," which, by linking admission to the decision, point clearly to the fact that the paragraph is solely concerned with the manner in which admission is effected, and not with the subject of the judgment of the Organization, nor with the nature of the appreciation involved in that judgment, these two questions being dealt with in the preceding paragraph. Moreover, this paragraph, in referring to the "recommendation" of the Security Council and the "decision" of the General Assembly, is designed only to determine the respective functions of these two organs which consist in pronouncing upon the question whether or not the applicant State shall be admitted to membership after having established whether or not the prescribed conditions are fulfilled.

The political character of an organ cannot release it from the observance of the treaty provisions established by the Charter when they constitute limitations on its powers or criteria for its judgment. To ascertain whether an organ has freedom of choice for its decisions, reference must be made to the terms of its constitution. In this case, the limits of this freedom are fixed by Article 4 and allow for a wide liberty of appreciation. There is therefore no conflict between the functions of the political organs, on the one hand, and the exhaustive character of the prescribed conditions, on the other.

It has been sought to base on the political responsibilities assumed by the Security Council, in virtue of Article 24 of the Charter, an argument justifying the necessity for according to the Security Council as well as to the General Assembly complete freedom of appreciation in connexion with the admission of new Members. But Article 24, owing to the very general nature of its terms, cannot, in the absence of any provision, affect the special rules for admission which emerge from Article 4.

The foregoing considerations establish the exhaustive character of the conditions prescribed in Article 4.

*   *   *

The second part of the question concerns a demand on the part of a Member making its consent to the admission of an applicant dependent on the admission of other applicants.

Judged on the basis of the rule which the Court adopts in its interpretation of Article 4, such a demand clearly constitutes a new condition, since it is entirely unconnected with those prescribed in Article 4. It is also in an entirely different category from those conditions, since it makes admission dependent, not on the conditions required of applicants, qualifications which are supposed to be fulfilled, but on an extraneous consideration concerning States other than the applicant State.

The provisions of Article 4 necessarily imply that every application for admission should be examined and voted on separately and on its own merits; otherwise it would be impossible to determine whether a particular applicant fulfils the necessary conditions. To subject an affirmative vote for the admission of an applicant State to the condition that other States be admitted with that State would prevent Members from exercising their judgment in each case with complete liberty, within the scope of the prescribed conditions. Such a demand is incompatible with the letter and spirit of Article 4 of the Charter.

For these reasons,

THE COURT,

by nine votes to six,

is of opinion that a Member of the United Nations which is called upon, in virtue of Article 4 of the Charter, to pronounce itself by its vote, either in the Security Council or in the General Assembly, on the admission of a State to membership in the United Nations, is not juridically entitled to make its consent to the admission dependent on conditions not expressly provided by paragraph 1 of the said Article;

and that, in particular, a Member of the Organization cannot, while it recognizes the conditions set forth in that provision to be fulfilled by the State concerned, subject its affirmative vote to the additional condition that other States be admitted to membership in the United Nations together with that State.

The present opinion has been drawn up in French and in English, the French text being authoritative. . . .

Judges ALVAREZ and AZEVEDO, whilst concurring in the opinion of the Court, have availed themselves of the right conferred on them by Article 57 of the Statute and appended to the opinion a statement of their individual opinion.

JUDGES BASDEVANT, WINIARSKI, MCNAIR, READ, ZORICIC and KRYLOV, declaring that they are unable to concur in the opinion of the Court, have availed themselves of the right conferred on them by Article 57 of the Statute and appended to the opinion a statement of their dissenting opinion. . . .

Appendix 18

VANDENBERG RESOLUTION—THE POLICY OF THE UNITED STATES TO ACHIEVE PEACE AND SECURITY THROUGH THE UNITED NATIONS, JUNE 11, 1948 [1]

Whereas peace with justice and the defense of human rights and fundamental freedoms require international cooperation through more effective use of the United Nations: Therefore be it

Resolved, That the Senate reaffirm the policy of the United States to achieve international peace and security through the United Nations so that armed force shall not be used except in the common interest, and that the President be advised of the sense of the Senate that this Government, by constitutional process, should particularly pursue the following objectives within the United Nations Charter:

(1) Voluntary agreement to remove the veto from all questions involving pacific settlements of international disputes and situations, and from the admission of new members.

(2) Progressive development of regional and other collective arrangements for the individual and collective self-defense in accordance with the purposes, principles, and provisions of the Charter.

(3) Association of the United States, by constitutional process, with such regional and other collective arrangements as are based on continuous and effective self-help and mutual aid, and as affect its national security.

(4) Contributing to the maintenance of peace by making clear its determination to exercise the right of individual or collective self-defense under article 51 should any armed attack occur affecting its national security.

(5) Maximum efforts to obtain agreements to provide the United Nations with armed forces as provided by the Charter, and to obtain agreement among member nations upon universal regulation and reduction of armaments under adequate and dependable guaranty against violation.

(6) If necessary, after adequate effort toward strengthening the United Nations, review of the Charter at an appropriate time by a General Conference under article 109 or by the General Assembly.

[1] Senate Resolution 239, 80th Congress, 2d Session, June 11, 1948.

Appendix 19

UNIVERSAL DECLARATION OF HUMAN RIGHTS, RESOLUTION OF GENERAL ASSEMBLY, DECEMBER 10, 1948 [1]

Whereas recognition of the inherent dignity and of the equal and inalienable rights of all members of the human family is the foundation of freedom, justice and peace in the world,

Whereas disregard and contempt for human rights have resulted in barbarous acts which have outraged the conscience of mankind, and the advent of a world in which human beings shall enjoy freedom of speech and belief and freedom from fear and want has been proclaimed as the highest aspiration of the common people,

Whereas it is essential, if man is not to be compelled to have recourse, as a last resort, to rebellion against tyranny and oppression, that human rights should be protected by the rule of law,

Whereas it is essential to promote the development of friendly relations between nations,

Whereas the peoples of the United Nations have in the Charter reaffirmed their faith in fundamental human rights, in the dignity and worth of the human person and in the equal rights of men and women and have determined to promote social progress and better standards of life in larger freedom,

Whereas Member States have pledged themselves to achieve, in co-operation with the United Nations, the promotion of universal respect for and observance of human rights and fundamental freedoms,

Whereas a common understanding of these rights and freedoms is of the greatest importance for the full realization of this pledge,

Now therefore

The General Assembly,

Proclaims this Universal Declaration of Human Rights as a common standard of achievement for all peoples and all nations, to the end that every individual and every organ of society, keeping this Declaration constantly in mind, shall strive by teaching and education to promote respect for these rights and freedoms and by progressive measures, national and international, to secure their universal and effective recognition and observance, both among the peoples of Member States themselves and among the peoples of territories under their jurisdiction.

Article 1. All human beings are born free and equal in dignity and rights. They

[1] U.N. press release PGA/100, Pt. IV, pp. 11–16.

429

are endowed with reason and conscience and should act towards one another in a spirit of brotherhood.

Article 2. Everyone is entitled to all the rights and freedoms set forth in this Declaration, without distinction of any kind, such as race, colour, sex, language, religion, political or other opinion, national or social origin, property, birth or other status.

Furthermore, no distinction shall be made on the basis of the political, jurisdictional or international status of the country or territory to which a person belongs, whether it be independent, trust, non-self-governing or under any other limitation of sovereignty.

Article 3. Everyone has the right to life, liberty and the security of person.

Article 4. No one shall be held in slavery or servitude; slavery and the slave trade shall be prohibited in all their forms.

Article 5. No one shall be subjected to torture or to cruel, inhuman or degrading treatment or punishment.

Article 6. Everyone has the right to recognition everywhere as a person before the law.

Article 7. All are equal before the law and are entitled without any discrimination to equal protection of the law. All are entitled to equal protection against any discrimination in violation of this Declaration and against any incitement to such discrimination.

Article 8. Everyone has the right to an effective remedy by the competent national tribunals for acts violating the fundamental rights granted him by the constitution or by law.

Article 9. No one shall be subjected to arbitrary arrest, detention or exile.

Article 10. Everyone is entitled in full equality to a fair and public hearing by an independent and impartial tribunal, in the determination of his rights and obligations and of any criminal charge against him.

Article 11. 1. Everyone charged with a penal offence has the right to be presumed innocent until proved guilty according to law in a public trial at which he has had all the guarantees necessary for his defence.

2. No one shall be held guilty of any penal offence on account of any act or omission which did not constitute a penal offence, under national or international law, at the time when it was committed. Nor shall a heavier penalty be imposed than the one that was applicable at the time the penal offence was committed.

Article 12. No one shall be subjected to arbitrary interference with his privacy, family, home or correspondence, nor to attacks upon his honor and reputation. Everyone has the right to the protection of the law against such interference or attacks.

Article 13. 1. Everyone has the right to freedom of movement and residence within the borders of each state.

2. Everyone has the right to leave any country, including his own, and to return to his country.

Article 14. 1. Everyone has the right to seek and to enjoy in other countries asylum from persecution.

2. This right may not be invoked in the case of prosecutions genuinely arising

from non-political crimes or from acts contrary to the purposes and principles of the United Nations.

Article 15. 1. Everyone has the right to a nationality.

2. No one shall be arbitrarily deprived of his nationality nor denied the right to change his nationality.

Article 16. 1. Men and women of full age, without any limitation due to race, nationality or religion, have the right to marry and to found a family. They are entitled to equal rights as to marriage, during marriage and at its dissolution.

2. Marriage shall be entered into only with the free and full consent of the intending spouses.

3. The family is the natural and fundamental group unit of society and is entitled to protection by society and the State.

Article 17. 1. Everyone has the right to own property alone as well as in association with others.

2. No one shall be arbitrarily deprived of his property.

Article 18. Everyone has the right to freedom of thought, conscience and religion; this right includes freedom to change his religion or belief, and freedom, either alone or in community with others and in public or private, to manifest his religion or belief in teaching, practice, worship and observance.

Article 19. Everyone has the right to freedom of opinion and expression; this right includes freedom to hold opinions without interference and to seek, receive and impart information and ideas through any media and regardless of frontiers.

Article 20. 1. Everyone has the right to freedom of peaceful assembly and association.

2. No one may be compelled to belong to an association.

Article 21. 1. Everyone has the right to take part in the Government of his country, directly or through freely chosen representatives.

2. Everyone has the right of equal access to public service in his country.

3. The will of the people shall be the basis of the authority of government; this will shall be expressed in periodic and genuine elections which shall be by universal and equal suffrage and shall be held by secret vote or by equivalent free voting procedures.

Article 22. Everyone, as a member of society, has the right to social security and is entitled to realization, throught national effort and international co-operation and in accordance with the organization and resources of each State, of the economic, social and cultural rights indispensable for his dignity and the free development of his personality.

Article 23. 1. Everyone has the right to work, to free choice of employment, to just and favorable conditions of work and to protection against unemployment.

2. Everyone, without any discrimination, has the right to equal pay for equal work.

3. Everyone who works has the right to just and favourable remuneration insuring for himself and his family an existence worthy of human dignity, and supplemented, if necessary, by other means of social protection.

4. Everyone has the right to form and to join trade unions for the protection of his interests.

Article 24. Everyone has the right to rest and leisure, including reasonable limitation of working hours and periodic holidays with pay.

Article 25. 1. Everyone has the right to a standard of living adequate for the health and well-being of himself and of his family, including food, clothing, housing and medical care and necessary social services, and the right to security in the event of unemployment, sickness, disability, widowhood, old age or other lack of livelihood in circumstances beyond his control.

2. Motherhood and childhood are entitled to special care and assistance. All children, whether born in or out of wedlock, shall enjoy the same social protection.

Article 26. 1. Everyone has the right to education. Education shall be free, at least in the elementary and fundamental stages. Elementary education shall be compulsory. Technical and professional education shall be made generally available and higher education shall be equally accessible to all on the basis of merit.

2. Education shall be directed to the full development of the human personality and to the strengthening of respect for human rights and fundamental freedoms. It shall promote understanding, tolerance and friendship among all nations, racial or religious groups, and shall further the activities of the United Nations for the maintenance of peace.

3. Parents have a prior right to choose the kind of education that shall be given to their children.

Article 27. 1. Everyone has the right freely to participate in the cultural life of the community, to enjoy the arts and to share in scientific advancement and its benefits.

2. Everyone has the right to the protection of the moral and material interests resulting from any scientific, literary or artistic production of which he is the author.

Article 28. Everyone is entitled to a social and international order in which the rights and freedoms set forth in this Declaration can be fully realized.

Article 29. 1. Everyone has duties to the community in which alone the free and full development of his personality is possible.

2. In the exercise of his rights and freedoms, everyone shall be subject only to such limitations as are determined by law solely for the purpose of securing due recognition and respect for the rights and freedoms of others and of meeting the just requirements of morality, public order and the general welfare in a democratic society.

3. These rights and freedoms may in no case be exercised contrary to the purposes and principles of the United Nations.

Article 30. Nothing in this Declaration may be interpreted as implying for any State, group or person any right to engage in any activity or to perform any act aimed at the destruction of any of the rights and freedoms set forth herein.

Appendix 20

THE ROAD TO PEACE—A TWENTY-YEAR UNITED NATIONS PROGRAM— MEMORANDUM BY SECRETARY-GENERAL TRYGVE LIE, JUNE 6, 1950 [1]

As Secretary-General, it is my firm belief that a new and great effort must be attempted to end the so-called "cold war" and to set the world once more on a road that will offer greater hope of lasting peace.

The atmosphere of deepening international mistrust can be dissipated and the threat of the universal disaster of another war averted by employing to the full the resources for conciliation and constructive peace-building present in the United Nations Charter. The employment of these resources can secure eventual peace if we accept, believe, and act upon the possibility of peaceful co-existence among all the Great Powers and the different economic and political systems they represent, and if the Great Powers evidence a readiness to undertake genuine negotiation—not in a spirit of appeasement—but with enlightened self-interest and common sense on all sides.

Measures for collective self-defence and regional remedies of other kinds are at best interim measures and cannot alone bring any reliable security from the prospect of war. The one common undertaking and universal instrument of the great majority of the human race is the United Nations. A patient, constructive, long-term use of its potentialities can bring a real and secure peace to the world. I am certain that such an effort will have the active interest and support of the smaller Member states, who have much to contribute in the conciliation of Big Power differences and in the development of constructive and mutually advantageous political and economic co-operation.

I therefore venture to suggest certain points for consideration in the formulation of a 20-year United Nations Peace Program. Certain of these points call for urgent action. Others are of a long-range nature, requiring continued effort over the next 20 years. I shall not discuss the problems of the peace settlements for Austria, Germany, and Japan—because the founders of the United Nations indicated that the peace settlements should be made separately from the United Nations. But I believe that the progress of a United Nations Peace Program such as is here suggested will help to bring these settlements far closer to attainment.

[1] *United Nations Bulletin,* Vol. VIII, No. 12, June 15, 1950, pp. 510–513, 540.

1. *Inauguration of periodic meetings of the Security Council, attended by foreign ministers, or heads or other members of governments, as provided by the United Nations Charter and the rules of procedure; together with further development and use of other United Nations machinery for negotiation, mediation, and conciliation of international disputes.*

The periodic meetings of the Security Council provided for in Article 28 of the Charter have never been held.   Such periodic meetings should be held semi-annually, beginning with one in 1950.   In my opinion, they should be used for a general review at a high level of outstanding issues in the United Nations, particularly those that divide the Great Powers.   They should not be expected to produce great decisions every time; they should be used for consultation—much of it in private—for efforts to gain ground toward agreement on questions at issue, to clear up misunderstandings, to prepare for new initiatives that may improve the chances for definitive agreement at later meetings.   They should be held away from Headquarters as a general rule, in Geneva, the capitals of the permanent members, and in other regions of the world.

Further development of the resources of the United Nations for mediation and conciliation should be undertaken, including re-establishment of the regular practice of private consultations by the representatives of the five Great Powers, and a renewed effort to secure agreement by all the Great Powers on limitations on the use of the veto power in the pacific settlement procedures of the Security Council.

2. *A new attempt to make progress toward establishing an international control system for atomic energy that will be effective in preventing its use for war and promoting its use for peaceful purposes.*

We cannot hope for any quick or easy solution of this most difficult problem of atomic energy control.   The only way to find out what is possible is to resume negotiation in line with the directive of the General Assembly last fall "to explore all possible avenues and examine all concrete suggestions with a view to determining what might lead to an agreement."   Various suggestions for finding a basis for a fresh approach have been put forward.   One possibility would be for the Security Council to instruct the Secretary-General to call a conference of scientists whose discussions might provide a reservoir of new ideas on the control of weapons of mass destruction and the promotion of peaceful uses of atomic energy that could thereafter be explored in the United Nations Atomic Energy Commission.   Or it may be that an interim agreement could be worked out that would at least be some improvement on the present situation of an unlimited atomic arms race, even though it did not afford full security.   There are other possibilities for providing the basis for a new start; every possibility should be explored.

3. *A new approach to the problem of bringing the armaments race under control, not only in the field of atomic weapons, but in other weapons of mass destruction and in conventional armaments.*

Here is another area where it is necessary to re-activate negotiation and to make new efforts at finding some area of common ground.   It must be recognized that up to now there has been virtually a complete failure here and that the immediate prospects seem poor indeed.   Clearly disarmament requires an atmosphere of confidence in which political disputes are brought nearer to solution.   But it is also true that any progress at all toward agreement on the regulation of armaments of any kind would help to reduce cold war tensions and thus assist in the adjustment of political disputes. Negotiation on this problem should not be deferred until the other great political problems are solved, but should go hand-in-hand with any effort to reach political settlements.

4. *A renewal of serious efforts to reach agreement on the armed forces to be made available under the Charter to the Security Council for the enforcement of its decisions.*

A new approach should be made toward resolving existing differences on the size, location, and composition of the forces to be pledged to the Security Council under Article 43 of the Charter. Basic political difficulties which may delay a final solution should not be permitted to stand in the way of some sort of an interim accord for a small force sufficient to prevent or stop localized outbreaks threatening international peace. The mere existence of such a force would greatly enhance the ability of the Security Council to bring about peaceful settlements in most of the cases which are likely to come before it.

5. *Acceptance and application of the principle that it is wise and right to proceed as rapidly as possible toward universality of Membership.*

Fourteen nations are now awaiting admission to the United Nations. In the interests of the people of these countries and of the United Nations, I believe they should all be admitted, as well as other countries which will attain their independence in the future. It should be made clear that Germany and Japan would also be admitted as soon as the peace treaties have been completed.

6. *A sound and active program of technical assistance for economic development and encouragement of broad-scale capital investment, using all appropriate private, governmental, and inter-governmental resources.*

A technical assistance program is in its beginnings, assisted by the strong support of the President of the United States. Its fundamental purpose is to enable the people of the under-developed countries to raise their standard of living peacefully by specific and practicable measures. It should be a continuing and expanding program for the next 20 years and beyond, carried forward with the co-operation of all Member governments, largely through the United Nations and the specialized agencies, with mutual beneficial programs planned and executed on a basis of equality rather than on a basis of charity. Through this means, the opportunities can be opened up for capital investment on a large and expanding scale. Here lies one of our best hopes for combating the dangers and costs of the cold war.

7. *More vigorous use by all Member governments of the specialized agencies of the United Nations to promote, in the words of the Charter, "higher standards of living, full employment, and conditions of economic and social progress."*

The great potentialities of the specialized agencies to participate in a long-range program aimed at drastically reducing the economic and social causes of war can be realized by more active support from all governments, including the membership of the Soviet Union in some or all of the agencies to which it does not now belong. The expansion of world trade which is vital to any long-range effort for world betterment requires the early ratification of the Charter of the International Trade Organization.

8. *Vigorous and continued development of the work of the United Nations for wider observance and respect for human rights and fundamental freedoms throughout the world.*

It is becoming evident that the Universal Declaration of Human Rights, adopted by the General Assembly in 1948 without a dissenting vote, is destined to become one of the great documents of history. The United Nations is now engaged on a program that will extend over the next 20 years—and beyond—to secure the extension and wider observance of the political, economic, and social rights there set down. Its success needs the active support of all governments.

9. *Use of the United Nations to promote, by peaceful means instead of by force, the advancement of dependent, colonial, or semi-colonial peoples toward a place of equality in the world.*

The great changes which have been taking place since the end of the war among the peoples of Asia and Africa must be kept within peaceful bounds by using the universal framework of the United Nations. The old relationships will have to be replaced with new ones of equality and fraternity. The United Nations is the instrument capable of bringing such a transition to pass without violent upheavals and with the best prospect of bringing long-run economic and political benefits to all nations of the world.

10. *Active and systematic use of all the powers of the Charter and all the machinery of the United Nations to speed up the development of international law toward an eventual enforceable world law for a universal world society.*

These three last points deal with programs already under way to carry out important principles of the United Nations Charter. They respond to basic human desires and aspirations, and co-ordinated efforts by all governments to further these programs are indispensable to the eventual peaceful stabilization of international relations. There are many specific steps which need to be taken: for example, under point 10, ratification of the Genocide Convention, greater use of the International Court of Justice, and systematic development and codification of international law. More important is that governments should give high priority in their national policies to the continued support and development of these ideals which are at the foundation of all striving of the peoples for a better world.

What is here suggested is only an outline of preliminary proposals for a program; much more development will be needed. It is self-evident that every step mentioned, every proposal made, will require careful and detailed, even laborious, preparation, negotiation, and administration. It is equally self-evident that the necessary measures of agreement will be hard to realize most of the time, and even impossible some of the time. Yet the world can never accept the thesis of despair—the thesis of irrevocable and irreconcilable conflict.

Appendix 21

UNITING FOR PEACE—GENERAL ASSEMBLY RECOMMENDATIONS TO SECURITY COUNCIL, RECOMMENDATIONS TO PERMANENT MEMBERS, NOVEMBER 2, 1950 [1]

RESOLUTION A
UNITING FOR PEACE

The General Assembly,

Recognizing that the first two stated Purposes of the United Nations are:

"To maintain international peace and security, and to that end: to take effective collective measures for the prevention and removal of threats to the peace, and for the suppression of acts of aggression or other breaches of the peace, and to bring about by peaceful means, and in conformity with the principles of justice and international law, adjustment or settlement of international disputes or situations which might lead to a breach of the peace," and

"To develop friendly relations among nations based on respect for the principle of equal rights and self-determination of peoples, and to take other appropriate measures to strengthen universal peace,"

Reaffirming that it remains the primary duty of all Members of the United Nations, when involved in an international dispute, to seek settlement of such a dispute by peaceful means through the procedures laid down in Chapter VI of the Charter, and recalling the successful achievements of the United Nations in this regard on a number of previous occasions,

Finding that international tension exists on a dangerous scale,

Recalling its resolution 290 (IV) entitled "Essentials of Peace," which states that disregard of the Principles of the Charter of the United Nations is primarily responsible for the continuance of international tension, and desiring to contribute further to the objectives of that resolution,

Reaffirming the importance of the exercise by the Security Council of its primary responsibility for the maintenance of international peace and security, and the duty of the permanent members to seek unanimity and to exercise restraint in the use of the veto,

[1] *United Nations Bulletin,* Vol. IX, No. 10, Nov. 15, 1950, pp. 508–509.

Reaffirming that the initiative in negotiating the agreements for armed forces provided for in Article 43 of the Charter belongs to the Security Council, and desiring to ensure that, pending the conclusion of such agreements, the United Nations has at its disposal means for maintaining international peace and security,

Conscious that failure of the Security Council to discharge its responsibilities on behalf of all the Member states, particularly those responsibilities referred to in the two preceding paragraphs, does not relieve Member states of their obligations or the United Nations of its responsibility under the Charter to maintain international peace and security,

Recognizing in particular that such failure does not deprive the General Assembly of its rights or relieve it of its responsibilities under the Charter in regard to the maintenance of international peace and security,

Recognizing that discharge by the General Assembly of its responsibilities in these respects calls for possibilities of observation which would ascertain the facts and expose aggressors; for the existence of armed forces which could be used collectively; and for the possibility of timely recommendation by the General Assembly to Members of the United Nations for collective action which, to be effective, should be prompt,

A.

1. *Resolves* that if the Security Council, because of lack of unanimity of the permanent members, fails to exercise its primary responsibility for the maintenance of international peace and security in any case where there appears to be a threat to the peace, breach of the peace, or act of aggression, the General Assembly shall consider the matter immediately with a view to making appropriate recommendations to Members for collective measures, including in the case of a breach of the peace or act of aggression the use of armed force when necessary, to maintain or restore international peace and security. If not in session at the time, the General Assembly may meet in emergency special session within 24 hours of the request therefor. Such emergency special session shall be called if requested by the Security Council on the vote of any seven members, or by a majority of the Members of the United Nations;

2. *Adopts* for this purpose the amendments to its rules of procedure set forth in the annex [2] to the present resolution;

B.

3. *Establishes* a Peace Observation Commission, which for the calendar years 1951 and 1952 shall be composed of fourteen Members, namely: China, Colombia, Czechoslovakia, France, India, Iraq, Israel, New Zealand, Pakistan, Sweden, the Union of Soviet Socialist Republics, the United Kingdom of Great Britain and Northern Ireland, the United States of America and Uruguay, and which could observe and report on the situation in any area where there exists international tension the continuance of which is likely to endanger the maintenance of international peace and security. Upon the invitation or with the consent of the state into whose territory the Commission would go, the General Assembly, or the Interim Committee when the Assembly is not in session, may utilize the Commission if the Security Council is not exercising the functions assigned to it by the Charter

[2] The text of the annex is omitted.

with respect to the matter in question. Decisions to utilize the Commission shall be made on the affirmative vote of two-thirds of the Members present and voting. The Security Council may also utilize the Commission in accordance with its authority under the Charter;

4. *The Commission shall have* authority in its discretion to appoint sub-commissions and to utilize the services of observers to assist it in the performance of its functions;

5. *Recommends* to all governments and authorities that they co-operate with the Commission and assist it in the performance of its functions;

6. *Requests* the Secretary-General to provide the necessary staff and facilities, utilizing, where directed by the Commission, the United Nations Panel of Field Observers envisaged in resolution 297 B (IV);

C.

7. *Invites* each Member of the United Nations to survey its resources in order to determine the nature and scope of the assistance it may be in a position to render in support of any recommendations of the Security Council or of the General Assembly for the restoration of international peace and security;

8. *Recommends* to the states Members of the United Nations that each Member maintain within its national armed forces elements so trained, organized, and equipped that they could promptly be made available, in accordance with its constitutional processes, for service as a United Nations unit or units, upon recommendation by the Security Council or General Assembly, without prejudice to the use of such elements in exercise of the right of individual or collective self-defence recognized in Article 51 of the Charter;

9. *Invites* the Members of the United Nations to inform the Collective Measures Committee, provided for in paragraph 11, as soon as possible of the measures taken in implementation of the preceding paragraph;

10. *Requests* the Secretary-General to appoint, with the approval of the Committee provided for in paragraph 11, a panel of military experts who could be made available, on request to Member states wishing to obtain technical advice regarding the organization, training, and equipment for prompt service as United Nations units of the elements referred to in paragraph 8;

D.

11. *Establishes* a Collective Measures Committee consisting of fourteen Members, namely: Australia, Belgium, Brazil, Burma, Canada, Egypt, France, Mexico, Philippines, Turkey, the United Kingdom of Great Britain and Northern Ireland, the United States of America, Venezuela, and Yugoslavia, and directs the Committee, in consultation with the Secretary-General and with such Member states as the Committee finds appropriate, to study and make a report to the Security Council and the General Assembly, not later than September 1, 1951, on methods, including those in Section C of present resolution, which might be used to maintain and strengthen international peace and security in accordance with the Purposes and Principles of the Charter, taking account of collective self-defence and regional arrangements (Articles 51 and 52 of the Charter);

12. *Recommends* to all Member states that they co-operate with the Committee and assist it in the performance of its functions;

13. *Requests* the Secretary-General to furnish the staff and facilities necessary for the effective accomplishment of the purposes set forth in Sections C and D of this resolution;

E.

14. *The General Assembly*, in adopting the proposals set forth above, is fully conscious that enduring peace will not be secured solely by collective security arrangements against breaches of international peace and acts of aggression, but that a genuine and lasting peace depends also upon the observance of all the Principles and Purposes established in the Charter of the United Nations, upon the implementation of the resolutions of the Security Council, the General Assembly, and other principal organs of the United Nations intended to achieve the maintenance of international peace and security, and especially upon respect for and observance of human rights and fundamental freedoms for all and on the establishment and maintenance of conditions of economic and social well-being in all countries; and accordingly

15. *Urges* Member states to respect fully, and to intensify, joint action, in cooperation with the United Nations, to develop and stimulate universal respect for and observance of human rights and fundamental freedoms, and to intensify individual and collective efforts to achieve conditions of economic stability and social progress, particularly through the development of under-developed countries and areas.

RESOLUTION B

For the purpose of maintaining international peace and security, in accordance with the Charter of the United Nations and, in particular, with Chapters V, VI, and VII of the Charter,

The General Assembly

Recommends to the Security Council:

That it should take the necessary steps to ensure that the action provided for under the Charter is taken with respect to threats to the peace, breaches of the peace, or acts of aggression and with respect to the peaceful settlement of disputes or situations likely to endanger the maintenance of international peace and security;

That it should devise measures for the earliest application of Articles 43, 45, 46, and 47 of the Charter of the United Nations regarding the placing of armed forces at the disposal of the Security Council by the states Member of the United Nations and the effective functioning of the Military Staff Committee.

The above disposition should in no manner prevent the General Assembly from fulfilling its functions under resolution A.

RESOLUTION C

The General Assembly

Recognizing that the primary function of the United Nations organization is to maintain and promote peace, security, and justice among all nations,

Recognizing the responsibility of all Member states in promoting the cause of international peace in accordance with their obligations as provided in the Charter,

Recognizing that the Charter charges the Security Council with the primary responsibility for maintaining international peace and security,

Reaffirming the importance of unanimity among the permanent members of the Security Council on all problems which are likely to threaten world peace,

Recalling General Assembly resolution 190 (III) entitled "Appeal to the Great Powers to Renew their Efforts to Compose their Differences and Establish a Lasting Peace,"

Recommends to the permanent members of the Security Council that:

(a) They meet and discuss, collectively or otherwise, and, if necessary, with other states concerned, all problems which are likely to threaten international peace and hamper the activities of the United Nations, with a view to their resolving fundamental differences and reaching agreement in accordance with the spirit and letter of the Charter;

(b) They advise the General Assembly and, when it is not in session, the Members of the United Nations, as soon as appropriate, of the results of their consultations.

INDEX